Estate Management Law

Sixth Edition

Richard Card LLB LLM FRSA

*Professor of Law and Chairman of De Montfort Law School,
De Montfort University, Leicester*

John Murdoch LLB ACIArb

*Professor of Law
University of Reading*

Sandi Murdoch LLB LLM

*Senior Lecturer in Law
University of Reading*

OXFORD
UNIVERSITY PRESS

OXFORD
UNIVERSITY PRESS

Great Clarendon Street, Oxford OX2 6DP

Oxford University Press is a department of the University of Oxford.
It furthers the University's objective of excellence in research, scholarship,
and education by publishing worldwide in

Oxford New York

Auckland Cape Town Dar es Salaam Hong Kong Karachi Kuala Lumpur
Madrid Melbourne Mexico City Nairobi New Delhi Shanghai Taipei Toronto

With offices in

Argentina Austria Brazil Chile Czech Republic France Greece
Guatemala Hungary Italy Japan Poland Portugal Singapore
South Korea Switzerland Thailand Turkey Ukraine Vietnam

Oxford is a registered trade mark of Oxford University Press
in the UK and in certain other countries

Published in the United States
by Oxford University Press Inc., New York

British Library Cataloguing in Publication Data

Data available

Library of Congress Cataloging in Publication Data

Data available

ISBN: 978-0-406-96375-8

9 10 8

Printed in Great Britain by
CPI Antony Rowe
Chippenham, Wilts.

Preface

Like its previous editions, this book is intended to serve as a comprehensive textbook for estate management students studying courses in basic legal topics, particularly ones which treat the subject matter in some depth.

We have had in mind the syllabuses for examinations in basic legal subjects for degrees and diplomas in estate management, land management and allied fields, as well as those for the comparable examinations of the relevant professional bodies. Despite its title, this book should also prove useful for those following similar courses in law for other types of qualifications.

Besides the inevitable updating and associated rewriting, this edition sees a substantial restructuring of the book so as to reflect changes in the needs of our readership.

This book is divided into six parts. Part I outlines the English legal system. Parts II, III and IV deal with the law of contract, the law of tort and land law, respectively. Parts V and VI are new parts, dealing with landlord and tenant and planning law respectively.

In addition to the usual flood of case law, we have also had to deal with a number of pieces of new legislation, in particular the Human Rights Act 1998, the Contracts (Rights of Third Parties) Act 1999, the Unfair Terms in Consumer Contracts Regulations 1999 and the Land Registration Act 2002.

We thank Professor Anthony Lavers, until recently of Oxford Brookes University, who contributed the chapters on planning law.

We have tried to summarise and explain the law as it has been reported on 1 June 2003.

Richard Card
John Murdoch
Sandi Murdoch

1 June 2003

Contents

Part II

The law of contract

Chapter 4

Chapter 5

Chapter 12

Chapter 13

Part III

The law of tort

Chapter 16

Introduction   221

Part V

The law of landlord and tenant

Chapter 37

Landlord and tenant: the general law   525

Chapter 38

Landlord and tenant: statutory protection 563

Part VI

Planning law

Chapter 39

The operation of the planning system and its legal framework   595

Chapter 40

Table of abbreviations

AA 1971	Animals Act 1971
AA1996	Arbitration Act 1996
AHA 1986	Agricultural Holdings Act 1986
AJA 1982	Administration of Justice Act 1982
ANLA 1992	Access to Neighbouring Land Act 1992
ATA 1995	Agricultural Tenancies Act 1995
C(RTP)A 1999	Contracts (Rights of Third Parties) Act 1999
CA 1985	Companies Act 1985
CL(C)A 1978	Civil Liability (Contribution) Act 1978
CLRA 2002	Commonhold and Leasehold Reform Act 2002
CRWA 2000	Countryside and Rights of Way Act 2000
DPA 1972	Defective Premises Act 1972
ECA 1972	European Communities Act 1972
FAA 1976	Fatal Accidents Act 1976
HA 1988	Housing Act 1988
HA1985	Housing Act 1985
HA1996	Housing Act 1996
HRA 1998	Human Rights Act 1998
IA 1986	Insolvency Act 1986
LA 1980	Limitation Act 1980
LCA 1972	Land Charges Act 1972
LDA 1986	Latent Damage Act 1986
LP(MP)A 1989	Law of Property (Miscellaneous Provisions) Act 1989
LPA 1922	Law of Property Act 1922
LPA 1925	Law of Property Act 1925
LR(FC)A 1943	Law Reform (Frustrated Contracts) Act 1943
LRA 1925	Land Registration Act 1925
LRA 1967	Leasehold Reform Act 1967
LRA 2002	Land Registration Act 2002
LRHUDA 1993	Leasehold Reform, Housing and Urban Development Act 1993
LT(C)A 1995	Landlord and Tenant (Covenants) Act 1995
LTA 1927	Landlord and Tenant Act 1927
LTA 1949	Lands Tribunal Act 1949
LTA 195	Landlord and Tenant Act 195
LTA 1985	Landlord and Tenant Act 1985

LTA 1987	Landlord and Tenant Act 1987
MA 1967	Misrepresentation Act 1967
OLA 1957	Occupiers' Liability Act 1957
OLA 1984	Occupiers' Liability Act 1984
PA 1832	Prescription Act 1832
PA 1890	Partnership Act 1890
PAA 1971	Powers of Attorney Act 1971
PEA 1977	Protection from Eviction Act 1977
RA 1977	Rent Act 1977
RcA 1977	Rentcharges Act 1977
RTA 1988	Road Traffic Act 1988
SCA 1981	Supreme Court Act 1981
SG(IT)A 1973	Supply of Goods (Implied Terms) Act 1973
SGA 1979	Sale of Goods Act 1979
SGSA 1982	Supply of Goods and Services Act 1982
SSAA 1992	Social Security Administration Act 1992
TA 1996	Treasure Act 1996
TCPA 1990	Town and Country Planning Act 1990
TLATA 1996	Trusts of Land and Appointment of Trustees Act 1996
UCTA 1977	Unfair Contract Terms Act 1977

Table of statutes

Paragraph references printed in **bold** type indicate where
the Act is set out in part or in full.

Table of cases

PARA

PARA

J

PARA

PARA

O

PARA

Decisions of the European Court of Justice are listed below numerically. These decisions
are also included in the preceding alphabetical list.

Part I

Outline of the English legal system

Chapter 1

Introduction

1.1   This book is concerned with aspects of *English* civil law. The laws and legal systems of Scotland and, to a lesser extent, Northern Ireland are distinct from those of England and Wales.

1.2   A major distinction can be drawn between civil and criminal law. It is criminal law which occupies most of the attention of non-lawyers, but lawyers are frequently more concerned with non-criminal, ie civil, law. Civil law can be subdivided into categories, for example contract and tort. These categories of civil law are no less important than criminal law.

It is surprisingly difficult in theory, though not in practice, to distinguish between civil and criminal law. Criminal cases, which are called prosecutions, are normally initiated by the state, but they may be brought by a private citizen, although this is rare. If a prosecution is successful the accused, or defendant, is liable to punishment. This affords no direct benefit to the victim of the crime since he does not receive fines payable or the fruits of a criminal's labours in prison. The victims of some crimes, such as an attempted theft or blackmail, may have suffered no loss from the commission of the crime anyway. Some crimes can be committed without there being a victim, for example offences involving obscene publications. Although punishment does not compensate victims, it is possible for the criminal courts to order the criminal to make reparation directly to his victim. The victim of a criminal offence cannot prevent a prosecution nor order its discontinuance, however much he may wish to avoid a criminal trial.

In contrast, civil actions are brought by an individual (the claimant, until 1999 called 'the plaintiff') who is seeking to obtain compensation for the loss he has suffered or to establish his legal rights. If damages are awarded as the result of a successful civil action, they are payable to the claimant and are generally assessed on the basis that they should compensate him and not on the basis of punishing the defendant. A claimant can discontinue a civil action at any time before judgment.

Facts which disclose a criminal offence may also form the basis of a civil action. If A, a taxi driver, collides with C's car while driving B to the station, the civil law of contract, the civil law of tort and criminal law may all be applicable. A has certainly broken his contract to drive B to the station, and if his driving was careless this may occasion not only criminal liability for an offence of careless driving but also tortious liability to C for the damage caused to C's car.

Common law and legislation[1]

1.3   Common law and legislation are sources of law. Common law means judge-made law. It is contained in the decisions or judgments made by the English judiciary over many centuries. Legislation comprises Acts of Parliament, subordinate legislation (examples of which are byelaws and statutory instruments deriving their authority from Acts of Parliament) and the legislation of the European Community.

1   Chapter 3 below.

Common law and equity

1.4   The common law can be further subdivided into common law and equity. If both are branches of the common law and therefore both judge-made law, wherein lies the difference between them? The difference between them is that of their origins. Prior to the Judicature Acts of 1873–1875 there were two systems of courts in England, the common law courts and the Court of Chancery. Although the court system was fused in 1875, the law which they applied was not. Thus it is still possible to speak of common law and equity as distinct bodies of law.

1.5   The common law courts had evolved from the centralised system for the administration of justice developed by a powerful monarchy between the eleventh and thirteenth centuries. Therefore, common law is that body of law developed by the common law courts prior to the fusion of the administration of justice in 1875, and modifications and extensions effected since 1875. The common law is not static but subject to constant affirmation, revision and development by modern judges.

1.6   Equity is that body of law developed in the Court of Chancery prior to 1875 and its subsequent amendments and developments. The Court of Chancery developed later than the common law courts because of defects in those courts and in the law which they administered; the common law courts had entangled themselves in an extremely rigid procedure which made it difficult to initiate actions and severely limited the development of the common law, and the remedies available in the common law courts for the successful litigant were inadequate. Thus, the habit arose in the fourteenth and fifteenth centuries of petitioning the King to remedy injustice. After a while, the King delegated the task of determining these petitions to his Chancellor. Initially, the Chancellor decided cases in the name of the King but in 1474 he began to do so in his own name, and this marked the beginning of the Court of Chancery presided over by the Lord Chancellor. The procedure in the Court of Chancery was originally less rigid than that of the common law courts; and the basis of decisions was supposed to be the merits of each action and what was just between the parties, with little reference to previous cases. Subsequently, both procedure and substantive law became more rigid; the notion of creating a remedy to fit the particular case before the court disappeared and the Court of Chancery became as much influenced by previous cases as the common law courts.

   The rules of equity developed by the Court of Chancery were concerned either with entirely new rights totally unknown to the common law or with remedies (such as injunctions and specific performance)[1] designed to counter the inefficacy or injustice of the common law. Equity did not amend the common law but enabled a litigant who had failed to establish a claim at common law, or been disappointed by the remedies available there, to seek an equitable remedy which made good the defects of the common law in a particular case.

For example, if the parties to a contract agree to vary their agreement the common law provides that the variation cannot take effect unless it is supported by consideration, whereas equity may prevent the agreement being enforced in its unvaried form, for a time at least.[2]

1 Paras 11.29 and 11.32 below.
2 Para 6.17 below.

1.7 Even modern courts, which administer both common law and equity, will tend to consider the common law first and then see if it is affected by equity. This process is reversed where a case is concerned with a body of rules developed almost entirely by equity, for example the law of trusts. If there is a conflict between the rules of the common law and those of equity, the rules of equity prevail. It cannot be emphasised too much that the remedies developed by equity cannot be demanded as of right (unlike common law remedies) but, reflecting the origins of equity in conscience, are discretionary.

Chapter 2

Administration of the law

2.1 In this chapter we describe:

- the system of courts with a civil jurisdiction;
- specialist courts and tribunals;
- alternative methods of dispute resolution.

The civil courts

2.2 We describe below those courts with a civil jurisdiction which would be of relevance to a surveyor or valuer in his or her professional capacity. We shall not, therefore, describe magistrates' courts or the Crown Court which have jurisdiction over criminal matters; such jurisdiction as they have over civil matters (eg licensing and family proceedings in the case of a magistrates' court) is of no direct relevance to a surveyor or valuer. Overleaf is a chart which shows the outline of the civil court structure.

County courts
2.3 The jurisdiction of the county courts is exclusively civil. There are some 230 county courts in England and Wales.

The full jurisdiction of the county courts is typically exercised by circuit judges. Circuit judges are appointed by the Queen on the recommendation of the Lord Chancellor to serve in the Crown Court and in the county courts, and to carry out such other judicial functions as may be conferred on them. There are about 420 circuit judges. Generally, only circuit judges specifically assigned for the purpose sit in county courts.

To reduce delay in the administration of justice, the Lord Chancellor can appoint deputy circuit judges on a temporary basis. Deputy circuit judges can exercise the full jurisdiction of a county court judge, and so can another type of judge, a recorder. Recorders are part-time judges appointed by the Lord Chancellor.

Only barristers and solicitors with 10 years' post-qualification experience can be appointed as a circuit judge, deputy circuit judge or recorder.

There are also some 230 district judges, appointed and removable by the Lord Chancellor and a substantial number of part-time deputy district judges. To be appointed as a district judge (or a deputy district judge, hereafter the term 'district judge' includes a deputy), a person must have seven years' post-qualification experience as a barrister or solicitor. District judges deal with the interlocutory work of the county courts and also have

THE CIVIL COURT STRUCTURE

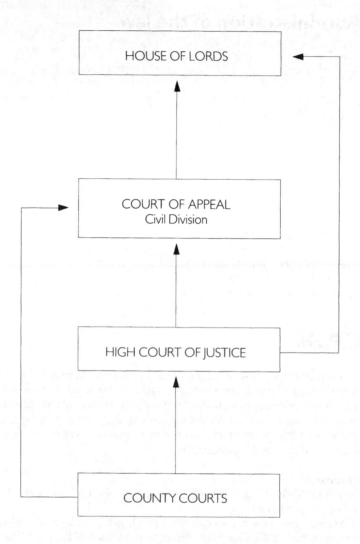

jurisdiction to try claims not exceeding £5,000 in value.[1] In addition, by leave of a judge of the court and with the consent of the parties, a district judge may try any other action. A district judge has the full jurisdiction of a circuit judge in all undefended actions.

1   See para 2.5 below.

Jurisdiction

2.4   County courts have jurisdiction over a wide range of civil matters. This jurisdiction includes:

a) *Jurisdiction over actions in contract or tort, except defamation, or for money recoverable by statute*   A county court has jurisdiction over defamation if the parties agree to accept its jurisdiction or if the High Court transfers the case to it.

An action in contract or tort may be *commenced* in a county court or in the High Court, save that a claim must be commenced in a county court where the value of a claim is £15,000 or less (or £50,000 or less where the proceedings include a claim for personal injury).

An action of which the value is less than £25,000 must be *tried* in a county court unless:

- where the action was commenced in a county court, the county court considers that it ought to be transferred to the High Court (and the High Court agrees), having regard to–
    - the importance of the action and, in particular, whether it raises questions of importance to people who are not parties or questions of public importance;
    - the complexity of the action;
    - the financial substance of the action, including the value of the counterclaim; and
    - whether a transfer will result in a speedier trial (although a transfer will not be ordered on this ground alone); or
- the case commenced in the High Court and the High Court, having regard to the above criteria, considers that it ought to try the action.

An action whose value is £50,000 or more must be tried in the High Court unless:

- it is commenced in a county court and the county court, having regard to the above criteria, considers that the action ought not to be transferred to the High Court; or
- where it is commenced in the High Court, the High Court, having regard to the same criteria as above, considers that it ought to transfer the action to a county court for trial.

In other words, there is a rebuttable presumption that actions whose value is less than £25,000 will be tried in a county court, and those whose value is £50,000 or more in the High Court.

b) *Jurisdiction over actions for the recovery of land.*

c) *An equity jurisdiction*, eg in cases of administration of estates, foreclosure of mortgages and specific performance of contracts for the sale of land, where the amount of the estate, the amount owing under the mortgage or purchase price, as the case may be, does not exceed £30,000.

d) *Bankruptcy and winding up of companies.*

e) *Matters under the Rent, Landlord and Tenant and Housing Acts.*

Small claims track

2.5   A defended action in the county court may be allocated by the court to the 'small claims track' if the amount involved is not in excess of £5,000. In the case of a personal injury claim the amount claimed for general damage for pain, suffering and loss of amenity must not exceed £1,000. If an action is so allocated the court can adopt any method of proceeding which it considers fair, including an inquisitorial approach under which it questions witnesses before the parties can. Proceedings are normally heard by a district judge.

If the amount in dispute exceeds the relevant limit a suitable claim can still be allocated to the 'small claims track' if the parties agree to this.

The advantage of the 'small claims track' is that it is eminently suitable for the litigant in person in small claims cases, which are mainly 'consumer disputes', since it is even more informal and inexpensive than trial in the county court. It can, for example, be held at the home or business premises of a party. Legal representation is discouraged by the fact that, contrary to the usual rule, a successful party cannot normally recover the costs of legal representation from his opponent.

Fast track claims and multi-track claims

2.6   The fast track is the normal track for any claim for which the small claims track is not used where the claim has a value of not more than £15,000. The 'multi-track' is the normal track for claims for which neither of the other two tracks is the normal track. Multi-track cases may also be heard in the High Court, depending on the relevant financial limits.

Fast-track cases must come to trial in 30 weeks. They have a cap on lawyers' costs, a standard fee for advocacy at trial and a maximum of one day for trial.

2.7   Appeal from a county court judge in multi-track cases and some other cases lies to the Court of Appeal. In other proceedings, appeal from a county court judge lies to the High Court rather than the Court of Appeal. Appeal from a district judge lies to a circuit judge but the permission of that judge or the circuit judge is required.

The High Court of Justice

2.8   The High Court is part of the Supreme Court of Judicature: the Crown Court and Court of Appeal are the other two constituent parts. The High Court was established by the Judicature Acts 1873–1875, replacing a number of separate courts. It is divided into three Divisions.

High Court judges are appointed by the Queen on the recommendation of the Lord Chancellor. Those qualified for appointment are persons who have for ten years had a right of audience in relation to all proceedings in the High Court (currently only barristers and some solicitors can have this right) or solicitors who do not possess High Court audience rights but who have been a circuit judge for at least two years. To reduce delay, the Lord Chancellor can appoint deputy High Court judges on a temporary basis. Because of the shortage of High Court judges, a significant number of cases, mainly in the Queen's Bench Division, are heard by deputy High Court judges.

As will be seen, the High Court has an extensive appellate jurisdiction. Except for isolated exceptions where an order affects the liberty of an individual, an appeal to the High Court requires the permission of the court or tribunal from whom it is sought to appeal or of the High Court.

Unless there are special circumstances where the interests of justice so require, an appeal will not be a rehearing but a review of the lower court or tribunal's decision.

Sometimes an appeal is required to be by case stated. An appeal by case stated is never reheard; the court simply hears legal arguments relating to the facts set out in the stated case.

An appeal will only be allowed where the decision of the lower court was wrong, or where it was unjust because of a serious procedural or other irregularity in the lower court. The same rule also applies to an appeal to a circuit judge from the decision of a district judge.

Chancery Division

2.9   The Chancery Division consists of the Lord Chancellor, as its nominal head, although he never sits at first instance, a Vice-Chancellor and, at present, 17 judges. The jurisdiction of the Chancery Division is exercised in London and in a number of regional towns.

2.10   The jurisdiction of the Chancery Division is entirely civil and can be split into original and appellate jurisdictions.

Original jurisdiction The Chancery Division has jurisdiction over a number of matters. These include:

- the administration of estates of deceased persons;
- the redemption and foreclosure of mortgages;
- the rectification and cancellation of deeds;
- partnership actions;
- bankruptcy;
- the sale, exchange or partition of land, or the raising of charges on land; and
- all causes and matters under enactments relating to companies.

As can be seen, there is some concurrence between the Chancery Division's original jurisdiction and that of the county courts (save for the financial limits which apply, for example, to their equity jurisdiction).

Appellate jurisdiction This covers appeals in 'Chancery matters' from a county court. In addition, a few appeals of other types may be heard, eg income tax appeals from the Commissioners of Inland Revenue.

Queen's Bench Division

2.11   This division is the largest of the three divisions and has the most varied jurisdiction. Its head is the Lord Chief Justice. At present, 74 judges are assigned to it. The original civil jurisdiction of this division is exercised in certain regional towns, as well as in London.

2.12   The civil jurisdiction of the Queen's Bench Division can be divided into three heads, the first of which is the busiest:

Original civil jurisdiction The principal aspects of this are actions in contract and tort. Commercial matters are dealt with by specialist judges in the Commercial Court which sits in London, and whose procedure is more flexible than the normal High Court procedure. Traditionally, cases in the Commercial Court were dealt with more speedily than elsewhere in the High Court. The success of the Commercial Court has meant that it has become inundated with work. Because of this, cases can take as long to get to trial as elsewhere, or even longer. To avoid the cost and inconvenience of advocates having to travel to the Commercial Court, commercial cases are also heard by High Court judges and specialist circuit judges in the Mercantile Courts which sit in a number of regional towns.

Appellate civil jurisdiction A single judge has jurisdiction to hear appeals from decisions in the county courts and from the decisions of certain tribunals, and certain other appeals. In addition, a single judge (or, if the court so directs, a divisional court) hears appeals by way of case stated on a miscellaneous collection of civil matters from magistrates' courts (excluding family proceedings), the Crown Court and certain other bodies. A divisional court consists of two or more judges, increasingly two, of whom one will normally be a Lord Justice of Appeal (a member of the Court of Appeal). An appeal by case stated must be on the ground that the determination or decision is wrong in law or is in excess of jurisdiction. The case is not re-heard, the judge or court merely hearing legal argument.

Judicial review jurisdiction This jurisdiction is exercised by the Administrative Court. In Wales it is exercised by the Administrative Court for Wales. Normally, the case is heard by a single judge, but if it is a particularly difficult one it may be heard by a divisional court.

Permission to claim judicial review must be obtained from a judge. Judicial review proceedings can be made in respect of the decisions of magistrates' courts, county courts, the Crown Court (except in respect of trials on indictment), tribunals and other decision-making bodies of a public nature, such as local authorities. As in an appeal by case stated, the court simply hears legal argument and decides on that basis. It is not concerned with the correctness of the decision on its merits but with whether it was lawfully and reasonably made.

On a claim for judicial review the court can make a mandatory order, a prohibitory order or a quashing order. A mandatory order is used to compel the body to whom it is directed to carry out a definite public duty imposed on it by law. The order cannot be used to compel the body to exercise its discretion in a particular way, but it may be used to compel it to hear and determine a case, or to state a case for the opinion of the High Court. A prohibitory order or a quashing order will only be issued in relation to an order or decision of a body which is under a public duty to 'act judicially' or 'act fairly' in making that decision, as opposed to purely administratively. This does not mean that a prohibitory order and a quashing order will be issued only to courts or tribunals, for many other bodies, such as local authorities, may sometimes be required to act judicially, and in other cases are required to act fairly. A prohibitory order is issued to *prevent* such a body from acting in excess of jurisdiction or otherwise acting improperly. A quashing order covers much the same area but after such a body has done something and it is desired to review it and, if necessary, quash it on the ground of excess of jurisdiction, denial of natural justice, or error of law on the face of the record.

Family Division

2.13   The Family Division deals with all aspects of family law, including:

*   proceedings for the determination of title to property in dispute between spouses; and
*   proceedings concerning the occupation of the matrimonial home and/or the exclusion of a violent spouse.

2.14   Appeals from the original jurisdiction of any division of the High Court lie to the Court of Appeal (Civil Division), as do appeals from the civil appellate jurisdiction of any Division.[1]

1   But note the 'leap-frogging' exception mentioned in para 2.18 below.

The Court of Appeal

2.15   The Court of Appeal is composed of the Master of the Rolls, the Lord Chief Justice, the President of the Family Division and, at present, 34 Lords Justice of Appeal. Lords Justice are appointed by the Queen on the advice of the Prime Minister who acts on the recommendation of the Lord Chancellor. They must have been judges of the High Court or for 10 years have had a right of audience in relation to all proceedings in the High Court. A High Court judge may be required to sit in the Court of Appeal if this is necessary. The Court of Appeal is divided into a civil and a criminal division. The Master of the Rolls is the President of the Civil Division, and the Lord Chief Justice is the President of the Criminal Division.

2.16   The Court of Appeal (Civil Division) hears appeals from:

- The decisions in civil matters of all three divisions of the High Court.
- The final decisions by a county court judge in a multi-track claim or in certain specialist proceedings and decisions by a county court judge when hearing an appeal.
- The decisions of the Lands Tribunal and certain other tribunals.[1]

Save for isolated exceptions where an order affects the liberty of an individual, an appeal to the Court of Appeal requires the permission of the court or tribunal from whom it is sought to appeal or of the Court of Appeal. There is no right of further appeal to the Court of Appeal from the determination of an appeal to a county court or the High Court unless the Court of Appeal considers that:

- the appeal would raise an important point of principle or practice; or
- there is some other compelling reason for the Court of Appeal to hear it.

Where in any proceedings in a county court or the High Court a person appeals, or seeks permission to appeal, to a court other than the Court of Appeal or House of Lords, the Master of the Rolls, or the court from which or to which the appeal is made, or from which permission to appeal is sought, may direct that the appeal be heard instead by the Court of Appeal. This is to enable unduly protracted or excessively complex appeals to be dealt with by the Court of Appeal as the most appropriate court.

1   Paras 2.23 and 2.24 below

The House of Lords

2.17   The House of Lords' appellate jurisdiction is discharged by its Appellate Committee. At the hearing of an appeal there must be present at least three of the following – the Lord Chancellor, the Lords of Appeal in Ordinary and such peers who hold or have held high judicial office (for example, ex-Lord Chancellors). Normally, five Lords of Appeal in Ordinary hear an appeal. Lords of Appeal in Ordinary (commonly called 'Law Lords', and not to be confused with Lords Justice of Appeal),[1] must have held high judicial office for two years or for 15 years have had rights of audience in the Supreme Court (ie the Court of Appeal, the High Court and the Crown Court). They are appointed by the Queen on the advice of the Prime Minister who acts on the recommendation of the Lord Chancellor. At present there are 12 Lords of Appeal in Ordinary. The House of Lords has both a civil and a criminal appellate jurisdiction.

1   Para 2.15 above.

2.18   Under its appellate civil jurisdiction, the House of Lords hears:

- Appeals from the Court of Appeal (Civil Division), provided that leave has been granted by that Court or by the House.
- 'Leap-frog' appeals from the High Court. To save cost and delay, in most civil cases appeal may be made direct from the High Court to the House of Lords. This procedure may only be used where:

- the parties agree to it;
- the High Court judge grants a certificate to sanction it (which he may only do if he is satisfied that a point of law is involved which is of general public importance and which either relates to a matter of construction of legislation or else is one in respect of which he considers that he is 'bound' by a decision of the Court of Appeal or of the House of Lords); and
- the House of Lords gives leave to appeal.

The 'leap-frog' procedure is used in comparatively few cases.

The House of Lords will not generally interfere with findings of fact on which the trial judge and appellate court are agreed, unless it can be shown that both courts were clearly wrong.

The Court of Justice of the European Communities (European Court)

2.19   The European Court operates under the treaties, including amending treaties, establishing the European Communities (ie the European Economic Community (EEC), the European Coal and Steel Community (ECSC) and the European Atomic Energy Community (EURATOM)) which make up the European Union. The EEC has now changed its name to the European Community (EC). The European Community is, of course, the pre-eminent Community. How many readers have heard of the other two Communities? It is the European Community and its legislation which have an increasing impact on everyday business and society.

The Court consists of 15 judges (which will increase from 2004, consequent on the enlargement of the European Union (EU)).[1] The Court sits in plenary session, ie as a 'court' (generally consisting of 11 judges), unless the decision has been made to hear the case in a 'chamber' of three or five judges. A court or chamber is assisted by Advocates-General, a type of official unknown to English law. The duty of an Advocate-General is, with complete impartiality and independence, to make reasoned submissions in open court on cases brought before the Court in order to assist in the performance of its functions.

Judges and Advocates-General are appointed for six-year periods by the governments of member states acting in agreement and are eligible for re-appointment. They are chosen from those who fulfil the conditions required for the holding of the highest judicial office in their respective countries or who are jurisconsults (persons learned in the law) of recognised competence.

Before 1973 the House of Lords was the final court of appeal in all cases in this country but the accession of the United Kingdom to membership of the European Community meant that the European Court became the ultimate court (ie its decisions are binding on the House of Lords and other United Kingdom courts) in matters within its jurisdiction. Nevertheless, in the great majority of cases arising within the United Kingdom the House of Lords remains the ultimate court. The fundamental point that the treaties under which the European Court operates are concerned only with those matters which have a European element must be firmly grasped in order to understand the relationship of the European Court to the rest of our legal system.

1   For the distinction between the EU and the EC, see para 3.37.

Jurisdiction

2.20   The jurisdiction of the European Court can be divided into the following principal categories:

- Matters concerning the conduct of member states or of the institutions of the Community, such as
  - the hearing of complaints brought by member states or by the Commission of the European Communities that a member state has failed to fulfil its obligations under the Treaties; and

- the review of the legality of the regulations, directives and decisions of the Council (of Ministers) of the European Union and of the Commission.

• Matters of direct concern to litigants or prospective litigants in a member state, which have been referred for a preliminary ruling by the European Court under Art 234 of the European Community (EC) Treaty by a court or tribunal in a member state. The European Court may give preliminary rulings on three matters
- on the interpretation of the EC treaty;
- on the validity and interpretation of the regulations, directives, decisions and other acts of the institutions of the Community or the European Central Bank; and on the interpretation of certain statutes of bodies established by an act of the Council.

The European Court may also give preliminary rulings on particular types of corresponding questions under certain other treaties. These other jurisdictions are narrower and rarely invoked.

The essence of a preliminary ruling is that it should precede the judgment of the referring court. Where a question of the above types of interpretation is raised before any court or tribunal of a member state, the court or tribunal *may*, if it considers that a decision on the question is necessary to enable it to give judgment, refer the matter to the European Court for a ruling. Where a court or tribunal of a member state intends to question the validity of a Community regulation (or other Community act), it *must* refer that question to the European Court for a ruling. In addition, where any type of interpretational question is raised in a case pending before a court or tribunal of a member state, against whose decisions there is no judicial remedy under national law, that court or tribunal *must* generally refer the matter to the European Court for a ruling. This provision refers to the House of Lords where an appeal lies to the House of Lords. On the other hand, it appears that, where there is no right of appeal at all from a lower court to a higher court in respect of the matter in issue, that court is the court of 'last resort'. The obligation to refer just mentioned does not apply if the question raised is not relevant to the outcome of the proceedings, or if it has already been answered by the European Court, or if the correct interpretation of the Community law is so obvious as to leave no reasonable doubt.

Where a matter is referred to the European Court for a preliminary ruling, only the request for interpretation or decision on validity is referred. The case itself is not transferred. Consequently, the court making the reference remains 'in charge' of it, although its procedure is suspended until the European Court has given its ruling on the reference.

In terms of the relationship between the European Court and English courts it is important to distinguish between the task of interpreting the Treaties, regulations etc – to see what they mean – and the task of applying them to the case in hand.

The English judges have the final say in applying the Treaties etc: only they are empowered to find the facts and give judgment for one side or the other. However, before they can apply the Treaties, etc they have to see what they mean, and in this task of interpretation English judges are not the final authority: the European Court is.[1]

1   See *H P Bulmer Ltd v J Bollinger SA* [1974] 2 All ER 1226, CA.

The Judicial Committee of the Privy Council
2.21   The Judicial Committee of the Privy Council is the final court of appeal from the courts of some Commonwealth countries. It also hears questions relating to the powers devolved to Wales, Scotland and Northern Ireland. The Committee is normally composed

of five Lords of Appeal, but Privy Councillors who are holders or past holders of high judicial office in this country or a Commonwealth country may, and do occasionally, sit.

The Technology and Construction Court

2.22   Some cases in the High Court are heard by the Technology and Construction Court, which consists of a High Court judge (who is in charge) and circuit judges assigned to it. The Court's business includes any Chancery or Queen's Bench cause or matter:

- which involves a prolonged examination of documents or accounts, or technical, scientific or local investigation, such as could more conveniently be conducted by a specialist judge in that court; or
- for which trial by a specialist judge is desirable in the interests of one or more of the parties on grounds of expedition, economy or convenience or otherwise.

The majority of cases in the Technology and Construction Court come from the construction industry and concern architects, engineers, surveyors, contractors, house-builders, developers and others involved in that industry. However, the Court also decides cases about computer hardware or software, and other disputes of a technical or scientific nature or of an environmental nature (such as pollution or noise).

The Lands Tribunal

2.23   The Lands Tribunal was established by the Lands Tribunal Act 1949. Its offices are in London but it also sits elsewhere to determine cases. Its membership is appointed by the Lord Chancellor. Lawyers and qualified surveyors are eligible for appointment. Its jurisdiction may be exercised by any one or more of its members, the composition of a tribunal in a particular case depending on the nature of the issues involved. The procedure at the hearing is less formal than in court proceedings.

The Lands Tribunal has jurisdiction over the following matters:

- appeals from local valuation courts (which are largely composed of local councillors and magistrates and which themselves hear appeals against assessments of the rateable value of land by local valuation officers);
- assessment of compensation for the compulsory purchase of land, where this has not been agreed between the acquiring authority and the property owner, or of compensation for certain other matters, such as compensation for planning restrictions restricting new development; and
- applications for the variation, modification or discharge of restrictive covenants under the Law of Property Act 1925, s 84,[1] and applications for certificates as to notice under the Rights of Light Act 1959.[2]

1   Paras 34.38–34.43 below.
2   Para 33.55 below.

Other tribunals

2.24   A large number of different tribunals have been created to deal with particular matters arising under modern legislation, especially social welfare legislation. The function of most administrative tribunals is to enable individual citizens to challenge the administrative decisions of a government department. For example, the Social Security Appeals Tribunal hears appeals against social security decisions. Some tribunals, however, adjudicate disputes between individuals; Employment Tribunals are an example. Tribunals are usually composed of a legally qualified chairman and lay members. Their hallmarks have traditionally been said to be informality, cheapness and freedom from technicality. For these reasons they have been compared favourably with courts.

The nature and powers of tribunals vary but they have the common function of determining the facts of a case and deciding it according to law rather than the dictates of policy. In the case of some 'first instance' tribunals there is a right to appeal to an appellate tribunal or to a minister. In addition, there is generally a right of appeal to the High Court, on a question of law only, from the decision of an appellate tribunal or (if there is not such a tribunal) a 'first instance' tribunal. Whether or not there is the possibility of an appeal, a tribunal's decision may be challenged by applying to the High Court for judicial review (which we mentioned in para 2.12 above).

Alternative Dispute Resolution

2.25   Alternative dispute resolution (ADR) refers to any method of resolving an issue capable of resolution by litigation in the civil courts without resorting to the courts. Examples of ADR are arbitration, early neutral evaluation, expert determination and conciliation. A court must encourage resort to ADR if it considers that appropriate. If the parties agree to refer a dispute, or a future dispute, to ADR, their agreement is binding.

ADR is a quicker and cheaper method than litigation in the courts. It is therefore of interest both to consumers and to businesses involved in commercial disputes. In addition to speeding up settlement, ADR has the advantage of making it possible to reach settlements reflecting commercial or personal interests, as well as strict rights. It also has the advantage of focusing on the issues rather than on the combat involved in the courts. It is, therefore, less destructive of relationships between the parties.

Arbitration
2.26   Particularly in commercial and consumer matters, the parties to a dispute may prefer to go straight to arbitration rather than become involved in court proceedings. Hence, they may voluntarily agree before or after the dispute to refer it to arbitration. Many construction contracts provide for such a reference, as do various codes of practice initiated by trade associations which are incorporated in their standard form contracts used by members.

The parties are free to agree on the number of persons whom they wish to act as arbitrators. They may appoint the arbitrators themselves or provide a procedure for the appointments to be made. They may, for example, provide that the appointment shall be made by the President of a relevant professional society, such as the Royal Institution of Chartered Surveyors.

Early neutral evaluation
2.27   Under this process a neutral person, commonly a lawyer, hears a summary of each party's case and gives a non-binding assessment of the merits. This can then be used as a basis for settlement or further negotiation.

Expert determination
2.28   Here a neutral person who is an expert in the subject matter is appointed to decide the dispute, the decision being binding on the parties.

Mediation
2.29   In mediation a neutral mediator helps the parties to reach a common position. It can be 'facilitative' or 'evaluative'. It is 'facilitative' if the mediator does not advise the parties of his own opinion of the merits of the dispute. It is 'evaluative' if he is expected to express his own opinion.

Mediation is particularly appropriate where the claim is small or not complex, or both. It is also appropriate where it is particularly important to reduce conflict and bitterness between the parties.

Conciliation

2.30   This is similar to mediation but differs in that the conciliator moves from one party to the other, discussing the merits of each side's case and the risks in litigation. Sometimes, if the conciliation does not directly lead to a settlement, the conciliator's role may extend to advising the parties of his assessment of the likely result of a trial. Of course, this is not binding, but it often leads to a settlement.

Chapter 3

Sources of English law

3.1   In this part we explain the direct means by which English law and, since it impacts on English law, European Community law are made. In the case of English law, they are

- legislation
- judicial precedent
- custom (which is now of very little relevance).

Legislation

3.2   Legislation plays an important part in the areas of company law, land law and employment law and of 'social legislation'. 'Social legislation' is concerned essentially with regulating the day-to-day running of the social system rather than with rights and duties between individuals. Examples of 'social legislation' are the Landlord and Tenant Acts, the Rent Act 1977, the Housing Act 1988 and the Town and Country Planning Act 1990. In these areas, legislation lays down the foundations of the relevant law which then has to be interpreted by the courts and applied by them and others involved. In the case of contract law and tort law, on the other hand, the foundations of that law are laid down by judicial precedent and legislation has only served to amend or add to it to a limited extent.

3.3   Sometimes a statute is described as a consolidating or codifying statute. Where a branch of statute law has evolved piecemeal, a consolidating statute may be passed, for the purpose of clarification, containing substantially the existing law in a consolidated form. An example of a modern consolidation Act is the Income and Corporation Taxes Act 1988. A consolidation Act only consolidates statute law: a codifying Act may codify both case law and statute law, a notable example being the Sale of Goods Act 1893 (which has now been consolidated with subsequent amending statutes in the Sale of Goods Act 1979). However, the object of both consolidation and codification is to simplify and clarify the existing law rather than to effect substantial alterations to it.

3.4   There are essentially three types of legislation: Acts of Parliament; subordinate legislation, which mainly consists of delegated legislation made by government ministers, local authorities and other bodies under powers derived from parliament; and the legislation of the European Community.

Acts of Parliament

3.5   Subject to an exception which we discuss in para 3.39 below, the validity of an Act of Parliament cannot be questioned in, or by, the courts; the Act has to be applied by them. In certain cases the validity of subordinate legislation and of most types of legislation of the European Community can be challenged.

3.6   The 'official' copies of Acts of Parliament are printed by the Queen's Printer and published by the Stationery Office which also publishes annual volumes of Public Acts. Various publishers publish annual volumes of Acts of Parliament verbatim, as well as in unbound parts soon after the Act is passed; a leading series is *Halsbury's Statutes of England*. Acts of Parliament are now available free on the Internet within days of royal assent. They are on http://www.hmso.gov.uk/acts.htm. They are also available on the LexisNexis electronic database.

Citation

3.7   Until 1963, statutes were cited by the date of the regnal year or years of the parliamentary session in which the Act was passed, the regnal year being assessed from the monarch's accession, together with a chapter number which denoted the order in which it received the royal assent. Thus, the Law of Property Act 1925 is cited '15 and 16 Geo 5, c 20'. Acts passed after 1962 are cited by reference to the calendar year, not the regnal year, in which they were passed. Thus, the Misrepresentation Act 1967 is cited '1967, c 7'.

Of course, the more usual way to refer to an Act is by reference to its short title, eg 'the Misrepresentation Act 1967'.

Commencement and repeal

3.8   An Act of Parliament comes into operation when it receives the royal assent unless, as frequently occurs, some other date is specified in the Act or it is to be appointed by a commencement order (which is normally made by a government minister). Sometimes a commencement order is not made for a considerable time. An extreme example concerns the Easter Act 1928; it provides a fixed date for Easter but a commencement order has not yet been made.

A commencement order may only relate to certain parts of an Act, so that the legislation is brought into force in a piecemeal fashion. For example, while most of the Estate Agents Act 1979 has been brought into force, a commencement order has not yet been made in relation to the requirement for bonding and the provisions on standards of competence.

An Act of Parliament may be repealed expressly by a subsequent statute, or impliedly by being inconsistent with it[1] (although there is a presumption against implied repeal).[2] Unless the contrary intention appears, repeal does not:

- revive a previously repealed rule of law; or
- affect existing rights and liabilities, or legal proceedings, civil or criminal.[3]

1   *Ellen Street Estates Ltd v Minister of Health* [1934] 1 KB 590, CA.
2   Para 3.24 below.
3   Interpretation Act 1978, ss 15 and 16.

Subordinate legislation

3.9   Various institutions, other than Parliament, have legislative powers. Such legislation is subordinate since it is made by bodies with limited powers and it is always subject to abrogation or amendment by Act of Parliament. Subordinate legislation can be quashed in appropriate cases if it is incompatible with a 'Convention right' under the Human Rights Act 1998.[1] In addition, subordinate legislation may be held invalid by the courts in the types of case described in para 3.13. In this respect, it may be contrasted with an Act of

Parliament. An Act of Parliament cannot be overridden by our courts, except to the extent that it is inconsistent with Community law which is directly applicable or of direct effect.[2]

Subordinate legislation can be of two types: delegated legislation and autonomic legislation.

1   Para 3.30 below.
2   Para 3.39 below.

Delegated legislation

3.10   Delegated legislation comprises the great bulk of subordinate legislation. Delegated legislation is legislation made by some executive body under powers delegated to it by Act of Parliament. An Act of Parliament often gives powers to some bodies, such as the Queen in Council (in effect the government), a minister or a local authority, to make regulations and prescribe for their breach.

There is a vast amount of delegated legislation – the number of pieces made annually being numbered in thousands, whereas the number of Public and Private Acts of Parliament a year rarely exceeds 70. An example of an Act giving very wide powers of delegated legislation is the European Communities Act 1972.[1] Delegated legislation made by the central executive may be required to be made by Order in Council made by the Queen in Council, otherwise it takes the form of regulations, rules or orders made by a minister or government department. Generally, delegated legislation of these types must be made by statutory instrument.

1   Para 3.45 below.

3.11   Statutory instruments are printed by the Queen's Printer and are published by the Stationery Office. They are available free on the Internet at http://www.hmso.gov.uk/stat.htm and they are also included in the LexisNexis database.

Statutory instruments are cited by calendar year and number and by a short title. For instance, the Land Registration (Official Searches) Rules 1993 are cited SI 1993, No 3276. A statutory instrument comes into effect when made unless, as is usual, it specifies a later date.

3.12   Another type of delegated legislation is the byelaw. Byelaws are made by local authorities, public corporations and certain other bodies authorised by statute. Although general in operation, they are restricted to the locality or undertaking to which they apply. They are not made by statutory instrument.

3.13   All forms of delegated legislation are invalid if they are proved to be ultra vires. Delegated legislation is ultra vires if it is in excess of the powers conferred by the enabling statute on the rule-making body (substantive ultra vires); or if it is made in breach of a mandatory part of the procedure concerning its making prescribed by that statute (procedural ultra vires); or, in the case of byelaws only, if it is patently unreasonable, or so uncertain as to have no ascertainable meaning, or so unclear in its effect as to be incapable of certain application in any given situation, or repugnant to the general law (in which cases it is regarded as substantively ultra vires).[1]

The invalidity of delegated legislation is either challenged directly before the courts on an application for judicial review or raised as a defence to a court action which concerns the application of the delegated legislation.

1   *Nash v Finlay* (1901) 85 LT 682, DC; *Powell v May* [1946] 1 All ER 444, DC; *Percy v Hall* [1996] 4 All ER 523, CA.

Autonomic legislation

3.14   Autonomic legislation is legislation made by the Queen by Order in Council, under the royal prerogative. There is no power under the prerogative to alter the general law of the land¹ but there is a limited prerogative power to legislate for the dependent territories, the armed forces and the civil service. The prerogative comprises those independent powers left to the Crown by Parliament, and legislation outside the prerogative powers of the Crown will be held invalid by the courts if it is not delegated legislation (ie made with statutory authority).

1   *Proclamations' Case* (1611) 12 Co Rep 74.

Interpretation

3.15   The courts are often faced with the question whether a particular matter or piece of conduct falls within the wording of a particular legislative provision. The exposition which follows is concerned with the interpretation of Acts of Parliament but, essentially, the same rules apply to the interpretation of subordinate legislation.

It is often said that in interpreting statutes, the courts are trying to discover Parliament's intentions from the words of the statute.¹ However, as Lord Reid observed in *Black-Clawson International Ltd v Papierwerke Waldhof-Aschaffenburg AG,²* 'that is not quite accurate. We are seeking the meaning of the words which Parliament used. We are seeking not what Parliament meant but the true meaning of what they said'. This does not mean that a court must give a statutory provision its historical meaning (ie interpret it as if it was doing so when it was enacted). Statutes are almost always intended to operate for many years and, unless they are not, a court is free to apply the current meaning of the provision to the context and conditions of the present day. In *Royal College of Nursing of the United Kingdom v Department of Health and Social Security,³* for example, the House of Lords interpreted the Abortion Act 1967 as applying to a medical method of inducing an abortion whose first reported use was in 1971, so that Parliament could not have had it in mind when it enacted the legislation.

Unfortunately, the courts have not adopted a consistent approach to the task of statutory interpretation. Instead, they have taken two, radically different, approaches to this task: the 'literal approach' and the 'purposive approach'.

Although the courts are increasingly taking the purposive approach, they are certainly not consistent in doing so. For example, although the House of Lords has taken a purposive approach in a number of recent cases,⁴ it took the literal approach to the question of whether a car park is a 'road' in the Road Traffic Act 1988 (and held that it was not) in *Cutter v Eagle Star Insurance Co Ltd,⁵* and the majority of their Lordships took the literal approach to the Data Protection Act 1984, s 5 in *R v Brown.⁶* It is impossible to know in advance which approach the court will adopt in a particular case. We shall consider them in turn, and then deal with various rules of interpretation which apply whichever of the two approaches is adopted.

1   But see para 3.27 below.
2   [1975] 1 All ER 810 at 814.
3   [1981] 1 All ER 545, HL.
4   See, for example, *Re C (a minor)* [1996] 4 All ER 871, HL; *Re Ismail* [1998] 3 All ER 1007, HL.
5   [1998] 4 All ER 417, HL.
6   [1996] 1 All ER 545, HL.

The two approaches to interpretation

The literal approach

3.16   The literal approach to statutory interpretation is otherwise known as the literal rule. This states that the meaning of the statute must be found by interpreting the words used in their ordinary, literal and grammatical sense. If the words can be so interpreted a judge must give effect to that interpretation, unless the statute or the legal context in which the words are used compels him to give the word a special meaning, even though he considers that it produces an undesirable, inexpedient or unjust result or that Parliament cannot have intended it.¹ In *IRC v Hinchy,²* the House of Lords had to interpret the Income

Tax Act 1952, s 25(3), which provided that a person who failed to deliver a correct income tax return should forfeit 'the sum of twenty pounds and treble the tax which he ought to be charged under this Act'. The House of Lords held that, in addition to the penalty of £20, a taxpayer who had declared only part of his Post Office interest was liable to pay treble the whole tax chargeable for the year, and not merely treble the tax on the undeclared income.

1   *Duport Steels Ltd v Sirs* [1980] 1 All ER 529, HL; *Leedale v Lewis* [1982] 3 All ER 808, HL.
2   [1960] 1 All ER 505, HL.

3.17   It may happen that to interpret statutory words according to their ordinary, literal and grammatical sense in their context would give rise to manifest absurdity, repugnancy or inconsistency *with the rest of the statute*. In such a case, the so-called 'golden rule' permits a judge to modify the literal interpretation so as to avoid such a result. The classical exposition of the golden rule was given by Lord Wensleydale in *Grey v Pearson*.[1]

> 'in construing... statutes ..., the grammatical and ordinary sense of the words is to be adhered to, unless that would lead to some absurdity or some repugnance or inconsistency with the rest of the instrument, in which case the grammatical and ordinary sense of the words may be modified so as to avoid that absurdity or inconsistency, but no further.'

A modern example is provided by the House of Lords' decision in *McMonagle v Westminster City Council*.[2] M was charged with the offence of using premises as a 'sex encounter establishment' without a licence, contrary to the Local Government (Miscellaneous Provisions) Act 1982. The definition of such an establishment was 'premises at which performances which are *not* unlawful are given, which ... comprise the sexual stimulation of persons admitted to the premises ...'. M's defence was that it had not been proved that the performances in question were *not* unlawful and that, if they were unlawful, a licence was not required under the plain words of the Act. The House of Lords rejected this interpretation as being absurd, and held that the words 'which are not unlawful' were mere surplusage which had been introduced by an incompetent draftsman solely to emphasise that a licence conferred no immunity from the ordinary criminal law. Thus, the prosecution did not have to prove that the performances were not unlawful and it was no defence that they were unlawful.

1   (1857) 6 HL Cas 61 at 106.
2   [1990] 1 All ER 993, HL.

Purposive approach

3.18   Under this approach to statutory interpretation, the words in a statute are interpreted not only in their ordinary, literal and grammatical sense but also with reference to their context and purpose. If the judge thinks that the interpretation of the words in their ordinary, literal and grammatical sense would produce a result contrary to the purpose of the statute as he understands it to be, the judge may construe them in any other way consistent with that purpose which the words are capable of bearing. This approach differs from the literal approach in that, while the court starts with a consideration of the ordinary, literal and grammatical meaning of the words, it can depart from that meaning not only in cases covered by the golden rule but also where that meaning would give rise to a result contrary to the purpose of the statute. In *Richard Thomas and Baldwins Ltd v Cummings*,[1] for example, a provision in the Factories Act 1937, which required the fencing of dangerous parts of a machine while it was in motion, was held not to apply where a worker turned the machine by hand. The machine could not have been repaired while it was fenced, and the purpose of the statute was to protect workers operating machines with dangerous parts.

1   [1955] 1 All ER 285, HL.

3.19 As part of the purposive approach, judges can correct obvious drafting errors in suitable cases by adding, omitting or substituting words. In *Inco Europe Ltd v First Choice Distribution*,[1] the House of Lords held that, before doing so, a court must be abundantly sure of three matters:

- the intended purpose of the statute;
- that by inadvertence, the draftsman and Parliament had failed to give effect to that purpose in the provision in question; and
- the substance of the provision that Parliament would have made, although not necessarily the precise words that it would have used, had the error in the Bill been noticed.

The House added that sometimes, even when these conditions are met, the court may find itself inhibited from interpreting the statute in accordance with what it is satisfied was Parliament's intention. The alteration in language required may be too far-reaching; the insertion must not be too big, or too much at variance with the language used by Parliament. Moreover, the subject matter of the legislation may call for a strict interpretation, as in the case of penal legislation.

On the other hand, if a court is faced with a factual situation for which the statute has not provided, for reasons other than a drafting error, even the purposive approach does not permit the court to fill the gap. To do so would be to attribute to Parliament an intention which it never had. Like the literal approach, the purposive approach is limited to giving effect to the words of the statute. It does not extend to reading words into it to rectify an anomaly or absurdity, *unless clear reason is found within the body* of the Act itself;[2] a judge cannot attribute to Parliament an intention which Parliament never had. For a judge to do so was condemned by Lord Simonds in *Magor and St Mellons RDC v Newport Corpn*,[3] as a 'naked usurpation of the legislative function under the thin disguise of interpretation'. His Lordship added that if a gap is disclosed the remedy lies in an amending Act.

1 [2000] 2 All ER 109, HL.
2 *Stock v Frank Jones (Tipton) Ltd* [1978] 1 All ER 948, HL.
3 [1951] 2 All ER 839 at 841.

General rules of interpretation
3.20 Whichever of the two approaches to interpretation is adopted, the court will be assisted by various general rules of interpretation. Indeed, if the provision proves to be uncertain or ambiguous, one or more of these rules may be determinative of the court's interpretation.

Words must be understood in their context
3.21 A word in itself does not have an absolute meaning; its meaning is relative to its context.[1] Part of this rule is the principle that a statute must be read as a whole. Every section must be read in the light of every other section,[2] including the interpretation section normally found towards the end of a statute. This can assist in resolving ambiguities, inconsistencies or redundancies in a particular provision.

1 See Lord Reid in *Pinner v Everett* [1969] 3 All ER 257 at 258.
2 *Beswick v Beswick* [1967] 2 All ER 1197, HL.

Ejusdem generis rule
3.22 An important example of this principle is the *ejusdem generis* (of the same class) rule. Enactments often list things which are so similar as to form a class to which a provision is to apply, following the list with some general words implying that some other similar things are intended to fall within the class. Whether something which is not specified in the

list of things falls within the general words depends upon whether or not it is ejusdem generis as the specified things. In *Powell v Kempton Park Racecourse Co Ltd*,[1] an Act prohibited the keeping of a 'house, office, room or other place' for betting with persons resorting thereto. The House of Lords held that Tattersall's Ring (an uncovered enclosure of a superior sort) at a racecourse was not ejusdem generis as the specified things, and was not therefore an 'other place' within the meaning of the Act, since the specific words 'house, office, room' created a *genus* (class) of indoor places. There cannot be a *genus* for the purposes of the present rule unless the 'other' thing is preceded by a list of at least two or more specific things which share the same common characteristics.[2]

1   [1899] AC 143, HL.
2   *Quazi v Quazi* [1979] 3 All ER 897, HL.

The mischief rule

3.23   The literal approach breaks down, in particular, in the case of an ambiguity. In such a case, a judge may apply the mischief rule, which is often called the rule in *Heydon's Case*[1] since it was formulated there. This rule, which may simply be another way of expressing the purposive approach, is best paraphrased by the statement by Lord Halsbury in *Eastman Photographic Materials Co Ltd v Comptroller-General of Patents, Designs and Trade Marks*: 'We are to see what was the law before the Act was passed, and what was the mischief or defect for which the law had not provided, what remedy Parliament appointed, and the reason for the remedy.'[2]

An example of the application of the mischief rule is *Gorris v Scott*.[3] The claimant claimed in respect of the loss of his sheep which were washed overboard and drowned while the defendant was engaged in carrying them by sea. The loss was due to the fact that, in breach of the statutory duty to do so, no pens had been provided. The claimant based his claim on the fact that the loss had been caused by the breach of the statutory duty. However, it was held that the purpose of the relevant provision was not to prevent loss overboard but to minimise the spread of contagious diseases, and that therefore the claim did not fall within the 'mischief' of the Act.

1   (1584) 3 Co Rep 7a.
2   [1898] AC 571 at 573.
3   (1874) LR 9 Exch 125.

Presumptions

3.24   There are a number of presumptions as to the intentions of Parliament, which may be rebutted by the express words of the Act or by necessary implication from the subject matter of the Act itself.

Against retrospective effect of legislation   This presumption is not concerned with when a statute comes into operation but with whether it affects factual situations which arose before that date. Parliament is presumed not to have intended to alter the law applicable to pre-existing events, contracts or other transactions in a manner which is unfair to those concerned in them, unless a contrary intention appears.[1] The greater the degree of unfairness, the stronger will have to be the evidence that Parliament intended the legislation to have retrospective effect.[1]

Against alteration of the law   Parliament is presumed not to intend to change the law, with the result that, unless the words of the statute unmistakably indicate that the law is changed, they must be interpreted so as not to alter it.[2] As part of the presumption against alteration in the law there are certain more specific presumptions: against the restriction of individual liberty; and against compulsory deprivation of property, at least without compensation.

Against the Crown being bound   The Crown is not bound by a statute unless there can be gathered from it an intention that it should be bound.[3] The presumption also extends to employees of the Crown, in the course of their duties, and to Crown property. However, statutes frequently provide that they are to bind the Crown. Even if a statute does not expressly bind the Crown, a court may construe it as doing so by necessary implication.

Other presumptions made in construing a statute are those against implied repeal of earlier legislation by later, apparently inconsistent, legislation (the earlier only being impliedly repealed if reconciliation is logically impossible); against ousting the jurisdiction of the courts; and against inconsistency with 'Convention rights' under the Human Rights Act 1998, European Community law or international law.

1   *L'Office Cherifien des Phosphates Unitramp SA v Yamashita-Shinnihon Steamship Co Ltd* [1994] 1 All ER 20, HL.
2   *Leach v R* [1912] AC 305, HL.
3   *Tamlin v Hannaford* [1950] 1 KB 18, CA; *Lord Advocate v Dumbarton District Council* [1990] 1 All ER 1, HL.

Aids to interpretation
Intrinsic aids
3.25   The rule that the enactment must be read as a whole makes it of obvious importance to know what parts of an Act may be regarded as intrinsic aids to interpretation.

Long title and short title   These are part of the Act, but, in practice, the courts do not refer to the short title and only refer to the long title to resolve an ambiguity; in other words the long title is not allowed to restrict the clear meaning of a provision. In *Re Groos*,[1] it was held that the Wills Act 1861, s 3, applied to the will of an alien, even though the long title read: 'An Act to amend the law with respect to wills of personal estates made by British subjects.'

Punctuation and headings to a section or group of sections are inserted into a Bill by the parliamentary draftsmen and can be altered any time up to royal assent. They are not debated by parliament and are therefore not part of the Act. The result is that they may only be looked at to determine the purpose, as opposed to the scope, of the section.[2]

Schedules which are used, for instance, to list repeals and set out transitional or more detailed provisions, are part of the Act, but they cannot affect the interpretation of a word in the body of the Act unless it is ambiguous or uncertain.[3]

1   [1904] P 269.
2   *DPP v Schildkamp* [1969] 3 All ER 1640, HL; *R v Kelt* [1977] 3 All ER 1099, CA.
3   *Ellerman Lines Ltd v Murray* [1931] AC 126, HL.

Extrinsic aids
3.26   Unlike most continental courts, an English or Welsh court may not generally look at material outside the four walls of the Act to find Parliament's intention. It cannot, for instance, generally look at reports of the parliamentary debates on the Bill which became the Act.[1] This may appear to fly in the face of common sense but it must be admitted that it might be difficult in some cases to determine a legislative intent from a two, or more, sided parliamentary debate, especially where the Bill has been subject to amendment in Parliament. However, the following extrinsic aids (including parliamentary debates) can be looked at for limited purposes:

Dictionaries can be consulted to ascertain the range of meaning, for the purpose of the literal rule, of words which have no particular legal meaning.[2]

Parliamentary debates   In 1992, the majority of the House of Lords in *Pepper v Hart*[3] held that the courts can refer to reports of debates or proceedings in Parliament relating to the provision in question as an aid to interpreting a statute if it is ambiguous or absurd or if its literal meaning would lead to absurdity. Even in such cases, it held, reference to parliamentary reports is only possible if:

- it discloses the mischief aimed at or the legislative intention behind the ambiguous or obscure words;
- the statements relied on were by a minister or other promoter of the Bill; and
- those statements are clear.

Pepper v Hart was concerned with a provision in the Finance Act 1976 whereby the cash equivalent of an in-house benefit was taxable. The Act provided that the cash equivalent of the benefit was 'an amount equal to the cost of the benefit' and by s 63(2) the cost of the benefit was 'the amount of any expense incurred in or in connection with its provision'. The in-house benefit in question was a reduced school fees scheme for members of staff at a school. The majority of the House of Lords held that s 63(2) was clearly ambiguous because the 'expense incurred in or in connection with' the provision of in-house benefits could be interpreted either as the marginal cost caused by the provision of the benefit or as a proportion of the total cost incurred in providing the service for all parents (the average cost). The majority of the House held that the requirements set out above were satisfied and that reference to a statement made by the government minister in Parliament made it clear that Parliament had intended to assess the expense incurred in the provision of in-house benefits, particularly concessionary fees, on the basis of the marginal cost to the employer, and not on the average cost of the benefit.

The admissibility of parliamentary materials is of obvious importance where a purposive approach is being taken to the interpretation of a statute.

Reports of committees or of the Law Commission containing proposals for legislation which have been presented to Parliament and resulted in the enactment in question can be looked at to discover the state of the pre-existing law and the mischief which the enactment was passed to remedy. An example is provided by the House of Lords' decision in *Black-Clawson International Ltd v Papierwerke Waldhof-Aschaffenburg AG*,[4] where their Lordships referred to the report of a committee, which had resulted in the passing of an Act, to discover what the pre-existing law was understood to be and what its mischief was. Two of the five Lords of Appeal, Viscount Dilhorne and Lord Simon, went further and stated that it was permissible to look at such a report for a direct statement of what the resulting enactment meant. This minority statement went further than our courts have been prepared to go in the past. Lord Reid and Lord Wilberforce disagreed with it expressly in *Black-Clawson,* and subsequent House of Lords' decisions have indicated that it is not correct.[5] However, in a more recent case the House of Lords was helped in determining the meaning of a section by reference to a Law Commission report which had resulted in the legislation in question.[6] We think that this approach will now prevail.

Judicial precedent   The interpretation given by a court to a statutory provision or word may be binding in relation to *that* provision or word in *that* Act, in accordance with the principles of the doctrine of judicial precedent (paras 3.47 to 3.59 below).

Interpretation Act 1978   The Act lays down various definitions which apply unless there is a contrary intention, express or implied, in a particular statute. For example, 'unless the contrary intention appears, (a) words importing the masculine gender shall include females; and (b) words in the singular shall include the plural and words in the plural shall include the singular'. Again, '"person" includes a body of persons corporate or unincorporate'.[7]

1   Assam Railways and Trading Co Ltd v IRC [1935] AC 445, HL; Davis v Johnson [1978] 1 All ER 1132, HL.
2   See, for example A-G's Reference (No 1 of 1988) [1989] 2 All ER 1, HL.
3   [1993] 1 All ER 42, HL.
4   [1975] 1 All ER 810, HL.
5   R v Ayres [1984] 1 All ER 619, HL; R v Allen [1985] 2 All ER 641, HL.
6   I v DPP [2001] UKHL 10, [2001] 2 All ER 583, HL.
7   Section 6 and Sch 1 respectively.

Cases where a Convention right is involved

3.27   The frequent but somewhat inaccurate statement that, in interpreting a statute, a court is trying to discover Parliament's intentions, is particularly hard to accept where a Convention right under the Human Rights Act 1998 is involved. The reason is that a court is required by s 3(1) of the Act to interpret legislation to comply with a Convention right so far as possible, which involves an approach to interpretation radically different from that described above, as we shall see in para 3.32 below.

Acts giving effect to international conventions

3.28   Increasingly, the purpose of an Act of Parliament is to put into domestic effect an international convention. In such a case recourse may be had to the terms of the convention if a provision of the Act is ambiguous or vague.[1]

Sometimes, an Act actually incorporates the convention. In such a case there are no limits on recourse to the terms of the convention because they have been made provisions of the Act. Conventions are apt to be more loosely worded than Acts of Parliament, and in James Buchanan & Co Ltd v Babco Forwarding and Shipping (UK) Ltd[2] the House of Lords held that a court must interpret the English text of an incorporated convention in a broad and sensible manner unconstrained by the technical rules of English law, and that if there is doubt about the true construction of the English text the court can look at an authorised text in a foreign language to resolve it. In the event of ambiguity or obscurity in the convention, the court can look at material in the public records of the international conference at which it was drafted provided that that material was intended to clear up the ambiguity or obscurity.[3]

1   Post Office v Estuary Radio [1967] 3 All ER 663, CA.
2   [1977] 3 All ER 1048, HL.
3   Fothergill v Monarch Airlines Ltd [1980] 2 All ER 696, HL.

European Convention on Human Rights and Human Rights Act 1998

3.29   The European Convention on Human Rights (ECHR), taken together with the Human Rights Act 1998, is of major importance. The provisions of the Act referred to below have great influence over the interpretation and development of the law by the judges and over new legislation.

Impact of the Act

3.30   The Human Rights Act 1998 'brings home' those Convention rights set out in Sch 1 to the Act. Essentially what this means is that remedies are available in courts and tribunals (hereafter simply 'courts') in England and Wales in respect of the Convention rights. This has not been achieved by the incorporation of the Convention rights into English law. Unlike directly applicable European Community legislation,[1] the Convention does not automatically take priority over English law. Our domestic courts have not been given a power to disapply an inconsistent Act of Parliament (primary legislation),[2] but the effect of the main provisions in the Act comes close to permitting disapplication without disturbing Parliamentary sovereignty. On the other hand, subordinate legislation incompatible with a Convention right can be quashed unless (leaving aside the possibility of revocation) primary legislation prevents removal of the incompatibility,[2] which it normally will.

1   Para 3.39 below.
2   Human Rights Act 1998, s 3(2).

3.31   The HRA 1998 gives teeth to the Convention rights:

*   by a special provision about statutory interpretation designed, so far as possible, to give effect to legislation in a way which is compatible with the Convention rights;
*   by providing for a court, other than a trial court, to make a declaration of incompatibility if legislation cannot be interpreted so as to be compatible; and
*   by making it unlawful for a public authority, such as a court or local authority, to act in a way incompatible with a Convention right.

Statutory interpretation
3.32   Section 3(1) of HRA 1998 provides that primary legislation (essentially Acts of Parliament) and subordinate legislation must, '*so far as it is possible to do so*, be read and given effect in a way which is compatible with the Convention rights'.[1] This is called 'reading down' the legislation. The courts, where necessary, will prefer a strained but possible interpretation which is consistent with Convention rights to one more consistent with the statutory words themselves. Where necessary to correct a defect in terms of ambiguity or omission the courts are able to insert words into a statute to give effect to a Convention right, although it remains to be seen how far the courts will go in this respect. An example of the operation of HRA 1998, s 3(1) is provided by *Cachia v Faluyi*.[2] This was concerned with the Fatal Accidents Act 1976, s 2(3), which provides that: 'Not more than one action [by a dependant in respect of a wrongful act causing death] shall lie for and in respect of the same subject matter of complaint'. The question for the Court of Appeal was whether this prevented three dependant children pursuing a claim by writ for damages for the death of their mother when a previous writ in the action had been issued but never served on the defendant. On a literal interpretation, the first writ could be regarded as constituting an action, in which case the children would have been prevented from pursuing their claim by the subsequent writ. The Court of Appeal, however, noting that Art 6 of the Convention gave the children a right of access to a court to claim damages for their loss of dependency, and noting HRA 1998, s 3, held that 'action' in the Accidents Act 1976, s 2(3) should be interpreted so as to refer to 'served process' (ie service of the writ) so as to give effect to Art 6. Consequently, the first writ not having been served, s 2(3) did not bar the children's pursuit of their claim by the writ in question.

The approach under HRA 1998, s 3(1) is radically different from traditional techniques of statutory interpretation. There are, however, limits, as indicated by 'as far as possible'. A court cannot construe a statute in a way which Parliament could not conceivably have intended. Perverse interpretation or extensive redrafting is not permissible. In the rare case where the mismatch between Convention rights and the statute is this great, the court will have to make a declaration of incompatibility.

This strong interpretative provision is the lynchpin of HRA 1998.

1   Emphasis added. For differing approaches to the extent of s 3, see *R v A (No 2)* [2001] UKHL 25, [2001] 3 All ER 1.
2   [2001] EWCA Civ 998, [2001] 1 All ER 192, CA.

Declaration of incompatibility
3.33   If a trial court is unable to interpret a statutory provision compatibly with a Convention right, it will have to proceed as normal. The issue of incompatibility can then be raised on appeal or in judicial review proceedings. The High Court, Court of Appeal and House of Lords, if satisfied that a provision of primary legislation is incompatible with

a Convention right, may then make a declaration of incompatibility (and presumably will feel obliged to do so).[1] They may also make such a declaration in respect of a provision of subordinate legislation which is so incompatible if satisfied that (disregarding the possibility of revocation) the primary legislation prevents removal of that incompatibility.[1]

If a declaration of incompatibility is made, the Government and Parliament are not required to take remedial action, although almost certainly they will. A fast-track route for doing so via a ministerial order is provided by HRA 1998, s 10.

1   HRA 1998, s 4.

Unlawful actions

3.34   It is unlawful for a public authority, such as a court or local authority, to act[1] in a way incompatible with a Convention right, unless:

- as the result of one or more provisions of primary legislation, the authority could not have acted differently; or
- in the case of one or more provisions of, or made under, primary legislation which cannot be read or given effect in a way which is compatible with the Convention rights, the authority was acting so as to give effect to or enforce those provisions.[2]

An individual may bring legal proceedings against any public authority in respect of any act which he considers to be unlawful in terms of the Convention rights. A court may grant such relief or remedy (including damages if this is necessary to afford just satisfaction to the person in whose favour they are made) or make an order as it considers appropriate within the terms of HRA 1998.

By HRA 1998, s 9(1), unlawful action of this sort by a court is normally remediable only by way of appeal or judicial review.

Because the prohibition on acting incompatibly with a Convention right only applies to a public authority, it does not in itself permit an individual citizen to enforce a Convention right in proceedings against another private citizen. It is, however, arguable that since the court is a 'public authority' subject to the prohibition it must apply such a right in a dispute between private individuals because it is prohibited from acting in contravention of such a right.

1   'Act' includes a failure to act: Human Rights Act 1998, s 6(6).
2   HRA 1998, s 6(1)-(3).

The Convention rights

3.35   The Convention rights specified in HRA 1998, Sch 1 include:

- the right not to be deprived of liberty save in specified cases, eg after conviction or lawful arrest, and in accordance with a procedure prescribed by law;
- the right to a fair trial (including the presumption of innocence);
- the right to respect for private and family life;
- the freedom of expression; and
- the freedom of assembly and association.

The exercise of the last three rights or freedoms mentioned may be restricted by the law on specified grounds if this is necessary in a democratic society in (for example) the interests of national security, for the prevention of disorder or crime, for the protection of health or morals or for the protection of the rights and freedoms of others.

Application of Convention rights

3.36   HRA 1998, s 2(1) provides that, in determining a question which has arisen in connection with a Convention right, a court must *take into account* the case law of the European Court of Human Rights and the European Commission of Human Rights[1] (which were effectively merged in 1998 in a restructured European Court of Human Rights). The terms of s 2(1) make it clear that these decisions are not binding; they are to be taken into account along with other relevant decisions. The right of individual petition to the European Court of Human Rights remains, however, and a failure by an English court to apply a decision of that Court could lead to an application to it.

1   The Commission decided on the admissibility of applications (ie complaints of a breach of the ECHR).

Legislation of the European Community

3.37   The fundamental legislation of the European Community is to be found in the treaties, including amending treaties, which established the three Communities - the European Economic Community (EEC), the European Coal and Steel Community (ECSC) and the European Atomic Energy Community (EURATOM). The EEC, now known as the European Community (EC) is easily the most important of the three. Although in strict law there are three distinct Communities, in practice they are administered as one, sharing a single Council and Commission.

The three Communities' structures and law are one of the three areas which make up the European Union established under the Treaty of Maastricht which came into force in 1993. The other two areas are inter-governmental co-ordination on matters of foreign policy and common external defence, and political inter-governmental co-operation on internal affairs such as policing, criminal justice and immigration.

Since 'European Union' is a wider concept than the legal order of the three Communities it is common to refer to that legal order as 'the Community' or 'the European Community', and this is the course adopted in this book. The singular, rather than plural, of the term is used because this reflects the practical reality of the situation.

The overwhelming mass of the Community legislation is found not in the treaties referred to above but in regulations, directives and decisions of the Community's organs. Community legislation is largely concerned with economic matters, such as agriculture, free trade and fair competition, but it also deals with other matters, such as immigration, employment and other social matters.

Regulations, directives and decisions

3.38   Regulations have general application and are made by the Council of Ministers of the European Union (a political body composed normally of foreign ministers) or the Commission (a supranational body composed of the highest officials) under the treaties.

Directives can be issued or decisions made by the Council or the Commission. Directives are directed to member states, who are obliged to implement them although they have a choice as to the form and methods of implementation. Decisions are addressed either to a member state or to an individual or institution. They are a formal method of enunciating administrative decisions effecting the policy of the Community and are binding on the addressee.

Regulations, directives and decisions are published in the *Official Journal of the European Communities*. The current forms of numerical citation can be exemplified as follows: Reg (EC) 2094 [1]/96[2]; Dec 96[2]/2[1]/EC; Dir 93[2]/13[1]/EEC.

1   Number in series for year made.
2   Year made.

Direct applicability and direct effect

3.39   In discussing the types of legislation of the Community, a fundamental point must be emphasised at the outset: regulations are *'directly applicable'* in the sense that they confer rights and duties on individuals and institutions which are enforceable in the courts of member states without being re-enacted by legislation in those states. This is provided by the treaties establishing the Community. However, although the treaties conclude the matter according to *Community law*, they do not in themselves give the concept of 'direct applicability' legal effect in the *law of the United Kingdom*. The reason is that treaty provisions do not become part of our law unless they have been incorporated into it by legislation. Such incorporation has been achieved by the European Communities Act 1972, s 2(1),[1] which provides that those rights and duties which are, as a matter of Community law, 'directly applicable' or 'directly effective' are to have legal effect in the UK.

Section 2(4) of the 1972 Act goes on to provide that Acts of Parliament passed or to be passed shall have effect subject to the rules of Community law which are directly applicable or of direct effect. According to the decisions of the House of Lords in *R v Secretary of State for Transport, ex p Factortame Ltd*[2] and *R v Secretary of State for Transport, ex p Factortame Ltd (No 2)*,[3] the effect of s 2(4) seems to be to imply into every piece of United Kingdom legislation a term that it takes effect subject to directly applicable or directly effective Community law and to require the United Kingdom courts to override a piece of United Kingdom legislation to the extent that it is inconsistent with Community law which is directly applicable or of direct effect.

It is inconceivable that a UK court would so act without first seeking a preliminary ruling from the European Court confirming the inconsistency.[4] Pending the preliminary ruling, a UK court may suspend the operation of the Act of Parliament by granting an interlocutory injunction.[5]

To the extent that directly applicable or directly effective Community law prevails over an Act of Parliament under United Kingdom law, the sovereignty of Parliament has been limited.

1   The European Communities Act 1972 has been stated by a divisional court to be a constitutional statute which cannot be impliedly repealed: *Thoburn v Sunderland City Council* [2002] EWHC 195 (Admin), [2002] 4 All ER 156.
2   [1989] 2 All ER 692, HL.
3   [1991] 1 All ER 70, ECJ and HL.
4   Para 2.20 above.
5   *R v Secretary of State for Transport, ex p Factortame Ltd* [1989] 2 All ER 692, HL.

3.40   No form of Community legislation, other than regulations, is expressly stated in the treaties establishing the Community to be directly applicable. It was once thought that these other forms could only take effect in member states if they were transposed into national law by them. However, in 1963 it was established by the European Court of Justice that the provisions of treaties of the Community could directly confer rights or impose obligations on individuals without transposition or proper transposition into national law.[1] This concept of *direct effect* has subsequently been extended to directives[2] and decisions.[3] In *Van Duyn v Home Office*,[4] for example, the European Court held that a directive was of binding effect so as to confer rights on the claimant against the United Kingdom government even though the UK had not implemented that directive. In order to have direct effect, a treaty provision, directive or decision must be unconditional and sufficiently precise.[5]

Where it exists, the direct effect of a directive is narrower than the direct applicability of a regulation or the direct effect of a treaty provision. The reason is that directives can only have 'vertical' direct effect (ie in favour of an individual against the state or an emanation of the state) and not, unlike regulations and treaty provisions, 'horizontal' effect (ie as between individuals in the state or in favour of the state or an emanation of the state against an individual). In other words, they can only confer rights on individuals, and not obligations on them. This was held by the European Court in *Marshall v Southampton and South West Hampshire Area Health Authority*,[6] where a woman who had been dismissed by an area health authority on reaching the retirement age for women (60, as opposed to 65 for men) succeeded in her claim that this constituted sexual discrimination contrary to a directive. The directive had not been incorporated into English law by United Kingdom legislation but the European Court held that it was directly effective vis-à-vis the employer, the area health authority, because it was an emanation of the state. In the most recent decision on the point, *Kampelmann v Landschaftverbond Westfalen-Lippe*,[7] the European Court held that there is more than one type of emanation of the state. It held that a directive had direct effect against any organisation or body which is subject to the control of the state *or* has special powers beyond those which result from the normal rules applicable to relations between individuals. The Court's decision also indicates that a directive has direct effect against any organisation or body, irrespective of its legal status, which the state has made statutorily responsible for providing a public service and which provides that service under the supervision (as opposed to the control) of the state. Directives have been held directly effective against local or regional authorities, police authorities and the governors of a voluntarily aided school, as well as public authorities providing public health services.

Whether or not a directive is directly effective depends on an examination of the nature, general scheme and wording of its provisions to see whether they are capable of producing direct effects.[3] In practice, very few directives are likely to be regarded as having direct effect.

1   *Algemene Transport-en Expedite Onderneming Van Gend en Loos v Nederlands Administratie Der Belastingadministratie* [1963] ECR 1, ECJ.
2   *Van Duyn v Home Office* [1975] 3 All ER 190, ECJ.
3   *Grad v Finanzamt Traunstein* [1971] CMLR 1, ECJ.
4   [1975] 3 All ER 190, ECJ.
5   *Becker v Finanzamt Münster-Innenstadt* [1982] 1 CMLR 499, ECJ.
6   [1986] 2 All ER 584, ECJ.
7   [1997] ECR I-6907, ECJ.

Untransposed directives: any effect in English law?

3.41   A directive which has not been transposed into the law of a member state and is not of direct effect in the circumstances is not devoid of all effect under that law. It may have effect in two ways. First, a national court can have regard to an untransposed directive in interpreting national regulations. Second, the failure of a member state to transpose a directive may give rise to a liability in damages.

3.42   As the European Court of Justice held in *Marleasing SA v La Comercial Internacional de Alimentación SA*,[1] national law, whenever passed, must be interpreted by a national court in such a way as to give effect to Community directives *so far as possible*. In this case, there was a dispute in a Spanish court between two Spanish companies. One sought to have the memorandum and articles of association of the other (company A) set aside on a ground prescribed by Spanish legislation. Company A argued in reply that its memorandum and articles were in accordance with a directive of the EC Commission. That directive had not been enacted into Spanish law. The European Court held that company A could not rely directly on the unenacted directive in an action with a private entity, but went on to state that the Spanish court was obliged to interpret the Spanish legislation 'in every way possible in the light of the text and aim of the directive to achieve the result envisaged by it'. This, the European Court held, required that in the particular case the Spanish court should ignore a specific provision of Spanish law which was inconsistent with the aim of the directive.

The ruling in *Marleasing* only requires a national court interpreting national law to do so *so far as possible* in such a way as to give effect to a directive which has not been transposed nationally. A national court cannot eliminate national provisions contrary to a provision of a directive which has not been implemented nationally and substitute the terms of the directive. To do so would be to introduce direct effect between individuals under the guise of interpretation.

The correct approach of an English court to the interpretation of untransposed directives has been stated in similar terms in our courts. It has been said that it is for an English court to construe an Act of Parliament so as to accord with a directive, if this can be done without distorting the meaning of the Act, whether the Act came after or before the directive.[2]

1   [1992] 1 CMLR 305, ECJ.
2   *Duke v GEC Reliance Ltd* [1988] 1 All ER 626, HL.

3.43   The European Court of Justice's decision in *Francovich v Italy*[1] indicates that a person may be able to claim from a member state in the courts of that state damages for loss suffered as a result of its failure to transpose (or correctly transpose) nationally a directive. In English law a breach of Community law is a tort tantamount to a breach of statutory duty.[2] In this case, the Italian government had failed to transpose a directive requiring a national institution to be established to ensure that employees of insolvent employers received arrears of salary. Employees of companies which had become insolvent owing substantial arrears of salaries brought proceedings in an Italian court against the Italian Republic, seeking payments under the directive. The European Court held that the directive was not of direct effect because it was insufficiently precise, in that it did not specify which organ of state was to bear the liability. Consequently, the employees could not rely on it in an action in an Italian court. However, the European Court held that the employees could succeed in their claim against the Italian Republic for damages for loss resulting from its failure to transpose the directive in breach of its obligation to do so under Community law. The court stated that three conditions must be fulfilled before such a claim could succeed:

- the objective of the directive must include the conferment of rights on individuals;
- the content of those rights must be ascertainable from the directive itself; and
- there must be a causal link between the state's failure to fulfil its obligations and the loss sustained by the individual.

Francovich concerned non-transposition of a directive. A member state can also be liable for damages where it has tried to transpose its obligations but has done so inadequately or erroneously.[3]

The above principles do not mean that a member state will always be liable if, for example, it fails to transpose by legislation its obligations under Community law, or does so inadequately or erroneously. The reason is that, where a member state is faced with a situation involving legislative choices comparable to those made by Community institutions when they adopt Community measures (legislation), the state will only be liable to individuals who have suffered loss for breach of the Community law if three conditions are met:

- the rule of law infringed must be intended to confer rights on the individuals;
- the breach must be sufficiently serious, in that the state or institution concerned has manifestly and gravely disregarded the limits on its discretion;[4] and
- there must be a direct causal link between the breach of the state's obligation and the loss sustained by the injured individuals.

It has now been established that these conditions also apply where the state has no legislative choices (as where it is obliged to legislate along certain lines by a set date) and has considerably reduced discretion, or even no discretion. In this type of case, the condition of a sufficiently serious breach is much more easily established. The mere infringement may in itself be enough to establish it.[5]

1   [1993] 2 CMLR 66, ECJ.
2   *R v Secretary of State for Transport, ex p Factortame (No 5)* [1998] 1 All ER 736n, DC, affd [1999] 4 All ER 906, HL; *R v Secretary of State for Transport, ex p Factortame (No 7)* [2001] 1 WLR 942. For breach of statutory duty, see ch 22.
3   Two cases are relevant: *Brasserie du Pêcheur SA v Germany; R v Secretary of State for Transport, ex p Factortame (No 4)* [1996] All ER (EC) 301, ECJ.
4   In *R v Secretary of State for Transport, ex p Factortame (No 5)* [1999] 4 All ER 906, HL, it was held that the breach was sufficiently serious to entitle the fishermen to damages for loss directly caused by the breach. The issue of causation was left to be tried.
5   *R v Ministry of Agriculture, Fisheries and Food, ex p Hedley Lomas (Ireland) Ltd* [1996] All ER (EC) 493, ECJ; *Dillenkofer v Germany* [1996] All ER (EC) 917, ECJ.

Supremacy of European Community law

3.44   In Community law, where there is a conflict between binding Community law and a national law of a member state, Community law takes precedence over that national law, whether the latter was enacted before or after the Community law in question.[1]

The position in English law, which is the law that an English court must apply, is more complicated.

Where a provision in an Act of Parliament is *followed* by an inconsistent directly applicable or directly effective provision of Community law, the latter has precedence.[2]

The same is true if the inconsistent directly applicable or directly effective Community law provision *preceded* the provision in the Act if both were made before the European Communities Act 1972. However, if the subsequent Act was made after the 1972 Act the position is as follows. If the Act of Parliament is unclear, an English court will seek to interpret it so as to be consistent with the directly applicable or directly effective Community law provision.[2] The reason is that, as already stated, a statute is presumed to be consistent with Community law. On the other hand, if the Act clearly conflicts with the prior Community law, then, unless the wording of the Act unambiguously compels the court to do otherwise, an Act of Parliament must be construed so as to be consistent with directly applicable or directly effective Community law, and if the Act is unintentionally inconsistent, precedence must be given to Community law.[3]

1   *Costa v ENEL* [1964] ECR 585, ECJ.
2   European Communities Act 1972, s 2.
3   *Macarthys Ltd v Smith* [1979] 3 All ER 325, CA.

Validity of legislation of European Community

3.45   Regulations, directives and decisions are subject to review by the European Court. They can be held invalid by it (but not by a court of a member state[1]) on the grounds of lack of competence, or infringement of any essential procedural requirement, or infringement of the treaties or of any rule of law concerning their application, or misuse of power. Where the validity of a piece of Community legislation is referred to the European Court, the referring court may adopt interim measures suspending the application of that law.[2]

Directives and decisions are transposed into law in the United Kingdom by delegated legislation made under powers given by the European Communities Act 1972, s 2(2), which also governs the implementation in further detail of regulations made by the Council or Commission. Orders in Council and departmental regulations made under these powers can include any provision which might be made in an Act of Parliament.[3] This power to make delegated legislation is the widest given to the executive in modern times apart from times of war. The power must be exercised by way of statutory instrument and presumably such an instrument will be ultra vires if it is not related to the affairs of the Communities. There are a number of limits on this power of delegated legislation; for instance, it cannot be used to impose taxation.

1   *Foto-Frost v Hauptzollamt Lübeck-Ost* [1988] 3 CMLR 57, ECJ.

2   *Atlanta Fruchthandelsgesellschaft mbH v Bundesant für Ernährung and Forswirtschaft* [1995] ECR I-3761, ECJ.
3   European Communities Act 1972, s 2(4).

Interpretation of the legislation of the European Community

3.46   The drafting of the legislation of the Community is quite unlike that of English legislation but, like the legislation of other European countries, is drafted in terms of broad principle, leaving the courts to supply the detail by giving effect to the general intention of the legislature.

The result of this difference in drafting is that the interpretation of the legislation of the Community, whether by the European Court or by an English court,[1] is not based on a slavish interpretation of the words or the grammatical structure of the sentences but on the purpose or intent of the legislation;[2] in other words, a purposive approach involving a preparedness to look at the policy underlying the words of the legislation is taken to the interpretation of such legislation.

1   *HP Bulmer Ltd v J Bollinger SA* [1974] 2 All ER 1226 at 1237–1238.
2   *Van Duyn v Home Office* [1975] 3 All ER 190, ECJ; *Litster v Forth Dry Dock and Engineering Co Ltd* [1989] 1 All ER 1134, HL.

Judicial precedent

3.47   This is the other important legal source and consists of the 'decisions' of courts made in the course of litigation. As will be seen, the 'decisions' of certain courts are more than just authoritative statements of the law since they can be binding (ie must be applied) in subsequent cases where the legally material facts are the same. Whether a particular statement of law made by a judge in one case is binding in a subsequent case depends partly on whether the statement formed the *ratio decidendi* (the reason of the decision) of the case or was merely an *obiter dictum* (something said by the way), and partly on the relative position of the two courts. Even if it is not binding, a judicial statement of the law has a persuasive effect in subsequent cases, the strength of its persuasiveness being a matter of degree, as we explain in para 3.59 below.

Ratio decidendi and obiter dictum

3.48   Only the ratio decidendi of a case can have binding effect. A judgment usually contains the following elements:

a.   A statement of the facts found with an indication, express or implied, of which of them are material facts.
b.   Statements by the judge of the legal principles which apply to the legal issues raised by the material facts and are the reason for his decision.
c.   The actual judgment, decree or order delivered by the judge after application of b. to a., eg that the defendant is liable coupled with an award of damages.

Part c. is binding only on the parties to the case and is not a precedent for the future, nor is part a. in itself. It is part b. of this process which constitutes the ratio decidendi.

3.49   Sometimes the statements of the applicable principles made by the judge may be wider than the material facts necessitate. In such a case the ratio of the decision will be limited to that part of it which applies to the material facts and, to the extent that the statement is wider, it will be obiter dictum.[1] There are two other types of obiter dictum.

First, a statement of legal principle is obiter if it relates to facts which were not found to exist in the case or, if found, were not material. For example, in *Central London Property*

Trust Ltd v High Trees House Ltd, which we discuss later in this book,[2] Denning J's principal statement about promissory estoppel was obiter since it applied to a set of facts which were not found to exist in the case.

Second, a statement of legal principle which relates to some or all of the material facts but is not the basis of the court's decision, eg because it is given in a dissenting judgment or because another material fact prevents the principle applying, is also obiter. A leading example is *Hedley Byrne & Co Ltd v Heller & Partners Ltd*.[3] The House of Lords expressed the opinion that the maker of a statement owes a duty of care, in certain circumstances, to persons who suffer loss in reliance on it. This opinion was obiter because, although it was based on material facts found to exist in the case, the actual decision – that there was no breach of such a duty – was based on another material fact, that the maker of the statement had made it subject to an effective disclaimer of responsibility.

1   *Cassidy v Ministry of Health* [1951] 1 All ER 574, CA.
2   Para 6.17 below.
3   [1963] 2 All ER 575, HL; para 17.25 below.

The hierarchy of the courts and judicial precedent

3.50   We saw earlier that the system of courts is a hierarchy. Essentially, one court is bound by the ratio decidendi of a case decided by another court if it is lower in the hierarchy than the latter and will not be bound by it if it is higher. Magistrates' courts and county courts are bound by the rationes decidendi in cases decided by a High Court judge or the courts above such judges. A High Court judge is bound by the rationes decidendi of cases decided by the Court of Appeal and the House of Lords, and the Court of Appeal is bound by those of the House of Lords. This basic statement will be expanded by taking courts in turn, starting from the top of the hierarchy. For convenience, the word 'decision' will be used to indicate 'ratio decidendi'.

The Court of Justice of the European Communities

3.51   As we said in para 2.20 above, the European Court is now the ultimate court in the following matters:

*   the interpretation of the EC Treaty;
*   the validity and interpretation of the acts of the institutions of the Community or the European Central Bank; and
*   the interpretation of the statutes of bodies established by an act of the Council of the European Union.[1]

Consequently, in these limited areas of jurisdiction the decisions of the European Court bind all English courts. Indeed, the European Communities Act 1972, s 3(1) provides that any question as to the meaning or effect of any of the Treaties, or as to the validity, meaning or effect of any Community instrument, shall be treated as a question of law (and, if not referred to the European Court, be for determination in accordance with the principles laid down by, and any relevant decision of, the European Court or any court attached thereto).

The European Court does not observe a doctrine of binding precedent and does not regard itself as bound by its previous decisions,[2] although it leans in favour of consistency with its previous decisions.

1   As stated in para 2.20 above, the Court is also the ultimate court in respect of corresponding questions under other treaties.
2   *Da Costa en Schaake NV v Nederlandse Belastingadministratie* [1963] CMLR 224, ECJ.

The House of Lords

3.52   A decision of the House of Lords binds all courts inferior to it. Until 1966, a decision of the House of Lords also bound that House. This principle meant that a legal rule might become unalterable by the House of Lords, in which case legislation was the only remedy if a change in the law was desired. In 1966, the House of Lords reversed this principle declaring that it would not be bound by its own decisions where it appeared right to depart from them.[1] The declaration added that in this connection the House would bear in mind the danger of disturbing retrospectively the basis on which contracts, settlements of property and fiscal arrangements have been entered into and also the special need for certainty as to the criminal law.

So far their Lordships have not made much use of their rediscovered freedom and have held that it is not enough that they should consider their previous decision was wrong; there must be an additional factor, such as a change of circumstances on which the decision was based or that it is productive of manifest injustice.[2] One of the few cases in which the House of Lords has overruled one of its previous decisions is *Murphy v Brentwood District Council*[3] where it overruled its decision in *Anns v London Borough Council of Merton*[4] that a local authority, exercising its statutory function of controlling building works, was under a common law duty to take reasonable care to ensure that the building complied with building regulations.

1   [1966] 3 All ER 77.
2   *Fitzleet Estates Ltd v Cherry* [1977] 3 All ER 996, HL.
3   [1990] 2 All ER 908, HL. See paras 21.26–21.27 below.
4   [1977] 2 All ER 492, HL.

The Court of Appeal
3.53   The Civil Division of the Court of Appeal is bound by the previous decisions of the House of Lords. It is also bound by the previous decisions of either division of the Court of Appeal. This was settled by the Court of Appeal in *Young v Bristol Aeroplane Co Ltd*.[1] The Court, however, recognised three exceptional situations where an earlier Court of Appeal decision is not binding on the Civil Division:

*   Where two of its previous decisions conflict. Normally, the Court of Appeal should follow the later of its two decisions, but it does not have to do so if it considers that that decision was wrongly decided.[2] The decision not followed will be deemed to be overruled.[2]
*   The Court must refuse to follow a previous decision of its own which, though not expressly overruled, is inconsistent with a later House of Lords decision.
*   The Court is not bound to follow its previous decision if that decision was given per incuriam (ie through lack of care). A decision is regarded as having been given per incuriam where some relevant statute or binding precedent, which would have affected the decision, was overlooked by the court making it.[3] Only in very rare instances can a case not strictly within this formulation be held to have been decided per incuriam, since such a case must involve a manifest slip or error and it must be likely to cause serious inconvenience in the administration of justice or serious injustice or some equally serious consequence.[4] The Court is not bound to follow another of its decisions (decision B) if, although not itself per incuriam, decision B was based solely on another Court of Appeal decision (decision A) which, unknown to the Court of Appeal when it made decision B, was per incuriam.[5]

While the per incuriam doctrine is also open to the House of Lords as a basis for rejecting one of its own previous decisions, the refusal of the Court of Appeal to follow the House of Lords decision in *Rookes v Barnard*,[6] on the basis that it had been reached per incuriam because of two previous House of Lords decisions, was rejected in strong terms by the House of Lords on appeal in *Cassell & Co Ltd v Broome*.[7]

In addition to the exceptions mentioned in *Young v Bristol Aeroplane*, five other exceptions have been indicated by subsequent cases: a decision by a two-judge Court of Appeal hearing an interlocutory appeal does not bind a court of three;[8] a Court of Appeal judgment on an application for permission to appeal does not have binding force;[9] a Court of Appeal decision in respect of a civil matter which has been subsequently disapproved by the Privy Council need not be followed by the Court of Appeal;[10] a Court of Appeal decision which is irreconcilable with a previous House of Lords decision need not be followed by the Court of Appeal;[11] and, if a Court of Appeal decision goes to the House of Lords and the House decides the appeal on a different ground from that argued in the Court of Appeal, being of the opinion that the issue decided in the Court of Appeal did not arise, the Court of Appeal's decision is not binding on a subsequent Court of Appeal.[12]

1   [1944] 2 All ER 293, CA.
2   *Starmark Enterprises v CPL Distribution Ltd* [2001] EWCA Civ 1252, [2002] Ch 306, CA.
3   See, for example, *R (on the application of W) v Lambeth London Borough Council* [2002] EWCA Civ 613, [2002] 2 All ER 901.
4   *Williams v Fawcett* [1985] 1 All ER 787, CA.
5   *Rakhit v Carty* [1990] 2 All ER 202, HL.
6   [1964] 1 All ER 367, HL.
7   [1972] 1 All ER 801, HL.
8   *Boys v Chaplin* [1968] 1 All ER 283, CA.
9   *Clark v University of Lincolnshire and Humberside* [2000] 3 All ER 752, CA.
10   *Doughty v Turner Manufacturing Co Ltd* [1964] 1 All ER 98, CA.
11   *Great Peace Shipping Ltd v Tsavliris Salvage (International) Ltd* [2002] EWCA Civ 1407, [2002] 4 All ER 689.
12   *R v Secretary of State for the Home Department, ex p Al-Mehdawi* [1989] 1 All ER 777, CA; reversed on appeal on another point [1989] 3 All ER 843, HL.

Divisional courts
3.54   Divisional courts are bound by decisions of the House of Lords and of the Court of Appeal, except, apparently, a Court of Appeal decision which is per incuriam, in that a relevant decision of the House of Lords was not cited.[1] A divisional court is bound by one of its own previous decisions unless the *Young v Bristol Aeroplane* principles apply.[2]

1   *R v Northumberland Compensation Appeal Tribunal, ex p Shaw* [1952] 1 All ER 122, CA.
2   *Huddersfield Police Authority v Watson* [1947] 2 All ER 193, DC.

High Court judges
3.55   A High Court judge is bound by the decisions of the courts mentioned above, but he is not bound by decisions of another High Court judge although he will treat such a decision as strong persuasive authority and will only refuse to follow it if he is convinced that it is wrong, and with a clear statement of the reason for doing so.[1] Where a High Court judge is faced with two conflicting decisions of other High Court judges, he should normally treat the legal point at issue as settled by the second decision, provided the judge in that case has reached his decision after full consideration of the first decision. The only, rare, exception is where the third judge is convinced that the second judge was wrong in not following the first.[2]

1   *Re Hillas-Drake, National Provincial Bank v Liddell* [1944] 1 All ER 375.
2   *Colchester Estates (Cardiff) v Carlton Industries plc* [1984] 2 All ER 601.

Other courts
3.56   County courts and other inferior tribunals are bound by the decisions of all the courts mentioned in the previous paragraphs, and by those of High Court judges sitting alone. The decisions of one of these courts are not binding on another mainly because they are not reported.

Effect of Human Rights Act 1998

3.57   Where a Convention right under the 1998 Act is involved, the strict rules of judicial precedent outlined above may have to be relaxed because, as we have seen in para 3.34 above, the courts must not act in a way incompatible with such a right. It was stated extra-judicially by the Lord Chancellor in 1998 that this means that a court of whatever level must overrule a judicial precedent, however longstanding and whatever its status, which it finds inconsistent with a Convention right.

Application of judicial precedents

3.58   The fact that a judicial precedent may be binding or merely persuasive in a subsequent case has already been touched on. It may also be noticed that a judicial precedent will become devoid of effect if it is overruled by a court competent to do so (normally, one higher in the hierarchy). As opposed to overruling by statute,[1] judicial overruling operates retrospectively, which may have the effect of disturbing financial interests or vested rights generally. For this reason the courts are reluctant to overrule a previous decision unless they consider it is clearly wrong.

Where a precedent is binding on a court, that court must follow it unless that court can distinguish it on the facts. Suppose that the House of Lords has held that if facts A and B exist, principle X applies, and that a case is heard by a High Court judge at first instance where facts A and B exist as well as fact E, which did not exist in the House of Lords' case. The judge may distinguish the House of Lords' case on its material facts and consequently, since that decision will not be binding in relation to the case before him, decide to apply some other principle or to apply principle X by analogy. Since the facts are never identical in any two cases there is wide scope for 'distinguishing'. However, a court inferior to that which gave the previous decision will not normally distinguish it on strained grounds.

1   Para 3.8 above.

3.59   There are various types of persuasive precedents:

- those decisions of courts inferior in the hierarchy to a court which subsequently hears a similar case. Into this category one can also put decisions of the Judicial Committee of the Privy Council on appeals from Commonwealth states, which do not bind English courts or the Privy Council itself. However, the decisions of the Privy Council are particularly persuasive;
- where an otherwise binding precedent is distinguishable; it will nevertheless have persuasive authority;[1]
- obiter dicta, the persuasiveness of which depends on the seniority of the court or prestige of the judge by whom the words were uttered and the relative position of that court and a subsequent court. One of the most significant examples is the 'neighbour principle' expounded by Lord Atkin in 1932 in *Donoghue v Stevenson*,[2] which was much wider than the actual case required but has become the basis of the modern tort of negligence and has been applied in numerous cases since;
- decisions of Irish, Scottish, Commonwealth and US courts, which are being referred to increasingly by our courts.

1   Especially if it is a House of Lords decision: *Re House Property and Investment Co* [1953] 2 All ER 1525.
2   [1932] AC 562, HL.

Literary sources of judicial precedent

3.60   Judicial precedent is discovered in the law reports. A law report does not simply contain the name of the parties, the facts and the decision of the court. It also contains the reasoning on which the result was based.

The publication of law reports began in about 1535. They were usually published under the names of the reporter. Altogether there were some hundreds of different series. Most of these private reports have been reprinted in a series known as the English Reports.

In 1865, the semi-official 'Law Reports' commenced. One or more volumes is published annually under each of the following titles 'Queen's Bench' ('QB') (covering cases decided in the Queen's Bench Division or by the Court of Appeal on appeal therefrom or from a county court), 'Chancery' ('Ch') (covering cases decided in the Chancery Division or by the Court of Appeal on appeal therefrom or from a county court), 'Family' ('Fam')[1] (covering family cases decided in the Family Division or by the Court of Appeal) and 'Appeals Cases' ('AC') (covering decisions of the House of Lords and Privy Council). Cases appearing in the Law Reports have often appeared previously in the Weekly Law Reports (WLR) published by the same organisation, the Incorporated Council of Law Reporting.

Although the Law Reports superseded most of the series of private reports, there are still a number of commercially owned reports. The All England Reports (All ER), a weekly publication, are a general series of reports, while others are more specialised. Mention may also be made of the Estates Gazette (EG), in which cases of special interest to the landed professions are reported.

Cases decided by the European Court of Justice and the European Court of First Instance may be found in the Official Reports of the Court and in the Common Market Law Reports (CMLR). Since 1996, they have also been reported in a separate volume of the All England Law Reports (All ER (EC)).

1   Until 1972 the citation was 'P' since what is now the Family Division was known as the Probate, Divorce and Admiralty Division until its name, and jurisdiction, were changed.

3.61   The transcripts of many recent judgments are now available on LexisNexis and other electronic databases.

Since November 1996, all decisions of the House of Lords have been available on the Internet via http://www.parliament.uk.

Custom

3.62   Local customs, ie customs operative in a particular locality or among a particular group of people in a particular locality, are occasionally recognised by the courts as establishing a local 'law' for the locality in question at variance with the general law of the land, although they must not be contrary to statute or to a fundamental principle of the common law.

Local customs are largely to be found in rights of way and common. Recognition of a local custom depends on a number of conditions being satisfied, the most important of which are that the alleged custom must:

*   have existed since 'time immemorial', which, theoretically, it will only do if it goes back to 1189 (for reasons of historical accident);
*   have been continuous. The custom must have been in existence continuously. This means that the right to exercise it must not have been interrupted; but the fact that the right has not actually been exercised for a period of time, even 100 years in one case,[1] does not negative the existence of a local custom (although if the evidence of custom is dubious it will go far to negative any customary right);
*   not be unreasonable;[2]
*   be certain; in other words the right claimed must be certain in nature and scope and prove to adhere to a defined locality or group of people;
*   be recognised as compulsory.[3]

The first condition is not as strict as may appear since the claimant can succeed in proving it if he can prove that the practice in question has existed in the locality for a substantial time: the oldest local inhabitant is often called as a witness in this context. If the claimant proves this, existence since 1189 will be presumed,[4] provided, of course, that such a practice was possible in 1189.

1   *New Windsor Corpn v Mellor* [1975] 3 All ER 44, CA.
2   *Wolstanton Ltd v Newcastle-under-Lyme Borough Council* [1940] 3 All ER 101, HL.
3   Blackstone's *Commentaries*: 'a custom that all the inhabitants shall be rated towards the maintenance of a bridge will be good, but a custom that every man is to contribute thereto at his own pleasure is idle and absurd, and indeed not custom at all'.
4   *Mercer v Denne* [1905] 2 Ch 538 at 577.

Part II

The law of contract

Chapter 4

Introduction

4.1 In this part of the book we adopt the following order:

- in this chapter and the next two we outline those basic elements of the law of contract which relate to the existence and enforcement of a valid contract;
- in the following five chapters (7–11) we deal with contractual obligations, with how they are discharged, and with the remedies available if they are broken;
- in Chapters 12 and 13 we deal with factors which may affect the validity of what would otherwise be a valid contract;
- in Chapter 14 we deal with the rights and obligations of third parties to a contract;
- in Chapter 15, the last chapter in this part, we deal with the law relating to agency.

Sometimes a contract may be tainted with illegality, either because it is prohibited by statute, or because it is performed in a way prohibited by statute, or because it involves an unlawful or immoral element. In such cases, one or both parties may be unable to enforce it. The relevant rules are outside the scope of this book, as are the rules whereby a wagering or gaming contract is void and unenforceable.

The essential elements of a contract

4.2 For there to be a contract (ie a binding agreement):

- there must be an agreement;
- the parties must have intended their agreement to be legally binding; and
- the contract must be supported by consideration or be made by deed.

Although it is usual to talk about enforcing a contract, it must not be forgotten that what is being enforced is a promise by one party to an agreement by the other party to it. A mere statement of present fact to which another person agrees cannot be enforced, even if it relates to the fact of the present intentions of the party making the statement. Thus, if a company says 'it is our policy to ensure that any of our subsidiaries is always in a position to meet its liabilities in respect of a loan made to it', there is not a breach of contract if one of the subsidiaries becomes unable to meet its liabilities in respect of a loan.[1]

Another point which must be made at the outset is that contracts may be either bilateral or unilateral. A bilateral contract is one in which a party (A) promises to do something if the other party (B) promises to do something in return and B makes that counter-promise. In such a case, the mere exchange of promises normally renders both promises binding immediately. A unilateral contract, on the other hand, arises where A promises to do something in return for an act by B, rather than a counter-promise, as where A promises to pay B a reward if he finds some lost property or where A promises to pay B £100,000 if he sails round the world in less than six months, and B responds by doing the requested act. In such a case B is not bound to do anything at all; only if he does the act will A's promise become binding (because only then will a unilateral contract between A and B come into being). A less obvious example of a unilateral contract, though one which is of great commercial importance, is the normal type of commission agreement entered into by estate agents, mortgage brokers and the like. According to the decision of the House of Lords in *Luxor (Eastbourne) Ltd v Cooper,*[2] an estate agent instructed by a client to find a purchaser is under no obligation to take any action at all; only when he satisfies the client's instructions (eg finding a purchaser) does the client's promise of commission become binding (because only then will a unilateral contract between the client and the estate agent come into being).

Sometimes a party to a binding contract has a statutory right to cancel it during a 'cooling off' period. For example, under the Consumer Protection (Cancellation of Contracts Concluded away from Business Premises) Regulations 1987, if a contract of sale or other agreement results from an unsolicited visit by a trader to a person's home, or place of work, for the purpose of soliciting sales of consumer goods or services, the consumer has a right to cancel within seven days of making the contract. The Consumer Protection (Distance Selling) Regulations 2000 make similar provision. In the case of a contract between a seller or supplier and a consumer made exclusively by means of distance communications, ie without the simultaneous physical presence of the parties, such as a contract made via the Internet, the 2000 Regulations provide that the consumer has a right to cancel the contract within seven working days of the goods being delivered. In the case of a contract of services the period is seven working days after the formation of the contract, but the right to cancel is lost if performance begins during that period. The cancellation period is extended to three months if specified information (eg about the seller or supplier, the goods or services, the price) has not been confirmed in writing or other durable form. The 2000 Regulations do not apply to certain types of contract, eg non-consumer contracts, contracts for the sale of an interest in land and contracts made via an auction.

Before discussing the basic requirement of any contract, agreement between the parties, something must be said about contractual capacity and about whether or not an agreement must be in writing in order to be a valid and enforceable contract.

1   *Kleinwort Benson Ltd v Malaysia Mining Corpn Bhd* [1989] 1 All ER 785, CA.
2   [1941] 1 All ER 33, HL.

Form

4.3   With the exceptions mentioned hereafter, English law does not require an agreement to be in writing in order to be a valid and enforceable contract, but there are obvious advantages in reducing it into writing.

Contracts which must be made by deed
Leases for three years or more
4.4   These are void at law and pass no legal estate unless made by deed. However, such a lease not made by deed can take effect as a contract to grant a lease, which can be

specifically enforced provided it complies with the provisions of the Law of Property (Miscellaneous Provisions) Act 1989, s 2, and will create the same rights between the parties for many purposes.[1]

1   See further, paras 31.3–31.5 below.

Contracts in which there is no consideration

4.5   If there is no consideration for the promise made by one party to the other the contract is invalid unless made by deed.[1]

1   *Rann v Hughes* (1778) 7 Term Rep 350n, HL.

What is a 'deed'?

4.6   A contract is not made by deed unless the instrument in which it is written:

*   makes it clear on its face that it is intended to be a deed by the person making it or, as the case may be, by the parties to it either because it describes itself as such or because it expresses itself to be executed or signed as such; and
*   it is validly executed as a deed by that person or, as the case may be, by one or more of those parties.[1]

An instrument is validly executed as a deed by an individual only if:

*   it is signed–
    -    by him in the presence of a witness who attests the signature, or
    -    at his direction and in his presence and the presence of two witnesses who attest the signature; and
*   it is delivered as a deed by him or a person authorised to do so on his behalf.[2]

A deed is no longer required to be sealed.

A deed is regarded as delivered as soon as there are acts which show that the person making it intends unconditionally to be bound by it: physical delivery of it to the other party is no longer required and a deed may be delivered even though it remains in the custody of its maker.[3]

There are special statutory provisions governing the execution of a deed by a company or a limited liability partnership.

A contract made by deed is known as a contract of specialty: all other contracts, whether written or not, are known as simple contracts.

1   Law of Property (Miscellaneous Provisions) Act 1989, s 1(2).
2   LP(MP)A 1989, s 1(3).
3   *Vincent v Premo Enterprises (Voucher Sales) Ltd* [1969] 2 All ER 941, CA.

Contracts which must be in writing

4.7   Some contracts are invalid or unenforceable unless they are in writing. For example, an agreement for the sale or other disposition of land or an interest in land is generally invalid unless it is made in writing, as we explain in para 30.2 below. By way of further example, consumer credit agreements and consumer hire agreements which are not executed in writing in the manner required by the Consumer Credit Act 1974 are enforceable against the debtor or hirer only on an order of the court.[1]

1   Consumer Credit Act 1974, s 65.

Contracts which must be evidenced in writing

4.8   Contracts of guarantee do not have to be written but if they are not there must be written evidence of their parties and terms; otherwise they cannot be enforced in legal proceedings.[1]

1   Statute of Frauds 1677, s 4.

Capacity

4.9   There are special rules about the capacity of the following to make contracts:

*   minors (ie people under 18);
*   mentally disordered and intoxicated persons;
*   partnerships; and
*   companies.

Those who are engaged in surveying or valuing are most unlikely to make contracts with people in the first two categories. Consequently, the contractual capacity of such people is not dealt with in this book. On the other hand, the contractual capacity of partnerships of the traditional type, companies and limited liability partnerships is of importance to surveyors and valuers.

Partnerships

4.10   A partnership will usually be governed by the rules laid down in the Partnership Act 1890, but it is possible to create limited partnerships, and they are governed by the Limited Partnerships Act 1907. The limited partnership, which is a partnership with some of the characteristics of a limited liability company, is not very popular in the United Kingdom, although much used in continental Europe. A 'partnership' or 'limited partnership' must not be confused with a 'limited liability partnership' referred to below which is a body corporate (ie a separate legal entity), and not a partnership in a legal sense. With a few exceptions, the law relating to partnerships does not apply to a limited liability partnership.[1]

Although a partnership and its partners are not separate legal entities, a partnership can usually sue and be sued in its own name.

The Partnership Act 1890, s 1 defines a partnership as 'the relation existing between two or more persons carrying on a business in common with a view to profit'. Because the partners and the partnership are not separate legal entities, unlike the shareholders and the company in which they hold shares, there are important differences between being a partner and being a shareholder. For example:

*   a partner is liable for the debts and liabilities of the partnership: a shareholder is not liable for the debts and liabilities of the company;
*   a partner has a legal interest in the assets of the partnership: a shareholder does not have any legally recognised interest in the assets of the company;
*   shares in a partnership are not transferable: shares in a company are; and
*   the death of a partner technically terminates the partnership, although the remaining partners may agree to carry on the partnership: the death of a shareholder leaves the company unaffected.

There is no longer a maximum number of partners.[2]

A limited partnership is a partnership where one or more partners has only a limited liability for the debts of the partnership. Every limited partnership must have at least one general partner[3] (ie with full liability for debts) and any limited partner who is active in the affairs of the partnership becomes a general partner.[4] The limited partnership is only suitable for those who wish to invest money in a partnership but take no part in its running; their lack of popularity seems hardly surprising.

It is unusual to find large businesses run as partnerships. While there are advantages over companies in that there is less publicity for the affairs of the partnership, and perhaps less tax to be paid, these benefits will probably be outweighed by the advantages enjoyed by a company (or limited liability partnership) of limited liability and tax saving once profits reach a certain size.

In making contracts, a partnership has to work through agents, usually the partners. In theory, a partnership can make any contract it wishes. Whether a contract entered into by a partner binds his fellow partners depends on the usual rules of agency,[5] with the additional rule that any contract entered into by a partner which would be within the usual practice of the partnership will bind his fellow partners.[6]

1   Limited Liability Partnerships Act 2000, s 1(5).
2   The Regulatory Reform (Removal of 20 Member Limit in Partnerships etc) Order 2002.
3   Limited Partnerships Act 1907, s 4.
4   Limited Partnerships Act 1907, s 6.
5   Chapter 15.
6   Partnership Act 1890, s 5.

Companies

Legal status
4.11   Under British law, a company (which is an artificial legal person) may be formed in any one of three ways:

- by registration under the Companies Act 1985, which simply involves submitting certain documents to the Registrar of Companies and paying a fee (registered companies); or
- by Private Act of Parliament (statutory companies); or
- by Royal Charter (chartered companies).

It is extremely rare (as well as difficult and expensive) to form a company other than under the Companies Act 1985. The Companies Act 1985 permits the formation of private companies and public companies. Only public companies can apply for listing on the Stock Exchange. Although company law usually applies equally to both types of registered company, there are important differences. One concerns company formation. A public limited company must reveal its status and its name, by using the words 'public limited company' (plc), or their Welsh equivalent, and must have a specified minimum amount of capital on its formation. A private limited company must use the word 'limited' (ltd) in its name (or the Welsh equivalent) and need not have capital exceeding two pence on its formation. Both types of registered company are easy to form and the costs of formation are modest, although flotation of a public company on the Stock Exchange is expensive.

Companies may be formed for any purpose which their progenitors or promoters choose but trading bodies will usually be in registered form. Statutory companies are often specialised trading bodies, for example building societies, friendly societies and insurance companies. Chartered companies are typically charitable or quasi-charitable associations or non-trading bodies, such as the Royal Institution of Chartered Surveyors.

In 2000 a new form of business entity, the limited liability partnership (LLP), was created by the Limited Liability Partnerships Act 2000. Despite its name the LLP is a body corporate and has more in common with a company than a partnership and is largely regulated by the provisions of company law rather than by partnership law. A LLP is formed by the submission of specified documents to the Registrar of Companies and the payment of a fee. One distinction between a LLP and most companies is that a LLP does not have shares held by shareholders in the same way.

4.12   Other associations of people may pursue some common purpose, such as trade unions, clubs and partnerships of the traditional type, but companies and limited liability partnerships can be distinguished from other associations in that they are themselves a legal person totally distinct from their shareholders (who are also called members) or partners and employees. Companies and limited liability partnerships are artificial legal persons. Even if a company is totally dominated by one shareholder, the company and that shareholder are distinct legal persons.[1] An example is provided by *Lee v Lee's Air Farming Ltd*,[2] where Lee, who was founder, principal shareholder, managing director, and chief pilot of a company, had been killed while engaged on the business of the company. The Privy Council held that Lee and the company were distinct legal persons. Consequently, Lee could enter into a contract of employment with the company and his widow could therefore claim compensation under a government scheme which was limited to widows of employees.

Two consequences of the separate legal identities of a company and its members are:

- a company can sue and be sued in its own name;
- a company can make contracts on its own behalf (and its members cannot claim the benefit nor be subject to the burden of such contracts[3]).

Likewise, a limited liability partnership can sue and be sued in its own name and can make contracts on its own behalf.

1   *Salomon v Salomon & Co Ltd* [1897] AC 22, HL.
2   [1960] 3 All ER 420, PC.
3   This is merely the effect of the doctrine of privity: ch 14.

Contractual capacity
4.13   Although a company is a legal person, it does not – except in the case of a chartered company[1] – have the contractual capacity of a natural person. The contractual capacity of registered and statutory companies is limited by the memorandum of association and the creating statute respectively.

1   *Sutton's Hospital Case* (1612) 10 Co Rep 23a; *Pharmaceutical Society of Great Britain v Dickson* [1968] 2 All ER 686, HL.

4.14   When a registered company is created, the people forming the company are required to lodge with the Registrar of Companies at Companies House in Cardiff the memorandum of association of the company. In addition, they may or, in some cases, must lodge articles of association. These documents are available for public inspection.[1] The memorandum of association can be described as the constitution of the company and the articles of association as the rulebook governing the relations of the participants in the company. The memorandum of association must state certain specific things including the objects of the company[2] (ie the purposes for which the company was formed and the aims and business it intends to pursue). The provision setting out the company's objects is known as the objects clause. A company can register its own specially drafted objects clause but the objects clauses of many companies created in the last few years adopt the wording of the Companies Act 1985, s 3A which permits a company 'to carry on business as a general commercial company'.

1   Companies Act 1985, ss 1, 7 and 10.
2   Companies Act 1985, s 2.

4.15   The contractual capacity of a registered company is defined by its objects clause. Traditionally, a contract unauthorised by that clause was void and unenforceable but that rule has been amended by statute. The Companies Act 1985, s 35(1), states that the validity of an act done by a registered company cannot be called into question on the ground of lack of capacity by reason of the fact that it is beyond the objects of the company stated in the memorandum. Consequently if a registered company enters into a contract with another person (X), which is not authorised by its objects clause, the contract binds the company and X. If s 35(1) stood alone, a registered company would in effect have been in the same position as if it had full contractual capacity. Section 35(1), however, does not stand alone.

By s 35(2), a shareholder (who has a right to have the memorandum enforced) can bring proceedings to restrain the company entering into a contract outside the scope of its objects clause. However, a shareholder cannot stop the carrying out of a contract which has already been made by a company, nor can a shareholder impugn its validity.

4.16   Although it is a person in law, a company obviously cannot negotiate contracts personally; it must act through agents. An agent, such as a director of the company, is subject to the usual rules of agency described in chapter 15. Hence, a contract entered into by an agent of a company is only binding on the company if he had actual, implied or ostensible authority to enter into it.

The authority which an agent of a company appears to possess may be restricted and that restriction may be capable of discovery. For example, the board of directors has actual, implied or ostensible authority to enter into almost any transaction on behalf of the company but the company's memorandum may say, for example, that transactions in excess of £500,000 in value must be approved by the shareholders. Can the board bind the company by a transaction which is in breach of such a restriction? The Companies Act 1985, s 35A provides that, in favour of a person dealing with the company, the power of the board to bind the company (or to authorise others to do so) is deemed to be free of any limitations contained in the company's memorandum or articles, provided that that person dealt with the company in good faith. Thus, a company cannot enforce a contract which was entered into by an unauthorised agent but the other party may be able to do so. A person does not manifest bad faith simply by knowing that there is a restriction on the powers of the directors or by failing to inquire whether their powers are limited.

4.17   A limited liability partnership has the same capacity to contract as a natural person.[1] As in the case of a company, a limited liability partnership will act through an agent and will be bound by an agent who has actual, implied or ostensible authority to make the contract. There is, however, no equivalent of the Companies Act 1985, s 35A in the case of a limited liability partnership. It is not necessary because such a partnership has the contractual capacity of a natural person.

1   Limited Liability Partnership Act 2000, s 1(3).

Chapter 5

Agreement

5.1   An 'agreement' is often said to require a meeting of the minds of the parties to it, but this is rather misleading. The reason is that the law tends to take an objective, rather than a subjective, approach to an agreement. It is concerned not so much with what is actually in the minds of the parties, but with what a reasonable person would infer, from their conduct and the circumstances, as being in their minds (ie did they agree and, if so, on what terms?). This approach is not surprising: when the question of whether or not there is agreement is raised it is not possible to look back into the actual minds of the parties.

The following quotation indicates the approach of the courts:

> 'In contracts you do not look into the actual intent in a man's mind. You look at what he said and did. A contract is formed when there is, to all outward appearances, a contract.'[1]

In this chapter we examine:

* the way in which an agreement is normally proved by proof that one person made an offer to another which the latter accepted;
* what constitutes an offer;
* what constitutes an effective acceptance of an offer;
* how offers may be terminated before acceptance;
* what the legal position is if an agreement is uncertain in its terms, or is inconclusive, or is subject to the operation of a condition.

1   *Storer v Manchester City Council* [1974] 3 All ER 824 at 828.

5.2   The agreement involved in most contracts can be reduced to an offer by one party which has been accepted by the other. However, not all agreements can easily be so reduced. This is the case, for example, where two parties agree to terms suggested by a third person. It may also be the case where several parties agree independently with X that they will be bound by terms stipulated by him. In such an event the parties may have entered into a contract not merely with X but with each other. In *Clarke v Dunraven*,[1] yachtsmen wrote to the secretary of a yacht club agreeing to be bound by certain rules during a yacht race. The House of Lords held that a contract containing those rules existed between the yachtsmen with the result that a yachtsman whose yacht was damaged was able to recover damages in accordance with the rules. While there was agreement between the yachtsmen to be bound by the rules, it cannot be analysed in terms of offer and acceptance between them.

Despite exceptional cases such as these, it is the law that generally, for there to be an agreement, what has occurred must be capable of analysis into an offer by one party accepted by the other. Some judges have taken a more liberal approach. For example, in *Gibson v Manchester City Council*,[2] Lord Denning MR said: 'To my mind it is a mistake to think that all contracts can be analysed into the form of offer and acceptance... You should look at the correspondence as a whole and at the conduct of the parties... and see therefore whether the parties have come to an agreement on everything that was material'. However, on appeal in that case, Lord Denning's approach was disapproved by the House of Lords. For example, Lord Diplock said: 'My Lords there may be certain types of contract, *though I think they are exceptional,* which do not fit easily into the normal analysis of a contract as constituted by offer and acceptance; but a contract alleged to have been made by an exchange of correspondence between the parties in which the successive communications other than the first are in reply to one another is not one of these... I venture to think that it was in departing from this conventional approach that the majority of the Court of Appeal was led into error'.[3] Lord Diplock's statement represents the weight of judicial opinion, although Lord Denning's approach is a more appropriate reflection of what happens in business than a strict 'offer and acceptance approach'.

1   [1897] AC 59, HL.
2   [1978] 2 All ER 583.
3   [1979] 1 All ER 972 at 974.

Offer

5.3   An offer is made where a person (the offeror) unequivocally expresses to another (the offeree) his willingness to make a binding agreement on the terms specified by him if they are accepted by the offeree.

An offer may be made to a specific person, to a group of people, or to the world at large.[1] An offer to a specific person cannot be accepted by anyone else.[2]

The fact that an offer requires an expression of unequivocal willingness to contract means that quotations of rates or prices are not offers.[3] It also means that inquiries and replies to inquiries are not offers, although sometimes they may resemble them. In *Harvey v Facey*,[4] one party inquired as to the lowest acceptable price for certain land, and the other party telegraphed his lowest acceptable price. This was held not to be an offer but merely a reply to the inquiry. Likewise, in *Gibson v Manchester City Council*,[5] where a letter had been sent saying that the council 'may be prepared to sell the house to you', it was held by the House of Lords that the letter did not constitute an offer to sell but merely an invitation to treat.

An offer must be distinguished from an 'invitation to treat' (ie an invitation to enter into negotiations which may lead to the making of an offer). In certain situations, what may appear to be an offer by X to Y will be regarded by a court merely as an invitation to treat, unless there is clear evidence that X was willing to be bound as soon as Y indicated his assent or satisfied a particular condition. The following examples of these situations can be given.

1   *Carlill v Carbolic Smoke Ball Co* [1893] 1 QB 256, CA.
2   *Cundy v Lindsay* (1878) 3 App Cas 459, HL.
3   *Scancarriers A/S v Aotearoa International Ltd* [1985] 2 Lloyd's Rep 419, PC.
4   [1893] AC 552, PC.
5   [1979] 1 All ER 972, HL.

Invitation to treat

Exposure for sale

5.4   An invitation to treat is a starting point for contractual negotiations and precedes the making of an offer. In *Fisher v Bell*,[1] a shopkeeper was charged with offering for sale a flick knife which was on display in his shop window.[2] A divisional court held that the display of goods in a shop window was not an offer to sell but an invitation to treat; it was for customers to make the offer. The rationale behind this decision is that a shop is a place for negotiation over the terms of a contract, including the price, and that the shopkeeper invites customers to make him an offer which he can accept or reject as he pleases. This is an unrealistic view of how shops operate today. Circulars sent to potential customers are also invitations to treat for the supply of goods, and not offers.[3]

Like the display of goods in shop windows, the display of goods in self-service shops is an invitation to treat. In *Pharmaceutical Society of Great Britain v Boots Cash Chemists (Southern) Ltd*,[4] statute required certain drugs to be sold only under the supervision of a qualified pharmacist. A pharmacist was at the cash desk but, if the sale of drugs had been made before a customer reached it, the statute would have been infringed. The Court of Appeal had no hesitation in finding that the display of goods was only an invitation to treat, that the offer to buy was made by the customer at the cash desk, and that the contract was concluded when the offer was accepted. Consequently, Boots were not in breach of the statute. It was not necessary to decide precisely when a customer's offer is accepted at the cash desk, but one member of the Court of Appeal agreed with the view that acceptance occurs when the price is accepted.[5]

1   [1960] 3 All ER 731, DC.
2   Contrary to the Restriction of Offensive Weapons Act 1959. The Restriction of Offensive Weapons Act 1961 reverses the actual decision in the case by extending the offence to cover 'exposing' a weapon for sale.
3   *Grainger & Son v Gough* [1896] AC 325, HL.
4   [1953] 1 All ER 482, CA.
5   [1953] 1 All ER 482, at 484.

Advertisements

5.5   Whether an advertisement is an offer or an invitation to treat depends on the intention with which it is made. Advertisements of rewards and the like are normally offers since the advertiser does not intend any further negotiation to take place. An example is provided by *Carlill v Carbolic Smoke Ball Co*,[1] where the defendants advertised that they would pay £100 to anyone catching influenza after using their product in a specified manner. The Court of Appeal held that, since no further negotiations on the defendants' part were intended, the advertisement constituted an offer made to all the world which would ripen into a contract with anyone who fulfilled the conditions.

On the other hand, an advertisement of goods for sale is presumptively an invitation to treat, and not an offer,[2] because otherwise the advertiser might find himself contractually obliged to supply the advertised goods to a greater number of people (those who had responded positively to the advertisement) than the number of specified goods which had been advertised.[3] Similarly, the advertising of an auction is not an offer; instead, those who bid at auction make an offer which the auctioneer is free to accept or reject, and an offer can be withdrawn at any time before the auctioneer accepts.[4] Because the advertisement of an auction is merely a declaration of an intention to hold the auction, potential buyers have no claim against the auctioneer if he fails to hold the auction.[5] These rules even apply where an auctioneer advertises an auction as 'without reserve' (ie that the bid of the highest bona fide bidder will be accepted and that the property will not be withdrawn if a reserve price is not reached), so that there is no contract *of sale* if the auctioneer refuses to accept the highest bid and withdraws the property. However, the auctioneer is liable in such circumstances for breach of a collateral contract *that the sale would be without reserve.*[6] This contract comes into existence as follows: by advertising the sale as without reserve the auctioneer makes an offer to this effect to whoever is the highest bona fide bidder, which is accepted by the person who makes the highest bona fide bid before the property is withdrawn.[7]

1   [1893] 1 QB 256, CA.
2   *Partridge v Crittenden* [1968] 2 All ER 421, DC.
3   This reason would not apply if the advertiser was the manufacturer of the goods advertised, because he could make more. In *Partridge v Crittenden* [1968] 2 All ER 421 at 424, Lord Parker CJ suggested that an advertisement or circular for the sale of goods by a manufacturer could be interpreted as an offer.
4   *Payne v Cave* (1789) 3 Term Rep 148; Sale of Goods Act 1979, s 57(2).
5   *Harris v Nickerson* (1873) LR 8 QB 286.
6   *Warlow v Harrison* (1859) 1 E & E 309; *Barry v Heathcote-Ball & Co (Commercial Auctions) Ltd* [2001] 1 All ER 944, CA.
7   If the auctioneer refuses to sell to the highest bidder, the damages will be assessed in the same way as if the vendor had wrongfully refused to deliver goods to the buyer: *Barry v Heathcote-Ball & Co (Commercial Auctions) Ltd.*

Tenders

5.6   An announcement that the provision of goods or services (or the purchase of goods or services) is open to tender is not an offer but only an invitation to treat. Consequently, a person who submits a tender makes an offer, which may be accepted or rejected by the person seeking tenders.[1] In *Spencer v Harding,*[2] for example, the defendant issued a circular offering by tender the stock in trade of X. This was held not to be an offer. Thus, the defendant was not required to sell the goods to the claimant who had submitted the highest tender.

A person seeking tenders who indicates that he will accept the highest or lowest tender, as the case may be, will be contractually bound to do so. The reason is that, in accompanying his request for tenders with such an indication, he thereby accompanies his invitation to treat with an offer of a unilateral contract to accept the highest or lowest tender, as the case may be. The highest or lowest tender, as the case may be, will constitute an acceptance of that offer, and the person seeking tenders will be contractually obliged to accept that tender.[3]

Where an invitation to tender is made only to a small, selected group of persons, it will be held to be accompanied by an offer to consider all conforming tenders submitted by the stipulated deadline, which offer is accepted by so submitting such a tender. Consequently, in such a case, it will be a breach of contract (a contract to consider a conforming tender submitted in time) to fail to consider such a tender.[4] It will not, of course, be a breach of contract to fail to accept a conforming tender after considering it.

1   For acceptance of tenders see para 5.11 below.
2   (1870) LR 5 CP 561.
3   *Harvela Investments Ltd v Royal Trust Co of Canada (CI) Ltd* [1985] 2 All ER 966, HL.
4   *Blackpool and Fylde Aero Club Ltd v Blackpool Borough Council* [1990] 3 All ER 25, CA.

Acceptance

Requirements

5.7   To convert an offer into a contract the offeree must unequivocally and unconditionally accept the offer; if, for example, A offers to sell B a computer for £5,000, payable in advance, B does not accept the offer when he replies purporting to accept the offer but saying that he will pay the £5,000 on delivery.[1] In addition, the offeree is normally required to communicate his acceptance to the offeror.

1   *Hyde v Wrench* (1840) 3 Beav 334; para 5.9 below.

5.8   It should come as no surprise to anyone to learn that one cannot accept an offer of which one is ignorant. This is important in the case where B offers a reward for the performance of a particular action, eg finding his lost dog. If A, who is ignorant of the offer, finds the dog, his action cannot constitute an acceptance of the offer and he cannot claim the reward successfully.[1] Moreover, if someone who knows of the offer performs the specified action for reasons entirely unconnected with that offer, there is no acceptance.[1] But, if his conduct is motivated partly by the offer and partly by other reasons there is a valid acceptance.[2]

A related point is that, if two offers which are identical in terms cross in the post, there can be no contract. The courts will not construe one offer as the offer and the other offer as the acceptance.[3] The practical basis for such a view would seem to be that neither party would know if he was bound, although if the terms of the offers were identical the parties would surely have no objection to being bound.

1   *R v Clarke* (1927) 40 CLR 227.
2   *Williams v Carwardine* (1833) 5 C & P 566.
3   *Tinn v Hoffmann & Co* (1873) 29 LT 271.

Counter-offers distinguished

5.9   As stated in para 5.7 above, for an acceptance there must be an unequivocal agreement to the terms proposed in the offer. If an offeree who purports to accept the offer seeks to introduce an entirely new term in his acceptance, eg as to the amount of goods to be delivered or the time of payment, this is not an acceptance. Instead, it is a counter-offer which may or may not be accepted by the original offeror.

A counter-offer puts an end to the original offer, so that it cannot subsequently be accepted by the offeree. In *Hyde v Wrench,*[1] for instance, the defendant offered to sell property to the claimant for £1,000. The claimant 'agreed' to buy the property for £950. This was rejected and the claimant then purported to accept the original offer of the property for £1,000. The Master of the Rolls held that the claimant's purported acceptance for £950 was a counter-offer which destroyed the original offer, so that it was no longer capable of acceptance when the claimant purported to accept it.

A counter-offer must be distinguished from an inquiry or request for information by an offeree. Such an inquiry or request, even if answered negatively by the offeror, does not destroy the offer. An example is *Stevenson, Jacques & Co v McLean.*[2] The defendant offered to sell iron to the claimants at 40 shillings a ton with immediate delivery. The claimants asked the defendant by telegram if he would sell at the same price if delivery was staggered over two months. On receiving no reply, the claimants accepted the original offer but the defendant failed to deliver and claimed the telegram was a counter-offer. The court rejected the defendant's claim and held that the telegram was a mere request for information, and not a counter-offer, so that the original offer could still be accepted.

A contract may arise in the course of long and complicated negotiations, during which one party offers to contract on certain terms (eg terms A, B and C contained in a document sent by him) and the other agrees to contract, but on different terms (eg terms A, B and D contained in a document sent by him), and so on. Even if it is expressed to be an acceptance, such a response will in law be a counter-offer and not an acceptance. If neither party expressly accepts the other's terms, what is the legal situation? The orthodox view is that if, after the communication of the last set of terms, the recipient does something which indicates a relevant agreement with the sender, for example by delivering the goods which the sender has ordered, the recipient will be held to have accepted[3] the sender's counter-offer and thus contracted on the sender's terms.[4] Of course, this approach does not produce a contract at all if the last set of terms are not followed by anything on the recipient's part which can be described as acceptance. An alternative approach, taken by Lord Denning MR in *Butler Machine Tool Co Ltd v Ex-Cell-O Corpn (England) Ltd*,[5] is that where there is a 'battle of the forms' a 'compromise' contract can be constructed by the court on reasonable terms. This does not yet represent the law but it would produce a contract in the type of case just mentioned.

1　(1840) 3 Beav 334.
2　(1880) 5 QBD 346.
3　Acceptance can be by conduct; see para 5.10 below.
4　*British Road Services Ltd v Arthur V Crutchley Ltd* [1968] 1 All ER 811, CA; *Butler Machine Tool Co Ltd v Ex-Cell-O Corpn (England) Ltd* [1979] 1 All ER 965, CA.
5　[1979] 1 All ER 965 at 968–969.

Acceptance by conduct

5.10　An acceptance may be express, as where the offeree accepts the offer by a written or oral statement intended to constitute an acceptance,[1] or it may be manifested by the offeree's conduct. For instance, a cover note issued by an insurance company is an offer to insure which would be accepted by using a car in reliance on it.[2] A more complicated case of acceptance by conduct is that of *Brogden v Metropolitan Rly Co*,[3] in which Brogden was sued for failing to deliver coal. Brogden regularly supplied the company with coal and they decided to draw up a contract for such supply. A draft contract was submitted to Brogden with a blank space for the name of a mutually agreeable arbitrator. This constituted an offer. Brogden filled in the name of an arbitrator, marked the draft 'approved', and returned it to the agent of the company (who put it in a drawer where it remained). Brogden's action was not an acceptance but a counter-offer,[4] because the company had to consider whether to accept his choice of arbitrator. Nevertheless, the parties bought and sold coal in accordance with the terms of the draft contract. Subsequently, Brogden refused to supply more coal and claimed that there was no binding contract for its supply. The House of Lords inferred from the conduct of the parties, the buying and selling of coal on terms exactly the same as those in the draft contract, that a contract had been concluded on the terms of the final draft, which came into effect either with the first order of coal by the company on the terms of the draft (since this conduct could be said to have manifested the company's acceptance of Brogden's counter-offer) or, at least, when Brogden supplied the coal. The first explanation is the more acceptable. The House of Lords stressed that mere mental acquiescence by the parties that the contract should exist would not have sufficed.

1　See, for example, *Wilson Smithett & Cape (Sugar) Ltd v Bangladesh Sugar and Food Industries Corpn* [1986] 1 Lloyd's Rep 378 (letter of intent to supply materials as per terms of offer held to constitute an acceptance, because it was found to have been intended to constitute an acceptance).
2　*Taylor v Allon* [1965] 1 All ER 557 at 559.
3　(1877) 2 App Cas 666, HL.
4　Para 5.9 above.

Acceptance of tenders

5.11　The acceptance of tenders illustrates another aspect of acceptance. Tenders can be in two forms:

- People may be invited to tender, for example by a local authority, for the supply of *specified* goods or services over a given period. In such a case, a contract for the supply of those goods or services is constituted when a person's tender (offer) is accepted.

- People may be invited to tender for the supply of *such* goods and services *as may be required* over a given period. In such a case, a contract is not immediately concluded with the successful tenderer. Instead, his offer is treated as a standing offer and each time an order is placed this constitutes acceptance of the standing offer and there is a contract for the goods or services ordered. Because the person making the successful tender has no definite contract, he can revoke his offer before any particular order is placed, and the person who invited tenders need never place an order.[1]

1 *Great Northern Rly Co v Witham* (1873) LR 9 CP 16.

Communication of acceptance

5.12 If an offer has been made and the offeree has decided to accept, there is normally no completed agreement until he (or his agent) has communicated his acceptance to the offeror (or his agent), by words or conduct which manifest his acceptance.[1] The reason for this is practical: if the offeror is not told that his offer has been accepted he does not know whether he has made a contract or can make offers to others.

Communication of acceptance usually requires actual communication. Consequently, an oral acceptance which is drowned by a passing aeroplane or is inaudible because of interference on the telephone is not effectively communicated.[2] It seems that fax messages sent during office hours are regarded as instantaneous communications and are subject to the same principles as oral acceptances; they take effect when printed out on the offeror's fax machine.[3] This rule would not apply where the communication was not instantaneous, as where a fax message is sent out of office hours; the time of acceptance in such a case would depend on the parties' intentions and sound business practice, and in some cases on a judgment as to where the risk should lie.

If an oral acceptance or one by fax does not completely reach the offeror and the party accepting does not realise this, there may be a valid communication of acceptance. But this will only be the case where the offeror realises he has missed some of what the offeree is seeking to communicate and does not attempt to discover what he has missed.[4]

It remains to be seen what rule applies to an acceptance by email. An email message is not always communicated to its addressee instantaneously. If the addressee has not logged into the network database, an email message is stored there until it is communicated to its addressee as a result of the addressee logging into the network. An email acceptance may be held by a court – when the occasion arises – to be subject to the same approach as the non-instantaneous communication of an acceptance by fax. Alternatively, the court may consider that committing the message to the network is akin to committing a letter of acceptance to the post office by posting and that the rules relating to postal acceptance, described in para 5.16, are applicable.

1 Para 5.10 above.
2 *Entores v Miles Far East Corpn* [1955] 2 All ER 493, CA.
3 In *Brinkibon v Stahag Stahl GmbH* [1982] 1 All ER 293, HL, this view was taken about messages sent by telex, a system now replaced by fax.
4 *Entores v Miles Far East Corpn* [1955] 2 QB 327 at 333.

Dispensation from need for communication of acceptance

5.13 The offeror may by the terms of the offer expressly or impliedly dispense with the need to communicate acceptance. In particular, dispensation with the need for communication will normally be implied where the alleged contract is of the unilateral variety. An example is provided by *Carlill v Carbolic Smoke Ball Co*,[1] where the vendors of a product argued that a user of it, who claimed a reward which they had offered to anyone catching influenza after using the product, should have told them of her acceptance of their offer of a reward. The vendors' claim was rejected, since it was clear they had not intended every purchaser of the product to write to them formally accepting the offer of a reward if illness was not avoided; consequently, they had impliedly dispensed with the need for communication of acceptance.

1   [1893] 1 QB 256, CA.

5.14   If the offeror does expressly or impliedly dispense with the need for communication of acceptance, the offeree's non-communication of acceptance does not enable the offeror successfully to deny that there is a contract enforceable against him.[1] In addition, there will be a contract enforceable against the offeree if he has unambiguously manifested his acceptance, as by driving a car in reliance on an offer of motor insurance.[2] On the other hand, an offeree is not bound simply because an offeror has framed his offer in such terms that a contract is presumed to exist unless non-acceptance is communicated. Contractual liability cannot be imposed on the offeree in this way; as against the offeree, silence is not assent. In *Felthouse v Bindley*,[3] the claimant offered to buy X's horse and said that he would presume his offer to be accepted unless he heard to the contrary. X did not reply. The horse was sold by the defendant, an auctioneer, to another. It was held that no contract binding on X had been formed: the claimant was not entitled to presume acceptance unless he heard to the contrary.

1   This is certainly the case in a unilateral contract, as *Carlill v Carbolic Smoke Ball Co*, para 5.5 above, shows.
2   *Taylor v Allon* [1965] 1 All ER 557 at 559.
3   (1862) 11 CBNS 869.

5.15   While some offers dispense with the need for communication of acceptance, others require a particular form of acceptance to be employed (as where the offer states: 'Please send acceptance in writing by first class post to our Liverpool branch'). If the offer states that the acceptance may only be made in the specified manner, an acceptance in any other way cannot be effective (unless the offeror waives the requirement).[1] On the other hand, if the offer does not state that only the specified method may be used, an acceptance made in some other way (eg by fax to the Liverpool branch in the above example) can be effective as long as it is no less disadvantageous to the offeror than the prescribed method;[2] but if it is not, it is ineffective[3] (unless the offeror waives the specified mode).

1   *Compagnie de Commerce et Commission SARL v Parkinson Stove Co* [1953] 2 Lloyd's Rep 487, CA.
2   *Yates Building Co Ltd v RJ Pulleyn & Sons (York) Ltd* (1975) 119 Sol Jo 370, CA.
3   *Financings Ltd v Stimson* [1962] 3 All ER 386, CA.

Postal acceptance

5.16   There is another exception to the general rule that acceptance must be actually communicated to be effective. It is that, subject to the qualifications referred to below, a posted acceptance is effective when it is posted, and this is so even if that acceptance is delivered late or is never delivered. This was first established in *Adams v Lindsell*,[1] where a letter of acceptance was posted the day that a postal offer to sell wool was received. The acceptance arrived two days later than expected and, after it had been posted but before it arrived, the offeror sold the wool to another. It was held that a contract had been formed as soon as the letter of acceptance had been posted. A letter is 'posted' when it is placed, correctly stamped, in an official box or into the hands of a Post Office employee or agent authorised to receive letters;[2] most postmen who deliver letters are not so authorised.

The offeror can exclude the special postal acceptance rule by specifying in his offer that acceptance must be actually communicated to him.[3] In addition, the postal acceptance rule will be disregarded, and the general rule requiring communication prevail, if it is not reasonable to accept by post[4] or if the special rule would give rise to 'manifest inconvenience or absurdity'.[5] For example, it would not be reasonable to accept by post an offer by fax to sell highly perishable goods.

The justification for the special rule for postal acceptances seems to be that the offeror, by expressly or impliedly (eg by making the offer by post) allowing an acceptance to be made by post, must stand the risk of failures of the postal system. However, if a postal acceptance is delayed in the post because of the negligence of the offeree, as where he wrongly addresses the letter, there seems no reason why the court should not decide the acceptance to have been effective at whatever time is least advantageous to the negligent offeree.

1 (1818) 1 B & Ald 681.
2 Re London & Northern Bank, ex p Jones [1900] 1 Ch 220.
3 For an example see Holwell Securities Ltd v Hughes [1974] 1 All ER 161, CA.
4 Henthorn v Fraser [1892] 2 Ch 27, CA.
5 Holwell Securities Ltd v Hughes [1974] 1 All ER 161, CA.

5.17 If an acceptance made by letter is effective when it is posted, then, logically, an attempt to withdraw the acceptance after the letter has been posted should be ineffective since the contract has been concluded. There are no English cases which support this view, although the principle stated is consistent with decisions in New Zealand and South Africa.[1] On the other hand, the Scottish case of Countess of Dunmore v Alexander[2] has been cited as authority for the view that, if a revocation of an acceptance is communicated before a postal acceptance arrives, the revocation is effective. However, the facts of this case are somewhat obscure and it is by no means certain that this is what the case decided.

1 Wenkheim v Arndt (1861–1902) 1 JR 73; A to Z Bazaars (Pty) Ltd v Minister of Agriculture 1974 (4) SA 392.
2 (1830) 9 Sh (Ct of Sess) 190.

Termination of offers

5.18 An offer may be terminated in several ways: by rejection (including a counter-offer[1]), by revocation, by lapse of time and by death.

1 Para 5.9 above.

Revocation
5.19 At any time until acceptance by the offeree, the offeror can withdraw his offer. The fact that the offeror has given the offeree time to make up his mind does not mean that the offeror is required to keep the offer open for that length of time. In Routledge v Grant,[1] an offer to lease premises was expressed to be open for acceptance for six weeks; it was held that nevertheless the offer could be withdrawn within that period.

There is an exception to the rule that the offer need not be kept open for a specified period. This is where there is a separate contract whereby the offeror contracts to keep the offer open for a given time. If there is such a contract the offer can be accepted at any time within the specified period. An example of such a contract is the granting of an option.

The revocation of an offer only becomes effective when it is communicated to the offeree. In Byrne v Van Tienhoven,[2] the defendants in Cardiff wrote on 1 October to the claimants in New York, offering to sell them goods. The claimant received the offer on 11 October and accepted it by telegram on the same day. Meanwhile, on 8 October the defendants had sent a letter to the claimants revoking their offer; this letter reached the claimants on 20 October. It was held that the revocation was ineffective because the claimants' acceptance had taken effect on 11 October (acceptance by telegram being treated in the same way as acceptance by letter) and therefore the defendants' offer was no longer capable of being revoked when their letter of revocation reached the claimants. Consequently, there was a contract between the claimants and defendants for the sale of the goods. There is no parallel rule to that which treats a posted acceptance as a communicated acceptance; a revocation must always be actually communicated.

This raises a question which has yet to be authoritatively determined. Does communication by letter, fax or email require that the revocation is actually read by the offeror[3] or does it occur when the letter is delivered, or the fax is printed out, at his premises, or notice of the email appears on his screen, regardless of whether it comes to his attention[3] at that time? In the case of a business, the latter is probably the answer provided that the delivery, print-out or appearance is during normal business hours.[4] The answer in other cases is less certain.

Communication of revocation may be indirect, in that, if the offeree hears from a reliable source that the offer has been withdrawn (and thereby knows beyond all question of the withdrawal), the courts will regard this as an effective revocation.[5] The difficulty inherent in this is that it is difficult to know what constitutes a reliable source.

1   (1828) 4 Bing 653. For a more recent example, see *Scammell v Dicker* [2001] 1 WLR 631, CA: offer to settle an action expressed to remain open for 21 days; held offeror entitled to withdraw offer within that period.
2   (1880) 5 CPD 344.
3   Or his agent.
4   Suggested by the decision in another context in *Tenax Steamship Co Ltd v Reinante Transoceania Navegacion SA, The Brimnes* [1974] 3 All ER 88, CA.
5   *Dickinson v Dodds* (1876) 2 Ch D 463, CA.

5.20   Special rules apply in the case of unilateral contracts, where A does something (eg returning lost property) in response to B's offer (promise) to do something (eg to pay a reward) if he does it. The general rule is that once the offeree has embarked on the performance of the stipulated act or acts necessary for acceptance, as where B has found lost property and is en route to return it in response to the offer of a reward for its return, the offer cannot be withdrawn.[1] The reason is that, when the offer is made which will mature into a unilateral contract when accepted, there is alongside that principal offer a collateral offer to keep the principal offer open once performance in relation to it has begun, which is accepted by the offeree starting to perform the stipulated act or acts.[2] In *Errington v Errington and Woods*,[3] a father purchased a house, partially by means of a mortgage, and allowed his daughter and her husband to live in it. The daughter and her husband paid the mortgage instalments in response to the father's offer that, if they did so, he would give them the house when it was paid for. The Court of Appeal held that this offer could not be revoked once the daughter and her husband had begun performance of the conduct specified in the offer. Of course, in the present type of case the offeror is not bound unless and until the offeree has fully performed the act or acts specified in the offer. This is subject to the important qualification that, if the offeror prevents performance of the necessary act or acts being completed, he cannot rely on the offeree's failure fully to perform as a defence to a breach of contract action by the offeree, because there is an implied obligation on the part of the offeror (which arises as soon as the offeree starts to perform) not to prevent performance by the offeree.[4]

What we have just said will not apply if the terms of the offer, or its surrounding circumstances, indicate that it was not intended to become irrevocable before the offeree had completely performed the envisaged act. A good example is the kind of commission agreement commonly used by estate agents. Although this is an agreement which will ripen into a unilateral contract if the estate agent satisfies the client's instructions (as we explained in para 4.2 above) it is well settled that the client may revoke his instructions at any time, notwithstanding that the agent may have expended time and money in attempting to find a purchaser.[5] The courts take the view that a change of mind by a client is simply one of the business risks which an estate agent must bear, and his fees for successful negotiations should be at a level sufficient to cover other abortive work.

1   *Errington v Errington and Woods* [1952] 1 All ER 149, CA; *Daulia Ltd v Four Millbank Nominees Ltd* [1978] 2 All ER 557 at 561.
2   *Daulia Ltd v Four Millbank Nominees Ltd* [1978] 2 All ER 557 at 561.
3   [1952] 1 All ER 149, CA.
4   *Daulia Ltd v Four Millbank Nominees Ltd* [1978] 2 All ER 557 at 561.
5   *Luxor (Eastbourne) Ltd v Cooper* [1941] 1 All ER 33, HL.

Lapse of time

5.21   Obviously, an offer which is to remain open for a set time lapses at the end of that time and cannot thereafter be accepted. If no time limit is expressly set for the offer, it will normally lapse after a reasonable period.[1] In *Ramsgate Victoria Hotel v Montefiore*,[2] for example, it was held that an offer to buy shares, which was made in June, could not be accepted in November since the offer had lapsed by then. What is a reasonable period varies, depending on the facts of the case.

1   *Chemco Leasing SpA v Rediffusion* [1987] 1 FTLR 201, CA.
2   (1866) LR 1 Ex Ch 109.

Death

5.22   Death after an offer has been accepted cannot affect the validity of a contract.[1] There are, however, cases where either the offeror or the offeree dies before the offer is accepted. If the offeror dies the offer does not seem to terminate automatically (except where the offer is clearly of such a type that it must end on death, eg an offer to work for X). However, the offeree cannot accept the offer once he knows of the death of the offeror.[2]

The effects of the death of the offeree have not been decided conclusively but uncontradicted dicta suggest that the offer lapses. In *Reynolds v Atherton*,[3] it was suggested that an offer, being made to a living person, cannot survive his death and be accepted by someone else. This may be an illustration of the basic rule that an offer made to A cannot be accepted by B. On the other hand, if an offer is made to A or B there seems no reason why the death of B should prevent A accepting it.

1   But it may discharge the contract: see para 10.6 below.
2   *Bradbury v Morgan* (1862) 1 H & C 249; *Coulthart v Clementson* (1879) 5 QBD 42.
3   (1921) 125 LT 690, CA; affd by the House of Lords who did not comment on this point.

Uncertain, inconclusive and conditional agreements

5.23   Here we are concerned with cases where, although there is an agreement, there may not be a legally binding contract because the agreement is uncertain in its terms, or is merely an agreement to agree in the future, or is subject to the operation of a condition.

Uncertainty

5.24   Where particular terms in an agreement are vague or unclear, the courts will try to divine the intention of the parties and find a contract, but if such intention cannot be discovered the agreement is not a legally binding contract and cannot be enforced.[1] In *Bushwall Properties Ltd v Vortex Properties Ltd*,[2] for instance, A agreed to buy from B 51½ acres of land for £500,000. Under the terms of the agreement the price was to be paid in three instalments and on each payment a 'proportionate part' of the land was to be conveyed to A. The Court of Appeal held that the agreement was void for uncertainty because it did not provide the machinery for identifying the proportionate part to be conveyed in each phase, nor could a term (based on the parties' presumed intention) be implied as to how each proportionate part was to be identified. Another agreement which has been held not to be binding because of lack of certainty is an agreement to continue to negotiate in good faith for an unspecified period, since a party would never know whether he was entitled to withdraw from the negotiations and the court could not be expected to decide whether a proper reason existed for him to do so.[3] For similar reasons an agreement of unspecified duration not to negotiate with anyone else is void for uncertainty. We return to this type of agreement in para 5.29.

On the other hand, a court can supply the details of an apparently vague term, so that the agreement is a valid contract, if the parties have provided the machinery to ascertain its precise nature, as where there is an agreement for the sale of land at 'market price' (in which case the court can fix that price after making an inquiry),[4] or if the details which the parties must have intended can be implied by reference to the practices of a particular trade to which they belong or by reference to their previous dealings. In *Hillas & Co Ltd v Arcos Ltd*,[5] the parties had entered into an agreement for the sale and purchase of timber in 1930. The agreement contained an option to buy 100,000 standards of timber in 1931 but the size and quality of the timber were not specified. The House of Lords refused to find the agreement unenforceable, clarifying any uncertainties by reference to the previous dealings of the parties and usual practice in the timber trade. The judgment of the House is permeated by the view that the courts ought to strive to give effect to business arrangements and not zealously demand absolute certainty of all terms.

Another case where there can be a valid contract despite the apparent uncertainty of a term is where the parties have provided the machinery for one of them, or for a third party or third parties, to fix the precise nature of that term. This was recognised in *Sudbrook Trading Estate Ltd v Eggleton*,[6] where the House of Lords dealt with the situation where the price of a piece of property was left to be decided by two valuers, one to be appointed by each party. It held that if the task of the valuers, expressly or impliedly, was to fix a fair and reasonable price and that method proved ineffective, either because a party refused to appoint a valuer or because the valuers failed to agree, a court could substitute its own machinery to ascertain the price, eg by appointing its own valuers. On the other hand, it held, if the price was to be fixed by a named valuer or valuers, it could not be implied that the price was to be a fair and reasonable one because the implication was that the price was to be fixed by a specified means, the use of the named valuer or valuers. In such a case, it held, a court could not substitute its own machinery if for some reason the named valuer or valuers failed to fix the price, and there would not be an enforceable contract for the sale of the property.

There can be a valid contract for the sale of goods or the supply of a service, even though the price is not fixed, or left to be fixed in an agreed manner, and cannot be determined by a course of dealings between the parties. Statute provides that, in such a case, a reasonable price must be paid.[7]

Where an apparently uncertain term can be determined in one of the above ways, the contract is complete on the agreement of the parties even though the precise nature of that term remains to be fixed.[8]

If a transaction has been performed on both sides, it will be difficult for a party to submit successfully that there is no agreement or that there is not a legally binding contract on grounds of uncertainty or vagueness.[9]

1   *Scammell and Nephew Ltd v Ouston* [1941] 1 All ER 14, HL.
2   [1976] 2 All ER 283, CA.
3   *Walford v Miles* [1992] 1 All ER 453, HL.
4   *Bushwall Properties Ltd v Vortex Properties Ltd* [1976] 2 All ER 283 at 289.
5   (1932) 147 LT 503, HL.
6   [1982] 3 All ER 1, HL.
7   Sale of Goods Act 1979, s 8; Supply of Goods and Services Act 1982, s 15 (see para 7.22).
8   *Sudbrook Trading Estate Ltd v Eggleton* [1982] 3 All ER 1, HL.
9   *G Percy Trentham Ltd v Archital Luxfer Ltd* [1993] 1 Lloyd's Rep 25 at 27.

5.25 Sometimes it may be possible to ignore uncertainty in an agreement. This can be done, for instance, where the uncertainty relates to what is a meaningless term. In *Nicolene Ltd v Simmonds*,[1] the agreement contained the phrase 'I assume the usual conditions of acceptance apply'. There were no usual conditions of acceptance, but the Court of Appeal said the phrase was meaningless and, since it did not relate to an important term or part of the contract, it could be ignored. A distinction must be drawn between meaningless phrases and phrases which denote that terms are still to be agreed. A phrase is unlikely to be considered meaningless, and thus capable of being ignored, if it concerns an important term of the contract.

1 [1953] 1 All ER 822, CA.

Agreement to agree

5.26 If the parties have agreed the essential terms of an agreement and agreed to be bound immediately, there is a concluded agreement despite the fact that further terms must be negotiated.[1] On the other hand, if an essential term of an agreement is open to further negotiation, or if the parties have not agreed to be bound immediately because further negotiation is necessary before a binding agreement can be concluded, there is no concluded agreement, but merely an agreement to agree. An example is where an agreement for the sale of goods leaves the price to be fixed by agreement between the parties. In *May and Butcher Ltd v R*,[2] the price of surplus tentage which was being sold by a government department to the claimants was such as 'shall be agreed upon from time to time between the government department and the purchasers'. The House of Lords found that, because an essential term was left open for future negotiation, the agreement was not a legally binding contract.

However, if the agreement expressly or impliedly provides a method for resolving the lack of agreement, there will be a valid contract. An example is provided by *Foley v Classique Coaches Ltd*;[3] the Court of Appeal held that an agreement containing the words 'price to be agreed by the parties' was a binding contract. The court felt able to distinguish *May and Butcher Ltd v R* on two grounds. First, on the basis that the parties had acted on the agreement for three years and their implied belief that they had been contractually bound during that period must be given effect, and, second, because the contract provided that in the absence of agreement on price it was to be determined by arbitration. *Beer v Bowden*[4] provides another example. Premises were let for 10 years (later extended to 14) at a fixed rent for the first five years, but at a rent 'to be agreed' thereafter. The Court of Appeal implied a term that in the absence of agreement a reasonable rent determined by the court should be paid.

1 *Pagnan SpA v Feed Products* [1987] 2 Lloyd's Rep 601, CA.
2 [1934] 2 KB 17n, HL.
3 [1934] 2 KB 1, CA.
4 [1981] 1 All ER 1070, CA.

Operation of a condition
Condition precedent

5.27 An agreement which appears to be a binding contract may never come into operation because it is subject to a condition precedent which is not satisfied. An example is afforded by *Pym v Campbell*.[1] In this case an agreement to purchase a share in an invention was subject to the condition precedent that the invention be approved by X. X failed to approve and thus no binding contract to buy came into existence.[2]

An agreement subject to a condition precedent is not necessarily devoid of all effect. It all depends on the interpretation which the court gives to it.

On its true construction, the effect of an agreement subject to a condition precedent may be that, although the agreement containing it is not binding before the condition is satisfied, neither party can withdraw until it is clear whether or not the condition will be satisfied.[3]

Alternatively, or in addition, the effect of such an agreement may be that one party must do his best to fulfil the condition[4] or, at least, not obstruct its fulfilment.[5] For example, the phrase 'subject to survey' in an agreement for the sale of land has been construed as meaning that the purchaser must proceed with due diligence to obtain a surveyor's report and, having received it, consider it, and must act in good faith. If, in good faith, he is not satisfied with the report he is not obliged to proceed with the purchase, but in the meantime neither party can withdraw.[6]

Lastly, a condition precedent may be construed as imposing no obligation on either party. This is the prima facie construction[7] given to 'subject to contract' and similar conditions. We deal with these further in para 5.28.

A condition precedent may be void for uncertainty, in which case the agreement in which it is contained is also void. An example is an agreement for the sale of land 'subject to the purchaser obtaining a *satisfactory mortgage*', since such a condition is too vague for the courts to enforce.[8]

1   (1856) 6 E & B 370.
2   In fact, it was held that there was no agreement at all.
3   *Smith v Butler* [1900] 1 QB 694, CA. In *Smallman v Smallman* [1971] 3 All ER 717, CA, a buyer, who withdrew from an agreement to purchase which was subject to a condition precedent before it was clear whether the condition was satisfied, was unable to recover the deposit he had paid.
4   *Marten v Whale* [1917] 2 KB 480, CA.
5   *Mackay v Dick* (1881) 6 App Cas 251, HL.
6   *Ee v Kakar* (1979) 40 P & CR 223.
7   *Alpenstow Ltd v Regalian Properties plc* [1985] 2 All ER 545.
8   *Lee-Parker v Izzet (No 2)* [1972] 2 All ER 800.

'Subject to contract' and similar conditions

5.28   A 'subject to contract' condition is usually inserted initially in an agreement to buy land which is for sale by private treaty. Unless there are very exceptional circumstances which oust the prima facie meaning of the phrase,[1] such agreements are simply 'agreements to agree' and are not binding, nor are the parties required to try to ensure that a contract is concluded.[2] Phrases similar to 'subject to contract' have the same effect, except that where an agreement for the sale of land is made 'subject to the purchaser obtaining a mortgage *on terms satisfactory to himself*' a further term is implied that such satisfaction must not be unreasonably withheld.[3]

Because an agreement to buy land 'subject to contract' is not binding, it is legally permissible for the vendor to agree to sell the property to someone else offering a higher price. This is particularly common when property prices are rising; it is called 'gazumping'.

1   *Alpenstow Ltd v Regalian Properties plc* [1985] 2 All ER 545.
2   *Winn v Bull* (1877) 7 Ch D 29.
3   *Janmohamed v Hassam* (1976) 241 Estates Gazette 609.

5.29   The precarious position of a party to an agreement to buy property 'subject to contract' has led such parties, and their legal advisers, to seek ways of protecting their legal position by the use of 'lock-out agreements', with varying success. A lock-out agreement is one where, in return for consideration by the other party, one party agrees to give the other party an exclusive opportunity to conclude a contract with him, ie he agrees not to negotiate with anyone else. A lock-out agreement whose duration is unlimited in time is not binding, but one which is subject to a time limit is.

This was held by the House of Lords in *Walford v Miles*.[1] In this case the claimants agreed in March 1987 'subject to contract' to buy a business from the defendants. Later that month there was a further agreement between one of the claimants and one of the defendants that, if the claimants obtained a 'comfort letter' from their bank that it was prepared to provide the finance for the purchase, the defendants would terminate negotiations with any third party. The comfort letter was provided, but at the end of March the defendants notified the claimants that they had decided to sell the business to a third party.

The claimants claimed that, although there was no binding contract for the sale of the business, their lock-out agreement with the defendants was binding, since they had provided consideration for the defendants' lock-out promise by providing the comfort letter and by promising to continue negotiations with the defendants.

The House of Lords held that, although it was possible for a lock-out agreement to be binding, the agreement in question was not binding because it was indefinite in duration.[2]

Walford v Miles can be contrasted with *Pitt v PHH Asset Management Ltd*[3] where a lock-out agreement for a specified period was held to be binding. In this case the defendant company had put on the market a property which attracted the interest of the claimant and of another person, Miss B. The claimant and Miss B made a number of offers, in which in effect they bid each other up. The claimant then entered an agreement through the defendant company's estate agents that the defendant company would sell the property to the claimant for £200,000 and would not consider any other offer provided that the claimant exchanged contracts within two weeks of receipt of a draft contract.

The defendant company sent a draft contract to the claimant. Eight days later the claimant indicated that he was ready to exchange contracts. However, on the same day, the claimant was notified that it had been decided to go ahead with a sale to Miss B at £210,000 unless the claimant was prepared to exchange contracts that day at £210,000. The claimant refused to do so and the property was sold to Miss B.

The claimant's action for breach of its lock-out agreement with the defendant company succeeded since it was of a specified duration (two weeks) and the defendant company was in breach of it. Of course, the defendant company was not bound by the lock-out agreement to sell to the claimant; it was only bound not to negotiate during the specified period. If it had waited for the two weeks to elapse, and not exchanged during that period, it would have been perfectly entitled thereafter to sell to Miss B.

The appropriate remedy for breach of a lock-out agreement is an award of damages, and not an injunction, since the purpose of such an agreement is to protect a potential purchaser from wasting expenses incurred in getting ready to complete when the vendor elects to sell to another. The potential purchaser can recover as damages his costs which have been wasted.[4]

1   [1992] 1 All ER 453, HL.
2   The claimants had argued that the lock-out agreement was subject to an implied term that the defendants would continue to negotiate in good faith with the claimants. The House of Lords held that, even if such a term could be implied, it would not assist the claimants because an agreement to such an effect was void for uncertainty, as stated in para 5.24 above.
3   [1993] 4 All ER 961, CA.
4   *Tye v House* [1997] 41 EG 160.

Condition subsequent

5.30   An agreement may also be subject to the operation of a condition subsequent. In such cases an agreement will be a binding contract unless and until the condition occurs. If it does occur, either the contract will automatically cease to bind or one party will have the right to cancel it, depending on the construction of the condition. In *Head v Tattersall*,[1] a contract for the sale of a horse was subject to the condition subsequent that, if the purchaser found within a given time that the horse did not meet its contractual description, the horse could be returned and the contract terminated. During that period, the purchaser found that the horse did not correspond with its description. It was held that he could return it and recover the price, even though it had been injured in the meanwhile.

1   (1871) LR 7 Exch 7.

Payment for work done in anticipation of concluding a contract

5.31   Where, in anticipation of concluding a contract with the defendant, the claimant has commenced *at the defendant's request* to perform the work which would be required under the contract, but no contract is entered into, the defendant is liable to pay a reasonable sum for the work done pursuant to his request.[1] This is of obvious importance, for example, in the type of case where the defendant has given the claimant a 'letter of intent' to contract and asked him to start work immediately but never finally concluded a contract.

1   *British Steel Corpn v Cleveland Bridge and Engineering Co Ltd* [1984] 1 All ER 504; cf *Regalian Properties plc v London Development Corpn* [1995] 1 All ER 1005.

Chapter 6

Binding agreement

6.1 An agreement which complies with the rules specified in the previous chapter will constitute a contract (ie a legally binding agreement), provided

- it is supported by consideration; and
- the parties intend to enter into a legally binding agreement.

Alternatively, it will constitute a contract if it is made by deed. We defined the requirements for a deed in para 4.6 above.

Intention to create legal relations

6.2 If an agreement is supported by consideration there is usually an intention to create legal relations, although the parties to an agreement rarely state this intention expressly. If the parties do not wish their agreement to be legally binding, they may expressly state this and the courts will give effect to their intention. In the absence of an express indication of intention, the courts rely on two presumptions in deciding whether there was an intention to create legal relations, both of which can be rebutted expressly or impliedly by the parties:

- parties to social, domestic and family arrangements and other non-business or non-commercial agreements do not intend to be legally bound;[1] *and*
- parties to business and commercial agreements intend their agreements to be legally binding.[2]

An example of the first type of arrangement is an agreement to give lifts to work, even if it is on an organised basis and involves payment to the car owners for their petrol.[3] While arrangements made within the family or household are presumed not to be intended to be legally binding, the nature of the agreement may clearly indicate that the parties intended a particular arrangement to be legally binding. In *Ward v Warnke*,[4] X allowed her son-in-law and her daughter (J) to occupy her holiday home under an agreement with the son-in-law that he would pay a modest rent (£3.50, later £6.00, per week). X paid the money into a building society account which named J as the beneficiary. The Court of Appeal held that on the facts the agreement constituted a legally binding tenancy agreement between the parties; the fact that it was between members of a family did not prevent the creation of a legal relationship. An example of a non-commercial agreement which is not a social, domestic or family arrangement is provided by *Robinson v Customs and Excise Comrs*,[5] which concerned an agreement by Customs and Excise to pay an informer for information. It was held that, because this was not a commercial agreement where an intent to create legal relations would be presumed, the informer had to prove such an intent in order to be able to enforce the agreement.

In the case of a business or commercial agreement it is extremely difficult to rebut the presumption that the arrangement is to be legally binding, other than by clear words. A case where clear words led to the presumption being rebutted is *Rose and Frank Co v J R Crompton & Bros Ltd*,[6] in which the defendants appointed the claimants their agents to sell their products in America under an agreement which contained an 'honour clause', ie a clause which said the agreement was merely recording the intention of the parties and was binding in honour only and not in law. The claimants sued for alleged breach of contract. The Court of Appeal and the House of Lords held that the honour clause constituted a clearly expressed intention that the agency agreement was not to be legally binding and that effect had to be given to this intention.

Even where the presumption is rebutted by clear words, this does not prevent the subsequent conduct of the parties to the agreement constituting a legally binding agreement. In *Rose and Frank Co v J R Crompton & Bros Ltd*, the parties to the agency agreement ordered and supplied goods for sale in America. It was held that these orders and acceptances gave rise to legally binding agreements, even though the agency agreement was not legally binding.

An important statutory exception to the presumption that business and commercial agreements are intended to be legally binding is contained in the Trade Union and Labour Relations (Consolidation) Act 1992, s 179, which provides that collective agreements between employers and trade unions are presumed not to be legally enforceable unless they are made in writing and expressly state that the agreement is to be legally enforceable. However, if terms in a collective agreement are incorporated in an individual employee's contract of employment, they are presumed to be intended to be binding.[7]

1   *Balfour v Balfour* [1919] 2 KB 571, CA. This presumption does not apply where the two parties are married to each other but are, or are about to be, separated. They are presumed to have intended to create legal relations: *Merritt v Merritt* [1970] 2 All ER 760, CA.
2   *Edwards v Skyways Ltd* [1964] 1 All ER 494.
3   *Coward v Motor Insurers' Bureau* [1962] 1 All ER 531, CA.
4   (1990) 22 HLR 496, CA.
5   (2000) Times, 28 April.
6   [1925] AC 445, HL.
7   *Robertson v British Gas Corpn* [1983] ICR 351, CA.

Consideration

6.3   A promise in an agreement not made by deed[1] must be supported by consideration on the part of the party to whom it is made if it is to be legally binding. It is in the requirement of consideration that English law recognises the idea that a contract is a bargain.

In order to provide consideration for a promise, the promisee (the person to whom the promise was made) must have made a promise or done an act:

* in return for that promise; and
* at the express or implied request of the promisor (the person making that promise).

It follows from the requirement that the promisee's act or promise must have been requested by the promisor that a 'gratuitous' act or promise by a promisee is not consideration. This is shown by *Re Cory*.[2] The YMCA wished to build a hall. It needed £150,000 to do so. £85,000 had been promised or was available. However, the YMCA decided not to commit itself to going on with the project until it saw that its efforts to raise the whole sum were likely to succeed. C then promised a donation of 1,000 guineas (£1,050) for the purpose of building the hall. The YMCA subsequently entered into a building contract for the hall, which they alleged they were largely induced to do by C's promise. C then died and the question arose whether his promise to pay was legally binding, in which case his estate would be bound by it. It was held that C's promise was not binding; the YMCA had not provided any consideration for C's promise because C had not expressly or impliedly requested the YMCA to do (or promise to do) anything in return.

It also follows from the definition of consideration that a promise (not made by deed) to give property on condition that something occurs is not legally binding if the promisee is not expressly or impliedly requested by the promisor to do or promise anything in return. In *Dickinson v Abel*,[3] A told B that he was willing to pay £100,000 for a farm which was vested in a bank as trustees. B had no proprietary interest in the farm but had previously passed on to the bank offers for the farm. B asked A: 'What's in it for me?' and was told that he would be paid £10,000 if A bought the farm for £100,000 or less. A did not ask B to perform any specific services, but B telephoned the bank and told them that an offer of £100,000 was on its way and that he personally would accept it. The farm was sold to A for less than £100,000 and B was paid the £10,000. The question later arose as to whether the £10,000 was taxable, which it would be if paid under a contract. It was somewhat surprisingly found as a fact that A had not expressly or impliedly requested B to do anything. Consequently, it was held, what B had done was not consideration for A's promise and there was therefore no legally binding agreement (ie contract) between A and B but merely a conditional gift. While the finding on the facts is hard to accept, the important legal point is the judge's application of the law to those facts.

1   Para 4.6 above.
2   (1912) 29 TLR 18.
3   [1969] 1 All ER 484.

6.4   In a number of cases,[1] consideration has been defined as follows: that X provides consideration for Y's promise if he confers a benefit on Y, in return for which Y's promise is given, or if he incurs a detriment, in compensation for which Y's promise is given. Certainly if there is either a benefit or a detriment to the appropriate party that is good consideration, but this definition has been criticised and some cases cannot be explained in terms of benefit and detriment. A better definition of consideration is that if one party's action or forbearance, promised or actual, is the price for which the other's promise is bought, and without that price there would be no bargain, the former party has provided consideration for the latter's promise.[2]

1   See, for example, *Currie v Misa* (1875) LR 10 Exch 153. For a more recent reference to this type of definition, see *Barry v Heathcote Ball & Co (Commercial Auctions) Ltd* [2001] 1 All ER 944, CA.
2   See *Dunlop Pneumatic Tyre Co Ltd v Selfridge & Co Ltd* [1915] AC 847 at 855.

Executed and executory consideration

6.5   In the case of a unilateral contract, ie where a person does something at the request of another in return for a promise, such as finding a lost dog in return for the promise of a reward, the person doing the requested act thereby provides consideration for the other's promise. In a unilateral contract, consideration is only given by one party and only the other party is bound (hence the description 'unilateral contract'). The consideration provided in a unilateral contract is said to be 'executed' because it consists of the actual doing of something in response to a promise by the other party and at his request.

In the case of a bilateral contract, ie where a party to an agreement promises to do something in response to a promise by the other and at his request, as where X promises to pay for goods to be supplied by Y, a party provides consideration by giving his promise. Thus, in the above example, X provides consideration for Y's promise to supply the goods. In a bilateral contract, consideration is given by both parties and both parties are bound (hence the description 'bilateral contract'). The consideration here is said to be 'executory' because it consists of a promise by each party which need not be executed (ie the promise need not be carried out) in order for the promise of the other party, for which it is exchanged, to be binding. The concept of executory consideration illustrates the difficulty of the benefit or detriment theory of consideration. When no one has done anything and there are merely promises there is no benefit or detriment to anyone, but it is possible to say that the price of one party's promise was the promise made by the other party.

Both executed and executory consideration are good consideration in law, unlike 'past consideration'.

Past consideration

6.6 'Past consideration' is said to have been given by a person when, only *after* he has done something, a promise (eg to reward him) is made in return by another person. 'Past consideration' is an inaccurate expression, since it is not consideration at all and a person who has given it cannot enforce another's promise made in return for it.

The fact that past consideration is not good consideration illustrates the idea that consideration is the price of a promise. In *Re McArdle*,[1] work was done by X on a house which had been left to her and other members of her family. The other members then promised to reimburse the cost to her of the work but failed to keep their promise. X sued on the promise to pay but failed because she had provided no consideration for it, since her acts (doing the work on the house), which she alleged constituted consideration, pre-dated the promise by the relatives.

It would be wrong to think that all actions which are not preceded by an express promise constitute past consideration. If an act is done by X at the request of Y in circumstances where X and Y must have understood that the act was to be remunerated (so that a prior promise of remuneration by Y can be *implied*), the act by X is good consideration.[2] An act done in response to a request accompanied by an implied promise of remuneration may be followed by an express promise to pay a particular sum or confer a particular benefit. If this is so, the promise quantifies the amount due to the party who performed the requested act. If there is no subsequent promise, the amount due is determined on the basis of reasonable remuneration for the services provided or the things supplied. What transforms apparently past consideration into good consideration is the fact that the action is in response to a request which raises an implied promise of payment. The requested action is the price of the implied promise to pay. In *Re McArdle* there was no prior request or expectation of payment. However, in *Re Casey's Patents, Stewart v Casey*,[3] the claimants wrote to Casey saying that 'in consideration of your [past] services as practical manager' they would give him a one-third share in certain patents. This promise was fulfilled but subsequently the claimants sought to recover the patents, claiming that Casey had given no consideration for their promise. The Court of Appeal rejected this argument, saying that Casey's services as manager clearly raised an implication that they would be remunerated and thus Casey had provided consideration, the subsequent express promise merely fixing the amount of that remuneration.

1   [1951] 1 All ER 905, CA.
2   *Lampleigh v Brathwait* (1615) Hob 105; *Kennedy v Broun* (1863) 13 CBNS 677; *Re Casey's Patents, Stewart v Casey* [1892] 1 Ch 104, CA; *Pao On v Lau Yiu Long* [1979] 3 All ER 65, PC.
3   [1892] 1 Ch 104, CA.

6.7 In determining whether a contract is supported by consideration, the courts have regard to two factors:

- consideration must have some value but need not be adequate; and
- consideration must be real and sufficient, ie what is alleged to be consideration must be an action or promise which the law recognises as capable of being consideration.

Adequacy

6.8 Provided that the alleged consideration has some economic value in the eyes of the law, the courts will not question its adequacy, even though one party is apparently making a very good bargain and the other is not. In *Mountford v Scott*,[1] £1, paid for an option to purchase a house, was found to be good consideration. Money is always considered to have an economic value and the fact that the amount was small was irrelevant.

Although the courts will not question the adequacy of consideration, the fact that the consideration is clearly inadequate may indicate that the contract has been procured by fraudulent misrepresentation, undue influence or duress on the part of the party benefiting from the inadequacy, in which case the contract may be set aside if the rules described in chapter 12 are satisfied.

The next paragraph provides another illustration that the courts will not question the adequacy of consideration which has some value.

1 [1975] 1 All ER 198, CA.

Forbearance to sue

6.9 If a person who could sue another promises not to pursue his claim, that constitutes good consideration for a promise by the other person to pay a sum of money as a final settlement of the claim. In addition, the person promising to pay that sum thereby provides consideration for the other's promise not to pursue his claim. In such a case, the amount of the acknowledged liability is the sum agreed to be paid. It is important to distinguish this situation from that where the acknowledged liability is greater than the sum promised or actually paid;[1] a promise to accept part payment in such a case is not binding, as explained in para 6.15 below.

It might be thought that promising to abandon an invalid claim cannot be good consideration. However, the abandonment of an invalid claim will be good consideration if the party abandoning it can show that the claim was reasonable in itself, that he genuinely believed the claim had some chance of success and intended to pursue it, and that he was not concealing from the other party facts which would constitute a defence to the claim.[2] The argument is that abandoning a doubtful claim saves the parties from the uncertainties of litigation and its attendant expense.

1 The dividing line between the two can be fine: see *Ferguson v Davies* [1997] 1 All ER 315, CA.
2 *Miles v New Zealand Alford Estate Co* (1886) 32 Ch D 266; *Horton v Horton (No 2)* [1960] 3 All ER 649, CA.

Sufficiency

6.10 The law refuses to recognise certain types of action or promise as capable of constituting consideration, with the result that a person making such an action or promise cannot enforce another's promise given in return for it. Such an action or promise is said not to be sufficient consideration, which is rather confusing since in law it is not consideration at all.

Performance of, or promise to perform, an existing duty imposed by law

6.11 The law imposes obligations on all people, and it is necessary to discuss whether performing or promising to perform such an obligation can also be good consideration for the contractual promise of another. The basic position was stated in *Collins v Godefroy*,[1] in which the claimant gave evidence at the defendant's trial in response to a promise of payment. When he sued for the payment, it was held that he could not succeed because he had provided no consideration since he was obliged by law to give evidence. It is now clear that the principle in *Collins v Godefroy* has been refined by the principle in *Williams v Roffey Bros & Nicholls (Contractors) Ltd*, referred to in para 6.13 below. The result is that, except where the existing duty is to pay money,[2] where A makes a promise to B in return for B's performance of, or promise to perform, his existing duty imposed by law to do something (other than to pay money), B will provide consideration for A's promise if, as a result of B's performance or promise, A obtains a practical benefit (or avoids a 'disbenefit').

1   (1831) 1 B & Ad 950.
2   *Re Selectmove Ltd* [1995] 2 All ER 531, CA.

6.12   The principle in *Collins v Godefroy* does not apply if the party seeking to show that he provided consideration promised to do, or did, more than was required by law, as where he promises to pay (or pays) more than he is legally obliged, because that is good consideration. In *Glasbrook Bros Ltd v Glamorgan County Council*,[1] the company requested greater protection for its mine during a strike than the police thought necessary and offered to pay for the increased police presence. The company later refused to pay, claiming that, since the police were under a legal duty to protect property, they had provided no consideration for the company's promise of payment. The House of Lords held that the company was obliged to pay because the duty of the police was to take such steps as they reasonably thought necessary and, by providing protection beyond that level, they had done more than they were legally obliged to do and thus had provided consideration for the company's promise.

1   [1925] AC 270, HL.

Performance of, or promise to perform, an existing contractual duty owed to the other party

6.13   If a person is under a contractual duty to do something, the mere performance of that duty (or mere promise to perform it) cannot be good consideration for another promise by the person to whom the contractual duty is already owed. In *Stilk v Myrick*,[1] the crew of a ship were paid a lump sum for a voyage including all normal emergencies. During the voyage two of the crew deserted and the captain promised to pay the wages of the deserters to the rest of the crew if they would continue the voyage short-handed. Once returned to England, the extra wages were not paid and the seamen sued. Their claim failed, the court finding that they had provided no consideration since they were required to cope with normal emergencies by their existing contracts. Desertion or death of fellow crew members was a normal emergency so they had done no more than they had contracted to do. The court stressed, however, that, if the seamen had promised to do more than they were obliged to do by their existing contracts, they would have provided good consideration. For example, if they had promised to face exceptional hazards that would have been good consideration for their employer's promise.[2]

In *Williams v Roffey Bros & Nicholls (Contractors) Ltd*[3] the Court of Appeal propounded a major limitation on the principle in *Stilk v Myrick*. It held that, where A makes a further promise to B in return for B's promise to perform (or performance of) his contractual obligations already owed to A, and as a result of B's promise (or performance) A obtains a practical benefit (or avoids a 'disbenefit'), B provides good consideration for A's further promise. The facts of this case were that the claimant had been engaged by the defendants, who were the main contractors in refurbishing a block of flats, to carry out carpentry work for £20,000 which turned out to be unprofitable for him. The main contract contained a 'time penalty' clause and, fearful that the claimant would not complete the work on time, the defendants promised him an extra £10,300, payable at the rate of £575 per flat, if he carried out the work on time. The claimant promised to do so and completed the work in a number of flats, but was not paid the amount promised. The Court of Appeal held that the claimant could recover the unpaid amount; the defendants' promise was binding, consideration having been given for it by the claimant, since his promise benefited the defendants (apparently by avoiding the penalty for delay and avoiding the trouble and expense of engaging other people to complete the carpentry work). The Court of Appeal added that, if the defendant's promise had been obtained by duress or fraud, the contract could have been set aside on that ground.[4]

Since it is unlikely that A will make a further promise to B if he is not going to obtain some benefit from B's promise to perform (or performance of) his contractual obligations owed to A, the decision appeared to refine the principle in *Stilk v Myrick* almost out of existence. However, in the subsequent case of *Re Selectmove Ltd*[5] the Court of Appeal took a restrictive approach to its decision in *Williams v Roffey Bros*, saying that it did not apply where the existing obligation was one to pay money. It held that a promise to pay (or the payment of) money already due could not be consideration for the promise of another. The Court emphasised that the existing obligation in *Williams v Roffey Bros* was to do work and supply materials and distinguished that case on that ground.

1   (1809) 2 Camp 317. For an affirmation of this rule, see *Syros Shipping Co SA v Elaghill Trading Co, The Proodos C* [1981] 3 All ER 189.
2   *Hartley v Ponsonby* (1857) 7 E & B 872; *North Ocean Shipping Co Ltd v Hyundai Construction Co, The Atlantic Baron* [1978] 3 All ER 1170.
3   [1990] 1 All ER 512, CA.
4   Chapter 12 below.
5   [1995] 2 All ER 531, CA.

Performance of an existing contractual duty owed to a third party

6.14   If a party to a contract with X (the 'third party') is obliged by it to perform some action, a subsequent promise by him to perform that action (or his performance of it) can be good consideration for a promise by another person, whether or not there is any benefit to that person. The principle in *Stilk v Myrick*[1] has never applied to this situation. In *Scotson v Pegg*,[2] for example, the claimants had contracted to deliver coal to X, or wherever X ordered it to be delivered. X sold the coal to the defendant and told the claimants to deliver it to him. The defendant then promised the claimants that if they delivered the coal he would unload it at a given rate. The defendant failed to unload at this rate and, when sued, argued that the claimants had not provided consideration for his promise by delivering the coal, because they were obliged to do so under their contracts with X. The court held that the claimants had provided consideration.

In two modern cases, *New Zealand Shipping Co Ltd v A M Satterthwaite & Co Ltd, The Eurymedon*[3] and *Pao On v Lau Yiu Long*,[4] the Privy Council has affirmed that a promise to discharge, or the discharge of, a pre-existing contractual obligation to a third party can be valid consideration for another's promise. In the former case, consideration for the promise consisted of unloading a ship which the promisee was already bound to unload under a contract with a third party.

1   See para 6.13 above.
2   (1861) 6 H & N 295.
3   [1974] 1 All ER 1015, PC.
4   [1979] 3 All ER 65, PC.

Part payment of debts

6.15   *Position at common law*   It is not surprising that, if A is under a contractual obligation to pay B and B agrees to forego part of the debt, A's payment of the rest of the debt (ie his partial performance of his existing obligation to B) is not consideration for B's promise and, according to the common law, B can subsequently recover the remainder of the debt. In *Foakes v Beer*,[1] Mrs Beer was owed money under a judgment debt by Dr Foakes. She agreed to accept payment by instalments but the agreement did not refer to the question of interest, which is payable on a judgment debt. Dr Foakes paid the debt. Mrs Beer then sued for the interest. In reply, Dr Foakes pleaded the agreement between them, in which Mrs Beer had agreed to bring no further action on the judgment if he paid the debt by instalments. Mrs Beer contended successfully that there was no consideration for her promise and that, therefore, even if her promise had included a promise to waive the interest element, it was not binding. Dr Foakes' payment by instalments of the judgment debts could not be consideration for a promise by her to take no further action. He was merely paying less than what he was obliged to do. The House of Lords regretted that this decision had to be reached, but considered itself bound by previous cases.

There are exceptions to the rule that part payment of a debt is no consideration for a promise to remit the rest of the debt. In *Pinnel's Case*,[2] for instance, it was said that, provided it was done at the creditor's request, early payment of part of a debt, or part payment at another place than that specified for payment, or payment in kind, even if the value of the goods is less than the debt, is good consideration for a promise by the creditor to forego the remainder of the debt. Thus, if A owes B £100 payable on 1 January at Reading and, at B's request, A pays £1 on 31 December (or pays £1 at Leicester on the correct day, or gives B a rose or a scarf on the correct day), the debt is validly discharged. It used to be thought that a part payment by cheque was good consideration for a promise to remit a debt payable in cash. This has been rejected by the Court of Appeal who decided that nowadays there is no effective difference between cash and a cheque which is honoured.[3]

1   (1884) 9 App Cas 605, HL.
2   (1602) 5 Co Rep 117a.
3   *D & C Builders Ltd v Rees* [1965] 3 All ER 837, CA.

6.16   There are two somewhat anomalous areas where partial payment of a debt discharges it. Both areas concern debts. First, where a debtor makes an arrangement with all his creditors that they will all be paid a given percentage of what they are owed, no creditor who has been paid it can recover more than that given percentage.[1] Second, when a third party pays part of a debt in full settlement, that is a valid discharge of the whole debt, and the creditor cannot recover the balance from the debtor.[2] The reason which has been given is that it would be a fraud on the third party if the creditor could do so.[3]

Neither of these areas can satisfactorily be explained in terms of principle (ie consideration by the debtor for the creditor's promise) and are best explained as based on grounds of public policy.

1   *Good v Cheesman* (1831) 2 B & Ad 328.
2   *Hirachand Punamchand v Temple* [1911] 2 KB 330, CA.
3   *Hirachand Punamchand v Temple* [1911] 2 KB 330, CA.

6.17   *Position in equity* Apart from these exceptions it appeared that a debtor who paid part of a debt, believing that the creditor had agreed to remit the remainder of the debt, had no defence if the creditor sought to recover the amount foregone. However, in 1947 Denning J (as he was then) called upon equity to aid the debtor. In *Central London Property Trust Ltd v High Trees House Ltd*,[1] the claimants let a block of flats to the defendants in 1937 for 99 years at a rent of £2,500 per year. The defendants intended to sub-let the flats but, because of the war, found they had many vacant flats and could not pay the rent out of profits. The claimants agreed to accept a reduced rent of £1,250, which was paid quarterly from 1941 until September 1945, by which time all the flats were let. The claimants demanded full rent from September 1945.

The defendants had provided no consideration for the promise by the claimants to remit the rent, but Denning J found that, while the common law could provide no defence in respect of an instalment to which the promise applied, equity could. The judge, drawing on two little-known cases decided in the 19th century, said that where one party gave a promise which he intended to be binding and to be acted on, and which was acted on, that promise could be raised as a defence by the promisee if the promisor sought to enforce his strict legal rights. In this case the claimants had promised to reduce the rent; they intended their promise to be binding, they knew the defendants would act on it and the defendants did so act; therefore the rent underpaid in the past could not have been recovered by the claimants since this would be inequitable. However, the judge found that the promise was understood by the parties only to apply under the conditions prevailing at the time it was made, namely when the flats were only partially let, and that when the flats became fully let, early in 1945, the promise to remit part of the rent ceased to bind the claimants. As explained in para 6.20, where a promise to accept part payment in settlement of a debt satisfies the above tests, the promise can be terminated by notice.

This case illustrates the equitable doctrine known as promissory estoppel,[2] which applies to promises to remit debts (in whole or part) and also to promises not to enforce other contractual rights.

1   [1956] 1 All ER 256n.
2   Estoppel (as opposed to promissory estoppel) is a legal doctrine whereby if a person misrepresents to another an existing fact and intends this misrepresentation to be acted on, and it is acted on by the other who suffers detriment in consequence, he cannot subsequently deny the truth of that fact. The doctrine was inapplicable in the *High Trees* case because the representation was as to the future and not to an existing fact.

Promissory estoppel

6.18   Under the doctrine of promissory estoppel a promise not to enforce a contractual right is given some effect, despite the absence of consideration for it, where it would be inequitable for the promisor simply to go back on his promise and enforce that right. There is authority that the doctrine can even apply where the promise is made before the contract is entered into, as where a person who is negotiating to lease property to another promises not to enforce a repairing covenant in the draft lease.[1] This goes beyond the previous authorities, which required or assumed that there must be an existing relationship between promisor and promisee when the promise was made, and its compatibility with certain other rules of the law of contract is as yet unexplained.[2]

1   *Brikom Investments Ltd v Carr* [1979] 2 All ER 753 at 758.
2   Such as the law relating to pre-contractual misrepresentations: ch 12.

6.19   The precise scope of promissory estoppel is still not entirely clear; indeed, in *Woodhouse A C Israel Cocoa Ltd SA v Nigerian Produce Marketing Co Ltd*,[1] Lord Hailsham LC said that it may need to be reviewed and reduced to a coherent body of doctrine by the courts. Nevertheless, its requirements appear to be as follows:

Unequivocal promise   There must be an unequivocal promise[2] by one party that he will not, at least for the time being, enforce his strict contractual rights against the other. The promise may be either express or implied from conduct.[3] Silence and inaction cannot by themselves give rise to a promissory estoppel because they are by their nature equivocal, since there can be more than one reason why the party concerned is silent and inactive.[4]

Alteration of position   The promisor must have intended that his promise should be acted on by the promisee, and the promisee must have acted on it in the sense of altering his position in reliance on the promise by doing something he would not otherwise have done or not doing what he would otherwise have done.[5] This requirement was satisfied in *Hughes v Metropolitan Rly Co*,[6] where a tenant, who had been given six months' notice to repair the premises in accordance with a repairing covenant but who had been induced by the landlord's conduct soon afterwards to believe that the lease would not be forfeited for failure to repair, failed to repair in reliance on this belief. It is not so easy to discern an alteration of position in the *High Trees* case, but the requirement has been said to be satisfied by the fact that the lessees elected to pay a lower rent and to continue to be liable as lessees in reliance on the lessor's promise that a lower rent would be accepted in satisfaction.[7]

The present requirement means that promissory estoppel cannot arise if the promisee does nothing, by action or inaction, in reliance on the promise but simply does what he was going to do anyway regardless of whether or not the promise was made.[8] This is illustrated by *Fontana NV v Mautner*.[9] T, the tenant of a flat, refused to leave when his tenancy expired, on the grounds that he had been a model tenant for many years and that a move would be disastrous for the health of his chronically-ill wife. At a meeting with a representative of the landlord, T was assured by the representative that he could stay on in the flat as long as he wished, but he subsequently received a notice to quit. In proceedings for possession, Balcombe J rejected T's claim that the assurance gave rise to a promissory estoppel, and made an order for possession. The judge held that this was not a case of promissory estoppel because T had done nothing, by action or inaction, in reliance on the assurance but had simply done what he was going to do anyway (and that was to sit tight for as long as he possibly could).

Inequitable for promisor to resile   It must be inequitable for the promisor to go back on his promise, having regard to the course of dealings which has taken place between the parties.[10] This requirement is not onerous because it will normally be satisfied if the promisee has simply altered his position in reliance on the promise by doing something he would not otherwise have done or by not doing something he would otherwise have done. However, this will not always be the case, as is shown by *The Post Chaser*,[11] where the promisors resiled from their promise not to enforce their strict rights only two days after making it. It was held that this was not inequitable because, in this short period, the promisees had not suffered any prejudice, despite having relied on the promise.

The present requirement has another aspect; it is not inequitable for the promisor to go back on his promise, and the promisee is therefore not protected by promissory estoppel, if the promise has been procured by improper pressure or fraud on the part of the promisee or an associate (or by other similar conduct which would render it unfair to the promisor to hold him to his promise). In *D & C Builders Ltd v Rees*,[12] the claimants were owed £482 by the defendant who knew that they were in desperate need of money to stave off bankruptcy. The defendant's wife offered the claimants £300 in settlement of the debt, saying in effect that if they refused they would get nothing. The claimants accepted the £300 reluctantly in settlement of the debt but later sued successfully for the balance. Lord Denning MR refused to allow the defendant to rely on promissory estoppel; his wife's conduct had been improper and therefore it was not inequitable for the claimants to go back on their promise and insist on their strict contractual right to payment of the balance.

1   [1972] 2 All ER 271 at 282.
2   *Woodhouse A C Israel Cocoa Ltd SA v Nigerian Produce Marketing Co Ltd* [1972] 2 All ER 271, HL.
3   *Hughes v Metropolitan Rly Co* (1877) 2 App Cas 439, HL.
4   *Allied Maritime Transport Ltd v Vale do Rio Doce Navegaeao SA, The Leonidas D* [1985] 2 All ER 796, CA.
5   *Hughes v Metropolitan Rly Co* (1877) 2 App Cas 439, HL; *Central London Property Trust Ltd v High Trees House Ltd* [1956] 1 All ER 256n; *Tool Metal Manufacturing Co Ltd v Tungsten Electric Co Ltd* [1955] 2 All ER 657, HL; *Ajayi v R T Briscoe (Nigeria) Ltd* [1964] 3 All ER 556, PC.
6   (1877) 2 App Cas 439, HL.
7   Spencer Bower and Turner *Estoppel by Misrepresentation* (3rd edn) p 393.
8   *Scandinavian Trading Tanker Co AB v Flota Petrolera Ecuatoriana, The Scaptrade* [1983] 1 All ER 301, CA (affd [1983] 2 All ER 763, HL).

9   (1979) 254 Estates Gazette 199.
10 *Hughes v Metropolitan Rly Co* (1877) 2 App Cas 439, HL; *Tool Metal Manufacturing Co Ltd v Tungsten Electric Co Ltd* [1955] 2 All ER 657, HL.
11 *Société Italo-Belge pour le Commerce et l'Industrie SA v Palm and Vegetable Oils (Malaysian) Sdn Bhd, The Post Chaser* [1982] 1 All ER 19.
12 [1965] 3 All ER 837, CA.

6.20 *Effect of promissory estoppel* Generally, promissory estoppel only suspends, and does not discharge (ie does not wholly extinguish), an obligation. Where promissory estoppel operates to suspend an obligation, the promisor may, by giving reasonable notice to the promisee, revert to his strict contractual rights thereafter.[1] If a promise not to enforce a strict contractual right was clearly intended to be operative only for a certain period, as in the *High Trees* case, the promisor automatically reverts to that right on the expiry of the period, if he has not previously determined his promise by giving reasonable notice.[2]

Where an obligation has been suspended, the effect of the promisor's reversion to the strict contractual position varies. If the obligation is to pay a lump sum or to perform some other act, such as to repair under a repairing covenant in a lease, the effect of a reversion is that after the period of reasonable notice the promisee must then perform his strict contractual obligation. An example is provided by *Hughes v Metropolitan Rly Co*,[3] discussed above, where the House of Lords held that the six months' notice to repair which had been suspended ran from the time of the landlord's reversion to his strict contractual rights. On the other hand, where the obligation in question is to make periodic payments (such as the payment of rent) or to make some other performance by instalments, the effect of a reversion to the strict contractual position is as follows. The promisee is liable to make future payments (or other performance) in full in respect of instalments due after the period of reasonable notice, but (unless the promise otherwise provides) he is not liable to pay (or perform) what was due, and unpaid (or unperformed), during the currency of the estoppel.[4]

Exceptionally, the effect of promissory estoppel may be to make a promise irrevocable, and thereby to discharge, and not just suspend, the promisee's obligations. A promise subject to promissory estoppel becomes irrevocable if the promisee cannot revert to his strict contractual position.[5]

1   *Tool Metal Manufacturing Co Ltd v Tungsten Electric Co Ltd* [1955] 2 All ER 657, HL; *Ajayi v R T Briscoe (Nigeria) Ltd* [1964] 3 All ER 556, PC.
2   *Birmingham and District Land Co Ltd v London and North Western Rly Co* (1888) 40 Ch D 268 at 288.
3   (1877) 2 App Cas 439, HL.
4   *Central London Property Trust Ltd v High Trees House Ltd* [1956] 1 All ER 256n; *Tungsten Electric Co Ltd v Tool Metal Manufacturing Co Ltd* (1950) 69 RPC 108, CA; *Tool Metal Manufacturing Co Ltd v Tungsten Electric Co Ltd* [1955] 2 All ER 657, HL.
5   *Ajayi v R T Briscoe (Nigeria) Ltd* [1964] 3 All ER 556, PC.

6.21 *A shield, not a sword* Promissory estoppel only prevents the promisor from enforcing his strict rights (at least, without reasonable notice) despite the absence of consideration from the promisee for the promise; it cannot be used to found a cause of action. In *Combe v Combe*,[1] a husband promised to pay his wife maintenance shortly before they were divorced. In reliance on his promise she did not bring court proceedings for financial provision. He failed to pay and she sued him. She had provided no consideration for his promise because he had not requested her not to bring proceedings for financial provision. Consequently, she alleged that he was estopped from going back on his promise (so that it was binding on him) because she had relied on his promise. The Court of Appeal rejected her claim, on the ground that promissory estoppel was a shield and not a sword.

1   [1951] 1 All ER 767, CA.

Consideration: discharge and variation

6.22 We have seen that consideration is necessary for the formation of contracts which are not made by deed, and that a promise by the creditor to remit a debt is not binding at common law without the provision of consideration by the debtor.[1] Consideration is also necessary when the parties agree (otherwise than by deed) to discharge (ie end) or to vary their contract before it is completely performed. Otherwise, the agreement is not binding at common law.

1   For two cases which are probable exceptions, see para 6.16 above.

6.23 The discharge of a contract by agreement may be either mutual or unilateral. It will be mutual, subject to the rules discussed later, where both parties still have contractual obligations to perform, ie there is executory consideration on both sides; it will be unilateral, subject to what we say in para 6.25 below, where one party still has contractual obligations to perform but the other party has completed his performance of the contract.

Mutual discharge
6.24 If both parties still have contractual obligations to perform, any agreement to discharge the contract relieves both parties from further performance of it. In such a case, both parties have provided consideration, for each party promises not to require further performance of contractual obligations by the other party in return for being absolved himself from further performance.

Unilateral discharge
6.25 A unilateral discharge by agreement is only effective if the party to be absolved has provided separate consideration for the other's promise to absolve him. In other words, where one party has performed all his contractual obligations prior to the agreement, his promise to release the other party from further performance does not bind him unless that other party provides separate consideration. Unilateral discharge by agreement is also known as accord (agreement to discharge) and satisfaction (consideration for that agreement). In relation to whether simply performing (or promising) to perform the existing contractual obligation (in whole or part) in response to a promise of release can constitute consideration, the reader is referred to paras 6.13 and 6.15 above, in particular.

Accord without satisfaction is ineffective to discharge a contract. Satisfaction usually consists of doing something in return for the promise to discharge, but the satisfaction which is offered may be a promise to do something. If so, it is necessary to decide whether the original contract is discharged from the moment of the accord or only when the promise, which is the alleged satisfaction, has been translated into action. The original contract will be discharged if the accord indicates on its proper interpretation that the person promised the satisfaction accepted the promise in discharge of that contract.[1] Even if this is not so, the accord will presumptively discharge the original contract,[2] although that discharge will be avoided (and the original contract revived) if the promise is not honoured.[2] If the accord expressly states that discharge of the original contract depends on *performance* of the promise to do something, the original contract can only be discharged when the promise is performed.

Promissory estoppel[3] may be available as a defence to a person who has been promised a release from further performance in circumstances where his obligation has not been discharged by accord and satisfaction because he has not provided consideration for the promise.

1   See, for example, *Elton Cop Dyeing Co Ltd v Robert Broadbent & Son Ltd* (1919) 89 LJKB 186, CA.

2   *Jameson v Central Electricity Generating Board (No 1)* [1999] 1 All ER 193, HL.
3   Paras 6.17–6.21 above.

Variation

6.26   If the variation of a contract benefits both parties (or could benefit one or other of them[1] depending on the outcome of a contingency) it will have contractual effect because each party will provide consideration for the other's variation promise, but it will have no effect (because of lack of consideration) if it can only be of benefit to one party. Suppose that a contract between A and B requires A to deliver 100 tons of copper to B in Leicester on 1 June. If A and B agree that A should, instead, deliver 95 tons on 1 May (or 100 tons on 1 July in Reading) the variation has contractual effect because it benefits both parties; in contrast, a variation whereby B agreed to accept the delivery of 95 tons in Leicester on 1 June would have no contractual effect, because it could only be of benefit to A, except that it might have a limited effect by virtue of the doctrine of promissory estoppel.

1   As where the variation consists of the alteration of the currency of payment, whose exchange rate against the original currency of payment may go up or down by the time payment is due: *W J Alan & Co Ltd v El Nasr Export and Import Co* [1972] 2 All ER 127, CA.

Chapter 7

Contractual terms

7.1   The terms of a contract may be:

- express; or
- implied.

Express terms

7.2   Clearly, the ascertainment of its express terms is facilitated when the contract has been reduced into writing, particularly because under the 'parol evidence'[1] rule oral or other evidence extrinsic to the document is not admissible generally to add to, vary, or contradict, the terms of the written agreement.[2] However, this rule is not as harsh as might be supposed, since in a number of cases extrinsic evidence is admissible, either as an exception to the parol evidence rule or because the circumstances fall outside its bounds. The following can be mentioned as examples.

1   Parol evidence of a written document means extrinsic evidence, whether oral or otherwise.
2   *Jacobs v Batavia and General Plantations Trust Ltd* [1924] 1 Ch 287 at 295.

Implied terms
7.3   The fact that a contract has been reduced into writing does not prevent extrinsic evidence being given to support or rebut the implication of a term into it[1] under rules which are discussed shortly.

1   *Gillespie Bros & Co v Cheney, Eggar & Co* [1896] 2 QB 59.

Conditions precedent
7.4   Extrinsic evidence is admissible to show that, although a written contract appears absolute on its face, it was not intended that a binding contract should be created (or that, although there was an immediate binding contract, a party's obligation to perform would not arise) until the occurrence of a particular event, such as a surveyor's report or the availability of finance.[1]

1   *Pym v Campbell* (1856) 6 E & B 370; para 5.27 above.

Invalidating factors
7.5   Extrinsic evidence of a factor, such as mistake or misrepresentation, which invalidates the written contract is, of course, admissible.

Written agreement not the whole contract

7.6   While a document which looks like a contract is presumed to include all the terms of the contract, this presumption may be rebutted by evidence that the parties did not intend all the terms of their contract to be contained in the document.[1] If the presumption is rebutted, extrinsic evidence is admissible to prove the other terms of the contract. An example is provided by the case of *J Evans & Son (Portsmouth) Ltd v Andrea Merzario Ltd*, which is discussed in para 7.13 below.

1   *Gillespie Bros & Co v Cheney, Eggar & Co* [1896] 2 QB 59 at 62.

Collateral contracts

7.7   The parol evidence rule will also be circumvented if the court finds that the parties have made two contracts, the main written one and a contract collateral to it. An example is provided by *Birch v Paramount Estates Ltd*[1] where the defendants, who were developing a housing estate, offered a house they were then building to the claimant, stating orally that it would be as good as the show house. Subsequently, the claimant agreed to buy the house but the written contract of sale made no reference to this statement. The completed house was not as good as the show house. The Court of Appeal held that there was an oral contract, to the effect that the house would be as good as the show house, collateral to the contract of sale and upheld the award of damages for its breach.

In essence, a collateral contract exists where A promises B something certain[2] in return for B making the main contract. A's promise must have been intended by the parties to be legally binding and to take effect as a collateral contract, and not merely as a term of the main contract, and it must be supported by separate consideration, although this may simply be B's making of the main contract.[3] Provided these requirements are satisfied, a collateral contract will be valid and enforceable by B, even though it conflicts with a term in the main contract. This is shown by *City and Westminster Properties (1934) Ltd v Mudd*.[4] In 1941, the defendant became the tenant of a lock-up shop for three years. He was allowed by the landlords, the claimants, to sleep in the shop. In 1944, a second lease for three years was granted to the defendant. In 1947, during negotiations for a new lease, the claimants inserted in the draft lease a clause restricting the use of the premises to trade purposes only. The defendant objected and was told by the claimants' agent that, if he accepted the new lease as it stood, the claimants would not object to him residing on the premises. In consequence, the defendant signed the lease. Later, the claimants sought to forfeit the lease for breach of the covenant only to use the premises for trade purposes. It was held that the defendant could plead the collateral contract as a defence to a charge of breach of the main contract, the lease.

1   (1956) 167 Estates Gazette 396, CA.
2   *Wake v Renault (UK) Ltd* (1996) 15 Tr LR 514, CA.
3   *Heilbut, Symons & Co v Buckleton* [1913] AC 30, HL.
4   [1958] 2 All ER 733.

Effect of 'entire agreement clauses'

7.8   A written agreement which has been formally drafted may well contain an 'entire agreement clause'. The precise wording of such a clause varies but it will normally state that the written agreement contains the entire and only contract between the parties in relation to the subject matter in question, each party acknowledging that in entering into the agreement it has not relied on any representation or undertaking which is not expressly incorporated in the written agreement.

The incorporation of an entire agreement clause is intended to prevent a party being liable for breach of contract in respect of statements not included in the written agreement.

The effect of such a clause depends on its precise wording. However, one drafted in the way described above will prevent parol evidence being given to prove that the written contract is not the whole contract (and that a statement not included in it is nevertheless a term of the contract) or that such a statement takes effect as a term of a contract collateral to the main contract; it will deprive that statement of any effect which it would otherwise have had as a contractual term.[1] We consider the effect of an entire agreement clause on liability for misrepresentation in para 12.39.

1   Deepak Fertilizers & Petrochemical Corpn v Imperial Chemical Industries plc [1999] 1 Lloyd's Rep 387, CA; Inntrepreneur Pub Co (Co Ltd) v East Crown Ltd [2000] 2 Lloyd's Rep 611.

Determination of whether a written term is a term of contract

7.9   The determination of whether what purports to be a term of the contract is indeed a term of the contract can sometimes give rise to nice questions. It depends very much on whether or not the term is contained in a signed contractual document. If it is, the general rule is that it is a contractual term binding on a party who signed the document, even though he was unaware of it because he had not read the document.[1] This is so even though that party is, to the other's knowledge, illiterate or unfamiliar with the English language.[2] An exception is where the party seeking to rely on a term has misrepresented to the other its contents or effect. In such a case, the term is rendered ineffective to the extent that it differs from the misrepresentation.[3]

Where the term is not contained in a contractual document signed by the party against whom it is being relied, eg where it is printed on a ticket or an order form or a notice, the term will only be a contractual term if adequate notice of it is given. The law in this respect has largely been developed in relation to a particular type of term, an exemption clause, and we deal with it in relation to such a clause in paras 9.4 -9.7 below.

1   L'Estrange v F Graucob Ltd [1934] 2 KB 394, DC.
2   Barclays Bank plc v Schwartz [1995] CLY 2492, CA.
3   Curtis v Chemical Cleaning and Dyeing Co Ltd [1951] 1 All ER 631, CA.

Contractual terms and mere representations

7.10   Where contractual terms are oral they must be proved by the evidence of the parties and other witnesses in the event of a dispute.

Problems can sometimes arise concerning whether a written or oral statement, which is made in contractual negotiations and not explicitly referred to at the time the contract is made, is nevertheless a term of the contract instead of being a mere representation. The present issue can be exemplified as follows. At the time the contract was made A may simply have said to B: 'I offer you £3,000 for the car' to which B replied 'I accept'. These two sentences will probably be the culmination of previous, and perhaps lengthy, negotiations between the parties during which B will have given A a number of assurances as to the condition of the car, its mileage and so on. Whether these pre-contractual statements are contractual terms or undertakings, or simply mere representations, is of importance for the following reason. Breach of a contractual term results in liability in damages, and certain other remedies for breach of contract may also be available to the 'injured party'. On the other hand, if a mere representation turns out to be false there can be no liability for breach of contract, although it *may* be possible for the misrepresentee to have the contract set aside (rescinded) for misrepresentation; and in certain circumstances he can recover damages for misrepresentation. Generally speaking, the remedies for misrepresentation are inferior to those for breach of contract. We discuss the subjects of breach of contract, remedies for breach and misrepresentation in chapters 8, 11 and 12, and for the present we are concerned with the question of how it is ascertained whether a pre-contractual statement has become a contractual term.

7.11   A representation will be a contractual term if the parties intended that the representor was making a binding promise as to it.[1] Whether the parties did so intend can only be deduced from all the evidence. Of course, it is always possible for the parties actually to state that a particular representation is or is not a term of their contract. If they do not, then, if an intelligent bystander would infer from the words and behaviour of the parties that a binding promise was intended, that will suffice.[2] In approaching the question of the parties' intentions, the courts take into account factors such as the following.

1   *Oscar Chess Ltd v Williams* [1957] 1 All ER 325 at 327–328.
2   Ibid. See also *Howard Marine and Dredging Co Ltd v A Ogden & Sons (Excavations) Ltd* [1978] 2 All ER 1134 at 1140.

Execution of a written contract

7.12   If the representation was followed by a written contract in which it does not appear, it will probably (but not necessarily) be regarded as a mere representation[1] since, because of the parol evidence rule, it can only take effect as a contractual term if the court finds that the parties intended that the contract should not be contained wholly in the written document or that the representation should form part of a collateral contract. An example of a case where a pre-contractual representation was found to be a contractual term despite the subsequent execution of a written contract is *J Evans & Son (Portsmouth) Ltd v Andrea Morzario Ltd*, which is discussed in the next paragraph.

1   *Heilbut, Symons & Co v Buckleton* [1913] AC 30 at 50; *Oscar Chess Ltd v Williams* [1957] 1 All ER 325 at 329.

The importance of the representation

7.13   The more important the subject matter of the representation the more likely it is that the parties intended a binding promise concerning it. In particular, if the representation was so important that without it the representee would not have made the contract, the court is very likely to hold that it is a contractual term. In *J Evans & Son (Portsmouth) Ltd v Andrea Merzario Ltd*,[1] the claimants bought some machines from an Italian company. They had previously employed the defendants to arrange transport, and the machinery had always been packed in crates or trailers and carried below deck. On this occasion the defendants' representative told the claimants' that it was proposed that the machinery should be packed in containers. The claimants' representative replied that if containers were used they must be stowed below, and not on deck, in case the machinery rusted. He was assured by the defendants' representative that this would be done but this oral assurance was not included in the written agreement subsequently made between the claimants and the defendants. In fact, the containers were carried on deck and two fell into the sea. In the Court of Appeal, Roskill and Geoffrey Lane LJJ held that the oral assurance had become a term of the contract between the parties, which was not wholly written, and that the claimant could recover damages for its breach. Roskill LJ stated that in the light of the totality of the evidence it was clear that the claimants had only agreed to contract with the defendants on the basis that the containers were stowed below deck, and therefore the defendants' assurance concerning this had become a contractual term. Similarly, in *Bannerman v White*,[2] a representation that sulphur had not been used in the treatment of hops was found to have become a term of the subsequent contract. It related to a matter of great importance and the buyer would not have made the contract without it.

1   [1976] 2 All ER 930, CA.
2   (1861) 10 CBNS 844.

Invitation to verify

7.14   If a seller invites the buyer to check his representation it is very unlikely to be regarded as a contractual term. In *Ecay v Godfrey*,[1] for instance, the seller of a boat said that it was sound but advised a survey. It was held that this advice negatived any intention that the representation should be a contractual term. Conversely, if the seller assures the buyer that it is not necessary to verify the representation since he can take the seller's word for it, the representation is likely to be found to be intended to be a term of the resulting contract if the buyer contracts in reliance on it. In *Schawel v Reade*,[2] the claimant, who required a stallion for stud purposes, went to the defendant's stables to inspect a horse. While he was inspecting it, the defendant said: 'You need not look for anything: the horse is perfectly sound. If there was anything the matter with the horse I would tell you.' The claimant thereupon ended his inspection and a price was agreed three weeks later, the claimant relying on the defendant's statement. The House of Lords held that the jury's finding that the defendant's statement was a contractual term was correct.

1   (1947) 80 Ll L Rep 286.
2   [1913] 2 IR 64, HL.

Statements of fact, of opinion or as to the future
7.15   A statement of fact is more likely to be construed as intended to have contractual effect than a statement of opinion or as to future facts (eg a forecast).[1] A statement about something which is, or should be, within the promisor's control is very likely to be construed as a contractual term.[2]

1   *Esso Petroleum Co Ltd v Mardon* [1976] 2 All ER 5 at 20.
2   *Oscar Chess Ltd v Williams* [1957] 1 All ER 325 at 329.

Ability of the parties to ascertain the accuracy of the statement
7.16   If the representor had a special skill or knowledge, or was otherwise in a better position than the representee to ascertain the truth of the representation, this strongly suggests that the representation was intended to be a contractual term, and vice versa. An example is provided by *Dick Bentley (Productions) Ltd v Harold Smith (Motors) Ltd*.[1] The claimant purchased a Bentley car from the defendants in reliance on their statement that the car had been fitted with a new engine and gear box and had done only 20,000 miles since then. The representation as to mileage, although honestly made, was untrue. The Court of Appeal held that the representation had become one of the terms of the contract because it had been made by a dealer who was in a position to know or find out the car's history, and it could therefore be inferred that the representation was intended to have contractual effect. The Court distinguished its previous decision in *Oscar Chess Ltd v Williams*.[2] There, Williams, a private person, represented in negotiations for the part-exchange of his Morris car that it was a 1948 model. This representation was based on the logbook which had been falsified by a person unknown. The representation was held not to have become a contractual term on the ground that Williams had no special knowledge as to the car's age, while the other party, who were car dealers, were in at least as good a position to ascertain whether the representation was true.

1   [1965] 2 All ER 65, CA.
2   [1957] 1 All ER 325, CA.

7.17   It must be emphasised that the factors mentioned above are only guides, not decisive tests or the only factors, to determining the parties' intentions.[1] Sometimes, they can point in different directions.

On many occasions, judges, having found that the parties intended a pre-contractual representation to have contractual effect, have found that it has taken effect under a collateral contract rather than as a term of the main contract.

1   *Heilbut, Symons & Co v Buckleton* [1913] AC 30, HL.

Implied terms

7.18 In addition to its express terms, the contract may contain certain terms implied by custom or usage or by statute or by the courts.

Terms implied by custom or usage

7.19 Terms may be implied by the custom of a particular locality, as in *Hutton v Warren*,[1] or by the usage of a particular trade, as recognised in *Lancaster v Bird*.[2] Although the terms are often used interchangeably, 'usage' differs from 'custom' in that it need not be ancient or recognised as compulsory, but like custom it must be reasonable and certain in the sense that it is clearly established.[3] In *Hutton v Warren*, where a local custom was proved that a tenant was obliged to farm according to a certain course of husbandry for the whole of his tenancy and, on quitting, was entitled to a fair allowance for seeds and labour on the arable land, it was held that a term to this effect was implied in the lease. In *Lancaster v Bird*, the Court of Appeal recognised that in the case of a contract between those engaged in the building trade there was a term implied by usage that a price quoted was exclusive of value added tax, although it held that that usage did not apply to a contract between a builder and a consumer.

A term cannot be implied by custom or usage if the express wording of the contract shows that the parties had a contrary intention. This is shown by *Les Affréteurs Réunis SA v Leopold Walford (London) Ltd*.[4] Walford acted as a broker in effecting the time charter of a ship. The charterparty provided that commission should be payable to Walford 'on signing this charter (ship lost or not lost)'. Before the charterparty could be operated, and therefore before any hire could be earned, the French government requisitioned the ship. The House of Lords held that Walford could recover his commission, despite a commercial usage in the case of a time charterparty that commission was payable only in respect of hire earned, because the usage was inconsistent with the express terms of the charterparty.

1   (1836) 1 M & W 466. For the requirements of a valid local custom, see para 3.62 above.
2   [1998] 73 Con LR 22, CA. For another example, see para 9.5 below.
3   *Cunliffe-Owen v Teather and Greenwood* [1967] 3 All ER 561 at 572.
4   [1919] AC 801, HL.

Terms implied by statute

7.20 The best-known examples of such terms are those implied into contracts for the sale of goods by the Sale of Goods Act 1979.

Section 12(1) of the Act of 1979 provides that there is an implied condition[1] on the part of a seller of goods that he has a right to sell them. Section 12(2) provides, inter alia, that there is an implied warranty[1] that the goods are free, and will remain free until the property passes, from any charge or encumbrance not known or disclosed to the buyer before the contract is made.

Section 13(1) provides that, where there is a contract for the sale of goods by description, there is an implied condition[2] that the goods will correspond with the description.

Section 14(2) provides that, where the seller sells goods in the course of a business, there is generally an implied condition[2] that the goods supplied under the contract are of satisfactory quality (ie of the standard that any reasonable person would regard as satisfactory). Section 14(3) provides that, where the seller sells goods in the course of a business and the buyer expressly or impliedly makes known to him any particular purpose for which the goods are being bought, there is generally an implied condition[2] that the goods supplied are reasonably fit for that purpose, whether or not that is a purpose for which such goods are commonly supplied. Unlike ss 12 and 13, sub-ss (2) and (3) of s 14 only apply where goods are sold *in the course of a business*. 'Business' is not limited to commercial activities in the ordinary sense because it is defined by s 61 to include 'a profession and the activities of any governmental department, or local or public authority'.

A sale is 'in the course of a business' in the present context whenever the seller is a business, unless it is a purely private sale of goods outside the confines of the business carried on by the seller.[3] The seller's business need not be directed to sales of goods at all; a firm of surveyors which sells an obsolete PC sells it in the course of its business, for example. On the other hand, a sale of an obsolete PC bought for his children's use at home by a surveyor in sole practice would not be a sale 'in the course of business' because it would be a purely private sale outside the confines of his business.

If a private individual sells goods through an agent, such as an auctioneer, acting in the course of a business, the two subsections apply to the sale, unless the buyer knows that the seller is a private individual or reasonable steps have been taken to bring that fact to the buyer's attention before the contract is made.[4] This rule applies whether the private individual is a disclosed or undisclosed principal.[5] It follows that it is extremely important that an auctioneer acting on behalf of a private client should notify prospective bidders for the goods of this fact, so as to avoid exposing his client to the risk of liability under the two subsections.

Finally, s 15 provides that where goods are sold by sample there is an implied condition[2] that the bulk will correspond with the sample in quality, and an implied condition that the goods will be free from any defect, rendering them unsatisfactory, which would not be apparent on reasonable examination of the sample.

1   This classification is made by the Sale of Goods Act 1979, s 12(5A).
2   By the Sale of Goods Act 1979, the term is classified as a condition.
3   *Stevenson v Rogers* [1999] 1 All ER 613, CA.
4   Sale of Goods Act 1979, s 14(5).
5   *Boyter v Thomson* [1995] 3 All ER 135, HL. As to 'disclosed' and 'undisclosed', see paras 15.36-15.37.

7.21   Terms modelled on those implied into sale of goods contracts are implied:

- into contracts of hire purchase, by the Supply of Goods (Implied Terms) Act 1973, ss 8 to 11;
- into contracts of hire, by the Supply of Goods and Services Act 1982, ss 7 to 10; and
- into contracts analogous to sale under which a person transfers or agrees to transfer to another the property (ie ownership) in goods, by the Supply of Goods and Services Act 1982, ss 2 to 5. One example of a contract analogous to sale is a contract for work and materials, such as a building contract or a contract for double glazing; another is a contract of exchange.

Although the exclusion or restriction by the contract of one of the implied terms referred to in para 7.20 and this paragraph, or of liability for its breach, is permissible,[1] there are strict limitations on this under the Unfair Contract Terms Act 1977 (paras 9.20 to 9.23 below).

1   Sale of Goods Act 1979, s 55; Supply of Goods and Services Act 1982, s 11.

7.22   By way of a further example, it may be noted that in a 'contract for the supply of a service' certain terms are implied by the Supply of Goods and Services Act 1982. Such a contract includes, for example, a contract between a surveyor and his client (but does not include a contract of employment or apprenticeship[1]). The fact that goods are transferred or hired under the contract does not prevent it being a contract for the supply of a service.[2] Consequently, for example, while a contract for work and materials will be subject to the implied terms under ss 2 to 5 of the 1982 Act in relation to the materials element, the work element will be subject to the terms implied into a contract of service by that Act.

The following terms are implied by the 1982 Act into a contract for the supply of a service:

- by s 13, where the supplier of the service is acting *in the course of a business*,[3] there is an implied term that he will carry out the service with reasonable care and skill;[4]
- by ss 14 and 15, where the time for the service to be carried out (s 14), or the consideration for the service (s 15),

  - is not stated by the contract, or
  - is not left to be determined in a manner agreed by the contract, or
  - is not determined by the course of dealings between the parties,

  there is an implied term that the service will be carried out within a reasonable time or, as the case may be, that a reasonable charge will be paid. The implied term as to the time of performance only applies where the contract is for the supply of a service by a supplier acting *in the course of a business*.[3]

Section 16 of the 1982 Act permits the rights, duties and liabilities which may arise by virtue of ss 13 to 15 to be negatived or varied, subject to the relevant provisions of the Unfair Contract Terms Act 1977 (paras 9.14 to 9.18 below) and to any other legislation relating to the particular contract which defines or restricts rights, duties or liabilities.

1   Supply of Goods and Services Act 1982, s 12(2).
2   SGSA 1982, s 12(3).
3   Business includes a profession and the activities of any government department or local or public authority: Supply of Goods and Services Act 1982, s 18.
4   There are very limited exceptions under the Supply of Services (Exclusion of Implied Terms) Orders 1982, 1983 and 1985, the most notable being that the implied term under s 13 does not apply to the services rendered by an advocate in court or before any tribunal, inquiry or arbitrator or in carrying out certain preliminary work, nor to the services rendered by an arbitrator, nor to the services rendered by a company director to his company.

7.23   Under the Landlord and Tenant Act 1985 terms as to fitness for habitation and as to repairs are implied into certain types of leases. We discuss this in para 37.24 and 37.25 below.

Terms implied by the courts
7.24   In *Liverpool City Council v Irwin*,[1] the House of Lords recognised that terms could be implied by the courts in two distinct situations:

- where the term was a necessary incident of the kind of contract in question, and
- where it was necessary to give 'business efficacy' to the particular contract.

1   [1976] 2 All ER 39, HL.

Implication of a term which is a necessary incident of the type of contract in question
7.25   When a court implies this type of term for the first time it lays down a general rule for contracts of the same type, eg employment contracts or leases, or a distinct species of that type of contract. The term will, therefore, be implied in subsequent cases concerning that type of contract,[1] subject to the rules of precedent, unless it is inconsistent with the express terms of the contract[2] or the contract validly excludes it.[3] In implying a term of the present type, the court is not trying to put the parties' intentions, actual or presumed, into effect but is implying it as a necessary incident of the type of contractual relationship in question.[4] In deciding whether to make such an implication, the courts take into account

the reasonableness of the suggested term and whether it is called for by the nature of the subject matter of the type of contract in question.[5]

1   Lister v Romford Ice and Cold Storage Co Ltd [1957] AC 555 at 576; Liverpool City Council v Irwin [1976] 2 All ER 39 at 46.
2   The Unfair Contract Terms Act 1977 (paras 9.14–9.23 below) may have the effect of automatically invalidating an inconsistent express term, in which case the implication can be made: Johnstone v Bloomsbury Health Authority [1991] 2 All ER 293, CA.
3   Lynch v Thorne [1956] 1 All ER 744, CA.
4   Tai Hing Cotton Mill Ltd v Liu Chong Bank Ltd [1985] 2 All ER 947, PC.
5   Liverpool City Council v Irwin [1976] 2 All ER 39, HL.

7.26   It is only possible here to refer to a few of the terms implied into contracts under the present heading.

In contracts of employment a number of obligations on the employee are implied. The fundamental implied duty is that the employee will faithfully serve his employer (the implied duty of fidelity).[1] A number of more specific implied duties to which an employee is subject are merely instances of the duty of fidelity, for instance:

*   not to use or disclose a trade secret or confidential information relating to his employer's business contrary to his employer's interests;[2]
*   not to copy or memorise such information for use after his employment has ceased;[2]
*   not to act against his employer's interests;[3]
*   to use reasonable care and skill in performing his duties;[4] and
*   to indemnify his employer against any liability incurred by the employer as a result of his wrongful acts.[5]

There is a separate implied duty whereby an ex-employee must not use or disclose a trade secret or information relating to the former employer's business which is so confidential that it requires the same protection as a trade secret.[6]

Reciprocal terms are implied in the employee's favour, the employer being obliged, for instance:

*   not to require the employee to do any unlawful act;[7]
*   to use reasonable care to provide safe premises, to provide a safe system of work and not to injure the employee's health;[8] and
*   not, without reasonable and proper cause, to conduct his business in a manner likely to destroy or damage seriously the relationship of trust and confidence between employer and employee.[9]

Another example of an implied term of the present type is provided by Liverpool City Council v Irwin.[10] In that case, the House of Lords held that, where parts of a building have been let to different tenants (the case concerned a high-rise block of flats) and essential rights of access over parts of the building, such as stairs, retained by the landlord have been granted to the individual tenants, a term could be implied into the tenancy agreements that the landlord would take reasonable care to keep them reasonably safe and reasonably fit for use by tenants, their families and their visitors. Likewise, it has been held that, where a tenant has a right of way over a path which is an essential means of access to his premises, the landlord having retained control of the path, there is implied in the tenancy agreement a term that the landlord will take reasonable steps to keep the path in good repair.[11] In a lease of furnished premises there is an implied term that they are fit for human habitation when let,[12] but for some obscure reason such a term is not implied by the courts in a contract for the sale of land with a house on it or for the letting of land with unfurnished premises on it[13] (although if the vendor or lessor is the builder he may be liable in tort to the purchaser, lessee, or even a visitor, who is injured as a result of his negligent building[14]). Lastly, where a builder contracts to construct a dwelling there is a term implied by the courts that the dwelling, when completed, will be reasonably fit for human habitation.[15] However, this implication may be rebutted where the contract expressly specifies the way in which the work is to be done and the work is completed according to that specification.[16]

1   Hivac Ltd v Park Royal Scientific Instruments Ltd [1946] 1 All ER 350, CA.
2   Faccenda Chicken Ltd v Fowler [1986] 1 All ER 617, CA.
3   Wessex Dairies Ltd v Smith [1935] 2 KB 80, CA.
4   Lister v Romford Ice and Cold Storage Co Ltd [1957] 1 All ER 125, HL.
5   [1957] 1 All ER 125, HL.
6   Faccenda Chicken Ltd v Fowler, above.
7   Gregory v Ford [1951] 1 All ER 121.
8   Lister v Romford Ice and Cold Storage Co Ltd, above.
9   Malik v Bank of Credit and Commerce International SA [1997] 3 All ER 1, HL.
10 [1976] 2 All ER 39, HL.
11 King v South Northamptonshire District Council [1992] 1 EGLR 53, CA.
12 Para 37.24 below. For other examples of terms implied into leases as a necessary incident, see paras 37.22, 37.23 and 37.26-37.28 below.
13 Hart v Windsor (1843) 12 M & W 68. For possible liability for breach of statutory duty see para 21.28 below.
14 Para 21.27 below.
15 Hancock v BW Brazier (Anerley) Ltd [1966] 2 All ER 901, CA; Basildon District Council v JE Lesser (Properties) Ltd [1985] 1 All ER 20.
16 Lynch v Thorne [1956] 1 All ER 744, CA.

Implication to give business efficacy

7.27   The implication of a term under this heading is less common and can only be made when it is necessary in the particular circumstances to imply a term to fill an obvious gap in a contract[1] and thereby to give it business efficacy and make it a workable agreement in such manner as the parties would clearly have done if they had applied their minds to what has occurred. This power of judicial implication was recognised in The Moorcock,[2] which concerned a contract permitting the claimant to unload his ship at a jetty operated by the defendants. A warranty on the part of the defendants was implied into the contract that the river bed was, so far as reasonable care could provide, in a condition which would not damage the ship when she grounded at low tide, as both parties realised she would. Bowen LJ stated that, where the parties had not dealt with the burden of a particular peril, a court could imply a term which would give such efficacy to the contract as both parties must have intended it to have.

The test which the courts apply in deciding whether to imply a term to give the contract business efficacy is a strict one. A term cannot be implied unless it is necessary to give business efficacy to the contract and it can be formulated with a sufficient degree of precision; it is not enough that it is reasonable in all the circumstances to imply the term,[3] nor that the contract would be more efficient or effective if the term was implied.[4] A classic statement of the test is that of Scrutton LJ in Reigate v Union Manufacturing Co (Ramsbottom) Ltd:[5] 'A term can only be implied if it is necessary in the business sense to give efficacy to the contract, ie if it is such a term that it can confidently be said that if at the time the contract was being negotiated someone had said to the parties: "What will happen in such a case?" they would both have replied: "Of course, so and so will happen; we did not trouble to say that; it is too clear".'

1   Adams Holden & Pearson Ltd v Trent Regional Health Authority (1989) 47 BLR 34 and 39, CA.
2   (1889) 14 PD 64, CA.
3   Liverpool City Council v Irwin [1976] 2 All ER 39, HL.
4   Express Newspapers v Silverstone Circuits [1989] CLY 422, CA.
5   [1918] 1 KB 592 at 605.

7.28   Pursuant to these principles, the courts have, for instance, refused to imply terms in the following cases: where tariff booklets were supplied free to a hotel in consideration of its proprietors undertaking to circulate or display them for a specified period, a term to the effect that the proprietors' obligation should cease if the business was sold was not implied;[1] where a petrol company subsidised two neighbouring filling stations during a price cutting war, a term to the effect that it would not abnormally discriminate against the claimant's filling station in favour of competitors was not implied into a contract for the exclusive supply of petrol by the petrol company to the claimant;[2] where a contract between an estate agent and a vendor of property did not provide that the commission payable on completion of the sale should be paid out of the proceeds of sale, a term to that effect was not implied into the contract because it was held not to be necessary to give it business efficacy to provide any particular way in which the debt should be discharged.[3]

In contrast, the courts have, for example, implied a term: into a statutory tenancy containing an express term that the tenant would repair the interior of the premises, that the landlord would repair the exterior;[4] into a contractual licence, that the premises were of sound construction and reasonably suitable for the purpose required by the licensees;[5] into a contract of transfer of a footballer, which provided that an additional sum be paid when he had scored 20 goals for the first team, that he was entitled to a reasonable opportunity to score the goals;[6] and into a contract for the sale of land, where the vendor undertook to give the purchaser 'first refusal' of adjacent land, that the vendor should not defeat the purchaser's right of 'first refusal' by disposing of the adjacent land to a third party by way of *gift* without first offering it to the purchaser.[7] In addition, the courts have held that generally a term is necessarily implied in any contract that neither party shall prevent the other from performing it.[8]

Since the implication of a term under *The Moorcock* principle is always dependent on the particular circumstances of the case, the implication of a term under it does not lay down a general rule for the future.

1   *General Publicity Services Ltd v Best's Brewery Co Ltd* [1951] 2 TLR 875, CA.
2   *Shell UK Ltd v Lostock Garage Ltd* [1977] 1 All ER 481, CA.
3   *W A Ellis Services Ltd v Wood* [1993] 31 EG 78.
4   *Barrett v Lounova (1982) Ltd* [1989] 1 All ER 351, CA.
5   *Wettern Electric Ltd v Welsh Development Agency* [1983] 2 All ER 629.
6   *Bournemouth and Boscombe Athletic Football Club Co Ltd v Manchester United Football Club Ltd* (1980) Times, 22 May, CA.
7   *Gardner v Coutts & Co* [1967] 3 All ER 1064.
8   *William Cory & Son Ltd v London Corpn* [1951] 2 All ER 85 at 88.

Unfair contract terms

7.29   Under the Unfair Contract Terms Act 1977 and the Unfair Terms in Consumer Contracts Regulations 1999 (replacing regulations with the same name made in 1994), which implement the EC Directive on unfair terms in consumer contracts, Directive 93/13/EEC, there are special provisions relating to contract terms which are unfair. In some cases, these provisions render an unfair term of no effect. We deal with these provisions later.[1]

1   Paras 9.14-9.24 and 12.58-12.63 below.

Chapter 8

Performance and breach

8.1 In this chapter we examine the following issues:

- how a party to a contract can be discharged from his obligations under it by performing them;
- the legal effect of a tender of performance by a party;
- the legal effect of a breach of contract by a party.

Performance

8.2 A contract may be discharged by agreement between the parties, by being broken by one of them, or by being frustrated, if the rules described elsewhere in this book[1] are satisfied. However, a contract is most frequently discharged by both parties performing their obligations under it, both parties being released from further liability thereby. If only one party performs his contractual obligations he alone is discharged and he acquires a right of action against the other for breach of contract. Special rules govern the discharge of a party who has unsuccessfully tendered performance.

1   Paras 6.22–6.25 above; 8.12–8.31 and 10.3–10.12 below.

8.3 For a party to be discharged by performance he must have precisely performed all his obligations under the contract. Thus, to decide whether a party is discharged by performance, one must first ascertain and construe the terms of the contract, express and implied, to see what his contractual obligations were, and then look at what has happened to see whether what he has done precisely corresponds with those obligations. The requirement of precise performance is a strict one and, if it is not met, it is irrelevant that the performance effected is commercially no less valuable than that which was promised. In *Arcos Ltd v E A Ronaasen & Sons*,[1] the claimants contracted to supply the defendants with a certain quantity of timber which, as they knew, was to be used for constructing cement barrels. The contract specified that the timber should be half an inch thick but when it was delivered the defendants discovered that 95% of it was over half an inch thick, although none of it exceeded three-quarters of an inch in thickness. It was still perfectly possible for the defendants to use all the wood, as it had been delivered, for the construction of cement barrels but the House of Lords held that they were entitled to reject the whole consignment[2] since the claimants had not performed a contractual obligation which was a condition of the contract.[3] Lord Atkin stated, obiter, that only if a deviation from the terms of the contract was 'microscopic' could the contract be taken to have been correctly performed. An example of this is provided by *Shipton, Anderson & Co v Weil Bros & Co*,[4] where a contract requiring the delivery of 4,950 tons of wheat was held to have been performed by the seller although he had delivered 4,950 tons 55 lbs.

Generally, no demand for performance is necessary to render an obligation to perform operative.[5] Thus, a debtor is bound to seek out his creditor and pay him.[6]

1   [1933] AC 470, HL.
2   The decision that the defendants were entitled to reject might now be different because of the Sale of Goods Act 1979, s 15A: para 8.26 below.
3   The contractual obligation broken was the condition implied by the Sale of Goods Act 1979, s 13(1), viz, that in a sale of goods by description the goods must correspond with the description. See paras 7.20 above and 8.24–8.27 below.
4   [1912] 1 KB 574.
5   A demand will be necessary if there is an express agreement or trade usage requiring it.
6   *Walton v Mascall* (1844) 13 M & W 452.

Payment

8.4   Where the obligation of one party (the debtor) to the other (the creditor) consists of the payment of a sum of money, the contract is discharged by the payment of that sum. Payment should, primarily, be made in legal tender. Unless the creditor has expressly or impliedly agreed to do so, he is not obliged to accept payment by cheque.

By the Currency and Bank Notes Act 1954 and the Coinage Act 1954, legal tender is as follows:

• Bank of England notes, to any amount;
• gold coins of the Mint, to any amount;
• silver and cupro-nickel coins of the Mint of more than 10p, up to £10;
• silver and cupro-nickel coins of the Mint of not more than 10p, up to £5;
• bronze coins, up to 20p.

Where a cheque is given, and accepted,[1] in payment, its effect may be absolutely to discharge the debtor or only conditionally to discharge the debtor.

The discharge will be *absolute* if the creditor promises expressly or impliedly, in accepting the cheque, to discharge the debtor from his existing obligations. If this occurs the creditor loses his right of action on the original contract but can sue on his rights under the cheque if it is dishonoured.[2]

The presumption is that the creditor only accepts a cheque as a *conditional* discharge, in which case the debtor is not discharged unless, and until, the cheque is honoured; if it is honoured, payment is deemed to have been made at the time the cheque is received.[3] If it is dishonoured, the debtor may be sued on the original contract or on the dishonoured cheque.[4]

1   *Official Solicitor to the Supreme Court v Thomas* [1986] 2 EGLR 1, CA.
2   *Sard v Rhodes* (1836) 1 M & W 153.
3   *Homes v Smith* [2000] Lloyd's Rep Bank 139, CA.
4   *Re Romer and Haslam* [1893] 2 QB 286, CA.

Tender of performance

8.5   If a party makes a valid tender (ie offer) of performance of his contractual obligations and the other party refuses to accept performance, the party making the tender is freed from liability for non-performance of those obligations, provided that the tender is made under such circumstances that the other party has a reasonable opportunity of examining the performance tendered, eg the goods tendered, in order to ascertain that it conforms with the contract.[1]

1   *Startup v Macdonald* (1843) 6 Man & G 593 at 610. Also see Sale of Goods Act 1979, s 29.

Tender of payment

8.6   If a party makes a valid tender of payment of money which he owes by producing the amount owed in legal tender but the other party refuses to accept it, this does not discharge his debt but there is no obligation to make a further tender. If an action is brought for non-payment against a party who has tendered unsuccessfully, all he has to do is to pay the money into court.

Tender of acts

8.7   Where a party is obliged to perform some act, other than the payment of something, he will make a valid tender of performance if he attempts to perform the act in precise accordance with the terms of the contract. In the case of a contract for the sale of goods, the tender of them must be made at a reasonable hour.[1]

1   Sale of Goods Act 1979, s 29.

Time of performance

8.8   When a contract does not stipulate a time within which a party's contractual obligations must be performed, they must be performed within a reasonable time.[1]

1   *Postlethwaite v Freeland* (1880) 5 App Cas 599, HL. The Sale of Goods Act 1979, s 29 gives this rule statutory effect in relation to a seller's obligation to send goods to a buyer. The Supply of Goods and Services Act 1982, s 14, has the like effect in relation to the provision of services by a supplier acting in the course of a business: see para 7.22, above.

8.9   Whether a time is stipulated for performance of a party's obligations by the contract or whether it is implied that they must be performed within a reasonable time, the question arises whether time is 'of the essence of the contract'. If it is, the stipulation or implied obligation as to time will be classified as a condition[1] and a party's failure to perform in that time will not only constitute a breach of contract entitling the other party to maintain an action for damages but also a repudiatory breach of the contract, which the other party can accept as discharging him from his contractual obligations.[2] The rule is a strict one; it applies even though the party in default tenders performance shortly after a stipulated time for performance. This was re-affirmed by the Privy Council in *Union Eagle Ltd v Golden Achievement Ltd*,[3] where a purchaser of a flat was required to complete by 5 pm on a specified day, time being of the essence. The purchaser failed to complete by that time. The purchaser's vendor declared that the contract was terminated and the purchaser's deposit forfeited. Ten minutes after the time for completion, the purchaser tendered the purchase price. The Privy Council refused to intervene by ordering the specific performance of the contract of sale on the ground that it had no power to do so.

   If time is not of the essence but a party delays in performing the contract, it may be possible to infer that he does not intend to carry out his obligations under it. In such a case the other party will be entitled to accept this implied renunciation as discharging him from his contractual obligation (ie entitled to terminate the contract for repudiatory breach).[4]

1   This point was made by the majority of the Court of Appeal in *Bunge Corpn v Tradax SA* [1981] 2 All

ER 513 and is implicit in the leading speeches in the House of Lords in that case: [1981] 2 All ER 513. With regard to conditions, see para 8.24 below.
2   See, in particular, *Bunge Corpn v Tradax SA* [1981] 2 All ER 513, HL. See also paras 8.14–8.19 below.
3   [1997] 2 All ER 215, PC.
4   *Graham v Pitkin* [1992] 2 All ER 235, PC. See para 8.21 below.

8.10   Whether time is of the essence of a contract, other than a contract which is specifically enforceable (see para 8.11 below), depends on the parties' intentions when the contract is made. If they are not expressed in the contract, they must be inferred from the nature of the subject matter of the contract and of the obligation which has not been performed in time. In this context certain presumptions have been established. For instance, a stipulation as to time in a contract granting an *option* to purchase land is presumptively of the essence.[1] Likewise, a stipulation as to time in a commercial contract is presumptively of the essence of the contract.[2] However, the Sale of Goods Act 1979, s 10 provides that a term as to the time of payment for goods is deemed not to be of the essence of the contract, unless the contrary intention appears from the contract.

1   *Di Luca v Juraise (Springs) Ltd* [1998] 2 EGLR 125, CA.
2   *Bunge Corpn v Tradax SA* [1981] 2 All ER 513, HL.

8.11   Before the Judicature Act 1873, common law and equity had different rules about when the time for completion was of the essence in a contract which was specifically enforceable,[1] such as a contract for the sale[2] of an interest in land or for the sale of a unique chattel, but since that Act the equitable rules prevail.[3] The result is that time is not of the essence in such a contract unless it falls within one of the following three categories where equity treated it as of the essence:

•   where the contract expressly states that obligations as to time must be strictly complied with. In *Harold Wood Brick Co Ltd v Ferris*[4] for instance, a stipulation that the purchase of a brickfield should be completed by 31 August which added that 'the purchase shall in any event be completed not later than 15 September' was held to make time (15 September) of the essence of the contract;
•   where the contract does not expressly make time of the essence of the contract, but the stipulated or impliedly required time has passed by, the party who has been subjected to delay can make time of the essence by invoking a period of notice for performance (eg completion in the case of a contract for the sale of land) if one is specified in the contract or, if one is not specified, by giving a notice fixing a reasonable time for performance;[5]
•   where the subject matter of the contract, or the circumstances surrounding it, makes punctual compliance with an obligation as to time imperative, time must be taken to be of the essence of the contract. For example, under this heading time has been held to be of the essence of a contract for the sale of business premises as a going concern.[6]

Even if time is not of the essence of a contract for the sale of an interest in land or of some other specifically enforceable contract, a party who fails to complete within the required time is, of course, in breach of that term and liable in damages, provided that the failure was not due to some conveyancing difficulty or some difficulty with regard to title.[7] Inability to raise the necessary finance is no defence.[7]

1   Para 11.30 below.
2   As opposed to a contract granting an option to purchase; para 8.10 above.
3   Law of Property Act 1925, s 41.
4   [1935] 2 KB 198, CA.
5   *Stickney v Keeble* [1915] AC 386, HL.
6   *Lock v Bell* [1931] 1 Ch 35. Also see *Harold Wood Brick Co Ltd v Ferris* [1935] 2 KB 198, CA.
7   *Raineri v Miles* [1980] 2 All ER 145, HL.

Breach

8.12 Breach of contract occurs where a party does not perform one or more of his contractual obligations precisely, in the sense discussed in para 8.3 above, and this failure is without lawful excuse. Thus, a breach will occur where a party without lawful excuse refuses to perform one or more of his contractual obligations, or simply fails to perform them, or incapacitates himself from performing them, or performs them defectively. Consequently, to decide whether a party is in breach of contract, one must first ascertain and construe the terms of the contract, express and implied, to see what his contractual obligations were, and then look at what has happened to see whether he has failed without lawful excuse to perform one or more of them precisely.

A person has a lawful excuse for failing to perform his contractual obligations precisely in the following cases:

- if the contract has been discharged by frustration, a matter which we discuss in chapter 10;
- if there is impossibility of performance less than frustration; for instance, a temporary illness preventing an employee working provides a lawful excuse for his failure to work during the period of the illness;[1]
- if he has validly tendered performance of his obligations in accordance with the rules set out in paras 8.5 to 8.7 above, but this has been rejected by the other party;
- if the other party has made it impossible for him to perform his obligations.

1   *Poussard v Spiers and Pond* (1876) 1 QBD 410.

8.13 Subject to a valid exemption clause to the contrary, whenever a party to the contract is in breach of contract, he is legally liable to pay compensation (ie damages) to the other party (the 'injured party') for the loss sustained by him in consequence of that breach but, unless the breach can be classified as a repudiatory breach and the injured party elects to terminate the contract, the contractual obligations of the parties so far as they have not been fully performed remain unchanged. The injured party may claim damages for breach either by an action of his own or by way of a counterclaim in an action brought against him by the defaulting party, and even where no actual loss or damage to the injured party can be proved nominal damages (usually in the region of £2 to £20) will be awarded. Quite apart from damages, the injured party may be entitled, additionally or alternatively, to claim some other remedy, eg an order of specific performance of the contract or the recovery of an agreed sum. We consider the question of remedies in chapter 11.

In the case of certain serious breaches of contract, which are commonly described as repudiatory breaches, the injured party can elect to treat the contract as repudiated by the other, accept the repudiation, and recover damages for breach, both parties being discharged from performance of their primary obligations under the contract which would have been due thereafter. If the injured party does this, he is said to terminate (or rescind[1]) the contract for repudiatory breach.

An additional right is given to a buyer of goods who deals as consumer[2] by the Sale of Goods Act 1979, s 48A and ancillary sections, inserted by the Sale and Supply of Goods to Consumers Regulations 2002 (which implement an EC Directive, Directive 1999/44/EC). Section 48A of the 1979 Act provides that, if a buyer of goods deals as consumer and the goods do not conform to the contract of sale at the time of delivery, the buyer has the right:

- to require the seller to repair or replace the goods; or
- to require the seller to reduce the price of the goods by an appropriate amount, or to terminate the contract with regard to the goods in question.

If the buyer requires the seller to repair or to replace the goods, the seller must do so within a reasonable time but without causing significant inconvenience to the buyer; the seller must bear any necessary costs in repairing or replacing the goods.[3] The buyer must not require the seller to repair or to replace the goods if *that* remedy is impossible, or disproportionate to the other of *those* two remedies, or disproportionate in comparison to an appropriate reduction in the price or termination of the contract.[4]

The buyer may only require the seller to reduce the price, or may only terminate the contract, if he (the buyer) is precluded from requiring the repair or replacement of the goods or if the seller, having been required to repair or replace, has failed to do so within a reasonable time and without significant inconvenience to the buyer.[5]

1   Termination for repudiatory breach should not be confused with rescission for misrepresentation (discussed in chapter 12), the effects of which (and the rules concerning which) are different.
2   'Dealing as consumer' has the same meaning as that given in the Unfair Contract Terms Act 1977 (see para 9.16 below): Sale of Goods Act 1979, s 61(5A).
3   Sale of Goods Act 1979, s 48B(2).
4   Sale of Goods Act 1979, s 48B(3).
5   Sale of Goods Act 1979, s 48C.

Repudiatory breach

Option to terminate or affirm
8.14   A repudiatory breach does not automatically discharge the contract. Instead, the injured party has an option to terminate the contract or to affirm it.[1] We shall see in para 8.27 below that in one type of case an injured party can lose the option to terminate, even though he has not affirmed the contract.

1   *Heyman v Darwins Ltd* [1942] 1 All ER 337 at 340.

Termination
8.15   The injured party will terminate the contract if he indicates to the defaulting party that he regards himself as discharged by the repudiatory breach. No particular form of indication is required.[1] It is sufficient that by words or conduct the injured party clearly and unequivocally conveys to the repudiating party that he is treating the contract as at an end.[1] Thus, the contract will be terminated if the injured party refuses to accept defective performance, or refuses to accept further performance, or simply refuses to perform his own contractual obligations. Moreover, termination can be inferred if the injured party simply does something incompatible with his own continued performance of the contract, or simply fails to perform his side of the contract, provided that this unequivocally points to the fact that he is treating the contract as at an end.[1] Suppose, for example, that an employer at the end of a day tells a contractor that he, the employer, is renouncing the contract and that the contractor need not return the next day. This would constitute a repudiatory breach of contract by the employer.[2] The contractor does not return the next day or at all. The contractor's failure to return may, in the absence of any other explanation, convey a decision to terminate the contract.[3] The injured party need not personally, or by an agent, notify the defaulting party of his election to terminate. It is sufficient that the election comes to the defaulting party's attention. For example, notification by an unauthorised intermediary can suffice.[3]

1   *Vitol SA v Norelf Ltd* [1996] 3 All ER 193, HL.
2   Para 8.21 below.
3   *Vitol SA v Norelf Ltd* [1996] 3 All ER 193 at 200.

8.16   If the injured party elects to terminate the contract, he is discharged for the future from his obligations under the contract which would otherwise have been due or continuing thereafter. One result is that he is not obliged to accept or pay for further performance. Another result is that an injured party who has terminated a contract for breach can resist successfully any action for failing thereafter to observe or perform a continuing obligation or an obligation due thereafter, even if the contract purports to make the obligation applicable after a repudiatory breach by the defaulting party.[1] Consequently, for example, a wrongfully dismissed employee who has indicated that he regards himself as discharged by the repudiatory breach from his employment contract is no longer bound by terms in that contract restraining his future employment, even if his employment contract purports to make those terms applicable after a repudiatory breach by the employer.[2]

On the other hand, an injured party who has terminated is not generally discharged from his obligations which are already due at the time of termination, since rights and obligations which arise from the partial execution of the contract – as well as causes of action which have accrued from its breach – continue unaffected.[3]

1   *General Billposting Co Ltd v Atkinson* [1909] AC 118, HL.
2   *Rock Refrigeration Ltd v Jones* [1997] 1 All ER 1, CA.
3   *Hurst v Bryk* [2000] 2 All ER 193, HL.

8.17   An injured party who has terminated may be entitled to refuse to pay for partial or defective performance already received by him if complete and precise performance of the obligation broken by the defaulting party is a precondition of his right to be paid. However, if the injured party is in a position to return the partial or defective performance (eg faulty goods), and does not do so, he must pay a reasonable sum or pro rata for the work done or goods supplied. It was held in *Sumpter v Hedges*[1] that, on the other hand, there is no such obligation where the injured party's acceptance of the partial or defective performance was not voluntary, ie the injured party had no choice. In that case A agreed to build two houses and a stable on B's land for a lump sum payable on completion. A did part of the work to the value of about three-fifths of the contract price but then abandoned the contract (a repudiatory breach) because of lack of money. It was held that A could not recover a reasonable sum for his work because B had no option but to accept the partial performance, viz the partly erected buildings.

In addition, an injured party who has terminated can recover back under the law of restitution any money which he has deposited or paid to the defaulting party under the contract if there has been a total failure of consideration on the part of the latter.[2] There will be a total failure of consideration by the defaulting party if he has not performed any part of his contractual duties in respect of which payment is due under the contract.[3] It follows that, where the injured party has deposited or paid money in pursuance of a contract which is rendered ineffective by a total failure of consideration on the part of the defaulting party and the injured party terminates the contract for breach, he can recover back under the law of restitution the money which he has paid.[2] Thus, if P pays D £500 as a deposit on a car but D fails to supply the car, P can terminate the contract and recover back the £500 which he paid.

If the failure of consideration is not total but only partial, the action for the recovery of money paid is not available, so that, whether the contract is terminated or not, the appropriate remedy is an action for damages for breach of contract. Thus, if P employs D to build a house for him and pays in advance, and D starts the work but abandons it before it is finished, P cannot recover any part of his payment and must claim damages for breach of contract.[4] However, if:

• the partial performance is such as to entitle the claimant to terminate the contract, and he elects to do so; and

- he is able to restore what he has received under the contract, and does so before he has derived any benefit from it,[5]

he is said to bring about a total failure of consideration and is entitled to recover back any money which he has paid.[6] A common example of this is where the buyer of defective goods rejects them immediately and claims back his payment.

As a final point, it should be noted that, if the injured party has started to perform his contractual obligations but is unjustifiably prevented from completing them by the other party, he can bring an action for reasonable remuneration. This is called suing on a quantum meruit.[7]

1   [1898] 1 QB 673.
2   Wilkinson v Lloyd (1845) 7 QB 27.
3   Stocznia Gdanska SA v Latvian Shipping Co [1998] 1 All ER 883, HL.
4   Whincup v Hughes (1871) LR 6 CP 78.
5   Hunt v Silk (1804) 5 East 449.
6   Baldry v Marshall [1925] 1 KB 260, CA.
7   Para 11.28 below.

8.18   After termination by the injured party, the defaulting party's position is as follows:

- he is not discharged from his contractual obligations which are due at the time of the termination and have not been performed (so that, for instance, he is still obliged to pay a sum of money then due[1]); and he is also liable to pay damages to the injured party for loss sustained by him in consequence of the breach of any such obligations;[2]
- his contractual obligations, so far as they are due or continuing after the termination, are discharged and there is substituted for them an obligation arising from the contract to pay damages to the injured party for the loss sustained by him in consequence of their non-performance in the future.[2]

1   McDonald v Dennys Lascelles Ltd (1933) 48 CLR 457 at 476–477; Hyundai Heavy Industries Co Ltd v Papodopolous [1980] 2 All ER 29, HL.
2   R V Ward Ltd v Bignall [1967] 2 All ER 449, CA; Moschi v LEP Air Services Ltd [1972] 2 All ER 393, HL; Photo Production Ltd v Securicor Transport Ltd [1980] 1 All ER 556, HL.

8.19   Termination for repudiatory breach does not necessarily extinguish the contract completely in relation to obligations whose performance is due after the time of the election to terminate, since an obligation will survive termination if on proper interpretation of the contract the parties intended that it should.[1] Thus, for example, obligations relating to matters such as arbitration or jurisdiction may continue in existence if it was the intention of the parties, when they made the contract, that this should be so.[2] In addition, terms which validly 'liquidate' damages or which validly exclude or restrict liability remain in force.[3]

1   Duffen v FRA Bo SpA [2000] 1 Lloyd's Rep 180 at 194-195.
2   Heyman v Darwins Ltd [1942] 1 All ER 337, HL.
3   Photo Production Ltd v Securicor Transport Ltd [1980] 1 All ER 556, HL. For liquidated damages provisions, see para 11.20 below, and for exemption clauses: see ch 9. The proposition in the text has been given statutory force in relation to exemption clauses which must satisfy the requirement of reasonableness under the Unfair Contract Terms Act 1977 (see paras 9.14 to 9.23 below) by s 9 of that Act.

Affirmation

8.20   The injured party will affirm the contract if, with full knowledge of the facts and of his right to terminate the contract,[1] he decides to treat it as still in existence, as where he decides to keep the defective goods delivered or, if the defaulting party has not completed performance, where he calls on him to perform. The injured party does not affirm a contract simply because he does not immediately terminate the contract but delays while he considers whether or not to terminate it.[2]

If the injured party elects to affirm, the contract remains in force, so that both parties are bound to continue performing any outstanding contractual obligations. Each party retains the right to sue for past or future breaches. Thus, if a seller of goods affirms the contract after a repudiatory breach by the buyer, the seller remains liable to deliver possession of the goods to the buyer and the buyer remains liable to accept delivery of the goods and pay the contract price.[3] Another example is provided by *Bentsen v Taylor, Sons & Co (No 2)*,[4] where a charterparty described the ship as 'now sailed or about to sail' from a port to the United Kingdom. In fact, she did not sail for another month. This constituted a repudiatory breach of contract by the shipowner[5] but, instead of electing to terminate the contract, the charterers intimated to the shipowner that he was still bound to send the ship to the port of loading and that they, the charterers, would load her there, thereby affirming the contract. When the ship arrived, the charterers refused to load her. The Court of Appeal held that, since the contract had been affirmed, the shipowner was entitled to payment of freight, subject to a set-off for the charterers for damages for the shipowner's breach of contract referred to above.

1   *Peyman v Lanjani* [1984] 3 All ER 703, CA.
2   *Bliss v South East Thames Regional Health Authority* [1987] ICR 700, CA.
3   *R V Ward Ltd v Bignall* [1967] 2 All ER 449, CA.
4   [1893] 2 QB 274, CA.
5   Because the term broken was a condition: see paras 8.24 and 8.25 below.

Types of repudiatory breach
Renunciation
8.21   Where one party renounces his contractual obligations the other party is entitled to terminate the contract. A party is said to renounce his contractual obligations if he has evinced an unconditional intention not to perform them or otherwise no longer to be bound by the contract or one of its essential terms.[1] Such an intention is easily established where there has been an express and unequivocal refusal to perform. Thus, if an employee unqualifiedly refuses to carry out his contractual duties (or to carry out a duty which is an essential contractual term), his employer is entitled to dismiss him (ie terminate the contract of employment).[2] However, express refusal is not necessary; an intent no longer to be bound by the contract (or one of its essential terms) can also be implied by the words or conduct of a party. The actual intention of the party is not the crucial issue in such a case; the test is whether his words and conduct were such as to lead a reasonable person to believe that he did not intend to be bound by the contract.[3]

1   *Mersey Steel and Iron Co v Naylor Benzon and Co* (1884) 9 App Cas 434, HL.
2   *Gorse v Durham County Council* [1971] 2 All ER 666.
3   *Woodar Investment Development Ltd v Wimpey Construction UK Ltd* [1980] 1 All ER 571, HL.

Incapacitation
8.22   Even though he has not evinced an intention not to be bound by the contract, a party who, *by his own act or default*, incapacitates himself from performing his contractual obligations is treated as if he had refused to perform them.[1] As Devlin J said in *Universal Cargo Carriers Corpn v Citati*,[2] 'To say "I would like to but cannot" negatives intent to perform as much as "I will not"'. Where a party has incapacitated himself from performing, it is no defence to show that he might be able to recover the capacity to perform.[3] One example of a case where a party has made performance of his obligations impossible is where A has contracted to sell a specific thing to B but then sells it to C.

1   *Torvald Klaveness A/S v Arni Maritime Corpn, The Gregos* [1994] 4 All ER 998, HL.
2   [1957] 2 All ER 70.
3   *Omnium D'Enterprises v Sutherland* [1919] 1 KB 618, CA.

Defective performance

8.23   Unless the party in default has a lawful excuse the injured party can, of course, recover damages for breach of contract but, leaving aside termination for renunciation[1] or incapacitation,[2] he can only terminate for failure to perform an obligation in two cases:

- where it involves breach of a term of the contract which is a condition;
- where it involves breach of an 'intermediate term' and the effect of the breach deprives the injured party of substantially the whole of his intended benefit under the contract.

1   Para 8.21 above.
2   Para 8.22 above.

8.24   *Breach of condition*   Some contractual terms can be classified as conditions, others as intermediate terms, and others as warranties. A condition is an essential term of the contract,[1] or, as it is sometimes put, one which goes to the root of the contract. If it is broken, the injured party may[2] terminate the contract for breach of condition, as well as claiming damages, whether the effect of the breach is serious or trivial.[3] In this context the word 'condition' is used in yet another sense. It does not bear its orthodox meaning, discussed in paras 5.27, 5.28 and 5.30 above, of an event by which an obligation is suspended or cancelled but is used to describe a particular type of contractual term. It is certainly an odd word to use for this purpose.

An intermediate term is one whose breach may entitle the injured party to terminate the contract, depending on how serious the effect of the breach is. We explain this further in para 8.28 below.

A warranty is a contractual term concerning a less important or subsidiary statement of fact or promise.[4] If a warranty is broken this does not entitle the other party to terminate the contract. It simply entitles him to sue for damages or make a set-off and the party in breach is entitled to the contractual price less the damages or set-off.[5]

1   *Heyworth v Hutchinson* (1867) LR 2 QB 447 at 451.
2   Unless the failure in performance is microscopic: para 8.3 above.
3   In relation to contracts for sale of goods this rule is given statutory effect by the Sale of Goods Act 1979, s 11(3).
4   *Oscar Chess Ltd v Williams* [1957] 1 All ER 325 at 328; Sale of Goods Act 1979, s 11(3).
5   *Gilbert Ash (Northern) Ltd v Modern Engineering (Bristol) Ltd* [1973] 3 All ER 195, HL; Sale of Goods Act 1979, s 53(1)(a).

8.25   The classification of a term as a condition depends on the following considerations:

- Sometimes statute provides that particular terms are conditions, eg the implied conditions in sale of goods contracts, hire purchase contracts, contracts analogous to contracts for the sale of goods and hire contracts under ss 12 to 15 of the Sale of Goods Act 1979, ss 8 to 11 of the Supply of Goods (Implied Terms) Act 1973 and ss 7 to 10 of the Supply of Goods and Services Act 1982, respectively.[1]
- In other cases, a term which has been classified as a condition in judicial decisions will be so classified thereafter, subject to the rules of judicial precedent.[2] An example is a stipulation as to time (other than the time for payment) in a commercial contract.[3]
- In the absence of classification by statute or case authority, a court has to decide whether the broken term is a condition by ascertaining the intention of the parties as at the time the contract was made.[3] The parties' intentions are particularly important and it is open to them to agree that what is a condition according to a previous judicial decision shall not be so treated in their contract, and vice versa. Because of the drastic consequences, the courts lean against construing a term as a condition: in fact, they are increasingly reluctant so to construe a term unless compelled by clear evidence of the parties' intentions.[4]

The approach of the courts is as follows:

First, the court must seek to ascertain the intention of the parties as expressed in the contract. If, on its proper interpretation, the wording clearly reveals that the parties intended that any breach of the term should give rise to a right to terminate, that term will be regarded as a condition. But if the parties clearly did not so intend, the term will not be regarded as a condition even though it is described as a 'condition' in the contract. This is shown by *Schuler AG v Wickman Machine Tool Sales Ltd.*[5] A four-year distributorship agreement provided that the distributor should visit six named customers every week. The agreement described this provision as a 'condition'. The House of Lords held that the contract could not be terminated simply because of breach of this 'condition'. Its reasoning was that the parties could not have intended a mere failure to make one visit to result in a right to terminate. It thought that more probably 'condition' had been used simply to mean 'term'. The Court of Appeal went even further in *Rice v Great Yarmouth Borough Council.*[6] It held that breach of a particular term in a contract did not automatically entitle the injured party to terminate the contract even though the contract expressly provided that on breach of any of its terms the injured party could do so. In this case the defendant local authority had contracted with the claimant firm for it to provide leisure management and grounds maintenance for a four-year period. A clause in the contract in question provided that if the claimant committed a breach of any term of the contract the defendant could terminate the contract. The claimant committed a number of breaches of contract by substandard performance. The defendant terminated the contract, relying on the above clause. The Court of Appeal held that the defendant was not entitled to do so, and treated the term in question as an intermediate term. Its reason was that the clause should not be interpreted literally so as to give the defendant the right to terminate for breach of any of the terms in the contract. Instead, it had to be given a commonsense, commercial interpretation. It noted that the clause did not characterise any particular term as a condition or indicate which terms were to be considered so important that any breach would justify termination but purported to apply to any breach, however small, of any obligation, however minor. Consequently, it could not have the effect of making a term in the contract one for which termination for its breach was automatically available. While this decision, which ignores the unambiguous words of the clause, might have been supported as an extreme case of judicial intervention if the claimant had been a consumer, it seems insupportable where (as here) the contract was not a consumer contract. Clearly, an all-embracing termination clause relating to breaches of a variety of terms, some major and some minor, will be unlikely now to be interpreted as effective to make the terms conditions. It is necessary to relate the clause to particular terms; it was the failure to do so in *Rice v Great Yarmouth Borough Council* which was the telling factor for the Court of Appeal.

If the wording of the contract, as interpreted by the courts, does not conclude the matter, the court must ascertain the parties' intentions by inference from the nature, purpose and circumstances of the contract. If, in the context of the whole contract, it is clear that the term was so important that an injured party would always want to be entitled to terminate if it was broken it will be regarded as a condition. An example is *Behn v Burness,*[7] where one term of a charterparty was that the ship was 'now in the port of Amsterdam': the ship was not then there. The statement was held to be a condition because of the commercial importance attached to such a statement. On the other hand, a term in a charterparty that a ship is seaworthy has not been construed as a condition because it can be broken in a number of ways, in some of which the parties would clearly not intend that the charterer should be entitled to terminate.[8] As this decision indicates, if a term can be broken in a variety of ways it is unlikely that it will be inferred that the parties intended that the injured party should always be entitled to terminate the contract for breach of that term, since where a variety of breaches occur it is likely that some of them may not be serious. This can be compared with the situation where the term can only be broken in one way and that breach will always be serious.

1   Paras 7.20 and 7.21 above.
2   *Maredelante Cia Naviera SA v Bergbau-Handel GmbH, The Mihalis Angelos* [1970] 3 All ER 125, CA.
3   *Bunge Corpn v Tradax SA* [1981] 2 All ER 513, HL; para 8.10 above.
4   *Cehave NV v Bremer Handelsgesellschaft mbH, The Hansa Nord* [1975] 3 All ER 739 at 755; *Bunge Corpn v Tradax SA* [1981] 2 All ER 513 at 542, 551.
5   [1973] 2 All ER 39, HL.
6   [2001] 3 LGLR 4, CA.
7   (1863) 3 B & S 751.
8   *Hong Kong Fir Shipping Co Ltd v Kawasaki Kisen Kaisha Ltd* [1962] 1 All ER 474, CA.

8.26   In the case of a contract for the sale or supply of goods, the right to terminate for breach of condition is subject to statutory limitations.

First, s 15A of the Sale of Goods Act 1979 provides that, where in the case of a contract of sale:

•   the buyer would otherwise have the right to reject goods (ie terminate the contract) by reason of a breach by the seller of one of the terms implied by ss 12 to 15 of the Act; but
•   the seller proves that the breach is so slight that it would be unreasonable for him to do so,

then, if the buyer does not deal as consumer,[1] the breach is not to be treated as a breach of condition but only as a breach of warranty (with the result that there is no right to reject the goods).

Similar provision is made by s 11A of the Supply of Goods (Implied Terms) Act 1973 and s 5A of the Supply of Goods and Services Act 1982 in relation to hire purchase contracts and contracts analogous to contracts for the sale of goods, respectively.

1   'Dealing as consumer' has the same meaning as that given in the Unfair Contract Terms Act 1977 (see para 9.16 below): Sale of Goods Act 1979, s 61(5A).

8.27   Second, there is a special rule which (where it is applicable) prevents a buyer of goods terminating the contract of sale for breach of a condition of it, even though he has not affirmed it because he lacks the knowledge of the breach necessary for affirmation. This rule – which only applies to contracts for the sale of goods – is provided by s 11(4) of the Sale of Goods Act 1979. This states that, where a contract for the sale of goods is not severable and the buyer has accepted the goods or part of them, he can only treat a breach of condition as a breach of warranty, 'and not as a ground for rejecting the goods and treating the contract as repudiated', unless there is a term of the contract, express or implied, to that effect.

Section 11(4) only applies where the contract of sale is not severable, so that it is inapplicable to a contract under which goods are to be delivered by instalments, each of which is to be separately paid for, because this is a severable contract. On the other hand, a contract for a lump sum price payable after the completion of delivery is not severable where the seller has an option to fulfil his obligations by one delivery or two or more,[1] unless the seller exercises that option (whereupon the contract becomes a severable one).

By the Sale of Goods Act 1979, s 35(1), a buyer is deemed to have accepted goods:

•   when he intimates to the seller that he has accepted them; or
•   when the goods have been delivered to him and he does any act in relation to them which is inconsistent with the ownership of the seller.

However, by s 35(2), where goods are delivered to the buyer and he has not previously examined them, he is not deemed to have accepted them under s 35(1) until he has had a reasonable opportunity of examining them to see whether they conform with the contract or, in the case of a contract for sale by sample, to compare the bulk with the sample.

Section 35(4) of the 1979 Act provides that a buyer is also deemed to have accepted the goods when, after a lapse of a reasonable time, he retains the goods without intimating to the seller that he has rejected them. In determining whether a reasonable time has elapsed, account must be taken of whether the buyer had a reasonable opportunity to examine the goods.[2]

What constitutes a reasonable time varies according to the nature of the goods: 'What is a reasonable time for a bicycle would scarcely be adequate for a nuclear submarine'.[3]

A buyer may be deemed to have accepted goods under this heading even though the defect has not manifested itself during the 'reasonable time' and even though he has not had a reasonable time to discover the defect.[3]

By s 35(6) of the 1979 Act, a buyer is not deemed to have accepted the goods merely because:

- he asks for, or agrees to, their repair by or under an arrangement with the seller; or
- the goods are delivered to another under a sub-sale or other disposition.

If there has been a breach of the implied condition under the Sale of Goods Act 1979, s 12(1) that the seller has the right to sell the goods,[4] the buyer who is forced to hand them over to the true owner is entitled to recover back the price he has paid, on the grounds that there has been a total failure of consideration,[5] notwithstanding that he has used the goods for some time. Section 11(4) has no application to a breach of s 12(1) because there is not really a contract of sale at all if the seller has no right to sell the goods.[6]

1   J Rosenthal & Sons Ltd v Esmail [1965] 2 All ER 860, HL.
2   Sale of Goods Act 1979, s 35(5).
3   Bernstein v Pamson Motors (Golders Green) Ltd [1987] 2 All ER 220 at 230.
4   Para 7.20 above.
5   Para 8.17 above.
6   Rowland v Divall [1923] 2 KB 500, CA.

8.28   *Breach of an intermediate term*   If the term broken is not a condition, it must not be assumed that it is a warranty for which the only remedy is damages, unless statute or a judicial decision compels such a classification.[1] Instead, the contract must be construed and, unless the contract makes it clear (either by express provision or by necessary implication from its nature, purpose and circumstances) that the parties intended that no breach of the term should entitle the injured party to terminate the contract, the term will be classified as an intermediate (or innominate) term and not as a warranty. If it is so classified one must then ask whether the nature and effect of its breach is such as to deprive the injured party of substantially the whole benefit which it was intended that he should obtain under the contract.[2] If it is, the injured party is entitled to terminate the contract, as well as claiming damages. In applying this test, account must be taken not only of the actual consequences of the breach but also of those whose occurrence is reasonably foreseeable.[3] There is high judicial authority in a number of cases that the present doctrine, whereby termination for breach of a term depends on the effects of the breach, is preferable to making termination dependent on whether the term itself is classified as a condition or a warranty, since it is far more likely to ensure that termination is possible when it is appropriate.[4]

A leading authority for the present doctrine is *Hong Kong Fir Shipping Co Ltd v Kawasaki Kisen Kaisha Ltd.*[5] The claimants chartered a ship to the defendants for 24 months. The ship was old and needed to be maintained by an adequate and competent engine room crew but the claimants did not provide such a crew and thereby were in breach of a term of the charterparty to provide a ship 'in every way fitted for ordinary cargo service' (otherwise called a 'seaworthiness clause'). Because of the incompetence and inadequacy of the engine room crew and the age of the engines, the ship was held up for repairs for five weeks on her first voyage, and when she reached her destination it was found that further repairs, which would take 15 weeks, were necessary to make her seaworthy. The defendants purported to terminate the charterparty and the claimants sued for breach of contract on the ground that termination was wrongful. The defendants pleaded that the seaworthiness clause was a condition of the contract, and that therefore they could terminate the contract for breach of it. Having held that the clause was not a condition for the reason set out towards the end of para 8.25 above, the Court of Appeal held that the effect of the claimants' breach of the clause was not sufficiently serious to justify the defendants in terminating the charterparty. One reason which it particularly relied on was the fact that after the repairs the ship was still available for 17 of the original 24 months. The defendants' termination had therefore been wrongful.

The same decision was reached in *The Hansa Nord*.[6] Citrus pulp pellets were sold by a German company to a Dutch company, delivery to be made in Rotterdam. The contract included a term that shipment was to be made in good condition. Some of the pellets arrived damaged. The buyers rejected the whole consignment (ie terminated the contract) and the goods were sold by the order of a Dutch court to a third person. Subsequently, they were re-sold at one-third the original contract price to the original buyers who then used the whole consignment for a purpose (cattle food) similar to that for which they had originally bought it (animal feed) – though at a lower rate of inclusion in the case of the damaged pellets. The Court of Appeal held that the 'shipment in good condition' term was not a condition of the contract because it could not have been intended that any breach of it should entitle the buyers to terminate the contract.[7] The Court then turned to the present doctrine and held that the buyers were not entitled to terminate under it because, particularly in the light of the subsequent events, the effect of the breach was not sufficiently serious to justify termination. Thus, the buyers were only entitled to damages and could not treat themselves as discharged from their obligation to accept the pellets and pay the contract price.

Particularly in long-running contracts, such as that in *Rice v Great Yarmouth Borough Council*[8] or a charterparty or building contract, there may be a series of breaches, each of which may have relatively trivial effects but which cumulatively have an effect so serious as to satisfy the *Hong Kong* test. In *Rice v Great Yarmouth Borough Council* the Court of Appeal held that, in applying the *Hong Kong* test to a particular breach, account could be taken of the cumulative effect of past breaches. It also held that in a cumulative breach case account could also be taken in applying that test not only to whether the injured party had been substantially deprived of the whole of his intended benefit under the contract but whether it could be inferred that the cumulative breaches would continue; if it could, the inference might be that the injured party *would* be substantially so deprived, in which case he would be entitled to terminate before that eventuality materialises. On the facts of the case, the Court of Appeal concluded that the trial judge had been entitled to find that the breaches of contract in question had not had a sufficiently serious effect to satisfy the *Hong Kong* test.

1   *Hong Kong Fir Shipping Co Ltd v Kawasaki Kisen Kaisha Ltd* [1962] 2 QB 26 at 63–64; *Reardon Smith Line Ltd v Hansen-Tangen* [1976] 3 All ER 570 at 573–573.
2   *Hong Kong Fir Shipping Co Ltd v Kawasaki Kisen Kaisha Ltd* [1962] 2 QB 26 at 70.
3   [1962] 2 QB 26 at 64.
4   Eg *Reardon Smith Line Ltd v Hansen-Tangen* [1976] 3 All ER 570 at 577.
5   [1962] 1 All ER 474, CA.
6   *Cehave NV v Bremer Handelsgesellschaft mbH, The Hansa Nord* [1975] 3 All ER 739, CA.
7   The Court also held that there was no breach of the implied condition as to quality under the Sale of Goods Act 1979, s 14(2); see para 7.20 above.
8   [2001] 3 LGLR 4, CA; para 8.25.

8.29   These two cases can be contrasted with *Aerial Advertising Co v Batchelors Peas Ltd (Manchester)*.[1] The claimants agreed to conduct an aerial advertising campaign for the defendants. One term of the contract was that the pilot of the aeroplane should telephone the defendants each day and obtain their approval for what he proposed to do. On Armistice Day 1937, the pilot, in breach of this term, failed to contact the defendants and flew over Salford during the two minutes' silence. The aeroplane was towing a banner saying 'Eat Batchelors Peas'. Of course, the term broken was not a condition since breach of it might well only have had trivial consequences, so that the parties could not have intended that its breach should always entitle the defendants to terminate the contract. However, the effect of the particular breach was disastrous since it aroused public hostility towards the defendants and their products. It was held that the defendants were entitled to terminate the contract.

1   [1938] 2 All ER 788.

Anticipatory breach

8.30   So far we have been concerned with actual breaches of contract, ie breaches of contractual obligations whose performance is due at the time of the breach. An anticipatory breach of contract occurs where a party renounces[1] his contractual obligations, or incapacitates himself[2] from performing them, *before the time fixed for their performance*. If a party commits such an anticipatory breach, the injured party can accept the breach as discharging the contract (ie terminate it) and immediately bring an action for damages for breach of contract or a quantum meruit action: he does not have to wait for the time of performance to become due. An example is provided by *Lovelock v Franklyn*,[3] where the defendant agreed to assign his interest in a lease to the claimant for £140. Before the agreed date of performance arrived, the defendant assigned his interest to another person. It was held that the claimant could bring an action for damages immediately: he did not have to wait for the time of performance to arrive.

If the injured party validly terminates the contract for anticipatory breach, the other party is not permitted to change his mind and seek to perform his contractual obligations,[4] but he may do so at any time before there is a valid termination by the injured party.[5]

1   Para 8.21 above.
2   Para 8.22 above.
3   (1846) 8 QB 371.
4   *Xenos v Danube and Black Sea Rly Co* (1863) 13 CBNS 825.
5   *Norwest Holst Group Administration Ltd v Harrison* [1985] ICR 668, CA.

8.31   As in the other situations where a party can terminate a contract for the other's failure to perform, a contract is never automatically discharged by anticipatory breach; instead, the injured party has an election to terminate or affirm the contract. If he refuses to accept the anticipatory breach as discharging the contract and continues to insist on performance, he will affirm it. When a contract is affirmed after anticipatory breach the effects are as follows:

- the injured party loses his right to bring an action for damages for anticipatory breach;
- the contract remains in force. Each party remains liable to perform his obligations when they become due and will be liable if he fails to perform them then. Thus, the party who committed the anticipatory breach is given an opportunity to perform his obligations, and only if he fails to do so will he be liable. The contract remains in existence at the risk of both parties; consequently, if the party who has affirmed after anticipatory breach subsequently commits a breach of contract he will be liable,[1] and either party can take advantage of any supervening circumstance which would justify him in declining to perform;[2]

- as opposed to the case where the injured party immediately sues for damages for anticipatory breach, a party who affirms is under no duty to mitigate his loss before performance is due.[3] This may result in the recovery of larger damages in the event of ultimate non-performance by the other.[4]

1   *Fercometal SARL v Mediterranean Shipping Co SA, The Simona* [1988] 2 All ER 742, HL.
2   *Avery v Bowden* (1855) 5 E & B 714.
3   *Tredegar Iron and Coal Co Ltd v Hawthorn Bros & Co* (1902) 18 TLR 716, CA.
4   Para 11.18 below.

Chapter 9

Exemption clauses

9.1 A contract may contain an exemption clause. An exemption clause may:

- purport to exclude or restrict one of the parties' liability for breach of contract, or some other liability, such as for misrepresentation or for the tort of negligence, or both; or
- purport to exclude or modify the obligations of a party which would normally be implied by law from the legal nature of the contract.

Because exemption clauses can operate very unfairly in the case of standard form contracts, where one party has no real option but to accept the terms offered by the other, a number of restrictive rules have been introduced by the courts and by legislation, as explained below.

9.2 In this chapter we consider:

- the requirements that a person who wishes to rely on an exemption clause must prove that it is a term of a contract to which he is a party and that, as a matter of construction, it covers the liability in question;
- two limitations on the operation of exemption clauses, which have been introduced by the courts;
- various legislative limitations on the validity of exemption clauses.

Term of the contract

9.3 As in the case of any purported contractual term, the determination of whether what purports to be an exemption clause is a term of the contract depends very much on whether or not the clause is contained in a signed contractual document or not. If it is, it is a contractual term, binding on the party who signed the document, even though he was unaware of it (eg because he had not read it).[1]

1   *L'Estrange v Graucob* [1934] 2 KB 394, DC. For an exception, see para 9.12 below.

9.4 In other cases, eg where the clause is printed on a ticket or an order form or a notice, the clause will only be a contractual term if reasonable notice of it is given. If reasonable notice of it is given, it is irrelevant that the party affected by the term is unaware of it. The following rules apply in this connection.

Notice must be given before or at the time of the contract

9.5   The exemption clause is ineffective unless it was brought to the party's notice before or at the time the contract was made. This is shown by *Olley v Marlborough Court Ltd*.[1] The claimant and her husband were accepted as guests at a hotel. They paid for a week in advance and went to their room, on the wall of which was a notice exempting the hotel proprietors from liability for the loss or theft of property. Due to the negligence of the hotel staff, property was stolen from the claimant's room. The Court of Appeal held that the hotel was not protected by the exemption clause because the contract had been made before the exemption clause was communicated so that it formed no part of the contract.

There are two exceptions to the present rule. The first is that, if there has been a course of dealings between the parties on the basis of documents incorporating similar terms exempting liability, then, provided those dealings have been of a consistent nature,[2] the court may imply the exemption clause into a particular contract where express notice is given too late. In *J Spurling Ltd v Bradshaw*,[3] the defendant had dealt with the claimant warehousemen for many years. He delivered barrels of orange juice to them for storage. Later he received a document from them which acknowledged receipt and referred to clauses on its back, one of which excluded the claimants from any liability for loss or damage occasioned by their negligence. Subsequently, the defendant refused to pay the storage charges because the barrels were empty on collection. He was sued for these charges and counterclaimed for negligence. The Court of Appeal held that the exemption clause was incorporated into the contract, and the defendant was therefore bound by it, because in previous dealings he had received a document containing the clause, although he had never read it. Since incorporation of an exemption clause in this way depends on a previous consistent course of dealings between the parties it is less likely to occur in the case of contracts to which a private individual is a party, because normally he will have had insufficient dealings with the other party to constitute a course of dealings; three or four dealings over a five-year period, for instance, have been held insufficient to constitute a course of dealing.[4]

The second exception to the rule that an exemption clause is ineffective unless brought to the notice of the party affected before or at the time the contract was made is as follows. An exemption clause may be implied into a contract if both parties are in a particular trade and the clause is used so frequently in dealings in that trade that the party affected must (as a reasonable person in that trade) have known that it would be included in the contract.[5] This is an application of the rule that a term may be implied by trade usage.[6]

1   [1949] 1 All ER 127, CA.
2   *McCutcheon v David MacBrayne Ltd* [1964] 1 All ER 430, HL.
3   [1956] 2 All ER 121, CA.
4   *Hollier v Rambler Motors (AMC) Ltd* [1972] 1 All ER 399, CA.
5   *British Crane Hire Corpn Ltd v Ipswich Plant Hire Ltd* [1974] 1 All ER 1059, CA.
6   Para 7.19 above.

The notice must be contained in a contractual document

9.6   An exemption clause is ineffective if it, or notice of it, is contained in a document which a reasonable person would not assume to contain contractual terms. Thus, in *Chapelton v Barry UDC*,[1] it was held that an exemption clause contained in a ticket for a deck chair on a beach was ineffective because no reasonable person would expect the ticket to be more than a receipt whose object was to enable a hirer to show that he had paid: he would not assume it contained contractual terms.

1   [1940] 1 All ER 356, CA.

Reasonable notice of the exemption clause must be given

9.7   A leading authority is *Parker v South Eastern Rly Co.*[1] The claimant left his bag at a station cloakroom. He received a ticket which said on its face: 'See back'. On the back were a number of terms, one of which limited the railway company's liability to £10 per package. The claimant's bag was lost and he claimed its value of £24 10s (£24.50). It was held that the claimant would be bound by the exemption clause, even though he had not read it, if the railway company had given reasonable notice of its terms. Notice can be reasonable even though it involves reference to other documents or to a notice.[2] The test laid down in *Parker v South Eastern Rly Co* is objective, and if reasonable notice has been given, it is irrelevant that the party affected by the exemption clause was illiterate or otherwise unable to comprehend its meaning.[2] The only exception would be where the party relying on the clause was aware of the other party's inability to comprehend; in such a case the clause would not be a term of the contract.[3]

What amounts to reasonable notice depends in part on the nature of the exemption clause. If it is particularly onerous or unusual and would not generally be known to the other party, more will be required (eg that the clause be printed in different type or colour from the other terms) in order that the notice be held to be reasonable[4] than would be required in a clause of a less onerous or unusual type.

1   (1877) 2 CPD 416, CA.
2   *Thompson v London, Midland and Scottish Rly Co* [1930] 1 KB 41, CA.
3   *Geier v Kujawa, Weston and Warne Bros (Transport) Ltd* [1970] 1 Lloyd's Rep 364.
4   *Thornton v Shoe Lane Parking Ltd* [1971] 1 All ER 686, CA; *Interfoto Picture Library Ltd v Stiletto Ltd* [1988] 1 All ER 348, CA.

Interpretation

9.8   If an exemption clause is a term of the contract the next question is whether it applies to the liability in question.

It must be emphasised that there is no rule of law that an exemption clause is eliminated, or deprived of effect, regardless of its terms by a breach of contract, however fundamental that breach may be. The question whether, and to what extent, an exemption clause applies in the event of any breach of contract is answered by construing the contract to see whether the parties intended that the clause should apply to the loss or damage which has occurred in the circumstances in which it has occurred. This was stated by the House of Lords in *Photo Production Ltd v Securicor Transport Ltd.*[1]

In the *Photo Production* case, the claimant company employed the defendant company to check against burglaries and fires at their factory at night. One night, the defendant's patrolman deliberately started a fire in the factory. It got out of control and a large part of the premises was burnt down. The loss and damage suffered amounted to £615,000. By way of defence to the claimant's action to recover this amount as damages, the defendant relied principally on an exemption clause in its contract with the claimant which purported to exempt the defendant from liability for any injurious act by an employee unless it could have been foreseen and avoided by due diligence on its part. The clause added that the defendant was not to be liable for any loss suffered by the claimant through fire, except in so far as such loss was solely attributable to the negligence of the defendant's employees acting within the scope of their employment. The House of Lords held that, although the defendant would otherwise have been liable to the claimant, on its true construction the exemption clause clearly and unambiguously applied to what had occurred, and protected the defendant from liability.[2]

In case it should be thought that the rule that the application of an exemption clause depends on the construction of the contract is liable to cause injustice in consumer contracts and other contracts based on standard terms, we would point out that exemption clauses in such a contract made nowadays are rendered either totally invalid or invalid unless fair and reasonable by the Unfair Contract Terms Act 1977, as we explain in paras 9.14 to 9.24 below,[3] even though on their true construction they were intended to apply to what has occurred. It follows that the construction of an exemption clause is now generally of crucial importance only where the contract has been negotiated between businessmen capable of looking after their own interests and of deciding how the risks inherent in the performance of the contract can most economically be borne, which is usually by one or other party insuring against such risks.

We set out below certain rules of construction which are applied to exemption clauses by the courts and which tend to favour the party affected by such a clause.

1   [1980] 1 All ER 556, HL. See also *George Mitchell (Chesterhall) Ltd v Finney Lock Seeds Ltd* [1983] 2 All ER 737, HL.
2   The contract in this case was a standard form contract, but, since it was entered into before the Unfair Contract Terms Act 1977, the House of Lords was not concerned with the validity of the exemption clause under that Act.
3   An exemption clause may also not be binding if it is unfair: Unfair Terms in Consumer Contracts Regulations 1999; para 12.60.

Liability can only be excluded or restricted by clear words
9.9   The liability in question must be precisely covered by the exemption clause relied on. In *Andrews Bros (Bournemouth) Ltd v Singer & Co Ltd,*[1] the claimants entered into a contract to buy 'new Singer cars' from the defendants. One of the cars delivered by the defendants was not a new car, having run a considerable mileage. A clause in the contract exempted the defendants from liability for breach of all 'conditions, warranties and liabilities *implied* by common law, statute or otherwise' but the Court of Appeal held that this did not protect the defendants against liability for breach of an express term. A similar decision was reached in *Wallis, Son and Wells v Pratt and Haynes.*[2] The defendants sold by sample to the claimants seed described as 'common English sainfoin'. The contract stated that the defendants gave 'no *warranty* express or implied' as to any matter concerning the seed. The seed turned out to be the inferior and cheaper 'giant sainfoin'. The House of Lords held that the exemption clause did not apply because there had been a breach of the *condition* implied by the Sale of Goods Act 1979, s 13 (that goods sold by description correspond with it) and the clause did not purport to exclude liability for breach of condition.

This rule of construction is applied more rigorously in the case of clauses purporting to exclude liability than in the case of those purporting to restrict it.[3]

1   [1934] 1 KB 17, CA.
2   [1911] AC 394, HL.
3   *Ailsa Craig Fishing Co Ltd v Malvern Fishing Co Ltd* [1983] 1 All ER 101, HL; *George Mitchell (Chesterhall) Ltd v Finney Lock Seeds Ltd* [1983] 2 All ER 737, HL.

All ambiguities in the exemption clause are construed against the party relying on it
9.10   This is in accordance with the rule normally applied in the construction of contracts.[1]

1   *Houghton v Trafalgar Insurance Co* [1953] 2 All ER 1409, CA.

Exclusion of liability for negligence
9.11   The nature of liability for a breach of contract depends on the term broken. In the case of most terms, liability for their breach is strict (ie a party who does not comply with the term is liable despite the absence of any negligence on his part); in the case of others, liability for their breach only arises if the party in question has been negligent (ie he has failed to show reasonable care). This distinction depends upon whether the term broken

simply imposes an obligation to do something or that something be of a certain standard, or whether it imposes an obligation *to take reasonable care* (or the like) in relation to something. It should also be borne in mind that, where contractual liability for the breach in question is strict, the guilty party may also be liable in tort if he can be proved to have been negligent.

If an exemption clause clearly purports to exclude *all* liability, effect must be given to it[1] (subject to the general rules as to the validity of exemption clauses), but if the clause is not so clearly drafted the law is as follows.

Where contractual liability for the breach in question is strict, the clause is normally construed as being confined to that contractual liability, and not as extending to any tortious liability for negligence, with the result that the guilty party is not protected by it if he is proved to have been negligent.[2] A leading example is *White v John Warrick & Co Ltd*.[3] The claimant hired a tricycle from the defendants. While he was riding it the saddle tilted forward and he was injured. The contract of hire stated: 'nothing in this agreement shall render the owners liable for any personal injury'. The Court of Appeal held that the exemption clause would not protect the defendants from liability in tort if they were found to have been negligent. Its reason was that, in the absence of the exemption clause, the defendants could have been liable for breach of contract in supplying a defective tricycle[4] irrespective of negligence and the operation of the clause had to be restricted to that strict liability.

Where liability can be based on negligence and nothing else, the exemption clause will normally be construed as extending to that head of damage, because if it were not so construed it would lack subject matter.[5] This is shown by *Alderslade v Hendon Laundry Ltd*.[6] The defendants contracted to launder the claimant's handkerchiefs, the contract limiting their liability 'for lost or damaged articles' to 20 times the laundering charge. The handkerchiefs were lost through the defendants' negligence. The Court of Appeal held that the only way in which the defendants could be made liable for the loss of the handkerchiefs would be if they could be shown to have been guilty of negligence. It held that the exemption clause applied to limit the defendants' liability for negligence because otherwise the clause would be left without any content at all.

Both these rules are only rules of construction and, although they will normally be adopted, the court is free to construe the clause in another way if, on its wording or other evidence, it considers that the parties had some other intention.[7]

1   *Joseph Travers & Sons Ltd v Cooper* [1915] 1 KB 73, CA.
2   *Alderslade v Hendon Laundry Ltd* [1945] KB 189, CA.
3   [1953] 2 All ER 1021, CA.
4   The term broken would have been an implied term that the tricycle was reasonably fit for the purpose for which it was hired: paras 7.20–7.21 above.
5   *Alderslade v Hendon Laundry Ltd* [1945] KB 189 at 192; *Hollier v Rambler Motors (AMC) Ltd* [1972] 1 All ER 399, CA.
6   [1945] 1 All ER 244, CA.
7   *Hollier v Rambler Motors (AMC) Ltd* [1972] 1 All ER 399, CA.

General limitations on the application of an exemption clause

Misrepresentation

9.12   If the party favoured by an exemption clause induced the other party to accept it by misrepresenting its contents or effect, the clause is rendered ineffective to the extent that it is wider than the misrepresentation, even though the contract was signed by the other party and even though the misrepresentation was innocent. In *Curtis v Chemical Cleaning and Dyeing Co Ltd*,[1] the claimant took a dress to the defendants' shop for cleaning. The dress was trimmed with beads and sequins. The claimant was asked to sign a receipt exempting the defendants from all liability for any damage to articles cleaned. The claimant asked why her signature was required and was told that the receipt exempted the defendants from liability for damage to the sequins and beads. When the dress was returned it was badly stained. It was held that the defendants were not protected by the clause because through their employee they had innocently induced the claimant to believe that the clause only referred to damage to the beads and sequins and therefore the clause only protected them against liability for such damage.

1   [1951] 1 All ER 631, CA.

Inconsistent undertakings

9.13   If, at or before the time the contract was made, the party favoured by an exemption clause gives an undertaking which is inconsistent with it, the exemption clause is rendered ineffective to the extent that it is inconsistent with the undertaking, even though the undertaking does not form part of the contract or of a contract collateral to it. In *Mendelssohn v Normand Ltd*,[1] the claimant left his car in the defendants' garage on terms contained in a ticket, one of which was that the defendants would not accept any responsibility for any loss sustained by the vehicle or its contents, however caused. The car contained valuables and the claimant wanted to lock it, but the attendant told him that this was not permissible. The claimant told the attendant about the valuables and the attendant promised to lock the car after he had moved it. On his return, the claimant discovered that the valuables had been stolen. The Court of Appeal held that the defendants were not protected by the exemption clause because their employee had in effect promised to see that the valuables were safe, and this oral undertaking took priority over the exemption clause.

1   [1969] 2 All ER 1215, CA.

Validity

9.14   The Unfair Contract Terms Act 1977 contains a number of provisions greatly limiting the extent to which it is possible to 'exclude or restrict liability'. Generally these provisions only apply to the clauses seeking to exclude or restrict 'business liability', which is defined as liability (whether in tort or for breach of contract) which arises *from things done or to be done in the course of a business or from the occupation of premises used for business purposes of the occupier*.[1] In the 1977 Act, '*business*' includes a profession and the activities of any government department or public or local authority.[2] The meaning of the phrase 'in the course of a business' in the 1977 Act is discussed in para 9.16 below. The main impact of the 'business liability limitation' on the effect of the Act is that its provisions do not generally apply to exemption clauses in contracts made between private individuals. The exceptions are indicated at the appropriate points below. It must be noted that the Act is inappropriately named; it is not concerned with unfair contract terms in general but only with terms which are exemption clauses.

Although the Act uses the words 'contract term', we propose generally to use the more familiar expression 'exemption clause'.

1   Unfair Contract Terms Act 1977, s 1(3). The liability of an occupier of premises for breach of an obligation or duty towards a person obtaining access to them for recreational or educational purposes, being liability based on the dangerous state of the premises, is not a business liability of the occupier unless granting that person such access for the purposes concerned falls within the business purposes of the occupier: ibid. Thus, the potential liability of a farmer in the Pennines who grants free access to potholers is not a 'business liability', in so far as it relates to the dangerous state of the potholes and the rest of his premises.
2   Unfair Contract Terms Act 1977, s 14.

Avoidance of liability for negligence

9.15 Section 2(1) of the Act provides that a person cannot, by reference to an exemption clause or notice, exclude or restrict his liability for death or personal injury (including any disease or impairment of physical or mental condition) resulting from negligence.

In the case of other loss or damage, s 2(2) provides that a person cannot, by reference to an exemption clause or notice, exclude or restrict his liability for negligence, *except in so far as the clause or notice satisfies the 'requirement of reasonableness'.* Unlike s 2(1), s 2(2) does not apply where the negligence consists of breach of an obligation arising from a contract term and the person seeking to enforce that term is a third party to the contract acting in reliance on the Contracts (Rights of Third Parties) Act 1999, s 1.[1] In such a case, the exemption clause will be effective in the same way as any other exemption clause to which the 1977 Act does not apply.

Sections 2(1) and (2) do not extend to a contract of employment, except in favour of the employee.[2]

'Negligence' in s 2 means the breach:

- of any obligation, arising from the express or implied terms of a contract, to take reasonable care or exercise reasonable skill in the performance of the contract; or
- of any common law duty to take reasonable care or exercise reasonable skill; or
- of the common duty of care imposed by the Occupiers' Liability Act 1957.[3]

Section 2 does not prevent the parties to a contract (eg for the hire of industrial plant) agreeing between themselves which of them should bear liability in negligence for any injury to a third party (eg injury arising from the negligent use of the plant) since this merely *allocates* liability (as opposed to excluding or restricting it).[4]

The fact that s 2 applies to non-contractual notices (see para 21.4) as well as exemption clauses is another reason why the Unfair Contract Terms Act 1977 is inappropriately named.

1   Contracts (Rights of Third Parties) Act 1999, s 7(2); for s 1 of that Act, see para 14.3.
2   Unfair Contract Terms Act 1977, Sch 1.
3   Unfair Contract Terms Act 1977, s 1(1). The duty at common law to take reasonable care or exercise reasonable skill, and the duty under the 1957 Act, are discussed in chs 17 and 21 below.
4   *Thompson v T Lohan (Plant Hire) Ltd* [1987] 2 All ER 631, CA.

Avoidance of liability for breach of contract

9.16 Section 3(2) lays down a special rule which applies *as between the contracting parties where one of them deals as consumer or on the other's written standard terms of business.*[1] A person 'deals on the other's written standard terms' if the contract which he makes is on those terms; if it is, it is irrelevant that negotiations have taken place over those terms.[2] 'Deals' in this context means 'make a deal'.[2] It has been common for a party to contract on the basis of a standard form contract produced by his professional or trade association. In *British Fermentation Products Ltd v Compare Reavell Ltd,*[3] the judge held that s 3 does not apply to such 'standard terms', because they are not 'the other's' (ie the other party's) standard terms of business, although he suggested that it might be possible to prove that the other party has expressly or impliedly from practice adopted the association's standard terms as *his* standard terms and that this might make s 3 applicable. Clearly, the narrow interpretation in this case limits the extent of s 3, which is unfortunate. The narrow interpretation in *British Fermentation* of 'dealing on the other's standard written terms' can be contrasted with the liberal interpretation of 'dealing as consumer' in *Brigden v American Express Bank Ltd.*[4] In that case it was held that, in making an employment contract, an employee 'deals as consumer' for the purposes of the 1977 Act, which is difficult to square with the ordinary concept of a 'consumer' in terms of the English language, although it is not incompatible with the technical definition of a 'consumer' under the Act.

In the present context, a party to a contract 'deals as consumer' in relation to another party if he neither makes the contract in the course of a business nor holds himself out as doing so, and the other party does make the contract in the course of a business.[5] A dictum by Dillon LJ in *R & B Customs Brokers Co Ltd v United Dominions Trust*[6] provides an explanation of the meaning of the phrase 'in the course of a business':

> 'There are some transactions which are clearly integral parts of the business concerned, and these should be held to have been carried out in the course of those businesses; this would cover, apart from much else, the instance of a one-off adventure in the nature of trade where the transaction itself would constitute a trade or business. There are other transactions, however, ... which are at the highest only incidental to the carrying on of the relevant business; here a degree of regularity is required before it can be said that they are an integral part of the business carried on and so entered into in the course of that business.'

In *R & B Customs Brokers* the Court of Appeal held that a company operating as a freight forwarding agent, which had bought a car for the business and personal use of its two directors and sole shareholders, a husband and wife, had not made the purchase in the course of a business. The purchase was *not clearly* an *integral* part of the freight forwarding agency business. It was *only incidental* to it and there was *no regularity* of purchases of the type in question. The meaning given to 'in the course of a business' in *R & B Customs Brokers* is narrower than that given to the same phrase in s 14(2) of the Sale of Goods Act 1979 by the Court of Appeal in *Stevenson v Rogers*,[7] a later case referred to in para 7.20 above. We think it likely that the wider view in that case will be adopted in relation to the 1977 Act if the point ever goes to the House of Lords.

In the case of contracts for the sale, hire purchase or other supply[8] of goods there is an additional requirement in order for a party who is not an individual to be 'dealing as consumer', viz that the goods are of a type ordinarily supplied for private use or consumption (see further para 9.21 below).[5]

The definition of 'dealing as consumer' is subject to the following qualification. A buyer is not regarded as dealing as consumer:

- if he is an individual and the goods are second-hand goods sold at public auction at which individuals have the opportunity of attending the sale in person; or
- if he is not an individual and the goods are sold by auction or competitive tender.[9]

It is for those claiming that a party does not deal as consumer to show that he does not.[10]

Section 3 provides that, *as against the party dealing as consumer or on the other's written standard terms of business*, the other party cannot by reference to any contract term:

- exclude or restrict his liability for breach of contract; or
- claim to be entitled
    - to render a contractual performance substantially different from that which was reasonably expected of him, or
      in respect of the whole or any part of his contractual obligation, to render no performance at all,

except in so far as the contract term satisfies the 'requirement of reasonableness'. This provision is widely drawn; for example, a term permitting a holiday company to provide accommodation in a different hotel from that specified in the contract may be held invalid, and so may a term entitling a theatre company to cancel a performance without a refund.

1   Unfair Contract Terms Act 1977, s 3(1).
2   *St Albans City and District Council v International Computers Ltd* [1996] 4 All ER 481 at 491.
3   [1999] 2 All ER (Comm) 389.
4   [2000] IRLR 94.
5   Unfair Contract Terms Act 1977, s 12(1).
6   [1988] 1 All ER 847, CA.
7   [1999] 1 All ER 613, CA.
8   Ie those described in para 9.22 below.
9   Unfair Contract Terms Act 1977, s 12(2).
10   Unfair Contract Terms Act 1977, s 12(3).

Matters common to sections 2 and 3

Excepted agreements[1]

9.17   Sections 2 and 3 do not extend to:

- any contract of insurance;
- any contract *so far* as it relates to the creation, transfer or termination of an interest in land[2] or of any right or interest in any patent, trade mark, copyright or the like;
- any contract *so far* as it relates—
    - to the formation or dissolution of a company (which in this context means any body corporate or unincorporated association and includes a partnership), or
    - to its constitution or the rights or obligations of its corporators or members;
- any contract *so far* as it relates to the creation or transfer of securities or of any right or interest in securities.

Contracts of insurance are totally excepted, but the other contracts are only excepted *so far* as they relate to the specified matters. Presumably, only those parts of such a contract which relate to the specified matters (such as the transfer of an interest in land) are excepted from ss 2 and 3 and the rest of the contract is subject to those sections.

Other exceptions relate to charterparties and the like, and are outside the scope of this book.

1   Unfair Contract Terms Act 1977, Sch 1.
2   A mere contractual licence does not create or transfer an interest in land (see para 29.45 below) and therefore an exemption clause contained in it is subject to ss 2 and 3.

The 'requirement of reasonableness'

9.18   In relation to an exemption clause, the requirement of reasonableness is that the clause itself must have been a fair and reasonable one to be included having regard to the circumstances which were, or ought reasonably to have been, known or in the contemplation of the parties when the contract was made.[1]

Where a party seeks to restrict liability to a specified sum in reliance on an exemption clause, then, in determining whether the clause satisfies the requirement of reasonableness, regard must be had in particular to:

- the resources which that party could expect to be available to him for the purpose of meeting the liability should it arise; and
- how far it was open to him to cover himself by insurance.[2]

It is for the party claiming that an exemption clause satisfies the requirement of reasonableness to show on the balance of probabilities that it does.[3]

In *Smith v Eric S Bush; Harris v Wyre Forest District Council*,[4] Lord Griffiths was of the opinion that the following matters should always be considered in relation to the requirement of reasonableness:

- Were the parties of equal bargaining power? If they were the requirement of reasonableness is more easily discharged than if they were not.
- How difficult is the task being undertaken to which the exemption clause applies? If the task is very difficult or dangerous there may be a high risk of failure, which would be a pointer to the requirement of reasonableness being satisfied.
- What are the practical consequences of the decision on the requirement of reasonableness? This involves the amount of money potentially at stake and the ability of the parties to bear the loss involved, which in turn raises the question of insurance.

The courts also apply by analogy the factors in Sch 2, set out in para 9.23 below.

It cannot be over-emphasised that it is the clause which must be reasonable in relation to the particular contract; the question is not whether its particular application in the particular case is reasonable. If a clause is drawn so widely as to be capable of applying in unreasonable circumstances it will not be held to be reasonable, even though in the actual situation which has arisen its application would not be unreasonable.[5] A clause may well have various parts to it but, because the whole clause must be subjected to the test of reasonableness, it is not permissible to look only at that part of it which is relied on.[6] A court will be particularly unwilling to find a clause reasonable if it purports to exclude all potential liability.[7]

1   Unfair Contract Terms Act 1977, s 11(1).
2   Unfair Contract Terms Act 1977, s 11(4).
3   Unfair Contract Terms Act 1977, s 11(5); *Phillips Products Ltd v Hyland* [1987] 2 All ER 620, CA.
4   [1989] 2 All ER 514, HL.
5   *Walker v Boyle* [1982] 1 All ER 634; *Phillips Products Ltd v Hyland Ltd* [1987] 2 All ER 620 at 628.
6   *Stewart Gill Ltd v Horatio Myer & Co Ltd* [1992] 2 All ER 257, CA.
7   *Lease Management Services Ltd v Purnell Secretarial Services Ltd* (1994) 13 Tr LR 337.

Avoidance of liability arising from sale or supply of goods
9.19   Sections 6 and 7 of the Act of 1977 contain additional provisions dealing with attempts to avoid liability where the ownership or possession of goods has passed.

Sale and hire purchase
9.20   By s 6(1), liability for breach of the obligations arising from:

- the Sale of Goods Act 1979, s 12 (seller's implied undertakings as to title etc);[1]
- the Supply of Goods (Implied Terms) Act 1973, s 8 (the corresponding things in relation to hire purchase),

cannot be excluded or restricted by reference to an exemption clause.

1   These terms are described in para 7.20 above.

9.21   Section 6(2) provides that, *as against a person dealing as consumer,* liability for breach of the obligations arising from:

- the Sale of Goods Act 1979, ss 13, 14 or 15 (seller's implied undertakings as to conformity of goods with description or sample, or as to their quality or fitness for a particular purpose);[1]
- the Supply of Goods (Implied Terms) Act 1973, ss 9, 10 or 11 (the corresponding things in relation to hire purchase),

cannot be excluded or restricted by reference to an exemption clause. It must be emphasised that this provision is limited to the implied terms specified. The validity of a clause excluding or restricting liability for breach of any express term will depend on the application of the principles which we have mentioned in para 9.16 above.

Unlike s 6(1), s 6(2) only vitiates the exemption clause as against a person dealing as consumer. In the present context, a party to a contract 'deals as consumer' in relation to another party if:

- he (A) neither makes the contract in the course of a business nor holds himself out as doing so; and
- the other party (B) does make the contract in the course of a business.

Where A is not an individual, it is also necessary, in order for A to deal as consumer, that the goods passing under or in pursuance of the contract are of a type ordinarily supplied for private use or consumption.[2]

We dealt with the meaning of 'in the course of a business' in para 9.16 above. The upshot of the above provision is that, if a company buys from a dealer a Rolls Royce or a yacht for its chairman, it will 'deal as consumer' and liability for breach of the implied terms just mentioned cannot be excluded or restricted.

The definition of 'dealing as consumer' is subject to the following qualification. A buyer is not regarded as dealing as consumer:

- if he is an individual and the goods are second-hand goods sold at public auction at which individuals have the opportunity of attending the sale in person; or
- if he is not an individual and the goods are sold by auction or competitive tender.[2]

It is for those claiming that a party does not deal as consumer to show that he does not.[2]

Where a party does not deal as consumer, s 6(3) is the operative provision. Section 6(3) provides that, *as against a person dealing otherwise than as consumer*, liability for breach of the obligations arising from the Sale of Goods Act 1979, ss 13–15, or the Supply of Goods (Implied Terms) Act 1973, ss 9–11, can be excluded or restricted by an exemption clause, but *only in so far as the clause satisfies the 'requirement of reasonableness'*.

The provisions of s 6(1) and (3) are exceptional in that they are not limited to liabilities arising in the course of business. Section 6 replaces substantially similar provisions introduced by the Supply of Goods (Implied Terms) Act 1973.

1   These terms are described in para 7.20 above.
2   Unfair Contract Terms Act 1977, s 12.

Miscellaneous contracts under which the ownership or possession of goods passes

9.22   Section 7 of the Act of 1977 deals with exemption clauses purporting to exclude or restrict liability for breach of obligations implied by law[1] into other contracts under which the ownership or possession of goods passes, eg contracts of hire or exchange or for work and materials. Section 7 applies to these contracts a regime which is broadly similar to that just mentioned in relation to sale of goods and hire purchase.

Section 7(2) provides that, *as against a person dealing as consumer* (in the same sense as in sale of goods and hire purchase), liability in respect of the goods' correspondence with description or sample, or their quality or fitness for any particular purpose, cannot be excluded or restricted by reference to an exemption clause.

On the other hand, as against a person dealing otherwise than as consumer, s 7(3) provides that such liability can be excluded or restricted by reference to such a clause, but *only in so far as the clause satisfies the 'requirement of reasonableness'*.

In relation to an exemption clause purporting to exclude or restrict liability for breach of the various terms as to title which are implied into contracts of exchange, contracts for work and materials and analogous contracts by s 2 of the Supply of Goods and Services

Act 1982, s 7(3A) provides that liability for breach of these terms cannot be excluded or restricted by reference to an exemption clause.

On the other hand, by s 7(4), liability in respect of breach of the various terms as to title etc which are implied otherwise than under s 2 of the 1982 Act into contracts for the transfer or supply of goods can be excluded or restricted by such a clause, but *only in so far as the clause satisfies the 'requirement of reasonableness'*. Thus, a different rule applies where such a clause appears in a contract of hire or of pledge from that which applies where it appears in a contract for, say, work and materials.

I   Supply of Goods and Services Act 1982, ss 2–5 and 7–10; see para 7.21 above.

The 'requirement of reasonableness' in relation to ss 6 and 7
9.23   The provisions which we mentioned in para 9.18 above concerning the requirement of reasonableness also apply where that requirement is relevant under ss 6 and 7. However, in addition, in determining for the purposes of these two sections whether a contract term satisfies the requirement of reasonableness, regard must be had in particular to the guidelines specified in Sch 2 to the Act,[1] viz:

- the strength of the bargaining positions of the parties relative to each other;
- whether the customer received an inducement to agree to the term, or in accepting it had an opportunity of entering into a similar contract with other persons, but without having to accept a similar term;
- where the term excludes or restricts any relevant liability if some condition is not complied with, whether it was reasonable at the time of the contract to expect that compliance with that condition would be practicable;
- whether the goods were manufactured, processed or adapted to the special order of the customer;
- whether the customer knew or ought reasonably to have known of the existence and extent of the term (eg because it was in small print or was unlikely to be read in full by the customer). We saw in paras 9.3 to 9.7 above that an exemption clause may be a term of the contract even though the customer was unaware of it, especially if he has signed a contractual document containing it. This provision enables the court to hold an exemption clause which is undoubtedly a term of the contract unreasonable, and therefore invalid, because, for instance, the customer could not reasonably have known of its existence.

Although Sch 2 does not apply to the requirement of reasonableness as it applies to ss 2 or 3, the courts apply by analogy the factors in Sch 2 when considering the requirement of reasonableness in relation to those sections.[2]

1   Unfair Contract Terms Act 1977, s 11(2).
2   *Phillips Products Ltd v Hyland* [1987] 2 All ER 620, CA.

Varieties of exemption clauses
9.24   As we have shown, the Act repeatedly refers to the 'exclusion or restriction of liability'. These words are given a wide interpretation by s 13(1) which provides that, to the extent that the provisions mentioned above prevent the exclusion or restriction of any liability, they also prevent:

- making the liability or its enforcement subject to restrictive or onerous conditions (eg a term requiring 14 days' notice of loss);
- excluding or restricting rules of evidence or procedure (eg a term that failure to complain within 14 days is deemed to be conclusive evidence of proper performance of the contract); or

- excluding or restricting any right or remedy in respect of the liability,[1] or subjecting a person to any prejudice in consequence of his pursuing any such right or remedy.

Section 13(1) also provides that, to the extent that ss 2, 6 and 7 prevent the exclusion or restriction of liability, they also prevent excluding or restricting liability by reference to terms which exclude or restrict the relevant obligation or duty. It follows that a clause purporting to disclaim any potential liability is caught by this provision, even though it purports to prevent a duty arising in the first place (as opposed simply to disclaiming liability for breach of an acknowledged duty).[2]

   Whether or not a contract term has the effect of excluding or restricting liability within the above formulation is determined by looking at its effect and substance, and not at its form.[3]

1   Eg a term which allows recovery of damages but which purports to remove any right to terminate the contract for repudiatory breach, or a term which excludes a right to set-off a claim by a buyer for damages for breach against a claim for the price by a seller: *Stewart Gill Ltd v Horatio Myer & Co Ltd* [1992] 2 All ER 257, CA.
2   *Smith v Eric S Bush; Harris v Wyre Forest District Council* [1989] 2 All ER 514, HL.
3   *Phillips Products Ltd v Hyland* [1987] 2 All ER 620, CA.

Unfair Terms in Consumer Contracts Regulations 1999

9.25   These Regulations, which give effect to the EC Directive on Unfair Terms in Consumer Contracts, Directive 93/13/EEC, are intended to harmonise the law relating to unfair terms in contracts between a seller or supplier and a consumer. The Regulations replace Regulations of the same name made in 1994.

   We deal in more detail with the Regulations in chapter 12 but it should be noted here that they cover matters already covered by the Unfair Contract Terms Act 1977. However, as will be seen, in some respects the Act is wider than the Regulations since:

- the Regulations are limited to contracts made by a 'consumer', whereas the Act is not;
- to the extent that the 1977 Act has special provisions relating to 'consumers', 'consumer' has a wider meaning under the Act, because under the Regulations a 'consumer' means 'any natural person who ... is acting for purposes outside his trade, business or profession' (so that, for example, a company entering into a one-off contract which was not integral to its business would not be a 'consumer' under the Regulations, although it would be under the Act)[1];
- in the case of consumer contracts for the sale or supply of goods, liability for breach of statutorily implied terms as to description or quality cannot be excluded under the Act regardless of whether they are reasonable or not, nor can liability for breach of the implied term as to title in any sale or supply contract, whereas under the Regulations an exemption clause of such a type in a consumer contract will only be invalid if it is unfair;
- the Regulations only apply to contracts which have not been individually negotiated, whereas the Act generally applies to individually negotiated contracts as well.

   As will be seen in chapter 12, in some respects the Regulations are wider than the Unfair Contract Terms Act, since they are not limited to exemption clauses, but extend to any 'unfair term' (as defined by the Regulations).

   Despite these differences, there is a substantial area of overlap between the Act and the Regulations. It follows that, in many cases involving exemption clauses, the application of the Act and of the Regulations must be considered.

1   Para 9.16 above.

Chapter 10

Discharge by frustration

10.1 Under the doctrine of frustration a contract is automatically discharged 'whenever the law recognises that, without default of either party,[1] a contractual obligation has become incapable of being performed because the circumstances in which performance is called for would render it a thing radically different from that which was undertaken by the contract'.[2] This classic statement has been approved in a substantial number of cases.[3]

1   For a qualification see para 10.12 below.
2   *Davis Contractors Ltd v Fareham UDC* [1956] 2 All ER 145 at 160.
3   See, for example, *National Carriers Ltd v Panalpina (Northern) Ltd* [1981] 1 All ER 161, HL.

10.2 In this chapter we consider:

- the scope of the doctrine of frustration;
- certain limits on its application;
- the legal effect of the frustration of a contract.

Scope

10.3 A contract may be frustrated if, for example, *subsequent to its formation*:

- a thing essential to its performance is destroyed or becomes unavailable; or
- a fundamental change of circumstances occurs; or
- a party to a contract of a personal nature dies or is otherwise incapacitated from performing it; or
- performance of it is rendered illegal; or
- a basic assumption on which the parties contracted is destroyed.

A contract is not discharged by frustration simply because a subsequent event makes its performance more costly or difficult than envisaged when the contract was made. This is shown by *Davis Contractors Ltd v Fareham UDC*.[1] In 1946, the contractors entered into a contract with the council to build 78 houses for the fixed sum of £94,000. Owing to an unexpected shortage of skilled labour and of certain materials, the contract took 22 months to complete instead of the anticipated eight months and cost £115,000. The contractors contended that the contract had been frustrated by the long delay and that they were entitled to a sum in excess of the contract price on a restitutionary basis (ie reasonable recompense for the benefit which they had conferred). The House of Lords disagreed, holding that the mere fact that unforeseen circumstances had delayed the performance of the contract and made it more costly to perform did not discharge the contract.

1   [1956] 2 All ER 145, HL.

Supervening destruction or unavailability

10.4   A contract is discharged by frustration if performance of it is rendered impossible by the subsequent destruction or unavailability of a specific thing expressly or impliedly required by the contract for its performance. A leading authority is *Taylor v Caldwell*.[1] The defendants agreed to hire a music hall and gardens to the claimants on specified days for the purpose of concerts. Before the first of the specified days, the music hall was destroyed by fire without the fault of either party. The defendants were held not liable for breach of contract because performance of the contract had become impossible through the destruction of the hall and they were not at fault. The contract was therefore frustrated and both parties discharged from their contractual obligations.

The subsequent unavailability of a thing will frustrate a contract if it renders performance of the contract in accordance with its terms impossible. This is shown by *Nickoll and Knight v Ashton Edridge & Co*.[2] The defendants sold the claimants a cargo of cotton seed to be shipped 'per steamship *Orlando* during the month of January'. Before the time for shipping arrived, the ship was so damaged by stranding as to be unable to load in January. It was held that the contract was discharged by frustration.

The point that, for a contract to be frustrated under the present heading, the thing which has been destroyed or is otherwise unavailable must have been expressly or impliedly required by the contract for its performance is well illustrated by *Tsakiroglou & Co Ltd v Noblee Thorl GmbH*.[3] That case concerned a contract for the sale of groundnuts which were to be shipped from the Sudan to Hamburg during November or December 1956. Both parties contemplated that the ship would proceed via the Suez Canal but this was not stated in the contract. On 2 November 1956, the Canal was closed (and remained so for five months). The House of Lords held that the unavailability of the Canal did not frustrate the contract, one of its reasons being that there was no express provision in the contract for shipping via the Canal, nor could a provision be implied to that effect, because the route was immaterial to the buyers.

Even more conclusively, unavailability of a thing does not frustrate the contract if it merely affects the method of performance contemplated by one of the parties.[4] In *Nickoll and Knight v Ashton Edridge & Co*, for instance, the contract would not have been frustrated if, instead of the name of the ship on which the cargo was to be loaded being stated in the contract, the defendant sellers had merely intended to load on that ship.

1   (1863) 3 B & S 826.
2   [1901] 2 KB 126, CA.
3   [1961] 2 All ER 179, HL.
4   *Blackburn Bobbin Co v T W Allen & Sons* [1918] 2 KB 467, CA.

Fundamental change of circumstances

10.5   A contract is frustrated if an event occurs of such gravity that, although technically the contract could still be performed, it would be the performance of a radically different contract from that contemplated.

In *Metropolitan Water Board v Dick Kerr & Co Ltd*,[1] the company contracted with the Board to construct a reservoir within six years, subject to a proviso that time could be extended if delay was caused by difficulties, impediments or obstructions. After two years had elapsed the Minister of Munitions, acting under statutory powers, required the company to stop work on the contract and remove and sell their plant. The House of Lords held that the interruption created by the prohibition was of such a nature and duration that the contract, if resumed, would in effect be radically different from that originally made. Therefore it was frustrated.

This case can be contrasted with *Tsakiroglou & Co Ltd v Noblee Thorl GmbH.*[2] In that case, the House of Lords held that the contract was not frustrated by the closure of the Suez Canal because a voyage round the Cape of Good Hope would not be commercially or fundamentally different from shipping via the Canal, albeit it was more expensive for the sellers.

1   [1918] AC 119, HL.
2   Para 10.4 above.

Death or other personal incapacity

10.6   A contract of employment, or any other contract which can only be performed by a party personally, eg a contract to paint a portrait, is discharged by frustration if that party dies[1] or is otherwise rendered *permanently* incapable of performing it.[2]

If a person becomes *temporarily* incapable of performing such a contract, it may be discharged. Whether or not the temporary incapacity frustrates a contract depends on whether, in the light of the probable duration of the incapacity at its inception, performance after it has ceased would be radically different from what was envisaged by the contract and in effect be the substitution of a new contract. In *Morgan v Manser,*[3] the defendant, a comedian, entered into a contract with the claimant in 1938 whereby he engaged the claimant's services as manager for 10 years. In 1940, the defendant was called up and was not demobilised until 1946. It was held that the contract was discharged by frustration in 1940 since it was then likely that the defendant would have to remain in the forces for a very long time. Similarly, if the duration of an employee's illness is likely to be so lengthy as to make performance of a contract of employment radically different from that undertaken by him and accepted by his employer, the contract will be discharged by frustration, and so will a contract to perform at a concert on a specified day by an illness of short duration.[4] Conversely, a contract of a personal nature is not frustrated by the illness of a party where this is likely to last for only a small part of the period of the contract: further performance after the party becomes available again will not be the performance of a radically different contract.

1   *Stubbs v Holywell Rly Co Ltd* (1867) LR 2 Exch 311.
2   *Notcutt v Universal Equipment Co (London) Ltd* [1986] 3 All ER 582, CA.
3   [1947] 2 All ER 666.
4   *Robinson v Davison* (1871) LR 6 Exch 269.

Supervening illegality

10.7   A change in the law or in the circumstances may make performance of the contract illegal. If the change is such as to make it impossible to perform the contract legally it is discharged by frustration. In *White and Carter Ltd v Carbis Bay Garage Ltd,*[1] for instance, it was held that a contract made in 1939 to display advertisements for three years was frustrated by wartime Defence Regulations prohibiting advertisements of the type in question. On the other hand, in *Cricklewood Property and Investment Trust Ltd v Leighton's Investment Trust Ltd,*[2] the House of Lords held that a 99-year building lease was not frustrated by Defence Regulations prohibiting building for only a small part of that term: performance had merely been suspended, not made impossible.

1   [1941] 2 All ER 633, CA.
2   [1945] 1 All ER 252, HL.

Supervening destruction of a basic assumption on which the parties contracted

10.8   A contract is discharged by frustration if, although it is physically and legally possible for each party to perform his obligations under the contract, a change of circumstances has destroyed a basic assumption on which the parties contracted. In *Krell v Henry*,[1] the defendant agreed to hire a flat in Pall Mall from the claimant for 26 and 27 June 1902, on one of which days Edward VII was to be crowned. To the claimant's knowledge, the defendant hired the flat in order to view the Coronation processions, but this was not mentioned in their written contract. The processions were postponed because of the King's illness.

The Court of Appeal held that a view of the processions was not simply the purpose of the defendant in hiring the flat but the basis of the contract for both parties, and that since the postponement of the processions prevented this being achieved the contract was frustrated.

It is not enough that the purpose of one party in making the contract cannot be fulfilled; the basis on which both parties contracted must have been destroyed. This is shown by *Herne Bay Steam Boat Co v Hutton*,[2] which also reveals the difficulty in drawing the distinction. The defendant chartered a ship from the claimants for 28 and 29 June 1902, for the express purpose of taking fare-paying passengers to see the Coronation naval review at Spithead and to cruise round the fleet. The review was cancelled, but the fleet remained.

The Court of Appeal held that the charterparty was not frustrated because the holding of the review was not the basis on which both parties had contracted and it was irrelevant that the purpose of the defendant was defeated.

1   [1903] 2 KB 740, CA.
2   [1903] 2 KB 683, CA.

Limits

10.9   There are no limits on the type of contract to which, as a matter of law, the doctrine of frustration can apply. In relation to most types of contract, the applicability of the doctrine is long-established; but it was only in 1980 in *National Carriers Ltd v Panalpina (Northern) Ltd*[1] that the House of Lords finally decided, with one dissentient, that the doctrine of frustration is applicable to a lease, although on the facts the particular lease was not frustrated. Their Lordships stated that cases where a lease would be frustrated would be extremely rare. In the case of a long lease, and it must be remembered that a lease may often be for 99 years or 999 years, a prime reason is that, if the lessee is only deprived temporarily of the use of the premises, the interruption of use will almost never be for long enough to frustrate the contract. Moreover, in the case of the destruction, or the like, of the premises, the lease will normally expressly provide for that event by covenants as to insurance and rebuilding, and thereby exclude the doctrine of frustration.

A contract for a lease and a contract for the sale of land can, of course, be discharged by frustration.[2] However, it is clear that such a contract will only be frustrated in the most extreme cases, since it has been held, for example, that a contract for the sale of premises is not frustrated simply because, before completion of the contract by conveyance, they are destroyed[3] or made subject to a compulsory purchase order.[4] In these cases, at least, the purchaser will be compensated by the payment of insurance monies or compulsory purchase compensation. Much greater hardship will be suffered by the person who has contracted to lease or buy land for redevelopment but before completion the buildings on it are listed as being of special architectural interest, so that redevelopment becomes difficult or impossible and the land loses most of its value. It has been held that the contract is not frustrated in such a case,[5] and consequently the person who has contracted to lease or buy remains bound to go ahead with a venture which is financially disastrous.

1   [1981] 1 All ER 161, HL.

2   Contract for a lease: *Rom Securities Ltd v Rogers (Holdings) Ltd* (1967) 205 Estates Gazette 427; contract for sale of land: assumed in *Amalgamated Investment and Property Co Ltd v John Walker & Sons Ltd* [1976] 3 All ER 509, CA.
3   *Paine v Meller* (1801) 6 Ves 349.
4   *Hillingdon Estates Co v Stonefield Estates Ltd* [1952] 1 All ER 853.
5   *Amalgamated Investment and Property Co Ltd v John Walker & Sons Ltd* [1976] 3 All ER 509, CA.

Express provision for frustrating event

10.10   The doctrine of frustration does not apply if the parties have made provision to deal with the frustrating event which has occurred. There is one exception: a contract is frustrated by supervening illegality despite an express provision to the contrary.[1]

A provision concerned with the effect of a possible future event is narrowly construed and, unless on its true construction it covers the frustrating event in question, the doctrine of frustration is not ousted. This is shown by *Metropolitan Water Board v Dick Kerr & Co Ltd*,[2] discussed above, where the contract for the reservoir provided that in the event of delays 'however caused' the contractors were to be given an extension of time. The House of Lords held that this provision did not prevent the doctrine of frustration applying because it did not cover the particular event which had occurred. Although the event was literally within the provision, the provision could be construed as limited to temporary difficulties, such as shortage of supplies, and not as extending to events which fundamentally altered the nature of the contract and which could not have been in the parties' contemplation when they made the contract.

1   *Ertel Bieber & Co v Rio Tinto Co Ltd* [1918] AC 260, HL.
2   [1918] AC 119, HL.

Foreseen and foreseeable events

10.11   If, by reason of special knowledge, the risk of the particular frustrating event was foreseen or foreseeable by only *one* party the doctrine of frustration cannot apply. It is up to that party to provide against the risk of that event and, if he fails to do so and cannot perform the contract, he is liable for breach.[1]

On the other hand, where the risk of the frustrating event was foreseen or foreseeable by both parties, but they did not make provision to deal with it, the doctrine of frustration can apply.[2] In each case, however, it is a question of construction whether the failure to make provision for the event means that each party took the risk of it rendering contractual performance impossible or whether, in the absence of any such intention, the doctrine of frustration should apply to discharge the contract.[3]

1   *Walton Harvey Ltd v Walker and Homfrays Ltd* [1931] 1 Ch 274, CA.
2   *Ocean Tramp Tankers Corpn v V/O Sovfracht, The Eugenia* [1964] 1 All ER 161, CA.
3   *Chandler Bros Ltd v Boswell* [1936] 3 All ER 179, CA; *Ocean Tramp Tankers Corpn v V/O Sovfracht, The Eugenia* [1964] 1 All ER 161, CA.

Fault of a party

10.12   A party cannot rely on the doctrine of frustration if it is proved that the frustrating event was brought about by his fault, but (assuming that he has not also contributed to the event by his fault) the other party can.[1]

A deliberate election to pursue a course of conduct which renders performance of the contract impossible or illegal is clearly established as fault in this context; that conduct may in itself be a breach of contract,[2] but it is not necessary that it should be.[3] In *Maritime National Fish Ltd v Ocean Trawlers Ltd*,[4] the claimants chartered to the defendants a trawler fitted with an otter trawl. Both parties knew that the use of an otter trawl without a licence from a minister was illegal. Later, the defendants applied for licences for five trawlers which they were operating, including the claimants'. They were only granted three licences and were asked to specify the three trawlers which they wished to have licensed. The defendants named three trawlers other than the claimants'. They then claimed that they were no longer bound by the charterparty because it had been frustrated. The Privy Council held that the frustration was due to the defendants' deliberate act in not specifying the claimants' trawler for a licence and that therefore they could not rely on the doctrine of frustration. Consequently, the claimants could recover the hire under the charterparty.

Any deliberate choice of conduct which renders performance of the contract impossible or illegal suffices for present purposes, however reasonable it is to make that choice.[5]

It would seem that a negligent act by a party, as opposed to a deliberate choice of conduct, which renders performance of the contract impossible or illegal prevents him relying on the doctrine of frustration.[5]

The onus of proof where fault is alleged is on the party alleging it.[6]

1   *FC Shepherd & Co Ltd v Jerrom* [1986] 3 All ER 589, CA.
2   As in *Ocean Tramp Tankers Corpn v V/O Sovfracht, The Eugenia* [1964] 1 All ER 161, CA. In fact, the deliberate conduct in question may constitute a breach by both parties: *Paal Wilson & Co A/S v Partenreederei Hannah Blumenthal, The Hannah Blumenthal* [1983] 1 All ER 34, HL.
3   *Denmark Productions Ltd v Boscobel Productions Ltd* [1968] 3 All ER 513, CA.
4   [1935] AC 524, PC.
5   *J Lauritzen AS v Wijsmuller BV, The Super Servant Two* [1990] 1 Lloyd's Rep 1, CA.
6   *Joseph Constantine Steamship Line Ltd v Imperial Smelting Corpn Ltd* [1941] 2 All ER 165, HL.

Effect

10.13   Frustration does not merely make the contract terminable at the election of a party: the frustrating event *automatically* discharges the contract at the time that it is frustrated[1] (except that provisions intended by the parties to apply in the event of frustration, such as one dealing with its consequences, remain in force).[2]

As explained in the previous paragraph, where the frustrating event is brought about by the fault of one party, the other party may rely on it as discharging the contract but the party at fault cannot.[3]

Leaving aside the complicated question of the effect of frustration on money paid or payable under the contract, the effect of frustration on other obligations under the contract is governed by the common law and is as follows: the discharge of a contract by frustration releases both parties from further performance of any such obligations due after the frustrating event[4] but not from any such obligations due before that time, which remain enforceable.[4]

Turning to the effect of frustration on money paid or payable under the contract, the position is as follows.

1   *Hirji Mulji v Cheong Yue Steamship Co Ltd* [1926] AC 497, PC.
2   *Heyman v Darwins Ltd* [1942] 1 All ER 337, HL.
3   *F C Shepherd & Co Ltd v Jerrom* [1986] 3 All ER 589, CA.
4   *Chandler v Webster* [1904] 1 KB 493, CA.

Money paid or payable under the contract before the occurrence of the frustrating event

10.14   At common law, the original position was that an obligation to pay money due before the frustrating event remained enforceable and money paid under the contract before that event was irrecoverable.[1] However, in 1942, in *Fibrosa Spolka Akcyjna v Fairbairn Lawson Combe Barbour Ltd*,[2] a case where money payable in advance for machinery had been paid but the contract had been frustrated before any of the machinery had been delivered, the House of Lords held that the money could be recovered back on the ground of a total failure of consideration, in the sense that the sellers had not performed any part of their contractual duties in respect of which payment was due.[3]

The decision in the *Fibrosa* case left the law unjust in two ways:

•   The decision only permitted recovery if there had been a total failure of consideration. This could be unjust to the payer of the money because, if the payee had performed any part of his contractual duties, however small, in respect of which the money was due, the payer could not recover a penny of what he had paid.

•   The decision could also be unjust to a payee who was ordered to return a pre-payment because he might have incurred expenses in preparing to perform his contractual duties in respect of which the money was due.

1   *Chandler v Webster* [1904] 1 KB 493, CA.
2   [1942] 2 All ER 122, HL.
3   *Stocznia Gdanska SA v Latvian Shipping Co* [1998] 1 All ER 883, HL.

10.15   These injustices were removed by the Law Reform (Frustrated Contracts) Act 1943. Section 1(2) of the Act provides:

•   all sums *payable* under the contract *before* the frustrating event *cease to be payable* whether or not there has been a total failure of consideration;

•   all sums *paid* under the contract *before* the frustrating event are *recoverable* whether or not there has been a total failure of consideration;

•   the court has a discretionary power to allow the payee to set off against the sums so paid or payable a sum not exceeding the value of the expenses he has incurred before the frustrating event in, or for the purpose of, the performance of the contract.

If the court exercises this power, the last point above, it allows the payee to retain the amount stipulated by it (if he has been paid) or to recover the stipulated amount (if money was payable but not paid). The stipulated amount, which may include an element in respect of overhead expenses and of any work or services performed personally by the payee,[1] cannot exceed the sums paid or payable to him. The following illustrates the operation of these provisions. X contracts with Y to manufacture and deliver certain machinery by 1 March for £5,000, £1,000 to be paid on 1 January and the balance of £4,000 on delivery. The contract is discharged by frustration on 1 February before the machinery is delivered but after X has incurred expenses of £500 in making the machinery. Pursuant to s 1(2), Y need not pay the £1,000 if he has not paid it before 1 February or, if he has, he can recover the £1,000, but the court may order Y to pay X up to £500 for his expenses or may allow X to retain up to £500, as the case may be.

The only reported decision on s 1(2) of the 1943 Act is *Gamerco SA v ICM/Fair Warning (Agency) Ltd,*[2] where the judge held that the court has a 'broad discretion' under s 1(2) to allow the payee to set off expenses. A contract between the claimant and the second defendants for the claimant to promote a concert at which the defendants, the Guns N'Roses band, was to play was frustrated when its intended location (a stadium) was declared unsafe. The claimant had paid the second defendants $412,500 in advance, and both parties had incurred expenditure in preparing for the concert. The claimant succeeded in a claim to recover the whole of the advance payment under s 1(2). The judge did not allow any deduction in respect of preparatory expenses incurred by the second defendants because he considered that justice would be done by making no deduction. In reaching this decision, he was mindful of the relatively low level of the second defendants' expenses compared with the claimant's losses. In addition, it appears that the precise nature and amount of the second defendants' expenses was unclear. This may have influenced the judge.

1   Law Reform (Frustrated Contracts) Act 1943, s 1(4).
2   [1995] 1 WLR 1226.

Money payable under the contract after the occurrence of the frustrating event

10.16   Such money is not recoverable by the party to whom it was due, in accordance with the rule that frustration releases both parties from performing any contractual obligation due after the frustrating event. Thus, in *Krell v Henry*,[1] it was held that the owner of the flat could not recover a sum payable for the hire of the flat because it was not due until a time after the processions had been postponed (the frustrating event). Likewise, the balance of £4,000 referred to in the example in the previous paragraph is not recoverable by X because it was not due until after the frustrating event. In further contrast to the rules outlined in para 10.15 above, the courts do not have power to allow a claim in respect of his expenses by a party to whom money was payable only after the frustrating event, because the Law Reform (Frustrated Contracts) Act 1943 does not apply in such a case.

1   [1903] 2 KB 740, CA; para 10.8 above.

Award for valuable benefit obtained

10.17   At common law, a party who had benefited another by partly performing the contract before it was frustrated could not recover any sum of money for this.[1] This rule was particularly harsh where payment was not due to him until after the occurrence of the frustrating event because where money was paid or payable before that time he could retain or recover it, as the case might be.

The Law Reform (Frustrated Contracts) Act 1943, s 1(3), now makes a monetary award available to either party for a valuable benefit conferred on the other. It provides that, where a party to a frustrated contract has, by reason of anything done by any other party in, or for the purpose of, the performance of the contract, obtained a valuable benefit before the frustrating event (other than the payment of money to which s 1(2) applies), that other party may recover from him such sum, if any, as the court considers just, having regard to all the circumstances of the case.

In assessing the amount of an award under s 1(3), the court must first identify and value the benefit obtained by the benefited party (whom we will call B). Where services rendered by the other party (whom we will call A) have an end-product, B's benefit is the end-product of those services.[2] It follows, for example, that, in the case of a building contract which is frustrated when the building is partially completed, the benefit to be valued is the uncompleted building, not the work put in by the builder. This is important because occasionally a relatively small service performed under a contract may confer a substantial benefit, and vice versa. Sometimes services will have no end-product, as where they consist of transporting goods. In such a case the benefit is the value of the services.[2] Generally speaking, valuation of the benefit must be made as at the date of the frustration and not at an earlier time when the benefit was received.[2] In particular, the court must take into account the effect in relation to the benefit of the circumstances giving rise to the frustration,[3] so that if a builder (A) contracts to do building work on B's house and, when he has nearly finished, the house (including A's work) is seriously damaged by fire, and the building contract is thereby frustrated, the valuation of the benefit relates to the value of what remains of A's work as at the date of frustration. From the benefit valued in the above way there must be deducted any expenses incurred by the benefited party (B) before the contract was frustrated, including any sums paid or payable by him to A under the contract and retained or recoverable by A under s 1(2).[3]

The value of the benefit assessed by the court under the above principles forms the upper limit of an award under s 1(3) but not the award itself. This is because the court, having identified and valued the benefit, must then decide on a 'just sum' within that upper limit to award to A in respect of his performance. Here, the court should take into particular account the contract consideration, since in many cases it will be unjust to award more than that consideration or a rateable part of it. The fact that A has broken the contract in some way before the frustration has no bearing on the just sum to be awarded to him, although B's claim to damages for the breach may be the subject of a counterclaim or set-off if not statute-barred.[2]

1   *Appleby v Myers* (1867) LR 2 CP 651.
2   *BP Exploration Co (Libya) Ltd v Hunt (No 2)* [1982] 1 All ER 925; affd at 986, HL.
3   Law Reform (Frustrated Contracts) Act 1943, s 1(3).

10.18   The operation of the 1943 Act can be illustrated as follows: A, a jobbing decorator, contracts with B to paint the outside of B's house for £900, £300 to be paid on 1 September and the rest on completion. B pays A the £300 on 1 September. After A has painted most of the house the contract is frustrated, A having been seriously incapacitated in a car crash. Under s 1(2), A must return the £300 to B, unless and to the extent that the court exercises its discretion to allow A to retain some or all of it. Suppose that A's expenses were £50 and the court allows him to retain this, only £250 will be recoverable by B. The obligation as to the further £600 is, of course, discharged by frustration and A cannot claim this from B. However, as A has conferred a valuable benefit on B before the frustrating event, s 1(3) comes into play. Suppose that the value of the paintwork completed by A is £525 as at the date of the frustration, the court must then deduct what it has allowed A to retain under s 1(2) and the resulting sum (ie £475) will be the upper limit of the 'just sum' awarded by the court under s 1(3).

Scope of the Act of 1943
10.19   Where a contract to which the Act applies is severable,[1] eg a contract to work for a year at £2,400 a month, and a severable part of it is wholly performed before the frustrating event, or wholly performed except in respect of payment of sums which are or can be ascertained under the contract, that part is to be treated as if it were a separate contract and had not been frustrated, and the Act is only applicable to the remainder of the contract.[2] The result is that, if the employee under the above contract works for two months and two weeks and then dies before any salary has been paid, his executors can recover the two months' salary owing to him (each month being treated as a separate contract) plus an award under s 1(3) of the Act for any valuable benefit conferred by the deceased on the employer during the remaining two weeks.

1   le complete performance by one party is not a condition of the other party's obligations becoming due.
2   Section 2(4).

10.20   Where a contract contains a provision (such as one precluding any recovery of any award under the Act or one limiting such an award) which is intended to have effect in the event of circumstances arising which operate, or would but for the provision operate, to frustrate the contract, or is intended to have effect whether such circumstances arise or not, the court must give effect to that provision and only give effect to s 1(2) and (3) of the Act to such extent, if any, as is consistent with that provision.[1]

1   Section 2(3). See, further, *BP Exploration Co (Libya) Ltd v Hunt (No 2)* [1982] 1 All ER 925; affd at 986, HL.

10.21   The Act does not apply to the following types of contract:

*   a contract of insurance.[1] Generally, a premium is not returnable once the risk has attached;
*   a contract to which the Sale of Goods Act 1979, s 7 applies.[1] Section 7 provides that where there is an agreement to sell specific goods, and subsequently, without any fault on the part of the seller or buyer, the goods *perish before the risk passes to the*

buyer, the agreement is thereby avoided. Where a contract is avoided under s 7, the principles laid down by the House of Lords in the *Fibrosa* case[2] apply. Under these a buyer who has paid for the goods before they perished can recover his payment only if there has been a total failure of consideration, in which case the seller has no right of set-off for any expenses he may have incurred in seeking to perform the contract before the goods perished.

1   Section 2(5).
2   Para 10.14 above.

Chapter 11

Remedies for breach of contract

11.1   In the event of a breach of contract, the injured party may have one or more of the following remedies:

- He may, subject to any applicable and effective exemption clause,[1] and to the rules discussed in paras 11.2 to 11.24 below, recover damages for any loss suffered as a result of the breach by bringing an action for damages for breach of contract.
- If a breach consists of the other party's failure to pay a debt, ie the contractually agreed price or other remuneration, due under the contract, the appropriate course for the injured party is to bring an action for the agreed sum to recover that amount, rather than an action for damages. We discuss this further in paras 11.25 to 11.27 below. A person who recovers an agreed sum may also recover damages for any further loss which he has suffered.
- In the case of a repudiatory breach, the injured party may terminate the contract for breach, ie accept the breach as discharging the contract, thereby discharging himself from any obligation to perform the contract further. If the injured party elects to terminate for repudiatory breach, he may also bring an action for damages for any loss suffered. We have already discussed termination for repudiatory breach in detail in paras 8.14 to 8.31 above.
- Where the injured party has performed part of his own obligations, but is unjustifiably prevented from completing them by the other party, the injured party may sue under the law of restitution for the value of what he has done *if he terminates the contract for breach*. We discuss this further in para 11.28 below.
- Where the injured party has paid the contractual price, but the other party has not performed any part of his contractual duties in respect of which the payment is due under the contract, the injured party may sue under the law of restitution for the return of the money paid *if he terminates the contract for breach*. If the failure of consideration is not total but only partial, an action for the return of money paid is not available. However, if—
    - the partial performance is such as to entitle the claimant to terminate the contract, and he elects to do so, and
      he is able to restore what he has received under the contract, and does so before he has derived any benefit from it,

  he is said to bring about a total failure of consideration and is entitled to recover back what he has paid. A common example of this is where the buyer of defective goods rejects them immediately and claims back his payment. We dealt with these matters in slightly more detail in para 8.17 above.

- In appropriate cases, the injured party may seek a decree of specific performance or an injunction in addition to, or instead of, damages. We discuss this further in paras 11.29 to 11.36 below.
- Lastly, the injured party may sue under the law of restitution for an account of profits accruing to the other party through the breach of contract. We deal with this in para 11.37.[2]

1   Chapter 9.
2   In the case of breach of a contract of sale of goods, where the breach consists of the goods not conforming to the contract of sale, the buyer has additional remedies to those referred to in this paragraph: see para 8.13.

Damages

11.2   Damages for breach of contract are not awarded to punish the defendant (with the result that the amount awarded is not affected by the manner of the breach or the motive behind it[1]). Instead, damages for breach of contract are awarded to compensate the claimant for the loss or damage which he has suffered as a result of the breach of contract.[2]

This rule means that, where the injured party has not suffered any loss or damage as a result of the breach, the damages recoverable by him will as a general rule be purely nominal (usually in the region of £2 to £20).

As part of this rule a claimant cannot, as a general principle, recover damages on behalf of a third party. This was established by the House of Lords in *Woodar Investment Ltd v Wimpey Construction Ltd*.[3] However, in a few exceptional cases, a claimant can recover substantial damages for a loss which he has not suffered. One exception is where the claimant made the contract as agent or trustee for another. If the contract is broken in such a case and the claimant sues for damages on the other's behalf he can recover substantial damages for the loss suffered by the other as a result of the breach.[4]

Judicial awareness that the general principle can have unfortunate results has led to the creation of further exceptions to it in a number of modern decisions. One of these was established by the decision in *St Albans City and District Council v International Computers Ltd*,[5] where the Court of Appeal held that a claimant could recover substantial damages in respect of loss suffered by a third party if the claimant was under a duty to act in the best interests of the third party, although not strictly a trustee. In this case, the claimant council purchased from the defendant company a computer program for its collection of community charge payments. The program was defective. As a result of this breach of contract the number of chargepayers was overstated when the program was used to extract the number of chargepayers. One result was that the claimant council had to pay £685,000 to the county council by way of increased precept payments. It could not recover it from the county council, but it was obliged to recover it from chargepayers by setting a higher community charge for the following year. When sued for the £685,000, the defendant company argued that the claimant council had not itself suffered any loss as a result of its breach of contract because the council had recouped its loss, and the only loss remaining was that of the chargepayers. The Court of Appeal upheld an award of £685,000 on the ground that, although not strictly a trustee, the claimant council had no less a capacity than a trustee to recover damage for breach of contract for the chargepayers' benefit. Otherwise the chargepayers would be out of pocket.

Another modern exception, established by the House of Lords in *Linden Gardens Trust Ltd v Lenesta Sludge Disposals Ltd*,[6] relates to a contract concerning land or goods where the parties contemplated when they contracted that the proprietary interest in the property might be transferred, before the time for contractual performance, by one party to a third party who would not have a right of action for breach of the contract. Here, unless they had some other intention, the parties are treated as having made the contract on the footing that the party who subsequently transfers his interest would be entitled to enforce his contractual rights for the benefit of the third party transferee. Thus, if A makes a contract with B for B to do some repair work to a building, which (as B knows) A may transfer to a third party before the time the contract is to be performed, and B in breach of contract does the work defectively after the property has been transferred to C, A can sue B for substantial damages for the loss caused to C by the defective work, since A and B are treated as having contracted on the basis that A would be entitled to enforce his contractual rights for the benefit of the third party transferee who has no contractual right of action. This exception does not apply if the third party has a valid claim (ie the right to recover damages) for the loss suffered by him.[7]

In *Darlington Borough Council v Wiltshier Northern Ltd*,[8] the Court of Appeal extended *Linden Gardens* to a case where the party in question had never had a proprietary interest in the land, which was owned by the third party throughout on the basis that otherwise a meritorious claim would not be satisfied. In *Darlington Borough Council*, the council, in order to avoid government restrictions on borrowing, negotiated a complex scheme to carry out some construction work on land which it already owned. Under the scheme, a bank prepared to lend the required money made two parallel sets of contracts:

- two building contracts under which the bank was the employer and Wiltshier were the building contractors, the bank being obliged to pay Wiltshier under the contract; and
- a contract (of which Wiltshier was aware) under which the bank agreed with the council, in return for payment by the council, to procure the building, to pay all amounts due under the building contract, and to assign to the council the benefit of any rights they had against Wiltshier.

After the building had been completed, and the bank had paid Wiltshier, the council discovered serious defects in the building. It obtained from the bank an assignment of its rights against Wiltshier under the building contract. The Court of Appeal held that the council could recover substantial damages for the foreseeable loss caused to it by Wiltshier's breaches of the construction contracts. Its reason was that the bank could have recovered substantial damages against Wiltshier, even though it had not suffered any loss from Wiltshier's breaches of contract, and the bank's rights had been assigned to the council. The width of this decision appears to be particularly difficult to square with the general principle established in *Woodar*.

1 *Addis v Gramophone Co Ltd* [1909] AC 488, HL.
2 For a modern authority for this well-established rule, see *Surrey County Council v Bredero Homes Ltd* [1993] 3 All ER 705, CA.
3 [1980] 1 All ER 517, HL.
4 *Lloyd's v Harper* (1880) 16 Ch D 290, CA; *Woodar Investment Development Ltd v Wimpey Construction (UK) Ltd* [1980] 1 All ER 571, HL.
5 [1996] 4 All ER 481, CA.
6 [1993] 3 All ER 417, HL.
7 *Panatown Ltd v Alfred McAlpine Construction Ltd* [2000] 4 All ER 97, HL.
8 [1995] 3 All ER 895, CA.

For what can compensation be awarded?

11.3 The principal function of damages for breach of contract is to put the claimant into the same position, so far as money can, *as if the contract had been performed* as agreed.[1]

In achieving this, damages are awarded to compensate the claimant for the loss of his expectations under the contract.

1   *Wertheim v Chicoutimi Pulp Co* [1911] AC 301, PC.

11.4   Lost expectations may consist of a loss of profit which the claimant expected to make if the contract had been properly performed but which has been lost as a result of the breach. Suppose, for example, that X agrees to sell some machinery to Y, a manufacturer, who intends to use it to make goods for sale at a profit, and that X does not deliver the machinery on time. X's loss as a result of Y's breach is the profit he would have made from selling the goods if the machinery had been delivered on time.

Where the claimant did not contract with any expectation of making a profit, his loss of expectation in a case where the subject matter of the contract involved property will be quantified either by reference to the diminished value of what he has received (ie the difference between what the thing would have been worth if the contract had been properly performed and its actual value) or by the cost of cure/repair/reinstatement of the thing so as to make it as it would have been if the contract had been properly performed.

In the case of many contracts there is no significant (if any) difference in the amount quantified by the 'diminution in value' measure and the 'cost of cure' measure. However, in some contracts, the two measures may produce significantly different sums. This is particularly likely to happen in the case of building contracts. Normally, the claimant's loss of expectations in respect of defective or incomplete workmanship is assessed by the cost of cure, but the choice between the two measures is essentially based on whether or not it is reasonable to use the cost of reinstatement measure. This was affirmed by the House of Lords in *Ruxley Electronics and Construction Ltd v Forsyth*.[1] The defendant contracted with the claimant for the construction by the defendant of a swimming pool at the claimant's house. A term of the contract specifically required the pool to be 7'6'' deep at its deepest point. However, the defendant constructed a pool which was, at most, 6' deep. More importantly, at a point where the diving board was situated, the pool was less than 6' deep. As indicated above, the House of Lords was faced with a choice of two options as to the quantification of damages in respect of the defect:

- capital value of pool in a non-defective state minus its value in its defective state ('diminution in value' measure). This was favoured by the trial judge, who found that there had been no diminution in value because, despite its defects, the pool still enhanced the value of the claimant's property;
- cost of repair/reinstatement ('cost of cure' measure). This was favoured by the Court of Appeal and involved an award of damages in line with the expensive cost of digging up and extensively reconstructing the pool (£21,650).

The House of Lords took the same view as the trial judge who had awarded nothing as damages in respect of the defect to the pool itself and simply awarded the claimant £2,500 for loss of amenity[2]. It held that the cost of cure could only be recovered if it was reasonable to allow this. In assessing this, it was appropriate to consider the personal preferences of the claimant and whether or not he intended to cure the defect (since if the claimant did not intend to rebuild he would have lost nothing except the diminution in value). Moreover, the House held that, where the cost of cure was *less* than the diminution in value, the measure should be the cost of cure. On the other hand, where the cost of cure was *out of all proportion* to the good to be obtained, the appropriate measure was the diminution in value measure, and if there was no diminution in value substantial damages could not be awarded in respect of the defect in the pool itself.

1   [1995] 3 All ER 268, HL.
2   Para 11.9.

11.5   The fact that the precise assessment of the value of a lost expectation is difficult does not prevent an award being made, as is shown by *Chaplin v Hicks.*[1] The defendant advertised that he would employ, as actresses, 12 women to be selected by him out of 50 chosen as the most beautiful by the readers of various newspapers, in which the candidates' photographs appeared. The claimant was one of the 50 chosen by the readers but the defendant made an unreasonable appointment for an interview with her, and selected 12 out of the 49 who were able to keep the appointment. In an action for breach of contract, the defendant contended that only nominal damages were payable, since the claimant would only have had a one in four chance of being selected. Nevertheless, the Court of Appeal refused to disturb an award of £100 damages for the loss of her chance of being selected. Where damages are claimed for a lost chance, the claimant must prove that the chance was a real or substantial, and not merely speculative, one. The value of the lost chance will depend on where the chance lay on a range between a real or substantial one and a virtually certain one.[2]

1   [1911] 2 KB 786, CA.
2   *Allied Maples Group Ltd v Simmons & Simmons* [1995] 4 All ER 907, CA; *Stovold v Barlows* [1996] PNLR 91, CA.

11.6   Where damages are awarded to compensate the claimant for loss of his expectations, they are normally assessed as at the date of the breach. However, this is not an absolute rule since, if its observance would give rise to injustice, the court has power to fix such other date as may be appropriate in the circumstances.[1] For example, where the claimant could only reasonably have been expected to mitigate his loss at a point of time after the breach, damages should be assessed as at that point of time, or, if that point of time is not earlier, at the date of the judgment.[2] By way of further example, if, as has happened with house prices in the recent past, there has been a rapid and dramatic rise in the value of the subject matter of the contract, it may be more appropriate for damages to be assessed at the date of the judgment rather than the date of the breach.[3]

In the case of an anticipatory breach of contract, damages for loss of bargain or expectations are assessed by reference to the time when performance ought to have been made, and not by reference to the time of the anticipatory breach.[4]

1   *Johnson v Agnew* [1979] 1 All ER 883 at 896.
2   *William Cory & Son Ltd v Wingate Investments (London Colney) Ltd* (1978) 17 BLR 104, CA. For mitigation of loss, see paras 11.16 to 11.18 below.
3   *Suleman v Shahsavari* [1989] 2 All ER 460.
4   *Tai Hing Cotton Mill Ltd v Kamsing Knitting Factory* [1978] 1 All ER 515, PC; *Gebrüder Metelmann GmbH & Co KG v NBR (London) Ltd* [1984] 1 Lloyd's Rep 614, CA.

Reliance loss

11.7   In some cases, damages are awarded to compensate the claimant for expenditure which he has incurred in reliance on the contract and which has been wasted as a result of its breach. Damages of this type are called damages for reliance loss. Damages for reliance loss put the claimant into the position in which he would have been if *the contract had never been made*. By way of an extension, damages can even be recovered for expenses incurred prior to, and in anticipation of, the contract and wasted as a result of the breach. In *Lloyd v Stanbury*,[1] for instance, the claimant, who had made a contract to buy a farm, which was broken by the defendant's failure to complete, was awarded damages for (inter alia) the following losses incurred before there was a binding contract of sale: legal expenses incurred in carrying out pre-contract searches and drafting the contract, and the cost of moving a caravan to the farm, as a temporary home for the defendant, prior to and in anticipation of the contract.

Because they compensate for expenditure which has been *incurred in reliance on the contract and wasted as a result of its breach*, damages for reliance loss cannot be awarded if this would make the claimant better off than if the contract had been performed, as where the claimant has made a bad bargain by agreeing to pay more for something than it was worth. *C and P Haulage v Middleton*[2] provides an example of the operation of this limitation. A was granted by B a contractual licence (on a six-month renewable basis) to occupy premises as a workshop. A spent money in making the premises suitable, although the contract provided that fixtures installed by him were not to be removed. Ten weeks before the end of a six-month term, A was ejected in breach of the contractual licence. As a temporary measure, A was permitted by his local authority to use his own home as a workshop, which he did until well after the six-month term had expired. The Court of Appeal held that A could only recover nominal damages. He could not recover, as reliance loss, his expenditure in equipping the premises, because, it was held, if the contract had been lawfully terminated at the end of the six-month term, there would have been no question of him recovering that expenditure and, therefore, to award him such damages would leave him better off than if the contract had been wholly performed. His ability to use his home as a workshop meant that he suffered no loss in terms of the deprivation of his licence. In order to defeat a claimant's claim for wasted expenditure, the onus is on the defendant to prove that the expenditure would not have been recovered if the contract had been performed.[3]

1   [1971] 2 All ER 267. Also see *Anglia Television Ltd v Reed* [1971] 3 All ER 690, CA.
2   [1983] 3 All ER 94, CA.
3   *CCC Films (London) Ltd v Impact Quadrant Films Ltd* [1984] 3 All ER 298.

11.8   A claimant has an unfettered right to frame his claim as one for loss of expectations or as one for reliance loss resulting from the breach. Although a claim for reliance loss is particularly appropriate where a claimant cannot prove any loss of expectations or can only prove a small loss of this type or where the contract is aborted too early for the value of the eventual loss of bargain properly to be assessed, a claim for reliance loss is not limited to such cases.[1]

Although damages for loss of expectations and damages for reliance loss are not mutually exclusive, claims for both cannot be combined if this has the effect of compensating the claimant twice over for the same loss. For example, in *Cullinane v British Rema Manufacturing Co Ltd*,[2] the defendants sold to the claimants a machine. A term of the contract related to the machine's output rate. The claimants claimed damages for breach of this term under two headings:

- loss of profits (loss of expectations), and
- the capital cost of the machine and its installation (reliance loss).

It was held that the claimants could not recover damages for both types of loss, as a claim for loss of profits could only be based on the fact that money had been spent on acquiring and installing the machine.

1   *CCC Films (London) Ltd v Impact Films Ltd* [1984] 3 All ER 298.
2   [1953] 2 All ER 1257, CA.

Other loss
11.9   Subject to the rules of remoteness, a claimant can recover not merely for the above types of economic loss resulting from the breach of contract, but also for personal injury (including pain and suffering), injury to property, or inconvenience or discomfort, resulting from the breach. *Bailey v Bullock*[1] provides an example of damages being awarded for physical inconvenience or discomfort. There, the claimant and his wife and child were forced to live in discomfort with his in-laws for two years because of his solicitor's failure, in breach of contract, to take effective steps to obtain possession of a house.

Damages for disappointment or distress brought about by breach of contract may also be awarded, but only:

- where it is a consequence of injury or of physical inconvenience or discomfort caused by the breach;[2] or
- where a major or important object of the contract was the giving of pleasure or enjoyment or the prevention of disturbed peace of mind or of distress.[3]

In *Jarvis v Swans Tours Ltd*,[4] for instance, the claimant booked a 15-day winter sports holiday with the defendants. He did so on the faith of the defendants' brochure, which described the holiday as a house party and promised a number of entertainments, including excellent skiing, a yodeller evening, a bar, and afternoon tea and cakes. In the first week there were 13 guests; in the second the claimant was entirely alone. The entertainments fell far short of the promised standard. The Court of Appeal held that the claimant was entitled to damages for mental distress and disappointment due to loss of enjoyment caused by the breach of contract. A similar decision was reached in *Heywood v Wellers*,[5] where a solicitor's client suffered distress as a result of the solicitor's incompetent handling of an injunction designed to prevent molestation of the client. In *Ruxley Electronics and Construction Ltd v Forsyth*, referred to in para 11.4 above, the award of damages for loss of amenity was held by the House of Lords to be justified on the basis that the object of the contract was the provision of a pleasurable amenity and that the claimant's pleasure was not as great as it would have been if the pool had been 7'6" deep. The trial judge had awarded £2,500 for loss of amenity, and this amount had not been attacked in the House of Lords, who were consequently reluctant to interfere with it. The one Law Lord who considered the matter further justified an award for loss of amenity on the basis that it was a logical adaptation or application of the existing exceptions to the rule that generally damages for distress or disappointment cannot be awarded.

In contrast, damages for disappointment or distress cannot be awarded where the breach is of an employment contract (eg wrongful dismissal) or of a covenant for quiet enjoyment[6] in a lease, since the giving of pleasure or peace of mind or the like is not an object of such a contract or covenant.[7] For example, in *Hayes v James & Charles Dodd (a firm)*,[8] a married couple, who suffered anxiety and distress when their car repair business failed because their solicitors had incorrectly advised them (in breach of contract) that there was a right of access to the rear of the workshop they were purchasing, were held by the Court of Appeal not to be entitled to damages for that distress (although they recovered damages for the financial loss which they had suffered). This case makes an interesting contrast to *Heywood v Wellers* where the object of the contract was to prevent the client suffering distress.

It can be seen from the above that normally damages for disappointment or distress are not recoverable for breach of a contract of survey, because the giving of pleasure or peace of mind or the like is not an object of such a contract.[9] *Farley v Skinner*,[10] however, shows that if a contract of survey has one of these things as its major or important object damages for distress can be awarded for its breach. In *Farley v Skinner*, a contract between a chartered surveyor and the claimant, a prospective purchaser, to inspect and report on the condition of a property included a requirement to advise about whether the property might be affected by aircraft noise; the claimant did not want a property on a flight path. The surveyor negligently failed to discover that the property was from time to time badly so affected. The House of Lords held that the claimant could recover damages for distress and disappointment suffered after he had bought the property in reliance on the surveyor's report, because a major or important object of the contract was to give pleasure, relaxation and peace of mind.

Damages for distress are not available where the distress is caused by the *manner* of the breach, as opposed to the breach itself. Thus, an employee who has been wrongfully dismissed in a harsh or humiliating way cannot recover for the distress resulting from the harshness or humiliation.[11] He may, however, recover compensation for this as part of the compensatory award made by an Employment Tribunal in unfair dismissal proceedings (where special statutory concepts and remedies, not based on contract law, apply).

Damages for injury to reputation are not as a general rule recoverable in a breach of contract action[12] but, where the loss of reputation results from breach of a term (as opposed to the manner of the breach) and leads to financial loss, damages are recoverable for that loss. This was held by the House of Lords in *Malik v Bank of Credit and Commerce International SA*,[13] where the claimants had been employees of the defendant bank which, unknown to them, had been engaged in a massive fraud. The bank collapsed and went into liquidation. The claimants were made redundant by the liquidator. Their association with the bank made it difficult to obtain employment in the banking field, and they suffered financial loss in consequence. The House of Lords held that the defendant bank was in breach of its implied obligation not, without reasonable cause, to conduct its business in a manner likely to destroy or seriously damage the relationship of confidence between employer and employee,[14] that this breach had caused financial loss as a result of the injury which it had done to the claimant's reputation, and that therefore the claimants could recover damages for that loss. In addition, where damages for distress are recoverable, that distress (and therefore the amount recoverable for it) may be increased by the mental anguish suffered by the claimant as a result of the loss of his reputation.[15]

1　[1950] 2 All ER 1167.
2　*Watts v Morrow* [1991] 4 All ER 937, CA.
3　*Farley v Skinner* [2001] UKHL 49, [2001] 4 All ER 801.
4　[1973] 1 All ER 71, CA.
5　[1976] 1 All ER 300, CA.
6　Para 37.22 below.
7　*Bliss v South East Thames Regional Health Authority* [1987] ICR 700, CA (breach of employment contract); *Hayes v James & Charles Dodd (a firm)* [1990] 2 All ER 815, CA; *Branchett v Beaney, Coster and Swale Borough Council* (1992) 24 HLR 348, CA (breach of covenant for quiet enjoyment in a lease; for a description of this type of covenant, see para 37.22 below).
8　[1990] 2 All ER 815, CA.
9　*Watts v Morrow* [1991] 4 All ER 937, CA.
10　[2001] UKHL 49, [2001] 4 All ER 801.
11　*Addis v Gramophone Co Ltd* [1909] AC 488, HL; *Johnson v Unisys Ltd* [2001] UKHL 13, [2001] 2 All ER 801.
12　*Addis v Gramophone Co Ltd* [1909] AC 488, HL.
13　[1997] 3 All ER 1, HL.
14　Para 7.26 above.
15　*McLeish v Amoco-Gottfried & Co* (1993) 10 PN 102.

Remoteness of damage

11.10　In order to succeed in his action for damages, the claimant must, of course, prove that the loss or damage (hereafter simply referred to as 'loss') which he has suffered resulted from the defendant's breach of contract.[1] This requires that the claimant's loss would not have occurred but for the defendant's breach. The defendant's breach need not be the only cause of the loss, since the conduct of others or the occurrence of extraneous events may also contribute to it, but it must be an effective or dominant cause of the loss.[2]

Proof of a causal link between breach and loss is not in itself enough to entitle the claimant to damages for that loss, because a defendant will only be liable for it if it was not too 'remote'. Whether or not loss suffered is too remote is determined by applying the rule in *Hadley v Baxendale*[3] (as explained in *Victoria Laundry (Windsor) Ltd v Newman Industries Ltd*[4] and *Koufos v C Czarnikow Ltd, The Heron II*[5]).

The rule, as explained, provides that damage is not too remote if one of the two following sub-rules is satisfied:

- if the loss arises naturally, ie according to the usual course of things, from the breach of contract as a seriously possible result of it; or
- if the loss could reasonably be supposed to have been in the contemplation of the parties, when they made the contract, as a seriously possible result of the breach of it.

The first sub-rule deals with 'normal' damage which arises in the ordinary course of events, while the second sub-rule deals with 'abnormal' damage which arises from special circumstances.

1   *Weld-Blundell v Stephens* [1920] AC 956, HL.
2   See, for example, *Galoo Ltd v Bright Grahame Murray* [1995] 1 All ER 16, CA; *County Ltd v Girozentrale Securities* [1996] 3 All ER 834, CA.
3   (1854) 23 LJ Ex 179.
4   [1949] 1 All ER 997, CA.
5   [1967] 3 All ER 686, HL.

11.11   In the light of subsequent cases, a number of things can be said about both sub-rules.

First, the claimant can only recover for such loss as would, *at the time of the contract*, have been within the reasonable contemplation of the parties as a serious possibility as a result of its breach, *had they had their attention drawn to the possibility of the breach which has in fact occurred.*[1] It must be emphasised that the particular breach itself need not have been contemplated. Suppose that the loss has been caused by some defect in the subject matter of the contract which was unknown, or even unknowable, when the contract was made. The court has to assume, even though it is contrary to the facts, that the parties had in mind the breach which has occurred when it considers whether the claimant's loss was within their reasonable contemplation.[1]

Second, what was within the parties' reasonable contemplation depends on the knowledge 'possessed' by them at that time. For this purpose, knowledge 'possessed' is of two kinds: one imputed, the other actual. Under the first sub-rule, everyone is taken to know (ie knowledge is imputed) the 'ordinary course of things' and, consequently, what loss is a seriously possible result of a breach of contract in that ordinary course. In addition, 'knowledge possessed' may, in a particular case, include knowledge which the defaulting party (and the other party) actually possess of special circumstances, outside the ordinary course of things, of such a kind that the breach in these special circumstances would as a serious possibility be liable to cause more loss. Such a case attracts the second sub-rule so as to make the additional loss recoverable.[2]

Third, provided the *type* of loss caused by a breach of contract was within the reasonable contemplation of the parties as a serious possibility when the contract was made, the loss is not too remote, and damages can therefore be recovered for it, even though its extent was much greater than could have been reasonably contemplated[3] and even though it occurred in a way which could not have been reasonably contemplated.[4] An example is provided by *H Parsons (Livestock) Ltd v Uttley Ingham & Co Ltd.*[5] The defendants supplied the claimants with a hopper in which to store pig nuts. The hopper was not properly ventilated, and this constituted a breach of contract by the defendants; as a result, the pig nuts became mouldy and many of the claimants' pigs suffered a rare intestinal disease (E coli) from which 254 of them died. The claimants were awarded damages by the Court of Appeal for the loss sustained by the death and sickness of the pigs. The reasoning of the majority of the Court of Appeal was that, if the breach had been brought to the parties' attention and they had asked themselves what was likely to happen as a result, they would have contemplated the serious possibility that the pigs would become ill, and that, since the type of loss caused (physical harm) was within the parties' reasonable contemplation, it was irrelevant that its extent and the way in which it occurred were not.

1   *H Parsons (Livestock) Ltd v Uttley Ingham & Co Ltd* [1978] 1 All ER 525, CA.
2   *Victoria Laundry (Windsor) Ltd v Newman Industries Ltd* [1949] 1 All ER 997, CA.
3   *Wroth v Tyler* [1973] 1 All ER 897; *H Parsons (Livestock) Ltd v Uttley Ingham & Co Ltd* [1978] 1 All ER 525, CA.
4   *H Parsons (Livestock) Ltd v Uttley Ingham & Co Ltd* [1978] 1 All ER 525, CA.
5   [1978] 1 All ER 525, CA.

11.12   The degree of risk which is required to have been within the parties' reasonable contemplation in order to satisfy the test of remoteness has been variously described in the cases. In *Koufos v C Czarnikow Ltd, The Heron II*,[1] which can be taken as settling the point, the House of Lords made it clear that the degree of risk is more than mere possibility or a risk that is 'on the cards'. However, they were not unanimous in their terminology as to the degree of risk required. Lords Pearce and Upjohn favoured 'serious possibility' or 'real danger'; Lord Reid favoured 'not unlikely' (ie 'considerably less than even chance, but nevertheless not very unusual and easily foreseeable'). With the exception of Lord Reid, the House was prepared to accept the phrase 'liable to result', a rather colourless and vague term which two of them thought was a convenient term to describe 'serious possibility' or 'real danger'. We have used 'serious possibility' in this book on the basis that it best conveys the degree of risk required which emerges from the speeches in the House of Lords.

1   [1967] 3 All ER 686, HL.

11.13   The application of the contractual rule of remoteness can best be illustrated by reference to past decisions. In *Hadley v Baxendale*,[1] the claimant's mill at Gloucester was brought to a halt when a crankshaft broke. The shaft had to be sent to its makers in Greenwich as a pattern for a new one. The defendant carriers undertook to deliver it at Greenwich the following day, but in breach of contract delayed its delivery so that the duration of the stoppage at the mill was extended. The claimant's claim to recover damages for loss of profits caused by the defendants' delay was unsuccessful since this loss was held to be too remote. The basis of the court's decision was that the defendants only knew that they were transporting a broken shaft owned by the claimants. The court applied the two sub-rules in turn, and held:

•   the claimants might have had a spare shaft or been able to borrow one, and therefore the loss of profits did not arise in the usual course of events from the defendants' breach; and
•   on the facts known to the defendants (they were unaware of the lack of a substitute shaft), the loss of profits could not be supposed to have been within the reasonable contemplation of the parties at the time they made the contract as the probable result of the breach.

1   (1854) 23 LJ Ex 179.

11.14   In *Victoria Laundry (Windsor) Ltd v Newman Industries Ltd*,[1] the defendants agreed to sell to the claimants, who were launderers and dyers, a boiler to be delivered on a certain date. The boiler was damaged in a fall and was not delivered until five months after the agreed delivery date. The claimants claimed damages for loss of profits that would have been earned during the five-month period through the extension of their business, and also for loss of several highly lucrative dyeing contracts which they would have obtained with the Ministry of Supply. The Court of Appeal held that the claimants could recover for the loss of 'normal' profits (ie those which would have been earned through an extension of the business) but not for the loss of 'exceptional' profits (ie loss of the highly lucrative contracts), which it treated as a different type of loss. This decision was based on the following application of the two sub-rules:

- the defendants knew at the time of the contract that the claimants were laundrymen and dyers and required the boiler for immediate use in their business and, with their technical experience and knowledge of the facts, it could be presumed that loss of 'normal' profits was foreseeable by them, and therefore within both parties' reasonable contemplation, as liable to result from the breach; but
- in the absence of special knowledge, the defendants could not reasonably foresee the loss of the 'exceptional' profits under the highly lucrative contracts as liable to result from the breach.

The case was, therefore, remitted for a decision as to the amount of 'normal' profits which had been lost in the circumstances.

1   [1949] 1 All ER 997, CA.

11.15   In *Koufos v C Czarnikow Ltd, The Heron II*,[1] the claimant sugar merchants chartered a ship from the defendant to carry a cargo of sugar from Constanza to Basrah. The ship deviated in breach of contract and arrived in Basrah nine days later than expected. Because of a fall in the market price of sugar, the claimants obtained £3,800 less for the cargo than would have been obtained if it had arrived on time. The defendant did not know of the claimants' intention to sell the sugar in Basrah, but he did know that there was a market for sugar at Basrah and that the claimants were sugar merchants. The House of Lords held that the claimants' loss of profits (£3,800) was not too remote under the first sub-rule, since knowledge could be imputed to the defendant that the goods might be sold at market price on their arrival in Basrah and that market prices were apt to fluctuate daily, and therefore the loss of profits was within the reasonable contemplation of the parties at the time of the contract as a serious possibility in the event of the breach in question.

1   [1967] 3 All ER 686, HL.

Mitigation

11.16   The claimant cannot recover for loss which he could reasonably have avoided. Thus, the seller of goods which have been wrongly rejected by the buyer must not unreasonably refuse another's offer to buy them. Similarly, an employee who has been wrongfully dismissed must not unreasonably refuse an offer of employment from another.[1] If such refusals occur, the claimant is said to be in breach of his duty to mitigate his loss and cannot recover his unmitigated loss but only the loss which he would have suffered if the damage had been mitigated. If he would have suffered no loss at all, only nominal damages are recoverable.[1]

A leading case on the duty to mitigate is *Payzu Ltd v Saunders*.[2] A contract for the sale of goods by the defendant to the claimants provided that delivery should be as required over a nine-month period and that payment should be made within one month of delivery. The claimants failed to make prompt payment for the first instalment and the defendant, in breach of contract, refused to deliver any more instalments under the contract. He did, however, offer to deliver goods at the contract price if the claimants would pay cash with each order. The claimants refused to do so and brought an action for breach of contract, claiming the difference between the contract price and the market price (which had risen). The Court of Appeal held that the claimants should have mitigated their loss by accepting the defendant's offer; consequently, the damages which they could recover were to be measured by the loss which they would have suffered if the offer had been accepted, and not by the difference between the contract and market prices.

1   *Brace v Calder* [1895] 2 QB 253, CA.
2   [1919] 2 KB 581, CA.

11.17   The following points may be noted about the duty to mitigate:

- The phrase 'duty to mitigate' is somewhat misleading because the claimant is not legally obliged to do so. He is free to act as he judges to be in his best interest, but if he does so he cannot recover for loss which he could reasonably have avoided.[1]
- The duty to mitigate may require the claimant to do something positive. In the examples given in para 11.16, the seller and the employee would equally have been in breach of their duty to mitigate if they had not made reasonable efforts to seek other offers to buy the goods or alternative equivalent employment: it would not necessarily excuse them that no one had spontaneously made them an offer. Damages cannot be recovered for any loss which would have been avoided if such reasonable steps had been taken.[2]
- The duty to mitigate only requires the claimant to take reasonable steps to minimise his loss. He is not required to act with lightning speed, nor to accept the first or, indeed, any offer that is made (unless it is a reasonable one). For example, a wrongfully dismissed managing director is not expected to mitigate his loss by taking a job sweeping floors. Indeed, in one case it was held that it was reasonable for a person who had wrongfully been dismissed as managing director in an arbitrary and high-handed fashion to refuse the company's offer of a slightly lower post at the same salary.[3]

1   *Sotiros Shipping Inc v Sameit Solholt, The Solholt* [1983] 1 Lloyd's Rep 605 at 608.
2   *British Westinghouse Electric and Manufacturing Co Ltd v Underground Electric Rlys Co of London* [1912] AC 673 at 689.
3   *Yetton v Eastwood Froy Ltd* [1966] 3 All ER 353.

11.18   Where there is an anticipatory breach of contract, the injured party has an option either to terminate the contract and sue immediately for damages or to affirm the contract and await the time fixed for performance, in which case he can then bring an action for damages if the other party is still in breach. If the injured party elects to terminate he is under a duty to mitigate his loss.[1] On the other hand, the injured party is under no duty to mitigate his loss before performance is due if he affirms the contract.[2]

1   *Roth & Co v Taysen Townsend & Co* (1895) 1 Com Cas 240; *Gebrüder Metelmann GmbH & Co KG v NBR (London) Ltd* [1984] 1 Lloyd's Rep 614, CA.
2   Para 8.31 above.

Contributory negligence

11.19   Where a claimant has by his own fault contributed to his loss or the event causing it, his damages for breach of contract are not generally reduced in proportion to his degree of responsibility for that loss or event.[1] The doctrine of contributory negligence, under which a claimant in a tort action may have his damages reduced where he is partly at fault,[2] does not generally apply to an action for breach of contract.[3] There is one exception. If the defendant is liable in tort for negligence independently of the contract and also for breach of a contractual obligation to take reasonable care which was the same as the common law duty in the tort of negligence,[4] a court may apportion the blame and reduce the damages awarded to the claimant for breach of contract by reason of his contributory negligence.[5] Suppose that a surveyor's client is negligently given incorrect information by the surveyor, and relies on it when he should know better (ie is negligent in doing so), and suppose that, as a result of his and the surveyor's negligence, the client suffers economic loss. The doctrine of contributory negligence would apply to an action by the client for breach of contract because the surveyor's liability to the client in the tort of negligence and for breach of contract would be based on the same obligation to take reasonable care.

Of course, in any breach of contract case, if the claimant's contribution to his loss is so great as to prevent the defendant's breach of contract being an effective cause of the claimant's loss, the claimant will not be able to recover any damages at all for it.[6] Moreover, if the defendant successfully brings a counterclaim to a successful claim by the claimant, the effect on the damages awarded to each party may be the same as if there was an apportionment of liability on grounds of contributory negligence. In *Tennant Radiant Heat Ltd v Warrington Development Corpn*,[7] for instance, the claimants leased a unit in a warehouse owned by the defendants. Goods stored there by the claimants were damaged when the roof collapsed under an accumulation of rainwater. The roof would not have collapsed but for the facts that the claimants in breach of covenant had failed to repair the roof over their unit and that the defendants had failed to keep clear the water outlets on the roof as a whole (and were therefore liable in tort for negligence and nuisance).[8] The Court of Appeal held that the damages recoverable on the claim and the counterclaim should be assessed on the basis of the extent to which the damage to the goods (claimants' claim) and to the roof (defendants' counterclaim) were caused, respectively, by the defendants' tortious behaviour and by the claimants' breach of covenant.

1   *Basildon District Council v J E Lesser (Properties) Ltd* [1985] 1 All ER 20.
2   Law Reform (Contributory Negligence) Act 1945. See para 20.11 below.
3   *Barclays Bank plc v Fairclough Building Ltd* [1995] 1 All ER 289, CA.
4   As to when there may be concurrent liability in tort and in contract, see para 17.21 below.
5   *Forsikringsaktieselskapet Vesta v Butcher* [1988] 2 All ER 43, CA; affd on other grounds [1989] 1 All ER 402, HL.
6   Para 11.10 above; *Marintrans AB v Comet Shipping Co Ltd* [1985] 3 All ER 442.
7   [1988] 1 EGLR 41, CA.
8   See chs 17 and 24.

Liquidated damages and penalties

11.20   So far we have been concerned with unliquidated damages, ie damages which are assessed by the court and not by the agreement of the parties. It is, however, possible for the parties to agree in their contract that in the event of a breach of it the damages shall be a fixed sum or be calculated in a specific way. Such damages are called liquidated damages. Liquidated damages have the obvious advantage that the amount recoverable as damages is always certain, whereas in the case of unliquidated damages it is uncertain until the court has decided the matter. Provision for liquidated damages is often found in contracts which have to be completed within a certain time. Thus, contracts for building or civil engineering work normally provide for a specified sum to be paid for every day or week of delay.

It is customary to refer to penalty clauses and liquidated damages clauses as involving the payment of a sum of money, and for convenience we shall discuss them mainly in that context. However, it should not be forgotten that penalty clauses and liquidated damages clauses may involve the transfer of property, and not the payment of money.[1]

If a contract containing a liquidated damages provision is broken, the injured party can recover the specified sum, whether this is greater or less than the actual loss suffered. This rule may benefit a claimant who has suffered little or no loss but can be to his disadvantage if the loss suffered greatly exceeds the specified sum. In *Cellulose Acetate Silk Co Ltd v Widnes Foundry (1925) Ltd*,[2] the defendants agreed to build machinery for the claimants in 18 weeks and, in the event of taking longer, to pay 'by way of penalty £20 per working week'. The machinery was completed 30 weeks late and the claimants lost £5,850 in consequence. The House of Lords held that the provision for payment was one for liquidated damages and that the claimants could only recover 30 weeks at £20, ie £600.

1   *Jobson v Johnson* [1989] 1 All ER 621, CA; para 11.24.
2   [1933] AC 20, HL.

11.21   Liquidated damages provisions must be distinguished from two other provisions:

Exemption clauses restricting liability   A liquidated damages clause is not an exemption clause limiting liability because it fixes the sum payable for breach whether the actual loss is greater or less, whereas (assuming it is valid) such an exemption clause merely fixes the maximum sum recoverable and, if the actual loss is less than that sum, only the actual loss can be recovered.

Penalty clauses   Where the sum fixed by the contract is a genuine pre-estimate of the loss which will be caused by its breach, the provision is one for liquidated damages, but if instead the sum is intended to operate as a threat to hold a potential defaulter to his bargain it is a penalty.[1] The distinction between a penalty and liquidated damages is crucial because their effects are different.

1   *Law v Redditch Local Board* [1892] 1 QB 127 at 132.

Penalty
11.22   If the actual loss by a claimant is less than the sum specified in a penalty clause, he can only recover his actual loss.[1] Suppose that a broken contract contains a penalty clause providing for a £1,000 penalty but the claimant's actual loss is only £100, the claimant can only recover £100 (whereas if the clause had been one for liquidated damages the claimant could have recovered £1,000). On the other hand, if the penalty is less than the actual loss suffered by the claimant, eg because of inflation since the contract was made, he cannot recover more than the penalty if he sues for it, although if he sues instead for (unliquidated) damages he can recover the whole of his loss.[2] This option is not, of course, open in the case of a liquidated damages provision.

    Where a consumer is subject to a penalty clause and the Unfair Terms in Consumer Contracts Regulations 1999 apply to the clause, it is highly likely to be regarded as an unfair term, and therefore not binding on the consumer.[3]

1   *Wilbeam v Ashton* (1807) 1 Camp 78. A similar principle applies where the penalty involves the transfer of property whose value exceeds the claimant's actual loss: *Jobson v Johnson* [1989] 1 All ER 621, CA.
2   *Wall v Rederiaktiebolaget Luggude* [1915] 3 KB 66.
3   See paras 12.59-12.62 below. Note, in particular, the fifth entry in the indicative list of unfair terms in Sch 2 to the Regulations set out in para 12.61.

Parties' intention
11.23   Whether an agreed sum is liquidated damages or a penalty depends on the parties' intention and, as is shown by the *Cellulose Acetate* case,[1] the use of the words 'penalty' or 'liquidated damages' in the contract is not conclusive. The crucial question is whether the parties intended the specified sum to be a genuine pre-estimate of the damage likely to be caused by the breach or to operate as a fine or penalty for breach. This intention is to be gathered from the terms and inherent circumstances of the contract at the time it was made, and not at the time of its breach.[2] This does not mean that what has happened subsequently is irrelevant, since it can provide valuable evidence as to what could reasonably have been expected to be the loss when the contract was made.[3]

    The determination of the parties' intention is aided by a number of rebuttable presumptions of intention summarised by Lord Dunedin in *Dunlop Pneumatic Tyre Co Ltd v New Garage and Motor Co Ltd*:[4]

•   'It will be held to be a penalty if the sum stipulated for is extravagant and unconscionable in amount in comparison with the greatest loss that could conceivably be proved to have followed from the breach.'

- 'It will be held to be a penalty if the breach consists only in not paying a sum of money, and the sum stipulated is a sum greater than the sum which ought to have been paid.'
- 'There is a presumption (but no more) that it is a penalty when a single lump sum is made payable by way of compensation, on the occurrence of one or more or all of several events, some of which may occasion serious and others but trifling damage.' In *Kemble v Farren*,[5] for example, the defendant agreed with the claimant to appear at Covent Garden for four seasons at £3.6s.8d (£3.33) a night. The contract provided that if either party refused to fulfil the agreement, or any part of it, he should pay the other £1,000 as 'liquidated damages'. The defendant refused to act during the second season. It was held that the stipulation was a penalty. The obligation to pay £1,000 might have arisen simply on the claimant's failure to pay £3.6s.8d and was therefore quite obviously a penalty. It has been held that the court should be careful not to set too stringent a standard and should bear in mind that what the parties have agreed should normally be upheld, since any other approach would lead to undesirable uncertainty, especially in commercial contracts.[3]
- 'It is no obstacle to the sum stipulated being a genuine pre-estimate of damage, that the consequences of the breach are such as to make precise pre-estimation almost an impossibility.' This is illustrated by the *Dunlop* case itself. The claimants supplied tyres to the defendants subject to an agreement that the defendants would not sell below the list price and would pay £5 by way of liquidated damages for every tyre sold in breach of the agreement. The House of Lords held that the stipulated sum was one for liquidated damages. Clearly, the figure of £5 was, at most, only a rough and ready estimate of the possible loss which the claimants might suffer if their price list was undercut.

1 Para 11.20 above.
2 *Dunlop Pneumatic Tyre Co Ltd v New Garage and Motor Co Ltd* [1915] AC 79 at 868–7.
3 *Philips Hong Kong Ltd v A-G of Hong Kong* (1993) 61 BLR 41, PC.
4 [1915] AC 79 at 86.
5 (1829) 6 Bing 141.

11.24 In *Jobson v Johnson*,[1] a similar approach was taken to a clause providing for the re-transfer of property at a fixed price in the event of a breach. The claimant contracted to sell to the defendant 45% of the shares in Southend United Football Club for a total of £350,000, £311,000 of which was payable by six instalments. The contract contained a clause providing for the re-transfer of the shares at a fixed price (£340,000) if the defendant defaulted in payment of the second or any subsequent instalment. It was held that this was a penalty clause since it was equally applicable if the defendant defaulted on the second instalment (when the claimant's loss would be great) or on the last (when his loss would be relatively small); the provision that in the event of default the defendant should re-transfer to the claimant the shares at a fixed price could therefore not be regarded as a genuine pre-estimate of the claimant's loss.

1 [1989] 1 All ER 621, CA.

Action for price or other agreed sum

11.25 If a breach consists of a party's failure to pay a debt, ie the contractually agreed price or other remuneration, which is due under the contract, the appropriate course for the injured party is to bring an action for the agreed sum to recover that amount.

11.26   There is an important limitation on an action for the agreed sum in the case of a contract for the sale of goods. The Sale of Goods Act 1979, s 49 provides that, unless the agreed price is payable on a specified date irrespective of delivery, an action for it only lies if the property (ie ownership) in the goods has passed to the buyer.

Agreed sum not due at time of repudiatory breach

11.27   Where a repudiatory breach is committed, the injured party may, of course, recover an agreed sum already due at the time of the breach, whether he terminates or affirms the contract.

The position is more complicated where the agreed sum is not due at the time of the repudiatory breach but may become due subsequently:

*   If the injured party elects to terminate the contract, he cannot claim an agreed sum which might have become due to him subsequently.[1]
*   If the injured party elects to affirm the contract, then, as we have already said,[2] the contract remains in force, so that both parties are bound to perform any outstanding contractual obligations. Consequently, if the injured party affirms the contract, he may be able to recover the agreed sum when it becomes due in the future. Whether or not he will be able to recover that sum depends on the rules discussed in the rest of this paragraph.

It was recognised by the majority of the House of Lords in *White and Carter (Councils) Ltd v McGregor*[3] that, if further performance on the part of the injured party is required in order for the sum to become due, he will be unable to recover the agreed sum if his further performance depends on the co-operation of the other party and it is withheld. It is for this reason that a wrongfully dismissed employee cannot sue for his wages payable thereafter, even though he has subsequently indicated his willingness to go on working under the employment contract.[4] Instead he must sue for damages for breach of contract (this measure being the amount which he would have earned had the employment continued according to the contract, ie if contractual notice had been given, subject to the requirement to take reasonable steps to mitigate his loss by obtaining other employment) or seek payment under the law of restitution on a quantum meruit basis (see below) for the value of work already done.

It will not be often that the injured party can perform his side of the contract without the co-operation of the other party, although it was possible in *White and Carter (Councils) Ltd v McGregor*.[3] The claimants were advertising contractors. They carried on a business of supplying free litter bins to local authorities, the bins being paid for by businesses which hired advertising space on them. The claimants agreed with the defendant garage proprietor to display advertisements for his garage on bins for three years. On the same day, the defendant renounced the contract and asked the claimants to cancel it. They refused, thereby affirming the contract, and proceeded to prepare advertisement plates which they attached to bins and displayed. When the defendant failed to pay at the appropriate time, the claimants sued for the full contract price. The House of Lords held that they could recover the full contract price despite the fact that they had made no effort to mitigate their loss by getting other advertisers in substitution for the defendant and had increased their loss after the renunciation by performing their side of the contract.

Even if he can perform his side of the contract without the co-operation of the other party, and does so, an injured party cannot recover an agreed sum when it becomes due in the future (as opposed to such damages as would be available) if it is shown that he had no legitimate interest, financial or otherwise, in performing the contract rather than claiming damages. This was stated by one of the Law Lords in the *White and Carter* case,[5] where a lack of a legitimate interest was not shown, and has subsequently been adopted in other cases.[6] 'Legitimate interest' in this context means that the injured party 'must have reasonable grounds for keeping the contract open, bearing in mind also the interests of the [other party]'.[7] By way of example, a commitment to a third party has been held to be a legitimate interest.[8]

1   Para 8.18 above.
2   Paras 8.20 and 8.31 above.
3   [1961] 3 All ER 1178, HL.
4   *Denmark Productions Ltd v Boscobel Productions Ltd* [1968] 3 All ER 513, CA.
5   [1962] AC 413 at 431.
6   Eg *Attica Sea Carriers Corpn v Ferrostaal Poseidon Bulk Reederei GmbH, The Puerto Buitrago* [1976] 1 Lloyd's Rep 250, CA.
7   *Stoczma Gdanska SA v Latvian Shipping Co* [1996] 2 Lloyd's Rep 132, CA (revsd on another ground [1998] 1 All ER 883, HL).
8   *Gator Shipping Corpn v Trans-Asiatic Oil Ltd SA, The Odenfeld* [1978] 2 Lloyd's Rep 357.

Restitutionary claim: quantum meruit

11.28   In a particular situation, set out below, a claim on what is called a quantum meruit basis is available to a claimant as an *alternative* to a claim for damages for breach of contract.

If a party to a contract unjustifiably prevents the other party performing his contractual obligations, as where he states that he will not accept performance, or renders performance impossible, his conduct will normally constitute a repudiatory breach of contract and the injured party can recover damages for breach of contract, whether he elects to terminate or to affirm the contract. Alternatively, if the injured party has partly performed his obligations under the contract he can claim under the law of restitution the reasonable value of the work done, provided he has elected to terminate the contract.[1] *Lusty v Finsbury Securities Ltd*[2] provides an example of the rules. The defendant company contracted with the claimant for the claimant to act as its architect for an office block development. After the claimant had done some work under the contract, the defendant company decided to use the land for residential development instead and cancelled future performance by the claimant of his contract. This was clearly a repudiatory breach of contract. It was held that the claimant could recover reasonable remuneration for his work on a quantum meruit basis.

It must be emphasised that an award of damages and quantum meruit award are distinct remedies. As we have already stated, damages are compensatory, their object generally being to put the claimant into the same position, so far as money can do it, as if the contract had been performed. Thus, if the injured party in a case like *Lusty v Finsbury Securities* decides to sue for damages, the damages awarded will be equivalent to the sum payable to him on completion of his work, less any savings (eg on labour and materials) made through not completing performance. However, if it is shown that the claimant would in any event have been unable to perform his entire obligation, he will at most be entitled to nominal damages.[3] On the other hand, a quantum meruit award is restitutionary, its object being to prevent unjust enrichment to the defendant by awarding the claimant an amount equivalent to the value of the work which he has done. Generally, an award of damages will be more generous than a quantum meruit award, but the converse may be true if the claimant originally made a bad bargain or if only nominal damages would be awarded.

1   *Planché v Colburn* (1831) 8 Bing 14; *Lusty v Finsbury Securities* (1991) 58 BLR 66, CA.
2   (1991) 58 BLR 66, CA.
3   *Maredelanto Cia Naviera SA v Bergbau-Handel GmbH, The Mihalis Angelos* [1970] 3 All ER 125, CA.

Specific performance

11.29   The court may grant a decree of specific performance to the injured party, instead of, or in addition to, awarding him damages. Such a decree orders the defaulting party to carry out his contractual obligations.

11.30   Specific performance will not be granted in the following cases:

Where damages are an adequate remedy   It is for this reason that specific performance of a contract to sell goods is not normally ordered; the payment of damages enables the claimant to go out into the market and buy the equivalent goods.[1] However, in exceptional cases, eg where the contract is for the sale of specific goods of a unique character or of special value or interest, the contract is specifically enforceable.[2] By way of contrast, every plot of land is unique, with the result that contracts for the sale or lease of land are always specifically enforceable. This has produced the rule that, since the contract is specifically enforceable in favour of the purchaser or lessee, a vendor or lessor of land can obtain an order of specific performance for the purchase price even though, in the particular case, damages would be an adequate remedy.[3]

It is because damages are normally adequate that a contractual obligation to pay money is not normally specifically enforceable. However, in addition to the exception just mentioned, there are other exceptions. For instance, as the House of Lords held in *Beswick v Beswick*:[4]

- a contract to pay money to a third party can be specifically enforced in favour of a party where, as is normally the case, any damages awarded to the party would be nominal; and
- where the contract is for an annuity or other periodical payment it can be specifically enforced (thereby avoiding the need to sue for damages every time a payment is not made).

Where consideration has not been provided   The remedy of specific performance is an equitable one and, since equity does not recognise the making of a contract by deed as an effective substitute for consideration, specific performance cannot be awarded in favour of a person who has not provided consideration ('equity will not assist a volunteer') and he is left to his common law remedy of damages.[5]

Where the court's constant supervision would be necessary to secure compliance with the order   An example is provided by *Ryan v Mutual Tontine Westminster Chambers Association.*[6] In the lease of a flat in a block of flats the lessors agreed to keep a resident porter, who should be in constant attendance and perform specified duties. The person appointed got his duties done by deputies and was absent for hours at a time at another job. The court refused to order against the lessors specific performance of the agreement relating to the performance of the specified duties by the porter because such an order would have required its constant supervision. On the other hand, in *Posner v Scott-Lewis*,[7] specific performance was ordered against a lessor of a covenant to appoint a porter because what had to be done to comply with the order (appointing a porter) could be defined with sufficient certainty and enforcement of the order would not require the constant supervision of the court.

In *Co-operative Insurance Society Ltd v Argyll Stores (Holdings) Ltd*,[8] where the House of Lords allowed an appeal against the Court of Appeal's order for specific performance of a covenant in a lease of a supermarket which required it to be kept open for trade, the House of Lords held that specific performance should not be ordered if it would require a defendant to run a business (save in exceptional circumstances). One of the House's reasons was that to order someone to carry on a business would require the court's constant supervision.

Where the contract is for services of a personal nature   The obvious example of such a contract is one of employment. The Trade Union and Labour Relations (Consolidation) Act 1992, s 236 prohibits an order of specific performance against an employee to compel him to do any work or to attend at any place for the doing of any work. It is well established by the cases that contracts for personal services not covered by the Act (for example an agency contract)[9] cannot be specifically enforced either, nor can an order of specific performance be made against an employer (except, possibly, in very exceptional circumstances). Reasons given are that such contracts would require constant supervision and that it is contrary to public policy to force one person to submit to the orders of another.

Lack of mutuality   There is a rule that a claimant who has not performed his contractual obligations cannot obtain specific performance against the defendant if, in the circumstances, it would not be available to the defendant against the claimant. In *Flight v Bolland*,[10] for instance, it was held that a minor could not be awarded specific performance of the contract in question because such an order could not be made against him in the circumstances. While there is no doubting the present rule, its extent is uncertain.

1   Apart from its inherent jurisdiction to order specific recovery of goods, the court has power under the Sale of Goods Act 1979 to order the specific performance of contracts for the sale of specific or ascertained goods. This power has not been used more liberally than the inherent power.
2   *Behnke v Bede Shipping Co Ltd* [1927] 1 KB 649. Cf *Cohen v Roche* [1927] 1 KB 169.
3   *Cogent v Gibson* (1864) 33 Beav 557.
4   [1967] 2 All ER 1197, HL; para 14.11 below.
5   *Cannon v Hartley* [1949] 1 All ER 50.
6   [1893] 1 Ch 116.
7   [1987] Ch 25.
8   [1997] 3 All ER 297, HL.
9   *Clarke v Price* (1819) 2 Wils Ch 157.
10   (1828) 4 Russ 298.

11.31   If the case does not fall within one of the above cases, specific performance may be ordered, but it must not be forgotten that, since specific performance is an equitable remedy, its award does not lie as of right (unlike the common law remedy of damages) but lies in the court's discretion.

Factors which make it unlikely that the court will exercise its discretion in favour of specific performance include:

- a mistake on the part of the defendant such that it would be unjust specifically to enforce the contract against him;
- delay in bringing an action for specific performance which resulted in the defendant so changing his position that it would be unjust specifically to enforce the contract against him;[1]
- exceptional severity of the hardship to the defendant if the contract is specifically enforced against him;[2]
- breach by the claimant of his contractual obligations in circumstances where the grant of specific performance would be unjust to the defendant.[3]

Lastly, it is clearly established that the court will refuse specific performance of a contract for the sale of land in favour of a claimant who is in breach of a contractual stipulation concerning the time of completion where time is of 'the essence of the contract',[4] although it will normally grant it to such a claimant (subject to a condition that the claimant pays damages for his delay) where time is not 'of the essence' since this will not cause injustice to the defendant.

1   *Stuart v London and North Western Rly Co* (1852) 1 De GM & G 721.
2   *Patel v Ali* [1984] 1 All ER 978.
3   *Walsh v Lonsdale* (1882) 21 Ch D 9.
4   *Stickney v Keeble* [1915] AC 386 at 415–416.

Injunction

11.32   An injunction is a court order restraining a party to a contract from acting in breach of a negative stipulation contained in it. By way of comparison, specific performance is concerned with the enforcement of positive contractual stipulations.

11.33   While it is correct to say that injunctions are concerned with restraining breaches of negative contractual stipulations, it would be erroneous to assume that only an express negative stipulation can be remedied by an injunction. Generally, a breach of a positive stipulation can be enjoined if the stipulation can properly be construed as impliedly being a negative stipulation. Thus, in *Manchester Ship Canal Co v Manchester Racecourse Co*,[1] a stipulation for the grant of a 'first refusal' was construed as a stipulation, enforceable by injunction, not to sell to anyone else in breach of the stipulation. Similarly, in *Metropolitan Electric Supply Co Ltd v Ginder*,[2] where the defendant had undertaken to take all the electricity required for his premises from the claimants, it was held that this was impliedly an undertaking not to take electricity from any other person, which could be enforced by an injunction.

1   [1901] 2 Ch 37.
2   [1901] 2 Ch 799.

11.34   Although the courts are prepared to enforce negative stipulations in a contract for personal services, consistency with the rule that such a contract cannot normally be the subject of a decree of specific performance means that an injunction will not be issued to restrain an employee or the like from breaking a promise not to work for any other person, if this would indirectly amount to compelling him to perform his contract with his employer.[1] This is given statutory force in relation to contracts of employment by the Trade Union and Labour Relations (Consolidation) Act 1992, s 236, which provides that no court may, by an injunction restraining a breach or threatened breach of a contract of employment, compel an employee to do any work or to attend at any place of work.

On the other hand, a negative promise by an employee or the like will be enforced against him by injunction if it does not indirectly force him to work for his employer. For example, in *Lumley v Wagner*,[2] the defendant, an opera star, agreed to sing at the claimant's theatre for three months and in no other theatre during that time. An injunction was granted restraining her from singing for another theatre owner during the three-month period. The approach taken in *Lumley v Wagner* was followed in *Warner Bros Pictures Inc v Nelson*.[3] The defendant, whose stage name was Bette Davis, agreed with the claimant company not to work in a film or stage production for any other company for a year nor to be engaged in any other occupation. During the year she contracted to work for another film company. The judge stated that, while an injunction enforcing all the negative stipulations in the contract could not be granted (because it would force Bette Davis either to be idle or to perform her contract with the claimant company), the injunction requested would be granted because it was limited to prohibiting her from working in a film or stage production for anyone other than the claimant company; she would still be free to earn her living in some other less remunerative way. The judge was unimpressed by the argument that the difference between what the claimant could earn acting and what she could earn in any other capacity would be so substantial that the injunction would drive her to work for the claimant company. An argument of this type did, however, persuade the judge in *Page One Records Ltd v Britton*,[4] an employee against employer case referred to in para 11.35 below. In *Warren v Mendy*,[5] the Court of Appeal was also persuaded by such an argument on grounds of realism and practicality. Consequently, it is now the law that, contrary to the view of the judge in *Warner Bros v Nelson*, the question of whether an injunction against him would compel the defendant to work for the claimant is not answered in the negative simply because the defendant is not debarred from doing other work. If the nature of, or remuneration for, that work is so different that effectively the defendant would be driven to work for the claimant, it will be held that an injunction would so compel him and an injunction will not be ordered. Thus, if the facts of *Warner Bros v Nelson* arose today the decision on them would no doubt be against an injunction being ordered.

1   *Rely-a-Bell Burglar and Fire Alarm Co Ltd v Eisler* [1926] Ch 609.
2   (1852) 1 De GM & G 604.
3   [1936] 3 All ER 160.
4   [1967] 3 All ER 822.
5   [1989] 3 All ER 103, CA.

11.35   The law is similar where an employee seeks to enforce a negative stipulation against his employer. Thus, generally, an injunction will not be issued if its effect is to compel the employer to continue employment. But an injunction may be granted in exceptional cases where employer and employee retain their mutual confidence.

In *Page One Records Ltd v Britton*,[1] The Troggs, a pop group, appointed the claimant as their manager for five years, agreeing not to let anyone else act as their manager during that time. After a year, The Troggs dismissed the claimant, who sought an injunction restraining them from appointing anyone else as their manager. It was held that an injunction would indirectly compel The Troggs to continue to employ the claimant because pop groups could not operate successfully without a manager, and it would be bad to pressure The Troggs into continuing to employ a person in whom they had lost confidence. Therefore the injunction sought was not granted. In comparison, one may note the exceptional case of *Hill v C A Parsons & Co Ltd*.[2] The defendant employers were forced by union pressure to dismiss the claimant in breach of contract. An injunction was granted to restrain this breach, even though its effect was to compel the reinstatement of the claimant. As the Court of Appeal pointed out, the circumstances were special, in particular because the parties retained their mutual confidence. Mutual confidence has been stressed as a precondition in other cases; it can be shown either by evidence that the employer and employee have expressed confidence in each other or by inference from evidence of an established and satisfactory employment relationship.[3]

Despite the general reluctance of the courts to grant specific performance or an injunction in respect of a contract of employment, there are signs that, in cases where the employee's contract requires a specified procedure to be followed before dismissal can take place, the courts will grant an injunction to restrain a proposed dismissal in breach of that procedure.[4]

1   [1967] 3 All ER 822.
2   [1971] 3 All ER 1345, CA.
3   *Powell v Brent London Borough Council* [1987] IRLR 466, CA.
4   *Jones v Lee* [1980] ICR 310, CA.

11.36   An injunction is like specific performance in that:

- it may be granted with or without an order for damages;
- where it is applicable, the grant of an injunction is discretionary (since it is an equitable remedy) and is likely to be refused where, for example, the claimant is guilty of delay or is in breach of his own obligations under the contract. In particular, an injunction will normally be refused if damages would be an adequate remedy.

On the other hand, an injunction is a much wider remedy than specific performance, partly because it can be ordered in many situations other than contractual situations, and partly because it can be ordered in contractual situations where specific performance could not, eg where enforcement of the contract would require the court's constant superintendence or where the contract is one for personal services.

Restitutionary claim: account of profits from breach

11.37   In 2000, in *A-G v Blake (Jonathan Cape Ltd, third party)*,[1] the House of Lords held that in exceptional circumstances it is possible for the injured party to get an account of the profits accruing to the party in breach from that breach. Such an award is different from an award of damages, in that it requires the party in breach to surrender a benefit (ie a gain) whereas damages require him to compensate the injured party for his loss.[2]

In *A-G v Blake*, Blake had for many years been employed by the British secret intelligence service. Unknown to them he had also worked for the KGB. In 1961 he was convicted of official secrets offences and imprisoned. He escaped from prison in 1965. He went to Russia where he remained. Some 20 years later he contracted with Cape to write his autobiography. The contract provided for an advance of royalties of £150,000 to be paid; of this £60,000 had actually been paid.

Blake had committed a breach of contract in writing the book because, when he had entered the British secret intelligence service, he had made a life-long contract with the Crown to keep everything he learnt confidential. The majority (4-1) of the House of Lords held that the Crown was entitled, by way of an account of profits, to the amount due and owing to Blake from Cape under the publishing contract on the ground that that money was the gain accruing to Blake through breach of his contract with it.

The decision in *A-G v Blake* is of limited effect. Lord Nicholls, with whom the rest of the majority agreed, made it clear that an account of profits was only available as a remedy for breach of contract where the availability of damages (to compensate the claimant for loss), specific performance and injunction would provide an inadequate remedy. Moreover, as an equitable remedy the option of an account of profits is discretionary in the same way as specific performance or an injunction. Lord Nicholls stated that, in deciding whether to order an account of profits where damages, specific performance and injunction are inadequate, the court will have regard to all the circumstances, including the subject-matter of the contract, the purpose of the contractual provision broken, the circumstances in which the breach occurred, the consequences of the breach and the circumstances in which relief is sought. He said that a useful, but not exhaustive, guide is whether the claimant has a legitimate interest in preventing the defendant's profit-making activity and, hence, in depriving him of his profit.

No doubt further detail will be given to this application of the account of profits remedy in subsequent cases.

1   [2000] 4 All ER 385, HL.
2   *Portman Building Society v Hamlyn* [1998] 4 All ER 202 at 205.

Limitation of actions

11.38   An action will be barred if it is not brought within the relevant limitation period. The rules relating to these periods are statutory, the relevant Act being the Limitation Act 1980. If an action is statute-barred this does not extinguish the claimant's substantive right but simply bars the procedural remedies available to him. One consequence of this is that if a debtor pays a statute-barred debt, he cannot recover the money as money not due.[1]

1   *Bize v Dickason* (1786) 1 Term Rep 285 at 287.

Limitation periods
11.39   Under the Limitation Act 1980:

- Actions founded on a simple contract (ie one not made by deed) cannot be brought after the expiry of six years from the date on which the cause of action accrued[1], which is normally when the breach of contract occurs and never when the damage is suffered. However, if the damages claimed consist of or include damages for personal injuries caused by a breach of contract, the time limit is reduced to three years[2], although this period may be extended in respect of an action for personal injuries if it is equitable to so do.[3]
- Actions founded on a contract made by deed cannot be brought after the expiry of 12 years from the date on which the cause of action accrued[4]. The special rules mentioned above concerning personal injuries claims also apply here.

There are special rules, described in para 28.25, about when the limitation period begins to run where the claimant was a minor or mentally ill when his cause of action accrued or where fraud, concealment or mistake is involved. In the former case time does not begin to run until the removal of the disability.[5] In the latter, time does not begin to run until the fraud, concealment or mistake has been, or ought to have been, discovered by the claimant.[6]

1   Limitation Act 1980, s 5. For a special rule in relation to actions on certain contracts of loan, see Limitation Act 1980, s 6. If the claimant can establish a cause of action in tort for negligence, a cause of action accrues (and time runs from) when the damage is suffered, although there are numerous exceptions, eg in personal injury cases and claims based on the negligent construction of buildings; see further paras 28.23 and 28.24 below.
2   Limitation Act 1980, s 11(4).
3   Limitation Act 1980, s 33; para 28.25.
4   Limitation Act 1980, s 8.
5   Limitation Act 1980, s 28.
6   Limitation Act 1980, s 32.

Extending the limitation period

11.40   A written acknowledgement of liability to pay, or part payment of, a debt or other liquidated (ie agreed) pecuniary claim may start time running again, provided that the right of action has not previously become statute-barred (ie the acknowledgement or part payment must be made during the currency of the relevant limitation period).[1] A cause of action for unliquidated damages cannot be extended by an acknowledgement or part payment.[1]

1   Limitation Act 1980, ss 29-31.

Equitable relief

11.41   The provisions of the Limitation Act 1980 do not apply to claims for equitable relief.[1] However, in cases where, before the Judicature Act 1873, the same claim for relief could have been entertained in either the common law courts or in the Court of Chancery, the limitation periods under the Limitation Act are applied to equitable claims by analogy.[2] The same is true where, although a particular remedy, eg equitable compensation for breach of fiduciary duty, would only have been available in the Court of Chancery, there is also a remedy at common law which corresponds with the equitable one. An example would be where, in relation to the same factual situation, there can be a claim for damages for a fraudulent breach of contract (formerly only available in the common law courts) and also a claim for equitable compensation for breach of fiduciary duty (formerly only available in the Court of Chancery).[3]

The position is different in the case of a claim for equitable relief where there is no corresponding remedy at common law, so that a claim for the type of relief in question could only have been entertained by the Court of Chancery before the 1873 Act. Examples are claims for specific performance or an injunction. Here, the claim may fail under the equitable doctrine of laches (delay). The modern test of whether the claimant is barred by laches is whether, broadly considered, the claimant's actions were such as to render it unconscionable for him to be permitted to assert his rights.[4] The avoidance of fixed limitation periods in this area is obviously more appropriate to the discretionary nature of equitable remedies.

1   Limitation Act 1980, s 36(1).
2   Limitation Act 1980; *Knox v Gye* (1872) LR 5 HL 656 at 674.
3   Limitation Act 1980; *Cia de Seguros Imperio v Heath (REBX) Ltd* [2001] 1 WLR 112, CA.
4   *Frawley v Neill* [2000] CP Rep 20, CA.

Chapter 12

Misrepresentation, duress and undue influence

12.1 In this chapter we consider:

- when a contract can be set aside by one party because of a misrepresentation by the other party;
- when damages can be recovered for misrepresentation;
- when a contract can be set aside for non-disclosure of a material fact by a party;
- when a contract can be set aside for duress or undue influence;
- the effect of an unfair term in a consumer contract for the sale or supply of goods or the supply of a service.

Misrepresentation

12.2 A misrepresentation is a false or misleading statement.

In certain very rare cases a contract is void if it is made in circumstances where one or both parties are labouring under a mistake as to the facts existing at the time of their agreement. In these cases, the mistake may have been induced by a misrepresentation by one of the parties, but this is not essential. If a contract is void for mistake it has no legal effect; consequently, it is unenforceable by either party, money paid under it is recoverable back and title to property cannot pass under it. A party who has received goods under a void contract will be liable to the transferor in tort if he wrongfully interferes with them, and so will a third party who has bought them from him.

A contract may be void for mistake:

- if it relates to a matter as to which the law or contract does not allocate the risk or provide some other solution, both parties share the mistake and the mistake relates to the existence of the subject-matter, as to the possibility of performing the contract or as to a fundamental assumption underlying the contract; or
- if, because of a mistake which the parties do not share, they are fundamentally at cross-purposes because the mistake relates to:
    - the identity (as opposed to an attribute) of one of the other party;
    - the essence of the subject-matter of the contract; or
    - whether a particular matter is a term of the contract,

    provided that the mistake is an operative one, in that the party who does not share the mistake knows of it, or that the circumstances are so ambiguous that a reasonable party could not say whether the contract meant what one party thought it meant or what the other party thought it meant.

We are not concerned further in this chapter where a mistake induced by misrepresentation is such as to render the contract void. We repeat that cases where a mistake has this effect are very rare.

Unless a mistake induced by a misrepresentation is such as to render the contract void, it is the rules which follow which govern the situation. These rules are somewhat involved, and different rules apply depending on whether there has been an active misrepresentation or a misrepresentation through non-disclosure.

Active misrepresentation

12.3　When one is faced with a situation involving an 'active misrepresentation' one must first ask whether the representation has become a term of the contract or not, applying the rules set out in paras 7.10 to 7.17 above. The division between active misrepresentations which have remained precontractual representations (mere representations) and those which have become terms of a resulting contract is fundamental since the remedies are different.

Active misrepresentations which have remained mere representations

12.4　If the misrepresentation has not become a contractual term, and provided certain requirements are satisfied, two remedies may be available to the misrepresentee: rescission of the contract (unless this is barred) and (in many cases) damages. The requirements mentioned above are that:

- the misrepresentation must be one of fact;
- it must have been addressed to the person misled;
- it must have been intended to be acted on by that person; and
- it must have induced the contract.

Misrepresentation of fact

12.5　There must be a misrepresentation by words or conduct of a past or existing fact. An example of a misrepresentation by conduct would be where the vendor of a house covered up dry rot in it.[1] It follows from the requirement that there must be a misrepresentation of a past or existing fact that there are many misrepresentations for which no relief is available. The following must be distinguished from misrepresentation of fact.

1　See *Gordon v Selico Co Ltd* [1986] 1 EGLR 71, CA.

12.6　*Mere puffs*　A representation which is mere vague sales talk is not regarded as a representation of fact, as is shown by *Dimmock v Hallett*.[1] At a sale of land by auction, it was said to be 'fertile and improvable'; in fact it was partly abandoned and useless. The representation was held to be a 'mere flourishing description by an auctioneer' affording no ground for relief. It is a question of fact whether a particular statement is merely vague sales talk or the assertion of some verifiable fact.

1　(1866) 2 Ch App 21.

12.7　*Statements of opinion*　A statement which merely expresses an opinion or belief does not give grounds for relief if the opinion or belief turns out to be wrong. In *Bisset v*

Wilkinson,[1] the vendor of a farm which (as he knew) had never been used as a sheep farm, told a prospective purchaser that in his judgment the land would support 2,000 sheep. It was held that this statement was one of opinion, given that the farm had never been used for sheep, and that, since it was an honest statement, no relief was available. It would have been different if there had been a misrepresentation of its actual capacity since this would have been a misrepresentation of fact.

What has been said in the last paragraph must be qualified by pointing out that in two cases statements of opinion can involve an implied misrepresentation of fact and so give rise to relief:

- Where a person represents an opinion which he does not honestly hold he will at the same time make a misrepresentation of fact, viz that he holds the opinion.[2]
- Where a person represents an opinion for which he does not have reasonable grounds, he will at the same time make a misrepresentation of fact if he impliedly represents that he has reasonable grounds for his opinion. A classic example is *Smith v Land and House Property Corpn*.[3] The vendor of a hotel described it as let to 'Mr Frederick Fleck (a most desirable tenant) ... for an unexpired term of 27 plus years, thus offering a first-class investment'. Fleck had not paid the last quarter's rent and had paid the previous one by instalments and under pressure. The Court of Appeal held that the above statement was not merely of opinion but also involved a misrepresentation of fact because the vendor impliedly stated that he had reasonable grounds for his opinion. Too much should not be read into this decision because the court will only find such an implied representation where the facts on which the opinion is based are particularly within the knowledge of the person stating the opinion, and not when the facts are equally known to both parties.[4]

1   [1927] AC 177, PC.
2   *Brown v Raphael* [1958] 2 All ER 79 at 81.
3   (1884) 28 Ch D 7, CA.
4   *Smith v Land and House Property Corpn* (1884) 28 Ch D 7 at 15.

12.8   *Statements as to the future*   Such statements, the best example of which is a statement of intention, are obviously not statements of fact in themselves and no remedy is available if the future event does not occur. However, a statement as to the future will involve a misrepresentation of fact if its maker does not honestly believe in its truth. In the case of a misrepresentation of intention this rule is well summarised by the statement of Bowen LJ in *Edgington v Fitzmaurice*[1] that the state of a man's mind is as much a fact as the state of his digestion. In this case the claimant was induced to lend money to a company by representations made in a prospectus by the directors that the money would be used to improve the company's buildings and to expand its business. The directors' true intention was to use the money to pay off the company's debts. They were held liable in deceit (fraudulent misrepresentation) on the basis that their misrepresentation of present intentions was a misrepresentation of fact.

1   (1885) 29 Ch D 459, CA.

12.9   *Statements of law*   Traditionally, a person who is induced to contract by a misrepresentation of law (eg a misrepresentation as to the meaning or effect of a statute) has no remedy.[1] The only exceptions to this traditional rule are:

- where, as in the case of a statement of opinion or intention, the representor wilfully misrepresents the fact that he does not believe his statement of the law;[2] and
- where the misrepresentation relates to the existence or meaning of a foreign law, since such a misrepresentation is regarded by our courts as one of fact.[3]

In 2002, a High Court judge held that it was no longer the law that a misrepresentation of law cannot suffice for an action for misrepresentation,[4] but this statement is contrary to weighty case law. Until the statement is adopted by an appeal court competent to overrule the contrary case law, it remains true to say that a misrepresentation must be one of fact.

1   *Beattie v Lord Ebury* (1872) 7 Ch App 777, CA in Chancery.
2   The point has not yet been decided by a court. It was left open for future decision in *West London Commercial Bank v Kitson* (1884) 13 QBD 360 at 362–363.
3   *André & Cie v Ets Michel Blanc & Fils* [1979] 2 Lloyd's Rep 427, CA.
4   *Pankhania v Hackney London Borough Council* [2002] NPC 123.

12.10 *Silence* Not surprisingly, silence cannot generally constitute an active misrepresentation.[1] However, there are two exceptions:

- Where the representor's silence distorts an assertion of fact made by him there will be an active misrepresentation of fact if the representor knows or has reasonable grounds to believe that there has been the distortion. Thus, in *Dimmock v Hallett*,[2] it was said that if a vendor of land states that farms on it are let, but omits to say that the tenants have given notice to quit, his statement will be a misrepresentation of fact. A modern example is provided by *Spice Girls Ltd v Aprilia World Service BV*.[3] During negotiations for an agreement for the Spice Girls to promote a brand of motor scooter, the Spice Girls made a film and provided logos and images of the five of them in order that the other party should sign the agreement. They did so without informing the other party that one of them, Ginger Spice, intended to leave the group before the conclusion of the intended agreement. It was held that by their conduct they had represented that they had no knowledge or reasonable grounds to believe that one of them would be leaving the group during the term of the agreement, and that therefore there had been a misrepresentation by conduct.
- Where a representation of fact is falsified by later events, before the conclusion of the contract, there will be an active misrepresentation if the representor fails to notify the other of the change. This is shown by *With v O'Flanagan*.[4] Negotiations for the sale of a medical practice were begun in January 1934. The defendant vendor represented to the claimant that the practice was producing £2,000 per annum, which was then true. Between January and May, the defendant was seriously ill and the practice was looked after by a number of substitutes with the result that the receipts had fallen to £5 per week by 1 May 1934. On 1 May 1934, the claimant, who had not been informed of the change of circumstances, signed a contract to purchase the practice. The Court of Appeal rescinded the contract on the ground that the defendant ought to have communicated the change of circumstances to the claimant. It said that the representation made to induce the contract must be treated as continuing until the contract was signed and what was initially a true representation had turned into a misrepresentation.

1   See further paras 12.41–12.45 below.
2   (1866) 2 Ch App 21.
3   [2000] EMLR 478.
4   [1936] 1 All ER 727, CA.

The misrepresentation must have been addressed by the misrepresentor to the person misled
12.11   The present requirement is not as stringent as may appear at first sight because:

- It is possible for a representation to be made to the public in general, as in the case of an advertisement.

- A representation need not be made directly to the person misled, or his agent, in order to satisfy the present requirement. It suffices that the representor knew that the person to whom he made the misrepresentation would pass it on to the claimant. This is shown by *Pilmore v Hood*.[1] The defendant wished to sell a public house to X and fraudulently misrepresented that the annual takings were £180. X was unable to buy and with the defendant's knowledge persuaded the claimant to buy by repeating the defendant's misrepresentation. The defendant was held liable in damages to the claimant for his fraudulent misrepresentation. An important limit on the rule in *Pilmore v Hood* is that, if the person (A) to whom the misrepresentation is originally made by the defendant (D) contracts with D as a result, the misrepresentation is deemed to be exhausted. Thus, if A then contracts to sell the property to B, repeating D's misrepresentation, as D knew he would, B has no redress against D because D's misrepresentation, being exhausted, is not regarded as addressed to B.[2] Of course, in such a case B is not remediless because he can pursue the normal remedies for misrepresentation against A who passed on the misrepresentation.

1   (1838) 5 Bing NC 97.
2   *Gross v Lewis Hillman Ltd* [1969] 3 All ER 1476, CA.

The misrepresentation must have been intended by the misrepresentor to be acted on by the misrepresentee or by a class of person including the misrepresentee

12.12   *Peek v Gurney*[1] is the leading case on this point. The promoters of a company issued a prospectus which contained misrepresentations. The promoters' intention was to induce people to apply for shares on the formation of the company. The claimants purchased shares on the market (ie not on formation of the company). They sued to recover their losses, claiming that they had been induced to buy the shares by the misrepresentations in the prospectus. Their claim was unsuccessful because the promoters had not intended that the prospectus should be relied on by people dealing in shares after the original allotment.

1   (1873) LR 6 HL 377, HL.

The misrepresentation must have induced the misrepresentee to make the contract

12.13   The question of inducement is one of fact but, if the misrepresentor made a statement of a nature likely to induce a reasonable person to contract and with the intention of inducing this, it will normally be inferred that it did induce the misrepresentee to contract.[1] However, this inference is rebuttable and will, for example, be rebutted in the following three cases:

- if the misrepresentee actually knew the truth,[2] or if an agent acting for him in the transaction knew the truth as a result of information received by him while acting in the scope of his authority (since such knowledge is imputed to the misrepresentee). *Strover v Harrington*[3] provides an example. In the course of pre-contractual inquiries the solicitors of purchasers of land learned that, contrary to the representations of the vendors, the property was not connected to main drainage; the solicitors' knowledge was imputed to the purchasers;
- if the misrepresentee was ignorant of the misrepresentation when the contract was made. In *Re Northumberland and Durham District Banking Co, ex p Bigge*,[4] the claimant, who had bought some shares in a company, sought to have the purchase rescinded on the ground that the company had published false reports of its financial state. He failed; one of the reasons was because he was unable to prove that he had read any of the reports or that anyone had told him of their contents;
- if the misrepresentee did not allow the representation to affect his judgment. Thus, if

the misrepresentee investigates the truth of the representation (as where a prospective purchaser has a house surveyed) and relies on his investigation, rather than the representation, in making the contract the inference of inducement is rebutted, except in the case of fraud. In *Attwood v Small*,[5] the appellant offered to sell a mine, making exaggerated representations as to its earning capacity. The respondent agreed to buy if the appellant could verify his representations and appointed agents to investigate the matter. The agents, who were experienced, visited the mine and were given every facility. They reported that the representations were true and the contract was made. The House of Lords held that the contract could not be rescinded for misrepresentation because the respondents had not relied on the misrepresentations but on their own independent investigations. By way of contrast, the inference of inducement is not rebutted where the misrepresentee could have investigated and discovered the falsity of the representation but chose not to do so.[6]

1   *Smith v Chadwick* (1884) 9 App Cas 187 at 196.
2   *Begbie v Phosphate Sewage Co* (1875) LR 10 QB 491.
3   [1988] 1 All ER 769.
4   (1858) 28 LJ Ch 50.
5   (1838) 6 Cl & Fin 232, HL.
6   *Redgrave v Hurd* (1881) 20 Ch D 1, CA.

12.14   Before leaving the requirement of inducement two general points must be noted. First, provided that it was one of the inducements, the misrepresentation need not be the sole inducement. This is shown by *Edgington v Fitzmaurice*,[1] where the claimant was induced to take debentures in a company partly by a misrepresentation in the prospectus and partly by his own mistaken belief that debenture holders would have a charge on the company's property. He was held entitled to rescission.

Second, the misrepresentation must not only have induced the misrepresentee to contract but it must also have been material, in that it related to a matter which would have influenced the judgment of a reasonable person.[2] The point is not an important one because an immaterial misrepresentation is unlikely to cause substantial loss with the result that any damages awarded are likely to be nominal and rescission is likely to be refused under the court's discretion to do so (which is described in para 12.31 below).

1   (1885) 29 Ch D 459, CA.
2   *Pan Atlantic Insurance Co Ltd v Pine Top Insurance Co Ltd* [1994] 3 All ER 581, HL (see especially pp 600–610).

Remedies for active misrepresentations which have remained mere representations

12.15   Provided the above requirements are satisfied, one or more of the remedies set out below is or are available to the misrepresentee. Alternatively, the misrepresentee can refuse to carry out the contract and, provided (generally) that he returns what he obtained under it, successfully resist any claim for damages or specific performance.

Rescission

12.16   The effect of a misrepresentation is to make the contract voidable so that it remains valid unless and until the misrepresentee elects to rescind it on discovering the misrepresentation. Rescission entails setting the contract aside as if it had never been made, the misrepresentee recovering what he transferred under the contract but having to restore what he obtained under it. The effect of misrepresentation is important in relation to the rights of third parties. If A sells a car to B under a contract which is voidable for B's misrepresentation, a voidable title passes to B and, if C (an innocent purchaser) buys the car from B before A has decided to rescind, A loses the right to rescind and C obtains a valid title.[1] This must be distinguished from the situation where the contract is void for mistake. There, title to the goods never passes and they can always be recovered, or damages obtained in lieu, from the other party or a third person to whom they have been transferred.[2]

1   White v Garden (1851) 10 CB 919.
2   Cundy v Lindsay (1878) 3 App Cas 459, HL.

12.17   Rescission can be effected in two ways. First, by bringing legal proceedings for an order for rescission. This may be necessary where a formal document or transaction, such as a lease, has to be set aside by a court order. In other cases a court order is not essential but may be advantageous if the misrepresentor is likely to prove unwilling to return what he has obtained under the contract.

Second, rescission can be effected by the misrepresentee making it clear that he refuses to be bound by the contract. Normally, communication of this decision to the misrepresentor is required, but there is an exception. If a fraudulent misrepresentor absconds, it suffices that the misrepresentee records his intention to rescind the contract by some overt act that is reasonable in the circumstances. This was decided by the Court of Appeal in *Car and Universal Finance Co Ltd v Caldwell.*[1] The defendant sold his car to N in return for a cheque which was dishonoured when he presented it the next day.[2] The defendant immediately informed the police and the Automobile Association of the fraudulent transaction. Subsequently, N sold the car to X who sold it to Y who sold it to Z who sold it to the claimants who bought it in good faith. It was held that in the circumstances the defendant had done enough to rescind the contract before the claimants bought the car, title had therefore re-vested in him and the claimants had not got title.

1   [1964] 1 All ER 290, CA.
2   By his conduct in drawing the cheque, N had fraudulently misrepresented that the existing state of facts was such that in the ordinary course of events the cheque would be honoured: *R v Hazelton* (1874) LR 2 CCR 134 at 140.

12.18   There are four bars to the right to rescind:

Affirmation of contract by misrepresentee   This occurs if, after discovering that the misrepresentation is untrue and knowing of his right to rescind,[1] the misrepresentee declares his intention to waive his right to rescission or acts in a way that such an intention can be inferred. An inference of such an intention was drawn in *Long v Lloyd.*[2] The claimant bought a lorry as the result of the defendant's misrepresentation that it was in excellent condition. On the claimant's first business journey the dynamo broke and he noticed several other serious defects. On the next business journey the lorry broke down and the claimant, realising that it was in a very bad condition, sought to rescind the contract. The Court of Appeal held that the second journey constituted an affirmation because the claimant knew by then that the representation was untrue.

Lapse of time   This can provide evidence of affirmation where the misrepresentee fails to rescind for a considerable time after discovering the falsity. In addition, lapse of time can operate as a separate bar to rescission in cases where the misrepresentee has not delayed after discovering the falsity. This is shown by *Leaf v International Galleries,*[3] where the claimant bought from the defendant a picture of Salisbury Cathedral which the latter had innocently represented to be by Constable. Five years later, the claimant discovered that this was a misrepresentation and immediately sought to rescind the contract. The Court of Appeal held that his right to rescind had been lost through lapse of a reasonable time to discover the falsity.

This bar does not apply in the case of a fraudulent misrepresentation.

Inability to restore　The main objects of rescission are to restore the parties to their former position and to prevent unjust enrichment.[4] Thus, if either party has so changed or otherwise dealt with what he has obtained under the contract that he cannot restore it, rescission is barred.[5] So, for example, the purchaser of a cake cannot rescind the contract if he has eaten the cake.

There are three qualifications on the present bar:

* A fraudulent misrepresentor cannot rely on his own dealings with what he has obtained as a bar to rescission by the misrepresentee.[6]
* The fact that a seller has spent the money which he has received does not make restitution impossible since one bank note is as good as another and the seller can restore what he obtained under the contract by handing over other notes.
* Precise restitution is not required for rescission. Provided the property obtained under the contract can substantially be restored, rescission can be enforced even though the property has deteriorated, declined in value or otherwise changed. For example, in *Armstrong v Jackson*,[7] a broker fraudulently sold shares to the claimant. Later, when the shares had fallen to one-twelfth of their value at the time of sale, the claimant claimed rescission. It was held that, since the claimant could return the actual shares, rescission would be ordered, subject to the defendant's repayment of the purchase price being credited with the dividends received by the claimant. Reference can also be made to *Cheese v Thomas*.[8] Here a contract between the claimant and defendant for their joint purchase of a house had involved the claimant contributing £43,000 to the purchase of a house at a price of £83,000 but, because of a fall in property values, the house had subsequently been sold for only £55,400. Rescission of the contract was ordered on the basis that the claimant and defendant should share the loss brought about by the fall in value in the same proportions (43:40) as they had contributed to the price, and not on the basis of the claimant's contribution of £43,000 being repaid.

    The Court of Appeal in *Cheese v Thomas* emphasised that the basic object of rescission was to restore each party as near as possible to his original position. Where a deterioration or loss of value results from the voluntary dealings with it by the person who obtained it under the contract, he must not only account for any profits derived from it but also pay compensation for such deterioration or loss of value.[9]

Bona fide purchaser for value　As has been indicated in para 12.16 above, if, before the misrepresentee elects to rescind, a third party has innocently purchased the property, or an interest in it, for value from the misrepresentor, his rights are valid against the misrepresentee, who loses the chance to rescind. This is illustrated by *White v Garden*,[10] where a rogue bought 50 tons of iron from Garden by persuading him to take in payment a fraudulent bill of exchange. The rogue then sold the iron for value to White who acted in good faith (ie was unaware of the rogue's fraudulent misrepresentation) and Garden delivered the iron to White. The bill of exchange was subsequently dishonoured and Garden seized and removed some of the iron. Garden was held liable for what is now the tort of conversion; he had purported to rescind the contract with the rogue too late, the rogue's voidable title having been made unavoidable when White innocently bought the iron from him.

In *Car and Universal Finance Co Ltd v Caldwell*,[11] on the other hand, rescission was not barred because it occurred before the intervention of a bona fide purchaser for value.

1　*Peyman v Lanjani* [1984] 3 All ER 703, CA.
2　[1958] 2 All ER 402, CA.
3　[1950] 1 All ER 693, CA.
4　*Spence v Crawford* [1939] 3 All ER 271 at 288–289.
5　*Clarke v Dickson* (1858) EB & E 148.

6   *Spence v Crawford* [1939] 3 All ER 271 at 280–282.
7   [1917] 2 KB 822.
8   [1994] 1 All ER 35, CA.
9   *Erlanger v New Sombrero Phosphate Co* (1878) 3 App Cas 1218 at 1278–1279.
10   (1851) 10 CB 919.
11   Para 12.17 above.

12.19   Before leaving the bars to rescission it should be noted that the courts have power, in the case of non-fraudulent misrepresentations, to refuse rescission, or to refuse to recognise a purported rescission, and to award damages in lieu. This power is discussed in para 12.31 below.

Damages

12.20   We are concerned here with damages for misrepresentation and not with damages for breach of contract, discussed in chapter 11, which are a different species. Sometimes damages for misrepresentation can be recovered under the common law rules of tort: sometimes under the Misrepresentation Act 1967. Rescission and damages are alternative remedies in many cases, but if the victim of a fraudulent or negligent misrepresentation has suffered consequential loss he may rescind and sue for damages.

The duty to mitigate loss referred to in para 11.16 above, in respect of the assessment of damages from breach of contract also applies to damages for misrepresentation; the duty arises when the misrepresentee discovers the truth.[1]

1   *Smith New Court Securities Ltd v Scrimgeour Vickers (Asset Management) Ltd* [1996] 4 All ER 769, HL.

12.21   The discussion of the rules of assessment of damages for misrepresentation requires the division of the relevant law into five classes:

12.22   *Fraudulent misrepresentation*   Fraudulent misrepresentation gives rise to an action for damages for the tort of deceit. The classic definition of fraud in this context was given by Lord Herschell in *Derry v Peek*.[1] Lord Herschell stated that fraud is proved where it is shown that a misrepresentation has been made:

*   knowingly; or
*   without belief in its truth; or
*   recklessly, careless whether it be true or false.

A misrepresentation is not fraudulent if there is an honest belief in its truth when it is made, even though there are no reasonable grounds for that belief.[2] Motive is irrelevant: an intention to cheat or injure is not required.

1   (1889) 14 App Cas 337, HL.
2   (1889) 14 App Cas 337, HL. See also *Thomas Witter Ltd v TBP Industries Ltd* [1996] 2 All ER 573.

12.23   *Negligent misrepresentation under the Misrepresentation Act 1967*   Section 2(1) of the Act of 1967 provides that where a person has entered into a contract after a misrepresentation has been made to him by another party thereto and as a result of it has suffered loss, then, if the misrepresentor would be liable to damages for misrepresentation if it had been made fraudulently, he is to be so liable notwithstanding that the misrepresentation was not made fraudulently, unless he proves that he had reasonable grounds to believe and did believe up to the time the contract was made that the facts represented were true. In other words, the misrepresentor is deemed negligent, and liable to pay damages, unless he proves in the stated way that he was not negligent. Whether the misrepresentor can prove this will depend, for instance, on whether he was an expert or not, the length of the negotiations and whether he himself had been misled by another. The representor's burden of proof is a difficult one to discharge. This is shown by *Howard Marine and Dredging Co Ltd v A Ogden & Sons (Excavations) Ltd*.[1] During negotiations for the hire of two barges, Howard's agent misrepresented their capacity in reliance on an error in Lloyd's Register. The Court of Appeal held that the burden of proof had not been discharged, since a file in Howard's possession disclosed the real capacity.

Section 2(1) applies where the misrepresentation was made on behalf of a party to the subsequent contract by his agent,[2] but in such a case the misrepresentee only has an action under s 2(1) against that party and not against his agent.[3]

1   [1978] 2 All ER 1134, CA.
2   *Gosling v Anderson* (1972) 223 Estates Gazette 1743, CA.
3   *Resolute Maritime Inc v Nippon Kaiji Kyokai* [1983] 2 All ER 1; an agent may be liable for a fraudulent misrepresentation or for negligent misrepresentation at common law.

12.24   *Remoteness and measure of damages*   In the tort of deceit and under s 2(1) of the 1967 Act the rule of remoteness of damage is that the defendant is liable for all actual damage or loss directly flowing from the misrepresentation.[1] This is a more liberal rule than that of reasonable foreseeability of the possibility of the damage which applies in other torts, and also more liberal than the rule of remoteness which applies in the case of damages for breach of contract, where damages are limited to compensation for loss which was within the parties' reasonable contemplation, when the contract was made, as a seriously possible result of its breach.[2]

1   *Doyle v Olby (Ironmongers) Ltd* [1969] 2 All ER 119, CA; *Smith New Court Securities Ltd v Scrimgeour Vickers (Asset Management) Ltd* [1996] 4 All ER 769, HL (action for deceit); *Royscot Trust Ltd v Rogerson* [1991] 3 All ER 294, CA (action under Misrepresentation Act 1967, s 2(1)).
2   See paras 19.16–19.20 below (other torts) and paras 11.10–11.15 above (breach of contract).

12.25   Damages for deceit or under s 2(1) of the 1967 Act are assessed according to the 'out of pocket rule',[1] ie an amount is awarded which puts the misrepresentee into the position in which he would have been had the misrepresentation never been made and the contract had not been made. In other words, damages are assessed by reference to all the loss resulting from entering into the contract.

Where he has been induced to buy something by a misrepresentation, the claimant is entitled to recover as damages the full price paid by him, but he must give credit for any benefits which he has received as a direct result of the transaction.[2] As a general rule, the benefits received by him include the market value of the property acquired as at the date of acquisition, with the result that the damages awarded will be the difference between the price paid and the real value of the property at the date of the acquisition by the claimant.[2] However, this general rule is not inflexibly applied; it will not be applied where to do so would prevent the misrepresentee obtaining full compensation for the wrong suffered.[2] Examples of cases where the general rule will not apply are where:

- the misrepresentation has continued to operate after the date of the acquisition of the asset so as to cause the misrepresentee to retain the asset; or
- the circumstances are such that the claimant is, by reason of the fraud, locked into the property.[2]

One case where the general rule did not apply is *Smith New Court Securities Ltd v Scrimgeour Vickers (Asset Management) Ltd*,[3] where the claimants were induced to buy some shares in company X for £23m by the defendants' fraudulent misrepresentation. Because a fraud had been practised on company X before the claimants acquired the shares, the shares were doomed to tumble in value and were therefore a flawed asset.

There was a slump in their value and the claimants were only able to sell them by degrees and only received £11m for them in total. The claimants were awarded as damages the difference between what they had paid for the shares and what they had obtained by their sale of the shares, since the latter amount was to be regarded as the benefit received by them as a result of the transaction, because they could not have sold the shares at the value they had when they acquired them.

The principles set out above were stated in *Smith New Court* in relation to damages for fraudulent misrepresentation, but they are of equal application to damages under s 2(1) of the Misrepresentation Act 1967. In *Royscot Trust Ltd v Rogerson*[4] the Court of Appeal held that damages under s 2(1) should be assessed as if the misrepresentation had been made fraudulently.

The 'out of pocket rule' should be contrasted with the measure of damages for breach of contract. Here the 'loss of expectations rule' normally applies, as has been explained in para 11.3 above, and the injured party recovers an amount which puts him into the position in which he would have been if the representation had been true. Where the breach relates to the thing's quality, this amount is the difference between the 'represented value' and the actual value.

The application of the 'out of pocket rule' does not mean that recovery as damages for deceit or under s 2(1) can never be made in respect of loss of profits. This is shown by *East v Maurer*,[5] where the seller of a hairdressing salon fraudulently represented that he would no longer be working at another salon in the area, in order to induce the claimant to contract to buy the salon. The claimant was induced by the representation to buy the salon. As a result of the untruth of the representation, the claimant was unable to run a successful business at the salon. He was unable to sell it for three years. The Court of Appeal held that the damages for deceit were to be assessed on the basis that the claimant should be compensated for all losses which he had suffered, including his loss on the resale *and his loss of profits*. The profits lost were assessed not on the basis of the profits which would have been earned if the representation had been true (which would have been the amount under the 'loss of expectations' rule) but on the basis of the profits which the misrepresentee would have made if he had not been induced into buying the salon but had bought a different one in the area (because this was the amount by which he was out of pocket as a result of the defendant's deceit).

1   *Smith New Court Securities Ltd v Scrimgeour Vickers (Asset Management) Ltd* [1996] 4 All ER 769, HL (action for deceit); *Royscot Trust Ltd v Rogerson* [1991] 3 All ER 294, CA (action under Misrepresentation Act 1967, s 2(1)).
2   *Smith New Court Securities Ltd v Scrimgeour Vickers (Asset Management) Ltd* [1996] 4 All ER 769, HL.
3   [1996] 4 All ER 769, HL.
4   [1991] 3 All ER 294, CA.
5   [1991] 2 All ER 733, CA.

12.26   A person who has been induced into a contract by a misrepresentation which is fraudulent or which is negligent under s 2(1) of the Misrepresentation Act may also recover damages for any consequential loss or damage, such as expenses, personal injury, damage to his property,[1] which he may have suffered, provided it is not too remote.

1   Damages for distress or disappointment are also recoverable in an action in deceit: *Archer v Brown* [1985] QB 401.

12.27   The contributory negligence of the misrepresentee is not a ground for reducing damages awarded for deceit,[1] but it is such a ground if damages are awarded under s 2(1) of the Misrepresentation Act, provided that the defendant is also liable in tort for negligence, since the Law Reform (Contributory Negligence) Act 1945[2] applies in such a case.[3]

1   *Standard Chartered Bank v Pakistan National Shipping Corpn (No 2)* [2002] UKHL 43, [2003] 1 All ER 173.

12.28   Given that, where a fraudulent misrepresentation has been made, an action may normally be brought for the same amount of damages under s 2(1) of the Misrepresentation Act 1967 without the need to prove fraud, or indeed negligence, it makes sense in many cases of suspected fraudulent misrepresentation for an action to be brought under s 2(1) rather than for deceit.

12.29   *Negligent misrepresentation at common law*   The victim of a negligent misrepresentation may be able to sue the misrepresentor under the principles of the tort of negligence, particularly those enunciated in *Hedley Byrne v Heller & Partners*[1] which we discuss in paras 17.25 to 17.28 below. If the misrepresentee sues under the *Hedley Byrne* principles, he must prove:

- that the misrepresentor owed him a duty to take reasonable care in making representation, which duty only arises if there is a 'special relationship';
- that the misrepresentor was in breach of that duty; and
- that damage resulted from that breach.

The circumstances in which a court may find a 'special relationship' are the subject of a certain amount of dispute, as we explain in paras 17.25 to 17.27 below.

The *Hedley Byrne* principles were applied to a representation made in pre-contractual negotiations by the Court of Appeal in *Esso Petroleum Co Ltd v Mardon*.[2] In negotiations in 1963 for the tenancy of a filling station, Esso negligently told Mr Mardon that the station had an estimated annual throughput of 200,000 gallons. Mr Mardon was induced to take the tenancy but the actual annual throughput never exceeded 86,000 gallons and Mr Mardon was awarded damages against Esso. One reason for its decision given by the Court of Appeal was that Esso were under the duty of care imposed by *Hedley Byrne* – which applied to pre-contractual statements – and were in breach of that duty. In this case, Mr Mardon could not have relied on the Misrepresentation Act 1967, s 2(1) because the misrepresentation had occurred before the Act came into force.

In practice, it is normally better to rely on s 2(1) in the case of a negligent misrepresentation because the onus of disproving negligence is placed on the defendant under that section, whereas if he relies on the *Hedley Byrne* principles the claimant must prove that they are satisfied. In addition, no special relationship need be proved under s 2(1). However, the *Hedley Byrne* principles are still important in cases of pre-contractual misrepresentation in three situations: where the misrepresentation is made by a third party to the contract; where the contractual negotiations do not result in a contract between the defendant and the claimant but the claimant nevertheless suffers loss in reliance on the misrepresentation; and where the limitation period for an action under s 2(1) has expired but that for negligence at common law (which runs from the suffering of loss, and not the misrepresentation) has not. In these cases, assuming their requirements are satisfied, there can be tortious liability under the principles in *Hedley Byrne*, although there can be no rescission for misrepresentation nor damages under the 1967 Act.

The measure of damages under *Hedley Byrne* is governed by the 'out of pocket' rule[3] and questions of remoteness of damage by the test of reasonable foreseeability at the time of the breach of duty (ie recovery can be had for such loss as is the reasonably foreseeable consequence of the statement being wrong, as opposed to the reasonably foreseeable loss caused by entering into the contract).[4] This is a narrower test of remoteness than that under the Misrepresentation Act 1967, s 2(1), which is another reason for an action under s 2(1) being preferable to a claim based on negligent misrepresentation at common law when both actions are available.

1   [1963] 2 All ER 575, HL.
2   [1976] 2 All ER 5, CA.
3   See, for example, *JEB Fasteners Ltd v Marks, Bloom & Co Ltd* [1983] 1 All ER 583 at 587.
4   Paras 19.16–19.20 below.

12.30   *Innocent misrepresentation*   Subject to what is said in para 12.31 below, damages cannot be awarded for a misrepresentation which is not fraudulent or negligent, as defined above. However, an indemnity – which is different from damages – may be awarded.

12.31   *Damages in lieu of rescission*   The Misrepresentation Act 1967, s 2(2) provides that, where a person has entered into a contract after a non-fraudulent misrepresentation has been made to him which would entitle him to rescind the contract, then, if it is claimed in proceedings arising out of the contract that the contract ought to be or has been rescinded, the court or arbitrator may declare the contract subsisting and award damages in lieu of rescission, if of the opinion that it would be equitable to do so. The rationale for this power is that rescission may be too drastic in some cases, eg where the misrepresentation was trifling. An award of damages under s 2(2) is discretionary. In exercising his discretion, a judge or arbitrator is required by s 2(2) to have regard to the nature of the misrepresentation and the loss that would be caused by it if the contract was upheld, as well as the loss that rescission would cause to the other party.

It is uncertain whether the power to award damages in lieu of rescission can only be exercised if rescission has not been barred, eg by affirmation of the contract. A literal interpretation, adopted by judges in three High Court cases, indicates that the power can only be exercised if rescission has not been barred.[1] However, in an earlier High Court case, to which these judges referred (but did not follow), it was held by the judge that this is not so and that the power to award damages under s 2(2) does not depend on an extant right to rescind, but only on a right having existed at some time after the contract was made.[2] The former interpretation is consistent with the purpose of s 2(2), to provide compensation where a court has refused to order rescission (or to recognise a rescission) which it would otherwise have done; the latter interpretation is not.

Important distinctions between s 2(1) and s 2(2) are that damages cannot be awarded under s 2(1) if lack of negligence is proved, whereas they can be awarded in such a case under s 2(2); that damages under s 2(1) can be awarded in addition to rescission; that an award of damages under s 2(1) is not discretionary; and that s 2(3), described below, contemplates that the measure of damages under s 2(1) is different from, and more generous than, an award under s 2(2).[3]

In the light of this, obiter dicta in the Court of Appeal that, unlike damages under s 2(1), damages under s 2(2) cannot include damages for consequential loss, is not surprising, although the other part of the obiter dicta, that damages under s 2(2) in respect of the value of the thing are assessed on the basis of 'loss of expectations' is surprising and doubtful in the light of the generally less generous rule which applies to damages under s 2(1).[4]

Where a person has been held liable to pay damages under s 2(1) of the 1967 Act, the judge or arbitrator, in assessing damages thereunder, is required by s 2(3) to take into account any damages in lieu of rescission under s 2(2).

1   *Zanzibar v British Aerospace (Lancaster House) Ltd* [2000] 1 WLR 2333; *Floods of Queensferry Ltd v Shand Construction Ltd (No 3)* [2000] BLR 81; *Pankhania v Hackney London Borough Council* [2002] NPC 123.
2   *Thomas Witter Ltd v TBP Industries Ltd* [1996] 2 All ER 573.
3   *William Sindall plc v Cambridgeshire County Council* [1994] 3 All ER 932 at 954; *Thomas Witter Ltd v TBP Industries Ltd* [1996] 2 All ER 573 at 591.
4   *William Sindall plc v Cambridgeshire County Council* [1994] 3 All ER 932 at 954 and 961.

Indemnity
12.32   It has already been noted that the object of rescission is to restore the contracting

parties to their former position as if the contract had never been made. As part of this restoration the misrepresentee can claim an indemnity against any *obligations necessarily created by the contract.*[1] The italicised words must be emphasised since they indicate that an indemnity is far less extensive than damages, as was recognised by the Court of Appeal in *Newbigging v Adam.*[2] A classic example of this distinction is provided by *Whittington v Scale-Hayne.*[3] The claimants, breeders of prize poultry, were induced to take a lease of the defendant's premises by his innocent misrepresentation that the premises were in a thoroughly sanitary condition. Under the lease, the claimants covenanted to execute all works required by any local or public authority. Owing to the insanitary condition of the premises the water supply was poisoned, the claimants' manager and his family became very ill, and the poultry became valueless for breeding purposes or died. In addition, the local authority required the drains to be renewed. The claimants sought an indemnity for the following losses: the value of the stock lost; loss of profit on sales; loss of breeding season; rent, and medical expenses on behalf of the manager. The trial judge rescinded the lease and held that the claimants could recover an indemnity for what they had spent on rent, rates and repairs under the covenants in the lease, because these expenses arose necessarily out of the occupation of the premises or were incurred under the covenants in the lease and were thus obligations necessarily created by the contract. However, the judge refused to award an indemnity for the loss of stock, loss of profits, loss of breeding season or the medical expenses, since to do so would be to award damages, not an indemnity, there being no obligation created by the contract to carry on a poultry farm on the premises or to employ a manager, etc.

1   *Whittington v Scale-Hayne* (1900) 82 LT 49, adopting the view of Bowen LJ in *Newbigging v Adam* (1886) 34 Ch D 582, CA.
2   (1886) 34 Ch D 582, CA.
3   (1900) 82 LT 49.

12.33   Two further points may be made concerning the award of an indemnity:

- Being ancillary to rescission, an indemnity cannot be awarded if rescission is barred.
- The remedy of an indemnity is redundant where the court can, and does, award damages for misrepresentation. However, where there has merely been an innocent misrepresentation and the court decides not to award damages in lieu of rescission, the availability of an award of an indemnity is very important.

Active misrepresentations which have become contractual terms
12.34   Whether a misrepresentation made during pre-contractual negotiations has become a term of the resulting contract, or of a contract collateral to it, is determined in accordance with the rules set out in paras 7.10 to 7.17 above.

If the misrepresentation has become a contractual term the misrepresentee has a choice between two courses of action.

Breach of contract
12.35   As in the case of the breach of any other contractual term, the misrepresentee can sue for breach of contract. If he does so, he can recover damages for breach of contract (as opposed to damages for misrepresentation). Where the misrepresentation relates to the subject matter of the contract, damages will be assessed according to the normal contractual rule, the 'loss of expectations' rule, and recovery can also be had for all consequential loss, provided the loss was within the parties' reasonable contemplation, at the time the contract was made, as a seriously possible result of the breach. The relevant law has already been discussed in detail in chapter 11. In addition, if the misrepresentation has become a condition of the contract, or an 'intermediate term' and there has been a

sufficiently serious breach of it, the misrepresentee can also terminate the contract for breach, a matter which we discussed in paras 8.14 to 8.31 above.

Misrepresentation Act 1967, s 1(a)

12.36 The misrepresentee's alternative course of action is to make use of the Misrepresentation Act 1967, s 1(a). Under this provision a person who is induced to enter into a contract by a misrepresentation of fact, which has become a term of the contract, can elect to rescind the contract for misrepresentation subject to the bars to rescission mentioned in para 12.18 above.

However, if he does so rescind he cannot recover damages for breach of contract since rescission for misrepresentation sets the contract aside for all purposes, including his right to claim damages for its breach, although he may be able to recover damages for misrepresentation, depending on the circumstances, in accordance with the rules set out in paras 12.20 to 12.31 above.

12.37 The choice of a particular course of action will depend very much on whether greater damages will be obtained for breach of contract or for misrepresentation and on whether the claimant wishes, and is able, to rescind for misrepresentation.

Avoidance of provision excluding or limiting liability for misrepresentation

12.38 The Misrepresentation Act 1967, s 3 provides that if a contract contains a term which would exclude or restrict:

- any liability to which a party to a contract may be subject by reason of any misrepresentation made by him before the contract was made; or
- any remedy available to another party to the contract by reason of such a misrepresentation,

that term is of no effect, except in so far as it satisfies the requirement of reasonableness. It is for the person claiming that it satisfies that requirement to show that it does. The requirement of reasonableness is that the term must have been a fair and reasonable one to be included having regard to the circumstances which were, or ought reasonably to have been, known to or in the contemplation of the parties when the contract was made.[1]

It is important to note that what must be considered under the requirement of reasonableness is the term itself and its potential effect in respect of any liability for any misrepresentation covered by it, as opposed to its effect in respect of the particular liability for the actual misrepresentation made.[2]

1   Unfair Contract Terms Act 1977, s 11(1). See, further, para 9.18 above.
2   *Thomas Witter Ltd v TBP Industries Ltd* [1996] 2 All ER 573.

12.39 Section 3 is of great importance in relation to the purported exclusion or restriction of liability for misrepresentations made by estate agents. Where an estate agent makes a misrepresentation in respect of a property which he has been instructed to sell and thereby induces another to enter into a contract to buy it, it is his client who becomes liable for misrepresentation to the other party,[1] although the client may seek to recover an indemnity for his loss from the agent[2] and the agent himself may be held liable to the other party in tort if deceit or negligence can be proved.

Not surprisingly, in an attempt to exclude or restrict a client's liability for a misrepresentation made by his estate agent, auction conditions, conditions of sale by tender and the like often contain a contract term (exemption clause) purporting so to exclude or restrict. Such a term is caught by the Misrepresentation Act 1967, s 3 and is of no effect except in so far as it satisfies the requirement of reasonableness. In this context, a 'contract term' is not limited to one which expressly excludes or restricts liability or a remedy, since it has been held that it also includes a term of the contract purporting to nullify any representation altogether so as to bring about a situation in law as if there was no representation, such as a term that 'although the particulars are believed to be correct their accuracy is not guaranteed and any intending purchaser must satisfy himself by inspection or otherwise as to their correctness'.[3]

On the other hand, the wording of an 'entire agreement clause'[4] which states that the parties have not relied on any representation not set out in the written contract is sufficient to preclude the parties from asserting that they relied on any representation not contained in the written contract, and therefore to prevent any liability arising for any such misrepresentation actually made. In such a case, s 3 does not apply. The reason is that it would be bizarre to attribute to the parties an intention to exclude a liability which they must have thought could never arise.[5] In addition, a contract term which denies that an estate agent has any authority at all to make representations is not caught by s 3 and may therefore prevent the client from incurring liability for a misrepresentation by the estate agent.[6]

It must be emphasised that s 3 is solely concerned with 'contract terms' (ie exemption clauses contained in a contract), and has no application to non-contractual clauses of the type commonly found in estate agents' particulars. Although it has been held that such a non-contractual clause denying that an estate agent has any authority to make representations is effective to prevent the client incurring liability for a misrepresentation by the estate agent,[7] it has been suggested that other non-contractual clauses purporting to exclude or restrict the client's liability for misrepresentation are ineffective to do so.[8]

1   Para 15.29 below.
2   Para 16.15 below.
3   Cremdean Properties Ltd v Nash (1977) 244 EG 547, CA; Walker v Boyle [1982] 1 All ER 634, [1982] 1 WLR 495; South Western General Property Co Ltd v Marton (1982) 263 Estates Gazette 1090.
4   Para 7.8 above.
5   Watford Electronics Ltd v Sanderson CFL Ltd [2001] EWCA Civ 317, [2001] 1 All ER (Comm) 696. Such a statement would not prevent liability for deceit if there has been a fraudulent misrepresentation.
6   Overbrooke Estates Ltd v Glencombe Properties Ltd [1974] 3 All ER 511; cf South Western General Property Co Ltd v Marton (1982) 263 Estates Gazette 1090 (where s 3 was applied to such a term but without any consideration or mention of whether s 3 applied to an authority-denying term).
7   Collins v Howell-Jones (1980) 259 Estates Gazette 331, CA.
8   Cremdean Properties Ltd v Nash (1977) 244 Estates Gazette 547 at 551.

12.40   Section 3 not only applies where the relevant misrepresentation has remained a mere representation but also where it has become a contractual term, at least as far as rescission for misrepresentation and damages for misrepresentation are concerned, although it is uncertain whether it applies if the misrepresentee elects to treat it as a breach of contract.

Misrepresentation through non-disclosure

12.41   Generally, mere silence as to a material fact or tacit acquiescence in another's erroneous belief concerning such a fact does not constitute a misrepresentation. Thus, in Turner v Green,[1] where two solicitors arranged a compromise of certain legal proceedings, the failure of the claimant's solicitor to inform the defendant's of a material fact was held not to be a ground for relief, even though the defendant would not have made the compromise if he had known of that fact.

1   [1895] 2 Ch 205.

12.42   However, in certain situations there is a duty to disclose material facts, breach of which gives rise to relief. Two of these situations have been referred to already: where silence distorts a positive assertion and where a positive assertion is falsified by later events (see para 12.10 above). In these cases silence is deemed to be an active misrepresentation. In addition, in the case of contracts *uberrimae fidei* – of the utmost good faith – a duty to disclose fully all material facts is imposed, breach of which is regarded as a misrepresentation through non-disclosure for which relief is available.

Contracts uberrimae fidei can be divided into two main types:

* insurance contracts; and
* contracts where one party is in a fiduciary relationship with the other.

Insurance contracts

12.43   An intending insurer or insured is under a duty to disclose all material facts known to him.[1] In the case of an intending insured, a material fact is one which would have an effect, not necessarily a decisive influence, on the mind of a prudent insurer in deciding whether to accept the risk or as to the premium to be charged.[2] In the case of an intending insurer, a material fact is one relating to the nature of the risk to be covered or the recoverability of a claim, which a prudent insured would take into account in deciding whether or not to place the risk in question with that insurer.[3] The duty of disclosure only extends to those material facts which are actually known to an intending insurer or insured.[4] If a material fact is not disclosed as required, the other party cannot rely on it as a ground to avoid the contract if it did not induce him to make the contract.[5]

1   *Banque Financière de la Cité SA v Westgate Insurance Co Ltd* [1989] 2 All ER 952, CA; affd [1990] 2 All ER 947, HL.
2   *Pan Atlantic Insurance Co Ltd v Pine Top Insurance Co Ltd* [1994] 3 All ER 581, HL.
3   *Banque Financière de la Cité SA v Westgate Insurance Co Ltd* [1989] 2 All ER 952, CA; affd [1990] 2 All ER 947, HL.
4   *Joel v Law Union and Crown Insurance Co* [1908] 2 KB 863, CA.
5   See, for example *Pan Atlantic Insurance Co Ltd v Pine Top Insurance Co Ltd* [1994] 3 All ER 581, HL.

Contracts where one party is in a fiduciary relationship of confidence with the other

12.44   Where one prospective contracting party stands in a confidential relationship with the other (such as parent and child; solicitor or accountant and client; trustee and beneficiary; partner and partner and principal and agent)[1] he is under a duty to disclose any material fact known to him. The same duty of disclosure applies where one person has placed himself in such a position that he becomes obliged to act fairly and with due regard to the interests of the other party.[2]

1   See paras 12.50–12.51 below.
2   *Tate v Williamson* (1866) 2 Ch App 55.

12.45   The effect of a breach of the duty of disclosure in contracts uberrimae fidei is that the person to whom the duty was owed can have the contract rescinded, in which case an indemnity can be awarded where appropriate. The same bars to rescission apply as described above. Alternatively, the person to whom the duty was owed can refuse to carry out the contract and, provided (generally) that he returns what he obtained under it, successfully resist any claim for damages for breach of duty.[1] The Misrepresentation Act 1967 does not apply to misrepresentation through non-disclosure in contracts uberrimae fidei, nor do the common law rules relating to liability for negligent misrepresentation. However, in the case of non-disclosure by a fiduciary, the fiduciary can be ordered to pay equitable compensation for any resulting loss suffered by the other party.[2] This is important where the right to rescind has been lost.

1   *Banque Financière de la Cité SA v Westgate Insurance Co Ltd* [1989] 2 All ER 952, CA; affd [1990] 2 All ER 947, HL.
2   *Nationwide Building Society v Various Solicitors (No 3)* [1999] PNLR 606.

Duress and undue influence

12.46   In some situations a contract can be avoided on the ground that it has been procured by illegitimate pressure or that unfair influence over a contracting party has been proved or may be presumed. The first case is governed by the common law of duress, and the second by principles of equity relating to undue influence and to what may be called 'unconscionable bargains'.

Duress
12.47   At one time only duress to the person, ie actual or threatened personal violence or imprisonment, sufficed for duress at common law.[1] In recent times, however, it has been held that economic duress, eg a threat to goods or to a person's business or a threat to break a contract, can also constitute duress at common law.[2]

To constitute duress at common law, the pressure must be 'illegitimate'. Legitimate commercial pressure cannot constitute duress.[3] Pressure will be illegitimate if what is threatened is unlawful (ie a breach of contract, tort or crime).[4] Pressure can also be illegitimate, even though the threat is of lawful action, because of the nature of the pressure and of the demand to which it relates. Consequently, a threat to assault someone can amount to duress (because what is threatened is unlawful) and so can a threat to report a crime to the police unless a demand is complied with (because the pressure is illegitimate on the second ground).[4] Cases where a threat of lawful action amounts to illegitimate pressure will be rare in commercial dealings. The Court of Appeal has held that where parties are traders dealing at arm's length and one threatens lawful action (eg not to grant credit) thinking in good faith that his demand is valid, it will be particularly difficult to establish illegitimate pressure, and relatively rare if he did not consider his demand valid.[5]

Even if there is illegitimate pressure, it will not constitute duress unless the victim has been coerced by that pressure into doing something because he had no practical alternative to submission to the pressure, so that he cannot be regarded as having given his true consent to that act.[3]

If duress is proved, it is irrelevant that that was not the sole or predominant cause inducing the contract, provided that it was a cause.[6]

It appears that duress renders a contract voidable, so that it is valid unless and until rescinded by the coerced party,[4] not void.

1   Co Litt 353b; *Cumming v Ince* (1847) 11 QB 112 at 120.
2   *Pao On v Lau Yiu Long* [1980] AC 614, [1979] 3 All ER 65, PC.
3   *Pao On v Lau Yiu Long; Hennessy v Craigmyle & Co Ltd* [1986] ICR 461, CA.
4   *Universe Tankships Inc of Monrovia v International Transport Workers Federation, The Universe Sentinel* [1982] 2 All ER 67, HL.
5   *CTN Cash and Carry Ltd v Gallaher Ltd* [1994] 4 All ER 714, CA.
6   *Barton v Armstrong* [1975] 2 All ER 465, PC.

Undue influence
12.48   A contract which falls within the equitable doctrine of undue influence is voidable at the instance of the party influenced. Two types of case fall within the equitable doctrine:

*   where actual undue influence is proved;
*   where there is a confidential relationship, actual or presumed, between two people, of which the dominant person takes unfair advantage. A confidential relationship is

one where one party (the dominant party) has influence or ascendancy over the other, so that the other places trust and confidence in him.

Actual undue influence

12.49 The party alleging undue influence must prove that the other party actually exerted unfair or improper influence over him and thereby procured a contract that would not otherwise have been made, as where a bank procured a mortgage from a father by a threat to prosecute his son for forgery otherwise.[1] There is no need for him to prove that the contract is manifestly disadvantageous to him.[2]

Developments in the common law rules of duress mean that there is now little difference in coverage between those rules and the equitable rules on actual undue influence.

1   *Williams v Bayley* (1866) LR 1 HL 200, HL.
2   *CIBC Mortgages plc v Pitt* [1993] 4 All ER 433, HL.

Unfair advantage of confidential relationship by dominant party

12.50 In some types of relationship it is presumed that there exists a confidential relationship between the two parties, as a result of which the dominant party owes a duty to deal fairly with the other. Examples are the relationships of: parent and child;[1] solicitor or accountant and client;[2] and trustee and beneficiary;[3] in each of which the first-named party is presumed to be in a position to influence the other. While the list of relationships which can be presumed to be confidential is not closed, it has been held that the relationships between husband and wife[4] and between employer and employee[5] are not presumed to be confidential.

In the case of relationships presumed to be confidential, the relationship, coupled with the nature of the transaction and whether or not it is advantageous to the non-dominant party, may justify a rebuttable presumption of undue influence on the part of the dominant party. For example, if a solicitor has bought land from a client at an under-value, a rebuttable presumption of undue influence will arise, but not if he has made a reasonable charge for professional services to a client.[6] The presumption of undue influence is rebuttable by proof that the dominant party did deal fairly with the non-dominant party and that the latter's consent was given with knowledge of the true facts and was given freely, independent of any sort of influence. One, but not the only,[7] way of rebutting the presumption is by showing that the non-dominant party entered into the transaction only after its nature and effect were explained by an independent qualified person properly informed of the facts.[7]

1   *Bainbrigge v Browne* (1881) 18 Ch D 188.
2   *Wright v Carter* [1903] 1 Ch 27, CA.
3   *Beningfield v Baxter* (1886) 12 App Cas 167, PC.
4   *Howes v Bishop* [1909] 2 KB 390, CA.
5   *Mathew v Bobbins* (1980) 41 P & CR 1, CA.
6   *Royal Bank of Scotland v Etridge (No 2)* [2001] UKHL 44, [2001] 4 All ER 449 at 482.
7   *Inche Noriah v Shaik Allie Bin Omar* [1929] AC 127, PC.

12.51 Outside the relationships just mentioned, it is open to a party to prove that his relationship with the other was actually confidential (ie that the other has influence or ascendancy over him, so that he placed trust and confidence in the other) and that the other has abused that relationship by not dealing fairly with him and having proper regard for his interests. Whether or not there has prima facie been such an abuse, when such a relationship is proved, depends on the evidence, including the nature of the transaction and whether or not it is advantageous to the ascendant party. If there is prima facie evidence, undue influence will be inferred unless the dominant party adduces evidence to disprove that conclusion.[1]

Thus, although the relationship of husband and wife, of employer and employee, of banker and customer[2] and of creditor and debtor are not presumed to be confidential, undue influence can be established under the present heading if on the facts it can be proved that there was a confidential relationship between the parties and that the dominant party has abused that relationship.

1   *Royal Bank of Scotland v Etridge (No 2)* [2001] UKHL 44, [2001] 4 All ER 449.
2   *National Westminster Bank plc v Morgan* [1985] 1 All ER 821, HL.

Undue influence or misrepresentation in respect of a loan: attribution to lender

12.52   It can happen that a person under the undue influence of a third party (or of a co-contracting party) makes a contract in respect of a loan. An example is where someone under another's influence contracts with a bank to guarantee a loan by the bank to the third party. The unduly influenced person can have a contract which is not to his financial advantage rescinded if:

*   the third party was an agent of the other party to the contract, which is normally unlikely; or
*   when making the contract, the other contracting party had actual notice (ie actually knew) or constructive notice that there had been undue influence.[1]

The same rules apply where a dominant person in a confidential relationship has by misrepresentation induced the weaker one to contract with another.[2]

Whether or not there was constructive notice of any undue influence or misrepresentation depends on whether the other contracting party knew of facts which should have put him on inquiry. If he did, he will have constructive notice unless he proves that he took reasonable steps to satisfy himself that the agreement of the party in question had been properly obtained. The law has been developed in relation to the situation where a wife offers to guarantee her husband's debts to a bank. The following principles, however, are equally applicable where a husband guarantees his wife's debts or one sexual partner guarantees the other partner's debts. They were laid down by the House of Lords in *Royal Bank of Scotland plc v Etridge (No 2)*.[3] The principles which follow are those which apply to transactions entered into after the House of Lords' decision; previous transactions are dealt with by rather different principles which will become time-expired in due course.

A bank is put on inquiry whenever a wife offers to stand surety for her husband's debts because on its face such a transaction is not to the wife's financial advantage and there is a substantial risk in such transactions of undue influence or misrepresentation by the husband.

Once a bank is put on inquiry it must bring home to the wife the risks of the transaction which she is offering to guarantee. The bank does not have to do so by meeting with her personally as long as it is reasonable for it to assume that a solicitor has advised the wife on her own behalf.

Before the wife goes to a solicitor for advice, the bank must communicate directly with her, informing her that it will require written confirmation from him that he has fully explained to her the nature of the transaction and its practical consequences and telling her that the purpose of this requirement is the bank's own protection (ie that after receiving the independent legal advice she will not be able to dispute that she is legally bound by the guarantee). The bank must not proceed until it has received an appropriate response from the wife.

The solicitor must advise the wife at a meeting held in the husband's absence. The solicitor must explain to her the purpose for which he is involved, namely that, should it become necessary, the bank will rely on his involvement to counter any suggestion that the wife's will was overborne by her husband or that she did not properly understand the implications of the transaction. Typically, the solicitor should go on to:

*   explain the nature of the documents and their practical consequences for the wife if she signs them;

- point out the seriousness of the risks involved, the amount of her liability, under the guarantee, the amount and principal terms of the loan and the bank's ability to increase the loan or change its terms without reference to the wife;
- discuss the wife's financial means;
- state clearly that the wife has a choice about agreeing to the guarantee;
- check whether she wishes to proceed; and
- ask her whether she is content for him to confirm to the bank that he has explained the nature of the documents and their practical implications for her or whether, for instance, she would prefer him to negotiate on terms with the bank.

The solicitor must not give any confirmation to the bank without the wife's authority. On receipt of such confirmation in writing the bank will be regarded as being discharged from its obligation to take reasonable steps to ensure that the wife's agreement has been properly obtained and it will be difficult, if not impossible, for the wife later to assert against it a defence based on the undue influence of the husband or misrepresentation by him.

1   *Barclays Bank plc v O'Brien* [1993] 4 All ER 417, HL; *CIBC Mortgages plc v Pitt* [1993] 4 All ER 433, HL.
2   *Barclays Bank plc v Boulter* [1999] 4 All ER 513, HL.
3   [2001] UKHL 44, [2001] 4 All ER 449.

Unconscionable bargains

12.53   Acting under equitable principles, a court will rescind a contract on the basis that unfair advantage has been taken by one party (or his agent) of the other party who was poor, ignorant, weak-minded, illiterate, unfamiliar with the English language, or otherwise in need of special protection.[1] It is insufficient to prove that the terms of the contract were harsh or oppressive; it must also be shown that the 'dominant party' has imposed the terms in a morally reprehensible manner, ie in a way which affects his conscience.[2] In other words, the other party must show impropriety in both the terms of the agreement and the manner in which it was arrived at.[3]

The law on unconscionable bargains has the same basis as the other areas of equitable intervention which have just been mentioned: inequality of bargaining power. Although there are dicta in some cases that this 'common thread' permits the courts to intervene in contractual situations other than those involving pressure or influence, or the taking of an unfair advantage of a poor, ignorant or weak-minded party or one otherwise in need of special protection, fairly recent decisions have rejected the argument that inequality of bargaining power is in itself a ground for rescinding a contract.[4]

1   *Evans v Llewellin* (1787) 1 Cox Eq Cas 333.
2   *Crédit Lyonnais Bank Nederland NV v Burch* [1997] 1 All ER 144 at 152-153.
3   *Kalsep Ltd v X-Flow BV* [2001] All ER (D) 113 (Mar).
4   *Alec Lobb (Garages) Ltd v Total Oil GB Ltd* [1985] 1 All ER 303, CA.

Bars to rescission

12.54   Where a contract is voidable for duress or undue influence, or because it is an unconscionable bargain, it is valid unless and until it is rescinded. Rescission will be barred in three cases.[1]

1   Where a rescission is barred in a case involving a confidential relationship, equitable compensation for resulting loss is available because of the breach of the fiduciary duty: *Longstaff v Birtles* [2001] EWCA Civ 1219, [2002] 1 WLR 470.

Affirmation

12.55   Rescission is barred if, after the pressure or influence, or relationship giving rise to a presumption of undue influence, has ceased, the party influenced expressly or impliedly affirms the contract.[1] An unreasonable lapse of time after removal of the influence before seeking rescission of the contract is a particularly important evidential factor suggesting affirmation,[2] and so is the fact that the party influenced performs obligations under the contract without protest.[3] A person can be held to have affirmed even though he has not had independent advice after the removal of the influence[4] and did not know that he could have the contract rescinded, provided he was aware that he might have rights and deliberately refrained from finding out.[5]

1   *Allcard v Skinner* (1887) 36 Ch D 145, CA.
2   *Allcard v Skinner.*
3   *North Ocean Shipping Co v Hyundai Construction Co, The Atlantic Baron* [1978] 3 All ER 1170.
4   *Mitchell v Homfray* (1881) 8 QBD 587, CA.
5   *Allcard v Skinner* (1887) 36 Ch D 145 at 192.

Inability to restore
12.56   Since, as in the case of misrepresentation, the party seeking to rescind must restore what he obtained under the contract, an inability to do so is a bar to rescission.[1]

However, precise restitution is not necessary; where precise restitution is not possible the same principles apply as in the case of rescission for misrepresentation.[2]

1   *O'Sullivan v Management Agency and Music Ltd* [1985] 3 All ER 351, CA.
2   Para 12.18 above.

Purchasers without notice
12.57   The right to rescission is lost if a third party acquires an interest for value in the property transferred by the party influenced, without notice of the pressure or influence, or of the facts giving rise to a presumption of undue influence, in question.[1] Rescission is, of course, not barred if the third party does not provide consideration or, where he does, if he has notice of the facts.[2]

1   *O'Sullivan v Management Agency and Music Ltd* [1985] 3 All ER 351, CA.
2   *Lancashire Loans Ltd v Black* [1934] 1 KB 380, CA.

Unfair terms in consumer contracts

12.58   We saw in para 9.25 above, that the Unfair Terms in Consumer Contracts Regulations 1999 (replacing regulations of the same name made in 1994), which give domestic effect to EC Directive on Unfair Terms in Consumer Contracts, Directive 93/13/EEC, are concerned not only with exemption clauses but with unfair terms in general in *consumer* contracts relating to the sale or supply of goods or the supply of a service. The object of the Regulations is to protect consumers against the inclusion of unfair and prejudicial terms in standard form contracts. In para 9.25 above, we contrasted the coverage of the Unfair Contract Terms Act 1977 with that of the directive in relation to exemption clauses.
The Regulations deal with two separate issues:

•   unfair terms in consumer contracts; and
•   interpretation of written terms in consumer contracts,

provided in each case that the term is one to which the Regulations apply.

Terms to which the Regulations apply
12.59   Regulation 4(1) provides that the Regulations apply to unfair terms in contracts, whether written or oral, between 'a *seller or a supplier*' and 'a *consumer*'. 'Seller or supplier'

means any natural or legal person who, in contracts covered by these Regulations, is acting for purposes relating *to his trade, business or profession, whether publicly owned or privately owned.* 'Consumer' means any natural person who, in contracts covered by these Regulations, is acting for purposes which *are outside his trade, business or profession.*[1] A company or other legal person cannot be a 'consumer' for the purpose of the Regulations.

1   Reg 3(1).

Unfair terms

12.60   The Regulations subject any term to which they apply to a test of fairness, save for an exception set out in reg 6(2). This provides that, *in so far as it is in plain, intelligible language*, the assessment of the fairness of a term must not relate to:

*   the definition of the main subject matter of the contract, or
*   the adequacy of the price or remuneration as against the goods or services supplied in exchange.

In other words, terms of these types are excluded from the requirement of fairness. The meaning of these exceptions, especially the first, is obscure. In *Director General of Fair Trading v First National Bank plc,*[1] the House of Lords held that they should not be given a liberal interpretation; the object of the Regulations would be frustrated if reg 6(2) was interpreted so as to exclude from the assessment of fairness a term which did not fall plainly within it. The House held that a term in a credit agreement providing for the payment by the borrower of interest 'after as well as before' any judgment against him in the event of default plainly did not concern the adequacy of the interest earned by the bank as its remuneration but was designed to ensure that the bank's entitlement to interest did not come to an end on the entry of judgment, as otherwise it would have. The House of Lords concluded, however, that the term was not an unfair term on the facts.

1   [2001] UKHL 52, [2002] 1 All ER 97.

Test of fairness

12.61   By reg 5(1), a contractual term which has not been individually negotiated is to be regarded as unfair if, contrary to the requirement of good faith, it causes a significant imbalance in the parties' rights and obligations arising under the contract, to the detriment of the consumer.

Regulation 5(2) provides that a term is always to be regarded as not having been individually negotiated where it has been *drafted in advance and the consumer has not been able to influence the substance of the term.* Regulation 5(3) adds that, notwithstanding that a specific term or certain aspects of it in a contract has been individually negotiated, the Regulations apply to the rest of a contract if an overall assessment of the contract indicates that it is a pre-formulated standard contract.

If a *seller or supplier* claims that a term was *individually negotiated*, he has the burden of proving this.[1]

Two elements of unfairness can be derived from reg 5(1):

*   the term must cause significant imbalance to the parties' rights and obligations to the detriment of the consumer; and
*   this 'significant imbalance' must be 'contrary to the requirement of good faith'.

Regulation 5(1) lays down a composite test covering both the making and the substance of the contract; in applying it regard must be had to the object of the Regulations.[2]

In *Director General of Fair Trading v First National Bank plc*,[3] the House of Lords held that the requirement of significant imbalance was met if, looking at the contract as a whole, a term was so weighted in favour of the seller or supplier as to tilt the parties' rights and obligations under the contract significantly in his favour.

Turning to the requirement of good faith, it held that it was one of 'fair and open dealing'. 'Openness', it held, required that the terms should be expressed fully, clearly and legibly, containing no traps. Appropriate prominence should be given to terms potentially disadvantageous to the consumer. 'Fair dealing', it continued, required that a seller or supplier should not take advantage, even unconsciously, of the consumer's necessity, lack of money, lack of experience, unfamiliarity with the subject matter, weak bargaining position or any other factor listed in or analogous to those listed in Sch 2 to the Regulations referred to below.

Schedule 2 to the Regulations contains an indicative, non-exhaustive and lengthy list of terms which *may* be regarded as unfair. These are terms which have the object or effect of, for example:

- excluding or limiting the legal liability of a seller or supplier in the event of the death of a consumer or personal injury to the latter resulting from an act or omission of that seller or supplier;
- inappropriately excluding or limiting the legal rights of the consumer vis-à-vis the seller or supplier or another party in the event of total or partial non-performance or inadequate performance by the seller or supplier of any of the contractual obligations, including the option of offsetting a debt owed to the seller or supplier against any claim which the consumer may have against him;
- making an agreement binding on the consumer whereas provision of services by the seller or supplier is subject to a condition whose realisation depends on his own will alone;
- permitting the seller or supplier to retain sums paid by the consumer where the latter decides not to conclude or perform the contract, without providing for the consumer to receive compensation of an equivalent amount from the seller or supplier where the latter is the party cancelling the contract;
- requiring any consumer who fails to fulfil his obligation to pay a disproportionately high sum in compensation;
- irrevocably binding the consumer to terms with which he had no real opportunity of becoming acquainted before the conclusion of the contract;
- enabling the seller or supplier to alter unilaterally without a valid reason any characteristics of the product or service to be provided;
- giving the seller or supplier the right to determine whether the goods or services supplied are in conformity with the contract, or giving him the exclusive right to interpret any term of the contract;
- obliging the consumer to fulfil all his obligations where the seller or supplier does not perform his;
- giving the seller or supplier the possibility of transferring his rights and obligations under the contract, where this may serve to reduce the guarantees for the consumer, without the latter's agreement.

As with the test of reasonableness under the Unfair Contract Terms Act 1977,[4] the test of fairness is assessed as at the time of the conclusion of the contract. Regulation 6(1) provides that the unfairness of a contractual term must be assessed, taking into account the nature of the goods or services for which the contract was concluded and by referring, as at the time of the conclusion of the contract, to all circumstances attending the conclusion of the contract and to all the other terms of the contract or of another contract on which it is dependent.

Unlike the provisions relating to the requirement of reasonableness in the Unfair Contract Terms Act 1977,[4] no provision is made concerning the burden of proof. Thus, it is for the consumer to prove that the test of fairness is not satisfied.

1 Reg 5(4).
2 *Director General of Fair Trading v First National Bank plc* [2001] UKHL 52, [2002] 1 All ER 97 at para 17.
3 [2001] UKHL 52, [2002] 1 All ER 97.
4 Para 9.18 above.

12.62 *Consequence of inclusion of unfair term* An unfair term under the provisions of the Regulations is not binding on the consumer.[1] However, the rest of the contract continues to bind the parties if it is capable of continuing in existence without the unfair term.[2]

1 Reg 8(1).
2 Reg 8(2).

Interpretation of written terms in consumer contracts

12.63 By reg 7, a seller or supplier must ensure that any written contractual term to which the Regulations apply is expressed in plain, intelligible language. The only effect of a breach of this requirement is that, where there is doubt about the meaning of a written term, the interpretation most favourable to the consumer prevails, the term is not rendered ineffective.

Chapter 13

Contracts in restraint of trade

13.1 Contracts in restraint of trade may be void at common law or, in some cases (which are outside the scope of this book), by legislation.

In this chapter we describe:

- the principal types of restraints of trade caught by the common law rules;
- the effect where a restraint is void under those rules.

Contracts (or more commonly covenants, ie promises in them) in restraint of trade include:

- agreements restricting the subsequent occupation of an employee;
- agreements restricting the subsequent occupation of a partner;
- agreements between the vendor and purchaser of the goodwill of a business restricting competition by the vendor.

Such contracts are not necessarily void at common law. They are valid and enforceable at common law if certain tests are satisfied.

Tests of validity

13.2 The general tests of validity applicable to contracts falling within the restraint of trade doctrine are as follows:

- A contract in restraint of trade is prima facie void; but
- Such a contract will be valid and enforceable if–
  - the party seeking to enforce it shows that the restraint is reasonable between the parties to the contract in protection of a recognised interest of that party; and,

    the other party does not show that the restraint is unreasonable in the public interest.[1]

The tests of reasonableness must be applied as at the date the contract was made and in the light of the then existing facts and of what might possibly happen in the future. Anything else which has occurred subsequently must be ignored.[2] The tests must also be applied by reference to what the terms of the restraint entitle or require the parties to do, and not by reference to what they have actually done or intend to do.[3]

A restraint of trade which is not void is most commonly enforced by an injunction restraining the defendant from breaking it.

1   These tests have their foundation in *Nordenfelt v Maxim Nordenfeldt Guns and Ammunition Co Ltd* [1894] AC 535, HL and *Herbert Morris Ltd v Saxelby* [1916] 1 AC 688, HL.
2   *Putsman v Taylor* [1927] 1 KB 637 at 643; *Gledhow Autoparts Ltd v Delaney* [1965] 3 All ER 288 at 295.
3   *Watson v Prager* [1991] 3 All ER 487, CA.

Agreements restricting the subsequent occupation of an employee

13.3   A contract between employer and employee, normally the contract of employment, may contain a covenant (promise) by the employee that he will not be employed in, or conduct, a business competing with his employer's after leaving his employment. Although this is the common form of a covenant restricting subsequent occupation, such a covenant need not be formed in these terms. A covenant is also in restraint of trade where it contains a restriction which provides that after leaving his employer's employment an employee shall be paid a pension or arrears of commission provided that he does not take employment with a competitor of the employer.[1] A covenant restricting the subsequent employment of an employee will normally be limited in duration and area. Being in restraint of trade, it is prima facie void and will only be valid and enforceable if the tests of reasonableness referred to above are satisfied.

1   *Wyatt v Kreglinger and Fernau* [1933] 1 KB 793, CA (facts set out in para 13.7 below).

Reasonable between the parties

13.4   Two things must be proved to satisfy this test:

13.5   *The restriction must protect a legally recognised interest of the employer*   Only two types of interest are so recognised:

*   *Protection of employer's trade secrets or other confidential information equivalent to a trade secret concerning employer's affairs whose disclosure to a competitor would cause significant harm to the employer*[1]   An example of a case involving the protection of trade secrets is provided by *Forster & Sons Ltd v Suggett*.[2] The defendant was the claimant company's works manager. He was instructed in secret methods relating to the production of glass which the claimant company produced. He agreed that, during the five years after the end of his employment with the claimant company, he would not carry on in the United Kingdom, or be interested in, glass bottle manufacturing or any other business connected with glass making as carried on by the company. It was held that this restriction was reasonable to protect the claimant company's trade secrets and an injunction was ordered to restrain breach of it. Examples of information equivalent to a trade secret concerning the employer's affairs, whose disclosure to a competitor would cause significant harm to the employer, are detailed information on costing, customer accounts, profit margins and development plans.[3]
*   *Protection of employer's business connections*   An employer is entitled to prevent an employee misusing influence which he has obtained over the employer's customers and thereby enticing them away.[4] Thus, in *Fitch v Dewes*,[5] where the contract provided that a Tamworth solicitor's managing clerk (who was himself a solicitor) should never practice within seven miles of Tamworth Town Hall, the House of Lords held that the restriction was valid because it constituted a reasonable protection of the employer's business connections against an employee who could gain influence over his clients.

It is not enough merely to show that the restriction purports to protect trade secrets etc or business connections: it must also be shown that they require protection against the particular employee. Thus, the restriction will be invalid if the employee did not know enough about a trade secret to be able to use it or was insufficiently acquainted with customers to be able to influence them. This is shown, for example, by *S W Strange Ltd v Mann*,[6] where a restriction imposed on a bookmaker's manager was held to be void because the business was mostly conducted by telephone and the manager had no chance to get to know his employer's customers or to influence them.

No other interests can be protected validly by the present type of restriction.[7] Consequently, a restriction whose object is simply to protect the employer against competition is invalid,[7] and so is one whose object is to prevent the employee using in another job the skill, experience, know-how and general knowledge acquired as part of his job.[8]

1 *SJB Stephenson Ltd v Mandy* [2000] IRLR 233.
2 (1918) 35 TLR 87.
3 *Poly Lina Ltd v Finch* [1995] FSR 751.
4 *Herbert Morris Ltd v Saxelby* [1916] 1 AC 688 at 709.
5 [1921] 2 AC 158, HL.
6 [1965] 1 All ER 1069.
7 *Herbert Morris Ltd v Saxelby* [1916] 1 AC 688 at 710.
8 *FSS Travel and Leisure Systems v Johnson* [1998] IRLR 382, CA.

13.6 *Reasonableness* To be reasonable between the parties, the restriction must be no wider than is reasonably necessary to protect the employer's trade secrets (or other equivalent information) or business connections. Reasonableness is a matter of degree: the terms of the restriction must be measured against the degree of knowledge or influence which the employee has gained in his employment. A restriction will be void if it relates to a wider range of occupations than is reasonably necessary to protect the relevant protectable interests. Two other factors which are particularly important are the duration and area of restriction.

- *Duration* In *M and S Drapers v Reynolds*,[1] a collector-salesman of a credit drapery firm covenanted not to canvass his employers' customers for a period of five years after leaving their employment. The restriction was held to be void: in view of the lowly position of a collector-salesman it was for a longer period than was reasonably necessary to protect the employers' business connections. On the other hand, the restriction in *Fitch v Dewes* was upheld, even though it was to last for life, because of the degree of influence which the solicitor's managing clerk would gain over his employer's clients.

- *Area* In *Mason v Provident Clothing and Supply Co Ltd*,[2] a canvasser in the claimant company's Islington branch district covenanted not to work in any similar business for three years within 25 miles of London. The restriction was held to be void because it extended further than was reasonably necessary to protect the claimant company's business connections. On the other hand, a covenant by a sales representative employed by a small company that, for two years after leaving his employment, he would not canvass (in the same goods) people who had been customers of his employer during his employment, was upheld in *G W Plowman & Son v Ash*,[3] even though it was unlimited in area.

1 [1956] 3 All ER 814, CA.
2 [1913] AC 724, HL.
3 [1964] 2 All ER 10.

Reasonable in the public interest

13.7 The operation of this test is demonstrated by *Wyatt v Kreglinger and Fernau*.[1] The employers of a wool broker promised to pay him a pension on his retirement provided he did not re-enter the wool trade and did nothing to their detriment (fair competition excepted). The broker subsequently sued for arrears of pension but the Court of Appeal held that he could not succeed since the contract was void for two reasons:

- the restriction was unreasonable as between the parties;
- the contract was unreasonable in the public interest because the permanent restriction on the broker working anywhere in the wool trade deprived the community of services from which it might benefit.

Provided the restriction is reasonable between the parties, employer-employee restrictions will rarely be invalidated on the ground that they are unreasonable in the public interest. However, where the employee has a special skill of particular value to the community, the restriction may well be found unreasonable in the public interest, even though it affords reasonable protection for the employer's trade secrets or business connections.[2]

1   [1933] 1 KB 793, CA.
2   Bull v Pitney-Bowes Ltd [1966] 3 All ER 384.

13.8   It may be noted in passing that, even in the absence of an express restraint, where an employee uses or discloses an employer's trade secrets or confidential information concerning his employer's affairs, or where an employee solicits an employer's customers, the employer can obtain an injunction to restrain this.[1] An employer can also obtain an injunction, even in the absence of an express restraint, to restrain an ex-employee from using or disclosing a trade secret of the employer or confidential information relating to the employer's business equivalent to a trade secret,[2] such as customers' names, which if disclosed to a competitor would cause real or significant harm.[3]

The basis on which such conduct is restrained is that there has been a breach of an implied term of the contract of employment whereby the employee is obliged not to engage in such conduct.[4]

1   Wessex Dairies Ltd v Smith [1935] 2 KB 80; Faccenda Chicken Ltd v Fowler [1986] 1 All ER 617, CA.
2   Faccenda Chicken Ltd v Fowler [1986] 1 All ER 617, CA.
3   Intelsee Systems Ltd v Grech-Cini [1999] 4 All ER 11.
4   Para 7.26 above.

Agreements restricting the subsequent occupation of a partner

13.9   Partnership agreements commonly provide that a partner who ceases to be a partner shall not, for a specified period, act or deal with any client of the firm in the professional capacity in which he was a partner. Such a restraint is valid and enforceable only if it is reasonable as between the parties to protect some legitimate interest of the firm and is not unreasonable in the public interest.[1] What is a legitimate interest of the firm depends largely on the nature of its business and on the ex-partner's position in the firm, but an example of such an interest is a firm's goodwill, ie its commercial reputation, its customer connections and its potential customers through referrals by existing customers.[2]

An example of the present type of restriction is Bridge v Deacons,[3] which was concerned with a covenant in a Hong Kong solicitors' partnership agreement whereby a partner who ceased to be a partner was restricted for five years thereafter from acting as a solicitor in Hong Kong for anyone who had been a client of the firm when he ceased to be a partner or during the preceding three years. The Privy Council held that the covenant, which applied to all the partners, was reasonable as between the parties, since it went no further in extent or time than was reasonable to protect the firm's connections with its clients, and was not unreasonable in the public interest; the covenant was therefore held enforceable against an ex-partner. Likewise, in Espley v Williams,[4] a covenant in an estate agents' partnership agreement that Williams would not practice as an estate agent on his own account, or with any other person or company, within two miles of the partnership premises within two years of the termination of the partnership was held to be reasonable to protect the goodwill of the partnership and was not held to be unreasonable in the public interest.

1   *Bridge v Deacons* [1984] 2 All ER 19, PC; *Edwards v Worboys* [1984] AC 724n, CA.
2   *Allied Dunbar (Frank Weisinger) Ltd v Weisinger* [1988] IRLR 60.
3   [1984] 2 All ER 19, PC.
4   [1997] 08 EG 137, CA.

Agreements between the vendor and purchaser of the goodwill of a business restricting competition by the vendor

13.10   An agreement of the present type is prima facie void for restraint of trade but will be valid and enforceable if it is reasonable between the parties and not unreasonable in the public interest. The following can be said concerning the requirements of reasonableness between the parties.

The restriction must protect the goodwill of the business sold

13.11   An agreement whereby one business surrenders its liberty to trade in a particular field is void since mere competition is not a protectable interest.[1] The restriction must relate to an actual business which has been sold. Thus, even though it is contained in what purports to be a contract for the sale of a business, a restriction will be void if there is no actual business to protect. This is shown by *Vancouver Malt and Sake Brewing Co Ltd v Vancouver Breweries Ltd.*[2] One company held a licence to brew beer and other liquors but the only trade actually carried on by it under the licence was brewing sake. It purported to sell the goodwill of its licence, so far as it related to brewing beer, to the other company and covenanted not to brew beer for 15 years thereafter. The Privy Council held that the covenant was void because, if there was a sale, it was merely a sale of the former company's liberty to brew beer since there was no goodwill of a beer-brewing business to be transferred and the covenant was simply a bare restriction on competition.

Other aspects of the rule that the covenant must protect the goodwill of the business actually sold are demonstrated by *British Reinforced Concrete Engineering Co Ltd v Schelff.*[3] The defendant, who ran a small business for the sale of 'Loop' road reinforcements, sold it to the claimant company, a large company which manufactured and sold 'BRC' road reinforcements. In the contract of sale the defendant covenanted that, for three years after the end of the First World War, he would not 'either alone or jointly or in partnership with any other person or persons whomsoever and either directly or indirectly carry on or manage or be concerned or interested in or act as servant of any person concerned or interested in the business of the manufacture or sale of road reinforcements in any part of the UK'. It was held that this covenant was too wide because it extended to the manufacture of road reinforcements as well as their sale, and thus it sought to protect more than the actual business sold (the sale of road reinforcements) in that it sought to protect the purchaser's existing business (the sale and manufacture of road reinforcements).

1   *Vancouver Malt and Sake Brewing Co Ltd v Vancouver Breweries Ltd* [1934] AC 181, PC.
2   [1934] AC 181, PC.
3   [1921] 2 Ch 563.

The restriction must go no further than is reasonably necessary to protect the business sold

13.12   As was pointed out in *British Reinforced Concrete Engineering Co Ltd v Schelff,*[1] the reasonableness of the restriction must be judged by reference to the extent and circumstances of the business sold, and not by the extent and range of any business already run by the purchaser. Reasonableness is judged from the standpoint of both parties. For example, in the *Schelff* case it was held that the 'servant clause' was unreasonable because it would preclude the defendant from becoming the servant of a trust company which, as part of its investments, held shares in a company manufacturing or selling road reinforcements.

The amount of the consideration for the agreement is a relevant factor in assessing the reasonableness of the restriction.[2] In addition, the duration and area of the restriction are particularly important factors to be taken into account in assessing its reasonableness. The approach of the courts is more liberal here than in the case of employer-employee restrictions because buyers and sellers of businesses are more obviously equal bargaining partners. A good example of this liberality is provided by *Nordenfelt v Maxim Nordenfelt Guns and Ammunition Co Ltd*.[3] N, who had obtained patents for improving quick-firing guns, carried on, among other things, business as a maker of such guns and ammunition. He sold the goodwill and assets of the business to a company, entering into a covenant which restricted his future activities. The company later merged with another to become the claimant company and N's earlier covenant was substantially repeated with it. This covenant provided that for 25 years N would not engage, except on behalf of the company, directly or indirectly in the trade or business of a manufacturer of guns, gun mountings or carriages, gunpowder, explosives or ammunition, or in any business competing or liable to compete in any way with that for the time being carried on by the claimant company. The first part of the covenant, relating to engaging in a business manufacturing guns, etc was held by the House of Lords to provide reasonable protection for the business acquired by the company, even though the restriction was worldwide and was to last 25 years, and was therefore valid. It was recognised, however, that the second part of the covenant, relating to engaging in any business competing with that carried on by the company, was void because it went further than was reasonable to protect the business acquired by the company. Similarly, the restriction in the *Schelff* case, even in so far as it related to the management, etc of a business selling reinforcements, was held void because it applied to the whole of the United Kingdom, which was regarded as a wider area than was necessary to protect the actual business sold.

1   [1921] 2 Ch 563.
2   *Nordenfelt v Maxim Nordenfelt Guns and Ammunition Co Ltd* [1894] AC 535 at 565.
3   [1894] AC 535, HL.

Effect

13.13   Provided that the part of the contract which is void on grounds of public policy can be severed from the rest of the contract, the latter, as opposed to the void part, is enforceable. However, if the void part cannot be severed the whole contract is void and unenforceable. Severance can operate in two ways.

Severance of the whole of an objectionable promise

13.14   If this can be done the rest of the contract is valid and enforceable by the party who made the promise. Severance of a whole promise is not possible if it is the whole or substantially the whole of the consideration furnished by the claimant for the promise by the defendant which the claimant wishes to enforce. Thus, in *Wyatt v Kreglinger and Fernau*, which we discussed in para 13.7 above, it was held that the ex-employee could not enforce the promise to pay him a pension since he had given no valid consideration for it, his only promise – not to compete – being void under the restraint of trade doctrine. This can be contrasted with *Marshall v N M Financial Management Ltd*,[1] where the claimant's contract of employment stated that commission should be payable to him after the termination of his employment, provided that he did not compete with his former employer. This proviso was void under the restraint of trade doctrine. It was held, however, that the claimant could enforce his right to commission because his promise not to compete was not the whole or substantially the whole of the consideration given by him for the former employer's promise to pay it; the main consideration given by him for that promise was his provision of services during the period of his employment.

1   [1997] 1 WLR 1527, CA.

Severance of the objectionable part of a promise

13.15   If severance of part of a promise is possible, the rest of the contract, including the unsevered part of the promise, can be enforced against the party subject to it. Severance of this type is only possible if two tests are satisfied:

The 'blue pencil' test

13.16   This test is only satisfied if the objectionable words can be struck out of the promise as it stands. This was possible in relation to the offending part of the promise in the *Nordenfelt* case, which has been discussed in para 13.12 above. Another example is provided by *Goldsoll v Goldman*.[1] The defendant sold his imitation jewellery business in Old Bond Street to the claimant, another jeweller. The defendant covenanted that for two years he would not 'either solely or jointly with or as agent or employee for any person or company… carry on or be interested in the business of a vendor of or dealer in real or imitation jewellery in the county of London, England, Scotland, Ireland, Wales or any part of the UK and the Isle of Man or in France, the USA, Russia or Spain, or within 25 miles of Potsdamerstrasse, Berlin, or St Stephan's Kirche, Vienna'. The defendant joined a rival jeweller's in New Bond Street within two years and the claimant sought an injunction to restrain breach of the covenant. The Court of Appeal held that the covenant was unreasonably wide in respect of subject matter (for the defendant had not dealt in real jewellery) and also in respect of area (because the defendant had not traded abroad), but that the references to foreign places and real jewellery could be severed because it was possible to delete them from the covenant as it stood. After severance, the covenant merely prohibited dealing in imitation jewellery in the United Kingdom and the Isle of Man, and an injunction was granted to prevent such dealing.

A more recent example is provided by *Anscombe & Ringland v Butchoff*.[2] A & R, a firm of estate agents carrying on business in London, employed B under a contract containing a clause that, for one year after the termination of the contract, B would not undertake 'either alone or in partnership or as a member of a company nor be interested directly or indirectly in the business of an auctioneer, valuer, surveyor or estate agent within a radius of one mile of the firm's office'. B left the firm and soon afterwards set up in business as an estate agent only 150 yards away from A & R's office. It was held:

- that the clause was unreasonable in so far as it forbade B to be interested in the business of a surveyor or valuer, for he had never been a surveyor or valuer, and that part of the clause would be severed; but
- that part of the clause relating to the carrying on of business as an estate agent within the specified area was reasonable and would be enforced.

If the unreasonable part of the promise cannot be deleted from the promise as it stands, severance of it is not possible. The court cannot rewrite the promise by adding or altering even one word so as to make it reasonable. Thus, in *Mason v Provident Clothing and Supply Co Ltd*,[3] which has already been referred to,[4] where the contract in question contained a promise that the employee would not work within 25 miles of London after leaving his employment, the House of Lords held that the promise was too wide in area, and therefore unreasonable, and refused to redraft the clause so as to make it reasonable and enforceable. The whole promise was therefore held void and unenforceable.

1   [1915] 1 Ch 292, CA.
2   (1984) 134 NLJ 37.
3   [1913] AC 724, HL.
4   Para 13.6 above.

Severance of the objectionable part must not alter the nature (as opposed to the extent) of the original contract

13.17   This means that severance of part of a promise is impossible unless it can be construed as being divisible into a number of separate and independent parts. This rule is sensible – otherwise the mechanical deletion of the objectionable part of the promise could radically change the whole contract – but difficult to apply.

The application of this test can be illustrated by two cases. In *Attwood v Lamont*,[1] the claimants owned a general outfitter's business in Kidderminster. The business was divided into a number of departments. The defendant was the head of the tailoring department but had no concern with any other department. In his contract of employment the defendant had undertaken that, after the termination of his employment, he would not 'be concerned in any of the following trades or businesses, that is to say, the trade or business of a tailor, dressmaker, general draper, milliner, hatter, haberdasher, gentlemen's, ladies' or children's outfitter' within 10 miles of Kidderminster. Later the claimants sought to enforce this covenant. They admitted that it was too wide in terms of the trades covered but argued that the references to aspects of the business other than tailoring could be severed, leaving the tailoring restraint enforceable. The Court of Appeal rejected this course because such severance would have altered the whole nature of the covenant: the covenant as it stood was one indivisible covenant (or promise) for the protection of the whole of the claimants' business, not several covenants for the protection of the claimants' several departments, and to alter it would be to alter its nature.

This case can be contrasted with *Scorer v Seymour-Johns*.[2] The defendant was in sole charge of the claimant's estate agency in Kingsbridge, Devon; the main office was in Dartmouth, Devon. He contracted that, for three years after the end of his contract of employment, he would not 'undertake or carry on either alone or in partnership or be employed or interested directly or indirectly in any capacity whatsoever in the business of an auctioneer, surveyor or estate agent or in any ancillary business carried on by [the claimant] at 85, Fore Street, Kingsbridge or Duke Street, Dartmouth aforesaid within a radius of five miles thereof.' After the end of his employment with the claimant, the defendant set up his own estate agency business within five miles of the Kingsbridge office. The covenant in respect of Kingsbridge was held reasonable, but not the covenant in respect of Dartmouth. The latter was severed, and the claimants granted an injunction in relation to the Kingsbridge covenant.

1   [1920] 3 KB 571, CA.
2   [1966] 3 All ER 347.

Chapter 14

Third party rights or obligations under a contract

14.1   A long-established doctrine of contract law is the doctrine of privity of contract. This doctrine consists of two rules:

- only a party[1] to a contract can have rights under it, so that a third party (ie someone who is not a party to a contract) cannot enforce a contract; and
- a contract cannot impose obligations on a third party, so that a contractual obligation cannot bind a third party or be enforced against him.

Both rules are subject to exceptions or qualifications. In particular, the first rule has been made subject to a particularly significant exception by the Contracts (Rights of Third Parties) Act 1999.

1   Although 'party to a contract' normally refers to a person who actually made the contract, a person on whose behalf an agent made an authorised contract is a party to it. In some cases the agent can also still sue or be sued on the contract as well. See paras 15.40-15.45 below.

Contractual rights and third parties

14.2   Until the Contracts (Rights of Third Parties) Act 1999, a third party could not generally enforce a contract, even if it was intended to benefit him. This was affirmed by the House of Lords in a number of cases in the twentieth century.[1] It resulted from two rules:

- As stated in chapter 6, unless a contract is made by deed, a person can only enforce a contractual promise if he has provided consideration for that promise. It is not sufficient that there is consideration in the abstract; it is also necessary for a person seeking to enforce a promise to show that he (or his agent on his behalf) has provided consideration for it.
- Even if a person can be said to have provided consideration for the promise in question, he cannot enforce that promise unless he is a party to it (the doctrine of privity).[2]

These are the traditional rules which have to be satisfied (subject to the 1999 Act and other exceptions or qualifications) before someone can enforce a promise (ie have a right under a contract). Suggested reasons for these rules have been that mere donees should not be able to enforce a contract (relevant only to the first rule) and that the parties to a contract should not have their freedom to vary it restricted by the existence of third party rights. Nevertheless, until the 1999 Act, the law was open to criticism because – apart from the exceptions and qualifications mentioned in para 14.8 below – it prevented effect being given to the intention of the contracting parties (where they had intended to benefit a third party); it was unfair on a third party who had relied on a contract but could not enforce it; it caused difficulties in commercial life, and it was out of step with the position in most other countries in the EU and with the law in New Zealand and many of the jurisdictions in the United States and Australia.

1   Eg *Dunlop Pneumatic Tyre Co Ltd v Selfridge & Co Ltd* [1915] AC 847, HL; *Scruttons Ltd v Midland Silicones Ltd* [1962] 1 All ER 1, HL; *Beswick v Beswick* [1967] 2 All ER 1197, HL.
2   *Dunlop Pneumatic Tyre Co Ltd v Selfridge & Co Ltd* [1915] AC 847, HL.

Contracts (Rights of Third Parties) Act 1999

14.3   Section 1(1) of the Act provides that, subject to the provisions of the Act (described below), a third party to a contract may in his own right enforce a term of the contract if:

• the contract expressly provides that he may; or
• the term purports to confer a benefit on him (unless on a proper construction of the contract the parties did not intend the term to be enforceable by the third party)[1].

In both cases, the third party must be expressly identified in the contract by name, or as a member of a class (eg a reference to 'the employees' of a party) or as answering a particular description (eg a reference to a purchaser from a party in a sale of goods contract).[2] The third party need not be in existence when the contract is entered into.[2] Thus, s 1 can apply to someone who was unborn when the contract was made if he is identifiable in one of the three ways referred to.

For the purpose of exercising his right to enforce a term of the contract, a third party has any remedy (eg damages, an injunction or specific performance) which he would have had if he had been a party to the contract and was bringing an action for breach of contract, subject to the same rules as would have applied to that remedy in such a case.[3]

1   Contracts (Rights of Third Parties) Act 1999, s 1(2).
2   Contracts (Rights of Third Parties) Act 1999, s 1(3).
3   Contracts (Rights of Third Parties) Act 1999, s 1(5).

Exemption clauses: protection of third party

14.4   Where its terms are satisfied, s 1 of the 1999 Act does not simply permit a third party to assert a positive right to sue for damages or some other remedy. It also enables a third party to rely on a term of the contract as a defence to an action brought against him if the contract expressly provides that he may rely on it or purports to confer the benefit of the term on him and (in either case) he is identifiable from the contract, as explained above. This is made clear by s 1(6), which provides that references in the Act to a third party enforcing a term of the contract include references to his availing himself of an exemption clause.

Thus, for example, if a contract between A and B for the carriage of machinery by B provides that B's liability for damage to the machinery is limited to £x and the machinery is damaged by the negligent driving of C, one of B's lorry drivers, C is not protected by the clause if he is sued in negligence by A. On the other hand, if the clause had expressly provided that the liability of B or any of B's employees for loss or damage was restricted to £x, C would be protected by the clause.

Section 3(6) of the 1999 Act provides that where a third party seeks the protection of an exemption clause in reliance on s 1 of the 1999 Act, he may not do so if he could not have done so (whether by reason of any particular circumstances relating to him or otherwise) had he been a party to the contract. Thus, for example, if an exemption clause is of no effect between the parties because of the provisions of the Unfair Contract Terms Act 1977 it likewise cannot be effective in favour of the third party.

Although a person cannot directly take the benefit of an exemption clause if he falls outside the terms of s 1(6) of the 1999 Act, he may indirectly benefit from it in some cases. The reason is that an exemption clause in such a case may limit his duty of care to one of the contracting parties, and hence his liability in tort for negligence. For example, where an exemption clause in a building contract placed the risk of damage by fire on the employer (rather than the building contractor), it was held that it would not be just and reasonable to impose on a sub-contractor hired by the building contractor a duty of care to avoid causing damage by fire.[1]

1   *Norwich City Council v Harvey* [1989] 1 All ER 1180, CA.

Discharge and variation

14.5   Where a third party has a right under s 1 of the 1999 Act to enforce a term of the contract, the parties to the contract are denied by s 2(1) of the 1999 Act the right, by agreement, to discharge the contract, or vary it in such a way as to extinguish or alter his entitlement under that right, without his consent if:

- the third party has communicated[1] his assent to the term to the promisor party (s 2(1)(a));
- the promisor party is aware that the third party has relied on the term (s 2(1)(b)); or
- the promisor party can reasonably be expected to have foreseen that the third party would rely on the term and the third party has in fact relied on it (s 2(1)(c)).

However, by s 2(3), this is subject to any express term of the contract under which:

- the parties may by agreement discharge or vary the contract without the third party's consent; or
- the consent of the third party is required in circumstances specified in the contract instead of those set out in s 2(1)(a)-(c).

Where the third party's consent to a discharge or variation is required that consent can be dispensed with by a court or arbitral tribunal under s 2(4) or (5) of the 1999 Act in certain cases.

Section 2(4) provides that a court or arbitral tribunal may dispense with the third party's consent if satisfied that:

- his consent cannot be obtained because his whereabouts cannot reasonably be ascertained; or
- he is mentally incapable of giving consent.

In addition, by s 2(5), a court or arbitral tribunal may dispense with a consent required under s 2(1)(c) (reasonable foreseeability of, and actual, reliance on term by third party) if it is satisfied that it cannot reasonably be ascertained whether or not the third party has in fact relied on the term.

If the court or arbitral tribunal dispenses with a third party's consent, it may impose such conditions as it thinks fit, including a condition requiring the payment of compensation to the third party.[2]

1   This assent may be by words or conduct. If it is sent to the promisor party by post or other means, it is not regarded as communicated to the promisor until received by him: Contracts (Rights of Third Parties) Act 1999, s 2(2).
2   Contracts (Rights of Third Parties) Act 1999, s 2(6).

Defences etc available to the promisor

14.6   Where proceedings are brought by a third party under s 1 of the 1999 Act to enforce a term of a contract, the promisor party (ie the party against whom enforcement is sought) has available to him by way of defence or set-off any matter that:

- arises from or in connection with the contract and is relevant to the term, and
- would have been available to him by way of defence or set-off if the proceedings had been brought by the promisee party (ie the party who was promised that the benefit would be conferred on the third party).

This is provided by s 3(2) of the 1999 Act.

In addition, by s 3(4) the promisor party also has available to him:

- by way of defence or set-off, any matter; and
- by way of counterclaim, any matter not arising from the contract,

that would have been available to him by way of defence or set-off or, as the case may be, by way of counterclaim *against the third party* if the third party had been a party to the contract.

Sections 3(2) and (4) is subject to any express term of the contract as to the matters that are not to be available to the promisor party by way of defence, set-off or counterclaim.[1]

Lastly, s 3(3) of the 1999 Act provides that the promisor party also has available to him by way of defence or set-off against the third party any matter if:

- an express term of the contract provides for it to be available to him in proceedings brought by the third party, and
- it would have been available to him by way of defence or set-off if the proceedings had been brought by the promisee party.

It will be noted that s 3 does not permit a *counterclaim against the promisee party* to be raised against the third party.

1   Contracts (Rights of Third Parties) Act 1999, s 3(5).

Cases where s 1 of the 1999 Act does not apply

14.7   Section 1 does not apply in a handful of cases, two of which may be of interest to surveyors or valuers.

Section 1 does not confer any rights on a third party in the case of any contract binding on a company and its members (ie shareholders) under the Companies Act 1985, s 14.[1] Section 14 of the 1985 Act provides that the memorandum and articles of the company are to be regarded as creating a contract between the company and each member. Nor does s 1 confer any rights on a third party in the case of any incorporation document of a limited liability partnership or any limited liability partnership agreement.[2] The effect of the present exceptions is that any provision in the memorandum or articles of a company (or the corresponding documentation of a limited liability partnership), which might benefit someone other than the company (or limited liability partnership) or a member, is not enforceable by that third party.

Secondly, s 1 does not confer any right on a third party to enforce any term of a contract of employment against an employee or other worker.[3] Thus, if an employment contract requires an employee not to divulge a trade secret supplied by a third party, that term cannot be enforced by the third party, although it could be enforced by the employer.

1   Contracts (Rights of Third Parties) Act 1999, s 6(2).

2   Contracts (Rights of Third Parties) Act 1999, s 6(2A) (added by the Limited Liability Partnership Regulations 2001, Sch 5).
3   Contracts (Rights of Third Parties) Act 1999, s 6(3) and (4).

Other exceptions and qualifications

14.8   Section 1 of the 1999 Act does not affect any pre-existing exceptions or qualifications to the doctrine of privity of contract.

It is possible for a party to a contract to assign his rights to a third party.[1]

Statutes have given a third party the right to enforce an insurance contract of certain types. For instance, a third party who has been injured in a road traffic accident can enforce the driver's insurance policy against the insurance company.[2] Likewise, where a man has insured his life for the express benefit of his wife and/or children, they can enforce payment under the policy on his death.[3]

The requirements of land law have also necessitated some modifications of the strict rules of privity. For example, the benefits of covenants in leases are transferred to successors in title of the landlord and tenant, despite the absence of privity, but in the case of leases created before 1 January 1996 only if the covenants affect the land.[4]

1   See Card and James *Law for Accountancy Students* (7th edn) paras 17.13-17.27.
2   Road Traffic Act 1988, s 148(7).
3   Married Women's Property Act 1882, s 11.
4   Paras 37.52-37.60 below.

Collateral contracts

14.9   The above situations are exceptions or qualifications to the doctrine of privity. It may also be possible to outflank the rule. For example, if a collateral contract can be found, a person not a party to the principal contract can sue on the collateral contract instead. In *Shanklin Pier Ltd v Detel Products Ltd*,[1] the claimants employed contractors to paint their pier. They instructed the contractors to buy and use the defendants' paint, having been promised by the defendants that the paint would last for seven to ten years. The paint lasted for only three months. It was held that, while the claimants could not sue on the contract of sale of the paint, to which they were not parties, they could sue on a collateral contract between them and the defendants which contained a promise by the defendants that the paint would last seven to ten years, for which promise the claimants had provided consideration by requiring their contractors to use the defendants' paint.

1   [1951] 2 All ER 471.

Action in tort by third party

14.10   Where the doctrine of privity applies to prevent a third party to a contract being entitled by virtue of the contract itself to enforce a benefit arising under it, this does not mean that a contract can never indirectly benefit him. For example, if it is foreseeable that negligent performance of a contract by a party to it will cause physical injury to a third party, that party may owe a duty of care to the third party and be liable to him in the tort of negligence if he is in breach of that duty. By way of another example, accountants, surveyors and other professional people may be held liable in tort to people who are not their clients if they cause them foreseeable economic loss in negligently carrying out a contract made with a client. However, it is exceptional for a person to be held liable in tort for negligently causing foreseeable economic loss. We discuss liability in tort in Part III; chapter 17 is particularly relevant in the present context.

Enforcement by a party to the contract

14.11   Whether or not a third party could enforce a contract, the promisee party (the party who was promised that the benefit would be conferred on the third party) can enforce the contract if the promisor party does not carry out his contractual obligations.[1] Damages, the usual remedy for failure to perform contractual obligations, are available, but, unless the contracting party is suing as agent or trustee for the third party, he cannot normally recover any damages on behalf of the third party in respect of his loss.[2] The reason is that, generally, as already said,[3] a claimant can only recover damages for the loss which he has suffered.[4] If the contract was intended solely to benefit the third party, so that the contracting party has suffered no loss, only nominal damages (usually in the region of £2 to £20) will normally be recoverable by the contracting party.[5]

This being so, it is preferable for the contracting party to seek the enforcement of the contract by means of the equitable remedy of specific performance. The advantages of this remedy are illustrated by *Beswick v Beswick*.[6] In this case, in consideration of Peter Beswick transferring his business to his nephew, the nephew agreed to pay his uncle a pension and, after his death, a weekly annuity to his widow. The nephew paid his uncle the pension but only one payment of the annuity was made. The widow, in her capacity as the administratrix of her husband's estate, successfully sued her nephew for specific performance of the contract to pay the annuity. (Because the case was decided before the Contracts (Rights of Third Parties) Act 1999, the widow would not have succeeded if she had sued merely as the intended recipient.) Thus, if specific performance of a contract can be ordered, a party to a contract or his personal representative can ensure enforcement of the contract for the benefit of a third party. However, it would be wrong to think that specific performance will always be ordered in the present type of case. It is a discretionary remedy and is subject to a number of other limitations described in para 11.30 above.

1   The Contracts (Rights of Third Parties) Act 1999, s 4 expressly preserves the right of the promisee to enforce any term of the contract where a third party has a right of enforcement under s 1.
2   If the contracting party sues for, and recovers, damages for the third party as agent or trustee, he will be obliged as trustee or agent to hand over the damages to the third party. Although there is no binding authority on this point, it seems that, in any other case where the contracting party can, and does, recover damages in respect of the third party's loss, the third party may recover any damages obtained by the contracting party in respect of it, either under the law of restitution (*Jackson v Horizon Holidays Ltd* [1975] 3 All ER 92 at 96) or on the basis that the contracting party holds the damages in trust for the third party (*Darlington Borough Council v Wiltshier Northern Ltd* [1995] 3 All ER 895 at 902-903 and 908).
3   For the general rule, and some exceptions to it, see para 11.2 above.
4   If the contract is one to provide a contracting party with a benefit which others will also enjoy, such as a contract for a family holiday or a group coach trip, he is entitled to substantial damages for his loss (the family holiday or group coach trip) if the other party breaks the contract by failing to provide the benefit: *Jackson v Horizon Holidays Ltd* [1975] 3 All ER 92, CA, as explained in *Woodar Investment Development Ltd v Wimpey Construction (UK) Ltd* [1980] 1 All ER 571, HL.
5   *Beswick v Beswick* [1967] 2 All ER 1197, HL.
6   [1967] 2 All ER 1197, HL.

14.12   Section 5 of the Contracts (Rights of Third Parties) Act 1999 protects a promisor party from double liability where under s 1 of that Act a term of a contract is enforceable by a third party, and the promisee party has received from the promisor a sum in respect of:

•   the third party's loss in respect of the term, or
•   the expense to the promisee of making good to the third party the default of the promisor.[1]

Section 5 provides that in such a case, where proceedings are then brought by the third party in reliance on s 1, the court or arbitral tribunal must reduce any award to the third party to such extent as it thinks appropriate to take account of the sum recovered by the promisee.

I   Section 5 does not apply where a contractual term enforceable by a third party is not enforceable
     under s I but is enforceable under some other rule.

Contractual obligations and third parties

14.13   As we have already indicated, the general rule is that only a person who is a party
to a contract can be subject to any obligations contained in it; consequently, a third party
cannot generally be sued for contravening a provision in a contract made between others.[1]

Although there is good reason for generally refusing to allow a contract to impose
obligations on third parties, there are some cases where this is possible. The principal
exceptions or qualifications to the general rule can be summarised as follows:

- the burdens of covenants in leases are transferred to the successors in title of the
  landlord and tenant, despite the absence of privity of contract, but in the case of leases
  created before I January 1996 only if the covenants affect the land; we discuss this
  further in paras 37.52 to 37.60 below;
- the burdens of negative covenants affecting the use of land (ie covenants *not* to do
  specified things on the land), inserted in a contract of sale of land, bind subsequent
  purchasers of the land, provided certain conditions are satisfied; we discuss this further
  in paras 34.11 to 34.15 below;
- where someone hands over goods to another for repair, cleaning, carriage, loading or
  the like, the transaction gives rise to what is called a 'bailment', the transferor being
  the 'bailor' and the recipient the 'bailee'. If the bailee sub-contracts the work to someone
  else, the terms of the contract between the bailee and that person will bind the bailor
  (a third party to the contract, which involves a 'sub-bailment') if the bailee had the
  bailor's authority to make the sub-bailment and the bailor had expressly or impliedly
  authorised him to make the sub-bailment on the terms in question;[2]
- in certain cases, the rights of a person, by virtue of a contract to which he is party, to
  make use of a chattel are enforceable against a third party.

1   *McGruther v Pitcher* [1904] 2 Ch 306, CA.
2   *K H Enterprise (Cargo Owners) v Pioneer Container (Owners), The Pioneer Container* [1994] 2 All ER 250,
     PC; see, further, in respect of exemption clauses, para 14.15 below.

Third party generally not bound by an exemption clause
14.14   Because a third party who can enforce a term of the contract by virtue of the
Contracts (Rights of Third Parties) Act 1999, s I may only do so subject to the other
terms of the contract, his enforcement of that term will be subject to any applicable, valid
exemption clause.

14.15   On the other hand, a third party cannot be deprived of his right to sue in tort by
an exemption clause contained in a contract between others, even though it purports to
have that effect. An authority is *Haseldine v C A Daw & Son Ltd.*[1] The owners of a block of
flats employed the defendants to repair a lift in the block. The defendants repaired the lift
negligently and the claimant was injured when the lift fell to the bottom of the lift shaft. The
defendants were held liable to the claimant, it being irrelevant that the contract between
the defendants and the owners of the block purported to exempt the defendants from
liability for personal injury. Likewise, in *Leigh and Sillivan Ltd v Aliakmon Shipping Co Ltd, The
Aliakmon,*[2] where a contract of carriage by sea contained an exemption clause, the buyers
of the goods were not bound by it because they were not parties to that contract (whose
only parties were the sellers and the shipowners).

There is one exceptional type of case where an exemption clause can bind a third party who brings a tort action. This arises through the operation of the rule relating to sub-bailments referred to in para 14.13 above. If the sub-bailment contract contains an exemption clause it will bind the third party bailor if the requirements of the rule are satisfied.[3]

1   [1941] 3 All ER 156, CA.
2   [1986] 2 All ER 145, HL.
3   *Singer Co (UK) Ltd v Tees and Hartlepool Port Authority* [1988] 1 FTLR 442.

Chapter 15

Agency

15.1   Agency is the relationship between two legal persons, whereby one person, the principal, appoints another, the agent, to act on his behalf. The relationship is usually, though not necessarily, contractual.[1] The major importance of agency lies in the fact that an authorised agent[2] may affect the legal position of his principal vis-à-vis third parties. In most cases, the agent does this by making a contract on his principal's behalf, or by disposing of property which the principal owns. However, he may also bind his principal in other ways, for example by signing a document,[3] receiving notice,[4] or committing a tort.[5] With certain exceptions,[6] mostly statutory, a principal may do anything through the medium of an agent which he could lawfully do in person.

1   *Yasuda Fire and Marine Insurance Co of Europe Ltd v Orion Marine Insurance Underwriting Agency Ltd* [1995] 3 All ER 211.
2   Including one who, though not actually appointed, is given the appearance of authority by his principal: paras 15.31–15.35 below.
3   *LCC v Agricultural Food Products Ltd* [1955] 2 All ER 229, CA.
4   *Proudfoot v Montefiore* (1867) LR 2 QB 511.
5   Paras 27.18–27.20 below.
6   See *Clauss v Pir* [1987] 2 All ER 752.

Three issues
15.2   The three issues with which we are concerned in this chapter are:

- the relationship of principal and agent (ie the creation of agency, the duties and rights of agents and the termination of agency);
- the changes in the legal relationship of the principal and third parties which may be effected by an agent; and
- the legal relationship, if any, between the agent and third parties.

Principal and agent

Creation of agency
15.3   Agency may be created by agreement, express or implied, by ratification or by virtue of necessity. In determining whether a principal (P) has appointed another person to act as his agent (A), it is necessary to decide whether P had the capacity to appoint an agent and whether A had the capacity to act as an agent, before considering how an agent is appointed.

Capacity

15.4   An agent can be appointed to effect any transaction for which the principal has capacity.[1] However, an agent who lacks full contractual capacity can only be made personally liable on those contracts which he would have had capacity to make on his own behalf.[2] Further, the agent may well not be liable on the contract of agency itself. Companies, no less than natural legal persons, can be appointed as agents.

1   For the law relating to capacity to contract, see paras 4.9–4.17 above.
2   *Smalley v Smalley* (1700) 1 Eq Cas Abr 6; for when an agent is personally liable on contracts see paras 16.40–16.45 below.

Appointment by express agreement

15.5   An agent may be appointed by express agreement between principal and agent. This agreement is frequently, but not necessarily, a contract. If the appointment is by contract, the usual rules for the formation of contracts must be complied with. Normally, the appointment can be made informally, even if the agent is to transact contracts which must be made or evidenced in writing. All that is necessary is a desire to appoint A as agent and A's consent to act as such. However, in some cases certain formalities are necessary to create agency. For instance, if an agent has to execute a deed, his appointment must be by deed, and is known as a power of attorney.[1]

1   *Steiglitz v Egginton* (1815) Holt NP 141, and see also the Powers of Attorney Act 1971, ss 1 and 7.

Appointment by implied agreement

15.6   If the parties have not expressly agreed to become principal and agent, it may be possible to find an implied agreement based on their conduct or relationship.[1] Factors which have been found relevant in determining whether agency has been created by implied agreement are whether one party acts for the other at the other's request and whether commission is payable.

An implied agreement to agency by virtue of the relationship of the parties arises in the case of husband and wife. A wife has authority to pledge her husband's credit for household necessaries even if he has not expressly appointed her his agent.[2]

1   *Ashford Shire Council v Dependable Motors Pty Ltd* [1961] 1 All ER 96, PC.
2   *Debenham v Mellon* (1880) 6 App Cas 24, HL.

Ratification

15.7   In certain circumstances, the relationship of principal and agent can be created or extended retrospectively under the doctrine of ratification. What this means is that, if A purports to act as agent for B in a particular transaction (although he is not authorised to do so), B may subsequently 'ratify' or adopt what A has done. In such a case, A is deemed to have been acting as an authorised agent when he effected the transaction.[1] However, ratification only validates past acts of the 'agent' and gives no authority for the future,[2] although frequent acts of ratification by an alleged principal may create agency by implied agreement or confer ostensible authority on the agent.[3]

1   *Bolton Partners v Lambert* (1889) 41 Ch D 295.
2   *Irvine v Union Bank of Australia* (1877) 2 App Cas 366, PC.
3   *Midland Bank Ltd v Reckitt* [1933] AC 1, HL.

15.8   *Effects of ratification*   If a person ratifies a transaction entered into on his behalf he must be taken to have ratified the whole transaction, and not merely those parts which are to his advantage.[1] The effect of ratification is to make the transaction (which is usually a contract) binding on the principal from the moment it was made by the agent.[2] Since the acts of the agent are retrospectively validated, the agent cannot be liable to a third party for breach of warranty of authority, nor to his principal for acting outside the scope of his authority,[3] and can claim commission and an indemnity.[4] Once a contract is ratified, the agent generally ceases to be liable on the contract, but ratification cannot vary rights in property which had vested before ratification.[5]

Perhaps the most controversial effect of ratification is that it allows the alleged principal to decide whether to accept a contract or reject it. The third party may wish to repudiate an agreement with the agent because of the agent's lack of authority, but find himself bound by the contract if the alleged principal subsequently ratifies.[6] However, if a contract is explicitly made 'subject to ratification' the third party can withdraw prior to ratification and, if he does so, ratification cannot bind him.[7] Because the effects of ratification are at least potentially unfair to third parties, ratification is only possible in some circumstances.

1   *Cornwal v Wilson* (1750) 1 Ves Sen 509.
2   *Bolton Partners v Lambert* (1889) 41 Ch D 295.
3   *Smith v Cologan* (1788) 2 Term Rep 188n. For breach of warranty of authority see para 15.46 below.
4   *Hartas v Ribbons* (1889) 22 QBD 254, CA. For indemnities see para 15.20 below.
5   *Bird v Brown* (1850) 4 Exch 786.
6   *Bolton Partners v Lambert* (1889) 41 Ch D 295.
7   *Warehousing and Forwarding Co of East Africa Ltd v Jafferali & Sons Ltd* [1963] 3 All ER 571, PC.

15.9   *Who can ratify* Only the alleged principal can ratify the actions of his alleged agent and then only if the latter purported to act on his behalf.[1] Therefore, if an agent has not revealed he was acting as an agent, ie he has an undisclosed principal, the undisclosed principal cannot ratify.[2] A leading illustration of this is the case of *Keighley, Maxsted & Co v Durant.*[3] In this case an agent purchased wheat at a price which was higher than he had been authorised to pay. The agent had not revealed that he was acting as an agent when he bought the grain. Because of this the House of Lords found the defendant principal was not liable for breach of contract when he refused to accept delivery of the grain, even though he had purported to ratify the contract of sale.

Provided that an agent reveals that he is acting as agent, his principal, even though unnamed, can ratify his unauthorised actions.[4] However, an unnamed principal should be identifiable,[4] unless, perhaps, the third party has shown that he is uninterested in the identity of the principal. Further, there is a strange rule by which unnamed, and possibly unidentifiable, principals can ratify contracts of marine insurance.[5]

A company which is a disclosed principal can only ratify if it is in existence at the time the agent enters into any contract.[6] Even if a company takes the benefit of a pre-incorporation contract it is not liable on it, although it will be liable if it makes a new contract post-incorporation on the same subject matter.[7] An agent who makes a pre-incorporation contract on behalf of a non-existent company is personally liable on it unless personal liability has been excluded 'by contract or otherwise'.[8]

To be able to ratify, the disclosed principal must have had the capacity to make the contract himself at the date when his 'agent' contracted.[9]

1   *Wilson v Tumman* (1843) 6 Man & G 236.
2   However, an alleged principal who acts towards the third party as if his agent's act was authorised may become liable for it on the basis of estoppel: *Spiro v Lintern* [1973] 3 All ER 319, CA; *Worboys v Carter* [1987] 2 EGLR 1, CA.
3   [1901] AC 240, HL.
4   *Watson v Swann* (1862) 11 CBNS 756; *Southern Water Authority v Carey* [1985] 2 All ER 1077.
5   *Boston Fruit Co v British and Foreign Marine Insurance Co* [1906] AC 336, HL.
6   *Kelner v Baxter* (1866) LR 2 CP 174. However, a company may claim damages in tort for a negligent act committed before its incorporation: *Miro Properties Ltd v J Trevor & Sons* [1989] 1 EGLR 151.
7   *Howard v Patent Ivory Manufacturing Co* (1888) 38 Ch D 156.
8   Companies Act 1985, s 36C. The agent is also entitled to enforce the contract in his own name: *Braymist Ltd v Wise Finance Co Ltd* [2002] EWCA Civ 127, [2002] 2 All ER 333, CA.
9   *Boston Deep Sea Fishing and Ice Co Ltd v Farnham (Inspector of Taxes)* [1957] 1 WLR 1051.

15.10 *What can be ratified* Apparently any action can be ratified (even where the purported agent was seeking to benefit himself[1]) except those which are illegal[2] or otherwise void.

1　Re Tiedemann and Ledermann Frères [1899] 2 QB 66.
2　Bedford Insurance Co Ltd v Instituto de Resseguros do Brasil [1984] 3 All ER 766.

15.11 *How to ratify* Ratification may be made by express affirmation of the unauthorised actions of the agent by the principal.[1] It need not, as a rule, take any special form, except that, where the agent has without authority executed a deed, ratification too must be by deed.[2] Ratification must take place within a reasonable time.[3] What is reasonable is a question of fact in every case but, if the time for performance of a contract has passed, ratification is impossible.[4] However, where an agent without authority commences legal proceedings, the client may ratify the agent's act even after the expiry of the limitation period within which proceedings must be commenced.[5]

Ratification may also be effected by conduct,[6] although mere passive acceptance of the benefit of a contract may be insufficient,[7] but if the conduct of the alleged principal amounts to ratification he cannot repudiate the actions of his agent.[8] Examples of ratification are provided by the following cases. In *Lyell v Kennedy*,[9] A received rent from property for many years, although not authorised to do so. When the owner sued him for an account of the rents, it was held that the owner's action constituted ratification of A's receipt of the rents. Similarly, in *Cornwal v Wilson*,[10] A bought some goods in excess of the price authorised by P. P objected to the purchase but sold some of the goods; it was held that he had ratified the unauthorised act by selling the goods. An action by the alleged principal will only be implied ratification if he had a choice of whether or not to act. If the alleged principal had no real choice, other than to accept the benefit of the unauthorised actions of his agent, accepting such benefit is not ratification. For example, if an agent has had unauthorised repairs done on a ship, merely retaking the ship with these repairs is not ratification by the alleged principal. This is because if he wished to recover his property he had to have it with the unauthorised repairs.[11]

Ratification will, generally, only be implied from conduct if the alleged principal has acted with full knowledge of the facts.[12] However, if the alleged principal is prepared to take the risk of what his agent has done, he can choose to ratify without full knowledge. For instance, in *Fitzmaurice v Bayley*[13] an agent entered into an unauthorised contract for the purchase of property. The alleged principal wrote a letter saying he did not know what his agent had done but would stand by all that he had done. This was an express ratification by him; he had agreed to bear the risk of being bound by the unauthorised acts of his agent, whatever they were.

1　Soames v Spencer (1822) 1 Dow & Ry KB 32.
2　Hunter v Parker (1840) 7 M & W 322.
3　Re Portuguese Consolidated Copper Mines Ltd (1890) 45 Ch D 16, CA.
4　Metropolitan Asylums Board (Managers) v Kingham & Sons (1890) 6 TLR 217.
5　Presentaciones Musicales SA v Secunda [1994] 2 All ER 737, CA.
6　Lyell v Kennedy (1889) 14 App Cas 437, HL.
7　Hughes v Hughes (1971) 221 Estates Gazette 145, CA.
8　Cornwal v Wilson (1750) 1 Ves Sen 509.
9　(1889) 14 App Cas 437, HL.
10　(1750) 1 Ves Sen 509.
11　Forman & Co Pty Ltd v The Liddesdale [1900] AC 190, PC.
12　The Bonita, The Charlotte (1861) 1 Lush 252.
13　(1856) 6 E & B 868.

Agency of necessity
15.12 Agency of necessity is a limited exception to the concept that agency is based on a consensual relationship between the parties. When certain emergencies occur, immediate

action may be necessary and the courts may be prepared to find that the person taking such action was thereby acting as an agent of necessity. A common example of agency of necessity is that masters of ships faced with an emergency are agents of the shipowner, and have authority to enter into contracts with third parties on behalf of him.[1]

Frequently, agency of necessity will merely extend the authority of existing agents but in other cases it may create agency where none existed previously – for example, between masters of ships and cargo owners. In other cases, if a person claims to be an agent of necessity, such agency will only affect the relationship of the alleged principal and agent, and will confer no power on the 'agent' to deal with third parties on behalf of the 'principal'. This type of agency of necessity is more likely than the former if the parties were not already principal and agent; for example, someone who salvages a ship cannot make contracts on behalf of the shipowner.

Agency of necessity will only arise if the 'agent' has no practical way of communicating with the 'principal',[2] if the action of the 'agent' is reasonably necessary to benefit the principal[3] and if the agent has acted bona fide.

1   *The Gratitudine* (1801) 3 Ch Rob 240.
2   *Springer v Great Western Rly Co* [1921] 1 KB 257, CA.
3   *Prager v Blatspiel, Stamp and Heacock Ltd* [1924] 1 KB 566.

Duties of an agent

Duty to act
15.13   A paid agent is under a duty to act, and any loss suffered by the principal because of failure to act is recoverable by the principal.[1] If the agent does not intend to act he should inform his principal of this fact, but the agent cannot be made liable for failure to perform acts which are illegal or void.[2] A gratuitous agent does not appear to be under any positive duty to act, although if he chooses to act and does so negligently he is liable.[3]

1   *Turpin v Bilton* (1843) 5 Man & G 455.
2   *Cohen v Kittell* (1889) 22 QBD 680, DC.
3   *Wilkinson v Coverdale* (1793) 1 Esp 74, CA.

Duty to obey instructions
15.14   The primary obligation imposed on an agent is to act strictly in accordance with the instructions of his principal in so far as they are lawful and reasonable. An agent has no discretion to disobey his instructions, even in what he honestly and reasonably regards to be his principal's best interests.[1] If an agent carries out his instructions he cannot be liable for loss suffered by the principal because the instructions were at fault.[2] If the instructions which an agent receives are not complied with he will be responsible to his principal for any loss thereby suffered, even if the loss is not occasioned by any fault on his part.[3] However, if the instructions received by an agent are ambiguous, he is not in breach of his duty if he makes a reasonable but incorrect interpretation of them.[4] If instructions confer a discretion on the agent, he will not be liable for failure to obey instructions if he exercises the discretion reasonably.[5]

The instructions which an agent should obey may be clarified or extended by virtue of custom or trade usage applying in the trade or profession which the agent follows.

1   *Bertram, Armstrong & Co v Godfray* (1830) 1 Knapp 381.
2   *Overend Gurney and Co v Gibb* (1872) LR 5 HL 480, HL.
3   *Lilley v Doubleday* (1881) 7 QBD 510.
4   *Weigall & Co v Runciman & Co* (1916) 85 LJKB 1187, CA.
5   *Boden v French* (1851) 10 CB 886.

Duty to exercise care and skill
15.15   An agent, whether paid or gratuitous,[1] is required to display reasonable care in carrying out his instructions and also, where appropriate, such skill as may reasonably be

expected from a member of his profession.[2] If he fails to do so, the agent will be liable for any loss which his principal suffers thereby. A negligent agent may also forfeit the right to remuneration where his negligence renders his services to the principal worthless.[3]

1   *Chaudhry v Prabhakar* [1988] 3 All ER 718, CA; see para 17.27 below.
2   Supply of Goods and Services Act 1982, s 13. For examples, see paras 18.8 and 18.9 below.
3   *Nye Saunders v Bristow* (1987) 37 BLR 92, CA.

Fiduciary duties

15.16   Every agent owes fiduciary duties, ie duties of good faith, to his principal. These duties are based on the confidential nature of the agency relationship. However, it is important to appreciate that an agent may be in breach of these duties, and liable for the consequences, even where he acts innocently.[1] There are two main fiduciary duties – a duty to disclose any conflict of interest and a duty not to take secret profits or bribes.

a. *Conflict of interest*   Wherever an agent's own interests, or the interests of a third party, come into conflict with those of the principal, the agent must make a full disclosure to the principal of all relevant facts, so that the latter may decide whether to continue with the transaction. It is this rule which prevents an agent, in the absence of disclosure, from selling his own property to the principal,[2] purchasing the principal's property for himself[3] or acting as agent for both vendor and purchaser[4] or for two competing would-be purchasers.[5] Similarly, an estate agent instructed to sell property must not favour one potential purchaser at the expense of others, in the hope of reward from that purchaser.[6] If the agent is in breach of this duty, the principal may have any resulting transaction set aside, claim any profit accruing to the agent and refuse to pay commission.[7]

b. *Secret profits and bribes*   If an agent, in the course of his agency and without his principal's knowledge and consent, makes a profit for himself out of his position, or out of property or information with which he is entrusted, he must account for this property to the principal.[8] Thus, an agent may not accept commission from both parties to a transaction,[9] nor keep for himself the benefit of a trade discount while charging his principal the full price.[10] It makes no difference that the agent has acted honestly throughout, nor even that his actions have conferred substantial benefit upon the principal.[11] However, an agent who has his principal's informed consent may keep whatever profit he makes.[12]

Where the secret profit takes the form of a payment from a third party who is aware that he is dealing with an agent, it is called a bribe, even if the payment is not made with any evil motive and even if the principal suffers no loss thereby.[13] The taking of a bribe entitles the principal to dismiss the agent,[14] recover either the amount of the bribe or his actual loss (if greater) from the agent or third party,[15] repudiate any transaction in respect of which the bribe was given[16] and refuse to pay commission.[17]

1   *Keppel v Wheeler* [1927] 1 KB 577, CA.
2   *Gillett v Peppercorne* (1840) 3 Beav 78.
3   *McPherson v Watt* (1877) 3 App Cas 254, HL.
4   *Harrods Ltd v Lemon* [1931] 2 KB 157, CA.
5   *Eric V Stansfield v South East Nursing Home Services Ltd* [1986] 1 EGLR 29. An estate agent can of course act for more than one vendor, but must not disclose to one of them information which is confidential to another: *Brent Kelly v Cooper Associates* [1993] AC 205, PC.
6   *Henry Smith & Son v Muskett* [1979] 1 EGLR 13.
7   Para 15.19 below.
8   *Regal (Hastings) Ltd v Gulliver* [1942] 1 All ER 378, HL.
9   *Andrews v Ramsay & Co* [1903] 2 KB 635, CA.
10   *Hippisley v Knee Bros* [1905] 1 KB 1, DC.
11   *Boardman v Phipps* [1966] 3 All ER 721, HL.
12   See *Anangel Atlas Compania Naviera SA v Ishikawajima-Harima Heavy Industries Co* [1990] 1 Lloyd's Rep 167.

13   *Industries and General Mortgage Co Ltd v Lewis* [1949] 2 All ER 573.
14   *Boston Deep Sea Fishing and Ice Co v Ansell* (1888) 39 Ch D 339, CA.
15   *Mahesan S/O Thambiah v Malaysia Government Officers' Co-operative Housing Society Ltd* [1978] 2 All ER 405, PC.
16   *Shipway v Broadwood* [1899] 1 QB 369; *Logicrose v Southend United Football Club* [1988] 1 WLR 1256.
17   Para 15.19 below.

Other duties

15.17   An agent has a duty not to delegate his responsibilities to a sub-agent without the authority of the principal.[1] An agent must pay over to the principal any money received for the use of the principal in the course of the agency, even if it is claimed by third parties,[2] and must keep proper accounts. An agent must allow the principal to inspect his accounts and all documents and records relating to acts done by the agent on the principal's behalf.[3]

1   *De Bussche v Alt* (1878) 8 Ch D 286, CA.
2   *Blaustein v Maltz, Mitchell & Co* [1937] 1 All ER 497, CA.
3   *Yasuda Fire and Marine Insurance Co of Europe Ltd v Orion Marine Insurance Underwriting Agency Ltd* [1995] 3 All ER 211.

Rights of agents

Remuneration

15.18   Where there is a contract of agency, an agent may be entitled thereunder to be paid for his services. The right to be paid may be an express term of the contract of agency or, in the absence of such a term, may be implied if it was clearly the intention of the parties that the agent was to be paid.[1] The agent will only be entitled to remuneration where he has performed, precisely and completely, the obligations in the agency agreement. If an agent does less than he is contractually required to do he can recover nothing, unless the contract provides for payment for partial services.

If the contract of agency expressly provides the amount of remuneration for a given task, this is the amount payable. If the contract merely provides that the agent is to be paid without specifying an amount, he is entitled to recover a reasonable amount.[2] If the contract mentions remuneration, but on its true construction does not entitle the agent to payment, he can recover nothing. For instance, in *Kofi Sunkersette Obu v Strauss & Co Ltd*,[3] the Privy Council refused to allow an agent to recover any commission in a case where the contract of agency provided that the amount of commission, if any, was to be fixed by the principal. If there is an implied term providing for payment, the amount of such payment must be determined by the courts. Usually it will be on the basis of what is reasonable, but it may be possible to imply the fixed scale costs of professional men.[4]

In the absence of a contract of agency, an agent may be entitled to be paid on a *quantum meruit* ('reasonable sum') basis. However, where an agent is to be paid on the occurrence of a certain event, such as a commission on sale, there can be no claim for a quantum meruit if the event does not occur.[5]

1   *Reeve v Reeve* (1858) 1 F & F 280. Also see the Supply of Goods and Services Act 1982, s 15 and the Commercial Agents (Council Directive) Regulations 1993.
2   *Way v Latilla* [1937] 3 All ER 759, HL.
3   [1951] AC 243, PC.
4   For when the courts will imply terms into contracts see paras 7.24–7.28 above.
5   *Howard Houlder & Partners Ltd v Manx Isles Steamship Co Ltd* [1923] 1 KB 110.

15.19   The mere occurrence of the transaction which the agent is commissioned to effect does not entitle the agent to remuneration; the occurrence must be brought about by the agent[1] unless the contract provides that he is to be paid however the desired result occurs.[2]

If the principal hinders the earning of commission by the agent, the agent cannot recover any commission thereby lost or sue the principal, unless the latter's action amounts to a breach of contract. The contract of agency may contain a term that the principal will not hinder the agent in his efforts to earn his commission,[3] but if it is not an express term the courts are reluctant to imply such a term into the contract of agency.[4]

Even if an agent complies with his instructions, he cannot recover any commission in respect of a transaction rendered void or illegal by statute.[5] An agent who is in breach of his duties towards his principal normally forfeits his right to commission,[6] unless the breach is a technical one and the agent has acted honestly.[7]

1　Millar, Son & Co v Radford (1903) 19 TLR 575, CA.
2　See Brian Cooper & Co v Fairview Estates (Investments) Ltd [1987] 1 EGLR 18, CA; Barnard Marcus & Co v Ashraf [1988] 1 EGLR 7, CA.
3　A 'sole agency' is a good example of this.
4　Luxor (Eastbourne) Ltd v Cooper [1941] 1 All ER 33, HL; Marcan Shipping (London) v Polish Steamship Co [1989] 2 Lloyd's Rep 138, CA. See also para 16.24 below.
5　Chapter 13 above.
6　Salomons v Pender (1865) 3 H & C 639.
7　Keppel v Wheeler [1927] 1 KB 577, CA.

Indemnity

15.20　An agent who has suffered loss or incurred liabilities in the course of carrying out authorised actions for his principal is entitled to be reimbursed or indemnified by the principal.[1] However, he has no right to reimbursement or an indemnity for losses or liabilities arising because of breaches of duty (eg failing to comply with his instructions) or in carrying out an illegal transaction or a transaction rendered void by statute.[2] In ex p Mather,[3] a principal employed an agent to purchase smuggled goods. The agent was not entitled to recover the cost of these goods from the principal, even though the principal had obtained possession of them.

1　Hooper v Treffry (1847) 1 Exch 17.
2　Capp v Topham (1805) 6 East 392; Gasson v Cole (1910) 26 TLR 468.
3　(1797) 3 Ves 373.

Sub-agents

15.21　Even where an agent is authorised to appoint a sub-agent to carry out his instructions, it is presumed that the person appointed is merely an agent of the agent; he does not, in the absence of clear evidence, become an agent of the principal.[1] As a result, the sub-agent has no claim against the principal for remuneration or indemnity, nor does he owe the principal any duty to act or to obey instructions. It has further been held, somewhat controversially, that the sub-agent owes the principal no duty of care in tort, unless he is also a bailee of the principal's goods.[2] Whether the sub-agent owes fiduciary duties to the principal is unclear, for there are conflicting decisions of the Court of Appeal.[3]

1　Calico Printers' Association Ltd v Barclays Bank (1931) 145 LT 51.
2　Balsamo v Medici [1984] 1 WLR 951.
3　Powell and Thomas v Evan Jones & Co [1905] 1 KB 11, CA; cf New Zealand and Australian Land Co v Watson (1881) 7 QBD 374, CA.

Termination of agency

15.22　A contract of agency may be terminated, like any other contract, by agreement,[1] by performance,[2] by breach[3] or by frustration,[4] although it is important to remember that termination of agency between principal and agent need not terminate the agent's ostensible authority (which we discuss in paras 15.31 to 15.35 below). In addition, there are certain special rules applicable to agency, which we now discuss.

1　Paras 6.23–6.26 above.
2　Paras 8.2–8.11 above.
3　Paras 8.12–8.31 above.
4　Chapter 10 above.

Act of parties

15.23   A contract of agency will not be specifically enforced, because it is a contract for personal services.[1] As a corollary, either party may terminate the relationship at will. This may amount to a breach of contract, as where the agency was for a fixed period which has not expired, or where a required period of notice has not been given. If so, the innocent party is entitled to damages, but the agency itself is nonetheless determined.[2]

As to whether termination of an agency relationship without notice amounts to a breach of contract, we have already seen that, if an agent accepts a bribe, his contract of agency can be terminated without notice.[3] There are other contracts which on their true construction allow either principal or agent to terminate the agreement without any notice.[4] If an agent is employed on a commission basis, so that he is only entitled to remuneration when he does the act required by the agency agreement (eg sells a house), it would seem that such contracts can be terminated without notice.[5] Agency contracts which resemble contracts of employment, in that the agent is paid merely for being an agent, rather than for facilitating a particular transaction, require notice.[6]

There are some cases where the authority of an agent is irrevocable.[7] Under the Powers of Attorney Act 1971, s 4, a power of attorney expressed to be irrevocable, and given to secure a proprietary interest of the donee of the power, can be revoked neither by the donor of that power without the consent of the donee nor by the death, mental incapacity or bankruptcy of the donor. This is essentially a restatement of the common law rule that, if the agent is given authority by deed, or for valuable consideration, to effect a security or to protect an interest of the agent, that authority is irrevocable while the security or interest subsists.[8] Again, an authority coupled with an interest is not revoked by the death, mental incapacity or bankruptcy of the donor.

1   *Chinnock v Sainsbury* (1860) 30 LJ Ch 409; para 11.30 above.
2   *Page One Records Ltd v Britton* [1967] 3 All ER 822.
3   Para 16.16b below.
4   *Atkinson v Cotesworth* (1825) 3 B & C 647.
5   *Motion v Michaud* (1892) 8 TLR 253, affd by the Court of Appeal (1892) 8 TLR 447, CA.
6   *Parker v Ibbetson* (1858) 4 CBNS 346. Also see the Commercial Agents (Council Directive) Regulations 1993.
7   See the Enduring Powers of Attorney Act 1985 (para 15.26 below).
8   *Gaussen v Morton* (1830) 10 B & C 731.

15.24   A problem may arise where a principal, without actually revoking his agent's authority, effectively brings the agency to an end, for example by closing down the business to which it relates. In order to recover damages for loss of earnings, the agent must be able to prove that the principal's action amounts to a breach either of an express term of the contract of agency, or of one necessarily implied to give business efficacy.[1] The courts are slow to imply such terms. In *Rhodes v Forwood*,[2] a colliery owner appointed brokers as sole agents for the sale of his coal in Liverpool for seven years or as long as he did business there. After four years the colliery was sold. It was held that the owner had not contracted, either expressly or impliedly, to keep the brokers supplied with coal for sale, and he was therefore not liable for breach of contract. On the other hand, in *Turner v Goldsmith*,[3] a shirt manufacturer expressly agreed to employ a travelling salesman for five years, but his factory was destroyed by fire after only two years. It was held that the manufacturer was not released from his obligation, so that the agent was entitled to damages.

1   Paras 7.26, 7.27 above.
2   (1876) 1 App Cas 256, HL.
3   [1891] 1 QB 544, CA.

Death

15.25   The death of a principal or of an agent determines the agency.[1] An agent's right to remuneration ceases with the death of his principal, as does his right of indemnity.[2] Most importantly, the actual authority of an agent (and, probably, his ostensible authority) ceases on the death of his principal and any transactions entered into thereafter bind the agent, but not the principal's estate, even if the agent does not know of the death.[3]

1   *Blades v Free* (1829) 9 B & C 167; *Friend v Young* [1897] 2 Ch 421.
2   *Farrow v Wilson* (1869) LR 4 CP 744; *Pool v Pool* (1889) 58 LJP 67.
3   *Blades v Free* (1829) 9 B & C 167.

Mental incapacity

15.26   If a principal becomes mentally incapable the agency is terminated, and the agent can presumably claim no commission in relation to transactions entered into after his actual authority is determined. Where the agent has ostensible authority, this survives his principal's mental incapacity, and any contract entered into by him is binding upon the principal, unless the third party knew of the principal's incapacity.[1] Somewhat inconsistently, however, it has also been held that, provided that the third party did not know of the incapacity, the agent can be liable for breach of warranty of authority even if he was unaware of his principal's mental incapacity.[2]

Under the Enduring Powers of Attorney Act 1985, it is now possible for a principal to execute a power of attorney, the authority of which will survive his subsequent mental incapacity.[3] To achieve this effect, various prescribed formalities must be complied with and the agent, on realising that the principal is becoming mentally incapable, must register the power of attorney with the Court of Protection, having first given notice to certain of the principal's relatives.

1   *Drew v Nunn* (1879) 4 QBD 661, CA.
2   *Yonge v Toynbee* [1910] 1 KB 215, CA.
3   For the mental capacity required to execute such a power, see *Re K; Re F* [1988] 1 All ER 358.

Bankruptcy

15.27   The bankruptcy of a principal terminates a contract of agency.[1] On the other hand, the bankruptcy of an agent does not automatically determine the agency, unless it effectively prevents the agent from doing what he was appointed to do.[2]

1   *Elliott v Turquand* (1881) 7 App Cas 79, HL.
2   *McCall v Australian Meat Co Ltd* (1870) 19 WR 188.

Effects of termination

15.28 While the termination of agency cannot deprive the agent of any rights to commission or indemnity which have already accrued,[1] it prevents him from acquiring such rights in the future.[2] Furthermore, an agent who continues to act may become liable to a third party for breach of warranty of authority, even if he is unaware that his actual authority has been determined.[3]

In the absence of ostensible authority, a principal is not usually bound by anything which his agent does after termination of the agency. However, where the agency is created by deed, both an agent and a third party are given statutory protection in respect of transactions effected after termination, provided that they were unaware of this.[4]

1   *Chappell v Bray* (1860) 6 H & N 145.
2   *Farrow v Wilson* (1869) LR 4 CP 744; *Pool v Pool* (1889) 58 LJP 67.
3   *Yonge v Toynbee* [1910] 1 KB 215, CA.
4   Powers of Attorney Act 1971, s 5. See also the Enduring Powers of Attorney Act 1985 (para 15.26 above).

Principal and third parties

15.29   If an agent makes an authorised contract on behalf of his principal, then the principal is deemed to have made the contract. The principal may sue and be sued on authorised contracts made by the agent, and he may be sued for a pre-contractual misrepresentation made by his agent. If a principal is undisclosed then both principal and agent can sue or be sued on the authorised contract. If a contract or other transaction, such as a disposition of property, is not authorised then it does not bind the principal, but the agent may incur personal liability in respect thereof. An agent's authority may take various forms.

The authority of agents
Actual authority
15.30   An agent who has been expressly appointed may have both express and implied actual authority. An agent appointed by implied agreement has implied actual authority.

Express authority is the authority conferred by the agreement (which is usually a contract) creating agency. Implied authority consists of those terms which will be implied into the contract of agency by applying the usual rules for the implication of terms into contracts.[1] Certain types of implied actual authority are well recognised, for instance incidental and customary authority.

Incidental authority is implied authority to do all subordinate acts incidental to and necessary for the execution of the agent's express authority.[2] Thus, incidental authority supplements the express authority of the agent and gives the agent authority to undertake tasks which are incidental to his expressly authorised task. It is a question of fact in every case whether a particular action is incidental to the authorised purpose of the agent.

Customary authority means that an agent operating in a particular market or business has the authority which an agent operating in that market or business usually has.[3] If an agent has a particular position in his principal's business, such as company secretary or foreman, or in his own right, such as stockbroker or auctioneer, he has a type of customary authority commonly called usual authority, which confers on him the authority to undertake any tasks which an agent in that position usually has authority to undertake.[4] In *Panorama Developments Ltd v Fidelis Furnishing Fabrics Ltd,*[5] a company appointed X their company secretary. As such he was an agent of the company, and the company was liable to pay for cars hired by X, even though he used them for his own and not the company's purposes, because hiring cars was within the customary or usual authority of an agent holding the position of company secretary.

It should be noted that, as between principal and agent, express authority is paramount. An agent who disobeys an express instruction cannot avoid liability on the ground that his actions lay within, for example, his usual authority. However, as far as third parties are concerned, they are entitled to assume, until they have notice to the contrary, that the agent has whatever authority would usually be implied in the circumstances.

1   Paras 7.23–7.27 above.
2   *Collen v Gardner* (1856) 21 Beav 540.
3   *Bayliffe v Butterworth* (1847) 1 Exch 425.
4   *Hely-Hutchinson v Brayhead Ltd* [1967] 2 All ER 14; affd on other grounds [1967] 3 All ER 98, CA.
5   [1971] 3 All ER 16, CA.

Ostensible authority
15.31   Ostensible authority may result (for the benefit of a third party) in:

- a person who is not an agent being regarded as an agent of a person for whom he acts or appears to act in a particular transaction; or
- the extension of the authority of an agent.[1]

It does not create a real agency relationship, nor does it extend the actual authority of the agent in relation to his principal, but merely allows the third party to deal with someone as if he were an authorised agent. Thus, if a bank promises unequivocally and without qualification to honour cheques backed by a cheque guarantee card, a person (even a thief) in possession of both a cheque and a guarantee card has ostensible authority to bind the bank by forging a signature on the cheque, provided that a third party had no reason to believe that the signatory was not the genuine card-holder.[2]

1   The important case of *Freeman and Lockyer v Buckhurst Park Properties (Mangal) Ltd* [1964] 1 All ER 630, CA, reaffirmed that ostensible authority operates in these two ways.
2   *First Sport Ltd v Barclays Bank plc* [1993] 3 All ER 789, CA.

15.32   Ostensible authority can arise when the alleged principal makes to a third party a representation of fact, usually by conduct, which the third party relies on, that another person is authorised to act as his agent.[1] If the third party can show that such was the case, the principal cannot deny the authority of the person whom he has held out as being his agent. Ostensible authority can operate in a single transaction. For instance, if a person stands by and watches someone acting for him, he conveys the impression to a third party that the person is authorised to act for him.[1] However, ostensible authority can also operate in a series of transactions; if a person has frequently allowed an unauthorised person to act for him, he may be unable to deny that the person had ostensible authority to act for him in future transactions of a similar type. For example, if a company allows X to act as managing director, even though he has not been appointed as such, third parties are entitled to assume that he is managing director.

If there is a single transaction, the ostensible authority of the agent is to effect that transaction and no more. That is all the 'principal' has represented to the world that the agent has authority to undertake. If the 'principal' has allowed a person to act on his behalf more than once, that person has ostensible authority to effect such transactions and similar transactions in the future, and may also have ostensible usual authority. Ostensible usual authority means that where a person is held out as occupying a particular position, for example managing director, then he will have all the usual authority that a person would have if properly appointed to that position.[2] If a person has invested an agent with ostensible authority, it is not necessarily limited to exactly the same transactions as those from which the ostensible authority arose. In *Swiss Air Transport Co Ltd v Palmer*,[3] an agent who was held out as having authority to ship wigs was held to have ostensible authority to arrange the shipment of wigs and other items over the same route, but not to buy himself an air ticket.

1   See *Egyptian International Foreign Trade Co v Soplex Wholesale Supplies and Refson (PS) & Co* [1985] 2 Lloyd's Rep 36.
2   *Freeman and Lockyer v Buckhurst Park Properties (Mangal) Ltd* [1964] 1 All ER 630, CA.
3   [1976] 2 Lloyd's Rep 604.

15.33   Ostensible authority is of great importance where a principal has restricted or terminated the actual authority of his validly appointed agent. As between principal and agent, the restriction or termination is binding, and the agent will be liable to his principal if he acts without actual authority. However, third parties are not bound by any restriction, provided that they are unaware of the restriction or termination.[1]

Acts within the ostensible authority of an agent bind the principal even if they are entered into for the agent's own purposes or are fraudulent, provided the fraud occurs while the agent is purporting to carry out what he is ostensibly authorised to do.[2]

1   *Trickett v Tomlinson* (1863) 13 CBNS 663.
2   *Lloyd v Grace, Smith & Co* [1912] AC 716, HL.

15.34   Ostensible authority is based on the belief raised in the mind of the third party by the representation of the alleged principal that a particular person is his agent or that a properly appointed agent has authority in excess of his actual authority. It follows that a third party, who knows, or ought to know, that the principal has not invested with authority the person whom he appears to hold out as his agent, cannot rely on the doctrine of ostensible authority – because he cannot say that he was led to believe that that person was the principal's authorised agent.[1]

1   See, for example, *Overbrooke Estates Ltd v Glencombe Properties Ltd* [1974] 3 All ER 511; para 12.39 above.

15.35   It must be emphasised that ostensible authority depends upon a representation of fact made by the alleged principal. A statement by the 'agent' that he is authorised to carry out a particular transaction does not in itself give him ostensible authority to do so.[1] However, in exceptional circumstances an agent may have ostensible authority to describe his own authority (eg by assuring the third party that his actions have been approved by head office).[2]

1   *British Bank of the Middle East Ltd v Sun Life Assurance Co of Canada (UK) Ltd* [1983] 2 Lloyd's Rep 9, HL; *Armagas v Mundogas SA* [1986] AC 717, HL.
2   See *First Energy (UK) Ltd v Hungarian International Bank Ltd* [1993] 2 Lloyd's Rep 194, CA.

The disclosed principal

15.36   A disclosed principal is one whose existence, though not necessarily his identity, is known to the third party at the time of contracting. To put it another way, a principal is disclosed wherever the third party is aware that he is dealing with an agent.

If the agent of a disclosed principal makes an authorised contract, the principal can almost invariably sue and be sued upon it.[1] Whether the agent also can sue or be sued on the contract is a question which we discuss in paras 15.40 to 15.45 below.

Contracts made by deed formed an exception to the general rule, but statute now provides that, if an agent executes a contract made by deed on behalf of the principal, the principal can sue on it,[2] although there is authority to suggest that he must still be named in the deed.[3]

1   *Montgomerie v United Kingdom Mutual Steamship Association* [1891] 1 QB 370.
2   Powers of Attorney Act 1971, s 7.
3   *Harmer v Armstrong* [1934] Ch 65, CA.

The undisclosed principal

15.37   If the third party is unaware that he is dealing with an agent, the principal is called an undisclosed principal. An undisclosed principal can sue and be sued on authorised contracts entered into on his behalf.[1] The agent can also sue and be sued on such contracts.[2] It may seem odd that the third party can be sued by someone with whom he did not know he was contracting and with whom he may not have wished to contract. To protect the third party certain limitations have been placed on the right of the undisclosed principal to sue.

1   *Scrimshire v Alderton* (1743) 2 Stra 1182; *Thomson v Davenport* (1829) 9 B & C 78.
2   *Saxon v Blake* (1861) 29 Beav 438.

Limitations on the right of the undisclosed principal to sue
15.38   An undisclosed principal cannot sue in the following circumstances:

*   where he did not exist or lacked capacity at the time the agent contracted;[1]
*   where the contract expressly prohibits the intervention of an undisclosed principal;[2]
*   where the contract impliedly excludes the intervention of an undisclosed principal. For example, if the contract 'shows' the agent to be contracting as principal. In the controversial case of *Humble v Hunter*,[3] the agent of an undisclosed principal signed

a charterparty as 'owner' of the ship. This contract was found impliedly to regard the agent as owner, and the true owner (the principal) could not sue on the contract;
- where the third party can establish that he had some reason for wishing to deal with the agent personally. For example, if the agent was a man of fine reputation and acknowledged skill, and the contract involved reliance on such integrity and skill;[4]
- where the third party would have a defence to an action by the agent. This most commonly arises where the third party has paid the agent what is due under the contract (for example, by setting-off money which the agent owes the third party). However, this only prevents the undisclosed principal from suing where it is his conduct which has enabled the agent to appear to be dealing on his own account;[5]
- where the third party's legal position would be materially worse as a result of the principal's intervention.[6] For example, where two persons became protected tenants of a flat, it was held that evidence could not be brought to show that they had taken the lease as agents for an undisclosed principal (consisting of themselves and a third person), since this would increase the number of people who would be entitled to security of tenure under the Rent Act.[7]

Apart from these cases, an undisclosed principal can intervene on the contract, even where it is clear that the third party would have refused for personal reasons to deal with him, provided that there has been no positive misrepresentation.[8]

1   Para 15.4 above.
2   *United Kingdom Mutual Steamship Assurance Ltd v Nevill* (1887) 19 QBD 110, CA.
3   (1848) 12 QB 310.
4   *Greer v Downs Supply Co* [1927] 2 KB 28, CA.
5   *Cooke v Eshelby* (1887) 12 App Cas 271, HL.
6   *Collins v Associated Greyhound Racecourses Ltd* [1930] 1 Ch 1.
7   *Hanstown Properties Ltd v Green* [1978] 1 EGLR 185, CA.
8   *Dyster v Randall & Sons* [1926] Ch 932.

Election
15.39   Where the third party is in a position to sue either the agent or the principal (eg where the agent has acted on behalf of an undisclosed principal), the third party may, if he takes action against one party, be deemed to have elected to pursue that party exclusively. In such a case, even if the third party fails to obtain satisfaction, he cannot turn to the other party.[1] 'Election' in this sense may be express or implied. An implied election will only occur if a third party with full knowledge of all the relevant facts indicates clearly which party he intends to hold liable on the contract.[2] What constitutes implied election is a question of fact – beginning legal proceedings,[3] demanding payment, and debiting an account[4] are all relevant but not conclusive factors. Where principal and agent are jointly liable, the third party may even obtain judgment against one of them without forfeiting his right to sue the other.[5]

1   *Paterson v Gandasequi* (1812) 15 East 62.
2   *Thomson v Davenport* (1829) 9 B & C 78; *Chestertons v Barone* [1987] 1 EGLR 15, CA.
3   *Clarkson, Booker Ltd v Andjel* [1964] 3 All ER 260, CA.
4   *Young & Co Ltd v White* (1911) 28 TLR 87.
5   Civil Liability (Contribution) Act 1978, s 3: para 28.15 below.

Agents and third parties

15.40   As we have seen, where an agent makes an authorised contract on behalf of an undisclosed principal, the agent can sue and be sued upon the contract.[1] Where an agent makes an authorised contract on behalf of a disclosed principal, the general rule is that the agent cannot sue or be sued on the contract.[2] However, in certain cases the agent is liable and entitled on the contract, either alone or jointly with the principal.

1   *Saxon v Blake* (1861) 29 Beav 438.
2   See, for example, *Foalquest Ltd v Roberts* [1990] 1 EGLR 50.

Contracts made by deed

15.41   An agent who enters into a contract made by deed is liable on it, even if he is known to be contracting as an agent.[1]

1   *Schack v Anthony* (1813) 1 M & S 573.

Trade usage

15.42   If a trade custom, not inconsistent with the contract, makes an agent liable on a contract the courts will give effect to that custom.[1]

1   *Barrow & Bros v Dyster, Nalder & Co* (1884) 13 QBD 635, DC.

Where the agent is in fact principal

15.43   If an agent contracts on behalf of a non-existent principal then the agent must be contracting on his own behalf.[1] If someone purports to contract as agent but is in fact the principal, he can sue and be sued on the contract.[2] But, if X, a purported agent who is in fact a principal, appears to contract on behalf of a named principal, he cannot sue or be sued on the contract[3] (though he can be sued for breach of warranty of authority[4]). The agent can sue if he contracts on his own behalf and the contract indicates, but does not name, a principal and shows that the identity of the principal is not relevant.[5] The cases in this area are generally considered to be unsatisfactory.

1   See in relation to unformed companies, the Companies Act 1985, s 36C.
2   *Gardiner v Heading* [1928] 2 KB 284, CA.
3   *Fairlie v Fenton* (1870) LR 5 Exch 169; *Hector v Lyons* (1988) 58 P & CR 156, CA.
4   Para 15.46 below.
5   *Schmaltz v Avery* (1851) 16 QB 655.

Other cases

15.44   Apart from these special cases, an agent may be jointly or solely liable on the contract entered into on behalf of his disclosed principal, if the contract expressly or impliedly reveals this to be the intention of the parties.[1] Under the Partnership Act 1890, s 5, a partner who contracts on behalf of the partnership is jointly liable with the rest of the partners on that contract. In other cases, whether there is an implied intention that an agent shall be jointly or solely liable on the contract is a question of construction.

Particular note is taken of the description of the agent in a written contract and of how the agent signed a written contract. If either the description of the agent in the document or the form of his signature makes it clear that he is acting merely as an agent, he is not usually liable on the contract.[2] If neither the document nor the signature describes him as an agent, he is liable on the contract,[3] even if he is known to be acting as an agent. If the contract is oral and the agent is known to be an agent, the above rules for written contracts do not apply and every case is determined by reference to its particular facts.[4] If an agent is liable on a contract he will probably also have the benefit of that contract, unless, as a matter of construction, the contract reveals that the agent is to be liable without having the benefit of the contract.

1   See, for example, *Savills v Scott* [1988] 1 EGLR 20.
2   *Lucas v Beale* (1851) 10 CB 739. Cf *Punjab National Bank v de Boinville* [1992] 3 All ER 104, CA.
3   *Basma v Weekes* [1950] 2 All ER 146, PC.
4   *N and J Vlassopulos Ltd v Ney Shipping Ltd* [1977] 1 Lloyd's Rep 478, CA.

Rights of third parties against agents

On the contract

15.45   If the agent is jointly or solely liable on the contract, the third party can, subject to the doctrine of election,[1] sue the agent.

1   Para 15.39 above.

For breach of warranty of authority

15.46   If a person acts as agent, knowing that he has no authority, he is liable to the third party for breach of warranty of authority if he has represented to the third party that he had authority.[1] Purporting to act as agent constitutes a representation of authority, unless the third party knew or ought to have known of the lack of authority.[2]

Even if the agent genuinely and reasonably believes he has authority, when he has not, he may be liable to the third party.[3] In *Yonge v Toynbee*,[4] an agent acting on behalf of his principal was held liable for breach of warranty of authority when, entirely unknown to him, his authority had been terminated by the mental incapacity of his principal. The third party can sue even if he has not entered into a contract, provided he has altered his position in reliance on the representation.

If the representation made by the agent is one of law, not fact, he is not liable if it is untrue.[5] An action for breach of warranty cannot lie if the principal ratifies the unauthorised act.

The amount of damages which may be awarded under this head is the amount which would put the third party in the same position as if the representation (of authority) had been true.[6] Therefore, if the third party could have recovered nothing from the principal, even if the agent had had authority (for example because the principal is insolvent), he can recover only nominal damages for breach of warranty of authority.

1   *Collen v Wright* (1857) 8 E & B 647.
2   *Halbot v Lens* [1901] 1 Ch 344.
3   *Penn v Bristol and West Building Society* [1997] 3 All ER 470, CA.
4   *Yonge v Toynbee* [1910] 1 KB 215, CA.
5   *Beattie v Ebury* (1872) 7 Ch App 777, HL.
6   *Richardson v Williamson and Lawson* (1871) LR 6 QB 276; *Suleman v Shahsavari* [1988] 1 WLR 1181.

In tort

15.47   An agent may be liable even if his principal is also vicariously liable. Therefore, an agent may be liable in deceit, or under the rules in *Hedley Byrne & Co Ltd v Heller & Partners Ltd*[1] or, of course, for such actions as knocking down a third party by negligent driving. However, an agent may not be personally liable under the Misrepresentation Act 1967 unless he is a party to the contract which he makes on behalf of his principal.[2]

1   [1963] 2 All ER 575, HL; para 17.25 below.
2   *Resolute Maritime Inc v Nippon Kaiji Kyokai* [1983] 2 All ER 1; para 12.23 above.

Types of agent

Estate agent

15.48   The primary function of an estate agent is to effect an introduction between persons who wish to buy and sell land. His implied or ostensible authority, and thus the extent to which he can bind his principal, is very restricted. Unless expressly authorised, an estate agent cannot make a binding contract for the sale of his principal's property,[1] accept a pre-contract deposit,[2] or appoint a sub-agent.[3] In fact, his implied authority is limited to the making of statements about the property. If a third party relies on a misrepresentation made to him by an estate agent, the principal cannot enforce the contract[4] and may be liable in damages.[5]

The relationship between an estate agent and his client is a unilateral contract.[6] The agent is under no positive duty to act (except, perhaps, where he is a 'sole agent'[7]) but, if he does act, he must display reasonable care and skill.[8] In order to be entitled to his commission, the estate agent must fulfil precisely the terms of his instructions, which may vary from the mere introduction of a person who is willing to purchase the principal's property to the completion of a sale. The law on this matter is complex, but it may be said that the courts seldom award an estate agent his commission unless there is an actual sale.[9]

1   Chadburn v Moore (1892) 61 LJ Ch 674.
2   Sorrell v Finch [1976] 2 All ER 371, HL.
3   John McCann & Co v Pow [1975] 1 All ER 129, CA.
4   Mullens v Miller (1882) 22 Ch D 194.
5   Gosling v Anderson (1972) 223 Estates Gazette 1743, CA.
6   Luxor (Eastbourne) Ltd v Cooper [1941] 1 All ER 33, HL; para 4.2 above.
7   E Christopher & Co v Essig [1948] WN 461.
8   Prebble & Co v West (1969) 211 Estates Gazette 831, CA.
9   For further discussion, see Murdoch The Law of Estate Agency (4th edn, 2003), ch 3.

Auctioneer

15.49   Unlike an estate agent, an auctioneer has implied authority to effect an actual sale of his principal's land or goods,[1] as well as to make statements about the property.[2]

1   Pickering v Busk (1812) 15 East 38 at 43.
2   Smith v Land and House Property Corpn (1884) 28 Ch D 7, CA.

Mercantile agent or factor

15.50   A mercantile agent or factor is an agent 'having in the customary course of his business as such agent authority either to sell goods, or to consign goods for the purpose of sale, or to buy goods, or to raise money on the security of goods'.[1] Such an agent has ostensible authority to dispose of his principal's goods in the ordinary course of business.

1   Factors Act 1889, s 1.

Commercial agent

15.51   Statutory regulations[1] enacted to give effect to a 1986 EC Directive[2] define a 'commercial agent' as a self-employed intermediary who has continuing authority to negotiate, or to negotiate and conclude, the sale or purchase of goods on behalf of another person (the principal). The regulations lay down the basic rights and obligations of commercial agents and their principals, and provide that these cannot be contracted out of. Particular provision is made as to the circumstances in which a commercial agent becomes entitled to commission from the principal, the period of notice which must be given by either party to terminate their agency relationship and the entitlement of the commercial agent to compensation on such termination.

1   Commercial Agents (Council Directive) Regulations 1993.
2   Council Directive 86/653/EEC.

Part III

The law of tort

Chapter 16

Introduction

16.1 In this part of the book we adopt the following order:

- in this chapter we outline the nature, functions and main features of the law of tort, showing how it differs from other forms of legal liability;
- in the following four chapters (17-20) we deal with the most important tort, that of negligence;
- in the next six chapters (21-26) we deal with specific areas of the law of tort which are of particular relevance to the ownership or occupation of land;
- in chapter 27 we examine the legal principles of vicarious liability, that is the liability of one person, such as an employer, for torts committed by another person, such as an employee;
- the last chapter in this part is concerned with the legal remedies available where a tort is committed.

There are other areas of the law of tort which fall beyond the scope of this book. Among the more important of these are trespass to the person (including assault, battery and false imprisonment), interference with goods (including trespass to goods and conversion) and defamation (libel and slander).

16.2 Our main purpose in this introductory chapter is to describe the subject matter of the law of tort and to distinguish it from other fields of legal liability. We therefore examine the following issues:

- the main aims of the law of tort in providing a source of compensation for loss suffered, while at the same time seeking to strike a fair balance between the victim and the cause of harm;
- the essential elements of a tort, and how it differs from other kinds of legal liability;
- the various interests which are protected within the law of tort;
- the difficulty of relating the various torts to any general underlying principle;
- the alternative sources of financial compensation which exist for injury, damage or loss;
- the potential impact of the Human Rights Act 1998 upon the development of the law of tort.

16.3   Wherever people live together, the acts, activities or omissions of one may cause losses of various kinds to another. Compensation for such losses may take a variety of forms; unemployment benefit from the state, sick pay from one's employer, the proceeds of a private insurance policy and so on. Apart from these sources, it is the law of tort which decides whether the primary loss should remain where it has fallen (on the claimant) or be transferred to the person who caused it (the defendant). It is important to appreciate that this is all that the law of tort can do; the loss which has occurred cannot be repaired but only allocated. In reaching a decision on this question, the law takes into account both the kind and the severity of the claimant's loss, and the defendant's reason for causing it: in short, it is for the law of tort to implement social policy by laying down the circumstances in which the loss ought to be transferred from one party to the other.

If a single main function can be ascribed to the law of tort, therefore, it is the provision of compensation for loss suffered, within the general confines of attempting to strike a fair balance between claimant and defendant. This is not to say, however, that there are no other aims to be fulfilled. The very fact that a defendant is not usually liable unless he is 'at fault' (in the sense of having deliberately or carelessly caused harm to the claimant) indicates an element of punishment for misconduct. The same principle, by enabling a careful defendant to avoid liability, also has a deterrent effect which plays a part in helping to prevent accidents.

Balance of interests

16.4   Compensation may be described as the keynote of the law of tort, but it is not an end in itself. What the law of tort seeks to achieve is, in truth, a just balance between the many conflicting interests which are inevitably found in any society. These conflicts are sometimes obvious. For example, where the tort of private nuisance is concerned, the courts are asked to reconcile A's right to use his land as he pleases with B's right not to be interfered with in the enjoyment of his own land. Similarly, the tort of defamation seeks to balance C's interest in his reputation with D's freedom of speech.

The balancing process may, on occasion, result in a decision that A may cause harm to B carelessly, or even deliberately, without being legally liable for it. This is where the law is simply not prepared to give protection to the interests involved. For example, there is nothing tortious in our opening a supermarket next door to your established but uncompetitive grocer's shop, even if it is our earnest hope that this will quickly put you out of business.

On the other hand, the balancing process may in some circumstances bring about the imposition of liability upon a defendant who, far from wishing to harm the claimant, has in fact taken all reasonable steps to avoid doing so. Suppose, for example, that there is an explosion at a chemical plant (a highly dangerous and highly profitable enterprise) which causes severe damage in the neighbourhood. The law might well say that, provided all due care has been used in running the plant, the victims of the explosions will have no grounds on which to claim damages. But might it not say instead, and with equal justification, that the risk of such losses should lie upon those who run chemical plants for profit, rather than upon those who merely happen to live in their vicinity? If the latter view is taken, then it would be for the law of tort to impose strict liability upon those responsible for operating the plant.

16.5   A tort may be defined as the breach of a legal duty owed, independent of contract, by one person to another, for which a common law action for unliquidated damages may be brought. As we shall see in the next few paragraphs, this definition enables us to identify areas of legal liability which do not fall within the law of tort.

Perhaps the most important element of the definition is that of the 'common law action for unliquidated damages': unless this particular remedy is available, the defendant's liability (if any) does not lie within the law of tort. However, this is not to say that an action for damages is the only remedy available to a claimant in tort, nor even that it is necessarily always the most important. Some torts, such as nuisance, lend themselves readily to control by the grant of an injunction. A person who has been wrongfully dispossessed of land or goods may obtain an order for their return, and a limited amount of self-help (eg ejecting a trespasser) is tolerated by the courts in the interest of avoiding unnecessary litigation. Nonetheless, the possibility of damages on a common law basis must always be there and, further, these must be unliquidated, in the sense of being subject to assessment by the court rather than by prior agreement between the parties.[1]

1   As to liquidated damages, see para 11.20 above.

Tort and crime

16.6   A tort is the breach of a legal duty which is owed by one person to another; a crime, on the other hand, is the breach of a legal duty which is owed to, and enforceable by, society as a whole. Thus, the true distinction between these two fields of law lies, not in their subject matter (for such things as assault, theft and careless driving may be both crimes and torts), but in the purpose of the legal proceedings to which each gives rise. The main object of a criminal prosecution (which is usually instigated by the state) is to vindicate the rights of society against the offender by punishing him. Such compensation as he may be ordered to pay to his victim[1] is an afterthought; the court's attention is focused primarily upon the question of what should be done with the defendant. The usual aim of a tort action, on the other hand, is to secure compensation for harm suffered by an individual claimant. It is true that, in very limited circumstances, a court is empowered to punish a defendant by ordering him to pay an extra sum as 'exemplary damages', over and above what is needed to compensate the claimant,[2] but this is subsidiary to the main object of the proceedings.

1   Under the Powers of Criminal Courts Act 1973.
2   See para 28.3 below.

Tort and contract

16.7   It is sometimes said that duties in tort are automatically imposed upon a person by law, while contractual duties arise only out of his voluntary acceptance. Both sides of this distinction, however, require some qualification. In the first place, there are many tortious duties which come into effect only as a result of some voluntary act by the defendant (eg permitting another person to enter his land, or offering him some advice). Second, while the existence of a contract depends upon the parties' agreement (although even this may be a question of interpreting their conduct rather than their secret thoughts), much of its content may be decided on by the general law, as in contracts for the sale of goods, which we discuss in chapter 7.[1]

A better distinction, perhaps, lies in the purpose of each field of law. Tort, as we have seen, aims to compensate the claimant for harm done to him; it does this by awarding as damages a sum which will, as far as possible, restore him to his original position. In actions for breach of contract, by contrast, the claimant's basic complaint is that he has not received some benefit which he was promised, and damages are generally designed to fulfil the claimant's expectation, by putting him into the position in which he would have been had the contract been performed.[2]

Theory apart, there are some significant practical distinctions between a breach of contract and a tort, with regard to such matters as the liability of minors, the awarding of exemplary damages (available in tort alone) and claims against bankrupt defendants. Most important, the rules as to limitation of actions are different. The time within which a claimant must serve his writ (or automatically lose his case) generally runs, in contract, from the date of the breach, while in tort the relevant date is usually that on which damage is suffered.[3]

It sometimes happens that a defendant's conduct is capable of constituting both a tort and a breach of contract. For instance, a surveyor who, on inspecting a property for a prospective purchaser, negligently fails to discover defects in it, is guilty of both a breach of contract (an implied term that he will carry out his inspection with due skill and care) and the tort of negligence. In such circumstances, the law allows the client to frame his case in whatever way he chooses (usually in tort, so as to gain the advantage of more generous limitation rules).[4]

1   Para 7.20 above.
2   Para 11.3 above.
3   Paras 11.38–11.41 above, and 28.22–28.24 below.
4   *Henderson v Merrett Syndicates Ltd* [1994] 3 All ER 506, HL; see para 17.21 below.

Tort and restitution

16.8   In some circumstances, a person who has been unjustly enriched at the expense of another may be compelled by law to make restitution. For instance, if A pays money to B under certain mistakes of fact, B may be ordered to return it. This area of law falls outside the definition of a tort because A is not claiming unliquidated damages; nor, indeed, can it meaningfully be said that B has broken any legal duty in merely receiving the money.

Tort and breach of trust

16.9   The obligations which a trustee owes to a beneficiary arise out of the trust relationship and may, if broken, lead to an award of damages. The whole matter, however (including the principles on which these damages are assessed) is governed by equity, rather than by common law, and the administration of trusts is today a function of the Chancery Division of the High Court; tort, by contrast, is normally regarded as within the province of the Queen's Bench Division.[1]

1   Paras 2.9–2.12 above.

Scope of the law of tort

Interests protected

16.10   The most important interest to be recognised by any legal system is that of personal security which, broadly speaking, involves freedom from both physical injury[1] and wrongful deprivation of liberty. This particular interest also finds expression in other less obvious ways, such as the protection of a person's reputation and of certain status-based rights, eg the right to vote. Of rather less importance, though still well protected, are interests in the ownership and possession of land and goods.

As a general rule, since no person can own or possess another person, A is not allowed to sue in respect of an injury to B. However, an important statutory exception to this principle permits the dependants of a deceased person to sue the person responsible for his death for the loss of their breadwinner.[2]

It takes a fairly sophisticated legal system to recognise the possibility of compensating a claimant for those effects of the defendant's conduct which are purely financial. Even where protection is given to such economic interests (eg by the torts of conspiracy, intimidation and interference with contract) it is usually limited to cases where the defendant's conduct is deliberate. By and large, as we shall see, the causing of financial loss through mere carelessness is not actionable.[3]

1   Including psychiatric damage; para 17.37 below.
2   Fatal Accidents Act 1976; see para 28.12 below.
3   Paras 17.15–17.19 below.

The relevance of damage

16.11   Even though a claimant may have suffered injury, damage or loss, he cannot claim compensation under the law of tort unless some recognised interest has been infringed. There is, for example, no right of privacy as such; consequently, a person who wishes to protect himself against unwanted intrusions must, in order to succeed, show that the defendant has committed some recognised tort such as trespass or nuisance. Similarly, while injury to the claimant's feelings may aggravate the damages to which he is entitled in respect of a known tort, as where the defendant trespasses on the claimant's land in order to hurl abuse at him, it is not of itself an interest which the law will protect.

Examples of loss falling outside the scope of the law of tort are not difficult to find. In *Day v Brownrigg*,[1] the defendant, wishing to spite the claimant, his next-door neighbour, changed the name of his house to match that of the claimant's. It was held that, since there was no interference with any trading interest of the claimant, this conduct was not actionable. In *Bradford Corpn v Pickles*,[2] the defendant, irritated by the claimant's refusal to buy his land, excavated in such a way that water which would otherwise have percolated into the claimant's reservoir instead collected on the defendant's property. The House of Lords held that, since the defendant was absolutely entitled to this water (unlike water flowing in a defined channel), the claimants could not complain when he intercepted it. Finally, in *Perera v Vandiyar*,[3] a landlord harassed his tenant by cutting off the supply of gas and electricity to the flat. This was undoubtedly a breach of contract, but it was held by the Court of Appeal that, since the landlord did not actually enter the premises, he was not guilty of any tort.[4]

The other side of the coin consists of circumstances in which the defendant's conduct may be actionable as a tort, notwithstanding that it has caused no actual damage to the claimant. The torts which come within this principle are said to be actionable per se; they are trespass in all its forms and libel (but not usually slander). The reasons for treating these torts differently and imposing liability are purely historical.

1   (1878) 10 Ch D 294.
2   [1895] AC 587, HL.
3   [1953] 1 All ER 1109, [1953] 1 WLR 672, CA.
4   A tort claim may now arise in such circumstances, under the Housing Act 1988, s 27.

General principle of liability

Tort or torts?

16.12   An argument on which much has been written over the years is whether the whole field of tortious liability rests upon any general principle, or whether it consists simply of a random collection of civil wrongs, each with its own elements of liability. The dispute may be summed up by asking whether there is a 'law of tort' or merely a 'law of torts'.

The law of tort theory suggests that the law will presume any causing of injury or damage to be actionable, unless there is some legal justification for it. This, of course, provokes the obvious criticism that it gives no indication as to what is a sufficient justification. However, there are signs that modern courts do adopt this approach, albeit in a somewhat modified form; it is probably true to say that, where a defendant intentionally or negligently inflicts physical damage on the claimant or his possessions, he can expect to be liable unless there is some good reason (eg self-defence) for his action.

The law of torts theory, which compels every claimant to find an appropriate pigeonhole for his complaint, is perhaps attractive if the law is considered at any given moment, without any reference to its past or future development. In its extreme form, however, it fails to allow for what undoubtedly occurs, namely the creation by judges from time to time of new torts. Outstanding among these are *Lumley v Gye*,[1] in which the courts for the first time recognised that, if A induces B to break his contract with C, an action *in tort* will lie against A, and *Rylands v Fletcher*,[2] where liability even in the absence of negligence was imposed upon a landowner for the escape of dangerous objects from his property.

The law of tort theory may have some merits, but these should not be over-stressed; the very existence of different torts, each with its own elements of liability, serves to indicate that no simple principle can be found to underlie the whole field of law. Nor is this surprising; as we have already seen, the function of the law of tort is to resolve the conflicts of interest which necessarily arise between members of society and, since these interests may vary greatly in importance, so the appropriate balance to be struck between them will alter. Any attempt to reduce to a single sentence all the policy factors which may play a part in judicial decisions would result in a proposition so generalised as to be practically meaningless.

1   (1853) 2 E & B 216.
2   (1866) LR I Ex Ch 265.

Mental element

16.13   A major obstacle in the way of any attempt to deduce a general principle of liability from the law of tort is the fact that different torts depend upon different mental elements on the part of the defendant. Three levels are involved. In the first place, some torts (such as assault, false imprisonment and deceit) depend upon proof of intention, that is to say that the defendant was aware of the likely consequences of his act and in fact desired those consequences. It is of course impossible to be absolutely certain of what a person wants but this, like so much else, can be proved to the satisfaction of a court by evidence as to what he says and does. Further, for the purposes of the law of tort 'recklessness' is equivalent to intention. This covers cases where the defendant is well aware of the risks inherent in what he is doing and those where, while not actually wanting to injure the claimant, he is totally indifferent to the possibility that he will do so.

The second mental element which may be relevant to the law of tort is negligence, which normally signifies a blameworthy failure to appreciate and guard against the likely consequences of one's acts or omissions.[1] This concept, which today governs liability in the great majority of cases, involves testing the defendant's conduct against the objective yardstick of the hypothetical reasonable man; if it falls short of that standard, the defendant is liable, whatever his subjective state of mind.

Third, certain torts are based upon what is termed strict liability. This means that a defendant is liable for the consequences of his actions, even though he neither desired nor ought reasonably to have foreseen and avoided them. This kind of liability includes the rule in *Rylands v Fletcher*,[2] liability for animals[3] and breach of statutory duty;[4] the vicarious liability of an employer for torts committed by his employees is also strict.[5]

1   Chapter 18 below.
2   Paras 25.2–25.13 below.
3   Chapter 28 below.
4   Chapter 22 below.
5   Paras 27.4–27.16 below.

Motive

16.14   'Intention' signifies a person's desire for certain consequences; his 'motive', on the other hand, tells us why he wants them to occur. Broadly speaking, the law of torts is not concerned with motive; it asks only what the defendant has done, not why. Thus, if A is exercising a legal right, the law does not inquire why he chooses to do so. This principle, which helps to explain the case of *Bradford Corpn v Pickles*,[1] was also applied by a majority of the Court of Appeal in *Chapman v Honig*.[2] The defendant in that case was a landlord who, incensed that the claimant, his tenant, had given evidence against him on behalf of another tenant, served the claimant with a valid notice to quit. This, it was held, could not be regarded as wrongful, even though the defendant had clearly acted out of spite.

It is important to appreciate that bad motives are ignored only where the defendant is exercising an absolute legal right. In other cases, where his rights are qualified or limited, a bad motive may be the factor which tips his conduct over the line into what is unlawful. The tort of nuisance, for instance, permits a landowner to make some noise on his own land, provided that the interference which is thereby caused to his neighbours is not unreasonable; in deciding what noise level is acceptable, it is legitimate to ask why the noise is being made. In *Hollywood Silver Fox Farm Ltd v Emmett*,[3] the defendant fired guns near where his land adjoined that of the claimants, frightening the claimant's silver foxes and ruining their breeding season. A landowner is of course usually entitled to shoot over his own land; here, however, the defendant's actions were motivated by malice, and he was therefore held liable in nuisance.

1   [1895] AC 587, HL; para 16.10 above.
2   [1963] 2 All ER 513, CA.
3   [1936] 1 All ER 825.

Fault liability

16.15   Although, as we have said, it does not seem possible to reduce the law of tort to a single principle, one particular idea has, over the last century, come to occupy a dominant position. This is the notion that a person's liability should be related to his 'fault', in the sense of intentional or negligent causing of harm. This principle, and its important corollary, that a person should not be liable *unless* he is at fault, became prominent at the time of the Industrial Revolution, when its moral appeal coincided with important vested interests. The vast increase in both traffic and industrial activity which occurred at this time were bound to lead to more accidents and, if liability for these were strict, development would thereby be retarded. Accordingly, 'no liability without fault' became the popular cry, and casualties were regarded merely as an unfortunate but inevitable price of progress. Today, 'fault' is established as the major, though not the only, criterion of liability in the law of tort.

Tort in context

Other compensation systems

16.16   This part of the book is concerned with the law of tort, rather than with compensation as a whole. Nevertheless, the role of tort cannot be fully understood without at least a mention of other actual or potential methods of compensation for losses of various kinds. In this connection it should be noted that liability insurance, such as is carried by all drivers of motor vehicles, is not an alternative compensation system, but simply a method of ensuring that tort damages, once awarded, are actually paid; a claimant's recovery of compensation by this route depends upon his ability to make out a case in tort against the defendant.

Apart from the law of tort, there are two obvious sources of monetary compensation. In the first place, almost any kind of potential damage, from death to loss of business through bad weather, may be the subject of private (loss) insurance. Such insurance policies may be taken out privately by individuals, but they are often found (in the guise of sick pay or disablement benefits) as part of the benefits offered to an employee under his contract of employment.

The second major source of compensation is the social security system; this contains a large number of different benefits, most of which are designed to cover the financial consequences of accident or disease. The system is extremely complex and is constantly under review. However, an important general point is that injuries (including certain diseases) contracted at work are more generously compensated than the rest, which are simply dealt with in the same way as sickness.

A mixed system in operation

16.17   Of the compensation which is paid in the United Kingdom in respect of accidents causing personal injury or death, approximately one-half comes from the social security system, one-quarter from private insurance and one-quarter from the law of tort. Interestingly, however, the tort damages are shared among a mere 6% of accident victims, which means that these victims are a privileged minority. The discrepancy arises because tort, unlike social security, places no fixed monetary ceiling on awards, and also because tort damages on a generous scale may be awarded for such non-financial losses as pain and suffering. The favoured position of tort victims is accentuated by the fact that, broadly speaking, their damages are not reduced to take account of any private insurance benefits (except occupational sick pay) which accrue to them as a result of their injuries; some reduction in damages is made on account of social security benefits, but the overall position is nonetheless that, in financial terms at least, the victim of a tort may receive far more than he has lost.

In most people's scale of values, property damage ranks well below personal injury, and the case of the uncompensated victim is not regarded as such a pressing social problem. This has two practical consequences: little or no state aid is available to those whose goods or land are damaged, and liability insurance in respect of causing such loss is in general not compulsory.[1] It might be thought that these factors would render the law of tort vitally important in this area; in fact, however, its significance is greatly reduced by the widespread use of private loss insurance, such as 'comprehensive' motor cover and 'house and contents' policies, and by the fact that many liability insurance policies in fact cover property damage.

1   It is now compulsory for the user of a motor vehicle to be insured against liability of up to £250,000 for damage to property (including that belonging to his passengers): Road Traffic Act 1988, s 145.

Human rights

16.18   We described, in chapter 3, the role of the Human Rights Act 1998 in giving effect to certain rights enshrined in the European Convention on Human Rights.[1] Since October 2000, when the Act came into force, it has become clear that it will have a significant impact on the law of tort. As to the precise ways in which that impact will be felt, the most obvious is in relation to claims brought against local authorities and other public bodies, for harm caused by the manner in which they carry out (or fail to carry out) their statutory powers and duties. Since s 6 of the HRA 1998 makes it unlawful for a public authority to act in a way which is incompatible with a Convention right, it seems inevitable that torts such as negligence and nuisance should be redefined so as to ensure that they give adequate protection to those rights.

What is less obvious is the potential impact of the Human Rights Act upon tort claims between individuals or companies, since these are not specifically made subject to its operation. However, there is an argument to the effect that, since a court falls within the definition of 'public authority', the courts are therefore under a duty to interpret the law of tort in such a way that Convention rights are protected, even in cases where neither of the parties is a public authority. Whatever the merits of this argument, there are already signs that the UK courts are prepared to adapt the law of tort in this way.

1   Paras 3.29-3.36 above. The rights in question are those set out in Sch 1 to the HRA 1998.

Chapter 17

Negligence – duty of care

17.1 Negligence today is by far the most important ground of liability in tort. Surprisingly, however, the emergence of negligence as a tort in its own right is a comparatively recent development; attempts to deduce general principles in this area are largely confined to the last 70 years or so.

Many dictionary definitions of negligence concentrate on 'lack of proper care and attention' or 'carelessness', thus stressing the mental element involved. As we shall see, however, the law of tort is concerned with negligence *as conduct*. A person is considered to be negligent whenever his conduct falls below the standard which is set by the law, usually that of the 'reasonable man'. Thus a person may be held guilty of negligence in circumstances where he personally could not possibly have avoided causing the damage in question, for example, because he was not sufficiently intelligent to appreciate the risks inherent in his conduct, or because he could not afford to take the necessary steps to avert the danger.

17.2 As an independent tort, negligence may be defined as the breach of a legal duty to take care, owed by the defendant to the claimant, which results in damage to the claimant. There are thus three elements of liability, each of which must be proved by the claimant if his action is to succeed:

- a duty of care owed by the defendant to the claimant;
- breach by the defendant of his duty;
- damage to the claimant which is caused by the defendant's breach.

At first sight, this definition appears enormously wide, since it is not limited to any particular factual situation, nor to any particular interest of the claimant. However, the law does not suggest that a person should always and in all circumstances be liable for all the consequences of his carelessness; such a burden would, it is thought, be an intolerably heavy one. The problem, therefore, is one of exclusion, and two of the elements of liability mentioned above are used by the courts to keep the tort of negligence within reasonable bounds. In the first place, however careless a defendant may have been, he is not legally liable to the claimant unless he owed him a legal duty to be careful. Second, even where the defendant is in breach of a duty of care, certain of the consequences of his breach are regarded by the courts as too remote to be actionable in law.[2]

1   Paras 25.2–25.13 below
2   Remoteness of damage is dealt with in ch 19 below.

17.3   In this chapter we examine the following issues:

- the principles used by the courts in deciding whether a particular situation gives rise to a duty of care;
- the extent to which the law imposes liability on one person for failing to protect another, for example against harm deliberately caused by a third party;
- the reluctance of the courts to permit a claim in respect of losses which are purely financial;
- the way in which liability in the tort of negligence may be shaped by the existence of a contract;
- the extent to which liability for negligent words is different from liability for negligent acts;
- the problems involved in claims against a public authority for negligence in the exercise of its statutory powers;
- the extent to which judges, arbitrators, advocates and others are immune from liability in negligence;
- the extent to which damages may be claimed for injuries which are purely psychological.

Duty of care

17.4   We have already noted that a defendant is liable, not for all his careless conduct, but only for that which occurs when the defendant is under a duty to take care. This emphasis on the idea of duty arose because, when the law first began to create positive obligations to take care, it did so in the context of certain easily recognisable relationships, whose common feature was that one party reasonably relied on the other to exercise the care and skill appropriate to his trade or profession. In this way liability for negligence was imposed upon the 'common callings' such as innkeepers, surgeons and attorneys, all of whom were said to owe a duty of care to those with whom they dealt in the way of their business or profession.

At about the time of the Industrial Revolution, negligence as a basis of legal liability spread into areas where the relationship between the parties was far more tenuous than in the case of the common callings, for example between one highway user and another. In thus extending the scope of the tort, judges continued to speak in terms of 'duty'. A claimant who wished to sue in negligence was required either to show that his case fell within an existing category of duty, or to persuade the court that a new duty should be recognised to cover it. As a result, it has been said, this area of law was built up in disconnected slabs, as new duties were created to cover more situations.

A general principle
Donoghue v Stevenson
17.5   As the tort of negligence developed, the requirement of a duty of care served a useful practical purpose. If a court wished to exclude certain types of claimant who were regarded as lacking merit, such as trespassers, or certain types of injury which were not thought important enough to deserve protection, such as losses which were purely financial, it could simply declare that there was no duty of care to such a person or in respect of such harm. Conceptually, however, it was unsatisfactory, since there appeared to be no general principle underlying a judge's decision as to whether or not a duty of care existed.

An attempt to deduce such a general principle was eventually made in 1932 in the leading case of *Donoghue v Stevenson*.[1] The facts of that case were that the appellant was treated by a friend, in a café, to a bottle of ginger beer manufactured by the respondents.

Having poured out and drunk part of the contents, the appellant discovered that the bottle contained a partially decomposed snail; this discovery, she claimed, caused her severe nervous shock and, later, an attack of gastro-enteritis. Since the appellant had no contract with the proprietor of the café, she sued the manufacturers of the ginger beer, who argued that their duty in respect of products was owed only to those to whom they sold them. In rejecting this argument, a majority of the House of Lords laid down that, in normal circumstances, a manufacturer owes a duty of care to the ultimate consumer of his products, notwithstanding the absence of any contractual relationship between them. In short, whatever else it may have done, *Donoghue v Stevenson* undoubtedly added a new duty to the existing list.

1   [1932] AC 562, HL.

17.6   The main importance of *Donoghue v Stevenson* for present purposes, however, lies in the speech of Lord Atkin, in which an attempt was made to formulate a general test for ascertaining whether or not a relationship is sufficient to found a duty of care. Having pointed out that 'the rule that you are to love your neighbour becomes, in law, you must not injure your neighbour', Lord Atkin went on to consider the question of duty in these terms: 'Who, then, in law is my neighbour? The answer seems to be – persons who are so closely and directly affected by my act that I ought reasonably to have them in contemplation as being so affected when I am directing my mind to the acts or omissions which are called in question.'

17.7   If taken at face value, this approach would impose a duty of care upon a defendant whenever he ought reasonably to have foreseen injury, loss or damage to the claimant. This is manifestly not the real position for, as we shall see, there are a number of areas in which the question whether or not there is a duty depends, not upon some purely mechanical test, but upon wider considerations of public policy. Nevertheless, foreseeability is always relevant in an exclusionary sense for, if it is not foreseeable to the defendant that the claimant may suffer damage, then no considerations of policy can justify a court in imposing a duty of care upon him. Thus in *Bourhill v Young*,[1] where a motor cyclist carelessly collided with a car and was killed, an action by a woman who suffered nervous shock as a result of hearing the crash failed, since it was not foreseeable that she would suffer injury of any kind, either by impact or through shock alone. Similarly, in *Hewett v Alf Brown's Transport*,[2] where a worker's clothing became coated with lead oxide powder, his employers were held not liable to his wife, since it was not foreseeable that she would contract lead poisoning from washing the clothes.

1   [1942] 2 All ER 396, HL.
2   [1992] ICR 530, CA.

The current position

17.8   In the years since *Donoghue v Stevenson*, the courts have come to recognise that 'foreseeability' alone is not sufficient to justify the imposition of a duty of care. However, what more might be required is an issue which has been debated in a large number of cases in both the House of Lords and the Court of Appeal.[1] Not surprisingly, the judges in these cases have expressed a wide range of opinions as to the true legal position. The most extreme view is that the situations in which a duty of care exists cannot be explained by reference to any general principle at all, and that the question which a judge should ask, when faced with a novel type of claim, is simply whether it is sufficiently similar to a situation in which a duty of care has previously been held to exist. In this way, it is said, the law can expand 'incrementally and by analogy with established categories of liability'.

If correct, this view would effectively return the law to its position prior to *Donoghue v Stevenson*.[2] However, we believe that it is not correct, and that in truth there remains a general principle, albeit one which is vague and flexible. This principle[3] is that a duty of care in tort will be recognised where:

- it is foreseeable to the defendant that negligence on his part will cause injury, damage or loss to the claimant; and
- there is a relationship of sufficient 'proximity' between the parties; and
- it would be 'just and reasonable' to impose liability.

This three-fold test has been adopted and applied by the courts in a wide range of recent cases, dealing for example with negligent statements,[4] the causing of nervous shock,[5] the responsibilities of public authorities[6] and the liability of builders.[7] Moreover, despite suggestions that 'foreseeability' in itself is sufficient to found a duty of care in cases of physical damage,[8] it appears that the threefold test is equally applicable to such cases.[9]

1   The most important of these cases are *Home Office v Dorset Yacht Co Ltd* [1970] 2 All ER 294, HL; *Anns v Merton London Borough Council* [1977] 2 All ER 492, HL, *Peabody Donation Fund Governors v Sir Lindsay Parkinson & Co Ltd* [1984] 3 All ER 529, HL; *Caparo Industries plc v Dickman* [1990] 1 All ER 568, HL; *Murphy v Brentwood District Council* [1990] 2 All ER 908, HL and *Alcock v Chief Constable of the South Yorkshire Police* [1991] 4 All ER 907, HL.
2   [1932] AC 562, HL.
3   Which was adopted by the House of Lords in *Caparo Industries plc v Dickman* [1990] 1 All ER 568, HL.
4   *Smith v Eric S Bush; Harris v Wyre Forest District Council* [1989] 2 All ER 514, HL; *Caparo Industries plc v Dickman* [1990] 1 All ER 568HL.
5   *Alcock v Chief Constable of the South Yorkshire Police* [1991] 4 All ER 907, HL.
6   *Hill v Chief Constable of West Yorkshire* [1988] 2 All ER 238, HL.
7   *Murphy v Brentwood District Council* [1990] 2 All ER 908, HL.
8   See *Caparo Industries plc v Dickman* [1990] 1 All ER 568 at 585.
9   *Marc Rich & Co AG v Bishop Rock Marine Co Ltd* [1995] 3 All ER 307, HL.

17.9   In considering the three-fold test described above, it is important to understand that it cannot be, and is not intended to be, applied in a mechanical way. Even the element of 'foreseeability', which might appear to be a question of fact, involves a judge in evaluating what a reasonable person could be expected to foresee. As for 'proximity' and 'justice and reasonableness', the courts themselves have emphasised that these are not capable of precise definition, but are merely convenient labels used to describe the features of a particular situation which call for the imposition of a duty of care.[1] In effect, it appears that a court uses these labels to justify a decision which it has reached on pragmatic, even instinctive, grounds.

    In the remainder of this chapter we consider a number of areas in which the existence or scope of a duty of care is subject to important and difficult issues of policy. In such cases the courts, while applying the general principle described above (and especially the second and third elements), have also attempted to lay down guidelines more specifically relevant to the type of case under consideration.

1   See, for example, *Caparo Industries plc v Dickman* [1990] 1 All ER 568 at 574, 582, 585.

Omissions

17.10   Where one person owes a duty of care to another, a breach of that duty may take the form either of a positive act or of an omission, such as where a motorist fails to give a signal or a valuer does not check his figures. However, the law is extremely reluctant to impose liability for pure omissions, in the sense of creating a positive duty to act for the benefit or protection of others, except where those others have given something in return. It has, for example, often been said that, in the absence of a prior legal relationship, there will be no liability involved in watching a blind man walk over a cliff edge, or a child drown in shallow water. Thus in *Ancell v McDermott*,[1] where police officers discovered an oil spillage on a main road which was an obvious danger to traffic, it was held that they owed no duty of care to road users to remain at the scene and warn them of the danger.

Judicial reluctance to impose obligations in this area is at its strongest in cases where the claimant is effectively demanding to be protected from harm which is purely financial. Thus it has been held that an employer owes no general duty to an employee to advise him to join the company pension scheme.[2] Nor is an employer, who sends an employee to work in a country where there is no compulsory insurance in respect of road accidents, under a duty to advise him to take out his own personal insurance policy.[3] Similarly, a school is under no legal obligation to warn its pupils or their parents of the desirability of taking out personal accident insurance to cover the risk of being injured during sporting activities at the school.[4]

1   [1993] 4 All ER 355, CA.
2   *Outram v Academy Plastics Ltd* [2001] ICR 367, CA.
3   *Reid v Rush & Tompkins Group plc* [1989] 3 All ER 228, CA.
4   *Van Oppen v Clerk to the Bedford Charity Trustees* [1989] 3 All ER 389, CA.

17.11   The 'no liability for pure omissions' principle has led the courts to conclude, further, that a person who would not be liable for failing to act at all is equally not liable for acting negligently, provided that he does not actually worsen the claimant's position. In *East Suffolk Rivers Catchment Board v Kent*,[1] the claimant's farm was flooded by the bursting of a sea wall. The defendants, who had a statutory power but no statutory duty to repair the wall, adopted such inefficient methods of doing so that the land remained under water for an unnecessarily long time. A majority of the House of Lords held that the defendants were not liable in negligence, for they had not created any new source of loss to the claimant, but had simply failed to reduce a loss which had already occurred and for which they were not themselves responsible.

The principle laid down in the *East Suffolk* case was strongly endorsed in *Capital and Counties plc v Hampshire County Council*,[2] which concerned the legal position of the fire brigade. The Court of Appeal there held that a fire brigade would be liable if, in the course of fighting a fire at the claimant's premises, it negligently increased the risk of damage (eg by turning off a sprinkler system). However, the fire brigade owed no positive duty either to turn up at the scene of the fire or, once there, to exercise care and skill in fighting the fire.

1   [1940] 4 All ER 527, HL.
2   [1997] 2 All ER 865, CA.

Duties of protection

17.12   Notwithstanding what was said in the previous two paragraphs, a duty positively to act for the protection of another is sometimes found to exist. This is especially so where there is a pre-existing relationship between the parties. It has accordingly been held that, where a patient is known to have suicidal tendencies,[1] a duty of care to prevent him from harming himself may be imposed upon those who have care of him, whether it be the police[2] or a hospital.[3] On the other hand, where a prisoner sustained serious injuries in attempting to escape from police custody, it was held that the police owed him no duty of care to prevent this.[4]

The pre-existing relationship which has featured most frequently in cases of this kind is that of employer and employee. It has been held that an employer may owe a duty to prevent a mentally disturbed seaman from throwing himself overboard,[5] or to protect an employee (a soldier) from injuries sustained while returning, in a drunken rowdy group, from a party organised by their commanding officer.[6] In *Barrett v Ministry of Defence*,[7] where a naval airman died in a drunken stupor following a heavy drinking session on a naval base, it was held by the Court of Appeal that the defendants owed no duty of care to prevent him from consuming large quantities of cheap alcohol. However, they were held liable for their failure to take care of him once he had collapsed, on the basis that they had assumed responsibility for him but had not called a doctor.

Duties of protection have occasionally been found where any existing relationship is less obvious. In *Goldman v Hargrave*,[8] for example, a tall redgum tree on the defendant's land caught fire after being struck by lightning. The defendant could hardly be blamed for this, but he was held liable in negligence for leaving the fire to burn itself out, with the result that it spread to the claimant's land. Similarly, in *Barnett v Chelsea and Kensington Hospital Management Committee*,[9] the claimant's husband went to the casualty department of a hospital, complaining of vomiting and violent stomach pains, but the doctor on duty, who was himself feeling unwell, refused to examine him. In an action against the hospital authority for negligence,[10] it was held that on the facts a duty of care was owed, although the court left open the question of what the position would have been if the hospital had closed its doors altogether. Again, in *Smoldon v Whitworth*,[11] it was held that a referee in charge of an under-19 rugby match owed a duty of care to ensure the players' safety, and was accordingly liable to a player who suffered serious injuries when a scrum collapsed. And in *Watson v British Boxing Board of Control*,[12] the defendants were held liable in negligence to a professional boxer who suffered brain damage after being knocked out, for failing to ensure that immediate medical attention was available.

1   But not otherwise: *Orange v Chief Constable of West Yorkshire Police* [2001] EWCA Civ 611, [2002] QB 347, CA.
2   *Kirkham v Chief Constable of the Greater Manchester Police* [1990] 3 All ER 246, CA; *Reeves v Metropolitan Police Comr* [1998] 2 All ER 381, HL.
3   *Knight v Home Office* [1990] 3 All ER 237.
4   *Vellino v Chief Constable of the Greater Manchester Police* [2001] EWCA Civ 1249, [2002] 3 All ER 78.
5   *Ali v Furness Withy (Shipping) Ltd* [1988] 2 Lloyd's Rep 379.
6   *Jebson v Ministry of Defence* [2000] 1 WLR 2055, CA.
7   [1995] 3 All ER 87, CA.
8   [1966] 2 All ER 989, PC.
9   [1968] 1 All ER 1068.
10   Which failed on the ground of causation; see para 19.3 below.
11   [1997] ELR 249, CA; followed in *Vowles v Evans* [2003] EWCA Civ 318, [2003] 1 WLR 1607, which concerned an amateur rugby match between teams of adults.
12   [2001] QB 1134, CA.

Damage caused by third parties

17.13   One specific aspect of the principle of non-liability for omissions is that, in the absence of special circumstances, the defendant is not responsible for harm to the claimant which results from the unlawful (usually criminal) conduct of an independent third party, even where such harm is foreseeable. Thus a bus company is not liable if one of its vehicles, left unattended with its keys in the ignition, is stolen and then negligently driven so as to cause a fatal accident;[1] the management of a theatre owes no duty to actors to safeguard their belongings against theft from the dressing-room;[2] and the owner of an empty and dilapidated building cannot be held responsible if neighbours suffer when it is used as a means of access by thieves[3] or as a playground by vandals[4] or fire-raising children.[5] Moreover, this approach serves to exclude actions by the victims of crime which allege negligence on the part of the police in failing to arrest a suspected murderer[6] or failing properly to investigate a burglary.[7]

Given the absence of any duty to prevent physical injury or damage to property, it is hardly surprising that there is no duty to prevent financial loss resulting from fraud. Thus, where a finance company carelessly failed to register a hire purchase agreement concerning a car, it was held by a majority of the House of Lords that the company owed no duty of care to future purchasers; they were accordingly not liable when the hire purchaser, fraudulently concealing the existence of the agreement, 'sold' the vehicle to a dealer.[8] Even more extreme, it has been held that an insurance company is under no duty to inform a client that his broker is deliberately deceiving him as to the extent of his insurance cover,[9] nor to tell the assignee of a policy that the insured person is dishonestly jeopardising the cover.[10]

1   *Topp v London Country Bus (South West) Ltd* [1993] 3 All ER 448, CA.
2   *Deyong v Shenburn* [1946] 1 All ER 226.
3   *Perl (P) (Exporters) Ltd v Camden London Borough Council* [1983] 3 All ER 161, CA.
4   *King v Liverpool City Council* [1986] 3 All ER 544, CA.
5   *Smith v Littlewoods Organisation Ltd* [1987] 1 All ER 710, HL.
6   *Hill v Chief Constable of West Yorkshire* [1988] 2 All ER 238, HL.
7   *Alexandrou v Oxford* [1993] 4 All ER 328, CA.
8   *Moorgate Mercantile Co Ltd v Twitchings* [1976] 2 All ER 641, HL.
9   *Banque Financière de la Cité, SA v Westgate Insurance Co Ltd* [1989] 2 All ER 952, CA.
10 *Bank of Nova Scotia v Hellenic Mutual War Risks Association (Bermuda) Ltd* [1989] 3 All ER 628, CA.

17.14   The problem of damage caused by third parties was examined by the House of Lords in *Smith v Littlewoods Organisation Ltd.*[1] The defendants there owned a disused cinema which they intended to demolish in order to redevelop the site. While the building was empty and unguarded, children broke in and caused damage in various ways, including the attempted lighting of fires. However, neither the defendants nor the police were told of these attempts, and eventually a serious fire was started which got out of control and damaged neighbouring property.

In holding the defendants not liable for this fire, a majority of the House of Lords took the view that a landowner's responsibility for the deliberate actions of a third party can be determined on the basis of 'foreseeability', albeit by using that term in a special sense. It will not, it appears, be enough that the third party's intervention is foreseeable as a mere possibility or even on the balance of probabilities; it must be 'highly likely' to occur.

The view taken by Lord Goff in *Smith v Littlewoods*, although failing to attract support from the majority of the House of Lords, nonetheless offers a convincing rationalisation of the cases in this area of law. This suggests that a duty of care can only arise in special circumstances, of which the most important concern the defendant's relationship with either the claimant or the third party.[2] As to the relationships with the claimant which may be sufficient to create a duty of protection, it seems that an employer owes a duty not to expose his employee to a foreseeable wages snatch;[3] a police inspector owes a duty to help a fellow-officer attacked by a prisoner in a police station cell;[4] a decorator working alone in a client's house may be answerable for a theft which occurs when he leaves it empty and unlocked;[5] and the prison authorities may be liable for negligently revealing a sex offender's record to other prisoners, resulting in a foreseeable attack upon him.[6] As to relationships which are sufficient to create a duty to control the third party, it seems that an institution which assumes control of a potentially dangerous person such as a violent lunatic[7] or a borstal inmate[8] may be liable for negligently permitting its charge to escape and cause damage.

1   [1987] 1 All ER 710, HL.
2   Others mentioned are the negligent creation of a source of danger which might foreseeably be sparked off by other persons, and failure to take reasonable steps to create a known danger created on his land by other persons.
3   *Charlton v Forrest Printing Ink Co Ltd* [1980] IRLR 331, CA (on the facts, employers not negligent). However, the police authorities owe no duty to individual officers in deciding on the policing of a potential riot: *Hughes v National Union of Mineworkers* [1991] 4 All ER 278.
4   *Costello v Chief Constable of the Northumbria Police* [1999] 1 All ER 550, CA.
5   *Stansbie v Troman* [1948] 1 All ER 599, CA. As to possible liability under the Occupiers' Liability Act 1957, see *Cunningham v Reading Football Club* [1992] PIQR P141: para 21.13 below.
6   *Steele v Northern Ireland Office* [1988] 12 NIJB 1.
7   *Holgate v Lancashire Mental Hospitals Board* [1937] 4 All ER 19.
8   *Home Office v Dorset Yacht Co Ltd* [1970] 2 All ER 294, HL.

Economic loss

17.15   A person who is physically injured, or whose property is physically damaged, through the negligence of another, is entitled to recover damages in the tort of negligence for the financial consequences (eg loss of earnings if he is unable to work through injury, or the cost of repairing damaged goods). As a general rule, however, no damages may be recovered for "pure" economic or financial loss which results from the defendant's negligence, even where this is foreseeable. The leading case is *Cattle v Stockton Waterworks Co*,[1] where the claimant was employed under a fixed-price contract to build a tunnel through an embankment. His costs were greatly increased when the partly built tunnel was flooded by water escaping from the defendants' negligently laid main, and he sued in negligence to recover this loss. It was held that the claim must fail, since the claimant had not been injured; nor had any of his property been damaged.

The principle laid down in *Cattle* has been consistently applied by the English courts in subsequent cases. For example, in *Weller & Co v Foot and Mouth Disease Research Institute*,[2] it was held that a person whose negligence caused an outbreak of foot and mouth disease among cattle could not be made liable to auctioneers who lost business when the government ordered local markets to close; their liability, if any, would be restricted to farmers whose cattle were physically affected by the disease. Moreover, it has been extended to cases where the 'primary injury' is to a person, rather than to property. If an injury to A causes financial loss to B, who is dependent upon him, then that loss will not be recoverable in the tort of negligence.[3] This is demonstrated by the case of *Kirkham v Boughey*,[4] where the claimant and his wife were both injured in an accident caused by the negligence of the defendant. After the claimant had recovered from his injuries, he gave up his highly-paid job in order to be near his wife, who was still in hospital. It was held that, since this part of the claimant's loss of earnings resulted from his wife's injuries and not from his own, it was a purely financial loss; hence, even though it could be regarded as foreseeable, he could not claim for it.

1   (1875) LR 10 QB 453. Approved by the House of Lords in *Simpson v Thomson* (1877) 3 App Cas 279, HL.
2   [1965] 3 All ER 560.
3   The position is different if B's loss results from A's death, but only by virtue of a statutory right to claim: see the Fatal Accidents Act 1976, para 28.12 below.
4   [1957] 3 All ER 153.

The basis of the rule
17.16   The main reason for the 'economic loss' rule is the courts' fear of 'opening the floodgates' to large numbers of legal claims arising out of a single act of negligence. This could occur because, while the physical effects of an act of negligence are normally felt by a restricted number of victims, the financial consequences may be felt by a great number of people. To allow them all to recover damages might produce a total liability out of all proportion to the defendant's wrong; as the court pointed out in the *Cattle* case, to permit the builder's claim would mean opening the door to every employee who had lost wages as a result of the flooded tunnel.

While the reasoning of the English courts has generally been accepted throughout the common law world, some jurisdictions have been willing to adopt a more flexible approach and to permit a claim for pure economic loss where, on the facts of a case, there is no risk of opening the floodgates. This may be seen in two decisions, by the highest courts in Australia and Canada respectively. In the Australian case,[1] the defendants' dredger negligently damaged a submarine pipeline which was used to transport oil belonging to the claimants from the refinery to their depot. In the Canadian case,[2] the defendants' ship negligently damaged a railway bridge which carried the claimants' trains. In neither case did the claimants have any proprietary interest in the damaged property but the respective courts, emphasising that the claimants were the only users of the property in each case, found sufficient special factors to justify the imposition of a duty of care upon the defendants for the claimants' benefit.

1   *Caltex Oil (Australia) Pty Ltd v Dredge Willemstad* (1976) 136 CLR 529, HC of A.
2   *Canadian National Rly Co v Norsk Pacific Steamship Co Ltd* (1992) 91 DLR (4th) 289, Supreme Court of Canada.

'Pure' and 'consequential' economic loss

17.17   As mentioned earlier, it is only 'pure' economic loss that lies outside the tort of negligence; there is no bar to recovering damages for economic loss which is the result of physical injury or damage. This principle can sometimes lead to fine distinctions, as in the case of *Spartan Steel and Alloys Ltd v Martin & Co (Contractors) Ltd*.[1] The defendants there negligently severed an electricity cable laid under the highway, thus cutting off power to the claimants' foundry. Molten metal being processed in a furnace threatened to solidify, which would have damaged both the metal and the furnace, and so the claimants had to incur expense (and damage the metal) in removing it. Furthermore, the loss of power meant that four more 'melts' which were planned could not be carried out, so that the claimants lost their expected profits on these. The Court of Appeal by a majority held that, while the defendants were liable for the physical damage and consequential loss of profit on the melt which had already been in progress, the inability to go ahead with the other four melts was pure economic loss and was therefore irrecoverable. It should be noted however that, if the metal had solidified in the furnace and production had been held up while it was cleaned out, the loss of profits would then have been classed as consequential economic loss and would thus have been recoverable.[2]

1   [1972] 3 All ER 557, CA.
2   *SCM (UK) Ltd v WJ Whittall & Son Ltd* [1970] 3 All ER 245, CA.

Transferred loss

17.18   The 'floodgates' reasoning which underpins the pure economic loss rule is easy to appreciate in cases where one person's property is negligently damaged, and the claimant is just one of the many persons who is in some way financially dependent upon that property. However, the courts have extended the rule of non-recovery to cases where, because of some contractual arrangement between the owner of the damaged property and the claimant, the financial effects of the damage are felt by the claimant instead of by the owner. The net result is that the defendant's liability, far from being over-extensive, is actually less than it would have been if the owner of the property himself had sued for the damage done to it.

The pure economic loss principle, in this extended sense, has been used to prevent the time charterer of a ship (ie someone who has no interest in the vessel, but merely a contractual right to use it) from recovering damages in negligence from a person responsible for damaging it.[1] This is despite the fact that the time charterer must continue paying hire charges to the shipowner for a vessel which he is unable to use. Similarly, there can be no recovery of damages by an insurer who has to compensate an owner for his damaged property, or an employer who has to continue paying an employee's wages while the latter is injured and unable to work.[2]

In *Leigh & Sillivan Ltd v Aliakmon Shipping Co Ltd*,[3] the House of Lords held that, where a ship's cargo is damaged through the negligence of the carrier, only a person with legal ownership of or a possessory title to the goods can recover damages from the carrier in negligence. Hence, if the cargo is in the process of being sold, under a contract which leaves ownership with the seller but places the risk of damage on the buyer (in the sense that he must still pay the full price), the buyer cannot recover damages. This decision was based, not on any fear of opening the floodgates, but rather on the feeling that the carrier should not be made liable beyond what he has positively undertaken. Contracts of carriage usually incorporate exemption and limitation clauses, and it was felt that it would be unjust to allow the buyer to circumvent these by bringing an action in tort.[4]

1   *Candlewood Navigation Corp Ltd v Mitsui OSK Lines Ltd* [1985] 2 All ER 935, PC.
2   *Simpson v Thomson* (1877) 3 App Cas 279.
3   [1986] 2 All ER 145, HL.
4   See further para 17.21 below.

Defective products

17.19   In *Donoghue v Stevenson*,[1] it was clearly laid down that a manufacturer of defective goods, who was guilty of a breach of contract vis-à-vis the person to whom he supplied those goods, could at the same time be liable in the tort of negligence to a third party (the consumer) who suffered injury or whose property was damaged. What the House of Lords did not consider, far less decide, was whether a consumer could recover damages from the manufacturer where the goods in question did no actual harm to persons or property but were simply defective, in the sense of not being of the quality one would normally expect. In such a case, what the consumer had suffered would be perceived by the courts as pure economic loss, since he would not have received value for money.

It has now been clearly established that a manufacturer[2] owes no duty of care to a consumer to avoid causing pure economic loss of this kind.[3] Moreover, it makes no difference that the defect has caused physical damage to the product itself, nor even that it has rendered the product dangerous.[4] The manufacturer can, however, be made liable where a defective product causes damage to other property, although there may be some difficulty in deciding what constitutes 'other property' for this purpose.[5]

1   [1932] AC 562, HL; para 17.5 above.
2   Most of the cases have in fact concerned defective buildings, but the relevant legal principles are identical: see para 21.7 below.
3   *Muirhead v Industrial Tank Specialities Ltd* [1985] 3 All ER 705, CA.
4   *Murphy v Brentwood District Council* [1990] 2 All ER 908, HL.
5   Eg where defective packaging results in damage to what is inside it: see *Aswan Engineering Establishment Co v Lupdine Ltd* [1987] 1 All ER 135, CA.

The interaction of contract and tort

17.20   The context in which an act of negligence occurs may involve a contractual relationship, either between the claimant and the defendant or between one of them and a third party. Where this occurs, a court may well be called upon to decide whether it would be just and reasonable to impose a duty of care upon the defendant, in circumstances where a purely contractual analysis of the situation would suggest that none exists.

The problem can arise in two ways. First, where claimant and defendant are themselves linked by a contractual relationship, the question is whether a parallel claim in tort should be allowed to avoid the restrictions of that contract (exemption clauses, limitation periods and the like). Secondly, where either claimant or defendant has a contract with a third party, the question is whether a direct claim in tort for pure economic loss should be allowed to outflank the principle of privity of contract, under which contractual rights and duties do not affect third parties.[1]

These two situations we now consider.

1   Chapter 14 above.

Contracts between claimant and defendant

17.21   For many years, the question whether English law would permit 'concurrent liability' (that is, liability in tort between the parties to a contract) was one of considerable uncertainty. However, the issue was authoritatively settled by the decision of the House of Lords in *Henderson v Merrett Syndicates Ltd*,[1] which made clear that concurrent liability is in principle available. Provided that the relationship between the contracting parties is of sufficient proximity to found a duty of care in tort, the claimant is entitled to frame his action in whichever way he chooses.[2] However, this is subject to the important qualification that the contractual context must be closely examined, and may be found to exclude or restrict a potential duty of care in tort. Thus, where the contract lays down clear limitations upon the scope of a party's obligation, it will not be just and reasonable to imply a duty of care in tort which is of wider scope.[3]

Apart from the possibility of contract terms which clearly exclude or limit a duty of care, the terms of a contract may have a more subtle effect. This may be illustrated by the decision of the Court of Appeal in *Greater Nottingham Co-operative Society Ltd v Cementation Piling & Foundations Ltd*.[4] The defendants there were the nominated sub-contractors for piling work on a large construction project in which the claimants were the clients. The defendants entered into a collateral contract with the claimants, by which they undertook to use skill and care in the design of the work and the selection of material; however, this contract was silent as to the execution of the work. When, due to the negligent execution of the piling work by the defendants, the claimants suffered economic loss, the Court of Appeal held that this loss could not be recovered from the defendants by an action in tort. The parties, it was held, had set out their rights and duties in a contract which must be presumed to be exhaustive.

1   [1994] 3 All ER 506, HL.
2   In most cases, the only advantage to be gained by claiming in tort is that of the longer limitation period which applies.
3   *William Hill Organisation v Bernard Sunley & Sons* (1982) 22 BLR 8, CA.
4   [1988] 2 All ER 971, CA.

Contracts with third parties

17.22   The problem of 'third party' contracts may be illustrated by a hypothetical example from the construction industry. Suppose a sub-contractor, in carrying out construction work, negligently causes damage to the property of the client. Should the client's right to claim damages from the sub-contractor in the tort of negligence be affected by the presence of an exemption clause in either the sub-contract (to which the client is not a party) or the main contract (to which the sub-contractor is not a party)? A well-established rule of contract law states that an exemption clause in a contract can neither benefit nor bind an outsider,[1] but it would surely seem harsh to allow the client in such circumstances to outflank what was clearly intended to be a restriction on liability.

In several cases, the courts have accepted that the contractual background can indeed have an effect on a claim in tort. For example, where a sub-contractor negligently caused a fire which damaged the contract works, the Court of Appeal ruled that it would not be 'just and reasonable' to hold the sub-contractor liable for this, since the main contract stated clearly that the risk of damage by fire should lie on the employer rather than on the main contractor.[2] Similarly, in holding that an engineer in charge of a major construction project owed no duty of care to the contractor in issuing certificates, the Court of Appeal gave very detailed consideration to the terms of the main contract (to which of course the engineer was not party).[3]

1   See Chapter 14.
2   *Norwich City Council v Harvey* [1989] 1 All ER 1180, CA. Unless the main contract clearly allocates the risk in this way, the sub-contractor will of course be liable for his negligence: *British Telecommunications plc v James Thomson & Sons (Engineers) Ltd* [1999] 2 All ER 241, HL.
3   *Pacific Associates Inc v Baxter* [1989] 2 All ER 159, CA.

Negligent statements
Physical damage

17.23   Where physical damage is concerned,[1] there seems no reason why the law should distinguish between negligent acts and negligent words. A doctor's liability to a patient who is treated with the wrong drug should surely be the same, whether the doctor injects it himself or merely tells the patient to take the tablets. Indeed, the law has found little difficulty in imposing liability where a person suffers injury as a result of relying on negligent advice. In *Sharp v Avery*,[2] for example, the defendant motor cyclist offered to lead a second motor cycle, on which the claimant was a passenger, along a road which the defendant claimed to know. When the defendant went off the road at a bend and drove on to a piece of waste ground, the second motor cycle followed, and the claimant fell off and was injured. The Court of Appeal held that the defendant had assumed a duty of care towards the claimant, by his assurance that he knew the way and might safely be followed.

1   Including psychiatric injury: see *Farrell v Avon Health Authority* [2001] Lloyd's Rep Med 458: para 17.34 below.
2   [1938] 4 All ER 85, CA.

Financial loss

17.24   Where negligent words lead to purely financial loss, the position is more complicated. The courts' realisation that words may be used over and over again, reaching unsuspected audiences without losing their power, has led to concerns that a single careless remark might expose a defendant to wholly disproportionate liability. As a result, the law in this area has been slower to develop and is based on the idea of a restricted duty of care. Indeed, for some three-quarters of a century, the possibility of any legal development in this area was blocked by the decision of the House of Lords in *Derry v Peek*,[1] in which it was held that, in the absence of fraud, company directors were not liable for false statements made in a prospectus.[2] In *Candler v Crane, Christmas & Co*,[3] a majority of the Court of Appeal held that the neighbour principle laid down by *Donoghue v Stevenson*[4] made no difference to this situation, so that a duty of care in respect of words was restricted to cases of physical damage, contractual relationships and certain fiduciary relationships (eg that between trustee and beneficiary) which were recognised by equity.[5]

1   (1889) 14 App Cas 337, HL.
2   The actual decision was immediately reversed by statute; see now Companies Act 1985, ss 67 and 68.
3   [1951] 1 All ER 426, CA.
4   [1932] AC 562: para 17.5 above.
5   *Nocton v Lord Ashburton* [1914] AC 932, HL.

Hedley Byrne v Heller

17.25   The breakthrough, in the sense of judicial recognition that the tort of negligence might extend to statements leading to financial, came with the decision of the House of Lords in the leading case of *Hedley Byrne & Co Ltd v Heller & Partners Ltd*.[1] The claimants, a firm of advertising agents, were asked to arrange advertising space on behalf of a client. Since, in accordance with trade practice, the claimants would incur personal responsibility for paying for this space, they asked their bankers to check on the client's credit-worthiness. An inquiry was made of the defendants, the clients' bankers and financial backers, and they replied 'without responsibility' that the client was 'a respectably constituted company, considered good for its ordinary business engagements'. Relying on this reference, the claimants went ahead with the contracts; when, shortly afterwards the client became insolvent, the claimants lost some £17,000. It was held, at first instance and in the Court of Appeal, that the defendants were not liable because, although they had been careless, they did not owe the claimants any duty of care.

On appeal, the House of Lords held that the disclaimer ('without responsibility') prevented a duty from arising in the present case.[2] However, after an exhaustive review of the authorities, it was laid down that in an appropriate case a duty could arise. As to what would be an appropriate case, the test could not, it was said, be simply that of foreseeability, for this would impose an unacceptably heavy burden upon professional advisers. What was required was evidence of a special relationship between the parties, arising out of a voluntary assumption of responsibility by the defendant.

The circumstances in which a court might expect to find a special relationship and, with it, a duty of care were the subject of a wide range of opinions in the House of Lords; Lord Devlin, for example, took the narrow view that only a relationship which was 'equivalent to contract' would suffice. This apparently meant that all the elements of a valid contract, with the exception of consideration, must be present in the relationship. On the other hand, the decision may support a wider principle, namely, that a duty of care will arise whenever the defendant realises or ought to realise that his skill and care are being relied upon, provided both that there is such reliance and that the reliance is reasonable in the circumstances. However, even if this wider approach were adopted, it is highly unlikely that a person would be held liable in respect of words casually uttered on a social occasion. It may also be necessary to show that the defendant gave the advice with a particular transaction in mind.[3] Thus a person who issues a prospectus inviting shareholders to take up a special 'rights issue' of shares is not liable if they decide, on the basis of misleading information in the prospectus, to purchase more shares on the open market,[4] unless the prospectus was clearly intended to encourage such further purchases.[5]

1   [1963] 2 All ER 575, HL.
2   Such a disclaimer would now, at least in business circumstances, be subject to a test of 'reasonableness' under the Unfair Contract Terms Act 1977 (paras 9.14-9.24 above): *Smith v Eric S Bush; Harris v Wyre Forest District Council* [1989] 2 All ER 514, HL.
3   *Candler v Crane, Christmas & Co* [1951] All ER 426 at 435.
4   *Al-Nakib Investments (Jersey) Ltd v Longcroft* [1990] 3 All ER 321.
5   *Possfund Custodian Trustee Ltd v Diamond* [1996] 2 All ER 774.

17.26   The House of Lords in *Hedley Byrne v Heller* spoke in terms of a voluntary assumption of responsibility by the defendant, and a similar approach may be seen in many subsequent cases, including important decisions of the House of Lords.[1] In *Hood v National Farmers Union*,[2] for example, the defendants were sued by one of their members for failing to warn him of the strict time limits within which he must act if he wished to challenge the decision of a Milk Quota Tribunal. The reason they were held liable was specifically that they had taken upon themselves the role of adviser to their member in respect of such a challenge. Again, in *Verity and Spindler v Lloyds Bank*,[3] where the claimant sought a loan from the defendants in respect of a business venture, her bank manager took it upon himself to advise her as to the prudence of the venture. The advice was negligent and the bank was held liable for it.

The idea of a voluntary assumption of responsibility has been regarded as important in cases where a claim for negligence is brought, not against an organisation, but against the individual within that organisation who actually gave the offending advice. In *Williams v Natural Life Health Foods Ltd*,[4] where the managing director and major shareholder of a franchising company gave advice to a prospective franchisee, it was held that only the company, and not the individual, was liable, since the latter had not assumed personal responsibility for the advice which he gave. In *Merrett v Babb*,[5] by contrast, it was held that an employed valuer who signed a mortgage valuation report in his own name has assumed responsibility for it and therefore owed a duty of care to a house purchaser who relied on it.

Despite the attention paid to the need for an assumption of responsibility, it has been suggested in several cases that the idea is really a fiction. The important question, it is said, is not: 'did the defendant undertake, expressly or impliedly, to be responsible for his advice?' but rather 'in what circumstances will the law impose a duty of care upon him?'. In *Smith v Eric S Bush; Harris v Wyre Forest District Council*,[6] Lord Griffiths, having described the voluntary assumption of responsibility test as neither helpful nor realistic, suggested that the courts should approach this question as it would any other duty of care inquiry, by using a composite test involving foreseeability, proximity and 'justice and reasonableness'.[7] Nevertheless, it is only in rare cases that a duty of care in respect of financial loss will exist in the absence of a voluntary assumption of responsibility and/or reliance by the claimant on such an assumption.[8] All in all, the concept of assumption of responsibility remains a significant one.

In *James McNaughton Papers Group Ltd v Hicks Anderson & Co*,[9] an attempt was made in the Court of Appeal to identify those matters likely to be of importance when considering whether a duty of care arises in respect of an allegedly negligent statement. These are the purpose for which the statement was made; the purpose for which it was communicated; the relationship between the adviser, the advisee and any relevant third party; the size of any class to which the advisee belongs; the state of knowledge of the adviser; and reliance by the advisee.

1   See, for example, *Spring v Guardian Assurance plc* [1994] 3 All ER 129, HL; *Henderson v Merrett Syndicates Ltd* [1994] 3 All ER 506, HL.
2   [1994] 1 EGLR 1, CA.
3   [1996] Fam Law 213.
4   [1998] 2 All ER 577, HL.
5   [2001] EWCA Civ 214, [2001] QB 1174, CA.
6   [1989] 2 All ER 514 at 536.
7   See para 17.11 above.
8   *Banque Financière de la Cité SA v Westgate Insurance Co Ltd* [1989] 2 All ER 952 at 1009, CA; *Reid v Rush & Tompkins Group plc* [1989] 3 All ER 228 at 239, CA.
9   [1991] 1 All ER 134 at 144.

17.27   *Hedley Byrne v Heller* was undoubtedly a decision of major importance in expanding the frontiers of negligence, and subsequent courts have by and large adopted a liberal approach in basing new duties upon this broad principle. A striking exception, however, is the decision of the Privy Council in *Mutual Life and Citizens Assurance Co Ltd v Evatt*,[1] in which a policyholder in the defendant company asked for advice as to the financial stability of an associated company, in which he had invested money. The Australian courts regarded this as a 'special relationship', but a bare majority of the Privy Council held that, in the absence of an express undertaking to use care, a duty of care would only arise if either the defendant had a direct financial interest in the transaction on which he was advising[2] or the advice given was of a type which the defendant was in business to give. It should be noted, however, that, in a strong dissent, Lords Reid and Morris (both of whom had sat in *Hedley Byrne v Heller*) thought that a person giving advice outside the scope of his business or profession should still owe a duty of care, although the standard demanded of him might well be lower.

It is not easy to see why a person giving advice outside his normal field should owe no duty of care at all, and it is perhaps not surprising that the Court of Appeal has twice expressed a preference for the reasoning of the minority in *Evatt's* case.[3] Indeed, a car enthusiast who advised a friend on the purchase of a second-hand vehicle has been held liable in negligence,[4] although the case is not of great authority, since the defendant there actually conceded that he owed the claimant a duty of care.

1   [1971] 1 All ER 150, PC.
2   As in *Anderson (WB) & Sons Ltd v Rhodes (Liverpool) Ltd* [1967] 2 All ER 850.
3   *Esso Petroleum Co Ltd v Mardon* [1976] 2 All ER 5, CA; *Howard Marine and Dredging Co Ltd v A Ogden & Sons (Excavations) Ltd* [1978] 2 All ER 1134, CA.
4   *Chaudhry v Prabhakar* [1988] 3 All ER 718, CA.

17.28   The limits of the *Hedley Byrne* doctrine have been explored in a number of subsequent cases, and the courts have resisted attempts to use it as a basis for a positive duty to advise or warn of some danger.[1] Furthermore, the case of *Argy Trading Development Co Ltd v Lapid Developments Ltd*[2] suggests that, even for those who choose to speak, the duty of care is subject to strict limits. In that case a lease of part of a warehouse placed the obligation to insure against fire upon the tenants. In fact, however, the landlords had a block policy which covered the whole building and so the tenants, at the landlords' suggestion, simply paid the landlords a proportionate part of the premiums. Some time later the landlords allowed the policy to lapse without telling the tenants, who consequently found themselves uninsured when fire gutted the building. In an action for negligence it was held that, although the relationship between the parties was such that the landlords owed the tenants a duty of care, this merely meant that they must not give inaccurate information as to the insurance position at the time; they were under no positive duty to notify the tenants if circumstances changed.

Another controversial issue is how far liability extends beyond cases where information or advice is specifically requested by and given to the claimant. It appears that an inquiry from the claimant himself is not a prerequisite for the imposition of a duty of care, so that an employer who gives a reference for an ex-employee may owe him a duty of care, notwithstanding that the reference is requested by and given to a third party.[3] Indeed, a duty may occasionally arise without any request at all, so that a bank manager who takes it upon himself to explain to a customer the legal significance of a mortgage which she is about to execute in the bank's favour must do so with care and skill.[4] However, success in such cases is rare; the Court of Appeal has held that, where information had not been requested at all (it was contained in advertisements published by a manufacturer), the mere fact that a person might be expected to rely on it was not sufficient to establish a 'special relationship'.[5] Similarly, where a medical charity advised a man that, following a vasectomy operation, he need no longer use contraception, the charity was held to owe no duty of care to a future sexual partner who became pregnant when, most unexpectedly, the vasectomy spontaneously reversed itself.[6]

1   Para 17.10 above.
2   [1977] 3 All ER 785.
3   *Spring v Guardian Assurance plc* [1994] 3 All ER 129, HL.
4   *Cornish v Midland Bank plc* [1985] 3 All ER 513, CA.
5   *Lambert v Lewis* [1980] 1 All ER 978, CA.
6   *Goodwill v British Pregnancy Advisory Service* [1996] 2 All ER 161, CA.

Professional liability

17.29   The greatest impact of *Hedley Byrne v Heller* has undoubtedly been in the sphere of professional work, because it is here that one person's reliance on advice from another is most likely to be regarded as reasonable. In fact, the principle has been extended to situations in which there is no discernible 'advice' at all, but where the professional adviser can be said to have assumed responsibility for the services which he provides.

Of the various professionals who have been held liable in the tort of negligence to persons other than their clients, a number of examples may help to show what the courts regard as a 'special relationship' for this purpose. In *Shankie-Williams v Heavey*[1] a surveyor, who was instructed by the vendor of three flats in a converted house to investigate the ground floor flat, reported that it was free from dry rot. It was held by the Court of Appeal that the surveyor, although instructed and paid by the vendor, owed a duty of care to a purchaser of that flat, but not to the purchaser of one of the other flats, who saw his report and jumped to the conclusion that the whole property must be rot-free.

A valuer who carries out a valuation of commercial property for a potential borrower, knowing that it will be shown to and relied upon by a lender, will owe a duty of care to the lender.[2] However, if the valuer in such circumstances makes it clear that the valuation is for the use only of a named lender, he will owe no duty of care to any other lender to whom it is passed on without his consent.[3] In residential cases, a valuer who is instructed by a building society or other lender to value a house for mortgage purposes will owe a duty of care to the purchaser and, moreover, any attempt to disclaim liability is likely to be held unreasonable and thus invalid under the Unfair Contract Terms Act 1977.[4] However, a valuer or surveyor who advises a mortgage lender on the sale of a repossessed property owes no duty of care to the borrower to see that the property is sold at a reasonable price.[5]

The position of an estate agent who, while acting on behalf of a vendor, passes on false or misleading information about the property to a prospective purchaser, is not entirely clear. It has been held on two occasions[6] that, where the agent was responding to a specific inquiry form the purchaser, he had voluntarily assumed responsibility for the information and thus owed a duty of care. However, in *McCullagh v Lane Fox & Partners Ltd*[7] it was suggested by a majority of the Court of Appeal that, in normal circumstances, an agent would not be liable in negligence for false statements in sale particulars, since the purchaser would be expected to rely, not on this information, but on the investigations carried out by his own solicitor and surveyor.

Turning to the legal profession, it appears that a vendor's solicitor owes no duty to the purchaser in answering preliminary inquiries before the conclusion of a contract for the sale of land.[8] However, a solicitor acting for a small firm in a loan transaction was held to have assumed responsibility to the lender, a private individual, and was liable in negligence for failing to warn the lender that the security might well prove ineffective.[9] Moreover, a solicitor who, on behalf of his client, gives an express or implied undertaking to take certain measures for the protection of a known third party, will owe a duty of care to that third party to fulfil his undertaking.[10] Of more far-reaching effect, it has been held that a solicitor instructed to draft a client's will owes a duty of care to those who are intended to benefit under it.[11] This ruling is especially interesting in that liability may be imposed upon the solicitor, even though it cannot be said that the beneficiaries have 'relied' upon any 'advice' which he gives. However, the duty imposed upon a solicitor in such circumstances appears limited to ensuring that the will achieves the testator's purpose; he is under no duty towards a beneficiary to warn the testator that subsequent dealings with his property are likely to affect that beneficiary's interest,[12] nor to advise the testator of further steps which may be required if the gift to the beneficiary is to be effective.[13] Nor can this duty of care be extended beyond wills to a badly drafted and thus ineffective deed of gift, where the donor (the client's solicitor) refused to execute another deed.[14]

As for other professions, it has been held that accountants instructed by a company to audit its accounts owe a duty of care to its existing shareholders as a group, but not to an individual existing or potential investor[15] or a creditor,[16] unless they make a specific representation to an identified individual which is intended to be relied upon.[17] An architect or engineer undoubtedly owes a duty to his client in issuing certificates under a construction contract,[18] but it appears that he owes no comparable duty of care in tort to the contractor.[19] Finally, it has been held that a surveyor who certifies a ship as seaworthy[20] or an aircraft as airworthy[21] owes no duty of care to a prospective purchaser, nor to the owner of cargo lost when the ship subsequently sinks.[22]

1   [1986] 2 EGLR 139, CA.
2   *Cann v Willson* (1888) 39 Ch D 39.
3   *Omega Trust Co Ltd v Wright Son & Pepper* [1997] 1 EGLR 120, CA.
4   *Smith v Eric S Bush; Harris v Wyre Forest District Council* [1989] 2 All ER 514, HL.
5   *Raja v Austin Gray* [2002] EWCA Civ 1965, [2003] 13 EG 117, CA.
6   *Computastaff Ltd v Ingledew, Brown, Bennison and Garrett* [1983] 2 EGLR 150; *Duncan Investments Ltd v Underwoods* [1997] PNLR 521. A similar principle applies to an auctioneer: *McAnarney v Hanraham* [1993] IR 492.
7   [1996] 1 EGLR 35, CA. The agents were in any event protected by an effective disclaimer in their sales particulars.
8   *Cemp Properties (UK) Ltd v Dentsply Research and Development Corpn* [1991] 2 EGLR 197, CA; *Gran Gelato Ltd v Richcliff (Group) Ltd* [1992] 1 All ER 865.
9   *Dean v Allin & Watts* [2001] EWCA Civ 758, [2001] Lloyd's Rep PN 605, CA.

10   *Al-Kandari v JR Brown & Co* [1988] 1 All ER 833, CA.
11   *White v Jones* [1995] 1 All ER 691, HL.
12   *Clarke v Bruce Lance & Co* [1988] 1 All ER 364, CA.
13   *Carr-Glynn v Frearsons* [1997] 2 All ER 614.
14   *Hemmens v Wilson Browne* [1993] 4 All ER 826.
15   *Caparo Industries plc v Dickman* [1990] 1 All ER 568, HL; *James McNaughton Papers Group Ltd v Hicks Anderson & Co* [1991] 1 All ER 134, CA.
16   *Al Saudi Banque v Clark Pixley* [1989] 3 All ER 361.
17   *Morgan Crucible Co plc v Hill Samuel Bank Ltd* [1991] 1 All ER 148, CA.
18   *Sutcliffe v Thackrah* [1974] 1 All ER 859, HL: para 17.35 below.
19   *Pacific Associates Inc v Baxter* [1989] 2 All ER 159, CA.
20   *Reeman v Department of Transport* [1997] 2 Lloyd's Rep 648, CA.
21   *Philcox v Civil Aviation Authority* [1995] 27 LS Gaz R 33, CA.
22   *Marc Rich & Co AG v Bishop Rock Marine Co Ltd* [1995] 3 All ER 307, HL.

Public authorities

17.30   Public bodies such as local authorities operate against the background of detailed and complex statutory provisions. Parts of these statutory codes impose positive duties on the bodies in question, others confer discretionary powers. Where, in the exercise of its statutory functions, a public body causes injury, damage or loss to an individual, a question which arises is whether an action by the victim may lead to the recovery of damages.

The general principles of law governing such actions were subjected to detailed examination by the House of Lords in three important cases,[1] from which the following principles emerge:

- In certain limited circumstances, an action may lie for the breach by a public authority of a statutory duty, independent of any question of negligence. However, this requires the claimant to convince the court that Parliament intended the statute in question to create a civil right of action for damages.[2]
- The mere fact of carelessness by a public authority in the exercise of a statutory power or duty does not lead to liability. In order to succeed in an action for negligence, the claimant must establish a common law duty of care in accordance with the general principles described earlier.[3]
- Although a public authority may in principle owe a common law duty of care as to the manner in which it performs its statutory functions, it owes no such duty of care as to the way in which it exercises a statutory discretion; anything within the ambit of its discretion is a matter for the authority, not for the courts. Furthermore, if the factors relevant to the exercise of the discretion include matters of policy, the courts will not even consider whether or not the decision was within the ambit of the statutory discretion.[4]
- Where the claimant's complaint is that the public authority negligently failed to exercise a statutory power, the claimant can only succeed by showing that:
  - any rational public authority would have exercised the power in question (so that there was in effect a public law duty to act); and
    the policy of the statute requires compensation to be paid to persons who suffer loss because the power was not exercised.

1   *X v Bedfordshire County Council* [1995] 3 All ER 353, HL; *Stovin v Wise* [1996] 3 All ER 801, HL and *Barrett v Enfield London Borough Council* [1999] 3 All ER 193, HL.
2   See ch 22.
3   Paras 17.11–17.12 above.
4   The distinction between 'policy' and 'operational' decisions was given detailed consideration in *Anns v Merton London Borough Council* [1977] 2 All ER 492, HL.

17.31   The way in which the courts have applied these principles has made it difficult for a claimant to succeed in an action for negligence against a public authority. The courts have shown considerable reluctance to deal with the kind of claims put forward in *X v Bedfordshire County Council*[1] (inadequate handling of potential child abuse cases, and failure to cater sufficiently for children with special educational needs). This is perhaps not altogether surprising, in view of the delicate decision-making processes involved, but a similar judicial attitude may be found in other less delicate areas. *Stovin v Wise*,[2] for example, concerned a claim by a motor-cyclist who was seriously injured when struck by a car emerging from a road junction. The junction was known to be dangerous, and the claimant claimed that the highway authority should have exercised its statutory power to remove a bank of earth which obstructed visibility. However, this claim was rejected by the House of Lords (albeit by a bare 3–2 majority).

In adopting such a restrictive approach to claims against public authorities, the courts clearly recognise that such actions raise a number of difficult issues which are not present in other cases of negligence. For example, it is always necessary to examine the particular statute under which the public body was acting at the time of its alleged negligence, to see whether its purpose was to protect the claimant from the type of harm which he has suffered.[3] So too, the courts have shown an increasing awareness of the fact that, in many of these cases, the defendant has not positively caused harm to the claimant, but has merely failed to offer him protection against harm arising naturally or from the acts of some third party. The law is slow to impose affirmative duties of protection,[4] and actions of this kind have failed against financial regulators,[5] a local authority responsible for vetting nursing homes,[6] the Law Society in its function of controlling solicitors,[7] the police in their function of investigating and suppressing crime,[8] the fire brigade[9] and the coastguard.[10] By contrast, it has been held that, once an ambulance service "accepts" a call for assistance, it assumes a duty of care towards the person concerned.[11]

In a number of cases, claimants have sought to use the tort of negligence as a means in effect of challenging decisions reached by various officials or public bodies. In rejecting these claims, the policy grounds relied upon by the courts have included the availability of alternative remedies such as statutory appeal procedures, the need to avoid putting undue pressure on public decision-makers and the undesirability of attempts by the courts to 'second-guess' the valid exercise of a discretion specifically conferred upon some other person or body. A combination of these factors has proved fatal to actions brought against an adjudicating officer deciding on a social security claim,[12] an immigration officer dealing with an asylum seeker,[13] a government minister exercising a discretionary power over foreign investment,[14] a police authority conducting disciplinary proceedings against a constable,[15] the charity commissioners[16] and university examiners.[17]

1   [1995] 3 All ER 353, HL.
2   [1996] 3 All ER 801, HL.
3   *Curran v Northern Ireland Co-ownership Housing Association Ltd* [1987] 2 All ER 13, HL.
4   See paras 17.10–17.14 above.
5   *Yuen Kun-yeu v A-G of Hong Kong* [1987] 2 All ER 705, PC.
6   *Martine v South East Kent Health Authority* (1993) 20 BMLR 51, CA.
7   *Wood v Law Society* [1993] NLJR 1475.
8   *Hill v Chief Constable of West Yorkshire* [1988] 2 All ER 238, HL; para 17.16 below.
9   *Capital and Counties plc v Hampshire County Council* [1997] 2 All ER 865, CA.
10   *OLL Ltd v Secretary of State for Transport* [1997] 3 All ER 897.
11   *Kent v Griffiths* [2000] 2 All ER 474, CA.
12   *Jones v Department of Employment* [1988] 1 All ER 725, CA.
13   *W v Home Office* [1997] Imm AR 302, CA.
14   *Rowling v Takaro Properties Ltd* [1988] 1 All ER 163, PC.
15   *Calveley v Chief Constable of Merseyside* [1989] 1 All ER 1025, HL.
16   *Mills v Winchester Diocesan Board of Finance* [1989] 2 All ER 317.
17   *Thorne v University of London* [1966] 2 All ER 338, CA.

17.32   In contrast to the generally restrictive approach described above, the courts have shown much greater willingness to impose a duty of care owed by a public authority, where the authority can be said to have assumed responsibility towards the claimant as an individual.[1]

This is especially so where the authority offers specific advice to someone, in such circumstances as to indicate that it assumes responsibility for the accuracy of that advice.[2] The courts have thus accepted that a duty of care might be owed by a local planning authority which advised a property developer about the status of a highway;[3] an environmental health officer who advised the owners of a guest house that expensive building work was necessary to meet statutory requirements,[4] and by local authorities which offered specific psychological advice to children with special educational needs,[5] recommended a child minder who then mistreated children in her care;[6] assured prospective foster parents that they would not be sent any child suspected of committing sexual abuse;[7] and failed to inform prospective adopters that the child placed with them for adoption had very serious behavioural problems.[8]

1   Swinney v Chief Constable of Northumbria Police [1996] 3 All ER 449, CA; L v Reading Borough Council [2001] EWCA Civ 346, [2001] 1 WLR 1575.
2   Para 17.25 above.
3   Gooden v Northamptonshire County Council [2002] 1 EGLR 137, CA.
4   Welton v North Cornwall District Council [1997] 1 WLR 570, [1997] PNLR 108, CA.
5   X v Bedfordshire County Council [1995] 3 All ER 353, HL.
6   T (a minor) v Surrey County Council [1994] 4 All ER 577.
7   W v Essex County Council [2000] 2 All ER 237, HL.
8   A& B v Essex County Council [2002] EWHC 2707 (QB), [2003] 1 FLR 615.

Judicial process

17.33   It has been said that judges, barristers, solicitors, jurors and witnesses enjoy an absolute immunity from any form of civil action being brought against them in respect of anything they say or do in court during the course of a trial. Indeed, it has been held that a litigant is owed no duty of care, as to the way in which legal proceedings are conducted, by the opposing party,[1] nor by the opposing party's solicitor[2] or barrister.[3] This means that, for example, there is no liability for causing loss to another party by negligently serving a notice upon him at the wrong address. However, the immunity does not extend to persons less closely connected with legal proceedings. A sequestrator, for example, owes a duty of care to the owner of property which he administers, notwithstanding that he is acting as an officer of the court.[4]

We now consider the most important effects of this rule, and one very significant exception to it.

1   Business Computers International Ltd v Registrar of Companies [1987] 3 All ER 465. This includes the Crown Prosecution Service: Elguzouli-Daf v Metropolitan Police Comr [1995] 1 All ER 833, CA.
2   Al-Kandari v JR Brown & Co [1988] 1 All ER 833 at 835, CA.
3   Connolly-Martin v Davis [1999] PNLR 826, CA.
4   IRC v Hoogstraten [1984] 3 All ER 25, CA.

Judges and magistrates

17.34   A judge (at least one who sits in a superior court of record)[1] has total immunity from any form of civil action in respect of anything which he says or does within his jurisdiction.[2] Even if he exceeds his jurisdiction, it seems that he is still immune from civil action, provided that he acts in good faith.[2] Statute has now in effect brought the legal position of magistrates into line with that of judges.[3]

1   The Crown Court, High Court and higher courts.
2   Sirros v Moore [1974] 3 All ER 776, CA.
3   Courts and Legal Services Act 1990, s 108.

Arbitrators and valuers

17.35   The immunity of judges has been extended to certain other persons who exercise a judicial or quasi-judicial function. In particular, an arbitrator is not liable for anything which he does or fails to do unless the act or omission is shown to have been in bad faith.[1]

It was for a long time thought that a similar immunity was enjoyed by 'quasi-arbitrators', ie persons who occupied a similar position to arbitrators but who were not formally appointed. Indeed, it was even said that any person determining a question which compelled him to hold the scales fairly between two other persons would be immune from an action in negligence. If correct, this would include any case in which the parties agree to be bound by the decision of a valuer appointed jointly by them both.

Two decisions of the House of Lords indicate that the immunity of quasi-arbitrators is not as wide-ranging as had previously been thought, although the present limits are not altogether clear. In *Sutcliffe v Thackrah*,[2] the defendant, an architect, was employed to supervise the construction of a house which was being built for the claimant. The defendant negligently certified certain work as having been properly executed, whereupon the claimant paid the builder. The work had not in fact been properly done, but the claimant was unable to recover his money as the builder had become insolvent, whereupon the claimant sued the defendant in negligence. The defendant claimed to be entitled to immunity as a quasi-arbitrator, on the basis that he was deciding a question which affected the parties' rights, but the House of Lords held that this immunity exists only where a person is engaged in settling a specific dispute, present or future. Nor did it matter that, in issuing certificates, the architect owed a duty to the builder to act honestly; this duty, said the House of Lords, in no way conflicted with the duty of care which he owed to his client.

In *Arenson v Casson, Beckman, Rutley & Co*,[3] the claimant, on entering his uncle's business, was given a number of shares in the private company which operated it. It was agreed that, if the claimant left the business, he would sell the shares to his uncle at whatever the defendants, who were the company's auditors, decided was a fair value. This eventually fell to be done, but the claimant subsequently complained that the true value of his shares was six times the fair value placed on them by the defendants. The Court of Appeal by a majority held that the defendants owed no duty of care in making this valuation, but their decision was unanimously reversed by the House of Lords, who took the opportunity to consider the general question of 'quasi-arbitrators'. Their Lordships agreed that immunity in this area does not depend simply on whether or not the defendant is formally appointed as an arbitrator. What matters, according to the majority, is whether the defendant is appointed to settle an existing dispute by judicial means, so as to bind the parties by his decision. If not, there will be no immunity.[4]

In principle, there is much to be said in theory for linking immunity to function, rather than to the formal question of whether the defendant is an arbitrator or not. However, it should not be overlooked that a party who is dissatisfied with the result of an arbitration has a limited right of appeal to the courts,[5] and it might therefore be argued that he does not need to be able to sue the arbitrator in negligence. A valuation, on the other hand, cannot be challenged, even where the valuer gives reasons for his decision which are demonstrably wrong, provided only that the valuer has at least addressed the correct question.[6] In consequence, if the valuer were personally immune from liability this would leave a dissatisfied party without any effective legal remedy.

1   Arbitration Act 1996, s 29.
2   [1974] 1 All ER 859, HL.
3   [1975] 3 All ER 901, HL.
4   Thus a surveyor who is appointed as an independent expert under a rent review provision in a lease will owe a duty of care to both parties: *Zubaida v Hargreaves* [1995] 1 EGLR 127, CA.
5   Arbitration Act 1996, s 69.
6   *Campbell v Edwards* [1976] 1 WLR 403, CA; *Jones v Sherwood Computer Services plc* [1992] 2 All ER 170, CA.

Advocates
17.36   It was at one time the law that a barrister could not be held liable in negligence by a client, for the way in which he prepared and conducted a case in court.[1] Two main

reasons were given for this immunity: first, that an advocate's primary duty lies, not to his client, but to the court to secure the true administration of justice, which may compel him, on occasion, to disclose matters unfavourable to his case; and second, that there must at some point be an end to litigation (whereas an action against one's advocate would always in effect amount to a retrial of the original case, with the possibility of ending up with two conflicting decisions).

In *Arthur JS Hall & Co v Simons*,[2] the House of Lords decided that neither of these reasons was sufficient to justify giving advocates, alone among professional persons, immunity from liability for incompetence. Their lordships felt that the problem of conflicting duties was not a serious one, for the advocate's duty to the court would be taken into account in deciding whether or not he had acted with reasonable care and skill towards his client. As for the problem of conflicting decisions, the House of Lords felt that this could be avoided by a separate legal principle,[3] namely that no negligence action would be permitted if it would amount to a collateral attack upon a previous decision of a court of competent jurisdiction. An action by a disappointed litigant against his lawyer would normally fall foul of this principle, since the essence of the claimant's claim is that he should have won the previous case. However, there would be no bar to a negligence claim by a litigant who had, for example, successfully appealed against the original decision, but who claimed to have suffered loss in the time taken to appeal.

The exact scope of the 'no collateral attack' principle is far from clear, but it seems likely that it will in practice substantially reduce the effect of the removal of the advocate's immunity.

1   *Rondel v Worsley* [1967] 3 All ER 993, HL: the principle was extended to other advocates, such as solicitors, by s 62 of the Courts and Legal Services Act 1990.
2   [2000] 3 All ER 673, HL.
3   Laid down in *Hunter v Chief Constable of West Midlands* [1981] 3 All ER 727, HL.

Psychiatric injury

17.37   Where a person recovers damages for physical injury, some compensation in respect of any accompanying psychological trauma is normally recoverable under the heading of pain and suffering.[1] Where, however, there is no 'impact injury', the courts have proved much less sympathetic to a claim in respect of purely mental harm. This may be due in part to an instinctive feeling that psychiatric damage is in some way less important that physical damage, or from a sense that claims for purely psychiatric harm are easier to counterfeit. There is also, no doubt, a fear of opening the floodgates, in the sense that a negligent driver, say, might be liable, not only to someone whom he has physically injured, but to a large number of the victim's relative and friends, who claim to have suffered psychiatric harm on seeing or hearing about the accident.

Whatever the reasons, there is no doubt that the law has sought to restrict claims by persons who have suffered psychiatric damage but not physical harm. The relevant legal rules, deriving mainly from three decisions of the House of Lords,[2] are extremely complex and somewhat uncertain: only a brief summary can be given here.

First, it must be emphasised that a claimant is only entitled to damages in respect of a recognised psychiatric illness, not for other mental responses such as distress or grief. Moreover, with one exception (noted below) it must have been foreseeable to the defendant that his negligence might cause psychiatric harm to a person of reasonable fortitude. Thus, if the claimant is only affected because he is particularly susceptible to psychiatric harm, the defendant is not liable for this.

A claimant who is a 'primary victim' (ie someone directly involved in the event caused by the defendant's negligence) is entitled to claim damages where for psychiatric injury where it was foreseeable that he would suffer either physical or psychiatric injury. This is the exceptional case mentioned above in that, if someone is in physical danger (whether or not any physical injury actually results) he can recover for psychiatric injury, even if that injury is unforeseeable. The courts have extended the category of 'primary victim' to include such claimants as an employee negligently exposed to stress at work,[3] a client sent to prison through the alleged negligence of his solicitor,[4] or the father of a new-born baby who was negligently told that his child had died.[5] However, it is now clear that an accident witness is not to be regarded as a primary victim merely because he is an employee of the defendant, nor because he is a rescuer.

A claimant who is a 'secondary victim' (ie someone who suffers psychiatric injury merely from seeing or hearing injury to another[6]) must satisfy much more stringent requirements in order to recover damages. In *Alcock v Chief Constable of the South Yorkshire Police*[7] (a case arising out of the Hillsborough disaster, in which 95 Liverpool football supporters were crushed to death through the negligence of the police in controlling the crowd), the House of Lords stressed the importance of three criteria by which such cases were to be judged: the class of persons whose claims should be recognised; the proximity of such persons to the accident; and the means by which the shock is caused. Applying these criteria to the facts of *Alcock*, the House of Lords held:

*   there is no arbitrary list of relationships which are close enough to render it foreseeable that injury to or death of one partner may result in shock to the other. However, the only relationships close enough to raise a presumption that shock may be suffered are those of husband-wife and parent-child. In order for other relatives or friends to recover damages, they must positively prove an equivalent emotional tie.
*   as a general rule, proximity requires a claimant to be physically close to the accident in time and space.
*   as a general rule, proximity also requires the claimant to witness the accident or its immediate aftermath personally. It is not enough to be told of the accident by a third party, to see a televised recording of it or to read about it in a newspaper.

1   Para 28.6 below.
2   *Alcock v Chief Constable of the South Yorkshire Police* [1991] 4 All ER 907, HL; *Page v Smith* [1995] 2 All ER 736, HL; *White v Chief Constable of the South Yorkshire Police* [1999] 1 All ER 1, HL.
3   *Walker v Northumberland County Council* [1995] 1 All ER 737.
4   *McLoughlin v Jones* [2001] EWCA Civ 1743, [2002] QB 1312.
5   *Farrell v Avon Health Authority* [2001] Lloyd's Rep Med 458.
6   There is no liability for a defendant who causes psychiatric injury to a witness by negligently injuring himself: *Greatorex v Greatorex* [2000] 4 All ER 769.
7   [1991] 4 All ER 907, HL.

Chapter 18

Negligence – breach of duty

18.1 In deciding whether a defendant has breached the duty of care which he owed to the claimant, the test to be applied is whether the defendant acted reasonably in all the circumstances of the case. In legal theory, this standard of 'reasonableness' is a uniform one. However, in practice it is capable of great flexibility, so that subtle differences of fact between one case and another may lead the court to apparently conflicting conclusions. Moreover, since decisions on the issue of breach of duty are based on the facts, they are not of binding authority for the future. Thus, even though a car driver in one case is held to have been negligent in turning right without giving a signal, this does not mean that such conduct will automatically amount to negligence in another case.

As we shall see, the tort of negligence imposes an objective standard of conduct. What is required of a person, if he is to avoid liability, is not that he does his best, but that he does what is reasonable. At first glance, this may appear rather harsh, in that a defendant is sometimes held liable in circumstances where no moral blame attaches to him. However, it may be pointed out that a court which sympathised with such a defendant, to the extent of acquitting him of negligence, would in effect be condemning an equally innocent claimant to shoulder his own loss.

18.2 In this chapter we examine the following issues:

- the concept of the 'reasonable man', and the extent to which this allows for disabilities or age;
- the standards of skill and care which the law demands from members of established professions;
- the modern 'risk/benefit' approach which is often used to determine negligence;
- the way in which a breach of duty is proved, and the circumstances in which it may be presumed.

The reasonable man

18.3 A well-established approach to the question of whether a duty of care has been breached is to measure the conduct of the defendant against such hypothetical creatures as 'the reasonable man', 'the man in the street', 'the man of ordinary prudence' or, most famously, 'the man on the Clapham omnibus'. As Alderson B put it in *Blyth v Birmingham*

Waterworks Co:[1] 'Negligence is the omission to do something which a reasonable man guided upon those considerations which ordinarily regulate the conduct of human affairs, would do, or doing something which a prudent and reasonable man would not do.'

In considering whether the defendant's conduct has reached the requisite standard, various attributes of the defendant will be taken into account, and these we consider below. Further, modern courts frequently evaluate a person's conduct by reference to the risk which it creates, and this we discuss under the heading of 'The principle of risk'.

1　(1856) 11 Exch 781 at 784.

The objective standard

18.4　As a general rule, no allowance is made in law for any lack of intelligence or emotional restraint on the part of a particular defendant. Indeed, both judges and academic writers have expressed the view that, in an appropriate case, liability in negligence may be imposed upon a person who is mentally incapable, notwithstanding his obvious personal inability to reach the standard of reasonableness. This is on the ground that to excuse such a defendant would be unfair to the victims of his actions. Similar reasoning has been used where the defendant is merely inexperienced, rather than mentally incapable; it was held by the Court of Appeal in *Nettleship v Weston*[1] that a learner-driver is negligent if he or she does not achieve the standard of an ordinarily competent and experienced driver.

1　[1971] 3 All ER 581, CA.

Physical defects

18.5　Although a person's psychological make-up is irrelevant to liability in negligence, the courts are more prepared to make allowances in the case of a defendant who suffers from some recognisable physical impediment. For example, a person who is blind or who has only one leg will be judged by what may reasonably be expected from someone in that condition. However, a problem arises where a person is unaware of his disability. In *Mansfield v Weetabix Ltd*[1] a lorry belonging to the defendants crashed into the claimant's shop and caused extensive damage. It appeared that the driver was suffering from a medical condition, of which he was unaware, which rendered him incapable of driving safely. The Court of Appeal, having found that the driver would not have continued to drive had he known the truth, held that he could not be regarded as negligent. However, if the driver had ignored clear symptoms of possible danger, the decision might well have been different.

1　[1998] 1 WLR 1263, CA.

Age

18.6　Children are very seldom sued in negligence, for the practical reason that they would not normally be able to pay any damages awarded against them. Nevertheless, the courts are not infrequently called upon to consider the reasonableness or otherwise of a child's conduct, when an injured child's claim is met with a defence of contributory negligence.[1] In *Morales v Eccleston*,[2] for example, where an 11-year-old boy ran into the road without looking and was struck by a negligently driven car, the boy was held 75% responsible for his own injuries. It is clear that, in making this assessment, a court must take the child's age into account. Thus in *Foskett v Mistry*,[3] where a 16-year-old ran into the road without looking, he was held 75% responsible, but the Court of Appeal made it clear that an adult would have been held entirely to blame. On the other hand, in *Gough v Thorne*,[4] a 13-year-old girl was held not negligent in relying entirely upon a signal from the driver of a stationary lorry and stepping out into the road past the lorry, without looking for vehicles overtaking it. An extreme example is *C v Imperial Design Ltd*,[5] where a child deliberately lit a fire with a container of flammable liquid, which the defendants had negligently left outside their factory. The Court of Appeal reduced the claimant's contribution from 75% to 50%, on the ground that, though well aware of the dangers of fire, he had not realised that the chemical might cause an explosion.

In the few cases in which negligence actions have been brought against children, it has been made clear that allowance should again be made for the age of the child concerned. In *Mullin v Richards*,[6] two 15-year-old schoolgirls were fencing with plastic rulers when one of the rulers snapped, causing a serious eye injury to one of the girls. The Court of Appeal held that, when age was properly taken into account, it could not be said that a reasonable 15-year-old ought to have foreseen the likelihood of injury from what was nothing more than a children's game.

Of course, even a child is expected to achieve certain standards. In *Watkins v Birmingham City Council*,[7] a 10-year-old boy, while distributing school milk to various classrooms, left his tricycle in a position where a teacher fell over it. This was held to constitute negligence, a finding which was not challenged in the Court of Appeal, where the decision was reversed on another ground.[8]

Although there is less authority than in respect of children, it seems that an elderly litigant is also to be judged in the light of his age. In *Daly v Liverpool Corpn*,[9] where a collision occurred between the claimant, a 69-year-old pedestrian, and the defendants' bus, it was held that a charge of contributory negligence against the claimant must take her age into account.

1   Paras 20.11–20.16 below.
2   [1991] RTR 151, CA.
3   [1984] RTR 1, CA.
4   [1966] 3 All ER 398, CA.
5   [2001[Env LR 33, CA.
6   [1998] 1 All ER 920, CA. Also see *Etheridge v K* [1999] Ed CR 550 (13-year-old not negligent in throwing a basketball down school stairs during an informal game, resulting in injury to a teacher).
7   (1975) 126 NLJ 442.
8   See para 27.7 below.
9   [1939] 2 All ER 142.

Experience of others

18.7   In order to attain the standard which the law demands of the reasonable man, the defendant must make due allowance for those shortcomings of others which can be reasonably foreseen. Thus, for example, if it is foreseeable that blind persons will use a city pavement, anyone who excavates there must erect a barrier sufficient to protect them, and not merely one which is sufficient to safeguard those who can see it.[1] Similarly, the reasonable man may have to recognise that others do not always act reasonably towards him, and must thus take such precautions against their negligence as experience shows to be necessary. There may even be extreme cases in which a defendant ought to foresee and guard against even the criminal misconduct of others, although, as we have seen,[2] the law is reluctant to impose a duty of care in such circumstances.

1   *Haley v London Electricity Board* [1964] 3 All ER 185, HL.
2   Paras 17.13–17.14 above.

Professional status

18.8   A person's status within a trade or profession may mean that he has to achieve a higher standard than others, in the sense of displaying skill as well as care. As to the degree of skill which must be shown, this is whatever may be expected of a reasonably competent practitioner, rather than a leading specialist (although a defendant who sets himself up as a specialist will probably be judged accordingly[1]). In *Roe v Minister of Health*,[2] the claimant underwent minor surgery in 1947, during which he became partially paralysed as a result of being injected with a contaminated anaesthetic. The danger of such contamination was appreciated by very few doctors until about 1951, after which the profession in general took action to prevent it from happening again. In acquitting the hospital staff of negligence, Denning LJ pointed out that: 'We must not look at the 1947 accident with 1954 spectacles.'

Where a person acts in accordance with what is the generally accepted practice of his profession, he is unlikely to be found negligent,[3] although there have been occasions on which a court has declared such common practice to be unreasonable.[4] Conversely, a practitioner who ignores the usual procedures runs an increased risk of being judged negligent,[5] although failure to adhere to a professional institution's guidance notes is not conclusive evidence of negligence.[6] What, then, of the case in which professional opinion is split? In Bolam v Friern Hospital Management Committee,[7] McNair J made it clear that it was not for the court to select one body of opinion as correct and to discount all others; the question was simply whether it could be said that no reasonably competent practitioner could possibly hold the view which the defendant preferred. This statement of principle was approved by the House of Lords in Maynard v West Midlands Regional Health Authority.[8] However, the House of Lords has since made it clear that evidence from expert witnesses as to what is sound professional practice should not be followed blindly; a judge must be satisfied that it has a logical basis.[9]

It should always be remembered that a professional man's duty is to be skilful and careful, not necessarily to be correct. Nevertheless, it is not true to say that an error of judgment cannot amount to negligence; the vital question is whether the error is one which a reasonably competent practitioner would not have made.[10]

In deciding whether or not a charge of professional negligence has been established, the courts rely heavily upon evidence from expert witnesses as to what might reasonably be expected of a competent member of the profession. Such expert witnesses should be drawn from the same profession as the defendant; thus a structural engineer is not qualified to give evidence as to what a building surveyor should have seen or done.[11] Expert witnesses are almost always called by the parties, although a court has a power to appoint its own expert.[12]

1   Duchess of Argyll v Beuselinck [1972] 2 Lloyd's Rep 172; cf Wimpey Construction UK Ltd v Poole (1984) 27 BLR 58.
2   [1954] 2 All ER 131, CA.
3   Morton v William Dixon Ltd 1909 SC 807 at 809; Beaumont v Humberts [1990] 2 EGLR 166, CA.
4   See, for example, Edward Wong Finance Co v Johnson, Stokes and Master [1984] AC 296, PC.
5   See, for example, Clark v MacLennan [1983] 1 All ER 416.
6   See PK Finans International (UK) Ltd v Andrew Downs & Co Ltd [1992] 1 EGLR 172.
7   [1957] 2 All ER 118.
8   [1985] 1 All ER 635, HL.
9   Bolitho v City and Hackney Health Authority [1997] 4 All ER 771, HL.
10 Whitehouse v Jordan [1981] 1 All ER 267, HL. See also para 18.9 below.
11 Sansom v Metcalfe Hambleton & Co [1998] 2 EGLR 103, CA.
12 Under what is now Part 35 of the Civil Procedure Rules: see Abbey National Mortgages plc v Key Surveyors Nationwide Ltd [1996] 2 EGLR 99, CA.

Valuers and surveyors

18.9   In dealing with allegations of negligence against valuers and surveyors, it must be emphasised that valuation is not an exact science, and that to be wrong is not necessarily to be negligent. Nevertheless, a sizeable error in a valuation will normally require some explanation and justification from the valuer who made it. Indeed, it was said in one case that a valuation which departs from the 'correct' figure (as found by the judge with the help of expert witnesses) by more than 10% or 15% brings into question the competence of the valuer and the sort of care he gave to the task of valuation.[1] However, it has subsequently been doubted whether a single 'correct' value really exists, and it has been suggested that a better approach is to ask whether the defendant's figure lies within the 'bracket' of values which competent practitioners might reasonably have arrived at for the property in question.[2]

Even assuming that a valuer has reached a wrong conclusion, in the sense described above, damages for negligence can only be recovered if it is established that his error was due to a lack of reasonable care and skill. This has been found in such matters as failure to keep up to date with the principles of law which affect the type of valuation in question,[3] and, where the complaint was of an under-valuation, the overlooking of a potential market.[4] As far as the actual valuation process is concerned, the courts are careful not to lay down restrictive rules, since it is appreciated that an experienced valuer may often operate intuitively. Hence, the absence of comparables or detailed calculations does not of itself indicate negligence.[5] On the other hand, a valuer who does not trouble to visit the site which he is to value,[6] who clearly ignores the price at which the property has recently changed hands[7] or who (after only three months' experience, all of it limited to property worth less than £33,000) nonchalantly values a house at £100,000 without seeking confirmation from a more experienced colleague,[8] is unlikely to attract the sympathy of a judge when it is alleged that he was lacking in reasonable care and skill.

In relation to surveys and other inspections of property, the crucial question is normally whether the survey was too superficial to reveal obvious defects in the property.[9] This naturally depends, to some extent at least, on the type of survey carried out, although it has been held that the standard of skill and care required in carrying out a House Buyers Report and Valuation is identical to that for a structural survey.[10] In the case of a mortgage valuation ('a walking inspection by someone with a knowledgeable eye, experienced in practice, who knows where to look'[11]), a surveyor is not expected to move furniture or to lift floor coverings; however, if his limited inspection reveals clear evidence of a defect, it is then his duty to 'follow the trail'.[12]

1   Singer and Friedlander Ltd v John D Wood & Co [1977] 2 EGLR 84.
2   See Mount Banking Corpn Ltd v Brian Cooper & Co [1992] 2 EGLR 142.
3   Weedon v Hindwood, Clarke and Esplin [1975] 1 EGLR 82.
4   Bell Hotels (1935) Ltd v Motion (1952) 159 Estates Gazette 496.
5   Corisand Investments Ltd v Druce & Co [1978] 2 EGLR 86.
6   Singer and Friedlander Ltd v John D Wood & Co [1977] 2 EGLR 84.
7   Banque Bruxelles Lambert SA v Eagle Star [1995] 2 All ER 769.
8   Kenney v Hall, Pain and Foster [1976] 2 EGLR 29.
9   As it was in Philips v Ward [1956] 1 All ER 874, CA.
10 Cross v David Martin and Mortimer [1989] 1 EGLR 154.
11 Lloyd v Butler [1990] 2 EGLR 155.
12 Roberts v J Hampson & Co [1989] 2 All ER 504; Sneesby v Goldings [1995] 2 EGLR 102, CA.

18.10   An obligation to display professional skill as well as reasonable care is imposed, not only upon those who are actually members of that profession, but also on those who attempt to take on work which requires professional skill.[1] Indeed, some jobs so obviously require an expert that a defendant who attempts to carry them out himself is almost bound to be regarded as negligent.[2] In Freeman v Marshall & Co,[3] the claimant complained of a survey carried out for him by the defendant, which failed to diagnose rising damp. The defendant argued that, since he was unqualified and had little knowledge of structures, he had done all that could be reasonably expected of him. It was held, however, that, by advertising himself as an estate agent, valuer and surveyor, and by undertaking a structural survey, he had laid claim to the necessary expertise and must be judged accordingly.

Many jobs may as reasonably be undertaken by semi-skilled or unskilled persons as by professionals. Where this is so, the courts will not necessarily judge the defendant by the standard of the most skilled person who might be expected to do the work. In Philips v William Whiteley Ltd,[4] for example, a jeweller pierced a woman's ears. The instruments used were disinfected, although not to the standard which a surgeon would be expected to achieve, and she developed an abscess. It was held that, since this operation was frequently performed by jewellers, the defendants fell to be judged by the standards of a reasonable jeweller, and not those of a reasonable surgeon. A similar decision was reached in the case of *Wells v Cooper*,[5] where a door handle fitted by the defendant householder, who was an amateur carpenter of some experience, came off, with the result that the claimant was injured. The Court of Appeal held that, since this was the sort of job which the reasonable householder might be expected to do for himself the defendant was to be judged by amateur, and not professional, standards.

Some doubt is thrown on the latitude given to defendants in these two cases by the later decision in *Nettleship v Weston*.[6] There the Court of Appeal, no doubt influenced by their awareness of available insurance, held that the standard which a learner-driver must achieve, if he is not to be held negligent, is not that of a reasonable learner, but that of a reasonable experienced driver.

1   However, there is no concept of 'team negligence' under which all members of, say, a medical unit would be judged by the standard of the unit as a whole: *Wilsher v Essex Area Health Authority* [1986] 3 All ER 801, CA.
2   Eg lift maintenance: *Haseldine v C A Daw & Son Ltd* [1941] 3 All ER 156, CA.
3   (1966) 200 Estates Gazette 777.
4   [1938] 1 All ER 566.
5   [1958] 2 All ER 527, CA.
6   [1971] 3 All ER 581, CA.

The principle of risk

18.11   As an alternative to considering what the hypothetical reasonable man would have done in a particular situation, a court may choose to assess the defendant's conduct by asking whether the risks which it creates are such as to outweigh any value it may have, and the cost or difficulty of rendering it safe. In conducting this balancing operation a court will take into account one or both of the following matters:

*   the likelihood that the activity in question will cause injury or damage; and
*   the seriousness of the injury that may result if the risk materialises.

Against these factors may be set:

*   the value, social utility or other desirability of the activity; and
*   the cost and practicability of taking steps to reduce or eliminate the danger.

Likelihood of injury

18.12   As Lord Dunedin remarked in *Fardon v Harcourt-Rivington*:[1] 'People must guard against reasonable probabilities, but they are not bound to guard against fantastic possibilities'. This means that a risk may be so remote that the reasonable man is quite justified in ignoring it altogether. Perhaps the most famous example of this is the case of *Bolton v Stone*,[2] where the claimant was injured by a cricket ball which a visiting batsman had struck more than 100 yards, clearing a high fence on the way. The evidence indicated that shots of this kind had occurred on the ground no more than six times in 28 years. The House of Lords held that, while the risk was clearly foreseeable, from the very fact that there had been such shots in the past, it was sufficiently remote that the defendants might reasonably ignore it.

1   (1932) 146 LT 391 at 392.
2   [1951] 1 All ER 1078, HL.

Seriousness of consequences

18.13   Quite apart from the probability or improbability that a particular type of accident will occur, a court assessing a defendant's conduct may justifiably consider the gravity of the potential consequences. This principle was laid down by the House of Lords in *Paris v Stepney Borough Council*,[1] where a one-eyed garage hand was struck in his remaining eye by a metal chip and became completely blind. It was not the practice of the employers to supply their workmen with safety spectacles, since they regarded the risk of eye injury as extremely remote. The House of Lords held that, although this approach was justifiable in relation to the other employees, special precautions should have been taken in the claimant's case, since he had so much more to lose.

1   [1951] 1 All ER 42, HL.

Value of conduct

18.14   The number of accidents which occur every day could be drastically reduced if certain steps were taken. To take a simple example, it is obvious that road accidents would be far less likely to happen if everyone drove at no more than 10 mph. However, this does not mean that exceeding that speed is automatically negligent; most people would regard the increased risk as justified, in view of the enormous inconvenience which would be caused to the general public if all traffic were to move at a snail's pace.

The principle that important ends may be held to justify risky means was invoked in *Daborn v Bath Tramways Motor Co Ltd*,[1] where it was held that the use of a left-hand drive vehicle as an ambulance in wartime was reasonable in view of the shortage of suitable transport, notwithstanding the dangers which it created to other road users when turning right without giving any signal. In *Watt v Hertfordshire County Council*,[2] a heavy jack, which was needed to rescue a woman trapped under a bus, was carried on a lorry not suited to the purpose. During the journey the jack shifted, injuring the claimant, a fireman. The Court of Appeal held that the fire brigade's decision to use this unsuitable vehicle was a reasonable one, having regard to the emergency.

1   [1946] 2 All ER 333, CA.
2   [1954] 2 All ER 368, CA.

Cost of precautions

18.15   In deciding whether a defendant has dealt adequately with a particular risk, the courts will have regard to the ease with which that risk could have been reduced or eliminated. This is not simply a matter of money, although financial considerations are undoubtedly of importance; it also covers questions of convenience and practicability. In extreme cases, where the risk is a very serious one, it may be that the only course of action open to the reasonable man is to cease altogether the dangerous activity, although the courts are reluctant to impose such a heavy burden.[1] In *Withers v Perry Chain Co Ltd*,[2] for example, a woman who was susceptible to dermatitis (a skin complaint caused by contact with grease) was given the driest work which her employers had available; nevertheless, she again contracted the disease. Her argument that the defendants should have dismissed her for her own protection was rejected by the Court of Appeal, who held that such a drastic step could not possibly be justified by the relatively minor risk to which she was exposed.

At the other end of the scale, a person may be held liable for failing to eliminate even a small risk, if he could have done so with ease. As Lord Reid put it:[3] 'It does not follow that, no matter what the circumstances may be, it is justifiable to neglect a risk of such a small magnitude. A reasonable man ... would not neglect such a risk if action to eliminate it presented no difficulty, involved no disadvantage, and required no expense.'

By and large, the objective standard of reasonable care applies to questions of cost and inconvenience as it does to other factors in the assessment of negligence. Thus, once a court decides that a reasonable man would have taken certain precautions (ie that they were not too costly in relation to the risk) a defendant who did not do so is liable, even if he personally could not afford them. However, a degree of subjectivity has been introduced for the benefit of an occupier upon whose land a danger arises through natural causes (and for which he naturally cannot be blamed). Where this happens, it has been held that the occupier may avoid liability to a neighbour by establishing that the actions necessary to eliminate the danger would have been beyond his personal means.[4]

1   See *Bolton v Stone* [1951] 1 All ER 1078, HL; para 18.12 above.
2   [1961] 3 All ER 676, CA.
3   *The Wagon Mound (No 2)* [1966] 2 All ER 709 at 718.
4   *Goldman v Hargrave* [1966] 2 All ER 989: para 24.16 below.

The proof of negligence

18.16   The burden of proof in negligence actions, as in civil cases generally, lies on the claimant. This means that it is for the claimant to bring evidence which establishes on the balance of probabilities that the defendant has been careless. If he cannot do this, the claimant's claim fails.

In seeking to establish negligence, a claimant may be able to rely on the Civil Evidence Act 1968, s 11 which provides that a criminal conviction for an offence which involves negligence (eg driving without due care and attention) is to be regarded in subsequent civil proceedings as sufficient evidence of negligence. This means that, in subsequent civil proceedings, the defendant's negligence will be presumed, although it is still open to him to rebut this presumption.

Res ipsa loquitur

18.17   In many negligence actions, the claimant will have to rely on circumstantial evidence, since the full details of the accident will be known only to the defendant. In such circumstances, the claimant may gain assistance from the maxim *res ipsa loquitur*, meaning 'the thing speaks for itself'. The operation of this maxim is illustrated by the leading case of *Scott v London and St Katherine Docks Co*,[1] in which the claimant, who was walking past the defendant's warehouse, was injured when six bags of sugar fell on him. Neither party could offer any explanation of this occurrence, and the trial judge held that there was not enough evidence to allow the case to go to the jury. However, on appeal, this decision was held to be incorrect, and the following principle was laid down by Erle CJ:

> 'There must be reasonable evidence of negligence. But where the thing is shown to be under the management of the defendant or his servants, and the accident is such as in the ordinary course of things does not happen if those who have the management use proper care, it affords reasonable evidence, in the absence of explanation by the defendants, that the accident arose from want of care.'

It is clear, then, that for *res ipsa loquitur* to apply, it must be shown that:

- the thing which did the damage was under the management and control of the defendant or someone for whom the defendant was responsible; and
- the occurrence was such as would ordinarily indicate negligence.

1   (1865) 3 H & C 596.

Control by the defendant

18.18   The mere fact that an unauthorised person *could* have tampered with the thing which causes injury to the claimant will not preclude reliance on *res ipsa loquitur*, provided that such intervention is improbable. Thus, where a railway passenger fell from a moving train immediately after leaving the station, it was held that the carriage doors could be regarded as under the control of the railway company.[1] However, the opposite conclusion was reached in the case of a child falling from the corridor of a train which had travelled a considerable distance since its last stop.[2]

1   Gee v Metropolitan Rly Co (1873) LR 8 QB 161.
2   Easson v London North Eastern Rly Co [1944] 2 All ER 425, CA.

Inference of negligence

18.19   The facts from which an inference of negligence may be drawn are extremely varied. Apart from the obvious case of objects falling from the upper floors of buildings,[1] the doctrine has been invoked in cases of railway collisions,[2] an aircraft which crashed on taking off,[3] the sudden and violent skid of a motor vehicle[4] and a stone in a bun.[5] In Ward v Tesco Stores Ltd,[6] where a supermarket customer slipped on some yoghurt which had been spilled on the floor, a majority of the Court of Appeal reached the somewhat doubtful conclusion that, in the absence of further evidence as to how the yoghurt came to be on the floor, its presence there could be attributed to negligence on the part of the defendants.

In practical terms, res ipsa loquitur is of most benefit to a claimant who is injured by a process the details of which he does not understand, or who cannot show which of the defendant's employees has been guilty of negligence. Common cases include consumers injured by defective products[7] and patients whose condition is rendered worse rather than better by the medical treatment which they receive, as in Cassidy v Ministry of Health,[8] where hospital treatment of the claimant's two stiff fingers left him with four stiff fingers.

1   Scott v London and St Katherine Docks Co (1865) 3 H & C 596; para 18.17 above.
2   Skinner v London, Brighton and South Coast Rly Co (1850) 5 Exch 787.
3   Fosbroke-Hobbes v Airwork Ltd and British American Air Services Ltd [1937] 1 All ER 108.
4   Richley v Faull [1965] 3 All ER 109.
5   Chaproniere v Mason (1905) 21 TLR 633.
6   [1976] 1 All ER 219, CA.
7   Such victims may now hold the manufacturer strictly liable under the Consumer Protection Act 1987.
8   [1951] 1 All ER 574, CA. Also see Saunders v Leeds Western Health Authority [1993] 4 Med LR 355 (res ipsa loquitur where heart of fit child stopped under anaesthetic).

Effect of the maxim

18.20   The precise effect of res ipsa loquitur upon a negligence action is a matter of some controversy. As originally conceived, it did not necessarily lead to a decision in the claimant's favour. However, the courts in more recent times have appeared on occasion to treat the maxim as raising a legal presumption, and thus as shifting the burden of disproving negligence on to the defendant.[1]

The practical significance of this theoretical controversy is shown by cases in which, after an initial finding that something speaks for itself, the defendant is able to identify the true cause of the accident. The crucial question then becomes whether the defendant must go on to prove that he was not to blame for this cause, or whether the onus of proving negligence reverts to the claimant. In Henderson v Henry E Jenkins & Sons,[2] where a man was killed by a runaway lorry, the defendants, who were the owners of the lorry, proved that concealed corrosion in a pipe had caused the brakes to fail. The defendants also showed that they had complied with the recommended maintenance schedules in respect of this vehicle. But the House of Lords held that even this was not sufficient to preclude a finding that they were guilty of negligence. In order to do this, they would have had to establish that nothing had happened to the lorry throughout its history which would call for extra precautions to be taken.[3]

The decision in Henderson v Henry E Jenkins & Sons is thought by some writers to mean that the legal burden of proof in res ipsa loquitur cases is indeed shifted to the defendant. However, this was strongly denied by the Privy Council in Ng Chun Pui v Lee Chuen Tat.[4]

The defendants there were the owners of a coach which suddenly went out of control, crossing the central reservation of a dual carriageway and colliding with a bus. The Privy Council held that such an occurrence would normally speak for itself; however, once the defendants had shown that their driver had swerved to avoid an unidentified car which had suddenly cut in front of him, the onus of proving negligence was back on the claimants and they had failed to discharge it.

Even where the cause of an accident remains unknown, the defendant may avoid liability by showing that he has not been in any way guilty of negligence. Of course the burden of proof on the defendant in such a case is an extremely heavy one, especially where the evidence consists of little more than his word.[5]

1   The most important cases are *Moore v R Fox & Sons* [1956] 1 All ER 182, CA; *Henderson v Henry E Jenkins & Sons* [1969] 3 All ER 756, HL and *Colvilles Ltd v Devine* [1969] 2 All ER 53, HL. Authority for the opposite view (ie that the legal burden of proof remains throughout on the claimant) is to be found in *Lloyde v West Midlands Gas Board* [1971] 2 All ER 1240, CA; *Turner v Mansfield Corpn* (1975) 119 Sol Jo 629, CA; and *Ng Chun Pui v Lee Chuen Tat* [1988] RTR 298, PC.
2   [1969] 3 All ER 756, HL.
3   Rather less is expected of a private motorist: *Rees v Saville* [1983] RTR 332, CA.
4   [1988] RTR 298, PC.
5   See, for example, *Ludgate v Lovett* [1969] 2 All ER 1275, CA.

Chapter 19

Negligence – the causing of damage

19.1   The mere fact that a defendant acts carelessly towards a claimant is not enough to render him liable in tort. In order to succeed in an action, the claimant must prove that he has suffered damage of a kind which is actionable in the tort in question. For example, a claimant who brings an action for negligence must establish that he has suffered personal injury, damage to property or (in certain circumstances) pure financial loss.

It was held by the House of Lords in *South Australia Asset Management Corpn v York Montague Ltd*[1] that, in order to recover damages, a claimant must show that his loss falls within the scope of the defendant's duty. Thus, where a valuer is commissioned to provide a valuation of property, on the basis of which the claimant will decide how much to lend, the valuer's duty is merely to take reasonable care to provide accurate information. If he is negligent and thus inaccurate, he will be liable for the consequences of the information being wrong, but not for losses which the lender would have suffered even if the property had been worth as much as the valuer said.

In addition to proving that he has suffered damage, the claimant must show that the damage was caused by the defendant's breach of duty. In this connection it must be appreciated that 'causation' in legal terms has a rather more restricted meaning than that given to it in a purely factual sense. To take a simple example: A is walking past some scaffolding when a brick falls on his head. From the *factual* point of view, we might say that A's injuries are caused by his presence there; by the act of a workman who leaned against the stack of bricks; by the action of a labourer who placed the stack in that position; by the decision of the owners to have their building repaired at that time; and so on. Fortunately perhaps, the lawyer is not concerned to identify all the causes of an accident, but merely to consider whether any or all of a small number of identified conditions (normally the acts or omissions of the parties to a lawsuit) may be regarded as sufficiently important to rank as *legal* causes and thus to attract responsibility. This task, clearly, is one of selection in which the judge, aided by common sense and human experience, arrives at what in the end is a value judgement.

1   [1996] 3 All ER 365, HL.

19.2   Causation in law is really two problems in one. In the first place, there must be a factual inquiry in order to ascertain whether the conduct of the defendant *can* be regarded as a cause of loss; if it cannot be so regarded, there could be no justification for holding the defendant liable for the claimant's misfortune. Second, assuming that the first question receives an affirmative answer, the law must decide whether the defendant's conduct and the claimant's damage are sufficiently closely connected that liability *ought* to be imposed.

An example may make this clear. Suppose that A negligently breaks B's arm. Obviously A is liable for such consequences as B's loss of earnings and medical expenses, and also for the pain which B suffers. What is the position, however, if B is run over by a car on his way to hospital to have the arm set? Or if a post-operative infection causes the arm to be amputated? Or if a boat in which B is travelling a month later sinks, and B is drowned because he cannot swim to safety? Or if, in a fit of depression at being unable to play cricket for his country, B commits suicide? All these catastrophes can in factual terms be traced back to A's original negligence, but should he be legally responsible for them?

Where a court concludes that a particular consequence of the defendant's breach of duty is not sufficiently connected to it to found liability, it may express this by stating that the conduct is not a legal cause or, as is more common today, that the item of damage is too remote.

In this chapter we examine the following issues:

- the way in which the law seeks to decide whether or not a defendant's breach of duty has 'caused' the claimant's loss;
- the situations in which the 'chain of causation' is broken, either by the claimant himself or by a third party;
- the legal rules which govern 'remoteness of damage', that is, the range of consequences for which a defendant can be held responsible.

Causation in fact

The 'but for' test

19.3   In order to establish whether or not the defendant's act was a factual cause of the claimant's injury, a court will normally apply the 'but for' test. According to this test (which, as we show later, is subject to some important exceptions), the question to be asked is whether the damage would have happened but for the defendant's breach of duty. If the answer is that it would not, then that breach may be said, at least in a factual sense, to have been a cause of it.[1] If, however, it would have happened anyway, then the defendant's breach is not a cause.

The operation of the 'but for' test is strikingly shown by the case of *McWilliams v Sir William Arrol & Co Ltd*,[2] in which a steel erector fell to his death from a tower on which he was working. His employers had failed in their statutory obligation to provide him with a safety belt. Nevertheless, they defeated an action by the steel erector's widow by producing overwhelming evidence that, even if a belt had been provided, the deceased would not have worn it and would therefore in any event have fallen. Similarly, in *Barnett v Chelsea and Kensington Hospital Management Committee*,[3] a casualty doctor's negligent refusal to examine a poisoned night-watchman was held not to be a cause of his death, since the evidence established that accurate diagnosis would have been too late to save him.

It must be emphasised that the 'but for' test is essentially exclusive in nature. A cause which does not satisfy this requirement cannot be a legal cause; one which does satisfy it may be treated as legally operative, but only if a court regards it as sufficiently important. In *Rouse v Squires*,[4] for example, a negligently driven lorry jack-knifed and blocked two lanes of a motorway. In trying to avoid it, a second lorry, also negligently driven, skidded and killed a bystander. The accident would obviously not have happened but for the presence of both lorries, and the Court of Appeal held that both drivers were liable.[5] In *Dymond v Pearce*,[6] by contrast, where a motor cyclist injured his pillion passenger by negligently driving into a parked lorry, it was held that the lorry's presence, although again a necessary condition for the accident, was not a legal cause of it; responsibility here was attributed solely to the motor cyclist.

1   Note that the defendant is in no way excused merely because other factors were also necessary.
2   [1962] 1 All ER 623, HL.
3   [1968] 1 All ER 1068.
4   [1973] 2 All ER 903, CA.
5   As between the drivers, liability was apportioned at 25% to the first and 75% to the second.
6   [1972] 1 All ER 1142, CA.

Proof of causation

19.4   In matters of causation, as in all other elements of liability, it is for the claimant to prove his case on the balance of probabilities. In certain circumstances it may be enough to show that the defendant's breach of duty materially contributed to the claimant's damage, without proving that it was the only or even the main cause of it. This was accepted by the House of Lords in *Bonnington Castings Ltd v Wardlaw*,[1] where the claimant contracted pneumoconiosis from inhaling silica dust at work. This dust came from two sources, only one of which was due to a breach of duty by the employers, and there was no evidence as to the relative proportions. The claimant could not therefore prove that, but for the employers' breach, he would not have contracted the disease at all. Despite this, it was held that the employers, having made a material contribution to the disease, were liable. On the facts, this liability extended to the claimant's entire loss; where, however, it is possible to identify the extent of the defendant's contribution, he may be held liable only for that proportion which he has caused.[2]

The principle adopted in *Bonnington Castings v Wardlaw* was extended by the House of Lords in *McGhee v National Coal Board*,[3] where the claimant's job exposed him to abrasive brick dust. The claimant contracted dermatitis and claimed that this was due to the defendants' failure to provide washing facilities on site, as a result of which he had to cycle home each day still caked with dust and sweat. It was held that, although a positive connection could not be established between the defendants' failure and the claimant's injury (since his exposure to the brick dust might have been enough to cause dermatitis even if washing facilities had been provided), it was sufficient to impose liability upon the defendants that they had materially increased the risk.

The *McGhee* principle was severely criticised in *Wilsher v Essex Area Health Authority*,[4] where the House of Lords refused to apply it to a case where the defendants' medical negligence was only one of six possible causes of a premature baby's blindness. However, it was restored to favour by the House of Lords in *Fairchild v Glenhaven Funeral Services Ltd*,[5] where an employee had contracted mesothelioma (a form of cancer) through negligent exposure to asbestos fibres at work. The employee had worked for, and been exposed to, asbestos fibres by more than one employer, and it was impossible to say which exposure had caused the onset of the disease. The House of Lords, applying *McGhee*, ruled that any of the employers who had materially increased the risk could be made liable; to hold otherwise would be deeply offensive to notions of justice, since a claimant who could show that one employer was guilty, but not which one, would lose against all of them.

1   [1956] 1 All ER 615, HL.
2   *Holtby v Brigham & Cowan (Hull) Ltd* [2000] 3 All ER 421, CA.
3   [1972] 3 All ER 1008, HL. See also *Fitzgerald v Lane* [1987] QB 781, CA.
4   [1988] 1 All ER 871, HL.
5   [2002] UKHL 22, [2002] 3 All ER 305.

Loss of a chance

19.5   In *Hotson v East Berkshire Health Authority*,[1] the claimant, who had been injured in a fall, claimed that the defendants' negligent failure to make a correct diagnosis of his injuries had allowed a more serious medical condition to develop. The evidence established that, when the claimant was first examined by the defendants, there was already a 75% likelihood that this condition would develop. The trial judge and the Court of Appeal awarded the claimant 25% of the damages claimed, on the basis that the defendants' negligence had turned a 75% risk into an inevitability. However, this approach was rejected by the House of Lords, which ruled that the claimant in these circumstances could only recover by showing that the defendants were responsible for his medical condition, something which, on the balance of probabilities, he was clearly unable to do.

It should not be thought, on the basis of this decision, that damages can never be awarded for loss of a chance. In particular, such an award appears possible in cases where the claimant's loss depends on the hypothetical action of some third party. This was accepted by the Court of Appeal in *Allied Maples Group Ltd v Simmons & Simmons.*[2] The claimant company entered into a contract to purchase certain business property on the basis of advice from its solicitors, the defendants. The advice was negligent and, as a result, the claimants incurred liabilities. The claimants alleged that, had they been given the correct advice, they would have taken steps to protect themselves against these liabilities, but the defendants pointed out that the success of those steps would have depended upon negotiations with a third party. The Court of Appeal held that, once the claimants had proved that they would have taken the necessary steps, it was not necessary for them also to prove on the balance of probabilities that the negotiations with the third party would have succeeded; they were entitled to damages based on the chance that this would have been so.

I   [1987] 2 All ER 909, HL.
2   [1995] 4 All ER 907, CA.

Multiple causes

19.6   Where damage is the result of more than one cause, the 'but for' test becomes an inadequate tool. Suppose, for example, that two independent fires, negligently lit by A and B, together destroy C's house. To allow each defendant to evade liability, by arguing that the house would in any event have been destroyed by the other fire, would be intolerable, and the law does not allow it: both A and B would be liable in full. However, this does not mean that the claimant can recover double damages. He may take his compensation as he chooses (all from one defendant, or some from each) and, once he has done so, the defendants may seek contribution from each other in proportions assessed by the court.[1]

A slightly different problem arises where the same injuries, or injuries which overlap each other, are 'caused' on separate occasions. The rule here is that the first cause in time is treated as the legally operative one, to the exclusion of all others. This may be illustrated by *Performance Cars Ltd v Abraham,*[2] where the defendant damaged the claimants' car in such a way that it required a repaint. In fact, however, as the result of a previous accident, the car already required a repaint, and it was accordingly held that the defendant could not be said to have caused this item of damage.

The principle of this case is that the second tortfeasor takes his victim as he finds him (ie in a damaged state). The effect which this has upon the liability of the first tortfeasor was considered in the important case of *Baker v Willoughby,*[3] in which the defendant was responsible for negligently injuring the claimant's leg and thereby reducing his earning capacity. Some time later, but before the case came to trial, the claimant was shot by robbers and his injured leg had to be amputated. The question was whether the defendant's liability for loss of earnings ceased at the time of the amputation. The Court of Appeal held that it did, on the ground that the second injury effectively 'swallowed up' the first. The House of Lords, however, pointed out that since the robbers, if sued, would be liable only for depriving the claimant of an already damaged leg, this solution would leave him out of pocket. It was accordingly held that, in assessing the defendant's liability, the second injury was to be ignored.

It should be noted that the approach adopted in *Baker v Willoughby* does not apply where the other cause of injury is natural, rather than tortious. In *Jobling v Associated Dairies*

Ltd,[4] it was held that a claimant's damages for loss of earnings should only compensate him up to the date on which an earlier injury would in any case have rendered him totally disabled. The House of Lords there pointed out that any other result would over-compensate the claimant, and suggested that the *Baker v Willoughby* approach can only be justified by the need to prevent the claimant from falling between two tortfeasors, in the sense of being unable to obtain compensation from either of them.

1   Paras 28.15-28.16 below.
2   [1961] 3 All ER 413, CA.
3   [1969] 3 All ER 1528, HL.
4   [1981] 2 All ER 752, HL.

Intervening causes

19.7   Where the injury or damage to the claimant is separated from the defendant's wrongful act by what has been called 'the conscious act of another volition', a court must decide whether the intervening act, whether by a third party or by the claimant himself, is sufficient to 'break the chain of causation' and thus to free the defendant from liability. This decision in truth requires a value judgement as to whether, in spite of the intervening conduct, total or partial responsibility should still attach to the defendant. A good example of this evaluation process is the case of *Wright v Lodge*,[1] in which a lorry, travelling at an excessive speed on a foggy night, crashed into a car which had broken down and was stationary on a dual carriageway road. The lorry then veered out of control on to the opposite carriageway and caused a fatal accident. The Court of Appeal held that, although the negligence of the car driver in failing to push her car off the road was a partial (10%) cause of the original collision, it was not a cause of the subsequent accident, for which the lorry driver was wholly responsible.

We now examine a number of examples of intervening acts, before considering whether it is possible to reduce the question of intervening cause to a statement of legal principle.

1   [1993] 4 All ER 299, CA.

Conduct of a third party
'Innocent' conduct
19.8   The chain of causation will seldom, if ever, be held to have been broken by the act of a third party who, for one reason or another, cannot be regarded as fully responsible for his actions. Where, for example, the defendant's negligence consists of leaving his horse untethered in the street, he cannot avoid liability by pointing out that it was stampeded by mischievous children.[1] Similarly, the unthinking action of a person in an emergency will not be regarded as the conscious act of another volition. In *Scott v Shepherd*,[2] the defendant threw a lighted squib in a crowded market. Two people in turn, seeking to protect themselves and their goods, picked up the squib and threw it away; it finally exploded in the claimant's eye. The defendant was held liable.

The emergency principle can on occasion be extended beyond the instinctive reactions of an endangered person to cover also his reasonable, albeit mistaken, decisions. In *The Oropesa*,[3] one of the many maritime collision cases to have raised this point, the master of a badly damaged ship launched a boat in heavy seas towards the *Oropesa*, which had been responsible for the collision, in order to discuss salvage. The boat overturned and a seaman was drowned. It was held that the seaman's death could be attributed to the negligence of the *Oropesa*; the decision of the other ship's master, made when under severe pressure, could not be said to break the chain of causation.

It should not be thought from what has been said above that a decision taken in an emergency can never be challenged on the ground of negligence. In *Knightley v Johns*,[4] a police inspector, who was in control following an accident in a one-way road tunnel, ordered a police motor cyclist to ride through the tunnel against the traffic flow, in order to stop cars from entering the tunnel. When the motor cyclist was struck by a car and injured, it was held by the Court of Appeal that the inspector's order was negligent; moreover, this broke the chain of causation between the injury to the claimant and the negligence of the motorist who had caused the original accident.

1   *Haynes v Harwood* [1935] 1 KB 146, CA.
2   (1773) 2 Wm Bl 892.
3   [1943] 1 All ER 211, CA.
4   [1982] 1 All ER 851, CA.

'Guilty' conduct

19.9   As shown by *Knightley v Johns*,[1] the negligent act of a third party may be sufficient to exempt the defendant from liability. This was also the case in *Baxall Securities Ltd v Sheard Walshaw Partnership*,[2] where the negligent failure of surveyors to discover an obvious defect in roof guttering broke the chain of causation from the negligence of the architects who designed it. However, it must be emphasised that such decisions represent judicial value judgements, and it cannot be assumed that this will always be the case. In *Prendergast v Sam and Dee*,[3] for example, where a doctor's bad handwriting led a pharmacist negligently to dispense the wrong drug, both the doctor and the pharmacist were held liable in negligence to the claimant. Generally speaking, where A injures B and so causes him to undergo medical treatment, A will also be liable for any further injury which results from that treatment.[4] This applies even where the medical treatment is itself negligent, so long as it is not wholly inappropriate.[5]

<sA negligent intervention by a third party may or may not break the chain of causation, but it might be thought that any deliberate, conscious act by a person of full capacity, in circumstances where there is no emergency, would always do so. However, even here the courts are occasionally prepared to trace liability back to the defendant. In *Philco Radio Ltd v J Spurling Ltd*,[6] the defendants negligently misdelivered cases of highly inflammable material to the claimants' premises. A typist employed by the claimants (intending to do minor damage, although unaware of the true contents) touched a case with a lighted cigarette and a serious explosion and fire resulted. The defendants were held liable, notwithstanding the typist's act. Indeed, in extreme cases it has been held that even a deliberate criminal act may not break the chain of causation. This is shown by *Stansbie v Troman*,[7] where a decorator, who was working alone in the claimant's house, left it unlocked and unoccupied for two hours. He was held liable for a theft of jewellery which occurred during his absence.

1   [1982] 1 All ER 851, CA; para 19.8 above.
2   [2002] EWCA Civ 09, [2002] BLR 100.
3   [1989] 1 Med LR 36, CA.
4   *Robinson v Post Office* [1974] 2 All ER 737, CA.
5   *Rahman v Arearose Ltd* [2001] QB 351, CA; *Webb v Barclays Bank plc and Portsmouth Hospitals NHS Trust* [2001] Lloyd's Rep Med 500, CA.
6   [1949] 2 All ER 882, CA.
7   [1948] 1 All ER 599, CA.

Conduct of the claimant

19.10   Principles similar to those which govern the conduct of a third party may also apply to an intervening act of the claimant himself, which may be held by the court to be so unreasonable that the effect of the defendant's original wrongdoing is entirely wiped out. In *McKew v Holland and Hannen and Cubitts (Scotland) Ltd*,[1] for example, an accident for which the defendants were responsible left the claimant's leg with a tendency to collapse suddenly and without warning. When, a few days later, knowing of this tendency, the claimant attempted to descend a steep staircase without assistance, it was held that he was entirely to blame for his resulting fall.

Decisions on the effect of a claimant's conduct in such cases are frequently made on the basis of contributory negligence,[2] so as to give more flexibility. Using this approach, a court can hold that the claimant's conduct, while not so outrageous as to exonerate the defendant entirely, is nevertheless a sufficiently significant cause of his injury that he should, by suffering a reduction in the damages awarded, be made to bear a proportion of his own loss.

In a number of cases, it can safely be said that the claimant's conduct will not affect causation, nor indeed amount to contributory negligence; these are considered below.

1   [1969] 3 All ER 1621, HL.
2   Paras 20.11–20.16 below.

Rescue cases

19.11   The act of a person who knowingly courts danger in attempting to rescue persons or even property[1] will not normally break the chain of causation. In *Haynes v Harwood*,[2] for example, the owner of a runaway horse was held liable to a policeman, who was injured in attempting to stop it in a crowded street. However, where the rescue attempt is unreasonable, for example because the danger outweighs the value of what is threatened, the chain of causation may be broken. In *Cutler v United Dairies (London) Ltd*,[3] the claimant was injured in helping the driver of a milk float whose runaway horse had come to rest safely in a field. The Court of Appeal held that, since the danger was over at the time of the claimant's intervention, he must be regarded as having caused his own injury. A rescuer has also been held to be a partial cause of his own injury and thus to be guilty of contributory negligence,[4] although this related to the manner in which he went about the rescue rather than his initial decision to attempt it.[5]

1   *Hyett v Great Western Rly Co* [1947] 2 All ER 264, CA.
2   [1935] 1 KB 146, CA.
3   [1933] 2 KB 297, CA.
4   Paras 20.11–20.16 below.
5   *Harrison v British Railways Board* [1981] 3 All ER 679.

Emergencies

19.12   Like third parties, whom we discussed in para 19.8 above, claimants who are faced with an emergency are given considerable latitude by the courts, in the sense that an instinctive decision, albeit one which turns out to be wrong, will not break the chain of causation unless it is totally unreasonable. In *Jones v Boyce*,[1] the defendant's negligence led the claimant to believe that his stagecoach, in which the claimant was a passenger, was about to overturn. The coach did not in fact overturn but the claimant, in jumping to safety, broke his leg. The defendant was held liable.

1   (1816) 1 Stark 493. See also *Colvilles Ltd v Devine* [1969] 2 All ER 53, HL.

Legal rights

19.13   The generous treatment which is given by the courts to claimants in an emergency is also reflected in their attitude towards those who act in defence of their legal rights, where these are infringed by the defendant. In *Clayards v Dethick and Davis*,[1] for example, the defendant unlawfully dug a trench in such a way that the sole access to the claimant's stables became dangerous. When a horse which the claimant attempted to lead out was injured, the defendant was held liable; it could not be said that the claimant had caused his own loss, since this was a risk which he was perfectly entitled to take in exercising his right of way.

In the celebrated case of *Sayers v Harlow UDC*,[2] the Court of Appeal reached a compromise solution. The claimant there was trapped in a public toilet by the negligence of the defendant local authority, who were responsible for the fact that there was no handle on the inside of the toilet door. In trying to climb out in order to catch a bus, the claimant fell and was injured. It was held that, since the claimant's predicament was one of inconvenience rather than danger, her attempt to escape was unreasonable; she should, it was held, have endured her loss of liberty rather than run this risk. Nonetheless, her negligence could not be said to have wiped out altogether the effects of the defendants' negligence, and so the claimant was held to be 25% responsible for her injuries.

1   (1848) 12 QB 439.
2   [1958] 2 All ER 342, CA.

Test of intervening cause

19.14   It is clear, from the cases mentioned above, that the question whether or not an intervening act breaks the chain of causation and so exculpates the defendant cannot be answered simply by asking whether or not that act was 'the conscious act of another volition'. It must indeed be regarded as highly doubtful whether a single satisfactory test can be devised; most of the judicial attempts to do so have concentrated either upon the foreseeability of the intervening act or upon its reasonableness. In so far as these tests are designed to show what is an intervening cause, rather than what is not, they are patently inadequate. The conduct of the typist, for example, in *Philco Radio Ltd v J Spurling Ltd*[1] must, by any rational standards, be regarded as both unreasonable and unforeseeable; yet the chain of causation remained unbroken.

The converse proposition, that a foreseeable or reasonable act does not exonerate the defendant, is much closer to the truth. Even here, however, there are exceptions. In *Quinn v Burch Bros (Builders) Ltd*,[2] the claimant fell from an unstable trestle, which he was using because the defendants had failed in their contractual duty to provide him with a stepladder. The Court of Appeal held that the claimant's unreasonable decision to adopt this dangerous practice was the sole cause of his injury, even though it was foreseeable.

In truth it seems that no single legal test can be devised which will accurately predict the outcome of what is essentially a practical, common sense inquiry. The question is whether, in the opinion of the judge, the intervening cause can be regarded as arising in the ordinary course of things out of the risks created by the defendant's breach of duty, or whether it is so powerful and overwhelming that it relegates the defendant's conduct from the status of 'cause' to being merely part of the surrounding circumstances.

1   [1949] 2 All ER 882, CA; para 19.9 above.
2   [1966] 2 All ER 283, CA.

Remoteness of damage

19.15   Even where it can be shown that the defendant's breach of duty is a factual cause of the claimant's injury, and that the chain of causation has not been broken by an intervening cause, it is still not certain that the defendant will be held responsible for a particular consequence. In attempting to keep liability for a single act of negligence within bounds, the law regards certain consequences as too 'remote' from the original tort to found an action.[1]

In seeking to relate the question of remoteness to a legal principle, English law has wavered between two different tests. The first, laid down by the Court of Appeal in 1921 in the case of *Re Polemis and Furness, Withy & Co*,[2] held a negligent defendant liable for all the *direct* consequences of his negligence, whether or not they were *foreseeable*. However,

40 years later, in the case of *Overseas Tankship (UK) v Morts Dock and Engineering Co*[3] (commonly known as *The Wagon Mound*), the Privy Council declared that the 'directness' test was wrong, and that the true test was one based on foreseeability of the damage.

1   The same principle applies to actions for breach of contract, although the detailed rules are different; paras 11.10–11.15 above.
2   [1921] 3 KB 560, CA.
3   [1961] 1 All ER 404, PC.

The 'foreseeability' test

19.16   The facts of *The Wagon Mound* were that the defendants negligently spilled large quantities of fuel oil into Sydney Harbour while their ship was being bunkered. Wind and tide carried this oil to the claimants' wharf, where two ships were being repaired by means of oxy-acetylene welding. The claimants ceased welding because of the fire risk but, on being assured by experts that fuel oil spread thus thinly on cool water would not ignite, recommenced; as a result a catastrophic fire badly damaged both the wharf and the ships. The Australian courts held that, since some damage to the claimants' wharf (fouling of the slipways) was foreseeable, the defendants were also liable for the damage done by fire, notwithstanding that this was unforeseeable. However, on appeal, the Privy Council held that foreseeability must embrace, not only the fact of injury, but also its kind; therefore, in this case, the defendants were not liable for the damage done by fire, since it was unforeseeable.

In *Overseas Tankship (UK) v Miller Steamship Co Pty*,[2] (commonly known as *The Wagon Mound (No 2)*), a second action arose out of the same incident, this time brought by the owners of the damaged ships. The evidence which was put before the trial judge on this occasion indicated that a reasonable ship's officer would have regarded fire as a possibility, albeit a slight one. The Privy Council held that, so long as the risk was not so remote that a reasonable man would brush it aside as far-fetched, it was foreseeable enough; accordingly, the defendants were held liable.

The *Wagon Mound* principle has been said to be logically superior to that laid down in *Re Polemis*, in that it applies the same 'foreseeability' test to remoteness of damage as to the question of breach of duty. On closer examination, however, it may be doubted whether the foreseeability test is applied in quite the same way in these two areas. Where breach of duty is concerned, a court is concerned to assess how foreseeable the damage was, and to balance the degree of foreseeability against other factors.[3] Where remoteness of damage is concerned, the principle appears to be that the defendant is liable if the damage in question was foreseeable to any degree at all.

Apart from being arguably more logical than *Re Polemis*, the *Wagon Mound* principle is also said to be more just, since it is unfair to expose a defendant who is guilty of a trivial act of negligence to liability for the serious unforeseeable consequences of that act. This, however, prompts the question: given that the unforeseeable loss must fall on someone, is it more just to place it on the defendant, who is at least guilty of some negligence, or on the claimant, who is guilty of none at all? In truth, the answer is a matter of policy, and depends upon whether claimants or defendants are to be favoured.

The practical effects of the change from directness to foreseeability can best be measured by considering separately the three identifying characteristics of any particular consequence in respect of which damages may be claimed. These are the kind of damage, the manner of its infliction and its extent. As we shall see, the interpretation which since 1961 has been given to foreseeability in this area means that the change brought about by the *Wagon Mound* principle is less fundamental than might have been expected.

1   [1961] 1 All ER 404, PC.
2   [1966] 2 All ER 709, PC.
3   Paras 18.11–18.15 above.

Kind of damage

19.17 Since *The Wagon Mound*, it is clear that a defendant is liable only for the kinds of damage which he might reasonably have foreseen. Thus, for example, the fact that damage by fouling is foreseeable will not render the defendant liable for damage by fire, if this what actually occurs. However, the general trend of decisions since 1961 has undoubtedly been against the drawing of fine distinctions. In *Bradford v Robinson Rentals Ltd*,[1] for example, a van driver, sent by his employers on a long journey in exceptionally cold weather in an unheated vehicle, suffered frostbite. It was held that, even if frostbite itself was unforeseeable, it was insufficiently akin to other foreseeable injuries from cold and fatigue to permit recovery.

1   [1967] 1 All ER 267.

Manner of infliction of damage

19.18 The approach of judges to the question of how damage is caused is, by and large, to require foreseeability of the general outline, rather than precise details. For example, where the defendant negligently causes a ship to collide with a quay, the true test of remoteness is whether it is foreseeable that the ship will suffer damage to its hull, not whether it is foreseeable that its hull will be holed by a badly designed fender on the side of the quay.[1] Furthermore, there has been a readiness to impose liability upon the defendant where an injury which he has caused to the claimant leads to a second accident,[2] to medical treatment with adverse effects,[3] or to even more unlikely consequences.[4]

The general attitude of the courts is well illustrated by two cases decided by the House of Lords. In the first, *Hughes v Lord Advocate*,[5] employees of the Post Office had left an open manhole covered by a canvas shelter and surrounded by paraffin warning lamps. An eight-year-old boy took one of these lamps into the shelter, where he accidentally knocked it down the hole; there was a violent explosion and the boy was severely burned. The Scottish courts held that the defendants were not liable, on the ground that, while injury by burning was foreseeable, the explosion was not. The House of Lords, however, held that such a distinction was too fine to be accepted, and that the accident fell within the area of risk which the defendants had created.

The second case, *Jolley v Sutton London Borough Council*,[6] concerned a rotten wooden boat which had been abandoned on the defendants' land, near blocks of flats. The 14-year-old claimant and his friend, in attempting to repair the boat, jacked it up with a car jack, and the claimant was injured when the boat fell while he was working underneath it. The Court of Appeal held the defendants not liable, on the ground that the only foreseeable risk resulting from their failure to remove the boat was that children might climb on it and fall through the rotten deck. However, the House of Lords reversed this decision, ruling that the foreseeable risk was a more general one, of children meddling with the boat and being injured in the process.

Occasionally, a decision stands out as taking a much narrower line, although it may for that very reason be regarded with some doubt. One such is *Doughty v Turner Manufacturing Co Ltd*,[7] where the defendants' employee negligently dropped an asbestos cement cover into a cauldron of molten liquid. There was no splash, but two minutes later, due to an unforeseeable chemical reaction, the liquid erupted and the claimant was burned. The Court of Appeal held that, even if injury by splashing were foreseeable, this eruption was not; nor could it be treated as a mere variant of the foreseeable risk. The defendants were accordingly not liable.

1   *Prekookeanska Plovidba v Felstar Shipping Corpn, The Carnival* [1994] 2 Lloyd's Rep 14, CA.
2   *Wieland v Cyril Lord Carpets Ltd* [1969] 3 All ER 1006.
3   *Robinson v Post Office* [1974] 2 All ER 737, CA.
4   See the cases discussed in para 19.21 below.
5   [1963] 1 All ER 705, HL.
6   [2000] 3 All ER 409, HL.
7   [1964] 1 All ER 98, CA.

Extent of damage

19.19   While the kind of damage, and the manner in which it is caused, must both be reasonably foreseeable, albeit in only a general sense, it appears that the extent of the damage need not be foreseeable at all. In *Vacwell Engineering Co Ltd v BDH Chemicals Ltd*,[1] for example, the defendants negligently failed to warn the claimants that a chemical which they had supplied was liable to explode on contact with water. An employee of the claimants placed a large quantity of this substance in a sink. This resulted in a violent explosion, which extensively damaged the claimants' premises. It was found that, while a minor explosion was foreseeable, one of this magnitude was not; nevertheless, the defendants were held liable for all the damage.

1   [1970] 3 All ER 553n, CA.

The 'egg-shell skull'

19.20   It is well established that a defendant is fully liable to a claimant whose injuries are aggravated by some inherent defect such as a thin skull or haemophilia, notwithstanding that the defendant could not possibly have foreseen this. Where the aggravated injury is of the same type, the defendant could equally be held liable on the basis that the extent of damage need not be foreseeable.[1] However, the 'egg-shell skull' principle extends also to cases where the secondary injury is of a different kind, based on the rule that a tortfeasor takes his victim as he finds him, a rule which was held, in *Smith v Leech Brain & Co Ltd*,[2] to have survived *The Wagon Mound*. The defendants in that case negligently caused an employee's lip to be burned by molten metal. This burn activated an unsuspected pre-malignant cancerous condition which, three years later, led to the man's death. The defendants were held liable, not only for the initial burn, but also for the death.

Although the egg-shell skull principle has been applied to claimants with a weak heart,[3] an allergy to certain vaccine[4] and even an 'egg-shell personality',[5] the House of Lords ruled in 1933 that it could not be extended to a claimant's financial state.[6] Consequently, if the loss caused to a claimant was aggravated due to his lack of means, the additional loss could not be treated as having been caused by the defendant. More recently, the courts have retreated somewhat from this position;[7] on several occasions, the Court of Appeal has distinguished *Liesbosch Dredger v SS Edison* on grounds which are unconvincing. For example, in *Dodd Properties (Kent) Ltd v Canterbury City Council*,[8] the claimants sued the defendants for the cost of repairing their garage, which the defendants had negligently damaged. By the time the case came to court, the cost of repairs had escalated and the defendants claimed that they were liable only for what the repairs would have cost if put in hand at an earlier date. The Court of Appeal held that, while pure lack of funds would have given the claimants no excuse to delay, and would thus have restricted their claim to the lower figure, their decision to delay until they had recovered damages (based upon principles of cash flow) was a reasonable one. The defendants were therefore liable in full.

1   See para 19.19 above.
2   [1961] 3 All ER 1159.
3   *Love v Port of London Authority* [1959] 2 Lloyd's Rep 541.
4   *Robinson v Post Office* [1974] 2 All ER 737, CA.
5   *Malcolm v Broadhurst* [1970] 3 All ER 508.
6   *Liesbosch Dredger v SS Edison* [1933] AC 449, HL; para 19.16 above.
7   But see *Ramwade v WJ Emson & Co* [1987] RTR 72, CA.
8   [1980] 1 All ER 928, CA; para 28.14 below.

Policy considerations

19.21   Decisions on both legal causation and remoteness of damage are, in truth, value judgments in which a judge's personal experience, common sense and notions of public policy all play their part. Notwithstanding the lip service which is habitually paid to the test of reasonable foreseeability, it must be all too obvious that many problems arise which no legal system can possibly answer by the mechanical application of such a principle. For example, only policy, and not foreseeability, can justify the ruling by the House of Lords that the police may be held liable in negligence for failing to prevent a person in custody from attempting or committing suicide.[1]

In *Clunis v Camden and Islington Health* Authority,[2] the claimant, a mentally disordered person, was in the care of the defendants when he killed a stranger in an unprovoked attack, for which he was convicted of manslaughter. He sued the defendants for negligently failing to control him, but this claim was rejected by the Court of Appeal, which ruled that a person could not recover damages on the basis of his own criminal act, unless he either did not know the nature and quality of that act or did not know that it was wrong.

The court in *Clunis* was not faced in that case by a claim on behalf of the victim, but such a claim was rejected in the earlier case of *Meah v McCreamer (No 2)*.[3] The claimant in that case, who had suffered serious head injuries in a road accident for which the defendant was responsible, subsequently carried out a series of sexual assaults for which he was sentenced to life imprisonment. When the claimant was successfully sued by two of his rape victims,[4] it was held that public policy would not allow him to reclaim from the driver the damages which he had to pay, nor would it permit those victims to sue the driver directly.

1   *Reeves v Metropolitan Police Comr* [1999] 3 All ER 897, HL.
2   [1998] 3 All ER 180, CA.
3   [1986] 1 All ER 943.
4   *W v Meah* [1986] 1 All ER 935.

Chapter 20

Defences to negligence

20.1 In addition to arguing that the claimant has failed to establish the necessary elements of a case in negligence (or whatever tort is alleged), a defendant may seek to rely on certain specific defences to liability. The most important of these are illegality, where a claim too closely linked to an illegal act is ruled out on grounds of public policy; consent and assumption of risk, the rule that a person cannot complain of an act to which he has expressly or impliedly consented, or of which he has assumed the legal risk; and contributory negligence, which applies where the claimant is partly responsible for his own injury. A significant difference between these defences is that the first two, if successful, operate as a complete defence to liability. Contributory negligence, on the other hand, leads only to a reduction in the damages awarded. The added flexibility which contributory negligence thus gives the courts has led them to favour this defence, and it has consequently become most unusual to find assumption of risk successfully pleaded, at least in cases of negligence. However, in *Morris v Murray*,[1] where the claimant accepted a flight in the defendant's light aircraft in bad weather when both parties were drunk, the Court of Appeal held that the claimant's claim for injuries received in the ensuing crash must fail altogether. The court was asked merely to reduce the claimant's damages for contributory negligence but refused to do so, stating that 'the wild irresponsibility of the venture is such that the law should not intervene to award damages and should leave the loss where it falls'.

In this chapter we examine the following issues:

- the circumstances in which a claim will be defeated on the grounds that it is contrary to public policy;
- the extent to which a person is debarred from claiming damages in respect of an act to which he has consented, or of which he has voluntarily assumed the risk;
- the problems involved in applying the concept of 'assumption of risk' to cases of negligence;
- the power of the courts to divide responsibility between claimant and defendant where both are partly responsible for causing the claimant's loss.

1   [1990] 3 All ER 801, CA.

Illegality and public policy

20.2 In certain, not very clearly defined, circumstances, an action in negligence will fail on the ground that the claimant, when he suffered injury or damage, was engaged in some unlawful (usually criminal) activity. In some of the cases where this applies, a court will treat the illegality as a defence in itself; in others, as a reason for holding that it would not be fair and reasonable to impose a duty of care. Whichever approach is adopted, the underlying reasons are not always expressed in the same way. Sometimes the courts emphasise that a claim will fail if, to make it, the claimant has to 'rely' in some way on his own illegal act. At other times, the court will claim to apply a test of what would offend the public conscience. A third reason that is sometimes given is that the law should ensure that 'crime does not pay'.

Whatever the true basis of this defence, the negligence cases in which it has been held to operate have fallen into three main categories. The first is where the two parties are engaged in some joint criminal enterprise when the claimant is injured. Claims of this type which have been rejected include one by an escaping robber against the driver of the getaway car,[1] and by a pillion passenger who encouraged a motor-cyclist to ride recklessly and dangerously as part of a drunken spree.[2]

The second type of claim is one brought against the police, or medical authorities, alleging that their failure adequately to control or treat the claimant permitted him to harm himself or others (leading, in the latter case, to a criminal conviction and punishment). In Clunis v Camden and Islington Health Authority,[3] for example, the Court of Appeal rejected a claim by someone with a long history of mental illness who, having been discharged without after care by the defendants, had three months later killed a stranger in a vicious and unprovoked attack.[4] Similarly, in Vellino v Chief Constable of the Greater Manchester Police,[5] a majority of the Court of Appeal refused to award damages to someone injured in attempting to escape from police custody by jumping out of a window. However, where the defendant in question owes a duty of care to prevent the very act which causes the harm (such as suicide or attempted suicide), an action for breach of that duty will not be defeated by the defence of illegality.[6]

The third, and perhaps most controversial, type of case is where the defendant's alleged negligence occurs as a reaction (or over-reaction) to the claimant's own misconduct. Here the court will pay regard to the question of proportionality; illegality may not operate to bar a claim where the defendant's reaction is out of all proportion to the harm or threatened harm. An example is Revill v Newbery,[7] where a 76-year-old man, sleeping in a shed at his allotment because of previous criminal activity, fired his shotgun 'blind' through a hole in the door and injured the claimant, a youth who was attempting to break in. The Court of Appeal held the defendant liable in negligence, although the claimant's damages were reduced by two-thirds on the ground of contributory negligence.

1   Ashton v Turner [1980] 3 All ER 870.
2   Pitts v Hunt [1990] 3 All ER 344, CA.
3   [1998] 3 All ER 180, CA.
4   The claimant was charged with murder, but this was reduced to manslaughter on the grounds of diminished responsibility.
5   [2001] EWCA Civ 1249, [2002] 3 All ER 78.
6   Reeves v Metropolitan Police Comr [1998] 2 All ER 381, CA.
7   [1996] 1 All ER 291, CA.

Consent and assumption of risk

Consent to torts other than negligence
20.3   The idea of consent as a defence is easy to understand in relation to intentional torts such as assault and battery; a boxer cannot complain of a fair punch, for example, nor a patient of the invasion of his body which is inherent in a surgical operation.[1] Consent, however, has its limits; even a participant in a fist fight may not be precluded from claiming

damages if his antagonist inflicts serious injury with a savage blow which is quite out of proportion to the occasion.[2]

Consent is also relatively straightforward in relation to torts of strict liability, although the terminology here is different; the claimant will lose his case wherever it can fairly be said that he has assumed the legal risk of being injured. Thus, a person who keeps a dog which he knows to be vicious takes the legal risk that it will bite someone; but that legal risk will be transferred to the shoulders of anyone who ignores a clear 'Beware of the Dog' notice.[3]

1   See para 20.4 below.
2   *Lane v Holloway* [1967] 3 All ER 129, CA.
3   *Cummings v Granger* [1977] 1 All ER 104, CA.

Meaning of consent

20.4   Although knowledge of a risk does not in itself indicate consent to run it, there can be no consent by someone who lacks full awareness of the nature and extent of the risk involved. Actual knowledge is required; thus in *Sarch v Blackburn*,[1] where the claimant was bitten by the defendant's dog, his right to recover damages was held to be unaffected by a large 'Beware of the Dog' notice, since he could not read.

Some jurisdictions adopt a principle of 'informed consent', whereby a patient who is not given full information about the risks involved in a proposed operation is not treated as having consented to it. This means that the operation is then actionable as a battery, even if it is carried out with all due care and skill. In *Sidaway v Board of Governors of the Bethlem Royal Hospital and the Maudsley Hospital*,[2] the House of Lords held that this doctrine has no place in English law and that a doctor's duty to warn of risks is merely part of the general duty of care which he owes to his patient. As a result, a patient who seeks legal redress for a failure to warn must show that any reasonably competent doctor would have given a warning.

To be of legal effect, a person's consent to assume a risk must be fully and freely given, neither induced by fraud nor resulting from some pressure sufficient to override his free will. For example, in cases of employer and employee,[3] it is usually said that economic pressure on the employee not to lose his job prevents the implication that he assumes the risks inherent in it. Similarly, in rescue cases,[4] the defence of assumption of risk is ruled out by the moral obligation on the claimant to go to the aid of someone in danger. At one time the courts held that, where a person of sound mind committed or attempted suicide, any action against police or hospital authorities for failing to prevent this would fail on the ground that he had voluntarily assumed the risk. However, in *Reeves v Metropolitan Police Comr*,[5] the House of Lords held that the defence could not be raised in a case where the claimant's act was the very thing that the defendant was under a duty to prevent.

1   (1830) 4 C & P 297.
2   [1985] 1 All ER 643, HL.
3   Para 20.8 below.
4   Paras 20.9 and 20.10 below.
5   [1999] 3 All ER 897, HL.

Assumption of risk in negligence cases

Express consent

20.5   Where the claimant is alleged to have expressly agreed to assume the risk of negligence by the defendant, the case is usually concerned with an exemption clause, although a non-contractual waiver is in principle also effective.[1] However, statute has now deprived the latter of one of its most important practical applications, namely, 'Ride at your own risk' as regards passengers in motor vehicles.[2] Further, the extent to which liability for negligence may be excluded by a contract term or notice is heavily restricted,[3] and the Unfair Contract Terms Act 1977, s 2(3) makes it clear that a person's agreement to or awareness of a purported exemption clause does not in itself lead to the conclusion that he assumes any risk.

1   *Buckpitt v Oates* [1968] 1 All ER 1145.
2   Road Traffic Act 1988, s 149(3).
3   Paras 9.11 and 10.15 above.

Implied consent

20.6   Attempts to persuade a court that it is clear, from the claimant's conduct, that he assumed the risk of negligence by the defendant are seldom successful. Those which do succeed are usually cases in which the defendant's negligence takes place first, so that its full effects are visible to the claimant before he puts himself in danger. In *Cutler v United Dairies (London) Ltd*,[1] due to negligence for which the defendants were responsible, a horse ran away into a field. There was no danger, but the driver called for assistance in pacifying the animal, and the claimant was injured in helping him. The Court of Appeal held that the claimant had obviously assumed the risk and that he could not, therefore, recover damages.

The very idea of a claimant taking on the risk that the defendant will in future act negligently towards him is one which judges dislike; it has even been suggested that the defence can never apply to negligence in the simple sense of a duty of care based upon foreseeability.[2] This may overstate the case, but it is worth remembering that the vital question is not whether the claimant foolishly risked injury, but whether he agreed in effect that the legal risk of loss should be upon him and not upon the defendant. It may be that a court will only come to such a conclusion in cases where the parties are engaged on a thoroughly irresponsible (and possibly illegal) joint venture.[3]

1   [1933] 2 KB 297, CA; para 19.11 above.
2   *Dann v Hamilton* [1939] 1 All ER 59 at 60; *Wooldridge v Sumner* [1962] 2 All ER 978 at 990.
3   See, for example, *Morris v Murray* [1990] 3 All ER 801, CA; para 20.1 above.

Variable duties

20.7   In certain circumstances the courts, while reluctant to exonerate a defendant altogether, have suggested the relationship between the parties, and their appreciation of the risks involved in a particular enterprise, may make it appropriate to impose something less than a full duty of care upon the defendant. In *Wooldridge v Sumner*,[1] for example, a competitor at the National Horse Show took a corner too fast, injuring a photographer who was standing in the arena. In holding the defendant not liable, a majority of the Court of Appeal laid down that no duty of reasonable care was owed, and that, since neither the photographer nor any other spectator would expect a competitor to consider his interests, liability could only be imposed if the defendant had shown 'reckless disregard' for the spectator's safety.

Despite the use of the word 'reckless', it seems that what this really means is that a sporting competitor is as much subject to the tort of negligence as anyone else; however, in deciding whether or not he has fulfilled his duty to act with reasonable care, a court should take into account the fact that competitors in sporting events are entitled to concentrate their attention more on winning than on protecting either spectators or other competitors. This approach has been applied to cases involving a scramble event in which a motor cycle jumped a safety rope;[2] a footballer who broke an opponent's leg with an 'over the top' tackle;[3] and jockeys who injured another by 'careless riding'.[4]

The more relaxed approach to the duty of care shown by such cases is found only where the alleged negligence occurs in the flurry and excitement of competition. In *Harrison v Vincent*,[5] a sidecar passenger was injured when a mechanical defect caused the defendant to lose control of his motor cycle combination during a race. The Court of Appeal held that, while the actual riding of the machine should be judged on the *Wooldridge v Sumner* principle, the mechanical preparations were done in the calm of the workshop and accordingly fell within the normal rules of negligence. The court also stated that a similar approach would be taken in respect of defects in course design or safety. And in *Smoldon v Whitworth*,[6] where a collapsing scrum in a colts rugby match caused serious injury to one of the players, it was held by the Court of Appeal that the referee owed a duty of care to the players to enforce rules designed for their safety.

1 [1962] 2 All ER 978, CA.
2 *Wilks v Cheltenham Home Guard Motor Cycle and Light Car Club* [1971] 2 All ER 369, CA.
3 *Condon v Basi* [1985] 2 All ER 453, CA.
4 *Caldwell v Maguire and Fitzgerald* [2002] PIQR P6, CA.
5 [1982] RTR 8.
6 [1997] PIQR P133, CA.

Employees

20.8 In the early 19th century, when the growth of industry was regarded as more important than the safety of the workforce, it was repeatedly held that a workman who continued to do his job in the face of clear danger could not recover damages for either negligence or breach of statutory duty if he was subsequently injured. This trend was reversed in the leading case of *Smith v Baker & Sons*,[1] where the claimant, who was working in a cutting, was injured when a crane dropped a stone on him. For several months this crane had swung its loads over the claimant's head, and at no time had any warning been given that it was about to do so. The House of Lords held that the claimant could not be said to have accepted the risk merely by virtue of continuing to work for the defendant with knowledge of it.

Today, an employer who is guilty of negligence will today find it almost impossible to avoid liability by raising the defence of assumption of risk. Further, one who is personally in breach of a statutory duty will certainly not be allowed to do so, since it would be totally against public policy to permit someone to contract out of a duty imposed upon him by statute.[2] However, there may be extreme cases in which the use of the defence against an employee would not offend public policy, and one such was *ICI Ltd v Shatwell*.[3] That case concerned two shot-firers who, in flagrant breach of statutory duties which were imposed upon them personally, tested a firing circuit without taking cover. When an explosion injured one of the men, he claimed that his employers were vicariously liable for his colleague's breach of statutory duty. The House of Lords held that the employers, who were morally innocent in this matter (having done everything in their power to see that these regulations were obeyed) and who were personally not guilty of any tort, were entitled to avoid liability on the ground of assumption of risk.

1 [1891] AC 325, HL. See also *Burnett v British Waterways Board* [1973] 2 All ER 631, CA.
2 *Baddeley v Earl of Granville* (1887) 19 QBD 423, DC.
3 [1964] 2 All ER 999, HL.

Rescuers

20.9 At first sight, the defence of assumption of risk would seem highly applicable to the case of someone who exposes himself to danger in attempting to rescue another person.[1] However, such a rule would hardly encourage humanitarian conduct and, not surprisingly, the law does not apply it. In *Haynes v Harwood*,[2] for example, where a policeman was injured in stopping a runaway horse in a crowded street, it was held that the defendant, whose negligence had permitted the horse to run away, could not avoid liability by claiming that the policeman had voluntarily incurred the risk.

The theoretical basis for excluding the defence in rescue cases is that the rescuer's free will is overborne by the moral compulsion which drives him to take the risk. This applies, not only to those whose job might be seen as imposing an obligation to go to the rescue (such as the policeman in *Haynes v Harwood*), but also to members of the public whose intervention is entirely voluntary.[3]

1   Or property; *Hyett v Great Western Rly Co* [1947] 2 All ER 264, CA.
2   [1935] 1 KB 146, CA; para 19.11 above.
3   [1967] 2 All ER 945.

20.10   It is now settled that an action brought by an injured rescuer is quite independent of any claim by the person rescued. It rests on a separate duty of care which is owed to the rescuer personally by whoever causes the danger and hence also causes the need for rescue. As a result, a rescuer is not adversely affected by any defect in the claim of the person rescued, such as contributory negligence, or the fact that the person is a trespasser.[1]

The legal independence of the rescuer's claim has further consequences. For instance, a person who negligently endangers himself may be liable to a rescuer, if the circumstances are such as to render a rescue attempt foreseeable.[2] Moreover, the Supreme Court of Canada has held that a rescuer who so bungles the job that someone is induced to make a second attempt may be liable to the second rescuer if the latter is injured.[3]

1   *Videan v British Transport Commission* [1963] 2 All ER 860, CA.
2   *Harrison v British Railways Board* [1981] 3 All ER 679.
3   *Horsley v MacLaren, The Ogopogo* [1971] 2 Lloyd's Rep 410.

Contributory negligence

20.11   At common law, contributory negligence was a complete defence to liability. A claimant who contributed to his own injuries by failing to take reasonable care of himself could recover nothing at all from the defendant whose tort would otherwise have been regarded as the legal cause. Despite the obvious harshness of this rule, it was not removed until the enactment of the Law Reform (Contributory Negligence) Act 1945.

The 1945 Act
20.12   Section 1(1) of the 1945 Act provides that where a person suffers damage as the result partly of his own fault and partly of the fault of another person, the damages recoverable by him shall be reduced to such extent as the court thinks just and equitable having regard to the claimant's share in the responsibility for the damage.

Interestingly, the Act speaks not of negligence but of *fault*. According to s 4, this means 'negligence, breach of statutory duty or other act or omission which gives rise to a liability in tort or would, apart from this Act, give rise to the defence of contributory negligence'. Clearly, then, this defence is available not only in cases of negligence, but also in a number of other torts, including, it appears, assault and battery.[1] It has no application, however, to actions in deceit.[2]

The 1945 Act is inapplicable to actions based purely on a breach of contract,[3] so that, if the claimant in such a case is also at fault, the court must either hold him entirely responsible and thus deny him compensation altogether, or ignore his share of the blame and award him damages in full.[4] Where, however, a defendant's liability in contract is identical to what his liability would be in the tort of negligence, the claimant will not be able to avoid the operation of the 1945 Act by framing his action in contract; the court has the power to reduce the claimant's damages, whatever the action is called.[5]

1   *Barnes v Nayer* (1986) Times, 19 December, CA.
2   *Alliance and Leicester Building Society v Edgestop Ltd* [1994] 2 All ER 38.
3   *Barclays Bank v Fairclough Building Ltd* [1995] QB 214, CA; see para 11.19 above.
4   In *Tennant Radiant Heat Ltd v Warrington Development Corpn* [1988] 1 EGLR 41, CA, the Court of Appeal managed to award partial compensation in such a case, by ruling that the defendant had only caused part of the claimant's loss, but this seems wrong.
5   *Forsikringsaktieselskapet Vesta v Butcher* [1988] 2 All ER 43, CA; para 11.19 above.

Standard of care

20.13 When a defendant alleges that the claimant was contributorily negligent, he is not called upon to show that the claimant owed him a legal duty; contributory negligence consists simply of failing to take such care of oneself as is reasonable in all the circumstances of the case. Thus, a mortgage lender who claims damages from a negligent valuer may suffer a reduction in those damages if either it was unreasonable for the lender to rely on the valuation[1] or the decision to lend was negligent for other reasons.[2]

As to the standard which the claimant is required to reach, this is evaluated in much the same way as is a defendant's for the purpose of establishing a breach of a duty of care.[3] Indeed, many of the factors which we considered in that context, such as the standard of care demanded of children, and the extent to which the reasonable man must foresee negligence in others, are of special relevance here. So too, those cases where the claimant's conduct tends not be regarded as an intervening cause,[4] such as rescue attempts, or the claimant's instinctive reactions to an emergency, may well today give rise to a finding of contributory negligence.[5] It has been held by the House of Lords that suicide, at least by a person of sound mind, may amount to contributory negligence in a claim against a defendant who owes a duty of care to prevent it.[6]

In considering the defence of assumption of risk, we noted that knowledge of a risk does not necessarily imply acceptance of it.[7] Such knowledge may, however, lead a court to the conclusion that the claimant was contributorily negligent in failing to take avoiding action. In *Owens v Brimmell*,[8] for example, a passenger in a car who knew that his driver had been drinking heavily lost 20% of his damages when the driver negligently crashed the car and the passenger was injured. So too, in *Gregory v Kelly*,[9] the claimant was held to be contributorily negligent in travelling in a car when he knew that the footbrake did not work.

1   *Banque Bruxelles Lambert SA v Eagle Star* [1995] 2 All ER 769.
2   *Platform Home Loans Ltd v Oyston Shipways Ltd* [1998] 13 EG 148, CA.
3   Chapter 18 above.
4   Paras 19.10–19.14 above.
5   See *Harrison v British Railways Board* [1981] 3 All ER 679; para 19.11 above.
6   *Reeves v Metropolitan Police Comr* [1999] 3 All ER 897, HL.
7   Para 20.3 above.
8   [1977] QB 859, [1976] 3 All ER 765.
9   [1978] RTR 426.

Causation

20.14 It is not enough for a defendant to show that the claimant failed to take reasonable care of himself; the lack of care must also be shown to have contributed, at least in part, to the claimant's damage. This, however, does not mean that it must have contributed to the accident which caused the damage. For example, a moped rider who is in no way responsible for a collision may nevertheless lose part of his damages if his injuries are increased by the fact that he was not wearing a helmet[1] or that his chin strap was not fastened.[2] The same principle applies to seat belts in motor vehicles;[3] failure by a driver or front-seat passenger to wear a seat belt normally leads to a reduction in damages of between 15% and 25%, depending on whether the injuries would have been substantially or even totally avoided but ignoring the question of what other injuries the seat belt itself might have caused.[4]

Since the attribution of legal cause is really, as we have seen,[5] a matter in which the judge exercises a choice, no hard and fast rules can be laid down. An important factor, however, is that of risk; if the claimant's damage does not fall within the scope of the risk to which he unreasonably exposed himself, then his negligence is not contributory. In *Jones v Livox Quarries Ltd*,[6] an employee who stood, contrary to instructions, on the back of a moving traxcavator was injured when another vehicle collided with it. The claimant argued that his negligence did not contribute to his injuries, since the only risk he had undertaken was that of falling off. The Court of Appeal, while accepting that he would not have been in any way to blame if, during his unauthorised ride, he had been shot by a negligent sportsman, nevertheless felt that the actual accident was within the risk. Accordingly damages were reduced by 20%. A similar problem arose in *Westwood v Post Office*,[7] where an employee was killed when he ignored a notice which read: 'Authorised personnel only', entered a lift motor room and fell through a defective trapdoor. A bare (3–2) majority of the House of Lords held that, since the notice gave no indication of danger, let alone of the specific danger, the trespasser's only fault was disobedience, and not contributory negligence.

1   *O'Connell v Jackson* [1971] 3 All ER 129, CA.
2   *Capps v Miller* [1989] 2 All ER 333, CA.
3   *Froom v Butcher* [1975] 3 All ER 520, CA.
4   *Patience v Andrews* [1983] RTR 447.
5   Paras 19.7–19.14 above.
6   [1952] 2 QB 608, CA.
7   [1973] 3 All ER 184, HL.

Identification

20.15   In some circumstances, A may be 'identified' with B for the purposes of contributory negligence. Where this is so, it means that any damages which are awarded to A in an action against a third party may be reduced because of the contributory negligence of B. For example, if a lorry is involved in a collision with another vehicle due to the negligence of both drivers, any damages which the lorry driver's employers claim as owners of the lorry from the other driver may be reduced on the ground of their employee's contributory negligence.

This doctrine of identification applies wherever there is a relationship sufficient to impose vicarious liability.[1] It also applies to a claim by dependants under the Fatal Accidents Act 1976, where the deceased was partly to blame for his own death.[2]

1   Chapter 28 below.
2   Para 28.12 below.

Apportionment

20.16   Section 1(1) of the 1945 Act instructs the court to reduce the claimant's damages to such an extent as is just and equitable in view of the claimant's share in the responsibility for the damage. No statutory guidance is given for this process, but two factors are clearly regarded by the courts as relevant. The first of these, naturally, is the degree of fault which may be attributed to each party. This, however, cannot be the sole criterion for, in a case where the defendant is strictly liable, such as for a breach of statutory duty, it would lead to the absurd conclusion that a slightly negligent claimant receives nothing at all. Thus a second factor, that of 'causative importance', must also be considered.[1]

It should not be thought that equal carelessness compels equal division. For example, it is not unreasonable to place a greater burden upon a negligent motorist than upon an equally negligent pedestrian, since the conduct of the former entails grave risks to others as well as to himself. All that can be said is that the courts make full use of the discretion which they are given; reductions have ranged from a mere 5% in the case of a passenger injured by negligent driving, whose failure to wear a seat-belt was itself partly the driver's fault,[2] to 80% where safety regulations were deliberately flouted by a workman and his colleague.[3] In one case the Court of Appeal even held an injured workman 100% contributorily negligent,[4] although a differently constituted Court of Appeal described such a conclusion as 'logically unsupportable'.[5] It would be preferable in such a case to regard the claimant as the sole cause of his injuries.

Where an action is brought against more than one defendant, any contributory negligence by the claimant must be measured against the totality of the defendants' conduct, rather than against each of them separately. Thus, for example, if the claimant, defendant A and defendant B are all equally to blame, the claimant should be awarded two-thirds of his damages against each defendant rather than one-half.[6]

1   *Stapley v Gypsum Mines Ltd* [1953] 2 All ER 478 at 486.
2   *Pasternack v Poulton* [1973] 2 All ER 74. However, a passenger failed in her claim against a *non-negligent* driver for merely failing to advise her to wear a seat belt: *Eastman v South West Thames Area Health Authority* [1991] RTR 389, CA.
3   *Stapley v Gypsum Mines Ltd* [1953] 2 All ER 478, HL.
4   *Jayes v IMI (Kynoch) Ltd* [1985] ICR 155, CA.
5   *Pitts v Hunt* [1990] 3 All ER 344, CA.
6   *Fitzgerald v Lane* [1988] 2 All ER 961, HL.

Chapter 21

Liability for dangerous premises

21.1   Premises which, because of their dangerous condition, cause injury to persons or damage to property may be a source of liability in various ways. Where the injury or damage is caused to persons or property off the premises, a claim in respect of that damage may arise in nuisance.[1] This chapter is concerned with injury or damage which results on the premises themselves, and includes the following issues:

- the statutory duty which is owed by the occupier of premises to his lawful visitors;
- the lesser statutory duty which the occupier owes to those who are not lawful visitors (mainly trespassers);
- the liability which the law of tort imposes upon those who are negligent in the design or construction of buildings;
- the extent to which a person who sells or lets dangerous property can be held responsible for the consequences.

1   Chapter 24 below.

Lawful visitors

Scope of the duty
21.2   Section 2(1) of the Occupiers' Liability Act 1957 provides: 'An occupier of premises owes the same duty, the "common duty of care", to all his visitors, except in so far as he is free to and does extend, restrict, modify or exclude his duty to any visitor or visitors by agreement or otherwise.'

Most of the litigation in this area concerns personal injury or death, but s 1(3) of the Act provides that the statutory rules also apply to the obligations of a person occupying or having control over any premises or structure in respect of damage to property, including the property of persons who are not themselves his visitors. Further, where damage to property is proved, the occupier's liability extends also to consequential financial loss, such as the expense of salvaging damaged goods.[1]

1   *AMF International Ltd v Magnet Bowling Ltd* [1968] 2 All ER 789.

Exclusion of liability by contract
21.3   Section 2(1) suggests that an occupier may exclude or restrict the duty which he would otherwise owe to a visitor. However, the qualification 'in so far as he is free to'

indicates that there are circumstances in which the occupier is denied this freedom. It seems, for instance, that an innkeeper is not permitted to exclude liability for damage to the property of guests.[1] Further, while s 5 of the 1957 Act makes a contract between the occupier and a visitor decisive as to the rights of the latter, s 3 provides that a person entering premises under a contract to which he is not a party may not be adversely affected by the terms of that contract.[2]

Any attempt by an occupier to exclude or restrict his duty by means of a contractual term is subject to the rules which govern exemption clauses.[3] Of fundamental importance is the Unfair Contract Terms Act 1977. This, when it applies, prohibits the exclusion or restriction of liability for personal injury or death altogether, and makes the exclusion or restriction of liability for other kinds of damage subject to a test of reasonableness. The provisions of this Act are considered in detail elsewhere;[4] for present purposes it is sufficient to state that its operation is limited to duties which arise 'from the occupation of premises used for business purposes of the occupier'. However, a relaxation of the rules, which was introduced by the Occupiers' Liability Act 1984, s 2, permits a business occupier to exclude or restrict liability to those whom he permits to enter his land for recreational or educational purposes which do not themselves form part of his business. A private occupier is not affected by the Unfair Contract Terms Act, but any attempt which he makes to exclude or restrict his liability by means of a contract term must still satisfy the stringent requirements of common law.

1   *Williams v Linnit* [1951] 1 All ER 278, CA; see now the Hotel Proprietors Act 1956, s 2(3).
2   Para 21.12 below.
3   Chapter 9.
4   Paras 9.14–9.24 above.

Exclusion of liability by notice

21.4   Occupiers not infrequently seek to exclude or restrict their liability by displaying prominently on their premises notices which state, for example: 'No Liability is Accepted for any Injury or Damage'. It appears that, as a general principle, such notices can be effective. It was held by the Court of Appeal, in *Ashdown v Samuel Williams & Sons Ltd*[1] and *White v Blackmore*,[2] that, since an occupier is entitled to say: 'Keep Out', he is equally entitled to impose conditions upon which persons may enter.[3] However, the legal position has been substantially altered by the Unfair Contract Terms Act, at least where business premises are concerned.[8]

1   [1957] 1 All ER 35, CA.
2   [1972] 3 All ER 158, CA.
3   For this reason it seems that a notice excluding liability will be of no effect against a person who enters the premises by some legal right.
4   Section 2(4)(a): para 21.16 below.
5   Section 2(5): para 21.18 below.
6   [1973] 2 All ER 631, CA.
7   Paras 20.1–20.10 above, especially para 20.8.
8   Paras 9.14, 9.15 and 21.3 above.

Occupier

21.5   The Occupiers' Liability Act 1957 contains no definition of 'occupier', indeed, the common law position is expressly preserved by s 1(3). Traditionally, this question has been approached by the courts on a commonsense basis, looking to the practicalities of the situation rather than to the technicalities of land law. Thus, for example, on a large-scale building project, the main contractor may well be held to be the occupier of the site (either alone or jointly with the owner).[1] Similarly, in a Canadian case where an auction was conducted on a farm, both the farmer and the auctioneer were held to be occupiers of the barn in which it took place.[2]

The most important single factor used in deciding who is an occupier is that of *control*. This need be neither entire nor exclusive but, unless a person is sufficiently in control of premises to realise that carelessness on his part may lead to a visitor being injured, he cannot be regarded as an occupier.[3] Thus a married couple were not occupiers of the flat roof of a supermarket, even though the window of their flat gave access to this roof and they allowed their own children to play on it. They therefore owed no duty to another child, who climbed from the garden on to the roof and then fell from it.[4]

It is on the basis of control that liability has been imposed upon a fairground concessionaire (who had no interest in the property)[5] and upon a local authority which, having acquired a house by compulsory purchase, ordered the resident to leave by serving a notice of intention to enter, even though the authority did not then take possession of the property.[6] Similarly, where the owner of premises licenses another to use them, it may well be that he retains sufficient control to be treated as an occupier,[7] and it is then a question of fact whether the licensee is an occupier as well. On the other hand, where property is leased,[8] it is the tenant, and not the landlord, who is the occupier, although a landlord who is in breach of his repairing obligations may incur liability under a separate provision.[9] The landlord will also be regarded as the occupier of the common parts of premises, such as lifts and staircases in a block of flats, notwithstanding that he cannot deny access to these areas to his tenants' families or guests.[10]

1   *AMF International Ltd v Magnet Bowling Ltd* [1968] 2 All ER 789.
2   *Couch v McCann* (1977) 77 DLR (3d) 387.
3   See *Cavalier v Pope* [1906] AC 428 at 433.
4   *Bailey v Armes* [1999] EGCS 21, CA.
5   *Humphreys v Dreamland (Margate) Ltd* (1930) 144 LT 529, HL.
6   *Harris v Birkenhead Corpn* [1976] 1 All ER 341, CA.
7   *Wheat v E Lacon & Co Ltd* [1966] 1 All ER 582, HL.
8   For the distinction between a lease and a licence, see para 37.9 below.
9   Para 21.29 below.
10 *Moloney v Lambeth London Borough Council* (1966) 64 LGR 440.

Multiple occupation

21.6   The courts have repeatedly held that neither occupation, nor the control on which it is based, need be exclusive, and that consequently there may be more than one occupier of the same premises. In *Fisher v CRT Ltd (No 2)*,[1] for example, X owned a gaming club; a restaurant on the premises was held under licence by Y, who ran it as a separate business. Although detailed control over the restaurant was in the hands of Y, its sole entrance was through X's premises, and X had a right of entry. When a workman was injured in the restaurant, both X and Y were held liable as occupiers.

The leading case on the subject of multiple occupation, *Wheat v E Lacon & Co Ltd*,[2] concerned a public house with a resident manager. The brewery company which owned the public house permitted the manager and his wife (who occupied part of the premises as licensees) to take in paying guests, and one of these guests was killed when he fell down the unlighted back stairs. In an action by the guest's widow (which failed because she was unable to prove negligence), the House of Lords made some important comments on the question of occupation. The brewery, it was said, should be regarded as occupying the residential part of the premises, either vicariously (through its employee, the manager) or because it retained sufficient control. The manager, too, was an occupier of the relevant part. Both occupiers therefore owed visitors a duty of care; the content of their duties, however, might well differ. For example, the structure of the property would probably be the responsibility of the brewery, while liability for such matters as defective carpeting in the manager's flat would more appropriately be imposed upon the manager himself.

1   [1966] 1 All ER 88, CA.
2   [1966] 1 All ER 582, HL.

Premises

21.7   The Occupiers' Liability Act 1957 does not define what is meant by 'premises', although these clearly include land and buildings. In addition, it is provided by s 1(3)(a) that the statutory rules shall regulate 'the obligations of a person occupying or having control over any fixed or moveable structure, including any vessel, vehicle or aircraft', a list which seems apt to include both such permanent structures as grandstands[1] or pylons,[2] and more temporary erections such as scaffolding[3] or ladders.[4] However, in *Wheeler v Copas*,[5] it was held that the Act did not apply to a farmer who lent an unsuitable ladder to a bricklayer; the farmer could not be said to remain in occupation of the ladder once it was lent. As far as 'vessels, vehicles or aircraft' are concerned, it appears that the Act covers only damage caused by defective structure and not that which results from, say, negligent driving.

1   *Francis v Cockrell* (1870) LR 5 QB 501.
2   *Kenny v Electricity Supply Board* [1932] IR 73.
3   *Pratt v Richards* [1951] 2 KB 208, [1951] 1 All ER 90n.
4   *Woodman v Richardson* [1937] 3 All ER 866, CA.
5   [1981] 3 All ER 405.

Visitor

21.8   The simplification of occupiers' liability by the Act of 1957 leaves untouched one vital distinction, namely that between a lawful visitor and a trespasser; the statutory duty of care is owed only to the former. The most frequently cited definition of a trespasser is 'he who goes on the land without invitation of any sort and whose presence is either unknown to the proprietor or, if known, is practically objected to'.[1] This category embraces a wide variety of entrants, from the burglar or poacher to the lost rambler or wandering child. However, where bee-keepers complained that their bees had been killed by the chemical spray used by a neighbouring farmer on his crops, the judge refused to categorise the bees as either visitors or trespassers; he held nonetheless that a duty of care was owed.[2]

Whether or not a person is expressly permitted to enter premises is simply a question of fact. However, more difficulties arise where it is alleged that the occupier has *impliedly* given permission. As a general rule, the courts are reluctant to reach such a conclusion, as is illustrated by the case of *Great Central Rly Co v Bates*,[3] in which a policeman, seeing a warehouse door open at night and going in to investigate, was held to be a trespasser. On the other hand, the mere existence of a path across one's front garden is regarded as a tacit invitation to members of the public wishing to conduct lawful business with the occupier, although this licence extends no further than the front door.[4] Further, even this implication can be excluded, for example by a clearly displayed notice stating: 'No salesmen'. In the entertaining case of *Snook v Mannion*,[5] however, a householder's instruction to two police officers to 'F—— off' was held to constitute mere vulgar abuse, rather than a valid revocation of their implied permission to be on the premises.

Particular problems are caused by cases of repeated trespass, for instance where the occupier's land is frequently used by members of the public as a short cut, or for picnicking. No permission can be inferred if the occupier takes reasonable steps to keep such people out.[6] Even if he takes no steps, however, it seems that acquiescence, rather than mere knowledge, is what must be proved; as Lord Goddard put it: 'How is it to be said that he had licensed what he cannot prevent?'[7] Nonetheless, in extreme cases, failure to take action may amount to permission, as it did in *Lowery v Walker*,[8] where a farmer's field had been used as a short cut to the local railway station for some 35 years. The farmer occasionally turned people back but otherwise took no action until, without warning, he put a savage horse in the field. The claimant, who was attacked and injured by this horse, was held by the House of Lords to be a lawful visitor and therefore entitled to sue the farmer for damages.

Now that trespassers themselves receive a much greater measure of protection in law,[9] it may well be that the courts will no longer strain to infer a licence as they did in *Lowery v Walker*. The same may also be true of the old doctrine of 'allurement', under which a child enticed on to the defendant's land by something dangerous and attractive might be regarded in law as a licensee rather than as a trespasser. An example of this doctrine may be seen in *Cooke v Midland Great Western Rly of Ireland*,[10] where it was well known that children frequently played on the defendants' turntable; indeed, a well-worn track led to it through a gap in the hedge which bordered a nearby road. When the turntable, which was kept unlocked, moved and crushed a four-year-old boy, the House of Lords held that he was not to be regarded as a trespasser.

1   *R Addie & Sons (Collieries) Ltd v Dumbreck* [1929] AC 358 at 371.
2   *Tutton v AD Walter Ltd* [1985] 3 All ER 757.
3   [1921] 3 KB 578.
4   *Robson v Hallett* [1967] 2 All ER 407, DC.
5   [1982] RTR 321, DC.
6   *Hardy v Central London Rly Co* [1920] 3 KB 459, CA.
7   *Edwards v Railway Executive* [1952] 2 All ER 430.
8   [1911] AC 10, HL.
9   Paras 21.21–21.24 below.
10   [1909] AC 229, HL.

Limited permission

21.9   The permission, whether express or implied, by which a person enters premises may be limited in scope. If this is so, and the permission is exceeded, that person ceases to be a lawful visitor and becomes a trespasser.

The limitations which may be placed upon a licence to enter take various forms, of which the most common relates to area. A hotel guest, for example, becomes a trespasser if he chooses to go through a door marked 'Private'. In *Westwood v Post Office*,[1] an employee who disregarded a notice on a door which stated: 'Authorised personnel only' was held to be a trespasser when he fell through a defective trapdoor in the room and was killed. On the other hand, where a limitation is not clearly shown, a visitor is given a certain amount of leeway. Thus, in *Pearson v Coleman Bros*,[2] a little girl was held to be a licensee when, in searching for a lavatory at a circus, she strayed into the zoo area and was mauled by a lion.

Permission may also be limited as to time, in which case it seems that, to be effective, the limitation must be brought to the entrant's notice. In *Stone v Taffe*,[3] where the manager of a public house gave an unauthorised after-hours party, it was held that the brewers were not entitled to treat a guest as a trespasser, as he did not know that they objected to this practice. This seems surprising since, as a general rule, a person may be a trespasser without being aware of it.[4]

The third limitation which may be placed upon permission to enter premises relates to the purpose of entry; a person may become a trespasser by abusing his licence. This rule, which Scrutton LJ summarised by saying: 'When you invite a person into your house to use the staircase, you do not invite him to slide down the banisters',[5] was applied by the Court of Appeal in *R v Jones and R v Smith*.[6] The two defendants in that case, who were accused of stealing two television sets from the house of Smith's father, could only be convicted of burglary under the Theft Act 1968 if they had entered the house 'as trespassers'. Smith's father gave evidence that his son had unrestricted permission to enter it; it was held, however, that the father's general permission had been exceeded in this case, so that both defendants were trespassers.

1   [1973] 1 All ER 283, CA; revsd on other grounds [1973] 3 All ER 184, HL.
2   [1948] 2 All ER 274, CA.

3   [1974] 3 All ER 1016, CA.
4   Para 23.1 below.
5   *The Carlgarth* [1927] P 93 at 110.
6   [1976] 3 All ER 54, CA.

Entry as of right

21.10   It is provided by the Occupiers' Liability Act 1957, s 2(6) that 'persons who enter premises for any purpose in the exercise of a right conferred by law are to be treated as permitted by the occupier to be there for that purpose, whether they in fact have his permission or not'. As a result, the occupier owes the common duty of care to those officials, such as policemen, who have statutory powers of entry. Similarly, where a local authority provides such facilities as parks, playgrounds, lavatories or libraries, it seems that persons using these are lawful visitors.

An exception to the above rule is contained in s 1(4) of the 1957 Act, as amended. Persons who enter property under rights conferred by the Countryside and Rights of Way Act 2000, or by an access agreement or order made under the National Parks and Access to the Countryside Act 1949, are not trespassing; however, if injured, they are not to be treated as visitors.[1]

1   They will now come within the Occupiers' Liability Act 1984: see para 21.21 below.

Rights of way

21.11   Where a person uses a public right of way across land, he is, of course, not guilty of the tort of trespass. However, the common law did not regard him as a visitor to the land, with the result that the occupier owed him no positive duty to make the way safe. In *Greenhalgh v British Railways Board*,[1] it was held by the Court of Appeal that this rule had not been altered by the Occupiers' Liability Act 1957, so that a woman who was injured when she tripped in a pothole on a railway bridge could not recover damages from the owners of the bridge, notwithstanding that it was crossed by a public footpath. Furthermore, the user of a public right of way cannot even take advantage of the statutory duty which an occupier of land owes to trespassers and other uninvited entrants,[2] for the Occupiers' Liability Act 1984, s 1(7) specifically provides that that duty is not owed to persons using the highway.

The occupier's immunity in such cases is subject to two qualifications. In the first place there may be liability where the danger arises, not from the condition of the way itself, but from activities which are carried on by the occupier on the same or adjoining land. In *Thomas v British Railways Board*,[3] for example, the defendants were held liable when their failure to repair a stile allowed a two-year-old girl to stray on to a railway line, where she was struck by a train. Second, where a right of way is maintainable at the public expense, the relevant highway authority is now under a positive statutory duty to repair and maintain the way, and can be liable for damages to anyone injured by its failure to do so.[4]

A person using a private right of way across land is likewise not treated, either by the common law or under the Occupiers' Liability Act 1957, as a visitor to the land.[5] However, he is now entitled to the more limited protection which is afforded to trespassers and other uninvited entrants by the Occupiers' Liability Act 1984.[6]

1   [1969] 2 All ER 114, CA; affd in *McGeown v Northern Ireland Housing Executive* [1994] 3 All ER 53, HL.
2   See para 21.21 below.
3   [1976] 3 All ER 15, CA.
4   Highways Act 1980, Part IV.
5   *Holden v White* [1982] 2 All ER 328, CA.
6   *Vodden v Gayton* [2001] PIQR P52, where the claim failed on the facts.

Visitors under contract

21.12   Persons who enter premises by virtue of a contract are subject to two specific provisions of the 1957 Act. First, where the contract is made between the occupier and the visitor (eg where entry is by ticket), s 5 provides in effect that the visitor's rights depend upon the terms of that contract; if the contract is silent on this point, the common duty of care will apply. However, this provision must now be read subject to the Unfair Contract Terms Act 1977, which contains severe restrictions on the use of exemption clauses where premises are 'business premises'.[1]

Section 3 of the Act of 1957 deals with persons who enter premises under some contract to which they are not party. For instance, where an occupier employs a firm of builders to work on his house, the actual workmen are not normally parties to the contract under which the work is done. So too, a lease may grant access to 'common parts' of the landlord's building, such as staircases and lifts, not only to tenants, but also their families and guests. In all such cases, it is provided that, while the visitor may take the benefit of any additional obligations which the contract imposes upon the occupier, his rights may not be reduced below the level which is imposed by the common duty of care.

1   Paras 10.20 and 22.3 above.

The common duty of care

21.13   The duty which an occupier owes to his lawful visitors is defined by the Occupiers' Liability Act 1957, s 2(2) as 'a duty to take such care as in all the circumstances of the case is reasonable to see that the visitor will be reasonably safe in using the premises for the purpose for which he is invited or permitted by the occupier to be there'. This definition is a straightforward application of the rules of negligence and, in deciding whether or not an occupier's duty has been breached, a court will consider all the circumstances of the case. To take a few examples, liability was imposed upon a local authority for allowing a school path which was swept free of snow to remain in a dangerously slippery condition,[1] and a hotel whose balcony balustrades were several inches lower than the height recommended by the British Standards Institution.[2] On the other hand, an occupier was held not liable for failing to replace a glass door panel which, though not conforming to current building regulations, had complied with those in force at the time of building.[3] Moreover, there was held to be no duty on a local authority to put up warning notices in respect of obvious dangers such as a cliff path[4] or seaweed-covered rocks;[5] nor on the owners of a disused gravel pit[6] or a stately home with a lake[7] to erect a 'no swimming' sign, where the dangers of swimming were obvious.

A crucial issue in many cases is the extent to which an occupier should predict what people will do on his premises. In *Wheeler v Trustees of St Mary's Hall, Chislehurst*,[8] it was held that the trustees of a church hall, who hired it out for a martial arts training session, could not be expected to ensure that the experienced hirer had supplied mats to cover the concrete floor. The trustees were accordingly not liable to a participant who suffered serious head injuries when he fell on the floor. By contrast, in *Bell v Department of Health and Social Security*,[9] employers who knew that their employees frequently carried tea and coffee from the kitchen back to their offices in a four-storey building were held liable for a danger created by the spillage of drinks on pseudo-marble floors. It has even been held that a football club can be liable to visitors if, knowing of the risk, it fails to prevent visiting hooligans from tearing pieces of concrete from the terracing to use as missiles.[10]

The 1957 Act might well have left the courts to work out the details of the common duty of care; however, certain areas which had caused problems before 1957 are specifically dealt with, and these we consider in the next five paragraphs.

1   *Murphy v Bradford Metropolitan Borough Council* [1992] PIQR P68, CA.
2   *Ward v Ritz Hotel (London)* [1992] PIQR P315, CA.
3   *McGivney v Golderslea Ltd* (2001) 17 Const LJ 454, CA.
4   *Cotton v Derbyshire Dales District Council* (1994) Times, 20 June, CA.
5   *Staples v West Dorset District Council* (1995) 93 LGR 536, CA.

6   *Whyte v Redland Aggregates Ltd* [1998] CLY 3989, CA.
7   *Darby v National Trust for Places of Historic Interest or Natural Beauty* [2001] EWCA Civ 189, 3 LGLR 29.
8   (1989) Times, 10 October.
9   (1989) Times, 13 June.
10 *Cunningham v Reading Football Club* [1992] PIQR P141.

Children

21.14   In pointing out that the carefulness or otherwise which may be expected of a visitor is relevant to the occupier's duty towards him, s 2(3)(a) provides that 'an occupier must be prepared for children to be less careful than adults'. That children are especially at risk is obvious. For example, in *Moloney v Lambeth London Borough Council*,[1] the defendants were held liable to a four-year-old who fell through a gap in a staircase balustrade which was too small to have endangered an adult.

A particular problem with children is that, even when on premises lawfully, they may be tempted by some dangerous and attractive object to exceed the scope of their permission. If this leads to injury, it is well established that the occupier may not use the child's technical trespass as a ground for avoiding liability. Thus in *Glasgow Corpn v Taylor*,[2] where a seven-year-old boy stole some attractive berries from an unfenced bush in a public park, it was held that his death by poisoning disclosed a good cause of action.

In relation to very young children, to whom almost anything is dangerous but who cannot understand warnings, the law seeks to balance the duty of the occupier with that of the parent. The courts take the view that an occupier, in taking precautions for the safety of small children, is entitled to assume that their parents will also take care. This approach was adopted by Devlin J in *Phipps v Rochester Corpn*,[3] where a five-year-old boy went blackberrying with his sister, aged seven, on a large grassy space forming part of the defendants' building site. The defendants were well aware that children frequently played in this place, so that they were to be regarded as lawful visitors.[4] When the boy fell into a trench and broke his leg, it was held that the defendants were not liable, since this was the kind of danger from which the occupier might expect a reasonable parent to protect his child. On the other hand, the owners of a holiday camp were held liable to a three-year-old who fell on to a low wall with sharp-edged bricks, because they could expect children to be in the area without close parental supervision.[5]

1   (1966) 64 LGR 440.
2   [1922] 1 AC 44, HL.
3   [1955] 1 All ER 129. See also *Simkiss v Rhondda Borough Council* (1982) 81 LGR 460, CA.
4   See para 21.8 above.
5   *Perry v Butlins Holiday World* [1998] Ed CR 39, CA.

Specialists

21.15   It is provided by s 2(3)(b) that 'an occupier may expect that a person, in the exercise of his calling, will appreciate and guard against any special risks ordinarily incident to it, so far as the occupier leaves him free to do so'. One important effect of this is that an occupier whose property becomes dangerous will not normally be liable to persons who come for the very purpose of repairing it. It might be thought that this would apply to the case of a fireman who is injured in fighting a fire which is caused by the occupier's negligence, but it has twice been held that such a person may recover damages from the occupier, provided that his presence at the fire was foreseeable and that he would be at risk despite exercising all the skill of his calling. Unfortunately, the first ruling to this effect[1] did not mention s 2(3)(b) of the Occupiers' Liability Act; the second[2] did not mention the Act at all but dealt with the case on the basis of common law negligence.

Whether or not a risk is 'incident to a person's calling' is a question of fact, but some guidance may be obtained from a comparison of two decisions. In *Howitt v Alfred Bagnall*

& *Sons Ltd,*[3] a clerk of works fell from scaffolding on which he was standing to inspect roof repairs. The occupiers were held not liable, for the scaffolding was not defective; the only risk lay in using it at all, and this was inherent in the man's job. In *Woollins v British Celanese Ltd,*[4] on the other hand, a post office engineer fell through some hardboard roofing at the defendants' factory. It was held by the Court of Appeal that, while he could be expected to guard against live wires, the structure of the building was not connected with his job; he was therefore able to recover damages.

1   *Salmon v Seafarer Restaurants Ltd* [1983] 3 All ER 729.
2   *Ogwo v Taylor* [1987] 3 All ER 961, HL.
3   [1967] 2 Lloyd's Rep 370.
4   (1966) 1 KIR 438, CA.

Warnings

21.16   A reminder that an occupier's duty is to render the *visitor* safe, rather than the *premises,* is given by s 2(4)(a), which provides: 'Where damage is caused to a visitor by a danger of which he had been warned by the occupier, the warning is not to be treated without more as absolving the occupier from liability, unless in all the circumstances it was enough to enable the visitor to be reasonably safe'. The legal effect of compliance with this provision is that the common duty of care is fulfilled, which has two important consequences in deciding whether or not a warning is valid. First, the warning must come from the occupier himself,[1] although a warning from another source may lead to the conclusion that a visitor either assumes the risk of injury or is contributorily negligent. Second, it must be adequate, in the sense of both specifying the particular danger sufficiently clearly that the visitor can avoid it and being visible. In *Woollins v British Celanese Ltd,*[2] a warning hidden behind a door was held to be inadequate.[3]

1   *Bunker v Charles Brand & Son Ltd* [1969] 2 All ER 59.
2   (1966) 1 KIR 438, CA.
3   In *Rae v Mars (UK) Ltd* [1990] 1 EGLR 161, it was held that no sufficient warning of danger had been given to a surveyor who, in inspecting an unlighted storehouse in a factory, fell on to the sunken floor and was injured.

Independent contractors

21.17   Section 2(4)(b) provides:

'Where damage is caused to a visitor by a danger due to the faulty execution of any work of construction, maintenance or repair by an independent contractor employed by the occupier, the occupier is not to be treated without more as answerable for the danger if in all the circumstances he had acted reasonably in entrusting the work to an independent contractor and had taken such steps (if any) as he reasonably ought in order to satisfy himself that the contractor was competent and that the work had been properly done.'

This, in effect, gives statutory approval to two earlier decisions of the Court of Appeal. In *Haseldine v CA Daw & Son Ltd,*[1] the claimant was injured when a lift in the defendants' block of flats fell to the bottom of the shaft. The accident resulted from negligent work by the firm of specialist engineers employed by the defendants to service the lift and it was held that, since the defendants had no reason to doubt the competence of their contractors, they had in no way failed in their duty towards the claimant.

The wording of s 2(4)(b) also endorses the principle laid down in *Woodward v Hastings Corpn*[2] that, if an occupier chooses to leave to an independent contractor jobs which he could and should do for himself, he remains personally responsible for their proper execution. In that case a school cleaner (who was assumed to be an independent contractor) swept the snow from a step and carelessly left it in a dangerously icy condition. It was held that the local authority were liable in negligence to a person who slipped on the step, since this was not a specialist task.

Even where it is reasonable to entrust the work to an independent contractor, the occupier must take reasonable steps to see both that the contractor is competent[3] and that the work is properly done. It has been held that on a large-scale construction job, for instance, the occupier may be obliged to appoint a qualified architect or surveyor (who would himself be an independent contractor of the occupier) to supervise the work.[4] However, the courts do not demand very much from an occupier in this connection where he cannot be expected to understand the intricacies of the job, so that where a demolition contractor adopted an unsafe method of working and one of his employees was injured as a result, it was held that the occupier, who was unaware of what was happening, could not be liable.[5]

1 　[1941] 3 All ER 156, CA.
2 　[1944] 2 All ER 565, CA.
3 　This may involve checking that the contractor is insured: *Gwilliam v West Hertfordshire Hospital NHS Trust* [2002] EWCA Civ 1041, [2003] QB 443.
4 　*AMF International Ltd v Magnet Bowling Ltd* [1968] 2 All ER 789.
5 　*Ferguson v Welsh* [1987] 3 All ER 777, HL.

Assumption of risk

21.18　Section 2(5) makes it clear that an occupier is not liable to a visitor in respect of risks which the latter willingly assumes. Thus, in *Simms v Leigh Rugby Football Club Ltd,*[1] where a professional Rugby League player was thrown against a concrete wall which surrounded the defendants' pitch, it was held that he could not recover damages for the injuries received; since the ground satisfied the League rules, it had to be assumed that players had accepted the risks inherent in playing on it.

Since s 2(5), in effect, applies the common law defence of assumption of risk, the rules which govern that defence are applicable.[2] In particular, it will not protect an occupier if the visitor has no real choice in the matter; for example, where his employer orders him to enter the premises[3] or to incur the risk.[4]

It should also be noted that, although the Act is silent on the point, it has frequently been held that the defence of contributory negligence is available to an occupier.[5]

1 　[1969] 2 All ER 923. Cf *Harrison v Vincent* [1982] RTR 8, CA; para 20.7 above.
2 　Paras 20.2–20.10 above.
3 　*Burnett v British Waterways Board* [1973] 2 All ER 631, CA.
4 　*Bunker v Charles Brand & Son Ltd* [1969] 2 All ER 59.
5 　See, for example, *Rae v Mars (UK) Ltd* [1990] 1 EGLR 161.

Trespassers

21.19　The Occupiers' Liability Act 1957 applies only to lawful visitors; hence, injuries to trespassers were governed by the common law, which had to deal with two separate problems. First, there is the trespasser who is injured by the very steps which the occupier has taken to keep him out. The position here seems to be that static deterrents, such as broken glass or spikes on top of a wall, are permissible;[1] concealed instruments of retribution (such as man-traps or spring-guns), on the other hand, are not allowed,[2] although a trespasser who enters with full knowledge of their presence may be held to have assumed the risk of injury.[3]

The second issue concerns the trespasser who is injured by the condition of the premises or by an activity which takes place on them. In such a case one might expect the law to strike a balance between the right of anybody, even a trespasser, to expect civilised behaviour from others, and the freedom of a landowner to use and enjoy his property as he wishes. For many years this balance was heavily weighted in favour of landowners, as shown by the case of *R Addie & Sons (Collieries) Ltd v Dumbreck*.[4] A four-year-old trespasser there was killed when a haulage wheel on which he was playing was started up by colliery employees who, despite knowing that children often played on the wheel, did not bother to check that all was clear. The House of Lords, in holding that the colliery was not liable, said that a trespasser must take the land as he finds it, and that an occupier's duty is limited to not injuring the trespasser intentionally or recklessly.

The legal position regarding injuries to trespassers underwent a radical change in *British Railways Board v Herrington*,[5] in which a six-year-old boy went on to an electrified railway line and suffered severe burns from the live rail. The House of Lords decided that the time had come to impose a higher duty upon occupiers towards trespassers, albeit not as high as that owed to lawful visitors.[6] Their lordships stated that an occupier must act with 'common humanity' towards a trespasser and that, in deciding whether or not the occupier had fulfilled this obligation, a fairly subjective test would be applied; no more would be demanded of the occupier than might reasonably be expected of a person with his knowledge, skill and resources.

1   *Deane v Clayton* (1817) 7 Taunt 489.
2   *Bird v Holbrook* (1828) 4 Bing 628.
3   *Ilott v Wilkes* (1820) 3 B & Ald 304.
4   [1929] AC 358, HL.
5   [1972] 1 All ER 749, HL.
6   However, this does not mean that an occupier could be positively compelled by injunction to fence children out from dangerous land: *Proffitt v British Railways Board* [1985] CLY 2302, CA.

Occupiers' Liability Act 1984

21.20   Fears that 'common humanity' would prove vague and uncertain led to a recommendation from the Law Commission that the matter be governed by statute, and this was duly done with the enactment of the Occupiers' Liability Act 1984. It should be noted that this Act applies, not only to trespassers, but to all persons other than the occupier's visitors. It thus embraces persons entering under the National Parks and Access to the Countryside Act 1949[1] and the Countryside and Rights of Way Act 2000,[2] and also those using a private right of way, although persons using the public highway are specifically excluded. The result appears to be that, while *Greenhalgh v British Railways Board*[3] remains good law, the effect of *Holden v White*[4] is reversed.

1   See para 21.10 above.

2   See para 21.22 below.
3   [1969] 2 All ER 114, CA: para 21.11 above.
4   [1982] 2 All ER 328, CA: para 21.11 above.

Scope of the duty

21.21   In attempting to strike the right balance between the interests of an occupier[1] of premises[2] and those of uninvited entrants, s 1(3) of the Act provides that the occupier shall only owe a duty to such a person if:

- he is aware of a danger or has reasonable grounds to believe that it exists;
- he knows or has reasonable grounds to believe that the other person is in the vicinity of the danger or that he may come into that vicinity;[3] and
- the risk is one against which he may reasonably be expected to offer the other person some protection.

The overall effect of this formulation appears to be that, while the occupier is not bound to inspect his property to see whether or not it is safe for trespassers and other uninvited entrants, he is assumed to be able to recognise a danger whenever what he actually knows should lead him to the conclusion that one exists.

It is important to note that the new statutory duty applies only to 'injury', which is defined to include death, disease and any impairment of physical or mental condition. The Act specifically provides that there is no liability for any loss of or damage to property (s 1(8)).

There have been relatively few reported cases arising under the Occupiers' Liability Act 1984, and these have not suggested that the Act is a 'trespassers' charter'. The courts have rejected claims by youths injured in attempting to board moving freight trains,[4] and one by a student who climbed over the locked gate of an open-air swimming pool at night and dived into the shallow end.[5] Even where children are concerned, judges have shown little sympathy for those who are injured after overcoming considerable obstacles in order to gain access to well fenced property.[6] However, the Court of Appeal imposed liability upon an allotment owner who fired a shotgun through a hole in the door of his shed an injured a trespasser who was attempting to break in,[7] and also (by a majority) upon a local authority for failing to give sufficient warning to deter trespassers from swimming and diving in a park lake.[8]

1   'Occupier' bears the same meaning as it does for the purpose of the Occupiers' Liability Act 1957; see paras 21.5–21.6 above.
2   'Premises' bears the same meaning as it does for the purposes of the Occupiers' Liability Act 1957; see para 21.7 above.
3   See *White v St Albans City and District Council* (1990) Times, 12 March, CA.
4   *Scott v Associated British Ports* (18 March 1999, unreported).
5   *Ratcliff v McConnell* [1999] 1 WLR 670, CA.
6   See *Adams v Southern Electricity Board* (1993) Times, 21 October; *Swain v Puri* [1996] PIQR P442, CA; *Platt v Liverpool City Council* [1997] CLY 4864, CA.
7   *Revill v Newbery* [1996] 1 All ER 291, CA.
8   *Tomlinson v Congleton Borough Council* [2002] EWCA Civ 309, [2002] PIQR P573.

Injury suffered on access land

21.22   The Countryside and Rights of Way Act 2000, s 2 creates a public right to enter, for the purposes of open-air recreation, any open country which has been officially designated 'access land'. A person who is injured while exercising this right comes within the Occupiers' Liability Act 1984, but the occupier's duty under that Act is a very restricted one. Section 13 of the CRWA 2000 excludes any claim for injuries caused by natural features (which include all plants, shrubs and trees, whether natural or planted), and also those suffered when passing over, under or through any wall, fence or gate, other than by proper use of a gate or stile, except where the occupier has intentionally or recklessly created the risk. Moreover, in considering other OLA 1984 claims by persons injured while exercising their right to enter access land, a court must have regard to the fact that the occupier should not be subjected to an undue financial or other burden, and also to the importance of maintaining the character of the countryside, including features of historic, traditional or archaeological interest.

Defences

21.23   The OLA 1984 provides an occupier with two defences against liability similar to those which are available under the OLA 1957. First, s 1(5) provides that the occupier's duty may be discharged by taking such steps as are reasonable 'to give warning of the danger concerned or to discourage persons from incurring the risk'.[1] Second, s 1(6) makes it clear that the defence of assumption of risk is applicable.[2] Although it is not specifically mentioned, it seems likely that the defence of contributory negligence would also apply.[3]

1   See para 21.16 above.
2   See paras 20.2–20.10 and para 20.18 above. A trespasser failed on this ground in *Ratcliff v McConnell* [1999] 1 WLR 670, CA.
3   See paras 20.11–20.16 above.

Exclusion of liability

21.24 We have already considered the extent to which an occupier may, by putting up a notice, exclude or restrict his liability to lawful visitors.[1] The OLA 1984 gives no guidance whatever as to whether the rights of non-visitors may be similarly affected, and the arguments for and against seem fairly well balanced. On the one hand, since a trespasser has no permission to enter, it would be nonsensical to suggest that he enters subject to a condition that the occupier shall not be liable to him. Furthermore, there is the practical argument that a visitor is more likely than a trespasser actually to see a notice; after all, this will normally be placed at the entrance, while a trespasser may well climb over the fence. On the other hand, it would surely be odd if a lawful visitor were to be placed in a worse position, legally speaking, than a trespasser. A possible solution might be for the courts to hold that, while the rights of a lawful visitor may be excluded by an appropriate notice, the visitor would then be left with rights equivalent to those enjoyed by a trespasser under the 1984 Act, and that neither lawful visitor nor trespasser may suffer any further reduction of their rights.

1 Para 21.4 above.

Purchasers

Caveat emptor

21.25 By virtue of a legal doctrine known as *caveat emptor* or 'let the buyer beware', a vendor or lessor of real property owed no duty of care to the purchaser or tenant (or to anyone else) in respect of injury or damage resulting from defects in the property. In relation to defects which the vendor/lessor has not positively created, this is still the position.[1] At one time, the landowner's immunity even extended to dangerous defects which he had positively created. Notwithstanding *Donoghue v Stevenson*,[2] an action in negligence for injuries could not succeed against an owner-builder,[3] nor against a landlord whose tampering made the premises dangerous before they were let.[4] However, in 1972 this anomalous position was affected by both judicial decision and legislation, as we now explain.

1 *Rimmer v Liverpool City Council* [1984] 1 All ER 930, CA, where the Court of Appeal reluctantly followed the ruling by the House of Lords in *Cavalier v Pope* [1906] AC 428, HL. Also see *McNerny v Lambeth London Borough Council* [1989] 1 EGLR 81, CA.
2 [1932] AC 562, HL; para 17.5 above.
3 *Otto v Bolton and Norris* [1936] 1 All ER 960. By contrast, a builder who was not also the owner had no immunity: *Sharpe v ET Sweeting & Son Ltd* [1963] 2 All ER 455.
4 *Davis v Foots* [1939] 4 All ER 4, CA.

Common law developments

21.26 In *Dutton v Bognor Regis UDC*,[1] the claimant was the second owner of a house which, a mere two years after being completed, was discovered to have inadequate foundations for its location (the site of an old rubbish tip). She sued the local authority, alleging that their building inspector had been guilty of negligence in passing the house's foundations as satisfactory. In upholding this claim, a majority of the Court of Appeal stated obiter that the builder would, if sued, also have been liable. This apparent reversal of the previous position was heavily criticised on the ground that the claim was in truth one for pure economic loss.[2] However, it was unanimously approved by the House of Lords in the similar case of *Anns v Merton London Borough Council*.[3]

For the next 10 years or so, the decision in *Anns v Merton* was used to justify the imposition of liability for negligence upon builders, sub-contractors, architects and other design consultants and, perhaps most importantly,[4] local authorities approving plans and inspecting buildings in the course of construction. However, a remarkable about-turn in the 1980s resulted in a series of decisions indicating that the House of Lords was extremely uneasy about this area of liability,[5] so far as it covered damage to the building itself. Eventually, in *Murphy v Brentwood District Council*,[6] the House of Lords declared that *Dutton v Bognor Regis, Anns v Merton* and all the cases which had followed them must be regarded as having been wrongly decided.

1   [1972] 1 All ER 462, CA.
2   See para 17.19 above.
3   [1977] 2 All ER 492, HL.
4   Since all the other potential defendants might well be insolvent and thus unable to pay any damages awarded.
5   The most important of these decisions was that in *D & F Estates Ltd v Church Comrs for England* [1988] 2 All ER 992, HL.
6   [1990] 2 All ER 908, HL. The House of Lords immediately applied this ruling in *Department of the Environment v Thomas Bates & Son Ltd* [1990] 2 All ER 943, HL.

21.27   As a result of *Murphy v Brentwood District Council*, the ability of a purchaser or tenant of a defective building to recover damages in the tort of negligence from whoever is responsible has been drastically restricted. The present legal position is as follows:

- A negligent designer, contractor or sub-contractor will be liable if a dangerous defect for which he is responsible results in death, personal injury or physical damage to property other than the building itself (eg where a defective garage roof falls on a car). However, once such a defect is discovered, a decision by the occupier to continue using the building might break the chain of causation from the defendant's negligence,[1] or might be held to constitute contributory negligence by the occupier.[2]
- A local authority which is guilty of negligence in approving plans, or inspecting a building in the course of construction, is probably liable to the same extent as a designer or builder as regards personal injury or death. However, the local authority will not be liable for physical damage to other property, since its duty is limited to ensuring the health and safety of persons.[3]
- With two possible qualifications, there is no liability in negligence to a future owner in respect of damage to the building itself. This is perceived as pure economic loss and is therefore not recoverable. It makes no difference whether the building is merely defective or positively dangerous.
- The House of Lords in *Murphy v Brentwood District Council* suggested that, in two exceptional situations, a future owner might be able to recover damages in respect of damage to the building itself. Both of these have been recognised and applied in subsequent cases. The first is where the negligent work of one contractor or sub-contractor causes damage to other parts of the building which were not constructed by them (eg where a defective central heating boiler causes a fire); it appears that this may be treated as 'damage to other property', for which the negligent party would be liable.[4] Second, where a defective building constitutes a threat to adjoining property with the result that the owner is forced to incur the cost of repairing it, he may recover this cost from the person whose negligence caused the defect.[5]

1   See paras 19.7–19.14 above.
2   See *Targett v Torfaen Borough Council* [1992] 3 All ER 27, CA.
3   *Tesco Stores Ltd v Wards Construction (Investment) Ltd* (1995) 76 BLR 94.
4   *Jacobs v Morton and Partners* (1994) 72 BLR 92.
5   *Morse v Barratt (Leeds) Ltd* (1992) 9 Const LJ 158.

Defective Premises Act 1972

21.28   Section 1 of this Act creates a legal remedy in respect of defects in dwellings (ie houses and flats, but not commercial property) which will run with the property for the benefit of purchasers or tenants. It provides that a person taking on work for or in connection with the provision of a dwelling (whether the dwelling is provided by the erection or by the conversion or enlargement of a building[1]) owes a duty:

a.   if the dwelling is provided to the order of any person, to that person; and
b.   without prejudice to paragraph a. above, to every person who acquires an interest (whether legal or equitable) in the dwelling,

to see that the work which he takes on is done in a workman-like or, as the case may be, professional manner, with proper materials and so that as regards that work the dwelling will be fit for habitation when completed.

This provision applies, not only to builders, but also to architects and other design consultants, sub-contractors, and the developer who arranges for someone else to do the work;[2] in short, to anyone who by his work contributes to the completed dwelling. However, it does not extend to a manufacturer or supplier of standard components, nor to a builder who works entirely to a specification which he is given.[3]

The duty imposed by s 1(1) is not a duty of care, but rather a statutory version of the warranty which the common law implies into contracts to build and sell a dwelling.[4] It applies to omissions as well as to positive acts[5] and cannot be contracted out of.[6] However, it has been held to apply only to defects which are sufficiently serious to render the dwelling unfit for habitation,[7] an interpretation which considerably limits the usefulness of this statutory provision. It may also be noted that claims under the Act are subject to a limitation period of six years from the date on which the dwelling is completed.

1   This does not include works of mere rectification or refurbishment; there must be a new dwelling: *Jacobs v Morton and Partners* (1994) 72 BLR 92.
2   Section 1(4).
3   Section 1(2) and (3).
4   See *Hancock v B W Brazier (Anerley) Ltd* [1966] 2 All ER 901, CA; para 7.26 above.
5   *Andrews v Schooling* [1991] 3 All ER 723, CA.
6   Section 6(3).
7   *Thompson v Alexander* (1992) 59 BLR 81.

Landlords

21.29   The law governing premises which are defective when disposed of applies to landlords just as it does to vendors. In respect of defects which arise after disposal, however, the position of the landlord requires separate treatment, since he may be under a continuing obligation to repair. At common law, the breach of a landlord's repairing obligation was actionable by the tenant alone;[1] a visitor who was injured could neither recover damages for breach of the landlord's contractual obligation to repair the demised premises, nor treat the landlord as 'occupier' of these premises.[2] This unsatisfactory state of affairs was remedied by the Defective Premises Act 1972, s 4[3], which provides: 'Where premises are let under a tenancy which puts on the landlord an obligation to the tenant for the maintenance or repair of the premises, the landlord owes to all persons who might reasonably be expected to be affected by defects in the state of the premises a duty to take such care as is reasonable in all the circumstances to see that they are reasonably safe from personal injury or from damage to their property caused by a [defect within the repairing obligation].'

The effect of s 4 is that an injured person (who may be a visitor, trespasser or even someone off the premises) may sue the landlord for injury or damage caused by a defect which the landlord is under an obligation (express or implied) to repair. Further, while the landlord might be able to answer a claim by the tenant on the ground that the latter had failed to notify him of the defect,[4] this will be no defence against a third party,[5] provided that the landlord knew or ought to have known of the defect. It is important to note that s 4 also applies to the many cases where a landlord, although under no duty to repair the premises, nonetheless has an express or implied right to do so.[6]

1   *Cavalier v Pope* [1906] AC 428, HL; para 21.25 above.
2   Para 21.5 above.
3   Replacing the more limited provisions of the Occupiers' Liability Act 1957, s 4.
4   Paras 37.25 and 37.41 below.
5   Including a member of the tenant's family: see *B v Camden London Borough Council* [2001] PIQR P9.
6   See, for example, *Mint v Good* [1950] 2 All ER 1159. CA; *McAuley v Bristol City Council* [1992] 1 All ER 749, CA.

Chapter 22

Breach of statutory duty

22.1   It frequently happens that an act done by one person which causes injury or damage to another also constitutes a breach of some statutory obligation. This naturally renders the person concerned liable to whatever penalty is prescribed by the statute; but our present concern is with the effect, if any, which the statutory breach has upon his liability to pay damages to the claimant.

Many legal systems treat the fact that a defendant has or has not contravened a statutory rule as relevant only to the question whether or not he has acted negligently. By contrast, English law takes the view that a breach of statutory duty may be a tort in itself, quite independent of negligence on the part of the defendant, and with its own elements of liability and defences. However, it is not suggested that every statutory obligation gives rise to a civil action, for such is the bulk of modern legislation that the universal imposition of liability would, it is thought, be an unacceptably heavy burden. Thus, a preliminary task for a claimant who wishes to frame his action in this way (in order to recover damages without the need to prove negligence) is to satisfy the court that the rule or regulation in question is one for breach of which damages may be awarded.

In this chapter we examine the following issues:

- the way in which the courts decide whether Parliament intended to create a civil right of action for breach of a particular statutory provision;
- the matters on which an individual claimant must satisfy the court in order to succeed in an action for breach of statutory duty.

Existence of civil liability

22.2   In some cases, a particular statute or regulation states clearly that it either does[1] or does not[2] give rise to civil liability. Usually, however, the point is not specifically mentioned, and the question is therefore left for the courts to determine by interpreting the relevant provision. In carrying out this task, the courts claim to be giving effect to the intention of Parliament, but it is probably sensible to recognise this as a fiction: in reality, the lack of express provision in the statute indicates that there is no Parliamentary intention, so that what the courts are doing is based on their view of policy.

In their search for the intention of Parliament, the courts sometimes claim to gain assistance from a consideration of what sanction, if any, has been laid down for a breach of the provision in question. In particular, if there is a heavy criminal penalty attached, this may point to the absence of a civil action for damages.[3]

It has sometimes been said that statutes passed for the benefit of a particular class of persons give rise to a civil action, whereas those which benefit the public in general do not.[4] However, the House of Lords has emphasised[5] that the crucial question is not whether the claimant is in a 'protected class' but whether the legislature intended to create a civil right of action. Nor do the decided cases lend strong support to the 'class' theory. It has been held, for example, that no civil right of action arises under the Protection from Eviction Act 1977, s 1, which makes it a criminal offence to evict or harass a residential tenant;[6] nor for breach of the Prison Rules, which govern the conditions under which convicted prisoners are held;[7] nor for breach of the Prosecution of Offences (Custody Time Limits) Regulations 1987, which require the Crown Prosecution Service to bring an arrested person to court within a certain time;[8] nor for breach of a local authority's obligation to house a homeless person;[9] nor for breach by a local authority of generally worded statutory duties to protect the welfare and educational interests of children within its area.[10] Furthermore, while a person who commits a criminal offence by making an unauthorised recording of a live performance may be liable in damages to the performer,[11] there is no liability to a recording company which has an exclusive right to record that performance.[12]

1   Eg the Nuclear Installations Act 1965 and the Consumer Safety Act 1978.
2   Eg the Guard Dogs Act 1975.
3   See *Richardson v Pitt-Stanley* [1995] ICR 303, CA.
4   See, for example, *Lonrho Ltd v Shell Petroleum Co Ltd (No 2)* [1981] 2 All ER 456 at 461.
5   *R v Deputy Governor of Parkhurst Prison, ex p Hague; Weldon v Home Office* [1991] 3 All ER 733, HL.
6   *McCall v Abelesz* [1976] 1 All ER 727, CA. An express right to damages in such cases has now been conferred by the Housing Act 1988, s 27.
7   *R v Deputy Governor of Parkhurst Prison, ex p Hague; Weldon v Home Office* [1991] 3 All ER 733, HL.
8   *Olotu v Home Office* [1997] 1 All ER 385, CA.
9   *O'Rourke v Camden London Borough Council* [1997] 3 All ER 23, HL.
10   *X v Bedfordshire County Council* [1995] 3 All ER 353, HL.
11   *Rickless v United Artists Corpn* [1987] 1 All ER 679, CA.
12   *RCA Corpn v Pollard* [1982] 3 All ER 771, CA.

22.3   It seems that the courts are very reluctant to use this tort to create new types of civil right, by allowing an action where there is no common law duty of care.[1] In *Atkinson v Newcastle and Gateshead Waterworks Co*,[2] for instance, the defendants, in breach of a statutory rule for which they could be fined £10, failed to maintain the prescribed pressure of water in their mains. As a result, a fire in the claimant's property could not be extinguished. It was held by the Court of Appeal that Parliament could not have intended to make the defendants virtual insurers of every property in the city and that consequently no civil action lay for breach of this duty. A similar decision was reached by the House of Lords in *Cutler v Wandsworth Stadium Ltd*,[3] where an individual bookmaker unsuccessfully claimed damages from the defendants for breach of their statutory duty to make space available for bookmakers at their greyhound racing track. Again, the Court of Appeal in *F v Wirral Metropolitan Borough Council*[4] held that a local authority in breach of a statutory code governing children in care could not be held liable in damages for 'interference with parental rights'.

It has been acknowledged by the House of Lords that 'directly applicable' legislation of the European Community[5] may confer upon individuals a right of action similar to that for breach of statutory duty.[6] In deciding whether or not this is the case, the courts do not, of course, refer to the intention of Parliament, but they nonetheless give attention to the criteria mentioned above. However, an important restriction upon this new form of civil liability lies in the fact that, even where a right of this kind is held to exist, it does not necessarily entitle a person aggrieved to recover damages; some other remedy may be appropriate.[7]

1   This is especially so where the claimant's 'injury' is not of a kind for which damages will normally be awarded: see *Pickering v Liverpool Daily Post and Echo Newspapers plc* [1991] 1 All ER 622, HL.
2   (1877) 2 Ex D 441, CA.

3   [1949] 1 All ER 544, HL.
4   [1991] 2 All ER 648, CA.
5   See paras 3.39–3.40 above.
6   *Garden Cottage Foods Ltd v Milk Marketing Board* [1983] 2 All ER 770, HL.
7   *Bourgoin SA v Ministry of Agriculture, Fisheries and Food* [1985] 3 All ER 585, CA; *An Bord Bainne Co-operative v Milk Marketing Board* [1988] 1 FTLR 145, CA.

22.4   It is difficult to find any coherent principle by which to explain the intention of Parliament. However, the actual decisions reached by the courts on this issue tend to fall clearly into two groups. Industrial safety regulations are almost invariably interpreted as conferring a civil right of action for damages; outside the field of industrial safety, the attitude of the courts towards claims for breach of statutory duty has been one of considerable and increasing reluctance.

The two areas of road safety and consumer protection stand out as ones where the courts have declined the opportunity to use detailed statutory codes to create civil rights. In *Coote v Stone*,[2] for example, it was held that no damages could be awarded in respect of a breach of parking regulations. Likewise, it was held in *Biddle v Truvox Engineering Co Ltd*[3] that, while the seller of a dangerously unfenced machine was guilty of a criminal offence under the Factories Act, an injured workman was not entitled to recover damages for this breach.

1   [1923] 2 KB 832, CA.
2   [1971] 1 WLR 279, CA.
3   [1951] 2 All ER 835.

Elements of liability

Class protected

22.5   Where a statutory provision is seen as having been passed for the protection of a defined class of persons, only members of that class can recover damages for a breach. A good illustration of this point is the case of *Hartley v Mayoh & Co*,[1] in which a fireman was killed by electrocution while fighting a fire at the defendants' factory. In an action by the fireman's widow it was held that the breach by the defendants of wiring regulations was irrelevant, since these were expressed to be for the benefit of persons employed at a factory, and this did not include the fireman.[2]

Even where a statute does not expressly define a 'protected class', a court may decide that Parliament intended to limit its protection. For example, it has been held that district auditors may be liable for breach of statutory duty to a local authority whose accounts they audit, but not to individual officers of that authority.[3] However, the courts are generally slow to impose limitations on the ambit of a statute in cases where Parliament has not done so. In *Westwood v Post Office*,[4] for example, a defective trapdoor, the condition of which constituted a breach of the Offices, Shops and Railway Premises Act 1963, led to the death of an employee at a telephone exchange. The trapdoor was in fact in a part of the premises which the deceased was not permitted to enter and it was argued by the defendants that, while the statute protected most employees, it did not cover trespassers. It was held by the House of Lords, however, that the employee's trespass did not deprive him of statutory protection.

1   [1954] 1 All ER 375, CA.
2   The claimant nevertheless succeeded in recovering damages on the ground of negligence.
3   *West Wiltshire District Council v Garland* [1995] 2 All ER 17, CA.
4   [1973] 3 All ER 184, HL; para 22.9 above.

Type of injury

22.6   The claimant in an action for breach of statutory duty must show that the injury or damage suffered is of a type which the statute is designed to prevent. The classic example of this principle is *Gorris v Scott*,[1] in which the absence of pens on the deck of the defendant's ship allowed the claimant's sheep to be swept overboard in a storm. Although pens were required by statute, this was held to be of no assistance to the claimant, for their purpose was merely to reduce the spread of disease among the animals. This principle also led to a rather harsh decision in *Close v Steel Co of Wales Ltd*,[2] where it was held that, since the purpose of a duty to fence dangerous machinery is to keep the operator out, it is of no relevance where the absence of a guard allows part of the machine to fly out and cause injury to the operator.

It is obvious that, the more precisely the purpose of a statute is interpreted by judges, the fewer cases will fall within it. The modern tendency, however, is to define the protected risk in fairly broad terms, an approach rather similar to that adopted towards the questions of how damage is caused in the tort of negligence.[3] Thus, in *Grant v National Coal Board*,[4] where a statutory breach allowed rock to fall from a mine roof, it was held that a miner could sue for injuries received when the bogie in which he was travelling was derailed by the fallen rock. So too, in *Donaghey v Boulton and Paul Ltd*,[5] the defendants failed in their statutory duty to supply an employee with crawling boards when he was working on a fragile asbestos roof. The employee fell, not through the asbestos, but through a hole in the roof adjacent to it. It was argued that this was outside the object of the statute, which was limited to fragile roofs, but the House of Lords rejected so narrow an interpretation and held that damages should be awarded.

It is noticeable that, in identifying the purpose of a statutory provision, the courts are usually reluctant to hold that it is intended to protect the claimant against pure economic loss.[6] This has even led to the rejection of a claim by a person whose house suffered radioactive contamination from the discharge of nuclear waste, on the ground that the damage suffered was not physical damage, but rather the devaluation of the property.[7]

1   (1874) LR 9 Exch 125.
2   [1961] 2 All ER 953, HL.
3   See *Hughes v Lord Advocate* [1963] 1 All ER 705, HL; para 19.19 above.
4   [1956] 1 All ER 682, HL.
5   [1967] 2 All ER 1014, HL.
6   See *Wentworth v Wiltshire County Council* [1993] 2 All ER 256, CA.
7   *Merlin v British Nuclear Fuels plc* [1990] 3 All ER 711. Contrast *Blue Circle Industries plc v Ministry of Defence* [1998] 3 All ER 385.

Breach by defendant

22.7   Where a statutory rule is clear and exact, there is no liability for almost breaching it. In *Chipchase v British Titan Products Co Ltd*,[1] for example, the claimant fell from a working platform only 9 inches wide; had it been a few inches higher, statute would have required a width of 34 inches. On these facts the defendants were held not liable for either negligence or breach of statutory duty.

In deciding whether or not a particular obligation has been broken, it is important to realise that the standard of conduct required may vary, because of either the words used or their interpretation by the courts. For example, in *Ministry of Housing and Local Government v Sharp*,[2] the Court of Appeal differed as to whether the duty of a local land registrar in issuing certificates of search was absolute or, as the majority held, one of reasonable care. A duty qualified by such words as 'so far as is reasonably practicable' is, it appears, equivalent to one of reasonable care;[3] at the other extreme, an unqualified duty may be held to impose an absolute obligation. In *John Summers & Sons Ltd v Frost*,[4] for instance, it was held by the House of Lords that a grinding wheel could not be described as 'securely fenced', as required by statute, if any part of the wheel remained exposed, even though to cover it completely would render it unusable.

Between these two levels lies an obligation 'to take such steps as may be necessary'. In deciding what steps are necessary, the courts consider only such dangers as the defendant ought reasonably to have foreseen. If this test establishes that steps are necessary, however, the defendant's obligation to take those steps is an absolute one.[5]

1   [1956] 1 All ER 613, CA.
2   [1970] 1 All ER 1009, CA.
3   The onus of proof may well rest on the defendant: *Larner v British Steel plc* [1993] 4 All ER 102, CA.
4   [1955] 1 All ER 870, HL.
5   *Brown v National Coal Board* [1962] 1 All ER 81, HL.

Causation

22.8   As with any action in tort, the claimant must establish that the defendant's breach of duty was a legal cause of his injuries. With one exception the law on this matter, although complex, is no different from that which governs cases of negligence and which we have already considered.[1] The exception is where a statute is so drafted as to place identical duties on two parties (usually employer and employee) in such terms that an act or omission by one party constitutes a breach by both of them. In such a case, where a statute states simply that something 'shall be done', failure to do it puts both parties in breach, even though the moral blame may rest on only one of them. In *Ginty v Belmont Building Supplies Ltd,*[2] for example, it was provided by statute that, when work was being done on fragile roofs, crawling boards 'shall be used'. The defendants supplied such boards, together with full instructions as to their use, to the claimant, an experienced workman whom they employed, but he decided not to use the boards and consequently fell through the roof. This breach of statutory duty was undoubtedly one for which both claimant and defendants could have been criminally liable. However, it was held that the claimant was not entitled to claim damages from defendants, for their breach of statutory duty consisted entirely of his own breach.

It is important to note that the decision in *Ginty* can only exonerate a defendant where the claimant is the sole cause of his own misfortune; if any kind of independent or extra fault can be attributed to the defendant, he will be liable, although the claimant is likely in such a case to lose a substantial proportion of his damages on the ground of contributory negligence. In *Boyle v Kodak Ltd,*[3] for instance, the House of Lords held the defendant employers two-thirds to blame for an accident at work, since they had failed to provide the claimant with adequate supervision or instruction in the relevant regulations. And, in *McMath v Rimmer Bros (Liverpool) Ltd,*[4] where the claimant fell from a ladder which no-one was 'footing', his employers were held liable for 50% of his damages, since the absence of anyone to foot the ladder was attributable to their fault.

1   Chapter 19 above.
2   [1959] 1 All ER 414.
3   [1969] 1 WLR 661, HL.
4   [1961] 3 All ER 1154, CA.

Defences

22.9   In principle, the defence of *volenti non fit injuria*[1] is available in actions for breach of statutory duty. However, for reasons of public policy it has long been settled that an employer may not use it against his employee when the employer is personally in breach of his own statutory obligation.[2] In cases where the employer is not personally in breach, but is made vicariously liable for breach by his employees of statutory duties which are laid upon them, he may use the defence.[3]

There is no doubt that the defence of contributory negligence[4] is available (and it should be noted that the claimant's 'fault' for this purpose may itself consist of some breach of statutory duty). However, if too liberally used, this defence would deprive many employees of the benefit of regulations specifically designed for their protection. Consequently, in dealing with industrial accident cases, the courts are careful to make full allowance for problems of fatigue, repetition, boredom and the like.[5]

Where the defendant is personally under a statutory duty, it is no defence for him to show that he delegated its performance to the claimant. However, if the claimant's conduct is the sole cause of his injury, the defendant may avoid liability on the basis of the rule in *Ginty v Belmont Building Supplies Ltd.*[6]

1   Paras 20.2–20.10 above.
2   *Baddeley v Earl of Granville* (1887) 19 QBD 423, DC.
3   *Imperial Chemical Industries Ltd v Shatwell* [1964] 2 All ER 999, HL; para 20.8 above.
4   Paras 20.11–20.16 above.
5   See *Caswell v Powell Duffryn Associated Collieries Ltd* [1939] 3 All ER 722, HL; *Mullard v Ben Line Steamers Ltd* [1971] 2 All ER 424, CA.
6   [1959] 1 All ER 414; para 22.8 above.

Chapter 23

Trespass to land

23.1 This tort may be defined as a direct intrusion upon land in the possession of the claimant. It is actionable per se, which means that a claimant may succeed without having to prove that any damage has been done.[1] However, despite notices proclaiming that 'Trespassers will be prosecuted', trespass is not in itself normally a criminal offence.[2]

A defendant may commit trespass without meaning to, as in *Basely v Clarkson*,[3] where a man cutting his grass crossed an ill-defined boundary and cut some of the claimant's grass as well. However, where the actual intrusion on to the claimant's land is accidental, in the sense that the defendant did not intend it and took reasonable steps to prevent it, there will be a defence of inevitable accident. Thus in *League Against Cruel Sports Ltd v Scott*,[4] it was held that the master of a hunt would only be liable for trespass by the hounds if he either intended them to enter the claimant's land or negligently failed to prevent them from so doing.

1   *Entick v Carrington* (1765) 19 State Tr 1029.
2   Except where statute so provides, eg where the trespasser has an offensive weapon (Criminal Law Act 1977).
3   (1681) 3 Lev 37.
4   [1985] 2 All ER 489.

23.2 In this chapter we examine the following issues:

- the extent to which trespass can be committed above and below the surface;
- the range of acts and activities which may amount in law to a trespass;
- the question of who is entitled to bring an action for trespass;
- the circumstances in which the law permits one person to enter land belonging to another;
- the remedies which are available to a person whose land is trespassed upon.

Land
23.3 In normal circumstances, possession of land carries with it possession of all underlying strata and of the airspace above, in which case the possessor may sue in trespass for intrusion at any level. Where, however, horizontal divisions are made, such as in a block of flats,[1] or on a sale of mineral rights, the possessor of the affected area is alone able to sue. Thus, for example, Y has rights of pasture over X's land, X may sue anyone who drives tent-pegs into the soil;[2] but only Y may take action against a person who merely rides across the grass.[3]

As far as the airspace above the land is concerned, it is clear that an unauthorised invasion of this is trespass, at least where it is not above the maximum height necessary for the occupier's ordinary use and enjoyment of the property. This may include, for example, a projecting advertisement[4] or the swinging jib of a crane.[5] In *Bernstein v Skyviews and General Ltd*,[6] however, the defendants were held not liable when they flew several hundred feet above the claimant's house to take unauthorised photographs of it, with a view to selling these to the claimant.

Over-flight is also subject to s 76 of the Civil Aviation Act 1982 which, broadly speaking, prevents the landowner from establishing a claim in either trespass or nuisance for the mere fact of the flight, provided that it takes place at a height which is reasonable, having regard to wind and weather. In *Bernstein*'s case, notwithstanding the purpose of their flight, the defendants were allowed to rely on this provision. However, the Act imposes strict liability in respect of any physical damage to the property below which results from an over-flight.

1   The tenant of a top floor flat is entitled to the air space above unless the lease defines an upper boundary: *Davies v Yadegar* [1990] 1 EGLR 71, CA.
2   *Cox v Glue* (1848) 5 CB 533.
3   *Cox v Mousley* (1848) 5 CB 533.
4   *Kelsen v Imperial Tobacco Co (of Great Britain and Ireland) Ltd* [1957] 2 All ER 343.
5   *Anchor Brewhouse Developments Ltd v Berkley House (Docklands Developments) Ltd* [1987] 2 EGLR 173.
6   [1977] 2 All ER 902.

Intrusion

23.4   The most obvious form of trespass to land is entry by the defendant in person. The slightest crossing of the boundary, such as a hand across the threshold,[1] is sufficient but, in the absence of such a crossing (or at least some contact with the fabric of the property), there is no trespass. Thus a landlord who cuts off mains services to a tenant's flat from a point outside the flat may be guilty of both a breach of contract and a criminal offence,[2] but such conduct does not constitute the tort of trespass.[3]

A common form of trespass consists of causing objects to enter the claimant's land, for example by erecting a building which straddles the boundary. The most trivial invasion will suffice, such as leaning a ladder against the claimant's wall.[4] However, the invasion must be direct. Thus, someone who chops down a tree so that it falls into a neighbouring garden commits trespass; someone who merely allows roots or branches to grow across the boundary is guilty of nuisance.[5]

A person who is permitted or legally entitled to enter land may become a trespasser by exceeding or abusing the right of entry.[6] This rule is important in relation to rights of way, which permit only reasonable passage; thus, in *Hickman v Maisey*,[7] the defendant, who had patrolled a 15-yard stretch of highway across the claimant's land in order to spy on racehorse trials there, was held to be a trespasser. In such cases, action may be taken by the owner of the subsoil, which will in practice often be a highway authority.

1   *Franklin v Jeffries* (1985) Times, 11 March.
2   Protection from Eviction Act 1977, s 1.
3   *Perera v Vandiyar* [1953] 1 All ER 1109, CA.
4   *Westripp v Baldock* [1939] 1 All ER 279, CA.
5   *Lemmon v Webb* [1894] 3 Ch 1, CA.
6   Para 21.9 above.
7   [1900] 1 QB 752, CA.

Possession

23.5   Trespass to land is a wrong to possession rather than to ownership. As a result, where land is let, it is only the tenant who can take action against a trespasser, unless permanent damage is done to the property, in which case the landlord may sue.[1] For the same reason, a tenant who fails to quit the premises when the lease expires is not thereby guilty of trespass, since the landlord is not in possession.[2] Conversely, where land is occupied under licence, the licensee normally[3] lacks the exclusive possession of the property which is necessary to found an action in trespass;[4] this remains in the hands of the licensor.

The common law's emphasis upon the protection of possession (based on its historical concern with preserving the peace) is such that even someone whose possession is wrongful may sue in trespass any other wrongdoer who disturbs him,[5] and it is no defence for the latter to show that the true right to possession lies with a third party. The only person who may override such wrongful possession is the true owner, or someone acting on his behalf.[6]

The question of what constitutes possession in law receives different answers in respect of different types of property. It is the occupation of a house which counts, but the possession of open land may depend upon evidence of actual use, so that the mere erection of a fence round an area of disputed land may not be enough.[7] If, as frequently happens in trespass actions, possession is disputed,[8] the law presumes in favour of the person with title[9] even if, on investigation, that title proves to be defective.[10]

A person who is not actually in possession of land cannot sue for trespass, even if he has an immediate right to possession. However, when such a person eventually enters upon the land, he is deemed to have been in possession from the moment his right accrued, and he is therefore entitled to claim damages in respect of trespass committed in the interim.

1   Jones v Llanrwst UDC [1911] 1 Ch 393. If damage which is merely temporary causes financial loss to the landlord, there may be a claim in negligence: Ehlmer v Hall [1993] 1 EGLR 137, CA.
2   Hey v Moorhouse (1839) 6 Bing NC 52.
3   But see para 37.9 below.
4   Hill v Tupper (1863) 2 H & C 121.
5   Nicholls v Ely Beet Sugar Factory [1931] 2 Ch 84, CA.
6   Delaney v T P Smith Ltd [1946] 2 All ER 23, CA.
7   See Marsden v Miller (1992) 64 P & CR 239, CA.
8   Especially where one party claims to have acquired title against the other by adverse possession: paras 31.19–31.34 below.
9   Jones v Chapman (1847) 2 Exch 803.
10 Fowley Marine (Emsworth) Ltd v Gafford [1968] 1 All ER 979, CA.

Defences

23.6   An entry cannot be a trespass if it is legally justified, and justification in this context may arise in various ways. Statutory powers of entry are conferred not only on the police, but also on a myriad of officials, such as inspectors of the Health and Safety Executive, trading standards officers and VAT inspectors. More generally, an access agreement or order made under the National Parks and Access to the Countryside Act 1949 entitles any person to enter the land concerned, provided that the specified conditions are complied with.

A person who has a public or private right of way over land is not guilty of trespass unless the right in question is abused or exceeded.[1] Moreover, the exercise of certain other rights over land (such as easements, profits à prendre and local customary rights[2]) may entitle a person to do what would otherwise be a trespass. Indeed, even a bare permission or licence will also have this effect. Once such a licence is validly revoked,[3] any further intrusion is a trespass, although the licensee cannot be compelled to undo what has been done. Thus, in Armstrong v Sheppard and Short Ltd,[4] where the claimant withdrew the permission which he had given the defendants to lay and use a sewer under his land, it was held that further use of the sewer was a trespass, although the defendants could not be compelled to remove the sewer itself.

A person who discovers that goods belonging to him are on someone else's land is entitled to enter that land to retake them, at least if the other person is wrongfully responsible for their presence there.[5] Further, apparent acts of trespass may be justified by necessity (defence of the realm or the preservation of life or property) provided that they are in reasonable proportion to the threatened harm and that the need to trespass is not brought about by the defendant's own negligence.[6] However, the defence of necessity is kept within strict limits; it does not entitle homeless persons to 'squat' in vacant premises,[7] nor protesters against genetically modified crops to enter land on which such crops are growing.[8]

Finally, a person who acquiesces in a trespass cannot sue for it if it would be unconscionable to do so, for example where the defendant has been allowed or encouraged to incur expense. However, mere delay in complaining about a trespass does not itself amount to acquiescence.[9]

1   Paras 21.9 and 23.4 above.
2   Chapter 33, below.
3   For revocation of licences, see paras 29.44–29.45 and 31.8–31.18 below.
4   [1959] 2 QB 384, [1959] 2 All ER 651, CA.
5   *Patrick v Colerick* (1838) 3 M & W 483.
6   *Rigby v Chief Constable of Northamptonshire* [1985] 1 WLR 1242.
7   *Southwark London Borough Council v Williams* [1971] 2 All ER 175, CA.
8   *Monsanto plc v Tilly* [2000] Env LR 313, CA.
9   *Jones v Stones* [1999] 1 WLR 1739, CA.

Access to neighbouring land

23.7   At common law, a landowner's need to carry out repairs to property did not justify him in trespassing upon adjoining land. However, there has been statutory intervention in this area. Under the Access to Neighbouring Land Act 1992,[1] any person wishing to carry out works of preservation to his land for which access to adjoining land is necessary,[2] but who cannot obtain the necessary permission for entry to that land, may apply to the county court for an access order.[3] It is for the court to decide whether any proposed works are works of preservation for this purpose, but certain works are presumed to be so.[4] The Act does *not* permit entry for the carrying out of improvements, alterations, or demolition work, except where these are incidental to works of preservation.[5]

An order under the Act must specify the works to be carried out, the land which can be entered and the period during which entry is authorised.[6] The court can impose such terms and conditions as are reasonably necessary for limiting or avoiding loss, damage, inconvenience or loss of privacy to the respondent or any other person,[7] and may require the applicant to insure against specified risks.[8] An order will not be granted where the entry would cause either interference to the use or enjoyment of the servient land, or hardship to any person in occupation of that land, to a degree which would make it unreasonable to make the order.[9] Once the work has been completed all waste must be removed and the servient land must be made good; the applicant is not authorised to leave anything on the servient land such as cables, pipes or drains.[10]

An order under the Act may require the applicant to pay *compensation* for any loss, damage or injury, or any substantial loss of privacy or other substantial inconvenience which might be caused.[11] In addition, except in the case of works to residential land, the court may order the payment of *consideration* for the entry; this sum is to be based on the likely financial advantage of the order to the applicant and the degree of inconvenience to the respondent or any other person.[12]

1   See also the Party Wall etc Act 1996.
2   Or which would be substantially more difficult to carry out without such access: s 1(2)(b).
3   Section 1(1). It may well be that the mere existence of the court's power will in future mean that parties are more prepared to negotiate access agreements.
4   These works, defined as 'basic preservation works', include such matters as the maintenance, repair or renewal of any part of a building, and the felling of trees or shrubs which are damaged or dangerous: s 1(4).
5   Section 1(5). The Act does not therefore solve the problem of tower cranes: see para 23.9 below.
6   Section 2(1).

7   Section 2(2).
8   Section 2(4)(b).
9   Section 1(3).
10 Section 3(3).
11 Section 2(4)(a).
12 Section 2(5). 'Likely financial advantage' is defined in s 2(6).

Remedies

Damages

23.8   Where actual damage is caused to land, the claimant is entitled to damages, and these will normally be assessed by reference to the amount by which the value of the property is diminished or, more commonly, the cost of reinstating it to its former condition.[1] Even where the land itself is not damaged, the claimant is entitled to claim for the loss of use of his property, and here the appropriate measure is its normal letting value,[2] whether or not it appears likely that the claimant could have let it.[3]

A defendant who is guilty of a continuing trespass, for example by remaining in occupation of or leaving goods on the claimant's land, is liable to successive actions until the offence ceases. Damages in each action will therefore be awarded for the effects of the trespass up to the date of judgment.[4] Where, however, the trespass consists of a single act, such as the digging of a hole in the claimant's land, that fact that its effects continue does not lead to the same result; here damages are awarded only once, and will therefore take into account both past and future effects of the trespass.[5]

1   Para 28.13 below.
2   *Whitwham v Westminster Brymbo Coal Co* [1896] 2 Ch 538, CA.
3   *Swordheath Properties Ltd v Tabet* [1979] 1 All ER 240, CA; *Inverugie Investments Ltd v Hackett* [1995] 3 All ER 841, PC.
4   *Holmes v Wilson* (1839) 10 Ad & El 503.
5   *Clegg v Dearden* (1848) 12 QB 576.

Injunction

23.9   Where a trespass is continuous or repetitive, the claimant may seek an injunction to compel the defendant to cease the offending activity. Such an injunction will normally be granted as a matter of course, even though this may cause serious inconvenience or expense to the defendant. Thus, for example, the claimant can obtain an injunction ordering the demolition of an encroaching building[1] or the immediate cessation of oversailing by a tower crane.[2]

Although an injunction will normally be granted, it must be borne in mind that it is a discretionary remedy.[3] It may accordingly be refused in special circumstances, such as where the court disapproves of the claimant's conduct.[4] Moreover, the court has a statutory discretion to award damages in lieu of an injunction in any case where it is felt to be appropriate.[5]

1   *Daniells v Mendonca* (1999) 78 P & CR 401, CA.
2   *Anchor Brewhouse Developments Ltd v Berkley House (Docklands Developments) Ltd* [1987] 2 EGLR 173; *London and Manchester Assurance Co Ltd v O & H Construction Ltd* [1989] 2 EGLR 185.
3   *Woollerton and Wilson Ltd v Richard Costain Ltd* [1970] 1 All ER 483.
4   *Tollemache and Cobbold Breweries Ltd v Reynolds* [1983] 2 EGLR 158, CA.
5   See para 28.19 below.

Action of ejectment

23.10   This ancient action, more commonly known as the action for the recovery of land, enables the claimant to regain actual possession of his land.[1] It has often been said that, whereas a claimant seeking damages need only show that he was in possession of the land, one who seeks to recover the actual land must prove his title. However, in practice it seems that proof of prior possession by the claimant raises a presumption of title which the defendant who is not entitled to the land will find almost impossible to rebut.[2] Whether proof that true title rests with a third party will suffice to defeat the claimant's claim is a matter of great controversy; even if it does, however, it is of no avail to a defendant whose possession is either wrongful as against the claimant or derives from the claimant.

A person who seeks to recover his land in this way frequently also claims for mesne profits, that is, any profit gained by the defendant from his wrongful occupation, together with damages for any harm done.

1   Under RSC Ord 113, a special summary procedure is available against persons who are unidentified, such as 'squatters' or 'sitters-in': see *Wiltshire County Council v Frazer* [1986] 1 All ER 65.
2   *Asher v Whitlock* (1865) LR 1 QB 1.

Self-redress

23.11   As an alternative to taking legal action, a person in possession of land is entitled to use a reasonable degree of force either to eject or to deny entry to a trespasser.[1] Similarly, a person in possession of land may simply remove (or demolish) an encroaching object, but only in simple cases which do not justify the expense of legal proceedings or urgent cases which require an immediate remedy.[2] It has also been held that, so long as adequate notice is given, a person in possession of land may lawfully wheel clamp motor vehicles parked on that land without permission and charge the motorist a reasonable fee for releasing the vehicle.[3]

Where a person is wrongfully dispossessed of land, the use of reasonable force to recover that land will not amount to a tort. However, great care must be taken to avoid a breach of the criminal law. A residential tenant who refuses to quit, for example, cannot be evicted without a court order. Further, the Criminal Law Act 1977 makes it an offence for anyone except a 'displaced residential occupier' to use or threaten violence in order to secure entry to property.

1   *Hemmings v Stoke Poges Golf Club* [1920] 1 KB 720, CA.
2   *Burton v Winters* [1993] 3 All ER 847, CA.
3   *Arthur v Anker* [1996] 3 All ER 783, CA.

Chapter 24

Nuisance

24.1 The legal meaning of the word nuisance is surrounded by confusion. This is due, at least in part, to the fact that the term is used to describe different areas of liability, which have relatively little in common. First, and most important as far as the law of tort is concerned, a *private nuisance* consists of any unlawful interference which damages a person's land or adversely affects his use and enjoyment of it. Within this category there also falls any interference with a person's rights over land, such as easements or profits.[1] Second, and quite separate, a *public nuisance* is a criminal offence, consisting of an activity which endangers or inconveniences the public in general, or which obstructs people in the exercise of public rights. The relevance of this class of nuisance to the law of tort is that damages may be awarded to any individual who suffers loss or damage over and above that which is incurred by the general public. Third, and not within the law of tort at all, is a *statutory nuisance* under various Acts of Parliament, such as the Control of Pollution Act 1974, the aim of which is to protect the environment. Enforcement in respect of this type of nuisance is in the hands of public bodies such as local authorities, although some of the statutes also make provision for an aggrieved individual to recover damages.

In this chapter we examine the following issues:

- the range of activities which may amount to a private nuisance;
- the factors which will determine whether or not an interference is a nuisance in the legal sense;
- the persons who are protected against, and those who may be held liable for, the commission of a nuisance;
- the special defences which apply to the tort of private nuisance, and the range of remedies available to the claimant;
- the legal definition of a public nuisance, and the extent to which such a nuisance may found liability in tort.

1   Discussion of these rights belongs to land law; see ch 34 below.

Private nuisance

24.2 It has been said that 'private nuisances, at least in the vast majority of cases, are interferences for a substantial length of time by owners or occupiers of property with the use of enjoyment of neighbouring land'.[1] The main function of the law is to balance the conflicting interests of neighbours, and to decide at what point an interference becomes intolerable and therefore actionable.

1   *Cunard v Antifyre Ltd* [1933] 1 KB 551 at 557.

Interference
Damage to land
24.3   A person who *directly* causes something to enter the claimant's land is guilty of the tort of trespass.[1] Where the element of directness is lacking, however, the appropriate tort is private nuisance. Thus, for example, while it would be trespass to plant a tree in the claimant's garden, it is nuisance when the roots or branches of trees which the defendant has planted on his own land grow across the boundary.[2] Similarly, to build a wall on the claimant's land is a trespass, but to allow one's own wall to become so dilapidated that it falls on to the claimant's land is a nuisance.[3]

The simplest case of this type arises where something tangible is allowed to enter the claimant's property. A defendant has been held liable, for example, for causing water to overflow on to neighbouring land, both by carrying out filling operations on his own land[4] and by merely allowing his drain to become blocked.[5] However, damage may also be caused intangibly, as when vibrations shake the foundations of the claimant's building,[6] or fumes from a factory kill his shrubs.[7] It is clear from these cases that nuisance protects crops and buildings as well as the land itself; in *Farrer v Nelson*,[8] for instance, a person who overstocked his land with pheasants was held liable for the effect which these had upon his neighbour's crops.

In *Hunter v Canary Wharf Ltd*,[9] the House of Lords emphasised that private nuisance is a tort to land, rather than to those who own or occupy it. This means that no-one, not even the occupier, can recover damages in private nuisance for personal injury (for example where a person is made ill by fumes which render his house an unhealthy place in which to live). However, it seems that damage to an occupier's goods is regarded as consequential on the damage to the land, so that damages can be recovered for this.[10]

1   Chapter 23 above.
2   *Lemmon v Webb* [1894] 3 Ch 1, CA.
3   *Brew Bros Ltd v Snax (Ross) Ltd* [1970] 1 All ER 587, CA.
4   *Home Brewery Ltd v William Davis & Co (Leicester) Ltd* [1987] 1 All ER 637.
5   *Sedleigh-Denfield v O'Callaghan* [1940] 3 All ER 349, HL.
6   *Hoare & Co v McAlpine* [1923] 1 Ch 167.
7   *St Helen's Smelting Co v Tipping* (1865) 11 HL Cas 642.
8   (1885) 15 QBD 258.
9   [1997] 2 All ER 426, HL.
10   *Halsey v Esso Petroleum Co Ltd* [1961] 2 All ER 145.

Use and enjoyment
24.4   The feature of private nuisance which sets it apart from other torts is that it protects the amenity value of land, in the sense of the occupier's use and enjoyment of the property. Even where no physical damage is done, an occupier is entitled to complain if his intended use of the property (be it residential, agricultural or commercial) is unreasonably curtailed by the activities of the defendant. It is on this basis that action in nuisance may be taken in respect of smoke from a factory chimney,[1] offensive smells from stables[2] or the periodic emptying of a neighbour's cess-pit,[3] or the noise from a children's playground.[4] Examples of more subtle attacks on the enjoyment of his land or upon its amenity include the picketing of a person's premises from the highway[5] and the use of high-class residential premises for prostitution.[6]

In *Bridlington Relay Ltd v Yorkshire Electricity Board*,[7] it was suggested that an action in private nuisance could not be brought in respect of interference with television reception, since this would be a purely recreational use of land. However, the House of Lords in *Hunter v Canary Wharf Ltd*[8] took the view that television reception would in principle attract protection under this tort. Even so, the action there failed because the actual cause of the interference (the erection of a very large building on the defendants' land which blocked signals from the television transmitter) was held to be something which the defendants were fully entitled to do.

1   *Crump v Lambert* (1867) LR 3 Eq 409.
2   *Rapier v London Tramways Co* [1893] 2 Ch 588, CA.
3   *Penn v Wilkins* [1975] 2 EGLR 113.
4   *Dunton v Dover District Council* (1977) 76 LGR 87.
5   *Hubbard v Pitt* [1975] 3 All ER 1, CA.
6   *Thompson-Schwab v Costaki* [1956] 1 All ER 652, CA. See also *Laws v Florinplace Ltd* [1981] 1 All ER 659 (sex shop in predominantly residential area).
7   [1965] 1 All ER 264.
8   [1997] 2 All ER 426, HL.

Unlawfulness

24.5   Although private nuisance consists of an interference, not every interference constitutes a nuisance. The law does not demand absolute silence or absence of smell from neighbours; they must be allowed the occasional party or garden bonfire. Indeed, it has been held by the House of Lords that the tenant of a flat who uses the premises in the normal way cannot be guilty of nuisance by noise, even if the lack of sound proofing in the block means that other tenants are badly affected.[1] The law seeks to apply the broad principle of 'give and take', or 'live and let live'; as Lord Wright put it in *Sedleigh-Denfield v O'Callaghan*:[2] 'A balance has to be maintained between the right of the occupier to do what he likes with his own, and the right of his neighbour not to be interfered with'.

In striking this balance, the courts frequently refer to 'reasonableness'. However, the word is used in a different sense from that in which it features in negligence cases. There, the focus is on the conduct of the defendant, the question being whether or not he has acted 'reasonably'. In nuisance, by contrast, the court is concentrating on the interference with the claimant, and asking whether this is so 'unreasonable' that the law should not require him to put up with it.

In deciding whether a particular interference is 'unreasonable' in this sense, the courts have regard to a number of factors, which we now consider.

1   *Southwark London Borough Council v Mills* [1999] 4 All ER 449, HL.
2   [1940] 3 All ER 349 at 364.

Degree of interference

24.6   A matter of obvious importance is the seriousness of the interference in question. Where actual physical damage is caused, a fairly minor interference is sufficient to constitute nuisance but, where the claimant complains of interference with his use and enjoyment, rather more is required. It has been said that there must be 'an inconvenience materially interfering with the ordinary comfort physically of human existence, not merely according to elegant or dainty modes and habits of living, but according to plain and sober and simple notions among the English people'.[1] In accordance with this approach, the Court of Appeal held that fluctuating night time noise from the defendants' factory was not sufficient to constitute a nuisance, even though it exceeded the maximum level recommended by the World Health Organisation.[2]

The matter here is purely one of degree. Thus in *Heath v Brighton Corpn*,[3] a buzzing noise from a power station, which disturbed a church congregation in a poor area, was held insufficient to be a nuisance. In *Haddon v Lynch*,[4] on the other hand, the persistent and early ringing of church bells on Sunday mornings was held to be actionable.

1   *Walter v Selfe* (1851) 4 De G & Sm 315 at 322.
2   *Murdoch v Glacier Metal Co Ltd* [1998] Env LR 732, CA.
3   (1908) 98 LT 718.
4   [1911] VLR 230.

Sensitivity

24.7   A person who is abnormally sensitive, or who puts his property to an abnormally sensitive use, is not thereby entitled to a greater freedom from interference than anyone else. This rule, which is really no more than an application of the general principle outlined in the previous paragraph, is illustrated by *Robinson v Kilvert*,[1] in which heat from the defendant's premises damaged the claimant's stocks of brown paper. The amount of heat was not unreasonable; the damage was only caused because the paper was unduly sensitive, and the defendant was accordingly not liable. So too, in *Bridlington Relay Ltd v Yorkshire Electricity Board*,[2] it was held that a company which relayed television signals from their receiver to members of the public were not entitled to a greater freedom from interference than the average domestic user, on the basis that, unless they could offer a superior signal, they would have no customers.

Although the law gives no extra protection to those who are particularly sensitive, it does not abandon them altogether. If an interference is sufficiently substantial to constitute nuisance by ordinary standards, the claimant may claim damages for the full effect which it has upon the extra-sensitive use which he makes of his property, such as the growing of delicate orchids.[3]

1   (1889) 41 Ch D 88, CA.
2   [1965] 1 All ER 264.
3   *McKinnon Industries Ltd v Walker* [1951] 3 DLR 577 at 581.

Locality

24.8   In assessing the standard of comfort to which the claimant is legally entitled, the character of the neighbourhood is an important factor. In *Halsey v Esso Petroleum Co Ltd*,[1] for instance, where the claimant complained of the nightly noise of tankers driving in and out of the defendants' oil depot, the judge regarded it as crucial that the depot was situated in a quiet residential part of Fulham. This does not mean that a person in a noisy area is left without protection altogether. For example, in *Polsue and Alfieri Ltd v Rushmer*,[2] the claimant, who lived in Fleet Street, was held entitled to complain of the nightly noise from a new printing press which the defendants had installed.

In *Allen v Gulf Oil Refining Ltd*,[3] claims in nuisance were made where a massive oil refinery, constructed under the authority of an Act of Parliament, caused severe dislocation of the environment. It was pointed out by Lord Wilberforce that, even if these claims were not completely defeated by the defence of statutory authority,[4] the appropriate standard of comfort for this locality was to be based on what Parliament had clearly authorised it to become, rather than on what it had been before the refinery was built. However, the mere fact that planning permission has been granted for an activity does not automatically provide a defence to an action in private nuisance; it will only do so where there has been a strategic planning decision affected by considerations of public interest.[5]

It should be noted that, where physical damage is caused to the claimants property, the locality is irrelevant. Thus, in *St Helens Smelting Co v Tipping*,[6] where the claimant's shrubs were killed by fumes from the defendants' smelting works, the House of Lords regarded it as no defence that the area was devoted to such industrial activity.

1   [1961] 2 All ER 145.
2   [1907] AC 121, HL.
3   [1981] 1 All ER 353, HL.
4   Para 24.17 below.
5   *Wheeler v JJ Saunders Ltd* [1995] 2 All ER 697, CA.
6   (1865) 11 HL Cas 642.

Continuity

24.9 In most cases of private nuisance, especially those in which the claimant's use and enjoyment of land are affected, there is an element of continuity or repetition in the interference of which he complains. This does not mean that an isolated incident can never be a basis for liability (though a court is less likely to grant an injunction in such cases);[1] where actual damage results, as where a dilapidated building falls on to the claimant's land, there is no need for a repetition before action can be taken.

Cases in which there is a single occurrence of damage are sometimes explained as resulting from a continuing state of affairs for which the defendant is responsible. Thus in *Spicer v Smee*,[2] where defective wiring in the defendant's bungalow caused a fire which spread to the claimant's property, the defendant was held liable in nuisance. In *British Celanese Ltd v A H Hunt (Capacitors) Ltd*,[3] where light strips of metal foil, which were stored over a period of time on the defendants' land, blew on to adjoining property and caused damage, liability in nuisance was again imposed. In *SCM (UK) Ltd v W J Whittall & Son Ltd*,[4] on the other hand, where a workman negligently severed a cable and thus cut off the electricity supply to the claimant's factory, it was held that the defendants could not be liable in nuisance. Here there was nothing which could be described as a state of affairs, but merely an isolated act of negligence.

1   *Swan v Great Northern Rly* (1864) 4 De GJ & SM 211.
2   [1946] 1 All ER 489.
3   [1969] 2 All ER 1252.
4   [1970] 2 All ER 417, CA.

Utility of the defendant's conduct

24.10 A frequent plea of defendants in nuisance actions is that the offending activity is being carried on for the benefit of the public. This can undoubtedly have some bearing on the degree of interference which the claimant can be expected to put up with (the noise and dust which usually accompanies demolition and rebuilding, for example, would certainly be actionable if caused for no good reason). However, it cannot be a complete defence, for the courts will not allow the public interest to ride roughshod over private rights. In *Adams v Ursell*,[1] for instance, the smell from a fried-fish shop was held to be a nuisance, notwithstanding its value in supplying good food in a poor neighbourhood. Even more striking is the case of *Shelfer v City of London Electric Lighting Co*,[2] in which vibrations from the building of a power station damaged the claimant's house. The Court of Appeal held that the claimant was entitled to an injunction to stop the work, even though the laudable purpose of the building was to bring electric light to the City of London.

It may be that modern courts are more willing than their predecessors to give weight to the public interest, at least to the extent of refusing to stop a beneficial activity altogether. In *Miller v Jackson*,[3] for example, the claimant bought a new house next to the ground on which the village team had played cricket for some 70 years. The Court of Appeal held, by a majority, that the danger from cricket balls constituted a nuisance; nevertheless, in view of the social value of the ground to the community, the claimant was denied an injunction and left to his remedy in damages. Likewise, in *Dunton v Dover District Council*,[4] where the claimant complained of the noise from a children's playground next to his hotel, the judge refused to order its closure, but restricted its opening times and the age-group of children permitted to use it. By contrast, the Court of Appeal in *Kennaway v Thompson*[5] granted an injunction which drastically curtailed the activities of a motor boat racing club, preferring to protect the interest of a neighbouring resident who complained about the noise.

1   [1913] 1 Ch 269.
2   [1895] 1 Ch 287, CA.
3   [1977] 3 All ER 338, CA.
4   (1977) 76 LGR 87.
5   [1980] 3 All 329, CA.

Order of events

24.11 Surprisingly, perhaps, it seems settled that a claimant is not precluded from complaining of a nuisance merely because he came to it with his eyes wide open. In *Sturges v Bridgman*,[1] a doctor was held entitled to complain of the noise from machinery used by the defendant on adjoining premises, even though this caused him no inconvenience until he chose to build a consulting room at the end of his garden.

1 (1879) 11 Ch D 852, CA.

The defendant's state of mind

24.12 The question whether liability in nuisance depends upon proof of any particular mental element on the part of the defendant is one of the most difficult and complex aspects of this tort. All that may safely be said is that the more unreasonable the defendant's conduct, the less likely it is that the claimant will be required to tolerate the interference in question. Thus, in *Christie v Davey*,[1] where the defendant banged a tray on the party wall in order to disrupt the claimant's music lessons, his malice was held to render this noise actionable as a nuisance, even though the volume itself might not have done so. Even clearer is *Hollywood Silver Fox Farm Ltd v Emmett*,[2] where the defendant fired guns near the boundary of his land for the specific purpose of disturbing the breeding season of the claimants' silver foxes. This was held to be actionable, although it could hardly be said that the sound of gunfire would normally amount to a nuisance, unless unduly prolonged. However, it should be noted that malice cannot make unlawful something which the defendant has an absolute right to do, such as the abstraction of percolating water from beneath his own land.[3]

Of less weight than malice, although still relevant to this question, is the possibility that the defendant has been negligent in failing to keep the interference to a minimum. If building operations cause more dust and noise than necessary,[4] or children in a day nursery are permitted to make excessive noise,[5] the defendant's lack of care may lead a court to the conclusion that the claimant should not be expected to put up with the consequences.

Although malice and negligence may thus both be highly relevant to liability in nuisance, it seems that neither is essential. The courts have repeatedly stressed that, if the interference caused by an activity is substantial enough to be a nuisance, the defendant cannot evade liability merely by showing that he took all reasonable steps to reduce it. Defendants who have taken all reasonable care have nevertheless been held liable in respect of the smell from stables[6] or from a fried-fish shop[7] and the noise from a hotel kitchen.[8] The same principle applies where actual damage is caused; for example, where building works infringe a neighbour's right of support, it is no defence to show that the works were carried out without negligence.[9] In all these cases, however, the defendant was held liable as creator of the nuisance. As we shall see, where the defendant is sued as occupier of the land from which the nuisance emanates, proof that he has not taken reasonable care is normally essential to liability.[10]

The Privy Council in *The Wagon Mound (No 2)*[11] added to the confusion surrounding this issue by declaring that, while 'negligence in the narrow sense' might not always be needed for an action in nuisance, 'fault of some kind' is almost invariably necessary. What is meant by 'fault' in this context is far from clear. However, an important consequence of the decision is that, since fault involves foreseeability, the rules as to remoteness of damage in nuisance are identical to those in negligence.[12]

1 [1893] 1 Ch 316.
2 [1936] 1 All ER 825.
3 *Bradford Corpn v Pickles* [1895] AC 587, HL.
4 *Andreae v Selfridge & Co Ltd* [1937] 3 All ER 255, CA.
5 *Moy v Stoop* (1909) 25 TLR 262.
6 *Rapier v London Tramways Co* [1893] 2 Ch 588, CA.
7 *Adams v Ursell* [1913] 1 Ch 269.

8   *Vanderpant v Mayfair Hotel Co Ltd* [1930] 1 Ch 138.
9   *Brace v South-East Regional Housing Association Ltd* [1984] 1 EGLR 144, CA.
10   Para 24.15 below.
11   [1966] 2 All ER 709, PC.
12   *Cambridge Water Co Ltd v Eastern Counties Leather plc* [1994] 1 All ER 53 at 71–72, HL. We describe the relevant rules at paras 19.17–19.21 above.

Who is protected?

24.13   The tort of private nuisance is a means of protection for persons in possession or occupation of land.[1] This does not mean that only the freehold owner can sue; a limited interest, such as a weekly tenancy,[2] will suffice, although someone with such an interest is unlikely to be awarded an injunction except in very serious cases. In exceptional circumstances, a person who is in exclusive possession of land but who is unable to prove title to it may be entitled to sue in private nuisance,[3] as he can in trespass.[4] However, it is now settled that a person who has neither an interest in the land nor exclusive possession of it (such as a member of the occupier's family) is not entitled to maintain an action for private nuisance.[5]

The requirement that a claimant has possession of land serves to exclude actions by the landlord of property, at least in respect of temporary interference with its use and enjoyment, even if the effect of these is to reduce its letting value.[6] The landlord can, however, sue to protect his reversionary interest against either physical damage or such nuisances as may, by the doctrine of prescription,[7] operate to deprive him of rights or burden his land with obligations.[8]

Where a nuisance is continuous, its effects may be felt by successive owners or occupiers of the same property. In *Delaware Mansions Ltd v Westminster City Council*,[9] for example, the roots of trees for which the defendants were responsible encroached and damaged the foundations of property owned, at the time of the case, by the claimants. It was held by the House of Lords that, where there is a continuing nuisance of which the defendant knew or ought to have known, reasonable remedial expenditure may be recovered by the owner who has had to incur it.

1   This includes a permanently moored barge to which the claimant has a right of exclusive use and occupation: *Crown River Cruises Ltd v Kimbolton Fireworks Ltd* [1996] 2 Lloyd's Rep 533.
2   *Jones v Chappell* (1875) LR 20 Eq 539.
3   *Hunter v Canary Wharf Ltd* [1997] 2 All ER 426, HL. This includes a 'tolerated trespasser' under the Housing Act 1985, that is a tenant who is liable to be evicted as soon as the landlord obtains a warrant: *Pemberton v Southwark London Borough Council* [2000] 3 All ER 924, CA.
4   Para 23.5 above.
5   *Hunter v Canary Wharf Ltd* [1997] 2 All ER 426, HL. However, it is possible that this restriction might be in contravention of the Human Rights Act 1998: *McKenna v British Aluminium Ltd* (2002) Times, 25 April.
6   *Simpson v Savage* (1856) 1 CBNS 347.
7   Paras 33.40–33.51 below.
8   *Jones v Llanrwst UDC* [1911] 1 Ch 393.
9   [2001] UKHL 55, [2001] 4 All ER 737.

Who is liable?

Creator

24.14   In practice, most nuisance actions are brought against the occupier of the offending land. However, it seems that the person who actually creates a nuisance is always liable for it, whether he does this on his own land, someone else's land, or the public highway. This was assumed to be the case in *Hall v Beckenham Corpn*,[1] where the claimant complained of noise from model aeroplanes in a public park, although the individual enthusiasts were not in fact sued in that case. Further, where a person creates a nuisance on his own land, he remains liable for it, even where he subsequently parts with possession of the property and so becomes unable to prevent its continuance.[2]

1   [1949] 1 All ER 423.
2   *Thompson v Gibson* (1841) 7 M & W 456.

Occupier

24.15   An occupier of land may be held responsible for nuisances which exist on it, even those which he has not created. An extreme example of this is *Russell v London Borough Council of Barnet,*[1] in which a highway authority was held liable to a neighbouring householder for damage caused by the spreading roots of trees which were growing in the street, notwithstanding that the trees actually belonged to the householder!

The simplest case of this type of liability is where the nuisance is created by someone for whom the occupier is responsible, such as a visitor. Here it seems that the occupier will be liable, provided that the nuisance is a foreseeable consequence of what he has permitted the visitor to do. Thus in *A-G v Stone,*[2] the defendant, who had allowed gypsies to camp on his land, was held liable when the noise and insanitary conditions of their camp constituted a nuisance. A similar principle applies where work carried out on the occupier's behalf by an independent contractor causes a nuisance; if this consequence is foreseeable from the nature of the work, as where support is withdrawn from neighbouring property,[3] the defendant will be liable. In *Matania v National Provincial Bank Ltd,*[4] for instance, building operations carried on by a contractor on behalf of the occupier of a building's first floor involved a clear risk of nuisance by noise and dust to the occupiers of higher floors. When this happened, the occupier was held liable for it.

The general rule is that an occupier is only responsible for a nuisance which he has not created where he 'adopts' or 'continues' it. In effect, these terms mean having knowledge or the means of knowledge of the existence of a nuisance and then failing to take reasonable steps to abate it. In *Sedleigh-Denfield v O'Callaghan,*[5] for example, a drainage pipe, which had been negligently laid in the defendants' ditch by trespassers, became blocked, with the result that water overflowed on to the claimant's land. The defendants were held liable, for they had known of the pipe for three years and should have appreciated the danger. In *St Anne's Well Brewery Co v Roberts,*[6] on the other hand, part of the city wall of Exeter which was owned by the defendant collapsed and demolished the claimants' inn. The cause of this collapse was excavations which had been carried out by the defendant's predecessor. Since the defendant did not and could not know of these, he was held not liable.

There is one anomalous exception to the general rule that an occupier's liability is based on the foreseeability of the nuisance in question. It was laid down by the Court of Appeal, in the much-criticised case of *Wringe v Cohen,*[7] that, where premises abut upon a highway, the occupier (and landlord, if he is under a duty to repair) is strictly liable for damage resulting from disrepair, whether this is caused to neighbouring property or to the highway.[8] The extent of this liability is uncertain, since the court excluded cases in which the damage resulted from either the act of a trespasser or the secret and unobservable processes of nature.

1   [1984] 2 EGLR 44. A highway authority is generally responsible for all trees, whether self-sown or planted before or after adoption of the highway: *Hurst v Hampshire County Council* [1997] 2 EGLR 164, CA.
2   (1895) 12 TLR 76.
3   *Bower v Peate* (1876) 1 QBD 321.
4   [1936] 2 All ER 633, CA.
5   [1940] 3 All ER 349, HL.
6   (1928) 140 LT 1, CA.
7   [1939] 4 All ER 241, CA.
8   In the latter case the occupier would be liable for public nuisance; para 24.25 below.

24.16   At one time, an occupier could not be held responsible for a nuisance arising naturally on his land. However, since the decision of the Privy Council in *Goldman v Hargrave,*[1] it has been accepted that the occupier may be liable for failing to take reasonable steps to see that the condition of his property does not damage that of his neighbour. At the same time, the courts have sought to avoid the imposition of an unreasonable burden on an 'innocent' occupier. They have thus held that, in deciding whether the occupier has acted reasonably, regard should be had to his individual circumstances, including financial resources.[2] In this way, more may be demanded of a company or local authority than an individual, and more of a healthy and wealthy individual than of an infirm and impoverished one.

This principle, of a subjective or 'measured' duty of care, has been applied to cases of fire caused by lightning striking a tall tree,[3] earth falling from a geological mound;[4] a landslip of cliff land occupied by the defendants which withdraws support from the claimant's property;[5] and the deteriorating roof of a 'flying freehold' flat which permitted water to leak into the ground floor shop below.[6] The courts have also adopted it in relation to structures on the defendant's land which, though adequate when built, become a nuisance through increased usage. This has enabled the Court of Appeal to impose liability on a highway authority in respect of a culvert taking a stream under a road, when an increase in the flow of water made the culvert insufficient,[7] and on a water authority when a sewerage system could not cope with an increased usage and repeatedly flooded the claimant's property.[8]

We saw above that an occupier can be held liable for a nuisance created by a trespasser on his land, provided that he has 'adopted' or 'continued' it.[9] In cases involving nuisance caused by gypsies who were camping without permission on local authority land, it has been held that here, too, the local authority's duty of care is a 'measured' one.[10]

1   [1966] 2 All ER 989, PC.
2   This is unlike the normal standard of care in negligence, which is objective.
3   *Goldman v Hargrave* [1966] 2 All ER 989, PC.
4   *Leakey v National Trust for Places of Historic Interest or Natural Beauty* [1980] 1 All ER 17, CA.
5   *Holbeck Hall Hotel Ltd v Scarborough Borough Council* [2000] 2 All ER 705, CA.
6   *Abbahall Ltd v Smee* [2002] EWCA Civ 1831, [2003] 1 All ER 465.
7   *Bybrook Barn Centre Ltd v Kent County Council* [2001] BLR 55, CA.
8   *Marcic v Thames Water Utilities Ltd* [2002] EWCA Civ 65, [2002] 2 All ER 55.
9   *Sedleigh-Denfield v O'Callaghan* [1940] 3 All ER 349, HL.
10   *Page Motors Ltd v Epsom and Ewell Borough Council* (1981) 80 LGR 337, CA. See also *Lippiatt v South Gloucestershire Council* [1999] 4 All ER 149, CA (travellers).

Landlord
24.17   Where a nuisance arises from premises which are let, a claimant will normally take action against the tenant, who is the occupier. Whether or not the tenant is liable for the nuisance depends upon the rules discussed in the previous paragraph. In certain circumstances, however, the landlord may also be liable, although it is important to realise that this will not exonerate the tenant; it will simply provide the claimant with an additional person to sue.

In the first place, the landlord is legally responsible whenever he can be said to have 'authorised' his tenant to commit nuisance. This will be so where the nuisance arises from the normal use of the land by the tenant for the very purpose for which it is let, as in *Harris v James*[1] (blasting and smoke from a lime quarry) or *Tetley v Chitty*[2] (disturbance from a go-kart club which operated as tenants of the local authority). It should be emphasised, however, that it is authority, and not merely foreseeability, which must be established. Thus, in *Smith v Scott*,[3] where a local authority placed a problem family in the next house to that of the claimants, it was held that the local authority were not liable for the foreseeable nuisances which ensued; having made their tenants covenant expressly not to commit nuisance, it could hardly be said that they had authorised them to do so. Similarly, in *Hussain v Lancaster City Council*,[4] the defendant local authority were held not liable for a campaign of racial harassment and abuse carried out by some of their tenants, where the offending conduct took place outside the tenants' property.

Where nuisance arises not from the use to which the property is put, but from the state of repair in which it is let, the landlord is liable if he knows or ought to know of its state at the commencement of the tenancy.[5] Further, the landlord remains liable in this situation even though the tenant has covenanted to put the premises into repair; this is because a covenant between landlord and tenant cannot restrict the rights of third parties.[6]

In cases where the property falls into disrepair, and thus becomes a nuisance, during the currency of the lease, the landlord is only responsible if he has a duty to repair[7] or a right to enter and do repairs.[8] The common law on these points is somewhat uncertain, but s 4 of the Defective Premises Act 1972 contains similar principles which are rather more clearly expressed.[9]

The general rule is that a landlord, like an occupier, is only liable for nuisance by disrepair where he knows or ought to know of it. Once again, however, the case of *Wringe v Cohen*[10] lays down that, if the premises adjoin a highway, liability is strict.

1   (1876) 45 LJQB 545.
2   [1986] 1 All ER 663.
3   [1972] 3 All ER 645.
4   [1999] 4 All ER 125, CA.
5   *St Anne's Well Brewery Co v Roberts* (1928) 140 LT 1, CA.
6   *Brew Bros Ltd v Snax (Ross) Ltd* [1970] 1 All ER 587, CA.
7   This may be express or implied, eg under the Landlord and Tenant Act 1985, ss 11–14; para 37.25 below.
8   *Heap v Ind Coope and Allsopp Ltd* [1940] 3 All ER 634, CA. This may be implied, eg in a weekly tenancy: *Mint v Good* [1950] 2 All ER 1159, CA.
9   Para 21.29 above.
10   [1939] 4 All ER 241, CA.

Defences
Statutory authority
24.18   Many actions in private nuisance arise out of the activities of local authorities and other public or quasi-public bodies, which are carried on under the auspices of a statute. Such bodies may have a defence against liability where they can prove that the nuisance they have created is an inevitable consequence of what the statute ordered or empowered them to do, in the sense that it would occur despite the use of all reasonable care and skill, according to the state of scientific knowledge at the time.[1] However, the position may be further affected if, as frequently occurs, the statute in question contains a specific statement to the effect that liability for nuisance is, or is not, excluded.

The case law on statutory authority as a defence is complex, but an attempt was made to rationalise it in the case of *Department of Transport v North West Water Authority*,[2] where the following propositions, formulated by the trial judge, were endorsed by the House of Lords:

* In the absence of negligence, a body is not liable for a nuisance caused by its performance of a statutory duty.[3]
* This is so, even if the statute in question expressly imposes liability for nuisance.[4]
* In the absence of negligence, a body is not liable for a nuisance caused by its exercise of a statutory power, where the statute does not expressly impose liability upon it.[5]
* Even without negligence, a body is liable for a nuisance caused by its exercise of a statutory power, if the statute expressly imposes liability upon it.[6]
* In all cases, immunity depends upon proof that the work has been carried out, or the operation conducted, with all reasonable regard and care for the interests of other persons.[7]

Whether or not a particular nuisance has been expressly or impliedly authorised in this sense is a matter of statutory interpretation. In the leading case of *Hammersmith and City*

Rly Co v Brand,[8] for instance, where a railway company was expressly authorised to use railway engines, it was held by the House of Lords that no action in nuisance would lie against it in respect of damage caused by vibrations from passing trains. In *Allen v Gulf Oil Refining Ltd*,[9] the express authority of the defendants was limited to acquiring land and there *constructing* an oil refinery. A majority of the House of Lords, reversing the decision of the Court of Appeal, held that there was also implied authority to *operate* a refinery, so that no action in nuisance would lie in respect of the inevitable consequences (smell, noise, vibrations, etc) of its operation.

In the last two cases, the defendants were empowered to carry on the activity in question in a specific place. Frequently, however, this is not so, the defendants in question having a wide discretion under the statute as to the place and method of exercising their power. In such a case, a court is less likely to take the view that any nuisance arising from the exercise of the discretion is inevitable. Thus, in *Metropolitan Asylum District Managers v Hill*,[10] it was held that a general authority to build hospitals did not protect the defendants from liability when they chose to site a smallpox hospital in a residential area.

Where the statutory authority is to carry out not a specific undertaking, but such works of a particular kind as may from time to time be necessary, the courts have been somewhat reluctant to use private nuisance for the protection of private rights. This reflects the view that, if parliament has seen fit to confer an administrative discretion upon a public body, the bona fide exercise of that discretion should be challenged only through administrative channels and not through the ordinary courts of law.[11]

1   *Manchester Corpn v Farnworth* [1930] AC 171, HL.
2   [1983] 3 All ER 273, HL.
3   *Hammond v St Pancras Vestry* (1874) LR 9 CP 316.
4   *Smeaton v Ilford Corpn* [1954] 1 All ER 923.
5   *Dunne v North Western Gas Board* [1963] 3 All ER 916, CA.
6   *Charing Cross West End and City Electric Supply Co v Hydraulic Power Co* [1914] 3 KB 772, CA.
7   *Allen v Gulf Oil Refining Ltd* [1981] 1 All ER 353, HL.
8   (1869) LR 4 HL 171, HL.
9   [1981] 1 All ER 353, HL.
10 (1881) 6 App Cas 193, HL.
11 *Marriage v East Norfolk Rivers Catchment Board* [1949] 2 All ER 1021, CA.

Other defences

24.19   The defences of assumption of risk and contributory negligence, which we have already considered in relation to negligence,[1] are clearly capable of applying to nuisance, at least where the claimant sues in respect of a single incident which causes physical damage. Where, however, the gist of the claimant's complaint is the general effect upon him of the defendant's unreasonable use of land, these defences seem of little relevance. In particular, it is certainly no defence to prove that the claimant came to an existing nuisance,[2] nor that he could have reduced its effects, eg by shutting his windows against noise.

It seems in principle that the right to commit certain private nuisances may be acquired by 20 years' use, under the doctrine of prescription. For this to be so, however, the right in question must be capable of forming the subject matter of an easement,[3] such as the right to send smoke through flues in a party wall.[4] It is generally thought that this requirement would exclude the possibility of prescription in respect of such variable nuisances as noise and smells, although cases on long-standing nuisances of this kind have all been decided on other grounds.[5]

It is no defence to show that the defendant's interference only amounts to a nuisance when combined with interference by others.[6]

1   Chapter 20 above.
2   Para 24.11 above.
3   Paras 33.3–33.12 below.
4   *Jones v Pritchard* [1908] 1 Ch 630.

5 See, for example, *Sturges v Bridgman* (1879) 11 Ch D 852, CA.
6 *Lambton v Mellish* [1894] 3 Ch 163; *Pride of Derby and Derbyshire Angling Association Ltd v British Celanese Ltd* [1953] 1 All ER 179.

Remedies

Damages

24.20 Although private nuisance is in theory actionable only on proof that the claimant has suffered damage, the necessary damage will sometimes be presumed to exist. For example, the mere fact that the cornice of the defendant's house projects over the claimant's land is sufficient to found an action, without the need to prove that water falls from it.[1] So too, any interference with a proprietary right of the claimant is automatically actionable; this is important, since continued interference by the defendant might otherwise lead to the loss of the claimant's right altogether.[2]

Once it is established that the defendant is guilty of nuisance, the claimant is entitled to claim damages for consequential losses, provided that these are of a foreseeable kind.[3] As we have seen,[4] relevant losses include damage to goods and land,[5] together with the intangible 'use and enjoyment' of the claimant's property. The last category is obviously difficult to express in monetary terms; the courts have sometimes used the analogy of personal injury cases, so that damages for noise reflect those for deafness[6] and damages for smell reflect those awarded for loss of that sense.[7] However, the correctness of this approach was doubted in *Hunter v Canary Wharf Ltd*,[8] where it was stated that damages should be measured by the effect which the nuisance had on the value of the affected land.

1 *Fay v Prentice* (1845) 1 CB 828.
2 *Nicholls v Ely Beet Sugar Factory Ltd* [1936] Ch 343, CA.
3 *The Wagon Mound (No 2)* [1966] 2 All ER 709, PC.
4 Paras 24.3 and 24.4 above.
5 For what is included in damage to land, see *Midland Bank plc v Bardgrove Property Services Ltd* [1992] 2 EGLR 168, CA; para 33.50 n 3 below.
6 *Chadwick v Keith Marshall* [1984] CLY 1037.
7 *Bone v Seale* [1975] 1 All ER 787, CA.
8 [1997] 2 All ER 426 at 451, HL.

Injunction[1]

24.21 A commonly sought remedy in nuisance actions is that of injunction, whereby the claimant asks the court to order the termination of the offending activity. The award of this remedy lies in the discretion of the court, and it will seldom be granted in respect of injury which is trivial or temporary.[2] In more serious cases, however, the courts have displayed a notable tendency to grant an injunction even when the defendant's activity has public value,[3] which seems rather surprising in view of their statutory power to award damages in lieu of the injunction sought.[4]

1 Paras 28.17–28.19 below.
2 *A-G v Sheffield Gas Consumers Co* (1853) 3 De GM & G 304.
3 Para 24.10 above.
4 Para 28.19 below.

Abatement

24.22 The law has for centuries recognised the right of a person affected by a nuisance to take matters into his own hands and abate (ie remove) it. In a more sophisticated age, however, such self-help remedies are treated by the courts with suspicion and dislike, if for no other reason than that they may lead to a breach of the peace, and anyone claiming to exercise this right must therefore take great care not to exceed what the law permits. Where, for example, the defendant's tree overhangs the claimant's land, the claimant may lop off its branches;[1] he must not, however, keep the fruit.[2] Further, where abatement involves entry on to the defendant's land, notice must first be given, except in an emergency.[3] And the overall requirement that damage be kept to a minimum means that, where there are alternative methods of abating a nuisance, the less mischievous must be chosen.[4]

1   *Lemmon v Webb* [1895] AC 1, HL.
2   *Mills v Brooker* [1919] 1 KB 555.
3   *Jones v Williams* (1843) 11 M & W 176.
4   *Lagan Navigation Co v Lambeg Bleaching Co* [1927] AC 226, HL.

Public nuisance

24.23   Public nuisance covers an even wider area than private nuisance, partly because it is not limited to interference with land. Public nuisance falls into two broad categories. First, the kind of interference, such as noise or smoke, which is commonly a private nuisance, will also become a public nuisance if it affects a sufficiently substantial neighbourhood or section of the public. Whether or not this is so is a question of fact;[1] thus, in *R v Lloyd*,[2] where only three people complained of noise, the defendant was held not guilty of public nuisance. Second, public nuisance may consist of interference with the exercise of public rights, for instance by obstructing a highway or navigable river. Within these two classes, liability has been imposed on such diverse activities as blasting operations causing widespread vibrations, dust, splinters and noise,[3] organising a pop festival which causes noise, traffic congestion and general inconvenience,[4] selling impure food[5] or water,[6] and failing to prevent pigeons roosting under a railway bridge from fouling the footpath.[7]

It must be remembered that public nuisance is essentially a matter of criminal law.[8] However, as we shall see, a private individual may in some circumstances seek damages for the effect which a public nuisance has on him. Further, where the relevant criminal penalties are felt to be inadequate, the Attorney-General is empowered to obtain an injunction and thus to have the offending activity terminated.

1   *A-G v PYA Quarries Ltd* [1957] 1 All ER 894, CA.
2   (1802) 4 Esp 200.
3   *A-G v PYA Quarries Ltd* [1957] 1 All ER 894, CA.
4   *A-G for Ontario v Orange Productions Ltd* (1971) 21 DLR (3d) 257.
5   *Shillito v Thompson* (1875) 1 QBD 12.
6   *AB v South West Water Services Ltd* [1993] 1 All ER 609, CA.
7   *Wandsworth London Borough Council v Railtrack plc* [2001] EWCA Civ 1236, [2002] QB 756.
8   A very important consequence of this is that a public nuisance can never be legalised by prescription.

24.24   Public nuisance, like private nuisance, involves the court in the task of balancing conflicting interests in accordance with the general idea of reasonableness. Therefore, a person is not automatically liable when queues form outside his shop and obstruct the highway, since these may be due to circumstances beyond his control, such as wartime shortages.[1] Liability will be imposed, however, on a theatre proprietor who takes no steps at all to reduce large nightly queues,[2] or on a shopkeeper who, by selling ice cream from a window, instead of inside the shop, positively increases the likelihood of obstruction.[3] The test is whether the defendant knows or ought to know that there is a real risk that nuisance of the kind which in fact occurs will be caused.[4]

Again, as with private nuisance, the court must apply the principle of 'give and take'. A builder may erect hoardings or scaffolding in the street,[5] vans may load and unload outside business premises[6] and vehicles may break down,[7] without liability arising in public nuisance. Indeed, where personal injury results from such an obstruction, as where the claimant collides at night with a parked vehicle, the modern tendency is to impose liability upon the defendant only where he has been negligent in causing the danger,[8] although it is not clear whether it is for the claimant to establish negligence or for the defendant to disprove it. Where, however, the obstruction is unreasonable in size or extent, as where a vehicle which has broken down is left for a long period in an unlighted or otherwise dangerous condition, the defendant will be liable in public nuisance.[9]

1   Dwyer v Mansfield [1946] 2 All ER 247.
2   Lyons, Sons & Co v Gulliver [1914] 1 Ch 631, CA.
3   Fabbri v Morris [1947] 1 All ER 315, DC.
4   R v Shorrock [1993] 3 All ER 917, CA.
5   Harper v GN Haden & Sons Ltd [1933] Ch 298, CA.
6   Trevett v Lee [1955] 1 All ER 406, CA.
7   Maitland v Raisbeck and AT and J Hewitt Ltd [1944] 2 All ER 272, CA.
8   Dymond v Pearce [1972] 1 All ER 1142, CA.
9   Ware v Garston Haulage Co Ltd [1943] 2 All ER 558, CA.

Highways

24.25   It is obvious from the previous paragraph that public nuisance frequently concerns the highway. In the first place, any obstruction, whether total or partial, of the highway is actionable, except where it can be justified on the broad ground of reasonableness. It has even been suggested[1] that it would be a public nuisance for pickets to harass workers in their use of the highway without actually obstructing it, but this has been doubted.[2]

Second, it is a public nuisance to carry on any activity, or to allow property to fall into a state, whereby users of the highway are endangered. This includes the creation of such obvious hazards as a pool of acid[3] or a pile of rubbish,[4] and the emission of large clouds of smoke from neighbouring premises[5] or defective vehicles[6] which obscure the vision of drivers. In *Castle v St Augustine's Links*,[7] liability was imposed upon a golf club which so sited one of its tees that golfers often sliced balls on to an adjoining public road. A person may be liable for public nuisance even where the danger which he has created is not technically on the highway at all, provided that a passer-by may be endangered without making a substantial detour. Thus, for example, an unfenced excavation at the very edge of the road, or sharp outward-pointing spikes on a boundary fence,[8] can constitute a public nuisance.

Where danger arises from work which is being done on or in the highway itself, such as excavations, it is important to note that the defendant is liable even where he is not negligent and, further, that he is responsible for any default of his independent contractor.[9]

The mere fact that a person's building or tree projects over the highway does not render him guilty of a public nuisance, unless it is such as to interfere with reasonable passage. Where, however, it falls and does damage, there may undoubtedly be liability, although the basis of this is disputed. It seems that, where trees are concerned, the occupier is not liable unless he had reason to suspect the danger;[10] nor is he responsible for the negligence of his independent contractor, eg in felling operations.[11] Where buildings collapse, liability appears to be strict, whether these project over[12] or merely adjoin[13] the highway.

As regards dangers arising from the condition of the highway itself, such as potholes or uneven flagstones, common law imposed no liability upon anyone for a mere failure to repair. In relation to highway authorities, this immunity was anomalous, and it was removed by statute in 1961. Under this provision (which is now contained in the Highways Act 1980), a highway authority may be liable in negligence, nuisance or breach of statutory duty for damage caused by its failure to maintain or repair a highway, subject to a statutory defence of proving that all reasonable care had been taken, by independent contractors or employees of the highway authority, to make the particular highway safe for the type and volume of traffic which might reasonably be expected to use it.

1   Thomas v National Union of Mineworkers [1985] 2 All ER 1.
2   News Group Newspapers Ltd v Society of Graphical and Allied Trades 1982 (No 2) [1987] ICR 181.
3   Pope v Fraser and Southern Rolling and Wire Mills Ltd (1938) 55 TLR 324.
4   Almeroth v Chivers & Sons Ltd [1948] 1 All ER 53, CA.

5   *Holling v Yorkshire Traction Co* [1948] 2 All ER 662.
6   *Tysoe v Davies* [1984] RTR 88.
7   (1922) 38 TLR 615.
8   *Fenna v Clare & Co* [1895] 1 QB 199, DC.
9   *Holliday v National Telephone Co* [1899] 2 QB 392, CA; see paras 27.26 and 27.29 below.
10 *Caminer v Northern and London Investment Trust Ltd* [1950] 2 All ER 486, HL. See also *Quinn v Scott* [1965] 2 All ER 588.
11 *Salsbury v Woodland* [1969] 3 All ER 863, CA.
12 *Tarry v Ashton* (1876) 1 QBD 314.
13 *Wringe v Cohen* [1939] 4 All ER 241, CA.

Action for damages

24.26   The fact that a person is inconvenienced by a public nuisance does not of itself entitle him to recover damages in respect of it.[1] In order to claim damages, he must show that he has suffered some 'special' or 'particular' damage, over and above that which is sustained by the public in general. This requirement is obviously satisfied by personal injuries, and, in *Halsey v Esso Petroleum Co Ltd*,[2] it was held that the claimant was entitled to complain of smuts from the defendants' oil depot, since these had caused actual damage to the paintwork of his car, which was parked in the street outside his house. Similarly, where unlawful industrial picketing obstructs the highway, the costs incurred by an employer in 'bussing' in his workers and providing extra security for them are recoverable as damages for public nuisance.[3]

In all these cases, the damage to the claimant was of a different kind from that suffered by other persons, but it seems that a substantial difference in extent is also sufficient to found an action. In the Irish case of *Boyd v Great Northern Rly Co*,[4] for instance, a doctor with a busy practice recovered damages when he was delayed for 20 minutes at a level crossing, while in *Rose v Miles*,[5] where the defendant obstructed a creek and thus trapped the claimant's barges, the claimant was able to recover the considerable cost of unloading the cargo and transporting it by land. Again, in *Tate & Lyle Industries Ltd v Greater London Council*,[6] where the defendants caused serious siltation in navigable reaches of the River Thames, the claimants recovered for losses caused by the inability of large vessels to load and unload at their sugar refinery.

The obstruction of streets not infrequently leads to complaints by neighbouring tradesmen of loss of custom. Where access to the claimant's premises is blocked, this certainly gives rise to an action for damages.[7] Where the obstruction is further away, the legal position is less clear, although the better view is that an affected tradesman can sue,[8] provided that the effect of the obstruction upon his business is foreseeable and therefore not too remote.[9]

1   *Winterbottom v Lord Derby* (1867) LR 2 Exch 316.
2   [1961] 2 All ER 145.
3   *News Group Newspapers Ltd v Society of Graphical and Allied Trades 1982 (No 2)* [1987] ICR 181.
4   [1895] 2 IR 555.
5   (1815) 4 M & S 101.
6   [1983] 1 All ER 1159, HL.
7   *Fritz v Hobson* (1880) 14 Ch D 542.
8   *Wilkes v Hungerford Market Co* (1835) 2 Bing NC 281.
9   *The Wagon Mound (No 2)* [1966] 2 All ER 709, PC; paras 19.17–19.20 above.

Chapter 25

Strict liability

25.1 In this and the next chapter we consider several situations in which, unusually, liability may be imposed upon a defendant who is not guilty of any 'fault'. In these situations, the law in effect says that, while it is quite permissible to carry on high-risk activities, any losses which they cause must be borne by those who carry on the activities, and not by innocent members of society on whom those losses happen to fall.

From a purely logical point of view, there is much to be said for the view that all 'ultra-hazardous activities' should attract this form of liability. However, as will be seen, English law has never developed a general theory of strict liability; those parts of the law of tort in which liability is strict have grown up piecemeal, both at common law and under statute.

In this chapter we examine the following issues:

- the principle of strict liability laid down in the leading case of *Rylands v Fletcher*;
- the special defences available in cases falling within that principle;
- the extent to which damage caused by fire attracts special treatment under the law of tort.

Rylands v Fletcher

25.2 The defendants employed reputable independent contractors to construct a reservoir on their land, for the purpose of supplying water to their mill. In the course of construction, the contractors discovered some disused mine shafts on the reservoir site but negligently failed to seal these properly, with the result that water flowed down the shafts and flooded the claimant's mine, which connected with the disused workings. No negligence was found against the defendants themselves and, at first instance, they were held not liable for the damage caused. On appeal, however, the claimant was successful, upon grounds stated by Blackburn J:[1]

'We think that the true rule of law is, that the person who for his own purposes brings on his lands and collects and keeps there anything likely to do mischief if it escapes, must keep it in at his peril, and, if he does not do so, is prima facie answerable for all the damage which is the natural consequence of its escape. He can excuse himself by showing that the escape was owing to the claimant's default; or perhaps that the escape was the consequence of *vis major*, or the act of God; but as nothing of this sort exists here, it is unnecessary to inquire what excuse would be sufficient.'

This decision, together with the reasoning on which it was based, was expressly approved and upheld by the House of Lords,[2] although Lord Cairns LC rather complicated matters by stressing the importance of the fact that the defendants were at the relevant time putting their land to a 'non-natural use'.

1   (1866) LR 1 Exch 265 at 279.
2   (1868) LR 3 HL 330, HL.

Elements of liability

Land

25.3   An important part of the rule as laid down, and one which has helped to prevent it from developing to cover dangerous activities in general, is the requirement that the escaping object be something which the defendant has brought on to his land. This does not mean, however, that liability is imposed only upon the freehold owner, or even the occupier, of the land in question. If a licensee, for example, introduces a dangerous substance on to land which he is permitted to use, he may be liable under *Rylands v Fletcher* for its subsequent escape, provided that it is then still under his (ineffective) control.[1] In such a case, it seems that the owner who is not in occupation is only liable if he has expressly or impliedly authorised the accumulation.[2]

The requirement of occupation of 'land' has been slightly relaxed, so as to include those who have a right to lay pipes, cables etc under the land of others or under the public highway. Indeed, an escape in such circumstances may render the defendant liable, not only to neighbouring landowners,[3] but also to other public bodies with similar rights.[4]

Whether the rule is capable of any further expansion must be regarded as doubtful. However, it may possibly apply where a dangerous thing escapes from the highway on to which the defendant has brought it.[5] It has also been suggested that it might apply to accumulations of dangerous objects in a vessel moored on a river.[6]

1   *Rainham Chemical Works v Belvedere Fish Guano Co* [1921] 2 AC 465, HL.
2   *St Anne's Well Brewery Co v Roberts* (1928) 140 LT 1, CA.
3   *Northwestern Utilities Ltd v London Guarantee and Accident Co Ltd* [1936] AC 108, PC.
4   *Charing Cross West End and City Electric Supply Co v Hydraulic Power Co* [1914] 3 KB 772, CA.
5   *Rigby v Chief Constable of Northamptonshire* [1985] 2 All ER 985.
6   *Crown River Cruises Ltd v Kimbolton Fireworks Ltd* [1996] 2 Lloyd's Rep 533.

Accumulation

25.4   Blackburn J spoke of the person who 'for his own purposes brings on his lands and collects and keeps there' something which, if it escapes, will be dangerous. Subsequent cases support this idea that the defendant is strictly liable only for artificial accumulations, and not for either natural material, such as earth, or material which accumulates naturally, such as rainwater.[1] For instance, in *Giles v Walker*,[2] an occupier who ploughed up forest land was held not liable for the subsequent spontaneous crop of thistles which spread to the claimant's land.[3] So too, in *Pontardawe RDC v Moore-Gwyn*,[4] it was held that *Rylands v Fletcher* had no application to a fall of rock from an outcrop due to the natural process of erosion. Again, where water is naturally on the defendant's land, the claimant cannot complain that the defendant's normal working of mines[5] or building works[6] causes it to flow on to his land.

Not surprisingly, an occupier who actively causes natural material to escape will be liable under *Rylands v Fletcher*.[7] For example, in *Miles v Forest Rock Granite Co (Leicestershire) Ltd*,[8] liability was imposed upon the defendants for damage done by the escape of rock caused by their blasting operations. A similar decision was reached in *Baird v Williamson*,[9] where the defendant pumped water which was naturally in his mine to a level from which it flowed into the claimant's mine.

The requirement that the accumulation be for the defendant's own purposes should not be taken too literally, as restricting *Rylands v Fletcher* to cases where the defendant acquires some personal benefit. It has been held to apply, for example, to a local authority compelled by statute to receive sewage into its sewers,[10] although the liability of statutory undertakers was doubted by the Court of Appeal on precisely this ground in *Dunne v North Western Gas Board*.[11]

1   For the 'measured duty of care' which arises in respect of natural dangers, see para 24.15 above.
2   (1890) 24 QBD 656.
3   Contrast *Crowhurst v Amersham Burial Board* (1878) 4 Ex D 5, where the defendants actually planted a poisonous tree.
4   [1929] 1 Ch 656.
5   *Smith v Kenrick* (1849) 7 CB 515, approved in *Rylands v Fletcher*.
6   *Ellison v Ministry of Defence* (1996) 81 BLR 101.
7   If his act is deliberate, the appropriate tort is trespass: *Rigby v Chief Constable of Northamptonshire* [1985] 2 All ER 985.
8   (1918) 34 TLR 500, CA.
9   (1863) 15 CBNS 376, again approved in *Rylands v Fletcher*.
10 *Smeaton v Ilford Corpn* [1954] 1 All ER 923.
11 [1963] 3 All ER 916, CA.

Dangerous things

25.5   As originally stated, the rule in *Rylands v Fletcher* applies to anything 'likely to do mischief if it escapes'. Such things have been held to include water in bulk,[1] gas,[2] electricity,[3] sparks,[4] acid smuts[5] and poisonous vegetation.[6] *Rylands v Fletcher* has also been held to apply to fire[7] and explosions,[8] notwithstanding that the thing which escapes in such cases is not necessarily the same as that which the defendant has accumulated.

All these seem to fall fairly within the rule as originally laid down, but some other candidates for inclusion are more questionable. In *Firth v Bowling Iron Co*,[9] for example, the defendants were held liable for a rusty wire fence which flaked on to the claimant's land and poisoned his cattle, while, in *Hale v Jennings Bros*,[10] the principle was invoked where a chair from a fairground 'chair-o-plane' became detached from the roundabout and, complete with its occupant, flew off and injured the occupier of a nearby booth. Even a falling flagpole[11] has been held to come within *Rylands v Fletcher*, although its application to vibrations,[12] where the invasion is intangible, has been criticised. Most extreme of all is the case of *A-G v Corke*,[13] where the doctrine was applied to human beings so as to justify the grant of an injunction against a man who allowed caravan dwellers to use his field, when these committed various acts of nuisance in the neighbourhood. The dubious nature of this decision is emphasised by the fact that liability could in any case have been imposed on the simple ground of nuisance.[14]

1   *Ryland v Fletcher* itself.
2   *Northwestern Utilities Ltd v London Guarantee and Accident Co Ltd* [1936] AC 108, PC.
3   *National Telephone Co v Baker* [1893] 2 Ch 186.
4   *Jones v Festiniog Rly Co* (1868) LR 3 QB 733.
5   *Halsey v Esso Petroleum Co Ltd* [1961] 2 All ER 145.
6   *Crowhurst v Amersham Burial Board* (1878) 4 Ex D 5.
7   *Mason v Levy Auto Parts of England Ltd* [1967] 2 All ER 62.
8   *Rainham Chemical Works v Belvedere Fish Guano Co* [1921] 2 AC 465, HL.
9   (1878) 3 CPD 254.
10 [1938] 1 All ER 579, CA.
11 *Shiffman v Hospital of the Order of St John of Jerusalem* [1936] 1 All ER 557.
12 *Hoare & Co v McAlpine* [1923] 1 Ch 167.
13 [1933] Ch 89.
14 *A-G v Stone* (1895) 12 TLR 76; para 24.15 above.

Escape

25.6   A major reason why *Rylands v Fletcher* has not been used as the basis for a general principle of liability for ultra-hazardous activities is the courts' insistence that there must be an escape, in the sense that the damage complained of is suffered outside the land on which the defendant accumulates the dangerous thing. In *Ponting v Noakes*,[1] for instance, the claimant was unable to recover damages when his horse reached over the boundary of the defendant's land, ate some poisonous vegetation which grew there, and died. This principle was unanimously endorsed by the House of Lords in *Read v J Lyons & Co Ltd*,[2] where a munitions inspector was injured by the explosion of a shell at the defendants' weapons factory. It was admitted that such shells were 'dangerous things'; nevertheless it was held that, in the absence of either negligence or an escape, the defendants were not liable.

In deciding whether there has been a sufficient 'escape' for this purpose, the courts are concerned, not with the niceties of land law, but with the simple question of fact whether something has travelled from a place where the defendant has control to a place where he has not. As a result, a landlord may be liable to his own tenant (or, possibly, his licensee) when something escapes from one part of the property, which he has retained, to another part which is in the occupation of the claimant.[3]

1   [1894] 2 QB 281.
2   [1946] 2 All ER 471, HL.
3   *Hale v Jennings Bros* [1938] I All ER 579, CA.

Non-natural use

25.7   In laying down the rule in *Rylands v Fletcher*, Blackburn J stressed the importance of the fact that the defendants had brought on to their land something which was not naturally there. This element of liability, like all the others, was expressly approved by Lord Cairns LC, in the House of Lords, but the additional point was made that the defendant must be engaged in a 'non-natural' use of his land.

The effect of this requirement has been to introduce a great deal of flexibility into this area of law, because the courts are free not to impose strict liability upon a person whose use of land, although artificial, is an ordinary and usual one. The result of this discretion has been to tie *Rylands v Fletcher* more closely to the idea of exceptional risk, and it has been suggested that a non-natural use is one which brings with it increased danger to others and is not merely the ordinary use of the land or such a use as is proper for the general benefit of the community.[1]

It is difficult to predict how the courts will make what is in effect a value judgment, although decided cases offer some insight into judicial attitudes. Thus, while a domestic water supply,[1] or a house's electric wiring,[2] or a fire in a grate,[3] have all been held to be natural, similar utilities carried in bulk have not.[4] So too, trees, whether planted or self-sown, have been regarded as natural,[5] except where they are poisonous.[6] Such decisions do not necessarily mean that the dividing line lies between domestic or agricultural uses, on the one hand, and industrial uses, on the other. A number of modern cases have used the idea of natural use to avoid imposing strict liability on industrial activities which are regarded as for the public benefit,[7] even to the extent of suggesting that an armaments factory is a natural use of land in wartime.[8] However, in the recent case of *Cambridge Water Co Ltd v Eastern Counties Leather plc*,[9] the House of Lords regarded the storage of substantial quantities of chemicals on industrial premises as 'an almost classic case of non-natural use', even though the premises were in an industrial village and the defendants' activity created much-needed employment in the locality.

1   *Rickards v Lothian* [1913] AC 263 at 279, PC.
2   *Collingwood v Home and Colonial Stores Ltd* [1936] 3 All ER 200, CA.
3   *Sochacki v Sas* [1947] I All ER 344; *Johnson v BJW Property Developments Ltd* [2002] EWHC 1131 (TCC), [2002] 3 All ER 574.
4   *Smeaton v Ilford Corpn* [1954] I All ER 923 (sewage).
5   *Noble v Harrison* [1926] 2 KB 332.
6   *Crowhurst v Amersham Burial Board* (1878) 4 Ex D 5.

7   Eg *Rouse v Gravelworks Ltd* [1940] 1 All ER 26, CA (working of mines and minerals); *British Celanese Ltd v A H Hunt (Capacitors) Ltd* [1969] 2 All ER 1252 (light engineering factory on an industrial estate); *Ellison v Ministry of Defence* (1996) 81 BLR 101 (construction of bulk fuel installations at airfield).
8   *Read v J Lyons & Co Ltd* [1946] 2 All ER 471 at 475, 478, 484.
9   [1994] 1 All ER 53 at 79.

Damage

25.8   It was said in *Rylands v Fletcher* that a defendant would be liable for 'all the damage which is the natural consequence' of the escape. This formulation does not indicate the appropriate test for remoteness of damage, but it is now established that the defendant can only be liable for damage of a type which could have been reasonably foreseen, even though foreseeability is irrelevant to liability itself.[1]

As to the *kinds* of damage which are actionable, the major question is whether *Rylands v Fletcher* is like private nuisance in protecting only those persons with an interest in or exclusive possession of land.[2] Until recently, the balance of authority suggested that *Rylands v Fletcher* is not so limited; thus in *Halsey v Esso Petroleum Co Ltd*,[3] the claimant was able to claim for damage caused to the paintwork of his car, which was parked in the street, by acid smuts from the defendants' oil depot. So too, in *British Celanese Ltd v A H Hunt (Capacitors) Ltd*,[4] where strips of metal foil blew from the defendants' land on to an electricity sub-station, and the resulting power cut caused damage in the claimants' factory, it was held to be no defence that nothing had 'escaped' on to the claimants' land. However, these decisions may be open to doubt in the light of *Cambridge Water Co Ltd v Eastern Counties Leather plc*,[5] where the House of Lords placed great emphasis on the close relationship between *Rylands v Fletcher* and private nuisance.[6]

It is uncertain whether damages may be recovered in respect of personal injuries, especially those suffered by a non-occupier. There is some authority in favour of such claims, whether by an occupier[7] or a non-occupier.[8] However, dicta in *Read v J Lyons & Co Ltd*[9] suggest that a claim for personal injury is always dependent on proof of negligence. Furthermore, the views expressed by the House of Lords in *Cambridge Water*, which were noted above, would appear hostile to such claims.

Whether or not it may accurately be described as a natural consequence, it is settled that no damages may be claimed under *Rylands v Fletcher* for pure economic loss.[10]

1   *Cambridge Water Co Ltd v Eastern Counties Leather plc* [1994] 1 All ER 53.
2   Para 24.13 above.
3   [1961] 2 All ER 145.
4   [1969] 2 All ER 1252.
5   [1994] 1 All ER 53 at 69–71.
6   In *McKenna v British Aluminium Ltd* (2002) Times, 25 April, it was accepted by the judge that restricting claimants in this way might be challenged under the Human Rights Act 1998.
7   *Hale v Jennings Bros* [1938] 1 All ER 579, CA.
8   *Miles v Forest Rock Granite Co (Leicestershire) Ltd* (1918) 34 TLR 500, CA; *Shiffman v Hospital of the Order of St John of Jerusalem* [1936] 1 All ER 557; *Perry v Kendricks Transport Ltd* [1956] 1 All ER 154, CA.
9   [1946] 2 All ER 471 at 478, 480, 481.
10   *Cattle v Stockton Waterworks Co* (1875) LR 10 QB 453; *Weller & Co v Foot and Mouth Disease Research Institute* [1965] 3 All ER 560. See paras 17.15–17.17 above.

Defences

Consent of the claimant

25.9   The defence of assumption of risk[1] means that, where the claimant consents to the presence of the source of danger, the defendant is not liable unless he is negligent. The claimant may consent expressly;[2] however, it is more commonly implied from the circumstances. As to when consent will be implied, the legal position is confused; many of the cases have concerned an escape of water from an upper floor to a lower floor, and these could have been decided on an alternative ground, namely, that the installation in question was a natural use of land.[3] Apart from this, two main threads emerge from the cases as reasons for holding that the claimant has consented. First, and despite its apparent conflict with the principle that 'coming to a nuisance' is no defence,[4] the claimant (at least where he is the defendant's tenant) cannot complain of the condition of his or the landlord's property at the commencement of the lease.[5] Second, consent to a dangerous installation will more easily be implied where it is maintained for the benefit of the claimant as well as the defendant.[6] This latter factor, however, is not conclusive, so that a consumer of gas is not precluded from suing the statutory undertakers by the fact that he benefits from the supply.[7]

It should be emphasised that the consent which is implied in these cases merely precludes the claimant from bringing an action under the rule in *Rylands v Fletcher*. Where the defendant is guilty of negligence, he remains liable,[8] unless the circumstances are so extreme that the claimant can be said to have assumed the risk of this.

1   Paras 20.2–20.4 above.
2   As in *A-G v Cory Bros & Co Ltd* [1921] 1 AC 521, HL.
3   *Rickards v Lothian* [1913] AC 263, PC; para 25.7 above.
4   Para 24.11 above.
5   *Kiddle v City Business Properties Ltd* [1942] 2 All ER 216.
6   *Gill v Edouin* (1895) 72 LT 579, CA.
7   *Northwestern Utilities Ltd v London Guarantee and Accident Co Ltd* [1936] AC 108, PC.
8   *A Prosser & Son Ltd v Levy* [1955] 3 All ER 577, CA.

Default of the claimant and hypersensitivity

25.10   If the true legal cause of damage is some act or default of the claimant himself, no action will lie. In *Dunn v Birmingham Canal Navigation Co*,[1] for example, where a mine-owner, fully aware of the danger, worked his mine directly under the defendants' canal, he was held unable to sue in respect of the resulting flood. It also appears that, if the claimant is partly responsible for the damage, his damages may be reduced on the ground of contributory negligence.[2]

Where injury or damage results from the hypersensitivity of the claimant or his property, it seems, by analogy with nuisance,[3] that the defendant should not be liable. In *Eastern and South African Telegraph Co Ltd v Cape Town Tramways Companies Ltd*,[4] where the escape of minute electric currents from the defendants' tramway system interfered with the claimants' submarine telegraph cable, the claimants failed to recover damages. Where, however, the claimant is not actively responsible for his sensitivity, the position is less clear. For example, in *Hoare & Co v McAlpine*,[5] it was said to be no defence to an action for causing damage by vibrations that the claimants' building was old and unstable.

1   (1872) LR 7 QB 244.
2   Paras 20.11–20.16 above.
3   Para 24.7 above.
4   [1902] AC 381, PC.
5   [1923] 1 Ch 167.

Act of God

25.11   The law recognises that there may be a natural catastrophe so overwhelming that even a system of strict liability should not hold the defendant responsible. Thus, where the escape is due to an operation of natural forces 'which no human foresight can provide against, and of which human prudence is not bound to recognise the possibility',[1] there is no liability. In *Nichols v Marsland*,[2] the defendant created artificial lakes on his land by damming a natural stream. A rainstorm of unprecedented violence broke down the banks which he had built, and the resulting flood swept away the claimant's bridges. The defendant was held not liable, on the basis that the storm constituted an act of God.

Nichols v Marsland appears to be the only reported English case in which the defence has succeeded, and even that decision has subsequently been heavily criticised. In *Greenock Corpn v Caledonian Rly Co*,[3] it was held by the House of Lords that, whatever the English position might be, an extraordinary rainfall in Scotland was no act of God!

1   *Tennent v Earl of Glasgow* (1864) 2 M 22 at 26.
2   (1876) 2 Ex D 1, CA.
3   [1917] AC 556, HL.

Act of a stranger
25.12   Although difficult to reconcile with the theory of strict liability, it is well established that a defendant is not liable under *Rylands v Fletcher* where the escape is due to the deliberate and unforeseeable intervention of a 'stranger', that is, someone over whom he has no control. This may be some unknown person who blocks up the waste-pipe of a washbasin and leaves the taps running,[1] a trespassing child who drops a lighted match into the petrol tank of a motor vehicle,[2] or even a neighbour who, by emptying his reservoir into the stream which feeds the defendant's reservoir, causes the latter to flood the claimant's land.[3] The defendant is responsible, however, for the acts of his employees, unless they go where they are expressly forbidden[4] and, of course, for his independent contractors.[5] Further, it appears that he may be liable for the actions of anyone lawfully on his land. For example, in *Hale v Jennings Bros*,[6] where a chair flew off a fairground 'chair-o-plane' and injured a stallholder, it was held to be no defence that this was due to tampering by the person who was riding in it.

A defendant is responsible, even for the intervention of a 'stranger', if he ought reasonably to have anticipated the danger and taken steps to prevent the accident. In *Northwestern Utilities Ltd v London Guarantee and Accident Co Ltd*,[7] for example, the claimants' hotel was destroyed by fire after gas escaped from the defendants' mains and exploded. The mains had fractured when support was withdrawn from it during the construction of a sewer. The Privy Council held the defendants liable, for they were aware of the construction work and should have appreciated the very grave danger which this involved.

1   *Rickards v Lothian* [1913] AC 263, PC.
2   *Perry v Kendricks Transport Ltd* [1956] 1 All ER 154, CA.
3   *Box v Jubb* (1879) 4 Ex D 76.
4   *Stevens v Woodward* (1881) 6 QBD 318, DC (employee caused a flood by leaving the taps running in a lavatory which he was not permitted to use).
5   *Rylands v Fletcher* itself.
6   [1938] 1 All ER 579, CA.
7   [1936] AC 108, PC.

Statutory authority
25.13   A person whose activity is authorised by statute is not liable under *Rylands v Fletcher* for any damage which it causes unless he is negligent.[1] Thus in *Pearson v North Western Gas Board*,[2] where an explosion of gas which had escaped from the defendants' mains seriously injured the claimant, killed her husband and destroyed her home, the defendants were not liable, since they had not been negligent.

Whether or not an activity is authorised depends upon the statute in question, and the principles of interpretation used by the courts are similar to those which apply in cases of nuisance.[3] In *Green v Chelsea Waterworks Co*,[4] for example, the defendants were under a statutory duty to maintain a certain pressure of water in their mains, and the statute, unlike many of its kind, did not expressly state that they would be liable for any nuisance caused.[5] When a mains burst, it was held that they were not liable in the absence of negligence. By contrast, in *Charing Cross West End and Electric Supply Co v Hydraulic Power Co*,[6] the defendants merely had a statutory power to carry water in mains, and they were specifically made liable for nuisance. It was held that the statute did not exempt them from strict liability under *Rylands v Fletcher* in respect of a burst main.

1   *Manchester Corpn v Farnworth* [1930] AC 171, HL.
2   [1968] 2 All ER 669.
3   Para 24.17 above.
4   (1894) 70 LT 547, CA.
5   Even if there had been such a provision, the defendants would probably not have been liable: *Department of Transport v North West Water Authority* [1983] 3 All ER 273, HL.
6   [1914] 3 KB 772, CA.

##

25.14   Common law has for centuries imposed a form of strict liability upon anyone from whose property fire is allowed to spread and cause damage,[1] except where this is due to an act of God[2] or the intervention of a 'stranger'. The latter defence covers only those over whom the occupier has no control, so that liability has been imposed upon an occupier for the negligence of an employee who allowed a fire to spread,[3] an independent contractor who used a blowlamp to thaw frozen pipes and set fire to their lagging;[4] another contractor who negligently installed a fireplace in a party wall;[5] an individual tenant of a bedsit in a hostel who dropped a cigarette;[6] and even a golf club guest who dropped a lighted match.[7] In *H and N Emanuel Ltd v Greater London Council*,[8] a demolition contractor, on the defendants' land with their permission, lit a bonfire to burn rubbish; this was known to be his normal practice, although the contract specifically prohibited the lighting of fires on site. When sparks carried to the claimants' property and caused damage, the defendants were held liable.

Actions for the spread of fire are today usually governed by statute. Where this is not so, however, the common law rule still applies. Thus, for example, in *Mansel v Webb*,[9] the defendant was held strictly liable for the escape of sparks from his steam engine on the highway.

1   *Beaulieu v Finglam* (1401) YB 2 Hen 4, fo 18, pl 6.
2   *Turberville v Stamp* (1697) 1 Ld Raym 264.
3   *Musgrove v Pandelis* [1919] 2 KB 43, CA.
4   *Balfour v Barty-King* [1957] 1 All ER 156, CA.
5   *Johnson v BJW Property Developments Ltd* [2002] EWHC 1131 (TCC), [2002] 3 All ER 574.
6   *Ribee v Norrie* [2001] PIQR P8, CA.
7   *Boulcott Golf Club Inc v Engelbrecht* [1945] NZLR 556.
8   [1971] 2 All ER 835, CA.
9   (1918) 88 LJKB 323, CA.

25.15   The Fires Prevention (Metropolis) Act 1774, s 86 provides that no action shall be brought against any person in whose premises, or on whose estate, any fire shall accidentally begin. In view of the way in which this provision (which, in spite of its title, applies throughout the country) has subsequently been interpreted, the extent to which it modifies the common law rule is somewhat uncertain. In *Filliter v Phippard*,[1] 'accidentally' was said to refer only to a fire produced by mere chance or incapable of being traced to any cause. This rules out protection where a fire either begins or spreads through the negligence of the defendant[2] or someone for whom he is responsible, such as an independent contractor;[3] but it seems that a person may avoid liability, even for a fire which he has deliberately lit, provided that there is no negligence. Thus in *Sochacki v Sas*,[4] a lodger who left his room for two or three hours with a fire burning was held not liable when a coal jumped out and set the house alight, since there was no evidence that the fire was too large for the grate. The operation of the statute is also shown by *Collingwood v Home and Colonial Stores Ltd*,[5] in which fire broke out at the defendants' shop as a result of defective electric wiring. In the absence of any negligence on the part of the defendants, they were held not liable.

It should be noted that, even where a fire is caused by an act of God or of a 'stranger', the defendant may still incur liability if, with knowledge of the danger on his land, he fails to take reasonable steps to abate it.[6]

1 (1847) 11 QB 347.
2 *Musgrove v Pandelis* [1919] 2 KB 43, CA.
3 *Johnson v BJW Property Developments Ltd* [2002] EWHC 1131 (TCC), [2002] 3 All ER 574.
4 [1947] 1 All ER 344.
5 [1936] 3 All ER 200, CA.
6 *Goldman v Hargrave* [1966] 2 All ER 989, PC.

25.16 Apart from the special rules outlined above, it is established that either fire itself,[1] or the combustible material on which it feeds,[2] may be treated as a dangerous thing for the purposes of the rule in *Rylands v Fletcher.* This might appear to be of great significance in view of the much-criticised decision of the Court of Appeal, in *Musgrove v Pandelis,*[3] that the Fires Prevention (Metropolis) Act 1774 provides no defence to such an action. In practice, however, the benefits to the plantiff may be more apparent than real. In the first place, either fire[4] or its cause[5] may be held to be a natural use of land, in which case *Rylands v Fletcher* does not apply.[6] Second, where the defendant accumulates materials, it has been held that liability under *Rylands v Fletcher* requires proof both that they were likely to ignite and that the resulting fire was likely to spread.[7] If this is correct, liability in such cases appears no different from ordinary negligence.

1 *Jones v Festiniog Rly Co* (1868) LR 3 QB 733.
2 *Mason v Levy Auto Parts of England Ltd* [1967] 2 All ER 62.
3 [1919] 2 KB 43, CA.
4 *Sochacki v Sas* [1947] 1 All ER 344.
5 *Collingwood v Home and Colonial Stores Ltd* [1936] 3 All ER 200, CA (electric wiring).
6 Para 25.7 above.
7 *Mason v Levy Auto Parts of England Ltd* [1967] 2 All ER 62.

Statutory liability

25.17 One of the features of an industrialised urban society is that a single accident may disastrously affect an enormous number of people. A collapsing slag-heap, an explosion at a chemical plant or a crippled oil tanker, all may cause severe injury and damage over a wide area. In recent years, governments have sought by various statutes to provide for the possibility of certain of these incidents, and the provisions have often included the imposition of some form of strict liability for the consequences. Of special importance in this connection are the Nuclear Installations Act 1965 (injury or damage resulting from the radioactive, toxic, explosive or otherwise hazardous properties of nuclear matter, or from radiations emitted from waste); the Control of Pollution Act 1974 (injury or damage caused by the deposit of poisonous, noxious or polluting waste on land); the Water Act 1981 (escape of water from mains); and the Merchant Shipping Act 1995 (damage caused by the escape or discharge of persistent oil from a ship). The forms of liability, and the defences available, vary from one statute to another, but they may all be regarded as strict, in the sense that the absence of negligence provides no defence.

Chapter 26

Animals

26.1 Unlike other goods, animals have minds and instincts of their own, which may lead them to cause damage in various ways. Not surprisingly, therefore, the common law has for centuries adopted special rules of liability for harm done by animals, in addition to actions which may arise from the application of ordinary tort principles. In 1967, a Law Commission Report on these special rules concluded that the basic forms of strict liability should be retained, although it recommended numerous changes of detail. Most of these changes were put into effect by the Animals Act 1971.

In this chapter we examine the following issues:

- the extent to which the activities of animals may lead to a person becoming liable under the ordinary law of tort;
- the special statutory provisions governing liability for dangerous animals, straying livestock and the worrying of livestock by dogs.

Liability at common law

26.2 Most torts are capable of arising out of the acts of an animal. It is, for example, an undoubted assault and battery to set one's dog on somebody, and there seems no reason why teaching a parrot to repeat slanderous material should not lead to liability in defamation. Of more practical importance, the action of fox hunters in riding across a farmer's land in spite of his protests has been held to constitute trespass[1] and, while direct authority is lacking, the application of *Rylands v Fletcher*[2] to both vegetation and human beings suggests that it could also be used in cases of escaping animals, subject to the question of non-natural user.[3]

1 *Paul v Summerhayes* (1878) 4 QBD 9, DC. See also *League Against Cruel Sports Ltd v Scott* [1985] 2 All ER 489; para 23.1 above.
2 Paras 25.2 to 25.13 above.
3 Para 25.7 above.

Nuisance
26.3 The tort of nuisance is one in which animals frequently play a part. The smell of pigs[1] or the crowing of cockerels[2] may be actionable, while the obstruction of a highway by 24 cows has been held to be a public nuisance.[3] Where there is an invasion of the claimant's

land by numbers of wild animals, such as rats or rabbits, escaping from the defendant's property, liability has traditionally turned upon whether the defendant is in any way responsible for their accumulation.[4] However, it is now clear that a defendant may become liable for a nuisance where, with knowledge of a danger, he fails to take reasonable steps to avert it,[5] and this principle has been applied so as to render the owners of a railway bridge liable in public nuisance, for the fouling of the pavement under it by the large numbers of pigeons roosting there.[6]

1   Aldred's Case (1610) 9 Co Rep 57b.
2   Leeman v Montagu [1936] 2 All ER 1677.
3   Cunningham v Whelan (1917) 52 ILT 67.
4   Farrer v Nelson (1885) 15 QBD 258; cf Seligman v Docker [1948] 2 All ER 887.
5   See para 24.15 above.
6   Wandsworth London Borough Council v Railtrack plc [2001] EWCA Civ 1236, [2002] QB 756.

Negligence

26.4   Damage done by animals, like other kinds of damage, is most likely to give rise to a claim in negligence.[1] There is no doubt that a person in charge of an animal is under a general duty of care to keep it from causing harm, and this can be of great assistance to a claimant who is unable to establish the necessary elements of strict liability under the Animals Act.[2] In Gomberg v Smith,[3] for example, a defendant who took his St Bernard for a walk in the street without a lead was held liable when it collided with and damaged the claimant's van. The dog in that case was merely clumsy, but the same principle may apply to a deliberate attack. For example, in Aldham v United Dairies (London) Ltd,[4] the defendants were held liable in negligence for leaving their pony unattended in the street for so long that it became restive and bit a passer-by. So too, in Draper v Hodder,[5] where a three-year-old child was attacked and seriously injured by a pack of Jack Russell terrier puppies, the defendant, a neighbouring breeder, was held negligent for allowing the dogs (which are known to be dangerous when in a pack) to wander both on his own property and on that of the claimant's family.

In a case of this nature, the claimant must show that there was a foreseeable risk of the type of injury suffered. This requirement proved fatal to two claims by persons injured when using public footpaths across fields. It has been held unforeseeable that a Limousin-cross cow with its calf would charge and butt a walker,[6] or that several horses would surround and push to the ground a person walking with his dog.[7]

There is no strict liability for livestock which stray from the highway,[8] but anyone who brings an animal on to the highway owes a duty of care to adjoining landowners. Thus in Gayler and Pope Ltd v B Davies & Son Ltd,[9] where the defendants left their pony and milk van unattended in the street they were held liable when it bolted and crashed through a draper's shop window. In Tillett v Ward,[10] by contrast, where an ox which was being driven along a street strayed into an ironmonger's shop, the defendant was found to have taken all reasonable care and was therefore not liable.

The old common law rule, that an occupier of land could not be held liable in negligence for failing to prevent domestic animals from straying on to the highway, was abolished by the s 8(1) of the Animals Act 1971. However, it is provided by s 8(2) that a person is not to be regarded as negligent by reason only of placing animals on unfenced land if:

• the land is common land; or
• it is situated in an area where fencing is not customary; or
• it is a town or village green;

and he has a right (which includes permission from someone else who has a right[11]) to place the animals on that land.

This is not a return to the old immunity since, even in these areas, road and traffic conditions may be such that it is negligent to allow one's animals to stray.

1   An attack by an animal on a visitor to premises might also found a claim under the Occupier's Liability Act 1957: see *Hill v Lovett* 1992 SLT 994.
2   Para 26.7 below.
3   [1962] 1 All ER 725, CA.
4   [1939] 4 All ER 522, CA.
5   [1972] 2 All ER 210, CA.
6   *Ostle v Stapleton* [1996] CLY 4443.
7   *Miller v Duggan* [1996] CLY 4444.
8   Para 26.9 below.
9   [1924] 2 KB 75.
10   (1882) 10 QBD 17.
11   *Davies v Davies* [1975] QB 172, [1974] 3 All ER 817, CA.

Animals Act 1971

Dangerous animals
Classification of species
26.5   The Animals Act 1971, like the rules of common law which it replaced, makes the keeper of a dangerous animal strictly liable for all the damage it causes. The Act also follows the common law in treating two different kinds of animal as 'dangerous' for this purpose. First, certain species (lions, tigers etc) are regarded as so obviously dangerous that all their members automatically attract strict liability. Second, members of other less dangerous species may attract strict liability as individuals by exhibiting dangerous tendencies, but only when their keepers are aware of these tendencies.

The classification of species is thus clearly of prime importance, and this is dealt with by s 6(2), which provides that a dangerous species is a species:[1]

*   which is not commonly domesticated in the British Islands; and
*   whose fully grown animals normally have such characteristics that they are likely, unless restrained, to cause severe damage or that any damage they may cause is likely to be severe.

The wording of this definition seems apt to include both animals which are normally fierce, such as bears, tigers and gorillas, and animals which, though normally docile, are likely to cause severe damage if they cause damage at all. An elephant, for instance, is unlikely to cause damage, but its sheer bulk makes it dangerous on the occasions when it does get out of control. It also appears that a species may be classified as dangerous on account of the threat which it poses to property; this could even include, for example, rabbits, squirrels and Colorado beetles, provided that the damage which they are likely to cause can be described as severe.

It is important to appreciate that, once a species is classified as dangerous, no allowance is made for the amiable nature of a particular individual. A circus elephant may be as tame as a cow and, because of its training, much easier to control; nevertheless, since the species satisfies s 6(2), the individual is dangerous in law.[2]

A species which does not satisfy the statutory definition contained in s 6(2) is automatically a non-dangerous species.

1   This includes sub-species and variety: s 11.
2   *Behrens v Bertram Mills Circus Ltd* [1957] 1 All ER 583.

Dangerous species

26.6 Section 2(1) provides that where any damage is caused by an animal which belongs to a dangerous species, any person who is a keeper of the animal is liable for the damage, except as otherwise provided by the Act. This wide form of strict liability is not limited to damage which results from the animal's dangerous characteristics, since it also includes, for example, injuries caused by the blunderings of a frightened elephant, or a disease transmitted by an infected rat. So too, a person who suffers nervous shock on being faced by an escaped tiger, or who falls and breaks his leg in running away from it, can recover damages under this provision. It has even been held applicable to someone falling from a swaying camel, although the claimant's claim under s 2(1) failed on the ground that she had voluntarily assumed the risk.[1]

Liability under s 2 is imposed upon the animal's keeper, defined in s 6(3) as someone who 'owns the animal or has it in his possession; or is the head of a household of which a member under the age of 16 owns the animal or has it in his possession'. That subsection further provides that a person who loses the ownership or possession of an animal continues to be its 'keeper' unless and until someone else fulfils the definition. Thus, if a person's pet fox escapes and reverts to the wild, he remains responsible for its activities. Where, however, a person takes possession of an animal merely to prevent it from causing damage or to return it to its owner, he does not thereby become its 'keeper'.[2]

1   *Tutin v Mary Chipperfield Promotions Ltd* (1980) 130 NLJ 807. The claimant recovered damages on the ground of negligence.
2   Section 6(4).

Non-dangerous species

26.7 The strict liability which attaches to dangerous species also encompasses other individual animals with known dangerous characteristics, although in such a case the keeper is liable, not for all the damage done, but only for that which results from those dangerous characteristics. This is laid down by s 2(2), which provides that where damage is caused by an animal which does not belong to a dangerous species, a keeper of the animal is liable for the damage, except as otherwise provided by the Act, if:

- the damage is of a kind which the animal, unless restrained, was likely to cause or which, if caused by the animal, was likely to be severe; and
- the likelihood of the damage or of its being severe was due to characteristics of the animal which are not normally found in animals of the same species (ie the particular breed of dog, rather than dogs generally[1]) or are not normally so found except at particular times or in particular circumstances; and
- those characteristics were known to the keeper or were at any time known to a person who at that time had charge of the animal as the keeper's servant or, where the keeper was the head of a household, were known to another keeper of the animal who was a member of that household and under the age of 16.

The essence of this provision is that strict liability is imposed on the keeper of an animal where he, or someone for whom he is responsible, knows of some abnormal (ie not common to the species as a whole) characteristic which renders the animal dangerous. This abnormality (which applies to nervous unpredictable animals as well as vicious ones[2]) may be permanent or periodic, such as the tendency of certain breeds of dog to show unusual aggression when defending their territory,[3] that of a bitch to be aggressive towards humans when she has pups,[4] or that of horses to panic and bolt into vehicles if they are frightened into escaping from their field on to the highway.[5] It may also be noted that the damage for which the keeper is liable may extend beyond the direct results of an attack; thus a person injured in a fall when his dog is attacked by the defendant's dog may recover damages under s 2(2), provided of course that the requirements of that provision are satisfied.[6] However, where horses were maliciously released from their field by an unidentified trespasser, their owner was held not liable for a traffic accident, since this was caused by the mere presence of the horses in the road rather than by any 'abnormal characteristic' which they possessed.[7] Moreover, it has been held than an Alsatian trained by the police to attack in certain circumstances does not then have an abnormal characteristic; its characteristic is its ability to respond to training, and this is common to the breed in general.[8]

A keeper is only liable under s 2(2) where he, or certain of his family or his employees, knows that the animal in question is dangerous.[9] Such knowledge is usually gained as the result of a previous attack, but this is not the only possibility. For example, in *Worth v Gilling*[10] it was sufficient that the defendant's dog habitually ran at passers-by to the limit of its chain, barking and trying to bite them. A horse's tendency to bite other horses, however, is not necessarily evidence that it is dangerous to people.[11]

Where the conditions of s 2(2) are satisfied, reasonable care is no defence; the defendant keeps the animal at his peril. The question of negligence may, however, be highly relevant in cases where, for some reason, s 2(2) does not apply.[12]

1   *Hunt v Wallis* [1994] PIQR P128.
2   *Wallace v Newton* [1982] 2 All ER 106.
3   *Curtis v Betts* [1990] 1 All ER 769, CA.
4   See *Barnes v Lucille Ltd* (1907) 96 LT 680.
5   *Mirvahedy v Henley* [2001] EWCA Civ 1749, [2002] QB 769.
6   *Smith v Ainger* (1990) Times, 5 June, CA.
7   *Jaundrill v Gillett* (1996) Times, 30 January, CA. Cf *Mirvahedy v Henley* [2001] EWCA Civ 1749, [2002] QB 769, where the horses panicked and bolted into the claimant's vehicle.
8   *Gloster v Chief Constable of Greater Manchester* [2000] PIQR P114, CA.
9   Where an animal has more than one 'keeper', there is no reason why one should not be liable to the other: *Flack v Hudson* [2001] QB 698, CA.
10   (1866) LR 2 CP 1.
11   *Glanville v Sutton & Co Ltd* [1928] 1 KB 571.
12   See *Draper v Hodder* [1972] 2 All ER 210, CA; para 26.4 above.

Defences
26.8   Liability under s 2 in respect of both dangerous and non-dangerous species is strict (ie independent of negligence). However, the liability is not absolute, since the Act expressly recognises four possible defences:

- Section 5(1) provides that a claimant cannot claim in respect of any damage which is due wholly to his own fault, as where he provokes a fierce dog, or reaches into a leopard's cage.
- A claimant who is partly responsible for his own injuries may suffer a reduction of his damages on the ground of contributory negligence.[1]
- The defence of assumption of risk[2] is made applicable to actions under s 2 by s 5(2). The scope of this defence is, however, restricted by s 6(5), which provides that a keeper's employee is not to be treated as voluntarily accepting any risk which is incidental to his employment.
- Section 5(3) lays down special rules for injured trespassers by providing that, where damage is caused by 'an animal kept on any premises or structure to a person trespassing there', the keeper is not liable under s 2 provided either that the animal was not kept there for the protection of persons or property or that, if it was so kept, it was reasonable to keep it there. Thus, a trespasser injured by an animal in a zoo or a safari park would probably not succeed in a claim under s 2,[3] for the animal would not be kept for protection. As to animals which it is reasonable to keep for protection, this is in practice most likely to apply to dogs. The Guard Dogs Act 1975, which makes it a criminal offence to have a guard dog on premises unless it is either

secured or under the control of a handler, does not give rise to civil liability. However, it is thought that a court would regard someone as unreasonable for the purpose of the Animals Act 1971, s 5(3) if he kept a dog in circumstances which contravened the Guard Dogs Act.

All the defences mentioned above were considered in the case of *Cummings v Granger*[4] where an untrained alsatian, kept by the defendant to guard his scrapyard, attacked the claimant who, despite seeing a large 'Beware of the Dog' notice and knowing that the dog was there, entered the yard as a trespasser. The trial judge held that keeping the dog in these circumstances was unreasonable and that the defendant was accordingly liable, although he reduced the claimant's damages on the ground of contributory negligence. The Court of Appeal, however, held that keeping the dog was reasonable[5] and that the claimant had in any case voluntarily accepted the risk of injury.

1 Section 10; paras 20.11–20.16 above.
2 Paras 20.2–20.10 above.
3 An action might nevertheless lie under the Occupiers' Liability Act 1984; paras 22.21–22.24 above.
4 [1977] 1 All ER 104, CA.
5 These events preceded the coming into force of the Guard Dogs Act 1975.

Straying livestock

26.9 Section 4(1) of the Act provides that where livestock belonging to any person strays on to land in the ownership or occupation of another and:

• damage is done by the livestock to the land or to any property on it which is in the ownership or possession of the other person; or
• any expenses are reasonably incurred by that other person in keeping the livestock while it cannot be restored to the person to whom it belongs or while it is detained in pursuance of s 7 of the Act, or in ascertaining to whom it belongs;

the person to whom the livestock belongs is liable for the damage or expenses, except as otherwise provided by the Act.

For the purpose of this provision, s 11 defines 'livestock' as 'cattle, horses, asses, mules, hinnies, sheep, pigs, goats and poultry [which means the domestic varieties of fowls, turkeys, geese, ducks, guinea-fowls, pigeons, peacocks and quails], and also deer not in the wild state'.

The right of action under s 4, which protects both owners and occupiers of land, but which imposes liability only upon a possessor of livestock, covers not only damage to the claimant's land and crops, but also damage to his goods, including other animals. As a result, the claimant is entitled to damages, not only where his own animals are attacked, but also for other consequences such as infection[1] or the serving of a thoroughbred heifer by a bull of low birth.[2]

Where livestock stray on to the highway, it seems that the owner or occupier of the land across which the highway passes may claim under s 4(3).[3] A mere user of the highway, however, has no such right and must, in order to recover damages (eg where straying livestock cause a road accident), establish negligence.[4] Further, where livestock which are lawfully on the highway[5] stray from it, liability again depends on negligence; s 4 is expressly excluded.[6]

1 *Theyer v Purnell* [1918] 2 KB 333.
2 *McLean v Brett* (1919) 49 DLR 162.
3 *Durrant v Child* (1611) 1 Bulst 157.
4 See Animals Act 1971, s 8; para 26.4 above.
5 But not those which have strayed on to it: *Matthews v Wicks* (1987) Times, 25 May, CA.
6 Section 5(5).

Defences

26.10 Liability under s 4 is strict, but certain defences are recognised by the Act. A claimant will fail altogether in his claim if the damage he suffers is wholly due to his own fault;[1] if it is partly due to his fault, his damages may be reduced on the ground of contributory negligence.[2]

The question of duties to fence is dealt with by s 5(6), which provides that a mere failure on the claimant's part to fence out the defendant's livestock does not amount to 'fault' on his part. However, the section goes on to provide that a defendant is nonetheless not liable where it is proved that the straying of the livestock on to the land would not have occurred but for a breach by any other person, being a person having an interest in the land, of a duty to fence. This, it should be noted, is not limited to the obvious case of the claimant who owes a fencing obligation to the defendant, since it also provides a defence where the claimant owes a legal duty to a third party, or where the duty is owed by a third party with an interest in the claimant's land, such as his landlord.

The defences of act of God, intervention by a 'stranger' and assumption of risk, all of which previously applied at common law, are not available in an action under s 4.

1 Section 5(1).
2 Section 10; paras 20.11–20.16 above.

Detention and sale

26.11 Section 7 of the Act provides that an occupier may detain any livestock which strays on to his land and which is not under anyone's control, provided he gives notice within 48 hours to the police and to the possessor of the livestock, if known. He must also treat the livestock with reasonable care, which includes feeding and watering it. The person entitled to possession of the livestock may demand its return but, if the detainor has a claim under s 4 for damage done by straying cattle, or for expenses incurred, this must first be met. It has been held that a local authority on to whose land animals frequently strayed was justified in making standard charges to cover its costs, rather than working out the exact expense caused by each stray.[1]

Once livestock has been lawfully detained for 14 days, then, provided neither party has commenced legal proceedings, the detainor may sell it at a market or by public auction and keep the amount of his claim under s 4 out of the net proceeds of sale.

1 *Morris v Blaenau Gwent District Council* (1982) 80 LGR 793, CA.

Dogs worrying livestock
Liability for dogs

26.12 The worrying of livestock by dogs has long been a special problem and the Animals Act 1971, s 3, which deals with this, merely repeats with some modifications the rules laid down by earlier statutes. Section 3 provides that, where a dog causes damage by killing or injuring livestock, any person who is a keeper of the dog is liable for the damage, except as otherwise provided by the Act. For this purpose, 'livestock' includes the same animals as for the purpose of s 4,[1] but also includes pheasants, partridges and grouse in captivity; the meaning of 'keeper' is the same as it is under s 2.[2]

As with the other forms of strict liability under the Act, a claimant's claim may fail wholly under s 5(1),[3] where his loss results entirely from his own fault, or partly under the doctrine of contributory negligence. Section 5(4) also provides a defence where the attack takes place on land to which the livestock have strayed, so long as the presence of the dog there is authorised.

1 Para 26.9 above.
2 Para 26.6 above.
3 Para 26.8 above.

Protection of livestock

26.13   At common law, a person whose animals were under attack from another animal could in certain circumstances act immediately in the defence of his property, even if this involved killing or injuring the attacker. The common law rules on this matter, which were laid down in the case of *Cresswell v Sirl*,[1] apply to all kinds of animal, provided only that the latter belong to the person acting in their defence; there is therefore no right to shoot a dog which is attacking wild animals on the defendant's land.[2]

The common law rules remain in force but, in relation to a somewhat narrower area, namely the worrying[3] of livestock by dogs, the Animals Act 1971, s 9 confers even greater protection upon a person who takes matters into his own hands. According to this provision, it is a defence to an action for killing or injuring a dog that the defendant was entitled to act for the protection of livestock, that he did so act and that, within 48 hours of the incident, he notified the police.

A person is entitled to act for the protection of livestock if and only if either the livestock or the land on which it is belongs to him, or if he is acting with the authority of such a person. However, if the circumstances in which a dog attacks livestock are such that the dog's keeper would have a defence under s 5(4),[4] then s 9 does not permit anyone to act for the protection of the livestock by killing or injuring the dog. The conditions under which the defendant may otherwise act are clearly stated by s 9, with the proviso that the defendant is protected if he reasonably believes them to be satisfied. These conditions are that either:

- the dog is worrying or is about to worry the livestock and there are no other reasonable means of ending or preventing the worrying; or
- the dog has been worrying livestock, has not left the vicinity and is not under the control of any person and there are no practicable means of ascertaining to whom it belongs.

1   [1947] 2 All ER 730, CA.
2   *Gott v Measures* [1947] 2 All ER 609, DC.
3   This probably includes not only an actual attack, but also chasing in such a way as is likely to cause injury.
4   Para 26.12 above.

Chapter 27

Vicarious liability

27.1 Vicarious liability arises when X is made answerable for a tort committed by Y, on the grounds that:

- there is a particular relationship between X and Y; and
- the tort is in some way connected to that relationship.

The only relationship which routinely gives rise to vicarious liability is that of employer and employee. Relationships of principal and agent[1] and between partners[2] may also create vicarious liability in limited circumstances. However, a superior employee is not vicariously liable for the torts of his subordinate,[3] nor a parent for those of his child.

1   Paras 27.18–27.20 below.
2   For torts committed 'in the ordinary course of the business of the firm': Partnership Act 1890, s 10.
3   *Stone v Cartwright* (1795) 6 Term Rep 411.

27.2   In this chapter we examine the following issues:

- how the law defines the relationship of employer and employee for the purposes of vicarious liability;
- the scope of an employer's liability for the torts of his employee;
- the extent to which the employer may be held liable for prohibited acts or deliberate misconduct;
- the limited form of vicarious liability which exists between principal and agent;
- the extent to which damage caused by an independent contractor may result in liability for the client.

27.3   Quite apart from the doctrine of vicarious liability, there are other circumstances in which X may be responsible in tort for damage caused by Y:

- where X specifically authorises or incites Y to commit a tort;
- where Y without authority purports to act on behalf of X, and X, with full knowledge of all material facts, ratifies or accepts what Y has done;
- where X asks Y (who is not his employee) to carry out some task, but is then personally guilty of negligence in selecting, instructing or supervising Y;
- where X is under a duty of care to control Y.[1]

1   Paras 17.13-17.14 above.

Employer and employee

27.4   As we have already seen, the relationship of employer and employee is the only one to which the law attaches a general principle of vicarious liability. It may be said that an employer is responsible for any tort which is committed by his employee in the course of his employment. This raises two questions, which we consider below:

*   who is an employee? and
*   what is the course of employment?

Who is an employee?

27.5   Since an employer is not usually responsible for the torts of an independent contractor to whom he entrusts work, it is obvious that the distinction between an employee and an independent contractor is of paramount importance. The wording of the contract under which someone is working is relevant, but it is not decisive; if the court decides that the relationship as a whole falls into one category, it will be treated as such, notwithstanding that the parties have called it by another name. Thus, for example, in *Ferguson v John Dawson & Partners (Contractors) Ltd*,[1] where a building worker was expressly described as a 'labour only sub-contractor', a majority of the Court of Appeal held that the relationship between the parties was in reality that of employer and employee.

It is worth stating that, while the formulation of a precise yet simple test for distinguishing employees from independent contractors has caused serious problems, it is not usually difficult to see on which side of the line a particular case falls. As Lord Denning has said,[2] it is often easy to recognise a contract of service when you see it, but difficult to say wherein the distinction lies. A ship's master, a chauffeur and a reporter on the staff of a newspaper are all employed under a contract of service; but a ship's pilot, a taxi driver, and a newspaper contributor are employed under a contract for services.

Of the many attempts made by judges and writers to lay down some criteria by which a contract of service may be recognised, one of the best known is that of Lord Thankerton to *Short v J and W Henderson Ltd*:[4]

*   the employer's power of selection of his employee;
*   the payment of wages or other remuneration;
*   the employer's right to control the method of doing the work; and
*   the employer's right of suspension and dismissal.

It should always be borne in mind, however, not only that this list is far from exhaustive (one writer has identified no fewer than 15 relevant factors), but also that the feature which is in one case decisive may in the next be overwhelmed by other features which point to the opposite conclusion.

1   [1976] 3 All ER 817, CA.
2   *Stevenson, Jordan and Harrison Ltd v Macdonald and Evans* [1952] 1 TLR 101 at 111.
3   (1946) 62 TLR 427 at 429.

Control and other criteria

27.6   There is no simple test by which employees and independent contractors may be distinguished. It used at one time to be thought that the crucial factor was the degree of control which the employer was entitled to exercise over each category. An independent contractor, it was said, could be told only what he was to do, whereas an employee was also subject to the command of his employer as to the *manner* in which he should do his work.[1] However, modern conditions, especially the widespread employment by corporations of highly skilled and qualified personnel, have shown up the inadequacy of this test. For example, it cannot be doubted that a ship's captain works under a contract of service, but it would be ludicrous to suggest that his employers are in a position to tell him exactly how to do his job.

If control alone cannot be regarded as decisive, the same applies even more strongly to the other criteria mentioned above. The employer's rights of appointment and dismissal, which were regarded as characteristic of a contract of service in *Short v Henderson*, seem equally applicable to independent contractors, while the type of remuneration paid, although helpful, is far from conclusive.

1   *Yewens v Noakes* (1880) 6 QBD 530 at 532.

Function of employee

27.7   It has been suggested that, instead of looking at the individual rights and duties which make up a contract of service or one for services, the courts should consider the *function* of the particular worker.[1] It is argued that, under a contract of service, a man is employed as part of a business, and his work is done as an integral part of the business; whereas, under a contract for services, his work, although done for the business, is not integrated into it but is only accessory to it. This 'organisation' test certainly serves to explain a number of cases in which a contract of service has been held to exist despite the lack of any real control by the employer, especially those in which, contrary to earlier authority, hospitals were held liable for the negligence of highly qualified staff.[2] However, in marginal cases, it seems merely to replace one difficult question: 'Is the person an employee?' with another: 'Is he part of the employer's organisation?'

Concentration upon the actual work which is done by a particular individual should not be allowed to obscure the fact that vicarious liability depends upon the existence of a contract of service. In *Watkins v Birmingham City Council*,[3] where a schoolteacher was injured due to the negligence of a 10-year-old milk monitor, the trial judge held the local authority vicariously liable on the ground that the boy was doing a job which would otherwise have been done by a paid employee. However, the Court of Appeal reversed this decision, holding that the boy was delivering the milk as a pupil and not as an employee.

1   *Stevenson, Jordan and Harrison Ltd v Macdonald and Evans* [1952] 1 TLR 101 at 111.
2   *Cassidy v Ministry of Health* [1951] 1 All ER 574, CA.
3   (1975) 126 NLJ 442, CA; para 18.6 above.

'Business' test

27.8   In a number of cases, the courts have adopted a slightly different approach to this problem, by considering whether it may fairly be said that the worker is in business on his own account.[1] Although this has links with the function test described above, it seems that the courts are concerned, not so much with the nature of the work done, but more with such questions as whether the person works on his own premises or with his own equipment, whether he hires his own helpers and can delegate the task to them, whether he works for a number of employers, what degree of financial risk he takes, what degree of responsibility he has for investment and management, and to what extent, if at all, he has an opportunity to profit from his own sound management.

Many of these factors were considered in *Ready-Mixed Concrete (South-East) Ltd v Minister of Pension and National Insurance*[2] a case concerning the drivers of lorries designed for the delivery of concrete. The drivers bought their own vehicles, although they could not alter or sell them without the company's consent, and they were obliged to maintain them and to use them exclusively for the company. The company was responsible for obtaining orders and supplying concrete, and it paid the drivers a rate based on mileage. After a thorough review of the authorities, MacKenna J held that the drivers were not employees of the company, but independent contractors, so that the company was not responsible for the payment of their national insurance contributions.

1   *Market Investigations Ltd v Minister of Social Security* [1968] 3 All ER 732.
2   [1968] 1 All ER 433.

Borrowed employees

27.9   A particular problem may arise in cases where an individual employee is lent (or, more commonly, hired) by his general employer to a third party. If the employee commits a tort while working for the third party, the question is where the burden of vicarious liability is to fall. It might have been thought that both employers should be liable, but the law insists that the responsibility falls upon one alone.

In *Mersey Docks and Harbour Board v Coggins and Griffith (Liverpool) Ltd*,[1] a mobile crane, complete with its driver, was hired by the harbour board to a firm of stevedores. The driver was paid by the board but, for the period of hire, was subject to the detailed control of the stevedores. When the driver negligently injured a third party, the House of Lords held that vicarious responsibility must rest with the harbour board; this primary liability could, it was said, be transferred in an appropriate case, but the burden of proof upon a general employer would be a heavy one. This heavy burden is perhaps most likely to be satisfied in cases where the employee in question is an unskilled labourer, since it is then more realistic to treat control as having been passed on.

Where the contract of hire provides that any vicarious liability shall attach to the special employer, this cannot operate so as to deprive an injured third party of his rights against the general employer; its effect is merely to govern the position of the two employers.[2] Even to this extent, the provision may be subject to the test of reasonableness under the Unfair Contract Terms Act 1977.[3]

1   [1946] 2 All ER 345, HL.
2   *White (Contractors) Ltd v Tarmac Civil Engineering Ltd* [1967] 3 All ER 586, HL.
3   See *Phillips Products Ltd v Hyland* [1987] 2 All ER 620, CA; *Thompson v T Lohan (Plant Hire) Ltd* [1987] 2 All ER 631, CA; paras 9.15, 9.18 and 9.24 above.

What is the course of employment?

27.10   An employer is not liable for every tort committed by an employee. However, the employer's liability is not restricted to torts which he has specifically authorised the employee to commit. The rule is that, for an employer to be liable, the employee must be shown to have committed the tort in the course of his employment. As to what is meant by this expression, the test which has often been judicially approved explains that an employer, as opposed to the client of an independent contractor, is liable even for acts which he has not authorised, provided they are so connected with acts which he has authorised that they may rightly be regarded as modes – although improper modes – of doing them. In other words, an employer is responsible not merely for what he authorises his employee to do, but also for the way in which the employee chooses to do it. On the other hand, if the unauthorised and wrongful act of the employee is not so connected with the authorised act as to be a mode of doing it, but is an independent act, the employer is not responsible: for in such a case the employee is not acting in the course of his employment, but has gone outside it.

Authorised acts

27.11   The idea that an unauthorised act may found vicarious liability if it can be treated as a mode of performing an authorised act means that a court, in seeking to determine the scope of an employee's employment, must first discover what acts are authorised and then consider what, if any, connection exists between an authorised act and the tort in question. The decision of the House of Lords in *Century Insurance Co Ltd v Northern Ireland*

Road Transport Board[1] provides a good illustration of this approach in operation. The employee in that case was the driver of a petrol tanker who, while delivering petrol to a garage, lit a cigarette and dropped the match. The driver's employers sought to avoid liability for the resulting fire by claiming that they did not employ men to smoke. Not surprisingly, this argument was rejected for, given that the driver was specifically authorised to deliver petrol, it would be difficult to think of a more negligent mode of doing so. By contrast, in *General Engineering Services Ltd v Kingston and St Andrew Corpn*,[2] where firemen operating a 'go slow' policy in support of a pay claim took 17 minutes to reach a fire instead of the normal 3 or 4 minutes, it was held that their conduct was outside the course of their employment. Their employers, the local authority responsible for the fire brigade, were thus not liable to the owners of property destroyed by the fire.

The need to find an authorised act, with which the unauthorised tort can be linked, may be illustrated by cases in which a vehicle owned by the employer is driven by an employee who has no specific authority to do so. In *Beard v London General Omnibus Co*,[3] where a conductor took it upon himself to turn a bus round for its return journey, it was held that his negligent driving which caused an accident was outside the scope of his employment, since he was not permitted to drive. His employers were therefore not vicariously liable. In *Ilkiw v Samuels*,[4] on the other hand, where a lorry driver allowed an incompetent person to drive it, it was held that the *lorry driver's* negligence fell within the course of his employment, for his job involved taking care of the vehicle. As a result, the lorry driver's employers were liable to a person injured in the ensuing accident.

1   [1942] 1 All ER 491, HL.
2   [1988] 3 All ER 867, PC.
3   [1900] 2 QB 530, CA.
4   [1963] 2 All ER 879, CA.

Implied authority

27.12   In considering exactly what acts of an employee may be regarded as authorised, it is important to realise that an employer's permission may be implied rather than express. To take a simple example, a person at work has implied authority to use lavatories, washbasins and so on. If he negligently leaves a tap running and thereby floods adjoining premises, his employer will be vicariously liable; he cannot argue that the employee was not in the course of his employment because he was not actually working at the time.[1] For example, in *Harvey v RG O'Dell Ltd*,[2] an employee sent out on an all-day job was held to be within the course of his employment when riding his motor-cycle into a neighbouring town to have lunch.

As far as travel to and from one's place of work is concerned, the course of employment will normally include those parts of the journey which take place on the employer's premises[3] and also journeys off the premises which are undertaken on the employer's business and in the employer's time.[4] However, ordinary commuting journeys are excluded, so that in *Nottingham v Aldridge*,[5] for example, an apprentice was held to be outside the scope of his employment while driving to a GPO training establishment after a weekend at home, even though, by giving a lift to a fellow-apprentice, he qualified for a mileage allowance from his employers. Occasionally, this distinction is not maintained. In *Harrison v British Railways Board*,[6] for example, a station foreman who attempted to board a moving train in order to leave work before his shift officially ended was held not be acting within the course of his employment.

1   *Ruddiman & Co v Smith* (1889) 60 LT 708, DC.
2   [1958] 2 QB 78, [1958] 1 All ER 657.
3   *Staton v National Coal Board* [1957] 2 All ER 667.
4   *Smith v Stages* [1989] 1 All ER 833, HL.
5   [1971] 2 All ER 751.
6   [1981] 3 All ER 679.

Ostensible authority

27.13   In certain circumstances an employer may incur vicarious liability where he had not expressly or even impliedly authorised his employee to commit a particular act. This is where the employer has given third parties the impression that the employee is authorised, and a third party relies upon this appearance of authority. In such circumstances the employer will in effect be estopped (prevented) from denying that authority exists. As a result, liability for a tort of the employee may be attributed to the employer, notwithstanding that it was committed purely for the employee's own benefit, or that it had been specifically prohibited by the employer.

The leading case on the subject of ostensible authority is *Lloyd v Grace, Smith & Co,*[1] in which the claimant, a widow, sought advice from a firm of solicitors about certain property which she had inherited. She dealt entirely with the solicitors' managing clerk, who fraudulently induced her to sign documents which transferred the property to him. The clerk then misappropriated it. It was held by the House of Lords that the solicitors were responsible for this fraud; having permitted their employee to deal unsupervised with clients, they were liable for any tort which he might commit in what appeared to be the course of his employment.

1   [1912] AC 716, HL.

Prohibitions

27.14   Where an employee commits a tort by doing something which the employer has forbidden, one might instinctively feel that the employer should never be held vicariously liable. However, the true legal position is more complex, turning on the question whether the employer has prohibited the act itself (in which case the employee cannot be within the course of his employment when performing it) or whether he has merely prohibited a particular mode of carrying it out. As was stated by Lord Dunedin, in *Plumb v Cobden Flour Mills Co Ltd,*[1] 'There are prohibitions which limit the sphere of employment, and prohibitions which only deal with conduct within the sphere of employment.'

Recognition that an employer may be legally responsible, even for conduct of his employee which he has banned, came as long ago as 1862, in the leading case of *Limpus v London General Omnibus Co.*[2] There, a bus driver, in attempting to obstruct a bus belonging to a rival company (a practice which his employers had expressly forbidden), caused an accident. Notwithstanding the prohibition, the employers were held vicariously liable, since the driver's negligence was undeniably committed in the course of performing an authorised act, namely, driving the bus. By contrast, where the prohibition is such as to remove all authority from the employee, he cannot then be said to act within the course of his employment. In *Kooragang Investment Pty Ltd v Richardson and Wrench Ltd,*[3] for example, a staff valuer was held to have gone outside the course of his employment in carrying out valuations for a client whom his employers had blacklisted. Likewise, in *Stevens v Woodward,*[4] an employee entered a washroom on the employer's premises, which he was not permitted to use, and, by leaving a tap running, caused a flood. The employer was held not liable because, if the employee's very presence in the washroom was forbidden, there was no authorised act in the course of which his tort could be committed. The effect of the prohibition in this case was to prevent any implication of authority.[5] However, it should be noted that ostensible authority cannot be removed by a prohibition unless the third party is aware of it.

The difference between prohibiting a class of acts, and prohibiting a mode of carrying out permitted acts, depends upon how precisely a court defines the scope of the employee's employment in the first place, and the modern tendency is to adopt a fairly liberal approach. In *LCC v Cattermoles (Garages) Ltd,*[6] for example, a garage hand was expressly forbidden to drive customers' vehicles, although he was allowed, and indeed expected, to push them around the premises. When he drove a customer's car and caused an accident, his employers argued that he was acting outside the course of his employment. The Court of Appeal, however, held the employers vicariously liable, on the grounds that their employee was authorised to move cars; the prohibition applied only to the method which he used.

1   [1914] AC 62 at 67.
2   (1862) 1 H & C 526.
3   [1981] 3 All ER 65, PC.
4   (1881) 6 QBD 318, DC.
5   Cf *Ruddiman & Co v Smith* (1889) 60 LT 708, DC, para 27.12 above.
6   [1953] 2 All ER 582, CA.

27.15   Particular problems have been raised by cases in which a driver has negligently injured someone to whom he has given a lift contrary to his employer's instructions. Clearly the invitation is unauthorised, but the injury is actually caused by negligent driving, which is precisely what the man is employed to do. In *Twine v Bean's Express Ltd*,[1] the Court of Appeal held the employer not liable since, while the employee could be regarded as within the course of his employment vis-à-vis other road users, he must be treated as outside it vis-à-vis his unauthorised passenger. Once again, however, the modern approach seems to be a rather broader one. In *Rose v Plenty*,[2] a milk roundsman took a young boy on the float to help with deliveries, strictly against the instructions of his employers. When, due to the milkman's negligent driving, the boy was injured, a majority of the Court of Appeal held the employers liable on the ground that, in taking him on, the employee was doing in an unauthorised way what he was authorised to do, namely, deliver the milk.

1   (1946) 175 LT 131, CA.
2   [1976] 1 All ER 97, CA.

Intentional wrongdoing
27.16   An intentional wrong may be held to fall within the course of an employee's employment, provided that the employee can be said to be doing wrongfully what he is employed to do lawfully. Thus, in *Moore v Metropolitan Rly Co*,[1] where a railway official arrested the claimant in the mistaken belief that he had not paid his fare, the railway company were held liable. In *Abrahams v Deakin*,[2] on the other hand, it was held that a barman had no implied authority to give someone into custody on a mistaken charge of attempting to pass bad money. In taking this step, the barman was not protecting the interests of his employer, for the attempt to defraud him had failed; he was rather furthering the course of justice.

A similar distinction can be found in cases of assaults committed by employees. There may well be vicarious liability in respect of excessive corporal punishment administered by a schoolteacher;[3] a blow given by a driver to a boy whom he suspects of stealing sugar from a cart;[4] an over-zealous ejection of a troublemaker by a dance-hall doorman;[5] or an assault by a railway ticket inspector suspicious that a passenger was travelling without a ticket.[6] On the other hand, the short-tempered petrol pump attendant[7] or bus conductor[8] who strikes a customer in the course of an argument will not normally render his employer responsible, even where the original cause of the dispute is connected with the employer's business.

The most difficult cases are those in which the employee has quite clearly acted (usually dishonestly) for his own benefit. While such conduct will normally be held to fall outside the scope of employment,[9] we have already seen from the case of *Lloyd v Grace, Smith & Co*,[10] that it will not always do so. Indeed, the *Lloyd* principle has been applied to torts other than deceit. In *Morris v C W Martin & Sons Ltd*,[11] the defendants, a firm of specialist cleaners, entrusted the claimant's mink coat to one of their employees. Instead of cleaning the garment, the employee stole it, and the defendants were held liable for this act of conversion. However, it should be noted that, had a third party or even another employee been guilty of the theft, the defendants would not have been liable; only in relation to the employee to whom the coat had actually been entrusted could it be said that he had done wrongfully what he was employed to do. Similar reasoning led to the imposition of vicarious liability in such cases as *Photo Production Ltd v Securicor Transport Ltd*,[12] where a patrolman employed by the defendants deliberately started a fire in one of the factories which it was his duty to visit, and *Lister v Hesley Hall Ltd*,[13] where the warden of a residential home was guilty of sexually abusing children in his care.

1   (1872) LR 8 QB 36.
2   [1891] 1 QB 516, CA.
3   *Ryan v Fildes* [1938] 3 All ER 517.
4   *Poland v John Parr & Sons* [1927] 1 KB 236, CA.
5   *Daniels v Whetstone Entertainments Ltd* [1962] 2 Lloyd's Rep 1, CA; *Vasey v Surrey Free Inns* [1996] PIQR P373, CA.
6   *Fennelly v Connex Southeastern Ltd* [2001] IRLR 390, CA.
7   *Warren v Henlys Ltd* [1948] 2 All ER 935.
8   *Keppel Bus Co Ltd v Sa'ad bin Ahmad* [1974] 2 All ER 700, PC.
9   *Heasmans v Clarity Cleaning Co* [1987] ICR 949, CA (office cleaning contractors not liable for their employee's unauthorised use of client's telephone); *Irving v Post Office* [1987] IRLR 289, CA (Post Office not liable for racist remarks written on mail by a sorter).
10   [1912] AC 716, HL; para 27.13 above.
11   [1965] 2 All ER 725, CA. See also *Nahhas v Pier House (Cheyne Walk) Management Ltd* [1984] 1 EGLR 160.
12   [1980] 1 All ER 556, HL. On the facts, a term in the contract between the parties was effective to exclude the defendants' liability; see para 9.8 above.
13   [2001] UKHL 33, [2001] 1 All ER 769.

Liability of employee

27.17   It is important to emphasise that, although a claimant will normally choose to make an employer vicariously liable, the employee who actually commits a tort may always be held personally responsible for it. Thus in *Merrett v Babb*,[1] where a valuer's employer became insolvent, the house purchaser successfully sued the individual valuer for his negligence in carrying out a mortgage valuation. Moreover, an employer who has been forced to pay damages on the basis of vicarious liability is legally entitled to recover those damages from the guilty employee.[2] However, employers hardly ever exercise this right of indemnity, except in cases of collusion or wilful misconduct by the employee.

1   [2001] EWCA Civ 214, [2001] QB 1174.
2   *Lister v Romford Ice and Cold Storage Co Ltd* [1957] 1 All ER 125, HL.

Principal and agent

27.18   As stated at the beginning of this chapter, there is no general rule of law by which a principal is responsible for the torts of his agent, unless the relationship of employer and employee exists between them. Nevertheless, in two specific instances, and for widely differing reasons, the courts have imposed such liability.

Statements

27.19   From the legal point of view, the most important characteristic of an agent is that he is authorised to make contracts or dispose of property on behalf of his principal, and thereby to create obligations which the principal is bound to honour. Central to this function is the agent's role in making statements for his principal and, as a result, it has long been established that the principal is liable when these statements turn out to be false, even though the cause of action to which they give rise is tortious in nature rather than contractual.

The principle is well settled, but its extent is rather less clear. It has been used to make the landlord of a block of flats liable to an incoming tenant for the fraud of a managing agent who allowed a builder to deliberately cover up dry rot,[1] and to render an estate agent's client liable for a fraudulent statement made about his property to a prospective purchaser.[2] In *Gosling v Anderson*,[3] another estate agent's client had to pay damages in respect of a negligent statement. It may even be that a principal would be held liable for defamatory statements made by his agent.[4]

1   *Gordon v Selico Co Ltd* [1986] 1 EGLR 71, CA.
2   *Mullens v Miller* (1882) 22 Ch D 194.
3   (1972) 223 Estates Gazette 1743, CA.
4   *Colonial Mutual Life Assurance Society Ltd v Producers and Citizens Assurance Co of Australia Ltd* (1931) 46 CLR 41.

Vehicles

27.20   In an attempt to ensure that the victims of road accidents do not go uncompensated for the lack of a defendant who is solvent or insured, English law treats the owner of a motor vehicle as vicariously liable for the negligence of anyone who is driving it with his consent and on his behalf.[1] Although the owner's presence in the vehicle is not required, he will not be liable unless the so-called 'agent's' journey is undertaken both with the owner's consent and for his benefit. Thus, in *Morgans v Launchbury*,[2] where a husband, too drunk to drive home in his wife's car, asked a friend to drive it, it was held by the House of Lords that the wife was not liable to passengers who were injured for the friend's negligent driving.

1   *Ormrod v Crosville Motor Services Ltd* [1953] 2 All ER 753, CA.
2   [1972] 2 All ER 606, HL.

Independent contractors

General principle

27.21   As a general rule, a person (hereafter referred to as the client) who entrusts work to an independent contractor is not legally responsible for any torts committed by the contractor or the contractor's employees in the course of carrying out that work. Where, for example, the police arrange for an abandoned car to be towed away, and the car is damaged due to the negligence of the garage to whom the job is entrusted, the police cannot be held responsible; it is the garage alone which is liable.[1] Likewise a local authority is not vicariously liable for injuries to a child caused by negligence on the part of foster-parents which it has selected.[2] The client will, of course, be liable for any tort which he authorises or ratifies, and he may also be liable if he has been personally negligent in selecting an incompetent contractor[3] or in giving him inadequate instructions.[4] Whether the client may be liable for failing to exercise reasonable supervision over the independent contractor depends on whether he owes any duty of care in this respect. Such a duty has been imposed upon an occupier of land in respect of work carried out there by a building contractor;[5] however, the House of Lords has held that a building contractor owes no duty of care in tort to a subsequent owner of the building to supervise the work of a sub-contractor.[6]

1   *Rivers v Cutting* [1982] 3 All ER 69, CA.
2   *S v Walsall Metropolitan Borough Council* [1985] 3 All ER 294, CA.
3   *Pratt v George J Hill Associates* (1987) 38 BLR 25, CA.
4   *Robinson v Beaconsfield RDC* [1911] 2 Ch 188, CA.
5   *AMF International Ltd v Magnet Bowling Ltd* [1968] 2 All ER 789; see para 21.17 above.
6   *D & F Estates Ltd v Church Comrs for England* [1988] 2 All ER 992, HL.

Non-delegable duties

27.22   Apart from these possibilities, there are a number of cases in which the law is prepared to say that the client owes a personal, non-delegable duty to third parties. In such cases the client, while entitled to delegate the performance of his duty to another, remains responsible for its due fulfilment. These exceptions to the general rule of non-liability for an independent contractor's torts do not appear to be based upon any coherent principle, but rather to have evolved to meet particular situations. Nevertheless, the main categories (which we describe in paras 28.23 to 28.28 below) are well established.[1]

It should be emphasised that the standard of liability which is imposed by these non-delegable duties is not entirely uniform. In some instances, such as the rule in *Rylands v Fletcher* and under many statutes, the client's duty is a strict one, in the sense that it can be broken even when there is no negligence on anyone's part. Other cases, such as the duty of a bailee of goods, depend upon proof that someone is negligent; the client here may be said to owe a duty that reasonable care be taken. The choice as to which standard is imposed by any particular duty does not appear to be based on any clear principle.

1   See *Alcock v Wraith* (1991) 59 BLR 20 at 23.

Statutory duties
27.23   Many, if not most, of the statutory duties which give rise to civil liability[1] are non-delegable. In *Gray v Pullen*,[2] for example, where the defendants were obliged by statute to reinstate the highway after laying a drain in it, they were held liable when their independent contractor failed to do so.

Furthermore, it seems that a person with a statutory power to do something which would otherwise be unlawful delegates the exercise of this at his peril. Thus, in *Darling v A-G*,[3] where the Ministry of Works employed a contractor to drill trial bore holes on the claimant's land, the Ministry was held liable for the contractor's negligence in leaving a pile of timber there which injured the claimant's horse.

1   Paras 22.2–22.4 above.
2   (1864) 5 B & S 970.
3   [1950] 2 All ER 793.

Withdrawal of support
27.24   Where a landowner has a right to have his land or buildings supported by those of his neighbour,[1] he may sue if that support is withdrawn by the neighbour himself or by his independent contractor. This principle, which was established in *Bower v Peate*,[2] was perhaps the first non-delegable duty to be recognised by common law. It extends to cases in which work on an adjoining property damages a party wall and, by analogy, to work negligently done on a roof above a party wall which permitted damp to penetrate the claimant's property.[3]

1   Para 33.50 below.
2   (1876) 1 QBD 321.
3   *Alcock v Wraith* (1991) 59 BLR 20, CA.

Strict liability
27.25   In Chapters 25 and 26 we considered a number of areas in which the common law imposes strict liability, notably the rule in *Rylands v Fletcher*, the escape of fire and damage of various kinds caused by animals. In all these cases a client may be held responsible for the default of his independent contractor.

Operations on the highway
27.26   Where work is done by an independent contractor on or under the highway, the client is liable if the contractor negligently causes damage to a highway user, for example by leaving an unlighted heap of soil in the road,[1] or to the occupier of adjoining premises, for example by fracturing a gas main and thus causing an explosion.[2] This principle extends to the negligent repair by a contractor of an overhanging lamp which consequently falls on

a passer-by;[3] it does not, however, cover the negligent felling of trees near a highway,[4] nor the obstruction of the highway by a contractor working on the client's property,[5] nor the negligent repair by a contractor of a motor vehicle which the employer then drives along the road.[6]

1   *Penny v Wimbledon UDC* [1899] 2 QB 72, CA.
2   *Hardaker v Idle District Council* [1896] 1 QB 335, CA.
3   *Tarry v Ashton* (1876) 1 QBD 314.
4   *Salsbury v Woodland* [1969] 3 All ER 863, CA.
5   *Rowe v Herman* [1997] 1 WLR 1390, CA.
6   *Phillips v Britannia Hygienic Laundry Co Ltd* [1923] 1 KB 539, DC.

Extra-hazardous acts

27.27   In *Honeywill and Stein Ltd v Larkin Bros Ltd*,[1] the defendants, a firm of photographers, were employed by the claimants to take pictures inside a cinema owned by third parties. Due to the negligence of the defendants in the use of magnesium flares (which were then necessary for indoor photography), the premises were damaged by fire. It was held by the Court of Appeal that, since this was a 'dangerous operation', the claimants' duty in respect of it was a non-delegable one, and they were accordingly liable. A similar line of thinking can be found in *Matania v National Provincial Bank Ltd*,[2] where noise and dust from building works caused a nuisance; the builders' clients were held liable, since this was no mere ordinary building operation, but an extensive job involving a high risk of nuisance.

Perhaps because it is so difficult to say precisely when an operation becomes 'dangerous' or an act 'extra-hazardous', the courts have shown no great enthusiasm for this particular category.[3]

1   [1934] 1 KB 191, CA.
2   [1936] 2 All ER 633, CA.
3   See, for example, *Alcock v Wraith* (1991) 59 BLR 20, CA.

Other cases

27.28   Of the other situations in which courts have declared a person's duty to be non-delegable, so as to fix him with responsibility for the default of his independent contractor, three worthy of note are the duty of a contractual bailee to safeguard his bailor's goods;[1] the duty of every employer to take care for the safety of his employees;[2] and (probably) the duty of a hospital to look after its patients.[3] The emphasis in all these cases is on the relationship between the *client* and the victim, and it may well be that courts will be increasingly ready to find that a client has 'undertaken' a non-delegable duty, at least where he and the victim are parties to a contract.[4]

1   *British Road Services Ltd v Arthur V Crutchley & Co Ltd* [1968] 1 All ER 811, CA.
2   *McDermid v Nash Dredging and Reclamation Co Ltd* [1987] 2 All ER 878, HL.
3   *Cassidy v Ministry of Health* [1951] 1 All ER 574, CA.
4   See *Rogers v Night Riders* [1983] RTR 324, CA.

Collateral negligence

27.29   Even in circumstances where the law recognises a non-delegable duty, it is usually said that the client is not responsible for *casual* or *collateral* negligence of the independent contractor, but only for negligence in the very act which he is employed to carry out. Thus in *Padbury v Holliday and Greenwood Ltd*,[1] where a workman employed by sub-contractors negligently left an iron tool on a window-sill and it fell on to a passer-by, the clients of the sub-contractors were held not liable.

The difficulty of deciding when negligence is collateral in this sense is well illustrated by *Holliday v National Telephone Co*,[2] where the defendants, who were laying telephone wires under a street, employed a plumber to make certain connections. The plumber negligently dipped his blow-lamp into molten solder, and a passer-by was injured by the resulting explosion. The Divisional Court thought that this was about as typical a case of casual negligence as it was possible to imagine, but the Court of Appeal held that this was negligence in the very act which the contractor was engaged to perform.

1   (1912) 28 TLR 494, CA.
2   [1899] 2 QB 392, CA.

Chapter 28

Remedies

28.1 The foregoing chapters have concentrated on the elements of liability in a number of different torts, analysing what a claimant must establish in order to secure a verdict against the defendant. Here we are concerned rather with what it means in practical terms to have secured such a verdict.

In this chapter we examine the following issues:

- the extent to which an award of damages in tort may depart from its main aim, that of compensating the claimant for loss suffered;
- the way in which damages are assessed in cases of personal injury, death and damage to property;
- the statutory mechanism for allocating liability where responsibility for the claimant's loss is shared by more than one person;
- the availability of remedies other than an award of damages, especially that of injunction;
- the time limits within which actions in tort must be commenced if they are not to be statute-barred.

Damages

28.2 The availability of an action for damages is the hallmark of a tort; the absence of such a remedy is what serves to distinguish other civil wrongs, such as breach of trust. Moreover, it should be emphasised that damages are available even in respect of those torts which are actionable without the need to prove that the claimant has suffered any actual loss. In such a case, the sum awarded may, but need not, be nominal. Where other torts are concerned, the claimant is called upon to establish his loss and, having done so, he is entitled to be compensated for it.

Kinds of damages
28.3 As a general rule, the sole object of awarding damages to a claimant is to compensate him for the loss which he has suffered as a result of the defendant's tort. With a few minor exceptions, matters such as the punishment of the defendant, or the restoration of benefits which he has wrongfully obtained, have no place in the law of tort. It should also be noted that, whereas damages for breach of contract generally endeavour to put the claimant, in monetary terms, into the position in which he would have been had the

contract been performed,[1] and thus take into account any profit which he would have made from the bargain, damages for tort attempt to restore the claimant to his original position, as if the tort had not been committed at all.

In a number of instances, the courts may depart, or appear to depart, from the principle of compensation in assessing the amount of damages to be awarded to a successful claimant. For example, where the claimant has a bare legal claim, but the court feels that he is morally wrong to pursue it, he may be awarded *contemptuous* damages, usually the smallest coin of the realm. In such a case the defendant may well not be ordered to pay the claimant's costs, in which case the claimant will end up out of pocket to a considerable extent.

Not to be confused with contemptuous damages are *nominal* damages, which are awarded in respect of torts actionable per se to mark the infringement of the claimant's legal rights, in cases where no actual loss has been incurred. An award of, say, £2 for trespass in no way signifies that the court is critical of the claimant for bringing the case; on the contrary, such an award is frequently accompanied by an injunction restraining the defendant from committing further acts of trespass.

In torts such as trespass or assault, where damages are incapable of precise assessment in money terms, the manner in which the defendant commits the tort may be taken into account by the court; if this is such as to injure the claimant's dignity or pride, *aggravated* damages may be awarded. Indeed, even where the claimant has suffered a quantifiable financial loss, as where he has been defrauded by the defendant, he may receive an additional sum for injury to his feelings.[2] However, a claimant cannot recover damages for his indignation at the high-handed attitude displayed by the defendant following the commission of a tort.[3]

Quite apart from any question of aggravation, there remains the possibility that, where the defendant's conduct is particularly outrageous, the court may order him to pay *exemplary* or *punitive* damages, over and above what is necessary to compensate the claimant, for the explicit purpose of punishing the defendant and of teaching him that tort does not pay. Such awards are open to criticism on the grounds that the defendant is being punished for something which is not a crime, and without the protection of a criminal trial. It might also be argued that what is in effect a fine should be paid to the state rather than to the claimant, since the latter has, after all, already received sufficient to compensate him for his loss. Nevertheless, the power to award exemplary damages is well established, although in *Rookes v Barnard*[4] the House of Lords laid down that it should only be exercised in three classes of case:

- where statute authorises such an award;
- in cases of oppressive, arbitrary or unconstitutional acts by the servants of the government, such as assault or wrongful arrest by police officers, who are regarded for this purpose as the servants of the government;[5] or
- where the defendant has quite cold-bloodedly decided to infringe the claimant's rights after calculating that his profit in doing so will outweigh any compensation he may be ordered to pay. This has been held to include such cases as the publication of a book[6] or a newspaper[7] containing sensational libels in order to boost sales, and the eviction of a protected tenant by a landlord[8] anxious to turn his flat to more profitable use.[9]

1   Para 12.3 above.
2   *Archer v Brown* [1984] 2 All ER 267.
3   *AB v South West Water Services Ltd* [1993] 1 All ER 609, CA.
4   [1964] 1 All ER 367, HL.
5   Exemplary damages may be awarded for wrongful arrest, even where the behaviour is not 'oppressive': *Holden v Chief Constable of Lancashire* [1986] 3 All ER 836, CA.
6   *Cassell & Co Ltd v Broome* [1972] 1 All ER 801, HL, in which it was held to be irrelevant that no profit was in fact made.
7   As to the assessment of exemplary damages where a newspaper article libels a group of claimants, see *Riches v News Group Newspapers Ltd* [1986] QB 256, CA.

8   But not the landlord's agent, unless he stands to benefit personally from the eviction: *Daley v Ramdath* (1993) Times, 21 January, CA.
9   *Drane v Evangelou* [1978] 2 All ER 437, CA (trespass); *Guppys (Bridport) Ltd v Brookling* [1984] 1 EGLR 29, CA (nuisance). The Housing Act 1988, s 28 entitles an unlawfully evicted tenant to a measure of damages which effectively consists of the profit which the landlord makes from the eviction.

Personal injury

28.4   The rules which govern the assessment of damages for personal injury are complex; no more than an outline can be given here. One of the major problems is that the loss which flows from an injury falls into two very different categories. In the first place, the claimant may suffer monetary losses, such as medical expenses or loss of earnings; the guiding principle here is that he is entitled, so far as is possible, to full restitution of what he has lost. Secondly, however, there is non-monetary loss, which includes such matters as pain and suffering and loss of amenity. It is obviously impossible to place a precise value upon such things, and the law's aim here is simply to ensure that compensation should be fair and reasonable. This involves attempting to devise a scale of injuries (so that, for example, a lost leg is treated as worth more than a lost eye) and also maintaining some degree of consistency between the amounts awarded in similar cases.[1] With these points, and especially these two categories, in mind, we may now consider the various heads of damage under which personal injury awards are usually itemised.

1   See *Heil v Rankin* [2000] 3 All ER 138, CA.

Loss of amenity

28.5   The claimant is entitled to an award of damages in respect of the extent to which his injuries render him unable or less able to do what he previously enjoyed. Under this heading compensation may be awarded, for example, in respect of a lost limb or the impairment of senses or of sexual function. The seriousness of the deprivation, the claimant's degree of awareness of it, and the period for which he is likely to have to endure it, are all factors which influence the size of the award. In *Daly v General Steam Navigation Co Ltd*,[1] a woman whose injuries made it difficult and painful to keep house for her family recovered under this heading for the period preceding the trial; as to the future, she was held entitled to the estimated costs of employing a housekeeper, whether or not she in fact intended to employ one.

Although this category appears to be based on a person's lost enjoyment of life, it was laid down by the House of Lords, in *H West & Son Ltd v Shephard*,[2] that it represents an objective loss. Consequently, even someone rendered immediately and permanently unaware of his loss may be entitled to a considerable sum. Of course, a claimant who is aware of his loss may be compensated for this under the heading of 'pain and suffering'.[3]

1   [1980] 3 All ER 696, CA.
2   [1963] 2 All ER 625, HL.
3   Para 28.6 below.

Pain and suffering

28.6   This head of damage includes not only the physical pain of the injury and subsequent surgical operations, but also mental anguish arising out of disability or disfigurement. It cannot by definition apply to claimants rendered permanently unconscious; nor, where a person is killed by a tort, can damages be awarded to the estate for that 'pain and suffering' which is really part of the death itself.[1]

As a general rule, the courts do not separate 'pain and suffering' from 'loss of amenity', but award a global sum to cover both categories. Where very severe injuries are involved, this can be a considerable amount.

1   *Hicks v Chief Constable of the South Yorkshire Police* [1992] 2 All ER 65, HL.

Loss of expectation of life

28.7   A claimant is not entitled to damages for the fact that his life expectancy has been reduced.[1] However, this does not prevent him from claiming in respect of the suffering caused by his awareness of his reduced lifespan,[2] nor for the money which he could have earned during the lost years.[3]

1   Administration of Justice Act 1982, s 1(1).
2   S 1(1)(b).
3   S 1(2).

Medical and other expenses

28.8   The claimant is entitled to claim the cost, both past and future, of medical and nursing care including, where appropriate, the expense of living in a suitable institution or of adapting his own home to his needs. If he has to live in an institution, a sum representing his normal living expenses must be deducted from the damages awarded under this head, since these will no longer be incurred.[1] The claimant cannot recover damages for any expenses which ought reasonably to have been avoided, but it is not unreasonable to care for a severely injured person at home just because he could be catered for more cheaply than in an institution,[2] nor to seek private medical treatment rather than making use of the National Health Service facilities.[3]

Where necessary nursing services have been rendered to a seriously disabled claimant by a close relative, as where a mother has given up a job in order to look after her crippled child, it is established that he can recover a reasonable sum in respect of them from the defendant.[4]

1   *Lim Poh Choo v Camden and Islington Area Health Authority* [1979] 2 All ER 910, HL.
2   *Rialas v Mitchell* (1984) Times, 17 July, CA.
3   Law Reform (Personal Injuries) Act 1948, s 2(4).
4   *Donnelly v Joyce* [1973] 3 All ER 475, CA. However, this does not apply where the defendant himself renders the services: *Hunt v Severs* [1994] 2 All ER 385, HL.

Loss of earnings

28.9   Earnings which the claimant has lost up to the date of the trial are relatively easy to measure, but loss of future earnings[1] must also be compensated, and here assessment is far less certain, especially where it appears that the claimant will never be able to work again. In such cases, the courts, having firmly refused to enter into detailed actuarial calculations,[2] simply multiply their prediction of the claimant's average annual income (net of income tax and national insurance contributions) by an appropriate multiplier. This is not simply the number of years' earnings which have been lost, but is discounted to reflect the chance of an earlier death and the benefit of having an immediate lump sum. It is not increased, however, to mitigate the effect which high rates of taxation will have upon the income produced by investing a large award of damages.[3] In *Wells v Wells*,[4] the House of Lords held that the multiplier should be calculated on the basis that the claimant would invest the damages in index-linked government securities and would thus be protected in inflation.

Where a person's life expectancy is substantially reduced as a result of a tort, it is of course likely that he will thereby be deprived of the opportunity to earn money during the lost years. Under the Administration of Justice Act 1982, s 1(2), a living claimant[5] can recover for prospective earnings during the lost years, although a deduction must be made in respect of what he would have spent on his own support during that time. However, the courts will not make an award of this kind to a very young claimant on the grounds that his loss is too speculative.[6]

Much of the uncertainty which surrounds this particular head of damage arises from the fact that, since damages are paid as a lump sum, they must be assessed in advance. The courts do not yet have power to award damages in the form of periodic payments, although section 32A of the Supreme Court Act 1981 provides that, in cases where there is a chance that the claimant's condition will deteriorate at some time in the future, the court may make an initial lump sum award on the basis that this will not happen, the claimant being at liberty to seek additional damages if it does.[7]

1   Including loss or reduction of future pension rights: *Auty v National Coal Board* [1985] 1 All ER 930, CA.
2   *Mitchell v Mulholland (No 2)* [1971] 2 All ER 1205, CA.
3   *Hodgson v Trapp* [1988] 3 All ER 870, HL.
4   [1998] 3 All ER 481, HL.
5   The claim does not pass to the deceased's estate: see para 28.11 below.
6   *Croke v Wiseman* [1981] 3 All ER 852, CA.
7   See *Willson v Ministry of Defence* [1991] 1 All ER 638.

Collateral benefits

28.10   A person who is injured in an accident may, as a result of this, receive sums of money from a wide variety of sources, such as insurance, sick pay or a pension from his employer or social security benefits. To what extent, if at all, should this be regarded as relevant when the claimant comes to claim damages from the defendant in respect of his loss of earnings? Should the claimant be allowed to recover full damages and to keep his other benefit, and thereby be doubly compensated? Should damages be reduced, so that the defendant reaps the benefit of a payment designed to help the claimant? Or should the law seek to ensure that the money is in some way returned to the collateral fund?

To these questions, English law has no simple answers, largely because it has dealt with each type of collateral benefit as it has arisen, without attempting to lay down any general principles. Very broadly, the position now is that most state benefits received in the five years after the accident are deducted from the damages and then recovered from the defendant by the state.[1] Also deducted, but not recovered, are wages, sick pay,[2] redundancy payments[3] and the like to which the claimant is actually entitled, together with any saving on living costs where the claimant is maintained at public expense in an institution.[4] The product of private insurance,[5] or a charitable payment, on the other hand, is non-deductible.[6] On the very borderline is a pension; in *Parry v Cleaver*,[7] this was held by a bare majority of the House of Lords to be non-deductible, on the ground that it is not intended to be an equivalent of wages lost and cannot therefore be said to reduce the loss which the claimant has suffered.

1   Social Security Administration Act 1992, Part IV, as amended by the Social Security (Recovery of Benefits) Act 1997. After five years there is neither deduction nor recovery.
2   *Hussain v New Taplow Paper Mills Ltd* [1988] 1 All ER 541, HL.
3   *Colledge v Bass Mitchells & Butlers* [1988] ICR 125, CA.
4   Administration of Justice Act 1982, s 5.
5   Even where paid for by the defendant employer: *McCamley v Cammell Laird Shipbuilders Ltd* [1990] 1 All ER 854, CA.
6   *Bradburn v Great Western Rly Co* (1874) LR 10 Exch 1.
7   [1969] 1 All ER 555, HL; followed unanimously by the House of Lords in *Smoker v London Fire and Civil Defence Authority; Wood v British Coal Corpn* [1991] 2 All ER 449, HL.

Death

28.11   The Law Reform (Miscellaneous Provisions) Act 1934 provides that most tort actions survive for and against the estates of the parties.[1] However, the Administration of Justice Act 1982, s 4 provides that a deceased person's estate may not be awarded damages for bereavement,[2] exemplary damages[3] or damages for loss of earnings during the lost years.[4] Apart from this, where an action is brought on behalf of a deceased person, the damages awarded are such as he could have recovered if he had not died, which means that the headings considered above under 'personal injury' are again relevant, at least as regards the period between the tort and death.

1   Actions for defamation do not survive.
2   Para 28.12 below.
3   Para 28.3 above.
4   Para 28.9 above.

Fatal accidents

28.12   At common law, no tort action could be brought by A on the ground that the death of B had caused him loss. However, a statutory right of action for the dependants of a person who is killed by a tort has long been in existence and is currently governed by the Fatal Accidents Act 1976, as amended by the Administration of Justice Act 1982, s 3. Dependants for this purpose bears a wide meaning, including spouses, all ascendants and descendants, brothers and sisters, uncles and aunts and their issue, provided, of course, that they truly were dependent upon the deceased. Moreover, since 1982, the Act has extended to a former spouse or cohabitee of the deceased, although the amount of damages payable must reflect the fact that he or she had no legal right to financial support by the deceased.

The cause of action given by the Fatal Accidents Act is quite separate from that which may have survived for the benefit of the estate itself. Normal practice is for the action to be brought by the personal representative of the deceased, on behalf of all the dependants; the court will then assess the total liability of the defendant before apportioning the damages between the various dependants. Since the action is an independent one, it has its own limitation period of three years from the date of death. Further, it seems that where a dependant has through his own fault contributed to the causing of death, for example by negligent driving, his damages, though not those of other dependants, may be reduced on the ground of contributory negligence.

Although the action is thus separate, it is still subject to the principle that it can only be brought where the deceased himself could have sued if he had been injured rather than killed. As a result, if the deceased had already sued to judgment or settled his claim against the defendant, or if his action was barred by time or by an exemption clause, the dependants' rights are also defeated. So too, if the deceased was guilty of contributory negligence, damages awarded under the Fatal Accidents Act will suffer an appropriate reduction.

It is important to appreciate that the main purpose of this statutory cause of action is to compensate the dependants, not for their grief at losing a loved one, but for the loss of some benefit which has a monetary value (including, for example, services performed by a wife and mother[1] or unpaid help given by a son to his father's work[2]) and which would have come to the dependants because of their relationship with the deceased.[3] However, since 1982 there has been a limited exception to this principle, in that damages for bereavement (a fixed sum laid down by statutory instrument[4]) may be awarded to the widow(er) or, where the deceased is an unmarried minor at the date of death, to his parents.

In deciding how much to award for loss of dependency, the court must try to assess what the position would have been had the deceased lived and, in carrying out this task, the prospects of both the deceased and the dependants are of course relevant. However, the court is not to consider a widow's prospects of remarriage.

Section 4 of the 1976 Act provides that, in assessing damages, no account is to be taken of any benefits which accrue to the dependant in question as a result of the death, for example by way of inheritance or insurance policies.[5]

1   *Mehmet v Perry* [1977] 2 All ER 529, DC.
2   *Franklin v South Eastern Rly Co* (1858) 3 H & N 211.
3   Funeral expenses incurred by the dependants are also recoverable: Fatal Accidents Act 1976, s 3(3).
4   This is currently £10,000: Damages for Bereavement (Variation of Sum) (England and Wales) Order 2002.
5   See *Pidduck v Eastern Scottish Omnibuses Ltd* [1990] 2 All ER 69, CA.

Damage to property

Measure of damages

28.13 A person whose property (whether land or goods) is destroyed or damaged as a result of a tort is in principle entitled to full restitution in money terms of what he has lost. Where property is totally destroyed (which will hardly ever apply to land), the usual measure of damages is at least the full value to the claimant of that property at the time and place of its destruction. This value, in the case of a profit-earning chattel such as a ship, should take into account its profitability at the time, in the light of its current engagements.[1] However, if the claimant receives this sum he may yet be out of pocket, in that the acquisition of a suitable replacement may take time; in such a case, damages for loss of profit, or simply loss of use, may also be recovered.

Where the claimant's property is damaged by the defendant, the court has a choice of at least two possible measures[2] to award (which may or may not be the same): either the amount by which the value of the property has been reduced, or the cost of repairing it. In the case of goods, the courts have usually been prepared to award the cost of repair, unless this would be unreasonable. For example, the owner of a badly damaged car will not normally be allowed the cost of repair where this exceeds the write-off value of the vehicle.[3] A similar principle applies in respect of damage to land and buildings, so that the cost of reinstatement is usually appropriate, provided that the claimant's decision to repair is a reasonable one. Thus, in *Hollebone v Midhurst and Fernhurst Builders*,[4] where the claimant's house was damaged by fire, the judge held that the claimant was fully entitled to decide to rebuild what was in effect a unique property. That case also laid down that a claimant need not suffer any deduction from his damages in respect of 'betterment', ie the amount by which the value of the restored property exceeds its pre-accident value.

Where the claimant has no intention of repairing the building (as in *C A Taylor (Wholesale) Ltd v Hepworths Ltd*,[5] where fire damaged a disused billiards hall on a site which the claimants had always intended to redevelop) damages should only reflect the diminution in value of the property. This is also true of cases where the cost of reinstatement would be out of all proportion to the loss suffered. In *Jones v Gooday*,[6] for example, where the defendant wrongfully removed soil from the claimant's field, the claimant was awarded only the amount by which the value of the field was reduced, and not the much greater cost of restoring it to its original condition. In *Heath v Keys*,[7] where the defendant wrongfully dumped spoil on a small area of woodland owned by the claimant, the award was something of a compromise; not the full cost of restoring the site to its original condition, but enough to pay the costs involved in removing most of the spoil and tidying the site, in addition to the diminution in value which would remain when this had been done.

Quite apart from the damages discussed above, a claimant is entitled to compensation for loss of profits or loss of use during the time taken to effect repairs, which may be assessed on the basis of the cost of hiring a reasonable substitute. What is reasonable is a question of fact, and may even include a prestige car.[8] It is important to note that the claimant is not required to show that he has actually suffered from the non-availability of his property. Consequently, in *The Mediana*,[9] where a damaged lightship was replaced for a time by a substitute which the claimants kept for just such an emergency, they were nevertheless awarded substantial damages for loss of use.

It is worth noting that, where a purchaser brings an action for negligence against a surveyor on whose advice he relied in deciding to purchase, the basic measure of damages will be not the cost of repairing defects which the surveyor ought to have discovered, but the difference between what the purchaser has been led to pay for the property and its actual value. This is because the surveyor has not actually damaged the property; his offence consists of leading the purchaser to pay more than it is worth.[10]

1   *Liesbosch Dredger v SS Edison* [1933] AC 449, HL.
2   These are not the only possible measures; the court will select whatever is the most appropriate measure

of compensation in all the circumstances. See *Dominion Mosaics and Tile Co Ltd v Trafalgar Trucking Co Ltd* [1990] 2 All ER 246, CA; *Farmer Giles Ltd v Wessex Water Authority* [1990] 1 EGLR 177, CA.
3   *Darbishire v Warran* [1963] 3 All ER 310, CA.
4   [1968] 1 Lloyd's Rep 38. Also see *Dominion Mosaics & Tile Co Ltd v Trafalgar Trucking Co Ltd* [1990] 2 All ER 246, CA.
5   [1977] 2 All ER 784.
6   (1841) 8 M & W 146.
7   [1984] CLY 3568.
8   *Daily Office Cleaning Contractors v Shefford* [1977] RTR 361, DC.
9   [1900] AC 113, HL.
10 *Watts v Morrow* [1991] 4 All ER 937, CA.

Date of assessment

28.14   Where damages fall to be based on the cost of repair, this is normally assessed as at the date on which the claimant ought reasonably to have repaired the property. In *Dodd Properties (Kent) Ltd v Canterbury City Council,*[1] where the claimants' garage was seriously damaged by building works carried on by the defendants on adjoining property, the claimants chose for sound financial reasons not to start repairs until they had recovered damages from the defendants. Despite the defendants' plea that lack of funds could not excuse the claimants' failure to put the repairs in hand at an earlier date,[2] it was held by the Court of Appeal that they were entitled to the much higher sum which represented this cost at the time of the trial.

1   [1980] 1 All ER 928, CA.
2   Based on *Liesbosch Dredger v SS Edison* [1933] AC 449, HL; para 19.20 above.

Multiple tortfeasors

28.15   Where the claimant is harmed by the tortious conduct of more than one person, the first question to be asked is whether each tortfeasor has caused a separately identifiable part of the claimant's overall damage. If this is so, then each is liable only for the part which he has caused. More commonly, however, the damage to the claimant will be indivisible; if so, the claimant is entitled to recover damages in full from any or all of the tortfeasors, subject to the proviso that he cannot recover more in total than he has lost. Thus, for example, if the claimant is injured by the combined negligence of A and B in such circumstances that the court regards A as three-quarters and B as one-quarter to blame, the claimant may nevertheless choose to sue B alone and may recover full damages. The importance of this principle is seen in cases where A is insolvent and uninsured; the loss then falls upon B, who is after all guilty of some fault, rather than upon the claimant who is completely innocent.

In practice, it is desirable that the claimant should bring all the defendants into court in one action. To encourage him to do so, s 4 of the Civil Liability (Contribution) Act 1978 provides that a claimant who brings successive actions against different tortfeasors will be unable to recover his costs in all but the first action, unless the court finds that there were reasonable grounds for bringing the subsequent ones.

Contribution between tortfeasors

28.16   Section 1(1) of the Civil Liability (Contribution) Act 1978 provides that any person liable[1] in respect of any damage suffered by another person may recover contribution from any other person liable in respect of the same damage.[2] The recovery of contribution may be sought as part of the original action by the claimant (so long as both tortfeasors are parties to that action), or in a separate action between the tortfeasors.

The right of one tortfeasor (D1) to claim contribution from another (D2) is independent of the claimant's right of action. Thus, the fact that the claimant's claim against D2 would have been barred by lapse of time[3] is irrelevant, provided that D1 himself brings his action for contribution within two years of the date on which his right arises (normally the date on which D1 pays compensation to the claimant).

In assessing the amount of contribution, the court is instructed to do what is just and equitable, and it seems that, in arriving at a fraction or percentage, it will rely on the same factors as in cases of contributory negligence.[4] However, it should be noted that D2 cannot be ordered to pay more to D1 than he would have had to pay the claimant (eg where his contract with the claimant contained a clause which limited his liability): nor does the Civil Liability (Contribution) Act prevail against a right of indemnity which is contained in a contract between the tortfeasors.

1   This includes liability in 'tort, breach of contract, breach of trust or otherwise'.
2   The phrase 'the same damage' requires both persons to be liable to the same third party: *Birse Construction Ltd v Haiste Ltd* [1996] 2 All ER 1, CA.
3   Paras 28.21–28.25 below.
4   Para 20.16 above.

Injunction

28.17   An injunction is a specific decree of the court which orders the defendant to do or, more commonly, not to do something. Like all equitable remedies it is not available as of right, but lies in the discretion of the court. As a result, it is unlikely to be granted where damages would be an adequate remedy, where the harm suffered by the claimant is of a very trivial or temporary nature,[1] or where the claimant has actually or apparently acquiesced in the defendant's tort. For example, in *Armstrong v Sheppard and Short Ltd*,[2] the claimant assented in principle to the laying of a sewer by the defendants under certain land near his house, unaware that he in fact owned it; upon discovering the truth, he sued the defendants in trespass. The Court of Appeal held that, since the defendants had been misled and the harm was trivial, the claimant was not entitled to an injunction but only to damages.

1   *A-G v Sheffield Gas Consumers Co* (1853) 3 De Gm & G 304.
2   [1959] 2 All ER 651, CA.

Kinds of injunction

28.18   A *prohibitory* injunction, the most common kind, is an order to the defendant to stop certain conduct which represents a continuing or repetitive infringement of the claimant's legal rights (eg by the commission of trespass or nuisance). In the absence of special circumstances, the grant of such an injunction is almost automatic, though its operation may on occasion be suspended for a period to enable the defendant to make alternative arrangements.

By contrast, a *mandatory* injunction, which orders the defendant to take positive steps to repair the wrong he has done, is reserved for those few cases in which the claimant will suffer very serious harm unless the injunction is granted. Further, unless the defendant has acted in flagrant disregard of the claimant's rights, the court must weigh up what it will cost the defendant to comply with the order. Thus, in *Redland Bricks Ltd v Morris*,[1] where the defendants' excavations on their own land had caused subsidence of part of the claimant's land and danger to the rest, the House of Lords refused to order the defendants to restore support, since the cost of doing this would be greater than the total value of the claimant's land.

In matters of urgency, where the preservation of the status quo is important to save the claimant from further loss, the court may grant him an *interlocutory* injunction, a provisional order until a full trial takes place. Since the defendant may lose money because of this order, and then turn out to have been in the right all along, the claimant may be compelled to give an undertaking that in such circumstances he will pay compensation. The principles on which a court should exercise its discretion in relation to interlocutory injunctions were laid down by the House of Lords in the case of *American Cyanamid Co v Ethicon Ltd*.[2] Briefly, these are that, if there is a serious question to be tried, the court must consider all the circumstances, particularly whether the preservation of the status quo is important, and whether the defendant will be adequately protected by the claimant's undertaking to pay damages.

In rare cases, where the claimant's cause of action depends on proof of damage, the court may issue an injunction *quia timet* ('because he is afraid') before such damage had actually occurred. In effect, this means that the defendant is held liable before a complete tort has been committed; not surprisingly, therefore such an order is only granted where damages is almost certain to occur and where it is imminent.

1   [1969] 2 All ER 576, HL.
2   [1975] 1 All ER 504, HL.

Damages in lieu of injunction

28.19   In any case where an injunction is claimed, the court has a discretion to refuse the injunction and award damages in substitution for it. In effect, such an order allows the defendant to purchase the right to commit a tort against the claimant, and the discretion is consequently to be used sparingly. It has been suggested that the court should only act in this way where it is shown that the injury to the claimant is small, capable of estimation in money terms and adequately compensated by damages, and that an injunction would cause great hardship to the defendant.[1]

In *Jaggard v Sawyer*,[2] the owners of a private road sought an injunction to prevent the occupiers of a new house from trespassing along the road. However, the Court of Appeal held that this was a case where damages should be awarded instead, since to award an injunction would in effect render the house uninhabitable. By contrast, in *Elliott v Islington London Borough Council*,[3] the Court of Appeal awarded an injunction compelling a local authority to cut down a tree which was encroaching on to the claimant's land, notwithstanding that the tree was an ancient horse chestnut which the local authority passionately wanted to preserve.

1   *Shelfer v City of London Electric Lighting Co* [1895] 1 Ch 287 at 322, CA.
2   [1995] 2 All ER 189, CA.
3   [1991] 1 EGLR 167, CA.

Other remedies

28.20   In the vast majority of tort cases which come to court, the claimant is seeking either damages or an injunction. However, in some circumstances other remedies may be of greater value, particularly an order for the specific restitution of goods or land.[1]

Although not popular with the courts, and therefore strictly controlled, a certain amount of self-help is tolerated, in the interest of avoiding unnecessary litigation. Examples of this principle, all of which we have considered at the appropriate place, are the ejection of a trespasser and re-entry on to land,[2] the abatement of a nuisance,[3] the detention of straying livestock[4] and the killing of a marauding dog.[5]

1   Para 23.10 above.
2   Para 23.11 above.
3   Para 24.22 above.
4   Para 26.11 above.
5   Para 26.13 above.

Limitation of actions

28.21   Any civil action will be barred by lapse of time unless it is commenced within the prescribed limitation period. The rules which govern this matter are entirely statutory and are contained in the Limitation Act 1980. For present purposes, the main limitation periods are 12 years (recovery of land and contracts made by deed); six years (breach of simple contracts and tort); and three years (actions for both tort and breach of contract in respect of personal injuries). Special periods apply to certain types of claim, for example those arising under the Defective Premises Act 1972.[1]

1   Para 21.28 above.

Commencement of limitation period

28.22   Whichever period is applicable, the basic rule is that it starts on the day when the claimant's cause of action accrues. In contract cases, this is almost invariably the date of the defendant's breach, and the same is true of those torts which are actionable per se, such as trespass. On the other hand, where proof of damage forms part of the tort itself, as in cases of negligence or nuisance, the cause of action does not arise until the damage occurs and, accordingly, time does not start to run until that date.

Clearly, it may sometimes be to a claimant's advantage to be able to sue in tort rather than in contract, and this is what gives such importance to those decisions which have held professional men liable to their clients in the tort of negligence as well as for breach of contract.[1] However, the advantage of a tort action is not always as marked as might be supposed. For example, where a solicitor gives negligent advice to a client, as a result of which the client executes an imprudent mortgage of her property, it has been held that the damage is suffered as soon as the mortgage is executed, since the property is immediately rendered less valuable, rather than when the property is later seized by the mortgagee.[2] Similarly, where a surveyor negligently advises his client to purchase a badly constructed building, the client is regarded as having suffered loss at the date of purchase, rather than at the later date when the building itself suffers physical damage.[3] By contrast, where the mortgage lender sues the valuer on whose valuation he relied when deciding to lend, the lender's loss is deemed to occur at the first moment when the amount of the outstanding mortgage debt (including any accrued interest) exceeds the value of the property.[4]

Continuing torts, such as certain kinds of trespass[5] or nuisance, give rise to a fresh right of action every day until they are abated. The consequence of this is that a claimant is entitled to sue for everything which has occurred during the past six years, even if the tort was first committed outside that period or, indeed, before he acquired the property in question.[6]

1   Para 17.21 above.
2   *Forster v Outred & Co* [1982] 2 All ER 753, CA.
3   *Secretary of State for the Environment v Essex, Goodman & Suggitt* [1986] 1 WLR 1432.
4   *Nykredit Mortgage Bank plc v Edward Erdman Group Ltd (No 2)* [1998] 1 All ER 305, HL.
5   Para 23.8 above.
6   See *Masters v Brent London Borough Council* [1978] 2 All ER 664.

Personal injury

28.23   A particular problem may arise in cases where an injury, such as a progressive industrial disease, is not discovered (or, indeed, discoverable) by the claimant until some considerable time after it first occurs. It was held by the House of Lords in *Cartledge v E Jopling & Sons Ltd,*[1] a case concerning a lung disease contracted over a long period of time by workers in a particular industry, that the limitation period in such circumstances began to run as soon as the disease passed beyond the merely trivial, notwithstanding that this might mean that a victim's cause of action was barred by time before he could possibly have known that it existed.

The obvious harshness of this ruling in the context of personal injury cases led swiftly to its alleviation by statute. The Limitation Act 1980, s 11 now provides that the limitation period in cases of personal injury based on 'negligence, nuisance or breach of duty'[2] shall be three years and shall not begin until the claimant has knowledge of a number of material facts, of which the most important are the significance of his injury (that is, that it is serious enough to justify taking legal action) and its attributability to an identified defendant. The claimant's 'knowledge' for this purpose includes knowledge which he might reasonably have been expected to acquire from his own observations or from such expert advice as he ought reasonably to have sought, taking account of his age, background, intelligence and disabilities.[3]

1   [1963] 1 All ER 341, HL.
2   This does not include trespass to the person: *Stubbings v Webb* [1993] 1 All ER 322, HL.
3   *Davis v City and Hackney Health Authority* [1989] 2 Med LR 366.

Latent damage

28.24   The problem of hidden damage is not confined to personal injury cases; negligence in building houses is another obvious example. In *Pirelli General Cable Works Ltd v Oscar Faber & Partners*,[1] the House of Lords laid down that, as with personal injuries before statute intervened, the correct starting-point is when the building actually suffers damage, not when it becomes visible. Indeed, it was said obiter that, if the building could be shown to have been 'doomed from the start',[2] then time would run from an even earlier moment, namely, that at which the building was completed.

Once again, the harshness of this rule led to statutory change. Section 14A of the Limitation Act 1980, added by the Latent Damage Act 1986, effectively extends the limitation period for claims in tort for negligence,[3] other than in respect of personal injury.[4] It also permits an action for negligent damage to property[5] to be brought by a person who acquires that property after it has suffered damage but before the damage has become apparent.

The time limit on claims falling within s 14A is either:

*   six years from when the cause of action accrued;[6] or
*   three years from when the claimant (or his predecessor in title, if property has changed hands) had both the right to bring an action and knowledge of material facts.[7]

However, s 14B of the Act imposes an overriding time limit of 15 years from the defendant's breach of duty on which the action is based. After this, the action is barred whether or not the damage has become known or has even occurred.

1   [1983] 1 All ER 65, HL.
2   A possibility which subsequent courts have consistently rejected: see, for example, *Ketteman v Hansel Properties Ltd* [1988] 1 All ER 38, HL.
3   The Act does not apply to claims based on a contractual duty of care: *Société Commerciale de Réassurance v ERAS (International)* [1992] 2 All ER 82n, CA.
4   Thus including both claims for both damage to property and pure financial loss.
5   But not for other types of claim, eg for negligent professional advice.
6   Ie when damage is suffered; see para 28.22 above.
7   'Knowledge' is defined in a similar way as for personal injury claims; see para 28.23 above. For the operation of the Act in respect of a negligent survey, see *Hamlin v Edwin Evans* [1996] 2 EGLR 106, CA.

Extension of time

28.25   It is provided by the Limitation Act 1980 that in certain circumstances the limitation period may either begin to run from a later date than normal or may simply be extended.

- Where there is fraud, concealment or mistake,[1] the limitation period does not begin to run until this has been or ought to have been discovered by the claimant. The question of concealment has arisen in a number of cases where defects in a building which are due to negligence by the builder have been covered up in the course of the construction work and have not come to light until many years later. It has been held that the mere fact that a builder continues with his work after something shoddy or inadequate has been done does not necessarily amount to concealment for this purpose.[2] The question is whether in all the circumstances it was unconscionable for the builder to proceed with the work so as to cover up the defect.[3]
- Where the claimant is a minor or is mentally ill, the limitation period does not begin to run until the removal of his disability or his death.[4] This provision has been held to apply where the claimant's unsoundness of mind is caused by the accident in respect of which he sues.[5]
- A sweeping change in the law governing limitation of actions was introduced by the Limitation Act 1980, s 33. This provision, which applies to all actions brought in respect of personal injuries, empowers the court simply to override the normal three-year period if it appears equitable to do so. In deciding how to exercise its discretion in this way, the court is instructed to have regard to all the circumstances of the case, and in particular to the extent to which each party would be prejudiced by an adverse decision, to the conduct of each party since the accident, and to the length and reasons for the delay.[6]

1 Para 11.39 above. 'Concealment' for this purpose may take place either when the cause of action first accrues or at any time thereafter: *Sheldon v RHM Outhwaite (Underwriting Agencies) Ltd* [1995] 2 All ER 558, HL.
2 *William Hill Organisation Ltd v Bernard Sunley & Sons Ltd* (1982) 22 BLR 8, CA.
3 *Applegate v Moss* [1971] 1 All ER 747, CA.
4 Limitation Act 1980, s 28.
5 *Kirby v Leather* [1965] 2 All ER 441, CA.
6 See *Thompson v Brown Construction (Ebbw Vale) Ltd* [1981] 2 All ER 296, HL; *Hartley v Birmingham City District Council* [1992] 2 All ER 213, CA.

Injunctions

28.26 Injunctions are equitable remedies and their award, therefore, is not subject to the provisions of the Limitation Act. However, equity has its own rules concerning delay, and these we discussed in para 11.41 above.

Part IV

Land law

Chapter 29

Land, its ownership and use

29.1   The study of land law is the study of the law relating to the rights and interests (ie 'bundles of rights') which people may have in respect of land. It deals with the nature of these rights and interests and with how they are created, transferred to other people, and enforced against them. Theoretically, when speaking of land being bought, sold or valued, we are not referring to the physical entity itself, but rather to the abstract interests which people have in the property. However, although land law is, in principle, concerned with abstract rights and interests, its practical context of houses and flats, offices and shops, factories and farms should always be borne in mind when studying its rules.

29.2   Rights to enter, use, occupy or own land can be infinitely variable in extent; they range from a short-lived permission for a child to come into a neighbour's garden to retrieve a ball, to a right to stay in a hotel for a week, to a right of way across neighbouring land, to a right to 'own' land either for a limited period or in perpetuity. Where all the elements of a contract are present[1], the law will enforce such rights as between the parties who created them. However, the doctrine of privity of contract[2] may confine enforcement to the contracting parties. Such an approach is unsatisfactory in the context of land since the effective use and enjoyment of land often needs to be supported by rights which remain permanently enforceable. So, for example, if the only access to Whitelands is across part of Blacklands, it is essential that the right of access does not cease to be enforceable once the owner of Blacklands who first conferred the right of access either dies or ceases to own Blacklands.

For this reason, the law has long recognised that certain rights to land are 'proprietary' in nature, with the result that they are legally capable of being enjoyed by, and being enforced against, not simply those parties who first created the rights, but also against future owners of the land to which they relate. It is with these proprietary rights that land law is largely concerned. However, we shall also briefly discuss non-proprietary, that is 'personal', rights to use land[3]. This not only helps to explain the distinction between proprietary and personal rights to land, it also demonstrates that personal rights to use land play an important practical role in the use and enjoyment of land.

1   See chs 4, 5 and 6 above.
2   But note the effect of the Contract (Rights of Third Parties) Act 1999; see ch 14 above.
3   See paras 29.41–29.45 below.

29.3   Proprietary interests in land may, broadly, be divided into two groups: those in respect of one's own land and those in respect of land belonging to another person. The former category we shall call 'ownership interests'; it may be further divided into that which in effect gives absolute ownership of the land, popularly referred to as the freehold interest, and those which give rise to a more limited ownership, of which the main modern example is the leasehold interest. The two main ownership interests are the freehold and the leasehold; although other forms of ownership can exist, there are rarely encountered today. These ownership interests may be enjoyed by a single owner or concurrently with other owners.[2]

As well as these ownership interests, a person may have interests in respect of land which is owned by another. These are usually referred to as 'third party' rights. Examples of such interests include a private right of way over neighbouring land (a species of easement[3]), a right to prevent a neighbour building on his land (an example of a restrictive covenant[4]), or a mortgage on land granted as security for a loan to its owner.[5]

1   Chapter 32 below.
2   Chapter 33 below.
3   Chapter 34 below.
4   Chapter 35 below.

29.4   What makes land law a subject of some complexity, and what makes buying and selling interests in land potentially more complicated than buying and selling a car is that it is usual for a number of interests to exist simultaneously in respect of one piece of land. For example, A may have a freehold interest in the property, and, at the same time, B may have a 21-year lease of the property. Meanwhile X, a neighbour, may have the benefit of a covenant restricting development on the property, Y may have a private right of way across it and Z may have a mortgage on A's freehold interest. The rules of land law are concerned with the extent of the rights enjoyed by each of these various people and with the protection of those rights, particularly in the event of the freehold of the land in question being sold.

29.5   In this chapter we examine the following issues:

- the way in which the law defines 'land' and the physical limits of land ownership;
- how and why the law classifies proprietary rights to land as estates or interests;
- how the law treats personal rights to use land.

What is land?

29.6   For a whole variety of reasons it may be crucial to know what exactly the law means by 'land'. For example, unlike most other contracts, contracts for the sale or disposition of an interest in 'land' must be in writing[1]. 'Land' is protected by the tort of trespass for which it is not necessary to prove damage[2]; while this strict protection has caused problems in the past over essential access to carry out repairs[3], it has also proved useful elsewhere, notably in the airspace cases considered at para 29.17 below. The meaning of 'land' is also important because items which are treated as part of land[4] will be included in a contract for the sale or lease of land and pass to the purchaser or tenant on a conveyance of land unless expressly excluded[5], and will form part of the security where land is mortgaged[6]. Furthermore, the question of whether or not an item is 'land' will dictate whether or not it can be the subject matter of a lease[7] and its treatment under the taxation regime[8].

1   Law of Property (Miscellaneous Provisions) Act 1989; para 30.2 below.
2   See para 23.1 above.
3   See para 23.7 above.
4   See paras 29.9-29.15 below.
5   Law of Property (Miscellaneous Provisions) Act 1989 s 2, Law of Property Act 1925 (LPA), s 62.

6   This was the issue in *TSB Bank plc v Botham* [1996] EGCS 149, CA: see para 29.12 below.
7   See *Chelsea Yacht & Boat Co Ltd v Pope* [2001] 2 All ER 409, CA and para 29.10 below.
8   See *Melluish (Inspector of Taxes) v BMI (No 3) Ltd* [1995] 4 All ER 453, HL.

General definition of land

29.7   Both common law[1] and statute[2] accept that the expression 'land' covers more than just the surface of the earth. Not only does 'land' include airspace and subsoil, it also includes physical things attached to it such as structures, buildings, fixtures and things growing naturally on the land (which we consider in the following paragraphs). Furthermore, in addition to these physical elements, 'land' also refers to intangible ('incorporeal') rights to use or restrict the use of the land such as easements; these we consider later.

1   *Mitchell v Mosley* [1914] 1 Ch 438, CA.
2   LPA 1925, s 205(1)(ix).

Physical extent

29.8   The notion that 'the grant of land includes the surface and all that is [above] – houses, trees and the like – ... and all that is [below], ie mines, earth, clay, etc'[1], is beyond doubt. On this basis, in *Grigsby v Melville*,[2] where the conveyance to the plaintiff of his semi-detached house was of 'all that dwelling-house and premises situate on the west side of Church Hill', it was held that the plaintiff acquired ownership of the cellar beneath his house, even though it could not be reached from the house but only from the adjoining property. He became owner of all the land above and below the surface.

That said, this principle that ownership of land extends above and below its surface is, as we shall see, subject to important limitations[3]. Furthermore, it should not be taken to preclude an owner from expressly splitting up his land by means of horizontal boundaries[4], as may occur where the ownership of a building is divided, say, into separate office units or into individual flats. However, as we shall see, while English law has no problem with the theory of stratified ownership, it has until recently found it impossible to accommodate the many practical problems which flow from the horizontal division of land[5]. For this reason a stratified freehold title (often referred to as a 'flying freehold') has been virtually unknown and the ownership of horizontally divided land has invariably been conferred by way of a long lease. This is now set to change. The Commonhold and Leasehold Reform Act 2002 introduces a new form of stratified freehold ownership known as commonhold; this is designed to replace the use of the long lease as a mechanism for the ownership of parts of buildings, especially but not exclusively in the context of residential properties.[6]

1   *Mitchell v Mosley* [1914] 1 Ch 438, CA.
2   [1973] 3 All ER 455, CA.
3   See paras 29.16-29.21 below.
4   Law of Property Act 1925, s 205(1)(ix). It may, of course, not always be easy to decide exactly where those horizontal boundaries are located; see *Davies v Yadegar* [1990] 1 EGLR 71, CA and para 29.24 below.
5   See para 34.4 below.
6   The commonhold aspects of Commonhold and Leasehold Reform Act 2002 will probably not come into force until 2004; see further para 29.35 and 34.5 below.

Artificial things brought onto land

29.9   It has been held by the House of Lords[1] that items brought onto land fall into one of three categories. They either become part and parcel of the land, or they are fixtures (in which case they are treated as part of the land), or they remain as chattels (goods) and are, therefore, regarded as quite separate from the land[2].

1   *Elitestone Ltd v Morris* [1997] 2 All ER 513, HL. In many instances there is no practical consequence of the distinction between an item that becomes part and parcel of the land and one that is a fixture. However, this is not always the case; for example, an item attached to property by a tenant which

becomes part and parcel of the land cannot be removed. As we shall see in para 29.14 below, tenants, on leaving the property, are allowed to remove many of the fixtures which they have attached to the property during the course of the lease.

2   While the ownership of chattels is, in principle, quite separate from that of the land on which they happen to be located, where the ownership of a chattel is unknown, there are circumstances in which the landowner may have first claim; see para 29.19 below.

29.10   *Items which are part and parcel of land*   Whether or not something becomes part and parcel of the land is 'as much a matter of common sense as precise analysis'[1]. So, in *Elitestone Ltd v Morris*[2] the House of Lords decided that a wooden bungalow resting on, but not attached to, concrete pillars had become part of the land. As a dwelling house, which the evidence showed could not be removed and re-erected elsewhere without destroying it, it must, objectively, be regarded as having been intended to serve a permanent purpose. It did not matter that the bungalow was not physically attached to the land, nor was it relevant that the parties themselves believed that the bungalow was owned separately from the site on which it stood. By way of contrast, a building which is designed to be taken apart and re-assembled elsewhere will retain its character as a chattel[3]; equally, an item such as a houseboat which could readily be moved somewhere else, will not be regarded either as part and parcel of the land or as a fixture[4].

1   Lord Lloyd in *Elitestone Ltd v Morris* [1997] 2 All ER 513, HL.
2   [1997] 2 All ER 513, HL.
3   See *Potton Developments Ltd v Thompson* [1998] NPC 49 where it was held that portable units of bedroom accommodation erected at a public house had not become part of the land but remained chattels; the units had been put together off-site, transported by lorry and put in place by crane and could be removed in the same way.
4   See *Chelsea Yacht & Boat Co Ltd v Pope* [2001] 2 All ER 409, CA where it was held that a houseboat which, although attached to its mooring and having connected services, was not regarded as part and parcel of the land because it was designed to, and could readily be, moved.

29.11   *Fixtures*   It is sometimes said that whatever is attached to the land becomes part of the land, but the law is not as straightforward as this. Whether or not something which is attached to the land is a fixture and thus treated as part of the land depends on all the circumstances. Two of these are particularly important: the degree of annexation and the purpose of annexation[1] (or, in other words, how securely the thing is attached to the land and the reasons behind its being attached). The law appears to be that if something is fixed to the land it is presumed to be land, and the more firmly it is fixed the stronger this presumption becomes. However, this presumption may be rebutted by evidence that it was not the intention behind fixing the thing to the land that it should become a permanent part of the land. For example, a poster pinned to the wall of a student's room would not be intended to become a permanent part of the land, and would not be a 'fixture'. If an item is resting on land by its own weight it is presumed to retain its own independent character and not to become part of the land, although this may be rebutted by evidence of intention. It is important to note that intention must be objectively assessed; the fact that parties may have agreed that an item is a chattel will be ignored by the courts in assessing whether or not it is a fixture[2]. This does not prevent parties agreeing, eg in the context of a sale, that an item which is a fixture may nevertheless be removed[3].

1   *Holland v Hodgson* (1872) LR 7 CP 328.
2   See *Elitestone v Morris* [1997] 2 All ER 513, HL; *Melluish (Inspector of Taxes) v BMI (No 3) Ltd* [1995] 4 All ER 453, HL.
3   See para 29.13 below.

29.12   Illustrations of whether a chattel fixed to the land has retained its chattel nature or has become a fixture are provided by the following cases. *Leigh v Taylor*[1] concerned tapestries which were put on the walls of a house by being fixed to a framework of wood and canvas which was nailed to the walls, each tapestry then being surrounded by a moulding, itself attached to the wall. The House of Lords held that the tapestries did not become part of the land and thus pass with it as fixtures, but remained chattels, since the reason they were fixed to the wall was so that they might be better enjoyed as chattels. The case of *TSB Bank plc v Botham*[2] provided the court with a rare opportunity to consider whether a range of modern household items were fixtures or chattels. The Court of Appeal ruled that fitted kitchen units and bathroom fittings (taps, showerheads, towel rails etc) were fixtures; all were necessarily attached to the property to enable those rooms to be used for their respective purposes. On the other hand, the following items were all considered to be chattels: fitted carpets, curtains, light fittings which were not part of the electrical installation, gas and electric fires, a 'slot-in' electric cooker, a plumbed-in washing machine and a refrigerator. Although all of these were in some way attached to the property, they could all be detached or disconnected without doing any damage to the fabric of the building. Furthermore, the purpose for which they were attached to the property was to enable the items themselves to function.

In contrast, in *Reynolds v Ashby & Son*,[3] the House of Lords held that machines which were let into concrete beds in the floor of a factory and fixed by nuts and bolts, but which could be removed without difficulty, became fixtures, since the purpose of annexation was to complete and use the building as a factory. Similarly, in *Aircool Installations v British Telecommunications*,[4] it had to be decided whether air-conditioning equipment had become a fixture. The internal units were bolted to the walls and were linked by pipework to external units which simply rested on their own weight; the system could have been removed and installed elsewhere. The court was nevertheless satisfied that the equipment had become a fixture. It was physically attached to the premises and the purpose of the annexation was manifestly for the better enjoyment of the building to which it was fixed.

It should also be noted that, on occasion, things not attached to land and resting purely by their own weight may, nevertheless, be treated as fixtures. Where items form part of a carefully integrated garden or interior design this may be treated as evidence of an overwhelming intention that they should form a permanent part of the land despite the absence of any physical attachment[5].

1   [1902] AC 157, HL.
2   [1996] EGCS 149, CA.
3   [1904] AC 466, HL.
4   [1995] CLY 821.
5   See *D'Eyncourt v Gregory* (1866) LR 3 Eq 382 (statues forming part of a landscaping scheme); *Hamp v Bygrave* [1983] 1 EGLR 174 (a collection of co-ordinated garden ornaments).

29.13   While the legal principles governing the distinction between fixtures and chattels may be relatively straightforward, their day-to-day application is notoriously difficult. The potential for disputes, especially on the sale of property, is well recognised. For this reason it has become usual for the vendor and purchaser to agree, prior to the exchange of contracts, a list of which items are to be taken by the vendor and which are to be left for the purchaser. This then is incorporated into the contract and, in so far as any item is, objectively speaking, a fixture, amounts to an agreement that it can be removed by the vendor.

29.14   *Fixtures added by a tenant*   In principle it is immaterial who paid for or who previously owned items which have become fixtures. Accordingly, fixtures added by a tenant under a lease are treated as part of the land and are therefore regarded as belonging to the freeholder, who has absolute ownership of the land. However, in practice, the effect of this last rule is modified in many instances since it has long been recognised that it operates as a disincentive, particularly for tenants who use premises for commercial purposes. Accordingly, when leaving the premises at the end of a lease, a tenant is permitted[1] to remove any domestic or ornamental fixtures[2] that he has attached and which can be removed without substantial[3] damage to the fabric of the building, together with any fixtures[2] which he has attached for the purposes of his business.[4]

1 Unless the lease clearly and unequivocally excludes the right to remove fixtures: see *Lamboum v McLellan* [1903] 2 Ch 268, CA.
2 The right of removal attaches only to fixtures, not to items which have become part and parcel of the land: see para 29.10 above.
3 In *Young v Dalgety plc* [1987] 1 EGLR 116 it was held that light fittings could be removed by a tenant even though this would cause minor damage. Such minor damage as is caused must be made good so as to leave the premises in a reasonable condition: see *Mancetter Developments Ltd v Garmanson Ltd* [1986] 1 All ER 449, CA.
4 The common law did not allow farm tenants to remove agricultural (as opposed to trade) fixtures. The right of a tenant of an agricultural holding to remove agricultural fixtures is currently governed by the Agricultural Holdings Act 1986, s 10. The right of a tenant under a farm business tenancy to remove *any* fixture is governed by the Agricultural Tenancies Act 1995, s 8.

Things growing on the land
29.15   Things which grow naturally on the land such as grass, plants and trees which, though they may need attention when first planted, do not need attention each year to produce a crop, such as apple trees, are known as *fructus naturales* and are regarded as part of the land. On the other hand, cultivated crops, such as wheat and potatoes, which are known as *fructus industriales*, are not regarded as part of the land.

Limitations on the physical extent of a landowner's rights
29.16   We saw in para 29.8 above that land includes not only the surface but also what is above and what is below the surface and that, on the face of it, the rights of a landowner extend over all the land as so defined. However, this must not be regarded as a rigid legal definition of land but rather as being a somewhat imprecise expression of the rights of a landowner[1]. While the principle at least makes it clear that the rights of a landowner normally extend above and below the surface, it is obviously fanciful to treat it as meaning that the landowner's rights literally extend upwards to the heavens and downwards to the centre of the earth, a notion which would lead to the absurdity of a trespass at common law being committed every time a satellite passes over a suburban garden.[2] On the other hand, the limits which may realistically be put on the height and depth to which the landowner's rights extend are not easy to determine. Those which can be identified will be dealt with briefly here.

1 *Railways Comr v Valuer-General* [1974] AC 328, [1973] 3 All ER 268, PC.
2 *Bernstein v Skyviews and General Ltd* [1977] 2 All ER 902 at 907.

Airspace
29.17   We have suggested in para 23.3 above, that, following *Bernstein v Skyviews and General Ltd*,[1] the rights of a landowner as regards the airspace above the surface of his land are restricted to such a height as is necessary for the ordinary use and enjoyment of the land and the structures on it. However, this begs the question of how high that is in any particular case. This means that whether or not a trespass to airspace has been committed in any particular instance depends on the facts of each case. However, it seems likely that, whenever the intrusion emanates from a structure on adjoining land such as a building or tower crane, this will virtually always constitute a trespass[2]. However, intrusion into the upper airspace by a flying object, such as a hot air balloon, will not, of itself, amount to trespass[3]. Furthermore, statute ensures that the ordinary overflight of civil aircraft at a reasonable height is not a trespass[4]; however, this immunity will not apply to extraordinary activities such as unwarranted surveillance[5].

1 [1977] 2 All ER 902.
2 See, for example, *Anchor Brewhouse Developments Ltd v Berkley House (Docklands Developments) Ltd* [1987] 2 EGLR 173 in which it was held that a trespass occurred where the jib of a tower crane 'oversailed' neighbouring land.
3 *Pickering v Rudd* (1815) 4 Camp 219.
4 Civil Aviation Act 1982, s 76(1).
5 In *Bernstein v Skyviews and General Ltd* [1977] 2 All ER 902 it was held that the statutory immunity applied to a flight at a reasonable height involving ordinary commercial aerial photography.

Minerals

29.18 The conventional view is that the landowner's rights do indeed extend to the earth's core, and as mining techniques improve this may turn out to be of practical importance. It certainly constitutes a trespass to tunnel into adjoining land to exploit minerals.[1] Although the general rule is that mineral are part of the soil and thus belong to owner of the surface, there are exceptions, of which the following are examples. All gold and silver in gold and silver mines belong to the Crown; therefore such a mine cannot be worked by an individual even on his own land without a licence from the Crown.[2] Oil and natural gas in underground strata belong to the Crown.[3] Coal is vested in the Coal Authority[4]. It should also be borne in mind that, even where a landowner does own minerals, he will require planning permission in order to be able to extract them[5].

1 See *Bulli Coal Mining Co v Osborne* [1899] AC 351, PC.
2 *A-G v Morgan* [1891] 1 Ch 432, CA.
3 Petroleum Act 1998, ss 1(a), 2(1).
4 Coal Industry Act 1994, ss1(1), 7(3).
5 Town and Country Planning Act 1990, s 55(1); see para 40.2 below.

Things found on or under the land

29.19 In the absence of evidence as to their true owner, the law presumes that the landowner, if he is in possession of the land, is entitled as against the finder to:

- things fixed or buried in the land[1];
- things on the land *where the landowner obviously intends to exercise control over the property and the things in it;*[2] and
- things on the land where the finder is a trespasser.[2]

However, finds of 'treasure'[3] belong to the Crown (or any franchisee of the Crown)[4] except where any rightful owner can be identified. Treasure may be returned to the landowner or finder;[5] this is likely to occur where the find is of little historical or archaeological significance. Where it is subsequently transferred by the Crown to a museum a reward may be payable to the finder, to the landowner on whose property the treasure was found, or may be shared between such persons.[6]

1 *Waverley Borough Council v Fletcher* [1995] 4 All ER 756, CA is modern authority confirming the important distinction between items found *in* the land, and those found *on* the land. In the former case the landowner has the superior claim even in situations where he has no obvious intention to exercise control over the property and the things in it.
2 *Parker v British Airways Board* [1982] QB 1004, [1982] 1 All ER 834, CA.
3 'Treasure' is widely defined in the Treasure Act 1996, s 1 with the aim of covering all finds of historical and archaeological importance; it is no longer confined to items of gold and silver, as was the case under the old law of treasure trove.
4 Treasure Act 1996, s 4.
5 Treasure Act 1996, s 6.
6 Treasure Act 1996, s 10. The Code of Practice drawn up under s 11 of the Act clearly envisages that finders who were trespassing at the time of their find may receive either no reward at all, or a reduced reward.

Wild animals

29.20   Wild animals cannot, while alive, be owned but, once killed on the land, they become the property of the landowner,[1] whether killed by the landowner in the exercise of his common law right to kill and take wild animals found on his land[2], or by a trespasser such as a poacher.[3]

1   *R v Townley* (1871) LR I CCR 315.
2   Statute makes it an offence to kill certain wild animals: see, for example, Wildlife and Countryside Act 1981, s 9.
3   *Blades v Higgs* (1865) 11 HL Cas 621.

Water

29.21   Water standing on the land in a pond or lake is part of the land and belongs to the landowner. Water percolating in undefined channels or flowing in defined channels through or past his land cannot be the subject of ownership but, although the landowner does not own the water, he has certain rights in relation to it. The most important of these is the right of abstraction. The Water Resources Act 1991,[1] s 24 lays down the general rule that the landowner may only abstract water from a 'source of supply' in pursuance of a licence obtained from the National Rivers Authority (NRA). Rivers, streams and water in underground strata all constitute 'sources of supply', as do those lakes, ponds or reservoirs which discharge into rivers or streams. However, a licence is not required for certain limited purposes.[2]

Where no NRA licence is required, a landowner is quite at liberty to abstract water percolating in undefined channels through underground strata even if this prevents any reaching his neighbour's land.[3] There is no remedy for damage to neighbouring property caused by such abstraction.[4]

Where the owner of land contiguous with a river or stream (the riparian owner) needs no NRA licence for his proposed abstraction, he is nonetheless limited in what he may take by the common law. He is free to abstract what he needs for his domestic purposes and for his cattle without regard to the effect which his use will have on landowners downstream,[5] but abstraction for other purposes (which must be connected with the land) is subject to the requirement that the water is put back in substantially the same volume and quality. The reason for this limitation is that at common law each riparian owner has the right to the flow of the river or stream unaltered in quantity and quality, and may enforce this right against owners upstream by an action in nuisance.[6] If water is abstracted in pursuance of an NRA licence, the riparian owner has a defence to such an action.[7]

The riparian owner also has the right to fish in non-tidal waters, even where they are navigable rivers.[8]

1   Which re-enacts the rules previously laid down in the Water Resources Act 1963, as amended by the Water Act 1989.
2   Water Resources Act 1991, s 27
3   *Bradford Corpn v Pickles* [1895] AC 587, HL; para 16.11 above.
4   *Langbrook Properties Ltd v Surrey County Council* [1969] 3 All ER 1424; *Stephens v Anglian Water Authority* [1987] 3 All ER 379, CA.
5   *Miner v Gilmour* (1859) 12 Moo PCC 131.
6   *John Young & Co v Bankier Distillery Co* [1893] AC 691, 1 IL; *Tate and Lyle Industries Ltd v Greater London Council* [1983] 1 All ER 1159, HL.
7   Water Resources Act 1991, s 48.
8   *Cooper v Phibbs* (1867) LR 2 HL 149; *Pearce v Scotcher* (1882) 9 QBD 162, DC.

Demarcating the physical extent of land: boundaries

The general law

29.22   Clearly it is important for a landowner to know the exact extent of his land, in order to know precisely what he has bought and can sell, or to prevent neighbours encroaching, or to know how much space is available for building. As a matter of law a boundary is simply an imaginary line which marks the confines or line of division of two contiguous parcels of land; in practice, the location of a boundary is often marked by some physical object such as a wall, hedge or fence. Unfortunately, despite the obvious importance of ensuring that the line of the boundary is clearly delineated, this is often not achieved, with the result that the question remains to be settled after the property has been transferred, often as a result of a boundary dispute between neighbours.

29.23   When the title to land is first registered at the Land Registry[1], the land is generally described in the transfer deed merely as 'the land comprised in Title Number ... ', a form of words which thereby incorporates the verbal description of the land in the Property Register of the register of title. This description normally gives only the postal address and refers to the filed plan. Although this plan is an accurate Ordnance Survey plan, it has two drawbacks. First, it is small scale, usually on a scale of 1:1250 in urban areas and 1:2500 in rural areas[2]. Second, in law, it normally only fixes a 'general boundary' (in effect the the land's location); it does not establish the exact line of the boundary[3]. Often, this causes no difficulty. The limits of the property are usually demarcated by a fence, wall or hedge which the adjoining owners never have cause to dispute. However, where the precise line of the boundary is for some reason crucial (eg where one of them needs to build right up to the edge of their land) the filed plan may not be sufficiently detailed, exact or authoritative.

Where the Land Register leaves the matter of the boundaries unclear the court will have regard to extrinsic evidence, such as the contract itself,[4] pre-registration deeds, auction particulars,[5] photographs and surveyors' oral evidence,[6] planning permission,[7] and any acts of ownership in relation to some boundary feature by one of the parties, such as the erection and maintenance of a boundary fence.

In a number of cases, where evidence is lacking as to the line of the boundary, the courts resort to certain rebuttable presumptions[8], which we consider in the following paragraphs.

1   As to which see para 30.14 below.
2   It should be noted that the Land Registry will always consider the use of a larger scale plan, notably where the topography of the land makes this desirable.
3   Land Registration Act 2002, s 60.
4   *Spall v Owen* (1981) 44 P & CR 36.
5   *Scarfe v Adams* [1981] 1 All ER 843, CA.
6   *Mayer v Hurr* (1983) 49 P & CR 56, CA.
7   *Stock v David Wilson Homes (Anglia)* [1993] NPC 83, CA.
8   Ie rules which apply only in the absence of evidence to the contrary.

Presumptions
29.24   *Walls and floors*   The outside of any external wall is presumed to be included in a sale or lease of the property[1]. Thus in one case[2] it was held to constitute trespass for a landlord to affix advertising hoardings to the outside wall of premises which he had let on the second floor of his property. As to where the legal boundary lies between two floors of a building, which have been separately let, it has been held that the ordinary expectation is that the lease entitles the tenant to occupy all the space between the floor of his flat and the underneath of the floor of the flat above.[3] Where a dispute concerns the upper boundary of a top floor flat, its resolution may require resort to general principles governing the ownership of airspace[4]. So, in *Davies v Yadegar*[5] it was held by the Court of Appeal that the tenant of a top floor flat was entitled to insert dormer windows into the roof above his flat. His lease, which had expressly included the roof and roof space, had not specified an upper boundary to his property and, consequently, he was a tenant not only of the flat but of the airspace above the flat, into which the proposed new windows could legitimately intrude.

1   *Sturge v Hackett* [1962] 1 WLR 1257, CA.
2   *Re Webb's Lease* [1951] Ch 808
3   *Graystone Property Investments Ltd v Margulies* (1983) 47 P & CR 472, CA.
4   See paras 29.8 and 29.17 above
5   [1990] 1 EGLR 71, CA.

29.25   *Hedges and ditches*   Where parties are disputing the exact line of a boundary along which runs a hedge or bank together with a ditch, the presumption of the law is that the boundary runs along the edge of the ditch furthest from the hedge or bank. This presumption derives from the quaint notion that the ditch was originally dug by the landowner at the furthest edge of his land and then, to avoid trespass, the resulting earth was thrown behind him onto his own land.[1] This presumption only applies where there is a hedge (or bank) and a ditch together. It would appear to apply to registered land even though the filed plan is based on the Ordnance Survey map on which boundaries are treated as running down the middle of any hedge.

1   *Vowles v Miller* (1810) 3 Taunt 137. For more recent applications of the presumption see *Hall v Dorling* (1997) 74 P & CR 400, CA and *Alan Wibberley Building Ltd v Insley* [1999] 2 All ER 897, HL.

29.26   *Highways*   It is presumed that, wherever land abuts a highway, the boundary line lies down the middle of the highway.[1] This presumption, which applies only where there is no other evidence as to the boundary, is easily rebutted, for example in the case of a building estate where the developer might intend to retain ownership of the roads for construction purposes and for dedication to the public. Where the highway has been adopted by the highway authority,[2] there vests in that authority the surface and so much above and below the surface as is necessary for the carrying out of their duties as highway authority; thus, in such cases the issue relates only to the ownership of the subsoil. In the case of registered land, it is not the practice of the Land Registry to show ownership of the subsoil where the highway is adopted.

1   *Central London Rly Co v City of London Land Tax Comrs* [1911] 1 Ch 467 at 474.
2   Ie under the Highways Act 1980.

29.27   *Rivers, etc*   In the case of non-tidal rivers which form a boundary to land, it is presumed that the boundary runs down the middle of the river bed. The rights of fishing and abstraction, described in para 29.21 above, would therefore be divided midstream between opposite riparian owners. In the case of land bounded by a tidal river or by the seashore, the boundary lies at the medium high water mark, the foreshore being vested in the Crown. There appears to be no presumption to assist in determining the boundary where the land of several owners is bounded by a lake.

Alteration of boundaries

29.28   The line of a boundary may be altered by agreement of the parties. Since this will involve the transfer of land from one party to the other such an agreement should be by deed and completed by registration, so as to comply with the formalities required for the transfer of an interest in land[1]. Where, as is often the case, such formalities are not complied with, the courts may be able to give effect to the agreement by the operation of the doctrine of estoppel.[2] The line of a boundary may also be changed by the alteration of the title register where the Land Registration Act applies,[3] or as a result of the rules relating to adverse possession (as where a landowner moves the boundary fence so as to incorporate some of his neighbour's land and remains in adverse possession for the requisite period).[4]

If a boundary dispute arises, it is possible that the parties may, informally, agree where the boundary between their properties lies. Such an agreement does not involve the transfer of any land and so it is not necessary for a deed to be used. However, it is likely that no consideration is provided with the result that the agreement has no contractual force. Nevertheless, the courts will strive to give effect to the parties' intentions, either by resorting to the doctrine of estoppel,[2] or by treating the agreement as evidence of where the boundary lies. So, in *Davey v Harrow Corpn*,[5] where adjoining landowners had agreed to the erection of a post and wire fence along the boundary, the Court of Appeal ruled that this rebutted any presumption which might otherwise have been relevant in determining the boundary line between the two properties, which were separated by a hedge and a ditch but had been conveyed by reference to the Ordnance Survey map.

1   See Chapter 30 below.
2   As in *Hopgood v Brown* [1955] 1 All ER 550, CA. See further paras 31.11-31.15 below.
3   Para 36.37 below.
4   Paras 31.19-31.34 below.
5   [1957] 2 All ER 305, CA.

Boundary structures

29.29 Obviously any boundary structure exclusively on one side of the boundary belongs to the owner of that side, even though the neighbour may have the right that it be maintained.[1] It may be that the owner of land is unable to repair or maintain a boundary structure which belongs to him (or other parts of his property) without going onto adjoining land. As we have seen, at common law, there is no automatic right of access for such purposes so that in the absence of an express right of access, or a temporary permission from the neighbour, the landowner would be committing a trespass which can be restrained by an injunction. This unsatisfactory state of affairs has been remedied by the Access to Neighbouring Land Act 1992.[2]

In practice many boundary structures straddle the line of the boundary. Irrespective of the nature of the structure it is known, in law, as a 'party wall'. In the ordinary case, party walls are regarded as being vertically severed, each side having the right to support from the other.[3] The Party Wall etc Act 1996 provides a scheme under which works can be carried out to party structures, and any disputes over such works resolved by a surveyor, without recourse to the courts.

1   See para 33.12 below.
2   Discussed at para 23.7 above.
3   LPA, s 38.

Legal nature of proprietary rights to land

29.30 Having considered the legal nature of land and the physical extent of a landowner's rights, we now turn to a further discussion of those rights to occupy or use land which the law recognises as proprietary, rather than personal. As we have mentioned[1] these can largely be categorised as either[2] 'ownership' interests, ie those which are enjoyed in respect of one's own land, or third party interests, ie those which are enjoyed in respect of land owned by another.

1   See para 29.3 above
2   However a leasehold ownership interest is hybrid in nature. Although it confers on a tenant the right to exclusive possession of the land in question for the duration of the lease, the land to which a lease relates is also 'owned' by another, ie the landlord.

Ownership interests: estates and tenure

29.31 We start by addressing the nature of ownership interests in land. As a matter of legal theory, under English law, only the Crown can 'own' land[1]; individual subjects of the

Crown merely 'hold' land from the Crown. This is the doctrine of tenure. While Crown land is held absolutely and in perpetuity, other land is held for a period of time. This 'holding' of land is categorised according to the length of time for which it will last, a notion which finds expression in the doctrine of *estates*. Thus, rather than speaking of owning land in perpetuity or for life, we speak of owning a particular 'estate'[2] in the land which will last for ever, or for the lifetime of its owner. We shall now briefly consider these two historical building blocks of English land law, the doctrine of *tenure* and the doctrine of *estates*.

1   Land owned directly by the Crown is known as 'demesne' land.
2   The term is here used in its technical land law sense, rather than as a synonym for 'land'.

Tenure

29.32   Feudalism, in which tenure (from the Latin, *tenere*, to hold) was the fundamental element, formed the basis of society after the Norman Conquest. The social structure was based on grants of land by the king (to whom all land was regarded as belonging as the spoils of victory) to his followers, not as theirs to own, but to 'hold of' him (or 'have possession of' from him) as their superior lord in return for their performing certain services, such as furnishing the king with armed horsemen or with provisions. These 'tenants-in-chief' in their turn granted some of this land to other 'tenants' to hold of them as superior lords in return for services, and so on. Each tenant, then, held land in return for providing services to his lord[1]. However, over time there has been a gradual decline in the practical significance of the system of tenure, with the benefits and obligations of tenure gradually disappearing, so that all that remains today is the legal theory that land is not owned outright but held of the Crown. That said, the theory remains alive; not only is there a tenurial relationship between the landlord and tenant of a lease, but the new strata title system which will be introduced[2] utilises a new form of tenure – commonhold.

1   We are here using the term 'tenant' in the feudal sense of someone who holds land by way of tenure, rather than in its modern connotation of someone who owns land by way of a lease.
2   By the Commonhold and Leasehold Reform Act 2002. See further para 29.35 below.

Estates

29.33   Although we referred in the last paragraph to the tenant holding land, it is more accurate to speak of the tenant holding the land for a particular estate, ie having possession of the land for an interest of a particular duration. The two most important estates are popularly referred to as the freehold and the leasehold. Historically, the law recognised other estates, in particular the fee tail and the life estate; however, these are rarely encountered today and no further discussion of them is necessary.

29.34   *Freehold: the fee simple absolute in possession*   The technical legal term for the freehold estate is the estate in fee simple absolute in possession.[1] The owner of a fee simple absolute in possession is equivalent to an absolute owner. He has the complete freedom to dispose of his rights to the land either during his lifetime or under his will; in other words, he can transfer ownership of his property as he wishes. He can also carve lesser ownership interests out of his freehold, for example by granting a lease, and can grant rights over it (such as easements or mortgages) to others.

1   LPA, s 1.

29.35   *Freehold estate in commonhold land*   The Commonhold and Leasehold Reform Act 2002[1] will introduce a new form of ownership – commonhold – which is designed to provide a form of landholding appropriate to those whose properties are necessarily interdependent. Classically it will apply to the ownership of flats, but it should be appreciated that commonhold is not confined to residential properties. It is intended that commonhold will replace the use of the long lease as a method of dealing with the ownership of physically interdependent properties. Such leases have become increasingly unpopular and discredited, especially in the residential context. They are a wasting asset and thus, over time, become unmortgageable; furthermore, tenants often believe that landlords do not manage and maintain their buildings in an efficient and cost-effective way.

It will be possible to register a freehold[2] estate in land as being a freehold in commonhold land, provided that there is in place a memorandum of association of a commonhold association and a commonhold community statement ('CCS')[3]. Once the development is completed[4] and the first unit sold, the initial title will be divided into what is effectively a community of freehold titles. The title to the common parts[5] will be held by the commonhold association and the purchaser of each unit will have a freehold title to that unit. Once the commonhold is active, only unit owners can be members of the commonhold association[6]. The CCS must define the units within the commonhold[7]; contain provisions governing the use, insurance, repair and maintenance of each unit[8]; and regulate the use of the common parts and oblige the commonhold association to insure, repair and maintain the common parts[9]. This new system is designed to ensure that unit holders have a freehold title (thus eliminating the problem of the wasting asset); that the use, repair and maintenance of both the units and the common parts are governed by provisions[10] contained in a single document (the CCS); and that the unit holders (as the only members of the commonhold association) are in charge of the management and maintenance of the common parts.

1   The Commonhold and Leasehold Reform Act 2002 ('CLRA') is due to come into force in 2004.
2   Commonhold can exist only in relation to freehold land, CLRA 2002, s 1.
3   CLRA 2002, s 1(1).
4   It is possible to convert an existing leasehold scheme (of which there are very many) into a commonhold; however, the consent of all leaseholders holding a registered lease of more than 21 years, and all mortgagees is required, CLRA 2002 s 3(1). It is felt that this will usually block the conversion to commonhold of many large leasehold schemes. Hence in the early years it is expected that commonhold will tend to be confined to new developments and refurbishments.
5   'Common parts' are all parts of the commonhold which are not defined by the CCS as a commonhold unit, CLRA 2002, s 25(1).
6   CLRA 2002, s 34, Sch 3.
7   CLRA 2002, s 11(2). There must be at least two units.
8   CLRA 2002, s 14.
9   CLRA 2002, s 26.
10 Which are likely to become standardised so that the provisions governing all commonholds will become very similar.

29.36   *Leasehold: the term of years absolute*[1] The leasehold interest is the second of the two estates recognised at law. The terminology used in the Law of Property Act 1925 (LPA), s 1 for the leasehold interest is 'the term of years absolute'. This phrase need not detain us; it can be regarded as having no meaning other than to denote a leasehold interest. A person has a leasehold interest in land where another, the landlord or lessor, grants him exclusive possession of property, as tenant or lessee, for a definite or certain period.[2]

The leasehold interest acquired by the tenant or lessee is known variously as a 'tenancy' – generally where it is of short duration, as in weekly, monthly or yearly tenancies – or as a 'lease', 'demise', 'term of years' or 'term certain' – generally where it is of longer, fixed, duration, perhaps of 21 or 99 years. Having granted a lease (or 'let', 'leased' or 'demised' the property) the landlord is said, somewhat inaccurately, to retain the 'reversion' on the lease, on the basis that physical possession of the land will revert to him on the ending of the lease. In the eyes of the law, of course, he is still regarded as being in possession during the course of the lease because he is in receipt of the rents and profits of the land.[3]

Since a leaseholder can usually[4] carve a further lease out of his own lease, there can be more than one lease in respect of the same piece of land. For example, A the freeholder may grant a 99-year lease of Whitelands to B and B then may grant a 10-year sub-lease to C. This means that, for the next 10 years C will actually occupy Whitelands and pay the rent fixed in the sub-lease to B; B will receive that rent from C and pay the rent agreed in the head-lease to A. B's expectation will be that the rent he receives from C will exceed that which he has to pay to A. At the end of the 10 years B will become entitled to physical possession of Whitelands although he may, of course, choose either to renew the sub-lease to C or to grant an new sub-lease to D.

1   Leaseholds interests are considered in more detail in chs 37 and 38, below.
2   See paras 37.2–37.10 below.
3   LPA, s 205(1) (xix).
4   The right to sublet may, however, be forbidden under the terms of a lease.

Third party rights: interests in land

29.37   We have already mentioned[1] that the law recognises not only ownership rights in respect of land, but also rights which one person may have over land which belongs to another, such as private rights of way. Where such rights fall within certain legally defined categories[2] they are regarded as interests in land. Interests in land, which are usually referred to, somewhat confusingly, as 'third party' rights, are 'proprietary' in nature. This means that they are capable of binding future owners of the land to which they relate, in other words that future owners can be obliged to recognise such rights.[3]

1   See para 29.3 above.
2   The most important of which are dealt with in chs 33–35 below.
3   The circumstances in which third party rights actually bind future owners are dealt with in ch 36 below.

Legal and equitable rights to land

29.38   The Law of Property Act 1925, s 1 distinguishes between legal estates and interests on the one hand, and equitable interests on the other. The freehold[1], or fee simple absolute in possession, and the leasehold, or term of years absolute, are now, by virtue of that section, the only estates that can exist at law. They are the two legal estates. Other forms of ownership, such as the life estate, which were formerly recognised by the law, today can only take effect as equitable interests (although they are rarely encountered today and are not further discussed).[2] The section also provides that only certain third party rights can exist at law[3]. The more important of these are easements[4] (rights of way, rights of support and the like) which have been granted for a period equivalent to a fee simple absolute in possession or term of years absolute, and charges by way of legal mortgage,[5] the most common device for mortgaging land. These are referred to as legal interests. Those third party rights which cannot take effect as legal interests now do so as equitable interests.

1   Includings its new variant, the freehold estate in commonhold land, see para 29.35 above.
2   LPA, s 1(3).
3   LPA, s 1(2), para 29.37 above.
4   Chapter 33 below.
5   Para 35.4 below.

What is an equitable interest?

29.39   An equitable interest is either (as explained in the previous paragraph) an interest which, after 1925,[1] can no longer exist at law, or it is one which is derived from the rules of equity (ie those principles of law which originated in the decisions of the former Court of Chancery[2]). As we shall see, apart from recognising rights for which the common law could find no place (such as restrictive covenants), equity was prepared to give effect to transactions which do not comply with the strict formalities demanded by the common law.[3] Whether a right is legal or equitable often makes little difference to its substance; however, the distinction can be crucial in determining its actual enforceability against future owners.[4]

1   As a result of LPA 1925, s 1(3).
2   Para 1.6 above.
3   Chapter 31 below.
4   Chapter 36 below.

29.40   *The trust*   One equitable concept which plays a particularly important part in the English law of property (both real and personal) is that of the 'trust'. The idea which lies behind the trust is that of separating the management of property from the enjoyment of its benefits, such as possession of it and income from it. The device is said to have originated in the practice of those going on crusades of transferring their land to trusted friends to hold for the benefit of their wives and children while they were away, and in the practice of granting land to be held for the benefit of Franciscan friars who, by the rules of their Order, could not themselves hold land. In the eyes of the common law, only those to whom the land had been formally conveyed had rights in respect of it; those for whose benefit the land was supposed to have been held were viewed as having no rights. The Court of Chancery, however, took a very different approach, and recognised that the persons to whom the land was conveyed (who are today known as trustees) were in conscience bound to observe the trust placed in them. This court obliged the trustees to deal with the land in accordance with the wishes of the person whom it was intended to benefit (whom we now call the beneficiary), and to permit him to use or take the income of the land. That the beneficiary had these rights against the trustees effectively meant that the trustees had only the bare legal ownership of the land, whilst the beneficial ownership lay with the beneficiary.

The trust has always been, and still is, used as a protective device under which the legal title and management responsibilities can be placed in the hands of an experienced and responsible trustee in order to guard the interests of a young and vulnerable (or, perhaps, not so young but irresponsible) beneficiary. However, it has always had other roles. From earliest times it was used as a pure conveyancing device. For example, it was possible to create a greater range of ownership rights in respect of the equitable interest in land than in the legal interest; further, it was possible to leave an equitable interest in land by will long before this was permitted at law. In more modern times, it became usual to create a trust of land where it was desired to give a number of different people ownership and other interests in the same piece of land, either in succession, or concurrently. In this way the legal title to the land, which would be held by a limited number of trustees, could be kept relatively straightforward; the complex equitable interests being kept 'behind' the trust. This latter use of the trust was greatly extended by the 1925 property legislation and is a topic to which we return in chapter 32. Finally, equity has come to employ the trust as a means of compelling a common law owner of land, in appropriate circumstances, to hold 'his' land for the benefit of another. So, for example, as we shall see,[1] where land is conveyed to A alone but B has contributed to the purchase price, equity may insist that A holds the land on trust for himself and B.

1   See para 31.9 below.

Personal rights to use land: licences

29.41   An owner of land is free to confer on others a right to use his land which does not amount to an interest in land. Such rights, although infinitely variable in content, are collectively known as 'licences'. The classic definition of a licence relating to land states that a licence passes no interest in the land but only makes lawful what would otherwise be unlawful.[1] It would appear, then, that a licence to enter on, or to occupy, property is a personal arrangement between the licensor and the licensee under which the licensee acquires no interest in the property. If a licence creates no property interest but is dependent on the permission of the licensor, why is the topic of licences included in the study of land law? First, because occupation of land by virtue of a licence has been common as a substitute for occupation by virtue of a tenancy, as a means of avoiding legislation which protects the rights of tenants[2], so that the courts have frequently been called upon to draw the fine line between a licence (which is not a property interest) and a lease (which is).[3] Second, because the courts may, in certain circumstances, recognise certain types of use and occupation of land which are, on the face of it, enjoyed merely by licence as having proprietary characteristics, in particular that of being enforceable against subsequent owners of the land.[4]

Most licences fall into one of the following two categories:

- gratuitous licences (sometimes referred to as 'bare' licences); or
- contractual licences.

The characteristics and nature of these types of licence will be discussed in the following paragraphs.

1   *Thomas v Sorrell* (1673) Vaugh 330 at 351.
2   Eg Rent Act 1977, Landlord and Tenant Act 1954.
3   See paras 37.9 and 37.10 below.
4   Paras 31.8–31.18 below.

Gratuitous licences

29.42   A gratuitous licence is, in essence, a permission to be on land for which no consideration[1] has been provided. The guest whom you invite to dinner has, when he comes to dinner, a gratuitous licence to be on your property. Your young neighbour, who with your permission enters your garden to retrieve his ball, is a gratuitous licensee. When a householder who lives in a dwelling-house which has a front garden garden in front and does not lock the gate of the garden, this amounts to an implied licence to any member of the public who has a lawful reason for doing so to proceed from the gate to the front door or back door, and to inquire whether he may be admitted to conduct his lawful business.[2] Although most gratuitous licences are of the relatively trivial variety just mentioned, it should be remembered that this category is a residual one; consequently any licence not falling within one of the other categories is a gratuitous licence.[3]

In each of the above examples the right of the licensee to be on the land is dependent entirely on the permission, express or implied, of the landowner/licensor. Without that permission, the licensee would be a trespasser. The licensee has no right to prevent the revocation of his licence and the landowner may revoke the permission to be on the land at any time. A withdrawal of permission does not mean that the licensee immediately becomes a trespasser. The law allows him a reasonable time to leave the premises; what is reasonable will vary according to the circumstances of the case.[2]

Clearly a gratuitous licence, being entirely dependent on the permission of the landowner, is neither assignable by the licensee nor, in the absence of additional factors, enforceable against successors of the licensor.[4]

1   See para 6.3 above.
2   *Robson v Hallett* [1967] 2 All ER 407 at 414.
3   See, for example, *Horrocks v Forray* [1976] 1 All ER 737; para 29.44 below.
4   Discussed at paras 31.8–31.18 below.

Contractual licences

Nature

29.43   A licence to enter land is a contractual licence if it is conferred by contract; hence, unless a deed is used, consideration must have been provided for the permission to be on the land. It is immaterial whether the right to enter the land is the primary purpose of the contract or is merely secondary.[1] An example of the former would be a contractual licence to hire a room for a function, or to occupy a room in a house as a lodger. (As we shall see,[2] in neither of these cases does the occupier have exclusive possession, hence there is no tenancy, merely a licence.) An example of a licence conferred as a secondary object of a contract is provided by *Hounslow London Borough Council v Twickenham Garden Developments Ltd,*[3] in which the primary object of the contract was that the defendants should build a housing estate for the plaintiffs; it was held that this necessarily conferred on the defendants a licence to enter the site.

Not surprisingly, in order for a contractual licence to be valid, it must be shown that the essential requirements of a contract are present. In certain cases where there has been no express agreement between the parties, the courts have been able to discern the presence of the requirements of a contract and thereby imply the existence of a contractual licence between the parties. In *Chandler v Kerley*[4], the Court of Appeal was satisfied that an arrangement under which the defendant, a former co-owner of the property, agreed to sell it to the plaintiff for two-thirds of the asking price on the understanding that she and her children could continue to live there, amounted to a contractual licence. However, it is often impossible, particularly in a family context, to infer the necessary ingredients of a contract, notably any intention to create legal relations. So, in *Horrocks v Forray,*[5] the court was unable to treat an arrangement between a man and his mistress, whereby the former had for many years provided accommodation for the latter, as a contractual licence. In the absence of any additional factors[6] she was regarded as having only a bare licence and could not resist his executors' claim for possession of the house in which she lived.

1   *Hounslow London Borough Council v Twickenham Garden Developments Ltd* [1970] 3 All ER 326 at 343.
2   Para 37.8 below.
3   [1970] 3 All ER 326.
4   [1978] 2 All ER 942, CA.
5   [1976] 1 All ER 737, CA.
6   Paras 31.8–31.18 below.

Revocability

29.44   A contractual licence is not an entity distinct from the contract which brings it into being, but merely a provision of that contract.[1] Thus the extent to which the licensor is free to revoke the licence depends on the terms, express or implied, of the contract. It is a question of construction of the particular contract whether a purported revocation by the licensor is or is not in breach of contract.[2] In the absence of express terms there is no general rule as to the revocability of a contractual licence,[3] although (where there is no other evidence of the parties' intentions) it appears that the courts will readily imply a term that the licence is revocable on reasonable notice being given;[4] what is 'reasonable' depending on the circumstances of the case.

If the licensor purports to revoke the licence in breach of contract, what is the licensee to do? He has a contractual right to remain on the property despite the wrongful revocation by the licensor and cannot be treated as a trespasser[5] (and, if he is forcibly removed as a trespasser, he may sue for damages for assault).[6] If it is practicable for the licensee to seek the assistance of the court, he may obtain an injunction to prevent his being turned out or, in a case where the licensor refuses to let him enter in the first place, an order of specific performance.[7] However, these orders are available only at the discretion of the court, and, for example, the court will not specifically enforce an agreement for two people to live peaceably under the same roof.[8] A licensee who cannot obtain an order enforcing the contractual licence, either because in the circumstances it is not practicable for him to seek one[9] or because the licence is not regarded as specifically enforceable, must, unless he can otherwise secure peaceable entry to the property, accept the termination of the licence as a fait accompli and sue for damages for breach of contract.

1   *Hounslow London Borough Council v Twickenham Garden Developments Ltd* [1970] 3 All ER 326 at 343.
2   *Millennium Productions Ltd v Winter Garden Theatre (London) Ltd* [1946] 1 All ER 678, CA; rvsd sub nom *Winter Garden Theatre (London) Ltd v Millennium Productions Ltd* [1947] 2 All ER 331, HL.
3   *Australian Blue Metal Ltd v Hughes* [1963] AC 74 at 99.
4   *Winter Garden Theatre (London) Ltd v Millennium Productions Ltd* [1947] 2 All ER 331, HL; *Chandler v Kerley* [1978] 2 All ER 942, CA.
5   *Winter Garden Theatre (London) Ltd v Millennium Productions Ltd* [1947] 2 All ER 331, HL.
6   See *Hurst v Picture Theatres Ltd* [1915] 1 KB 1, CA.
7   *Verrall v Great Yarmouth Borough Council* [1980] 1 All ER 839, CA.
8   *Thompson v Park* [1944] 2 All ER 477 at 479.
9   As where a customer is threatened with eviction from a theatre performance, or from a restaurant.

Enforceability against third parties

29.45   In principle, the modern view that a contractual licence has no existence independent of the contract which creates it[1] means that the licensee cannot enforce his contractual right to remain on land against a successor of the licensor, for the arrangement between licensor and licensee is a personal contractual arrangement giving the licensee no interest in the land capable of binding the third party.[2] Thus, for example, the occupier of a university hall of residence room under a contractual licence could not insist on remaining in the hall were it sold by the university to a third party; his remedy would lie in damages against the licensor.[3] It follows that, although a person may enjoy under the terms of a contractual licence rights which appear to be very similar to a lease or easement, the contractual licence does not possess that most important characteristic of an interest in land, that of being capable of binding third parties. This is confirmed by the decision of the Court of Appeal in *Ashburn Anstalt v Arnold*,[4] where it was held that a mere contractual licence to occupy land is not binding on a purchaser of the land even though he has notice of the licence. In reaching this decision, the Court of Appeal held that its earlier decision in *Errington v Errington and Woods*,[5] in which the contrary view was taken, could not stand with the decisions of the Court of Appeal in *Clore v Theatrical Properties Ltd*[6] and of the House of Lords in *King v David Allen & Sons Billposting Ltd*.[7]

However, there are cases in which a person who occupies or uses property under a licence which may have been gratuitous or contractual at the outset is protected by equity from having his enjoyment of the property terminated by the licensor. In some instances the courts have even been prepared to enforce the licensee's rights against a subsequent purchaser.[8] The devices used include the doctrine of proprietary estoppel and the constructive trust. These are discussed more fully at paras 31.8–31.18, below.

1   Para 29.41 above.
2   *Clore v Theatrical Properties Ltd* [1936] 3 All ER 483, CA.
3   *King v David Allen & Sons Billposting Ltd* [1916] 2 AC 54, HL.
4   [1988] 2 All ER 147, CA.
5   [1952] 1 All ER 149, CA. It appears that in *Street v Mountford* (para 37.9 below) the House of Lords treated this case as being concerned not with a licence at all but with an estate contract. The disapproval of *Errington v Errington and Woods* in *Ashburn Anstalt v Arnold* would appear to apply with equal force to another decision of the Court of Appeal, in *Midland Bank Ltd v Farmpride Hatcheries Ltd* (1980) 260 Estates Gazette 493.
6   [1936] 3 All ER 483.
7   [1916] 2 AC 54.
8   See, for example, *Inwards v Baker* [1965] 1 All ER 446, CA. Para 29.41 above.

Chapter 30

The formal acquisition of rights to land

30.1   The context in which most people experience the operation of land law is that of the transfer or creation of rights to land. The most commonly encountered transactions relate to ownership rights such as the transfer of freehold ownership, the transfer (technically 'assignment') of the remainder of an existing lease, or the creation of a new lease. As part and parcel of any of these arrangements it will be usual for lesser *interests* in land such as easements or mortgages to be transferred or created, although such interests can, of course, be created quite independently of any transfer of ownership.

Many land transactions can, legally speaking, be broken down into three stages:

- a binding agreement to carry out the agreed deal (the contract);
- the actual creation or transfer of the interest in land (the conveyance or transfer); and
- registration at the Land Registry (where necessary).

As we shall see, the contract and the conveyance or transfer must *each* comply with *different* formal requirements; registration is applied for by the purchaser (or lessee or assignee where appropriate) and is effected by the Land Registry.

Not surprisingly, the common law always demanded that the *actual disposition* of interests in land should comply with strict formalities; however, these rules have long been enshrined in statutory provisions.[1] Furthermore, ever since the 17th century, legislation has dictated that *contracts* for the sale or other disposition of land should also satisfy formal requirements, albeit that these are different from those required for actual dispositions.[2] In practice, given the importance of such transactions to those involved, these formalities are normally observed, if only because it is usual for the parties to employ legal advisers. However, in those cases where these rules are not complied with, equity will sometimes intervene and give effect to the parties' intentions.[3] Furthermore, as we shall see, there are occasions where the law is prepared to acknowledge that, even in the absence of any documentary evidence, freehold ownership[4] or an easement[5] has arisen on the basis of long unchallenged possession or use.

The rules governing the creation and transfer of interests in land are further complicated by the process of registration of title. As we shall see,[6] many titles to land are already entered on a central Land Register. Any dealings with such land not only must comply with the general law, but must also be carried out in accordance with the specific rules laid down for registered land[7]. In cases where title is not yet registered, most transactions now trigger a requirement for the title to be registered so that compliance with registered land rules is also necessary[8]. Hence it is only in respect of transactions relating to unregistered land which do not trigger registration of title, or the creation of titles to registered land which do not require registration (eg short leases) that the Land Registry procedures can be ignored.

It should also be noted that major reforms to the process of creating and transferring interests in land are currently underway. The Government is committed to a move to electronic conveyancing and the preliminary stages of this project have been completed. The new Land Registration Act 2002 is about to come into force and it is expected that, over the next few years, the building blocks of the new system – notably the establishment of a secure intranet through which the process can be conducted – will be put into place.

In this chapter, we shall consider:

- the formalities with which contracts for the sale or other disposition of land must comply;
- the formalities with which the actual transfer or creation of legal or equitable rights to land must comply;
- the circumstances in which the transfer or creation of legal rights to land must be completed by registration at the Land Registry;
- where appropriate, the current proposals relating to the introduction of electronic conveyancing; and
- the typical process of negotiating and then transferring the ownership of freehold land from one person to another.

1   Paras 30.10 and 30.11 below.
2   Para 30.2 below.
3   Paras 31.2–31.18 below.
4   Paras 31.19–31.34 below.
5   Para 31.19 and paras 33.40-33.51 below.
6   Para 30.12 below.
7   Para 30.17 below.
8   Para 30.14 below.

Formal requirements governing contracts for the sale of land

The statutory requirements

30.2   A contract for the sale or other disposition of land is a legally binding agreement under which an owner of an interest in land becomes committed to transfer that interest, at some future date, to the purchaser. It is *not* the actual transfer of the interest in question; this takes place at the second and third stages of the transaction.[1] Such contracts must, of course, satisfy all the usual legal requirements relating to the formation of a contract.[2] In particular (and self-evidently), any agreement for the sale of land will fail to meet the contractual prerequisite for certainty unless it identifies the parties, the price or other consideration, and the property which is being sold. However, land contracts must also comply with additional rules governing the form in which they must be made. Since the Law of Property (Miscellaneous Provisions) Act 1989,[3] such[4]contracts[5] must comply with the following requirements:

- the agreement must be in writing; and
- the document must be signed by or on behalf of each party; and
- all the terms expressly agreed by the parties must either
  − be incorporated in one document; or
  − where contracts are exchanged, be set out in each of the identical documents; or
  − set out in a 'secondary' document which is expressly referred to in the signed 'master' document.

1   See para 30.10 below.

2   See chs 4, 5 and 6 above.
3   Law of Property (Miscellaneous Provisions) Act 1989, s 2(1).
4   The Law of Property (Miscellaneous Provisions) Act 1989, s 2(5) provides that the following three
    types of land contract do not have to be in writing in order to be valid: contracts made in the course
    of a public auction; contracts to grant a lease not exceeding three years taking effect in possession at
    the best rent reasonably obtainable; and contracts regulated under the Financial Services Act 1986.
    Furthermore, the Act does not affect the creation of implied, resulting or constructive trusts. It should
    also be noted that a 'lock-out' agreement under which a vendor agrees not to negotiate with anyone
    else for a specified period (as to which see para 5.29 above) is not a contract for the disposal of an
    interest in land and does not, therefore, have to be in writing: see *Pitt v PHH Asset Management Ltd*
    [1993] 4 All ER 961, CA.
5   The same formal requirements also apply to the variation of an existing written contract: see *McCausland
    v Duncan Lawrie Ltd* [1996] 4 All ER 995, CA.

Amplification by the courts

30.3   In the vast majority of cases these statutory provisions give rise to no difficulties at
all. Parties rarely embark on land transactions without professional advice and the procedures
routinely followed[1] involve the signing and exchanging of standard-form, written documents
which almost invariably meet the requirements of s 2. That said, and although the 1989
Act was intended to eliminate the uncertainties which had come to surround the previous
law, the new legislation has spawned an unwelcome amount of litigation. This has clarified
the following points.

1   See paras 30.21–30.37 below.

Signatures

30.4   The signature of all parties must appear on the same document, except where the
standard conveyancing procedure of exchanging identical copies of the contract is followed,
in which case the Act allows for each party to sign one copy. So, in *Commission for the
New Towns v Cooper (Great Britain) Ltd*,[1] the Court of Appeal ruled that an exchange of
letters each signed by one party did not amount to a contract. This decision appears to
rule out the possibility of a contract arising as a result of the exchange of correspondence.
The requirement for a signature is not met by the mere insertion of the name of a party;
each must write his name on the document in his own handwriting.[2]

1   [1995] 2 All ER 929, CA.
2   *Firstpost Homes Ltd v Johnson* [1995] 4 All ER 355.

More than one document

30.5   It is perfectly possible for a contract for the sale or disposition of land to comprise
more than one document. Section 2 requires that, in such a case, there must be incorporation
by reference. This means that there should be a 'master' document which has to be signed
by both parties; this 'master' document must refer to the other document(s) (which
themselves do not need to be signed[1]). The application of these rules is well illustrated by
the case of *Firstpost Homes Ltd v Johnson*[2]. Here, a vendor agreed, in a letter addressed
to the purchaser, to sell land which the letter identified by reference to an enclosed plan.
The letter was signed by the vendor; the plan was signed by both parties. The court held
that the letter and the plan must be treated as two separate documents. It therefore
followed that, since the signed document (ie the plan) did not refer to the letter, there was
no incorporation by reference and thus no contract had come into being.

    The courts have been rather more generous in their approach where parties to a contract
for the sale or lease of land have entered into additional agreements which have not been
referred to in the main contract. In the cases to date it has been held that these do not
render the main contract invalid. Despite the argument that these 'side' agreements are, in
reality, terms of the main contract which have not been included in the one document, the

courts have ruled the 'side' agreements to be either collateral contracts,[1] entirely separate contracts,[3] or have ordered the main contract to be rectified so as to include the omitted terms.[4]

1   *Record v Bell* [1991] 4 All ER 471.
2   [1995] 4 All ER 355.
3   *Tootal Clothing Ltd v Guinea Properties Management Ltd* (1992) 64 P & CR 452, [1992] 2 EGLR 80, CA. It should, however, be noted that in *Grossman v Hooper* [2001] EWCA Civ 615, [2001] 2 EGLR 82 a different Court of Appeal expressed grave misgivings about such an approach.
4   *Wright v Robert Leonard (Developments) Ltd* [1994] NPC 49, CA.

Non-compliance

30.6   Where the requirements of section 2 are not satisfied there will, in most circumstances, be no contract[1]. However, an important issue concerns the position of a person who erroneously believes that he is party to a contract for the sale of land. It is now clear that, where such a person acts to his detriment in reliance on the agreement, he may sometimes be able to overcome the lack of writing and acquire an interest in the land. In *Yaxley v Gotts*[2] the Court of Appeal accepted that the principles of either proprietary estoppel[3] or constructive trust[4] could be used as a means of giving effect to an agreement which does not comply with s 2. Here the claimant had orally agreed with the defendant's father that, if the latter bought a house and the claimant carried out work on it to convert the property into flats, then Mr Yaxley would own the ground floor flats. Unknown to the claimant, the house was transferred to the defendant and it was the son who, after Mr Yaxley had carried out the work and moved into the ground floor, was now trying to evict him. It was held that Mr Yaxley had an interest in the land – the court awarded him a 99-year lease free of any rent – on the basis of either a constructive trust or proprietary estoppel[5].

1   *United Bank of Kuwait v Sahib* [1997] Ch 107.
2   [2000] 1 All ER 711, CA .
3   See further paras 31.11-31.16 post.
4   See further para 31.10 post.
5   The court is unlikely to find that, even where the claimant has acted on the agreement, the requirements of either proprietary estoppel or constructive trust are satisfied where the oral agreement was made on a 'subject to contract' basis: see *James v Evans* [2000] 3 EGLR 1, CA.

Reform: electronic documents

30.7   It is accepted that, once the second and third stage of the conveyancing process (ie the transfer and   registration) becomes electronic[1], the same should be true of the contract phase. Accordingly, draft amendments to s 2 have already been drawn up[2]. While these have not been finalised and will not come into force for some time, they extend the ambit of s 2 so that its requirements will be satisfied by an agreement in electronic form[3].

1   See para 30.19 below.
2   See the draft Law of Property (Electronic Communications) Order 2001, drawn up under the Electronic Communications Act 2000, s 8.
3   See Article 4.

Options and rights of pre-emption

30.8   Two particular forms of land contract merit specific mention. An option to purchase a freehold or leasehold interest in land is traditionally viewed as a continuing offer to sell the land which the person to whom the option is granted has the right, if he so chooses, to convert into a contract for sale by notifying his acceptance of that offer.[1] While this analysis is not universally accepted,[2] it is clear that the initial grant of the option is itself a contract[3] to which s 2 of the 1989 Act applies. The difficulty is whether the exercise of an option gives rise to a second contract to which s 2 also applies. This question came before the court in *Spiro v Glencrown Properties Ltd*[4] where it was held that it is *only* the initial grant which needs to satisfy s 2; the actual exercise of the option, which usually takes the form of a unilateral notice signed only by the grantee, is not caught by the Act.

A right of pre-emption, or right of first refusal, is rather different. Here the grantee does not have a *right* to require the land to be transferred to him; all that is required is that the potential vendor will not sell the land without first giving the holder of the right of pre-emption the opportunity to buy on the agreed terms. Although it has been held that a right of pre-emption confers no immediate rights to the land,[5] in the same case it was indicated that such rights do arise as soon as the prospective vendor takes some steps indicating a desire to sell; at this point the right of pre-emption effectively converts into an option. Where this is the case, it would seem that, so long as the initial grant of the right of pre-emption satisfies section 2, its exercise can be by unilateral notice, as with an option. However, it has recently been made clear that, where the initial grant does not set out the terms on which the right of pre-emption is to be exercised, there is no contract of sale unless the exercise of the right results in an agreement which satisfies section 2.[6]

1   *Helby v Matthews* [1895] AC 471, HL. In order not to be void for uncertainty an option must be subject to an overall time limit and must either be at a fixed price or must contain a formula under which a price can be arrived at, eg open market value at the date of exercise.
2   Alternative views are that an option is a conditional contract which the grantee is entitled to convert into a concluded contract, or that an option comprises two contracts, the first a unilateral contract and the second a concluded contract of sale.
3   If the *initial grant* of the option is not supported by consideration as required under ordinary contractual principles it will need to take the form of a deed; see para 6.3 above. For the meaning of a deed, see para 30.10, below.
4   [1991] 1 All ER 600.
5   *Pritchard v Briggs* [1980] Ch 338, [1980] 1 All ER 294, CA. It should be noted that it is now provided that, in relation to registered land, rights of pre-emption are to be treated as giving rise to an interest in land at the date of its creation, Land Registration Act 2002, s 115.
6   *Bircham & Co Nominees (No 2) Ltd v Worrell Holdings Ltd* [2001] EWCA Civ 775, 82 P & CR 34.

Estate contract

30.9   Once a valid contract to convey or create a legal estate has been entered into, the purchaser has more than simple contractual rights. As we have seen,[1] the law regards every piece of land as unique, with the result that contracts for the sale or lease of land can normally be enforced by way of specific performance by either a purchaser or a vendor. For this reason the purchaser is regarded as having a right to the land from the moment the contract is entered into.[2] This equitable proprietary right is known as an estate contract. This means that if, for example, V contracts to sell to P[3] and then, in breach of that contract, conveys the land to X, P will usually[4] be able to compel X to convey the land to him rather than simply claim damages from V.

1   Para 11.30 above.
2   *Lysaght v Edwards* (1876) 2 Ch D 499.
3   Or grants either an option or a right of pre-emption to P.
4   For an explanation of the circumstances in which P's rights *will* bind X, see para 36.34 below.

Formal requirements governing the creation of legal and equitable interests

Legal estates and interests: the general law

30.10   In the preceding paragraphs we have dealt with the legal formalities governing the contract stage of a land transaction. We now turn to its second phase, that where the interest in question is created or transferred. The general rule governing the creation or transfer of legal estates and interests, which is laid down by the LPA, s 52(1), is that they must be created and conveyed by means of a deed. Traditionally, a deed was a document which was 'signed, sealed and delivered'. Many features of this old definition of a deed had long been unsatisfactory and, in 1989, reforms were enacted by s 1 of the Law of Property (Miscellaneous Provisions) Act. A deed is now defined as an instrument which makes it clear on its face that it is intended to be a deed (eg 'signed as a deed') and which is validly executed as a deed. The requirements of valid execution vary according to whether the deed is being entered into by an individual or by a company. A deed is validly executed by an individual provided it is both signed (in the presence of a witness who attests the signature) and delivered as a deed by him or a person authorised to do so on his behalf[1]. The term 'delivery' is misleading since no physical handing over of the document is necessary. Any act or words by the maker of the document showing an intention to be bound constitutes 'delivery' even though the document remains in the possession of the grantor.[2] There is no longer any need for an individual to seal a deed.

In the case of a deed entered into by a company, execution can be effected by the affixing to the document of the company seal.[3] Equally, it is now perfectly valid for a company to execute a deed without the use of a seal; in this case the document must be expressed to be executed by the company and must be signed by a director and the company secretary, or by two directors.[4] Once a deed has been executed by a company, there is a presumption that it has been delivered unless a contrary intention is shown.[5]

It should be noted that s 91 of the Land Registration Act 2002 makes provision for 'electronic deeds' in connection with dispositions of registered land[6]. This section is not scheduled to come into force for some time; when it does, there will be no need for paper-based documents.

1   A solicitor or licensed conveyancer acting in the course of a conveyancing transaction is conclusively presumed to have the necessary authority to deliver a deed, Law of Property (Miscellaneous Provisions) Act 1989, s 1(5).
2   *Vincent v Premo Enterprises (Voucher Sales) Ltd* [1969] 2 All ER 941, CA.
3   Companies Act 1985, s 36A(2).
4   CA 1985, s 36A(4).
5   CA 1985, s 36A(5).
6   See para 30.19 below.

Short lease exception

30.11   One important exception to the general rule that a deed must be used is that new leases taking effect in possession[1] for a term not exceeding three years (a definition which covers periodic leases such as yearly or weekly tenancies) may be created[2] orally or in writing so long as they are at the best rent reasonably obtainable and not for a lump sum payment. This is provided for by the LPA, s 54(2). Within this exception also falls the creation of a periodic tenancy by implication, arising from going into possession and paying rent which is accepted.[3]

1   Ie the lease must come into effect immediately. If it is to come into operation at a future date it will not fall within the exception and must be created by deed: see *Long v London Borough of Tower Hamlets* [1996] 2 All ER 683.
2   All transfers (assignments) of an existing lease must be by deed, irrespective of the length of the lease: see *Crago v Julian* [1992] 1 All ER 744, CA and para 37.37 below.
3   Para 37.13 below.

Legal estates and interests: registration of title

30.12   Prior to 1925 compliance with the rules laid down in the preceding two paragraphs would have ensured that the purchaser or lessee immediately acquired the relevant legal estate or interest. This is no longer always the case. In 1925 a system for registering the title[1] to land was introduced by the enactment of the Land Registration Act 1925. This Act used only to apply to certain parts of England and Wales, known as areas of compulsory registration; however, by 1990 it had come to apply to the whole country. The 1925 Act is about to be replaced by the Land Registration Act 2002 (hereafter 'LRA')[2], and it is to the provisions of this new Act that the following text refers as if that Act is already in force. The main aims of the 2002 Act are to achieve universal registration[3] and to provide the framework for the introduction, in the future, of electronic conveyancing. While the Act retains most of the underlying principles of the existing system, there have been some significant changes.

The system involves the registration of the title to the major legal interests in land, in the main the freehold and leases for terms in excess of 7 years. We explain the rules governing which titles must be registered at para 30.14. However, it should be appreciated from the outset that it is perfectly possible (and, indeed, commonplace) for one piece of land to be the subject of two or more registered titles; for example if A, the registered proprietor of the freehold title to Blacklands, grants a 25-year lease of it to B, then B will also have to be registered as proprietor of a leasehold title to Blacklands; if B then grants a 10-year sublease of the property to C, C will also have to register his title.

1   The registered system of conveyancing is usually known as the 'registered land' scheme; this is, however, something of a misnomer, for what is registered is not the land itself, but the title to the land, ie the evidence of the owner's right to the land.
2   The Land Registration Act 2002 will come into force on 13 October 2003.
3   Although the current scheme of registration has been in place since the beginning of 1926 many titles are not yet registered. This is because, until recently the system did not apply to all parts of England and Wales and the requirement to register a title was only triggered by a transaction on sale. Thus if the land is located in the 'wrong' area, or it is owned by a corporate body (which includes large landowning entities such as local authorities, the Church Commissioners and Oxford and Cambridge colleges) there may never have been any transaction (especially relating to the freehold) to provoke registration of title. In 2001 it was estimated that some 17 million titles are registered with in the region of 5 million as yet unregistered.

The Land Register

30.13   The Land Register comprises the collection of all registered titles. It operates through district registries. A file of each title is kept[1] at the appropriate District Land Registry. Any person may inspect and make copies of the register, together with any documents to which it refers, and any other document relating to an application which is held by the Registry.[2] The file of each title is divided into three parts: the Property Register, the Proprietorship Register and the Charges Register.

*   *Property Register* This part of the register contains a description of the land, states whether it is freehold or leasehold, and refers to a filed plan of the land. Where the land is leasehold, brief particulars of the lease are set out. The Property Register also contains notes of any rights which benefit the land, such as easements.
    The filed plan is prepared from the plans and description of the land in the title deeds and is based on the Ordnance Map. It denotes the land comprised in the title by red edging. Boundaries shown in the filed plan are general, not fixed, boundaries; that is they do not purport to show the exact line of the legal boundary.[3]
*   *Proprietorship Register* This part states the class of title with which the land is registered, the name and address of the registered proprietor, the price paid or rent reserved, together with any restrictions[4] affecting the proprietor's right to deal with the land.
*   *Charges Register* This part contains entries and notices of rights and interests which adversely affect the title, such as restrictive covenants, easements, mortgages and registered leases.

It used to be the case that, on registration, a proprietor would be issued with a land certificate which was a copy of the register and filed plan relating to his title. Although this document afforded some evidence of title, it did not necessarily correspond exactly with the register itself because some entries could be made on the register without the certificate being lodged at the registry for amendment. Its limitations are now recognised and henceforth it will merely be a certificate of ownership without any details of the title. It is the register which is the proof of title.

1   The Register was originally filed on a card index. Since 1988 all new titles have been computerised; virtually all existing titles have now been transferred onto this system.
2   LRA, s 66. It is, however, possible to apply for an exemption in respect of commercially sensitive information (which does not include the price paid for the property).
3   LRA, s 62; para 29.23 above.
4   Para 36.33 below.

Title not yet registered: first registration

30.14   *Compulsory registration of title* LRA, s 4 requires that, where title to land has not yet been registered the following specified transactions (which can be on sale, by order of the court or by way of gift or bequest) now always trigger a first registration of title:

- the transfer of a freehold estate;
- the transfer (ie the assignment) of a lease having more than seven years to run;
- a grant of a lease or sub-lease of more than seven years;
- the grant of a lease or sublease of *any length* where the lease will not take effect in possession until more than three months after the date of grant;[1]
- the grant of a first legal mortgage.

Neither the creation or transfer of leases not exceeding 7 years, nor the creation of legal interests (apart from a first legal mortgage) relating to unregistered land, lead to a requirement to register title.

On the occurrence of a transaction within s 4, the legal estate will pass to the transferee or grantee on due execution of the deed[2]. However, the new owner or tenant is required to apply for first registration within two months of completion (or by such later date as is specified by the Registrar provided there is good reason for an extension of time)[3]. If no application for registration is made, the transaction becomes void as to the passing or creation of the legal estate[4]. In the case of a transfer of a freehold or of an existing lease, the legal estate reverts to the vendor who will hold it on trust for the purchaser[5]. Where the transaction comprises the grant of a new lease or a first mortgage, the grant takes effect as a contract to ccreate the lease or mortgage[6]. In any event the purchaser/tenant/mortgagee has the right to require the legal estate to be transferred to him again and this time he should have his title to it registered; he will however be liable to the vendor/landlord/mortgagor for the additional costs[7].

1   Such leases are a form of future ('reversionary') lease; see para 37.18 below.
2   See para 30.10 above.
3   LRA, s 6.
4   LRA, s 7(1).
5   LRA, s 7(2)(a).
6   LRA, s 7(2)(b).
7   LRA, s 8.

30.15   *Voluntary registration of title* It is not necessary to wait until one of the transactions specified in s 4 occurs before first registration. The owner of the following unregistered estates and interests may apply at any time to have his title registered[1]:

- a freehold estate;
- a lease with more than seven years left to run;

- a lease of any length where the term is discontinuous (eg a time share lease);
- a rentcharge (a sum of money charged on land);
- a franchise (eg a right granted by the Crown to hold a market or a fair);
- a profit a prendre in gross (such as a right to hunt game)[2].

1 LRA, s 3. This process is further encouraged by a significant reduction in the fees charged for voluntary registration.
2 See para 33.20 below.

30.16 *The effects of first registration* An application to the Registrar for first registration of title to land is made for one of three classes of title[1]: absolute, good leasehold, or possessory[2]. A fourth class, qualified title, may be given where the Registrar is unable to grant the class of title originally applied for.

In the vast majority of cases involving freehold land, and in an increasing number of those relating to leaseholds, absolute title can be granted[3]. Absolute title will be given where the applicant proves his title to the satisfaction of the Registrar. It is not quite accurate to say that registration with absolute title affords an unqualified state guarantee of the registered proprietor's title, for there exists the possibility that the register may be altered, ie amended if it does not show what should be the true state of affairs[4]. However, subject to this possibility, registration with absolute title effectively guarantees that the registered proprietor is entitled to the legal estate, together with all the existing rights which benefit that estate (such as, for example, easements like rights of way)[5]. The only adverse interests to which the new registered proprietor will be subject[6] are:

- interests protected by an entry on the register;
- 'overriding interests' within Sch 1;
- interests acquired under the Limitation Act 1980 (ie squatter's rights) of which the proprietor has notice[7];
- where, the proprietor is a trustee, those rights of the beneficiaries of which he has notice; and
- in the case of leaseholds, the express and implied covenants in the lease[8].

In a few rare cases, the Registrar may decide that he is unable to grant the title applied for because of some specific defect in the title. In such a case, the applicant for registration may be registered with a qualified title. The effect of registration with a qualified title is the same as the effect of registration with absolute title except that in addition to entries on the register and overriding interests, the registered interest is also subject to a specified qualification stated in the register, for example any rights arising before a specified date or under a specified document.[9]

1 LRA, ss 9 and 10.
2 Possessory title is only appropriate where there are no documents of title. Occasionally this will be because title deeds have been lost or destroyed; more likely is the case where the claim to title is based on adverse possession (as to which see paras 31.19-31.34 below). Possessory title provides no guarantee of title at the date of registration but, after an appropriate period, an application can be made to upgrade the title to absolute.
3 The proprietor of a lease can only be registered with an absolute title where the Registrar is satisfied both as to the title to the lease and as to the title to the freehold and any intermediate leasehold interests. This will only be the case where either the landlord's title and any intermediate titles are themselves registered, or where the applicant can produce proof of his landlord's unregistered title. Where an absolute title cannot be granted, a good leasehold title will be awarded: this offers the same guarantee as an absolute title save that the proprietor takes subject to any rights or interests affecting the landlord's title to grant the lease, LRA, s 12(6). Where, at a later date, the Registrar can be satisfied as to the landlord's title, a good leasehold title can be upgraded to absolute.
4 LRA, s 65 and Sch 4; see para 36.37 below.
5 LRA, ss 11(3), 12(3).

6   LRA, ss 11(4),(5), 12(4) and (5).
7   Note that, where a squatter is in actual occupation of the land, he may have an overriding interest under Sch 1: see para 36.29 below. In such a case the proprietor will be bound irrespective of whether he has notice.
8   LRA, s 12(4)(a).
9   LRA, ss 11(6), 12(6).

Title already registered

30.17   Once title to an estate in land has already been registered (as is usually the case) dealings in respect of it are thereafter governed by the LRA. A registered proprietor has the power to make any disposition permitted under the general law[1] and a purchaser is entitled to assume that the registered proprietor has the power to make a disposition, save where those powers are restricted by an entry on the register[2]. Most dispositions affecting a registered estate have to be completed by registration[3]. So

1   Any subsequent transfer of the estate itself must be carried out by a registered disposition which must be completed by registration, ie by the Registrar entering the transferee of the land on the register as proprietor.[4]
2   Where the registered proprietor of the estate creates an interest which is required to be registered with its own independent title[5] this again must be carried out by registered disposition. So, for example, where a lease of more than 7 years is created out of a registered estate, the lessee will be registered as proprietor of the leasehold interest which is accorded its own separate title. The grant of such a lease will also be noted on the landlord's title[6].
3   Where a registered proprietor of either a freehold or leasehold estate creates a legal *interest* affecting his land which does not itself have to be registered with its own independent title[7], again it is not enough simply to use a deed; the disposition must be completed by registration if it is to be fully effective.[8] Here, 'completion by registration' means that the interest is noted on the titles of any properties to which it relates[9].

Unless and until such dispositions are completed by registration, no legal estate or interest is created or transferred[10]. The purchaser acquires only an equitable interest which is capable of being overridden if not protected under other provisions in the LRA.[11]
An important exception to the rule that the creation or transfer of legal estates and interests relating to registered land must be completed by registration arises where a registered proprietor grants a lease of seven years or less. Save for the exceptional case where such leases do have to be registered with their own independent title[12], a legal estate is created immediately on grant, provided that the general law on formalities has been complied with[13]. Where the lease is for a term of more than three years it can be (but does not have to be) protected by an entry against the landlord's title[14].

1   LRA, s 23.
2   LRA, s 26. As we shall see where, for example, a registered proprietor is a trustee with restricted powers to dispose of the land, a restriction to that effect can be entered in the register – see para 36.33 below.
3   At the moment there is, inevitably, a gap between the making of the disposition (ie executing the deed) and its completion by registration. One of the important benefits of the introduction of electronic conveyancing (see para 30.19 below) is that the making of a disposition (which will then no longer be paper-based) and completion by registration will become simultaneous.
4   LRA, s 27(2)(a) and Sch 2, para 2.
5   LRA, s 27(2)(b) and Sch 2 para 3(2)(a). In some instances there is a requirement for a lease of 7 years or less to be registered with its own title; this is where the lease will not take effect in possession until more than 3 months after it is granted (a form of future or reversionary lease – see para 37.18 below) and where the lease is for a discontinuous term (eg a time share lease).
6   LRA, Sch 2 para 3(2)(b).
7   Notable examples are expressly created legal easements and legal charges.

8   LRA, s 27(1).
9   LRA Sch 2, para 7(2).
10   LRA, s 27(1).
11   See para 36.32 below.
12   See para 30.14 above.
13   See paras 30.10 and 30.11 above.
14   See para 36.4 below.

30.18 *The effect of a registered disposition*   Where a disposition is duly completed by registration a purchaser for valuable consideration of a registered estate[1] is well protected. He takes free from any interest affecting the land[2] except:

–   a registered charge (mortgage)[3];
–   any interest protected by way of a notice entered on the register[4];
–   any 'overriding' interest within Sch 3[5];
–   any interest excepted from the effect of registration[6];and
–   where the estate being disposed of is leasehold, the obligations contained in the lease.

1   Ie any estate that has been registered with its own title, LRA, s 132.
2   LRA, s 29.
3   See Ch 35.
4   See para 36.34 below.
5   As we shall see, these are the only interests affecting registered land that will routinely bind a purchaser even though there is no entry on the register; see para 36.20 below.
6   Where, unusually, a proprietor is registered with either a possessory or qualified title (see para 30.16 above) neither he, nor any purchaser from him, is protected against existing rights affecting the land.

conveyancing
30.19   The Land Register itself is already computerised and there is increasing on-screen access for both searches and the transmission of information. However, the Government is committed to the further step of introducing electronic conveyancing during the next 5–10 years. The intention is that the whole transfer process from contract to registration will take place on-line, via a secure intranet. This will mean that those professional advisers who have access will be able to monitor their own transfer but also the progress of related transactions, notably those in the same chain of sales and purchases[1]. It is clear that the actual transfer and its completion by registration will become both electronic and simultaneous, so that there will no longer be any gap between transfer and registration. Furthermore, related matters such as the discharge of the vendor's mortgage, the completion of the purchaser's mortgage, and the payment of Stamp Duty will also be automatically and electronically effected at the same time.

1   See para 30.22 below.

Equitable interests
30.20   The LPA, s 53 states the general rule that equitable interests, although not requiring the formality of a deed, must nevertheless be created or transferred by signed writing. Classically, s 53 applies to the express creation of trusts of land although, in practice, a deed is often employed. While s 53 must be complied with where equitable interests are deliberately created, as has already been indicated,[1] equity has traditionally given effect to some transactions which were intended to give rise to legal estates or interests but which failed to do so because the correct formalities[2] were not complied with. Here, as we shall see,[3] it is not necessary to comply with s 53. Equally there are other circumstances in which equitable interests can arise without the need to comply with s 53. The LPA specifically provides that the section does not affect the creation of resulting, implied or constructive

trusts.[4] Furthermore, certain equitable interests may come into existence as a result of the operation of other equitable principles without any need for writing.[5]

1   See para 30.39 above.
2   See paras 30.10 and 30.11 above.
3   See paras 31.2–31.6 below.
4   LPA, s 53(2). See further paras 31.8-31.10 below.
5   See paras 31.11–31.18 below.

A typical sale of land

30.21   In order to place the legal rules governing the creation, transfer and registration of estates and interests into their practical context, we now outline the steps involved in a typical sale of a freehold interest in land. The sale of a leasehold interest follows essentially the same path.

Initial negotiation

30.22   The typical private sale[1] begins when the parties, introduced probably by an estate agent, discuss and agree on a price for the property. Although it might appear that vendor and purchaser are now parties to a binding contract, this is not the case. As we have seen, even if it were their intention to be legally bound at this early stage, which is unlikely, a contract for the sale or lease of land must be in writing[2]. It is normal practice for this written contract to come into existence by exchange of contracts.[3]

The period between the initial agreement and the exchange of contracts is one during which either side can withdraw[4]. Such a withdrawal may be for perfectly legitimate reasons (eg an unsatisfactory survey, an unexpected lack of finance, or the loss of a purchaser for a party's existing property). However, one particularly irksome cause is where, in a rising market, a vendor backs out in order to achieve a higher price than that which has already been agreed with the present purchaser – a practice usually referred to as 'gazumping' (although it should be noted that the reverse can occur in a falling market, ie the purchaser can back out in order to force a lower price than that which has been agreed). Whatever the cause, a withdrawal after an agreement has been reached is not only distressing to the innocent party, it can also cause the loss of any expenditure already incurred in the expectation that the deal would go through (notably solicitor's and surveyor's fees).

Where the chances of a withdrawal are greater than usual, for example because the risk of gazumping is high because the market is volatile or where it is known that the period between initial agreement and exchange of contracts may become protracted, it is possible for the parties to enter into an option[5] or a 'lock-out' agreement.[6] The latter requires less formality[7] and is often the more realistic course since the vendor merely agrees not to negotiate with anyone else for a specified period. While a lock-out agreement cannot be used to compel the vendor to exchange contracts,[8] its breach will give rise to a claim in damages; this, at least, compensates the innocent party for wasted expenditure.

However, such safeguards are not usually regarded as appropriate in the case of a routine transaction and it is in this regard that a number of initiatives are currently taking place. At the time of writing the Government has signalled its intention to introduce a requirement that a vendor of residential property must supply to prospective purchasers a Home Information Pack[9]. The pack is likely to include responses to local searches[10], a home condition report, information as to title, copies of planning consents, any warranties and guarantees and a draft contract. The expectation is that the provision of much fuller information before the parties even begin to negotiate an agreement will reduce the number of transactions which currently fall through once the full picture becomes known to the purchaser. It will also facilitate a more rapid exchange of contracts which will reduce the risk of gazumping. However, it should be appreciated that the most usual stumbling block to a swift exchange of contracts is not the legal procedures but rather the financing practices under-pinning the purchase of property, especially those in the domestic residential sector. A purchaser who already owns a house is rarely able to afford to purchase another until his existing property is sold. As a result, the sale of a residential property is seldom an isolated transaction but rather one in a chain of similar deals; if any one of these falls through, the chain breaks down so that the exchange of contracts on all the other dependent sales has to be delayed. However, the Government's major project – the introduction of electronic conveyancing[11] will also have a significant impact. The expectation is that, once in place, electronic conveyancing will also allow the details of the progress of each transaction in such chains can be viewed, on-line, by all involved in related sales; in this way problems can be spotted, and resolved, at an earlier stage.

1   Ie one concluded by negotiation rather than by auction.
2   Law of Property (Miscellaneous Provisions) Act 1989, s 2; para 30.2 above.
3   Para 30.26 below.
4   The Government estimates that nearly 30% of transaction fail after terms have been agreed.
5   See para 30.8 above.
6   See *Pitt v PHH Asset Management Ltd* [1993] 4 All ER 961, CA and para 5.29 above.
7   Unlike an option, a lock-out agreement is not a contract for the sale of land and thus does not need to comply with the Law of Property (Miscellaneous Provisions) Act 1989, s 2; see *Pitt v PHH Asset Management Ltd* [1993] 4 All ER 961, CA.
8   *Tye v House* [1997] 2 EGLR 171.
9   Outlined in Part 5 of a draft Housing Bill published by the Office of the Deputy Prime Minister in March 2003.
10   See para 30.24 below.
11   See para 30.19 above.

Enquiries and searches

30.23   Until such time as the Home Information Pack becomes compulsory (and even when it does, where the property involved is non-residential), the period between initial agreement and the exchange of contracts provides an opportunity for the purchaser to take further steps, some of which ought to be completed to his satisfaction before it is sensible to become legally committed to the transaction. At this stage the wise purchaser will usually put matters in the hands of professional advisers: a surveyor to report to the purchaser on the structural state of the property and solicitors to carry out the transaction. Where, as is usually the case, the purchaser wishes to finance the purchase by means of a mortgage, this will need to be arranged. Apart from assessing the purchaser's personal creditworthiness, the lender will require a valuation of the property to be carried out, at the purchaser's expense. The purchaser or his solicitor will also now institute the local searches' described in the following paragraph. In the case of non-domestic property the purchaser will send to the vendor a set of preliminary enquiries about the property, dealing with such matters as boundaries, the fixtures and fittings included in the sale, and asking whether the vendor is aware of any adverse interests affecting the property. Where the property is domestic, under the Law Society's National Conveyancing Protocol, the vendor now provides the purchaser with a completed Property Information Form and Fixtures, Fittings and Contents Form which covers these matters.

Local land charges and supplementary enquiries

30.24   A search of the local land charges register (not to be confused with the Land Register), maintained by the district council (or London borough council) under the provisions of the Local Land Charges Act 1975, will reveal such matters as revocations of planning permission, orders requiring the discontinuance of an existing use, building preservation notices, listings of buildings of special architectural or historical interest, and (charges of a private rather than a public character) light obstruction notices under the Rights of Light

Act 1959.[1] Registrations of these matters are made against the land in question. A search may be personal or official (ie carried out by officials of the registry). By virtue of the Local Land Charges Act 1975, s 10, charges of a public character which are not registered nevertheless remain enforceable. However, if a personal search fails to turn up the existence of a charge because it was not registered, or an official search fails to reveal an existing charge, the purchaser will be entitled to compensation for any losses he has thereby suffered.[2]

At the same time as an official search of the local land charges register is sought, a list of additional enquiries is also submitted to the district council.[3] While these supplementary enquiries form an essential adjunct to a search of the local land charges register, the procedure has no statutory basis. The district councils merely voluntarily answer the enquiries; nevertheless they may be liable to be sued for negligence in answering them. These enquiries cover such matters as whether the roadways abutting on the property are maintained at the public expense, whether it is proposed to construct any road or flyover close to the property, whether the property is drained to a sewer, whether the property is in a slum clearance area and other matters within the knowledge of the district council.

1   Para 33.55 below.
2   Local Land Charges Act 1975, s 10.
3   Or London borough council.

Draft contract

30.25   Meanwhile, the vendor or his solicitor will be preparing a draft contract of sale, usually based on the Standard Conditions of Sale. At this stage of the transaction it has become normal, where title is already registered,[1] for the vendor to send to the purchaser, along with the draft contract, official copies of his register of title (ie those provided and authenticated by the Land Registry), title plan and any documents referred to on the register which are filed at the Registry. Thus, the vendor, in practice, takes the first step in fulfilling his contractual obligation to prove his title[2] before the contract is formally entered into.

1   See para 30.17 above.
2   Explained further in para 30.36 below.

Contract
Exchange

30.26   Once both sides are ready to be legally committed to the transaction they will enter into a formal contract. As we have seen, since 1989 most contracts for the sale or disposition of an interest in land must be made in writing.[1]

It is almost invariable conveyancing practice for the contract to come into being by 'exchange of contracts', more accurately the exchange of identical copies of the contract signed by each party. In the past 'exchange' was effected in person but today it is usual practice to exchange by post or, increasingly, by telephone. Where exchange takes place through the post, it would seem that the contract is formed not when each party receives the other's copy of the contract, but when the second (vendor's) copy is posted.[2] In the case of sales of houses there is often a chain of transactions in which each purchaser needs to sell his property before he can buy the vendor's and each vendor needs to sell in order to buy another property. Here it is often vital that there be as near as possible simultaneous exchanges of contract in respect of each of these transactions. One method of achieving this object, sanctioned by the Court of Appeal[3] and regulated by the Law Society is the 'telephonic exchange'. In this case, either each solicitor holds his own client's signed part of the contract or one solicitor holds both parts, and they then, by telephone, deem the contracts to be exchanged, the date of exchange then being entered on each part.[4] Actual physical exchange by post follows.

1   Law of Property (Miscellaneous Provisions) Act 1989, s 2; para 30.2 above.
2   Para 5.16 above. The Standard Conditions of Sale explicitly provide that this shall be the case.

3   *Domb v Isoz* [1980] 1 All ER 942, CA.
4   In 1989 the Law Society authorised a more complex procedure which was specifically designed to deal with 'chain' transactions; this has not proved popular in practice, conveyancers preferring to use one or other of those described in the text.

Deposit

30.27   At exchange of contracts it is usual for the purchaser to pay a deposit. The purpose of this is that, in effect, it gives the vendor a remedy, which is available without bringing a court action, in the event of the purchaser failing to complete. This is because the vendor is normally entitled to keep the deposit where such a failure to complete amounts to a breach of contract. The court does, however, have an unqualified discretion to order the repayment of the whole deposit under the LPA, s 49(2).[1] It is usual for the contract to fix the amount of the deposit at 10% of the purchase price although, increasingly, the amount of the deposit is negotiable.

The deposit is normally paid not to the vendor but to his solicitor. The general rule is that the solicitor holds it as agent for the vendor[2] unless the contract provides that it should be held by the solicitor as stakeholder. In practice, except where the vendor is to be allowed to use the whole or part of the deposit towards the deposit on any property he is buying in a related transaction, it is usual for the contract to require it to be held by the vendor's solicitor as stakeholder.

1   *Universal Corpn v Five Ways Properties Ltd* [1979] 1 All ER 552, CA. Where, for no particular reason, an unusually large deposit has been paid this may be regarded as a penalty, in which case the court may order the repayment of the whole sum; see *Workers Trust and Merchant Bank Ltd v Dojap Investments Ltd* [1993] 2 All ER 370, PC. On penalties generally see para 11.22 above.
2   *Ellis v Goulton* [1893] 1 QB 350, CA; *Tudor v Hamid* [1988] 1 EGLR 251, CA.

Terms

30.28   As we have said, the terms of the contract are largely based on those contained in the Standard Conditions of Sale, modified by any special conditions agreed to by the parties. So, for example, it is usual to specify a date for completion; any failure to meet that deadline would then be a breach of contract entitling the innocent party to damages.[1] He would only be entitled to terminate for breach where time is made of the essence;[2] it is normally provided that, while time is not automatically of the essence, either party can render it so by serving a notice to complete on the other party.

1   *Raineri v Miles* [1980] 2 All ER 145, HL.
2   Para 8.9 above.

Vendor's liability for defects

30.29   It is said that an underlying rule in contracts for the sale of land is *caveat emptor*, let the buyer beware; in other words, it is for the buyer to discover defects in the property he is buying, and not for the seller to warn him of them. However, this rule is subject to a number of important exceptions:

*   The vendor may be liable for misrepresentation, which we discussed at paras 12.2 to 12.40 above.
*   The vendor may be liable for breach of contract where the property is misdescribed; for example, if the contract describes his interest in the property or the size of the property as being greater than it is.
*   The vendor is under an implied contractual duty to disclose all latent defects in his *title* to the property, ie defects which the purchaser could not discover on a reasonable inspection of the property. Thus, for example, the vendor is obliged to disclose that his title is dependent on adverse possession, or that the property is subject to restrictive covenants.

The vendor's liability under each of these three heads is likely to be modified by the terms of the contract. Under the Standard Conditions of Sale, for example, the vendor is to disclose to the purchaser all adverse interests of which he knew and the purchaser is to accept the property in the physical state it is in when the contract is made. Furthermore, albeit that property information will have been provided by the vendor, the contract provides that the onus remains on the purchaser to make all the searches, enquiries and inspections which a prudent buyer would make and that he buys the property subject to such defects as they would reveal. As to liability for misrepresentation, the Misrepresentation Act 1967, s 3[1] should be borne in mind when drafting any clause restricting or excluding liability.

It will be appreciated from this that the vendor is not normally liable to the purchaser for *physical* defects in the property.[2] To guard against these the purchaser needs to have a structural survey carried out before he enters into the contract.

1   Paras 12.38–12.40 above.
2   However, as we have seen, a vendor/builder may, in appropriate circumstances, be liable to his purchaser under the provisions of the Defective Premises Act 1972; see para 21.28 above.

Remedies

30.30   The contractual remedies of particular relevance to sales of land are of course applicable to contracts in general and little need be said here additional to our earlier discussion of these remedies.

30.31   *Rescission*   It is open to a purchaser to rescind the contract in the face of misrepresentation by the vendor,[1] although it should be remembered that he may be debarred from so doing after completion has taken place in a case where the property is purchased with the aid of a mortgage, for the mortgagee will be a purchaser of an interest in the property for value.[2]

1   Para 12.16 above.
2   Para 12.18 above.

30.32   *Termination of the contract for repudiatory breach*[1]   The injured party may not only accept the repudiatory breach of the defaulting party as terminating the contract but may also sue for damages for loss of the bargain or wasted expenditure and any other loss which is not too remote.[2]

1   Para 8.14 above.
2   Paras 11.2–11.19 above.

30.33   *Damages*   As in the general case, a breach of the contract for the sale of the land entitles the innocent party to sue for damages for loss of the bargain or for wasted expenditure, at his option, and any other loss which is not too remote. The date at which damages for loss of bargain are assessed is normally the date of breach though some other date may be chosen where otherwise injustice might be caused.[1]

A vendor who cannot show good title may have represented otherwise in answer to enquiries. Where there has been any misrepresentation by the vendor, the purchaser may choose to sue for damages for misrepresentation, rather than for breach of contract, a matter which we discussed in paras 14.19 to 14.30 above.

1   Para 11.6 above.

30.34   *Specific performance*   It will be remembered that the law regards every plot of land as unique, with the result that contracts for the sale or lease of land are always on the face of it specifically enforceable by both a purchaser and a vendor.[1] This does not mean that the remedy will always be granted, since it is discretionary. Where the court refuses to grant specific performance to either party, it has a discretion to order the repayment of the deposit,[2] wherever this is the fairest course between the parties.[3] Further, the court has a discretion to award damages in addition to, or in substitution for, specific performance. Where the innocent party obtains specific performance, but the order is not complied with by the party in breach, the innocent party, having elected to affirm the contract, cannot then unilaterally terminate for breach. He must return to the court, under whose supervision the performance of the contract now is, to seek enforcement of the order or dissolution of the order and termination of the contract.[4]

1   Paras 11.30 and 30.9 above.
2   LPA, s 49(2).
3   *Universal Corpn v Five Ways Properties Ltd* [1979] 1 All ER 552, CA; *Workers Trust and Merchant Bank Ltd v Dojap Investments* [1993] 2 All ER 370, PC. See para 30.27 above.
4   *GKN Distributors Ltd v Tyne Tees Fabrication Ltd* (1985) 50 P & CR 403.

Sale by auction

30.35   Where a sale is conducted by public auction there is a legally binding contract as soon as the property is knocked down[1] to the highest bidder, despite the absence of writing.[2] A person wishing to bid for a property may make pre-contract enquiries and searches before the auction but it is more usual either for the vendor to produce the relevant evidence at the auction, or for the contract to provide for the searches to be made after the auction, giving the purchaser the right to rescind if the searches produce adverse results. In *Rignall Developments Ltd v Halil*,[3] where the contract deemed the purchaser to have made the relevant searches and to have knowledge of what would thereby be disclosed, it was held that the vendor, who was aware of the defect in the title which the searches would disclose, could nonetheless not require the purchaser to complete the transaction since he had not made full and frank disclosure of the known defect.

1   See para 5.5 above.
2   Law of Property (Miscellaneous Provisions) Act 1989, s 2(5); para 30.2 note 4 above.
3   [1987] 3 All ER 170.

Transfer stage

Registered land

30.36   *Proving title*   During the period between contract and transfer it is for the vendor to carry out his contractual obligation to prove his title, ie to prove that he is in a position to sell what he has contracted to sell. It is increasingly the case that the first stage of this process will already have taken place in that the vendor will have furnished the purchaser with official copies of his register of title, etc.[1] These official copies can be relied on to the same extent as the originals[2] and do not need to be verified against them.

The vendor should also provide the purchaser with any available documentary evidence relating to any interests which do not appear on the register.[3] The purchaser's solicitor will inspect the official copies and any documents required to be furnished to ensure all is well. He may also raise requisitions on title, that is, make enquiries of the vendor for further particulars, for example as to adverse entries on the register, or, more likely, simply point them out and require their removal.[4] A failure by the vendor to answer a proper requisition on title may lead to the purchaser terminating the contract for breach or may lead to him applying to the court to require an answer under the summary procedure provided by the LPA, s 49(1).

At this stage, also, the purchaser's solicitor should draft the transfer of title, using the prescribed form.[5]

The next stage of the procedure is for the purchaser or his solicitor to request an official search of the register. This search is, in effect, to check for any further entries which may have been made since the date of the official copies already provided by the vendor.[6] The official certificate of search which results ensures that, provided the transaction is completed and the purchaser applies to be registered as proprietor within 30 working days, the purchaser will not take subject to entries made in the register during that time.[7]

Where a person suffers loss as a result of an error in an official search he is entitled to an indemnity.[8] He is still bound by any entry which the search fails to reveal.[9]

1   Para 30.25 above.
2   LRA, s 67.
3   Such as overriding interests; see para 36.20 below.
4   See Re Stone and Saville's Contract [1963] 1 All ER 353, CA.
5   LRA, s 25.
6   If any such entries are discovered, it may be necessary to raise further requisitions, for example requiring their removal.
7   See further para 36.35 below.
8   LRA, s 103, Sch 8, para 1(1)(c); para 36.43 below.
9   Parkash v Irani Finances Ltd [1969] 1 All ER 930.

30.37   *Completion and registration*   Completion now takes place. The transfer is executed and the purchase price paid. The transfer is in simple form but it must, of course, be validly executed as a deed.[1] As we have seen, the deed of transfer itself does not pass the legal estate in registered land to the purchaser. Only registration of the purchaser as proprietor vests in him the legal estate.[2] The purchaser should therefore apply to the Registry for registration as proprietor.

Where the vendor's title was not registered, the sale to the purchaser will invariably trigger first registration. In this case the legal estate will pass to the purchaser on completion but he must, within two months, apply to the Land Registry to be registered as proprietor[3].

1   Para 30.10 above.
2   Para 17 above.
3   Para 30.14 above.

Chapter 31

The informal acquisition of rights to land

31.1 In the previous chapter we considered the formal rules which govern the creation and transfer of legal and equitable interests in land. As we have said, in practice the vast majority of land transactions satisfy those requirements. However, situations do arise, often in family or domestic situations, where parties fail to act in accordance with strict legal niceties. Furthermore, landowners may exercise rights over their neighbour's land, or people use land as if it were their own, for very many years but without any proper documentary evidence of their legal right to do so. In such circumstances, the lack of paperwork and the absence of entries on the Land Register make it difficult for solicitors to spot the possibility that rights to land may nevertheless be in existence. This makes it vital that those professionals who do regularly carry out physical inspections of land, notably surveyors, are aware that those who actually occupy or use land may have acquired proprietary rights despite the lack of any paperwork. In this chapter, therefore, we deal with:

- the effect of transactions which ought to have been made by deed;
- the circumstances in which effect will be given to informal arrangements relating to land; and
- the operation of the statutory rules under which title to land can be acquired as a result of its use over a long period of time.

Informal transactions

31.2 Where parties make a positive attempt to create an estate or interest in land which fails in the eyes of the law because the formality of a deed is not gone through, their efforts may nonetheless give rise to an interest in the eyes of equity. The same principles apply whatever the type of estate or interest was intended to be created or transferred; hence, the same approach is taken to attempts to transfer a freehold, or to create a lease, an easement, or a mortgage. However, in order to demonstrate the application of the relevant principles, we will use the example of an informal lease, ie a lease which has not been created in accordance with the formality required by law.

An example: informal leases
31.3 Suppose that L grants to T a seven-year lease which is simply in writing (ie a document which does not comply with the legal requirements of a deed).[1] Such a lease is not within

the exception to the general rule for legal estates under the LPA, s 54(2),[2] and should therefore have been made by deed.[1] The result, at common law, is that this document does not create a seven-year lease. However, suppose further that, because the parties were not aware that they have failed to comply with the proper formalities, T goes into possession and pays rent which L accepts. At common law, this gives rise to a periodic tenancy by implication.[3] Accordingly, the operation of the common law rules leaves T with a markedly inferior interest, a periodic tenancy (which can be terminated at any time by the landlord serving an appropriate notice to quit[4]), rather than the seven-year lease which the parties had meant to create.

Equity, however, regards the matter differently; it will, where possible, treat the purported lease as if it were a contract to create a lease.[5] So, if court proceedings are actually brought, equity will usually grant specific performance of the contract. This has the effect of remedying the initial failure to comply with the formal rules, since the court order compels the landlord to draw up (or the tenant to accept) a proper deed granting a seven-year legal lease.

However, what is T's position if, as is more likely, neither party goes to court to seek any remedy? (The parties' failure to use a deed may well have arisen from the fact that they did not appreciate that one was necessary, in which case they will have no cause to realise that they need a remedy because both will have acted as though a legal lease had been created.) In such circumstances equity applies one of its basic principles; ie it 'looks on that as done which ought to be done'. Since, in equity's view, the informal lease is treated as a contract to grant a lease, what ought to be done is that this contract should be performed. Equity therefore regards the situation *as if* the agreement had been complied with and a seven-year lease granted. Accordingly, in the eyes of equity, an informal lease is regarded from the outset as a lease.[6] But this lease is only recognised by equity; thus T has an *equitable* seven-year lease, which, as we shall see, falls short of a legal lease in some respects.

1   Para 30.10 above.
2   Para 30.11 above.
3   Para 37.13 below.
4   See para 37.76 below. It may be that L's right to serve a notice to quit is restricted by statute (see Chapter 38 below), in which case the implied periodic tenancy may be less of a disadvantage to T.
5   Since this contract is one which creates an interest in land, it must be in writing sufficient to satisfy the requirements of the Law of Property (Miscellaneous Provisions) Act 1989, s 2 (see para 30.2 above). Accordingly, equity cannot be of assistance to T where the informal lease is oral since an oral agreement to create an interest in land cannot, since 1989, amount to a contract.
6   As we have seen, equity treats a 'genuine' agreement (ie a formal contract) to grant a lease in the same way; see para 30.9 above.

31.4   This means that where T has gone into possession and paid rent he, in effect, has two parallel leases – the implied periodic tenancy recognised by the common law and the seven-year equitable lease. The potential conflict between these two leases was addressed by the courts in the case of *Walsh v Lonsdale*.[1] Here, the parties entered into an agreement that Lonsdale would grant Walsh a seven-year lease of a mill. The agreement provided that Walsh was to pay rent annually in advance. No deed was ever drawn up, but Walsh went into possession, paying rent quarterly in arrears. On the basis of the principles explained in the previous paragraph Walsh held two 'parallel' leases; at common law the absence of a deed meant that he was a periodic tenant, in equity he held a seven-year lease. The essential dispute in this case was whether Lonsdale was entitled to demand the payment of rent annually in advance (in accordance with the terms of the equitable lease) or whether Walsh could continue to pay rent in arrears (as was his right under the legal periodic tenancy). It was held that Lonsdale could demand the rent in advance since, where the rules of equity and law conflict, those of equity must prevail.[2] Accordingly, *as between the parties themselves,*[3] the terms of their equitable lease prevailed over the common law periodic tenancy. The principle of this decision, although adverse to the tenant on the facts, could have been of benefit to him (and to any tenant in his position) in other circumstances. If, for example, Lonsdale had been seeking to turn him out by notice appropriate to ending the periodic tenancy, this would not have been allowed. His seven-year equitable lease, which could not be terminated during its fixed term, would have prevailed over the periodic tenancy.

1   (1882) 21 Ch D 9.
2   Supreme Court of Judicature Act 1873, s 25(11); now re-enacted in Supreme Court Act 1981, s 49(1).
3   As we shall see in para 31.5 and in Chapter 35, the equitable lease does not always prevail over a purchaser.

31.5   It has been said that, as a result of the decision in *Walsh v Lonsdale*,[1] a written agreement for a lease is as good as a lease. There are, however, some important differences between a legal lease and an equitable lease. First, equity will only look on the parties to an informal lease or an agreement for a lease as having a lease where it considers that specific performance ought to be granted. Specific performance is a discretionary remedy.[2] So, for example, should the tenant go into possession under the agreement and immediately break one of its terms, equity would refuse him specific performance of the agreement.[3] He would not then have a lease in the eyes of equity, although he would still have a legal periodic tenancy where rent has been paid and accepted.

Second, an informal lease is only an equitable interest. Thus, unlike a legal lease, it is not necessarily binding on subsequent purchasers of the landlord's estate.[3] In particular, as we shall see, in some circumstances (notably where the tenant does *not* occupy the premises) the tenant may need to protect his lease by an entry on the Land Register.[4] Since the parties to an informal lease may well have been unaware of the legal requirement for creating a legal lease, the tenant is unlikely to know that an equitable lease should be protected in this way. Thus, where a tenant should have secured an entry on the Land Register and has failed to do so, and the landlord subsequently sells the freehold to a third party, the third party will not be bound by the tenant's equitable lease. The new landlord will be bound by any legal periodic tenancy which has arisen by implication, as this does not require to be entered on the Register; however, except where prevented by landlord and tenant legislation, this periodic tenancy can be terminated by notice.[5]

Further, legal and equitable leases differ in that certain easements which may, by virtue of the LPA, s 62, be implied on the grant of a formal lease may not be implied where there is only an informal lease.[6]

1   (1882) 21 Ch D 9, CA.
2   Para 11.31 above.
3   See generally Chapter 35 below.
4   Under the Land Registration Act 2002; see para 36.34 below. This cannot be done where the lease is for three years or less, LRA, s 33.
5   This discussion is subject to the caveat that if the tenant is in actual occupation under the lease, his rights under the equitable lease will bind the purchaser as an overriding interest, see para 36.23 below.
6   Para 33.38 below.

The overall principle

31.6   In summary, where parties try to create a legal estate or interest without using a deed, equity will often[1] be able treat them as having created the equitable equivalent. As we have seen in the preceding paragraphs, an attempt to create a lease for more than three years which does not employ a deed, results in an equitable lease. Similarly, any attempt to create a legal mortgage or a legal easement without using a deed will often result in an equitable mortgage or an equitable easement.

1   Provided that, as explained at para 31.3, note 5 above, the attempt takes the form of a written document
    which satisfies the requirements of the Law of Property (Miscellaneous Provisions) Act 1989, s 2.

Informal arrangements

31.7   In the foregoing paragraphs we have been explaining how equity may give effect
to *positive* attempts to create interests in land, ie those which have, at the least, got to the
stage of being formulated in a written document which satisfies the requirements of the
Law of Property (Miscellaneous Provisions) Act 1989, s 2. We now turn to those situations
where matters have never reached this point; the parties may merely have a spoken or
unspoken understanding that one has, or will have, some right to property owned by the
other, or the words or actions of the landowner may have given rise to an expectation
that another has, or is to have, a right to his land. In such circumstances, equity may
sometimes either

- accept that the parties intended a trust[1], or
- impose a trust, or
- order that either a legal, equitable or some personal interest in land be conferred.

In many of these cases the connecting thread is that the owner of the legal estate in land
has acted in such a way that, in fairness, he should either be regarded as holding the land
(either wholly or partially) in trust for another, or that he must formally grant an estate or
interest in the land to that other.

1   See para 29.40 above for an outline of the concept of a trust.

Implied, resulting and constructive trusts
31.8   As we have seen,[1] s 53 of the LPA requires that equitable interests, including trusts,
be created by a written and signed document. However, the section expressly provides
that this rule does not apply to the creation or operation of resulting, implied or constructive
trusts.[2] Accordingly, the courts have been able to use the implied trust (of which the resulting
and constructive trust are now usually regarded as the two constituent species) as a
mechanism for conferring an equitable interest in land even in the absence of any written
evidence at all.

1   Para 30.20 above.
2   LPA, s 53(2).

Resulting trusts
31.9   Traditionally, a resulting trust arises where land is conveyed to A alone but where
B has contributed either all or part of the purchase price. In such a situation it is presumed[1]
that it was the intention that A should hold the land on trust for B to the extent of the
latter's contribution.[2] Thus B will be regarded as either the sole or part owner in equity. So,
in *Sekhon v Alissa*[3] a mother gave her daughter £22,500 (a sum representing most of the
mother's savings) towards the purchase of a house which was conveyed into the daughter's
name. Later, when the daughter wished to sell the property she claimed that the property
was solely hers and that the mother's contribution had been a gift. It was held that, in the
absence of any evidence that a gift had been intended, a resulting trust would be presumed;
accordingly, the parties were entitled to share the proceeds of sale in proportion to their
initial contributions.

Not surprisingly, the possibility of a resulting trust arises most commonly in the domestic
situation where spouses or co-habitees make financial contributions to the purchase of a

home which is registered in the sole name of their partner. It is usual that, following the application of resulting trust principles, the parties are regarded as co-owners in equity; accordingly, this is a topic to which we shall return when dealing with co-ownership in chapter 32.[4]

1   Unless a contrary intention is proved. It may, for example, be shown that B was making a gift or a loan; see *Re Sharpe (a bankrupt)* [1980] 1 All ER 198.
2   *Dyer v Dyer* (1788) 2 Cox Eq Cas 92.
3   [1989] 2 FLR 94.
4   At para 32.12 below.

Constructive trusts

31.10   Under the doctrine of constructive trusts, the courts may in certain circumstances preclude a landowner from enjoying all or part of the beneficial interest in his land by constructively treating him as trustee for another person. Although modern courts sometimes use the terms 'resulting' and 'constructive' trust indiscriminately, it would appear that, in order to establish a constructive trust the following elements must be present:

- an agreement, arrangement, understanding or common intention that a property right has been or will be created; and
- detrimental reliance on that agreement, arrangement, understanding or intention.[1]

Again, the constructive trust is often used to confer equitable co-ownership in domestic cases where a spouse or co-habitee, who is not named as a legal owner of the family home, has not made direct financial contributions to the purchase price. Although unable to establish a true resulting trust, the claimant may, in certain circumstances, satisfy the requirements of a constructive trust. Again, we deal with this specific application of the constructive trust later.[2]

However, the constructive trust has been employed in a very much wider context. Thus, in *Bannister v Bannister*,[3] the defendant had conveyed the freehold of two cottages to the claimant, her brother-in-law, at an under-value on the understanding that she would be allowed to live in one of the cottages, rent-free, for the rest of her life. When he sought to evict her, the Court of Appeal held that he was unable to do so; he was a constructive trustee with his sister-in-law having an equitable life interest in the property. In *Lyus v Prowsa Developments Ltd*[4] it was held that a purchaser, by expressly agreeing with the vendor to honour the claimant's existing contract to purchase part of the land,[5] thereby became a constructive trustee and was obliged to complete that contract. More controversially, it has been suggested that a purchaser of land may find himself bound by a contractual licence by virtue of the imposition of a constructive trust. In *Ashburn Anstalt v Arnold*[6] the Court of Appeal opined that, where a purchaser expressly agrees to be bound by[7] an existing contractual licence, this stipulation may independently give rise to a constructive trust under which the purchaser must give continued effect to the rights of the licensee.[8]

1   See, in particular, *Lloyds Bank plc v Rosset* [1991] 1 AC 107, [1990] 1 All ER 1111, HL.
2   At para 32.12 below.
3   [1948] 2 All ER 133.
4   [1982] 1 WLR 1044.
5   Which was not otherwise binding on the purchaser because it had not been registered, see para 35.35 below.
6   [1989] Ch 1.
7   The court made clear that merely taking with notice of a contractual licence is insufficient to give rise to a constructive trust; it must be shown that the purchaser was agreeing to be bound by the licensee's rights.
8   It is worth noting that, today, claimants may, in such circumstances, be able to utilise the Contracts (Rights of Third Parties) Act 1999; see Chapter 14 above.

Proprietary estoppel

31.11　An early statement of the equitable doctrine of proprietary estoppel is to be found in the judgment of Lord Kingsdown in *Ramsden v Dyson*:[1] 'If a man ... under an expectation, created or encouraged by the land[owner], that he shall have a certain interest, takes possession of such land, with the consent of the land[owner], and upon the faith of such ... expectation, with the knowledge of the land[owner], and without objection by him, lays out money upon the land, a court of equity will compel the land[owner] to give effect to such ... expectation'. Whilst the development of this doctrine was greatly restricted for over a century by the very much stricter rules laid down in *Wilmott v Barber*,[2] it re-emerged following the decision in *Taylor's Fashions Ltd v Liverpool Victoria Trustees Co Ltd*.[3] There, Oliver J identified as the primary question for the court 'whether, in particular individual circumstances, it would be unconscionable for a party to be permitted to deny that which, knowingly or unknowingly, he has allowed or encouraged another to assume to his detriment'.[4] Having returned to its more broadly based roots the doctrine has, as we shall see, come to be used more widely.

However flexible the court's approach may have become, certain elements must be present if the doctrine is to be established in any given case. These we consider in the following paragraphs.

1　(1866) LR 1 HL 129 at 170.
2　(1880) 15 Ch D 96.
3　[1982] QB 133n.
4　See also *Habib Bank Ltd v Habib Bank AG Zurich* [1981] 2 All ER 650, CA. This approach has recently been endorsed by the Privy Council in *Lim Teng Huan v Ang Swee Chuan* [1992] 1 WLR 113.

Assurance

31.12　First, the landowner must have made a representation or created an expectation that the claimant has, or is to have, rights over the land in question[1]. Whilst this will normally involve proof of some positive statement to such effect, the courts may infer the necessary assurance where the landowner has remained silent and allowed the claimant to incur expenditure or otherwise act to his detriment in the mistaken belief that he has rights to the land in question.

1　The claimant's belief that he is to have rights over the land must be justified; in particular it is unlikely that the courts will regard explicitly non-binding undertakings, such as a 'subject to contract' agreement, as giving rise to a claim to rights by way of proprietary estoppel: see *James v Evans* [2000] 3 EGLR 1, CA.

Acts in reliance

31.13　Second, it must be shown that the claimant acted in reliance on that representation. While it has been suggested that, once it is proved that a representation has been made and that the claimant has acted to his detriment, there is a rebuttable presumption that those acts were in reliance on the representation,[1] the Privy Council has expressed the view that such reliance must either be strictly proved, or that this must be a matter of 'inevitable inference'.[2] Thus, in the normal event, the claimant must show that his subsequent actions were induced or influenced by the landowner's assurance.

These acts often, in practice, comprise expenditure on, or improvements to, the land in question. So, in *Pascoe v Turner*,[3] the claimant, on leaving the defendant for another woman, represented to the defendant that the house in which they had been living as man and wife was hers. On the faith of this, the defendant spent money on repairs and decoration. When the claimant subsequently sought to determine what he alleged was a mere licence to occupy, the Court of Appeal held that he could not do so because the doctrine of proprietary estoppel gave rise to an 'equity' in favour of the defendant. In *Inwards v Baker*,[4] a father allowed his son to build a bungalow for himself on the father's land, which the son did, by his own labour, and sharing the expense with his father. The father had, by an old unrevoked will, left the land to someone else, and on his death his executors claimed possession of the land from the son. This the Court of Appeal refused, holding that the son, having spent money on the land in the expectation of being allowed to stay there, was entitled to remain on the property.

However, it is equally clear that other acts will suffice, for example, expenditure on one's own land in expectation of being granted some right over another's land. This is shown by the application of the doctrine in *ER Ives Investments Ltd v High*,[5] where the defendant had spent money constructing a garage on his own land in a position where it could be reached only across the yard of the neighbouring property. The neighbouring owners at that time (predecessors of the claimant) had stood by and, indeed, encouraged the defendant so to build his garage, knowing that he believed, as a result of prior transactions, that he had a right of way across the yard. The decision in *Crabb v Arun District Council*[6] demonstrates that the doctrine also extends to the situation where the claimant merely acts to his detriment in reliance on the expectation encouraged by the landowner. Here, the claimant, believing himself entitled, as a result of negotiations with the defendant, to a right of way across the defendant's adjoining land, sold part of his land, leaving the remainder accessible only via this disputed right of way. The Court of Appeal held that the actions of the defendant, in encouraging the claimant so to act to his detriment, raised an 'equity' in favour of the claimant.

1   *Greasley v Cooke* [1980] 3 All ER 710, CA.
2   *Lim Teng Huan v Ang Swee Chuan* [1992] 1 WLR 113.
3   [1979] 2 All ER 945, CA.
4   [1965] 1 All ER 446, CA.
5   [1967] 1 All ER 504, CA.
6   [1975] 3 All ER 865, CA.

Detriment

31.14   Finally, it is clear that, in order to found a claim based on proprietary estoppel, it must be shown that the claimant will suffer a detriment unless the court intervenes to offer protection. This detriment lies not simply in the expenditure that has been incurred, or the acts that the claimant has carried out, but rather in the prejudice which he will suffer if the landowner is allowed to insist upon his strict legal rights and, thereby, to deny the expected rights. This means that the claimant must satisfy the court that 'the defendant, by setting up his right, is taking advantage of him in a way which is unconscionable, inequitable or unjust'.[1]

1   *Crabb v Arun District Council* [1975] 3 All ER 865, CA.

Effect of the doctrine

31.15   The doctrine of proprietary estoppel operates to prevent what the court regards as the true arrangement envisaged by the parties being frustrated by their being left to their rights and duties at law.[1] Its effect is to give rise to what is often referred to as an 'equity' in favour of the claimant, which the court satisfies by making an appropriate order. It is clear that the court has a wide discretion in deciding what is a suitable remedy, but there is considerable debate as to the exact basis of this discretion. In most cases it appears that the remedy is designed to give effect to the claimant's expectations. However, there may be circumstances, especially where the value of the claimant's reliance is far less than that of his expectation, or where it is difficult to measure the extent of the expectation, the remedy may be suitably modified and may be more closely linked to the claimant's reliance or expenditure. The nature of the remedy may also be dictated by practicalities; it may, for example, be inappropriate to order the defendant to share property with the claimant where the two could not live happily under one roof[2]. Furthermore, it is possible that, by the time the matter comes to court, the circumstances may be such that it is no longer equitable for the court to intervene, so that the owner is entitled to recover possession of the land free from any further claim.[3]

Where the court decides to confer rights to the property itself, it is now more usual for these to take the form of a recognised proprietary right. It is relatively rare for the court to order the outright transfer of the freehold, but it can happen. Thus, in *Pascoe v Turner*[4] the court decided that, in the circumstances, the equity could be satisfied only by declaring that the freehold of the property was vested in the defendant.[5] More likely is a declaration that the claimant is entitled to some lesser proprietary right such as a share in the ownership of the property,[6] or a right akin to an easement.[7] A common course of action in the past was for the courts to give the claimant an irrevocable licence for life.[8] While this had the attraction of representing fairly accurately the true arrangement envisaged by the parties, it did give rise to uncertainties as to the legal effect of the rights conferred. For this reason, the court will now usually try to devise some alternative solution.[9]

However, the court may decide not to confer rights to the property. For example, in *Dodsworth v Dodsworth*[10] the court merely protected the defendants' occupation until such time as they had been compensated by the claimant for their improvements to the property. In *Wayling v Jones*[11] the specific property which had been promised to the claimant had been sold and he was given a money award instead.

1   *Chandler v Kerley* [1978] 2 All ER 942 at 946.
2   *Dodsworth v Dodsworth* (1973) 228 Estates Gazette 1115, CA.
3   *Sledmore v Dalby* (1996) 72 P & CR 196, CA. Here, by the time of the hearing, the defendant had already occupied the property rent-free for 18 years and the claimant's need for the property was now very much greater than his. The court therefore decided that it was no longer equitable to fulfil the defendant's expectation that he would be allowed to remain in the property for the rest of his life, and the claimant was permitted to regain possession.
4   [1979] 2 All ER 945, CA, para 31.13 above.
5   See also *Dillwyn v Llewelyn* (1862) 4 De GF & J 517; *Voyce v Voyce* (1991) 62 P & CR 290, CA.
6   *Lim Teng Huan v Ang Swee Chuan* [1992] 1 WLR 113.
7   *Crabb v Arun District Council* [1975] 3 All ER 865, CA; *ER Ives Investment Ltd v High* [1967] 1 All ER 504, CA.
8   Eg *Inwards v Baker* [1965] 1 All ER 446, CA; *Greasley v Cooke* [1980] 3 All ER 710, CA.
9   In *Griffiths v Williams* (1977) 248 Estates Gazette 947, CA the court suggested that the parties should agree to the grant of a long lease, terminable on the death of the claimant, and subject to an absolute covenant against assignment.
10   (1973) 228 Estates Gazette 1115, CA. See also *Baker v Baker* (1993) 25 HLR 408, CA.
11   (1993) 69 P & CR 170.

Conveyancing problems

31.16   The doctrine of proprietary estoppel gives rise to potential conveyancing problems. A major difficulty is whether, prior to any determination of the matter by a court, the claimant has a proprietary right at all. His equity arises from the estoppel and is not created by the court.[1] It thus dates from the moment when the landowner unconscionably sets up his own rights against the legitimate expectations of the claimant.[2] It remains uncertain whether the claimant can, at this stage (ie prior to any ruling by a court) transfer the benefit of his estoppel rights to someone else. In some instances, it may be clear that the rights are personal and non-assignable[3], in other cases the suggestion is that the benefit is transferable[4]. The position as to the other side of the coin, ie whether estoppel rights can bind a purchaser of the affected land, is rather clearer. This equity was assumed to be capable of binding purchasers in *Ives v High*[5] and *Inwards v Baker*[6], and it has now been confirmed that this is indeed the case in relation to registered land.[7] Thus, a purchaser may[8] be bound to give effect to a right, which may be difficult to detect and the full extent of which will not be known until the court decides on the appropriate remedy.

Once a court has determined how the 'equity' arising from proprietary estoppel should be satisfied further conveyancing problems should not arise. In the past, the court sometimes decided to satisfy the equity negatively, by holding merely that the claimant had an irrevocable licence to occupy for life. This did cause difficulties. However, where a right to the property is awarded, the courts are now more likely to ensure that a recognised proprietary right is granted.

1   Re Sharpe (a bankrupt) [1980] 1 All ER 198.
2   Lim Teng Huan v Ang Swee Chuan [1992] 1 WLR 113 at 117.
3   Maharaj v Chand [1986] 3 All ER 107, PC.
4   Brikom Investments Ltd v Carr [1979] 2 All ER 753, CA.
5   [1967] 1 All ER 504, CA.
6   [1965] 1 All ER 446, CA.
7   LRA, s 116.
8   We discuss the exact circumstances in which the equity will bind a purchaser in Chapter 35 below.

Proprietary estoppel and constructive trusts

31.17   It will be apparent from the foregoing paragraphs that there are strong similarities between the doctrine of proprietary estoppel and the constructive trust. Although the former doctrine has a quite distinct legal pedigree from the constructive trust and the two principles have developed separately without cross-fertilisation between them, it is clear that the two have come to bear a close resemblance, particularly when applied in the context of co-ownership.[1] That said, there remain important differences. Particularly in its more recent formulations,[2] the constructive trust appears to be based firmly on some sort of express or implied *agreement* between the parties. Proprietary estoppel is more firmly directed towards fulfilling *expectations* created by the landowner. It is also possible that, under the doctrine of proprietary estoppel, the courts may accept a wider range of acts in reliance[3] than is acceptable as a basis for imposing a constructive trust.[4] Finally, there is little doubt that the doctrine of proprietary estoppel affords the court a far wider range of remedies. As we have seen,[5] the court can confer a range of rights from a temporary licence through to full legal ownership. Where a constructive trust is imposed the almost invariable result is that the claimant has an equitable interest in the property which amounts either to sole or, more likely, a share in the beneficial ownership of the property.

In those cases where the facts do lend themselves to alternative claims based on either constructive trusts or proprietary estoppel (usually those involving claims to shared ownership), there are circumstances in which the claimant might prefer to rely on proprietary estoppel. This is because estoppel rights can be more effectively enforced against a purchaser or mortgagee than those arising under constructive trusts[6]. Where this issue has come before the courts, the claimant has not been allowed to resort to proprietary estoppel as a way of avoiding the consequences of the trust[7].

1   As to which see para 32.12 below.
2   In Lloyds Bank plc v Rosset [1990] 1 All ER 1111, HL.
3   See, for example, Greasley v Cooke [1980] 3 All ER 710, CA and Re Basham [1986] 1 WLR 1498 in both of which the continued contribution of domestic labour and services were held to be sufficient.
4   It remains highly unlikely that the courts will regard the performance of 'ordinary' domestic duties as sufficient; see further para 32.12 below.
5   Para 31.15 above.
6   As we shall see in paras 32.31, 36.13 and 36.27, beneficial interests under a trust can be overreached, in which case they are transferred to the purchase money and do not bind a purchaser.
7   See Birmingham Midshires Mortgage Services Ltd v Sabherwal (1999) 80 P & CR 256. This is not the case with proprietary estoppel.

The doctrine of benefit and burden

31.18   Further illustrating equity's flexibility in this area, other aspects of the case of *ER Ives Investment Ltd v High*[1] demonstrate how the doctrine of benefit and burden,[2] originally limited to those taking the benefit of a deed, may be pressed into service to protect rights arising from informal arrangements. High's original neighbour W built a block of flats on his land, the foundations of which encroached on High's land by about one foot. High and W agreed that the foundations could remain where they were and that in return High could have a right of way across the yard of W's flats to gain access to a side road. W subsequently sold his property to X. While X owned the flats, High, to X's knowledge, built a garage in such a way that it could only be reached across the yard, and also contributed to the cost of resurfacing the yard. Later X sold the flats to Ives Ltd, expressly subject to High's right to cross the yard. Ives Ltd brought this action to restrain High from crossing the yard. The Court of Appeal, in addition to upholding High's right on the basis of proprietary estoppel,[3] held that, on the principle that 'he who takes the benefit must accept the burden', so long as the owners of the blocks of flats had the benefit of having their foundations in High's land, they had to allow High and his successors to have access over their yard. The converse equally applies: so long as High took the benefit of access across the yard, he had to permit the foundations to remain. This would suggest then that should High, for example, decide to abandon using the access across the yard, he could demand that the foundations be removed from his land, no doubt necessitating the demolition of the flats. Thus, where the doctrine of benefit and burden does apply, it operates to render a licence irrevocable for so long as the corresponding benefit is enjoyed.

It has been made clear by the House of Lords in *Rhone v Stephens*[4] that the doctrine does not mean that any party deriving *any* benefit from a conveyance has to accept *any* burden imposed by that conveyance; the burden must be relevant to the exercise of the right. Accordingly, in that case, the defendant could not be required to repair a roof which overhung the adjoining cottage simply because she had the benefit of a right of support from that property.

1   [1967] 1 All ER 504, CA.
2   See also para 34.10 below; and see *Tito v Waddell (No 2)* [1977] 3 All ER 129.
3   Para 31.13 above.
4   [1994] 2 All ER 65, HL.

Adverse possession

31.19   Finally, we turn to the circumstances in which legal estates and interests may be acquired despite the absence of any formal grant, agreement or even an understanding between the parties. Here we are considering those situations in which, due to possession or user enjoyed by the claimant over a long period of time, the law is prepared to validate the claim to the estate or interest in question. The only legal rights to land which can be acquired in this way are ownership rights (both freehold and leasehold) and an easement (such as a right of way). Ownership may be established by long use (or, more accurately, adverse possession). A claim to an easement is made under the rules relating to prescription. In this section we shall deal only with the acquisition of ownership by way of adverse possession; prescription is more conveniently dealt with in chapter 33. It should be noted that the LRA 2002 introduces radical changes to the law governing the acquisition of title by adverse possession where land is registered. The following paragraphs deal almost exclusively[1] with these new rules. For a full consideration of the position regarding claims to unregistered estates, reference should be made to the standard texts on land law[2].

1   A brief summary of the law governing unregistered land is provided at para 31.21 below.
2   Eg Megarry and Wade *The Law of Real Property* (6th edn) pp 1303 – 1335.

Introduction
31.20   Where a landowner's possession is interrupted he is entitled to take steps against the trespasser.[1] However, where the trespasser takes possession, rather than simply intruding on a temporary basis, he is often referred to as a 'squatter' rather than just a trespasser; here the landowner will need to recover possession of the land rather than simply suing in

trespass.[2] Traditionally the law has placed a limit on the time within which he should take action to recover possession, for it is the policy of the law, first, to protect undisturbed possession and, second, that a person should pursue his lawful claims with diligence. This is the principle of 'limitation of actions'.[3]

The effect of the limitation principle was that a person who had the right to possess land could lose that right if someone else took possession of the land in a way which was inconsistent with his possession (ie took 'adverse possession') and remained in possession for the statutory 'limitation period', which was, generally, 12 years.[4] In such a case, not only was the original owner's right to take action to recover possession terminated, but also his title to the land was extinguished.[5]

It should be appreciated that, while this principle sometimes operated to deprive a landowner of title to the whole of his land, its more usual application was far less dramatic (and rather more acceptable). Suppose, for example, that a boundary structure between A and B's properties was inadvertently erected in the wrong place so that A's garden included a strip of B's land. If this situation remained undisturbed for a period of 12 years, B's title to that strip was extinguished. In this way, minor boundary discrepancies were often resolved in a relatively straightforward manner.[6]

1   Para 23.1 above.
2   Should he choose self-help rather than seeking a court order for possession he should take care to avoid transgressing the criminal law; see para 23.11 above.
3   Currently embodied in the Limitation Act 1980, as amended. As we shall see, this Act no longer applies where the title to the estate being claimed by the squatter is registered, LRA, s 96. The 1980 Act still applies where title to the estate being claimed is not registered, see para 31.21 below.
4   Limitation Act 1980, s 15(1).
5   LA 1980, s 17.
6   See para 29.28 above. Although, generally speaking, the changes introduced by the LRA make it more difficult for a squatter to acquire title, the role of adverse possession as a mechanism for resolving such minor boundary discrepancies is retained, see para 31.31 below.

31.21   *The law governing unregistered land* The Limitation Act 1980 still applies to unregistered land. It provides[1] that no action may be brought to recover land after the expiration of 12 years from the date on which the right of action accrued. The right of action is deemed to accrue on the date on which the person in possession was dispossessed or discontinued possession and continues only so long as another person is in adverse possession of the land.[2] Hence, in order for time to start running it must be established that

•   the 'paper' owner has either been dispossessed or has discontinued possession; and
•   that the squatter has gone into adverse possession.

The adverse possession must continue, unbroken, for the full 12-year period. However, it is not essential that the same person is the squatter for the whole of that period.[3] So, if A (the 'paper' owner) is dispossessed by B for five years and then B is himself dispossessed by C, A's title will be extinguished once C has been in adverse possession for seven years. However, C will remain vulnerable to an action for possession brought by B for a further five years; only at that point does C's title become secure. Equally, B could have voluntarily transferred his rights to the land to C; in that case C's title would become unimpeachable after seven years.

In the case of unregistered land, the title of the person entitled to bring an action for possession is extinguished on the expiration of the limitation period.[4] The effect of the Limitation Act 1980 is not to convey from one to another but to extinguish;[2] hence, the squatter does not acquire the title or estate of the owner whom he has dispossessed,[5] but acquires a new freehold title of his own. However, it is important to remember that the only rights extinguished for the benefit of the squatter are those of persons who might, during the statutory period, have brought, but did not in fact bring, an action to recover possession of the land.[6] Thus the squatter has no answer to the claim of a third party seeking to enforce, for example, an easement or a restrictive covenant over the land;[7] these rights continue to bind the land in accordance with normal principles.

1   Limitation Act 1980, s 15(1).
2   LA 1980, Sch 1, paras 1 and 8. As we shall see in para 31.25 below, 'adverse' possession is very much more than simple trespass.
3   *Mount Carmel Investments Ltd v Peter Thurlow Ltd* [1988] 3 All ER 129, [1988] 1 WLR 1078, CA.
4   Limitation Act 1980, s 17.
5   *Tichborne v Weir* (1892) 67 LT 735.
6   *Fairweather v St Marylebone Property Co Ltd* [1962] 2 All ER 288, HL.
7   *Re Nisbet and Potts' Contract* [1906] 1 Ch 386 at 409.

Land Registration Act 2002: claims to registered land

Introduction

31.22   The LRA has made radical changes to the law in this area. The Limitation Act 1980 no longer applies where a squatter is claiming title, by way of adverse possession, to a registered estate[1]. Such claims are now governed by LRA 2002, s 97 and Sch 6. In summary, these provide that, where a squatter can establish adverse possession[2] for the immediately preceding 10-year period[3], he can apply to be registered as proprietor[4]. This will prompt the registrar to notify the registered proprietor of the squatter's application[5]. If, as is likely, the registered proprietor objects within three months then, save in exceptional circumstances, the squatter's application will be rejected[6]. If there is no objection within three months to the squatter's application, he will be registered as the new proprietor[7].

1   LRA, s 96. However, where a squatter has already completed a period of 12 years adverse possession by 13 October 2003 (ie the date on which LRA 2002 comes into force), the old rules will still apply, LRA Sch 12, para 18.
2   For the meaning of 'adverse possession' see paras 31.23-31.29 below.
3   See para 31.28 below.
4   LRA, Sch 6, para 1(1), see para 31.30 below.
5   LRA, Sch 6, para 2, see para 31.30 below.
6   LRA, Sch 6, para 3(1), 5, see para 31.31 below.
7   LRA, Sch 6, para 4.

Adverse possession

31.23   A squatter can only apply for registration once he has established that he has been in adverse possession for the requisite period. LRA 2002 expressly provides that the meaning of 'adverse possesion' is to be the same as under s 15 of the Limitation Act 1980[1]; thus, those statutory provisions and the pre-existing case law remain relevant to the new law. These establish that a period of adverse possession only commences when:

–   the 'paper' owner has either been dispossessed or has discontinued possession; and
–   the squatter has gone into 'adverse possession'; this requires proof that the squatter has taken factual possession (as opposed to a temporary incursion or occupation) and that he has the requisite intention to possess.

The House of Lords has recently made it clear that although the term 'adverse possession' is used by statute, it should not be regarded as meaning anything different from ordinary possession[2]. It is, however, to be contrasted with a temporary incursion onto, or intermittent use of, land. It should also be appreciated that a squatter's initial use of land may not amount to adverse possession but can, over time, so develop. So, for example, in *Powell v McFarlane*[3] the court concluded that, although for a number of years the claimant had done some clearing of the defendant's land and had grazed animals on it, these acts had not amounted to adverse possession. Only later, when his activities on the property had become more extensive and his intention to possess more formulated, could it be said that he was in adverse possession and it was only from this later date that the requisite period could be said to run.

1   LRA, Sch 6, para 11(1).
2   *JA Pye (Oxford) Ltd v Graham* [2002] UKHL 30, [2002] 3 All ER 865.
3   (1977) 38 P & CR 452.

31.24   *Discontinuance or dispossession* The requisite period cannot start to run until the paper owner has either been dispossessed or he has discontinued his possession. Dispossession refers to a person coming in and putting another out of possession, while discontinuance refers to the case where the person in possession abandons possession and another takes it.[1] Abandonment of possession may be difficult to establish. The smallest act by the paper owner will be sufficient to show that there was no discontinuance[2] since the owner with the right to possession will be readily assumed to have the requisite intention to possess.[3] Thus, the acts of the paper owner, in *Leigh v Jack*[4] in repairing a fence on the land, and, in *Williams Bros Direct Supply Ltd v Raftery*[5] in measuring the land for development and depositing rubbish on it, were sufficient to show no discontinuance. However if, for example, the paper owner erects a fence which prevents *his own* access to the disputed land, this will be strong evidence of abandonment, particularly in the case of urban property.[6]

The fact that there is no discontinuance or abandonment of possession by the paper owner means only that the squatter's case must be based on his having 'dispossessed' the paper owner. As has now been made clear by the House of Lords, this term carries no suggestion that the paper owner has been ousted or ejected. It means no more than that it has to be shown that it is now the squatter who is in possession of the land rather than the paper owner; 'if the squatter is in possession the paper owner cannot be'[7].

1   *Powell v McFarlane* (1977) 38 P & CR 452.
2   *Leigh v Jack* (1879) 5 Ex D 264, CA.
3   *Powell v McFarlane* (1977) 38 P & CR 452.
4   (1879) 5 Ex D 264, CA.
5   [1957] 3 All ER 593, CA.
6   *Hounslow London Borough v Minchinton* (1997) 74 P & CR 221, CA.
7   *JA Pye (Oxford) Ltd v Graham* [2002] UKHL 30, [2002] 3 All ER 865, 875 per Lord Browne-Wilkinson.

31.25   *Factual possession*   Whether a person has factual possession depends on the circumstances, particularly the nature of the land and the way in which land of that nature is commonly used or enjoyed. Basically, however, what is required is that the squatter's use of the land should amount to more than persistent trespass. He must have been exercising sufficient physical control over the land to amount to exclusive possession and must have dealt with the land in the same way as any occupying owner might have done. Clearly building on land, occupying and using a building,[1] or fencing[2] and then incorporating land into land already owned by the claimant[3] will amount to factual possession. Equally, acts falling short of such obvious control for example, rough shooting,[4] grazing and storage,[5] weeding, tending and putting a compost heap on land,[6] have all been regarded as sufficient to show factual possession, in the light of the nature of the land in question.

Contrary to the view taken in a number of earlier authorities,[7] it is not the case that a squatter can only be said to take possession against a paper owner who has no present use for the land but who plans to use the land for a particular purpose in the future (eg redevelopment), where the squatter's acts are inconsistent with those future plans.[8] It is possible that, in such circumstances, the acts of a would-be squatter are too trivial to amount to factual possession[9] or that, particularly if the squatter is aware of the owner's plans, he has not demonstrated the requisite intention.[10] However, it is clear that, as *Buckinghamshire County Council v Moran* shows, a squatter's claim can succeed, despite the fact that his possession does not interfere with the paper owner's future plans for the land.

1   *Mount Carmel Investments Ltd v Peter Thurlow Ltd* [1988] 3 All ER 129, CA.
2   A claimant who fences the disputed land will almost always have done enough to demonstrate factual possession since this is viewed as 'the strongest possible evidence' (*Seddon v Smith* (1877) 36 LT 168). However, in some circumstances fencing will not provide proof of factual possession eg in *Boosey v Davis* (1987) 55 P & CR 83 (incomplete fence) and *Marsden v Miller* (1992) 64 P & CR 239 (fence in place for only 24 hours).
3   *Buckinghamshire County Council v Moran* [1989] 2 All ER 225.
4   *Red House Farms (Thorndon) Ltd v Catchpole* (1977) 244 Estates Gazette 295.
5   *Treloar v Nute* [1976] 1 WLR 1295.
6   *HounslowLondon Borough v Minchinton* (1997) 74 P & CR 221, CA.
7   Commencing with a dictum of Bramwell LJ in *Leigh v Jack* (1879) 5 Ex D 264 at 273; see also, in particular, *Williams Bros Direct Supply Ltd v Raftery* [1957] 3 All ER 593, CA.
8   *Buckinghamshire County Council v Moran* [1989] 2 All ER 225, CA, a view that has been emphatically endorsed in *JA Pye (Oxford) Ltd v Graham* [2002] UKHL 30, [2002] 3 All ER 865.
9   See, for example, *Boosey v Davis* (1987) 55 P & CR 83, CA.
10 See, for example, *Pulleyn v Hall Aggregates (Thames Valley)* (1992) 65 P & CR 276, CA, where there was held to be no adverse possession since the squatter's acts were consistent with the paper owner's present plans for the land. However, it should be noted that in *JA Pye (Oxford) Ltd v Graham* [2002] UKHL 30, [2002] 3 All ER 865 it was made clear that this would rarely be the correct inference where the paper owner has been physically excluded from the land. For a further discussion of the role of the squatter's intention, see para 31.26 below.

31.26   *Intention*   However, factual possession alone is not enough; the squatter must prove the requisite intention. The law requires the squatter to demonstrate, by his actions, an intention, in his own name and for his own benefit, to exclude the world at large, including the owner with the paper title,[1] so far as is reasonably practicable and so far as the processes of the law will allow. What is required, according to *Buckinghamshire County Council v Moran*, is not that the squatter must intend to own or even to acquire ownership of the land but rather that he must intend to possess it for the time being[2]. Thus the fact that Mr Moran's intention was to use land belonging to the council (which he had incorporated into his garden and access to which he had barred by a padlocked gate) only unless and until a proposed bypass was built on it did not preclude his having the requisite intention. Equally, the fact that it can be shown that the squatter would be willing, if asked, to pay for the use of the land is not inconsistent with his being in possession in the meantime[3].

Evidence of the squatter's intention is likely in most cases to be derived from his actions. As in *Buckinghamshire County Council v Moran*, enclosure of the land by the squatter, for example by putting up a fence, is strong evidence not only of factual possession but also of the requisite intention. However, even fencing may be equivocal. It may, for example, be that, as in *Littledale v Liverpool College*,[4] it is done to protect a right of way enjoyed over the paper owner's land from interference by the world at large, rather than to establish possession of the land by the squatter[5]. That said, the House of Lords has expressed the view that where a squatter has occupied and made full use of the land in the way that an owner would, he does not need to prove any intention to possession; positive proof of intention is only necessary where his acts are equivocal[6].

1   It is not fatal that the squatter erroneously believes the land to be his own since the intention required is to *possess* rather than to *dispossess*; see *Hughes v Cork* [1994] EGCS 25, CA.
2   These views have recently been affirmed by the House of Lords in *JA Pye (Oxford) Ltd v Graham* [2002] UKHL 30, [2002] 3 All ER 865.
3   *JA Pye (Oxford) Ltd v Graham* [2002] UKHL 30, [2002] 3 All ER 865.
4   [1900] 1 Ch 19, CA.
5   See also *Fruin v Fruin* [1983] CA Transcript, where a claimant who had erected a fence to prevent an elderly member of the family wandering off was held not to have been in adverse possession.
6   *JA Pye (Oxford) Ltd v Graham* [2002] UKHL 30, [2002] 3 All ER 865, at p 887 per Lord Hutton.

31.27   *Occupation as a licensee*   Occupation cannot amount to adverse possession if it has a lawful basis. If therefore a person's use of land is with the permission of the paper owner, it cannot found a claim to title. However, there must be a genuine factual basis for any finding by the court that there is such a licence from the paper owner. In *BP Properties Ltd v Buckler*[2] the paper owner wrote to the squatter unilaterally permitting her to remain in the property; although the squatter ignored this letter, incorrectly believing she was entitled to remain as of right, it was held that her continued occupation was attributable to the licence and could not therefore amount to adverse possession. This case suggests that the unilateral grant[2] to the squatter of a short-term licence to remain in the property is a speedy, cheap and effective way of stopping time running in the squatter's favour. By way of contrast, sending a letter which merely asserts the paper owner's right to possession, without more, is ineffective to prevent the squatter acquiring title.[3]

1   [1987] 2 EGLR 168, CA.
2   There must he an outright *grant* of permission; merely inviting the squatter to agree to a licence will not, where the squatter fails to respond, stop time running; see *Pavledes v Ryesbridge Properties* (1989) 58 P & CR 459.
3   *Mount Carmel Investments Ltd v Peter Thurlow Ltd* [1988] 3 All ER 129, CA.

31.28   *Adverse possession for the requisite period*   The LRA requires that the squatter must establish that he has been in continuous adverse possession for a period of 10 years ending on the date of his application for registration[1]. It is not necessary for the applicant himself to have been in adverse possession throughout this period since any period during which the land has been in the adverse possession of a predecessor in title can be added to his own, provided that there has been continuity[2]. However if, during the 10-year period, there has been any action which stops the squatter's occupation from amounting to possession (such as the granting of a licence[3]) time will stop running; if the squatter's possession later re-commences he must complete a fresh period of 10 years.

1   LRA, Sch 6, para 1(1). A squatter who has completed a period of 10 years adverse possession and is then evicted by the registered proprietor can still apply for registration provided that he does so within six months of the eviction.
2   LRA, Sch 6, para 11. This will not be the case where the applicant has *dispossessed* (as opposed to have taken title from) a previous squatter.
3   See para 31.27 above.

31.29   *The position prior to completing the requisite period of adverse possession*   Once the squatter has commenced adverse possession[1] he is regarded at common law as having a freehold interest in the land, albeit one that can be defeated by the paper owner taking steps to recover possession. Given that the paper owner's title continues to be registered, this means that there are two competing freehold estates. The squatter's rights are, of course, proprietary and are capable of binding anyone to whom the paper owner sells[2]. So if, for example, the paper owner transfers the land to a purchaser when the squatter has been in adverse possession for five years, that purchaser has only five years in which to regain possession. If he does not do so, the squatter will have the right to apply for registration. As we shall see[3], the new rules mean that only rarely will a squatter be registered as proprietor; however, if he is, he becomes the proprietor of the paper owner's estate and his 'parallel' freehold interest is extinguished[4].

1   Note that a squatter's initial use of the land may not always amount to adverse possession, see para 31.23 above.
2   Provided the squatter is in occupation of the land he will have what is known as an 'overriding interest' which will normally bind any purchaser, see para 36.23 below.
3   See para 31.30 below.
4   LRA, Sch 6, para 9(1).

The effect of completing the requisite period of adverse possession

31.30   Completion of the requisite period of adverse possession confers no additional rights to the land; it merely entitles the squatter to apply to be registered as proprietor[1]. On receiving such an application the registrar must notify the existing registered proprietor and certain parties with interests in the land, such as the proprietor of any registered charge over the land[2]. If, within three months[3], there is no objection from those notified, the squatter is entitled to be registered as the new proprietor of the paper owner's estate[4], subject to all existing third party rights such as easements or covenants[5]. In practice, those notified are highly likely to object in which case the squatter's application for registration will normally be refused[6], save in the exceptional cases dealt with in the following paragraph.

1   LRA, Sch 6, para 1(1).
2   LRA, Sch 6, para 2.
3   LRA, Sch 6, para 3(2).
4   LRA, Sch 6, para 4.
5   LRA, Sch 6, para 9(2).
6   LRA, Sch 6, para 5. Note that, following such a refusal, the applicant is entitled, in some circumstances, to make a further application, LRA, Sch 6, para 6 and para 31.32 below.

31.31   *Exceptional cases*   Where objection is made to the squatter's application, registration will normally be refused. However, there are three instances where the squatter will be registered as the new proprietor even in the face of objections:

–   where it would be unconscionable because of an equity by estoppel for the applicant to be dispossessed;
–   where the applicant is for some other reason entitled to be registered as proprietor; and
–   where the land in question is adjacent to land owned by the applicant, the line of the boundary between the two pieces of land has not been determined, and during the ten years of adverse possession the applicant has reasonably believed that the land belongs to him[1].

In the first two of these exceptional cases, it is clear that the applicant also has a quite independent claim to the land which could be pursued through the courts. It appears to have been envisaged[2] that an application under Sch 6 might afford such applicants an easier and cheaper way of achieving a remedy. However, it is arguable that anyone who occupies land by virtue of either proprietary estoppel or some other right cannot be in adverse possession[3] and is not therefore entitled to make an application under Sch 6.

That said, it is the third exception that is likely to prove the most important. This effectively preserves at least some aspects of one of the most useful and uncontroversial benefits of the law of adverse possession, namely that of giving effect to the mis-placed boundary feature[4]. It is not uncommon for fences to be erected which do not accord with the legal boundary; where these remain unchallenged for over 10 years, this exception will often allow the existing state of affairs to be preserved.

1   LRA, Sch 6, para 5(2).
2   By the Law Commission, see Law Com No 271, para 14.36.
3   Because they occupy with the consent of the paper owner, see para 31.27 above.
4   See paras 29.28 and 31.20 above.

31.32   *Further application for registration*   As has already been pointed out[1], where objections are raised to a squatter's application for registration, it will normally be refused save in the exceptional cases discussed in the previous paragraph. However, the policy underlying the new provisions requires that the paper owner (or other objector) does more than simply object; he is expected to take steps to recover possession. If this is not done, and the squatter remains in undisturbed adverse possession for a further two years, he is entitled to make a fresh application for registration[2]. In such a case the paper owner will not be notified, he cannot object and the squatter has an automatic right to be registered as the new proprietor[3].

1   See para 31.30 above.
2   LRA, Sch 6, para 6. Such an application cannot be made if the applicant is the defendant in current legal proceedings being taken to regain possession of the land, or if judgment for possession of the land has been obtained in the last two years or if he has been evicted from the land under a judgment for possession.
3   LRA, Sch 6, para 7.

possession and leases
Adverse possession against a tenant of an unregistered lease
31.33   Where a person occupies land adversely to a tenant holding under an unregistered lease for the 12-year statutory limitation period, the tenant's title is extinguished.[1] There is no transfer of the tenant's lease to the adverse possessor since the title acquired by the latter is to a freehold estate[2]. It follows that the squatter is not directly bound by covenants in the original lease[3] but, where (as is usual) there is a provision in the lease allowing the landlord to terminate in the event of any breach of covenant (known as a right of re-entry), this right is binding on the squatter.[4] Thus, unless the squatter complies with the covenants, the landlord will be able to re-enter the land and regain possession.[5]

1   Limitation Act 1980, s 17.
2   See para 31.29 above.
3   *Tichborne v Weir* (1892) 67 LT 735.
4   A right of re-entry in a lease is a legal interest binding on all-comers.
5   Paras 37.44–37.49 below.

The position of the landlord of an unregistered lease
31.34   Although adverse possession by a squatter will extinguish the tenant's title, time only begins to run against the landlord when the lease expires.[1] So, for example, where T, the tenant under a 20-year lease[2] is dispossessed by S in the fifth year of the lease, T's title will be extinguished 12 years later (ie in the 17th year of the lease). Just over three years later, when the lease would have expired, the landlord becomes entitled to regain possession against S; only then does time start to run against the landlord. Accordingly, S is not secure against the landlord until he has been in adverse possession for a further 12 years.

Furthermore, it has been held, by the House of Lords in *Fairweather v St Marylebone Property Co Ltd*,[3] that where a tenant's title is extinguished as a result of 12 years' adverse possession, that title is only extinguished as against the squatter. As between the landlord and the tenant the lease remains on foot. Accordingly, in that case it was held that the tenant whose title had been extinguished could, nevertheless, surrender the lease to the landlord before the expiration of the term. This brought the lease to an end and enabled the landlord to take immediate action to recover the land from the squatter, since time then immediately began to run against the landlord.

1   Limitation Act 1980, Sch 1, para 4.
2   It should be noted that it has only become compulsory to register leases of more than seven years under LRA 2002. see para 30.14 above. Prior to the commencement of this Act leases of 21 years and less were not registered.
3   [1962] 2 All ER 288, HL.

Adverse possession against tenants of registered leases
31.35   Where a squatter takes adverse possession of land held by way of a registered lease the LRA rules apply in much the same way as for freeholds[1]. On completion of the 10-year period the squatter can apply for registration; the registered proprietor of the

lease (ie the dispossessed tenant) and the landlord will be notified and will normally make objections which, save in exceptional circumstances, will prevent the squatter from being registered. If no objections are made, or any of the exceptional circumstances apply, or the squatter is able to make a further application, the squatter will be registered as proprietor of the existing lease[2]. Because the squatter effectively takes a transfer of the lease, unlike the position with unregistered leases, he will be directly bound by the covenants in the lease. However, during the period of adverse possession (ie prior to any registration as proprietor), the squatter's rights are to a freehold[3] and he will not be directly bound by the covenants in the lease; as with unregistered leases, the landlord may be able to enforce the covenants indirectly[4]. Furthermore, as with unregistered leases, it would appear that, unless and until the squatter is registered as proprietor of the lease, the dispossessed tenant can surrender the lease to the landlord who will then be entitled to take immediate steps to regain possession[5].

1   See paras 31.30-31.32, above. It is clear that there is, in effect a transfer of the existing lease, see LRA, Sch 6, paras 4, 5(1) and 7.
2   See para 31.29 above. If and when the squatter is registered as proprietor of the lease his freehold estate is extinguished, LRA, Sch 6, para 9(1).
3   See para 31.32 above.
4   See para 31.33 above.

Chapter 32

Concurrent ownership

32.1 So far, we have tended to speak of 'an' owner of land or an interest in land. This over-simplistic view of land ownership must now be examined more closely since the ownership of a piece of land can be enjoyed by more than one person. It is possible to carve up the ownership of land so that limited 'slices' of it are enjoyed successively, ie by one person after another. While the practice of successive ownership was very common in the past, it is extremely rare today and we devote no space to this area of the law. Far more prevalent is the concurrent ownership of land, ie where it is enjoyed by two or more persons at the same time. Concurrent or co-ownership poses particular problems; notably how to balance the sometimes competing interests of the various owners, and how to facilitate the sale and management of land in which a number of ownership interests co-exist. In this chapter we shall consider the following topics:

- the forms of concurrent ownership;
- the circumstances in which such ownership exists;
- the potential problems posed where the ownership of land is shared and the ways in which these are addressed by the law; and
- the legal machinery for giving effect to co-ownership.

The forms of concurrent ownership

Introduction
32.2 The law has long recognised both successive and concurrent ownership of land. Successive ownership, usually in the form of settlements, was widely employed until the middle of the nineteenth century since it provided a mechanism by which the major form of wealth and route to political power (ie land) could be tied to a particular family for very lengthy periods of time. However, as the economy changed and diversified, social and political attitudes changed, and taxation bit, this type of ownership became increasingly unattractive. In sharp contrast, modern social, political and economic conditions provide an environment in which the concurrent ownership of land thrives. It is now[1] usual for domestic residential property to be co-owned; equally, in the commercial sphere, where a business is run as a partnership, its property will often be co-owned by the partners.

1   Whereas the 'family' home always used to be owned solely by the husband, the picture has changed dramatically in the last 40 or so years. The norm is now for a matrimonial home to be in the names of

both husband and wife. This is increasingly the case where property is bought by those in other forms of relationship. Even where this is not so it is likely that, where any financial contribution is made to the purchase of property which is owned by another, the contributor will be accorded a share in its ownership; see para 32.12 below.

32.3   In the past there were various forms of concurrent ownership. Today, there are only two: joint tenancy and tenancy in common. ('Tenancy' in this context effectively means 'ownership'.) Both forms of co-ownership may exist in relation to freehold or leasehold interests.

Joint tenancy
32.4   The essential characteristics of joint tenancy are:

* the right of survivorship; and
* the 'four unities'.

The right of survivorship
32.5   Where co-ownership takes the form of joint tenancy, a joint tenant's interest in the land passes automatically on his death to the surviving joint tenants (and so on, until there is one survivor who is then the sole owner of the land). This is the right of survivorship; the ultimate survivor takes all. Should a joint tenant try to leave his interest in the land by will, this disposition has no effect. Nor do the rules of intestacy, which apply where a person dies leaving no effective will, take precedence over the right of survivorship.

Although the right of survivorship might be thought to render the joint tenancy something of a lottery and therefore an unattractive form of co-ownership, this is not necessarily the case. It is very appropriate for those whose ownership allows them no financial stake in the land, notably trustees. Furthermore, for co-owners who wish their fellow co-owner(s) to succeed to the property on their death, the joint tenancy is simple and convenient; for this reason it is often used by married couples or by those in a stable relationship.

The four unities
32.6   The 'four unities' are the unities of possession, interest, title and time; if one of them is missing there cannot be a joint tenancy. Joint tenants share possession of the land, together having one interest in the land, deriving the one title to the property at the same time.

* *Unity of possession*   Joint tenants enjoy unity of possession; each has the right to possession of all of the co-owned land. No one joint tenant can exclude the others from any part of the land. A co-owner cannot, by the very nature of co-ownership, point to one part of the land and say 'that is mine and no one else's'.
* *Unity of interest*   Where there is joint tenancy, each co-owner is entitled jointly with the other joint tenants to the entire interest in the property. Each tenant's interest must, therefore, be the same and, necessarily, equal. There is one interest, freehold or leasehold, to which they are all entitled. This means that the joint tenancy is not appropriate where co-owners are to have unequal shares in the land.
* *Unity of title*   Joint tenants derive title to the property under the same document (or by simultaneously taking possession and acquiring it by adverse possession).
* *Unity of time*   For a joint tenancy to exist the co-owners must not have interests commencing at different times.

Tenancy in common
No right of survivorship
32.7   If co-ownership takes the form of tenancy in common, the interest of each co-owner does not automatically pass to the surviving co-owners. The reason is that each tenant in

common has a fixed share in the land which may or may not be equal. On his death this may be passed on, by his will, to whomsoever he chooses (or, in the event of his leaving no will, pass to the person(s) specified by the rules of intestacy). Thus, unlike the joint tenancy, the tenancy in common is appropriate for those who do not necessarily wish their fellow co-owners to become entitled to their share on their death. Accordingly, the tenancy in common is likely to be used where friends are buying property together or by business partners. It must also be used where the shares of each co-owner are to be unequal. Although each tenant in common has a fixed share, the land is not, of course, physically divided to give effect to those shares; land subject to tenancy in common is referred to in the LPA 1925 as being held 'in undivided shares'.

Four unities not essential

32.8 Unity of possession is an essential characteristic of co-ownership, whatever form it takes, for there is clearly no co-ownership where a person possesses land to the exclusion of all others. However, the other unities are not essential to tenancy in common, although they are usually present.

The circumstances in which concurrent ownership exists

Express creation

32.9 In most instances concurrent ownership is expressly created. Prospective purchasers or tenants who wish to co-own the property ensure that the property is explicitly transferred, or leased, in the name of both (or all) of them. Where a testator leaves property by will to two or more beneficiaries, his executor will ensure that there is an express transfer to all. Where a donor gives land to more than one person, again, the documentation will be explicitly so drafted. Whenever land is transferred to two or more persons as co-owners, statute requires that a trust be created; this we discuss later in this chapter[1].

1   See para 32.25 below.

How to recognise whether an express transfer to co-owners is a joint tenancy or a tenancy in common

32.10 *Express declaration* In most instances where concurrent ownership is expressly created the relevant documentation (ie the transfer or will) will specify which form of co-ownership is intended, by declaring that the co-owners are to hold as 'joint tenants' or as 'tenants in common'; in the case of tenancies in common, the size of the shares of the parties may also be stated.[1] This declaration is conclusive, in the absence of fraud or collusion[2].

It may be, however, that wording other than these technical terms is used. In such cases a different approach is necessary. Where wording other than 'joint tenancy' or 'tenancy in common' (or 'undivided share') is used the courts will have to decide on their meaning and effect. Any words which demonstrate that each co-owner is to take a particular share to the property, such as 'to A and B in equal shares' or 'to be divided among A and B' are known as 'words of severance'[3] and give rise to a tenancy in common. In Re North, North v Cusden[4] land was left in a will to two sons on condition that they paid to their mother the sum of ten shillings weekly 'in equal shares'. It was held that the sons should likewise hold the property 'in equal shares', ie as tenants in common. In addition, of course, words which confer unequal shares (eg 'two-thirds to A, one-third to B') create a tenancy in common.

1   Where, as is now almost invariable (see para 30.17 above), the co-owners are subsequently registered as proprietors it should be appreciated that this declaration of trust is not entered on the Register; it should, therefore, be retained as evidence, should this ever prove necessary.
2   *Goodman v Gallant* [1986] 1 All ER 311, CA.

3   Since they destroy the essential unity which characterises a joint tenancy.
4   [1952] I All ER 609.

32.11   *No declaration*   Where the documentation merely makes clear that the parties are to be co-owners, but gives *no indication* as to the *form* of co-ownership, common law would always assume a joint tenancy.[1] In certain cases, however, equity infers the existence of a tenancy in common despite the presence of the four unities and the absence of words of severance. The rationale is that the right of survivorship, which benefits the co-owner who lives longest, might operate particularly unfairly in the following instances:

- where the purchase price for the land was provided by the co-owners in *unequal*[2] shares. The co-owners are then regarded as holding the land in undivided shares proportionate to their contributions;
- where the land was acquired by business partners as part of the assets of the partnership;
- where money is lent by co-mortgagees. As between themselves, co-mortgagees are regarded as being tenants in common in relation to their interest in the land; the loan is repaid however into a joint account and the survivor can thus give a complete discharge for all money due;[3]
- where the co-owners hold the land for their separate individual business purposes.[4]

In each of these cases, equity presumes that each co-owner will wish to have the fullest ability to realise his investment. However, there is only a presumption of tenancy in common, which can be rebutted.

1   *Morley v Bird* (1798) 3 Ves 628.
2   Note that there is no equitable presumption of a tenancy in common where the contributions are *equal*.
3   LPA, s 111.
4   *Malayan Credit Ltd v Jack Chia-MPH Ltd* [1986] I All ER 711, PC.

Co-ownership by implication

32.12   Co-ownership usually arises expressly because the co-owners opt to have property transferred to them both, or because a testator or donor choose to bequeath or give land to more than one person to share. However, this is not the only situation in which co-ownership arises. As we have seen,[1] in certain circumstances, where land is conveyed to one person alone, the courts may nevertheless imply that another has ownership rights. Much of the case law in this area has arisen in the context of a matrimonial home or one shared by a couple living together in a stable relationship where the property was transferred into the name of one partner only but the other claims a share. There is no principle in English law of community of property or family assets whereby property belonging to either of a couple is regarded as family property. Consequently, the claim to a share must, in general, be based on a claim to an interest arising under an implied trust.[2]

We have already discussed the basic principles governing resulting and constructive trusts.[1] Here we shall simply demonstrate how these principles are likely to be applied in the particular context of implied co-ownership cases. Where there have been *direct* financial contributions either to the initial purchase price or, more likely these days, to mortgage repayments, the principles of resulting trust will accord to the contributing party a share commensurate to that contribution unless it can be shown that no share in the property was intended.[3]

Where there have been no direct financial contributions to the acquisition of the property, or where it is desired to establish a share greater than that gained under ordinary resulting trust principles, resort must normally be had to the constructive trust. The operation of constructive trust principles has been considered by the House of Lords on a number of occasions, but most recently in *Lloyds Bank plc v Rosset*.[4] This ruling appears to establish that there must, at some time prior to the acquisition of the property (or exceptionally, at some later date), be *evidence* of some agreement, or arrangement or understanding between the parties that the property is to be shared beneficially. Once a finding to this effect is made, the partner asserting a claim to land registered in the name of the other partner must show that he or she has acted to his or her detriment or significantly altered his or her position in reliance on the agreement in order to give rise to a trust.[5] The House pointed out that, in considering the claims of a partner to have acted to his or her detriment, the court must distinguish between reliance on an expectation of sharing the practical benefits of occupying the home whoever owns it, and an expectation of sharing the ownership of the property asset which the home represents. Only in the latter case will a trust arise.

If there is *no evidence* to support a finding of an actual agreement or arrangement to share, the court may be able to rely on the behaviour of the parties both as the basis on which to infer a common intention to share the property beneficially and as the conduct relied on to give rise to a trust. In such a case only direct contributions to the purchase price by the partner who is not the legal owner, whether initially or by payment of mortgage instalments will readily justify the inference necessary to the creation of a constructive trust. It is extremely doubtful whether anything less will do; 'merely' keeping house and raising a family will not suffice to give a non-owner a share in the home.[6] In the case of *married* couples it is specifically provided, by the Matrimonial Proceedings and Property Act 1970, s 37, that, subject to any contrary agreement between the spouses, a substantial contribution in money or money's worth to the improvement of the property entitles a spouse to a share (or, as the case may be, an enlarged share) in the beneficial interest in the property.

In the *Rosset* case, Mrs Rosset alleged a constructive trust in her favour based on an express agreement with her sole proprietor husband that the property was to be jointly owned and detrimental reliance in the form of work that she had undertaken in the course of renovation of the property. The court found no evidence of such an agreement and felt that any work of renovation was trifling. As Mrs Rosset had made no financial contribution to the acquisition of the property, there was no basis on which the court could infer a common intention to share the property. Accordingly she was not a beneficial co-owner of the house.

1   Paras 31.8–31.10 above.
2   Occasionally such interests have arisen on the basis of proprietary estoppel; see para 31.11.
3   See para 31.8 above.
4   [1990] 1 All ER 1111.
5   See, for example, *Eves v Eves* [1975] 3 All ER 768, CA and *Grant v Edwards* [1986] 2 All ER 426, CA.
6   *Gissing v Gissing* [1970] 2 All ER 780, HL; *Burns v Burns* [1984] 1 All ER 244, CA.

The conversion of a joint tenancy into a tenancy in common: severance

32.13   Severance is a process by which a joint tenant can convert his joint tenancy into a tenancy in common *during his lifetime*; he cannot sever *by will* since a will only comes into effect after his death, by which time the joint tenant's rights have already passed to his fellow joint tenant(s) under the right of survivorship[1].

As we shall see, co-ownership can now only exist in the form of a trust under which the trustees always hold the legal estate as joint tenants.[2] This legal joint tenancy can never be severed; the severance of a legal joint tenancy would create a *legal* tenancy in common, which cannot now exist.[3] Accordingly, severance affects only an *equitable* joint tenancy, converting it into an *equitable* tenancy in common.

The most important practical effect of severance is to defeat the right of survivorship since, once the joint tenant has become a tenant in common, his interest will, on his death, pass either under his will or under the rules of intestacy.

There are five methods of severing an equitable joint tenancy. In the first two methods, severance is effected by destroying one of the four unities.[4]

1 Para 32.5 above
2 Para 32.25 below.
3 LPA, s 1(6); para 32.26 below.
4 Para 32.6 above.

Acquiring a greater interest in the land

32.14 All the joint tenants have one identical interest in the land; if one acquires another interest, the unity of interest is destroyed. This is rarely encountered in practice.

By disposition of the equitable interest

32.15 A disposition of his equitable interest by the joint tenant during his lifetime effects a severance by destroying the unity of title, since the assignee derives title under a different document from the original co-owners. Thus, if A, a joint tenant with B and C, assigns his equitable interest in the land to X, X takes as tenant in common. As between themselves, B and C remain joint tenants, for between them the four unities remain. X becomes a tenant in common, having a one-third share, with B and C who are joint tenants of a two-thirds share. The disposition in question need not be an outright transfer; severance may result, for example, where a joint tenant mortgages his interest.[1]

1 *First National Securities Ltd v Hegerty* [1985] QB 850.

By mutual agreement to sever

32.16 Equitable joint tenants may by mutual agreement sever that joint tenancy. The agreement may be one to sever, or one to deal with the property in a way which involves severance, for example where joint tenants agree that one will sell his share to the other. The agreement itself converts the joint tenancy into a tenancy in common. It would appear that the agreement itself need not be in writing, nor be specifically enforceable since it is not necessary for it to *bind* the parties; it needs merely to demonstrate a mutual intention to sever.[1]

1 *Burgess v Rawnsley* [1975] 3 All ER 142, CA; see also *Hunter v Babbage* (1994) 69 P & CR 548.

By notice in writing

32.17 An equitable joint tenant may sever the joint tenancy by giving a notice in writing to that effect to the other joint tenant(s).[1] In practice this is by far the simplest method of severance; it does not require the agreement of the other joint tenant(s) but they are, by definition, informed of the position, which removes the possibility of subsequent disputes. Such a notice will readily be served by legal advisers where the relationship between joint tenants has broken down; in such circumstances the right of survivorship becomes inappropriate. A notice will also often be served where a married couple, who have hitherto held their property as joint tenants, wish to arrange their affairs so as to utilise a variety of schemes designed to reduce their liability to inheritance tax. Even where a 'formal' notice has not been served it is sometimes possible that documentation, which has been drawn up for other purposes, can also constitute a notice of severance[2].

1 LPA, s 36(2).
2 *Re Draper's Conveyance, Nihan v Porter* [1967] 3 All ER 853.

Course of dealings

32.18 In *Burgess v Rawnsley*[1] Lord Denning took the view that the negotiations which had taken place between the parties were a sufficient 'course of dealing' to bring about severance. The other members of the Court of Appeal thought, despite the unsatisfactory evidence, that there had been a mutual agreement to sever.[2] In that case, all were agreed that an uncommunicated declaration of an intention to sever, and realise one's share, is insufficient to bring about severance, but that a course of dealings between the parties sufficient to indicate a *shared* intention to sever will bring about severance.

1 [1975] 3 All ER 142, CA.
2 Para 32.16 above.

Ending co-ownership

32.19 In practice, where concurrent owners no longer wish to co-own a particular property, they usually agree to sell it; their co-ownership of it will then cease[1]. However, co-ownership may also be ended by physical partition of the land or by union of the concurrent interests in a single co-owner.

Partition of the land destroys the unity of possession without which there can be no co-ownership. The parties agree physically to divide the land between them, the trustees conveying a part to each.[2] Sale may be ordered under the Trusts of Land and Appointment of Trustees Act 1996, s 14[3] as a substitute for partition and this will be particularly appropriate if partition is impractical, as where the property consists of a single house.

Union of the interests in the land in a sole tenant may occur by survivorship or by one tenant acquiring the interests of the others.

1 We consider the sale of co-owned land in more detail at paras 32.31–31.32 and 32.36 below.
2 LPA, s 28.
3 Para 32.35 below.

The potential problems arising from concurrent ownership

Some of the problems
32.20 Where more than one person has ownership rights in the same property the potential for difficulties exists. Suppose, for example, that A, B and C concurrently own the freehold of Blacklands and that X wishes to buy the property. In theory X will have to investigate three different titles to Blacklands; furthermore, A, B and C may not all want Blacklands to be sold. These difficulties will rapidly multiply if A, B and C are tenants in common and A dies, leaving his share to his four children P, Q, R and S; there are now six titles to investigate and six people to agree to any sale.

The old solutions
32.21 The problems faced by co-owners were not tackled until 1925 (largely because co-ownership was not, before that date, very often encountered as a way of owning land on a long term basis). It was then decided that a particular form of trust, the trust for sale, should be the mechanism for co-ownership. The Law of Property Act 1925 required all concurrent ownership to exist in the form of a trust for sale. If land was conveyed[1] to co-owners without the express use of a trust for sale, one was imposed by statute. Briefly, by requiring that, to revert to the example used in the previous paragraph, A, B and C must hold the legal estate, on a joint tenancy, as trustees on trust for sale for themselves as beneficiaries, the Act ensured that the legal title to the land was a single indivisible[2] one which could easily be investigated by any purchaser. In this way any sale of co-owned property was rendered more straightforward.

1 We have seen (at para 32.12 above) that co-ownership can arise by implication as a result of the

operation of the doctrines of resulting or constructive trusts, or proprietary estoppel; where this occurred a trust for sale would also be imposed.

2   It will be remembered that a joint tenancy must have unity of title (see para 32.6 above), that the right of survivorship (see para 32.5 above) means that the number of joint tenants can only diminish, and that there can be no severance of a joint tenancy of the legal estate (see para 32.13 above).

32.22   A fundamental feature of the trust for sale (and just as important to the new trust of land) is the concept of overreaching. Overreaching was an existing principle which applied where trustees of land exercised a power to sell that land. The LPA 1925 merely extended and regulated its operation. Where the trustees under a trust for sale, actually sold the land then, provided the purchase money was paid to at least two trustees,[1] the interests of the beneficiaries ceased to relate to the land and attached henceforth to the proceeds of sale. In this way any purchaser who dealt with at least two trustees was certain to acquire the land free from the claims of the beneficial co-owners (ie A, B, and C in the example used above). The usefulness of this concept in freeing the title to land of equitable ownership interests is very clear and has been carried over into the new trust of land[2].

1   LPA, s 2(2).
2   See further para 32.31 below.

32.23   However, the imposition of a trust for sale in the co-ownership context came to pose its own difficulties. Even after 1925 concurrent ownership was not widespread, especially in circumstances where the co-owned land was to be retained; at that time co-ownership was either a means by which the income from property (as opposed to its occupation) could be shared, or a temporary state of affairs pending its sale (eg where property was given, or bequeathed to children). In the early 20th century many family homes would have been leased rather than held in freehold ownership; in either event, it would have been owned by the husband alone. Co-ownership by husband and wife only started to become commonplace well after the Second World War and has only become standard practice in the last 40 or so years. It was only then that the drawbacks of the trust for sale became really apparent. The imposition of a duty to sell (albeit theoretical) in the case of property which had been purchased for the purpose of occupation was not only confusing to purchasers who were buying a property in which to live, it gave rise to technical legal difficulties. The courts had to adopt some deft footwork in order to provide workable rules on rights to occupy co-owned property and on its sale where the co-owners were in dispute as to whether it should be kept or disposed of. Reform of the mechanism for concurrent ownership has long been advocated.

The modern mechanism for owning land concurrently: trusts of land

32.24   Although the trust *for sale* had proved an increasingly unsatisfactory mechanism for the co-ownership of land, the basic idea of requiring concurrent ownership to take the form of a trust has been retained by the Trusts of Land and Appointment of Trustees Act 1996 (TLA 1996). This Act implemented proposals for reform made by the Law Commission in 1989 and came into effect on 1 January 1997. Broadly, the Act:

- leaves existing settlements untouched;
- converts existing trusts for sale into 'trusts of land';
- ensures that concurrent ownership (and any other trust of land[1]) arising on or after 1 January 1997 takes the form of 'trusts of land' within the TLA 1996;[2] and
- allows for the express creation of a trust for sale but subjects such trusts to the same regime as the 'trust of land'.[3]

We now examine in a little more detail the machinery for creating concurrent ownership.

1   Such as a an implied, resulting or constructive trust: see TLA 1996, s 1(2)(a).
2   TLA 1996, ss 1,2 and 5 and Sch 2.
3   TLA 1996, s 4. Hence, there will be little point, in practice, in creating an express trust for sale.

The imposition of a trust of land

32.25   In cases of concurrent ownership a trust of land is imposed by the Law of Property Act 1925; the relevant provisions have been amended by the TLA 1996 so that what previously were references to a trust for sale are now references to a trust of land.[1] The amended LPA 1925 requires that, in all cases of co-ownership, a trust of land must be used under which the trustees *must* hold the legal estate as joint tenants. Where co-ownership arises expressly it is normal practice to create an express trust. Where this is not done (and also where co-ownership arises by implication) the LPA 1925 automatically imposes a trust.[2] In the following paragraphs we explain the operation of the trust of land in the context of concurrent ownership.

1   TLA 1996, s 5 and Sch 2, paras 3 and 4.
2   LPA, ss 34 and 36 (as amended by the TLA 1996).

32.26   *Tenancy in common*   A tenancy in common cannot exist in relation to a legal estate;[1] consequently, it takes effect only in equity. If land is conveyed to a number of people as tenants in common, the LPA 1925 provides that the conveyance takes effect as if it were a conveyance of the legal estate to the co-owners (or, if there are more than four, to the first four named in the conveyance) *as joint tenants on trust* to give effect to the rights of the co-owners *as tenants in common in equity*.[2] Thus a tenancy in common can only exist behind a trust; it takes effect in relation to the beneficial, equitable interest in the land, but not the legal estate. It will be seen that the key to an understanding of the machinery of co-ownership is to consider separately the position of the co-owners in relation to the legal estate in the land (be it freehold or leasehold) and their position in relation to the equitable interests existing behind the curtain of the trust.

Thus, if land is granted to A, B and C in equal shares they will hold the legal estate as joint tenants and as trustees; the wording used[3] gives rise to a tenancy in common which will take effect in equity.

Should C die, his individual share under the tenancy in common may pass under his will or on intestacy (say to X); but the right of survivorship operates in respect of the joint tenancy of the legal estate:

A, B – legal JT
_____
A, B, X – equitable TiC

1   LPA 1925, s 1(6).
2   LPA 1925, ss 34 and 35.
3   Being words of severance; see para 32.10 above.

Joint tenancy

32.27   As in the case of tenancy in common there is a splitting of the legal and equitable ownership whenever a joint tenancy is created. The co-owners (or the first four of them) hold the legal estate as joint trustees for themselves as joint tenants in equity:[1]

A, B, C – legal JT
_____
A, B, C – equitable JT

Should C die, the right of survivorship operates in respect of the joint tenancy both at law and in equity:

$$A, B - \text{legal JT}$$

$$\overline{A, B - \text{equitable JT}}$$

1   LPA, s 36.

The position of the trustees

Powers and duties

32.28   There will normally be between two and four trustees of a trust of land[1]. In relation to the land, they have all the powers of an absolute owner of land.[2] This means that they can sell,[3] lease or mortgage the land. In doing so they must, under the general law of trusts, act in the best interests of the trust and have regard to the rights of the beneficiaries.[4] Where either the whole or part of the land is sold, or capital money is raised by the creation of other interests (eg the grant of an option or lease at a premium) the trustees must invest that money. They can do so by purchasing investments in accordance with the provisions of the Trustee Act 2000. Equally, they are empowered to purchase other land as an investment, for occupation by a beneficiary, or for any other purpose.[5] Where all of the beneficiaries are of full age and capacity, the trustees can compel the beneficiaries to take a conveyance of the land irrespective of whether the beneficiaries wish this to happen.[6]

When exercising any of their functions relating to land[7] the trustees are under an obligation, so far as is practicable, to consult all the beneficiaries who are entitled to a present interest in the land. They should, in so far as is consistent with the best interests of the trust, give effect to the wishes of the majority of the beneficiaries.[8]

The trustees can choose[9] to delegate all or any of their functions relating to the land[10] to any beneficiary(ies) of full age who are entitled to an interest in possession in the land, either for a limited time, or indefinitely. Such a delegation must be made by way of power of attorney (ie formally by deed) which must be given by all of the trustees jointly. This power of attorney may be revoked by any one of the trustees, and will automatically be revoked by the appointment of a new trustee. Any beneficiary to whom the functions of a trustee have been delegated has the same duties and liabilities as regards the exercise of those functions as a trustee.

1   There need to be a minimum of two in order that overreaching can take place (see para 32.22 above; there can be no more than four trustees of land, Trustee Act 1925, s 34(1).
2   TLA 1996, s 6(1).
3   It should be noted that, in sharp contrast to the position of a trustee under the old trust for sale, there is merely a *power* to sell, not an obligation. Even if a trust of land contains an express provision *obliging* the trustees to sell, this can safely be ignored since the trustees always have a power to postpone sale for an indefinite period: TLA 1996, s 4.
4   TLA 1996, s 6(5) and (6).
5   TLA 1996, s 6(3) and (4), s 17(1).
6   TLA 1996, s 6(2). Where all the beneficiaries are of full age and capacity it has always been possible for the *beneficiaries* to compel the trustees to convey the land to them: *Saunders v Vautier* (1841) 10 LJ Ch 354. The TLA now allows the trustees the same freedom. Provided the beneficiaries *consent*, the trustees can, instead, partition the land between them: TLA 1996, s 7.
7   The trustees' functions relating to land do not extend to their powers and duties in respect of capital monies, such as investment.
8   TLA 1996, s 11.
9   Delegation is a matter of discretion for the trustees and, in deciding whether or not to delegate, they must bear in mind that they will become liable for the consequences of any negligent delegation. Any beneficiary to whom they refuse to delegate could apply to the court under TLA 1996, s 14; see para 32.35 below.
10 Again (see note 7 above) the power to delegate does not extend to the trustees' powers and duties in respect of capital monies. So, for example, any capital monies received as a result of the sale of the trust property must be paid to the trustees.

Restrictions on powers

32.29   In the case of an express trust of land (as opposed to one which is *imposed* by statute[1] or the courts[2]) certain of the trustees' power can either be expressly excluded,[3] or their exercise made subject to the consent of some person(s)[4] by the terms of the instrument creating the trust. The powers which can be restricted in this way are only those conferred by the TLA 1996, ss 6 and 7. So, the all-important power to dispose of the land can be restricted, as can the power to require adult beneficiaries to take a conveyance of the land or the power to invest in other land. However, neither the other powers of investment, nor the power to delegate, can be excluded.

1   Such as is imposed by the LPA 1925, ss 34 and 36 wherever co-ownership is created without the use of an express trust of land; see para 32.25 above.
2   Such as a resulting or constructive trust in the case of implied co-ownership.
3   TLA 1996, s 8.
4   TLA 1996, s 10.

The position of the beneficiaries

32.30   There can be any number of beneficiaries of a trust of land and, naturally, the interest of each one will be equitable. Any co-owner has the right to occupy the trust land provided that

- the purposes of the trust include the provision of land for the occupation of the beneficiary(ies); and
- the property is not unavailable or unsuitable for occupation.[1]

Where more than one beneficiary is entitled to occupation they can, of course, occupy the property together. Where joint occupation is not feasible, the trustees (and, if necessary, the courts) can resolve disputes over which of them should occupy.[2]

As we have seen,[3] any beneficiary of full age and capacity with a present interest in the land is entitled to be consulted when the trustees exercise any of their functions relating to the land. Where there is an express provision requiring their consent,[4] a beneficiary may be able to prevent the trustees exercising any of their functions relating to the land. Where delegation has taken place,[5] a beneficiary will be able to exercise all those functions which have been delegated to him, although in doing so he must act in the best interests of the trust.

The beneficiaries under a trust of land are not entitled to receive capital monies directly from a purchaser even where there has been full delegation of the trustees' functions.[6] Furthermore, they have no right to control[7] the trustees in the exercise of their functions relating to the investment of capital monies.

1   TLA 1996, s 12.
2   TLA 1996, ss 13 and 14. See para 32.37 below.
3   See para 32.28 above.
4   See para 32.29 above.
5   See para 32.28 above.
6   See para 32.28 above. It should be remembered that a purchaser would not wish to pay capital monies to anyone other than the trustees since this would prevent the overreaching of the beneficial interests under the trust: see paras 32.22 above and para 32.31 below.
7   Either by way of consultation, consent or delegation since all of these relate only to the trustees' functions in so far as they relate to the land.

The sale of trust land

The basic principles

32.31   One of the major purposes of using the trust to give effect to concurrent ownership is to avoid complexity in conveyancing. The ready marketability of land would be seriously inhibited if purchasers (and, in law[1], 'purchasers' include mortgagees[2] and lessees) could not be sure that the interest which they are acquiring is free from the claims of others (save where those claims are readily detectable and then either reflected in the price paid or otherwise dealt with to the satisfaction of the purchaser). We have seen[3] that, without the device of the trust, a purchaser of land which is owned concurrently would have a multiplicity of titles to investigate, and would take subject to the rights of any owner who would not co-operate in the sale or other transaction. The trust avoids these difficulties.

Trustees always hold an unfragmented legal estate, be it freehold or leasehold. They hold that estate as joint tenants; this means that there is unity of title, so that there is only one register of title for the purchaser to investigate.

Furthermore, a purchaser of land held on trust need not concern himself with the equitable ownership[4] interests behind the 'curtain' of the trust, no matter how many.[5] They are not part of the legal title to the property; they are 'off the title' and neither the existence of the trust nor its details are recorded in the Land Register.[6] A purchaser need only ensure that any purchase money (or loan or other capital monies) is paid to the trustees, who must be at least two in number (or a trust corporation)[7]; this ensures that the beneficial interests under the trust are overreached by the conveyance.[8] This does not mean that those beneficial interests are destroyed; it means that they cease to relate to the land and are transmuted into equivalent rights to the proceeds of sale. We can illustrate this fundamental principle with two examples.

EXAMPLE 1
Suppose Blacklands is conveyed to H and W as joint tenants. This takes effect in the following way:

$$H, W - \text{legal JT}$$
$$\overline{}$$
$$H, W - \text{equitable JT}$$

On a sale of Blacklands a purchaser only needs to investigate the single legal register of title of H and W. He would not be concerned with their beneficial interests; he does not have to check whether H or W have, for example, severed the equitable joint tenancy and disposed of their interest to X, or whether Y has acquired a beneficial interest by way of financial contribution to the mortgage on Blacklands. By paying the purchase price to H and W *as trustees* any potential complexity in relation to the beneficial ownership of the land need not concern him, for the conveyance overreaches the beneficial interests. H and W's beneficial rights (and any rights which X and Y may have) are now rights to a share in the monies paid by the purchaser.

EXAMPLE 2
Suppose Whitelands is conveyed to A, B, C, D and E as tenants in common. This takes effect as follows:

$$A, B, C, D - \text{legal JT}$$
$$\overline{}$$
$$A, B, C, D, E - \text{equitable TiC}$$

Suppose A dies, leaving his interest in Whitelands to Z. The position now is:

$$B, C, D - \text{legal JT}$$
$$\overline{}$$
$$Z, B, C, D, E - \text{equitable TiC}$$

On a sale of Whitelands, a purchaser would only be concerned to investigate the single title of B, C and D. He would not be concerned with the beneficial interests in general or with what has happened to A's interest in the land, in particular. If he deals with and pays the purchase price to the trustees (B, C and D) the complexity in relation to the beneficial ownership of Whitelands need not concern him, for the conveyance overreaches the beneficial interests. The rights of Z, B, C, D and E are now rights to a share of the proceeds of sale.

However, it should be appreciated that, while the principle of overreaching is highly convenient for those purchasing, or lending on the security of land, it can operate unfairly to deprive beneficiaries of their right to occupy trust property. In cases where the trustees and beneficiaries are different persons, the trustees can sell or mortgage the property without the knowledge or consent of the beneficiaries; their interests are automatically overreached and while, in certain circumstances, the beneficiaries may be able to sue the trustees for breach of trust, they will certainly not regain their rights to the land. This is well illustrated by the decision in *City of London Building Society v Flegg*.[9] Here the defendants had contributed to the purchase of a property in which they, and their daughter and son-in-law were to live. This was transferred into the names of the younger couple, with the result that they were trustees under a trust of land; they and the parents (by way of resulting trust[10]) were the beneficiaries. Some time later and unknown to the Fleggs, the young couple granted a mortgage on which they subsequently defaulted. When the claimant mortgagee sought possession, the Fleggs claimed that their rights as equitable co-owners were binding. The House of Lords held that this was not so; the Fleggs' rights had been overreached because the mortgage had been granted by the trustees. In 1989, the Law Commission proposed that the rights of adult beneficiaries who are occupying the property should not be overreached by transactions conducted without their consent,[11] but this suggestion has now been abandoned.[12]

1   LPA 1925, s 205(1)(xxi).
2   A mortgagee of land is a person who makes a loan on the security of land; he is a person to whom a mortgage is granted by the landowner/mortgagor.
3   See para 32.2 above.
4   A purchaser does, of course, need to be concerned about equitable interests which are *not* ownership interests, eg restrictive covenants, since these may can continue to affect the land (see generally ch 35 below).
5   LPA 1925, s 27(1).
6   Any purchaser's lawyer checking title will, of course, realise that there is always a trust wherever there is more than one owner of the legal estate; however, the details of the trust is of no concern.
7   Overreaching also occurs where capital monies are not paid to the trustees at the time of the conveyance but later. In *State Bank of India v Sood* [1997] 1 All ER 169, CA the trustees executed a charge over trust property in favour of the bank, as security for present and future indebtedness on certain bank accounts. No loan was advanced at the time of the charge but the accounts became further overdrawn. When the bank wished to exercise its power of sale (as to which see para 39.35 below) it was held that it could do so free from the claims of the beneficiaries; their interests had been overreached at the time of the charge.
8   LPA 1925, ss 2(1)(i) and 27(2).
9   [1987] 3 All ER 435, HL.
10 See para 32.12 above.
11 In Law Com No 188 (1989), the sentiments of which were echoed by Peter Gibson LJ in *State Bank of India v Sood* [1997] 1 All ER 169, CA.
12 Press notice, 19 March 1998.

32.32   It may, of course, happen that a sale cannot proceed in the straightforward manner suggested by the examples given in the previous paragraph. The trustees may not agree that the land should be sold, or the beneficiaries may disagree with the trustees' decision to sell. In the typical co-ownership situation outlined in Example 1, it may be that H and W disagree as to whether a sale should take place, a state of affairs which completely rules out the possibility of overreaching since the purchaser would be unable to pay the money to at least two trustees. We discuss how these difficulties may be resolved in paragraph 32.36.

Furthermore, in the examples so far employed, the existence of the trust has been apparent on the title because each property was expressly conveyed to more than one person. What is the position where there is no indication on the title of the existence of any trust? This situation will arise when land has been conveyed in the name of one person only but where that person is regarded by equity as holding it on trust either wholly, or partly for another. The most commonly encountered example of this is where equity implies co-ownership.[1] As we have seen, there is no doubting the existence of a trust of land in such circumstances,[2] the problem is that a purchaser (or mortgagee) may unwittingly hand over purchase money or otherwise deal with someone who is in reality a *sole* trustee. This means that the purchaser is deprived of the protection of overreaching which only applies to dealings with *two* trustees. As we shall see,[3] in such circumstances the purchaser or mortgagee may be bound by the interests of the implied (co) owner (who is a 'hidden'[4] beneficiary under the trust) unless careful investigations are carried out.

1   See para 32.12 above.
2   See para 32.25 above.
3   See para 35.22 and 36.23 below.
4   By 'hidden' we mean undetectable on the paper title; such beneficiaries are often, in practice, detectable since they are usually in occupation of the trust land. As we shall see in para 35.22 and 36.26 below, the purchaser's (and mortgagee's) best protection is the careful inspection of the property and the investigation of the property rights of anyone who is occupying the property either with, or instead of, the vendor/mortgagor.

Disputes over trusts of land

32.33   Inevitably, there will be times when there are disputes over the operation of a trust of land. The trustees may disagree with each other over whether or not the land should be sold or retained, on whether (or which of) the beneficiaries should occupy the property, or on how it should be managed. The beneficiaries may be at odds with the trustees, or with each other.

These difficulties produce a total stalemate in the very common situation where the trustees and the beneficiaries are one and the same and where there are only two of them. Classically, this will occur where property is co-owned by a married couple or by co-habitees whose relationship has broken down. In practice, the legal title to their home will be vested in the two of them as trustees, and they will also be the only beneficiaries, holding either as joint tenants or tenants in common in equal shares (see Example 1 in para 32.31 above). Obviously, they may be able to agree on what should happen to the property; for example that it should be sold and the proceeds divided between them, or that one should buy the other out. Often, however, they will be unable to reach agreement, if only because their respective interests will have become diametrically opposed. One may wish to remain in the house with any children; the other will need to realise their share in the property in order to fund the purchase of another home.

Matrimonial property

32.34   Where the dispute concerns matrimonial property (eg where, in the scenario described in the previous paragraph are a married couple), it will be resolved by the courts under the Matrimonial Causes Act 1973,[1] as part of any divorce proceedings. The MCA 1973 gives the court wide powers to make orders relating to what was matrimonial property; it can order that the property be sold, or retained (especially where there are young children still living at home) and it can adjust the parties' rights to the property. So, it can order that one party transfer their share to the other.

1   Matrimonial Causes Act 1973, ss 23–25.

Other trust property

32.35 Where disputes concern trust land which is not co-owned by a married couple, they must be resolved by the application of ordinary property principles. The TLA 1996 has sought to rationalise and improve the approach to differences arising in the context of trusts of land.[1] The courts have been given a wide jurisdiction to entertain applications from trustees or those with an interest in a trust of land.[2] They may make any order 'relating to the exercise by the trustees of any of their functions, including an order relieving them of any obligation to obtain the consent of, or to consult, any person in connection with the exercise of their functions'.[3] They may also make an order 'declaring the nature or extent of a person's interest' in the trust land.[4]

The Act sets out matters which the court should take into account when making *any* order;[5] there are also specific provisions dealing with a dispute as to which beneficiary(ies) should occupy the trust property.[6] Many of these principles are derived from the case law which was developed by the courts prior to 1997 so that, as we shall see, some pre-1997 cases provide an indication of how the courts are likely to apply these new statutory provisions.

In practice, most of the disputes concerning trust land concern one (or both) of two issues; whether the land should be sold or, which of the beneficiaries should occupy the trust property. We shall, therefore, address each of these in the following paragraphs.

1   It should be remembered that the provisions of the Act which we are about to deal with apply to *all* trusts of land. In practice, however, most of the disputes arise in connection with *co-owned* land.
2   TLA 1996, s 14(1).
3   TLA 1996, s 14(2)(a).
4   TLA 1996, s 14(2)(b). It should be noted that, in sharp contrast to the position regarding *matrimonial property* (see para 32.34 above), the court has no power to *vary* the interests of the beneficiaries.
5   TLA 1996, s 15.
6   TLA 1996, ss 13 and 15(2).

32.36 *Sale.* Where there is an application to court under the TLA 1996, s 14 because there is a dispute as to whether or not the trust land should be sold, it is clear that the court can

- order a sale; or
- order a sale but suspend the order for the time being; or
- refuse a sale; or
- refuse a sale and make an order as to the occupation of the property.

When making its decision the court is required to take into account:[1]

- the intentions of the person(s) creating the trust;
- the purposes for which the trust property is held;
- the welfare of any child who occupies or might reasonably be expected to occupy the trust property as his home;
- the interests of any secured creditor of any beneficiary; and
- the wishes (of the majority by value) of any beneficiaries of full age and capacity.

Where an application under TLA 1996, s14 is made by a trustee in bankruptcy, the above principles do not apply. So where, for example, one of the co-owners becomes bankrupt and their trustee in bankruptcy applies for an order of sale, it is the insolvency regime which applies.[2] Broadly, where the property is the home of the bankrupt or the bankrupt's spouse or former spouse, one year's grace following the bankruptcy is given; thereafter, on any application for sale by the trustee in bankruptcy the interests of the creditors are paramount so that, in practice, an order of sale will virtually always be made.[3]

1   TLA 1996, s 15. The section makes it clear that what follows is not an exhaustive list, so that the court is free to take account of other matters as well.
2   TLA 1996, s 15(4).
3   Insolvency Act 1986, s 335A; Re Citro [1990] 3 All ER 952, CA.

32.37   *Occupation*   As we have seen,[1] beneficiaries often have the right to occupy the trust property and, in the case of concurrent ownership where the property was purchased for joint occupation, this will invariably be the case. Where two or more beneficiaries are entitled to occupy at the same time, but do not wish to occupy the property together and cannot agree a solution, the trustees are given the power to decide which of them can occupy and on what terms.[2] If a beneficiary is dissatisfied with the trustees' decision, an application to court under the TLA 1996, s 14 can, of course, be made. However, the more likely circumstance of an application to court will be where the trust arises as a result of co-ownership. Here, the trustees are usually the very same beneficiaries who no longer wish to share occupation and who cannot agree as to which of them should stay. Here, a court's intervention will be necessary. As can be seen from the cases considered in the previous paragraph, it may well be the case that the court considers the question of sale and occupation together.

The TLA 1996, s 13 sets out the powers of the trustees and the circumstances which they must take into account when arriving at a decision about the occupation of trust property. If the matter goes to court it would appear that the court is not so constrained since, by virtue of s 14, it can make *any* order. That said, it seems likely that the matters set out in the Act will be particularly influential in any decision as to occupation, whether that decision is made by the trustees or by the court.

Section 13 provides that the trustees may exclude or restrict the right to occupy where it is reasonable to do so. Where this is done, the occupying beneficiary can be required to make payments to the excluded beneficiary.[3] Equally, the trustees can subject a beneficiary's occupation to reasonable conditions (such as, in particular, the payment of compensation to other beneficiaries and responsibility for any outgoings or expenses in respect of the land). In reaching any decision the trustees should have regard to the intentions of the person who created the trust, the purposes for which the land is held and the circumstances and wishes of the beneficiaries who are entitled to occupy.

1   See para 32.30 above.
2   TLA 1996, s 13.
3   It is worth noting that where a co-owner *voluntarily* goes out of occupation, he is not entitled *as of right* (ie in the absence of an express agreement) to 'rent' or compensation from any other co-owners: see, for example, *Jones v Jones* [1977] 1 WLR 438.

Chapter 33

Easements

33.1 In this and the following two chapters, we turn our attention to the more important of third party rights, ie those proprietary rights that are enjoyed over land belonging to another. Some such rights, notably easements and restrictive covenants, can only exist between neighbouring properties, so that they are a benefit to one and a burden on the other. These rights are particularly important in dictating the way in which each piece of land can be used and enjoyed. Other third party rights, such as mortgages, options and rights of pre-emption, can be enjoyed by those who do not themselves have any rights to other land; these are therefore simply a burden on the land to which they relate, their benefit attaches to a person (who can, of course, usually transfer their rights to another) rather than to other land.

33.2 We start by considering one of the most important of the third party rights to land, the easement. As we shall see, there are a number of different types of easement (such as rights of way, rights of support, rights of drainage, rights of light) but they all share the same basic characteristics. Easements are irrevocable rights which one landowner enjoys in respect of his neighbour's land and, as such, they provide what is often an essential basis for the full enjoyment of land ownership. Many pieces of land or buildings or parts of buildings cannot be properly utilised without the existence of rights over adjoining property: for example, the tenant of a first floor flat will need a right of way over the ground floor of the premises; the owner of a semi-detached house needs support from the adjoining 'semi'.

In this chapter we consider:

* the essential legal characteristics of an easement;
* the methods by which easements can be created or acquired; and
* certain specific easements.

The nature of easement

33.3 An easement is a right which one landowner enjoys in respect of his neighbour's land; it may be legal or equitable.[1] Some idea of the nature of easements may be gathered from the following dictum of Lord Denning:[2] 'There are two kinds of easements known to the law: positive easements, such as a right of way, which give the owner of land *a right himself to do something* on or to his neighbour's land: and negative easements, such as a right of light, which give him *a right to stop his neighbour doing something* on his (the neighbour's) own land.'

The nature of an easement is best explained by reference to Cheshire's[3] four essential characteristics of an easement, approved by the Court of Appeal in *Re Ellenborough Park, Re Davies, Powell v Maddison*.[4] In this case, the Court held that the right to use a park or garden adjacent to a group of houses was an easement attaching to those houses. The Court reached its decision by considering whether the following four requirements were satisfied:

- there must be a dominant and a servient piece of land;
- the easement must 'accommodate' the dominant land;
- the dominant and servient owners must be different persons; and
- the right must be capable of forming the subject matter of a grant.

Each of these will now be considered.

1   Para 33.12 below.
2   *Phipps v Pears* [1964] 2 All ER 35 at 33.
3   *Cheshire and Burn's Modern Law of Real Property* (15th edn) pp 520-524.
4   [1955] 3 All ER 667, CA.

The essential characteristics of an easement

There must be a dominant and servient piece of land

33.4   This is another way of saying that there must be land which enjoys the right (the dominant land) and land which is subject to the right (the servient land). An easement takes effect for the benefit of *land*; it is annexed to that land and passes automatically on its transfer. An easement cannot exist independently of the ownership of land; it exists in respect of, and in amplification of, an owner's enjoyment of some estate or interest in a piece of land.[1] Thus there can be no grant of an easement at a time when the dominant land has not yet been identified, so that it is not possible to create easements in favour of land which has yet to be acquired.[2] Furthermore, where an easement exists for the benefit of one piece of land, it cannot later be used for the benefit of another, subsequently acquired, piece of land[3], save where the use of the easement for the extra land is genuinely ancillary[4].

1   *Alfred F Beckett Ltd v Lyons* [1967] 1 All ER 833, CA.
2   *London and Blenheim Estates Ltd v Ladbroke Retail Parks Ltd* [1993] 4 All ER 157, CA. See also *Voice v Bell* (1993) 68 P & CR 441, CA.
3   *Jobson v Record* (1997) 75 P & CR 375, CA; *Peacock v Custins* [2001] 2 All ER 827, CA; *Das v Linden Mews Ltd* [2002] EWCA Civ 590, [2002] 2 EGLR 76.
4   *Massey v Boulden* [2002] EWCA Civ 1634, [2003] 2 All ER 87 and see para 33.53 below.

The easement must 'accommodate' the dominant land

33.5   This means that an easement must be of benefit to the dominant land. There must be a clear connection between the enjoyment of the right and the enjoyment of the dominant land. In *Re Ellenborough Park*,[1] the court held that the park became a communal garden for the benefit and enjoyment of those whose houses adjoined it or were in its close proximity; it was the collective garden of the neighbouring houses. The necessary connection between the right and the land was thus shown. In contrast, a right given to the purchaser of a house to attend Lord's cricket ground without payment would not constitute an easement, for, although it would confer an advantage on the purchaser and doubtless would increase the value of the property, it would be wholly extraneous to, and independent of, the use of the house as a house.[2]

This is not to say that a right which primarily benefits a business may not also be held to accommodate the land from which that business is operated. Thus, in *Moody v Steggles*,[3] it was held that the right to affix an inn sign on adjoining property accommodated the claimant's public house. The question would seem to depend on whether the court is prepared to find an intimate connection between the land and the business carried on there.[4]

However, where the right in question actually constitutes the business, there can be no easement. So, in *Hill v Tupper*,[5] the tenant of premises on the bank of the Basingstoke Canal was given the 'sole and exclusive right' by the owners to put pleasure boats on the canal. He subsequently brought an action against the defendant, who had also started to hire out pleasure boats on the canal, alleging that the latter was interfering with his easement. This claim failed; the court held that the claimant's right to put boats on the canal was merely a contractual licence, giving him rights against the licensors (the owners of the canal) but not against the defendant. The claimant was trying to set up, under the guise of an easement, a monopoly which had no normal connection with the ordinary use of his land but which was merely an independent business enterprise. Far from the right claimed accommodating the land, the land was but a convenient incident to the exercise of the right.

1   [1955] 3 All ER 667, CA.
2   [1955] 3 All ER 667 at 680.
3   (1879) 12 Ch D 261. See also *William Hill (Southern) Ltd v Cabras Ltd* [1987] 1 EGLR 37, CA where the right to erect the name of a business on adjoining property was held to be an easement.
4   In *Clapman v Edwards* [1938] 2 All ER 507 a *general* right to advertise on adjoining premises was held not to be an easement since there was no connection with the land.
5   (1863) 2 H & C 121.

33.6   It may not be possible to demonstrate the necessary connection between enjoyment of the right and the dominant land where the dominant and servient properties are at some distance from each other: 'a right of way over land in Northumberland cannot accommodate land in Kent'.[1] On the other hand, it is not necessary that the properties be adjoining. In *Re Ellenborough Park*,[2] a few of the houses having the benefit of the use of the park were some 100 yards from it: nonetheless, the court held that the necessary connection between dominant and servient tenement existed. Again, in *Pugh v Savage*,[3] the owner of field C was held entitled to an easement of way across field A to reach the nearby highway despite the existence of field B, which he had a licence to cross, between the two properties.

1   *Bailey v Stephens* (1862) 12 CBNS 91.
2   [1955] 3 All ER 667, CA.
3   [1970] 2 All ER 353, CA.

The dominant and servient owners must be different persons
33.7   Clearly, as an easement is a right over another's land, one cannot have an easement over one's own land. However, the freehold owner of two plots may grant an easement over one plot to the tenant of the other, and a tenant may expressly or impliedly grant an easement to another tenant of the same landlord. Where the owner of two plots of land uses a way across one plot to reach the other, he is clearly doing so as owner rather than by virtue of an easement; nevertheless, it is sometimes said that he enjoys a 'quasi-easement'. We consider the relevance of quasi-easements in para 33.31 below.

The right must be capable of forming the subject matter of a grant, ie be capable of being granted
33.8   This requirement comprises a number of elements some of which are 'technical' and others of which are more policy based. It ensures that the right claimed must be one which can be formulated in a deed of grant by a capable grantor to a capable grantee. For

example, a tenant cannot grant an easement in fee simple, nor can an easement be granted to a fluctuating group of persons.

However, this requirement also, and perhaps more importantly, acts as a filter for the recognition of new types of easement, a question that raises policy issues. Although there is no fixed list of easements, the courts do control the rights which will be recognised as easements. Easements are powerful rights which last for as long as the interest to which they are attached. So, an easement for the benefit of a freehold estate is, in reality, indefinite; an easement attached to a leasehold estate will continue for as long as the lease. Furthermore, as we shall see, easements do not always originate in an express agreement between neighbouring landowners; they can arise by implication or as a result of prescription (long use). For these reasons a court, when deciding whether a type of right *which has never previously been accepted as an easement,*[1] should be so recognised, will consider a variety of matters. However, it will often take into account four particular factors which are accepted as delimiting the nature of an easement.

1   Once a type of right has been accepted by the courts as *capable* of being an easement, these policy issues will not normally be re-visited should the same type of right be litigated in future cases.

33.9   *Sufficiently definite* The first factor is whether the right claimed is one which is of too wide and vague a character,[1] rendering it difficult to define in a deed of grant. Thus a right to a view over neighbouring land cannot be an easement[2]. It is on this basis that the courts have also refused to allow as an easement a claim to a general right of light for one's land;[3] such rights can only exist as an easement in respect of a defined aperture.[4] Similarly, the right to the general passage of air over one's land cannot exist as an easement,[5] but a right to air to a defined aperture can.[6] The extent of the right claimed can in the latter case be expressed with some precision.

1   *Re Ellenborough Park* [1955] 3 All ER 667, CA.
2   *William Aldred's Case* (1610) 9 Co Rep 57b.
3   See *Roberts v Macord* (1832) 1 Mood & R 230.
4   Para 33.54 below.
5   *Webb v Bird* (1861) 10 CBNS 268.
6   *Bryant v Lefever* (1879) 4 CPD 172.

33.10   *No new negative easements*   The second matter that will affect a court's consideration of whether to recognise a new right as an easement will be the question of whether the right is negative or positive. Although negative easements (ie those which operate to restrict what the servient owner can do on his own land[1]) do exist, notably easements of light and easements of support for buildings, those that do have been recognised for hundreds of years. Today, the law is reluctant to recognise new ones, largely because it is felt that rights which prevent the servient owner using his land in some way are better dealt with by way of expressly agreed restrictive covenants[2]. So, in *Phipps v Pears*,[3] the Court of Appeal had to decide whether the right to have one's property protected from the weather could exist as an easement. One of two houses, which were very close together but which did not actually support each other, was demolished, thereby exposing to the elements the wall of the other house, which had never been rendered or plastered. Reflecting the policy considerations which must always be present when a claim to a new type of easement is decided, the court rejected the claim to an easement on the basis that this was a claim to a *negative* easement, new examples of which the law should be chary of creating since they restrict the servient owner in the enjoyment of his own land and hamper legitimate development[4]. Similarly, in *Hunter v Canary Wharf Ltd*[5], it was held that the right to receive an uninterrupted television signal could not exist as an easement.

1   See para 33.3 above.
2   See ch 34.

3   [1964] 2 All ER 35, CA.
4   It should be noted that, today, the claimant may well have been able to base a claim in tort, in either
     negligence or nuisance, see *Rees v Skerrett* [2001] EWCA Civ 760, [2001] 1 WLR 1541.
5   [1997] 2 All ER 426, HL.

33.11   *No joint possession*   A third relevant factor in the decision whether to recognise
a claim to an easement is that it must not amount to a claim to use and enjoy the servient
land either exclusively, or jointly with the servient owner. An easement is a right which is
compatible with the servient owner's right to exclusive possession of his own land. In *Copeland
v Greenhalf,*[1] the defendant claimed that he was entitled to an easement to store vehicles
awaiting and undergoing repair on a strip of land opposite his premises. Upjohn J rejected
the claim as being virtually a claim to possession of the servient land, since it involved the
defendant and his employees being able to carry out repair work on the land and involved
the defendant leaving as many vehicles on the land as he wished, thereby effectively treating
the land as his own.[2] Similarly, in *Grigsby v Melville*[3] it was held that an unlimited right to
store items in an adjoining cellar could not amount to an easement.

It does not follow, however, that an easement to store articles on another's land cannot
exist. The possibility was recognised in *A-G of Southern Nigeria v John Holt & Co (Liverpool)
Ltd,*[4] and in *Wright v Macadam*[5] it was held, without argument on the point, that the right
to store coal in a coal shed was clearly an easement. The question is, no doubt, one of
degree. Thus, in *Miller v Emcer Products Ltd,*[6] a case demonstrating that the categories of
easements are not closed, the Court of Appeal held that a right to use a neighbour's
lavatory could exist as an easement. The Court pointed out that, although at the times
when the dominant owner exercised his right the owner of the servient tenement would
be excluded, this was a common feature to a greater or lesser extent of many easements,
such as a right of way, and in any case this did not amount to so complete an ouster of the
servient owner's rights as was held to be incompatible with an easement in *Copeland v
Greenhalf.* In *London and Blenheim Estates Ltd v Ladbroke Retail Parks Ltd*[7] the view was
expressed that a right to park a car anywhere within a defined area can be an easement
whereas a right to park in a particular slot, to the exclusion of the servient owner, would
not be. This approach seems to be confirmed by two more recent cases. In *Hair v Gillman*[8]
it was held that a right to park one car anywhere within an area in which four cars could
be parked was an easement; by way of contrast, in *Batchelor v Marlow*[9] an exclusive right
to park six cars on a strip of land during working hours was held to be too extensive to
be an easement.

1   [1952] 1 All ER 809.
2   Such facts might provide a basis for a claim to the *ownership* of the land under the principles of adverse
     possession: see paras 31.19–31.34 above.
3   [1973] 1 All ER 385.
4   [1915] AC 599, PC.
5   [1949] 2 All ER 565, CA.
6   [1956] 1 All ER 237, CA.
7   [1993] 1 All ER 307, affirmed by the Court of Appeal on another point.
8   (2000) 80 P & CR 108.
9   [2001] EWCA Civ 1051, 82 P & CR 459.

33.12   *No expense for servient owner*   A fourth factor to be considered is that the
easement claimed must not automatically involve the servient owner in expenditure. An
easement is either a right to do something or a right to prevent something. A right *to have
something done* is not an easement, nor is it an incident of an easement.[1] Thus an agreement
by a landlord to supply hot water and heating to the tenants of a block does not give rise
to an easement;[2] rights such as these can only exist as express contracts or covenants.
However, both a right to a supply of water,[3] and a supply of electricity,[4] through meters
located on the servient land and for payment of which the servient owner was responsible,

have been analysed as easements for the passage of water and electricity respectively. In both instances the dominant owner would, by implication, be liable to reimburse the servient owner for the costs of the supply to the dominant tenement.

An exception to the rule that the right claimed must not involve the servient owner in expenditure is provided by the long recognised easement of fencing. 'The right to have your neighbour keep up the fences is a right in the nature of an easement which is capable of being granted by law'.[5] The cases suggest that such easements are restricted to fencing against straying livestock. If this is so, an obligation to maintain a fence between two neighbouring houses does not amount to an easement; it will therefore bind only the contracting parties and cannot affect a new owner of the 'servient' property[6].

There is long-standing authority that the owner of the servient tenement, though he must not act positively to interfere with the enjoyment of the easement by the dominant owner, is not bound, in the absence of an express or implied contractual obligation,[7] to carry out any repairs necessary to ensure the enjoyment of the easement by the dominant owner. It may now be the case, however, that the servient owner may be liable in negligence or nuisance if he fails to take reasonable steps to repair defects of which he is aware or ought to have been aware which threaten to interfere with the dominant owner's easement.[8] It should be noted that the grant of an easement does, ordinarily, confer on the *dominant* owner the right to enter the servient property to effect necessary repairs[9] and, where this is necessary to the enjoyment of the right, to make improvements (eg to a right of way).[10]

1   *Jones v Price* [1965] 2 All ER 625 at 628, CA.
2   *Regis Property Co Ltd v Redman* [1956] 2 All ER 335, CA.
3   *Rance v Elvin* (1985) 50 P & CR 9, CA.
4   *Duffy v Lamb* [1997] NPC 52, CA.
5   *Crow v Wood* [1970] 3 All ER 425 at 429, CA.
6   See *Jones v Price* [1965] 2 All ER 625, CA.
7   See *Liverpool City Council v Irwin* [1976] 2 All ER 39, HL and *King v South Northamptonshire District Council* (1991) 64 P & CR 35, CA, two cases in which the courts were prepared to imply a contractual obligation on the part of a landlord to repair and maintain an essential means of access to the demised property; see para 37.25 below.
8   *Bradburn v Lindsay* [1983] 2 All ER 408; see also para 24.16 above and para 33.50 below.
9   *Jones v Pritchard* [1908] 1 Ch 30.
10   The dominant owner may not, however, carry out works which amount to an improvement which increases the burden on the servient land where the right has been acquired by prescription (for which see paras 33.40–33.51 below). See *Mills v Silver* [1991] 1 All ER 449, CA where it was held that the dominant owner was not entitled to improve the surface of a right of way.

Rights similar to easements

33.13   Under this heading we further explain the nature of easements by considering rights which are similar to easements and, in each case, what it is which differentiates them from easements.

Natural rights

33.14   Every landowner enjoys certain natural rights against neighbouring landowners. Unlike easements, these rights flow automatically from the ownership of land; they do not depend on any form of creation. Every landowner has the right to receive support for his land from that of his neighbour.[1] Further, as we have seen,[2] all landowners have certain limited right to water.

1   See further para 33.50 below.
2   Para 29.21 above.

Restrictive covenants[1]

33.15   A similarity between easements and restrictive covenants can be seen in that both require dominant and servient land.[2] Indeed, restrictive covenants were described by Sir

George Jessel MR[3] as being an extension in equity of the doctrine of negative easements, such as the easements of light and of support. However, there are important differences. Restrictive covenants must be expressly created; as we shall see, easements may be implied, and can be acquired as a result of long use (ie by prescription).[4] Again, as we shall see, restrictive covenants are equitable only, whereas easements may be legal or equitable. Furthermore, it may be that the content of a restrictive covenant is not limited in the same way as that of easements. So, for example, while the right to a view is too vague to exist as an easement,[5] the same objective may be achieved by the imposition of a restrictive covenant preventing development which obstructs the view.[6] Certainly, save for the requirement that a restrictive covenant be negative,[7] the courts do not exercise control over the type of rights which can exist by way of restrictive covenant; as we have seen,[8] policy considerations do dictate the nature of rights which will be accepted as easements. Finally, as we shall see,[9] there are recognised circumstances in which both the common law and, more particularly, statute allows for restrictive covenants to be modified or discharged. There is no such provision for the removal of easements; indeed, once created, the law is most reluctant to extinguish an easement.[10]

1   See ch 34.
2   See para 34.13 below.
3   *London and South Western Rly Co v Gomm* (1882) 20 Ch D 562.
4   See paras 33.40–33.51 below.
5   *Aldred's Case* (1610) 9 Co Rep 57b.
6   *Wakeham v Wood* (1981) 43 P & CR 40, CA, para 34.30 below; and see *Gilbert v Spoor* [1982] 2 All ER 576, CA, para 34.42 below.
7   See para 34.12 below.
8   Para 33.8 above.
9   See paras 34.31–34.44 below.
10 See para 33.52 below.

Public rights

33.16   An easement is a private right which one landowner can exercise against the land of another. Some rights to land can be exercised by any member of the public and one of the most commonly encountered is a public right of way. Those entitled to exercise such rights do so in their capacity as members of the public, they do not have to own dominant land. Public rights of way can be created expressly by statute, or at common law by dedication and acceptance[1]. The rights of the public to have access over privately owned land has recently been greatly extended by the Countryside and Rights of Way Act 2000.[2]

1   Highways Act 1980, s 31(1).
2   Part I of the Act confers a public right to roam over certain designated land (largely open country and registered common land) while Part II contains new provisions governing the classification and recording of public rights of way.

Licences[1]

33.17   The right to walk across another's field, for example, may exist either as an easement, a public right of way, or a licence. A licence differs from an easement in that it can, in general, be revoked. Moreover, a licence is a personal right not a proprietary right; it requires no dominant land and, unless supported by some equity, can only be enforced against the licensor, and not against any subsequent owner of the licensor's land.[2]

1   Paras 29.41–29.45 above.
2   See para 29.45 above.

Non-derogation from grant[1]

33.18   Where a person conveys or leases land *for a specific purpose*, he is under an obligation not to use the land retained by him in such a way as to render the land conveyed or leased unfit, or materially less fit, for the particular purpose for which the conveyance or lease was made.[2] *Aldin v Latimer Clark, Muirhead & Co*[3] illustrates how this principle may confer greater rights than may be conferred as an easement. Land was let to the claimant to enable him to carry on the business of a timber merchant. It was held that the landlord could not build on his retained land so as to interrupt the free passage of air to the claimant's timber-drying sheds. A general right to air such as this could not have existed as an easement; the easement to the free passage of air is limited to one through a defined aperture.[4]

1   See, in the specific context of leases, para 3723 below.
2   *Browne v Flower* [1911] 1 Ch 219 at 226.
3   [1894] 2 Ch 437.
4   Para 33.9 above.

Profits à prendre

33.19   A profit à prendre is a right to take from another's land the natural produce of the land, minerals, or wild animals on the land. The most important modern day examples of profits are: the profit of pasture (ie a grazing right), whereby grass (a natural product of the land) is taken from the land by being eaten by the profit-owner's animals; the rights to take gravel and minerals from the land; the rights to catch fish and shoot game.

33.20   A profit may be legal or equitable.[1] In the case of registered land a profit which is not entered on the register is an overriding interest whether it is legal or equitable.[2]

A profit may be several or in common. A 'several' profit is owned by one person to the exclusion of others. A profit in common (or simply 'common') is owned in common with others. A common pasture is perhaps the most important type of profit in common. This is often encountered in hill-farming areas whereby a number of farms may enjoy the right to graze stock on the adjoining hills and mountains.

A profit may be appurtenant or in gross. If appurtenant, it is, like an easement, annexed to a dominant tenement. If so, the profit is limited to the needs of the dominant land. For example, an appurtenant profit of pasture will be limited to the number of cattle or sheep which the dominant land is capable of supporting. A several profit in gross is owned independently of land and is unconnected with any dominant tenement. Nevertheless, it is still a right in land and, indeed, the owner of such a right may now register his title to it[3].

Profits are acquired in much the same way as easements,[3] with some variations as to detail. In particular, a profit in gross cannot be acquired by prescription.

1   The rules outlined in para 33.24 below apply also to profits.
2   Para 36.30 below.
3   LRA 2002, s 3(1)(d); see para 30.15 above.

33.21   Under the Commons Registration Act 1965, any common right or common land (ie land subject to common rights) existing before 2 January 1970 must have been registered in the appropriate county council's register of commons before 31 July 1970, otherwise it ceased to be exerciseable. Should any new common land come into existence, registration under the Act is again required.

Customary rights

33.22   Customary rights are not public rights, available to the general public at large, but are confined to the inhabitants of a particular locality. They differ from easements in that there is no necessity for dominant land and in that they are not capable of forming the subject matter of a grant, since a fluctuating body of inhabitants is not a capable grantee. A customary right must be ancient, continuous, certain and reasonable.[1] Examples include the right of fishermen of a particular parish to dry their nets on private land[2] and the right of the inhabitants of a village to hold a fair on private land.[3]

1   Para 3.62 above.
2   *Mercer v Denne* [1905] 2 Ch 538, CA.
3   *Wyld v Silver* [1962] 3 All ER 309, CA.

Acquisition of easements

33.23   It is not sufficient for an easement to exist that a right exhibit the characteristics outlined above. It must also be created or acquired in a manner recognised by the law. In practice, most easements are created expressly by deed in the context of a sale or lease of part of the vendor's or lessor's land. However, it is important to note that easements can also be created by implication and as a result of prescription (ie long use).

We will first consider the difference between legal and equitable easements and then deal, in turn, with the various methods by which an easement can be created.

Legal and equitable easements

33.24   An easement is legal if it is created in fee simple or for a term of years absolute,[1] and is made by deed.[2] Easements created by implication, or by prescription are also legal easements. This is because, in such cases, it is either implied or presumed that a deed has been used.

An easement is necessarily equitable if it is created for a lesser interest than a fee simple or term of years, eg for life. Furthermore, an easement in fee simple or for a term of years will, if not created by deed, be equitable if created by means of an agreement which satisfies the requirements of the Law of Property (Miscellaneous Provisions) Act 1989, s 2.[3]

Where a proprietor of registered land expressly grants an easement, the disposition must be completed by registration in order for the easement to exist as a legal interest[4]. This means that the right will be entered in the property register of the dominant land (if title to that land is also registered) and a notice will be entered in the charges register of the servient land.[5] Any legal easement affecting the title at the time of first registration will similarly be entered on the register of the servient land.[6] Certain legal easements are not required to be entered on the register; in practice, these are easements arising by implication, or by virtue of section 62 of the Law of Property Act 1925, or as a result of prescription.[7] These take effect as overriding interests.[8]

All equitable easements must be protected by the entry of a notice on the title of the servient land; if this is not done, the equitable easement will not bind a purchaser of the servient land.[9]

1   LPA 1925, s 1(2).
2   LPA 1925, s 52.
3   Para 33.31 above.
4   LRA 2002, s 27(2)(d).
5   LRA 2002, s 27, Sch 2, para 7.
6   LRA 1925, ss 37, 71.
7   See paras 33.27-33.51 below.
8   LRA 2002, ss 29, 30, Sch 3, para 3. See para 36.30 below.
9   LRA 2002, ss 29,30. See para 36.34 below.

Expressly created easements

33.25   An easement is usually created expressly on the transfer or lease by a landowner of part of his land. It can, however, be created, independently of the transfer of land, by two neighbouring landowners. It was made clear by the Court of Appeal in *IDC Group Ltd v Clark*[1] that, even where a right displaying all the features of an easement has been expressly created, there will be no easement unless the parties *intended* to create an easement. Accordingly, in that case, a right to use a fire escape route through a neighbouring building which the two neighbouring owners had created by deed, was held not to be an easement because it had been clearly described as a licence. This meant that the right was not intended to be proprietary and did not bind a purchaser of the 'servient' land.

1   (1992) 65 P & CR 179, CA.

Grants and reservations

33.26   An easement is said to be *granted* where the vendor or lessor confers an easement over the land he is retaining in favour of the land he is selling or leasing. An easement is *reserved* where the vendor or lessor of land reserves to himself a right over the land sold or leased in favour of his retained land. Any ambiguity in the terms of a grant will be resolved in favour of the purchaser/lessee and against the vendor/lessor; any ambiguity in the terms of a reservation is to be resolved in favour of the vendor/lessor. [1]

1   *St Edmundsbury and Ipswich Diocesan Board of Finance v Clark (No 2)* [1975] I All ER 772, CA.

Implied easements

33.27   There are circumstances in which, despite the fact that a transfer or lease does not expressly create an easement, the law will do so by implication[1]. This method of creation is applicable only where a landowner is selling or leasing a part of his land and is retaining the remainder (or disposing of the whole in parcels), because only in such a case is there a transaction into which the grant or reservation of an easement can be implied.

1   Where an easement is implied into a deed, the easement will be legal rather than equitable.

Implied grants

33.28   The common law will fairly readily imply the grant of easements in favour of a purchaser or tenant. The underlying approach is that a purchaser or tenant is entitled to the benefit of such easements over the vendor's or landlord's retained land as he might reasonably have expected to receive. However, this broad policy is applied through the medium of three[1], sometimes overlapping, mechanisms:

- easements of necessity;
- intended easements; and
- easements within the rule in *Wheeldon v Burrows*.

We consider each of these in turn.

1   Purchasers and tenants can also acquire easements that have not been expressly mentioned in their transfer of lease by virtue of LPA 1925, s 62; see paras 33.35-33.38 below.

33.29   *Easements of necessity*   Where a vendor sells land which, as a result, is left without any legally enforceable means of access, ie which is 'landlocked', the law will imply from those circumstances that the parties intended a right of way of necessity to be granted.[1] It is for the vendor to select the route but it must, however, provide convenient access. Such a right of way is limited to what was necessary in the circumstances of the original transaction. Thus, in *London Corpn v Riggs*,[2] following a sale, the defendant's agricultural land was left without access; since there was no mention of any easements of way in the conveyance this meant that he was entitled to a right of way of necessity. However the defendant later sought to build refreshment rooms open to the public on his land.

The claimant was held to be entitled to prevent him using the right of way for any purposes other than those connected with the agricultural use of the land.

1   *Nickerson v Barraclough* [1981] 2 All ER 369, CA. Such an intention cannot be implied where there is any alternative access, even solely by water; see *Manjang v Drammeh* (1990) 61 P & CR 194, PC.
2   (1880) 13 Ch D 798.

33.30 *Intended easements* The law will imply the grant of easements in order to give effect to the common intention of the parties as to the purposes for which the land granted is to be used. However, it is essential that the parties intend that the land sold should be used in some definite and particular manner;[1] it is, however, sufficient to establish the intended use on the balance of probabilities.[2]

It is arguable that the categories of easements of necessity and intended easements overlap. For example, reciprocal easements of support will be implied on the sale by their owner of one of two adjoining properties. This may be regarded as an easement of necessity, although some regard it as an intended easement.[3] Conversely, the case of *Wong v Beaumont Property Trust Ltd*[4] was held to concern an implied easement of necessity, although it could equally well be regarded as concerning an intended easement. Here, cellar premises were let to a tenant who covenanted that he would carry on business as a restaurateur, would not cause any nuisance, and would control and eliminate all smells and odours in conformity with the health regulations. The tenant subsequently assigned to Wong. In order to comply with the health regulations, Wong sought the landlord's permission to affix a ventilation duct to the outside wall of the landlord's premises. The landlord refused but Wong obtained a declaration that he was entitled to attach the duct. The Court of Appeal held that, where a lease is granted which imposes a particular use on the tenant and it is impossible for the tenant so to use the premises legally unless an easement is granted, the law does imply such an easement as of necessity.

1 *Pwllbach Colliery Co Ltd v Woodman* [1915] AC 634, HL.
2 *Stafford v Lee* (1992) 65 P & CR 172, CA. Note that the test for implied reservations is stricter, see para 33.33 below.
3 *Jones v Pritchard* [1908] 1 Ch 630.
4 [1964] 2 All ER 119, CA.

33.31 *Easements within the rule in Wheeldon v Burrows* In addition to the two bases of implication just discussed, there has evolved an extension of the doctrine of non-derogation from grant[1] known as the rule in *Wheeldon v Burrows*.[2] The rule states that where a landowner sells or leases part of his land, the *grant* (but *not* the reservation) of certain quasi-easements[3] will be implied into the conveyance (or into any contract to convey[4]). The quasi-easements which will pass to the purchaser or tenant as full easements are those which are 'continuous and apparent', necessary to the reasonable enjoyment of the property granted, and which have been and are at the time of the grant used by the owners of the entirety for the benefit of the part granted.[5] Thus, where, prior to the sale or leasing of part of his property, the owner has exercised some right over the part he is retaining which is necessary to the reasonable enjoyment of the part he is selling, that right will pass to the purchaser or lessee as an easement, provided it is continuous and apparent.

It is said that, strictly, a 'continuous' easement is one that is enjoyed passively, without the need for action on the part of the dominant owner, such as the right of light.[6] Something is 'apparent' if it is discoverable on a careful inspection by a person ordinarily conversant with the subject.[7] Thus the presence of a window on the dominant tenement receiving light from the adjoining land suggests a continuous and apparent easement of light. However, the courts have extended the concept of what is 'continuous and apparent' beyond these narrow confines; the phrase is regarded as being 'directed to there being on the servient tenement a feature which would be seen on inspection and which is neither transitory nor intermittent'.[8] Thus, it is well established that a right of way over a made-up road or worn track can pass as an easement under the rule in *Wheeldon v Burrows*, provided it is necessary to the reasonable enjoyment of the property.[9] Similarly, a right to use drains running through the vendor's retained land may also be created as an easement under this rule.[10]

It is clear that the requirement that the easement be necessary to the reasonable enjoyment of the property granted is less strict than that for easements of necessity.[11] In *Millman v Ellis*[12] it was held that the claimant, who had expressly been granted a right of way over part of a layby on the defendant's retained land which provided access to the road, was also entitled to an implied right of way over the remainder of the layby. The more extended right was reasonably necessary to the enjoyment of the claimant's property since, without it, access to the highway was dangerous. This can be compared with the decision in *Wheeler v JJ Saunders Ltd*[13] that a right of way over the defendant vendor's retained land would not be implied; given that there was a perfectly adequate alternative access, this second access was not necessary to the reasonable enjoyment of the claimant's land.

1   Para 37.18 above and para 37.23 below.
2   (1879) 12 Ch D 31.
3   Para 33.7 above.
4   *Borman v Griffith* [1930] 1 Ch 493; *Sovmots Investments Ltd v Secretary of State for the Environment* [1976] 1 All ER 178.
5   (1879) 12 Ch D 31 at 49.
6   Megarry & Wade *Law of Real Property* (6th edn) p 1110.
7   *Pyer v Carter* (1857) 1 H & N 916 at 922.
8   *Ward v Kirkland* [1967] [1966] 1 All ER 609 at 616.
9   *Borman v Griffith* [1930] 1 Ch 493.
10 *Ward v Kirkland* [1966] 1 All ER 609.
11 Para 33.29 above.
12 (1995) 71 P & CR 158, CA.
13 [1995] 2 All ER 697, CA.

Implied reservations

33.32   Easements in favour of a vendor or landlord can also be implied. However, the courts are far more reluctant to imply reservations than they are to imply grants (ie easements in favour of the purchaser or tenant). The reason for this is that, where a vendor or landlord sells or leases part of his land and wishes to reserve rights over the part sold or leased, in favour of the land he is keeping, he should make this clear. Reservations ought therefore to be express. To imply reservations imposes an unexpressed (and possibly unexpected) burden on the purchaser or lessee. However, in very limited circumstances, the courts will imply reservations, namely:

*   easements of necessity; and
*   intended easements.

It should be emphasised that neither the rule in *Wheeldon v Burrows*[1], nor LPA 1925, s 62[2] applies to reservations.

1   See para 33.31 above.
2   See paras 33.34-33.38 below.

33.33   *Easements of necessity and intended easements*   The rules governing implied easements of necessity are the same for reservations as they are for grants[1]. However, where a landlord or vendor is seeking to show the *reservation* of an intended easement the test is stricter than it is for grants[2], since it must be shown that the facts are not reasonably consistent with anything but a common intention. In *Re Webb's Lease, Sandom v Webb*,[3] where a landlord sought to show that he had the right to use the outside wall of demised premises for displaying advertisements, the court held that the mere fact that the tenant knew of the presence of the advertisements at the time of the lease was insufficient to show an intention common to both parties that the landlord was to have a reserved right to maintain the advertisements. However, in *Peckham v Ellison*[4] the facts were strong enough for the Court of Appeal to imply the reservation of a right of way; the right had been exercised for many years and had been believed by all concerned to be legally valid.

1   See para 33.29 above.
2   See para 33.30 above.
3   [1951] Ch 808, [1951] 2 All ER 131, CA.
4   (1998) 31 HLR 1030, CA.

Creation of easements by the operation of the LPA 1925, s 62

33.34   The creation of easements under the LPA 1925, s 62 does not come about by implication in the conveyance; rather the words creating the easement are deemed by virtue of the section to have been expressed in the conveyance from the outset. However, it is convenient to treat s 62 here, because of the interrelation of the section and the rule in *Wheeldon v Burrows.*

The ambit of s 62

33.35   The section provides that a conveyance of land shall be deemed to include and shall by virtue of the Act operate to convey, with the land, all liberties, privileges, easements, rights and advantages, whatsoever, appertaining or reputed to appertain to the land or any part thereof, or, at the time of the conveyance, enjoyed with the land or any part thereof. This provision applies to dispositions of registered land by virtue of the LRA 1925, ss 19(3) and 22(3).

Section 62 makes it clear that *existing* easements enjoyed with the land pass on a conveyance of the land. However, the section has a further most important effect, namely that it operates to convert mere privileges and advantages into *new* legal easements. In effect s 62 states that a conveyance of a piece of land operates to convey with that land all advantages appertaining to, or, at the time of the conveyance, enjoyed with the land, so as to convert such advantages into legally enforceable rights.[1] These rights and privileges must actually be enjoyed at the time of the grant with the land granted or a part of it.[2] Furthermore, they must have been enjoyed by an occupier of the land other than the grantor, over other land of the grantor.[3] It follows that, while the dominant and servient lands must have been in *common ownership* prior to the transaction creating the easement, they must have been in *separate occupation.*

It should be noted that the section does not operate to create easements out of rights not capable of existing as such; thus the right to protection from the weather,[4] or to the provision of hot water and heating,[5] cannot pass under s 62.

1   *Nickerson v Barraclough* [1981] 2 All ER 369 at 381–382.
2   *Payne v Inwood* (1996) 74 P & CR 42, CA. However, actual user must be judged not by reference simply to the moment of the conveyance, but rather in relation to a reasonable period leading up to that conveyance; see *Green v Ashco Horticulturist Ltd* [1966] 1 WLR 889. Furthermore, the operation of s 62 is *not* prevented where the use of the right has been *temporarily* interrupted at the date of the conveyance; see *Pretoria Warehousing Co Ltd v Shelton* [1993] NPC 98, CA.
3   *Sovmots Investments Ltd v Secretary of State for the Environment* [1977] 2 All ER 385, HL; *Long v Gowlett* [1923] 2 Ch 177.
4   *Phipps v Pears* [1964] 2 All ER 35, CA.
5   *Regis Property Co Ltd v Redman* [1956] 2 All ER 335, CA.

The operation of s 62

33.36   The operation of s 62 is illustrated by *International Tea Stores Co v Hobbs.*[1] A tenant, with the landlord's permission, made use of a roadway on the landlord's property. Subsequently, the tenant acquired the freehold and it was held that the right to use the roadway passed to him as an easement under s 62. Similarly, in *Wright v Macadam,*[2] a tenant was given permission by the landlord to use a coal shed belonging to the landlord. The Court of Appeal held that on the renewal of the lease the right to use the coal shed passed as an easement, although previously depending on permission. These cases constitute a warning to landlords to revoke all licences granted to a tenant prior to renewing the lease or selling the reversion, or, preferably, positively to exclude the operation of s 62.[3]

1 [1903] 2 Ch 165. see also *Hair v Gillman* (2000) 80 P & CR 108.
2 [1949] 2 All ER 565, CA.
3 Para 33.39 below.

33.37 Another warning as to the possible effect of the section appears from *Goldberg v Edwards*.[1] Edwards leased an annexe at the rear of her house to Goldberg. This annexe could be reached by an outside passage at the side of the house. Goldberg was allowed into possession before the lease was executed and was given permission to use a passage through the landlord's house to reach the annexe. The lease was executed some time later. Edwards subsequently let her house to Miller, the second defendant, who barred the door to Goldberg. Goldberg claimed he was entitled to a right of way either under the rule in *Wheeldon v Burrows*[2] or under s 62.

The Court of Appeal held that the claimed right of way had not passed under *Wheeldon v Burrows* since it was not necessary for the reasonable enjoyment of the annexe, which could conveniently be reached via the outside passage. However, the right did pass as an easement under s 62 since, at the time of the conveyance (ie when the lease was finally executed), the privilege of going through the house was being enjoyed with the annexe and thus passed as an easement when the lease was executed.

1 [1950] Ch 247, CA.
2 Para 33.31 above.

33.38 Section 62 operates only in respect of a 'conveyance', ie the transfer or creation of a *legal* estate; accordingly it will not operate to pass easements in an equitable lease.[1] Just as *Goldberg v Edwards* illustrates how an easement may pass by virtue of s 62 where *Wheeldon v Burrows* is inapplicable, so *Borman v Griffith*[1] shows how easements within the rule in *Wheeldon v Burrows* may pass where s 62 is inappropriate. Borman occupied a house in the grounds of Wood Green Park under an agreement for a seven-year lease. He made use of the main drive of the park which ran past the front of his house although the agreement contained no reference to a right of way and despite the fact that his house could be reached by an unmade track at the rear. Borman claimed a right of way along the main drive in this action against the tenant of the remainder of the park who had prevented Borman's use of the drive. The court rejected the claim based on s 62 as Borman had only an equitable lease. However, the court in effect held that, just as easements within the rule in *Wheeldon v Burrows* will be implied in the grant of a legal estate, so continuous and apparent easements necessary for the reasonable enjoyment of the property will be implied in an agreement for such a grant,[2] and, since the drive was plainly visible and was necessary for the reasonable enjoyment of the property, a right of way over it passed to Borman.

1 *Borman v Griffith* [1930] 1 Ch 493. In this case the claimant occupied on the basis of a contract for a seven-year lease; as we have seen in Note 6,para 31.3 above, this gives rise not to a legal lease but to an equitable one.
2 *Sovmots Investments Ltd v Secretary of State for the Environment* [1976] 1 All ER 178, HL.

Exclusion of s 62 and the rule in Wheeldon v Burrows

33.39 Neither the rule in *Wheeldon v Burrows* nor s 62 will apply in the face of a contrary intention and it is common for their operation to be expressly excluded by making it clear that rights which might otherwise pass are not intended to be conveyed.[1] Where there is no explicit exclusion, the courts may decide that other provisions in the conveyance necessarily exclude the implication of any easements. So, for example, it is possible that, where a purchaser covenants to erect a fence, this will prevent the implication of any access through that fence.[2] However, this will depend on the particular facts; in some circumstances it will be proper to treat the covenant to fence as permitting the inclusion of a gate, so that a right of access can still be implied.[3]

1   *Squarey v Harris-Smith* (1981) 42 P & CR 118, CA.
2   *Wheeler v JJ Saunders Ltd* [1995] 2 All ER 697, CA.
3   *Hillman v Rogers* [1997] NPC 183, CA.

Prescription

33.40   Prescription is the method whereby the law confers legality on the long enjoyment of a right, by presuming it had a lawful origin in a grant. An easement acquired by prescription is, therefore, a legal easement. The law of prescription has been described as unsatisfactory, uncertain and out of date,[1] particularly because there exist side by side three methods by which a claim to have acquired an easement by prescription may be made: at common law, under the doctrine of lost modern grant, and under the Prescription Act 1832. Whichever method is being relied on as the basis of a claim (and it may be advisable to rely on more than one method) it must be shown that there has been:

- continuous enjoyment of the alleged right,
- in fee simple,
- as of right.

1   Law Reform Committee, 14th Report, Cmnd 3100 (1966).

Continuous enjoyment

33.41   This requirement does not mean that the right claimed must have been used ceaselessly day and night throughout the prescriptive period. What is continuous depends on the nature of the right being claimed and the circumstances of the case. In *Diment v NH Foot Ltd*,[1] the use of a path between six and ten times a year was considered sufficient in regularity and extent to constitute continuous enjoyment. The claim to a right of way by prescription was, however, unsuccessful for other reasons.

1   [1974] 2 All ER 785.

In fee simple

33.42   An easement (other than one of light[1]) may only be acquired by prescription by a freehold owner against a freehold owner.[2] Hence prescription cannot be established during any period when the freeholds of the dominant and servient lands are in common ownership.

This requirement also means that, where the *servient* land is held by a tenant under a lease throughout the period of enjoyment on which the dominant owner's claim to have acquired an easement is based, the claim will usually be unsuccessful.

Furthermore, long enjoyment of a right by a tenant of the *dominant* land is treated as being on behalf of the freeholder; the easement is thus acquired by the freeholder and not by the tenant. This, coupled with the fact that a person cannot have an easement over his own land, means that a tenant cannot acquire a prescriptive right against his own landlord, nor can a tenant acquire an easement by prescription against another tenant of the same landlord.[3]

1   Para 33.55 below.
2   *Wheaton v Maple & Co* [1893] 3 Ch 48, CA.
3   *Kilgour v Gaddes* [1904] 1 KB 457, CA. Note, however, that the position is different in the case of claims to a right to light under the Prescription Act 1832, see para 33.55 below.

As of right

33.43   A person claiming to have acquired an easement by prescription must show that he has thus far enjoyed the right on the basis that he was entitled to do so on a permanent basis. This he does by showing that his enjoyment was neither by force, nor secretly, nor by permission. Furthermore, the user on which a prescriptive claim is based must not be prohibited by statute.[1] This latter rule has given rise to considerable difficulties to those whose rights of access to their properties (often, but not exclusively, over common land) have never been formally granted. Access by motor vehicle across the land of another without the consent of that person has long been a criminal offence[2] and the *Hanning* decision confirmed that even long enjoyed rights of *vehicular* access could not, therefore, be acquired by prescription. The situation has now been rectified by statute and those who, but for the illegality, would otherwise have been entitled to their right of vehicular access by prescription, can now compel the servient owner to grant such rights at a statutorily fixed price[3].

1   *Hanning v Top Deck Travel Group Ltd* (1993) 68 P & CR 14, CA.
2   Currently by virtue of LPA 1925, s 193(4) and the Road Traffic Act 1988, s 34.
3   Countryside and Rights of Way Act 2000, s 68.

33.44   *Without force*   There can be no claim to an easement by prescription where the alleged right has been exercised by force or in the face of open and continuous opposition from the servient owner.

33.45   *Without secrecy*   Where the servient owner does not know, or cannot discover, that a right over his land is being used,[1] that enjoyment cannot be said to be acquiesced in; the use cannot therefore be as of right. So, it was not possible to claim by prescription an easement in respect of the support of a dry dock where none of the supporting rods was visible on the alleged servient land.[2] Similarly, the intermittent discharge of borax at night into a sewer could not, even over a long period, ripen into an easement; the servient owner clearly could not discover such a use.[3]

1   *Dalton v Angus* (1881) 6 App Cas 740 at 801, HL.
2   *Union Lighterage Co v London Graving Dock Co* [1902] 2 Ch 557 at 571, CA.
3   *Liverpool Corpn v H Coghill & Son* [1918] 1 Ch 307.

33.46   *Without permission*   To succeed in a claim to have acquired an easement by prescription, the dominant owner must show that the servient owner acquiesced in his enjoyment as if it were an established right, ie that the latter knew, or had the means of knowing, that the right was being exercised and stood by and allowed the use to continue.[1] However, if a claimant's use is with the positive permission of the servient owner, or is subject to the control of the servient owner, this makes it clear that the latter did not regard the enjoyment as an established and irrevocable right, but merely as a licence which could be terminated at any time by the withdrawal of the permission.[2]

1   *Mills v Silver* [1991] 1 All ER 449, CA.
2   See *Goldsmith v Burrow Construction Co* (1987) Times, 31 July, CA: here the fact that the gate to a footpath was periodically locked by the alleged servient owner rendered the use of path permissive.

The three methods of prescription
33.47   *Common law* Thus far we have said that a claim to have acquired an easement by prescription depends on showing long enjoyment as of right. Strictly, at common law, it is necessary to show enjoyment as of right since before 1189 which, for historical reasons, is regarded as 'time immemorial'. Obviously, a need positively to prove continuous enjoyment since before 1189 would in most cases be impossible. Accordingly, where it is proved that a right has been enjoyed during living memory (usually treated as about 20 years) the courts will presume that enjoyment has been since time immemorial. However, this presumption can easily be rebutted, and the claim will fail, if it is shown that at some time

since 1189 the right either did not exist or could not have existed. So, for example, in the case of a claim to an easement of support, or an easement of light, there can be no prescription at common law if there was no building on the land in 1189. Equally, there can be no prescription at common law where it can be shown that the dominant and servient lands have been in common ownership at any time since 1189.

Because common law prescription is often impossible to establish, the doctrine of lost modern grant was developed.

33.48   *Lost modern grant*   By this pretence, the court presumes that there was a comparatively recent deed granting the easement which has since been lost. In this way a lawful basis for long enjoyment is presumed without the need to show user since 1189. A lost modern grant will be presumed on evidence of 20 years' continuous use in fee simple[1] as of right, even where this period of user took place at some time in the past. So, in *Tehidy Minerals Ltd v Norman*,[2] the fact that, during part of the 20 year period preceding the court action, the right could not be used because the servient land had been requisitioned by the Government was not fatal to a claim based on lost modern grant[3]. More than twenty years user, prior to the date of requisition could be shown, and this was sufficient.

Lost modern grant is a strong presumption which cannot readily be rebutted. It cannot be defeated by evidence that no deed was ever drawn up[4] . but only by evidence showing that a grant could not possibly have been made, eg where the grant was prohibited by statute.[5]

1   Thus a tenant cannot acquire an easement under the doctrine of lost modern grant, nor can an easement be acquired on this basis by one tenant against a tenant of the same landlord: *Simmons v Dobson* (1991) 62 P & CR 485, CA; see para 33.42 above.
2   [1971] 2 All ER 475, CA.
3   This would, however, prevent a claim under the Prescription Act 1832, see para 33.50 below.
4   *Dalton v Angus* (1881) 6 App Cas 740.
5   *Neaverson v Peterborough Rural District Council* [1902] 1 Ch 557.

33.49   *Prescription Act 1832*   'The Prescription Act 1832 has no friends. It has long been criticised as one of the worst drafted Acts on the Statute Book'.[1] The Act was apparently drafted with the aim of avoiding the pitfalls involved in a claim at common law. In view of its complexity, the Act provides few advantages over the other two methods with which it co-exists. Nonetheless, it may, in fact, be of some utility to those claiming an easement by prescription.

The Act provides for a claim to an easement other than light to be based either on 20 years' enjoyment as of right without interruption, or on 40 years' such enjoyment. It deals separately with claims to easements of light and these provisions are dealt with in a later paragraph.[2]

1   Law Reform Committee, 14th Report, Cmnd 3100 (1966).
2   Para 33.55 below.

33.50   Where a claim under the Act to an easement other than light is based on 20 years' enjoyment as of right without interruption, it cannot be defeated by evidence that enjoyment began later than 1189, although it may be defeated in any other way in which a claim at common law may be defeated.[1] Thus it is still necessary to show that enjoyment was continuous, in fee simple, and as of right.

There must be some court action to confirm the embryonic right as an easement. This can take the form either of an action by the dominant owner for a declaration that he is entitled to an easement, or an action by the servient owner to prevent continued enjoyment, in which the dominant owner relies on the Act as a defence. The Act requires that the period of enjoyment must have *immediately preceded* the court action relating to the claim.[2]

If there has been no enjoyment for some time prior to the court action, then even if there has been 20 years' enjoyment, a claim under the Act cannot, subject to the question of an interruption, succeed.[3]

Although the Act requires the enjoyment to be 'without interruption', it does define an interruption as an act which has been acquiesced in for one year.[4] So, if a landowner has enjoyed a right of way over his neighbour's land for 15 years and the neighbour then physically bars the way, this will only constitute an interruption after the elapse of one year. If the use of the way recommences in less than twelve months and the 20-year period is completed, a claim will succeed. However, if the exercise of the right is interrupted for a full year, a fresh period of 20 years user will then have to be established before an easement can be acquired. It also follows that, if that landowner had already enjoyed the right of way for 20 years before it was barred, he would still be able to claim an easement under the Act provided he brings an action to claim the right within one year of the commencement of the obstruction.

1 Prescription Act 1832, s 2.
2 Prescription Act 1832, s 4.
3 A claim can, however, be based on the doctrine of lost modern grant, see para 33.48 above
4 Prescription Act 1832, s s 7.

33.51 A claim to an easement under the Act based on 40 years' enjoyment as of right without interruption is deemed to be absolute and indefeasible unless it is shown that the enjoyment depended on written consent.[1] Again, the 40-year period must immediately precede some court action. 'Interruption' has the same meaning as in relation to the 20-year period.

Although a claim based on 40 years' enjoyment will only be defeated by proof of written permission, the enjoyment must nevertheless be 'as of right'. Therefore, enjoyment which depends on regular permission (written or oral) – as in *Gardner v Hodgson's Kingston Brewery Co*[2] where an annual payment of 15 shillings had to be made for the use of a right of way – will not ripen into an easement even if the permission is oral and the enjoyment has continued for 40 years, because the enjoyment is permissive and not as of right.[3] Oral permission given at the outset and not renewed will not defeat a claim based on the 40-year period, though it will defeat a claim based on 20 years' enjoyment.

1 Prescription Act 1832, s 2.
2 [1903] AC 229, HL.
3 See also *Jones v Price and Morgan* (1992) 64 P & CR 404, CA.

Extinguishment of easements

33.52 At common law easements may only be extinguished by being released, expressly or impliedly, by the dominant owner, or by ownership and possession of the dominant and servient properties falling into the same hands. In practice, implied release is extremely difficult to establish. It is not enough to show that the dominant owner is not using the right and has not used it over a long period,[1] or to prove that the obstruction of some aspects of the right has been acquiesced in.[2] It must be shown that the dominant owner intends to abandon the right, and abandonment of an easement can only be treated as having taken place where the person entitled to it has demonstrated a fixed intention never at any time thereafter to assert the right himself or to attempt to transmit it to anyone else.[3]

Unlike the case of restrictive covenants, there is no statutory scheme for the modification or discharge of easements.[4] Easements may, however, be expressly extinguished by specific statutes (as happened under the old Inclosure Acts). They can also be effectively suspended by a number of Acts under which land can be compulsorily acquired[5]; in such cases the owner of the dominant tenement can claim compensation.

1   See *Benn v Hardinge* (1992) 66 P & CR 246, CA where it was held that there was no abandonment of an easement simply because no one had occasion to use the right during the previous 175 years.
2   See *Snell & Prideaux Ltd v Dutton Mirrors Ltd* [1995] 1 EGLR 259, CA, where it was held that a right to use a passageway *both* as a right of way *and* for loading and unloading had not been abandoned simply because its use as a right of way had long been obstructed by the erection of a brick pillar.
3   *Tehidy Minerals Ltd v Norman* [1971] 2 All ER 475 at 492, CA.
4   Paras 34.38-34.43 below.
5   See *R v City of London Corpn, ex p Mystery of the Barbers of London* (1997) 73 P & CR 59 where easements were suspended when the servient land was acquired for planning purposes under the Town and Country Planning Act 1947.

Particular easements

Rights of way

33.53   A right of way may be limited in extent, for example, as to the times it may be used or as to the purposes for which it may be used (eg agricultural purposes only) or as to the modes of enjoyment (eg on foot only), or it may be unlimited.

Disputes can often arise as to whether the dominant owner is making excessive use of his right of way. In resolving these, the method of creation of the easement is highly relevant. Where the easement was expressly granted or reserved, the question turns on the construction of the relevant deed in the light of the circumstances surrounding its making, in particular the nature of the road or track over which the right was granted.[1] However, in the absence of any special factors, the dominant owner is not confined to using the right of way for the purposes which existed at the date of grant but is entitled to use it for any lawful purposes to which the dominant tenement is later put.[2] Where the wording of the deed is unclear, ambiguities are resolved in favour of the person having the benefit of the easement.[3] In the case of easements of way arising by implication, enjoyment is limited by the situation prevailing at the time of the grant.[4]

The extent of enjoyment permitted in the case of an easement of way acquired by prescription is determined by the nature of the enjoyment during the prescriptive period;[5] however an increase in the frequency of use is unobjectionable unless it produces a change in the nature of the enjoyment.[6] For example, where a right of way had been acquired by prescription to a site used by a small number of caravans, the servient owner could not object to a considerable increase in the number of caravans using the site.[6]

Enlargement of the dominant tenement by the acquisition of additional land will not affect entitlement to a right of way to the original dominant tenement. However, the use of that right of way for the additional land will not be permitted save where that use is genuinely ancillary to that in respect of the dominant land.[7]

Where a dominant owner is using a right of way in a manner or to an extent which exceeds that to which he is entitled, his action amounts to a nuisance and the servient owner may seek an injunction to limit the use to the permitted level.[8] However, where the express terms of a right of way permit a level of use which, in other circumstances, might amount to a nuisance the servient owner has no remedy.[9]

1   *Cannon v Villars* (1878) 8 Ch D 415; see also *Jelbert v Davis* [1968] 1 All ER 1182, CA; *National Trust for Places of Historic Interest or National Beauty v White* [1987] 1 WLR 907.
2   *Alvis v Harrison* (1991) 62 P & CR 10, HL.
3   *St Edmundsbury and Ipswich Diocesan Board of Finance v Clark (No 2)* [1975] 1 All ER 772, CA.
4   *London Corpn v Riggs* (1880) 13 Ch D 798.
5   *Mills v Silver* [1991] 1 All ER 449, CA.

6   *British Railways Board v Glass* [1964] 3 All ER 418, CA.
7   *Harris v Flower* (1904) 74 LJ Ch 127, CA; *Peacock v Custins* [2001] 2 All ER 827, CA; *Das v Linden Mews Ltd* [2002] EWCA Civ 590, [2002] 2 EGLR 76; *Massey v Boulden* [2002] EWCA Civ 1634, [2003] 2 All ER 87, CA.
8   *Rosling v Pinnegar* (1986) 54 P & CR 124, CA.
9   *Hamble Parish Council v Haggard* [1992] 4 All ER 147.

Rights of light

33.54   There is no natural right to light. The right of light can exist only as an easement and then only in respect of a defined aperture, usually a window.[1]

1   See *Levet v Gas Light and Coke Co Ltd* [1919] 1 Ch 24.

Acquisition by prescription

33.55   Although a right to light can be created expressly or by implication, it is more usually acquired by prescription and is then sometimes referred to as 'ancient lights'. Ancient lights can be acquired by all three methods of prescription, though acquisition at common law is highly unlikely since it is often easy to prove that there was no building with windows on the site in 1189.[1]

Where reliance is placed on the Prescription Act 1832, special rules apply. Under the Act, a claim to an easement of light based on 20 years' enjoyment immediately preceding a court action, without interruption, gives rise to an absolute and indefeasible right, unless the light was enjoyed by written consent.[2] There is no requirement that enjoyment be as of right, so the fact that the light was enjoyed by virtue of regular oral permission is no bar to a claim to have acquired a prescriptive right. Furthermore, since it is not necessary to show enjoyment in fee simple, a tenant may acquire an easement of light against his own landlord or against another tenant of the landlord.[3]

The existence of a right to light can severely restrict the servient owner's ability to build on his land so it is particularly important for owners of undeveloped land to be able to prevent their neighbours from acquiring rights to light. Enjoyment of the light could, of course, be interrupted[4] by the erection of a structure blocking the light to the particular window, and traditionally this was done by the erection of a hoarding. However, this method may now fall foul of the planning laws, and so, as an alternative, the servient owner may apply under the Rights of Light Act 1959 for registration in the local land charges registry[5] of a notice, which is treated as being equivalent to an actual obstruction of the light. The application for registration must state the size and position of the opaque structure which the notice is intended to represent.[6] Before such a notice can be registered, the Lands Tribunal must certify that all those likely to be affected by the registration have been notified.[7] Registration is effective for one year, which is sufficient to constitute an interruption; this means that, in order to acquire an easement of light, a further 20 years' enjoyment must be established which can, where necessary, be interrupted by a further registration of a right to light notice.

1   Para 33.47 above.
2   Prescription Act 1832, s 3.
3   *Morgan v Fear* [1907] AC 425, HL.
4   An act does not constitute an interruption for the purpose of the Act unless submitted to or acquiesced in for one year; Prescription Act 1832, s 4; see para 33.50 above.
5   Para 30.24 above.
6   Rights of Light Act 1959, s 3.
7   Rights of Light Act 1959, s 2.

Extent of right

33.56   An owner of a right to light is not necessarily entitled to maintain the level of light which he currently enjoys; generally speaking, he is entitled to sufficient light 'according to the ordinary notions of mankind' for the comfortable use and enjoyment of his house as a dwelling-house, if it is a dwelling-house, or for the beneficial use and occupation of the building if it is a warehouse, a shop, or other place of business.[1] Where there is a right of light, a dominant owner may only bring an action in respect of a reduction in the amount of light received where the reduction constitutes a nuisance; this will only be the case if the light received is reduced below what is sufficient according to the ordinary notions of mankind. In determining this question, the court may take into account the nature of the locality and may have regard to the fact that higher standards may be expected as time goes by.[2] A right of light exists in respect of a defined aperture in a building; the internal arrangement of the rooms in the building is not necessarily relevant to ascertaining the extent of the right.[3]

It is sometimes possible to have a right to a higher than usual level of light. In *Allen v Greenwood*,[4] the claimants, who for at least 20 years had had a greenhouse in their garden, close to the boundary with the neighbouring property, sought an injunction restraining their neighbours from obstructing the light to the greenhouse. The obstruction was caused by a fence which the neighbours had erected and by the neighbours' caravan which was parked close to the greenhouse. Although the greenhouse still received enough light to read by, the Court of Appeal held that this was insufficient for the ordinary purposes of mankind for the use and enjoyment of a greenhouse as a greenhouse (which is regarded as a building with apertures). The question of the amount of light necessary for ordinary purposes is determined by the nature and use of the building, and thus a high degree of light may be necessary in a particular case. Alternatively, the Court held that it is possible to acquire a prescriptive right to a greater than ordinary amount of light. Just as the extent of enjoyment during the prescriptive period determines the extent of a prescriptive right of way, so it determines the extent of a right of light acquired by prescription. The greenhouse having enjoyed an extraordinary amount of light for 20 years, to the knowledge of the servient owner, a prescriptive right to that amount of light had been acquired.

1   *Colls v Home and Colonial Stores Ltd* [1904] AC 179 at 208,HL.
2   *Ough v King* [1967] 3 All ER 859, CA.
3   *Carr-Saunders v Dick McNeil Associates Ltd* [1986] 2 All ER 888.
4   [1979] 1 All ER 819, CA.

Rights of support

33.57 All landowners automatically have a natural right of support[1] which means that they may bring an action in nuisance should the support to their *land* be removed. For example, in *Redland Bricks Ltd v Morris*,[2] the claimant successfully sought damages when part of his market garden slipped into the defendants' land as a result of their digging for clay for their brickworks,[3] and, in *Lotus Ltd v British Soda Co Ltd*,[4] the claimant was held to be entitled to damages when the pumping of brine from boreholes on adjacent land resulted in withdrawal of support from and consequent subsidence of the claimant's land, with resultant damage to the buildings on it. In addition, in certain circumstances at least, landowners can expect their neighbours to take reasonable steps to prevent the potential removal of support to their land.[5]

There is no natural right of support in respect of *buildings*. Such a right of support must be acquired as an easement. However, as *Lotus v British Soda* shows, damages may be claimed in respect of damage to buildings which results from infringement of the natural right of support to the land on which they stand.

An easement of support for buildings may be acquired expressly, by implication or by prescription. A servient owner who by a positive act interferes with a right of support does so at his peril;[6] if he removes the support he must provide an equivalent. There is, however, established authority that he is under no strict obligation to repair that part of his building which provides support for his neighbour; he can let it fall into decay. However, it is becoming clear that a servient owner may be liable in the tort of either negligence or nuisance where he should reasonably have taken steps to prevent interference with his neighbour's right of support. It should be noted that the owner of the *dominant* land may always enter the servient land in order to carry out repairs so as to ensure the support continues.[7]

1   See para 33.14 above.
2   [1969] 2 All ER 576, HL.
3   He also sought, and failed to obtain, a mandatory injunction: para 28.18 above. Where the withdrawal of support causes no immediate collapse but merely the certainty of subsidence in the future, no action can be taken: *Midland Bank Ltd v Bardgrove Property Services Ltd* (1992) 65 P & CR 153, CA.
4   [1971] 1 All ER 265.
5   *Holbeck Hall Hotel Ltd v Scarborough Borough Council* [1997] 2 EGLR 213.
6   *Brace v South East Regional Housing Association Ltd* (1984) 270 Estates Gazette 1286, CA.
7   *Bradburn v Lindsay* [1983] 2 All ER 408; *Rees v Skerrett* [2001] EWCA Civ 760, [2001] 1 WLR 1541.

Chapter 34

Restrictive covenants

34.1 In the property context a covenant is a contractual agreement, usually occurring in a transfer or a lease, in which one party, the *covenantor*, agrees to do or not to do something for the benefit of another, the *covenantee*. Typical covenants which might be entered into between the parties to a transfer include covenants preventing building on the land transferred, or preventing the building of more than one house, or requiring the building of a boundary wall. The parties to a lease may enter covenants requiring the payment of rent and the carrying out of repairs, or preventing sub-letting[1]. All these covenants, being contractual agreements, are enforceable between the original parties according to the ordinary law of contract. However, a covenant may also be a right in land, which is enforceable not only between the original parties to it, but also by and against their successors in title to the property concerned.

In this chapter, we shall be considering the circumstances in which:

- covenants arise where there is no relationship of landlord and tenant;
- the burden of such covenants will pass to a successor in title of the covenantor;
- the benefit of such covenants will pass to a successor in title of the covenantee;
- restrictive covenants will be discharged or modified.

1   Para 37.19 below.

Covenants where there is no relationship of landlord and tenant

34.2 We leave until a later chapter our consideration of the circumstances in which covenants imposed between landlord and tenant will bind parties to whom the lease or reversion is transferred.[1] Here, we consider the question of the extent to which the *benefit* of a covenant 'runs' (ie passes) with the land of the covenantee, and the extent to which the *burden* of it runs with the land of the covenantor where there is no relationship of landlord and tenant. Suppose that P purchases 100 hectares of farmland from V and covenants with V that he will use the land for agricultural purposes only. If V then sells the remainder of his land to R, R will wish to know whether he can enforce the covenant entered into by V and P, ie whether the benefit of the covenant has run, with the land, to him. Were P subsequently to sell his land to A, A would wish to know if he was bound by P's covenant, ie whether the burden of the covenant has run with the land to him.

<sp>We are here dealing with the enforcement of covenants between persons who are

not, either as original parties or as assignees, in the relationship of landlord and tenant. In other words, we are mainly concerned with the enforcement of covenants between freeholders, although it should be noted that these same rules apply should a landlord wish to enforce covenants against a sub-tenant since there is no direct relationship of landlord and tenant between such parties.[2]

In this area, common law and equity have separate rules. Both permit the benefit of a covenant to run with the land. Common law, however, does not allow the burden of a covenant to run, while equity allows the burden of negative covenants, which restrict the use of the land, to run. This means that the burden of positive covenants, which require the covenantor to do something in connection with the land, will not run with freehold land.

1   Paras 37.52 – 37.67 below.
2   Para 37.70 below.

34.3   Clearly, covenants entered into between freeholders, usually on the sale of part of his land by one to another, are mutually enforceable between the original parties on the basis of the contract between them. Furthermore, like other contractual rights, the benefit of a covenant may be assigned to a third party who may then enforce the benefit in his own right.[1] In certain exceptional cases the LPA 1925, s 56 allows a person to enforce a covenant relating to property *as if he were* a party to it, even though he is not named as a party to the covenant; this will be allowed so long as he is in existence at the time of the covenant, identified by it, and the covenant purports to be made *with* him.[2] Such a person is then assumed to be a covenantee. Furthermore only those who, *at the time the covenant was made*, were owners of adjoining land are deemed to be covenantees by virtue of s 56. In the case of covenants entered into after May 2000, it is possible that a wider range of persons might be regarded as having the benefit of a covenant as a result of the Contracts (Rights of Third Parties) Act 1999. As we have seen[3], under this Act a party may sue on a covenant either where it is expressly provided that he can, or where the covenant purports to confer a benefit on him. However, the 1999 Act can be expressly excluded and the signs are that, in the property context, this practice is widespread with the result that it is not as yet having much of an impact.

1   See para 14.8 above.
2   *White v Bijou Mansions Ltd*   [1937] 3 All ER 269.
3   See ch 14.

The running of the burden

Positive covenants

34.4   Where the parties are not in the relationship of landlord and tenant, the burden of a covenant does not run with the land at common law.[1] Since, as we shall see, equity allows the burden of restrictive (negative) covenants to run with the land of the covenantor, the practical effect of the common law rule is that the burden of positive covenants will not run with freehold land. This rule, 'the greatest and clearest deficiency' in the law of covenants,[2] is of considerable significance since it means that covenants which impose positive obligations, such as to keep premises in repair, to erect boundary walls, and to contribute to the maintenance of roads, cannot be enforced against successors of the original covenantor. Despite the criticisms of the rule, the House of Lords has recently declined to overrule it in *Rhone v Stephens*,[3] expressing the view that such a significant departure from long-established principles should be implemented by legislation rather than by judicial decision.[4]

An inability to ensure compliance with positive obligations to repair or to contribute to the cost of maintenance and other services is a grave disadvantage in the case of certain types of property such as a block of flats, an estate with common facilities or a commercial building in multiple occupation. Indeed, the rule has, in the words of the Law Commission,[5] cast a blight on developments of freehold flats which for this reason (among others) are not considered to be a particularly good security for a mortgage. It has therefore become the usual practice for units within buildings in multiple occupation (such as blocks of flats) and estates with shared facilities to be sold on long leases, thus ensuring that positive covenants are enforceable[6]. However, over the years, long leasehold ownership has become very unpopular and after lengthy political pressure, things are set to change.

1   *Austerberry v Oldham Corpn* (1885) 29 Ch D 750, CA, approved *Rhone v Stephens* [1994] 2 All ER 65, HL. Section 33 of the Local Government (Miscellaneous Provisions) Act 1982 provides that local authorities may enforce positive covenants made by deed against successors of the covenantor.
2   Law Commission Report on the Law of Positive and Restrictive Covenants; Law Com No 127.
3   [1994] 2 All ER 65, HL.
4   For a discussion of proposals for reform see para 34.45 below.
5   Law Com No 127.
6   On the principles expounded in paras 37.52 – 37.67 below.

Commonhold

34.5   It is the difficulties over the enforcement of positive covenants which have helped to provoke the eventual implementation of a new type of land holding – commonhold – designed to facilitate the freehold ownership of flats in particular. The commonhold provisions of the Commonhold and Leasehold Reform Act 2002[1] are unlikely to come into operation before 2004 and when they do will, in practice, apply only to new buildings. However, once in place, it will be possible to register a scheme as a 'commonhold'. Individual units therein (eg flats) will be owned freehold, but the common parts will be owned by the commonhold association (which is made up of the unit owners). That association is to be responsible for the maintenance of the common parts and for major expenditure; the positive obligation to contribute to the cost of such work will be enforceable against the original unit holders and anyone to whom they sell their unit. In this way, albeit without any general reform of the law on positive covenants[2], it will be possible for positive obligations to bind future owners of units within a commonhold.

1   Contained in Part I of the Act; see para 29.35 above.
2   As to which see para 34.45 below.

Devices to achieve the enforcement of positive covenants

34.6   Not surprisingly, legal ingenuity has sought to devise methods of achieving the enforcement of positive obligations against successive freehold owners without transgressing the rule preventing the enforcement of positive covenants against successors of the covenantor. However, as the Law Commission has pointed out,[1] none of the devices used to achieve enforcement of positive obligations can be said to provide an effective general solution to the problem. However, since they are to some extent encountered in practice, we give a brief summary of them in the following paragraphs. It should be appreciated that, while some of these could be useful in enabling a developer or management company to enforce positive obligations against successive residents of a housing estate or block of flats, they do not enable the individual residents to enforce such obligations against each other.

1   Law Com No 127.

34.7   *Chain of indemnity covenants*   By virtue of the LPA 1925, s 79, unless a contrary intention is expressed, a covenantor covenants that both he *and* subsequent owners will abide by the covenant. Should a subsequent owner fail to do so, the covenantee may sue the original covenantor for breach of contract. The covenantor (and each successive owner) should therefore ensure that purchasers from him undertake to indemnify him in the event of his being sued for their non-performance of an obligation. Such a chain of indemnity provides an indirect method of enforcing covenants, but like all chains it is only as strong as its weakest link.

34.8 *Rights of entry* A right of entry may be used to secure compliance with positive covenants even though the covenants themselves are not enforceable as such.[1] A person having a right of entry has the right to enter property should certain conditions occur and take possession of it, thereby ending the interest of the person holding the land. For example, a vendor of property might insert in the conveyance a covenant requiring the purchaser and his successors to keep the property in repair and reserve to himself a right of entry should the property fall into disrepair. The threat that this right will be exercised will ensure that the purchaser and his successors comply with a positive covenant to repair. However, such a right of entry suffers two disadvantages: first, it is equitable, and must, therefore, be positively protected by the entry of a notice in the Land Register.[2] Second, it is subject to the rule against perpetuities; that is, there is a limit to how far in the future the right may be exercised. To overcome these two disadvantages, it should be annexed to, ie incorporated with, an estate rentcharge, which we discuss in the next paragraph.

1   *Shiloh Spinners Ltd v Harding* [1973] 1 All ER 90, HL.
2   See para 36.32 below.

34.9 *Estate rentcharges* A rentcharge is any annual or other periodic sum charged on or issuing out of land, except rent reserved by a lease or tenancy or any sum payable by way of interest.[1] If it is perpetual or for a term of years it is a legal interest.[2] The Rentcharges Act 1977 prohibits the creation of rentcharges for the future, subject to the important exception of the estate rentcharge.

An estate rentcharge may be of two kinds. The first is one created for the purpose of making positive covenants enforceable by the person to whom the rentcharge is paid (the rent owner) against the owner for the time being of the land. Such a rentcharge must not be of more than a nominal amount.[3] This kind of estate rentcharge achieves its object of making positive covenants enforceable against successive landowners by having a right of entry annexed to it. A right of entry annexed to a rentcharge is a legal interest and is not subject to the rule against perpetuities.[4] Essentially, annexing a right of entry to this kind of estate rentcharge cures it of the defects which it suffers when not so annexed. Nonetheless, the remedy remains 'clumsy and draconian' and although the device of the estate rentcharge comes closest to providing a solution to the unenforceability of positive covenants, it is undoubtedly artificial and technical in the extreme.[5]

The Rentcharges Act 1977 also provides for a second kind of estate rentcharge, defined as one created for the purpose of meeting, or contributing towards, the cost of the performance by the rent owner of covenants for the provision of services, or for the carrying out of maintenance or repairs, or for the effecting of insurance or the making of any payment by him for the benefit of the land affected by the rentcharge. Such a rentcharge must be reasonable in relation to the cost to the rent owner of performing the covenant.[6] Examples of this kind of rentcharge are where the developer of a housing estate reserves to himself a rentcharge from each purchaser to provide him with a fund to maintain the estate roads until adoption by the local authority; or where the management company of a block of flats reserves a rentcharge in respect of each flat to provide a fund for the maintenance of the common parts.

1   Rentcharges Act 1977, s 1. A legal rentcharge created out of registered land is noted together with the right of entry in the Charges Register of the landowner's register of title, and the rent owner may be substantively registered as the proprietor of a rentcharge LRA, s 27(2)(e), Sch 2, para 7

2 LPA 1925, s 1(2).
3 Rentcharges Act 1977, s 2.
4 LPA, ss 1(2) and 4(3).
5 Law Commission Report on the Law of Positive and Restrictive Covenants; Law Com No 127.
6 Rentcharges Act 1977, s 2.

34.10 *Doctrine of benefit and burden*   Another possible method of securing the enforcement of positive obligations against successive landowners is the doctrine of benefit and burden elaborated in the case of *Halsall v Brizell*.[1] Here, the developers of a private housing estate imposed a covenant on each purchaser, under which the latter covenanted to contribute towards the cost of maintaining the roads and footpaths of the estate, which were retained by the developer. Upjohn J held that as this covenant was positive it could not be enforced as such against successors of the original purchasers. However, by applying the doctrine that a person who takes the benefit of a deed is bound by any conditions in it, he held that if successors of the original purchasers wished to take advantage of the benefit of the roads and footpaths, which, of course, they had to do, they must also accept the burden of paying for their maintenance. It has recently been made clear that this doctrine does not mean that *any* condition can be rendered enforceable by attaching it to a right; the condition must be relevant to the right.[2] Furthermore, it is clear that the subsequent purchasers must have a real option to decline to take the benefit and thereby escape the burden[3]. This doctrine is, therefore, only of utility where the obligation is linked to a corresponding benefit of which the successors wish to take advantage.

1   [1957] 1 All ER 371; para 31.18 above.
2   *Rhone v Stephens* [1994] 2 All ER 65, HL.
3   *Thamesmead Town Ltd v Allotey* [1998] 3 EGLR 97, CA.

Restrictive covenants

34.11   The particular contribution of equity, originating in the case of *Tulk v Moxhay*,[1] is to allow the burden of restrictive covenants, those which restrict the uses to which the land may be put, to run with the land. Consequently, although a vendor may not ensure that successors of his purchaser act positively in relation to the land, he may ensure that they refrain from acting in particular ways: he may, for example, restrict building on the land or the carrying on of any trade. Equity will allow the burden of a covenant to run with the land of the covenantor if:

* it is essentially negative;
* the covenantee retains land capable of being benefited by the covenant;
* the parties intend that the covenant should run with the land; and
* the requirements of registration or of the doctrine of notice are complied with.

Each of these will now be considered in turn.

1   (1848) 18 LJ Ch 83.

The covenant must be essentially negative

34.12   The essence of the covenant, whether positively or negatively worded, must be negative or restrictive. The case of *Tulk v Moxhay*[1] provides an example. Tulk owned Leicester Square. He sold off the gardens in the centre and retained the surrounding land. The purchaser of the gardens covenanted that 'his heirs and assigns… would… at all times… keep and maintain the said piece of ground… in an open state'. This covenant was held to be binding on a successor of the purchaser. Although the covenant was phrased in terms of a positive obligation, 'keep and maintain in an open state', it was essentially negative, prohibiting building on the land. Conversely, a covenant 'not to let the premises fall into disrepair' is a positive covenant since the covenantor must take positive steps to carry out repairs.

Why did equity confine its intervention to negative covenants? As we have seen,[2] equity does not override a common law rule, thus it could not compel positive compliance with a contractual obligation entered into by the current owner's predecessor. However, the court of equity could take the view that, where land is sold subject to a *restriction*, this means that the purchaser, and anyone who subsequently purchases the land with notice of that restriction, simply never acquires that right to use the land which he would otherwise have had.[3] If he tries to act in a way which contravenes the restriction, equity can restrain him by the issue of an injunction, a remedy which is particularly suitable for the enforcement of negative obligations, on the basis that he has no right to do so.

1   (1848) 18 LJ Ch 83.
2   Para 1.6 above.
3   See *Rhone v Stephens* [1994] 2 All ER 65 at p 68.

The covenantee must retain land capable of being benefited

34.13   The requirement that the covenant must have been imposed for the benefit of land retained by the covenantee is effectively the same as that   in the law relating to easements, for there to be dominant land which is benefited by the easement.[1] It means that restrictive covenants are only enforceable as between neighbouring landowners. The rule was established in *LCC v Allen*,[2] where a developer covenanted with the London County Council (LCC) not to build on a plot which lay across the end of a proposed street. It was held that the LCC could not enforce this covenant against a successor of the developer since at no time did the council have any interest in any land capable of being benefited by the covenant.

It has been held that the reversion on a lease gives the landlord a sufficient retained interest in the land to enable him to enforce against a sub-tenant a restrictive covenant made by the tenant and contained in the head-lease.[3] Such a covenant may be enforced by the landlord against a sub-tenant having notice of it, despite the absence of a contract or privity of estate between a landlord and sub-tenant. A mortgagee's (lender's) interest has also been held sufficient to enable him to enforce restrictive covenants against successors of the mortgagor/covenantor.[4]

The courts will readily assume that the retained land is capable of being benefited by the covenant unless the defendant can show that the restriction cannot reasonably be said to be of value to the land.[5] Furthermore, the courts have been prepared to hold that a covenant restraining a purchaser from carrying on a business which competes with that carried on by the vendor on his retained land benefits the vendor's land. Both these points are illustrated in *Newton Abbot Co-operative Society Ltd v Williamson and Treadgold Ltd*[6] where a covenant imposed by the vendor prohibiting dealing in articles of ironmongery in the property sold was held to benefit the vendor's retained ironmonger's shop. Upjohn J stressed the enhanced price the vendor would realise on selling together the land and the business, as a result of the covenant.

There are some circumstances in which the requirement that the covenantee must retain land which is benefited by the covenant is manifestly inconvenient. For this reason statute expressly permits local authorities, local planning authorities, the National Trust and the Nature Conservancy Council to enforce restrictive covenants despite the absence of any retained land.[7]

1   Paras 33.5 above.
2   [1914] 3 KB 642, CA.
3   *Hall v Ewin* (1887) 37 Ch D 74.
4   See *Regent Oil Co Ltd v J A Gregory (Hatch End) Ltd* [1965] 3 All ER 673, CA.
5   *Wrotham Park Estate Co v Parkside Homes Ltd* [1974] 2 All ER 321. Contrast *Re Ballard's Conveyance* [1937] 2 All ER 691.
6   [1952] 1 All ER 279.

7   See Housing Act 1985, s 609, Town and Country Planning Act 1990, s 106(3), National Trust Act 1937, s 8 and Countryside Act 1968, s 15(4).

The parties must intend that the covenant should run

34.14   By the LPA 1925, s 79, which applies unless a contrary intention is expressed,[1] the parties are assumed to intend that the covenant should run with the land, rather than being merely personal to the parties.

1   See *Re Royal Victoria Pavilion, Ramsgate* [1961] 3 All ER 83.

Registration and notice

34.15   In the case of registered land, the covenant must be protected by the entry of a notice in the Charges Register of the burdened land in order to bind the land of the covenantor.[1] The details of the covenant are set out in full on the register of the burdened land. It should be noted that a restrictive covenant entered into between landlord and tenant cannot be registered[2]. Consequently, enforcement of such a covenant by the landlord against a *sub-tenant* depends on whether or not the title of the headlease is registered. If it is, the covenant is automatically binding[3]. Where it is only title to the sub-lease which is registered, the doctrine of notice would appear to dictate whether or not restrictive covenants in the (unregistered) headlease bind the sub-tenant.[4]

1   LRA, s 29(2); para 36.32 below.
2   LRA, s 33(c).
3   LRA, s 29(2)(b).
4   In such circumstances the sub-lessee could only have been accorded a good leasehold title which does not guarantee that his landlord had the right to grant the lease free from incumbrances; see para 30.39 above and LRA, s 12(6).

The running of the benefit

34.16   As with the running of the burden, there are certain divergences between the rules of common law and of equity on this topic. To the extent that equitable rules differ from common law rules, they apply only to restrictive covenants. For our purposes therefore it is appropriate to retain the division of the subject matter into positive and restrictive covenants.

Positive covenants

34.17   At common law the benefit of a covenant will run with the land to a successor of the original covenantee if it is annexed to the land, that is incorporated with it so that on a transfer of the land the benefit automatically passes without the need for any mention being made of it. A covenant will be annexed and the benefit will run where the conditions set out in the following paragraphs are met.

The covenant must touch and concern the land of the covenantee

34.18   The covenant must either affect the way in which the land is occupied or it must be such that in itself, and not merely as a result of collateral circumstances, it affects the value of the land.[1]

In *Smith and Snipes Hall Farm Ltd v River Douglas Catchment Board*,[2] the Catchment Board covenanted with the owner of the land adjoining a brook that the Board would maintain the banks of the brook. The Court held that the covenant touched and concerned the adjoining land, in that it affected the value of the land by converting it from flooded meadows to land suitable for agriculture.

A difficulty can arise where the benefited land is large, with the result that it may successfully be argued that the whole of that land cannot be benefited from the imposition of a covenant relating to land which adjoins only part.[3] While it is possible to prove that the whole of a very large property does in fact benefit from the covenant,[4] the problem can be avoided altogether by the inclusion of an express provision that the covenant is imposed for the benefit of 'all or any part of' the covenantee's land.[5]

1   Rogers v Hosegood [1900] 2 Ch 388 at 395; see also P & A Swift Investments v Combined English Stores Group plc [1988] 2 All ER 885, HL.
2   [1949] 2 All ER 179, CA.
3   As in Re Ballard's Conveyance [1937] Ch 473.
4   Marten v Flight Refuelling Ltd [1962] Ch 115.
5   Marquess of Zetland v Driver [1938] 2 All ER 158, CA.

It was intended that the benefit should run

34.19   In the *River Douglas Catchment Board* case, the Court of Appeal held that it was plain from the language of the covenant, under which the Board undertook to maintain the banks of the brook 'for all time', that it was intended to take effect for the benefit of successive owners of the land. While in this case evidence of intention was sought and found in the language of the document creating the covenant, we shall explain in para 34.26 below that this may no longer be necessary.

The land to be benefited should be identifiable

34.20   In the *River Douglas Catchment Board* case, the document creating the covenant referred only to 'certain land situate between the Leeds and Liverpool Canal and the River Douglas and adjoining the Eller Brook'. This was, however, regarded as sufficient; extrinsic evidence was admissible to prove the precise extent and situation of the relevant land.

The successor must acquire a legal estate

34.21   The common law used to require that the person seeking to enforce the covenant should have the same legal estate as the original covenantee. However, in *Smith and Snipes Hall Farm Ltd v River Douglas Catchment Board*, the Court of Appeal held that the covenant could be enforced against the Board not only by Smith who purchased the freehold from the original covenantee, but also by Snipes Hall Farm Ltd to whom Smith had leased the land. The Court held that the LPA 1925, s 78 permits the benefit of a covenant to run to lessees and sub-lessees as well as to successors of the covenantee's legal estate. A further, more radical effect, of s 78 is considered in para 34.26, below.

It should be noted that it is not necessary that the covenant should have any connection with the land of the covenantor.

Restrictive covenants

34.22   As with the common law rules, the first requirement of the equitable rules, which apply to restrictive covenants, is that the covenant should touch and concern the land of the covenantee; this has already been discussed.[1] A successor in title of the original covenantee must then go on to show that the benefit has passed to him either:

- by annexation, or
- by assignment, or
- under a scheme of development.

1   See para 34.18 above.

Annexation

34.23   We have already considered the common law rules on annexation. In practice these are rarely encountered for the very good reason that they apply only where the burdened land has not yet changed hands. Once that has occurred, the assistance of equity must be sought for both the running of the burden and the running of the benefit. In truth, the equitable rules as to annexation are almost certainly a more fully developed version of the common law rules.

34.24 *Annexation by express words* Where a positive obligation is imposed, it is often clear from the circumstances that it is intended to benefit particular identifiable land. This is not always the case with obligations imposed by restrictive covenants. The original approach was, therefore, that in order to annex the benefit of a restrictive covenant in equity express wording must be used which clearly identifies the land and indicates the parties' intention that the covenant is for the benefit of that land; that is, words which demonstrate either that the covenant has been entered into for the benefit of identifiable land or that it was made with the covenantee in his capacity as owner of that land[1]. As we shall see in the following paragraphs, it is now clear that it is not essential to use express words of annexation. Nevertheless, it is good conveyancing practice to put the matter beyond argument by formulating a restrictive covenant in a way which does itself achieve annexation[2].

It is also desirable for the wording to make clear that the covenant is intended to benefit *each and every part* of the covenantee's property. This serves two purposes. First, as we have seen, it ensures that, where the land to be benefited is unusually large, there will be no argument over the question of whether the land is in fact benefited.[3] Second, it also means that, as well as the benefit of the covenant passing by annexation to subsequent owners of the *entire* benefited land, it will, if the benefited land is divided up rather than remaining as an entity, pass also to the purchasers of *those parts*. However, where the wording of the covenant is unclear, the courts will now presume that annexation is to each and every part; hence if it is intended that the benefit of the covenant should pass only to successors to the whole of the benefited land this needs to be made explicit[4].

1 *Renals v Cowlishaw* (1878) 9 Ch D 125; *Reid v Bickerstaff* [1909] 2 Ch 305.
2 *Rogers v Hosegood* [1900] 2 Ch 388, CA.
3 See *Marquess of Zetland v Driver* [1938] 2 All ER 158, CA and para 34.18 above.
4 *Federated Homes Ltd v Mill Lodge Properties Ltd* [1980] 1 All ER 371, CA.

34.25 *Annexation by implication* However desirable, it is clear that the use of express words is not essential to bring about the annexation of the benefit of a covenant. It is a question of construction of the particular covenant. There is authority that annexation can be implied where, from the document creating the covenant, the land intended to be benefited and an intention to benefit the land can be clearly established.[1] As we have explained, these two matters, together with evidence that the covenant touches and concerns the land, themselves establish annexation.

1 *Marten v Flight Refuelling* Ltd [1962] Ch 115; *Shropshire County Council v Edwards* (1982) 46 P & CR 270; *J Sainsbury plc v London Borough of Enfield* [1989] 2 All ER 817.

34.26 *Annexation under LPA 1925, s 78* A more important erosion of any requirement for express wording is the ruling by the Court of Appeal in *Federated Homes Ltd v Mill Lodge Properties Ltd*[1] that the LPA 1925, s 78 can cause the benefit of a covenant to be annexed, and hence to run with the land.

Section 78 provides that a covenant relating to any land of the covenantee shall be deemed to be made with the covenantee and his successors in title, including the owners and occupiers for the time being of the land of the covenantee intended to be benefited, and the persons deriving title under him or them, and shall have effect as if such successors and other persons were expressed.

Prior to the *Federated Homes* case, s 78 was regarded, like its mirror provision s 79, as merely a word saving provision with no substantive effect.[2] However, this view was rejected by the Court of Appeal which held that s 78 operates to annex the benefit of any post-

1925 covenant which touches and concerns (ie 'relates to') the land of the covenantee. It seems that it is not necessary for the covenant to express any positive intention that the benefit should run and it may not even be necessary for the covenant itself to identify the benefited land.[3] However, where the covenant makes it clear that there is no intention for the covenant to run, as where it provides that it should not take effect for the benefit of successors unless the benefit is expressly assigned to them, s 78 does not cause the benefit to be annexed.[4]

Although the decision in *Federated Homes* has been heavily criticised, it has now remained unchallenged for over twenty years. It radically simplifies the law relating to annexation which is of considerable assistance both to students learning the law and to those claiming the benefit of covenants. However, this simplification has its disadvantages; it is now much more difficult than hitherto for those ostensibly subject to the burden of covenants to escape liability on the grounds that there was no adequate annexation and thus no-one entitled to enforce the covenant.

1   [1980] 1 All ER 371, CA.
2   A view which still prevails in relation to s 79; see *Tophams Ltd v Sefton* [1967] 1 AC 50, HL; *Rhone v Stephens* [1994] 2 All ER 65, HL.
3   The answer to this important question is left unclear in the judgment of Brightman LJ and was not alluded to at all by Megaw LJ who delivered the only other judgment.
4   *Roake v Chadha* [1983] 3 All ER 503.

Assignment
34.27   The traditional view of the law was that if the benefit of a covenant was not originally annexed to the land by the use of appropriate wording, it was necessary for a successor of the covenantee to show that the benefit of it had been separately expressly assigned to him at the same time as the land was transferred to him. However, as we explained in the preceding paragraphs, it now appears to be the law that annexation may either be implied or be brought about by the LPA 1925, s 78. Thus the circumstances in which it will be necessary to resort to the law of assignment are limited. However, where there is no express or implied annexation of a pre-1926 covenant, assignment must be considered,[1] likewise where, as in *Roake v Chadha*,[2] annexation is expressly excluded.

Briefly, the rules as to the assignment of the benefit of a covenant are as follows. The assignment of the benefit of the covenant must be contemporaneous with the assignment of the land; once the covenantee has transferred the land he can no longer enforce the covenant[3] and he thus has no enforceable covenant to assign.[4] To be capable of assignment, a covenant must have been taken for the benefit of ascertainable land which is capable of being benefited by it. The existence and situation of the land to be benefited need not – and, since assignment is being resorted to in the absence of annexation, usually will not – be indicated in the terms of the covenant itself but it is sufficient that, on a broad and reasonable view, it can otherwise be shown with reasonable certainty.[5] The benefit of an assignable covenant may be assigned separately and at different times with parts of the benefited land.[6]

1   *J Sainsbury plc v London Borough of Enfield* [1989] 2 All ER 817.
2   [1983] 3 All ER 503; para 34.26 above.
3   *Chambers v Randall* [1923] 1 Ch 149.
4   *Re Union of London and Smith's Bank Ltd's Conveyance, Miles v Easter* [1933] Ch 611, CA.
5   *Marten v Flight Refuelling Ltd* [1961] 2 All ER 696.
6   *Chambers v Randall* [1923] 1 Ch 149.

Scheme of development
34.28   Where a developer wishes to impose a set of mutually enforceable restrictions on a number of plots of land, the rules of annexation and assignment cannot achieve the desired result. This can be illustrated by the following example:

Plot 1	Plot 2	Plot 3	Plot 4
A	B	C	D

Elm Avenue

Plot 5	Plot 6	Plot 7	Plot 8

When the developer sells Plot 1 to A, subject to a number of restrictive covenants, the benefit of those covenants can be annexed to, or assigned with, the developer's retained land (ie Plots 2, 3 and 4); when Plot 2 is sold to B, subject to the same restrictions, these can only be annexed to, or assigned with the developer's retained land (ie Plots 3 and 4); the benefit of restrictions imposed on Plot 3 (sold to C) can only be for the benefit of Plot 4 and, by the time Plot 4 is sold to D, there is no longer any retained land to benefit. Hence it can be see that annexation and assignment do not allow the land of earlier purchasers to benefit from covenants imposed on land purchased later. So, in our example the restrictions imposed on A's land can be enforced by B, C and D, those imposed on B's land by C and D but not A, those on C's land by D but not A and B, and so on. This pattern would be extended by the sale of plots 5 to 8.

For this reason the rules relating to schemes of development were devised. A scheme of development exists where a landowner has disposed of his land in parcels, imposing, on each transfer of a parcel of land, restrictive covenants intended not simply for his advantage as owner of the land but for the advantage of each parcel purchased. Such schemes may be imposed to maintain the character of an area such as a housing estate. The scheme of covenants gives rise to what is in effect a local 'planning' law for the area of land disposed of, which is based on *reciprocal* rights and obligations.[1] However, the use of a scheme of development secures only the passing of the benefit of the covenants; in order to achieve the necessary reciprocity, it is essential that the restrictive covenants be properly registered[2] in order to ensure that they are mutually *binding*. If this is not done the whole scheme may collapse. As soon as the original vendor sells the first parcel of land, the scheme crystallises, and all the land within the area of the scheme (there must be a clearly defined area[3]) is bound, becoming subject to the 'local law'.[4]

Species of scheme of development which may be encountered include the building scheme, designed to provide for and regulate building development, and the letting scheme, under which a common set of restrictions is imposed on leasehold interests whether in relation to flats in a particular block, or houses on an estate, or a group of commercial premises[5].

1   *Reid v Bickerstaff* [1909] 2 Ch 305 at 319, CA.
2   See Preston and Newsom *Restrictive Covenants Affecting Freehold Land* (7th edn, 1992). See para 34.26 below.
3   *Reid v Bickerstaff* [1909] 2 Ch 305, CA. The defined area of the scheme must be clear to both vendor and all the purchasers, see *Emile Elias & Co Ltd v Pine Groves Ltd* [1993] 1 WLR 305, PC.
4   *Brunner v Greenslade* [1970] 3 All ER 833.
5   In *Williams v Kiley* [2002] EWCA Civ 1645, [2003] 1 P & CR D 38 the principles of a letting scheme were, apparently for the first time, applied to a small arcade of shops. In this way the tenant of one shop was able to prevent the tenant of another breaching the user covenants in the lease in a way which competed with the claimant's business.

34.29   In the case of *Elliston v Reacher*,[1] Parker J laid down four requirements of a scheme of development:

- both claimant and defendant in the action to enforce the particular covenant must derive title from the same vendor;
- this vendor must have laid out his estate, or a defined part of it, for sale in lots, subject to restrictions which were intended to be imposed on all the lots, and which are consistent only with some general scheme of development;
- these restrictions must have been intended to be, and be, for the benefit of all the lots; and
- the lots must have been purchased from the common vendor on the basis that the restrictions to which they were subject were to take effect for the benefit of all the other lots. This is an important requirement.

More recent cases have shown that this list does not constitute an inflexible definition. For example, in *Baxter v Four Oaks Properties Ltd*,[2] the estate was not laid out in lots by the original vendor, rather he sold the land in parcels of whatever size the particular purchasers required. Nonetheless the area was held to be the subject of a scheme. In *Re Dolphin's Conveyance, Birmingham Corpn v Boden*,[3] the original owners of an estate, having sold off part in lots, gave the rest to their nephew who continued the process of selling the estate off in lots, imposing the same restrictions. Again, there was held to be a scheme of development, despite the absence of a common vendor. In these cases the intention to impose a scheme was evident in the conveyancing documents. Where such an intention is not evident, it is more necessary to consider whether Parker J's four requirements are complied with. Thus in *Emile Elias & Co Ltd v Pine Groves Ltd*,[4] where there was no evidence of a common intention to produce mutually enforceable covenants, the absence of a clearly defined area to which the alleged scheme applied and the lack of uniformity between the restrictions imposed on different plots, proved fatal to the existence of a scheme of development.

It must be remembered that a scheme of development is a scheme for the reciprocal enforcement of restrictive covenants and that for the burden to be enforceable restrictive covenants require protection by registration. Thus, every time a parcel is sold, the common vendor must have the covenants noted on the charges register of the purchaser's register of title,[5] as appropriate. Furthermore, since the nature of the scheme is such that the vendor is impliedly bound by the restrictions (even if he has not expressly covenanted), each purchaser should register the restrictions against the common vendor. Only if this is done can each purchaser enforce the restrictions against subsequent purchasers.

1   [1908] 2 Ch 374.
2   [1965] 1 All ER 906.
3   [1970] 2 All ER 664.
4   [1993] 1 WLR 305, PC.
5   Para 34.15 above and 36.32 below.

Remedies

34.30   The equitable remedy of an injunction is particularly suitable for enforcing negative obligations such as restrictive covenants. Such a remedy achieves exactly what the claimant normally desires, namely the cessation of the activity which breaches the covenant, as opposed to mere compensation. Indeed, equitable remedies are, in principle, the only remedies available for the enforcement of restrictive covenants against a successor of the original covenantor. However, in such cases, the court has a discretion to award damages, as an alternative to granting an injunction.[1] A 'good working rule' for deciding whether to grant damages instead of an injunction was put forward in *Shelfer v City of London Electric Lighting Co*.[2] According to this an injunction will be granted unless:

- the injury to the claimant's legal rights is small;
- it is capable of being estimated in terms of money;
- it can adequately be compensated for by a small payment; and
- it would be oppressive to the defendant to grant an injunction.

It should be noted that this is only a good working rule and the court always retains its discretion to refuse an injunction.[3] In practice such a refusal is increasingly likely where the claimant fails to take immediate legal steps to protect his rights, eg by seeking an interlocutory injunction to stop any building in breach of covenant. Where damages are awarded on a discretionary basis, as an alternative to an injunction, they can be based on the profit which has accrued to the defendant as a result of the breach of covenant.[4]

Nonetheless, in the majority of cases an injunction is the remedy which is sought and that which is granted. In appropriate cases, a mandatory injunction will be granted; for example requiring the demolition of a building, as in *Wakeham v Wood*,[5] where the defendant erected a house blocking the claimant's sea view in flagrant disregard of a covenant prohibiting him so doing.

In the event of a breach by an original covenantor, damages at common law will be available as of right; unlike damages awarded as an alternative to an injunction, these cannot be based on the profit which has been gained as a result of the breach; accordingly, in the absence of actual loss by the claimant, damages will only be nominal.[6] Where the breach is of a positive covenant damages will normally be the appropriate remedy, though specific performance may be granted in certain circumstances.[7] Where the breach is of a restrictive covenant the claimant will normally seek, and be granted, an injunction.

1   Supreme Court Act 1981, s 50.
2   [1891–4] All ER Rep 838.
3   See, for example, *Wrotham Park Estate Co v Parkside Homes Ltd* [1974] 2 All ER 321.
4   *Wrotham Park Estate Co v Parkside Homes Ltd* [1974] 2 All ER 321; *Surrey County Council v Bredero Homes Ltd* [1993] 3 All ER 705, CA; *Jaggard v Sawyer* [1995] 2 All ER 189, CA.
5   (1981) 43 P & CR 40, CA.
6   *Surrey County Council v Bredero Homes Ltd* [1993] 3 All ER 705, CA.
7   See, for example, *Jeune v Queens Cross Properties Ltd* [1973] 3 All ER 97.

Discharge of restrictive covenants

Development, planning law and restrictive covenants

34.31   Planning law and restrictive covenants exist side by side as a means of controlling development.[1] 'From the individual's point of view, control by private covenant has obvious advantages over planning control, in that it can cover matters of important detail with which a planning authority would not be concerned and the procedure of enforcement is available to a person who is entitled to the benefit of a covenant and is aggrieved by a breach, instead of depending on the planning authority's decision to act'.[2] In the words of a leading textbook on the subject, 'one thing that is abundantly plain is that there is no prospect whatever that restrictive covenants will become unnecessary and that their place will be taken by the planning laws. For planning standards are still too often below the standards imposed by restrictive covenants'.[3] Another point is that, as the Law Commission says,[4] certain changes of use and certain building operations to which a neighbour might reasonably object do not require planning permission. It is important to realise that the fact that an individual has planning permission for a particular project in no way permits or excuses the breach of a restrictive covenant burdening his land, though the grant of planning permission may be relevant, but far from decisive, in relation to an application to the Lands Tribunal for the modification or discharge of the covenant.[5] However, as we shall see,[6] where land is acquired for planning or other statutory purposes, a restrictive covenant will not be allowed to impede those purposes.

1   For an outline of the law of development control and its enforcement, see Chapter 40 below.
2   Law Commission, Report on Restrictive Covenants No 11, para 8.
3   Preston and Newsom *Restrictive Covenants Affecting Freehold Land* (7th edn, 1982).
4   Report on Positive and Restrictive Covenants, Law Com No 127.
5   *Re Martin's Application* [1989] 1 EGLR 193, CA; para 34.29 below.
6   See para 34.37 below.

34.32   A purchaser or would-be purchaser of land, discovering that the land is apparently subject to some long-standing restriction preventing intended development, may make an application to the Chancery Division for a declaration as to whether or not the land is, or would in any given event be, affected by the restriction; or as to the nature and extent of the restriction and whether it is enforceable and if so by whom.[1] Such a declaration, which will only be made after due publicity of the proceedings has been circulated to all nearby owners who might have the benefit of the covenant,[2] is conclusive; anyone not named in the declaration will lose the benefit of the covenant. It should be noted also that it is possible to take out a 'relatively inexpensive'[3] insurance policy against one's plans being thwarted by the enforcement of a restrictive covenant.

1   LPA 1925, s 84(2).
2   *Re Sunnyfield* [1932] 1 Ch 79; *Re Elm Avenue* [1984] 3 All ER 632.
3   Law Commission, Report on Positive and Restrictive Covenants, Law Com No 127.

34.33   There are various circumstances in which a person claiming the benefit of a restrictive covenant may be prevented from enforcing the covenant. At common law, there are four main possibilities:

•   a change in the character of the neighbourhood;
•   release of the covenant;
•   unity of ownership; and
•   acquisition for planning or statutory purposes.

Under statute, we consider applications to the Lands Tribunal to discharge or modify the covenant, and (briefly) applications under the Housing Act 1985.

Discharge at common law
Change in character of neighbourhood
34.34   In *Chatsworth Estates Co v Fewell*,[1] Fewell had opened a guest house contrary to a covenant that his house should be used as a private dwelling only. The estate company having the benefit of the covenant sought an injunction against him. Fewell claimed that the covenant was not enforceable on the ground that the character of the neighbourhood had completely changed since the covenant was made because some houses in the area were now used as guest houses, and some as schools. Farwell J rejected this argument holding that to succeed on this basis a defendant would have to show so complete a change in the character of the neighbourhood that there was no longer any value left in the covenant at all. This was clearly not so in this case.

1   [1931] 1 Ch 224.

Release of the covenant
34.35   Release may be express or implied. In *Chatsworth Estates Co v Fewell*, the defendant also argued that the estate company, by allowing others to open guest houses, etc had

impliedly released the benefit of the covenants. This, said Farwell J, was a matter of degree, to be decided in this case by reference to the question, 'have the claimants by their acts and omissions represented to the defendant that the covenants are no longer enforceable and that he is therefore entitled to use his house as a guest house?' Again, this was not so in this case.

Unity of ownership

34.36   If the burdened and benefited land come into the same ownership, any restrictive covenants are extinguished.[1] This follows from the fact that a person cannot have a third party right over his own land. Land subject to a scheme of development, however, forms an exception to this rule. Plots within the area of a scheme, which have fallen into common ownership, remain subject to the scheme and continue to do so if they are later sold off separately.[2] Thus, if the common vendor sells, subject to the scheme, a number of lots to a builder, who subsequently sells the lots to separate purchasers, the restrictions are enforceable between those purchasers even though their land had for a period been in common ownership.

1   Re Tiltwood, Sussex, Barrett v Bond [1978] 2 All ER 1091.
2   Texaco Antilles Ltd v Kernochan [1973] 2 All ER 118, PC; Brunner v Greenslade [1970] 3 All ER 833.

Acquisition for planning or statutory purposes

34.37   Where land is acquired by a local authority for planning purposes, restrictive covenants will not be allowed to impede the carrying out of works in accordance with planning permission,[1] whether these works are carried out by the local authority or by someone to whom the local authority has later transferred the land.[2] Equally, restrictive covenants will not be allowed to prevent the use of land acquired by other bodies for statutory purposes.[3] It matters not whether the acquisition was made under compulsory powers, or by agreement.[3] It is usual for the person entitled to the benefit of the restriction to be entitled to the payment of compensation.[4]

Technically, the covenant remains in existence; it is merely the right to enforce which is taken away. However, the covenant will still be enforced where it does not directly prevent the statutorily authorised use. So, where a covenant prevented the carrying out of building works to a hospital without prior approval, it was held that such approval must be sought. Only if that approval was actually refused would the statutory powers (to operate a hospital) be impeded and the right to further enforce the covenant be denied.[5]

1   Town and Country Planning Act 1990, s 233.
2   R v City of London Corpn, ex p Masters, Governors and Commonlity of the Mystery of the Barbers of London [1996] 2 EGLR 128.
3   Kirby v School Board of Harrogate [1896] 1 Ch 437.
4   Usually under the Compulsory Purchase Act 1965, s 10.
5   Cadogan v Royal Brompton Hospital National Health Trust [1996] 2 EGLR 115.

Application to the Lands Tribunal

34.38   Under the LPA 1925, s 84(1) the Lands Tribunal[1] has jurisdiction on certain grounds to discharge, wholly or partly, or to modify, restrictive covenants affecting freehold or leasehold land. In the case of leasehold land, the power is limited to where the term is of more than 40 years of which at least 25 years have expired.[2] The majority of applications made to the Tribunal under this section are to modify a covenant; for example, to enable the owner of the land affected to build at a higher density than that permitted in the covenant, or to carry out such projects as the conversion of a house into flats,[3] the building of a house in the garden of an existing house, or the erection of a public house. The fact that an applicant has planning permission for his intended development is in no way decisive of an application under s 84, although the Tribunal must take into account the development plan for the area and the pattern of grants and refusals of planning permission in the area.[4]

Provision is made for those having the benefit of the relevant covenant to lodge an objection to the application. If the applicant considers that any objector is not entitled to the benefit of the covenant the Tribunal may make a preliminary determination of the matter,[5] the onus being on the objector to prove his entitlement.[6]

There is no rule preventing the original covenantor making an application under s 84, nor preventing modification of a covenant which has only recently been imposed.[7] These are merely factors to be taken into account in the exercise of the Tribunal's discretion.

The Tribunal may, in modifying a covenant, add other reasonable restrictions which are acceptable to the applicant.[8]

The Tribunal may exercise its jurisdiction to discharge or modify a covenant on one or more of the grounds outlined in the following paragraphs.

1   Para 2.36 above.
2   LPA 1925, s 84(12).
3   See also para 34.44 below.
4   LPA 1925, s 84(1B).
5   LPA 1925, s 84(3A); Lands Tribunal Rules 1975, r 20.
6   Re Edis's Application (1972) 23 P & CR 421.
7   Ridley v Taylor [1965] 2 All ER 51, CA; Cresswell v Proctor [1968] 2 All ER 682, CA; Jones v Rhys-Jones (1974) 30 P & CR 451, CA.
8   LPA 1925, s 84(1C).

Obsolescence

34.39   A restrictive covenant may be modified or discharged on the basis that it ought to be deemed obsolete by reason of changes in the character of the property or the neighbourhood, or other material circumstances.[1]

In Re Truman, Hanbury, Buxton & Co Ltd's Application[2] the applicant brewers applied on this ground to have a covenant modified to permit the erection of a public-house. The covenant was imposed under a scheme to preserve the character of an estate as a residential area. On appeal from the Lands Tribunal, the Court of Appeal held that only when the original purpose of a covenant can no longer be achieved can it be said to be obsolete. In this case it would be necessary to show that what was intended to be a residential area had become a commercial area, which was not the case. Furthermore, it was clear that the object of the covenant was still capable of fulfilment since the Lands Tribunal had expressly found that the proposed development would injure the objectors.

1   LPA 1925, s 84(1)(a).
2   [1955] 3 All ER 559, CA.

Agreement

34.40   The second ground for modification or discharge is that the persons entitled to the benefit of the restriction have agreed either expressly or by implication, by their acts or omissions, to the discharge or modification.[1]

This ground is rarely relied on by an applicant at the outset for, if there is evidence of agreement to the discharge or modification, an application to the Tribunal is probably not worthwhile. However, an individual may amend his application to include this ground once it has become clear that those who are entitled to the benefit of the covenant have failed to object to the application or have withdrawn their objection. The application will then be granted, since the persons entitled to the benefit have shown by their acts or omissions that they agree to the proposals.[2]

1   LPA 1925, s 84(1)(b).
2   Re Dare's and Beck's Application (1974) 28 P & CR 354.

No injury
34.41 A restrictive covenant can be discharged or modified where this will not injure the persons entitled to the benefit of the restriction.[1] This ground has been described as a long-stop against frivolous or vexatious objections,[2] and is limited to cases where there is no merit in the objections.

1 LPA 1925, s 84(1)(c).
2 *Ridley v Taylor* [1965] 2 All ER 51 at 58.

Impedes reasonable use
34.42 The final and most widely used ground is where the restriction impedes some reasonable use of the land, and either:

• does not secure to persons entitled to the benefit of it any practical benefits of substantial value or advantage to them; or
• is contrary to the public interest;

provided that

• money will be an adequate compensation for the loss or disadvantage (if any) which any such person will suffer from the discharge or modification.[1]

The majority of successful applications are made on this ground. The leading case is *Re Bass Ltd's Application*.[2] The company wished to use a site, which was subject to a restriction limiting its use to dwelling-houses, as a loading area for articulated trucks. The site was zoned in the development plan for industrial use and planning permission had been granted. A large number of those having the benefit of the covenant, imposed under a scheme of development, objected. The Tribunal rejected the company's application, giving its decision in the form of answers to questions formulated by counsel. These have come to provide the usual approach to applications on this ground.

• *Is the proposed use which is impeded by the restriction reasonable?* This question is to be answered leaving aside for the moment the restrictions. Where planning permission has been granted it will be difficult to find the proposed use unreasonable.
• *Does impeding the proposed use secure practical benefits to the objectors?* The expression 'practical benefits' is very wide: the Tribunal is to consider the adverse effects of the applicant's proposal on a broad basis. Thus, in *Gilbert v Spoor*,[3] the preservation of a pleasant rural view enjoyed not from the benefited land but from a point a short distance away was held to be a practical benefit. The Tribunal in the *Bass* case answered this second question affirmatively, in view of the fact that the proposed development would give rise to increased noise, fumes, vibration, dirt and risk of accidents.
• *If yes, are the benefits of substantial value or advantage?* The Tribunal has stressed that the benefits are not to be assessed in terms only of financial value. In the *Bass* case the benefits were held to be of substantial advantage, as have been, in other cases, peace and quiet, an unobstructed view[4] and the advantage of not being overlooked.
• *Is impeding the proposed use contrary to the public interest?* Again, planning permission is relevant, but it must be remembered that planning permission does not necessarily imply that the proposed development is positively in the public interest. In the *Bass* case in view of the noise and amenity problem the development would cause, the economic interest of Bass Ltd could not be equated with the public interest. It is worth noting that the Tribunal has normally interpreted the requirement of public interest

strictly and has rejected claims that impeding particular development is contrary to the public interest because, for example, housing land is in short supply or government policy favours high density development.

- *If the restriction does not secure benefits of substantial value and/or the proposed use is not contrary to the public interest, would money be an adequate compensation?* This question was not relevant to the *Bass* case and so was not dealt with. It is clear that a restriction can be discharged or modified without the payment of any compensation where no loss or disadvantage is suffered.[5] By definition, even where a loss or disadvantage is suffered, the levels of compensation are likely to be modest since a restriction which secures substantial benefits will not be modified or discharged in the first place. Equally, there are cases where money is not adequate compensation, for example where the application is being opposed by a local authority acting in the interest of the local community.[6]

1   LPA 1925, s 84(1)(aa), (1A).
2   (1973) 26 P & CR 156.
3   [1982] 2 All ER 576, CA.
4   [1982] 2 All ER 576, CA.
5   See LPA 1925, s 84(1) and para 34.40 below.
6   *Re Martin's Application* [1989] 1 EGLR 193, but note *Re Willis' Application* [1997] 28 EG 137.

34.43   The Tribunal may order that the applicant pay to the objectors a sum by way of compensation intended either:

- to make up for any loss or disadvantage suffered in consequence of the discharge or modification of the restriction; or
- in an appropriate case to make up for any effect the restriction had, at the time when it was imposed, in reducing the price then received by the objector for the land affected by it.[1]

1   LPA 1925, s 84(1).

Housing Act 1985, s 610
34.44   Application may be made under this section to a county court to vary a restrictive covenant to enable a house to be converted into two or more dwellings. The applicant must either have planning permission for the proposed conversion or prove to the court that (owing to changes in the character of the neighbourhood) the house cannot readily be let as a single dwelling but could if converted. The court must give interested parties an opportunity of being heard, and may vary the covenant (subject to such conditions and on such terms as it thinks just).

Proposals for reform

34.45   In 1984 the Law Commission produced a report and draft legislation[1] aimed at comprehensive reform of the law of covenants. The mainspring of their report was the need to deal with the unsatisfactory state of the law concerning positive covenants,[2] but they were equally unhappy with the complex and uncertain law relating to restrictive covenants. Their proposal was to introduce for the future a new interest in land, the land obligation. However, in 1998 it was announced that the report will not be implemented.[3]

This does not mean that no change to the law is envisaged. As we have seen[4], in the context of buildings in multiple occupation and other discrete schemes, commonhold will provide a ready means of enforcing positive obligations. Furthermore, the Law Commission is currently in the process of conducting a review of the law on easements and analogous rights in which there may be a fresh look at the concept of the land obligation.

1   The Law of Positive and Restrictive Covenants (1984) Law Com No 127.
2   Para 34.4 above.
3   Press Notice, 19 March 1998.
4   Para 34.5 above.

Chapter 35

Mortgages

35.1 A mortgage of land is a transfer of an interest in the land as security for a debt. It enables the creditor, in the event of the debtor being unable or unwilling to pay off the debt, to enforce the debt against the land, usually by selling the land and recouping what he is owed. Mortgages are created most commonly where a building society or other institutional lender lends money towards the acquisition of either residential or commercial property. A mortgage may, however, be granted by a landowner to secure (ie as security for) a bank loan, or a loan from a finance company, or to secure a current account, as well as, in the commercial sphere, to secure a loan to finance the development of property or the expansion of a business. The creditor, the lender of the money to whom the mortgage is granted, is called the mortgagee, the debtor or borrower is called the mortgagor.

35.2 The law of mortgages is still heavily influenced by its historical development. This means that, in many respects, its provisions can appear artificial and out-dated. That said, the actual operation of the law, especially in respect to registered land (on which this chapter concentrates) works reasonably well; this is in no small part due to the intervention of equity which has done much to ensure that, despite appearances, mortgages retain their essential character as security for a loan.

In this chapter we consider:

- the ways in which mortgages of registered land can be created;
- the rights of the mortgagor;
- the mortgagee's remedies; and
- the order in which mortgages will be paid off where the security proves to be insufficient.

Creation of mortgages

Historical background

35.3 For several hundred years prior to the 1925 property legislation mortgages were created by the mortgagor (the borrower) transferring his ownership of the land to the mortgagee (the lender). Provided that the loan was repaid by the due date, the land would be re-transferred to the borrower; if not, the land would remain in the ownership of the lender subject, as we shall see, to the increasingly important equitable right to redeem[1]. Thus the form of the mortgage was not that of a mere security, but rather of a change of ownership.

In 1925 the creation of mortgages was modified by the LPA 1925. Mortgages by outright transfer could no longer be created. Henceforth they were to be created either by the grant of a 3000-year lease (which would automatically come to an end when the loan was repaid) or by means of a charge by way of legal mortgage. While the grant of a long lease might have been preferable to an outright transfer of ownership, it still conferred on the mortgagee very considerable ownership rights which distorted the nature of a mortgage as a security.

1   See para 35.8 below.

Modern mortgages
Legal mortgages
35.4   Today, mortgages of unregistered land are invariably created by way of a charge by way of legal mortgage. While this gives the mortgagee 'the same protection, powers and remedies' as if the mortgage had been created by long lease[1], it at least gives a more accurate impression of the mortgage as a security since the freehold remains vested in the mortgagor. Mortgages of registered land must now be created by legal charge[2]; in order to be legal the charge must be completed by registration which means that the mortgagee is entered in the register as proprietor of the charge[3]. A registered charge takes effect as a charge by way of legal mortgage[4]; this means that the mortgagee has the benefit of the legal remedies afforded to mortgagees by the LPA 1925[5]. In law, any number of mortgages can be created in respect of one property; in practice, the number of mortgages that can be created will be limited by the value of the property[6].

1   LPA 1925, s 87(1).
2   LRA, ss 23(1)(a), 27(2)(f).
3   LRA 1925, s 27, Sch 2 para 8.
4   LRA 1925, s 51.
5   Notably the statutory power of sale and the right to appoint a receiver; see paras 35.26 and 35.33 below.
6   For the order in which a series of mortgages are paid off, see para 35.40 below.

Informal mortgages
35.5   It is possible to create informal mortgages of registered land by way of an agreement to create a mortgage. Such an agreement falls within the Law of Property (Miscellaneous Provisions) Act 1989, s 2 and must therefore be made in writing and be signed by all parties[1]. Such a mortgage will not bind future purchasers of the land (including subsequent mortgagees) unless it is protected by the entry of a notice in the Land Register[2]. It is no longer possible to create an informal mortgage of registered land by way of a deposit of the Land Certificate[3].

1   See para 31.6 above.
2   LRA 2002, s 29(2); see para 36.32 below.
3   This used to be permitted under LRA 1925, s 66; this has not been repeated in LRA 2002.

Mortgagor's right to redeem (repay)

Commercial arrangements for repayment
35.6   Provisions in mortgages for the repayment of the debt, ie the principal sum borrowed plus interest and costs, vary considerably. In the traditional 'standing' mortgage, in relation to which the law of mortgages originally developed, the principal is repaid in a lump sum, although provision will normally be made for regular payments of interest in the interim. The modern endowment mortgage is a variety of this type of mortgage. Under this scheme,

the mortgagor makes regular monthly payments of interest to the mortgagee while at the same time paying premiums on an endowment assurance policy[1] which, on maturity (usually in 20–25 years), will provide a lump sum for the repayment of the principal. Today, the most common form of mortgage in the domestic market is the true instalment mortgage (sometimes somewhat misleadingly described as a 'repayment' mortgage) under which both the principal and interest is repayable in monthly instalments spread over a lengthy period – again, usually 20–25 years.

Traditionally, mortgage interest rates have been variable, with the result that mortgagees have been able to change their rate of interest during the course of the mortgage in order to keep pace with general interest rates. Thus, if interest rates rise, a mortgagor's liability can increase in an often unpredictable and dramatic fashion. Recently, there has been a move towards mortgage loans at fixed rates for the early part of the loan period; this provides mortgagors with a greater degree of certainty as to their liabilities. The Government is currently investigating the possibility of encouraging far greater use of fixed rate mortgages.

1   It is the poor stock market performance of such 'with profits' endowment policies that has led to the declining popularity of this type of mortgage.

The differing approaches of the common law and equity to repayment
Legal date of redemption
35.7   As we pointed out in para 35.3 above, prior to 1926 a legal mortgage of land was effected by an outright transfer of the mortgagor's estate to the mortgagee, subject to a provision for re-transfer on payment of the moneys due. The mortgage would provide that redemption (repayment) should take place on a fixed date. At common law, if the moneys due under the mortgage were not repaid on that date, there could be no re-transfer. Further, the mortgagor, despite having lost the right to have his land re-transferred, remained liable to repay the money he owed.

The equity of redemption and the equitable right to redeem
35.8   This harsh common law rule was radically limited by equity. In equity, despite an apparent transfer of ownership to the mortgagee, the essence of a mortgage was always seen to be simply the provision of security for a debt; if that was repaid the mortgagee's rights to the land should cease. Equity recognised that, despite having transferred the legal estate to the mortgagee, the mortgagor still had an interest in the land. This interest, known as his 'equity of redemption', is best described as the sum of the mortgagor's interest in the property. It can be represented in purely financial terms as the value of the mortgaged property minus the amount owing to the mortgagee. (So, if a house is worth £200,000 and there is an outstanding mortgage of £150,000, the mortgagor's equity of redemption is £50,000.) One of the vital rights attaching to the equity of redemption is the continuing right of the mortgagor to redeem the mortgage. Accordingly, even though the contractual (or legal) date for redemption had passed, the mortgagee would be compelled to re-transfer the land on payment of what was owed to him, ie the principal plus interest (and costs).

Once it was established that redemption was possible after the contractual date for repayment, that contractual date came to be fixed at a token date, conventionally six months from the date of the mortgage. This clearly did not affect the mortgagor's equitable right to redeem thereafter, but enabled him to redeem at that early date if he wished. The reason why the contractual provision for redemption was retained was because, once the legal date fixed for repayment has passed, the mortgage money is regarded as due and the mortgagee is thereafter in a position to exercise his remedies for non-payment[1].

This remains the situation, despite the fact that, today, a mortgage cannot be created by an outright transfer.[2] Although the mortgagor now retains the legal estate, he is nevertheless still regarded as also having an equity of redemption in respect of the land, giving him the right to redeem the mortgage despite the passing of the contractual date for redemption. In a standing mortgage and in certain instalment mortgages, an early date for redemption is still fixed, commonly at six months from the date of the mortgage. Neither party intends that the mortgage should be repaid at that date, the provision is inserted simply to bring into play the mortgagee's remedies, as the mortgage money is then due. In those instalment mortgages which do not provide for an early contractual date, it is usual for the parties to provide that the entire mortgage moneys become due should the mortgagor default in respect of one or two instalments.

Where the contractual date for redemption has passed, the mortgagor is entitled, subject to any express provision in the mortgage providing otherwise,[3] to redeem the mortgage by paying the principal plus interest on giving the mortgagee six months' notice or six months' interest in lieu of notice.[4]

1   Para 35.27 below.
2   Paras 35.3 and 35.4 above.
3   But see paras 35.10–35.12 below.
4   *Browne v Lockhart* (1840) 10 Sim 420; *Cromwell Property Investment Co Ltd v Western and Toovey* [1934] Ch 322.

Impediments to full redemption

35.9   Equity is careful to preserve the essential nature of a mortgage as a transaction involving the giving of security for a loan by protecting the mortgagor's equity of redemption. In particular, it requires that there should be 'no clogs or fetters on the equity of redemption', that is, that the mortgage should not contain terms which impede the ability of the mortgagor to redeem his property free of the conditions of the mortgage. We shall see that the case law in the following paragraphs establishes that the court will declare void any provision in a mortgage which either is inconsistent with the mortgagor's right to redeem his property unfettered by any term of the mortgage, or is unfair and unconscionable.

It should also be noted that, like any other contract, a mortgage transaction may be set aside on the basis of misrepresentation or undue influence. Many of the modern cases on this subject have involved mortgages, notably where a mortgagor has persuaded his spouse or co-habitee to participate in a mortgage; as we have seen, this may mean that the victim can have the mortgage set aside.[1]

1   Paras 12.48-12.52.

Provisions excluding redemption

35.10   It follows from what we said in the preceding paragraph that a provision excluding redemption in a mortgage granted by an individual[1] is of no effect.[2] Thus where the mortgage deed confers on the mortgagee an option to purchase[3] the mortgaged property, that provision is void[4] because, of course, at the option of the mortgagee, the mortgagor may be forced to sell his property and thus lose his opportunity to redeem. However, there is nothing to prevent the parties, by a separate transaction genuinely independent of the mortgage, agreeing that the mortgagee should have an option to purchase the property[5]. A subsequent variation of a mortgage under which the mortgagee is given an option to purchase will be viewed not as a separate arrangement but as part of the original transaction and the option will, therefore, be void.[6]

A provision will be regarded as excluding the right to redeem where this is its real effect. Thus, in *Fairclough v Swan Brewery Co Ltd,*[7] F mortgaged his 17½-year lease to the brewery, the mortgage containing a clause prohibiting redemption until six weeks before the expiry of the lease. This clause was held to be void since, for all practical purposes, it rendered the mortgage irredeemable.

1   Under the provisions of the Companies Act 1985, s 193, a company may create an irredeemable mortgage.
2   *Re Wells, Swinburne-Hanham v Howard* [1933] Ch 29 at 53.
3   Para 30.8 above.
4   *Samuel v Jarrah Timber and Wood Paving Corpn Ltd* [1904] AC 323, HL; *Lewis v Frank Love Ltd* [1961] 1 All ER 446.
5   *Reeve v Lisle* [1902] AC 461, HL.
6   *Jones v Morgan* [2001] EWCA Civ 995, [2002] 1 EGLR 125.
7   [1912] AC 565, PC.

Oppressive or unconscionable terms

35.11   Equity[1] has long regarded itself as having a broad jurisdiction to strike down any provision in a mortgage which impedes full redemption of the mortgaged property unfettered by the terms of the mortgage or which is unfair, oppressive or unconscionable. This is well illustrated by *Cityland and Property (Holdings) Ltd v Dabrah*[2] where the mortgage provided for the repayment by instalments over six years of a sum representing the capital sum advanced together with a premium of 57%. On the mortgagor's default, the court refused to permit the mortgagee to enforce payment of the stated sum, allowing him only the principal plus interest, which (in 1967) was fixed at what, in 1967, was a moderate 7%. In the circumstances, the provision for the payment of a premium was unconscionable, particularly as this was not a bargain between trading concerns but a case of house purchase by a mortgagor of limited means.

However, the limits of this general jurisdiction were explained in *Multiservice Bookbinding Ltd v Marden*.[3] Here the mortgage provided for the repayment by instalments of the capital sum plus interest at 2% above the bank rate payable on the whole sum throughout the term of the loan. Further, each instalment was subject to index-linking in the form of a 'Swiss franc uplift'; that is, the amount payable was then to be increased (or, theoretically, decreased) in proportion to the variation in the rate of exchange between the pound and the Swiss franc after September 1966. (Furthermore, the loan could not be called in, nor was the mortgage redeemable, for 10 years.) Browne Wilkinson J held that although the mortgage might be unreasonable this is not the relevant test; the question is whether any of the terms of the bargain are unfair and unconscionable which requires that the terms have been imposed in a morally reprehensible manner. In this case the parties were businessmen, who entered the agreement with their eyes open, with the benefit of independent legal advice and without any compelling necessity on the part of the company to accept the loan on these terms. The company was therefore bound to comply with the mortgage[4].

The general power to strike out unconscionable terms has been resorted to in two particular types of case which we consider in the following paragraphs.

1   We have seen that statute, in the form of the Unfair Terms in Consumer Contracts Regulations 1999, controls unfair terms in consumer contracts; see paras 12.58-12.63 above. These Regulations may impact on terms in residential mortgages but it should be noted that they do not allow a challenge to price (which includes interest).
2   [1967] 2 All ER 635.
3   [1978] 2 All ER 489.
4   A similar approach was adopted in *Jones v Morgan* [2001] EWCA Civ 995, [2002] 1 EGLR 125 where the court held that a mortgagor who had taken advice from his own solicitor could not escape 'unwise and improvident' mortgage terms by arguing that they were unconscionable.

35.12   *Provisions postponing redemption* We have seen that provisions which render a mortgage irredeemable will be struck out.[1] Terms which merely *postpone* the right to redeem are not automatically void; their validity depends on whether or not they are unfair or unconscionable. In *Knightsbridge Estates Trust Ltd v Byrne*,[2] the claimant company, wishing to pay off an existing debt, sought a loan of £310,000 from the friendly society of whom the defendants were trustees, at 5% interest repayable over 40 years. The society agreed and a mortgage was executed providing for repayment in half-yearly instalments over 40 years.

Five-and-a-half years later the claimant company brought an action claiming to be entitled to redeem the mortgage, on the basis that the postponement of redemption for 40 years was a clog on the right to redeem. The Court of Appeal rejected their claim, holding that equity is concerned to see only two things – one that the essential requirements of a mortgage transaction are observed and the other that oppressive or unconscionable terms are not enforced. Equity does not interfere with mortgage transactions merely because they are unreasonable, which, in any event, this transaction was not.

Most instalment mortgages of the traditional building society repayment variety, although providing for repayment over 20 or 25 years, do not prevent early redemption; however, they often insist upon a period of notice or the payment of interest instead. The recently introduced fixed rate interest mortgages do tend to prevent repayment of the mortgage within, say, 2–5 years; these provisions are designed to stop mortgagors moving to new providers should a better deal be offered and would not appear to be unreasonable.

1   Para 35.10 above.
2   [1938] 4 All ER 618, CA; affd on other grounds [1940] 2 All ER 401, HL.

35.13   *Provisions conferring collateral advantages*   The parties may by their agreement confer on the mortgagee some advantage additional to repayment of the principal plus interest plus costs. Where such an additional advantage, such as an option to purchase, renders the mortgage irredeemable, it is clearly void, unless contained in some separate and independent transaction.[1] More complex are those cases in which mortgages impose some type of commercial tie such as that the mortgagor should only buy, and sell on the premises, beer or petrol supplied by the mortgagee. Originally the courts took the view that such provisions would be valid if limited to the period of the mortgage;[2] if designed to continue beyond redemption they would be invalid because they would then fetter the right to full redemption. Thus, in *Noakes & Co Ltd v Rice*,[3] a provision in a mortgage tying the mortgaged leasehold property to the mortgagee brewery not only for the duration of the mortgage but for the duration of the entire lease, was held void, for its effect would have been to permit the mortgagor, who mortgaged a free house, to redeem only a tied house thus fettering his right to redeem.

However, it is clear that the courts have become uncomfortable at the prospect of interfering with the terms of a bargain entered into by business people, often with the assistance of professional advice. Accordingly, various devices have been used to retreat from the position where the enforceability of a collateral adavantage hinges entirely on the technicality of whether or not they last beyond redemption. As with provisions excluding the right to redeem, in some cases the court may be able to construe a provision contained in a mortgage deed which confers some additional advantage on the mortgagee as in fact being a separate transaction even though it is contained in the same deed.[4] In this way the advantage will not be struck down as being inconsistent with, or a clog on, the right to redeem. Thus, in *Kreglinger v New Patagonia Meat and Cold Storage Co Ltd*,[5] the mortgage between the claimant woolbroker and the defendant meat packers provided that for a period of five years, whether or not the loan was paid off earlier, the defendants would give the claimant the right to buy all sheepskins. The mortgage was redeemed after two years and the defendants disputed the claimant's right thereafter to the sheepskins. The House of Lords held that the claimant remained entitled to the skins. The grant of the right to purchase sheepskins was in substance independent of the mortgage.

However, certain of the judgments in the *Kreglinger* case went rather further, suggesting that, in any event, an advantage collateral to the security will not be held void unless it is:

•   unfair or unconscionable; or
•   in the nature of a penalty clogging the equity of redemption; or

• inconsistent with or repugnant to the contractual and equitable right to redeem.[6]

If this wider approach is accepted, the validity of a collateral advantage may now quite simply depend on whether or not it is unfair, oppressive or unconscionable, rather than on the period for which it is imposed.[7]

1   Para 35.10 above.
2   *Biggs v Hoddinott* [1898] 2 Ch 307, CA.
3   [1902] AC 24, HL.
4   *Kreglinger v New Patagonia Meat and Cold Storage Co Ltd* [1914] AC 25, HL; *Re Petrol Filling Station, Vauxhall Bridge Road, London, Rosemex Service Station Ltd v Shell Mex and BP Ltd* (1968) 20 P & CR 1.
5   [1914] AC 25, HL.
6   [1914] AC 25 at 61.
7   Subject to what is said in the following paragraph concerning the doctrine of unreasonable restraint of trade.

Restraint of trade

35.14   In *Esso Petroleum Co Ltd v Harper's Garage (Stourport) Ltd*[1] the House of Lords held that the restraint of trade doctrine, which we discuss in ch 13 above, applies to provisions in a mortgage. Thus collateral advantages contained in a mortgage, perhaps providing for a commercial tie, may not only be invalidated as preventing full redemption or as being unfair and unconscionable, but also as being in unreasonable restraint of trade.

1   [1967] 1 All ER 699, HL.

Consumer Credit Act 1974

35.15   Under ss 137 to 139 of this Act, power is conferred on the county court to 're-open extortionate credit bargains' and to 'do justice between the parties' in consequence. Thus any mortgage where the mortgagor is an individual may be re-opened if it provides for the mortgagor to make 'grossly exorbitant' repayments or if it otherwise grossly contravenes ordinary principles of fair dealing. In determining whether the agreement is extortionate, the court is to take into account only the statutory criteria, without regard to any general principles of unconscionability;[1] these include interest rates prevailing at the time the agreement was made, the age, experience and business capacity of the mortgagor and the extent to which he was under financial pressure. In reopening the agreement, the court may, among other things, alter its terms or set aside the whole or part of any obligation imposed by it.

The Act further regulates mortgages granted to secure loans not exceeding £25,000, other than loans by banks, building societies, local authorities and certain bodies (including insurance companies and friendly societies) specified in subordinate legislation. The provisions of the Act relating to such mortgages (which, notably, cover second mortgages to finance companies), include that which provides for the prospective mortgagor to be given an opportunity to withdraw from the transaction, those providing for the form and content of the agreement, that which prevents a higher rate of interest being charged on default, and particularly (and to be borne in mind in relation to the mortgagee's remedies) that providing that a mortgage regulated by the Act may only be enforced by order of the court.

1   See *Davies v Directloans Ltd* [1986] 2 All ER 783.

Mortgagee's remedies

Possession of the mortgaged property

35.16   Strictly speaking, the right to take possession of the mortgaged property is not a *remedy* of the mortgagee. This is because, as a matter of legal theory, which has little relation to practical reality, the mortgagee rather than the mortgagor, has the legal *right* to possession right from the outset of the mortgage. In the absence of agreement to the contrary, the mortgagee may go into possession before the ink is dry on the mortgage. He has this right because he has, in effect, a long lease of the property.[1] Thus the right of the mortgagee to possession has nothing to do with default on the part of the mortgagor and is not, therefore, properly described as a remedy. The rigour of this apparently harsh rule, that the mortgagee may have possession of the property at any time, is in fact mitigated in a number of respects; as a result, in practice, possession is almost invariably resorted to only as a remedy in the event of default and, even then, only as a preliminary step to an exercise of the power of sale, so that the sale may be made with vacant possession.

A legal mortgagee may take physical possession by peaceably entering on the property.[2] It is usual, however, in the case of a dwelling-house, to seek a possession order from a county court, requiring the delivery of vacant possession within a specified time. It is likely, but not absolutely certain, that possession of a dwelling-house can only be obtained by a court order.[3]

1   *Four-Maids Ltd v Dudley Marshall (Properties) Ltd* [1957] 2 All ER 35 at 36. See para 35.3 and 35.4 above.
2   For regulated credit agreements, see para 35.15 above.
3   A mortgagor who is in occupation of a dwelling may qualify for protection under the Protection from Eviction Act 1977, s 1. Furthermore, it has been suggested that, although the Administration of Justice Act 1970, s 36 (see para 35.23 below) does not explicitly require court proceedings to be taken in order to take possession of a dwelling, this requirement is implicit. Finally, anyone taking possession of premises, irrespective of their nature, needs to beware of falling foul of the Criminal Law Act 1977, s 6(1).

Restrictions on the mortgagee's right to possession
35.17   The mortgagee's right to possession may be restricted in a number of ways. It may be limited

- by an express provision in the mortgage;
- by an implied provision in the mortgage;
- (indirectly) by the obligation to account strictly while in possession;
- as a result of someone else's prior claim to possession; and
- (in the case of a dwelling) by the court.

Each of these will be examined in the following paragraphs.

Express restriction
35.18   The terms of the mortgage may expressly provide that the mortgagee may only go into possession in the event of default. This is increasingly the case in building society and similar mortgages.

Implied restriction
35.19   Although the legal mortgagee's right to possession should not be lightly treated as restricted,[1] the court may find that the mortgagee has by implication contracted out of his right to possession. In particular, the court will be ready to find an implied term that the mortgagor may remain in possession until default in an instalment mortgage. However, there must be something on which to hang such a conclusion other than the mere fact that it is an instalment mortgage;[2] this will be the case where, for example, the mortgage speaks of the mortgagee having the power to eject the mortgagor in the event of default.[3]

1   *Western Bank Ltd v Schindler* [1976] 2 All ER 393 at 396.
2   *Esso Petroleum Co Ltd v Alstonbridge Properties Ltd* [1975] 3 All ER 358.
3   *Birmingham Citizens Permanent Building Society v Caunt* [1962] 1 All ER 163.

Duty to account strictly

35.20   A mortgagee who goes into possession is liable to account *strictly* to the mortgagor. This goes well beyond a natural requirement that he must account for any income which he has actually received since taking possession; the duty to account *strictly* means that he is also liable to the mortgagor for money which he *ought* to have received. Thus, where a mortgagee in possession (a brewery) leased[1] the mortgaged premises (a public-house) on the basis that it was tied to the brewery, the mortgagee was held liable to account to the mortgagor not only for the rent actually received but also for the (higher) rent which would have been received had the property been let as a free rather than a tied house.[2] While this duty to account strictly does not directly restrict a mortgagee's right to possession, any mortgagee who would have taken possession in order to receive the income of the mortgaged property so as to cover unpaid instalments is very much better advised not to do so and instead to appoint a receiver, a remedy which we consider at para 35.41 below.

1   For powers of leasing, see para 35.37 below.
2   *White v City of London Brewery Co* (1889) 42 Ch D 237, CA.

The existence of a prior claim to possession

35.21   *Existing leases*   Where the mortgaged property is subject to a lease that was in existence prior[1] to the creation of the mortgage, this lease will normally bind the mortgagee[2] with the result that he will not be able to obtain physical possession of the property. The tenant cannot waive any statutory rights such as his protection under either the Rent Act 1977 or the Housing Act 1988[3]. The mortgagee can merely take legal possession by requiring the tenant of the mortgagor to pay rent to him[4].

1   For the position with regard to lease granted *after* the mortgage, see para 35.37 below.
2   An existing lease of registered land will bind a mortagee either because it will itself be registered with its own independent title and thus noted on the freehold title (leases of more than 7 years) or will usually rank as an 'overriding' interest under LRA, Sch 3, para 1 or para 2 (leases of 7 years or less); see para 36.22 below.
3   *Woolwich Building Society v Dickman* [1996] 3 All ER 204.
4   See *Davies v Law Mutual Building Society* (1971) 219 Estates Gazette 309, DC.

35.22   *The claims of implied co-owners* [1]   One of the most serious impediments to the mortgagee's right to possession can occur where, unknown to the mortgagee, there is someone occupying the property – usually a spouse or cohabitee – whom equity regards as a co-owner of the property with the mortgagor. The rights of that implied co-owner can bind the mortgagee. So, for example, in *Williams & Glyn's Bank Ltd v Boland*[2] a matrimonial home was in the sole name of the defendant; however his wife had contributed to the purchase and was therefore an implied co-owner in equity. He mortgaged the house to the claimant and then defaulted on the repayments. When the bank sought possession, the House of Lords held that the wife's equitable interest in the property was binding[3] on the bank and that it could not obtain possession against her.

Subsequent case law[4] has established that the courts will not normally regard the rights of an implied co-owner as having priority over a mortgagee where that co-owner knew that the mortgage was being obtained to *acquire* the property to which the co-owner has a claim. The mortgagee is also secure where the mortgage is granted by at least two legal co-owners of the property. The claims of any additional, implied, co-owners are not regarded as binding on the mortgagee because they are said to be 'overreached'[5].

Hence the mortgagee is only at risk in the case where a mortgage (often a second mortgage or a re-mortgage[6]) is created *after* the acquisition of the property. Here, it is vital that, prior to taking the mortgage, the mortgagee makes enquiries of any adult occupying the property in order to satisfy itself that such persons are not implied co-owners. If they are, the mortgagee will require them to agree that their rights will not take priority over the mortgage[7].

1   For implied co-ownership see para 32.12 above.
2   [1980] 2 All ER 408, HL.
3   As an 'overriding' interest; see para 36.28 below.
4   Bristol and West Building Society v Henning [1985] 2 All ER 606, CA; Abbey National Building Society v Cann [1990] 1 All ER 1085, HL. See para 36.24 below.
5   See City of London Building Society v Flegg [1987] 3 All ER 435, HL; see para 36.27 below.
6   A re-mortgage occurs where the mortgagor grants a replacement mortgage, the proceeds of which are used to repay and discharge the existing loan. This practice is becoming more widespread as lending institutions compete for business by offering more favourable terms to mortgagors who wish to change providers.
7   See para 36.26 below.

Restrictions on claims to possession of dwellings

35.23   The fact that a mortgagee's claim to possession is strictly a *right* rather than a *remedy* made it difficult for the courts to control the circumstances in which it was exercised. This was particularly important in the context of residential property where the consequence of a mortgagee taking possession is that the mortgagor loses his home. For this reason, in the 1970s, legislation was passed which gave the courts powers to ensure that mortgagees could not take possession where there was any chance that the mortgagor could repay his loan. The Administration of Justice Act 1970 applies where the mortgagee of a dwelling house is seeking possession. Section 36 provides that the court can adjourn the proceedings, or make an order but suspend its operation, or make an order postponing the date for possession, if it appears to the court that the mortgagor is likely within a reasonable period to pay any sums due under the mortgage or to remedy any other default under the mortgage.

35.24   *The problem of instalment mortgages* A problem which rapidly emerged out of the original drafting of s 36 concerned the usual provision in instalment mortgages that, in the event of default, the *entire sums* due under the mortgage become immediately payable. It was obviously not Parliament's intention to give the court the power to delay possession only where the mortgagor could pay off the *whole* mortgage debt within a reasonable period, but this was all the original section achieved.[1] The Administration of Justice Act 1973, s 8 seeks to alleviate the problem. This provides that in the case of instalment mortgages, or other mortgages providing for deferred payment of the principal, which contain such a default clause, the sums due under the mortgage are to be regarded, for the purposes of s 36, as being the arrears of instalments or deferred payments. In such cases the court may exercise its power to delay possession where it appears likely that within a reasonable period the mortgagor will pay the *instalments* owing and that he will keep up with the *instalments*.

Unfortunately, the wording of s 8 is far from ideal and litigation has been necessary to establish exactly what types of deferred payment mortgages fall within its ambit. It is now settled that the section applies to endowment mortgages,[2] but not to mortgages which secure an overdraft repayable 'on demand'.[3]

1   Halifax Building Society v Clark [1973] 2 All ER 33.
2   Bank of Scotland v Grimes [1985] 2 All ER 254, CA.
3   Habib Bank Ltd v Tailor [1982] 3 All ER 561, CA.

35.25   *The court's discretion* Clearly the court will delay possession where there is a reasonable prospect of paying off the arrears within a reasonably short period. In practice, however, by the time proceedings are actually brought the mortgagor is often in substantial default. The decisions of the courts have been notoriously inconsistent and it is difficult to discern a principled approach. However, it is clear that the court cannot postpone possession for an indefinite period[1]. Furthermore, in *First National Bank plc v Syed*[2] the Court of Appeal ruled that, in order to justify a postponement, the mortgagor must have a realistic ability to make payments which will cover current instalments and make some inroads into the arrears. In this case the mortgagor was only able to afford payments which fell below the interest charges and a postponement was refused.

A crucial issue is often the period over which the repayment of the arrears can be made; in other words, what is the reasonable period within which payment of the sums owing must take place? Initially, the courts seemed to take the view that this would be no more than two to four years (and, often very much shorter).[3] However, the position was reviewed by the Court of Appeal in *Cheltenham and Gloucester Building Society v Norgan*.[4] Here, most importantly, the court has taken the view that, in principle, the outstanding period of the loan should be regarded as a reasonable period within which any arrears should be paid off, at least in a case where the property is still adequate security for the loan. Accordingly, it would now seem that, where the mortgagor can make payments which will cover current instalments and pay off the arrears by the end of the loan period (which can be anything up to 25 years), possession will be postponed.

The court may also delay possession in order to give the mortgagor an opportunity to sell the property himself (in order to produce the funds to pay off the debt), since such a sale will normally result in a better price than one earned out by the mortgagee;[5] the court will not adopt this approach unless there is a realistic prospect of a speedy sale.[6] Furthermore, where the proceeds of sale will not discharge the debt, and where the mortgagee would prefer to conduct the sale itself, possession will not normally be postponed since the objective of the mortgagor in such a situation is not usually to obtain a better price but to hold up the eventual sale of the property.[7]

1 *Royal Trust Co of Canada v Markham* [1975] 3 All ER 433, CA.
2 [1991] 2 All ER 250.
3 See the comments of Waite LJ in *Cheltenham and Gloucester Building Society v Norgan* [1996] 1 All ER 449, CA.
4 [1996] 1 All ER 449, CA.
5 *Target Home Loans Ltd v Clothier* [1994] 1 All ER 439, CA.
6 *Town and Country Building Society v Julien* (1991) 24 HLR 312, CA.
7 *Cheltenham and Gloucester plc v Krausz* [1997] 1 All ER 21, CA. The position will be rather different where the mortgagee is *not* wishing promptly to sell the property; see *Palk v Mortgage Services Funding plc* [1993] 2 All ER 481, CA which we consider at para 35.31 below.

Sale

35.26   While it is possible for a mortgage to provide expressly for a power of sale, it is usual to rely on the statutory power conferred by the LPA 1925, or that power as modified by the terms of the mortgage. The major attraction of the statutory power is that there is no requirement for the mortgagee to obtain court approval for its exercise although, as we have just seen, where the mortgaged property is a dwelling-house, the mortgagee will, in practice, need to obtain a court order for possession[1] in order to be able to sell with vacant possession.

1 Paras 35.23–35.25 above.

The power of sale

35.27   Where the mortgage is made by deed and contains no expressed contrary intention, the LPA 1925, s 101 confers on the mortgagee the power to sell the mortgaged property when the mortgage money has become due. The mortgage money becomes due when the contractual date for redemption has passed, if such a date is fixed or, in the case of mortgages providing for repayment in instalments of principal and interest, when an instalment is due and unpaid. The contractual date of six months or earlier usually fixed in standing mortgages is incorporated therefore, not with the object that the mortgage should be redeemed at that time, but in order that the remedy of sale and other remedies for enforcing the security should become available at an early opportunity. As to mortgages providing for repayment by instalments of principal and interest, the mortgagee may only exercise his power of sale to enforce his security in respect of instalments in arrear,[1] unless, as is normal, it is provided that failure to pay one or more instalments causes the entire sum to become due. In endowment mortgages it is likewise usual for a default clause to provide that failure to pay instalments of interest makes the entire sum, principal and interest, due[2].

Although the mortgagee's power to sell *arises* when the mortgage money has become due, he may not, by virtue of the LPA 1925, s 103, *exercise* the power, unless and until:

- notice (in writing) requiring payment of the mortgage money has been served on the mortgagor, and he has not, within three months thereafter, paid the sums due; or
- some interest under the mortgage is in arrear and unpaid for two months after becoming due; or
- there has been a breach of some provision contained in the mortgage deed or in the LPA other than the covenant for repayment.

The provisions of the mortgage deed itself may, and commonly do, vary or extend the statutory provisions,[3] for example by providing that the power of sale should be exerciseable as soon as it arises.

1   *Payne v Cardiff RDC* [1932] 1 KB 241.
2   See para 35.8 above
3   LPA 1925, s 101(3).

Exercise of the power

35.28   The power of sale is exercised, and the mortgagor's right to redeem thus barred, as soon as the mortgagee enters into a binding contract to sell.[1] The mortgagee may not purport to sell the land to himself.[2] There is, however, no hard and fast rule that a mortgagee may not sell to a company in which he is interested. Where he does so, the mortgagee and the company seeking to uphold the transaction must show that the sale was in good faith and that the mortgagee took reasonable precautions to obtain the best price reasonably obtainable at the time.[3]

Although the mortgagee has only a term of years or equivalent charge in respect of the land, he has full power to convey the mortgaged freehold or leasehold together with fixtures attached to the land.[4]

The purchaser takes the estate subject to rights having priority to the mortgage, but freed from subsequent rights. The Act provides that the purchaser's title may not be challenged on the ground that the mortgagee's power was not, in fact, exerciseable, or due notice was not given, or the power was otherwise improperly or irregularly exercised. The Act further provides that the purchaser is not concerned to inquire as to these matters.[5] It would thus appear that, unless the power of sale has not even arisen (in which case the purported sale takes effect as a transfer of the mortgage) the purchaser takes a valid legal title to the mortgaged land. However, it has been suggested that, if the purchaser becomes aware of any facts showing that the power is not exerciseable, or that there is some impropriety in the sale, he does not get a good title.[6] In any event a person affected by an improper or irregular exercise of the power of sale has a remedy in damages against the mortgagee.[5]

1   *Property and Bloodstock Ltd v Emerton* [1967] 3 All ER 321, CA.

2   *Farrar v Farrars Ltd* (1888) 40 Ch D 395 at 409; *Williams v Wellingborough Borough Council* [1975] 3
    All ER 462, CA.
3   *Tse Kwong Lam v Wong Chit Sen* [1983] 3 All ER 54, PC; see para 35.29 below.
4   LPA, ss 88 and 89, and see LRA 2002, s 23(2).
5   LPA 1925, s 104.
6   *Lord Waring v London and Manchester Assurance Co Ltd* [1935] Ch 310 at 318.

35.29   *Price* In exercising its power of sale, a building society is under a statutory duty to
take reasonable care to ensure that the price at which the property is sold is the best price
which can reasonably be obtained.[1] In any event it was established in *Cuckmere Brick Co
Ltd v Mutual Finance Ltd*[2] that all mortgagees are under a duty to the mortgagor to take
reasonable care to obtain 'a proper price' or 'the true market value'. In that case the duty
was framed as one in the tort of negligence; this suggested that a mortgagee's professional
adviser could owe a similar duty[3] and that a mortgagee could owe such a duty to third
parties, such as guarantors.[4] However, later cases have made it clear that the duty is one
imposed by equity on the mortgagee alone, and is owed only to the mortgagor.[5]

Case law indicates that sale by auction does not necessarily show that reasonable care
has been taken to obtain the proper price.[6] A mortgagee proposing to sell should consult
professional advisors such as estate agents as to the method of sale and the measures
which should be taken in order to secure the best price. However, this does not mean
that the mortgagee must exercise his power of sale as a trustee would. On the contrary,
he is entitled to exercise it for his own purposes whenever he chooses. It matters not that
the moment may be unpropitious and that, by waiting, a higher price could be obtained.[7]
However, and by way of example, should the mortgagee, in advertising the property for
sale, negligently fail to mention that it has the benefit of planning permission, he will be
liable to account to the mortgagor for the difference between the price obtained and 'a
proper price' or 'the true market value'.[2] A purchaser in such a case would appear to be
protected by the LPA 1925, s 104,[8] unless, perhaps, he was aware of the irregularity.

1   Building Societies Act 1986, Sch 4, para 1.
2   [1971] 2 All ER 633, CA; see also *Predeth v Castle Phillips Finance Co Ltd* [1986] 2 EGLR 144, CA.
3   See remarks in *Cuckmere Brick Co Ltd v Mutual Finance Ltd* [1971] 2 All ER 633, CA.
4   *Standard Chartered Bank Ltd v Walker* [1982] 3 All ER 938, CA.
5   *China & South Sea Bank Ltd v Tan* [1989] 3 All ER 839, PC; *Parker-Tweedale v Dunbar Bank plc* [1990]
    2 All ER 577, CA.
6   *Tse Kwong Lam v Wong Chit Sen* [1983] 3 All ER 54, PC.
7   *Bank of Cyprus (London) Ltd v Gill* [1980] 2 Lloyds Rep 51.
8   Para 35.28 above.

35.30   *Proceeds*   The LPA 1925, s 105 provides that, first, any prior mortgages to which
the sale was not made subject must be discharged. Then the proceeds are held by the
selling mortgagee in trust:

* to pay the costs and expenses of the sale;
* to pay off the principal plus interest and costs due under the mortgage;
* to pay the surplus to any subsequent mortgagee of whom he has notice (he should
  therefore search the Land Charge Register or register of title as appropriate), or, if
  there is no subsequent mortgagee, to the mortgagor.

Court's power to order sale
35.31   It will be appreciated from the foregoing paragraphs that the mortgagee's statutory
power to sell is almost invariably more than adequate to allow the realisation of the security
once the mortgagor is in default. However, there may be situations in which the mortgagee
does not have a statutory power to sell because the mortgage is not by deed; in such a
situation, a mortgagee wishing to sell will need to seek a court *order* of sale.[1] Further, as

we shall see, where a mortgagee is seeking to foreclose,[2] the court may well choose to order a sale instead.[3]

In addition, there have been recent illustrations of applicants asking the court to exercise its jurisdiction to order a sale, despite the existence of a statutory power to sell. In *Arab Bank plc v Merchantile Holdings Ltd*[4] the mortgagee had already negotiated a sale which was the best that could be hoped for in the light of the fall in the property market. It asked the court to order a sale rather than rely on its statutory power because of strong evidence that the mortgagor would try, unjustifiably, to prevent the transaction going ahead. The court agreed to do so, especially given that the sale might well fall through unless the purchasers were confident that it could not be challenged.

Palk v Mortgage Services Funding plc[5] was a case in which, most unusually, it was the *mortgagor* asking the court to order a sale. Here, again, the value of the mortgaged property had fallen dramatically. The mortgagors wished to sell, albeit at a price well below their outstanding debt, in order to reduce the amount of capital owed and so to stem the ever-increasing interest charges. The mortgagee was refusing to co-operate,[6] taking the view that it would be better to let the property (even though the rent would not meet the interest payments) and wait for the market to improve. In these exceptional circumstances the Court of Appeal was prepared to order a sale. However, it has recently been made clear that the court will not allow the mortgagor to conduct a sale where it is clear that the mortgagee does wish to exercise its statutory power of sale (which was not the case in *Palk*); in such a situation, the mortgagor's motive is normally to delay the sale for as long as possible.[7]

1   Under LPA 1925, s 91(2).
2   See paras 35.34–35.36 below.
3   See para 35.36 below.
4   [1994] 2 All ER 74.
5   [1993] 2 All ER 481, CA.
6   A sale by the mortgagor could not, in practice, go ahead without the mortgagee undertaking to discharge the mortgage.
7   *Cheltenham and Gloucester plc v Krausz* [1997] 1 All ER 21, CA and para 35.25 above.

Action on the personal covenant

35.32   It should not be forgotten that a mortgage is a loan under which the mortgagor covenants to repay. Hence, in the event of any default, the mortgagee can sue on this personal covenant. In practice, a defaulting mortgagor will not usually have the funds to pay off the debt and the mortgagee will normally choose to rely on his security by taking possession and selling the property. However, there are occasions where the right to sue can be valuable. First, it can be utilised in addition to the mortgagee's other rights; thus, where the sale of the property fails to raise enough money to pay off the debt, the mortgagor can be sued for the balance. Since such an action can be brought up to 12 years after the initial default[1], this means that the mortgagee can wait to see if the mortgagor's financial position improves[2]. The other circumstance in which the right to sue can be useful is where the mortgagee is unable to sell the property because he cannot obtain possession due to another (eg an impled co-owner) having priority[3]. Although the mortgagor in such a situation would be most unlikely to be able to pay, the mortgagee can then have him declared bankrupt. The trustee in bankruptcy will then usually, after a year, be able to obtain an order for the sale of the property[4] and the mortgagee will recover more of its money[5] than might otherwise be the case.

The date on which the right to sue arises depends on the form of the covenant to pay. Where the mortgage provides for repayment on a fixed contractual date, the mortgagee's right to sue arises in the event of failure to pay on that date. Where the mortgage provides for repayment in instalments, the mortgagee may sue for unpaid instalments. However, as we have seen[6], it is usual to include a default clause providing that the whole sum becomes due in the event of failure to pay, perhaps, two instalments. Where the mortgage makes the whole sum payable on demand, the right of action accrues at the start of the mortgage unless, as is common, there is provision for notice to be given.[7] However, where a default clause in an instalment mortgage provides for default to result in the mortgage money becoming payable on demand, the demand must first be made before the right to sue accrues.[8]

1 Limitation Act 1980, s 20. The limitation period for claims to interest is six years.
2 In *Bristol & West plc v Bartlett* [2002] EWCA Civ 1181, [2002] 4 All ER 544 the mortgagee had, some eight years previously, sold three properties at prices which did not clear their mortgage debt. It was held to be entitled to sue the three mortgagors, each of whom still owed in the region of £60,000.
3 See para 35.22 above.
4 Insolvency Act 1986, s 335A. See para 32.36 above.
5 The implied co-owner's prior claim means that they must be paid before the mortgagee can take its share of the proceeds.
6 See para 35.8 above.
7 *Re Brown's Estate, Brown v Brown* [1893] 2 Ch 300.
8 *Esso Petroleum Co Ltd v Alstonbridge Properties Ltd* [1975] 3 All ER 358.

Appointment of a receiver

35.33 In the case of commercial or tenanted properties, the mortgagee may wish to secure payment of any instalment due to him without taking action to sell, by appointing a receiver to manage the property and receive its income or rents. The statutory power to appoint a receiver arises and is exercisable on the same conditions as the power of sale,[1] again subject to any extension or variation in the mortgage deed. The appointment and removal of the receiver must be in writing. A receiver appointed under the statutory power is deemed to be the agent of the mortgagor.[2] The mortgagee will be liable to account to the mortgagor only for what he receives from the receiver, and not for what, without wilful default, might have been received.[3] The receiver has power to demand and recover rents due but may not himself grant leases unless he has the sanction of the court[4] or the mortgagee has delegated his power of leasing to him. The receiver is to apply money received by him in the following order:

- in discharge of all outgoings affecting the mortgaged property;
- in making payments under prior mortgages;
- in payment of his own commission, of insurance premiums payable under the mortgage, and of the cost of carrying out repairs required by the mortgagee;
- in payment of interest due under the mortgage;
- in or towards paying off the principal if required by the mortgagee; and
- in paying the residue to the mortgagor.[5]

1 LPA, ss 101 and 109; paras 35.27 and 35.28 above.
2 LPA 1925, s 109.
3 Which would be the position if the mortgagee himself took possession, see para 35.20 above.
4 *Re Cripps* [1946] Ch 265, CA.
5 LPA 1925, s 109.

Foreclosure

35.34 As soon as the mortgage money is due, or in the event of a condition of the mortgage being broken,[1] the mortgagee may apply to the court for foreclosure. When foreclosure is granted to the mortgagee it has the effect of putting an end to the mortgagor's right to redeem and vests the mortgaged property in the mortgagee, subject to any prior mortgages but freed from any subsequent ones[2]. On the face of it, this is, from the point of view of the mortgagor and any subsequent mortgagees, a harsh remedy; their rights in the property are extinguished, in theory, even where the value of the property exceeds the value of the debt owed to the foreclosing mortgagee[3]. For this reason both the mortgagor and any subsequent mortgagees must be made parties to the foreclosure action.

Because of the severity of the remedy it is in fact made subject to a number of restrictions which have had the effect that foreclosure is rarely sought; mortgagees usually prefer to enforce their security by seeking vacant possession of, and subsequently selling, the mortgaged property.

1   Eg a covenant to pay instalments of interest: *Twentieth Century Banking Corpn Ltd v Wilkinson* [1976] 3 All ER 361.
2   LPA 1925, s 88(2).
3   But see para 35.36 below.

35.35   On an application for foreclosure, the court will first grant an order nisi. This requires accounts to be taken of what is due to the mortgagee in respect of principal, interest and costs, and orders the mortgagor, within (usually) six months thereafter, to pay the sums due or be foreclosed in default. In the event of non-payment an order absolute for foreclosure may be made. Where there are subsequent mortgagees, they too have the opportunity to redeem but in default will be foreclosed.

The court has a discretion to extend the period given for repayment of the sums due or even to 'open the foreclosure' after an order absolute has been made. Furthermore, in cases of instalment (or other deferred payment) mortgages of dwelling-houses, power is conferred on the court by the Administration of Justice Act 1973, s 8 to adjourn the proceedings or suspend its order, where it appears likely that the mortgagor will pay the instalments owing and keep up with future instalments.[1]

1   Paras 35.23–35.25 above.

35.36   Perhaps more influential than the foregoing in reducing the importance of foreclosure as a remedy is the fact that, under the LPA 1925, s 91(2), the court has power on the application of any interested party to order sale of the property instead of foreclosure.[1] Clearly, the court will be particularly willing to exercise this power where it is shown that the value of the property exceeds the amount due under the mortgage since, otherwise, the mortgagee reaps a windfall profit. Sale may be ordered on such terms as the court thinks fit; for example, it may even require that the mortgagor pay into court a sum sufficient to protect the mortgagee against loss. While it may order immediate sale, it may equally provide time for redemption of the mortgage. Conduct of the sale will usually be given to the mortgagor since he will be most concerned to realise the highest price for the property. A reserve price will be fixed, and the purchase money must be paid into court.

Given that sale of the mortgaged property is highly likely as a result of an application for foreclosure, it will be preferable for the mortgagee to exercise his statutory power of sale to realise his security. However, that power must have arisen and must be exerciseable.[2]

In *Twentieth Century Banking Corpn Ltd v Wilkinson*,[3] the mortgage provided that, for the purposes of the LPA, the mortgage money was not due until the end of the mortgage term. The mortgagor defaulted on his obligation in the meantime to pay instalments of interest and the mortgagee sought an order for sale or foreclosure. The court held that the mortgagee's statutory power of sale would not arise until the mortgage money became due, but that the mortgagee was entitled to seek foreclosure because the mortgagor was in breach of a condition of the mortgage. Since the mortgagee was entitled to foreclosure the court had a discretion to order sale instead, which it did.

1   Para 35.31 above.
2   Paras 35.27 and 35.28 above.
3   [1976] 3 All ER 361.

Leasing

35.37 Both the mortgagor, while in possession, and the mortgagee, if he has taken possession or has appointed a receiver,[1] are empowered by the LPA 1925, s 99[2] to grant leases in accordance with that section. The leases authorised by the section are agricultural or occupation leases for a term not exceeding 50 years, and building leases for a term not exceeding 999 years. Such leases must take effect in possession not later than 12 months from their date, must reserve the best rent reasonably obtainable, and must contain a covenant for payment of rent and a condition of re-entry in the event of breach.[3] The lessee must execute a counterpart of the lease. If in good faith a lease is granted which does not comply with these requirements, it takes effect in equity as a contract to grant an equivalent lease in accordance with the statutory power.[4]

Save in relation to mortgages of agricultural land[5] and the grant of new tenancies of business premises under the Landlord and Tenant Act 1954, Part II,[6] the statutory power applies only to the extent that it is not excluded by the parties. In fact it is normal practice to exclude the mortgagor's statutory power of leasing altogether. In this way the mortgagor is prevented from creating (without the positive consent of the mortgagee), for example, an assured tenancy within the Housing Act 1988,[7] which would devalue the mortgagee's security. Where the mortgage terms exclude the power to create any tenancy, any breach is commonly expressed to give rise to the mortgage money becoming due, and hence to the mortgage's remedies becoming available. Where the mortgagor's power of leasing is so excluded then any purported tenancy granted by the mortgagor is binding on the parties to it by estoppel[8] but does not bind the mortgagee.[9]

1 To whom the power of leasing may be delegated.
2 See also LRA 1925, s 23(2).
3 Further conditions are imposed in respect of building leases.
4 LPA 1925, s 152(1).
5 Agricultural Holdings Act 1986, Sch 14, para 12.
6 Para 38.22 below.
7 Para 38.4 below.
8 Para 37.17 below.
9 *Iron Trades Employers Insurance Association v Union of House and Land Investors Ltd* [1937] 1 All ER 481; *Dudley and District Benefit Building Society v Emerson* [1949] 2 All ER 252, CA; *Britannia Building Society v Earl* [1990] 2 All ER 469, CA; and see *Quennell v Maltby* [1979] 1 All ER 568, CA.

Insurance

35.38 The mortgagee is empowered by the LPA 1925, s 101 to insure the mortgaged property against loss or damage by fire up to the amount specified in the deed or up to two thirds of the amount which would be required to reinstate the property in the event of total destruction.[1] The premiums become part of the mortgage debt. It is common expressly to provide that the mortgagor shall insure the property for a specified sum or the full value of the property or, particularly in building society mortgages, that the society will effect the insurance for a specified sum but the premiums will be payable by the mortgagor.

The mortgagee may require that all moneys received under an insurance of the mortgaged property effected under the terms of the Act or the mortgage deed be applied by the mortgagor in making good the loss or damage or be applied in or towards the discharge of the mortgage money.[1] Should the mortgagor independently of any obligation in the mortgage insure the property the mortgagee is not entitled to any money received, but where the money is payable in the event of fire he can require that it be used towards reinstatement,[2] and in any event it is common to exclude the mortgagor's power independently to insure the property.

1   LPA 1925, s 108.
2   Fires Prevention (Metropolis) Act 1774, s 83.

Priorities

35.39   The issue of priorities between competing mortgagees arises where the value of the mortgaged property is insufficient to provide security for all the mortgages to which the property is subject. The incidence of this problem is rare in times of rapidly increasing property values, so long as mortgagees act with care. However, as the property recession of the early 1990s has shown, should the value of property decline the difficulty may well arise. In such a case, if the property is sold to realise the security, the various mortgagees do not share in the proceeds equally or rateably in proportion to the size of their mortgage; the mortgagee having priority is paid in full before any money is passed to the second in priority, and so on. We shall only consider the rules governing the priority of mortgages of registered land.

Priority
35.40   Registered charges[1] rank for priority as between themselves in order of registration.[2] A charge which has not yet been registered takes effect in equity only; it will be overridden by a subsequent registered charge but, being the first in time, it will take priority over any other unregistered charge[3].

1   Para 35.4 above.
2   LRA 1925, s 48.
3   LRA 1925, s 30.

Tacking of further advances
35.41   Where a mortgagee makes a further loan, or advance, to the mortgagor, in certain circumstances it may be 'tacked on' to the original mortgage so as to enjoy the priority of that mortgage. Tacking of further advances is particularly important where a person mortgages property to a bank to secure his overdrawn current account. The overdraft at the time of the mortgage represents the original debt for which the mortgage is security: each subsequently honoured cheque represents a further advance. The bank will, of course, wish to ensure that it does not lose priority in respect of these further advances to any intervening mortgage of the property created by the debtor.

The circumstances in which tacking will be permitted are:

- if there is an arrangement to that effect with the subsequent mortgagee[1];
- if the mortgagee has received no notice from a subsequent mortgagee of the creation of the subsequent charge[2];
- where the mortgagee is obliged to make further advances and that fact is noted on the register at the time the subsequent mortgage is created[3];
- where the parties to the first mortgage have agreed a maximum amount for which the charge is security and that fact is noted on the register and the further advance is within that limit[4].

1   LRA 2002, s 49(6).
2   LRA 2002, s 49(1). In practice a subsequent chargee will always give notice to a prior mortgagee.
3   LRA 2002, s 49(3).
4   LRA 2002, s 49(4).

Chapter 36

Enforceability of interests in land

36.1 We have already seen[1] that one of the essential features of any proprietary right to use and enjoy land is that it must be *capable* of binding, not just the landowner who created the right, but also subsequent purchasers of the land to which the right relates. Rights, such as licences, which cannot in themselves[2] bind a purchaser are, by definition, purely personal. However, the fact that a right is proprietary does not mean that it will *automatically* bind a purchaser of the land. Now that we have discussed many of the most important proprietary rights to land, we turn to the final piece in the jigsaw and examine the circumstances in which such rights *will actually bind* a future owner. This is an issue that is of prime importance. The value, and indeed the very marketability, of land depends on a purchaser or lender[3] being able to discover exactly what rights relating to the land will continue to operate after the sale or mortgage since this can profoundly affect the decision to purchase or to lend (or the price to be paid or the amount of any loan). Equally, those who have the benefit of rights over land which belongs to another, wish to ensure that any transfer of that land will not result in the loss of their rights.

In this chapter we consider:

- the background to the current rules relating to the enforceability of proprietary rights affecting land; and
- the rules governing the enforceability of proprietary rights relating to registered land.

1   Para 29.2 above.
2   Additional factors may persuade a court to invoke the constructive trust or the doctrine of proprietary estoppel as a means of protecting a licensee against a subsequent purchaser; see paras 29.45 and 31.10 – 31.16 above.
3   A 'purchaser' includes 'a lessee, mortgagee or other person who for valuable consideration acquires an interest in property…'; LPA 1925, s 205(1)(xxi).

The background

The pre-1926 rules
36.2 The pre-1926 rules governing the enforceability of proprietary rights depended simply on whether the right in question was *legal* or *equitable*.

Legal rights
36.3 It was always a basic principle of English land law that legal rights to land 'bind the whole world'. Thus a legal right always bound a purchaser irrespective of whether the

purchaser knew of the right in question. So, for example, if A (a freeholder) granted a legal lease to B and then sold his freehold reversion to C, C was always bound by the lease. The same would be true if, instead of selling the freehold, A had granted a legal mortgage to D; D would also be bound by B's lease. This rule rarely caused unfairness because it was easy for a purchaser to discover the existence of legal rights to land. As we have seen, common law usually required rights to land to be created by deed[1] with the result that there was documentary evidence of such rights which formed part of the title to the land. In those instances where the common law recognises rights despite the absence of a deed,[2] the owner of those rights was either in occupation of the land, or was openly exercising his rights; accordingly they would be revealed by the physical inspection of the land which every prudent purchaser is assumed by the law to make.

1   Para 30.10 above.
2   Eg leases not exceeding three years (para 30.11 above), freehold ownership based on adverse possession (paras 31.19–31.31 above) and easements acquired by prescription (para 31.19 above and paras 33.40–33.51 above).

Equitable interests
36.4   We have seen that equity's first foray into English land law was when the Court of Chancery started enforcing the trust by requiring the trustees, the legal owners of the land, to abide by the terms of the trust, thus recognising that it was the beneficiary who was entitled to the benefits of the land.[1] However, the beneficiary's rights against the trustees would be of little use if he could be deprived of these benefits should the trustees transfer their ownership of the land to someone else. Gradually, the Chancellor came to hold that there were others besides the original trustees who were in conscience bound to give effect to the rights of the beneficiary. Thus, these rights came to be enforceable against a trustee's heir, against someone to whom a trustee left the land by will, against someone to whom the trustees gave the land, and against someone who bought the land knowing that the beneficiary was entitled to the benefit of it. As the class of persons against whom the beneficiary could enforce his rights was extended the effect was that his equitable interest became almost as good as the legal estate which was held by the trustees. However, the Court of Chancery stopped short of enforcing the beneficiary's rights against the whole world; equitable rights came to be enforceable against the whole world *except* a 'bona fide purchaser of a legal estate for value without notice of the equitable interest'.

In addition to beneficial interests under a trust, equity, over the years, came to recognise a number of rights in respect of land which were not recognised by the common law; for example the restrictive covenant.[2] Furthermore, as we have seen,[3] equity will sometimes give effect to rights despite the fact that they were created in ways which failed to comply with the formalities demanded by the common law and statute. The decision in *Pilcher v Rawlins*,[4] in 1872, made it clear that the rule that equitable rights were not enforceable against a bona fide purchaser of a legal estate without notice of their existence applied to all equitable interests, not just beneficial interests under a trust.

1   Para 29.4035 above.
2   Chapter 34 above.
3   See paras 31.2–31.6 above.
4   (1872) 7 Ch App 259.

The bona fide purchaser of a legal estate for value
36.5   In order to appreciate the differences between the rules governing the enforceability of legal and equitable rights to land, we need briefly to examine the notion of the bona fide purchaser of a legal estate for value without notice. To fall within the exception and thus take free from prior equitable interests in the land, a purchaser must have acted bona fide, 'in good faith'; he must have acted honestly, and genuinely be without notice. As we

have seen, the term 'purchaser' bears an extended meaning in law encompassing all those who acquire an interest in land[1] and includes a lessee and a mortgagee. However, the purchaser must have acquired the legal estate 'for value', ie for valuable consideration[2] or in consideration of marriage. Thus, where a person acquired the legal estate as a gift or under a will or on an intestacy[3] he would be bound by any equitable interests, even if he had no notice of them.

1 Para 36.1 above.
2 See ch 6 above.
3 Ie where a person dies leaving no effective will.

36.6 *The doctrine of notice* We now turn to the concept of notice itself, of which three varieties came to be recognised: actual notice, constructive notice and imputed notice. A purchaser has actual notice of rights of which he knows.

If actual notice were the only type of notice, a purchaser could have avoided knowledge of an equitable interest, and thus take the land free from it, by refraining from inspecting the land he was buying or by failing to investigate the title to it. However, equity also recognised that a purchaser has constructive notice of an equitable interest if its existence would have come to his knowledge if reasonable inquiries and inspections had been made. The onus was thus on the purchaser to make such reasonable inquiries and inspections as would be made by any prudent purchaser. A further aspect of constructive notice was the doctrine of *Hunt v Luck*,[1] whereby a person's occupation of property (or, it may be, notice of a person's occupation of property[2]) constituted constructive notice to others of his rights in respect of the property. Thus, a purchaser, on inspecting the property, needed to make inquiries of any person in occupation in order to establish whether that person had any rights in the property. Failure to do so would give him constructive notice of those rights.

Finally, we should mention imputed notice. For fairly obvious reasons, equity also took the view that any notice, actual or constructive, which was acquired or deemed to be acquired by a solicitor or other agent acting for the purchaser in the transaction was imputed to the purchaser.

1 [1901] 1 Ch 45; affd [1902] 1 Ch 428, CA.
2 *Kingsnorth Trust Ltd v Tizard* [1986] 2 All ER 54.

36.7 *The problems caused by the doctrine of notice* The application of the fully developed doctrine of notice undoubtedly came to cause problems for both a purchaser of land and an owner of any equitable interest. A purchaser was at risk of being bound by an undiscovered equitable interest since he could be deemed to have notice unless he had made 'proper' pre-purchase inquiries. Furthermore, and conversely, an equitable interest in land could be lost if the legal estate was acquired for valuable consideration by someone without notice of its existence. If these difficulties were not seriously to hinder dealings in land (which were, of course, by the end of the 19th century starting to increase quite dramatically) changes in the law were necessary, and it is to these which we now turn.

The solutions adopted in 1925
36.8 Two solutions were adopted in 1925 to ease the problems outlined in the previous paragraph. In the case of some equitable interests which might loosely be regarded as 'commercial',[1] the concept of registration was introduced. The essence of this is that if such interests are protected by being registered they will bind a purchaser; if they are not, they will not bind. A purchaser thus knows that, prior to his purchase, he must search the relevant register to discover the existence of those interests which will bind him; equally, the owner of the interest knows that, by registering his interest, they will be enforceable against all purchasers.

The second solution relates to those equitable interests of a 'family' nature, such as interests arising under a settlement or as a result of co-ownership.[2] We have already seen that, after 1925, all such interests are necessarily equitable and can now only exist behind a trust.[3] In the case of these trust interests it was felt unnecessary that they should bind a purchaser at all, and undesirable that the legal estate should for ever be encumbered with a string of beneficial interests. Consequently, the existing notion of 'overreaching' was extended. As we have seen,[4] this is the process whereby, on the sale of the trust land, the beneficial interests cease to bind the land, and are satisfied thenceforth out of the proceeds of sale instead.

1   Eg estate contracts (para 30.9 above), restrictive covenants (ch 34 above) and mortgages (ch 35 above).
2   Chapter 32 above.
3   Para 32.25 above.
4   Paras 32.22 and 32.31 above.

Two systems of registration

36.9   The detailed implementation of the policy of registering 'commercial' type proprietary rights was further complicated by the simultaneous introduction of the system of registration of *title*. While the introduction of a radically different system for the protection and enforcement of interests in land was a vital aspect of registration of title, the LRA 1925 had a much wider remit. As we have seen,[1] the 1925 Act put in place a scheme for the central registration of title to land which resulted in quite different procedures for the transfer and creation of rights to land once registration has taken place. For practical reasons which we have already explained, this had to be implemented on a gradual basis which, even now, is not yet complete.

Accordingly, in 1925 the legislators had to decide whether to leave unregistered land subject to the existing, unsatisfactory, rules on notice, or whether to introduce essentially temporary reforms, designed to apply until such time as the title to any particular piece of land was actually registered. In the event, the latter course was adopted with the result that there are two *quite separate and mutually exclusive* systems of registration. The first and far more limited scheme, is that which applies *only* to unregistered land and is contained in what is now the Land Charges Act 1972 (hereafter LCA 1972). The second is that which is now governed by the LRA 2002. We have already dealt with the conveyancing aspects of the LRA;[2] in this chapter we concentrate on the rules governing the protection and enforceability of third party rights to registered land.

Before providing a very brief summary of the Land Charges Act scheme of registration, we first consider the impact of registration on the traditional division of proprietary rights to land as either legal or equitable.

1   Paras 30.12–30.18 above.
2   Paras 30.12–30.18 above.

36.10   It will become very clear that the introduction of systems of registration has diminished the importance of a proprietary right being legal or equitable. As we shall see, the LCA and the LRA each classify proprietary rights in their own distinct way and it is that classification which then dictates the enforceability of those rights against future owners. However it remains fair to say that whether a right is legal or equitable will often determine the category into which a right falls under each Act.

Unregistered land

36.11   Before concentrating on the position of registered land, we first summarise the rules relating to the protection of interests in land where the LRA does not apply because the title to land has not yet been registered. As we have just indicated, the key to understanding the rules governing the enforceability of rights in unregistered land lies in grasping the way in which such rights are now classified. The rights of third parties will fall into one of two categories; they will either be registrable under the LCA or they will not be so registrable. This second category can itself be further divided into two groups; those rights which are legal and those which are equitable. Again this second group, ie equitable rights which are not registrable under the LCA, can be further divided into those which are overreachable and those which are not. A different rule on enforceability applies to each category and we shall deal with each in turn.

36.12   *Rights made registrable by the Land Charges Act 1972*   The policy of reducing the impact of the doctrine of notice, both to enable a purchaser more readily to discover interests affecting the land and to enable those entitled to those interests to fix the purchaser with notice of their existence, was given effect by the Land Charges Act 1925, now repealed and consolidated by the Land Charges Act 1972. The fundamental objective of this Act is to mechanise the doctrine of notice by requiring rights governed by the Act to be registered[1]. Such registration constitutes actual notice[2], while a failure to register renders the right void against most purchasers; a failure to register does not however render the right void against a donee, a devisee (ie a beneficiary under a will) or a squatter[3]. If a right is void against a purchaser for non-registration then it is irrelevant that the purchaser actually knew about it.[4]

The rights made registrable by the LCA are mostly equitable and include estate contracts (ie contracts for the sale of land, options and rights of pre-emption), post 1925 restrictive covenants and some equitable easements.

1   The LCA obliges the Land Registry, in addition to operating the system of registration of title under the LRA, also to maintain a Land Charges department operating the Land Charges Act 1972. This department keeps the Land Charges Register on computer at Plymouth.
2   LPA 1925, s 198(1).
3   LCA 1972, s 4(5) and (6).
4   LPA 1925, s 199.

36.13   *Interests outside the Land Charges Act* As explained at the outset, the LCA system of registration was never intended to apply to all third party rights affecting unregistered land. In particular, it was always anticipated that virtually all *legal* interests, and those equitable interests to which the *overreaching* provisions apply, should not be registrable.

1   On the whole *legal* third party rights are not registrable under the LCA. For such rights the pre-1926 rules apply; namely that, as legal rights, they bind the whole world. Thus a purchaser is bound by such rights irrespective of whether he knows about them or not; as we have already explained, in practice, it is generally quite easy for a purchaser to discover the existence of legal rights.[1]
2   We have already seen that certain *equitable interests arising under trusts* are overreachable. This means that, on a sale of unregistered land, the rights of beneficiaries do not bind a purchaser even where the purchaser is fully aware of them. In the event of a sale or mortgage the rights of the beneficiaries are transferred from the land to the purchase or loan money. It must be remembered that, in order for overreaching to take effect, the purchaser or lender must pay the money to trustees who must be at least two in number (or a trust corporation).[2] If this is not done,[3] no overreaching occurs; in such a situation whether or not the purchaser takes free from the rights of the beneficiaries depends on the old doctrine of notice.
3   The LCA itself envisages that some other *equitable* interests are not registrable, eg pre 1926 restrictive covenants. Case law has made clear that certain other equitable interests, such as those arising by way of proprietary estoppel, are also not registrable[5]. In these cases also the doctrine of notice governs whether the rights are enforceable against a purchaser.

A good example of the modern operation of the doctrine of notice is provided by *Kingsnorth Finance Ltd v Tizard*.[6] Here the matrimonial home (title to which was not registered) had been conveyed in the name of the husband only, although the wife had made a financial contribution and so was an implied co-owner in equity. Unknown to the wife the husband applied for a mortgage, indicating that he was not married; he arranged for the mortgagees' valuer to inspect the property at a time when she was not present. The valuer reported that the property appeared to be occupied only by the applicant and his two children and the loan was duly made. When the husband disappeared with the money the claimants sought possession. The wife argued that the mortgagees were bound by her rights as a beneficiary under the statutory trust; they had dealt with a single trustee when granting the mortgage so that no overreaching could have taken place and the doctrine of notice therefore applied. Since she was in occupation of the property they had constructive notice of her rights. The judge agreed and possession was refused. Thus, although the Land Charges Act has considerably reduced the importance of the doctrine of notice as the vehicle for the protection of equitable interests in unregistered land, it has not totally superseded it.

1   Para 36.3 above.
2   Paras 32.22 and 32.31 above and 36.8 above.
3   As already explained, this is most likely to occur in cases of implied co-ownership, where the title deeds often give the purchaser the impression that the property is solely owned so that he does not realise that any question of overreaching arises; see para 32.32 above.
4   *Caunce v Caunce* [1969] 1 All ER 722.
5   *E R Ives Investments Ltd v High* [1967] 1 All ER 504, CA.
6   [1986] 2 All ER 54.

Registered land

Introduction
36.14   As we have said[1] the introduction of a new system of registration of title by the LRA 1925 offered an opportunity to adopt a fresh approach to the question of the enforceability and protection of third party rights and this process has now been refined and taken further by the LRA 2002. In order to be covered by the 2002 Act at all a third party right must relate to or be parasitic on an interest to which title has been registered[2]. So, for example, a restrictive covenant, a short lease or a mortgage, will only fall within the ambit of the LRA if the title to the freehold or lease to which it relates has been registered. First registration of title[3] provides a chance for the Land Registry to check all the existing evidence of rights affecting that title, to classify those rights and to record their existence by way of an entry in the register. By definition this initial investigation by the Land Registry will reveal, and result in the registration of, a far wider range of rights than are covered by the much more limited system of registration set up by the LCA. Since virtually all dealings with the land thereafter should be completed by registration[4] the register can be kept up to date by the addition, where necessary, of fresh entries.

1   Para 36.8 above.
2   We have discussed the circumstances in which title either must or can be registered at paras 30.14 and 30.15 above.
3   Para 30.14 above.
4   Para 30.17 above. Note that the grant of leases for seven years or less is an important exception to this requirement, see para 30.17 above and note 1, para 36.17 below.

The classification of rights to registered land
36.15   The classification of rights to land by the LRA is its own. As we have seen[1], title can only be registered to certain interests, largely but not exclusively, either freehold or

leasehold estates; these are registrable interests. Rights affecting any interest to which the title has been registered are either registered charges, interests which will override first registration or a registered disposition, or minor interests which should be protected by an entry on the register. The enforceability against subsequent purchasers of rights affecting registered interests to which the title has been registered flows from the LRA classification and system of protection and not from whether the rights are legal or equitable.[2]

1   Para 30.14 and 30.15 above.
2   Although their LRA classification may hinge on whether they are legal or equitable.

The effect of registration of title

36.16   *First registration*   Although the effects of registration of title have already been dealt with[1], it might be helpful to remind ourselves of these. When a title is registered (with absolute title[2]) for the *first* time that first registered proprietor is entitled to the legal estate, together with all the existing rights which benefit that estate (such as easements and restrictive covenants). More importantly for present purposes, the only adverse interests to which that first registered proprietor will be subject are:

*   interests protected by an entry on the register;
*   'overriding interests' within Sch 1 to the LRA;
*   interests already acquired under the Limitation Act 1980 (ie squatter's rights) of which the proprietor has notice;
*   where, the proprietor is a trustee, those rights of the beneficiaries of which he has notice; and
*   in the case of leaseholds, the express and implied covenants in the lease.

1   See paras 30.16 and 30.18 above.
2   As is usually the case, see para 30.16 above.

36.17   *Subsequent dealings*   Once a title has been registered for the first time, any *subsequent* dealing with that registered interest must normally be carried out by way of a disposition which must be completed by registration[1]. A purchaser[2] for valuable consideration under a registered disposition of an interest with absolute title will take the registered estate together with the rights by which it is benefited. However, as compared to a *first* registered proprietor, a purchaser of an *already registered estate* takes subject to a *narrower* range of adverse interests, namely:

*   a registered charge
*   interests protected by an entry on the register;
*   'overriding interests' within Sch 3[3] of the LRA;
*   in the case of leaseholds, the covenants in the lease.

1   Note that where a registered proprietor grants a lease for seven years or less he does not normally have to complete the process by registration (see para 30.14 above). This means that such leases do not normally appear on the register (although leases of more than three years *may* be protected by the entry of a notice – see para 36.32 below). Where a lease is not entered on the register it will normally be an overriding interest – see para 36.22 below.
2   Note that a purchaser includes a mortgagee; see note 3 para 36.1 above.
3   As we shall see, the overriding interests within Sch 3 are a narrower group than those within Sch 1 which bind a *first* registered proprietor, see para 36.21 below.

36.18   We now consider in more detail the circumstances in which registered charges, 'overriding interests', and those interests that can be protected by an entry on the register will bind either a first registered proprietor or a purchaser for valuable consideration of an already registered estate.

Registered charges

36.19　As we have seen, a mortgage of registered land must now be created by way of a legal charge[1]. It constitutes a 'registered disposition'[2] and must be completed by registration, ie the lender is registered as proprietor of the charge.[3] By definition, a registered charge cannot be in existence at the time of a first registration of title; they can only be created where title is already registered. A purchaser of an already registered title and a subsequent mortgagee will always be bound by an existing registered charge[4]. In practice, particularly in the case of residential property, existing registered charges are usually paid off by the vendor immediately prior to a sale so that a purchaser will not then be bound by the vendor's mortgage. It is likely, of course, that the purchaser will immediately create his own registered charge in order to finance the purchase.

1　See para 35.4 above.
2　LRA 2002, s 27(2)(f).
3　LRA 2002, s 27, Sch 2, para 8.
4　LRA 2002, s 29(2)(a)(i).

Overriding interests

Introduction

36.20　The land registration system has always accepted that there must be some interests that must bind a purchaser or lender despite not being entered on the register. The LRA 1925 referred to such rights as 'overriding interests'. While the LRA 2002 discards this label (and makes some radical changes to this area of the law) the term remains a useful description and we retain the expression. At first sight, the existence of a category of rights, which bind the purchaser despite not being entered on the register, may appear surprising; it clearly invalidates any idea that the registered land scheme ensures that all interests affecting the land should be discoverable from an inspection of the Land Register. However, we have seen a number of situations where the law recognises that rights to land can be created outside the context of a formal transaction and without the use of documents[1]. In such instances the owner of the right would be most unlikely to be aware of any need to register their right if this were required. Accordingly, a registration system either has to decide that such rights effectively disappear in the event of a sale or mortgage – a stance that would inevitably reproduce the very unfairness that the informal conferment of rights was designed to eliminate – or it is accepted that, in certain circumstances at least, unregistered rights can bind a purchaser or mortgagee. It is the latter course that was followed by the LRA 1925. This approach has been accepted by the LRA 2002 although that Act has cut down the number of overriding interests and drawn a new distinction between unregistered rights that can bind a *first* registered proprietor, and those that can bind purchasers and mortgagees of an *already registered estate*. The aim is to strike a balance between fairness to the owner of what are often informally created or longstanding rights and the imposition of an unreasonable requirement to expect purchasers to discover the existence of unregistered rights.

1　For example, the conferment of interests in land by the use of resulting or constructive trusts (see paras 31.8-31.10 above) or under the doctrine of proprietary estoppel (see paras 31.11-31.16 above). We have also seen that easements can be created by implication (se paras 33.27-33.33 above) or by prescription (see paras 33.40-33.51 above) and that squatters can acquire rights by way of adverse possession (se para 31.19-31.34 above); in none of these situations will documents have been used.

36.21　*The distinction between first registration and subsequent dealings*　The LRA 2002 has, for the first time, drawn a distinction between those overriding interests that bind a first registered proprietor and those that bind on any subsequent dealings with the registered estate. While the overriding interests themselves are broadly the same, those that bind on a first registration are more widely defined and are listed in Sch 1 to the Act[1]. Those that bind on subsequent dealings are more narrowly defined and are listed in Sch 3. The reason for the distinction is that first registration can take place voluntarily without the need for any transaction. Thus, there is not necessarily any purchaser or mortgagee to be burdened by the need to discover the existence of overriding interests; they are therefore more widely defined. In the case of subsequent dealings, the needs of a purchaser are given greater consideration with the result that overriding interests are, in this case, drawn more narrowly; in particular, account is often taken of how readily the rights can be discovered by a purchaser.

In practice, the vast majority of transactions are dealings with already registered estates. In the following paragraphs we will, therefore, deal primarily with those overriding interests that will bind a purchaser or mortgagee of such estates, ie those listed in Sch 3. However, where appropriate, we will draw attention to the way in which the Sch 1 equivalent differs.

1   It should be noted that an applicant for first registration is obliged to inform the Land Registry of any known interests to which their estate is subject, LRA 1925, s 71. Where such interests fall within Schedule 1 and are not excluded by s 33 (as to which see para 36.34 below) the registrar is obliged to protect them by the entry of a notice. In this event the interests take their protection from the entry of the notice and are not then overriding.

Short legal leases

36.22 Most legal leases exceeding seven years are overriding interests under Sch 3, para 1. The only exceptions are those few leases for seven years or less that are required to be registered with their own independent title[1]; of these, the most important are reversionary leases of any length that are to start at least 3 months after the date of grant[2]. The reasons why it is felt unnecessary to require short leases either to be registered with their own title, or protected by notice[3] are various. Such leases are often not transferred or mortgaged; there are very many of them (so that registration would have considerable resource implications); and tenants are usually in occupation so that the existence of the lease is readily discoverable.

1   LRA 2002, s 4; see para 30.14 above.
2   LRA 2002, s 4; see para 30.14 above.
3   See para 36.34 below.

Rights of persons in actual occupation

36.23 Schedule 3, para 2 provides that 'interests belonging at the time of the disposition to a person in actual occupation of the land' will bind a purchaser of a registered estate. It replaces s 70(1)(g) of the LRA 1925, one of the most heavily litigated provisions in that Act. While there are important differences between s 70(1)(g) and para 2, some at least of the existing case law on the former provision will remain relevant.

This is the most controversial and extensive category of overriding interest. Any proprietary right affecting registered land can fall within para 2 provided only that its owner is in actual occupation of the land to which it relates[1]. (It should be stressed that it is the *right* that is the overriding interest, not the occupation; occupation by someone without a proprietary right to the land can never give rise to an overriding interest.) While the LRA seeks to eliminate the doctrine of notice, para 2 may be regarded as affording very similar protection under the registered land system to that conferred by the doctrine in *Hunt v Luck*.[2] Indeed, para 1 may be regarded as even more extensive; while constructive notice cannot save an interest in unregistered land which should have been registered under the LCA,[3] para 2 can operate to protect a right which could have been entered on the Land Register; it makes no difference that the right protected by occupation might also have been protected by the entry of a notice on the register.[4]

1   Thus, the right must relate to the land that is occupied; this means that the occupation of part of land cannot render overriding an interest over a larger whole. This overturns previous case law – *Wallcite Ltd v Ferrishurst* Ltd [1999] 1 All ER 977.

2   [1902] I Ch 428, CA. Ie whereby a purchaser has constructive notice of the rights of any person in occupation of land; para 36.6 above.
3   Land Charges Act 1972, s 4(5) and (6); see para 36.12 above.
4   Williams and Glyn's Bank Ltd v Boland [1980] 2 All ER 408, HL; see para 36.28 below.

36.24   *Rights with reference to land*   The only rights which can be protected by actual occupation under para 2 are 'rights with reference to land which have the quality of being capable of enduring through different ownerships of the land according to normal conceptions of title to real property', in other words, recognised proprietary interests.[1] Examples include unregistered estate contracts such as contracts for the sale of land and options [2], rights of pre-emption[3], interests under any trust of land,[4] rights in the course of being acquired by a squatter[5], and interests arising by way of proprietary estoppel[6].

However, proprietary rights that are not intended to take priority over the purchaser cannot be overriding. So, where an implied co-owner knows that a mortgage is necessary in order to acquire the very property to which she will have rights, those rights cannot override the rights of the mortgagee, even though she is in actual occupation[7]. Rights to land that are not proprietary, such as contractual licences[8], cannot be overriding interests. It is expressly provided that certain interests are not covered by para 2; these are beneficial interests under an old strict settlement,[9] a spouse's rights of occupation under what is now the Family Law Act 1996,[10] reversionary leases that are not to commence for at least three months and have not yet taken effect[11], and overriding leases under the Landlord and Tenant (Covenants) Act 1995[12]. These must be protected by other means; either by registration in their own right (reversionary leases) or by the entry of a notice[13] or restriction[14].

I   National Provincial Bank Ltd v Ainsworth [1965] AC 1175 at 1226.
2   Bridges v Mees [1957] 2 All ER 577 (contract of sale); Webb v Pollmount [1966] 1 All ER 481 (option to purchase).
3   Specifically dealt with by LRA 1925, s 115.
4   Williams and Glyn's Bank Ltd v Boland [1980] 2 All ER 408, HL.
5   Ie where a squatter has been in adverse possession of registered land for, say, five years and the land is then sold by the registered proprietor, the new registered proprietor will usually be bound by the five years of adverse possession. Time does not begin afresh for the squatter; he can apply for registration after a further five years adverse possession. See para 31.29 above.
6   Specifically dealt with by LRA 1925, s 116.
7   Bristol and West Building Society v Henning [1985] 2 All ER 606; Paddington Building Society v Mendelsohn (1985) 50 P & CR 244; see para 35.22 above.
8   See para 29.41 above.
9   LRA 2002, Sch 3, para 2(a).
10   Family Law Act 1996, s 31(10)(b).
11   LRA 2002, Sch 3, para 2(d).
12   Landlord and Tenant (Covenants) Act 1995, s 20(6). For the confusingly named overriding lease, see para 37.67 below.
13   See para 36.34 below.
14   See para 36.33 below.

36.25   *Actual occupation*   It is expressly provided that, for the purposes of Sch 3, the occupation (*not* the right) must, except where the purchaser has actual knowledge, be 'obvious on a reasonably careful inspection of the land at the time of the disposition'. This is a new requirement which settles a long standing debate on whether, under the previous law, actual occupation was purely a question of fact or whether it should be readily discoverable by a purchaser. Under the new law it is clear that discoverability is now a key question.

This does not mean that there will not still be difficult questions to answer. There are bound to be issues over what amounts to a 'reasonably careful inspection'. It will also be necessary to clarify whether the occupation must be obvious to *a* purchaser, or to *the* purchaser. Equally there will continue to be issues over what constitutes actual occupation. Clearly, where the adult[1] owner of the right is in permanent occupation of the property, eg a wife or cohabitee living in the home to which she has implied rights of co-ownership, she will be in actual occupation[2]. The position would be the same were a permanent occupier be away on holiday or in hospital for a short time[3]. What of a more intermittent presence in the home? Would the wife in *Kingsnorth Finance Co Ltd v Tizard*[4] be regarded as being in actual occupation under para 2? What of a long holiday away from home, or leaving the property empty save for furniture[5]? Can actual occupation take place through an agent or employee[6]?

Under the previous law, there was for a long time uncertainty as to whether the actual occupation had to exist at the date of the disposition, ie completion of the purchase or mortgage, or at the date when the purchaser or mortgagee is registered[7]. Paragraph 2 makes it explicit that actual occupation must exist at the date of completion. This means that anyone going into occupation after completion but before registration (classically, a cohabitee who, unknown to a mortgagee financing the purchase, goes into occupation with the registered proprietor immediately after the mortgage is created but before it can be registered) cannot claim priority over that mortgagee.

1   It has been held that minor children cannot be in actual occupation, see *Hypo-Mortgage Services Ltd v Robinson* [1997] 2 FLR 71.
2   *Williams and Glyn's Bank Ltd v Boland* [1980] 2 All ER 408.
3   *Chhokar v Chhokar* [1984] FLR 313.
4   [1986] 2 All ER 54. For the facts of this case see para 36.13 above.
5   The decision in *Strand Securities v Caswell* [1965] 1 All ER 820 held that leaving furniture would not be sufficient.
6   Possibly. Compare *Strand Securities v Caswell* [1965] 1 All ER 820, where occupation by a step daughter was held not to be on behalf of her stepfather with *Lloyds Bank plc v Rosset* [1989] Ch 350 where the Court of Appeal held that actual occupation by builders employed by the wife was sufficient for her to be so. (Note that this issue was not discussed by the House of Lords' ruling in that case.)
7   Finally resolved in favour of the date of completion by the House of Lords in *Abbey National Building Society v Cann* [1990] 1 All ER 1085 at 1101.

36.26 *Inquiry*   A purchaser or mortgagee of registered land should inquire of all those who are or appear to be in actual occupation of the property as to whether they have any rights in the land; the vendor's word should not be accepted.[1] Where such an inquiry is made of an occupier and that person does not disclose the right when he could reasonably have been expected to do so, that right will not then be an overriding interest.[2]

Particular care needs to be taken where a spouse or co-habitee whose name is not on the register is in occupation; a prospective purchaser or lender should ensure that a reasonable inspection of the property is undertaken[3] and where this reveals the presence of such an occupier, inquiries should be made of him or her. If, as in *Williams and Glyn's Bank Ltd v Boland*,[4] the occupier has rights (in that case as a beneficial co-owner of the property) and the purchaser or lender fails to make inquiry of him or her, the purchaser or lender takes subject to them. Where potential lenders become aware that persons other than the registered proprietor are in occupation of the property being offered as security, it is now standard practice for them to require those occupiers to sign a declaration under which any rights that they may have are postponed to the rights of the mortgagee.

1   *Hodgson v Marks* [1971] Ch 892 at 931.
2   LRA 2002, Sch 3, para 2(b).
3   See para 36.25 above.
4   [1980] 2 All ER 408, HL.

36.27 *Overreaching*   Many of the cases concerning the LRA 1925, s 70(1)(g) involved the claims of implied co-owners and this is likely to continue under the new Sch 3. As we have seen[1] co-ownership gives rise to a trust of land with the result that, in many instances of implied co-ownership, the person who appears to be a sole registered proprietor is in law a trustee holding the property on trust for himself and the implied co-owner. We have also seen that, where a purchaser deals with a sole trustee, the overreaching machinery is not triggered[2] so that the implied co-owner's rights may bind the purchaser. In unregistered land this will only be the case where the purchaser has *notice* of the rights of the co-owner.[3] In registered land those rights can, but are unlikely to be, protected by an entry in the register[4] or, where the implied co-owner is in actual occupation, they can bind a purchaser as an overriding interest under Sch 3. However, it has been made clear by the House of Lords in *City of London Building Society v Flegg*[5] that, where a purchaser (in that case a mortgagee) deals not with a sole trustee but with the trustees who are at least two in number, the rights of any other implied co-owners will be overreached even where the latter are in actual occupation.[6]

1   Para 32.32 above.
2   Para 32.32 above.
3   Para 36.13 above.
4   Para 36.34 below.
5   [1987] 3 All ER 435, HL. For the facts of this case, see para 32.31 above.
6   See also *State Bank of India v Sood* [1997] 1 All ER 169, CA.

36.28   *The operation of Schedule 3*   There is, of course, no experience yet of the operation of Sch 3. However, some flavour of how the new provision will work can be gained from looking at three cases under the old s 70(1)(g) since, if the facts of these were to be repeated today, the outcome would be the same. In *Hodgson v Marks*[1] Mrs Hodgson, the freehold owner of a house, transferred it, for nothing, to her lodger, Evans. This was not intended to be an outright gift, for the parties agreed that although Evans was to become the registered proprietor, the beneficial (equitable) ownership was to remain in Mrs Hodgson; in other words, Evans was to hold the land on (resulting) trust for Mrs Hodgson. The parties continued to live in the house as if nothing had changed: Mrs Hodgson as if owner and Evans as if lodger. Evans then sold the house to Marks who became registered proprietor. Marks was aware of Mrs Hodgson's presence in the house but not of any rights she might have in respect of it. Mrs Hodgson's interest under the trust could only bind Marks if either it was protected by an entry on the register, which it was not, or if it was an overriding interest by virtue of her occupation of the property. The Court of Appeal held that she was in actual occupation of the property and her rights under the trust constituted an overriding interest. The court held that simply because the vendor is, or appears to be, in occupation of the property does not mean that no one else can be in actual occupation.

In *Strand Securities Ltd v Caswell*[2] the defendant was the tenant under a sublease which, as the law then stood, was not required to have its title registered. He later allowed his stepdaughter and her family to live in the flat rent free. When his landlord's registered lease was later transferred to the claimants the latter claimed to take free from the defendant's sublease. The Court of Appeal held that the defendant could not have an overriding interest under s 70(1)(g)[3] since, although he owned a right having reference to land (ie the sublease), he was not in actual occupation of the flat. He did not live there and neither the presence of his furniture nor the occupation of his stepdaughter ranked as his actual occupation. Equally his stepdaughter did not have an overriding interest; although she was in actual occupation, she did not have a right with reference to land since she was only a licensee.[4]

In *Williams and Glyn's Bank Ltd v Boland*[5] Mrs Boland was, by virtue of her substantial contribution to its purchase price, an equitable tenant in common of the house which had been transferred into the sole name of her husband.[6] In order to raise money for his business, he later mortgaged the house to the bank which made no inquiries of Mrs Boland. On the husband defaulting, the bank started possession proceedings. It was held, however, that the wife had an interest with reference to land and was in actual occupation; she therefore had an overriding interest which had priority over the bank's mortgage and it could not therefore obtain possession against her.

1   [1971] 2 All ER 684, CA.
2   [1965] 1 All ER 820, CA.
3   The sublease did not meet the requirements of s 70(1)(k).
4   The court went on to hold that, for other reasons, the defendant's sublease bound the claimants.
5   [1980] 2 All ER 408, HL.
6   Para 32.12 above.

36.29   *Rights of persons in actual occupation under Schedule 1*   Because a first registration can take place voluntarily without the occurrence of any transaction, the definition in Sch 1 of the rights of persons in actual occupation is slightly different from that in Sch 3. Such rights will bind the first registered proprietor, even though the occupation is not obvious and even though inquiries may have been made of the occupier and the rights have not been disclosed[1]. This seems fair enough in the case of a voluntary registration, where there will normally have been no disposition and the new registered proprietor will be the existing owner. It seems less justifiable where there is a transaction and the first registered proprietor is a new owner; in such circumstances there seems no good reason for the new registered proprietor not being given the same protection as under Sch 3.

1   LRA 2002, Sch 1, para 2.

Easements and profits a prendre

36.30   *Schedule 3*   Paragraph 3 of Sch 3 makes certain legal easements[1] and profits[2] overriding interests. It will be remembered[3] that expressly created easements and profits are dispositions that must be completed by registration[4]; this means that such rights will be noted on the register[5] and will not therefore be overriding interests. Accordingly, the only legal easements and profits that can be overriding interests under Sch 3 are those created under LPA s 62[6], those created by implication[7], and those acquired by prescription[8]. Even then, unless the dominant owner proves that the easement or profit has been exercised during the year preceding the disposition[9], it will not be overriding unless it was known to the purchaser and obvious on a reasonable inspection of the servient land[10]. However, these limitations will not apply to those easements and profits within Sch 3 that are created after the commencement of LRA 2002 (ie 13 October 2003) and during the following three years (ie prior to 13 October 2006)[11], with the result that all[12] legal easements and profits arising during that period will be overriding. It should be noted that, unlike LRA 1925, the 2002 Act makes it clear that equitable easements and profits cannot be overriding interests; these will only bind a purchaser for valuable consideration where they are protected by the entry of a notice[13].

1   See Ch 33.
2   See para 33.19 above.
3   See para 30.17 above.
4   LRA 2002, s 27(1).
5   LRA 2002, Sch 2, para 7(2).
6   See para 33.34-33.38 above. LRA 2002, s 27(7) specifically provides that in such circumstances there is no requirement for there to be a disposition completed by registration; hence such easements can fall within para 3.
7   See paras 33.27-33.33 above.
8   See paras 33.40-33.51 above.
9   LRA 2002, Sch 3, para 3(2).
10   LRA 2002, Sch 3, para 3(1).
11   LRA 2002, Sch 12, para 10.
12   Save those that are expressly created; these must be created by registered disposition, LRA 2002, s 27.
13   See para 36.34 below.

36.31   *Schedule 1*   In the case of a first registration any existing legal easement or profit, whether created expressly or impliedly or acquired under LRA 1925 s 62 or by prescription, will bind a first registered proprietor of the servient land[1]. As with Sch 3, it is now clear that equitable easements cannot bind a first registered proprietor unless it was already registered under the LCA[3].

1   LRA 2002, Sch 1 para 3.
2   See para 36.12 above.

Miscellaneous overriding interests

36.32   Both Schs 1 and 3 make a range of other rights overriding[1]; these include customary rights[2], public rights[3] and local land charges[4]. A further series of somewhat archaic rights (eg manorial rights and rights to payment in lieu of a tithe) are retained as overriding interests for the next 10 years[5]; after that period they will cease to have effect[6].

1   LRA 2002, Sch 1, paras 4–9; Sch 3, paras 4-9.
2   See para 33.22 above.
3   See para 33.16 above.
4   See para 30.24 above.
5   LRA 2002, Sch 1, paras 10-14; Sch 3, paras 10-14.
6   LRA 2002, s 117(1).

Interests that require protection by an entry on the register

36.33 Virtually all interests affecting a registered estate *can* be protected by an entry on the register, including those that, in the absence of such an entry, will be overriding interests. As we have seen[1], most of the rights that can be overriding interests are, in practice, unlikely to be protected by way of an entry on the register and the owners of such rights will usually need to depend for their protection on the overriding status of their rights. However, it should be appreciated that such rights *are capable* of being protected by an entry on the register.

For most practical purposes we are here concerned with third party rights affecting a registered estate which cannot be overriding interests. Such interests must be protected by entry on the register; however, the function of such an entry is not always to render the right binding on a purchaser. In some instances, notably entries in relation to the rights of beneficiaries under a trust of land, the purpose of the entry is to make any purchaser aware that the registered proprietors are trustees and that the overreaching machinery (ie payment of the purchase money to at least two trustees) needs to be complied with if the purchaser is to take free from the rights. In the other cases the function of the entry is indeed to inform the purchaser of rights which will bind him. There are now two methods of protecting interests by entry on the register.

1   Para 36.20 above.

Methods of protection

36.34   *Restriction* A restriction can be entered in the Proprietorship Register of the register of title by, or with the consent of, the registered proprietor himself[1]. They can also be entered by the registrar[2], by order of the court[3], or on the application of any person with a sufficient interest in the making of an entry[4]. A restriction does not operate to make interests binding on a purchaser. Rather, its object is to prevent dealings with the land unless a specified requirement has been complied with[5], such as the payment of the purchase money to trustees who must be at least two in number, or the obtaining of the consent of a particular person. It is also used to stop the registered proprietor dealing with the land, eg where the registered proprietor has been declared bankrupt. It can be used to protect any type of interest but one of its main uses is to protect beneficial (equitable) interests under a trust of land by ensuring that the overreaching provisions are complied with.[6]

1   LRA 2002, s 43(1)(a) and (b).
2   LRA 2002, ss 42 and 44.
3   LRA 2002, s 46.

4   LRA 2002, s 43(1)(c).
5   LRA 2002, s 40.
6   See para 32.32 above.

36.35   *Notice*   A notice is an entry in the register in respect of the burden of an interest affecting a registered estate.[1] It can be used to protect any right except certain specified rights[2]. The most important of the excluded rights are: beneficial interests under a trust (which as we have seen[3] are more appropriately protected by a restriction); any lease for a term of three years or less that is not required to be registered with its own title[4]; restrictive covenants between landlord and tenant. All other interests such as estate contracts, restrictive covenants between freeholders and adverse easements can be protected by notice. There are two alternative types of notice that can be entered; and agreed notice or a unilateral notice.

1   An agreed notice will be entered where either the registered proprietor makes the application (or consents to the application) or where the registrar is satisfied as to the validity of the interest[5]. Its normal use is, therefore, where the registered proprietor acceptes the validity of the interest (which he often does).

2   However, there are times when the registered proprietor disputes the validity of the interest being claimed and will not agree to the entry of a notice. In this event the owner of the interest can apply for the entry of a unilateral notice[6]. Where a unilateral notice is entered the registered proprietor must be informed and he can apply for the entry to be cancelled[7]; where this happens, the owner of the interest will have to prove the validity of his claim in order to prevent the removal of the entry. Since the entry of a unilateral notice can damage the registered proprietor (it may, for example, prevent a sale of the property going ahead) the entry of such a notice without reasonable cause gives rise to a liability in damages[8].

The effect of the entry of a notice is to render the right binding on a subsequent purchaser for valuable consideration since a disposition by a registered proprietor takes effect subject to all rights protected by a notice;[9] however, it does not confer priority over an earlier, unregistered minor interest since, in such a situation, priority is governed by the order in which the interests are created.[10] The entry of a notice does not confer validity on an otherwise invalid interest.[11]

1   LRA 2002, s 32(1).
2   LRA 2002, s 33.
3   See para 36.33 above.
4   This means, in effect, that leases for a term exceeding three years but not more than seven years *can* be protected by an entry on the register. This is, of course, not necessary since such leases are overriding interests and will therefore bind a purchaser in any event. Leases of three years or less cannot be protected by the entry of a notice and will thus depend for their protection on their overriding status, save in those cases where such leases have to be registered with their own independent title (for which see para 30.14 above).
5   LRA 2002, s 34(3).
6   LRA 2002, s 34(2).
7   LRA 2002, s 35.
8   LRA 2002, s 77.
9   LRA 2002, s 29(2).
10   LRA 2002, s 28.
11   LRA 2002, s 32(3).

The search procedure
36.36   As we have seen,[1] an intending purchaser (which, as always, includes a mortgagee) can request an official search of the register in order to discover the existence of interests protected by an entry on the register.[2] Once in receipt of an official certificate of search the

purchaser has the benefit of a 30-day priority period in which to complete his transaction and apply for registration; provided he does so, he will not be bound by any adverse entries made on the register during that period.

1 Para 30.36 above.
2 LRA 1925, s 70.

Failure to register

36.37 The scheme of the LRA is designed to ensure that, in the case of interests that can be protected by an entry on the register, the state of the register should be paramount and that the doctrine of notice has no application. All a purchaser has to do is consult the register; he will take free from any interest not entered on the register. To this, as we have seen[1], there is one exception. Where the owner of an unregistered interest that could have been protected by an entry but has not been, is in actual occupation of the land to which the right relates, that interest will be regarded as an overriding interest within Sch 3. As such it will bind any purchaser.

The intention that the enforceability of interests affecting a registered estate should hinge solely on either an entry in the register or their overriding status, is made clear by LRA 1925, s 29. This provides that the purchaser of registered land for valuable consideration is bound only by entries on the register and overriding interests. However, there are always difficult issues where a purchaser either knows or ought to have known of an interest which ought to have been entered on the register but which has not been. Under the LRA 1925, there were situations in which the courts held that a purchaser was bound by an interest which was neither overriding nor entered on the register. These included cases of fraud[2], bad faith[3], and circumstances in which a constructive trust was imposed on the purchaser[4]. The LRA 2002 does not deal with this question explicitly; however, the Law Commission, in the Report containing the draft of the LRA 2002, has made it clear that neither actual notice nor bad faith will affect the statutory protection of the purchaser[5]. While it seems unlikely that a fraudulent purchaser will retain the protection of s 29, the clear intention is that, in all other cases, the owner of the unprotected interest will be left to any personal claims that he might have against the purchaser. These could include contractual rights, tortious liability for interference with contractual rights, or equitable liability for knowing receipt of trust moneys. The ambit of these liabilities in this context are at present unknown and it remains to be seen how ready the courts are to intervene. Too enthusiastic an approach would undermine the protection of purchasers and the whole system of registration of title.

1 Para 36.20 above.
2 *Jones v Lipman* [1962] 1 WLR 832. It should be appreciated that a purchaser will not be regarded as fraudulent simply because he knows of the unregistered minor interest; see *De Lusignan v Johnson* (1973) 230 Estates Gazette 499.
3 *Peffer v Rigg* [1978] 3 All ER 745.
4 *Lyus v Prowsa Developments Ltd* [1982] 2 All ER 953. See para 31.10 above.
5 Law Com 271 (2001).

Alteration, rectification and indemnity

Alteration

36.38 It was pointed out earlier[1] that registration with absolute title does not, despite the name, absolutely guarantee the title, for there remains the possibility that the register of title may be altered (either by court order[2] or by the Registrar[3]). It is inevitable that errors can be made and that there should be the power to put these right. In some circumstances, where a person suffers loss as a result of a change in the register (or a refusal to change the register) there is an entitlement to an indemnity from state funds[4]. Broadly speaking, although the structure and terminology of the provisions governing alterations has been changed by LRA 2002, the substance of the law remains much as it was under LRA 1925. Thus previous case law will remain relevant.

LRA 2002 introduces the term 'alteration'; this applies to any change to the register. Some alterations, ie ones that involve correcting a mistake and which prejudicially affect the title of a registered proprietor, are known as 'rectification'. Thus rectification is narrower than alteration and, as we shall see, it is usually only rectification that gives rise to a right to an indemnity[4]. Under LRA 2002, s 65 and Sch 4 either the court or the registrar can order the alteration of the register in three circumstances:

- to correct a mistake;
- to bring the register up to date; and
- to give effect to any interest excepted from the effects of registration.

In addition, the registrar has the power to remove superfluous entries. Where a case falls within any of these heads the register must be altered, unless the circumstances are exceptional[5].

1 Para 30.16 above.
2 LRA 2002, Sch 4, para 2.
3 LRA 2002, Sch 4, para 5.
4 See para 36.43 below.
5 LRA 2002, Sch 4, paras 3(3) and 5(3).

36.39 *Mistake* One of the most obvious mistakes that can be made is where someone who is not entitled to the land (or not to all of it) is wrongly registered as its proprietor[1]. Similarly, a fraud practised on the registry, as where a conveyance or mortgage is forged,[2] will also be regarded as a mistake. In these instances the register will be rectified (and an indemnity may well be payable[3]). However, where a *transferor* (as opposed to the registry) is defrauded, it will not be regarded as a mistake and the register will not be *rectified*[4] (although the register will be *altered* under the jurisdiction to bring the register up to date.[5]) In such a case, no indemnity will be payable.

1 *Re 139 High Street, Deptford* [1951] Ch 884.
2 *First National Securities v Hegerty* [1984] 1 All ER 139.
3 See para 36.44 below.
4 *Norwich and Peterborough Building Society v Steed* [1993] 1 All ER 330, CA.
5 See para 36.40 below.

36.40 *Bringing the register up to date* This covers the entry on the register of rights that arise after registration, such as easements acquired by prescription. As indicated in the previous paragraph, it will also cover cases where it was the transferor who was defrauded rather than the registry.

36.41 *Exceptions from registration* We have seen that, where a person is registered with a title less than absolute (eg he is registered with a possessory or qualified title), he does not take free from any existing rights[1]. If such rights become known to the registry they will be entered on the register.

1 See para 30.16 above.

36.42 *Removal of superfluous entries* The registrar has jurisdiction to remove entries that cease to have effect. For example, a restriction[1] on all dealings with the land may have been imposed due to specific circumstances. If these come to an end, the restriction can be removed.

1 See para 36.33 above.

36.43 *Limits on the right to alter*   Although the circumstances in which the register can be altered or rectified appear to be very wide, as under the LRA 1925, the 2002 Act limits the right to alter the register against a registered proprietor who is in physical possession[1]. (A registered proprietor who is a landlord, mortgagor, licensor or trustee is to be treated as being in possession where the land is occupied by his tenant, mortgagee, licensee or beneficiary respectively[2].) In these circumstances the register cannot be altered without his consent unless either the registered proprietor has by fraud or lack of proper care caused or substantially contributed to the mistake, or where it would be unjust not to rectify[3].

1   LRA 2002, s 131(1).
2   LRA 2002, s 131(2).
3   LRA 2002, Sch 4, paras 3(2) and 6(2).

Indemnity

36.44   Schedule 8 governs the payment of an indemnity. It is now tied to rectification, ie the correction of a mistake that adversely affects the title of the registered proprietor (and to a refusal to rectify that causes loss)[1]. A close consideration of the other alterations that can be made to the register show that these do not, in fact, cause loss to the registered proprietor. This is because they give effect to rights that would in any event have bound him; the alteration is being made in order to ensure that the register truly reflects the existing position. An indemnity is also available if loss is caused where the registry has made certain specified errors, notably if a mistake in making an official search[2] is made by the registry.

The indemnity payable where the applicant has caused or substantially contributed to the loss by fraud or lack of proper care may be reduced to such extent as is just and equitable.[3]

1   LRA 2002, Sch 8, para 1(1)(a).
2   LRA 2002, Sch 8, para 1(1)(b)-(g).
3   LRA 2002, Sch 8, para 5.

Part V

The law of landlord and tenant

Chapter 37

Landlord and tenant: the general law

37.1 We have, so far, given only passing consideration to leasehold ownership when dealing with the doctrine of estates[1] and the formal[2] and informal[3] creation of interests in land. This may have given a misleading impression for such ownership is widespread in England and Wales. The lease obviously provides an important medium through which essentially short-term occupation of both residential and commercial property can be enjoyed without the need for a capital contribution to its purchase. However, the long-term lease (eg for 99 years or even 999 years) for which a capital sum (known as a 'premium') is normally paid is commonplace. Such leases have become, in the 20th century, a popular device for financing the development of land and for investing in land. In addition, they are still the usual mechanism for the occupation of a unit within a building (notably flats); this is because, as we have seen, obligations imposed under a lease are more readily enforceable against future owners of that lease than they would be if imposed on a freeholder.[4] However, as we have also seen[5], the Commonhold and Leasehold Reform Act 2002 is to introduce a new form of ownership – the commonhold – which is specifically (but not exclusively) aimed at facilitating the freehold ownership of flats. This is not expected to come on stream until 2004 and, even then, it will take many years before existing long leases of flats disappear.

In this chapter we deal with:

- the essential features of leasehold ownership;
- the most commonly encountered of the obligations (ie covenants) imposed in a lease;
- the remedies available to both landlord and tenant in the event of a breach of covenant;
- the circumstances in which lease covenants are enforceable against those to whom either the lease or the landlord's interest (the reversion) may be transferred; and
- the termination of leases at common law.

1 Para 29.33 above.
2 Paras 30.10 and 30.11 above.
3 Paras 31.3–31.5 above.
4 Para 34.4 above and para 37.53, note 1 below.
5 Para 29.35 above

Characteristics of leasehold interests

37.2 In order for a lease to arise, exclusive possession of a defined area of land for a certain or ascertainable period of time must be conferred. Any occupation of land which fails to display these characteristics cannot be a lease and the occupier is a mere licensee.[1] While it is usual for rent to be paid this is not legally essential.[2] As will become apparent, the distinction between a lease and a licence has been fraught with difficulties because landowners have sought to devise agreements to occupy which do *not* amount to leases in order to avoid the statutory protection which is conferred on many tenants (but not on licensees).[3]

If a lease is to confer a legal estate it must comply with the required formalities; as we have seen, for leases in excess of three years a deed must be used, while those for three years or less may be created orally or in writing, provided that they take effect in possession[4] and are at the best rent reasonably obtainable.[5] A lease for a term in excess of seven years must always be registered with its own independent title[6]. Leases which fail to comply with these formal requirements may nevertheless take effect in equity.[7]

1   Paras 37.3–37.10 below.
2   *Ashburn Anstalt v Arnold* [1988] 2 All ER 147, CA.
3   The problem has diminished since the implementation of the Housing Act 1988; this Act has significantly reduced the protection given to residential tenants with the result that, since 1989, landowners have been happy to grant short-term tenancies of residential property. See ch 38.
4   A lease not exceeding three years which is to take effect on a future date must be created by deed; see *Long v London Borough of Tower Hamlets* [1996] 2 All ER 683 and para 30.7, note 1 above. Furthermore if it is to commence more than three months after the date on which it is created, it must also be registered with its own title.
5   Paras 30.10 and 30.11 above.
6   LRA 2002, s 4 and para 30.14 above.
7   Paras 31.3–31.5 above.

Certainty of term

37.3   The requirement that a lease must be of certain duration means that, at the outset, it must have a certain commencement date[1] and a certain or ascertainable maximum duration (often referred to as 'certainty of term'). These days most leases are for a fixed term, eg for five years, and no problems of certainty of term arise. However, from time to time cases arise where leases have been granted for a period measured by reference to an uncertain event. Periodic tenancies have also given rise to difficulties on the question of certainty. In addition, the LPA 1925 deals specifically with some unusual types of lease which might otherwise be regarded as uncertain, in order to bring them within the framework of modern leasehold ownership.

1   *Harvey v Pratt* [1965] 1 WLR 1025.

Fixed-term leases

37.4   A fixed-term lease is one which is granted for a predetermined period of time. It is not necessary for the term to be continuous; thus there is a valid lease where a holiday home is let on a 'time-share' basis for one week per year for 80 years.[1] A fixed-term lease cannot be certain if it is expressed to last until an event which either may or may not happen, or which will happen but at an unpredictable date. So for example, a lease which was expressed to last for the duration of the war was declared to be void by the Court of Appeal in *Lace v Chantler*.[2] This rule has recently been affirmed by the House of Lords in *Prudential Assurance Co v London Residuary Body*.[3] Here a lease granted until the land was required for road widening was held to be void for uncertainty.[4] Their Lordships emphatically rejected any suggestion[5] that a term can be certain where the event which is to bring about the termination of the lease is within the control of one of the parties.

Where a fixed-term lease is held to be void for uncertainty of term, the agreed 'lease' is of no effect but, provided the tenant has taken up occupation and paid rent, an implied periodic tenancy will arise.[6] This tenancy can be terminated by the service of an appropriate notice to quit. The courts will *not* imply that such a notice can only be served in the circumstances which would have brought about the end of the intended fixed term, since this would render the periodic tenancy uncertain. So, in the *Prudential* case, the tenants were held to be yearly tenants; the defendant landlords were entitled immediately to serve six months' notice to quit and were not obliged to wait until the land was required for road widening before serving such a notice.

1   *Cottage Holiday Associates Ltd v Customs and Excise Comrs* [1983] QB 735. Note that such discontinuous leases *may* now be registered with their own title.
2   [1944] 1 All ER 305, CA.
3   [1992] 3 All ER 504, HL.
4   It is worth noting that the desired object can be achieved in such cases without offending the rule on certainty of term by including a 'break' provision (as to which see para 37.76 below); for example, in *Prudential*, the parties could have expressed the lease to be for, say, 99 years subject to a landlord's right to break when the land was required for road widening.
5   See *Ashburn Anstalt v Arnold* [1988] 2 All ER 147, CA.
6   See para 37.13 below.

Periodic tenancies
37.5   Periodic tenancies – for example, weekly, monthly or yearly tenancies – do not determine (end) automatically at the end of the period, be it week or month or year, but continue from week to week, month to month, year to year, until ended by appropriate notice.[1] Thus, in one sense, at the outset of the tenancy its maximum duration is unknown and it has been said that the simple statement that the maximum duration of a term must be certainly known in advance of its taking effect does not directly apply to periodic tenancies.[2] However, this view has now been rejected by the House of Lords in the *Prudential* case.[3] Here it was held that periodic tenancies are subject to the same rule on certainty as fixed terms. A periodic tenancy is normally sufficiently certain because each party has the right to terminate it at the end of any period of the tenancy. Equally, such a tenancy will be valid where, at the beginning of the tenancy, it is agreed that one side cannot serve a notice to quit until after a *certain* time limit has elapsed (eg that the landlord will not serve a notice to quit for at least one year).[4] However, any agreement preventing one side determining the tenancy for an *uncertain* period will render the tenancy void (eg that the landlord will only serve a notice to quit if he requires the property for his own personal use).[5] A provision purporting to prohibit absolutely the giving of notice by one party is repugnant to the nature of the tenancy and therefore invalid.[6]

1   Para 37.76 below, and note, in particular, ch 38 as to the statutory regulation of the termination of tenancies.
2   *Re Midland Rly Co's Agreement* [1971] 1 All ER 1007; see also *Ashburn Anstalt v Arnold* [1988] 2 All ER 147, CA.
3   *Prudential Assurance Co v London Residuary Body* [1992] 3 All ER 504, HL, overruling *Midland Rly Co's Agreement* [1971] 1 All ER 1007 and *Ashburn Anstalt v Arnold* [1988] 2 All ER 147, CA on this point.
4   *Prudential Assurance Co v London Residuary Body* [1992] 3 All ER 504, HL.
5   {1992] 3 All ER 504, HL.
6   *Centaploy Ltd v Matlodge Ltd* [1973] 2 All ER 720.

Leases for life
37.6   Prior to 1926, it was possible to create a lease for life, despite the fact that such a term is far from certain. As a result of the LPA 1925, s 149(6), an attempt to create such a lease, at a rent or for a premium, now results in the grant of a 90-year term which may be ended after the death of the lessee by one month's notice in writing given on one of the usual quarter days (25 March, 24 June, 29 September, and 25 December).[1] This same rule applies to leases determinable on the marriage of the lessee.

1   For a recent application of this provision see *Skipton Building Society v Clayton* (1993) 25 HLR 596, CA; here it was held that an arrangement whereby, in return for the grant of an option to purchase at one-third market value, a couple were to be given a right to occupy a property for their joint lives fell within s 149(6).

Perpetually renewable leases

37.7   Again, prior to 1926, it was permissible to grant a lease conferring on the lessee the right to have the lease renewed on the expiry of the existing term over and over again. Such leases were, by the Law of Property Act 1922, s 145 and Sch 15 converted into terms of 2,000 years commencing with the beginning of the then existing term. Any perpetually renewable lease granted since 1926 is likewise to take effect as a 2,000-year term. The term created by the statute is subject to the provision that the tenant may terminate the lease on 10 days' notice ending on a date on which it would have expired had it not been converted. It is, of course, highly unlikely that a landlord would deliberately create a perpetually renewable lease and the court leans against finding that a lease contains a perpetual right of renewal.[1] However, this may be the only possible conclusion, as is demonstrated by *Re Hopkin's Lease, Caerphilly Concrete Products Ltd v Owen*,[2] where a landlord granted a lease, for a term of five years at a rent of £10 per annum, containing a covenant to renew the lease at the same rent and subject to the same covenants, including the covenant to renew, with the result that the lease was perpetually renewable; the landlord had inadvertently created a 2,000-year term at a rent of £10 per annum.

1   *Marjorie Burnett v Barclay* (1980) 258 Estates Gazette 642.
2   [1972] 1 All ER 248 CA.

Exclusive possession

37.8   For a person to be regarded as having a leasehold interest in property, it is essential that he should have exclusive possession of it. That is, he must have the right to exclude all others from the property, even the landlord himself. It is a fundamental principle that the landlord may only enter the property either with the permission of the tenant or under a right of entry[1] accorded to him by the lease. Without exclusive possession there can be no lease, only a licence. The latter confers only a personal permission to occupy property but does not give the occupier a stake in the property.[2]

1   Such a right is of a limited nature and allows entry only for specified purposes, eg to inspect for repairs.
2   *Marchant v Charters* [1977] 3 All ER 918, CA; para 29.41 above.

The distinction between a lease and a licence

37.9   The issue we are concerned with here is not simply an academic question of the difference between a personal right and a proprietary right, but also the practical question of whether in a given case a person is in occupation of property as a licensee or as a tenant. In some cases, particularly of shared occupation of residential premises, the grant of a licence to each occupier is more appropriate than the grant of a tenancy. However, the issue has more often arisen where a landowner has deliberately sought to 'dress up' a lease as a licence in order to prevent the occupier qualifying for the statutory protection which is conferred on many tenants. This used to be a particular problem in the residential sector because of the extremely beneficial nature of the protection conferred by the Rent Act 1977 and its precursors;[1] this legislation has now been supplanted[2] by the Housing Act 1988[3] and landlords are not now seeking to use residential licences to the same extent. However, landlords of commercial property will sometimes seek to avoid the provisions of Pt II of the Landlord and Tenant Act 1954 by granting purported licences; furthermore, the application of other statutory regimes often distinguish between leases and licences[4].

In considering whether a transaction constitutes a licence or a tenancy, the court is to have regard not to the label ('lease' or 'licence') which the parties give to the document but to the substance of the transaction.[5] As Lord Templeman pointed out in a now famous dictum in *Street v Mountford*,[6] 'The manufacture of a five-pronged implement for manual digging results in a fork even if the manufacturer ... insists that he intended to make and has made a spade.'[7] In other words, if the parties' agreement has the hallmarks of a tenancy, it is a tenancy, even if the parties by their agreement 'intend' to enter into a licence.

The hallmarks of a tenancy are, according to the House of Lords, exclusive possession, for a fixed or periodic term, at a rent.[8] Since Mrs Mountford's agreement with Mr Street was admitted to give her exclusive possession of rooms owned by Mr Street at a rent for a term, she was a tenant even though she had signed an agreement under which she expressly accepted that it was only a licence which gave her no protection as a Rent Act tenant. Accordingly, subject to limited exceptions,[9] since *Street v Mountford*, the courts need only inquire whether or not an agreement to occupy confers exclusive possession (for a fixed or periodic term).

However, once it was made clear that the absence of exclusive possession precluded the grant of a tenancy, it became common for landlords wishing to avoid the provisions of protective legislation to make use of agreements which either stated that exclusive possession was not conferred, or which contained provisions which were designed to have the effect of taking away exclusive possession. So, for example, there might be included a term under which the owner was given the right to share the property with the occupier, or one which prevented the occupier from using the property during, say, the hours of 12 noon and 2 pm. Where a court is satisfied that terms of this kind do not truly represent the intentions of the parties (ie that they are 'sham' terms), they will be ignored and the occupier will be a tenant.[10] However, where, for example, the landlord provides attendance or services[11] which require the landlord or his employees to exercise unrestricted access to and use of the premises, or where access is genuinely needed in the particular circumstances,[12] the occupier will not have exclusive possession and will be a mere licensee.

1   See para 38.2 below.
2   The RA 1977 continues to apply to tenancies granted prior to 15 January 1989; accordingly the lease/licence distinction remains vital in such cases.
3   See para 38.4 below.
4   See ch 38 below.
5   *Shell-Mex and BP Ltd v Manchester Garages Ltd* [1971] 1 All ER 841 and 845.
6   [1985] 2 All ER 289, HL.
7   [1985] 2 All ER 289 at 299.
8   [1985] 2 All ER 289 at 306. That is not to say that the payment of rent is an essential prerequisite of a tenancy, but rather that if the three hallmarks are present there is a tenancy: *Ashburn Anstalt v Arnold* [1988] 2 All ER 147, CA. 'Rent' does not include a mere contribution to the household expenses (eg to gas and electricity bills) of the property owner: *Bostock v Bryant* (1990) 22 HLR 449, CA.
9   In *Street v Mountford* [1985] 2 All ER 289 it was acknowledged that there may be occasions when an occupier has exclusive possession yet is merely a licensee. Two situations referred to in that case were that of a service occupier (ie an employee who occupies his employer's premises in order better to perform his duties as an employee) and where occupation has been conferred as an act of friendship or generosity (which negatives any intention to enter into legal relations and hence negatives the existence of a tenancy).
10   See, for example, *Aslan v Murphy (Nos 1 and 2)* [1989] 3 All ER 130, CA.
11   Such as cleaning the room and changing the linen: *Marchant v Charters* [1977] 3 All ER 918, CA.
12   *Westminster City Council v Clarke* [1992] 1 All ER 695, HL.

37.10   *Sharers*   In one particular situation the courts faced further difficulties in determining whether or not an occupier enjoyed exclusive possession. Where the use of accommodation was to be shared, landowners commonly required each sharer to sign a separate (but often identical) agreement conferring a right to occupy the whole of the premises, subject to the rights of the other occupiers. In this way it could be argued that none of the sharers had exclusive possession; each destroyed the others' exclusive possession. Not surprisingly, this matter came before the House of Lords in 1988 when appeals in two cases, *AG Securities v Vaughan* and *Antoniades v Villiers* were heard together.[1] Here it was decided that, in such instances, the approach should be two-stage. First, it should be decided whether or not the signing of *separate* agreements was genuine. If so, each sharer would have an individual, but not exclusive, right to use the property and could only be a licensee. However, if the signing of separate agreements was itself a pretence, then the sharers should be regarded as having together signed a single agreement; if this agreement genuinely conferred exclusive possession the sharers would be joint tenants.

In *AG Securities* four individuals sharing a four-bedroomed flat in a London mansion block, signed separate licence agreements at different times on different terms. They had not known each other prior to moving in to the flat. In these circumstances there was no artificiality about the separate agreements; it was clear that the purpose and intention of both parties to each agreement was that it should confer an individual right on the licensee named. Each was individually liable for the amount of rent to which he had agreed which, in that case, differed from the amounts paid by the others. There had been no grant of exclusive possession of any identifiable part of the flat to any individual and so each was a licensee.[2]

By way of contrast, in the *Antoniades* case, the defendant and a woman friend each signed a separate agreement for the occupation of a small one-bedroomed flat. Each agreement provided that the licensee was to have the use of the flat 'in common with the licensor and such other licensees or invitees as the licensor may permit from time to time to use the rooms'. The House of Lords found that there was an air of total unreality about these 'separate' documents, given the fact that the appellants were together seeking a flat as a quasi-matrimonial home. The documents were a pretence designed to disguise the true character of the agreement which, their Lordships held, should be regarded as a single contract. As the parties' subsequent conduct indicated, there was never any intention on the part of the landlord to share possession (either by himself or by introducing others) with the couple, who together had exclusive possession and were, therefore, joint tenants.

1   [1988] 3 All ER 1058, HL.
2   See also *Stribling v Wickham* (1989) 21 HLR 381, CA.

Particular types of tenancy

37.11   The great majority of leases are created expressly and tend, these days, to be for a fixed term. That said, periodic tenancies remain common, particularly in the residential sector. While many of these are expressly created, they also often come into being by way of implication. In this section we also consider a number of anomalous forms of tenancy and, finally, we explain forms of lease under which the tenant does not necessarily take an immediate entitlement to physical occupation.

Fixed-term leases

37.12   This is the simplest and most common form of lease. It arises where the tenancy is granted for a pre-determined period, eg for six months, for five years or for 99 years. The law sets no minimum or maximum period for such leases; all that is required is that the period of time for which the lease is to last is certain or ascertainable at the outset.[1] When the term for which the lease has been granted expires, the lease comes to an end automatically without the need for notice.[2] A fixed term lease must, in principle, run its course; it can only be brought to an end before the end of the term:

*   by the agreement of the parties (ie a surrender[3]);
*   where the tenant is in breach, by the exercise by the landlord of a right of re-entry (ie forfeiture[4]); or
*   by the exercise, where present, of an option to terminate (usually known as a 'break clause')[5].

1   See para 37.4 above.
2   See para 37.75 below, but note that statutory protection may mean that the tenant does not have to leave the premises, see ch 38.
3   See para 37.73 below.
4   See paras 37.44–37.47 and 37.72 below.
5   Para 37.76 below.

Periodic tenancies

37.13   A periodic tenancy is one which continues automatically from period to period until terminated by either side serving an appropriate notice to quit.[1] It is not a series of renewed tenancies but one continuous term which will run until brought to an end.[2] The most commonly encountered periodic tenancies are weekly, monthly and yearly tenancies. Such tenancies must, by definition, have a minimum duration of the initial period; as we have seen,[3] its maximum duration remains unknown until a notice to quit is actually served.[4]

Periodic tenancies can be created expressly but, in practice, many arise by implication.[5] Where a person is allowed into occupation of property as a tenant, without any express agreement as to the duration of the tenancy, he will be treated initially as a tenant at will.[6] If rent is then paid and accepted, an implied periodic tenancy, based on the periods by reference to which that rent is calculated, may then arise. Thus if the rent is fixed at £1,000 per annum, a yearly tenancy arises even if the rent is paid at more frequent intervals; if rent is fixed at £20 per week, a weekly tenancy arises.[7] As the case of *Manfield & Sons Ltd v Botchin*[8] shows, there is no room for the implication of a periodic tenancy where the parties expressly provide that the tenancy should remain at will. Furthermore, modern cases stress that whether or not a periodic tenancy arises as a result of the payment of rent depends on the intention of the parties.[9] Such an intention is particularly difficult to establish where a tenant holds over on the determination of a previous tenancy; where he is entitled to do so by virtue of statutory protection it is now more usual for the court not to imply a periodic tenancy.[10]

1   For notices to quit see para 37.76 below.
2   *Hammersmith and Fulham London Borough Council v Monk* [1992] 1 All ER 1, HL.
3   Para 37.5 above.
4   However, the fact that either side can ascertain the maximum term by serving a notice to quit is sufficient to render periodic tenancies sufficiently certain; see para 37.5 above.
5   Periodic tenancies are almost invariably legal. Provided the period on which the tenancy is based does not itself exceed three years (which would be very unusual) no formalities are required; LPA 1925 s 54(2), para 30.11 above.
6   See para 37.14 below.
7   See *Ladies' Hosiery and Underwear Ltd v Parker* [1930] 1 Ch 304.
8   [1970] 3 All ER 143.
9   *Javad v Aqil* [1991] 1 All ER 243, CA.
10 *Harvey v Stagg* (1977) 247 Estates Gazette 463, CA; *Longrigg, Burrough and Trounson v Smith* (1979) 251 Estates Gazette 847, CA.

Tenancy at will

37.14   A tenancy at will occurs where a person is let into, or allowed to remain in, possession of property as a tenant by the landlord on the basis that either side may terminate the arrangement whenever he wishes. It may arise where a purchaser of the freehold is permitted to occupy the property prior to completion of the transaction or where a prospective lessee is allowed into occupation while the parties continue negotiating the detailed terms of the lease,[1] or where a fixed-term tenant is permitted to remain in occupation after the expiry of the term.[2] Consequently, it has been suggested by Scarman LJ in *Heslop v Burns*,[3] that it may be that the tenancy at will can now serve only one legal purpose, and that is to provide for occupation of property during a period of transition. It was certainly made clear in *Javad v Aqil*[4] that, in such a transitional situation, the court may conclude that the parties only intended a tenancy at will even though rent has been paid and accepted.[5]

Although a tenancy at will often arises by implication, such a tenancy may be expressly granted, as in *Manfield & Sons Ltd v Botchin*[6] where such a tenancy was granted pending the landlord's application for planning permission to develop the site. An express tenancy at will may provide for the payment of rent by the tenant, in which case there will be no implication of a periodic tenancy.[7] If no provision is made for rent to be paid, the landlord is entitled to compensation for the use and occupation of the property.

1   *Javad v Aqil* [1991] 1 All ER 243, CA.
2   Unless the tenant is staying in occupation by virtue of statutory protection; see ch 38 below.
3   [1974] 3 All ER 406 at 416.
4   [1991] 1 All ER 243, CA.
5   As opposed to a periodic tenancy; see para 37.13 above.
6   [1970] 3 All ER 143.
7   Para 37.13 above.

Tenancy at sufferance

37.15   A tenant at sufferance is, at common law, someone who wrongfully remains in possession ('holds over') without the landlord's consent after his tenancy has come to an end. Such a person is in effect a trespasser. The landlord may at any time claim possession of the property. The tenant at sufferance is essentially in the position of a 'squatter',[1] though liable under statute[2] to pay either a payment calculated at double the rental value of the property or, in certain circumstances, double the rent which he paid under the lease, for holding over in the face of a notice to quit. In practice, many tenants who hold over after the end of their tenancies do so by virtue of statutory protection[3] and are not, therefore, tenants at sufferance.

1   Paras 31.32-31.34 above.
2   Landlord and Tenant Act 1730; Distress for Rent Act 1733.
3   Chapter 38 below.

Tenancy by estoppel

37.16   Where a person who has no power to do so purports to grant a lease or tenancy, he and his 'tenant' are estopped (ie prevented by the rules of evidence) from denying the validity of the 'lease'. Thus, as between the parties, a tenancy by estoppel has all the features of a valid tenancy; it will similarly bind assigns of the parties but will not bind third parties. A tenancy by estoppel could arise where a purchaser of land is allowed into possession prior to completion of the transaction and then purports to grant a lease, or where a mortgagor (borrower) purports to grant a lease where his power to do so has been excluded.[1] In the former case, the subsequent acquisition of the freehold estate by the purchaser is said to 'feed the estoppel' and confers on the tenant a valid tenancy.
1   Para 35.37 above.

Concurrent leases

37.17   A concurrent lease (sometimes called a 'side-by-side' lease, or a lease of the reversion) arises where a lease is granted which is to commence before the expiry of an existing lease of the same premises granted to another person. Accordingly the concurrent lessee becomes the landlord of the existing lessee. He is entitled to receive the rent and to enforce the tenant's covenants; equally he is obliged to honour the landlord's obligations under the existing lease. If the existing lease expires before the concurrent lease then the concurrent lessee becomes entitled, at that time, to physical possession of the property. If not, the concurrent lessee is only ever entitled to receive the income produced by the existing lease. The concurrent lease is thus a device by which income under an existing lease can be assigned for a fixed period of time, with or without any right to future physical occupation.

Reversionary leases

37.18 A reversionary lease is one which is granted now but which is to take effect at a future date, eg a lease for five years granted on 1 September 1998, to commence on 1 September 1999. A person may not create, or make a contract to create, a lease which is to take effect in possession more than 21 years after the date of the lease.[1] In order to create a legal estate, such a lease must always be made by deed[2]. Where the lease is not to commence for at least three months, it must always[3] be registered with its own title.[4]

1   LPA 1925, s 149(3).
2   The 'short lease' exception, whereby leases of three years or less can be created orally or in writing applies only to leases taking *immediate* effect; see *Long v London Borough of Tower Hamlets* [1996] 2 All ER 683 and para 30.11, note 1 above.
3   Even if for a term of seven years or less, see para 30.14 above.
4   LRA 1925, s 4.

Rights and obligations of the parties to a lease

Introduction

37.19 In practice a lease does much more than simply confer ownership for a limited period. Where it is of very short duration the landlord will wish to impose strict controls on the tenant, but will invariably have to accept responsibility for the upkeep of the property. Where a lease is relatively long and at a market rent, the landlord will wish to impose such restrictions as are necessary to protect the value of his investment while, where possible, imposing substantial obligations on the tenant for the repair and maintenance of the property. Where a lease is granted at a premium for a very long term (and thus very similar in economic terms to a freehold), the restrictions on the tenant will tend to be minimal; in this case substantial obligations will be imposed on the tenant, who will expect to carry all the responsibility for the upkeep of the property.

The primary source of the rights and obligations of the landlord and the tenant is, of course, the lease itself. The terms of the lease are referred to as 'covenants', whether or not the lease was made by deed, even though, strictly speaking, that word is reserved for contractual terms contained in a deed.[1] It is possible, but increasingly less likely, that nothing will be expressly agreed by the parties to the lease, other than its duration and the rent. In such a case, only the most minimal terms will be implied by the law[2]. It is therefore preferable that the parties should agree terms for themselves even where the tenancy is only to be of very short duration.

It should be borne in mind that, when negotiating the terms of a lease, both legal and commercial factors will affect the outcome, as will the state of the market. Equally, other influences may need to be taken into account. The Government is encouraging the landlords of commercial property to be more flexible in the lease terms that are offered to tenants. To this end a Code of Practice has been issued[2]; this contains a range of recommendations as to the terms that might be included in such leases. So far as leases of residential property are concerned, the impact of the Unfair Terms in Consumer Contracts Regulations 1999[3] should not be overlooked since it is clear that these do apply to such leases.

1   See paras 37.21-37.29 below.
2   Code of Practice for Commercial Leases in England and Wales (2nd edn, 2002).
3   See paras 12.58-12.63 above.

Absolute, qualified and fully qualified covenants

37.20 While some of the covenants imposing restrictions on the tenant will be absolute, ie the tenant is totally prevented from carrying out the activity, others are merely subject to the landlord's consent. In some instances the landlord agrees that his consent will not unreasonably be withheld. So, for example, a lease may state that a tenant cannot erect signs on the outside of the demised premises; this is known as an 'absolute' covenant. If the covenant states that the signs cannot be erected without the landlord's consent, it is known as a 'qualified' covenant. If it provides that the signs cannot be put up without the landlord's consent which cannot unreasonably be withheld, the covenant is known as a 'fully qualified' covenant. As we shall see in the following paragraphs, a tenant is significantly more restricted by a covenant that is in the absolute form than he is by one that is fully qualified.

37.21   We consider first the position of the parties to a lease that either contains no express terms governing their rights and obligations, or contains very limited provisions[1]. As we shall see, save where statute requires the implication of terms[2], the courts are reluctant to imply covenants into leases. They will only do so where either this is an essential incident of the type of lease in question[3],or where it is necessary in order to give business efficacy to the agreement.[4]

1   Paras 37.21-37.29 below.
2   See para 7.20 above and para 37.25 below.
3   See para 7.25 above and para 37.25 below.
4   See para 7.27 above and para 37.35 below.

Where no express terms
The landlord
37.22   *Implied covenant for quiet enjoyment*   This obligation on the part of the landlord is implied into all leases as being essential to the relationship of landlord and tenant. Its primary purpose is to ensure that the tenant enjoys the use of the leased property free from disturbance by adverse claimants to the property and free from substantial physical interference by the landlord.[1] The implied covenant for quiet enjoyment extends only to the acts of the landlord and those claiming under him (such as other tenants of the same landlord). It does not apply to protect the tenant from any adverse rights arising from a title superior to the landlord's or granted by the landlord's predecessor in title.[2]

The covenant will be breached if it emerges that the landlord had no right to grant the lease, or if he fails to give vacant possession to the tenant at the outset of the lease[3], or if he interferes with the tenant's access to the premises during the course of the lease[4]. It is also clear that, even when carrying out his other obligations under the lease (notably that to repair) the landlord must have regard to the covenant for quiet enjoyment; so he must take reasonable precautions to ensure that the tenant's use of the premises is not unduly disrupted[5]. The covenant may also be broken where the landlord (or his agents) carry out excessively prolonged and intrusive works in the vicinity of the demised premises.[6] Furthermore, it is apparent that, at least where the landlord undertakes a management role in respect of a community of tenants, he may be held responsible – under the covenant for quiet enjoyment – for failing to take steps against tenants whose activities are causing excessive disturbance to other of his tenants. So, for example a landlord has been held liable where the way in which one of its tenants was operating her business seriously disrupted that of another tenant[7]. In another case, a landlord was required to compensate one of its tenants where it failed to enforce lease covenants restricting parking against the other neighbouring tenants[8].

However, there are limits to a landlord's liability. In particular, the covenant for quiet enjoyment does not protect a tenant from disturbance by other tenants arising from the state of the premises as they existed at the start of the lease. So, a landlord will not be liable to upgrade sound-proofing in a block of flats in order to prevent one tenant from being disturbed by a neighbouring tenant's normal use of his flat[9]. Furthermore, the covenant only protects a tenant from interference with his rights under the lease; it does not guard him from interference with privacy or his amenities[10].

A particular use of this covenant is as a means of gaining compensation for unlawful eviction and harassment. Thus, the landlord was held liable in damages for breach of this covenant in *Perera v Vandiyar*[11] where, with the object of driving the tenant out, he cut off the electricity and gas supplies to the premises. It should be noted that a landlord of a residential occupier who indulges in such harassment will often be guilty also of a criminal offence under the Protection from Eviction Act 1977, s 1,[12] as will a landlord who unlawfully evicts a tenant. Furthermore, acts of harassment often also amount to a tort such as trespass or nuisance, in which case there may, in appropriate circumstances, be an award of exemplary damages.[13] However, such claims are diminishing because, under the Housing Act 1988, s 27, a residential occupier now has a statutory right to damages, based on the difference in value of the landlord's interest with and without the occupier being in occupation, where he is driven to give up occupation as a result of harassment or eviction. This section is being widely used and the cases indicate that it is producing awards of damages which far outstrip those gained for breach of the covenant of quiet enjoyment or in the tort of trespass or nuisance.[14]

1   *Hudson v Cripps* [1896] 1 Ch 265.
2   *Jones v Lavington* [1903] 1 KB 253, CA; *Celsteel Ltd v Alton House Holdings Ltd (No 2)* [1987] 2 All ER 240, CA.
3   *Miller v Emcer Products Ltd* [1956] 1 All ER 237.
4   *Hilton v James Smith & Sons (Norwood) Ltd* [1979] 2 EGLR 44, CA.
5   *Goldmile Properties Ltd v Lechouritis* [2003] EWCA Civ 49, [2003] 2 P & CR 1.
6   See *Mira v Aylmer Square Investments Ltd* [1990] 1 EGLR 45, CA.
7   *Chartered Trust plc v Davies* [1997] 2 EGLR 83, CA.
8   *Nynehead Developments Ltd v RH Fibreboard Containers Ltd* [1999] 1 EGLR 7.
9   *Southwark London Borough Council v Mills* [1999] 4 All ER 449, HL.
10 See *Browne v Flower* [1911] 1 Ch 219 (landlord not in breach of this covenant where another tenant, with landlord's consent, erected an iron staircase outside the plaintiff tenant's window seriously affecting the plaintiff's privacy); contrast *Owen v Gadd* [1956] 2 QB 99, [1956] 2 All ER 28 (landlord in breach of this covenant where he erected scaffolding outside the entrance to tenant's shop).
11 [1953] 1 All ER 1109, CA.
12 As amended by the Housing Act 1988. This does not, in itself give the tenant the right to any financial compensation.
13 See para 28.3 above.
14 See, for example, *Tagro v Cafane* [1991] 2 All ER 235, [1991] 1 WLR 378, CA where a monthly tenant was awarded damages of £31,000 under s 27.

37.23   *Non-derogation from grant*   It is a principle of general application that a grantor may not take away with one hand what he has given with the other.[1] Accordingly, a covenant is implied into all leases that the landlord will not derogate from his grant. Thus, if the landlord leases land to be used in a particular way, he must not so act in relation to land retained by him as to make the demised premises materially less fit for their intended use.[2] It has been accepted that there is often an overlap between this obligation and a landlord's liability under the covenant for quiet enjoyment[3].

Examples of liability under non-derogation from grant include where a landlord, who leased to the tenant two floors of a block of flats for residential purposes, then leased the remainder to another tenant for business purposes.[4] It has also been held that a landlord who let retail premises was liable to the tenant under the principle of non-derogation where a neighbouring tenant of the same landlord used his premises in a way which amounted to a nuisance.[5] Similarly, a landlord who closed off an access, thereby restricting the flow of people going past a sales kiosk let to his tenant, was held to have breached this obligation[6]. The conversion of part of a mall in a retail centre into an additional unit could also incur liability to the other tenants in the centre.[7] However, letting adjacent or nearby property for a competing use will not normally amount to a breach[8], nor will moderate changes to the tenant-mix in a shopping centre found liability[9].

1   Birmingham, Dudley and District Banking Co v Ross (1888) 38 Ch D 295 at 313.
2   Aldin v Latimer Clark, Muirhead & Co [1894] 2 Ch 437; Browne v Flower [1911] 1 Ch 219.
3   Southwark London Borough Council v Mills [1999] 4 All ER 449, HL.
4   Newman v Real Estate Debenture Corpn Ltd and Flower Decorations Ltd [1940] 1 All ER 131. See also Aldin v Latimer Clark, Muirhead & Co [1894] 2 Ch 437, para 33.18 above.
5   Chartered Trust plc v Davies [1997] 2 EGLR 83, CA. It was of some significance that the landlord retained control of the common parts of the arcade in which both shops were located since this was why the court concluded that the landlord had a duty to act against the tenant whose activities were causing the problem. See also Nynehead Developments Ltd v RH Fibreboard Containers Ltd [1999] 1 EGLR 7.
6   Platt v London Underground Ltd [2001] 2 EGLR 121.
7   Petra Investements Ltd v Jeffrey Rogers plc [2000] 3 EGLR 120.
8   Port v Griffith [1938] 1 All ER 295; Romulus Trading v Comet Properties [1996] 2 EGLR 70.
9   Petra Investements Ltd v Jeffrey Rogers plc [2000] 3 EGLR 120.

37.24   *Fitness for habitation*   The courts have not taken the step of implying, as a legal incident of the relationship of landlord and tenant, any covenant on the part of the landlord that the premises are and/or will remain fit for habitation.[1] There is one exception: where premises are let furnished, a condition is implied that they are fit for human habitation at the commencement of the tenancy.[2] Further, in one other situation, of little practical relevance because of ridiculously low rental limits and restrictive interpretation by the courts, a covenant is implied under statute.[3] It is worth noting that, under the Housing Act 1985, Part VI,[4] local authorities have power to require landlords to render their property fit for human habitation if this can be done at reasonable cost. A tenant may thus call upon the local authority to exercise its powers rather than rely on any covenant in the lease. The Law Commission has proposed that there be a new statutorily implied obligation in leases of less than seven years that the landlord must keep residential property in a state fit for human habitation[5]. This seems unlikely to be implemented and consideration is currently being given to the provision of individual health and safety ratings for dwellings[6].

1   Hart v Windsor (1844) 12 M & W 68.
2   Smith v Marrable (1843) 11 M & W 5.
3   Under the Landlord and Tenant Act 1985, s 8, there is an implied condition in any letting of a dwelling-house at a rent not exceeding, in Greater London, £80 per annum, or elsewhere, £52, that the house is fit for human habitation both at the commencement of, and during, the tenancy. In Quick v Taff-Ely Borough Council [1986] QB 809, [1985] 3 All ER 321, the Court of Appeal remarked that this section must have remarkably little application.
4   As amended by the Local Government and Housing Act 1989, s 165 and Sch 9.
5   Responsibility for the State and condition of Property, Law Com 238, 1996.
6   Health and Safety in Housing 2001, DETR.

37.25   *Repairs*[1]   There is no generally implied covenant that the landlord shall carry out repairs. A statutory exception is contained in the Landlord and Tenant Act 1985, ss 11 to 14, which provide that where a dwelling-house is let for less than seven years, the landlord impliedly covenants:

*   to keep the structure and exterior in repair; and
*   to keep in repair and proper working order the installations in the house for the supply of water, gas and electricity, for sanitation, and for space- and water-heating.

The landlord is only liable for defects of which he has notice.[2] The landlord has the right, on giving 24 hours' written notice, to enter and view the premises at all reasonable times. The landlord's obligations under these provisions may, in the case of leases entered into on or after 15 January 1989, extend beyond the structure and exterior of the particular dwelling-house or the installations in it. Where the dwelling-house is a part only of a building, as in the case of a flat, then, in the case of breaches affecting the tenant's enjoyment of the dwelling-house or the common parts, the landlord's obligation to keep in repair the structure and exterior extends to any part of the structure and exterior of the building in which the landlord has an estate or interest, eg the common parts of a block of flats. Likewise, the obligation to keep in repair and proper working order the utility installations applies also to all those installations serving the flat or dwelling-house which the landlord owns or controls or which are in a part of the building in which the landlord has an estate or interest.[3]

There are other specific situations in which a landlord may be held responsible to the tenant for the physical state of the premises. It was held in *Liverpool City Council v Irwin*[4] that where parts of a building (in this case, a high-rise block of flats) have been let to different tenants and the essential means of access, such as stairs and lifts, are retained by the landlord, a term may be implied that the landlord will take reasonable care to keep those parts reasonably safe and reasonably fit for use. It has also been held that, where a tenant was expressly obliged to keep the interior of a dwelling in repair, a term could be implied on the grounds of business efficacy[5], that the landlord must keep the exterior in repair[6]. In *Rimmer v Liverpool City Council*[7] it was held that a landlord who designed and built the demised premises owed, in his capacity as designer and builder, a duty in the tort of negligence to the tenant (among others) to take reasonable care to ensure he would not suffer personal injury as a result of dangerous defects in the design and construction of the premises.[8] Third, the reader should also note the obligations of a landlord under the Defective Premises Act 1972, s 4 which we discuss at para 21.29 above.

1   For the meaning of 'repair' see para 37.42 below.
2   *O'Brien v Robinson* [1973] I All ER 583, HL.
3   Landlord and Tenant Act 1985, s 11(1A),(1B), added by the Housing Act 1988. For leases entered into prior to 15 January 1989, the landlord's obligation is limited to the structure and exterior of the particular flat and the installations therein: *Campden Hill Towers Ltd v Gardner* [1977] I All ER 739, CA, and see *Douglas-Scott v Scorgie* [1984] I All ER 1086, CA.
4   [1977] AC 239, [1976] 2 All ER 39. See also *King v South Northamptonshire District Council* [1992] I EGLR 53, CA.
5   See para 7.27 above.
6   See *Barrett v Lounova (1982) Ltd* [1989] I All ER 351, CA, although it now appears that this decision may be confined to its own particular facts: *Adami v Lincoln Grange Management Ltd* [1998] 17 EG 148, CA.
7   [1984] I All ER 930, CA.
8   In *Targett v Torfaen Borough Council* [1992] I EGLR 275, CA it was expressly held that this liability has survived despite the House of Lords' decision in *Murphy v Brentwood District Council* [1990] 2 All ER 908;.

The tenant

37.26   A freeholder's rights of disposition and of enjoyment of his property are remarkably wide.[1] In the absence of an express covenant, a tenant is equally free to assign his interest, ie transfer his entire interest to another (the assignee) thus putting the latter in the position of tenant vis-à-vis the landlord,[2] or he may sub-let (ie carve a shorter lease out of his own, putting himself in the position of landlord to the sub-lessee).[3] However, these rights are almost invariably subject to restriction, absolute or qualified, by the express terms of the lease.[4] As to the tenant's use of the premises, in the absence of express covenants, there are two restrictions imposed by the law; he must not commit waste, and, in the case of periodic tenancies, he is bound by an implied covenant to use the premises in a tenant-like manner.

1   See para 29.34 above.
2   Note that assignment must be by deed (LPA 1925, s 52(1)) even where the lease itself was not required to be created by deed (LPA 1925, s 54(2)); see *Crago v Julian* [1992] I All ER 744, CA.
3   A purported sub-lease which passes the residue of the term takes effect as an assignment; see *Milmo v Carreras* [1946] I All ER 288, CA.
4   Para 37.37 below.

37.27 *Waste*   'Waste' has been defined as 'any act which alters the nature of the land, whether for the better or for the worse'.[1] It is an ancient, tortious liability imposed on owners of limited interest in land in order to protect the interests of those with rights to the subsequent occupation of the property; those most likely to be affected are tenants for life under a settlement[2] and tenants under leases. It is rarely encountered in modern times, largely because both settlements and leases tend to contain express provisions which obviate the need to rely on the doctrine.[3]

Common law recognised two forms of waste, voluntary and permissive. Voluntary waste would be constituted by carrying out substantial alterations to the property, for example by pulling down a building, or, as in *Marsden v Edward Heyes Ltd*,[4] by gutting the ground floor of a building to convert the entire area into a shop. Permissive waste is damage caused by omission or neglect, as by letting the premises go to ruin. All tenants are liable for voluntary waste. A tenant holding under a periodic tenancy is not liable for permissive waste but the point is probably covered by his obligation to use and deliver up the premises in a tenant-like manner.

1   Megarry and Wade *The Law of Real Property* (6th edn) p 80.
2   See para 32.2 above.
3   That said, for various technical reasons, the doctrine was resorted to in *Mancetter Developments Ltd v Garmanson Ltd* [1986] 1 All ER 449, CA.
4   [1927] 2 KB 1.

37.28   *To use the premises in a tenant-like manner*   This covenant is implied in all periodic tenancies.[1] According to Denning LJ, as he then was, in *Warren v Keen*, 'The tenant must take proper care of the place ... he must do the little jobs about the place which a reasonable tenant would do. In addition, he must, of course, not damage the house, wilfully or negligently, and he must see that his family and guests do not damage it, and if they do, he must repair it.'[2]

1   *Marsden v Edward Heyes Ltd* [1927] 2 KB 1; *Warren v Keen* [1954] 1 QB 15, [1953] 2 All ER 1118, CA.
2   [1954] 1 QB 15 at 20, [1953] 2 All ER 1118. For example, the covenant does not necessarily oblige the tenant to lag water pipes. This depends on the circumstances, including the severity of the cold and the length of contemplated absences from home, see *Wycombe Health Authority v Barnett* (1982) 47 P & CR 394.

37.29   *Right to fixtures*   For the tenant's right to remove fixtures at the end of the lease, see para 29.14 above.

Express terms

37.30   Covenants commonly found in leases include:

- a covenant to pay rent (including rent review);
- a covenant to pay a service charge;
- a covenant restricting assignment, sub-letting or parting with possession;
- a covenant restricting alterations;
- user covenants;
- repairing covenants;
- covenants restricting the use of the premises;
- a covenant to insure. Either the landlord will covenant to insure the property on the basis that the tenant will pay the premiums, or the tenant will be required to insure the property, often with a named company, to its full value. Failure to keep the property insured constitutes a breach.[1]

We shall briefly consider these covenants in the ensuing paragraphs; for a more detailed treatment readers are advised to consult a specialist textbook on the law of landlord and tenant.[2]

1   *Penniall v Harborne* (1848) 11 QB 368.
2   See, for example, P F Smith *The Law of Landlord and Tenant* (6th edn) 2002.

Rent

37.31   The payment of rent, although a normal feature of leases, is not an essential legal requirement.[1] The rent payable by a tenant will generally take the form either of a market rent or a ground rent. A market rent is sometimes described as a 'rack' rent. A ground rent, commonly paid in the case of long leases, is paid where the land has been leased partly in consideration of a lump sum payment (ie a premium) at the commencement of the lease, or in consideration of the tenant building on the land, this being reflected in the rent which is, in essence, a rent for the land only and not the buildings thereon. It is normally expressly provided that rent is payable in advance; if this is not done, rent is payable in arrears.

1   *Ashburn Anstalt v Arnold* [1988] 2 All ER 147, CA.

Rent reviews

37.32   It is usual in the case of longer[1] commercial leases to provide for the level of rent to be revised at prescribed intervals, for example every five years. The object of a rent review clause is to give the landlord the benefit of increases in property values and to protect him from the effects of falls in the value of money by increasing the rent payable in line with the market. It has become the widespread practice for rent review to take the upwards-only form[2]. Under such a provision, the rent at each review can only either stay the same or move up in line with market rents. Such clauses play a vital role in preserving for the landlord the value of the income stream produced by commercial property and do much to enhance the attraction of property as an investment. They can, however, cause substantial hardship to tenants during a recession. When market rents fall significantly and for a lengthy period, as they did in the early 1990s, tenants can find themselves locked into leases which cause their premises to be over-rented.

A well-drafted rent review clause should contain both a formula for determining the revised rent and machinery for agreeing the rent and resolving disputes between the parties (generally by way of reference to a chartered surveyor acting as expert or arbitrator[3]). Rent review clauses vary in their details with the result that each clause is, in principle, unique. What follows is, therefore, merely a brief indication of features that are commonly encountered in rent reviews.

1   In recent years the length of commercial leases has been reducing. There are now many more leases of five years or less; such leases often do not contain any rent review at all or, where they do, the rent review may take the form of simple index-linking.
2   Despite Government efforts to discourage such forms of review and its current threat to introduce legislation to outlaw them: ODPM Press Release on the launch of the Code of Practice for Commercial Leases in England and Wales, April 2002.
3   See para 2.26 above and para 37.35 below.

37.33   *The machinery of review*   It is usual for the rent review process to be initiated by the serving of a landlord's notice (a 'trigger' notice). Sometimes (but less often in modern forms of rent review clause) the tenant must respond with a counter-notice. The function of such counter-notices varies; some require a counter-proposal as to the rent, others provide a mechanism under which the tenant can elect to have the rent fixed by a third party where the parties are unable to agree. Any rent review notice must be intended to have legal effect[1] and should convey its meaning in a manner that is clear to the other side[2]. In older forms of lease, it is usual to find that rent review notices are required to be served within specified time limits. It is now settled that time is not normally 'of the essence' (ie these time limits are not strict)[3] except where the parties have expressly or impliedly provided that this is to be the case[4].

1   So that a 'subject to contract' notice will usually be invalid, see *Shirlcar v Heinitz* (1983) 268 Estates Gazette 362 and on 'subject to contract' generally, see para 5.28 above.

2   *Amalgamated Estates v Joystretch Manufacturing* (1980) 257 Estates Gazette 489. CA. So, for example,
     where a counter-notice is required to operate as an election to have the rent decided by a third party,
     a notice must clearly do this; a letter that merely objects to the landlord's proposed rent will not be a
     valid notice, see *Fox & Widley v Guram* [1998] I EGLR 91.
3   *United Scientific Holdings v Burnley Borough Council* [1978] AC 904, HL.
4   *United Scientific Holdings v Burnley Borough Council* [1978] AC 904, HL. The parties may include the
     phrase 'time to be of the essence' or employ other wording that has this effect. In addition, the use of
     a series of strictly timetabled requirements, coupled with provisions that deal with the consequences
     of a failure to comply with the time limits will usually make time of the essence: see *Starmark Enterprises
     Ltd v CPL Distribution Ltd* [2001] EWCA Civ 1252, [2002] Ch 306. It is also likely that where provisions
     for which time is always of the essence, notably tenant's break provisions, are linked to a rent review,
     this will also make time of the essence for the review: see *Central Estates Ltd v Secretary of State for the
     Environment* [1997] I EGLR 239, CA. For a discussion of time of the essence generally, see paras 8.8-
     8.11 above.

37.34   *The valuation basis*   The essence of a rent review is that, as at each review date[1],
a current open market rental value for the premises is assessed and, where that exceeds
the rent currently payable (ie the passing rent), the new figure is substituted as the new
rent for the next review period. This process inevitably requires the hypothesis that the
premises are vacant and available to let when, in reality, the property is being occupied by
the current tenant. This means that, in order to ease the task of the valuer, the clause
normally contains a variety of assumptions (eg as to the length and terms of this hypothetical
letting and the state of the property) and 'disregards', ie matters which should be ignored
(eg any improvements carried out and paid for by a tenant). So, for example, a very basic[2]
rent review clause would usually provide that the reviewed rent is to be the rent that
would be agreed, in the open market between a willing landlord and a willing tenant, for
the demised premises with vacant possession, on a lease equal in length to the unexpired
residue of, and on the same terms as, the actual lease[3]. It will be assumed that the premises
are fitted out and ready for occupation[4] and that the tenant has complied with his covenants[5];
any improvements carried out by someone who was at the time[6] a tenant of the property
will be disregarded. It should be appreciated that, while assumptions and disregards are
usually designed to do no more than create a fair basis for the rent review valuation, they
can be used to manipulate a rental advantage (usually, but not exclusively, for the landlord).
The courts will strive to avoid interpreting these in a way that departs from the underlying
purpose of a review clause, namely to align rents with current market levels[7].

I   Note that although rent reviews are usually not settled until after the review date, it is that date which
     is invariably the valuation date for fixing the new rent.
2   It must be stressed that we here highlight only the main valuation elements of a rent review clause; in
     practice, all rent reviews will be more detailed and wide ranging.
3   Thus, at rent review, the valuer must assess the rental impact of the actual lease terms so that, for
     example, if a tenant is subject to an unusually onerous repairing obligation, or a very narrow user
     clause, the reviewed rent will be discounted: see *Norwich Union Insurance Society v British Railways Board*
     [1987] 2 EGLR 137 (25% reduction in the reviewed rent due to an onerous repairing covenant), *Plinth
     Property Investments Ltd v Mott, Hay and Anderson* (1978) 38 P & CR 361, CA (36% reduction due to
     a very tight user clause).
4   This is to ensure that a tenant cannot argue that, at review, he is entitled to a discount to reflect the
     benefit of a rent free period for fitting out which is normally given to new tenants at the beginning of
     their lease: see *London and Leeds Estates Ltd v Paribas Ltd* [1993] 2 EGLR 149, CA.
5   The most important of which is any tenant's covenant to repair; this means that, if the tenant has not
     complied with his repairing obligations, the rent will not be reduced to reflect the disrepair. Even in the
     absence of any express provision to this effect, the courts will imply a requirement that the premises
     be valued as if in repair: see *Harmsworth Pension Fund Trustees Ltd v Charringtons Industrial Holdings Ltd*
     [1985] I EGLR 97. Note that if it is the *landlord* who is in breach of his repairing obligations, the
     premises will be valued in their existing state; to hold otherwise would be to allow the landlord to
     benefit from his own wrong: see *Fawke v Viscount Chelsea* (1979) 250 Estates Gazette 855.
6   It is not usually necessary for the improvements to have been carried out by the *current* tenant; thus
     where a tenant carries out improvements and then assigns the lease, the assignee will have the benefit
     of the disregard at the next rent review.

7   So, in a series of conjoined appeals – *Co-operative Wholesale Society Ltd v National Westminster Bank plc* [1995] 1 EGLR 97, CA – the Court of Appeal strove to avoid holding that provisions in a rent review clause entitled the landlords to claim the headline, as opposed to the effective, rent for the properties.

37.35   *Resolving rent review disputes*   Where the parties are unable to agree a rent review it is usual for the rent review clause to provide that the matter will be referred to a third party, usually a chartered surveyor (or sometimes a lawyer), acting as either an arbitrator or expert[1]. The capacity in which the third party is to act can have a significant impact on both the procedure and outcome of a rent review dispute.

An arbitrator acts in a quasi-judicial capacity[2]. He must act impartially and give a fair hearing to both sides[3]; although he is now empowered to make his own investigations[4], he should normally base his decision on the evidence put to him by the parties (although this does not necessarily have to comply with the strict rules of evidence[5]). He must normally give reasons for his decision[6]. He is entitled to use his expertise to evaluate the arguments put to him by the parties, but not to substitute his own views (unless he puts these to the parties and allows them to comment)[7], or to make rulings on points not raised before him[8]. An arbitrator's decision ('award') is open to limited challenge in the courts. With the leave of the court, it can be set aside, varied or remitted where the arbitrator has made an error of law that is either obviously wrong or, where the issue is of general public importance, open to serious doubt[9]. An award can also be set aside or remitted where there has been a serious irregularity in the conduct of the arbitration, but only where this would give rise to a substantial injustice[10]. An arbitrator has a wide range of powers conferred by the Arbitration Act 1996, notably that to order disclosure of documents[11] and to award costs[12].

An expert is not governed by the Arbitration Act and has none of the statutory powers accorded to arbitrators; he cannot therefore order disclosure or, save where the lease gives him power to do so, make an award of costs. He does not act in a quasi-judicial capacity but merely as a professional person appointed to carry out a specific task – to fix the rent. He is not required to hear submissions from the parties (unless the rent review clause requires him to). In practice experts will usually invite the parties to put their case to him, but he is not obliged to base his decision on their evidence. Although an expert may be required to give reasons for his decision, he will normally opt to give only a non-speaking valuation (ie one without reasons. He can be held liable in negligence should he act without due care[13] (although, to date, no expert has been found to have been negligent when determining a rent at rent review). A court will not readily disturb a determination made by an expert where the lease has given him the exclusive jurisdiction to deal with the matter[14]. Exactly what aspects of the rent determination process are within the exclusive remit of the expert, will depend on the exact wording of the rent review clause. It will usually be the case that the courts will always regard the valuation approach as a matter for the expert alone. However, it may be that the legal interpretation of the clause and what it properly requires the expert to take into account in his valuation is an area that the court will not necessarily regard as his exclusive territory[15]. Where this is the case, the court may set aside a determination where an expert has misinterpreted the rent review clause[16].

1   The rent review clause will almost invariably be specific as to the capacity of the third party; if it is not, the courts tend, in rent review cases, to assume that the appointment is as an expert: see *Safeway Food Stores Ltd v Banderway Ltd* (1983) 267 EG 850.
2   This means that he is immune from any action in negligence, see para 17.35 above and Arbitration Act 1996, s 29.
3   Arbitration Act 1996, s 33.
4   AA 1996, s 34(1)(g).
5   AA 1996, s 34(2)(f).
6   AA 1996, s 52(4).
7   *Fox v PG Wellfair Ltd* [1981] 2 Loyd's Rep 514, CA. In *Checkpoint Ltd v Strathclyde Pension Fund* [2003]

EWCA Civ 84, [2003] 14 EG 124, CA, the Court of Appeal made it clear that an arbitrator may have more leeway to use his own experience where the rent review clause specifically requires him to have expertise of a particular type.

8   See *Guardcliffe Properties Ltd v City and St James* [2003] EWHC 215 (Ch), 147 Sol Jo LB 693.
9   Arbitration Act 1996, s 69.
10 AA 1996, s 68 and see *Checkpoint Ltd v Strathclyde Pension Fund* [2003] 14 EG 124, CA.
11 AA 1996, s 34(2)(d).
12 AA 1996, s 59–65.
13 *Palacath v Flanagan* (1985) 274 Estates Gazette 143.
14 *Jones v Sherwood Computer Services plc* [1992] 2 All ER 170, CA.
15 *Mercury Communications Ltd v Director General of Telecommunications* [1996] 1 All ER 575, HL; *British Shipbuilders v VSEL Consortium plc* [1997] 1 Lloyd's Rep 106; *National Grid plc v M 25 Group Ltd* [1999] 1 EGLR 65, CA.
16 *National Grid plc v M 25 Group Ltd* [1999] 1 EGLR 65, CA, where the Court of Appeal held that it could either rule on the meaning of the rent review clause before the expert had made his determination (as was the case there) or, where an expert had made an error as to the meaning of the clause, set aside the determination after it had been made. However, it should be noted that in *Morgan Sindall plc v Sawston Farms (Cambs) Ltd* [1999] 1 EGLR 90, a different Court of Appeal held that, in the case of a non-speaking determination, a court should not set aside an expert's determination after the event.

Service charges

37.36   Where buildings or complexes such as shopping centres are in multiple occupation, it is usual for the landlord to undertake responsibility for the repair and maintenance[1] of the structure and exterior and other common parts, to insure, and to provide the services since this is the only practicable way of dealing with such matters. The tenants then covenant to pay the landlord's costs of carrying out these obligations. Service charges are a fertile source of disputes between landlords and tenants since the latter are always concerned that they may be being over-charged, or charged for works carried out to too high a standard. A service charge will define the items that fall within the service charge and provide a mechanism for allocating payments between the various tenants (eg based on relative floor space or rateable value); ideally it should also prescribe the information to be provided to tenants and lay down a procedure for resolving disputes. The courts will strictly construe service charge provisions and will not allow recovery for items unless they are clearly covered by the terms of the lease[2]. Where a lease allowed for the recovery of sums 'properly expended' by the landlord, the court took the view that although works of repair were an item within the service charge, they could not be charged to one of the tenants; its short lease was approaching its expiry date and the repairs had not been carried out for its benefit[3].

Service charges relating to residential property are the subject of strict statutory control. Briefly, service charges must be held on trust in a separate account[4]. Service charges[5] cannot be recovered unless they have been reasonably incurred and the work or services provided to a reasonable standard[6]. Either the landlord or the tenant can ask the leasehold valuation tribunal to make a determination on reasonableness[7]. Where works costing over a prescribed amount, or to be carried out under a contract for over 12 months, are planned, the landlord must consult the tenants[8]. Tenants are also entitled to a regular statement of account and have wide rights to inspect estimates and accounts[9].

Service charges relating to commercial property are not subject to any statutory controls[10]. It was thought that there would always be an implied term that such service charges must be reasonable[11]. However, there is now some doubt as to whether or not this is the case[12].

1   See paras 37.40-37.42 below.
2   See, for example, *Mullaney v Maybourne Grange (Croydon) Management Co* [1986] 1 EGLR 70; *Jollybird Ltd v Fairzone Ltd* [1990] 1 EGLR 253; *Morgan v Stainer* [1993] 2 EGLR 73.
3   *Scottish Mutual Assurance plc v Jardine Public Relations Ltd* [1999] EGCS 43.
4   Landlord and Tenant Act 1987, ss 42, 42A and 42B.
5   As defined by the Landlord and Tenant Act 1985, s 18, as amended by the Commonhold and Leasehold Reform Act 2002.

6   Landlord and Tenant Act 1985, s 19.
7   LTA 1985, s 19(2A) and (2B).
8   LTA 1985, s 20 (as substituted by the Commonhold and Leasehold Reform Act 2002).
9   LTA 1985, ss 21, 21A (as substituted and added by the Commonhold and Leasehold Reform Act 2002).
10   There is a voluntary code of practice in place, but this is not widely adhered to: *Service Charges in Commercial Property: A Guide to Good Practice* (2nd edn, 2000).
11   *Finchbourne v Rodrigues* [1976] 3 All ER 581, CA.
12   *Havenridge Ltd v Boston Dyers Ltd* [1994] 49 EG 111, CA; *Berrycroft Management Co Ltd v Sinclair Gardens Investments (Kensington) Ltd* [1997] 1 EGLR 47, CA.

Assignment, sub-letting, or parting with possession

37.37   At common law a tenant is free to deal with his lease by way of assignment[1] (ie an outright transfer of the remainder of his lease) or subletting (the carving of shorter lease out of his own lease). In practice it is usual for the lease to restrict the tenant's rights. An absolute[2] covenant against assignment or sub-letting, etc is usually only found in short tenancies. In longer[3] leases it is common to allow assignment or sub-letting provided that the tenant first obtains the landlord's consent which is not to be unreasonably withheld.[4] Should the landlord unreasonably refuse consent the tenant may go ahead with the proposed assignment or sub-lease, or may apply to court for a declaration that the refusal is unreasonable and, as we shall see, claim damages for any losses suffered.

The Landlord and Tenant Act 1988 imposes certain statutory duties on a landlord whose consent to an assignment or sub-letting is required. He must respond in writing, within a reasonable time[5], to the tenant's written application for consent, giving consent unless it is reasonable not to do so. Where his consent is conditional, he must specify those conditions (which must be reasonable). Where he is refusing consent he must give his reasons for that refusal (which must be reasonable). Breach of any of these duties gives rise to liability in tort for breach of statutory duty. This means that the tenant can obtain either damages or a mandatory injunction against a dilatory or unreasonable landlord.

In any case where the reasonableness of a landlord's refusal is in issue it is now[6] for the landlord to show that consent was reasonably withheld. In considering this question it is assumed that the purpose of such a covenant is to protect the lessor from having his premises used or occupied in an undesirable way or by an undesirable tenant or assignee. The court will take account of the purpose of the covenant and all the circumstances, including the statutory background, at the time when the consent is sought. It is acceptable that the landlord should give priority to his own interests although, where the consequences of a refusal for the tenant are particularly serious, this may not be the case[7]. Whether or not the landlord is acting unreasonably is a question of fact in every case; previous case law should, therefore, be regarded as laying down guidelines rather than binding precedents[8]. That said, a landlord's refusal of consent will usually be regard as reasonable where he has genuine doubts about the proposed assignee's ability to pay the rent[9], or to remedy serious breaches of covenant committed by the current tenant[10]. A refusal will normally be justified if the assignee intends to use the premises in breach of the user covenant[11]. However, the landlord will be regarded as unreasonable where the refusal is designed to achieve 'collateral' objectives outside those secured by the terms of the lease[12]. So, a refusal was held to be unreasonable where a landlord was seeking to obtain possession[13], as was one where the proposed assignee was occupying other premises owned by the same landlord which would be difficult to re-let[14].

In the case of leases of commercial and industrial[15] entered into on or after 1 January 1996 the landlord is now permitted to specify in the lease any objectively verifiable circumstances[16] in which his consent to an *assignment*[17] will be withheld; where consent is later withheld, or subjected to conditions, in those circumstances the landlord's refusal (or any condition subject to which a consent has been given) is deemed to be reasonable.[18] A refusal of consent on a ground which has not been pre-specified in the lease can still be challenged as unreasonable. It is clear that landlords are making full use of their new ability to control assignments more tightly; it is now standard practice to include in commercial and industrial leases a list of circumstances in which consent to an assignment can be refused, and conditions to which any consent may be subject. In particular, it is now usual to insist that the outgoing tenant will always enter into an authorised guarantee agreement[19].

An assignment or sub-letting in breach of covenant does not affect the validity of the assignment or sub-lease, but may expose the assignee or sub-lessee to the risk of forfeiture.[20]

1   As to the liability of the assignee on the covenants in the lease, see paras 37.52-37.67 below.
2   See para 37.20 above.
3   In very long leases, ie those for which a premium was paid and only a ground rent reserved, the lease will often do no more than require the tenant to inform the landlord of any assignment.
4   Where a covenant requires the landlord's prior consent to any disposition, but does not expressly provide that this consent is not to be unreasonably withheld, the Landlord and Tenant Act 1927, s 19(1) operates to achieve this effect.
5   What is a reasonable time will depend on the facts of every case. In *Dong Bang Minerva v Davina Ltd* [1995] 1 EGLR 41 it was held that 28 days was sufficient and this has become an approximate rule of thumb. The Court of Appeal has recently emphasised that, in unusual or complex cases, a reasonable time may sometimes have to be measured in weeks rather than days, but should always be measured in weeks rather than months, see *Go West Ltd v Spigarolo* [2003] EWCA Civ 17, [2003] 2 All ER 141.
6   Landlord and Tenant Act 1988, ss 1(6) and 3(5).
7   *International Drilling Fluids Ltd v Louisville Investments (Uxbridge) Ltd* [1986] 1 All ER 321, CA.
8   *Ashworth Frazer Ltd v Gloucester City Council* [2001] UKHL 59, [2002] 1 All ER 377.
9   *British Bakeries (Midlands) Ltd v Michael Testler & Co Ltd* [1986] 1 EGLR 64.
10 *Orlando Investments Ltd v Grosvenor Estate Belgravia* [1989] 2 EGLR 74, CA.
11 *Ashworth Frazer Ltd v Gloucester City Council* [2001] UKHL 59, [2002] 1 All ER 377.
12 *Bromley Park Garden Estates Ltd v Moss* [1982] 2 All ER 890. CA.
13 *Bates v Donaldson* [1896] 2 QB 241, CA.
14 *Re Gibbs and Houlder Bros' Lease* [1925] Ch 575, CA.
15 The new law does not apply to residential or agricultural leases.
16 Ie circumstances which are essentially factual and which do not involve any value judgment, eg 'consent to an assignment to a company will not be given unless that company is a plc'.
17 The new law applies only to consent to *assignments*; it does not apply to sub-lettings and other types of disposition.
18 Landlord and Tenant Act 1927, s 19(1A), added by the Landlord and Tenant (Covenants) Act 1995, s 22.
19 For authorised guarantee agreements, see para 37.61 below.
20 *Old Grovebury Manor Farm Ltd v W Seymour Plant Sales & Hire Ltd (No 2)* [1979] 3 All ER 504, [1979] 1 WLR 1397, CA; and see paras 37.44–37.47 below.

Covenants against alterations
37.38   It is usual for a lease to restrict the tenant's ability to make alterations to the premises. The lease may differentiate between different types of work. So structural alterations may be absolutely prohibited, while those to the internal layout may be permitted with the landlord's consent. All depends on the terms of the particular lease. A tenant may nevertheless be able to carry out works that are absolutely prohibited by his lease. A tenant of business premises who wishes to carry out improvements[1] can go ahead where he complies with the requirements of Part I of the Landlord and Tenant Act 1927 and where either the landlord fails to object or the court certifies the improvements as 'proper'[2]. Furthermore, alterations required by Part III of the Disability Discrimination Act 1995[3] can be undertaken by the tenant, irrespective of any provisions in the lease.

Where a lease provides that alterations cannot be undertaken without the consent of the landlord, statute ensures that consent cannot unreasonably be withheld where the alteration amounts to an improvement[4]. The landlord can, however, require as a condition of his consent that the tenant pays reasonable compensation for any damage or diminution in value to either the demised premises or the landlord's neighbouring property. Where the improvement does not add to the letting value the landlord can also, where it is reasonable to do so, require the tenant at the end of the lease to reinstate the premises to their former condition.

1   Landlord and Tenant Act 1927, ss 1, 3. The improvements must add to the letting value of the premises, be suitable in character and must not be carried out under an obligation to the landlord.
2   LTA 1927, s 3.
3   This will come into effect on 1 October 2004 and will require the removal or alteration of any physical feature which makes it impossible or reasonably difficult for a disabled person to gain access to business premises offering goods facilities or services.
4   Landlord and Tenant Act 1927, s 19(2). The Act does not define an improvement but, given the landlord's entitlement to claim compensation for any diminution in value, the courts have held that whether or not work amounts to an improvement must be looked at from the tenant's point of view and does not depend on whether the work adds to the letting value; see *FW Woolworth & Co v Lambert* [1937] Ch 37. In practice this makes it very difficult for a landlord to argue that alterations are not an improvement.

User covenants

37.39   Virtually all leases include provisions that restrict the way in which the tenant may use the premises. Such covenants vary enormously and their complexity will depend upon the nature of the premises in question. So, a lease of residential premises may simply restrict use to that of a single dwelling, whereas that of a retail unit in a shopping arcade or centre may strictly limit the use of the property to a narrow range, while forbidding certain specified uses[1]. Even where positively worded, user covenants are usually interpreted as imposing only a negative obligation restricting the tenant to the permitted use but without positively requiring the tenant to use the premises in that way[2]. However, in some retail centres tenants may be required positively to 'keep open' for their particular trade[3]. The words of a user covenants must be interpreted according to the meaning that they carried when the lease was first drafted; so a covenant in a lease drafted in the 1950s to use premises only for the purposes of selling 'groceries' may prevent the current tenant from using the property as a modern supermarket selling a significant proportion of non-food items[4].

User covenants can be framed as absolute, qualified or fully qualified obligations[5]. Where the covenant is absolute the landlord is free to refuse any request for a change of use or he can charge the tenant, either by way of a premium or an increase in rent for any change to which he chooses to agree. Where the covenant is qualified or fully qualified, statute does provide that where the change of use does not involve any structural alteration the landlord is not permitted to charge for any consent[6]. He can however require the payment of a reasonable sum to compensate for any diminution in value of the demised premises or of the landlord's neighbouring premises.

Where the covenant is merely qualified (ie subject to the landlord's consent) there is no statutory requirement that the landlord can only refuse consent where this is reasonable. Such a requirement must be expressly set out in the lease[7]. Where the landlord is specifically required to act reasonably, the approach to the test of reasonableness is much the same as for disposition covenants[8]. However, it should be noted that the Landlord and Tenant Act 1988 does *not* apply to applications for consent to a change of use. Accordingly, it is for the *tenant* to prove that the landlord is acting unreasonably in refusing consent and the landlord is not under the obligations imposed by that Act; the landlord is not, therefore required to respond to a tenant's application within a reasonable time and nor is he liable in damages for any losses caused by an unreasonable refusal.

1   It should be noted that a very restrictive user clause may have a serious impact on rent at rent review, see *Plinth Property Investments Ltd v Mott, Hay and Anderson* (1978) 38 P & CR 361, CA (36% reduction due to a very tight user clause) and para 37.34, note 3 above.
2   *Montross Associated Investments SA v Moussaieff* [1990] 2 EGLR 61, CA.
3   Where such covenants are broken, eg by a retailer closing down its operation, the courts will not enforce the covenant by way of a mandatory injunction: see *Cooperative Insurance Society Ltd v Argyll Stores (Holdings) Ltd* [1997] 3 All ER 297, HL. In appropriate circumstances, notably where an 'anchor'

tenant in a shopping centre closes, the landlord may obtain substantial damages, see *Costain Property Developments Ltd v Finlay & Co Ltd* [1989] 1 EGLR 237; *Transworld Land Co Ltd v J Sainsbury plc* [1990] 2 EGLR 255.
4   *St Marylebone Property Co Ltd v Tesco Stores Ltd* [1988] 27 EG 72.
5   See para 37.20 above.
6   Landlord and Tenant Act 1927, s 19(3). Where the covenant is qualified rather than fully qualified this does not prevent the landlord simply refusing consent outright and then, say, offering to grant the tenant a new lease at a higher rent.
7   *Guardian Assurance Co Ltd v Gants Hill Holdings Ltd* [1983] 2 EGLR 36.
8   See para 37.37 above.

37.40   A variety of covenants providing for the liability of the landlord or the tenant to repair either the demised premises, the common parts of a building or complex, or the landlord's adjoining premises may be encountered. In the case of longer leases of whole buildings, it is often provided that the full legal and financial responsibility for repairing the demised premises is placed on the tenant. Equally, the repairing obligations may be split between landlord and tenant, with the landlord being liable for repairs to the structure and exterior of the property and the tenant being obliged to repair the interior. In such cases great care must be taken to ensure that the parts of the building for which each party is responsible is very carefully defined. Also common, where premises are occupied by a number of tenants, are so-called 'clear leases'. These are leases in which the landlord covenants to carry out all works of repair and maintenance to the common parts of the building or complex including the structure and exterior and to provide all services; however the tenants bear all the costs of these works (by way of service charges[1]). The tenants are each responsible for the repair of the interior of their respective parts. As a result the rent reaches the landlord clear of all expenses and overheads. In the case of shorter tenancies, the tenant's liability tends to be restricted to an obligation to keep, and deliver up at the end of the term, the interior of the premises in a good and tenantable state of repair, perhaps 'fair wear and tear excepted'. In the case of short residential tenancies, the landlord is always liable under the Landlord and Tenant Act 1985,[2] to keep in repair the structure and exterior and service installations.

1   Para 37.36 above.
2   Para 37.25 above.

37.41   *To keep in repair*   Where the obligation imposed is to 'keep' in repair (which it usually is) this means that, where necessary, any *existing* disrepair must be remedied.[1] It is thus vital, where such a repairing obligation is being imposed on a tenant, that the property is structurally surveyed before the lease is entered into in order to identify the extent of any disrepair. It will then be a matter for negotiation whether the landlord puts the premises into repair (or pays the incoming tenant to do so), whether the tenant accepts the responsibility of carrying out the repairs, or whether the repairing obligation is modified so that the tenant is only required to maintain the premises in their existing state. In this latter case, it is essential that the existing state of the premises is properly recorded – usually by way of a schedule of condition – so as to avoid future disputes.

In any case where the landlord is under an obligation to keep in repair the demised premise, his liability to the tenant does not arise until he has notice of the defect;[2] however, where the landlord is obliged to keep either his own adjoining premises, or common parts, in repair, his liability arises as soon as the disrepair occurs[3]. This is also the case where it is the tenant who is covenanting to keep in repair.

1   *Proudfoot v Hart* (1890) 25 QBD 42, CA.
2   *McCarrick v Liverpool Corpn* [1946] 2 All ER 646, HL.
3   *British Telecommunications plc v Sun Life Assurance Society plc* [1995] 4 All ER 44, CA.

37.42   *The meaning of repair*   Where the obligation imposed is one to 'repair' or keep in 'repair' it can often be a highly technical issue as to whether or not the premises are, legally speaking, in disrepair. 'Repair' connotes the idea of making good damage so as to leave the subject so far as possible as though it had not been damaged.[1] There can be no disrepair unless a part of the building to which the covenant relates has physically deteriorated since the date of its construction.[2] Thus the rectification of a defect arising in the course of construction (an 'inherent defect') will only fall within the ambit of a repairing covenant if it has given rise to some physical deterioration in the part of the building to which the covenant applies[3]. An inherent defect that gives rise to a loss of amenity (however severe) is not disrepair[4]. A covenant to repair may require renewal of subsidiary parts, but not renewal of the whole.[5] Repair will, inevitably, involve some element of improvement, but it must not result in premises which are wholly different in character from those which were demised.[6] Within these limits, a covenant to repair will cover works necessitated by inherent defects in the premises.[7] It is always a question of fact and degree whether the work in question can properly be described as repair; in coming to any conclusion the court will take account of many factors including the age of the building, its expected lifespan, the extent of the works required and their cost compared to the value of the building or its replacement cost.[8]

1   Anstruther-Gough-Calthorpe v McOscar [1924] I KB 716, CA. It should be noted that where positive damage to premises is caused, eg destruction by fire, an obligation to repair requires the damage to be put right even if this involves complete re-building. It is, therefore important that such disasters are covered by insurance, in which case the obligation to repair will exclude insured risks.
2   Quick v Taff-Ely Borough Council [1985] 3 All ER 321, CA. See also Post Office v Aquarius Properties Ltd [1987] I All ER 1055, CA.
3   Stent v Monmouth District Council [1987] I EGLR 59, CA.
4   Quick v Taff-Ely Borough Council [1985] 3 All ER 321, CA, Lee v Leeds City Council [2002] EWCA Civ 06, [2002] I WLR 1488.
5   Lurcott v Wakely and Wheeler [1911] I KB 905, CA.
6   Ravenseft Properties Ltd v Davstone (Holdings) Ltd [1979] I All ER 929.
7   [1979] I All ER 929.
8   See, for example, Brew Bros v Snax (Ross) Ltd [1970] I QB 612 and Ravenseft Properties Ltd v Davstone (Holdings) Ltd [1979] I All ER 929.

Remedies for breach of covenant

For breach of covenants other than for payment of rent

37.43   For breach of covenants other than for payment of rent the injured party may pursue his normal contractual remedies, ie he can sue for damages[1] or seek an injunction to restrain the breach. These have already been discussed[2]. Peculiar to leases is the landlord's remedy of forfeiture of the lease. It should be noted that, where the breach is of the covenant to repair important variations to the basic rules sometimes apply.[3]

1   It should be appreciated that such an action may be brought not only against the current tenant, but also against a former tenant who remains liable either under the terms of the lease or as a result of entering into an authorised guarantee agreement, or any other guarantor; see paras 37.52 – 37.69 below.
2   See paras 11.2-11.18 and 11.32-11.36 above.
3   See para 37.48 below.

Forfeiture[1]

37.44   *The right to forfeit*   The landlord normally has a right to claim forfeiture of the lease because a proviso for re-entry in the event of a breach of covenant is invariably expressly included in the lease.[2] Such a right of re-entry is a proprietary right and as such is enforceable not only against the tenant but also against assignees and sub-tenants (including mortgagees). In claiming forfeiture and exercising a right of re-entry the landlord is choosing to put an end to the tenant's interest in the property because of the breach. It is a remedy that needs to be exercised with some thought, especially in a depressed market, where the lease is at a market as opposed to a ground rent. In such circumstances, the tenant may regard the termination of his lease as a blessing and the landlord may be left with a property that he cannot readily re-let[3].

1   It should be noted that the Law Commission has published a report incorporating a draft bill, which proposes sweeping changes to the law on forfeiture; see Termination of Tenancies Bill 1994 Law Com No 221. This has been further modified in 1998 and 1999 in respect of the proposals relating to the right of peaceable re-entry. There is no indication of when, if ever, this Bill will be put before Parliament.
2   In those rare cases where the lease does not contain an express right of re-entry for breach, the landlord can only forfeit for breaches of those covenants which are framed as conditions (eg by the use of wording such as 'on condition that').
3   See, for example, GS Fashions Ltd v B & Q plc [1995] 4 All ER 899.

37.45   *Waiver*   The landlord may lose his right to forfeit for a breach of covenant where he has expressly or impliedly waived his right to do so. Implied waiver can only occur where the landlord (or his agent), knowing of the breach, does some unequivocal act which, considered objectively without regard to the landlord's motive or intention, is consistent only with the continued existence of the lease.[1] The onus is on the tenant to show that waiver has occurred. The act most commonly relied on as constituting waiver is the acceptance of future rent. The very fact of acceptance of rent,[2] even as a result of a clerical error, amounts, as a matter of law, to waiver of the right to forfeit.[3] Whether or not other acts amount to waiver is a question of fact.[4] If the breach is of a continuing nature, for example a failure to insure or to repair, continued breach after the waiver revives the right of re-entry. Waiver only deprives the landlord of his right to forfeit; he can still pursue other remedies for the breach.

1   Matthews v Smallwood [1910] 1 Ch 777 at 786; Central Estates (Belgravia) Ltd v Woolgar (No 2) [1972] 3 All ER 610, CA; Expert Clothing Service and Sales Ltd v Hillgate House Ltd [1985] 2 All ER 998, CA.
2   A demand for future rent is similarly treated as waiver as a matter of law; see David Blackstone Ltd v Burnetts (West End) Ltd [1973] 3 All ER 782.
3   Central Estates (Belgravia) Ltd v Woolgar (No 2) [1972] 3 All ER 610, CA.
4   Expert Clothing Service and Sales Ltd v Hillgate House Ltd [1985] 2 All ER 998, CA.

37.46   *Procedure*   The LPA 1925, s 146 provides that a right of re-entry or forfeiture for breach of a covenant or condition *other than one for payment of rent* may not be enforced unless and until the landlord serves on the tenant a notice which is designed to give the tenant reasonable information about what, if anything, he has to do to avoid forfeiture. In the case of a long lease (ie one for more than 21 years) of a dwelling, a landlord cannot issue a s 146 notice until either the tenant has admitted the breach, or a leasehold valuation tribunal has determined that a breach has occurred[1].

A s 146 notice must;

*   specify the particular breach complained of;
*   require the lessee to remedy it (if the breach is capable of remedy[2]); and
*   if desired, require the lessee to make compensation in money for the breach (if required).

Having served a s 146 notice, the landlord is compelled then to allow the tenant sufficient time to remedy the breach and to make reasonable compensation (where that was required) before he can take any further steps. Even where the breach is not capable of remedy, the tenant must still be given a short time in which to consider his position before the landlord proceeds to forfeiture.[3]

The landlord should normally forfeit by bringing a court action for possession. Although, theoretically, he may have the alternative of forfeiting by peaceably re-entering on the land, this is not to be recommended, for the following reasons. First, in the case of residential lettings, forfeiture must be effected by court proceedings while any person is lawfully residing in the premises.[4] Second, the landlord runs the risk of contravening the Criminal Law Act 1977, s 6 (which prohibits the use or threat of violence to secure entry) or some other provision of the criminal law. Third, forfeiting by way of peaceable re-entry does not give the landlord an unchallengeable right to possession since a tenant, sub-tenant or mortgagee may still be able to claim relief.[5]

It should also be noted that a landlord of residential premises is not entitled to re-enter[6] for non-payment of a service charge unless its amount has been admitted, agreed, or determined.[7] This is designed to prevent landlords threatening tenants (or their mortgagees) with the termination of their lease for non-payment of what might well be disputed service charge payments.

1   Commonhold and Leasehold Reform Act 2002, s 168.
2   Certain breaches are, legally speaking, regarded as incapable of remedy. These include the breach of a covenant against immoral user (see *Rugby School (Governors) v Tannahill* [1935] 1 KB 87, CA) and that of a covenant against assignment or sub-letting (see *Scala House and District Property Co Ltd v Forbes* [1973] 3 All ER 308, CA). See generally *Expert Clothing Service and Sales Ltd v Hillgate House Ltd* [1985] 2 All ER 998, CA and *Savva v Hussein* [1996] 47 EG 138, CA. Where a breach is incapable of remedy the landlord may proceed to forfeit more rapidly (see note 3 below); furthermore, the tenant is less likely to be given relief, see para 37.47 below.
3   *Horsey Estate Ltd v Steiger* [1899] 2 QB 79, CA. Fourteen days' notice has been held sufficient in such cases: *Civil Service Co-operative Society Ltd v McGrigor's Trustee* [1923] 2 Ch 347.
4   Protection from Eviction Act 1977, s 2.
5   *Billson v Residential Apartments Ltd* [1992] 1 AC 494, [1992] 1 All ER 141, HL; see para 37.47 below.
6   The landlord can serve a s 146 notice provided that this informs the tenant that the landlord cannot take the matter further (ie by actually re-entering) until the service charge amount is admitted, agreed or determined, Housing Act 1996, s 82.
7   Housing Act 1996, s 81.

37.47   *Relief*   At any time from the service of the s 146 notice until the landlord has recovered possession of the property under an unassailable court order,[1] the tenant may apply to the court for relief from forfeiture.[2] The court has a complete discretion as to whether or not to grant relief and on what terms, if any, it thinks fit,[3] although the tenant will, invariably, be required to remedy the breach.

Where a lease is terminated by forfeiture this necessarily destroys any sub-leases and mortgages granted by the lessee. This, of course, would involve considerable hardship to an innocent sub-lessee or mortgagee and so, under the LPA 1925, s 146(4), they are entitled to apply to court for relief. This will normally only be given where the sub-tenant (or mortgagee) is prepared to remedy the tenant's breach. Where relief is given, a new lease, held direct of the landlord, will be vested in the applicant.

1   *Billson v Residential Apartments Ltd* [1992] 1 AC 494, [1992] 1 All ER 141, HL. This means that, should a landlord forfeit by way of peaceable re-entry, a tenant (and, presumably a sub-tenant or mortgagee) can still apply to court for relief. It is this which makes it unwise for a landlord to re-enter peaceably.
2   Under LPA 1925, s 146(2).
3   LPA 1925, s 146(2).

For breach of repairing covenants
37.48   We have already mentioned that certain special rules apply in cases where the covenant which has been breached is that to repair. Where it is the *landlord* who is seeking a remedy the following restrictions apply.

First, he cannot normally obtain an *injunction* or *specific performance* in order to enforce a tenant's obligation to repair since damages will usually be an adequate remedy.[1]

Second, where a landlord is seeking *damages*, two special rules apply. In certain cases he cannot commence an action for damages without serving a s 146 notice[2] and, where the tenant so requires, without obtaining the leave of the court.[3] Even where he does obtain damages, the measure of those damages is limited by statute; they can, in no event, exceed the amount by which the value of his reversion is diminished and, where the landlord is planning to demolish or re-develop the premises at the end of the lease, he cannot recover damages at all.[4]

Third, where a landlord is seeking to *forfeit* for breach of a repairing covenant a number of special rules apply. In certain instances[5] the s 146 notice must inform the tenant of his right to claim the benefit of the Leasehold Property (Repairs) Act 1938 by serving a counter-notice within 28 days. The landlord must prove that the tenant actually knows that the s 146 notice has been served.[6] Where the tenant does claim the benefit of the LP(R)A 1938 the landlord cannot proceed to forfeit without the leave of the court. This will not be given unless he proves that the tenant is in breach and that the case is covered by one of the 1938 Act grounds.[7]

Finally, where the s 146 notice relates to internal decorative repairs, the tenant may apply to court for relief from all liability for such repairs, which the court may grant if in all the circumstances it considers the notice unreasonable.[8]

Where it is the *tenant* who is seeking a remedy for the landlord's breach of his repairing obligations, not surprisingly, there are no special restrictions but, rather, additional rights. In the case of residential tenancies, there is no bar to the tenant being awarded specific performance,[9] and in any case the court has a general jurisdiction, which should be carefully exercised, to order a landlord to do some specific work pursuant to his covenant to repair.[10] It may also be noted at this point that the court has the power, at the suit of a tenant, to appoint a receiver to receive the rent and exercise the duties of the landlord,[11] a power which has been used where a landlord is in breach of a repairing covenant and has persistently failed to remedy the breach.[12] In the case of tenancies of flats, this general jurisdiction has been superseded by the right, given by Pt II of the Landlord and Tenant Act 1987, to apply to the leasehold valuation tribunal for the appointment of a manager where the landlord is in breach of an obligation, such as a repairing covenant, which is likely to continue[13]. Where this remedy does not solve the problem the tenants can apply for the compulsory acquisition of the landlord's interest under Pt III of the 1987 Act.

1   The first reported case in which an order for the specific performance of a repairing covenant has been made against a tenant has just occurred: *Rainbow Estates Ltd v Tokenhold Ltd* [1998] 2 All ER 860. Unusually, the lease contained neither a forfeiture provision, nor any right for the landlord to enter and carry out the repairs himself; in these circumstances it was clear that damages would not be an adequate remedy.
2   Ie all leases (except agricultural holdings) granted for a term of seven years or more, of which at least three years remain unexpired; Leasehold Property (Repairs) Act 1938, s 1(2).
3   Where the tenant serves a counternotice within 28 days of receiving the s 146 notice the landlord must then obtain the leave of the court;LP(R)A 1938, s 1(3).
4   Landlord and Tenant Act 1927, s 18.
5   Ie where the lease is covered by the Leasehold Property (Repairs) Act 1938; see note 2 above.
6   Landlord and Tenant Act 1927, s 18(2).
7   Leasehold Property (Repairs) Act 1938, s 1(5); see *Associated British Ports v CH Bailey plc* [1990] 1 All ER 929, HL.
8   LPA 1925, s 147.
9   Landlord and Tenant Act 1985, s 17.
10 *Jeune v Queens Cross Properties Ltd* [1974] Ch 97, [1973] 3 All ER 97.
11 Supreme Court Act 1981, s 37.
12 See, for example, *Hart v Emelkirk* [1983] 1 WLR 1289; *Daiches v Bluelake Investments Ltd* [1985] 2 EGLR 67.
13 Landlord and Tenant Act 1987, s 24.

For non-payment of rent

37.49   In the event of non-payment of rent, the remedies available to the landlord are distress, an action to recover the rent[1], and forfeiture.

I It should be appreciated that such an action may be brought not only against the current tenant, but also against a former tenant who remains liable either under the terms of the lease or as a result of entering into an authorised guarantee agreement, or any other guarantor; see paras 37.52-37.69 below.

Distress[1]

37.50 This is an ancient remedy which the Law Commission has recommended should be abolished.[2] Its attraction to landlords is that it is available without recourse to the courts[3] and without prior notice to the tenant, thus making it extremely effective in practice. For this reason it appears likely that the Government will accede to pressure that it should be retained for commercial property[4]. Currently, the landlord's right of distress entitles him, or rather his certificated bailiff, to enter the demised premises and impound goods found there[5] to provide security for the outstanding rent. Provided that notice is given to the tenant these goods may be sold after five days. It is proposed that this procedure, or rather lack of it, should be reformed, notably so that a tenant should be given some warning that distress is imminent in order to give him an opportunity to challenge its legality in court[6].

1 Distress for Rent Acts 1689 and 1733.
2 Landlord and Tenant: Distress for Rent (1991) Law Com No 194.
3 Save in relation to tenancies of dwelling-houses falling within the Rent Act 1977 or Housing Act 1988, where leave of the county court is required; Rent Act 1977, s 147, Housing Act 1988, s 19.
4 Distress for Rent Consultation Paper, 2001.
5 Subject to certain limited exceptions.
6 Distress for Rent Consultation Paper, 2001.

Forfeiture

37.51 The landlord may claim forfeiture of the lease for non-payment of rent where the lease contains an express proviso for re-entry.[1] However, in the case of long leases (ie those of more than 21 years) of dwellings, a landlord cannot forfeit for non-payment of small amounts of rent or service charges[2] unless these have not been paid within a prescribed period. At common law, the landlord cannot claim forfeiture without having first made a formal demand for the exact sum due, on the demised premises, between sunrise and sunset. The technicality of a formal demand is invariably dispensed with by an express provision in the lease.[3] A s 146 notice is not required in the case of forfeiture for non-payment of rent. (Thus, in theory at least, a landlord is usually able to forfeit for non-payment of rent without giving any prior warning to the tenant; in practice he is likely to have been chasing the tenant for payment for some time.) The law as to waiver and as to the exercise of the right of re-entry explained in paras 37.45 and 37.46 applies equally in cases of non-payment of rent.

Most applications for relief from forfeiture for non-payment of rent are heard in the county court[4]. If the tenant pays off all the arrears and the landlord's costs at least five days before the hearing date, the proceedings are automatically terminated[5]. Where this is not done and an order for possession is granted, this must be suspended for at least four weeks (or, at the court's discretion, for longer). If the arrears are paid off within this period (or within any extension granted by the court) then relief will be granted[6]. If this is not done then the order for possession will be enforced[7]. Even then the tenant has one further chance to obtain relief by applying to court within six months of the date on which possession was recovered by the landlord[8]. Mortgagees and sub-tenants may apply for relief either under LPA 1925, s 146(4) or under the County Courts Act. In the latter instance relief must be applied for within six months[9].

1 Where this is not the case, the landlord will still be able to forfeit if the covenant to pay rent is framed as a condition of the lease.
2 Commonhold and Leasehold Reform Act 2002, s 167.
3 In any event, in cases where half a year's rent is in arrear and insufficient distrainable goods are available

on the premises, there is no need for a formal demand: Common Law Procedure Act 1852, s 210. See also County Courts Act 1984, s 139(1), for actions brought in the county court.

4   It should be noted that, where an application for relief is made to the High Court, the rules are slightly different; we do not deal with these.
5   County Courts Act 1984, s 138(2).
6   CCA 1984, s 138(3).
7   CCA 1984, s 138(7).
8   CCA 1984, s 138(9A).
9   *United Dominions Trust Ltd v Shellpoint Trustees Ltd* [1993] 4 All ER 310, CA.

Enforceability of covenants by and against assignees

37.52   We have indicated that, subject to any controls imposed by the lease,[1] a tenant may assign his lease to another, ie transfer the whole of the remainder of the term[2]. The longer the lease the more likely this is to happen and, in practice, assignments are commonplace. Equally, during the continuance of a lease, the landlord is completely free to transfer his interest in the land. We now need to consider the effect which such transfers will have on the enforceability of the covenants contained in the lease. To what extent will a new landlord be able to enforce the lease covenants against either the original tenant, or an assignee of the lease? Can a new tenant insist that the original landlord, or an assignee of the reversion, perform the obligations imposed by the lease terms?

The law in this area has recently been radically overhauled by the Landlord and Tenant (Covenants) Act 1995 ('LT(C)A 1995'). This introduces a new regime on the enforceability of leasehold covenants, but only for leases entered into on or after 1 January 1996 ('new' leases); the existing rules, with limited modifications, continue to apply to leases granted before that date ('old' leases). Since 'old' leases will remain in existence for very many years to come, those dealing with property need to be equally familiar with both regimes. We turn first to the enforceability of covenants contained in 'old' leases.

1   Paras 37.26 and 37.37 above.
2   This should not be confused with the situation where a tenant sublets, ie carves a shorter lease out of his own interest. For subleases, see para 37.70 below.

Leases entered into before 1 January 1996

37.53   The rules relating to the enforceability of covenants in 'old' leases are essentially two-fold. First, and obviously, all covenants, whether imposing positive or negative obligations, are mutually enforceable between the original parties to the lease as a matter of basic contract law. Second, as we shall see, where there has been an assignment of the lease or the reversion, or both, all covenants (whether positive or negative[1]) which 'touch and concern' the land which is the subject of the lease are mutually enforceable between the persons who are now in the relationship of landlord and tenant. This relationship is known as 'privity of estate' and is the very basis on which such covenants remain enforceable.

1   Thus, where property is held by way of a lease, positive obligations will pass on to an assignee. This is in sharp contrast to covenants affecting freehold land where, as we have seen at para 34.4 above, only negative covenants can bind transferees.

Touching and concerning

37.54   Before examining the operation of these two rules, we must first consider what is meant by the phrase 'touch and concern'. It means that the covenant should relate to either the demised land, or to the reversion; it must be reasonably incidental to the relationship of landlord and tenant rather than merely of personal advantage to the particular covenantee and must affect the nature, quality, mode of enjoyment or value of the land[1].

Examples of covenants which have been held to touch and concern the property are a covenant to pay rent, a covenant to repair the property, a covenant not to assign, the landlord's covenant for quiet enjoyment, a covenant by a surety guaranteeing the rent and a covenant giving the tenant an option to renew the lease. Covenants which have been held not to touch and concern the land include a covenant not to open a public house within half a mile of the demised public house, a covenant to pay the tenant £500 unless the lease is renewed, a covenant to pay rates on other land, and a covenant giving the tenant an option to purchase the reversion.

I   *P & A Swift Investments v Combined English Stores Group plc* [1988] 2 All ER 885, HL.

Assignment of the lease

37.55   *A single assignment*   We now turn to consider the operation of the two basic rules relating to the enforceability of covenants in 'old' leases.

We first consider the case where the tenant has assigned his entire leasehold interest:

Here, T has assigned his leasehold interest to A. L and A are now in the relationship of landlord and tenant; they have 'privity of estate'. Therefore covenants in the lease which touch and concern the land are enforceable by L against A, and by A against L.[1] Thus, for example, A will be bound by a covenant to pay rent and L will be liable to A on the covenant for quiet enjoyment.

If A is in breach of a covenant touching and concerning the land, such as the covenant to pay rent, L could, and normally would, take action against A to remedy the breach.[2] However, it must be remembered that there is still a contract between L and T; under this contract T remains liable on the covenants for the rest of the lease[3]. This means that, should a successor of the tenant fail to perform a covenant, the original tenant is in breach of his *contractual* obligation. So, instead of, or as well as,[4] suing A, L may also sue T in respect of A's breach of covenant. This continuing liability of T is often referred to as 'original tenant liability'.

It is to be noted that T will not be liable for the breach of any *new or changed* covenant inserted into the lease by L and A after the assignment from T to A.[5] However T is liable in respect of any changes which occur after the assignment but which are the result of the operation of the terms of the lease as they existed at the date of the assignment; this means that, in particular, T is liable for rent which has been increased after the assignment in accordance with a rent review clause which was already in the lease.[6]

If L does sue T, T may then sue A in an attempt to recover money paid to L. This will be on the basis of a term implied by statute[7] that A will perform the covenants in the lease and, if he does not, will then indemnify T for any losses that T suffers as a result of A's breach of the lease covenants.

In practice, L is only likely to sue T where A has failed to pay rent and is insolvent. However, during the recent recession, it became commonplace for landlords to utilise their rights against original tenants and it was the latter's complaints which eventually persuaded the government to implement a reform of this area of the law.

In the event, most of the provisions of the LT(C)A 1995 apply only to leases entered into after 1 January 1996, leaving tenants under existing leases to the rigours of the old law. However, two of the new measures introduced by the 1995 Act do apply to 'old' leases. First, in order to be able to recover a 'fixed charge'[8] from a former tenant, the landlord must serve on him a default notice within six months of those sums becoming due.[9] This notice must specify the sums due. Second, where a former tenant pays all the sums specified in a default notice, he is then entitled to require the landlord to grant him an overriding lease.[10] Broadly, this lease sits between the current tenant, A, and L; thus T becomes A's landlord and is able to take steps to enforce the covenants which A is breaking, and in particular, to forfeit A's lease[11]. This at least means that T then has the right either to occupy the premises, or to re-assign them to a more reliable assignee than A has proved to be.

1   *Spencer's Case* (1583) 5 Co Rep 16a.
2   Paras 37.43–37.51 above.
3   LPA 1925, s 79.
4   He may not recover twice in respect of the same loss.
5   *Friends' Provident Life Office v British Railways Board* [1995] 48 EG 106, CA, LT(C)A 1995, s 18.
6   LT(C)A 1995, s 18.
7   LPA 1925, s 77(1)(c) and Sch 2.
8   Broadly, rent and service charge payments; LT(C)A 1995, s 17(6).
9   LT(C)A 1995, s 17(2), para 37.66 below.
10   LT(C)A 1995, s 19(1), para 37.67 below.
11   See para 37.44 above.

37.56   *A further assignment*

Here T has assigned his lease to A (as in the previous example) but A has then later assigned the lease to B. This allows us to demonstrate the fundamental difference between T's liability, which is based on privity of contract, and that of A, which is based on privity of estate. Once A assigns the lease he ceases to be in a relationship of landlord and tenant with L; since there is no longer any privity of estate between them, A cannot be made liable for any subsequent breaches committed by B.[1] However, T's liability remains unaltered; he is still bound by his original contract and can be sued in respect of breaches committed by B (or any subsequent assignee).

However, it should be noted that, particularly in the case of commercial leases, it has become the widespread practice for the basic rule concerning the liability of assignees to be varied by express agreement. It is usual for a landlord to require that an assignee enters into a direct contract with him under which the assignee agrees to be bound by the covenants contained in the lease for the remainder of the term; in this way the assignee accepts a contractual liability which is identical to that of an original tenant.[2] Thus, in our example, both A and B may have entered into a direct contract with L; if, and only if, this is the case, L can sue A in respect of breaches committed by B. If B assigns on, L can sue B in respect of subsequent breaches.

An assignee who remains liable to the landlord following a further assignment because of the imposition of a direct covenant is entitled to the limited benefits introduced by the LT(C)A 1995. Accordingly, he must be served with a default notice and, if he has paid the sums specified in that notice, he is entitled to call for an overriding lease.[3]

1   *Onslow v Corrie* (1817) 2 Madd 330. For the same reason A is not liable for breaches which occured before he became the tenant, *Grescot v Green* (1700) 1 Salk 199.
2   *J Lyons & Co Ltd v Knowles* [1943] 1 All ER 477.
3   See para 37.55 above and paras 37.566 and 37.567 below.

Assignment of the reversion
37.57

In this case, the landlord has assigned his reversion to R. R and T are now in the relationship of landlord and tenant. Covenants which touch and concern the subject matter of the lease are mutually enforceable between R and T.[1] Indeed *only* R can sue T; L is unable to enforce the lease covenants once he has assigned the reversion[2].

As with an original tenant, L remains contractually liable to T even after an assignment of the reversion (even though he can no longer enforce covenants *against* T).[3] However, since landlords do not, generally speaking, undertake obligations which are as onerous as those imposed on tenants, the continuing liability of landlords has not given rise to the same pressure for reform.[4]

1   LPA 1925, s 141 provides that the *benefit* of such covenants passes to an assignee of the reversion; s 142 passes the *burden*.
2   LPA 1925, s 141, *Re King, Robinson v Gray* [1963] 1 All ER 781, CA; *London and County (A & D) Ltd v Wilfred Sportsman Ltd* [1970] 2 All ER 600, CA.
3   *Stuart v Joy* [1904] 1 KB 362, CA.
4   Although, as we shall see in para 37.64 below, landlords under new leases can apply to be released from their obligations following an assignment of the reversion.

Assignment of both the lease and the reversion
37.58

Here both landlord and tenant have assigned their interest in the property. All covenants which touch and concern the land are mutually enforceable between R and A, the new landlord and tenant. In addition, where A is in default, R can also sue T whose contractual liability for the remainder of the lease[1] is owed to R just as much as it was to L.

It should be noted that it is provided by s 3 of the Landlord and Tenant Act 1985 that in the case of leases of dwellings, on assignment of the reversion, L remains liable to the current tenant (T or, as the case may be, A) in respect of any breach of covenant until either he or R gives written notice of the assignment and of R's name and address to the current tenant.

1   See para 37.55 above.

Leases entered into on or after 1 January 1996
The broad effect of the LT(C)A 1995
37.59   The broad effect of the LT(C)A 1995, which applies to all[1] leases entered into on or after 1 January 1996[2] is as follows:

* the requirement that covenants should 'touch and concern' the land is abolished;[3]
* all tenants, whether original tenants or assignees, are automatically released from future liability on an assignment of their lease;[4]

- however, a landlord can often require an assigning tenant to enter into an agreement guaranteeing that the assignee will perform the obligations imposed by the lease;[5]
- while landlords are not *automatically* released from future liability when transferring their reversion, they can seek release from the tenant or from the court;[6]
- where landlords are able to hold a former tenant liable for breaches committed by the current tenant, they must serve a default notice within six months of any sums becoming due and, where these sums are paid, must if required to do so by that former tenant, grant an overriding lease;[7] and
- landlords are given greater control over the assignment of leases. This aspect of the 1995 Act has already been dealt with.[8]

We now deal, in outline, with each of these changes.

1   The provisions of the Act cannot be avoided; any attempt to 'exclude, modify or otherwise frustrate the operation of any provision of this Act' is void; LT(C)A 1995, s 25(1).
2   The major exception to this is where a lease is granted after 1 January 1996 as a result of the exercise of an option granted prior to that date; such leases are subject to the old rules.
3   See para 37.60 below.
4   See para 37.61 below.
5   See para 37.62 below.
6   See para 37.64 below.
7   See paras 37.66 and 37.67 below. As we have seen in paras 37.55 and 37.56 above, these provisions also apply to 'old' leases.
8   See para 37.37 above.

The transmission of covenants on assignment of the lease or the reversion
37.60   When either a lease or a reversion is assigned the benefit and burden of all landlord and tenant covenants passes to the assignee.[1] There is no longer any requirement that the covenants should 'touch and concern' the land, but covenants which are expressed to be personal will not pass.[2] A landlord or tenant covenant includes any term, condition or obligation, whether contained in the lease or in any collateral agreement entered into before or after the lease, which has to be complied with by either the landlord or tenant respectively.[3]

1   LT(C)A 1995, s 3(1); the benefit of a landlord's right of re-entry also passes to the assignee of the reversion; LT(C)A 1995, s 4.
2   LT(C)A 1995, s 3(6)(a).
3   LT(C)A 1995, s 28(1). Covenants which require third parties to discharge any function in respect of the demised premises (eg where a management company is required to carry out repairs, maintenance, etc) are treated as landlord or tenant covenants, as appropriate, and can, therefore, be enforced by assignees; LT(C)A 1995, s 12.

Release of tenant on assignment of the lease
37.61   Where a tenant assigns a lease he is released from the tenant covenants from the date of the assignment.[1] The only circumstances in which this release does not occur is where the assignment is 'excluded'; an assignment is excluded if it is made in breach of covenant (eg without consent where consent is required) or by operation of law (eg where a lease transfers automatically, on bankruptcy, to the tenant's trustee in bankruptcy).[2] As we shall see in the following paragraph, the practical benefits of this release are reduced where the landlord can, and does, require the assigning tenant to guarantee the obligations of the assignee.

1   LT(C)A 1995, s 5 (2).
2   LT(C)A 1995, s 11.

Authorised guarantee agreements
37.62   Although a tenant is released from the *tenant covenants* on assigning the lease, the Act expressly permits him to enter into an agreement under which he guarantees that

his assignee will perform the tenant covenants.[1] This means that, if the assignee is in breach of those covenants, the former tenant can then be sued under the *guarantee*. Such agreements are known as 'authorised guarantee agreements' ('AGAs'). A crucial restriction on AGAs is that they cannot impose liability on a former tenant once his assignee has been released by a further, non-excluded, assignment.[2]

A landlord is entitled to require an assigning tenant to enter into an AGA in the following circumstances:[3]

- where the lease contains an absolute covenant against assignment (but the landlord is prepared to allow the assignment);
- where the landlord's consent is required in a lease of *commercial or industrial* premises and the lease contains an express requirement that, on assignment the tenant must enter into an AGA;[4] and
- in the case of any lease where the landlord's consent is required and a condition that the tenant enter into an AGA is *reasonable*.

In the period since the 1995 Act came into force, it has become clear that landlords of commercial and industrial premises are, as a matter of standard practice, including in their leases provisions which require their tenants to enter into an AGA as a condition of consent to any assignment; the *automatically* imposed AGA has therefore become a fact of life for such tenants. Accordingly, the normal pattern of liability following the assignment of a business lease is that the outgoing tenant is released from the tenant covenants but will remain liable (under the AGA) for any breaches committed by his own immediate assignee; only when that assignee further assigns will the original tenant be entirely free from any further obligation.

1   LT(C)A 1995, s 16(1).
2   LT(C)A 1995, s 16(4)(b).
3   LT(C)A 1995, s 16(2) and (3).
4   As we have seen in para 37.37 above, the LT(C)A 1995, s 22 has inserted a new s 19(1A) into the Landlord and Tenant Act 1927; as a result it is now possible for landlords of commercial and industrial premises to specify in advance the conditions to which any consent to an assignment will be subject. Where this is done, any condition is deemed to be reasonable.

Illustrations
37.63   It may be helpful to illustrate the principles outlined in the previous two paragraphs by three examples.

EXAMPLE 1

$$T \longrightarrow A_1$$

Provided T's assignment to A_1 is not excluded, T is released from the tenant covenants. However, if he has entered into an AGA, he will be liable on that agreement if A_1 breaches any tenant covenant.

EXAMPLE 2

$$T \longrightarrow A_1 \longrightarrow A_2$$

Provided both assignments are not excluded, T is now free from any further liability. Any AGA which T entered into when assigning to A_1 cannot have any further effect after A_1's assignment to A_2. A_1 will be released from the tenant covenants on assigning to A_2 but, if he entered into an AGA he will be responsible, under that AGA, for any breaches committed by A_2; A_1 will only be free from all liability when A_2 lawfully assigns.

EXAMPLE 3

$$T \longrightarrow A_1 \longrightarrow A_2$$

Here let us assume that T's assignment to A_1 is excluded because he assigned without consent. This means that T is *not* released from the tenant covenants; should A_1 breach those covenants, T is *directly* liable to the landlord. If A_1 lawfully assigns to A_2, T is then released from the tenant covenants (as is A_1). However, T may be required to enter into an AGA guaranteeing A_2's performance of the tenant covenants (as may A_1); in such a case T is not free from all liabilities until A_2 lawfully assigns.

Release of landlord on assignment of the reversion
37.64 A landlord is not automatically released from the landlord covenants when the reversion is assigned. Thus each successive landlord is, in principle, liable on the landlord covenants for the remainder of the lease.[1] It should be remembered that the continuing liability of a landlord is nothing like as onerous as that of a tenant; indeed, there has, as yet, been no reported decision in which a former landlord has been sued in respect of breaches committed by the current landlord.

That said, the 1995 Act does permit[1] a landlord who assigns the reversion to apply, in the first instance to the tenant, for release from the landlord covenants[2] within four weeks of any assignment. Where the tenant objects to such a release, the landlord can apply to court.[3] Where a landlord fails to apply for a release, or fails to achieve a release, he can re-apply should his assignee further assign.[4]

This procedure is cumbersome and may, in itself provoke tenants into objecting to any release. It is clear that the parties are free simply to agree a release following an assignment by the landlord;[5] what is not clear is whether this allows a landlord to insert into a lease from the outset a provision under which the landlord *will* be released following any assignment.

1   LT(C)A 1995, s 6(2). This differs from the position under an 'old' lease where only the original landlord continues to be liable following the assignment of the reversion; see para 37.45 above.
2   This will not include covenants that are stated to be personal; see *BHP Petroleum Great Britain Ltd v Chesterfield Properties Ltd* [2001] EWCA Civ 1797, [2002] 1 All ER 821 where it was held that a landlord could obtain release from a personal warranty against defects in the new building leased to the tenant.
3   LT(C)A 1995, s 8.
4   LT(C)A 1995, s 7.
5   LT(C)A 1995, s 26(1)(a).

Default notices and overriding leases
37.65 Despite the radical changes introduced by the 1995 Act, it is clear that the device of the AGA permits a former tenant to be liable for breaches committed by his immediate assignee; indeed, as we have seen, emerging practice suggests that in the case of commercial and industrial leases, this liability is turning out to be automatic.[1] However, the Act does contain provisions designed to alleviate the position of a former tenant who is being, or has been pursued, by the landlord. Landlords must now serve default notices wherever they wish to pursue a former tenant; furthermore, where a former tenant pays all the sums due under a default notice, he is entitled to require the grant of an overriding lease. As we have seen, these provisions apply not only to 'new' leases but also to 'old' leases to which the Act does not otherwise apply.[2]

1   See para 37.62 above.
2   See paras 37.55 and 37.56 above.

37.66   *Default notices*   No former tenant can be held liable for a 'fixed charge' unless, within six months of that charge becoming due the landlord serves on him a prescribed form of notice which informs him that the sum is now due, and the amount which is due, together with any interest thereon.[1] A 'fixed charge' is defined so as to cover rent, service charge payments and any other fixed sum payable in the event of a breach of covenant.[2] This prevents landlords allowing arrears to build up (on which a penal rate of interest is normally payable) without informing the former tenant. Where arrears continue to accrue the landlord must, of course, serve further default notices every six months in order to be able to pursue the former tenant.[3]

1   LT(C)A 1995, s 17(2).
2   LT(C)A 1995, s 17(6).
3   The service of regular default notices is a matter which will normally be left to a landlord's managing agent.

37.67   *Overriding leases*   A major defect in the law as it stood prior to 1995 was that a former tenant had no rights in respect of the demised premises. All original tenants, and any assignee who had signed a direct covenant,[1] could be held liable for all the obligations under the lease for the remainder of the lease, yet the current tenant could remain in occupation of the property.[2] The former tenants could sue the current tenant under their indemnity covenant (which would be worthless if the current tenant has no money) but could not regain the property. This has now been changed for all leases, 'old' and 'new'.

   Where a former tenant pays all sums due under a default notice,[3] he is entitled to require the landlord to grant to him an overriding lease.[4] This overriding lease is, in effect, a concurrent lease (or lease of the reversion)[5], which sits between the landlord's reversion and the current tenant's lease; thus the former tenant becomes a direct tenant of the landlord and the landlord of the current tenant. This means that the former tenant can now take steps, as landlord, against the current tenant. In particular, he can forfeit the current tenant's lease and then either occupy the premises himself on the basis of the overriding lease, or assign the overriding lease to a reliable assignee who will thus take over its obligations.

1   See para 37.56 above.
2   Obviously the *landlord* can forfeit the lease, but may choose not to do so where there is a former tenant who is liable and able to meet all its obligations. This will particularly be the case where the premises are let on terms which are better than those which could now be achieved.
3   See para 37.65 above.
4   LT(C)A 1995, s 19(1).
5   See para 37.17 above.

Sureties and sub-tenants
37.68   To conclude this section on the transmission of covenants we briefly consider the position of sureties and sub-tenants.

Sureties
37.69   For many years it has been the widespread practice of landlords to require a lease to be executed not just by the tenant but also by a surety (or guarantor). This does not make the surety a tenant, rather it commits the surety to the obligations imposed by the covenant of guarantee which is then included within the lease. The broad effect of such a covenant is to render the surety liable to the landlord in virtually[1] the same circumstances as the tenant would be liable; in other words the liability of the surety 'mirrors' that of the tenant he is guaranteeing. In particular this means that, where the tenant remains liable following the assignment of the lease, so does his surety. So, the surety of an original tenant

under an 'old' lease will remain liable for the whole of the lease term, even after 'his' tenant has assigned. So far as 'new' leases are concerned, the 1995 Act has been drafted so as to ensure that sureties incur no greater liability than the tenant whom they are guaranteeing, and enjoy the same benefits. So, where a tenant is released from the tenant covenants, so is his surety;[2] where a former tenant is entitled to a default notice or an overriding lease, so is his surety.[3]

1   There are circumstances where a surety is released from liability where his principal is not, notably where, without his consent, the terms of the lease are varied in a material way.
2   LT(C)A 1995, s 24(2).
3   LT(C)A 1995, s 17(3), s 19(1). Note that these rights are accorded to sureties under 'old' leases as well.

Subtenants

37.70   The position where a tenant sub-lets is quite different from that where a tenant assigns:

Here T has created a sub-lease out of his own lease. In this case while there is a contract (and a relationship of landlord and tenant) between L and T and a contract (and a relationship of landlord and tenant) between T and S, there is no contract between L and S, nor are L and S in a relationship of landlord and tenant. Therefore enforcement between L and S of covenants contained in the head-lease between L and T depends not on the foregoing rules but on the rules described in chapter 34. It should be noted that any covenant in a post-1995 head lease that restricts the use of the demised premises can be enforced against a subtenant even though there is no express mention of this in his own lease[1].

1   LT(C)A 1995, s 3(5), *Oceanic Village Ltd v United Attractions Ltd* [2000] 1 All ER 975.

Bringing leases to an end: the common law

37.71   At common law a lease may come to an end in a number of different ways. Those which we have not already dealt with, we outline in the following paragraphs. We consider how the common law concerning termination of leases has been altered by statute in chapter 38.

Forfeiture

37.72   So long as there is an express provision within the lease (known as a right of re-entry) a landlord can terminate a lease where the tenant is in breach of covenant. We have already considered forfeiture in paras 37.44 to 37.47 and 37.51 above.

Surrender

37.73   A lease comes to an end where it is 'swallowed up' by the immediate landlord's reversion and is thus extinguished. Surrender of a fixed term lease[1] may be effected by an express agreement[2] that the tenant is giving up his lease; this agreement should be in the form of a deed.[3] Surrender can also take place by operation of law. This will occur where the tenant gives up possession and the landlord accepts[2] this as surrender, or where the tenant takes a new lease from the landlord during the currency of the existing tenancy–this existing lease disappears.

1   In practice, surrender is only applicable to fixed-term leases that would otherwise continue until their contractual term date (see para 37.75 below). Where either party wishes to terminate a periodic tenancy they can (subject to statute) simply serve a notice to quit (see para 37.76 below).
2   It must be stressed that a surrender is *not* a unilateral act. A tenant cannot simply 'decide' that he no longer wishes to hold the lease; the landlord must agree that the lease is at an end.
3   LPA 1925, s 52(1), see para 30.10 above.

Merger
37.74   This occurs where either the landlord's and the tenant's interests are acquired by a third party in the same capacity, or where the tenant acquires the landlord's reversion.

Expiry
37.75   At common law a lease for a fixed term of years comes to an end when that term expires without the need for notice from either party. The common law position is, however, much affected by statute.[1]

1   See Chapter 38 below.

Notice
37.76   A lease for a fixed term may not be determined by notice unless there is an express provision to that effect. Such options to terminate are known as break options or rights to break. Depending on the terms of the lease, they may be operated by either the landlord or the tenant. Tenants' rights to break are becoming increasingly common as they mitigate the effect of a long lease by providing the tenant with an opportunity for earlier termination. It is usual for rights to break to be operable by the giving of a specified period of notice at a given point; so, a 10-year lease may contain a tenant's right to break on the giving of six months' notice expiring at the end of the fifth year of the term. It should be noted that any time provisions relating to break options must be strictly adhered to, ie time is always of the essence[1]. Any preconditions to the right to break, eg that the rent is fully paid up, must also be strictly complied with.

As we have seen,[2] periodic tenancies continue automatically until terminated by a notice to quit served by either party.[3] In the absence of any agreement to the contrary, a yearly tenancy may be determined by the service of no less than six months' notice expiring at the end of a period of the tenancy. In the case of other periodic tenancies, again in the absence of any agreement to the contrary, the minimum notice required at common law is equal to one full period of the tenancy; once again the notice must expire at the end of a period of the tenancy. So, a monthly tenancy can be terminated by the service of one month's notice expiring at the end of a month. These rules are subject to the overriding statutory requirement that, in the case of tenancies of residential premises, a notice to quit must be in writing[4] and must be for a minimum of four weeks.[5] Furthermore, the termination of leases by notice is also considerably affected in other respects by various statutes.[6]

1   For a discussion of time of the essence generally, see paras 8.8-8.11 above. That concept is also referred to in the context of rent review at para 37.33 above.
2   See para 37.13 above.
3   Where there are joint tenants or joint landlords, a notice to quit served by one only, without the knowledge or consent of the other(s), is effective to terminate the tenancy: *Hammersmith and Fulham London Borough Council v Monk* [1992] 1 AC 478, HL. It should be noted that this rule only applies where the notice is a valid notice to quit of the required length expiring at the end of a period of the tenancy. Any other notice will, in law, operate as a break notice; this requires the co-operation of all

joint owners, *Hounslow London Borough Council v Pilling* (1993) 25 HLR 305, CA.
4   Protection from Eviction Act 1977, s 5(1)(a).
5   PEA 1977, s 5(1)(b). It should be noted that, as a result of an amendment introduced by the Housing
     Act 1988, s 5 no longer applies to tenancies where the tenant shares the home of the landlord or his
     immediate family.
6   See Chapter 38 below.

Enlargement

37.77   The LPA 1925, s 153 provides that where a lease has been granted for a term
of not less than 300 years, of which not less than 200 years are left unexpired, and either
no rent or no rent having any money value is payable, the term of years may be enlarged
into a fee simple (freehold) by the tenant executing a deed to that effect. Such a combination
of circumstances is no doubt unlikely.

Frustration

37.78   A lease can occasionally be terminated as a result of the operation of the contractual
doctrine of frustration, a matter which is discussed in para 10.9 above.

Repudiation

37.79   We have seen that there are circumstances in which the breach of a contract by
one of the parties can entitle the other party to repudiate, ie terminate, the contract[1]. Although
a lease is a contract, it also creates an estate in land and, for this reason, it used to be
thought that a lease could not be repudiated. However, it does now appear to be accepted
that the principle can apply to leases[2]. Since a landlord can normally achieve the same
effect by forfeiture[3], this development is of greatest interest to tenants who otherwise have
no right to terminate in the face of substantial breaches of covenant by their landlords.
However, it is clear that the only circumstances in which repudiation by a tenant will be
allowed is where the landlord's breach effectively deprives the tenant of the benefit of the
whole of the remainder of the lease. Breaches that do not have this effect should be
remedied by an award of damages[4].

1   See paras 8.14-8.29 above.
2   See *Hussein v Mehlman* [1992] 2 EGLR 87 where a landlord's very serious breach of its repairing
     covenants was held to entitle the tenants to repudiate the lease. See also *Chartered Trust plc v Davies*
     [1997] 2 EGLR 83, CA where a landlord's breach of its obligation not to derogate from its grant was
     similarly treated, see para 3723 above.
3   See paras 37.44-37.47 above.
4   See *Nynehead Developments Ltd v RH Fibreboard Containers Ltd* [1999] 1 EGLR 7.

Disclaimer

37.80   Where a tenant becomes insolvent the tenant's trustee in bankruptcy or, in the
case of a company tenant, liquidator (to whom the lease passes by operation of law) may
disclaim it where the lease is not readily saleable.[1] This terminates the lease as against the
insolvent tenant; however, the lease remains on foot for other purposes so that others,
such as former tenants, or sureties will remain liable to the landlord.[2]

1   Insolvency Act 1986, ss 178, 315.
2   *Hindcastle Ltd v Barbara Attenborough Associates Ltd* [1996] 1 All ER 737, HL.

Chapter 38

Landlord and tenant: statutory protection

38.1   Our exposition of the law of landlord and tenant in the previous chapter deals with only half the story, for today the law relating to leases is much modified and qualified by statute. This statutory regulation is divided broadly into three areas: residential tenancies, business tenancies and agricultural tenancies. The hallmark of much of the legislation in all three sectors for a large part of the 20th century was the imposition of security of tenure, ie the right of the tenant to remain in occupation after the termination of their contractual lease, and, in the private residential sector, rent control. This approach is changing. Fearful that security of tenure (and, in the private residential sector, rent control) was discouraging landowners from letting their property, legislation in the late 1980s and 1990s heralded a much greater emphasis on freedom of contract in both private residential and agricultural tenancies, a move on which there appears to be political consensus. It is perhaps ironic that, on its face, it is the regime affecting tenants of business premises which now appears to confer the greatest security of tenure. However, as we shall see, it is possible for the parties to commercial leases to opt out of the scheme of protection.

It should also be appreciated that, during the last century, Parliament has had to tackle the problem posed by long leases of residential property. Ever since 19th century, the grant of such leases has been commonplace. This was partly because the long lease provided an effective mechanism for the large landowners to control the development of our cities. However, as we have seen, leasehold ownership was also the only practical basis for the ownership of flats. By the 1960s a significant number of these long leases had diminished to a length that was having a serious economic impact, notably that they were now too short to offer sufficient security for mortgage lending. This stirred the political conscience and it was then that the first steps down the thorny path of conferring on tenants a statutory right to enfranchisement (ie to acquire the freehold or a new long lease) were first taken. While this now horribly complex legislation will eventually be displaced if commonhold takes root, it will take many years before existing long leases are phased out.

A knowledge of the impact of the statutory regulation of the landlord and tenant relationship is an important part of the study of estate management. Although, in a book of this nature, we cannot deal with this in great detail, in this chapter we will give an outline of:

- the statutory regulation of residential tenancies;
- the statutory protection of business tenants; and
- the statutory schemes applying to agricultural tenancies.

Residential tenancies

Introduction

38.2   Although, inevitably, residential tenancies come in all shapes and sizes, for the purposes of statutory regulation one key practical distinction is usually that between long leases, ie those for more than 21 years, and those of a shorter duration. Most (but not all) leases of more than 21 years are granted at a premium, with the result that the rent is a low ground rent. Where the rent is low, neither the Rent Act 1977 nor the Housing Act 1988, can apply. This is no great disadvantage to the tenants under such leases since neither security of tenure nor rent levels are an immediate problem. The relationship between the landlord and the tenant at the outset of such leases is much more akin, at least in economic terms, to that between a vendor and purchaser of a freehold. However, there are problems for the tenants and these stem from the nature of their ownership, ie they hold a wasting asset and, where the property is a flat, it is usually the landlord who maintains the whole property and who provides services often, from a tenant's perspective, in an unsatisfactory way. These difficulties are addressed not by a regulatory scheme designed to protect tenants during and at the end of short leases, but by the prospect of enfranchisement and self-management. Accordingly, there has come to be a complex statutory framework allowing for the enfranchisement of long leases of both houses and flats. The management problem has also been tackled by a variety of measures, including the control of service charges affecting residential property[1] and by the rights of tenants of flats to apply for the appointment of a manager and, in extreme cases, compulsorily to acquire the landlord's interest[2]. Most recently, a right to take over the management of the building has been introduced.[3]

The regimes governing tenancies where the rent is not low (and where lease lengths are usually, but not necessarily, short) are very different. Originally, the aim was to confer both security of tenure and rent control and this was the remit of a series of Rent Acts spanning the period 1915-1977. The change came in the late 1980s. The Housing Act 1988 in its original form abandoned rent control for new tenants but did still confer significant security of tenure. However, that Act made provision for a form of tenancy – the assured shorthold tenancy – under which tenants enjoyed little security. Subsequent amendments to the HA 1988 have ensured that the assured shorthold tenancy has become the dominant form in the private sector. Thus the traditional twin pillars of residential tenant protection – rent control and security of tenure – have all but disappeared, a trend that looks set to continue under the reform agenda currently being pursued.

Another key factor in the statutory framework is the divide between private and public sector provision. However, this is not, in terms of numbers, as significant as it used to be. As we shall see[4], much of the former public sector housing function has been handed over to housing associations and tenancies granted by these bodies are governed by the legislation relating to tenancies granted by private landlords.

Another important area of statutory provision in residential tenancies relates to harassment and unlawful eviction and the provision of information to tenants. In this section we will deal with:

- private sector regulation – the Rent Act 1977 and the Housing Act 1988;
- public sector regulation – the Housing Act 1985;
- leasehold enfranchisement;
- miscellaneous statutory provision – harassment, unlawful eviction, and information to tenants; and
- the agenda for reform.

1   See para 37.36 above.

2 See para 37.48 above.
3 Para 38.15 below.
4 Para 38.16 below.

Rent Act tenancies

38.3 The Rent Act 1977 applies to certain lettings[1] of dwelling-houses, granted *before* 15 January 1989. Excluded from its application are, for example, houses with an annual rent above £25,000 or of £1,000 or less in Greater London (or £250 or less elsewhere),[2] tenancies where the rent includes an element for board or attendance, lettings to students by universities and colleges, holiday lettings and tenancies where the landlord resides in another part of the same building (so long as this is not a purpose-built block of flats).

Rent Act tenancies terminate in accordance with the common law rules explained in Chapter 37; however, on the termination of a protected contractual tenancy, provided the tenant is occupying the premises as his residence, there immediately arises a statutory tenancy,[3] on the same terms. This confers on the tenant, not an estate in the land, but a 'status of irremovability'.[4] The landlord under either a protected or statutory tenancy (known collectively as 'regulated tenancies') may not recover possession save by order of a county court which will only be granted in accordance with the provisions of the Rent Act 1977, s 98 and Sch 15. Possession will only be granted where the court considers it reasonable to do so and either there is suitable alternative accommodation available to the tenant or the landlord makes out one of the discretionary cases for possession set out in the Act. The Act also provides for mandatory grounds for possession,[5] which, if made out, entitle the landlord as of right to regain possession.

On the death of a Rent Act tenant, the tenancy will not necessarily come to an end since a successor may be entitled to take over the tenancy[6]. On the death of an original tenant, a surviving spouse[7] can succeed to the tenancy and will continue to pay a fair rent[8]. If there is no surviving spouse, any member of the family[9] who was living with the deceased tenant for the previous two years can succeed but, in this case, the successor takes an assured tenancy[10] and must pay a market rent. It is these rights of succession which mean that it will still be some time before Rent Act tenancies disappear[11].

The Rent Act also imposes rent control. The landlord or tenant may apply to the rent officer for the area for the determination and registration of a fair rent,[12] which must not thereafter be exceeded and which takes effect for two years. Either party can, after two years (or earlier if the premises have been improved), apply for a re-registration of the rent; this is, in effect, the only means by which a landlord can achieve an increase in the rent. While it is now clear that fair rents must usually be fixed by reference to market rents in the locality[13], the Act requires that any element of scarcity must be ignored[14]. It is this disregard of scarcity which means that, although fair rents are now more closely linked to the market than used to be the case, they are still nearly always noticeably lower than market rents. Furthermore, anxious that the link to market rents meant that fair rents were rising too quickly, and mindful that the remaining Rent Act tenants tend to elderly and on low incomes, the Government has now introduced a cap on increases to fair rents[15].

1 There must be a lease and not a licence; it is this requirement that provoked much of the litigation on the distinction between a lease and a licence referred to at para 37.9 above.
2 Tenants under long tenancies (ie those in excess of 21 years) at a low rent qualify for the rights conferred by the Leasehold Reform Act 1967 and the Leasehold Reform, Housing and Urban Development Act 1993, paras 38.13 and 38.14 below.
3 Rent Act 1977, s 2.
4 *Keeves v Dean* [1924] 1 KB 685 at 686.
5 These mandatory grounds usually only apply where the landlord has served notice to this effect on the tenant at the commencement of the tenancy.
6 Rent Act 1977, s 2(1), Sch 1.
7 RA1977, Sch 1, para 2 defines surviving spouse so as to include any person living with the tenant as his or her wife or husband; it has been held that the Human Rights Act 1998, s 3 requires this to be

interpreted so as to include a same-sex partner in a stable relationship, see *Ghaidan v Mendoza* [2002] EWCA Civ 1533, [2002] 4 All ER 1162.

8   On the death of a surviving spouse who has succeeded to a statutory tenancy there can be one further succession to a member of both the original tenant's and the successor's family who was living with the survivor for two years before his or her death. Any second successor takes an assured tenancy and must pay a market rent.

9   While this will include blood relatives and adopted family, it will not normally extend to those who are not related to the tenant, see *Carega Properties SA v Sharratt* [1979] 2 All ER 1084, HL.

10   Ie a tenancy governed by the Housing Act 1988, see paras 38.8-38.10 below.

11   Although no new Rent Act tenancies have been created since 1989, it was estimated in 2000 that there were then about 150,000 such tenancies still remaining (some 6% of the private rented sector), although they do appear to be declining fairly rapidly, DETR Housing Statistics, 2000.

12   The basis on which a 'fair rent' is to be ascertained is defined in the Rent Act, 1977, s 70.

13   *Spath Holme Ltd v Chairman of Greater Manchester and Lancashire Rent Assessment Panel* (1995) 28 HLR 107, CA; *Curtis v London Rent Assessment Committee* [1997] 4 All ER 842, CA.

14   Rent Act 1977, s 70(2).

15   Rent Acts (Maximum Fair Rent) Order 1999. This limits increases to the increases in the RPI plus a further percentage.

Housing Act tenancies

Introduction

38.4   Where a tenancy of a separate dwelling house is granted *on or after 15 January 1989* it will be governed by the Housing Act 1988, so long as the tenant is an individual who occupies the property as his only or principal home.[1] As with the Rent Act, certain tenancies are excluded, such as those of dwelling-houses let at a rent above or below prescribed limits or let by educational institutions to students; also excluded are holiday lettings and tenancies granted by a resident landlord (the definition of which is much the same as under the Rent Act).[2] Housing Act tenancies are either assured shorthold tenancies[3] or assured tenancies[4]. Neither type of tenancy can be brought to an end by the landlord except in accordance with the Act[5]. Landlords are not restricted as to the rent they can charge, although a tenant under an assured shorthold tenancy can, in limited circumstances, ask a rent assessment committee to ensure that the initially agreed rent is no more than a market rent[6]. The Act provides a mechanism under which rent can periodically be increased in line with market rents[7], but the parties are not required to use the statutory scheme and can make their own provision for rent reviews. In the event of the death of a tenant holding under either an assured shorthold, or an assured, periodic tenancy there is a single right of succession to any spouse[8] of the deceased tenant who, at the date of the death was occupying the premises as his or her only or principal home[9].

1   Housing Act 1988, s 1. In the case of joint tenants, each must be an individual, though only one need occupy the premises as his home. There has been considerable litigation, both under the Rent Acts and the Housing Act, as to the meaning of a separate dwelling house. Suffice to say that the thrust of this is that the premises should be capable of providing all the necessary attributes of a home; it has, however, been acknowledged that, in modern times, accommodation can be a home even though it is a single room (with ensuite facilities) that has no cooking amenities, see *Uratemp Ventures Ltd v Collins* [2001] UKHL 43, [2002] 1 All ER 46.

2   HA 1988, s 1 and Sch 1.

3   See paras 38.5-38.7 below.

4   See paras 38.8-38.10 below.

5   HA 1988, ss 5, 7.

6   HA 1988, s 22.

7   HA 1988, ss 13, 14.

8   A 'spouse' is defined so as to include a person who was living with the tenant as his or her wife or husband, HA 1988, s 17(4). This expression will now be taken to include a same-sex partner in a stable relationship, see *Ghaidan v Mendoza* [2002] EWCA Civ 1533, [2002] 4 All ER 1162,.

9   HA 1988, s 17.

Assured shorthold tenancies

38.5   *The creation of an assured shorthold tenancy*   Right from the outset the HA 1988 envisaged a form of assured tenancy under which tenants would enjoy minimal security of tenure and which landlords could terminate simply by serving notice – the assured shorthold tenancy. However, initially, the Act required that such tenancies could only arise where criteria additional to that for assured tenancies were satisfied. So, for tenancies created *on or after 15 January 1989 and before 28 February 1997* it was essential, in order for there to be an assured shorthold, that the tenancy was for a term of not less than six months (and did not contain any provision - other than a forfeiture provision - allowing the landlord to terminate the tenancy within six months) and that the landlord had served on all the tenants a statutorily prescribed form of prior notice stating that the tenancy was to be an assured shorthold tenancy. These preconditions caused problems. Many landlords found that, either through ignorance or incompetence, these requirements had not been met and that the tenancy was, as a result, a fully assured tenancy under which it was very difficult to regain possession[1].

The HA 1988 was therefore amended in 1997[2] and, for Housing Act tenancies created *on or after 28 February 1997*, the position is now very different. All tenancies that satisfy the basic criteria of the Act[3], whether fixed term or periodic, are now assured shorthold tenancies unless the landlord gives notice that they are to be assured tenancies[4]. Accordingly the assured shorthold has now become the norm.

1   See para 38.9 below.
2   By the Housing Act 1996.
3   See para 38.4 above.
4   HA 1988, s 19A, Sch 2A as inserted by the Housing Act 1996, s 96.

38.6   *Termination of assured shorthold tenancies* An assured shorthold tenancy can now[1] be either fixed term or periodic. Neither can be brought to an end by the landlord except in accordance with the Act[2]. The tenant is free to terminate the tenancy in accordance with the common law, subject to any express provisions in the agreement; accordingly he can, as appropriate, treat a fixed term tenancy as at an end on its contractual term date, or serve a notice to quit a periodic tenancy.

A landlord cannot regard a fixed-term assured shorthold tenancy as expiring on its contractual term date[3]. Unless the tenant chooses to leave, the tenancy is automatically replaced by a statutory periodic tenancy[4] under which the tenant can remain in possession until the tenancy is terminated in accordance with the Act. Where the assured shorthold tenancy is periodic from the outset, the landlord cannot serve a notice to quit[5]. The landlord will normally terminate an assured shorthold tenancy by serving notice under the Act[6]. He can also end the tenancy by obtaining a court order based on one of the statutory grounds for possession but will rarely need to opt for this method given the simple alternative of serving notice[7].

The great attraction of the assured shorthold for landlords is the ability to regain possession[8] following the simple service of a statutory notice, without the need to prove any statutory ground. In order to terminate the tenancy in this way the landlord must serve at least two months' notice in writing[9]. While this can be served during the currency of any fixed-term tenancy, no order for possession can be obtained until such fixed term has expired[10]. A landlord's notice to terminate a periodic tenancy can, subject to any express provisions in the agreement, be served at any time; it must expire at the end of a period of the tenancy[11]. However, no order for possession will be granted until six months after the assured shorthold tenancy (whether fixed term or periodic) was first granted[12]; this is designed to ensure that all assured shorthold tenants have, if they choose, a minimum of six months' security of tenure.

1   Ie for tenancies granted on or after 28 February 1997, see para 38.5 above.
2   Housing Act 1988, ss 5, 7.
3   HA 1988, s 5(1).
4   HA 1988, s 5(2).
5   HA 1988, s 5(1).
6   HA 1988, s 21.
7   HA 1988, ss 5, 7, 21. The notice method of termination can only be used at the expiry of a fixed-term

tenancy. If a landlord wishes to terminate *during* a fixed term (eg where the tenant is in default) he will then have to use a statutory ground, see para 38.9 below.

8   It should be appreciated that, where a tenant refuses to leave following the service of a proper notice, the landlord will then need to obtain a court order for possession since it is a criminal offence simply re-enter residential premises: see Protection from Eviction Act 1977, s 3(1), para 38.19 below.

9   HA 1988, s 21.

10   HA 1988, s 21(1)(a).

11   HA 1988, s 21(4)(a).

12   HA 1988, s 21(5).

38.7   *Rent referral and rent review* The only theoretical drawback of an assured shorthold tenancy for landlords is that a tenant is entitled to refer the *initial* rent to a rent assessment committee during the first six months of the tenancy[1]; however, the committee's jurisdiction is limited and is designed only to ensure that the landlord does not charge a rent which is *in excess* of market rents and there is little evidence that such references are often made. The landlord of an assured shorthold tenancy can, if he chooses, make use of the statutory provisions governing rent increases[2]. In practice, where a landlord does allow assured shorthold tenants to remain in occupation for a relatively lengthy period, he either includes express rent review provisions in the original agreement[3], or he grants a series of short fixed term tenancies and negotiates a new rent at the beginning of each.

1   Housing Act 1988, s 22.

2   HA 1988, ss 13, 14, see para 38.10 below.

3   Which necessarily excludes the statutory machinery, HA 1988, s 13(1).

Assured tenancies

38.8   *Creation of assured tenancies* Where a tenancy complying with the basic criteria of the Act[1] is entered into on or after 28 February 1997, it will only be an assured tenancy (as opposed to an assured shorthold tenancy[2]) where a notice to that effect is served on the tenant.[3] Accordingly, Housing Act tenancies granted by private landlords will now invariably be assured shorthold rather than assured tenancies; however, those granted by housing associations will often be fully assured since such bodies are encouraged to confer long term security wherever possible[4].

1   See para 38.4 above.

2   See paras 38.5-38.7 above.

3   Housing Act 1988, s 19A.

4   *Tenant's Guarantee* issued by the Housing Corporation.

38.9   *Termination of an assured tenancy* Where a fixed-term assured tenancy expires, a statutory periodic tenancy arises (the periods of which are those in respect of which rent was payable under the fixed term).[1] A periodic assured tenancy, including one arising on the ending of a fixed term, cannot be terminated by the landlord serving a notice to quit.[2] In contrast to an assured shorthold tenancy, a landlord cannot bring an assured tenancy to an end simply by serving notice; he must obtain a court order based on a statutory ground for possession[3]. To do this he must first serve on the tenant a statutory notice in prescribed form specifying the ground(s) on which possession will be sought and stating that proceedings will commence within a specified period.[4] As with the Rent Act, the HA 1988 provides for discretionary and mandatory grounds for possession, though some of these grounds are new or differ in detail[5]. Most of the mandatory grounds are not available to the landlord until the expiry of any fixed-term tenancy[6] and also require the service of a prior notice on the tenant at or before the grant of the tenancy[7]. Most of the grounds that are available during the currency of any fixed term are based on tenant default (and thus effectively replace forfeiture as a method of termination); however, virtually all of these are discretionary grounds. However, a vitally important exception is Ground 8. This is a mandatory ground of possession based on at least two months' rent arrears. This is widely used in practice as it provides the only opportunity for a landlord, whose tenant is in default, to recover possession as of right during any fixed term assured or assured shorthold tenancy.

1   Housing Act 1988, s 5(2).
2   HA 1988, s 5(1).
3   HA 1988, s 5(1).
4   HA 1988, s 8.
5   HA 1988, s 7, Sch 2.
6   HA 1988, s 7(6).
7   HA 1988, Sch 2, Part 1.

38.10   *Rent review*   The Housing Act 1988 does not in any sense impose rent control in the case of assured tenancies. The tenant has no right to refer the rent to a rent assessment committee[1]. The parties are free to include their own provisions for rent review, provided that these are genuine[2]. Wherever an assured periodic[3] tenancy does not contain its own provisions for rent review the Act provides a statutory mechanism under which a landlord can, by the service of a prescribed form of notice, seek to increase[4] the rent; such a notice can be served every year.[5] A tenant who objects to the landlord's proposed rent may refer the notice to a rent assessment committee, usually within one month of receiving the landlord's notice; where this is done the committee will determine the new rent by reference to open-market rental value.[6]

1   Compare the position of an assured shorthold tenant: see para 38.7 above.
2   If the tenancy agreement includes a rent review provision that is manifestly not intended to operate as a review but merely as a mechanism to force the tenant to quit, the provision will not be enforced. See *Bankway Properties Ltd v Pensfold-Dunsford* [2001] EWCA Civ 528, [2001] 2 EGLR 36 where there was a provision that, as from the last review date, the rent (of just over £4,500 pa) should automatically increase to £25,000 pa.
3   The statutory machinery does not apply during the currency of a fixed-term tenancy; it will, however, kick in once the fixed term expires and is replaced by a statutory periodic tenancy (see para 38.9 above), provided the tenancy agreement does not set out its own rent review provisions.
4   Since only the landlord can serve the statutory notice it is inherently unlikely that there will ever be a proposal that the rent goes down.
5   Housing Act 1988, s 13.
6   HA 1988, s 14.

Long residential tenancies

Security of tenure

38.11   Tenants of residential premises let on leases in excess of 21 years at a low rent (ie an annual rent of £1,000 or less in Greater London, £250 or less elsewhere) are given security of tenure at the expiry of the term, by virtue of Schedule 10 to the Local Government and Housing Act 1989.[1] Their existing lease is automatically continued on the same terms, including as to rent. The continued tenancy may be terminated by the landlord giving to the tenant between six and twelve months' notice either offering an assured monthly tenancy, or stating that the landlord will seek a possession order from the court on grounds stated in the Act, which are essentially the same as the discretionary grounds provided for under the Housing Act 1988. This protection will now rarely be necessary since such tenants will often, in practice, exercise the rights to enfranchise or to extend their existing leases discussed in the following paragraphs.

1   This replaces the previous scheme contained in Part 1 of the Landlord and Tenant Act 1954.

Enfranchisement

38.12   *Introduction*   Residential tenants under long leases of both houses and flats now have extensive rights to enfranchise. Enfranchisement for tenants of houses was the first to be introduced – by the Leasehold Reform Act 1967 ('LRA 1967'). This scheme is necessarily more straightforward since the problems posed by the rules under which the burden of positive covenants cannot pass to a purchaser of freehold land[1] is not so acute in the case of houses.

It took nearly thirty years to devise rules under which tenants of flats – for whom the running of positive covenants is essential – could be given the right to enfranchise[2]. This was achieved by Part I of the Leasehold Reform, Housing and Urban Development Act 1993 ('LRHUDA 1993'). This complex piece of legislation was initially hampered by poor drafting and has been subjected to numerous amendments, most recently in 2002[3]. As we shall see[4], it conferred two alternative rights: either a significant majority of the tenants in the building could, collectively, acquire the freehold and thus effectively become their own landlord or, where such agreement could not be achieved, individual tenants could exercise a right to acquire a new extended lease.

It is now recognised by all political parties that the use of the lease as a mechanism for the long-term ownership of residential property is no longer acceptable. The introduction of commonhold[5] is seen as the correct approach for the future. However, although it is theoretically possible to convert the ownership of a building from long leasehold to a commonhold, this is very unlikely to occur to any great extent[6]. Accordingly, enfranchisement is the only realistic prospect for the current owners of long leases.

1 See paras 34.4, 34.5 and 37.53 above.
2 Some tenants of flats had been given a right of first refusal by virtue of Part I of the Landlord and Tenant Act 1987.
3 By the Commonhold and Leasehold Reform Act 2002.
4 Para 38.14 below.
5 Para 29.35 and 34.5 above.
6 Largely because the conversion to commonhold requires the consent of 100% of those with any existing interest in the property, see Commonhold and Leasehold Reform Act 2002, s 3; thus the dissent of just one tenant will prevent any change.

38.13 *Leases of houses* The Leasehold Reform Act 1967, as amended, applies where a tenant has held[1], either for the last two years, or for periods amounting to at least two years during the last 10 years[2], a lease of a *house*[3] which was originally granted for a fixed term of over 21 years[4]. In these circumstances[5] the tenant[6] can, by serving notice on the landlord, require that the freehold of the house and premises[7] be transferred to him, or alternatively that he be granted a new lease in substitution for his existing lease, for a term expiring 50 years from the end of the existing lease[8]. This latter alternative is rarely sought.

The price or rent to be paid is to be determined in accordance with a formula laid down in the Act. The price to be paid on the acquisition of the freehold is calculated on one of two alternative bases, depending on the rateable value[9] of the property on the appropriate day[10]. For lower value properties the formula is very favourable to tenants; it is assumed that the vendor is selling subject to the tenancy as extended by 50 years and that any higher bid that might be expected from the sitting tenant (ie marriage value) is excluded[11]. For higher value property it is not assumed that the tenancy has been extended and the sitting tenant bid is not excluded (although the landlord's share of that is limited to 50%); the price is to be diminished by any increase in value attributable to improvements carried out and paid for by the present or previous tenants[12]. Furthermore the landlord has more extensive compensation rights, eg for diminution in value to other land, including loss of development value[13].

1 There used to be a requirement that the tenant must have occupied the house as his residence. This has now been abolished, Commonhold and Leasehold Reform Act 2002, s 138.
2 This period used to be three years and has now been reduced to two: CLRA 2002, s 139.
3 A house is any building designed or adapted for living in and reasonably so called whether or not it is structurally detached; where a building is divided horizontally, the flats or units into which it is divided are not 'houses': LRA 1967, s 2. The meaning of a house is to be construed in a flexible and non-technical way, see *Malekshad v Howard de Walden Estates Ltd* [2002] UKHL 49, [2003] 1 All ER 193. It has been held to include a purpose built shop with living accommodation above (*Tandon v Trustees of Spurgeon's*

Homes [1982] 1 All ER 1086, HL), a house comprising two flats occupied as a single residence (*Malpas v St Ermin's Property Ltd* [1992] 1 EGLR 109) and a house where a small part of its basement lay beneath adjoining property (*Malekshad v Howard de Walden Estates Ltd* [2002] UKHL 49, [2003] 1 All ER 193), but not a house the whole of whose basement lay below neighbouring freehold property (*Duke of Westminster v Birrane* [1995] 3 All ER 416, CA).

4   There used to be a requirement that the rent be 'low'; this requirement has now gone, CLRA 2002, s 141.

5   It should be noted the tenants of some types of landlord cannot enfranchise, eg the National Trust, local authorities and registered housing associations.

6   A surviving spouse and certain other member's of a deceased tenant's family who succeed to the tenancy can take the benefit of that tenant's accrued rights: LRA 1967, s 7.

7   The freehold can be acquired not only of the house but also of any garage, outhouse, yard, or garden which are let to the tenant with the house: LRA 1967, s 2(3).

8   LRA 1967, s 8.

9   For tenancies granted after 1 April 1990 (when domestic rates were abolished) rateable value limts have been replaced by a statutory formula based on the premium paid on the grant of the tenancy.

10   These vary according to the date on which the tenancy was first rated.

11   LRA 1967, s 9(1).

12   LRA 1967, s 9(1A), (1B), (1C).

13   LRA 1967, s 9A.

38.14   *Leases of flats* Tenants under long leases of *flats* now have, in certain circumstances, a right, together with other tenants in the same building, to form an RTE (right to enfranchise) company in order collectively to acquire the freehold of that building. Alternatively, a tenant may exercise an individual right to acquire an extended lease; this takes the form of a new lease for 90 years plus the outstanding period of the old lease.

The right to collective enfranchisement applies only to residential flats within a self-contained building or part of a building comprising at least two flats that are owned by 'qualifying tenants'[1]. At least two thirds of the total number of flats in the building must be occupied by tenants who qualify.[2] Buildings where more than 25% of the internal floor area is occupied for non-residential purposes are outside the Act, as are those comprising not more than four units where there is a resident landlord[3].

The right to collective enfranchisement can be exercised where at least half of the qualifying tenants wish to do so[4]. In order to 'qualify' the tenant must hold a lease for more than 21 years[5]; there is no longer a low rent requirement or any residence qualification[6]. They must form an RTE company and it is this company that must obtain a valuation of the freehold and then carry out the various procedures laid down by the Act[7]. The process is started by the service of a claim notice; this must specify the premises to be acquired, propose the price to be paid and provide the landlord with details of the qualifying tenants participating in the notice[8]. The landlord must respond within a strict time limit[9] and can either: admit the right to enfranchise and state which of the proposals are accepted; challenge the right to enfranchise, giving reasons; or indicate that the landlord intends to redevelop so that there is then no right to enfranchise. Following this exchange of notices the parties may well be able to agree the terms of the acquisition. If not, any dispute will be resolved by the leasehold valuation tribunal[10]. The price to be paid is governed by a statutory formula[11]. This is based on the open market value, assuming that the freehold is encumbered by the existing leases. The landlord is entitled to a 50% share in any marriage value. Once the process is completed the freehold is vested in the RTE company which becomes the landlord to all the tenants in the building.

It may be that there are tenants under long lease of flats who cannot participate in collective enfranchisement. This may be because the building does not qualify or because insufficient other qualifying tenants wish to acquire the freehold. Such tenants, provided they have held their existing lease for at least two years, are given an individual right to acquire a new long lease[12]. The procedure is similar to that for collective enfranchisement. The tenant must serve a claim notice, giving details of the flat, proposals as to the terms of the new lease, and the premium to be paid[13]. The landlord must respond to this in much the same way as for collective enfranchisement and any disputes as to the terms of the new lease, or the premium to be paid can be referred to the leasehold valuation tribunal[14]. The new lease will be for a term of 90 years from the expiry date of the existing lease at a peppercorn rent[15]. A premium, calculated by reference to a statutory formula, must be paid[16]. Again, this is based on market value and the landlord is entitled to a 50% share of any marriage value. The terms of the lease are to be the same as the existing lease save where this does not contain any provision for variable service charges; the new lease must provide for such service charges and their enforcement[17].

1   LRHUDA 1993, s 3(1).
2   LRHUDA 1993, s 3(1)(c).
3   LRHUDA 1993, s 4(4).
4   LRHUDA 1993, s 13(2)(b).
5   LRHUDA 1993, s 5(1).
6   Commonhold and Leasehold Reform Act 2002, ss 117 and 120.
7   CLRA 2002, ss122-124 and Sch 8.
8   LRHUDA 1993, s 13.
9   The date for the landlord's response must be set out in the claim notice; this must be not less than two months after the date on which the claim notice was served.
10   LRHUDA 1993, s 24(1).
11   LRHUDA 1993, s 32 and Sch 6.
12   LRHUDA 1993, s 39.
13   LRHUDA 1993, s 42.
14   LRHUDA 1993, s 48(1).
15   LRHUDA 1993, s 56.
16   LRHUDA 1993, s 56(2) and Sch 13.
17   LRHUDA 1993, s 57.

Right to manage

38.15   We have seen that where the landlord of a block of flats is guilty of failing to carry out his repairing and insuring obligations, the tenants can apply for the appointment of a manager and, where this proves not to be an adequate remedy, they can compulsorily acquire the landlord's interest[1]. Part II of the Commonhold and Leasehold Reform Act 2002 introduces a new right for long leaseholders of flats to take over the management of their building despite the fact that their landlord is not in breach of his obligations. This right to manage arises in much the same circumstances as the right to collective enfranchisement[2]. It is exerciseable by an RTM (right to manage) company which must be set up by the qualifying tenants[3]. Following the service of a notice of claim[4] and the elapse of the stated period of notice, the RTM company will take over the landlord's management functions, notably those with respect to services, repairs, maintenance, improvements, insurance and management[5].

1   See para 37.48 above.
2   See para 38.14 above.
3   Commonhold and Leasehold Reform Act 2002, s 74.
4   CLRA 2002, s 79.
5   CLRA 2002, ss 96, 97.

Secure tenancies in the public sector

38.16   The Housing Act 1985, Pt IV, confers security of tenure on public sector tenants. It should be appreciated that the traditional housing function of local authorities is diminishing. Much social housing provision is now undertaken by housing associations; since 1989, new tenancies granted by such bodies are usually assured tenancies governed by the Housing Act 1988[1]. The secure tenancy regime is thus largely confined to the remaining tenants of local authorities and housing action trusts. Furthermore these bodies are now allowed to grant introductory tenancies under which the tenant has less security.

1   See paras 38.8-38.10 above.

Secure tenancies

38.17 Subject to certain exclusions[1], where a dwelling house is let as a separate dwelling it will be a secure tenancy whenever both the landlord and the tenant condition are satisfied[2]. The landlord condition limits the type of landlord to a local authority, a new town corporation, an urban development corporation and certain housing co-operatives[3]. The tenant condition requires that the tenant is an individual who occupies the dwelling house as his only or principal home[4]. The provisions as to security apply not only to tenancies but also to licences[5]; however, it is clear that the only licences covered by the HA 1985 are those that confer exclusive possession[6].

The landlord of a secure tenancy cannot recover possession without serving a notice on the tenant and then obtaining a court order based on one of the statutory grounds for possession. Thus, any fixed-term tenancy does not end by expiry but is automatically replaced by a periodic tenancy[7], and the landlord cannot serve a notice to quit in respect of a periodic tenancy[8]. In order to terminate a tenancy the landlord must serve a notice on the tenant that specifies the grounds of possession on which the landlord will rely and which states a date after which proceedings will be commenced[9]. The grounds for possession are set out in Sch 2. Some, based largely on tenant default are discretionary, others are mandatory provided that suitable alternative accommodation is available to the tenant, and a third group is discretionary and also subject to the availability of suitable alternative accommodation. Not surprisingly, given the role of public sector landlords, the courts are reluctant to order possession. Even when granted, orders for possession are usually suspended especially where this will give the tenant a further opportunity to pay off arrears of rent. However, once an order is granted (whether suspended or not), the secure tenancy comes to an end. If the landlord allows the former tenant to remain in possession the latter does so as a tolerated trespasser[10]. In particular, the continued acceptance of 'rent' payments will not lightly be regarded as giving rise to a new tenancy[11]. To hold otherwise would be to discourage landlords from giving their former tenants a last chance. This means that, if any arrangement as to the payment of arrears is not kept, the landlord will be able to enforce the order for possession without commencing new proceedings.

Where a secure periodic tenant dies the tenancy will pass to any qualifying successor[12]. Priority is given to a surviving spouse[13]; where there is no surviving spouse the tenancy can pass to any member of the deceased tenant's family who resided with him for the 12 months preceding the death[14]. The expression family is defined and includes a person living with the tenant as husband or wife[15]; this expression will now include a same-sex partner in a stable relationship[16].

In addition to the rights conferred by the terms of their tenancy agreement, secure tenants have the benefit of the Secure Tenant's Charter which sets out a list of basic tenant's rights and the level of service they can expect from their landlords[17]. Most secure tenants also have a right to buy the freehold or acquire a long lease at a substantial discount[18]. The details of this scheme are outside the ambit of this book. They are listed in the Housing Act 1985, Sch 1.

1 The exceptions include, for example, land acquired for development and accommodation for homeless persons.
2 Housing Act 1985, s 79(1).
3 HA 1985, s 80.
4 HA 1985, s 81.
5 HA 1985, s 79(3).
6 See *Parkins v Westminster City Council* [1998] 1 EGLR 22, CA, *Westminster City Council v Clarke* [1992] 1 All ER 695, HL.
7 HA 1985, s 86(1).
8 HA 1985, s 82(1).
9 HA 1985, s 83.
10 *Burrows v Brent London Borough Council* [1996] 4 All ER 577, HL.
11 [1996] 4 All ER 577, HL.
12 HA 1985, s 89(1).

13   HA 1985, s 89(2)(a).
14   HA 1985, s 87(b).
15   HA 1985, s 113(1)(a).
16   *Ghaidan v Mendoza* [2002] EWCA Civ 1533, [2002] 4 All ER 1162.

Introductory tenancies

38.18   In 1996 a scheme was introduced under which local authorities and housing action trusts can grant introductory rather than secure tenancies[1]. This appears to be designed to ensure that new tenants[2] are effectively 'on probation' for a one-year period before becoming secure tenants. If they prove themselves to be difficult or anti-social they can readily be evicted; if not, after the expiry of the one-year period, the tenancy will automatically convert into a secure tenancy. Once the scheme is adopted by a local authority or housing action trust, any periodic tenancy which it then grants will be an introductory one rather than a secure tenancy[3]. This introductory tenancy will last for one year[4]; during this period the tenancy cannot be a secure one[5] but, after the expiry of the one-year period, it automatically becomes secure[6] unless the landlord has commenced possession proceedings[7]. During the introductory period the landlord can readily regain possession without having to prove a statutory ground[8]. Before seeking possession, the landlord must serve a preliminary notice[9]. This must set out the reasons why the landlord has decided to retake possession, tell the tenant of his right to ask the landlord to review its decision and specify a date after which court proceedings for possession can be commenced. Provided any review has been properly undertaken, the court must then order possession[10]; it has no power to review the landlord's decision[11].

1   Housing Act 1996, s 124.
2   Existing secure tenants cannot be granted an introductory tenancy, HA 1996, s 124(2)(a).
3   HA 1996, s 124(2).
4   HA 1996, s 125(1), (2).
5   Housing Act 1985, Sch 1, para 1A inserted by HA 1996.
6   Provided the conditions for a secure tenancy are then satisfied, see para 38.17 above.
7   HA 1996, ss 127, 130.
8   HA 1996, s 127(2).
9   HA 1996, s 128(1).
10   HA 1996, s 127(2).
11   *Manchester City Council v Cochrane* [1999] L & TR 190, CA. It can adjourn the possession proceedings in order to allow the tenant to seek judicial review of the landlord's decision.

Miscellaneous statutory provisions

Harassment and unlawful eviction

38.19   The Protection from Eviction Act 1977, as amended, confers basic protection against eviction and harassment on a wide range of residential occupiers[1]. It creates three criminal offences[2] and ensures that, in most circumstances, possession cannot be obtained without a court order while anyone is in residential occupation of the premises[3]. The Housing Act 1988 introduced a new statutory tort under which the victims of unlawful eviction can claim damages which are calculated at a penal rate[4].

The offence of unlawful eviction is committed where any person unlawfully deprives, or attempts to deprive, a residential occupier of his occupation of the whole or any part of the premises, unless he proves that he believed, and had reasonable cause to believe, that the occupier had ceased to reside on the premises[5]. The first offence of harassment is committed where any person does acts likely to interfere with the peace or comfort of the residential occupier or members of his household or persistently withdraws or withholds services reasonably required for the occupation of the premises as a residence, with the intent to cause the residential occupier of any premises to give up occupation, or to refrain from exercising any right or remedy in respect of the premises[6]. The intention required for this offence has made convictions difficult to secure. To overcome this, the Housing Act

1988 added a further offence of harassment which is designed to be easier to prove. This can be committed only where a landlord or his agent carries out any of the above acts; the intention required is merely that he knows, or has reasonable cause to believe, that this conduct is likely to cause the residential occupier to give up occupation or to refrain from exercising his rights or remedies[7]. There is, however, an absolute defence where the landlord or his agent can prove that he had reasonable grounds for carrying out the conduct which would otherwise constitute the offence[8].

Conviction for a criminal offence does not in itself afford a remedy to the victim[9]. This is now provided by the Housing Act 1988 which creates a new statutory tort[10]. This imposes civil liability on a landlord wherever he unlawfully evicts a residential tenant or where such a tenant leaves the premises because of the landlord's attempt to unlawfully evict him or as a result of the landlord's harassment[11]. It is not a pre-requisite of this civil liability that the landlord be convicted of the criminal offences of unlawful eviction or harassment. The measure of damages awarded is set out in the Act. Damages are to be assessed on the basis of the difference in value of the landlord's interest in the building in which the premises are situated subject to the occupier's right of occupation and the value of the landlord's interest free from that right[12]. Thus the more secure the occupier's rights, the greater the level of damages to which he will be entitled; an unlawfully evicted assured tenant – against whom possession cannot readily be recovered – would obtain a much higher award of damages than an assured shorthold tenant.

1   Covering both tenants and licensees, see Protection from Eviction Act 1977, s 1(1).
2   PEA 1977, s 1(2), (3) and (3A).
3   PEA 1977, ss 2 and 3. Tenants or licensees who share accommodation with their landlord, or a member of his family are excluded from this protection: PEA 1977, s 3A.
4   Housing Act 1988, ss 27, 28.
5   Protection from Eviction Act 1977, s 1(2).
6   PEA 1977, s 1(3).
7   PEA 1977, s 1(3A).
8   PEA 1977, s 1(3B).
9   *McCall v Abelesz* [1976] 1 All ER 727, CA.
10 Housing Act 1988, s 27.
11 HA 1988, s 28.

Information for tenants

38.20   Various statutory provisions require the landlord of residential premises to provide their tenants with certain information, either at the request of the tenant, or by way of inclusion in the tenancy agreement or on notices or demands. Landlords and managing agents need to be very aware of these since non-compliance may mean that payments under the lease are not, as a matter of law, due from the tenant and, as a result, remedies for non-payment cannot be pursued.

A residential tenant is entitled to request and be provided with the landlord's name and address. Failure to comply with such a request amounts to a criminal offence[1]. Where the reversion on a lease which includes residential premises has been assigned, the new landlord must, within two months, give the tenant notice of the assignment and of his name and address[2]. Failure to comply amounts to a criminal offence; furthermore until such notice is given the former landlord remains liable on the lease covenants[3].

The landlord of residential premises must, by notice[4], provide the tenant with an address in England or Wales at which notices may be served on him[5]. Until this is done neither any rent or service charge is treated as legally due[6]. Any written *demand* for rent or other payments due under the lease must also contain the name and address[7] of the landlord; if it does not, any service charge will be treated as not due until this information is provided[8]. Any tenant or licensee of residential premises who is obliged to pay their rent on a weekly basis is entitled to be supplied with a rent book[9]. Where the tenancy is a Rent Act tenancy or an assured tenancy the rent book must contain prescribed information. A failure to comply with these requirements is a criminal offence. The tenant of an assured shorthold tenancy granted on or after 28 February 1997 can require his landlord to provide information on any of the terms of his tenancy that have not previously been evidenced in writing[10]. A failure to comply amounts to a criminal offence.

1   Landlord and Tenant Act 1985, s 1.
2   LTA 1985, s 3(1).
3   LTA 1985, s 3(3A) and (3B).
4   The inclusion of the landlord's name and address in the tenancy agreement is sufficient, see *Rogan v Woodfield Building Services Ltd* [1995] 1 EGLR 72, CA.
5   Landlord and Tenant Act 1987, s 48(1).
6   LTA 1987, s 48(2).
7   Which must be in England or Wales: LTA 1987, s 47(1)(b).
8   LTA 1987, s 47(1).
9   Landlord and Tenant Act 1985, s 4(1).
10   Housing Act 1988, s 20A.

The agenda for reform

38.21   It is clear that the law governing residential leases not exceeding 21 years is facing a radical overhaul. For much of the last century the law in this area has been a political football; the sharp differences of approach between the major political parties have meant that changes of government have resulted in dramatic amendments to the law, many of which have been achieved by the introduction of legislation on a piecemeal basis. Over the past 20 years, these differences of approach have been replaced by a large degree of consensus; in particular, rent control is regarded as a thing of the past and the ready availability, to private landlords at least, of a form of letting under which the tenant is not given security of tenure beyond that conferred by his contract is now largely accepted. The stage is therefore set for a reformulation of the law, the principles of which (if not their detail) seem likely to meet with general approval. It must be stressed that what follows is merely a brief indication of what is currently being proposed; it is inevitable that this will, to a greater or lesser extent, be modified before emerging in legislative form.

In 2001 the Law Commission published a Scoping Paper which set out the issues[1]. This has been followed by a set of provisional proposals for the first stage of the reform programme[2]. The period for consultation on these is now over and the publication of a final report and a draft Bill is expected later in 2003. As things stand, the expectation is that most[3] of the essential features of the current law will remain unaltered, although it is envisaged that the new regime will be greatly simplified. It is planned that the differentiation between public sector landlords and those in the private sector will disappear and that the rules applying to each will be the same. Landlords will be able to grant one of two types of tenancy both of which will have to be written agreements in a largely standard form. A Type I tenancy, viewed as more appropriate for social landlords, will be the more secure of the two. In particular, under this type of agreement, a landlord will only be able to regain possession on statutory grounds, all of which will be discretionary. Type II agreements are the ones most likely to be used by private landlords and these will be very similar to the current assured shorthold tenancy. Not only will the landlord be able to regain possession simply by giving notice, he will also have available statutory grounds, some of which will be mandatory.

1   *Reform of Housing Law: A Scoping Paper* Law Commission, 2001.
2   *Renting Homes I: Status and Security* Law Commission Consultation Paper No 162, 2002.
3   However, it is being suggested that one basic tenet of the present law should disappear, namely the distinction between a lease and a licence. It is proposed that the new law should apply to any contractual agreement which confers the right to occupy premises as a home in return for a rent. Attention has also been given to ensuring that any new regime will satisfy the requirements of the Human Rights Act 1998.

Business tenancies

Introduction

38.22 The general law of landlord and tenant governs the parties to a business lease during its contractual term[1]. However, their rights and obligations once the tenancy agreement is approaching its expiry have been regulated by statute ever since the 1950s[2]. Part II of the Landlord and Tenant Act 1954 was first reviewed and then amended in 1969[3]. A second review was carried out by the Law Commission in 1992[4] and most[5] of the changes then proposed are in the process of being implemented by the Regulatory Reform (Business Tenancies)(England and Wales) Order 2003 ('RRO 2003'). The progress of this Order through Parliament is currently at a standstill as a result of concerns expressed by the House of Lords Select Committee as to the proposed new contracting out procedure. At the time of writing it is expected that these can be satisfactorily addressed and that the RRO 2003 will come into force during 2004. The following text states the law as it stands today but draws attention to the proposals for reform; these are summarised at paras 38.40-38.45. Broadly speaking, Pt II of the Landlord and Tenant Act 1954 provides that a tenancy under which the tenant occupies premises for business or professional purposes[6] does not come to an end until terminated in accordance with the Act[7]. Until that happens the tenant is entitled to remain in the premises under a continuation tenancy on the same terms and at the same rent as under the contractual tenancy. Even when the current tenancy has been properly terminated the tenant is entitled to a new tenancy as of right (provided certain procedural steps are taken within the prescribed time limits)[8] unless the landlord can establish one or more of the statutory grounds of opposition[9]. The new tenancy will be on such terms as the parties agree; if they are unable to agree, both the terms and the rent will be fixed by the court (or, at the option of the parties, by an arbitrator or expert[10]) in accordance with the provisions of the Act[11].

1   See Chapter 37 above.
2   Ie by Part II of the Landlord and Tenant Act 1954.
3   By the Law of Property Act 1969.
4   *Landlord and Tenant: Business Tenancies: A Periodic Review of the Landlord and Tenant Act 1954 Part II* Law Com No 208 1992.
5   Some relatively minor changes have been made to the original proposals, see *Business Tenancies Legislation in England and Wales: The Government's Proposals for Reform* DETR 2001.
6   Paras 38.22 and 38.23 below.
7   Paras 38.25-38.27 below.
8   Para 38.28 below.
9   Paras 38.31-38.33 below.
10 Ie under the voluntary PACT scheme set up by the Law Society and the RICS, see para 38.35 below.
11 Paras 38.35-38.39 below.

Tenancies within the Act

38.23 *The requirement for an occupying tenant* Part II of the LTA 1954 applies to any tenancy where the property comprised in the tenancy is or includes premises[1] which are occupied by the tenant and are so occupied for the purposes of a business carried on by him or for those and other purposes[2]. It is essential that the occupation is by virtue of either a fixed term or periodic tenancy; occupation as a licensee or tenant at will is not sufficient[3]. It matters not whether the tenancy is a head lease or a sublease or even that it is a lease that has been granted in breach of covenant[4]. In principle, it is the tenant[5] who must be in occupation since it is the policy of the Act is to provide security of tenure for tenants who have established themselves in a business located at the premises in order that they can continue to carry on their business there. Thus a tenant who has parted with exclusive possession (usually by subletting)[6], or ceased trading[7] or vacated the premises[8] will not be protected. However, a tenant who has ceased trading or vacated for reasons beyond his control and who intends to resume his business as soon as possible retains protection[9]. A tenant will also be protected where, despite allowing another to occupy the premises, he retains enough control (usually by the provision of services which require his continued access to the demised premises) to be regarded as in occupation[10]. Furthermore, the Act makes specific provision for occupation in the case of leases held by trusts and by groups of companies[11].

1   In practice business premises usually comprise buildings or other structures; however, where a business is carried out on open land, the Act will apply: see *Bracey v Read* [1962] 3 All ER 472.
2   Landlord and Tenant Act 1954, s 23.
3   *Shell-Mex & BP Ltd v Manchester Garages Ltd* [1971] 1 All ER 841, CA (a licence held not to be within the Act); *Wheeler v Mercer* [1956] 3 All ER 631, HL (a tenancy at will held not to be within the Act).
4   *D'Silva v Lister House Development Ltd* [1970] 1 All ER 858; *Parc Battersea Ltd v Hutchinson* [1999] 2 EGLR 33.
5   Acting either personally or through employees or agents. However, as the law stands, a tenant who allows a separate company to occupy the premises for the purposes of its business will not be protected, even where it is the tenant who has a controlling interest in that company, see *Cristina v Seear* [1985] 2 EGLR 128, CA. RRO 2003 changes the law on this, see para 38.45 below.
6   *Graysim Holdings Ltd v P & O Property Holdings Ltd* [1995] 4 All ER 831, HL.
7   *Aspinall Finance Ltd v Viscount Chelsea* [1989] 1 EGLR 103, CA.
8   *Esselte AB v Pearl Assurance plc* [1997] 2 All ER 41, CA.
9   See *Morrison Holdings Ltd v Manders Property (Wolverhampton) Ltd* [1976] 2 All ER 205 and *Flairline Properties Ltd v Hassan* [1999] 1 EGLR 138. In both of these cases the tenants had only vacated because their premises had been seriously damaged by fire and the court held that protection was retained because it was satisfied that the tenant intended to resume business occupation once the premises were reinstated.
10   See *Lee-Verhulst (Investments) Ltd v Harwood Trust* [1972] 3 All ER 619, CA; *Linden v Department of Health and Social Security* [1986] 1 All ER 691; *Groveside Properties Ltd v Westminster Medical School* (1983) 47 P & CR 507, CA.
11   Landlord and Tenant Act 1954, s 41(1) ensures that where a lease is held on trust, occupation by any of the beneficiaries qualifies for protection; ibid s 42 provides that, where a lease is held by one group in a company, occupation by another company in the same group also suffices. Note that RRO 2003 extends the meaning of a group of companies: see para 38.45 below.

38.24   *The meaning of business* The term 'business' is very widely defined. Where the tenant is an individual the expression includes any trade, profession or employment[1]. It has been held that this means that where such a tenant carries on any undertaking of a non-commercial nature or something in the nature of a hobby, he will not be protected[2]. However, where the tenant is a body of persons, the statutory definition is widened so as to include any 'activity'. While this term has been held to carry some of the connotations of a business[3], it is clear that it covers non-profit making enterprises[4]. Where the terms of the tenancy prohibit all business use, the LTA 1954 cannot normally apply; where the tenancy permits a business use and, in breach of covenant, the tenant uses for another business use, the Act still applies[5]. The Act does not require the premises to be used only for business purposes, so that where premises are used for mixed business and residential use, the tenancy will be covered by the LTA 1954[6] rather than by any of the residential codes[7]. However, where the business use is incidental to any residential use, the LTA 1954 will not apply and the tenant will then be governed by the appropriate residential scheme[8].

1   Landlord and Tenant Act 1954, s 23(2).
2   See *Lewis v Weldcrest* [1978] 3 All ER 1226, CA (where a tenant who took in lodgers was, perhaps, surprisingly, held no to be conducting a trade; note that she did then qualify for protection under the Rent Act), *Abernethie v AH & J Kleiman Ltd* [1969] 2 All ER 790 (a tenant running a Sunday School for which no charge was made, was held to be engaging in a hobby and not a business).
3   *Hillil Property and Investment Co Ltd v Naraine Pharmacy Ltd* (1979) 39 P & CR 67, CA.
4   Such the running of a members' tennis club (*Addiscombe Garden Estate Ltd v Crabbe* [1957] 3 All ER 563, CA) a hospital (*Hills (Patents) Ltd v University College Hospital Board of Governors* [1955] 3 All ER 365, HL) and the provision of accommodation for students of a university medical school (*Groveside Properties Ltd v Westminster Medical School* (1983) 47 P & CR 507, CA).
5   Landlord and Tenant Act 1954, s 23(4).
6   *Cheryl Investments Ltd v Saldanha* [1979] 1 All ER 5, CA.
7   Tenancies governed by Part II of the Landlord and Tenant Act 1954 are positively excluded by the

Rent Act 1977, s 24(3), by the Housing Act 1985, s 79, Sch 1, para 11 and by the Housing Act 1988, s 1, Sch 1, para 4.

8 *Gurton v Parrott* [1991] 1 EGLR 98, CA.

38.25 *Excluded tenancies* A variety of tenancies are expressly excluded from the protection of the LTA 1954[1]. These are: tenancies of an agricultural holding[2], farm business tenancies[3], mining leases, service tenancies[4], and tenancies granted for a fixed term not exceeding six months provided that the tenancy does not include any provision for renewal and that the tenant has not either been in occupation for a period exceeding 12 months, or has not succeeded to a business which has operated from the premises for such a period[5].

1 Landlord and Tenant Act 1954, s 43.
2 See para 38.47 below.
3 See para 38.48 below.
4 Ie any tenancy granted due to the fact that the tenant was an employee of the landlord.
5 This means that the landlord cannot grant a series of short-term tenancies to the same tenant without the tenant automatically becoming protected once he has occupied for more than 12 months.

38.26 *Contracted out tenancies* Originally, the LTA 1954 did not permit the parties to exclude ('contract out') its application to their tenancy. The Act was amended in 1969[1] so as to permit the parties to agree that the Act should not apply provided only that the approval of the court was obtained prior[2] to the grant of the tenancy (which had to be for a fixed term). It appears that it was expected that this would only be done where a landlord wished to let on a very temporary basis[3]; however, no restrictions were imposed on the length of lease which could be contracted out and nor was the court given any power to refuse approval where the proper procedure had been followed and where both parties are properly advised[4]. Over the years, the practice of contracting out has certainly increased dramatically in numerical terms[5], although it is impossible to say whether or not there is any real increase in the proportion of contracted out tenancies relative to the number of new leases in the market place. RRO 2003 contains provisions which change the procedure for contracting out[6]; as we have noted, it is these which are currently delaying the implementation of the whole package of reforms[7].

1 Landlord and Tenant Act 1954, s 38(4) inserted by the Law of Property Act 1969. These provisions also apply to agreements to surrender: see note 3, para 38.25 below.
2 *Essexcrest Ltd v Evenlex Ltd* [1988] 1 EGLR 69, CA.
3 Law Com No 17, 1969.
4 *Hagee (London) Ltd v AB Erikson and Larson* [1975] 3 All ER 234, CA.
5 Judicial statistics indicate that by 1989 the number of leases contracted out of the Act each year amounted to approximately 18,000; by 2000, this figure had increased to about 54,000.
6 See para 38.41 below.
7 See para 38.22 above.

Termination of tenancies governed by the LTA 1954

38.27 The LTA 1954 provides that business tenancy does not come to an end by expiry or by a common law notice served by the landlord. Save where the tenant ceases business occupation by the end of the term,[1] it is statutorily continued[2] until terminated in accordance with the Act. The Act specifically recognises certain common law methods of termination. So, the parties can agree a surrender, the tenant can serve a notice to quit, and the landlord can forfeit the lease[3]. In all other circumstances, a statutory notice must be served in order to bring the tenancy to an end. It is important to appreciate that termination does not necessarily (and does not usually) mean that the tenant must leave the premises since, on the termination of his tenancy, the tenant is entitled to apply for a new tenancy[4]. Only if the landlord successfully opposes that application[5] will the tenant have to vacate. Accordingly, taking steps to terminate a tenancy is often simply the first stage of putting in place a new tenancy at a current open market rent[6].

1   The cessation of business occupation means that the Act can no longer apply (see para 38.22 above), hence the tenancy will come to an end by effluxion: see *Esselte AB v Pearl Assurance plc* [1997] 1 EGLR 73, CA. This case (which is to be confirmed by RRO 2003) recognises the important practical point that a fixed-term business tenant can walk away from the tenancy at the end of the lease without warning (see para 38.27 below).

2   Landlord and Tenant Act 1954, s 24(1).

3   LTA 1954, s 24(2). Note that while the parties can enter into a deed of surrender, a binding agreement to surrender at a future date is not effective without prior court approval (see para 38.24 above). Note also that a notice to quit is defined by ibid s 69 as including a contractual notice to terminate; this means that a tenant can not only terminate a periodic tenancy but also operate a break notice in a fixed term tenancy.

4   See para 38.28 below.

5   See paras 38.31-38.33 below.

6   In most cases, by the time a business lease is at contractual term date the rent will last have been fixed by a rent review which took place five years previously. Thus, in a rising market, a landlord will normally be anxious to terminate the current tenancy and put a new lease in place simply in order to achieve a current open market rent.

38.28   *Termination by the landlord* The landlord[1] can only terminate the lease by serving on the tenant a section 25 notice in a prescribed form[2]. Such a notice cannot be served if the tenant has already served a section 26 request[3]. It must require the tenant to serve, within two months, a counter notice, stating whether or not he is willing to give up possession[4]. A tenant who fails to serve such a counter notice within the strict two-month time limit will lose any right to apply for a new tenancy[5]. A section 25 notice must state a date for termination which must be no earlier than the date on which the tenancy could be brought to an end at common law and give between six and twelve months' notice[6]. So, where the tenancy is for a fixed term, the earliest a section 25 notice can be served is 12 months prior to contractual term date. If the current tenancy is to end on contractual term date the latest date by which it can be served is six months before contractual term date. However, it must be stressed that there is no latest date for the service of a section 25 notice. Provided that a section 26 request has not been served and that no other termination method has been employed, a section 25 notice can be served at any time; the existing tenancy will simply continue until the date specified in that notice. As has already been mentioned[7], a section 25 notice is often served where the landlord is quite willing for the tenant to take a new tenancy. However, where this is not the case and the landlord wishes the tenant to leave, he must state in his section 25 notice that he will oppose any application for a new tenancy and enumerate the statutory grounds on which he is intending to rely[8]. A failure to do so means that the landlord will be unable to oppose a renewal.

1   In order to be able to serve a section 25 notice, the landlord must be the 'competent' landlord: Landlord and Tenant Act 1954, s 44. Where the immediate landlord is the freeholder, he will always be the competent landlord. Where the immediate landlord is himself a leaseholder, he must hold a reversion which will last for a further 14 months; if this is not the case, the competent landlord is the next landlord up the chain whose reversion will continue for at least 14 months.

2   LTA 1954, s 25.

3   LTA 1954, s 26(4):, see para 38.27 below.

4   LTA 1954, s 25(5).

5   The trap posed for tenants by this requirement to serve a counter notice has been recognised; it is to be abolished by RRO 2003: see para 38.42 below.

6   LTA 1954, s 25(1), (2), (3), (4).

7   See para 38.25 above.

8   LTA 1954, s 25(6).

38.29   *Termination by the tenant* We have already seen[1] that, where a periodic tenant wishes to leave the premises, he can serve a common law notice to quit; similarly, a fixed-term tenant who wishes to operate a break can serve an effective break notice. A fixed-term tenant who wishes to leave *at contractual term date* now has two options. He can either simply quit the premises by that date without any need to give notice[2], or he can serve a notice giving at least three months' notice expiring on contractual term date[3]. However, where a fixed-term tenancy *has already been continued by the Act* (ie where the tenant has stayed on in business occupation beyond contractual term date) the tenant can only bring the tenancy to an end by serving a notice on the landlord giving three months' notice expiring on a quarter day[4].

Where a fixed-term tenant wishes to remain in the premises there is normally no need for him to take any positive steps. In the absence of any action by the landlord[5], his tenancy will be continued on the same terms and at the same rent[6] and, in a rising market, this will be to his obvious advantage. The position will be very different in a falling market, or where there are specific reasons for him to want to have a new tenancy in place. Here the tenant will need to take the initiative and can do so by serving a request for a new tenancy[7]. Such a request has the effect of terminating the existing tenancy[8]. The statutory requirements for a section 26 request largely mirror those for a section 25 notice[9]. The request (which cannot be served if the landlord has already served a section 25 notice[10]) must be in a prescribed form and must be served by the tenant[11] on the competent landlord. It must give between six and 12 months' notice and specify a date for the commencement of the new tenancy which must be no earlier than the contractual term date of the existing tenancy. It must set out the tenant's proposals as to the terms of the new tenancy[12]. The landlord can, within two months of being served with a section 26 request, serve a counter notice stating that he will oppose renewal and the grounds on which he intends to do so[13]. If the landlord does not do this he cannot oppose renewal[14].

1   Para 38.25 above.
2   See note 1 para 38.25 above. It appears that this option is open to the tenant even where he has given the landlord the impression that he wishes to stay by applying for a new tenancy: see *Single Horse Properties Ltd v Surrey County Council* [2002] EWCA Civ 367, [2002] 2 EGLR 43.
3   Landlord and Tenant Act 1954, s 27(1).
4   LTA 1954, s 27(2). The requirement in this instance that the three months' notice must expire on a quarter day is to be replaced, under RRO 2003, by one for a straight three months' notice: see para 38.42 below.
5   Such as the service of a section 25 notice.
6   See para 38.25 above.
7   LTA 1954, s 26.
8   Immediately before the date specified in the request for the commencement of the new tenancy: LTA 1954, s 26(5).
9   See para 38.26 above.
10   LTA 1954, s 26(4).
11   Certain tenants – those who hold under either a periodic tenancy or for a fixed term not exceeding one year – cannot serve a s 26 request: LTA 1954, s 26(1). This does not mean that such tenants cannot obtain a new tenancy, merely that they must wait for the landlord to initiate the process.
12   LTA 1954, s 26(3).
13   LTA 1954, s 26(6).
14   Para 38.31 below.

The renewal process

38.30   *Application to court* It is in the area of the procedure for renewal that RRO 2003 is to make the most significant changes; these are explained at para 38.43 below. What follows is a very brief account of the current system. Once either a section 25 notice or a section 26 request has been served the tenant must, within a strict period of between two and four months, apply to court[1] for a new tenancy[2]. If an application is not made within these time limits the tenant loses any right to a new tenancy[3]. In practice, the application to court is often a token step taken merely to preserve the tenant's legal rights. The proceedings are normally adjourned[4] to allow the parties to negotiate and the result will be that either the tenant's application is withdrawn or that a court order by consent is made. The parties are usually able to reach agreement either that the landlord has made out a good ground of opposition, or that the tenant no longer wishes to take a new tenancy, or as to the terms of the new tenancy. The most usual reason for a court hearing is that the tenant challenges his landlord's ground(s) for opposing renewal[5].

1   Usually to the county court for the district in which the premises are located.
2   Landlord and Tenant Act 1954, s 24(1).
3   LTA 1954, s 29(3).
4   While this is less easy under the new Civil Procedure Rules, it is now usual for proceedings to be adjourned virtually automatically for a period of three months.
5   See paras 38.31-38.33 below.

38.31   *Interim continuation*   It is common for the tenant's position still to be unclear by the date specified for the termination of the existing tenancy in either the section 25 notice or section 26 request. This may be because the parties are still carrying out their own negotiations, or they may be waiting for a court hearing or an appeal. The Act makes provision for this. By definition, by the date specified for termination, the tenant must have made an application to court[1]. The Act therefore provides that, once an application to court has been made, the current tenancy will not terminate on the date specified in the notice or request but will, where necessary, continue until three months after the date on which the tenant's application is either withdrawn or finally disposed of by the court[2]. This is known as 'interim continuation'.

1   Since such an application must be made within two to four months of the service of a section 25 notice or section 26 request and the minimum period for such a notice is six months.
2   Landlord and Tenant Act 1954, s 64.

38.32   *Interim rent*   Under the original provisions of the Act, the tenant would continue to pay the existing rent throughout any period of interim continuation. The landlord would not get rent at a current open market level until the commencement of any new tenancy. Not surprisingly, this encouraged tenants to drag their feet when negotiating new leases. This resulted in an amendment to the Act, which introduced the concept of interim rent[1]. Again, this is an area in which the RRO 2003 is to make significant changes[2]. As things stand, a landlord[3] can apply to court for an interim rent. If the court so decides[4] (or the parties agree), this will be payable from either the date specified for termination in the section 25 notice or the section 26 request, or the date of the landlord's application, whichever is the later[5]. Interim rent is payable until the date when the current tenancy actually ends. The level of interim rent is determined in accordance with the Act. This provides that interim rent is to be the open market rent, as at the commencement of the interim period, but taking account of the existing rent and on the assumption of a yearly tenancy[6]. This has the effect of cushioning the tenant from a substantial increase in the rent[7].

1   Landlord and Tenant Act 1954, s 24A inserted by the Law of Property Act 1969.
2   See para 38.44 below.
3   Currently, a tenant cannot apply for interim rent. It was not appreciated by those drafting LTA 1954, s 24A that, in a falling market, a tenant could wish to apply for interim rent; this is to be rectified by RRO 2003, see para 38.44 below.
4   The award of an interim rent is at the court's discretion, LTA 1954, s 24A(1).
5   LTA 1954, s 24A(2).
6   LTA 1954, s 24A(3).
7   This, of course, means that a dilatory tenant is still at an advantage. This is a matter which is addressed by RRO 2003: see para 38.44 below.

Opposing renewal
38.33   Provided that a landlord has stated, in either his section 25 notice, or in a counter notice to the tenant's section 26 request, that he intends to oppose renewal on one or more of the statutory grounds, he can do so. He[1] is limited to the grounds specified and cannot add to his stated grounds[2]. The statutory grounds are set out in s 30(1)(a)–(g). Those most widely used in practice are the ones based on tenant default (para (a) – breach

of repairing covenant, para (b) – persistent delay in paying rent, and para (c) – breaches of other obligations), or para (f) – where the landlord intends to redevelop or para (g) where the landlord wishes to occupy the premises for his own business purposes. Grounds (e) – a more economic letting of the whole and ground (d) – the availability of suitable alternative accommodation – are rarely employed and have scarcely been litigated. The tenant default grounds are straightforward; they are, however, discretionary and the court tends to be generous towards tenants whenever there is any suggestion that they can retrieve the situation[3]. Paragraphs (f) and (g) are mandatory so that, where made out, the court must refuse to order a new tenancy. Where either is the sole basis on which the landlord has successfully opposed renewal, compensation must be paid to the tenant[4]. It is these two grounds that are the most frequently litigated.

1   It should be noted that where, after serving a section 25 notice or counter notice to a section 26 request, the landlord disposes of his interest, the new landlord can rely on any grounds of opposition stated by his predecessor.
2   See *Smith v Draper* [1990] 2 EGLR 69, CA.
3   See, for example, *Hurstfell Ltd v Leicester Square Property Co Ltd* [1988] 2 EGLR 105, CA. It is fair to say that, where a business tenant is in serious default, this may be an indication that his business is also in difficulties; in such cases the tenant may well choose not to take a new tenancy.
4   See para 38.34 below.

38.34   *Redevelopment by the landlord* It is not the policy of the LTA 1954 to impede development. Accordingly, where the landlord intends to demolish or reconstruct the premises (or a substantial part of them) or to carry out substantial works of construction, the court must refuse to order a new tenancy[1]. The works to be taken into account must affect the structure of the premises[2]; this is usually easy to establish in the case of demolition, reconstruction, or where a new building or extension is being built. It may be less easy to prove in cases of refurbishment where the core of an existing building is being left intact and where much of the work relates to the internal layout[3]. Demolition and reconstruction must affect the whole or a substantial part of the premises; works of reconstruction must themselves be substantial. Substantiality is, inevitably, a question of fact and degree to be decided by the trial judge; an appeal court will rarely intervene[4].

The landlord must satisfy the court that he has the requisite intention by the date of any court hearing[5]. This means he must show not simply a desire to carry out the works in question but rather a reasonable prospect of doing so[6]. Ideally, he should have taken a formal decision to undertake the project[7], have put in place the necessary finance and building contracts and obtained planning permission, where this is necessary. However, it is clear that a somewhat lesser state of preparedness can suffice. So, for example, where a landlord has not yet been given planning permission, or has had an application refused, he may still succeed in his opposition if he can show that he has a sufficient prospect of gaining planning permission that a reasonable landlord would persist with the proposal[8].

The project must be one for which the landlord requires possession of the premises; if he already has rights under the lease which allow him access to do the work in question, a new tenancy will be ordered[9]. The landlord must also show that it is he who is going to carry out the redevelopment. Manifestly, this will be satisfied by the employment of a building contractor – the landlord does not have to do the work personally[10]. However, para (f) is not made out where the landlord is intending to sell the premises outright to a developer; he must show that he retains control and this can be achieved by the grant to a developer of a building lease as opposed to selling the freehold[11] (unless, by the date of the hearing, the developer has become the competent landlord[12]).

Where a landlord has, in principle, satisfied all the requirements of paragraph (f) the tenant may turn to LTA 1954, s 31A. This allows the tenant to offer to take a new tenancy that gives the landlord rights of access to carry out the proposed works, or to take a letting of an economically severable part of his existing premises. However, the court will only allow this where the works will not interfere to a substantial extent, or for a substantial time, with the tenant's business at the premises[13]. What amounts to a substantial interference is a question of fact and degree; in one case[14] a new lease was ordered where the relevant works would take about two weeks to complete, in another[15] a new tenancy was refused where the works would take 12 weeks.

1   Landlord and Tenant Act 1954, s 30(1)(f).
2   See Percy E Cadle & Co Ltd v Jacmarch Properties [1957] 1 All ER 148, CA; Joel v Swaddle [1957] 1 WLR 1094, CA, Romulus Trading Co v Trustees of Henry Smith's Charity [1990] 2 EGLR 75, CA.
3   See Barth v Prichard [1990] 1 EGLR 109, CA, Global Grange Ltd v Marazzi [2002] EWHC 3010, [2002] All ER (D) 334 (Dec).
4   See Global Grange Ltd v Marazzi [2002] EWHC 3010, [2002] All ER (D) 334 (Dec).
5   Betty's Cafes Ltd v Phillips Furnishing Stores Ltd [1957] 1 All ER 1, CA.
6   Cunliffe v Goodman [1950] 1 All ER 720, CA – the landlord must have moved 'out of the zone of contemplation into the valley of decision'.
7   Eg, where the landlord is a company, by making a formal board decision.
8   See Cadogan v McCarthy & Stone (Developments) Ltd [2000] L & TR 249, CA; Gatwick Parking Services Ltd v Sargent [2000] 2 EGLR 45, CA. For a case where the court was satisfied that the landlord had no real prospect of obtaining planning permission: see Coppin v Bruce-Smith [1998] EGCS 55, CA.
9   Heath v Drown [1972] 2 All ER 561, HL.
10   Gilmour Caterers Ltd v St Bartholomews Hospital Governors [1956] 1 QB 387, CA.
11   PF Ahern & Sons Ltd v Hunt [1988] 1 EGLR 74, CA.
12   Morris Marks v British Waterways Board [1963] 1 WLR 1008, CA.
13   It is irrelevant that the tenant can relocate his business for the period of the work; what matters is the period and extent of the disruption at the demised premises: Redfern v Reeves (1978) 37 P & CR 364, CA.
14   Cerex Jewels Ltd v Peachey Property Corpn [1986] 2 EGLR 65, CA.
15   Blackburn v Hussain [1988] 1 EGLR 77.

38.35   *Occupation by the landlord* A landlord may oppose the grant of a new tenancy on the basis that he intends to occupy the premises[1] for the purposes of his business[2] or as his residence[3]. As with para (f)[4], the landlord must demonstrate the requisite intention, namely that he has a reasonable prospect of fulfilling his wishes[5]. So, he must show that he has a fair chance of obtaining planning permission[6], where this is necessary, and that he has the necessary finance to set up his business[7]. Provided that the court is satisfied that the landlord is intending to set up his business at the premises, it matters not that there is a real risk that the business may not survive on a long-term basis; the landlord is entitled to try[8]. It is not clear whether a landlord will satisfy para (g) where he intends only to occupy for a very short period before, say, selling the property. He will probably do so where the court accepts that the landlord is acting genuinely; the position may be different where the occupation appears to be a mere ploy in order to regain possession[9].

An important restriction on the right to rely on para (g) is the five-year rule. This prevents a landlord from using this ground where he acquired his interest in the property within five years of the date specified in the section 25 notice or section 26 request and where throughout that period there has been a business tenancy of the premises[10]. This rule is designed to prevent landlords buying up reversions subject to business tenancies that are about to expire and then using para (g) to evict the tenant at the end of his lease.

1   The test of occupation is the same as for tenants claiming the protection of the Act. So, for example, where a landlord was intending to run a business which involved subletting the premises, it was held that para (g) was not satisfied because the landlord would not be in occupation: see Jones v Jenkins [1986] 1 EGLR 113, CA.
2   The landlord must either solely own the business which is to operate from the premises, or he can be a partner in the business (in which case it is not essential for him to be intending to take an active part in it: see Skeet v Powell-Sheddon [1988] 2 EGLR 112, CA); or the business may to be operated by a company in which the landlord has a controlling interest (Landlord and Tenant Act 1954, s 30(3)).
3   LTA 1954, s 30(1)(g).
4   See para 38.31 above.
5   Much of the case law on intention can be used interchangeably for either para (f) or (g).
6   Gregson v Cyril Lord Ltd [1962] 3 All ER 907, CA.

7   The failure to provide evidence of the availability of finance needed to set up a restaurant business was fatal to the landlord in *Zarvos v Pradhan* [2003] EWCA Civ 208, [2003] 26 EG 180, CA.
8   *Cox v Binfield* [1989] 1 EGLR 97, CA; *Dolgellau Golf Club v Hett* [1998] L & TR 217, CA.
9   See *Willis v Association of Universities of the British Commonwealth* [1965] 1 QB 140, CA.
10 LTA 1954, s 30(2).

38.36   *Compensation for disturbance* Where a landlord successfully opposes the grant of a new tenancy on the basis of paras (e)[1], (f) or (g) he may become liable to pay compensation to the tenant[2]. Compensation is payable where the landlord has specified one or more of those grounds and no other and, as a result, the tenant either makes no application for a new tenancy, or withdraws his application, and then quits the premises; it matters not that, by the time the tenant leaves, the landlord has abandoned his opposition[3]. Compensation may also be payable where the landlord specifies one of the compensateable grounds along with other grounds; however, in this instance the tenant must obtain a ruling from the court that the only ground on which a new tenancy was refused was a compensateable one[4]. It is possible to include in the tenancy agreement a clause contracting out of compensation. However, this ceases to have effect where the tenant has been in occupation of the premises for at least five years preceding the date on which the tenant is to quit the premises[5].

The amount of compensation is the product of a statutorily prescribed 'appropriate multiplier' (currently set at 1) and either the rateable value or twice the rateable value[6]. The higher rate of compensation is only payable where the tenant has been in occupation of the premises[7] for the whole[8] of the 14-year period preceding the date specified for termination by either the section 25 notice or section 26 request[9]. A tenant who makes the mistake of moving out of the premises prior to the date specified for termination in the landlord's section 25 notice will lose his right to the higher level of compensation[10].

1   Which is very rarely used: see para 38.31 above.
2   Landlord and Tenant Act 1954, s 37(1).
3   As happened, for example, in *Bacchiocchi v Academic Agency Ltd* [1998] 2 All ER 241. The tenant must, however, have served a counter notice expressing his unwillingness to give up possession: *Re 14 Grafton Street, London W 1* [1971] Ch 935.
4   LTA 1954, s 37(1).
5   LTA 1954, s 38(2).
6   LTA 1954, s 37((2).
7   Or has taken over a business which has been operated at the premises by a business tenant for that period, LTA 1954, s 37(3)(b).
8   The court will ignore short periods of non-occupation which have occurred for sensible operational reasons: see *Bacchiocchi v Academic Agency Ltd* [1998] 2 All ER 241.
9   LTA 1954, s 37(3)(a).
10 *Sight and Sound Education Ltd v Books etc Ltd* [2000] L & TR 146.

The new tenancy

38.37   Unless the landlord succeeds in establishing a ground of opposition, the court must order the grant of a new tenancy[1]. The terms of the new tenancy (including the rent) are usually agreed by the parties. Where, or to the extent that, agreement is not possible, the court will settle them by applying ss 32-35 of the LTA 1954. Alternatively, the parties can opt to have the terms and the rent settled in accordance with the Act by a third party, appointed under the PACT scheme[2]. Accordingly, since the provisions of the Act will dictate the terms of the lease should the parties fail to agree, these must be borne in mind when seeking to negotiate out of court. Where the terms are settled by the court, or by a third party, the tenant has 14 days in which to decline the tenancy and to apply for the revocation of the order[3].

1   Landlord and Tenant Act 1954, s 29(1).
2   See para 38.21 above.
3   LTA 1954, s 36(2).

38.38 *The premises* Unless the parties agree otherwise, the tenant is entitled to a new tenancy of the 'holding' ie those parts of his existing premises which he occupies at the date of the hearing[1]. So, if the tenant has sublet part of the premises he has no right to a new tenancy which includes the sublet part, although the landlord can require this of him[2]. The tenant is entitled to have included in the new tenancy any rights such as easements which he has previously enjoyed in connection with the holding[3].

1   Landlord and Tenant Act 1954, ss 23(3), 32(1).
2   LTA 1954, s 32(2).
3   LTA 1954, s 32(3).

38.39 *Duration of the new tenancy* The parties can agree any length of term they choose. Where they are unable to agree, the court can order a new tenancy of up to 14 years[1]. The court will take into account a whole range of factors when deciding on the appropriate duration (or on the insertion of a landlord's break option): the length of the current lease, the business requirements of both parties[2], the wish of the landlord to reoccupy[3] and the prospects of redevelopment[4] have all been regarded as relevant. A vexed question in today's market, where lease lengths are getting shorter, is whether tenants can insist on a lease that is shorter than their existing lease, simply as a matter of policy. This appears only to have been considered once, and then only in the county court[5]. The view was expressed that this will all depend on the particular circumstances; the tenant in that case was given the shorter lease that it had requested. It should always be remembered that, at the end of a renewed lease, the LTA 1954 will still, in principle, apply. Thus, the tenant will be entitled to a further statutory renewal unless the landlord can successfully establish a ground of opposition.

1   Landlord and Tenant Act 1954, s 33. This upper limit will be increased to 15 years by RRO 2003.
2   For example, where a tenant was due to retire on a particular date, he was given a lease which would last until then in order to avoid him having to re-locate for a short period: see *Becker v Hill Street Properties Ltd* [1990] 2 EGLR 78, CA.
3   See *Upsons Ltd v E Robins Ltd* [1955] 3 All ER 348, CA where only a short new lease was granted because the landlord had only just failed to satisfy the five-year rule under para (g).
4   See, for example, *Adams v Green* [1978] 2 EGLR 46, CA and *National Car Parks Ltd v Paternoster Consortium Ltd* [1990] 1 EGLR 99. In both cases landlord's break provisions were included so that the landlord could then seek to terminate should he be in a position to redevelop.
5   See *Rumbelows Ltd v Tameside Metropolitan Borough Council* (1994) county court, noted at [1994] 15 EG 154.

38.40 *Lease terms other than rent* LTA 1945, s 35 gives the court a wide discretion to settle the terms of the lease other than rent. It does, however, require regard to be had to terms of the existing lease. It has been held that, where a party is proposing terms that are different from those in the current lease, it is for him to justify the changes and to prove that they are fair and reasonable in all the circumstances; it was also suggested that a term is not necessarily fair and reasonable simply because it accords with current market practices in lease drafting[1]. This has produced a tendency for the terms of statutorily renewed leases to follow that of the existing lease, save where the parties are able to agree the change. So, a landlord may not be able to substitute a variable service charge for a fixed charge[2]; it has been held that a user clause could not be varied so as to exclude a use which was important to the tenant's business[3]; a 'keep open for trade' covenant was not excluded from the new tenancy because of the benefit it conferred on the landlord[4]; and a user covenant cannot be altered for the sole purpose of either enhancing[5] or diminishing[6] the rental value of the premises. It is specifically provided that the court can take into account the operation of the Landlord and Tenant (Covenants) Act 1995[7]; this means that the court can now approve the inclusion of a new style disposition covenant under which the landlord can stipulate specific requirements that do not have to be reasonable[8]. It has been held that this does not mean that the landlord can insist on the inclusion of a requirement that a tenant cannot assign without automatically entering into an authorised guarantee agreement; such a requirement must be subject to the reasonableness test[9].

1   O'May v City of London Real Property Co Ltd [1982] I All ER 660, HL.
2   [1982] I All ER 660.
3   Gold v Brighton Corpn [1956] 3 All ER 442, CA.
4   Boots the Chemist v Pinkland Ltd [1992] 2 EGLR 98, county court.
5   Charles Clement(London) Ltd v Rank City Wall Ltd [1978] I EGLR 47.
6   Aldwych Club Ltd v Copthall Property Co Ltd (1962) 185 Estates Gazette 219.
7   Landlord and Tenant Act 1954, s 35(2).
8   Wallis Fashions Group plc v CGU Life Assurance Ltd [2000] L & TR 520. See para 37.37 above.
9   Wallis Fashions Group plc v CGU Life Assurance Ltd [2000] L & TR 520.

38.41   *Rent*   Once all the other terms of the new lease have been settled the rent can then be determined. This is required, by LTA 1954, s 34(1) to be that at which the premises might reasonably be expected to be let in the open market. It does not matter if this means that the rent is then set at a level that the tenant cannot afford to pay[1]. The appropriate valuation date is the commencement of the new lease[2]. The rent will usually be fixed by reference to appropriate comparable evidence; if this is not available account can be taken of general rent increases in the locality[3]. The rent will not be reduced to take account of disrepair where this is due to the tenant's default[4]; however, where it is due to the landlord's breach, the court can order that any increase in the rent cannot come into effect until repairs are carried out[5].

It is specifically provided that certain matters are to be disregarded when fixing the rent: any effect on rent attributable to the tenant's occupation; any goodwill attaching to the premises by reason of the business carried on there by the tenant; in the case of licensed premises; any increase in value attributable to any tenant's licence; and any increase in value attributable to certain tenant's improvements[6]. The improvements to be disregarded are defined as those carried out by anyone who was at the time the current tenant provided that these were not carried out under an obligation to the landlord. All such improvements that were carried out under the *current* tenancy are disregarded[7]. Where such an improvement was made during a *previous* tenancy it will only be disregarded if it was completed not more than 21 years before the date of the application for the new tenancy; in addition, the premises must have at all times after the completion of the improvements have been the subject of a 1954 Act tenancy and, at the end of any such tenancy, no tenant must have quit the premises[8].

1   Giannoukakis Ltd v Saltfleet Ltd [1988] I EGLR 73, CA.
2   Lovely and Orchard Services Ltd v Daejan Investment (Grove Hall) Ltd [1978] I EGLR 44. Since, technically, this is three months after the application is finally disposed of (see para 38.29 above) the valuation date is usually taken to be the hearing date.
3   National Car Parks Ltd v Colebrook Estates Ltd [1983] I EGLR 78.
4   Family Management v Gray [1980] I EGLR 46, CA.
5   Fawke v Viscount Chelsea [1979] 3 All ER 568, CA.
6   Landlord and Tenant Act 1954, s 34(1).
7   LTA 1954, s 34(2).
8   LTA 1954, s 34(2)(a), (b), (c).

The reforms proposed by RRO 2003

38.42   As we have already indicated, Part II of the LTA 1954 is scheduled to be amended by the RRO 2003. At the time of writing this process is stalled, but is expected to be restarted during the Autumn of 2003 with the RRO 2003 coming into force during 2004. Most of the reforms relate to procedural matters, but there are some changes to other areas. A number of the provisions of the RRO 2003 have been alluded to in the preceding paragraphs. What follows is a brief indication of the main thrust of what is to come.

38.43   *Contracting out* One of the most controversial elements of the reform package relates to the procedure for contracting out. As we have noted[1], it is clear that the present requirement for the parties to obtain prior court approval before entering into a contracted out tenancy has become a mere rubber-stamping process since the court has no power to withhold approval where the parties are properly advised. It is therefore being proposed that a new prior notice procedure be introduced[2]. The prospective landlord will always be required to serve on the prospective tenant a prescribed form of notice which contains a 'health warning' advising the tenant of the main consequences of taking a contracted out lease. A specific reference to this notice must then be contained in the tenancy agreement, so that it will be apparent on the face of any lease, that it is contracted out. After serving the prior notice the parties can opt for one of two alternative procedures. What is expected to be the norm is that the parties will wait at least 14 days before entering into the lease; this delay is designed to give the tenant time to consider his position. However, it is recognised that there may be circumstances in which a tenant needs to enter into a contracted out tenancy at very short notice (eg to obtain new premises after an emergency such as a fire or flood). In such a case, which is expected to be exceptional, the requirement to wait 14 days before entering into the tenancy or agreement to surrender can be avoided by the tenant making a statutory declaration (which has to be made in front of a solicitor) that he has received and read the prescribed form of notice and accepts the consequences of entering into a contracted out tenancy. As we have seen[3], these provisions have not yet been regarded as acceptable by the House of Lords Select Committee; while these concerns are expected to be overcome, there could yet be further modifications to the current proposals.

1   See para 38.24 above.
2   Which will apply equally to agreements to surrender.
3   See para 38.24 above.

38.44   *Notices* It is expected that a landlord's notice to terminate under LTA 1954, s 25[1] will in future have two alternative prescribed forms; one for when the landlord is opposing renewal and one for when he is not. In the latter case, he will be obliged to set out his proposals for the new tenancy. It is not intended that these will be binding, rather that the tenant should be given an early indication of what the landlord has in mind. A tenant will no longer be obliged to serve a counter notice stating his unwillingness to give up possession[2]; this removes a requirement that can be a trap for tenants without giving the landlord a reliable indicator of the tenant's intentions. Where a fixed-term tenant wishes to terminate a tenancy that has already been continued, his section 27(2) notice will no longer have to expire on a quarter day[3]; a straight three months' notice will be sufficient. The RRO 2003 confirms that a tenant who has ceased business occupation by contractual term date does not have to serve a section 27(1) notice[4]; he can, however, still choose to do so.

1   See para 38.26 above.
2   See para 38.26 above.
3   See para 38.27 above.
4   See para 38.27 above.

38.45   *Court applications* The procedure for termination and renewal is to be radically changed. In order to avoid the need to make token applications to court and to encourage parties to negotiate for themselves without court intervention, the very strict time limits for court applications are to be removed[1]. Henceforth, an application will simply have to be made before the date specified for termination in either the section 25 notice or the section 26 request. Furthermore, the parties will be able to make a written agreement to extend this deadline; further extensions can be agreed so long as they are entered into before a previous one expires. Only where no application to court has been made within any extended time limit will the tenant lose the right to apply for a new tenancy.

In order to give the landlord an opportunity to keep the process moving, he can now apply to court, either simply for a termination of the current tenancy (which will only succeed if he establishes a ground of opposition) or for the grant of a new tenancy. The tenant's right to apply for a new tenancy is, of course retained. In order to avoid multiple applications, only one application can be made.

1   See para 38.28 above.

38.46   *Interim rent*   Significant changes to the interim rent provisions[1] are to be made. Either the landlord or the tenant will be able to apply. Interim rent will henceforth be payable from the earliest date that could have been specified for termination in either the section 25 notice or the section 26 request. This is designed to prevent the current practice of seeking to preserve a rental advantage by serving a long section 25 notice or section 26 request. In certain circumstances, the basis on which interim rent is calculated will also change. In all cases where the landlord has not opposed renewal, where the tenant was in occupation of the whole of the demised premises, and where the landlord actually grants a new tenancy of the whole of the property to the tenant, the interim rent will be equal to the rent payable under and at the commencement of the new tenancy[2]. In all other circumstances, interim rent will continue to be assessed in the same way as at present[3].

1   See para 38.30 above.
2   Save where due to changes in the market, or in the terms of the new lease, this will produce a substantial difference. In such cases the 'new style' interim rent can be modified by the court.
3   Para 38.30 above.

38.47   *Other changes*   The RRO 2003 also makes other changes of which the following can be noted[1]. The rules defining business occupation are to be changed so as to ensure that the way in which either a landlord's or a tenant's business is structured will no longer affect their rights under the Act. So, for example, where a tenant incorporates his business and retains a controlling interest, with the result that it is now the company which occupies the premises, this will no longer cost the tenant his protection under the Act[2]. The definition of a group of companies has been widened; this will allow a greater variety of company structures to come within the business occupation rule[3]. The maximum length of new lease that can be ordered by the court is to be increased from 14 years to 15 years so as to fit more conveniently with modern rent review patterns[4].

1   It should be emphasised that this is not an exhaustive list of the changes to be made.
2   See para 38.22 above.
3   See para 38.22 above.
4   See para 38.37 above.

Agricultural tenancies

38.48   Most agricultural tenancies are regulated by one of two statutory schemes of protection. Those granted prior to 1 September 1995 are, where appropriate, governed by the Agricultural Holdings Act 1986. Those granted on or after that date are given very much more limited protection under the Agricultural Tenancies Act 1995.

Agricultural holdings

38.49   An agricultural holding is land (whether agricultural land or not), comprised in a contract for an agricultural tenancy. A contract for an agricultural tenancy is a contract of tenancy, other than one granted on or after 1 September 1995,[1] under which the whole of the land is let for use as agricultural land for the purposes of a trade or business. 'A contract of tenancy' is defined so as to include a lease or agreement for a lease for a term of years or from year to year; furthermore, it is provided that any letting of land less than a tenancy from year to year, or any licence to occupy such land, is to take effect as if it were an agreement for a tenancy from year to year.

A tenancy for a fixed term of two years or more[2] continues, on expiry, as a tenancy from year to year unless and until either party serves a notice to quit; this provision is modified where the tenant dies before the term expires and may be contracted out of, with approval of the minister.[3] As a general rule, an agricultural tenancy may only be terminated by a notice to quit of at least 12 months. On the service of such notice by the landlord, the tenant may serve a counter-notice, the effect of which is to prevent the notice to quit operating without the consent of the Agricultural Land Tribunal. The Tribunal is to withhold consent if satisfied that in all the circumstances a fair and reasonable landlord would not insist on possession, but subject to this it may consent to the notice operating if, for example, the landlord proposes to terminate the tenancy in the interest of good husbandry or the sound management of the estate.[4] In a number of cases the tenant may not serve a counternotice and thus has no security, for example where the land is required for a non-agricultural use for which planning permission has been granted.[5] The AHA 1986 confers some protection in respect of rent; either the landlord or the tenant may apply for the rent to be submitted to arbitration.[6] Such applications cannot be made more frequently than every three years.

1   Agricultural Tenancies Act 1995, s 4(1). This section does provide for the Agricultural Holdings Act 1986 to apply in certain exceptional cases to tenancies granted on or after 1 September 1995.
2   It should be noted that, perhaps curiously, the scheme of the Act is such that a tenancy for a fixed term of at least 12 months but less than two years is a lease of an agricultural holding so that, for example, the other major statutory schemes of protection are excluded. However, it is *not* afforded any security of tenure under the AHA 1986 since it is not made to continue, after expiry, as a tenancy from year to year. See *Gladstone v Bower* [1960] 2 QB 384, [1960] 3 All ER 353, CA. A recent attempt to challenge this decision has been rejected in *EWP Ltd v Moore* [1992] QB 460, [1992] 1 All ER 880, CA.
3   AHA 1986, ss 1–5.
4   AHA 1986, ss 25–27.
5   AHA 1986, Sch 3.
6   AHA 1986, ss 12, 84 and Sch 2.

Farm business tenancies
38.50   The Agricultural Tenancies Act 1995 applies to farm business tenancies granted on or after 1 September 1995. A farm business tenancy is one[1] under which all or part of the land comprised in the tenancy is farmed for the purposes of a business and has been so farmed since the beginning of the tenancy.[2] It is essential that the character of the tenancy is, at all times, primarily or wholly agricultural,[3] with the result that the tenancy can move in and out of the ATA 1995. At any time when it is outside that Act, ie when the tenancy is not primarily or wholly agricultural, it could, provided that there is business use of part, move into the protection of Pt II of the Landlord and Tenant Act 1954.[4] This possibility can be avoided by each party giving notice to the other, at or before the beginning of the tenancy, that the tenancy is to be and to remain a farm business tenancy.[5]

A tenant under a farm business tenancy has only very limited statutory protection. Where the tenancy is a periodic tenancy other than a yearly tenancy, or where it is for a fixed term of two years or less, the tenancy comes to an end in accordance with the normal common law rules. Accordingly, it will either come to an end by expiry,[6] or by means of a normal notice to quit served by either party.[7] A tenancy for a fixed term of more than two years, can only be brought to an end by one of the parties serving a notice to terminate in writing at least 12 months and less than 24 months before it is due to take effect; in the meantime the tenancy continues as a tenancy from year to year.[8] Similarly, a yearly tenancy can only be brought to an end by the service of a notice to quit, in writing, given at least 12 months and less than 24 months before the end of a year of the tenancy.[9] In neither case is there a need for there to be any grounds for the termination of the tenancy.

Part II of the ATA 1995 sets out statutory provisions for rent review. These apply in all cases unless there is an express provision in a written lease which[10] either:

- states that the rent is not to be reviewed during the tenancy, or
- provides for the rent to be varied by a specified amount,[11] or
- provides for the rent to be varied in an upwards or downwards direction in accordance with a formula which does not require or permit the exercise by any person of any judgment or discretion in relation to the determination of the rent.[12]

1   Unlike the AHA 1986, the ATA 1995 does not apply to licences: see Agricultural Tenancies Act 1995, s 38(1).
2   ATA 1995, s 1.
3   ATA 1995, s 1(3).
4   See para 38.23 above.
5   ATA 1995, s 1(4).
6   See para 37.75 above.
7   See para 37.76 above.
8   ATA 1995, s 5.
9   ATA 1995, s 6.
10 ATA 1995, s 9.
11 Eg a stepped rent.
12 Eg a rent which moves upwards or downwards in line with a specified index such as the Retail Price Index.

Part VI

Planning law

Chapter 39

The operation of the planning system and its legal framework

39.1   The creation of the planning system, sometimes referred to as the Town and Country Planning system, was intended to secure public control over the use of land, including its development. Public control is seen as essential to ensure that land use and development are reasonably systematic, or at least not determined solely by commercial factors. This enables the interests of the community to be taken into account.

39.2   The modern planning system was created by the Town and Country Planning Act 1947, which came into force on 1 July 1948. Modern planning law can be said to begin at that date. The provisions of the TCPA 1947 contained four major elements which remain central to the planning system today:

*   Local planning authorities were created by giving new functions to councils. Among their obligations was the production of development plans[1].
*   All land was made subject to development control, whereby any person intending to carry out development would require planning permission from the local planning authority[2]. In making its decision, the planning authority would have regard to its development plan[3].
*   Local planning authorities were given powers to enforce development control[4].
*   Local planning authorities were given additional powers to control land use outside the basic development control system, including preservation of buildings of historic or architectural interest[5], tree preservation and display of advertisements.

In addition to these elements, there is also statutory provision for the compulsory acquisition of property and compensation; these are outside the scope of this book.

1   Paras 39.28-39.43 below.
2   Paras 39.14-39.19 below.
3   Paras 39.28 et seq below.
4   Paras 40.36-40.47 below.
5   Paras 40.29-40.31 below.

39.3   In this chapter we examine:

*   the legal framework of the planning system;
*   the planning institutions;
*   the forward planning process – development plans;
*   the legal liabilities of local planning authorities.

The framework for planning control

Legislation
General planning Acts
39.4   Since 1948, the main statutory landmarks have been the Town and Country Planning Act 1968, which instituted the type of development planning currently in operation, the Town and Country Planning Act 1971, which consolidated the then existing statutory provisions, and the present principal statute, the Town and Country Planning Act 1990 (which will be referred to as 'the TCPA 1990'). The TCPA 1990 was significantly amended by the Planning and Compensation Act 1991.

Currently then, the principal statute is the Town and Country Planning Act 1990. This was a consolidating statute, re-enacting and amending the provisions of the TCPA 1971 and subsequent legislation, although some of the benefit was lost by the passing soon after its enactment of the Planning and Compensation Act 1991, which made important, although miscellaneous, changes to the system, notably to the enforcement powers of local planning authorities.

At the time of writing (Spring 2003), major new legislation has been introduced in Parliament in the shape of the Planning and Compulsory Purchase Bill. A brief outline of the main provisions of the Bill is included at the end of Chapter 40[1].

1   Para 40.55 below.

Local government legislation
39.5   The TCPA 1947 swept away such piecemeal planning regulation as already existed. But it was grafted onto the then-existing system of local government. Subsequent legislation has effected more than one local government reorganisation and this has impacted on the planning system. The relevant statutes are the Local Government Act 1972, the Local Government Planning and Land Act 1980, and the Local Government Act 1985, which reorganised local government in London and the metropolitan counties. The Greater London Authority Act 1999 created the Greater London Authority, although it is still the London boroughs rather than the GLA which are the planning authorities.

1   Para 39.15 below for details of the position in London.

Specialist planning Acts
39.6   As well as the principal statute, there are specialist statutes dealing with discrete areas. The main ones are the Planning (Listed Buildings and Consolidation Areas) Act 1990, a consolidation of legislation relating to listed buildings and conservation areas and the Planning (Hazardous Substances) Act 1990, relating to the control of the presence on land of substances defined by the Planning (Hazardous Substances) Regulations 1992 as hazardous, as toxic, oxidising, explosive, inflammable or environmentally dangerous.

Subordinate legislation
39.7   Beyond the principal statute and the specialist statutes, there is extensive subordinate legislation in the form of numerous rules, regulations and orders. Because there are so many of these (they cover more than 20 aspects of planning law) and because they are subject to frequent amendment, it would not be useful to give a comprehensive account of the subordinate legislation. Instead, it will be referred to where necessary. Nevertheless, its importance should not be underestimated. For example, the Town and Country Planning (General Permitted Development) Order 1995 as amended (the GPDO) and the Town and Country Planning (Use Classes) Order 1987 as amended (the Use Classes Order) probably have proportionately greater significance over the outcome of more development

proposals than any part of the principal statutes. In planning law, subordinate legislation constitutes not so much small print as the sharp end of the system. In practical terms, it is in rules, regulations and orders, as well as in case law, that the answer is commonly to be found as to what may or may not be done.

Case law

39.8   A third important source of planning law is case law[1]. In the planning context, this tends to be of two main types: those cases that rule on the interpretation of statutory provisions and those that involve the application of public law principles in the decision-making process, such as the right to a fair hearing, or the rule against bias, or under general judicial review powers, by which the court is asked to rule on the legality of a procedure or a decision. The litigation leading to these cases may be brought either under specific provisions of the TCPA 1990[2] or under general judicial review procedures. A new trend in recent years has been litigation based on allegations of breaches of the European Convention on Human Rights, enacted in the United Kingdom by the Human Rights Act 1998, such as in the *Alconbury* case[3].

1   Students and practitioners can keep themselves up to date with developments in case law through specialist law reports like those in the Journal of Planning and Environment Law (JPL) and Estates Gazette (EG), as well as the main law reports (All England and Weekly Law Reports) and by using on-line services like LexisNexis, LawTel and EGI.
2   TCPA 1990, ss 287 (development plan challenges), 288 (planning appeals), 289 (enforcement notices).
3   Para 39.13 below.

Government policy: Planning Policy Guidance Notes

39.9   Although it is not law, government policy is particularly important in the planning system. This is partly because, as is explained in the section on decision-making in development control in Chapter 40[1], government policy is a material consideration to be taken into account in deciding whether or not to grant planning permission (as well as making other decisions) and partly because appeal from the decision of the local planning authority is, in effect, to central government, in the form of the Secretary of State. While policy, which is chiefly set out in Planning Policy Guidance Notes (PPGs), is not binding on any decision-maker, it is at least influential, and failure to pay due regard to it may lead to the decision being declared invalid in the courts[2].

There are over 20 PPGs at the time of writing which set out government policy on a whole range of planning issues. Some of the best known are PPG 1 on general planning policy, PPG 2 on green belts, PPG 6 on town centres and retail developments, PPG 13 on transport and, recently, PPG 25 on development and flood risk.

1   Para 40.20 below.
2   For example, in *Fulford v Secretary of State* [1997] JPL 163, the court stated that relevant national policy (in that case PPG 15) was one of the necessary material considerations in deciding an application to demolish buildings in a conservation area.

The planning institutions – a mixture of central and local government

Central government

39.10   At the central government level, the key player is the Secretary of State and the Department which he or she heads. Successive reorganisations of government have made this confusing. The names of planning law cases reported over the years refer to Ministers and Secretaries of State presiding over Housing and Local Government, Town and Country Planning, and Environment. Since 2001, the central government role has been led by the Secretary of State for Transport, Local Government and the Regions, previously Environment,

Transport and the Regions. Based on the experience of post-war government history, it is probable that this is not the final name-change or combination. What really matters is the concept, which has changed little. The Secretary of State (SoS) fulfils three very important functions in the planning system, as well as a number of others.

The role of the Secretary of State

39.11   *Policy* The making of PPGs and other circular advice has already been mentioned. The SoS may also 'call in' development plans and seek to ensure their compatibility with government policy[1]. This means that the SoS, on behalf of central government, scrutinises the content of the development plan, to identify any concerns he has about the planning authority's policies and proposals.

1   Para 39.39 below.

39.12   *Legislation* The SoS is responsible for the delegated legislation described above. Amendments may constitute significant changes in the substance of planning law, so the SoS possesses real power to effect legal change. For example, the 1995 amendments to the Use Classes Order of 1987 made by the GPDO permitted change of use from Class A1 or A2 (shops) to a mixed use of shop and flat without the need for planning permission. This was an attempt by central government to give increased flexibility of use in the then economically hard-pressed retail sector and it was achieved through the power of the SoS to make and amend delegated legislation.

39.13   *Appeals to the Secretary of State* The TCPA 1990 provides a mechanism for appeal[1] for applicants for planning permission who are dissatisfied with the decision of the local planning authority, for example because permission has been refused or granted subject to unacceptable conditions. There are other types of statutory appeal, such as those against enforcement notices[2] which are made similarly. Appeal is thus from a decision of local government to a central government decision-maker. In practical terms, this will nearly always mean to an inspector from within the Department's Inspectorate, although the SoS can also 'call in' appeals for personal decision-making, just as development plans can be called in. This process, although provided for by statute[3] is controversial because it seems to permit intervention on political grounds in an objective process. In *R v Secretary of State for Environment, Transport and the Regions, ex p Alconbury Developments*[4], an attempt was made to argue that the process of calling in an appeal by the SoS was contrary to the European Convention on Human Rights[5], as being inconsistent with the right to a fair trial. The House of Lords held that the call-in procedure was not incompatible with a fair hearing even where, as here, the SoS was deciding an appeal concerning government land.

1   TCPA 1990, s 78.
2   TCPA 1990, ss 174-177.
3   TCPA 1990, Sch 6, para 3.
4   [2001] UKHL 23, [2001] JPL 920.
5   Article 6 (1).

Local government: the local planning authority

Identifying the LPA

39.14   At local government level, the main institution is the local planning authority (LPA). However, just as central government reorganisation of ministries and departments has made tracing the predecessors of the SoS problematic, so local government reform has made the identification of an LPA much less straightforward than it used to be. Nevertheless, the basic concept is much as it was in 1947; the LPA is a local council with responsibility for the planning functions identified in para 39.2 above: development plans, development control enforcement and additional land-use regulation.

Local government re-organisation in 1974[1] and 1985[2], followed by the setting up of the Local Government Commission[3] to effect a wide-ranging review of local authorities, has meant that it is impossible to generalise about the *identity* of the councils which fulfil these functions in any specific part of the country. There is no longer anything approaching a uniform system of local government. The effect is rather of a patchwork quilt with several different arrangements; indeed, even this analogy does not fully reflect the complexity of the situation, because the work of the Local Government Commission has resulted in an ongoing state of transition. The following models can be identified; which of them has been adopted at any given date in a particular part of the country can only be ascertained by specific inquiry.

1   Local Government Act 1972.
2   Local Government Act 1985.
3   Local Government Act 1992, s 13.

39.15   *London* The position of London is unique. After the abolition of the Greater London Council[1], all planning functions were undertaken by the London borough councils, which were thus the first unitary ie 'one-tier' authorities.

Although London now has the Greater London Authority[2], it is still the London boroughs rather than the GLA which are the planning authorities. However, the boroughs' unitary development plans must now conform generally with the (elected) Mayor of London's Spatial Development Strategy. Furthermore, the TCPA 1990 has been amended[3] to allow the Mayor to direct a London borough, as planning authority, to refuse planning permission in certain circumstances[4]. Subject to these qualifications, for everyday purposes, the London borough councils are the sole planning authorities and are the LPAs.

1   Local Government Act 1985.
2   Greater London Authority Act 1999.
3   TCPA 1990, ss 74(1B) and 74(1C).
4   See Town and Country Planning (Mayor of London) Order 2000.

39.16   *Metropolitan areas* In the metropolitan areas (Greater Manchester, Merseyside, Tyne & Wear, West Midlands, South Yorkshire and West Yorkshire), the LPA is the relevant metropolitan borough council which, like the London boroughs, will also be a unitary authority.

39.17   *Non-metropolitan areas – 'traditional' model* Traditionally, most of England [1] had two tiers of planning authority. These were the county council, being the planning authority for the county, and, within the county, a number of borough councils, district councils and city councils which were the LPAs for their own area. (County planning authorities also have jurisdiction over certain miscellaneous areas, such as extraction of minerals. These are sometimes described as 'county matters'.) A significant number of areas of non-metropolitan England retain this two-tier model, which is, accordingly, explained in more detail below, although as a result of the Local Government Commission's work, a growing number of areas have moved from the 'traditional' to the 'unitary' model. An example will illustrate the traditional two-tier model. In Oxfordshire, the county planning authority for the whole county is Oxfordshire County Council. Within Oxfordshire are five LPAs: Cherwell District Council, South Oxfordshire District Council, Vale of the White Horse District Council, West Oxfordshire District Council and Oxford City Council.

1   TCPA 1990, s 1 (1B). In Wales, since 1996 the LPA has been the county or county borough council.
2   Para 39.20 below.

39.18   *Non-metropolitan areas – the unitary model.* Since 1994, ever-increasing numbers of areas of England have gone over to unitary local government, meaning that all planning functions are exercised by a single council. The first English non-metropolitan area to move to a unitary model was the Isle of Wight in 1994. This will provide an example of how the changeover works. Previously, the Isle of Wight had operated the two-tier model. The Isle of Wight County Council was the county planning authority and the two LPAs were Medina Borough Council and South Wight District Council. All three were replaced by the unitary Isle of Wight Council, which now exercises all planning functions.

39.19   *Special LPAs* In certain circumstances different bodies may exercise the functions of an LPA:

*   National parks, such as the Peak District and the Lake District, have their own arrangements, either in the form of the National Park Authority[1] or the county council's national park committee. The Norfolk and Suffolk Broads have the Broads Authority as the equivalent.
*   A number of enterprise zones were set up in the 1980s and 1990s. They retained this status for 10 years and so have gradually expired. The designated authority acts as the LPA within the enterprise zone.
*   Urban development areas, of which London Docklands, Cardiff Bay and Merseyside were among the most prominent, were set up with (much reduced) control over development exercised by a development corporation.

1   Established by the Environment Act 1995, s 63.

The operation of LPAs

39.20   LPAs, as has been indicated, are nearly all councils. Whether they are district councils, city councils, traditional or unitary authorities, does not matter for operational purposes. What does matter is that they have certain features and methods of operating which affect how they discharge their planning functions.

Any LPA is made up of two categories of people who play fundamental roles in the planning process:

*   councillors (members)
*   officers

Councillors

39.21   Councillors (who are also known as members) are elected by the voters of the area. They represent sub-divisions of their city or district, which are often called wards, each of which holds a mini-election, as part of the election of the council, every four years[1]. The councillors often stand as candidates on behalf of one of the major political parties: Labour, Conservative or Liberal Democrat, or on behalf of a special interest group (such as a campaign against an airport development or to protect the Green Belt), or as independents. The councillors are the decision-makers of the council. They are not paid salaries, although some receive quite substantial payments of expenses incurred while carrying out council business.

1   Some areas have elections for the whole council every four years, while others have one-third of the seats contested each year over a three-year cycle.

39.22   *The Planning Committee* Councillors meet periodically as a Full Council, ie all together, but most of their business is transacted in committees, of which the Planning Committee is one. This is a subdivision of the council as a whole, although attempts will have been made to ensure that the political parties are represented in approximately the same proportions as in the Full Council. If the Council has 50 members, of whom 20 are Labour, 20 are Conservative and 10 Liberal Democrat, the 10 members of the Planning Committee would be 4 Labour, 4 Conservative and 2 Liberal Democrat. Party politics is important in local government as it is in central government, because the members of a party group or bloc tend to vote together, so that support or opposition for a scheme by a party may well mean that all the party's councillors will support or oppose it. If the party has a majority, ie more than half the total councillors, it is in a position to ensure a particular outcome, assuming all councillors obey the party line. The Planning Committee meeting can be attended by members of the public and thus by applicants[1], unless, exceptionally, a compelling reason exists for holding it behind closed doors, eg because confidential matters have to be discussed, such as the content of a barrister's opinion on the council's legal position in an appeal.

1   Local Government (Access to Information) Act 1985.

Officers of the council
39.23   The officers of the council are not elected. They are members of the council's work-force and are paid salaries from the council's income. The officers' task is to *run* the council; in this respect they are rather like managers or executives in a company, implementing the decisions of the councillors (who are somewhat like the board of directors) and handling day-to-day business. However, they are more than mere employees and may take on significant responsibilities. A Chief Planning Officer, for example, will almost always be a well-qualified and experienced professional planner, with a degree and membership of the Royal Town Planning Institute (MRTPI). Other officers, such as a Deputy Development Control Officer, will also be qualified and experienced professionals.

39.24   *The role of planning officers in LPA decisions* In the past it was only councillors, as elected members, who could take decisions, which the officers would put into practice. Today a high percentage of planning decisions in LPAs are taken by planning officers. Senior officers in a modern LPA will take well in excess of 50% of planning decisions; in some LPAs it might be more like 80%. This has been made possible by statutory delegation of tasks by the council to its officers[1]. Usually, the council's established procedures, known as 'standing orders' will provide for a 'scheme of delegation', by which certain routine decisions will automatically go to named officers or others acting under their authority. Alternatively, a specific decision could be delegated to officers by a resolution of the council.

Not surprisingly, it tends to be only the more routine decisions which are delegated to officers, or ones where it is a purely technical input which is required. The councillors who make up the Planning Committee will still make the decision on any contentious proposals or ones where there may be political implications, eg because one group especially favours or opposes the scheme. So, even if the councillors decide the minority of decisions statistically, that numerical minority will contain almost all the planning applications and other decisions of most significance.

1   Under Local Government Act 1972, s 101.

39.25   *The role of planning officers: committee work* Even when not acting under delegated powers, officers are still centrally involved in the council's planning functions. All committees, including the Planning Committee, are serviced by officers, who provide research, background preparation, technical knowledge and advice on the matters on the agenda; indeed, the agenda will have been prepared by officers. With each planning application, the planning officer responsible for the area where the property is located will have obtained a summary of the planning history of the site, relevant council policy from the Local Plan (or UDP), strategic policy guidance from the Structure Plan (or UDP) and any government guidance in PPGs. Legal advice may have been obtained on doubtful or borderline questions from the council's legal department, where the Chief Officers will be solicitors or sometimes barristers. Crucially, the officers will send to the Committee meeting, or provide on request, recommendations as to the most eligible course of action open to the members, on technical grounds at least. Members come to trust and rely on good officers, so that the officer's recommendation to Committee is highly influential, statistically at least, in the eventual outcome. Sometimes the members will overturn recommendations on political grounds and occasionally for purely subjective reasons. These 'maverick' decisions are likely to be difficult to defend if the council's decision is challenged on appeal or by judicial review. Such challenges can place officers in the invidious position of trying to defend on appeal a decision of the council which was contrary to their own recommendation. Since this fact will be known to the appellant and inspector/judge, it is a mark of serious weakness in the council's position and may lead to heavy defeat and the award of costs to the appellant. More usually, of course, the Planning Committee follows the Planning Officer's recommendation.

39.26   *The role of planning officers: development plans* Officers have other significant planning functions besides their involvement in development control decisions. One has already been mentioned. The task of preparing development plans and going through the stages of consultation, draft, deposit, negotiation of objections, and EIP/public inquiry, falls almost entirely to officers. The members, while they will have some input into making policy choices, often reflecting their own political mandates, have neither the technical expertise nor the time for development planning. The structure plan, the local plan and the UDP are drafted by officers from the Forward Planning Section and the Legal Department.

39.27   *The role of planning officers: enforcement* Another major planning task of officers is enforcement of planning control and this is dealt with in Chapter 40 below[1].

1   Paras 40.36-40.47 below.

The planning process: development plans

39.28   The United Kingdom's planning system is often described as a 'plan-led' system. This means that the role of development plans is crucial in determining the outcome of applications for planning permission and other development decisions.
  There are two basic elements of the development plan:

• structure plans; and
• local plans.

However, as part of the movement to unitary local government[1], there is an alternative type of development plan, the unitary development plan (UDP), which combines the features of the structure and local plans into one plan.

1   Para 39.17 above.

Structure plans
39.29   A structure plan is prepared by the county planning authority, eg Oxfordshire County Council, for the whole county. It comprises a broad statement of strategic planning policies developed through studies and appraisals of the area and through consultation with the LPAs of the county, local authorities representing adjoining areas (say Buckinghamshire, in the case of Oxfordshire), the Environment Agency, the Countryside Agency, the Nature Conservancy Council and English Heritage. As will be seen below, further consultation takes place at subsequent stages of the structure planning process.

Public participation

39.30 *On deposit* The draft structure plan document is then put 'on deposit', meaning that it is made publicly available[1], for objection or other comment. This and the following stages of the plan-making process are known as 'public participation'. Public participation in plan-making is seen as very desirable in terms of giving credibility and legitimacy to the plan, although the reality is that the number of people involved in participation at structure plan level is often small.

1 In accordance with the Town and Country Planning (Development Plans) (England) Regulations 1999.

39.31 *Examination in public* Issues raised by the plan and the consultation and participation processes are then considered at an Examination in Public (EIP). The EIP is a unique model of public participation, bearing little resemblance to the public inquiry still used for local plans[1]. The SoS selects the Chair and Panel who will conduct the EIP. At least one member will be from the Department's Planning Inspectorate. Members are often senior lawyers, planners and specialists in disciplines relevant to property or transport. The EIP consists of what the official guide[2], calls a 'probing discussion' led by the panel. The EIP has been criticised as not offering genuine public participation, partly because objectors have no legal right to appear and partly because of the dominant role played by the plan-making authority and the SoS. Against this, it may be argued that the 'broad-brush strokes' of strategic policy would be beyond the capacity of ordinary citizens to discuss. The relatively restricted use of legal representation by participants is seen as a benefit in terms of keeping the EIP as short as possible. Critics regard the absence of legal representations as dangerous, since vital interests can be at stake, even if the policies which affect them are stated in general terms.

1 Para 39.35 below.
2 *Structure Plans: A Guide to Procedure* (2000).

Modification

39.32 The EIP Panel then produces a report containing recommendations as to modifications of the draft structure plan. The plan-making authority is not bound to accept or incorporate all these recommendations (or any of them, in theory) into the final plan as adopted, but in reality is obliged at least to consider them thoroughly. If this is done properly, the plan-making authority is entitled to prefer its own policy on any particular point. In *Steel v North Yorkshire County Council*[1], it was held that the council could reject an EIP Panel's recommendations on environmental grounds, having given a statement of their decisions on the recommendations; there was thus no breach of the duty to give reasons. Similarly, in *House Builders Federation v Royal County of Berkshire*[2], the council was held to be entitled to depart from the EIP Panel's recommendations, provided its reasons were proper, adequate and intelligible and reached after genuine consideration of the Panel's report.

However, a more serious supervisory role is exercised by the SoS, who can prevent the adoption of a Structure Plan until modified. The SoS can 'call in' any part of a structure plan at any time prior to adoption; this formidable power would normally only be exercised where the plan raised national or regional issues or where it was incompatible with the structure plan of an adjoining authority.

1 [1996] EGCS 139.
2 [1996] EGCS 79.

Local plans

39.33 Local plans are prepared by LPAs, eg Oxford City Council and South Oxfordshire District Council, for their areas. They set out detailed policies and specific proposals for the development and use of land. Although structure plans are important for the strategic policies they contain and are influential on local plans, it is to the local plans that developers and their professional advisers will refer for guidance on day-to-day planning decisions. Maps and diagrams within the local plan are especially useful in identifying specific sites. Structure plans are not intended to be site-specific.

Public participation

39.34   *On deposit and consultation* As with structure plans, local plans are produced in draft form from historical study, usually referring to the experience of the predecessor plan and from consultation with local interest groups and organisations. The draft will also need to take account of central government guidance as expressed in PPGs and must conform with the structure plan. Again, like the structure plan, the draft local plan is placed on deposit and the LPA, as plan-making authority, will receive objections and other representations. Often they will enter into discussions with objectors in the hope of negotiating an agreement. Typically, this might involve a modification of the draft plan in return for a withdrawal of the objection.

39.35   *Public inquiries* The procedure of consideration of objections to local plans is quite unlike that for structure plans, namely the EIP. Local plans are subject to a traditional public inquiry into objections. Presided over by an inspector appointed by the SoS, the inquiry is recognisably quasi-judicial and often somewhat adversarial, as objectors, frequently legally represented, challenge the local authority, almost always legally represented, employing techniques and procedures similar to those of the courts, as witnesses give evidence and are examined, cross-examined and re-examined. Since 1991, for reasons which will be explored further below[1], local plan inquiries have become a major focus of conflict between the plan-making LPA and developers seeking to loosen or remove the development control policies proposed in the draft plan. This may be adversarial, and usually is, but it is often not of the simple two-sided (bi-partisan) kind seen in a courtroom between claimant and defendant. The local plan inquiry may see conflict between two, or even several, rival developers, say for a town centre redevelopment, each seeking to advance one scheme at the expense of others and to secure the adoption of policies friendly to the favoured scheme. Furthermore, the presence of special interest groups advocating radical conservation or environmental policies may complicate the conflict. The LPA can become the 'meat in the sandwich' in a dispute, for example, over maximum housing densities. Attacked by developers arguing for higher densities of units per hectare than proposed in the draft plan, the LPA may find itself unsupported by residents' groups or, equally likely, urged by them to permit only lower densities or no development at all.

   The outcome of these volatile proceedings will be at least influential, and often decisive, in determining which development can and cannot occur within an area for the 10-year life of the plan. It is unsurprising that developers, large and small, commercial and amateur, invest substantial resources in retaining solicitors, barristers, chartered surveyors, planning consultants and other professional assistance to try to secure the outcome they require.

1   Para 39.41 below.

Modification

39.36   The inspector reports to the LPA, who must consider the report thoroughly and issue a statement on its attitude to the inspector's comments and any modifications proposed. As with the structure plan, the plan-making authority is not obliged to accept the inspector's recommendations but it is obliged to act properly and explain its reasons.

39.37   *Legal challenges: procedural* In *Hall Aggregates v New Forest District Council*[1],the court emphasised that a council's statement of reasons must be intelligible and adequate to permit the lawful rejection of an inspector's recommendation. It may in certain circumstances be necessary to reopen the inquiry to give objectors a further chance to be heard, although this will not be a right for the objectors. Given the interests at stake, it is not surprising that challenges to the LPA's response are frequently made in the courts. In *Stirk v Bridgnorth District Council*[2], the LPA was held to have acted unfairly in refusing to hold a second inquiry into local plan objections. In simply giving exactly the same reason for refusal to adopt the inspector's recommendations as in rejecting the original objections, the council had shown a failure to consider them properly. In *Harlowby Estates and Bryant Homes v Harlow District Council*[3], the LPA was held to have failed to have regard to government guidance on appropriate factors, such as the importance of independent scrutiny of objections, in deciding not to hold a second inquiry. However, in *Warren v Uttlesford District Council*[4] the Court of Appeal upheld the council's basic right to refuse to hold a further public inquiry, where the objectors' complaints were the same as before and where the council had taken the decision to adopt the plan with all due consideration.

1   [1996] EGCS 108.
2   [1996] EGCS 159.
3   [1997] JPL 541.
4   [1997] JPL 1130.

39.38   *Legal challenges: matters of law* It is not merely the procedure in the making of a plan which may be challenged. The TCPA 1990[1] gives a right to seek review in the High Court on matters of law. An example of this kind of challenge succeeding was *Westminster City Council v Great Portland Estates*[2], where developers objected to two elements of Westminster's local plan which would have the effect of obstructing Great Portland's office development proposals. The general policy of encouraging applications for redevelopment of industrial floor-space was made subject to an exception where proposed redevelopment would threaten existing established industries. Great Portland Estates unsuccessfully contended that individual occupiers should not be protected against market forces. The House of Lords held that harm to particular businesses was a relevant consideration in making planning policy. However, the challenge to the office policy element of Westminster's plan succeeded. It stated that no further office development would be permitted in designated areas, save in 'exceptional circumstances', which were not specified, since Westminster hoped to retain flexibility in defining them, by issuing non-statutory guidance. The House of Lords held that the plan was invalid if it omitted information vital for the guidance of developers.

1   TCPA 1990, s 287.
2   [1985] AC 661.

39.39   *Call in by the SoS* As with structure plans, local plans may be the subject of call-in by the SoS, similarly for restricted reasons of national or regional importance. Non-conformity with the structure plan or other neighbouring development plans might create such an issue.

Unitary development plans
39.40   Unitary development plans (UDPs) combine the features of both structure plans and local plans. Part I, in which the plan-making authority sets out its general policies in respect of development and land-use, which must make specific reference to conservation, improvement of physical environment and traffic, is the equivalent of the structure plan. Part II, which comprises a detailed written statement of proposals for development and land-use with a map and any relevant diagrams and reasoned justification for the policies, is the equivalent of the local plan. As with the other types of plan, UDPs must have regard to government guidance and must be consistent with regional policies and other plans. In

London, a UDP must be consistent with the Spatial Development Strategy prepared by the Mayor. Procedure for producing a UDP is similar to that for a local plan, in that a public inquiry will be held into objections and other representations, following the period of consultation and deposit. An EIP on Part I matters would normally only be held if there were no Part II objections, which is likely to be very infrequent.

The SoS enjoys similar call-in powers for UDPs to those for local plans, which can be exercised at any time prior to adoption. The plan-making authority will receive the inspector's recommendations on amendments arising from the inquiry into objections. As with local plans, the plan-making authority must consider them and give reasons for any decisions, particularly for any departure from the recommendations.

The significance of development plans
Section 54A

39.41   As has been stated, the planning system is often described as plan-led. The reason for this is encapsulated in a single section of the TCPA 1990, which was added by the Planning and Compensation Act 1991. This section is fundamental to understanding why so much effort is invested by LPAs in producing development plans and why resources are expended on such a scale by developers in trying to shape their content by objections, representations, negotiation, appearance in inquiries and even judicial challenge.

By s 54A of the TCPA 1990[1]:

'Where, in making any determination under the Planning Acts, regard is to be had to the development plan, the determination shall be made in accordance with the plan unless material considerations indicate otherwise.'

This section must be read in conjunction with TCPA 1990, s 70, which states: 'where an application is made to a local planning authority for planning permission ... in dealing with such an application the authority shall have regard to the provisions of the development plan, so far as material to the application, and to any other material considerations'.

I   As inserted by the Planning and Compensation Act 1991, s 26.

39.42   *The apparent purpose of TCPA 1990, s 54A* When s 54A was inserted retrospectively into the TCPA 1990, it was apparent that it was done so for a purpose. Section 70(2)(c) already required the LPA to *have regard to* both the provisions of the development plan and material considerations. The difference appeared to consist in two features of the new provision (that is, as well as applying to all those making determinations and not just LPAs considering applications for planning permission):

*   whereas under s 70 (2) the decision-maker's duty is only to have regard to the provisions of the development plan, the obligation under s 54A is to *follow* it (unless material considerations indicate otherwise);
*   whereas under s 70(2) development plan provisions are distinguished from *other* material considerations, obviously indicating that they are themselves material considerations, under s 54A the word 'other' is missing. The implication is that the development plan provisions have a status other than that of material considerations; the only logical conclusion being that they are accorded a *higher* status.

39.43   *The approach of the courts to TCPA 1990, s 54A* The general effect of case law since 1991 has been to confirm this interpretation of s 54A, although the courts have rejected some of the more extreme formulations proposed, which would have moved the development plan provisions towards an almost impregnable position. The Court of Appeal in *Loup v Secretary of State for Environment*[1], confirmed that s 54A was intended to give some degree of priority to the provisions of the development plan and the High Court in *St Albans District Council v Secretary of State for Environment*[2] went so far as to refer to a 'presumption' in favour of the development plan. However, in the latter case, the judge rejected the idea that material considerations would have to be particularly strong to outweigh the plan's provisions. Probably the most useful guidance to date on s 54A was the House of Lords decision of *City of Edinburgh v Secretary of State for Scotland*[3] in which the view was expressed that, although priority is to be given to the development plan, it is for the decision-maker to assess, having regard to all the material considerations, what weight should be given to it (and to them). Furthermore, the decision-maker's assessment could only be challenged on grounds of irrationality or perverseness.

In conclusion of the discussion on this provision, it must be emphasised that it must be interpreted carefully, although it is of vital importance as the link between development planning and development control decision-making. Old cases like *Simpson v Edinburgh Corpn*[4] and *London Borough of Enfield v Secretary of State for Environment*[5] established that 'shall have regard to', as in s 70(2), does not mean that the LPA can undertake 'slavish adherence' to the plan, meaning following it blindly and without thought. This has not been reversed by later case law and s 54A no more authorises 'slavish adherence' than s 70(2).

How the decision-maker uses the provisions of the development plan is often a delicate matter. In *London Borough of Hounslow v Secretary of State for Environment Transport and the Regions*[6] it was pointed out that, where relevant plan policies pull in different directions or apparently conflict, it is for the decision-maker to undertake a balancing exercise, to see whether the proposal could accord with the plan as a whole, which is in turn subject to balancing against material considerations. The court will not make strenuous efforts to overturn the decision-maker's attempt unless it is irrational or perverse, as the House of Lords explained in the *City of Edinburgh* case.

A plan-led system, which it is, must not be taken to mean one where the plan is slavishly adhered to, which it is not. Provided each decision is made after taking account of the development plan and material considerations, on a case-by-case basis, the courts will be reluctant to intervene, since this would be likely to involve them in making judgements on planning merits, which they are neither equipped nor inclined to do.

1   [1996] JPL 22.
2   [1993] 1 PLR 88.
3   [1998] 1 All ER 174. The decision was actually on the Scots equivalent but it is submitted that it represents English law too: see the Court of Appeal's decision in *R v Leominster District Council, ex p Pothecary* [1998] JPL 335.
4   1961 SLT 17.
5   [1975] JPL 155.
6   [1999] JPL 364.

The legal liabilities of LPAs

39.44   The planning functions of the LPA bring it into a greater degree of contact with the 'public' or 'outside world' than many council activities. This occurs to some extent in the consultation and participation stages of forward planning, but more often in the day-to-day business of development control and enforcement. Planning officers in particular are required to communicate and negotiate with would-be developers and their professional representatives and many other categories of inquirer. The question is therefore bound to arise – and does – as to the position of the LPAs in terms of liability for their actions or statements.

The power of planning officers to bind the LPA

39.45   In principle, the delegation of powers to officers of the council should be capable of carrying with it the power to bind the council. The courts, however, have not, with a few exceptions, viewed with much enthusiasm the proposition that a council should be deprived of its power to make a correct decision by an officer's indication that an incorrect one is appropriate.

39.46   *The doctrine of estoppel* In *Southend-on-Sea Corpn v Hodgson (Wickford) Ltd*[1] , it was held that an officer's incorrect statement to a purchaser to the effect that a builder's yard enjoyed established use rights did not prevent the council from taking enforcement action against the new owner when the true position was ascertained As appears from the *Western Fish Products* case below, this remains a correct statement of the basic position: incorrect statements by officers should not fetter the council's exercise of its powers. However, exceptionally, this basic position was modified by the doctrine of estoppel in limited circumstances, which must be considered briefly.

In *Wells v Minister of Housing and Local Government*[2] and *Lever Finance v Westminster City Council*[3], Lord Denning almost single-handedly developed the doctrine of estoppel, a concept more properly at home in the law of contract, as applied to planning law. The basic idea of estoppel is that where one is induced to act or alter one's position by reliance on the representation or assurance of another, that other should in equity be prevented (estopped) from denying the truth of the statement or withdrawing it if it will cause loss to the person relying on it. It is common for developers and their representatives to inquire whether planning permission is needed for their proposal and to proceed if assured that it is not. Lord Denning in *Lever Finance* thought that the LPA should be bound by an officer, acting with what he called 'ostensible authority' giving such an assurance, so that it could not take enforcement action if it subsequently discovered that the assurance was incorrect and that planning permission would be needed.

The Court of Appeal in *Western Fish Products v Penwith District Council*[4] endeavoured to redress the balance in favour of the local authority without completely denying the inquirer protection. They reaffirmed as correct the basic *Southend-on-Sea* position that a local authority should not be estopped from exercising its powers properly by any statement of its officers. They were prepared to concede two limited exceptions to this general principle, although the estoppel argument failed in *Western Fish* because the LPA had made no representation on which the property owner was entitled to rely. They accepted that in a case like *Wells*, if the landowner applied for planning permission and was told that none was necessary, the local authority should not subsequently take enforcement action. It must be doubtful whether this exception is of continued relevance today because, since the TCPA 1990, the owner can obtain a binding decision from the LPA as to whether he or she requires planning permission by applying for a Certificate of Lawfulness of Proposed Use or Development (known as a CLOPUD)[5]. The other exception, according to the Court of Appeal in *Western Fish*, should be confined to situations where an officer gave an assurance with *actual* (ie delegated) authority, rather than ostensible authority.

The House of Lords has recently doubted[6] whether the doctrine of estoppel should have any place in planning law, although since they also refer to parts of it being already assimilated into public law, it must be assumed that they would not wish those relying on statements of officers to be left completely unprotected. The exact position following the *Reprotech* case probably requires further clarification since there was held to be no possibility of estoppel in that case in any event.

1   [1962] 1 QB 416.
2   [1967] 2 All ER 1041.
3   [1971] 1 QB 222.
4   [1981] 2 All ER 204.
5   TCPA 1990, s 192.
6   *R v East Sussex County Council, ex p Reprotech* [2002] UKHL 8, [2002] 4 All ER 58; [2003] 1 WLR 348.

39.47   *Negligent misstatements*[1] It is theoretically possible for the LPA to incur liability in tort for negligent misstatement by its officers under the principle established in *Hedley Byrne* v *Heller*[2]. The possibility of this was stated in *Tidman v Reading Borough Council*[3], where an inquirer had sought information regarding the development potential of his land. He sued the council after his attempted sale of the land collapsed, when the prospective purchaser discovered the difficulties which would attend any attempt to develop the site. The court accepted that in principle an officer could vicariously incur civil liability for negligent misstatement on behalf of the LPA. However, on these facts there would be no such liability. It would not be just or reasonable to impose a duty of care on a planning authority responding to a casual telephone enquiry. To impose such a duty would hardly be in the public interest, since it would discourage officers from responding helpfully. For such liability to exist, the claimant would have needed to make a formal approach, making clear to the LPA what information was needed and for what purpose. In *Welton v North Cornwall District Council*[4], an environmental health officer was held to have created a duty of care by giving guest-house owners inaccurate information on the requirements which would be made of them.

1   For a general discussion of this area of the law , see paras 17.23-17.28 above.
2   [1964] AC 465.
3   [1994] 3 PLR 72.
4   [1997] 1 WLR 570.

39.48   *Liability in negligence*[1] Generally speaking, the trend in recent years has been against imposing duties of care on local authorities acting in a regulatory capacity. In *Murphy v Brentwood District Council*[2],the House of Lords refused to impose a duty of care on a local authority acting under its building control functions in favour of property owners claiming to rely on it for protection.

In particular, since the House of Lords decision in *Stovin v Wise*[3], it has been regarded as difficult to sue a local authority for failure to act. The allegation in that case was that a highway authority had negligently failed to act in dealing with an accident 'black-spot', resulting in a further accident. Lord Hoffman doubted whether a council would often be liable for omission to act, since it only had finite resources and could not act immediately in every case. However, there have been some indications that the courts may be willing to permit the Human Rights Act to be used as a way of avoiding *Stovin v Wise*. In *Peter Marcic v Thames Water Utilities Ltd*[4], the claimant, who had suffered flooding through the water company's neglect of its drainage system, was able to succeed in an action based on the Human Rights Act, even though Thames Water was only guilty of non-feasance, because under the European Convention 'an act' includes 'a failure to act'.

In the actual grant of planning permission, the LPA had seemed to be secure from liability by the decision in *Ryeford Homes v Sevenoaks District Council*[5],in which it was held that the LPA owed no duty of care to protect adjoining landowners when granting planning permission. The permission Sevenoaks had granted to one developer led to an overburdening of the drainage system and flooding of a development site adjoining owned by Ryeford. But Ryeford could not claim against the LPA; their only possible remedy would lie in nuisance against the owners of the site where development had already occurred.

However, to emphasise the continued volatility in this area, in *Kane v New Forest District Council*[6], the Court of Appeal distinguished *Stovin v Wise*, in holding the council liable for allowing a footpath to be opened before it was safe. The Court of Appeal, which does not appear to have overruled *Ryeford Homes*, nevertheless held that it was 'far from clear that a local planning authority would be immune from liability'.

1   For a general discussion of negligence liability in this area, see paras 17.30-17.32 above.
2   [1991] 1 AC 398.
3   [1996] AC 923.
4   [2002] EWCA Civ 65, [2002] QB 929, [2002] 2 All ER 55.
5   [1989] 2 EGLR 281.
6   [2001] EWCA Civ 878, [2001] 3 All ER 914.

Chapter 40

The law of development control and its enforcement

40.1 If, as stated in para 39.2 above, the requirement of planning permission is one of the central elements of the planning system, it is right at the heart of development control itself. At its simplest, it means that permission is needed to develop land.[1] The meaning of 'development' is given in statute[2] and elaborated in case law.

1   Town and Country Planning Act 1990, s 57.
2   TCPA 1990, s 55 (1).

Types of development

40.2   Under s 55(1) of the TCPA 1990, there are two basic types of development:

*   *operational development,*   meaning the carrying-out of building, engineering, mining or other operations in, on, over or under land; and
*   *change of use,*   meaning the making of any material change in the use of any buildings or other land.

Building operations
40.3   There is extensive case law on what constitutes building operations. In *Cheshire County Council v Woodward,*[1] Lord Parker CJ had to consider a coal merchant's coal hopper, some six metres in height and mounted on wheels. Its installation was held not to be development. Lord Parker stated that the definition meant 'any structure or erection which can be said to form part of the realty and to change the physical character of the land.... there is no one test; you look at the erection, equipment, plant, what it is, and ask: in all the circumstances is it to be treated as part of the realty?'

Normally, the change to the physical character of the land must have some degree of permanence. However, even this is not an infallible test, which emphasises Lord Parker's point about the need to look at all the circumstances. In *Skerritts of Nottingham Ltd v Secretary of State for Environment Transport and the Regions (No 2)*[2] the Court of Appeal held that the erection of a large marquee for nine months each year in hotel grounds constituted operational development.

1   [1962] 2 QB 126.
2   [2000] JPL 1025.

Demolition

40.4   It should be noted that demolition is included in the statutory definition of operational development. For many years, this was a doubtful question and the subject of much contention in the courts. The TCPA 1990[1] provides that 'for the purposes of this Act 'building operations' includes

a)   demolition of buildings
b)   rebuilding
c)   structural alterations of or additions to buildings
d)   other operations normally undertaken by a person carrying on a business as a builder'.

1   TCPA 1990, s 55(1A).

Change of use

40.5   The other basic type of development is change of use. The statutory definition refers[1] to 'any *material* change of use in the use of any buildings or other land' (emphasis supplied). In extreme cases, what is material could be an apparently minor change in the use. A classic example of this was *Bendles Motors Ltd v Bristol Corpn*[2] where the installation of a free-standing vending machine selling eggs on the forecourt of a petrol station was held to involve a material change of use and thus to constitute development.

What does amount to material development will depend to some extent on the facts of the individual case. There is also some scope for interpretation by the LPA. In *Bendles Motors*, the court upheld the right of Bristol Corporation to decide that the installation of the vending machine constituted a material change of use. It did not hold that every LPA must decide that every vending machine involves development, and many will not. However, the position is not completely open-ended; certain definite statements can be made about what will and what will not constitute a change of use.

1   TCPA 1990, s 55(1).
2   [1963] 1 WLR 247.

What constitutes change of use?

40.6   The TCPA 1990 states[1] that the following *do* constitute a change of use:

•   'the use as two or more separate dwelling houses of any building previously used as a single dwelling house'
•   'the deposit of refuse or waste materials on land.... notwithstanding that the land is comprised in a site already used for that purpose, if
    (a)   the superficial area of the deposit is extended or
    (b)   the height of the deposit is extended and exceeds the level of the land adjoining the site.'

Additionally [2] 'the use for the display of advertisements of any external part of a building which is not normally used for that purpose' will comprise a material change of use, and thus development. Such use would, in any event, fall within the Town and Country Planning (Control of Advertisements) Regulations 1992, the most important part of the regime for the control of outdoor advertising.

1   TCPA 1990, s 55 (3).
2   TCPA 1990, s 55(5).

What does not constitute change of use?

40.7   The TCPA 1990 also states[1] that certain uses *do not* constitute a change of use:

- 'the use of any buildings or other land within the curtilage of a dwelling house for any purpose incidental to the enjoyment of the dwelling house as such'. However, whether a use comes within this provision, thus avoiding the need for planning permission, will be arguable, especially in more extreme cases. Some of the more bizarre cases are found in this part of planning law. In *Croydon London Borough Council v Gladden*[2] the Court of Appeal refused to accept that keeping a life-size model of a Spitfire (and other World War II memorabilia) in a garden was use incidental to normal enjoyment of a dwelling house. The concept of 'normal' or 'reasonable' enjoyment to come within this provision was derived from *Wallington v Secretary of State for Wales*[3] where the Court of Appeal held that keeping 44 dogs in a house was not reasonably incidental to its enjoyment as a dwelling house.

- 'the use of any land for the purposes of agriculture or forestry... and the use for any of those purposes of any building occupied together with land so used'. This provision has also been the subject of litigation as owners explore the boundaries of what they might do as part of an agricultural use in particular. The association of retailing and the serving of refreshments with agriculture/horticulture at farm shops and garden centres has provided material for dispute with planning authorities seeking to control creeping commercial development in rural areas.

  In *Millington v Secretary of State for Environment Transport and the Regions*[4] the Court of Appeal took the view that wine production and associated activities were part of the farmer's grape-growing activities and not a separate business, as the LPA had maintained.

1   TCPA 1990, s 55 (2).
2   [1994] JPL 723.
3   [1990] JPL 112.
4   [2000] JPL 297.

Other changes where planning permission is not required
40.8   As well as uses incidental to the enjoyment of a dwelling-house and to agriculture, there are two other major categories of uses/activities where planning permission will not be required:

- a change of use within the same use class of the Use Classes Order 1987;
- certain uses which are permitted development under the General Permitted Development Order (GPDO) 1995. Note that this also contains permitted *operational* development, as well as changes of use; both will be referred to below.

The Use Classes Order
40.9   The Use Classes Order sets out a list of use classes. Under the TCPA 1990[1], change of use *within* one of the classes will not constitute development and thus will not require planning permission. For example, a change under Class A2 Financial and professional services (see below) from a building society to a bank would not be a material change of use, and so would not constitute development requiring planning permission. This assumes that the change could be made without structural works (other than internal fitting-out), which would be operational development and so would require planning permission.

The use classes are divided into four main groups of use (there are also several less important classes):

A   Retail/shopping uses;
B   Business and industrial uses;
C   Residential uses;
D   Non-residential/institutional uses.

The table below shows which uses fall within each use class:

Class A1 (shops)	Class A2 (financial and professional services)	Class A3 (food and drink)
retail sale of goods other than hot food; post office; ticket or travel agency; sale of cold food for consumption off the premises; hairdressing; direction of funerals; display of goods for sale; hire of domestic or personal goods; reception of goods for washing, cleaning or repair	financial services; professional services (other than health or medical services); any other services (including betting) appropriate to a shopping area, provided principally to members of the public	use for the sale of food or drink for consumption on the premises or hot food for consumption off the premises
Class B1 (business)	**Class B2[1] (general industrial)**	**Class B8 (storage/distribution)**
office (other than financial or professional services); research and development of products or processes; any industrial process which can be carried out in a residential area without detriment to amenity	use for the carrying out an industrial process not falling within B1	use for storage or a distribution centre
Class C1 (hotels)	**Class C2 (residential institutions)**	**Class C3 (dwelling houses)**
use as a hotel or boarding or guest house where no significant care element is provided	use for residential accommodation or care; hospital or nursing home; residential school, college, or training centre	occupied by a single person or family; or by not more than 6 residents living as one household
Class D1 (non-residential institutions)	**Class D2 (assembly and leisure)**	
for provision of medical or health services; as crèche, day nursery or day centre; for provision of education; for display of works of art; as a museum; as a public library or reading room; as a public hall or exhibition hall; for public worship or religious instruction.	a cinema; a concert hall; a bingo hall or casino; a dance hall; swimming bath, skating rink, gymnasium, or for indoor or outdoor sports (not involving motor vehicles or fire-arms).	

1　Classes B3-7 have been repealed.

40.10   *Classes E and F* Classes E and F are generally much less important. Classes F and G were introduced in 1995 by the GPDO amending provisions to permit change of use from Class A1 or A2 to a mixed shop/flat use (ie shop with flat above it) or from such a mixed use to wholly Class A1 or A2 (eg to allow the flat above to be used for shop storage).

40.11   The principle of the Use Classes Order, then, is that change *within* classes will not require planning permission because it is not a material change of use. Change *between* classes is a material change of use and will require planning permission. Not every type of use is covered by the Order. Change to a use not covered by the Order will almost always require planning permission. Uses outside the Order are known as *'sui generis'* uses.

40.12   Before leaving change of use, the following additional points should be noted. Existing use rights can be lost by *abandonment*, unless they are granted expressly by planning permission, where the circumstances justify such a conclusion. *Intensification* or increase of a use could constitute a material change of use; in *Wallington*, the owner's movement from a small number of dogs covered by 'use incidental to the enjoyment of a dwelling house' to a large number of dogs would constitute a material change of use.

A significant factor in change of use can be the extent of the *planning unit*. An hotel with a restaurant could be a single unit with mixed C1/A3 use or it could be a C1 and an A3 unit respectively; this depends on the facts relating to integration/separation, both physical and legal.

Permitted development
40.13   The Town and Country Planning (General Permitted Development) Order 1995 (the GPDO) specifies 31 categories of development which do not require application for planning permission. Strictly speaking, they *are* development, unlike changes of use that are not material, but the effect is similar: no permission is necessary.

As a generalisation, it can be said that much of the minor development activity, which would otherwise create a huge burden for LPAs across the country, is dealt with by the GPDO. This does not mean that it is all permitted; whether it is depends on whether it falls within the provisions of the GPDO. Nor does it mean that everything covered by the GPDO is minor; some permitted development can be quite significant. But it remains true that the GPDO avoids the need for planning permission for many types of development, especially operational development, but also some changes of use.

While it is not feasible to deal with the 31 categories of permitted development here, some examples of categories frequently encountered may be mentioned as illustrative of the content of the GPDO.

Development within the curtilage of a dwelling house (Part 1) Such development consists of:

- enlargement or extension (by up to 10% of cubic content for terraced houses and 15% for other houses);
- additions or alterations to roof;
- erection of porch;
- provision (within curtilage) of a building, enclosure or pool incidental to enjoyment of dwelling house;
- hard surface or container for oil storage;
- installation of satellite antenna.

The definition of 'curtilage' usually means the area immediately around the house, but need not be synonymous with 'garden': *McAlpine v Secretary of State for Environment.*[1]

Minor operations (Part 2) Such operations include:

*   gates, fences, walls or other enclosures;
*   means of access to highways (not trunk roads or classified roads);
*   external painting.

Changes of use (Part 3) The following changes of use within the Use Classes Order are automatically allowed as permitted development. They will almost always be one-way only, ie reversal would require an application for planning permission:

*   A3 (food and drink) to A2 (financial and professional services);
*   A2 (financial and professional services) to A1 (shops) where there is a ground level display window;
*   A3 (food and drink) to A1 (shops);
*   B3 (storage and distribution) to B1 (business);
*   B2 (general industrial) to B1 (business).

Agricultural buildings and operations (Part 6) Certain erections and extensions of buildings are permitted on agricultural land where reasonably necessary for the agriculture on that unit, although this basic provision is subject to significant exceptions and conditions.

1   [1995] JPL B43.

Variations: Article 4 directions

40.14   Certain variations to the basic GPDO regime should be mentioned briefly at this point. Article 4 of the GPDO empowers the Secretary of State, or the LPA with the SoS's approval, to make a direction (referred to as an 'Article 4 Direction'), withdrawing certain classes of permitted development rights in a specified area. This would be done where the LPA wished to tighten control on particular types of development, either to protect the character or amenity of a particular neighbourhood or to deal with a perceived problem.

Other regimes

40.15   Apart from the GPDO, there are certain other types of regime which can confer (or sometimes restrict) rights to permitted development:

*   A Special Development Order issued by the SoS could extend or limit GPDO rights within a designated area.
*   An Enterprise Zone is created by government to try to regenerate industry and business activity within an economically depressed area. It has the effect of granting planning permission automatically for particular types of development that are to be encouraged within the Zone.   Some 20 Enterprise Zones are in existence and they normally have 10-year lives; most will expire in 2005 or 2006.
*   Simplified Planning Zones are, in effect, zones where the LPA can operate its own GPDO, although it can only extend further rights locally; it must not withdraw generally available GPDO rights. It could only do that by Article 4 Direction.[1]

1   Para 40.14 above.

Other ways of obtaining planning permission

40.16   Having examined the meaning of 'development' and considered means by which, through the Use Classes Order and GPDO, permission will not be required in some situations, it is now necessary to consider how planning permission is obtained outside those situations. Generally speaking, it would be true to say that most major developments, especially building operations, will require planning permission.

Application procedure

40.17   Application for planning permission to carry out development is made to the LPA in whose area the site is located. It is made by completing the LPA's standard form. This is submitted, accompanied by any site plans, drawings or other documents required by the LPA and by any information which the applicant believes will support the application. The applicant has to pay the relevant application fee as prescribed by the Town and Country Planning (Fees for Applications and Deemed Applications) Order and also to submit a certificate under Article 7 of the General Development Procedure Order 1995. The GDPO (not to be confused with the GPDO – para 40.13 above) governs the procedure for application for planning permission. An Article 7 certificate contains a statement from the applicant concerning the ownership of the site. The four types of Article 7 certificate are:

- Certificate A, for use where the applicant is the sole owner of the site;
- Certificate B, for use where the applicant has identified the owner/s of the site and has notified them of the application;
- Certificates C and D, for use where the applicant cannot identify all or any of the owners of the site but can show reasonable steps taken to contact them.

The applicant must also submit an Agricultural Holdings Certificate, stating whether or not the site forms part of an agricultural holding.

The GDPO[1] requires the LPA to enter details of the application in the register and to publicise the application.[2] Failure to secure proper publicity may invalidate the procedure. In *R v Alnwick District Council, ex p Robson*,[3] a leaflet inviting members of the public to make representations regarding an application contained a number of errors and omissions as to time, date, place of meeting and the committee concerned. The effect was that the permission granted under the invalid procedure was rendered void.

1   Article 25.
2   Article 8.
3   [1997] EGCS 144.

Outline and detailed planning permission

40.18   The applicant has to choose whether to apply for outline or full/detailed planning permission and this is stated clearly on the application form. An outline consent establishes the principle that a development of the kind applied for is acceptable to the LPA and may be all that the applicant needs at that stage to sell the site at an enhanced price, to obtain funding for the development, or to decide whether to purchase the site. An outline application means that this stage can be reached without incurring the expense, which may be considerable, of having plans and drawings prepared. Outline planning permission does not, however, enable the developer to go ahead with the development. Where the application is for building, ie operational development, a further application will be necessary for full/detailed planning permission to obtain approval for such matters as siting of the building, design, external appearances (such as materials used) access and landscaping. Alternatively, the applicant can apply immediately for full/detailed planning permission, which, if granted, gives approval to both the principle of the development and the above detailed matters, and allows development to begin. The outline/detailed distinction does not apply where the permission sought is for change of use.

Material considerations

What can constitute a material consideration?

40.19   The LPA's obligation to have regard to the provisions of the development plan has already been explained.[1] But even if it is a situation where prima facie the provisions of the development plan are to be followed[2], the LPA, in making its decision, must also have regard to 'material considerations'. This covers a whole range of factors which may be relevant to the grant of planning permission and which may apply in any individual situation. What actually is a 'material consideration' in any given application will depend upon its facts. The classic statement of this principle was by Cooke J in *Stringer v Minister of Housing and Local Government*[3]: 'In principle it seems to me that any consideration which relates to the use and development of land is capable of being a planning consideration. Whether a particular consideration falling within that broad class is material in any given case will depend upon the circumstances.' Because of the range of possible material considerations which this entails, it is clearly not practical to deal with every possibility, but some examples will suffice.

1   Para 50.28 above.
2   TCPA 1990, s 54A.
3   [1970] 1 WLR 1281.

40.20   *Government policy* Government policy is a material consideration and will virtually always need to be taken into account. This does not mean that it will automatically prevail. In *London Borough of Camden v Secretary of State for Environment*[1] the court held that, while government policy, as set out in PPGs and other circulars, will normally be a material consideration, it must be weighed against others, which might include local factors, either within the development plan or outside it.

1   [1989] JPL 585.

40.21   *Local economic need* Local economic need can also usually be expected to be a material consideration, although, again, not one which will be decisive in all cases, especially not where the proposal is contrary to the provisions of the development plan.   Where, as in *R v Kingston upon Hull, ex p Kingswood District Council*[1], the development plan itself accorded high priority to economic development in the area, the LPA was held to be entirely justified in regarding the intended closure of a factory as a material consideration. In *R v Westminster City Council, ex p Monahan*[2], the Court of Appeal regarded the fact that profit from office development in a proposed scheme on the Royal Opera House site could subsidise the improvement of the Royal Opera House itself as capable of being a material consideration. In *Northumberland County Council v Secretary of State for Environment*,[3] the court even allowed the concept of profit from development on one site subsidising 'desirable' development on an otherwise unrelated site some distance away as a material consideration, although this may be regarded as an extreme example.

1   [1996] EGCS 200.
2   [1989] JPL 107.
3   [1989] JPL 700.

40.22   *Precedent* Another controversial material consideration is that of precedent. Strictly speaking, there is not supposed to be a doctrine of precedent within the development control system. The fact that two different decisions were made by the LPA on identical applications was said in R v Aylesbury Vale District Council, ex p Chaplin[1] not necessarily to invalidate either; neither need be irrational. Planning committees (and, presumably, even officers acting under delegated powers) are entitled to change their minds. However, the development control system would be unworkable if it was completely devoid of consistency or predictability. Thus other decisions by the LPA on identical or similar applications and especially appeal decisions by the SoS (more usually, his inspectors) can be material considerations. In Knott v Secretary of State for the Environment[2], the court held that previous decisions on appeal are properly taken into account and, while it is possible to depart from them, there would be need to be adequate reasons for deciding inconsistently with them.

1   [1996] EGCS 126.
2   [1996] EGCS 175.

40.23   *Private interests* As the *Stringer* case (above) made clear, private interests, as well as the public interest, could be material considerations. However, it does not mean that they always will be and they would have to be compelling to overcome the public interest, not to mention the development plan. In *Khan v Secretary of State for Environment*[1], the fact that a severely disabled child was accommodated in a residential extension was held not to be a material consideration capable of outweighing UDP guidelines on the dimensions of extensions.

1   [1997] JPL B126.

Planning gain

40.24   At this point, it is convenient to deal with another factor which may constitute a material consideration; namely, planning gain. The concept is simple enough. A developer offers, as part of the proposal which is the subject of the planning application, to provide certain benefits for the public or a section of the public, which the LPA would like to secure. An obvious example, and one which was common in the 1980s, is that of out-of-town retail developments; the supermarkets and shopping centres built on the outskirts of urban areas and beyond their limits. Hence, two of the leading cases on planning gain involve Tesco and the Co-op. The supermarket chains offered benefits such as a dedicated wildlife area, art centres and improved park-and-ride facilities, paid for by the chain on land adjoining, or near to, the supermarket site. The benefit would then be taken into account positively as a material consideration by the LPA in making the decision whether to grant planning permission.

If this sounds like a commercial process, or even one tinged with corruption, these are both criticisms levelled against planning gain. Another is that it is undemocratic. The details of the benefit are negotiated, invariably behind closed doors, between developer and representatives of the LPA.

Planning gain is criticised by developers, when it is exacted from them, particularly in the form of contributions to infrastructure costs. It is criticised by developers whose schemes are rejected when, as they see it, they are out-bid by rivals. It is criticised too by objectors who perceive their objections as overridden by offers of benefit from developers. Nor are these criticisms completely fanciful. The process by which the successful developers secured the planning agreement in *R v Plymouth City Council, ex p Plymouth and South Devon Co-operative Society Ltd*[1] was described by the Department of Environment's Head of Development Policy as 'the nearest thing to a Dutch auction we have seen in the context of planning obligations', while Hutchinson J commented that he could 'readily understand the train of reasoning that has led the applicants (for judicial review) to believe that this is a case where it can be said that planning permission was sold'.

Against this, defenders of planning gain argue that it affords opportunities to obtain benefits for the community which would be beyond the means of local authorities or other sources of public finance. In particular, it is seen as reasonable that developers should contribute to improve the infrastructure serving the developments they propose.

In *R v South Northamptonshire District Council, ex p Crest Homes plc*[2], Henry LJ in the Court of Appeal affirmed that 'where residential development makes additional infrastructure necessary or desirable, there is nothing wrong in the local planning authority having a policy that requires major developers to contribute to the costs of infrastructure related to their development. Such a policy is lawful and does not imply, or in itself amount to, the imposition of an illegitimate planning levy, nor does it offend against the principle that planning permissions must not be bought or sold.'

1   [1993] JPL 1099.
2   [1995] JPL 200.

40.25   *The purpose of planning gain* The purpose of planning gain, then, is that it enables developers to offer positive incentives, typically in the form of community facilities or financial contributions to infrastructure, which will then be taken into account by the LPA as a material consideration in deciding whether or not to grant planning permission, or which of two or more competing schemes should be accepted.

To be taken into account by the LPA, the commitment undertaken by the developer would have to pass the test referred to by Lord Hoffman in *Tesco Stores v Secretary of State for Environment*[1] namely that it would have to have a planning purpose and must not be unreasonable[2]. Provided the 'gain' offered passes these tests, the weight given to it is a matter for the LPA to decide, and the courts would be reluctant to interfere with their conclusion. In *R v West Dorset District Council, ex p Searle*[3], the LPA granted permission to a developer, who promised to spend substantial sums on a deteriorating mansion, for a five-flat conversion and eight new dwellings in the grounds. A majority of the Court of Appeal upheld the LPA's decision on the ground that it was entitled to give what weight it thought appropriate to the desirability of saving the mansion.

1   [1995] 1 WLR 759.
2   *Associated Provincial Picture Houses v Wednesbury Corpn* [1947] 2 All ER 680.
3   [1999] JPL 331.

40.26   *Planning obligations – by agreement* The mechanism for implementing planning gain is principally the planning obligation[1]. There are two types: the first is an agreement between the developers and the LPA, which is entered into in the form of a deed, enforceable as a contract by the LPA against the developers and their successors in title. This type of obligation is sometimes known by its former name: a 'planning agreement'. Enforcement can be problematic if the beneficiaries of the gain are third parties. In *Jelson Ltd v Derby City Council*[2], the developer had agreed with the LPA to transfer land for low-cost housing to a housing association. The s 106 deed was held to be insufficient to transfer the land to the housing association, since it was not a party to that deed. The transaction did not therefore meet the requirements of the Law of Property (Miscellaneous Provisions) Act 1989, s 2, that the contract should be signed by the transferee. Third party beneficiaries of planning obligations will be dependent upon the LPA to enforce them and usually would be without remedy if the LPA declined to do so. It has been suggested that the Contracts (Rights of Third Parties) Act 1999 might be used to give rights to third parties to enforce planning obligations against developers, but this is not at the time of writing a widespread practice.

1   TCPA 1990, s 106.
2   [2000] JPL 203.

40.27   *Planning obligations – unilateral* The other type of planning obligation used to enforce planning gain is known as a unilateral obligation or unilateral undertaking. Its distinctive characteristic is that it is *not* the result of agreement between LPA and developers; indeed, it is normally used only where no such agreement could be reached. The developers, despite having failed to persuade the LPA of the adequacy of the gain, may nevertheless unilaterally commit themselves to providing it. The purpose of this is to try to persuade an inspector hearing an appeal against refusal of planning permission that sufficient weight should be given to the obligation to overturn the LPA's decision. The unilateral obligation is otherwise created in the same way as an obligation by agreement and is similarly enforceable.

Special situations
Environmental impact
40.28 Before leaving the subject of material considerations to be taken into account by the LPA in deciding on an application for permission for development, reference should be made to what might be called special situations, where further considerations will be imported into the decision. Special considerations will apply where the proposed development is subject to the Environmental Impact Assessment (EIA) regime.

Where the proposed development falls within Sch 1 to the Regulations,[1] an EIA statement by the developer will be required in every case, giving details of the probable impact of the development upon the environment. This impact, and any proposals for reducing or remedying it, will be taken into account by the LPA in deciding whether or not to grant planning permission and no permission can be granted unless the EIA Procedure has been followed. Schedule 1 covers such developments as refineries, power stations, nuclear installations, smelting works, chemical plants, construction of railways, airports and roads, ports, water treatment plans, waste disposal installations, oil and gas extraction and storage pipelines, dams, mines and quarries and intensive pig/poultry units.

Where the proposed development falls within Sch 2, an EIA statement will be required if it is for a major development of more than local importance, or in a particularly environmentally sensitive location or has unusually complex or hazardous environmental effects. Schedule 2 could apply to developments in the following sectors: agriculture/aquaculture, extractive industries (including quarries and mining), energy, metal production and process, minerals, chemicals, food manufacture, textiles/wood/leather/paper production, rubber manufacture, infrastructure (including industrial estates and transport schemes), racing and testing of motor vehicles, tourism and leisure.

Developers and their professional advisers must therefore consider whether their proposal is caught by Sch 1 or Sch 2. If it is, they must provide the following information where appropriate:

*   description of the development, including any processes and emissions, giving expected qualities and levels;
*   alternatives considered and the reasons for the scheme selected;
*   description of effects on population, fauna, flora, soil, water, air, climate, architecture and archaeology;
*   measures proposed to deal with adverse environmental effects.

1   Town and Country Planning (Environmental Impact Assessment) (England and Wales) Regulations 1999 (as amended).

Listed buildings and conservation areas
40.29   Special considerations will also apply where the proposed development affects listed buildings or conservation areas, which are governed by the Listed Buildings and Conservation Areas in the Planning (Listed and Conservation Areas) Act 1990 (as

amended). It is not intended to describe here in full detail the regime for the protection of buildings of special interest and conservation areas, which comprises a whole area of specialist practice for planners and chartered surveyors. However, although specialised, these issues arise quite often in development in many parts of the country, and so must be considered in the context of how they are dealt with by the LPA handling an application for planning permission. Special consents may also be required in addition to those obtained by a normal planning application.

40.30 *Listed buildings* Listed buildings are those that have been listed as of special architectural or historic interest. Listing is the statutory responsibility of the Secretary of State, although in practice much of the listing is done by English Heritage (formerly the Historic Buildings and Monuments Commission for England).

Buildings are listed as:

- Grade I, being buildings of exceptional interest;
- Grade II, being particularly important buildings of more than special interest; and
- Grade II*, being buildings of special interest.

The listing is recorded in the local land charges register and so can be ascertained by obtaining a search from the local authority.

The purpose of listing is to oblige LPAs to treat in particular ways applications for development of the listed building or applications for adjoining development that would affect it. Specifically, the LPA is expected to give special consideration to listed buildings in deciding whether to grant permission for adjoining development. There is also a presumption against permitting demolition of a listed building, although in *Save Britain's Heritage v Secretary of State for the Environment*[1], the House of Lords held that it would always be possible to rebut this presumption if exceptional circumstances justified it. In that case, the outstanding quality of the design of the proposed development, produced by an architect of international reputation, was said to offer a greater contribution to architectural heritage than the retention of the listed buildings on the old Mappin & Webb site in the City of London.   Such exceptions will be relatively rare.

Where the application is to develop the listed building itself (which, of course, includes alteration and demolition), a separate consent is necessary, known as listed building consent. Planning permission does not give listed building consent and listed building consent does not give planning permission. Separate forms will be needed and separate decisions given by the LPA.

1   [1991] 2 All ER 10.

40.31 *Conservation areas* Unlike listed buildings, the designation of conservation areas is the responsibility of the LPA, although a county council and, in theory, the Secretary of State can also undertake this task. The purpose of designating a conservation area is to import additional, and stricter, criteria into the decision-making process by which the LPA deals with planning applications.

The most important factor in deciding on an application for development in a conservation area is the obligation that, in exercising its planning powers with respect to any buildings or other land in a conservation area, 'special attention shall be paid to the desirability of preserving or enhancing the character or appearance of that area'[1]. Because it is central to decision-making on development in conservation areas, in addition to the usual material considerations, the meaning of this obligation has been subject to close scrutiny by the courts on a number of occasions. In *Steinberg v Secretary of State for the Environment*[2], the High Court rejected the interpretation placed on it by a planning inspector in an appeal, that a vital question was 'whether the proposed development would harm the character of the conservation area'. The court regarded this as a negative duty, whereas the statute requires a positive one in the 'paying of special attention to the desirability of preserving or enhancing'.

In *Bath Society v Secretary of State*[3], the Court of Appeal established that the LPA has in all cases its usual duty to have regard to the development plan and other material considerations, and that the 'special attention' requirement should be a major consideration in conservation area cases, although not so as to outweigh the TCPA 1990, s 54A[4]. However, the Court also thought that if the proposal failed to 'preserve or enhance' the character or appearance of the conservation area it should be rejected unless it offered some other advantage.

This attempt at interpretation was disapproved by the House of Lords in *South Lakeland District Council v Secretary of State for the Environment*[5], where it was stated that the object of the statute of preserving the character or appearance of the conservation area could be achieved, either by a positive contribution to preservation, or by development which was neutral in its effect and which left the character or appearance unharmed, ie preserved. It is not the purpose of the statute to prevent development in conservation areas.

Although an application for planning permission in a conservation area is made in the usual way on the LPA's forms, where it involves total demolition (although not alteration or partial demolition), a further consent will be necessary, known as conservation area consent. Since the House of Lords decision in *Shimizu v Westminster City Council*[6], it has been established that conservation area consent would only be required for complete demolition of an unlisted building (because a listed building demolition would be considered under a listed building consent application[7]).

LPAs will operate policies, usually within the local plan, on the character and appearance of particular conservation areas that will offer guidance to developers (and objectors). They will typically have made Article 4 directions to remove or modify permitted development rights.[8]

1   Planning (Listed Buildings and Conservation Areas) Act 1990, s 72.
2   [1989] JPL 258.
3   [1991] JPL 663.
4   Para 39.41 above.
5   [1992] 2 AC 141, [1992] 1 All ER 573.
6   [1997] JPL 523.
7   Para 40.30
8   Para 40.14 above.

The making of the decision

40.32   As explained at para 39.22, the decision whether or not to grant planning permission will be made either by the LPA's Planning Committee in its regular (often monthly) meeting, or by an authorised officer acting under delegated powers. In either event, officers will have prepared the material needed for consideration of the applications[1]: relevant provisions of the local plan/structure plan/UDP, extracts from PPGs, details of the planning 'history' of the site (such as previous applications and decisions), and information relating to other material considerations. Objections and other representations from neighbours and local organisations, which are themselves material considerations, will be stated or at least summarised. If the application is controversial, and thus before the LPA Planning Committee, rather than delegated to an officer, after discussion, a vote may be taken among the members to produce a decision. There will have been a recommendation from the officer handling the application as to what the decision should be; the members are not bound to follow it, although it will normally be influential. If members ignored an officer's recommendation on weak grounds (or none), the LPA would be vulnerable to an appeal to the Secretary of State (and possibly a costs application[2]), or even to a judicial challenge in the courts. The decision must be given within eight weeks of the application unless the applicant agrees to an extension of time.

1   In R v Selby District Council, ex p Oxton Farms [1997] EGCS 60, it was held that, while a planning officer reporting to committee must have regard to s 54A, the report should not be subjected to textual analysis and the decision could not be challenged on the ground of defects in the presentation of the report.
2   Para 40.52 below.

The decision

40.33   There are three decisions which the LPA could make on a planning application:

- to grant planning permission unconditionally;
- to grant permission subject to conditions; or
- to refuse permission.

The first of these is self-explanatory[1], but the second and third require further explanation.

1   Except to say that ordinarily the development must be commenced within five years or such other period as the LPA decrees.

Conditions

40.34   Although the statute[1] gives the LPA power to grant permission 'subject to such conditions as they think fit', case law has placed certain restrictions on this apparently very wide discretion. The leading case is Newbury District Council v Secretary of State for the Environment[2], where the House of Lords laid down three tests for validity:

- the condition must have a planning purpose;
- it must fairly and reasonably relate to the development in question;
- it must not be unreasonable within the general public law meaning of the word[3]: 'Wednesbury unreasonableness'.

The LPA, then, can impose conditions where they are justified to guard against some perceived harm to the public interest or the private interests of neighbours, where the harm would be insufficient to justify outright refusal, or to secure development which is consistent with planning policy. But it cannot use conditions for extraneous purposes. An example of the kind of condition which would offend against the Newbury tests can be seen in R v London Borough of Hillingdon, ex p Royco Homes[4], where a condition was imposed on the grant of permission to build houses that a number of the units must be offered for rent by people on the council's housing waiting list. This was held to be an invalid condition, since it was an attempt by the council to force the developer to take on part of its housing obligations. A similar effect could be achieved lawfully by entering into a planning obligation by agreement[5] to make a number of units available, for example to a housing association. But to seek to impose such an obligation by condition invites a challenge on the ground that it is ultra vires, meaning beyond the council's powers.

Beyond the Newbury tests, the LPA must have regard to government guidance[6] as to the imposition of conditions. As well as being necessary, relevant and reasonable, the conditions must also be precise and enforceable. These requirements are especially important since the applicant may well appeal against the imposition of conditions which appear uncertain. Because the LPA takes action for breach of condition through a Breach of Condition Notice[7] against which there is no appeal, appeals against the imposition of conditions have become more likely; hence the increased onus on the LPA to get them right in terms of precision and enforceability.

Applicants who are dissatisfied with the potential effect of the conditions imposed should be advised to consider an appeal, which is done in the same way as appeal against refusal[8] and will need to pay careful attention to the LPA's reasons for imposing the conditions which it is obliged to give, including details of any policies on which it relies[9].

1   TCPA 1990, s 70(1).
2   [1981] AC 578.
3   *Associated Provincial Picture Houses v Wednesbury Corpn* [1948] 1 KB 223.
4   [1974] QB 720.
5   Para 40.26 above.
6   Circular 11/95 (Annex).
7   Para 40.42 below.
8   Para 40.48 below.
9   GDPO art 22, as amended by the Town and County Planning (General Development Procedure) (England) (Amendment) Order 2000.

Refusal

40.35   The LPA has statutory power to refuse planning permission[1]. However, it can only do so on the basis of the contents of the development plan and other material considerations. The LPA must justify the refusal by giving reasons in the refusal notice, which will enable the applicant to decide whether or not an appeal to the Secretary of State may be worthwhile. In recent years,[2] LPAs have been required to give fuller details of the policy reasons for a refusal: this also assists in the appeal process by focussing on the LPA's objection to the application. Note that failure by the LPA to issue a decision within the eight weeks allocated (unless an extension has been agreed with the applicant), will be regarded as a 'deemed' refusal, giving the same rights of appeal as an actual refusal.

1   TCPA 1990, s 70(1).
2   Since the Town and County Planning (General Development Procedure) (England) (Amendment) Order 2000.

Enforcement of development control

40.36   LPAs have an extensive range of powers[1] to enforce their control over development, by taking action against those who act without, or outside, planning permission. Enforcement powers were strengthened by amendments to TCPA 1990 by the Planning and Compensation Act 1991, as a result of the Carnwath Report, which highlighted weaknesses in the LPA's position in dealing with breaches of development control, leading to a loss of public confidence in the system. Specifically, there were few incentives for property owners to comply with the requirements of the LPA, which often lacked the necessary information to decide what action to take. The Planning Contravention Notice (PCN) was introduced to address this problem. Difficulties with enforcing conditions on permissions were dealt with by the introduction of the Breach of Condition Notice (BCN). Additionally, deficiencies in the use of Enforcement Notices were tackled by amendment and uncertainties over use of injunctions were resolved. Finally, rights of entry and sanctions were strengthened.

At the time of writing, these measures have been in operation for just over 10 years. They can be said to have improved enforcement without having altogether resolved its problems. There is still advantage for owners in using the appeal system to delay the ultimate outcome, ie 'buying time' while continuing the breach.

1   Under the TCPA 1990.

Enforcement action generally

40.37   Under the TCPA 1990, a breach of development control occurs when development is carried out without the requisite planning permission or when any condition or limitation attached to a permission is not complied with. When this occurs, in principle, the LPA is entitled to take enforcement action. However, before considering the powers that it might deploy, certain major qualifications to the right to take enforcement action must be examined. These are time limits and established use rights, which are separate but related issues.

40.38   *Time limits* There are two time limits for taking enforcement action[1]. After expiry, the LPA loses the right to do so.

The four-year rule
Where the breach of development control consists of either:

* operational development; or
* change of use of a building to use as a dwelling house,

the LPA must take enforcement action within four years of the date when the operational development was substantially complete or the change of use took place.

The 10-year rule
For all other material changes of use and for any breach of condition on a permission, the LPA must take enforcement action within 10 years of the date of the breach.

I   TCPA 1990, s 171B.

40.39   *Established use rights* This expression is used for convenience, even though it does not appear in the statute. The meaning that is intended is that, after the expiry of the relevant time limits[1], because the LPA has lost the right to take action against the breach, the development in question becomes 'lawful', ie the right is established. The mechanism by which it is possible to ascertain if a use has been established so as to be immune from enforcement is an important procedure in property development and land management.

An owner (or any other person wishing to find out, such as a prospective purchaser) can apply to the LPA[2] for a Certificate of Lawfulness of Existing Use or Development (a CLEUD). The application is made by using a LPA form (quite distinct from an application for planning permission) and supplying relevant evidence, particularly on the development in question and its dates of origin. The applicant has to prove, as in a civil case, on the balance of probabilities that the development is lawful. If the LPA is satisfied that it is, it will issue a CLEUD and cannot therefore take enforcement action in respect of that development. The effect is similar to the grant of planning permission. If the LPA refuses the application, the applicant has a right of appeal to the Secretary of State within six months of the refusal[3], an appeal similar to that against a refusal to grant planning permission.

A variation on the CLEUD is the Certificate of Lawfulness of Proposed Use or Development (CLOPUD). This has the same function as the CLEUD, namely ascertaining if a development is lawful and thus protected from enforcement action, with the obvious difference that it relates to future development or a state of affairs not yet in existence. The CLOPUD may enjoy something of a tactical advantage over the CLEUD, in that applying for the latter involves asserting an existing state of affairs. If this proves not to entitle the applicant to a CLEUD, it could furnish evidence on which the LPA might commence enforcement proceedings; it can at least have the effect of drawing the LPA's attention to the existing position on the site. The CLOPUD, because its essence is projected development, may not require the making of any damaging statements about the current use of the site.

I   Para 40.38 above.

2   Under TCPA 1990, s 191.
3   TCPA 1990, s 195.

Enforcement Powers

40.40   Subject, then, to enforcement action not being barred by time limits or the issue of a CLEUD (or CLOPUD), the LPA may use one, or a combination, of its enforcement powers which fall to be considered in turn.

40.41   *Planning Contravention Notice*[1] The purpose of a PCN is principally to obtain information. It may also have the ancillary benefit of alerting persons responsible for alleged contraventions to the need to comply with the requirements of development control. They might, for example, seek to regularise the position by coming forward with an application for planning permission or at least to discuss the matter with the LPA. This, however, is secondary to the LPA's main objective in issuing a PCN, which is to gain some insight as to what is happening as a preliminary to deciding whether or not further enforcement action will be necessary.

There is a degree of variation in practice between LPAs in their use of PCNs. Some are reticent in using them, while others resort to them with relatively little encouragement. However, PCNs cannot be used without some basic justification. In *R v Teignbridge District Council, ex p Teignmouth Quay Co*[2] the court held that there must be *some* basic evidence of a possible breach before a PCN could be served; a merely uncooperative attitude by a landowner would not be enough, of itself.

The PCN requires the occupier of land upon whom it is served to state:

- whether the land is being used as alleged;
- when any use or operation began;
- the identity of any persons responsible;
- information about existing planning permission or why none is necessary; and
- the identity of persons having an interest in the land.

The LPA may propose a meeting to discuss the alleged breach and this may be included in the notice.

The PCN has two sanctions to encourage the occupier to reply within the 21-day time limit: first, it is an offence to fail to reply or to reply misleadingly; and, second, the compensation which the occupier might claim if the LPA unjustifiably serves a stop notice[3] would be lost if it was discovered that the LPA was misled by receiving no response or partial information. The PCN will normally be used as a preliminary to some further enforcement measure, or to a decision to take no further action.

1   TCPA 1990, ss 171C and 171D.
2   [1995] JPL 828.
3   Para 40.45 below.

40.42   *Breach of Condition Notice (BCN)*[1] As its name suggests, the sole purpose of a BCN is to take action against an occupier alleged to be in breach of a condition attached to a planning permission. The BCN will specify the alleged breach and the steps which the LPA consider ought to be taken (including cessation of activities in some cases) in order to secure compliance with the condition. The BCN must give a time-limit for compliance and this must be not less than 28 days from the service of the BCN.

It is a formidable feature of the BCN that failure to comply with it is an offence and that there is no appeal.   This is a compelling reason why an applicant for planning permission should appeal to the Secretary of State promptly on receipt of permission if doubtful conditions are attached to it which the applicant is unlikely to be able to accept. To realise this when a BCN is served is too late to mount a challenge. The only defence to a prosecution for breach of a BCN is for the recipient to show that he took all reasonable measures to secure compliance or was not in control of the land.

1   TCPA 1990, s 187A.

40.43 *Enforcement notices* The standard method of taking action against breach of development control is for the LPA to serve an enforcement notice[1]. As with a PCN, the LPA must have some justification for serving an enforcement notice, and government guidance[2] makes clear that it is not for trivial breaches. Equally, an enforcement notice would be inappropriate if the unauthorised development is unobjectionable and would probably be granted planning permission. The enforcement notice will be served on owners, occupiers and any other persons having an interest in the land (such as mortgagees).

The notice must contain:

- the alleged breach;
- the steps required to remedy the breach (which could be less than the LPA is entitled to ask for: 'under-enforcement' is permitted);
- the date when the notice takes effect (at least 28 days from its service);
- the period for carrying out any remedial works;
- the reason for issuing the notice;
- delineation of the site affected by the notice; and
- notification of the right to appeal against the notice to the Secretary of State. (This right of appeal is significant because the effect of the enforcement notice is suspended during the appeal. Appeal is thus a favoured means of delaying the enforcement process, although a frivolous appeal could result in a costs order against the appellant.[3])

Once the time limit has expired, the enforcement notice is confirmed and is registered against the property by the local authority. Breach of it, or continuing failure to comply with it, which amounts to the same thing, is an offence punishable by heavy fines, which can take account of the benefit to the owner of the breach. A favourite tactic of defendants in enforcement proceedings was to reopen all the planning issues that had often been argued through planning application and appeal processes to try to persuade the court that the enforcement notice should never have been served. This defence was rejected by the House of Lords in *R v Wicks*[4], where it was held that the only thing to be decided was whether the enforcement notice had been breached. Its validity could only be challenged at the earlier stage of appeal to the Secretary of State. Similarly, in *Vale of White Horse District Council v Parker*[5], it was held that the defendants in a prosecution for breach of an enforcement notice would not be allowed to argue that the steps that it required were excessive. Again, this came too late in the day. The only valid defences to a prosecution would be for the owner to show that he had taken all reasonable steps to comply with the notice.

The proper means of responding to an enforcement notice is either to comply with it, to try to negotiate with the LPA a partial or complete withdrawal (in return for some concession, if they will accept it), or to appeal.

1   Under TCPA 1990, s 172 (1).
2   PPG 18.
3   Para 40.52 below.
4   [1997] JPL 1049.
5   [1997] JPL 660.

40.44 *Appeals against enforcement notices* These are procedurally similar to appeals against refusal of planning permission, which are considered below[1]. The principal differences are the time limit – appeal against an enforcement notice must be lodged before the notice takes effect – and the grounds for appeal.

The statutory[2] grounds for appeal against an enforcement notice are that:

- planning permission ought to be granted or the condition in question discharged;
- the matters alleged have not occurred or do not amount to a breach;
- the LPA has lost the right to enforcement (eg, through time limits);
- the enforcement notice was not validly served;
- the steps required were excessive;
- the period for compliance was inadequate.

The effect of success in an appeal against an enforcement notice is similar to that in an appeal against a refusal of planning permission, namely that permission is deemed to be granted for the development in question. For this reason, a fee is charged on appeal equivalent to the fee charged by LPAs with planning applications, so that appellants do not seek to avoid the application fees by this 'backdoor' route.

1   Para 40.48 below.
2   TCPA 1990, s 174(2).

40.45   *Stop Notices* As stated above[1], there is a problem (for the LPA) of delay in the implementation of an enforcement notice. This can even be utilised as a tactic, with legal challenges to the appeal decision lengthening the process. In *R v Kuxhaus*[2], the Court of Appeal would not allow an enforcement notice to be confirmed until the last legal challenge had been exhausted, although the court has the power[3] to permit confirmation of the notice pending appeal if it appears to be justified. This delay can be overcome by the LPA's use of another of its powers: the issue of a stop notice[4]. A stop notice can only be issued in conjunction with an enforcement notice (and must refer to it) but unlike the latter, it has almost immediate effect (within three days or even less if the LPA can justify it). The LPA can, therefore, use this powerful weapon to procure an immediate cessation of the activity alleged to constitute the breach. Failure to comply with the stop notice is an offence.

The appeal is against the enforcement notice and not the stop notice, but the difference, if the latter is used, is that the activity cannot continue pending the appeal. However, the LPA may have to pay a price for resorting to such an effective procedure. If the enforcement notice is subsequently withdrawn, or overturned on appeal to the Secretary of State, or declared invalid on appeal to the Secretary of State, or on judicial challenge, the LPA may be liable to pay compensation for the interruption to activity caused by the stop notice. The compensation may be considerable in some circumstances and this prospect can inhibit the use of stop notices by LPAs. In *Barnes and Co v Malvern Hills District Council*[5], it was held that compensation payable could include liquidated damages payable for delay under an interrupted building contract. Disputes as to compensation are settled by the Lands Tribunal. As has been mentioned[6], no compensation is payable if the enforcement action was erroneously taken because of non-compliance with a PCN.

1   Para 40.36 above.
2   [1988] 2 All ER 705.
3   TCPA 1990, s 289 (4A).
4   TCPA 1990, s 183.
5   [1985] 274 Estates Gazette 830.
6   Para 40.41 above.

40.46   *Injunctions* Although potentially the most powerful weapon available, being an order of the court, failure to comply with which would be a potentially imprisonable contempt, LPAs were, in the past, hesitant in applying for them. There was uncertainty as to whether they should be granted to restrain breaches of development control when enforcement notices were provided by statute for that purpose. The high standards of proof required to obtain an injunction generally were also a deterrent.

However, statute[1] and case law have combined to facilitate the use of injunctions by LPAs. In *London Borough of Croydon v Gladden*[2], the Court of Appeal upheld the use of an injunction under the TCPA 1990 with the encouragement that the standard of proof required to obtain it may not be as high as in the general law. In *Harborough District Council v Wheatcroft*[3], the court made clear that it was not necessary for every remedy (such as the enforcement notice and its appeal mechanism) to have been exhausted before resorting to an injunction. Indeed, an injunction could, in appropriate circumstances, be served at an early stage of enforcement proceedings.

1   TCPA 1990, s 187B.
2   [1994] JPL 723.
3   [1996] JPL B128.

40.47   *Rights of entry* To underpin the specific enforcement powers set out above, the LPA has powers of entry to land for purposes of investigation[1]. A person duly authorised in writing by the LPA can enter any land without warrant at any reasonable hour, provided it has reasonable ground for doing so, to ascertain whether there has been a breach of development control, whether enforcement action would be justified or whether it is being complied with. Twenty-four hours' notice has to be given if the premises are residential. Further powers of entry are obtainable by warrant from a magistrate if the LPA can justify them.

1   Under TCPA 1990, s 196A.

Appeals to the Secretary of State

40.48   An applicant for planning permission can appeal to the Secretary of State[1] in the following circumstances:

- LPA's refusal to grant planning permission;
- LPA's grant of planning permission subject to objectionable conditions;
- LPA's refusal to approve reserved matters following an outline permission;
- LPA's failure to decide application within eight weeks (or longer agreed period).

The appeal must be lodged within six months of the decision (or the failure to determine) and can only be lodged by the applicant. Third parties who have objected unsuccessfully cannot appeal against grant of planning permission, although they may be heard in an appeal made by the applicant, either as objectors or in support of the appeal.

There are three methods by which appeals are determined by inspectors appointed by the Secretary of State (referred to as 'planning inspectors', these are civil servants, usually with considerable experience of planning, either from private practice or local government service). These are:

- written representations;
- informal hearing;
- public inquiry.

Each has distinct characteristics and there are advantages and disadvantages for appellants (and LPAs) to consider.

1   Under TCPA 1990, s 78.

Written representations

40.49   This is the quickest and cheapest method of determining appeals. Over 80% of appeals are dealt with by 'written reps' (the proportion varies somewhat from year to year). The method consists of a limited exchange of written submissions and evidence by appellant and LPA. The inspector reaches a decision on the basis of these and a site visit. Third parties can also put in written representations, but this is the limit of their involvement. Either the LPA or appellant can refuse to proceed by this method, although many are glad to have it resolved as economically as possible. An unjustified insistence on one of the more expensive methods (see below) could result in an award of costs.

Informal hearing

40.50   If both appellant and LPA agree, this can be a more cost-effective alternative to a full inquiry (see below). As well as the initial written statement of grounds for appeal and the LPA's response, the parties will have a hearing before an inspector, but it will be conducted more like a discussion than the quasi-judicial formality of an inquiry. This places a greater burden on the inspector to take the lead. In *Dyason v Secretary of State for the Environment*[1], the inspector was said to have failed to take the necessary steps to inform himself, more necessary in the absence of quasi-legal procedures. The intervention of lawyers in hearings is strongly discouraged, although they may give the parties advice on how to proceed.

This method is rarely likely to be suitable where there is fundamental hostility between LPA and appellant, since it relies on a degree of co-operation and willingness to engage in dialogue to assist the inspector's deliberations. A hearing will typically be much shorter (one day or less) than an inquiry, but can rarely be completed as rapidly as the written representations method.

1   [1998] JPL 778.

Public inquiry

40.51   The most formal method of determining an appeal comprises a quasi-judicial process in which both appellant and LPA (and sometimes even third parties) are represented by lawyers and the inspector assumes the role (almost) of a judge. Procedures for presenting arguments and evidence are formal and errors may be subject to legal challenge. For example, in *West Lancashire District Council v Secretary of State for the Environment*[1], the absence, through illness, of a LPA expert witness on noise levels was fatal to an inspector's decision; the expert's evidence needed to be subjected to cross-examination and the absence of this meant that the inspector could not have weighed it properly.

The inquiry offers scope for open challenge to the other side's experts and is favoured by appellant developers in very contentious cases where the stakes are high. Lay appellants sometimes opt for this method because they feel that it gives them their 'day in court' – their chance to advance arguments about which they feel strongly. Third parties also favour the inquiry as their best chance to be heard, although they have no say in the method adopted. Either the appellant or the LPA can insist on an inquiry if they wish, although they may have to bear the consequences in costs if their insistence creates unjustified expense. A major inquiry, with legal representatives on both sides, and perhaps several expert witnesses each, may take several weeks rather than days and prove enormously costly both in terms of fees and time.

1   [1998] EGCS 33.

Costs in appeals

40.52   Inspectors have the power to award costs against parties to an appeal, either against the LPA or the appellant. Costs could be awarded against the LPA where:

•   it imposed unreasonable or unnecessary conditions on a planning permission;

- it ignored relevant legal authorities or government policies in its decision;
- it pursued unreasonable demands, eg for planning gain, in connection with an application; or
- it failed to follow proper appeal procedure.

Costs could be awarded against an appellant where:

- there was no reasonable prospect of success;
- the appellant introduced new grounds of appeal or evidence late in the proceedings; or
- the appellant failed to follow proper appeal procedure.

The inspector's decision

40.53   Whichever method of determining the appeal is used, the inspector's decision will be conveyed to the parties in the form of a decision letter. The inspector's decision letter will be scrutinised carefully by the appellant and the LPA (and by third parties) and by their legal advisers. This is not only for the most obvious reason – to understand the outcome – but to assess whether there is any prospect of success in mounting a challenge in the courts to the appeal decision.[1]

1   Under TCPA 1990, s 284.

Judicial challenge

40.54   Application must be made to the High Court within six weeks of the decision. There are only two grounds for judicial challenge by this means: that the decision is not within the powers of the Act (is ultra vires); or that the procedural requirements have not been met (eg, that the inspector has not acted with procedural fairness or within the rules of natural justice).

The only parties who can apply to the High Court to challenge the decision are 'persons aggrieved'[1]. This is meant to exclude, in particular, mere busybodies, who have no genuine involvement with the case. Third parties who have made representations (whether objecting or supporting) *may* be able to bring themselves within this definition. However, the courts are often strict in refusing standing to parties who are merely 'interested'. In *R v North Somerset District Council*[2] a group of local residents and environmentalists who lived three to four miles from the park which was the subject of the appeal, were refused standing to challenge the inspector's decision. The court paid particular attention to the facts that: the objectors were not owners; had no legal rights over the site; were not immediate neighbours; had no commercial interest; had no statutory rights of consultation; and were indistinguishable from other members of the public.

The scrutiny which is accorded to the decision letter by all parties means that inspectors have to draft them very carefully. To some extent, the courts are sympathetic with their position. In *Mobil Oil Co v Secretary of State*[3], the court held that the inspector is under no obligation to refer explicitly to opposition from third parties (such as the challenger to the decision). The inspector need do no more than deal with the principal important controversial issues and produce a decision which 'enables the reader to know what conclusion he has reached on them'. However, where the matter in question is fundamental, it must be dealt with. In *MJT Securities v Secretary of State for the Environment*[4] the importance of the matter was common ground between both parties: the inspector cannot omit to deal with such an issue.

Generally speaking, the courts endeavour to take a robust attitude to judicial challenges that are in reality only means to continue the battle. Thus in *John Clark Dealy v Secretary of*

State for the Environment[5] an unsuccessful appellant argued that the inspector had breached natural justice by allowing a third party objector to present extensive evidence without warning. The court upheld the inspector's decision; the third party, although represented by counsel, was not subject to the same strict rules on advance notice as the appellant and the LPA. Judicial challenge is not intended for such cases. It is intended to be a means for redress when serious procedural irregularity or absence of procedural fairness has occurred. In *London Borough of Havering v Secretary of State for the Environment*[6] the inspector, realising that the decision contained a serious omission, sought to remedy it by trying to insert a condition four weeks later. The decision was quashed for irrationality and for the procedural error in trying to affect the decision after the process had been completed.

As with any judicial process, a challenge under TCPA 1990, s 284 can in principle be subject to a further appeal to the Court of Appeal and House of Lords, but an appeal would only be entertained if there was a genuine point of law to decide. Leave would not be given if the appellant merely wished to continue to argue the merits of the decision. In particular, in the case of appeals against enforcement notices, the court would not allow the appeal process to be used as a means of delaying the enforcement of development control.

1   Under TCPA 1990, s 288.
2   [1997] JPL 1015.
3   [1996] EGCS 125.
4   [1996] EGCS 85.
5   [1999] JPL 273.
6   [1997] JPL B165.

The Planning and Compulsory Purchase Bill

40.55   In December 2002, following a Green Paper on the reform of the planning system, the Planning and Compulsory Purchase Bill was introduced. It passed through the Commons Committee stage in late January 2003 and is expected to become law in the latter part of 2003 or early in 2004. Although it had not become law at the time of writing and although it can be hazardous to attempt to forecast the final version of legislation, it is possible and necessary to highlight the key features of the Bill. At the outset it must be emphasised that the Bill does not rewrite planning law, nor revolutionise the planning system. However, some of its reforms will constitute significant changes to key elements of the system described in this chapter and Chapter 39 and require comment.

The first changes to note are structural, ie relating to the local government institutions. Parts I and II of the Bill include the removal of statutory planning powers from county councils (except the so-called 'county matters', relating basically to minerals and waste disposal). County councils will lose their structure planning function and the development plan system will become two-tier, with *regional spatial strategies* prepared by regional planning bodies and *local development frameworks* instead of local plans prepared by district and unitary authorities. The structure plan/local plan/UDP system will thus be replaced. It is not known exactly how the regional planning bodies will operate, or how much scope for public participation is envisaged.

Under Part III, the development plan will comprise the regional spatial strategy and the local development framework documents, and duties will be imposed upon the plan-making bodies to ensure that they contribute to the achievement of sustainable development (not defined by the Bill). Part IV is intended to give greater clarity as to which types of development are likely to be permitted through *local development orders* which will implement policies set out in the local development framework.

Some detailed changes to development control will also be introduced:

- LPAs will be allowed to decline to consider applications where the applicant is 'twin-tracking' with identical applications;
- planning permissions will have to be implemented within three years rather than the current five years;
- outline planning permission is to be replaced eventually by a *statement of development principles* by which the LPA indicates whether it agrees or disagrees with the basic principle of the proposed development.

The Bill also includes the concepts of *business planning zones* and *simplified planning zones* which can be designated by LPAs or the Secretary of State to encourage particular types of development in areas which need urban regeneration. The Secretary of State will receive powers to streamline the handling of applications for major infrastructure projects.

The Bill can be summarised as introducing significant changes to the planning system. However, it falls short of constituting wholesale reform. The expected proposals for a 'development tariff' to replace s 106 obligations have not materialised. The right to a public inquiry for major developments has not been abolished, as had been suggested, although new procedures for public inquiries may be introduced later.

While the effects of the new legislation will require a considerable period after its introduction to evaluate, it is safe to say that the *substance* of planning law, especially as described in this chapter, will remain substantially the same.

Index

[all references are to paragraph number]